Ⓢ 1772764

shakespearean criticism

"Thou art a Monument without a tomb,
And art alive still while thy Book doth
   live
And we have wits to read and praise to
give."

*Ben Jonson, from the preface
to the First Folio, 1623.*

Mr. WILLIAM
SHAKESPEARES
COMEDIES,
HISTORIES, &
TRAGEDIES.

Published according to the True Originall Copies.

LONDON
Printed by Isaac Iaggard, and Ed. Blount. 1623.

Frontispiece to the First Folio (1623). By permission of the Folger Shakespeare Library.

PIERCE COLLEGE LIBRARY
PUYALLUP WA 98374
LAKEWOOD WA 98498

ISSN 0883-9123

Volume 51

shakespearean criticism

Excerpts from the Criticism of
William Shakespeare's Plays and Poetry,
from the First Published Appraisals
to Current Evaluations

**Kathy D. Darrow
Michelle Lee**
Editors

Detroit
New York
San Francisco
London
Boston
Woodbridge, CT

STAFF

Kathy D. Darrow, Jelena Krstovic, Michelle Lee, *Editors*
Gianna Barberi, Elisabeth Gellert, *Associate Editors*
Andrea Henry, Tom Schoenberg, *Assistant Editors*

Lynn Spampinato, *Managing Editor*

Maria L. Franklin, *Permissions Manager*
Kimberly F. Smilay, *Permissions Specialist*
Kelly A. Quin, *Permissions Associate*
Erin Bealmear, Sandy Gore, *Permissions Assistants*

Victoria B. Cariappa, *Research Manager*
Corrine Boland, Tamara C. Nott, Tracie A. Richardson, *Research Associates*
Timothy Lehnerer, Patricia Love, *Research Assistants*

Dorothy Maki, *Manufacturing Manager*
Stacy Melson, *Buyer*

Michael Logusz, *Graphic Artist*
Randy Bassett, *Image Database Supervisor*
Robert Duncan, *Imaging Specialist*
Pamela A. Reed, *Imaging Coordinator*

Since this page cannot legibly accommodate all copyright notices, the acknowledgments constitute an extension of the copyright notice.

While every effort has been made to ensure the reliability of the information presented in this publication, The Gale Group neither guarantees the accuracy of the data contained herein nor assumes any responsibility for errors, omissions or discrepancies. Gale accepts no payment for listing; and inclusion in the publication of any organization, agency, institution, publication, service, or individual does not imply endorsement of the editors or publisher. Errors brought to the attention of the publisher and verified to the satisfaction of the publisher will be corrected in future editions.

This publication is a creative work fully protected by all applicable copyright laws, as well as by misappropriation, trade secret, unfair competition, and other applicable laws. The authors and editors of this work have added value to the underlying factual material herein through one or more of the following: unique and original selection, coordination, expression, arrangement, and classification of the information.

All rights to this publication will be vigorously defended.

Copyright © 2000 Gale Group, Inc.
27500 Drake Rd.
Farmington Hills, MI 48331-3535
Gale Group and Design is a trademark used herein under license.

This book is printed on acid-free paper that meets the minimum requirements of American National Standard for Information Sciences—Permanence Paper for Printed Library Materials, ANSI Z39.48-1984.

Library of Congress Catalog Card Number 86-645085
ISBN 0-7876-3146-9
ISSN 0883-9123

Printed in the United States of America
Published simultaneously in the United Kingdom
by The Gale Group International Limited
(An affiliated company of The Gale Group)
10 9 8 7 6 5 4 3 2 1

The Gale Group

Contents

Preface vii

Acknowledgments ix

List of Plays and Poems Covered in *SC* xii

Love and Romance in Shakespeare's Plays

    Introduction 1

    Romantic Comedy 1

    Love Tragedy 25

    Courtship and Marriage 30

    Further Reading 69

Pericles

    Introduction 71

    Love and Romance 71

    Genre 79

    Language and Structure 86

    Sexuality and Tradition 110

    Further Reading 137

The Phoenix and Turtle

    Introduction 138

    Overview 138

    Love and Romance 145

    Mortality 162

Religious and Mystical Elements	181
Further Reading	194

Romeo and Juliet

Introduction	195
Love and Romance	195
Death and Desire	219
Gender and Society	245
Further Reading	267

Sonnets

Introduction	269
Overview	270
Love and Romance	284
Self-Love	300
Further Reading	333

Venus and Adonis

Introduction	335
Overview	335
The Rhetoric of Desire	345
Themes	377
Further Reading	393

Guide to *Shakespearean Criticism* Series   397

Cumulative Character Index   399

Cumulative Critic Index   411

Cumulative Topic Index   449

Cumulative Topic Index, by Play   467

Preface

Shakespearean Criticism (SC) provides students, educators, theatergoers, and other interested readers with valuable insight into Shakespeare's drama and poetry. A multiplicity of viewpoints documenting the critical reaction of scholars and commentators from the seventeenth century to the present day derives from the hundreds of periodicals and books excerpted for the series. Students and teachers at all levels of study will benefit from *SC,* whether they seek information for class discussions and written assignments, new perspectives on traditional issues, or the most noteworthy analyses of Shakespeare's artistry.

Scope of the Series

Volumes 1 through 10 of the series present a unique historical overview of the critical response to each Shakespearean work, representing a broad range of interpretations. Volumes 11 through 26 recount the performance history of Shakespeare's plays on the stage and screen through eyewitness reviews and retrospective evaluations of individual productions, comparisons of major interpretations, and discussions of staging issues.

Beginning with Volume 27 in the series, *SC* focuses on criticism published after 1960, with a view to providing the reader with the most significant modern critical approaches. Each volume is ordered around a theme that is central to the study of Shakespeare, such as politics, religion, or sexuality. The topic entry that introduces the volume is comprised of general essays that discuss this theme with reference to all of Shakespeare's works. Following the topic entry are several entries devoted to individual works. Volume 51 is devoted to the topic of love and romance in Shakespeare's works, and provides commentary on that topic as well as on the plays and poems *Pericles, The Phoenix and Turtle, Romeo and Juliet,* Sonnets, and *Venus and Adonis.*

SC also compiles an annual volume of the most noteworthy essays published on Shakespeare during the previous year. The essays, reprinted in their entirety, have been recommended to Gale by an international panel of distinguished scholars. The most recent volume, *SC Yearbook 1998,* Volume 48 in the series, was published in October 1999.

Organization of the Book

Each entry consists of the following elements: an introduction, critical essays, and an annotated bibliography of further reading.

- The **Introduction** outlines modern interpretations of individual Shakespearean topics, plays, and poems.

- The **Criticism** for each entry consists of essays that are arranged both thematically and chronologically. This provides an overview of the major areas of concern in the analysis of Shakespeare's works, as well as a useful perspective on changes in critical evaluation over recent decades. Footnotes that appear with previously published pieces of criticism are reprinted at the end of each essay or excerpt. In the case of excerpted criticism, only those footnotes that pertain to the excerpted text are included.

- All of the individual essays are preceded by **Explanatory Notes** as an additional aid to students using *SC.* The explanatory notes summarize the criticism that follows.

- A complete **Bibliographical Citation** providing publication information precedes each piece of criticism.

- Each volume includes such **Illustrations** as reproductions of images from the Shakespearean period, paintings and sketches of eighteenth- and nineteenth-century performers, photographs of modern productions, and stills from film adaptations.

- The annotated bibliography of **Further Reading** appearing at the end of each entry suggests additional sources of study for the reader. Explanatory notes summarize each essay or book listed here.

- Each volume of *SC* provides the following indices:

    Cumulative Character Index: Identifies the principal characters of discussion in the criticism of each play and non-dramatic poem.
    Cumulative Critic Index: Identifies each critic that has appeared in *SC*.
    Cumulative Topic Index: Identifies the principal topics in the criticism and stage history of each work. The topics are arranged alphabetically, by topic.
    Cumulative Topic Index, by Play: Identifies the principal topics in the criticism and stage history of each work. The topics are arranged alphabetically, by play.

Citing *Shakespearean Criticism*

Students who quote directly from any volume in the Literature Criticism Series in written assignments may use the following general forms to footnote reprinted criticism. The first example pertains to material drawn from periodicals, the second to material reprinted from books.

[1]Gordon Ross Smith, "Shakespeare's *Henry V*: Another Part of the Critical Forest," in *Journal of the History of Ideas,* XXXVII, No. 1 (January-March 1976), 3-26; excerpted and reprinted in *Shakespearean Criticism,* Vol. 30, ed. Marie Lazzari (Detroit: Gale Research, 1996), pp. 262-73.

[2]Katherine Eisaman Maus, *Inwardness and Theater in the English Renaissance* (The University of Chicago Press, 1995); excerpted and reprinted in *Shakespearean Criticism,* Vol. 33, ed. Dana Ramel Barnes and Marie Lazzari, (Detroit: Gale Research, 1997), pp. 112-17.

Suggestions Are Welcome

The editors encourage comments and suggestions from readers on any aspect of the *SC* series. In response to various recommendations, several features have been added to *SC* since the series began, including the topic index and the sample bibliographic citations noted above. Readers are cordially invited to write, call, or fax the editors: *Shakespearean Criticism,* The Gale Group, 27500 Drake Rd., Farmington Hills, MI 48331-3535. Call toll-free at 1-800-347-GALE or fax to 1-248-699-8049.

Acknowledgments

The editors wish to thank the copyright holders of the excerpted criticism included in this volume and the permissions managers of many book and magazine publishing companies for assisting us in securing reproduction rights. We are also grateful to the staffs of the Detroit Public Library, the Library of Congress, the University of Detroit Mercy Library, Wayne State University Purdy/Kresge Library Complex, and the University of Michigan Libraries for making their resources available to us. Following is a list of the copyright holders who have granted us permission to reproduce material in this volume of SC. Every effort has been made to trace copyright, but if omissions have been made, please let us know.

COPYRIGHTED EXCERPTS IN *SC*, VOLUME 51, WERE REPRODUCED FROM THE FOLLOWING PERIODICALS:

Ariel: A Review of International English Literature, v. 12, April, 1981 for "Romeo and Juliet and the Art of Naming Love" by Barbara L. Estrin. Copyright © 1981 The Board of Governors, The University of Calgary. Reproduced by permission of the publisher and the author.—***Ball State Teachers College Forum,*** v. V, Autumn, 1964. Copyright © 1964, renewed 1993 Ball State University. Reprinted by permission of the publisher.—***Comparative Drama,*** v. 15, Spring, 1981. Copyright © 1981, by the Editors of *Comparative Drama*. Reproduced by permission.—***Contemporary Review,*** v. 227, December, 1975. Copyright © 1975 Contemporary Review Co. Ltd. Reproduced by permission.—***Criticism,*** v. XXXI, Winter, 1989. Copyright ©1989, Wayne State University Press. Reproduced by permission of the publisher.—***English Studies in Africa,*** v. 20, September, 1977 for "Love and Grace in Romeo and Juliet" by Geoffrey Hutchings. Copyright © Witwatersrand University Press 1977. Reproduced by permission of the publisher and the author.—***English Studies,*** v. 58, December, 1977; v. 67, February, 1986. Copyright © 1977, 1986 Swets & Zeitlinger. Both reproduced by permission.—***Essays in Criticism,*** v. XV, July, 1965 for "The Dead Phoenix" by Murray Copland. Reproduced by permission of the Editors of *Essays in Criticism* and the author.—***Forum For Modern Language Studies,*** v. XXXIII, October, 1997 for "Troping Desire in Shakespeare's 'Venus and Adonis'" by Goran V. Stanivukovic. Copyright © *Forum for Modern Language Studies* 1997. Reproduced by permission of the publisher and the author.—***Literature and Psychology,*** v. XXXXII, 1996. Copyright © Editor 1996. Reproduced by permission of the publisher.—***Mosaic: A Journal for the Interdisciplinary Study of Literature,*** v. XVIII, Summer, 1985. Copyright © *Mosaic* 1985. Acknowledgment of previous publication is herewith made.—***Papers on Language and Literature,*** v. 26, Spring, 1990. Copyright © 1990 by The Board of Trustees, Southern Illinois University at Edwardsville. Reproduced by permission.—***The Review of English Studies,*** v. XLVI, November, 1995 for "The Phoenix and Turtle: Requiem and Rite" by H. Neville Davies. Copyright © Oxford University Press 1995. Reproduced by permission of Oxford University Press and the author.—***The Sewanee Review,*** v. CX, Winter, 1997. Copyright © 1997 by David Solway. Reproduced with permission of the editor and the author.—***Shakespeare Quarterly,*** v. 41, Fall, 1990; v. 48, Fall, 1997. Copyright © The Folger Shakespeare Library, 1990, 1997. Both reproduced by permission of *Shakespeare Quarterly*. —***Shakespeare Studies: An Annual Gathering of Research, Criticism, and Reviews,*** v. VIII, 1975 for "Shakespeare's *The Phoenix and the Turtle* and the Defunctive Music of Ecstasy" by Vincent F. Petronella. Copyright © 1975 The Council for Research in the Renaissance. Reproduced by permission of the author.—***Shakespeare Survey: An Annual Survey of Shakespeare Studies and Production,*** v. 49, 1996 for "Ideology and Feud in *Romeo and Juliet*" by Susan Snyder / v. 49, 1996 for "'Death-Marked Love': Desire and Presence in *Romeo and Juliet*" by Lloyd Davis. Copyright © Cambridge University Press 1996. Both reproduced by permission of Cambridge University Press and the authors.—***Studia Neophilologica,*** v. 51, 1979; v. 68, 1996. Both reproduced by permission.—***Studies in Philology,*** v. 80, Summer, 1983; v. LXXXV, Summer, 1988. Copyright © 1983, 1988 The University of North Carolina Press. Both used by permission of the publisher.—***Style,*** v. 28, Spring, 1994 for "Since First Your Eye I Eyed: Shakspeare's Sonnets and the Poetics of Narcissism" by Jane Hedley. Copyright © *Style* 1994. All rights reserved. Reproduced by permission of the publisher and the author.

COPYRIGHTED EXCERPTS IN *SC*, VOLUME 51, WERE REPRODUCED FROM THE FOLLOWING BOOKS:

Bock, Philip K. From " 'Neither Two Nor One': Dual Unity in *The Phoenix and Turtle*" in ***The Undiscover'd Country: New Essays on Psychoanalysis and Shakespeare.*** Edited by B. J. Sokol. Free Association Books, 1993.

Copyright © B. J. Sokol 1993. Reproduced by permission.—Cook, Ann Jennalie. From *Making a Match: Courtship in Shakespeare and His Society*. Princeton University Press, 1991. Copyright © 1991 by Princeton University Press. All rights reserved. Reproduced by permission.—Dean, John. From "The Theme of Love in Shakespeare's Romances" in *Institut Für Anglistik Elizabethan and Renaissance Studies, Vol. 86: Restless Wanderers: Shakespeare and the Pattern of Romance*. Institut Für Anglistik Und Amerikanistik der Universitat Salzburg, 1979. Copyright © Institut Für Anglistik Und Amerikanistik der Universitat Salzburg, 1979. Reproduced by permission.—Gajowski, Evelyn. From *The Art of Loving: Female Subjectivity and Male Discursive Traditions in Shakespeare's Tragedies*. University of Delaware Press, 1992. Copyright © 1992 by Associated University Presses, Inc. All rights reserved. Reproduced by permission.—Hecht, Anthony. From an introduction to *The Sonnets*. Edited by G. Blakemore Evans. Copyright © Cambridge University Press, 1996. Reproduced by permission of Cambridge University Press and the author.—Hunt, Maurice. From *Shakespeare's Romance of the Word*. Bucknell University Press, 1990. Copyright © 1988 by Associated University Presses, Inc. All rights reserved. Reproduced by permission.—Kay, Dennis. From *William Shakespeare: Sonnets and Poems*. Twayne Publishers, 1998. Copyright © 1998 by Twayne Publishers. All rights reserved. Reproduced by permission.—Knight, G. Wilson. From *The Mutual Flame: On Shakespeare's Sonnets and The Phoenix and the Turtle*. Methuen and Co. Ltd., 1955. Reproduced by permission.—Levin, Richard A. From an introduction to *Love and Society in Shakespearean Comedy: A Study of Dramatic Form and Content*. University of Delaware Press, 1985. Copyright © 1985 by Associated University Presses, Inc. All rights reserved. Reproduced by permission.—Martin, Philip. From *Shakespeare's Sonnets: Self, Love and Art*. Cambridge University Press, 1972. Copyright © Cambridge University Press 1972. Reproduced by permission of Cambridge University Press and the author.—McCoy, Richard C. From "Love's Martyrs: Shakespeare's 'Phoenix and Turtle' and the Sacrificial Sonnets" in *Religion and Culture in Renaissance England*. Edited by Claire McEachern and Debora Shuger. Cambridge University Press, 1997. Copyright © Cambridge University Press, 1997. Reproduced with the permission of Cambridge University Press and the author.—Merrix, Robert P. From " 'Lo, in This Hollow Cradle Take Thy Rest': Sexual Conflict and Resolution in *Venus and Adonis*" in *Venus and Adonis: Critical Essays*. Edited by Philip C. Kolin. Garland Publishing, Inc., 1997. Copyright © 1997 by Philip C. Kolin. All rights reserved. Reproduced by permission.—Neely, Carol Thomas. From *Broken Nuptials in Shakespeare's Plays*. Yale University Press, 1985. Copyright © 1985 by Yale University. Reprinted in 1993 by University of Illinois Press. All rights reserved. Reproduced by permission of the author.—Schiffer, James. From "Shakespeare's *Venus and Adonis*: A Lacanian Tragicomedy of Desire" in *Venus and Adonis: Critical Essays*. Edited by Philip C. Kolin. Garland Publishing, Inc., 1997. Copyright © 1997 by Philip C. Kolin. All rights reserved. Reproduced by permission.—Skeele, David. From *Thwarting the Wayward Seas: A Critical and Theatrical History of Shakespeare's Pericles in the Nineteenth and Twentieth Centuries*. University of Delaware Press, 1998. Copyright © 1998 by Associated University Presses, Inc. All rights reserved. Reproduced by permission.—Smith, Hallett. From *The Tension of the Lyre: Poetry in Shakespeare's Sonnets*. Huntington Library, 1981. Copyright © 1981 The Huntington Library. All rights reserved. Reproduced by permission of the Henry E. Hutington Library.—Weiser, David K. From *The Mind in Character: Shakespeare's Speaker in the Sonnets*. University of Missouri Press, 1987. Copyright ©1987 by The Curators of the University of Missouri. Reproduced by permission.—White, R. S. From *Let Wonder Seem Familiar: Endings in Shakespeare's Romance Vision*. Humanities Press and the Athlone Press, 1985. Copyright © 1985 R. S. White. All rights reserved. Reproduced by permission of Humanities Press and The Athlone Press Ltd.—Wilson, John Dover. From An Introduction to *The Sonnets of Shakespeare for the Use of Historians and Others*. Cambridge University Press, 1964. Copyright © Cambridge University Press 1963. Reproduced with the permission of Cambridge University Press.—Witt, Robert W. From "Recognition of Beauty" in *Elizabethan and Renaissance Studies, Vol. 77: Of Comfort and Despair: Shakespeare's Sonnet Sequence*. Institut Für Anglistik Und Amerikanistik der Universitat Salzburg, 1979. Copyright © Institut Für Anglistik Und Amerikanistik der Universitat Salzburg, 1979. Reproduced by permission.

PHOTOGRAPHS AND ILLUSTRATIONS APPEARING IN *SC*, VOLUME 51, WERE RECEIVED FROM THE FOLLOWING SOURCES:

Act I, scene v, from William Shakespeare's *Romeo and Juliet*, from *Boydell - Shakespeare Gallery*, photograph. Special Collections Library, University of Michigan. Reproduced by permission.—Act II, scene v, from William Shakespeare's *Romeo and Juliet*, from *Boydell - Shakespeare Gallery*, photograph. Special Collections Library, University of Michigan. Reproduced by permission.—Act III, scene i, from William Shakespeare's *Pericles*, from *Gallerie des Personnages* . . . facing p. 103, photograph. Special Collections Library, University of Michigan. Reproduced by permission.—Act III, scene ii, from William Shakespeare's *Pericles*, from *Shakespeare's Works* (1714)

v. 8, photograph. Special Collections Library, University of Michigan. Reproduced by permission.—Act III, scene v, from William Shakespeare's *Romeo and Juliet,* from *Boydell - Shakespeare Gallery,* photograph. Special Collections Library, University of Michigan. Reproduced by permission.—Act IV, scene iv, from William Shakespeare's *Pericles,* from *Gallerie des Personnages* . . . facing p. 107, photograph. Special Collections Library, University of Michigan. Reproduced by permission.—Act V, scene iii, from William Shakespeare's *Romeo and Juliet,* from *Boydell - Shakespeare Gallery,* photograph. Special Collections Library, University of Michigan. Reproduced by permission.—Act V, scene iii, from William Shakespeare's *Romeo and Juliet,* from *Smirke's Illustrations,* photograph. Special Collections Library, University of Michigan. Reproduced by permission.—Act V, scene iv, from William Shakespeare's *Pericles,* from *Smirke's Illustrations,* photograph. Special Collections Library, University of Michigan. Reproduced by permission.—DiCaprio, Leonardo, with Claire Danes, in the movie *Romeo and Juliet,* 1996. The Kobal Collection. Reproduced by permission.—From a title page of *The Phoenix and Turtle* by William Shakespeare, photograph. The Folger Shakespeare Library. Reproduced by permission.—From the second title page of *The Phoenix and Turtle* by William Shakespeare, photograph. The Folger Shakespeare Library. Reproduced by permission.—Frontispiece from William Shakespeare's *Venus & Adonis,* from *Shakespeare's Works* (1714) v. 9, photograph. Special Collections Library, University of Michigan. Reproduced by permission.—Harvey, Laurence with Susan Shentall, in the movie *Romeo and Juliet,* 1954, photograph. The Kobal Collection. Reproduced by permission.—Phoenixes and Dragons, exterior of Temple of Heaven, Beijing, photograph. Wolfgang Kaehler/ Corbis. Reproduced by permission.—Shakespeare's Contemporaries from *Gallerie des Personnages* . . . , photograph. Special Collections Library, University of Michigan. Reproduced by permission.—Title page from *William Shakespeare's Venus & Adonis,* from *Shakespeare's Works* (1714) v. 9, photograph. Special Collections Library, University of Michigan. Reproduced by permission.—Ulanovna, Galina, and B. Bulgakov in Prokofiev's ballet *Romeo and Juliet,* c. 1952, photograph. The Library of Congress.—Whiting, Leonard, with Olivia Hussey, in the movie *Romeo and Juliet,* 1968. The Kobal Collection. Reproduced by permission.

List of Plays and Poems Covered in *SC*

Volumes 1-10 present a critical overview of each play, including criticism from the seventeenth century to the present. Beginning with Volume 11, the series focuses on the history of Shakespeare's plays on the stage and in important films. The Yearbooks reprint the most important critical pieces of the year as suggested by an advisory board of Shakespearean scholars. Beginning with Volume 27, each volume is organized around a theme and focuses on criticism published after 1960.

Volume 1
The Comedy of Errors
Hamlet
Henry IV, Parts 1 and 2
Timon of Athens
Twelfth Night

Volume 2
Henry VIII
King Lear
Love's Labour's Lost
Measure for Measure
Pericles

Volume 3
Henry VI, Parts 1, 2, and 3
Macbeth
A Midsummer Night's Dream
Troilus and Cressida

Volume 4
Cymbeline
The Merchant of Venice
Othello
Titus Andronicus

Volume 5
As You Like It
Henry V
The Merry Wives of Windsor
Romeo and Juliet

Volume 6
Antony and Cleopatra
Richard II
The Two Gentlemen of Verona

Volume 7
All's Well That Ends Well
Julius Caesar
The Winter's Tale

Volume 8
Much Ado about Nothing
Richard III
The Tempest

Volume 9
Coriolanus
King John
The Taming of the Shrew
The Two Noble Kinsmen

Volume 10
The Phoenix and Turtle
The Rape of Lucrece
Sonnets
Venus and Adonis

Volume 11
King Lear
Othello
Romeo and Juliet

Volume 12
The Merchant of Venice
A Midsummer Night's Dream
The Taming of the Shrew
The Two Gentlemen of Verona

Volume 13
1989 Yearbook

Volume 14
Henry IV, Parts 1 and 2
Henry V
Richard III

Volume 15
Cymbeline
Pericles
The Tempest
The Winter's Tale

Volume 16
1990 Yearbook

Volume 17
Antony and Cleopatra
Coriolanus
Julius Caesar
Titus Andronicus

Volume 18
The Merry Wives of Windsor
Much Ado about Nothing
Troilus and Cressida

Volume 19
1991 Yearbook

Volume 20
Macbeth
Timon of Athens

Volume 21
Hamlet

Volume 22
1992 Yearbook

Volume 23
As You Like It
Love's Labour's Lost
Measure for Measure

Volume 24
Henry VI, Parts 1, 2, and 3
Henry VIII
King John
Richard II

Volume 25
1993 Yearbook

Volume 26
All's Well That Ends Well
The Comedy of Errors
Twelfth Night

Volume 27
Shakespeare and Classical Civilization
Antony and Cleopatra
Timon of Athens
Titus Andronicus
Troilus and Cressida

Volume 28
1994 Yearbook

Volume 29
Magic and the Supernatural
Macbeth
A Midsummer Night's Dream
The Tempest

Volume 30
Politics
Coriolanus
Henry V
Julius Caesar

Volume 31
Shakespeare's Representation of Women
Much Ado about Nothing
King Lear
The Taming of the Shrew

Volume 32
1995 Yearbook

Volume 33
Sexuality in Shakespeare
Measure for Measure
The Rape of Lucrece
Romeo and Juliet
Venus and Adonis

Volume 34
Appearance versus Reality
As You Like It
The Comedy of Errors
Twelfth Night

Volume 35
Madness
Hamlet
Othello

Volume 36
Fathers and Daughters
Cymbeline
Pericles
The Winter's Tale

Volume 37
1996 Yearbook

Volume 38
Desire
All's Well That Ends Well
Love's Labour's Lost
The Merry Wives of Windsor
The Phoenix and Turtle

Volume 39
Kingship
Henry IV, Parts 1 and 2
Henry VI, Parts 1, 2, and 3
Richard II
Richard III

Volume 40
Gender Identity
The Merchant of Venice
Sonnets
The Two Gentlemen of Verona

Volume 41
Authorship Controversy
Henry VIII
King John
The Two Noble Kinsmen

Volume 42
1997 Yearbook

Volume 43
Violence
The Rape of Lucrece
Titus Andronicus
Troilus and Cressida

Volume 44
Psychoanalytic Interpretations
Hamlet
Macbeth

Volume 45
Dreams
A Midsummer Night's Dream
The Tempest
The Winter's Tale

Volume 46
Clowns and Fools
As You Like It
King Lear
Twelfth Night

Volume 47
Deception in Shakespeare
Antony and Cleopatra
Cymbeline
The Merry Wives of Windsor

Volume 48
1998 Yearbook

Volume 49
Law and Justice
Henry IV, Parts 1 and 2
Henry V
Measure for Measure

Volume 50
Social Class
Coriolanus
Julius Caesar
The Two Noble Kinsmen

Volume 51
Love and Romance
Pericles
The Phoenix and Turtle
Romeo and Juliet
Sonnets
Venus and Adonis

Future Volumes

Volume 52
Morality
Richard II
Richard III
Timon of Athens

Volume 53
Race
Othello
The Merchant of Venice

Love and Romance

INTRODUCTION

In Shakespeare's plays, love and romance are often treated in ambiguous ways. Romantic love frequently ends in death, as in the tragedies, but such love may be presented in an idealized manner, shown to be courageous and unconditional. In Shakespeare's romantic comedies, the traditional comic ending featuring one or more marriages is often tempered by a more serious note, which questions the finality of that ending. Additionally, the so-called "romantic" comedies may feature a certain degree of tension between romantic and antiromantic elements. Marriage—typically viewed as the goal of romantic love—is also treated ambiguously by Shakespeare. In many of Shakespeare's comedies and tragedies, marriages are frequently disrupted by the husband's usually irrational fear of being cuckolded. Despite the taint on marriage by the specter of cuckoldry or by other subversions, marriage nevertheless occupies a central role in Shakespeare's work.

Evelyn Gajowski (1992) examines the qualities shared by Juliet (*Romeo and Juliet*), Desdemona (*Othello*), and Cleopatra (*Antony and Cleopatra*), maintaining that all three women give themselves freely to their beloveds without expecting or demanding any reciprocal emotion. Gajowski notes that the women, like the speaker in Shakespeare's sonnets, possess "the courage to love despite awareness of the vicissitudes of human existence." The romantic comedies treat love a bit differently than these tragedies. R. S. White (1981) demonstrates the way in which the finality of comic endings is often questioned in Shakespeare's romantic comedies. In *Love's Labour's Lost*, for example, the courtships of the couples are postponed when a death is announced; the men are required by their beloveds to undergo a period of self-examination before the relationships may resume. Similarly, Richard A. Levin (1985) observes that in Shakespeare's mature comedies, romantic elements are challenged by "antiromantic" elements. In these works, the conflict between love and fortune is often emphasized, Levin notes. Fortune—as either money or social status—is a "constant temptation" to lovers in these plays. While marriage is usually seen as the happy consummation of romantic love, it is often viewed in less-than-optimistic terms, many critics assert. B. J. Pendlebury (1975) maintains that while the early plays do portray marriage in an optimistic manner, the later plays' treatment of marriage often focuses on the male fear of being deceived by an adulterous wife. Coppélia Kahn (1981) offers a similar assessment, but also notes that even in many of the earlier plays, the threat of cuckoldry "lurks in the wings." Such a fear of cuckoldry stems from a variety of factors, Kahn explains, including the patriarchal marriage itself, where women are viewed as the sexual property of their husbands, and the double standard that permits husbands to have extramarital sex, but makes the perception of the husband's virility dependent on his wife's chastity. Other critics analyze the relevancy of Elizabethan marriage laws and customs to Shakespeare's treatment of matrimony. Ann Jennalie Cook (1991) offers a detailed discussion of Elizabethan betrothal contracts, elopements, annulments, and divorces. Cook highlights the social, legal, and economic punishments exacted for participating in unsanctioned behavior related to betrothals and marriages and then explores Shakespeare's representation of such irregular behavior in his plays. In conclusion, Cook comments that as Shakespeare treats this type of behavior in both negative and positive ways, there is no easy way to assess his own opinions on the matter. Similarly, Margaret Loftus Ranald (1979) demonstrates how Elizabethan issues such as betrothals, contracts, premarital intercourse, impediments to marriage, and the marriage ceremony itself are examined by Shakespeare in many plays in a variety of ways. Ranald observes that marriages form the conclusion to every comedy and typically emphasize social harmony; that marriage is treated both humorously and tragically in Shakespeare's poems; that in the tragedies, the subversion of marital relationships results in some form of disaster; and that in the last plays, Shakespeare places less of an emphasis on the particulars of marital law and instead celebrates "the kind of virtuous love that ends in marriage."

ROMANTIC COMEDY

R. S. White (essay date 1981)

SOURCE: "Shakespeare's Mature Romantic Comedies," in *'Let Wonder Seem Familiar': Endings in Shakespeare's Romance Vision,* Humanities Press, Inc., 1985, pp. 35-66.

[*In the following essay, White studies the endings of Shakespeare's romantic comedies, maintaining that the playwright experiments with combining the finality of a comic ending with the "endless" nature of a romantic ending.*]

Love's Labour's Lost is another attempt by Shakespeare to write the kind of romantic comedy pioneered by Lyly, where the ending is qualified and open. The stroke he uses to solve the problems inherent in the form is daringly simple, for he simply denies the credibility of the conventional happy ending, almost gratuitously going out of his way to provide a complicating factor. The direction of our expectations in the play is clear and conventional. The action seems to be moving towards a declaration of marriage. From the opening, there is little doubt that the sterile vow will crumble before the shattering power of love, and this is what happens. The pageant of the Nine Worthies seems calculated to relax the mood into the festivity of betrothal. Little resistance poses itself to the courtships, since the ladies' coyness is, we find from their conversations, a teasing test of the men rather than a denial of their suits. The vitality lies not in true conflict, nor in the complexity of debate about love but in the fertility of language, and in the energetic release of the men when they fall in love. However, as if it is too easy for the dramatist to satisfy our expectations, and as if love should not be won so easily by men who have denied its existence, resistance is introduced in the form of a chilly message from the outside world:

> *Enter as messenger.* MONSIERU MARCADE.
> MARCADE. God save you, madam!
> PRINCESS. Welcome, Marcade;
> But that thou interruptest our merriment.
> MARCADE. I am sorry, madam; for the news I
>   bring
> Is heavy in my tongue. The King your
>   father—
> PRINCESS. Dead, for my life!
> MARCADE. Even so; my tale is told.
>   (V. ii. 703-9)

This strikes a grim note, intruding from a more distressing and succinctly-spoken world into the charm, chatter and hyperbole of the King's curious-knotted garden.[1] The King tries to sustain the spirit of gallant courtship, but he is quite roughly rebuffed:

> KING. Yet since love's argument was first on
>   foot,
> Let not the cloud of sorrow justle it
> From what it purpos'd . . .
> QUEEN. I understand you not; my griefs are
>   double.
>   (V. ii. 736-40)

Even after sober declaration of love from the men, the ladies are still not able to treat the proposals except as 'pleasant jest and courtesy, As bombast and as lining to the time.' In Lyly's fashion, a compromise is struck. The ladies will mourn for a year in France, the men are to undergo certain taxing experiences such as living in a hermitage or a hospital, to learn genuine self-denial and understanding of people's problems. After the educative process, the courtship may (or may not) begin afresh.

The play ends with chastened self-awareness on the part of the men and reluctant withdrawal on that of the women:

> BEROWNE. Our wooing doth not end like an
>   old play:
> Jack hath not Jill. These ladies' courtesy
> Might well have made our sport a comedy.
> KING. Come, sir, it wants a twelvemonth an' a
>   day
> And then 'twill end.
> BEROWNE. That's too long for a play.
>   (V. ii. 862-6)

Berowne's rueful comment is more than just a statement about form, since it points towards a moral lesson which the men ought to have learned during the action. They have throughout treated life as a play and other people as merely objects for their own amusement. After the vow to study has been taken, Berowne asks, "But is there no quick recreation granted?" (I.i.159), and the King replies that Armada the Spaniard will serve their turn:

> But I protest I love to hear him lie,
> and I will use him for my minstrelsy.
>   (I.i.173-4)

Longaville agrees, adding another human toy to their repertory:

> Costard the swain and he shall be our sport;
> And so to study three years is but short.
>   (I.i.177-8)

The low-born characters are eventually used mercilessly for the "sport" of the courtly, when their humbly offered entertainment of masque is mocked off the stage in derisive laughter and in a manner which is "not generous, not gentle, not humble" (V.ii.621). To emphasize the point, after this touching line from Holofernes, the shadows lengthen on the world of play: "A light for Monsieur Judas! It grows dark, he may stumble" (V.ii.622). The courtiers have played loose with their oaths, have attempted to play with the lives of the women, have condescendingly played with the low-born characters, and they have played with language, turning every word inside out for a joke. Of course, such things are appropriate to a stage comedy, but a life may not be responsibly led on such a basis. "That's too long for a play" uses the word in at least two senses. By drawing attention to the play as artifice, Shakespeare reminds the audience that it too is about to leave the playful world for one more serious.

The hints pointing to the necessity of leaving the golden world for the brazen gather as the end comes in sight. Armado sees his duty for the future through the little hole of discretion, and swears marriage to Jaquenetta, and she too is directed into the future, for she is 'quick, the child brags in her belly already'.[2]

When the action "doth not end like an old play", it is tempting to see the separation as Shakespeare's rejection of the conventions of literature itself, as if from this point onward he is not writing a work of art but somehow showing us "life" directly. It is worth remembering, however, that he could in fact find many prototypes for such an ending in romance. Apart from Gascoigne's *The Adventures of Master F. J.* and Lyly's *Euphues*, which give us saddened retreats, there are more clear-cut analogues. In Malory's *Le Morte d'Arthur*, Sir Marhaus, Sir Gawain, and Sir Uweyn make an oath to separate from their chosen damsels and to return "that day twelve monthe". "And so they kissed and departed."[3] (Gawain's lady is lost and the other two, at the end of the twelve months, effect a permanent separation, which shows that we cannot be so sure of happiness in the world of romance as in comedy.) At the end of *The Parliament of Fowls*, the female eagle, wooed by three males, asks Nature to allow her to postpone her choice for a year. She advises the lusty suitors:

> Beth of good herte, and serveth alle thre.
> A yer is nat so longe to endure.[4]

Book I of *The Faerie Queene* ends with the Redcross Knight leaving his newlywed Una in order to pursue his quest of the Blatand Beast, "The which he shortly did, and Una left to mourne."[5] Certainly Shakespeare in *Love's Labour's Lost* is exhibiting a general wariness about the authenticity and validity of fictions, yet he is ironically, also drawing on a fictional model in doing so. Romance includes in its vision many separations and reunions, and it is often arbitrary which of the two events will be chosen to end the work. Comedy, on the other hand, characteristically closes with happy harmony. With the arrival of Marcade, a messenger whose forebears lie in Greek tragedy, Shakespeare stops writing comedy and begins to write romance. It seems a paradox in the light of unashamed fictiveness of this genre, but he is also representing something more "realistic" than we find in a comedy where Jack hath Jill and all will be well.

The little songs sung by the Worthies after the action, a timely lightening of the tone, continue the disengagement from the play's golden world. Nothing could be further from the pontifical words of the King at the beginning when declaring the plan for the academe. Instead of lofty abstractions like fame, death, time, honour and eternity, the songs modestly depict rapid vignettes of real life: the sight of flowers and the sounds of birds in spring, physical hardship in winter, evidenced by cold hands, frozen milk and red noses, with their homely, cosy compensations like the prospect of roasted crab-apples sizzling in a pot of ale while greasy Joan keels the pot. The songs accept, without any attempt at evaluation, the contradictions in the seasons: delight and sexual uncertainty in the spring, adversity and warmth in the winter. The repeated syntax, 'When . . . then . . . ' suggests the underlying idea that everything is 'fit in his place and time' (I. i. 98).[6] A new attitude towards time's open-endedness, and a new mode of expression (a ballad statement by an uncourtly, rustic voice outside the play world, rather than the dramatic utterance of a character in context), takes us further outside the self-contained fictional world of the play about protected university-types. The direction is appropriate to the overall ideas presented by the play, for the men have discovered that the cloistered attempt to discover truth is barren and offending against the law of nature, because, if they had listened, they would have known that 'it is the simplicity of man to hearken after the flesh'. They must accept the brazen uncertainties of the future before committing themselves to the world-without-end bargain of marriage.

Love's Labour's Lost is Shakespeare's first successful attempt to square up the moral problems raised by the narrative with the necessity for an ending. It is also his first considered attempt to fuse the comic expectation of an ending with the romance tendency towards endlessness. Inconclusive as it is, the play-world is brought to an end with a regretful explanation that the future is too long for a play. The final comment, whatever its authorial sanction, is teasing. 'You that way; we this way' is perhaps the final separation of the play-world (where the characters either go back into their fictional world and visit hospitals, or they take off their play clothes and become people like us) and our own world, as we leave the theatre and walk home, or close the book and prepare supper. Since our own minds must still be partially engaged with the fate of the courtiers, speculating upon whether they will marry or not at the end of a year, endlessness rolls before the worlds of fiction and of fact, despite the attainment of a temporary resting-place in both, the end of the play.

After showing a delicate mastery of the Lylian presentation of romance, ending with a careful compromise that balances and sets against each other the conflicting tensions raised in the action, Shakespeare could conceivably have gone on to remain within such a dramatic world. Instead, he chooses to take a slightly different course. In *A Midsummer Night's Dream* he partly repeats the experience, but he extends radically an element which is present in *Love's Labour's Lost* but not emphatically. In the *Dream* we are faced with the curious sense that the play is functioning fully within the conventional assumptions of romance, and yet also contemplating itself, in a self-conscious way, inviting us to explore the boundaries between romance and the reality outside the work of art. The play achieves such a double perspective by centering around the metaphor of the dream, and by making the ending of the play highly elusive and shifting. Here, we have a new dimension added to the 'endless ending'. Convinced by the illusion, we may remain within the world of the artifice; and yet simultaneously we are encouraged to disengage ourselves from the action, and contemplate it from a more rational distance. With this play, Shakespeare develops a critique of romance expectations, as he did in *Love's Labour's Lost,* but not yet so drastic a questioning as to imply that he is losing faith in the potency and utility of fictions. A more radical challenge is to be posed in later plays.

The elusiveness of *A Midsummer Night's Dream* as a whole can be appreciated when we simply try to locate where the actual ending of the play lies, as a point in the action. Aristotle would have some trouble specifying the point 'which is naturally after something itself, either as its necessary or usual consequent, and with nothing after it.'[7] Does the resolution lie in the awakening of Titania, the awakening of the lovers, the rout of Peter Quince's play or the fairies' benediction pronounced upon the marriage house? In this play which has so many wonderfully overlapping qualities, it is possible to see the inherent tendency of romantic comedy to give a vision of endlessness sustained in one long ending. In his first three scenes, Shakespeare characteristically presents three little societies one by one—the court, the artisans and the fairies—and although unexpected twists will occur, there is never much doubt where each is leading. The need to draw the strings together becomes a matter of urgency as early as III. ii:

My fairy lord, this must be done with haste,
For night's swift dragons cut the clouds full
   fast.

(III. ii. 378-9)

At the very end the dramatist shows some solicitude for the audience, as he gently allows each society the courtesy of its own farewell, as if acknowledging that we are reluctant to leave his fictional world:

And farewell, friends;
Thus Thisby ends;
Adieu, adieu, adieu.

. . . . .

Lovers, to bed; 'tis almost fairy time

. . . . .

Trip away; make no stay;

Meet me all by break of day.

. . . . .

So good night unto you all.
Give me your hands, if we be friends,
And Robin shall restore amends.

(V. i. 335-427 *passim*)

The ripples of farewells move outwards until they wash around the audience. Having seen what, at the time, the audience thought would be the last performance of Peter Brook's production of the play, I can testify to the strange sense of exhilaration, nostalgia and reluctance to leave, inspired in the audience by this rocking, endless ending.

The atmosphere of the play is created largely by the sustained use of the dream metaphor, and the ending is marked by the repeated idea of awakening. Hippolyta's compressed prediction at the beginning sets the direction:

Four days will quickly steep themselves in
   night;
Four nights will quickly dream away the time.

(I. i. 7-8)

So quickly does this happen that the four nights are telescoped into one, and the events packed into that night are 'swift as a shadow, short as any dream' (I. i. 144). There is even a trace of the medieval dream vision of the *Roman de la Rose*. The lovers, after entering the woods contemplating those doctrines of love that they 'could ever read, Could ever hear by tale of history' are confronted with situations which bring fictional statements to life in such an explicit way that we are reminded of Chaucer falling asleep over 'the Dreem of Scipioun' and dreaming of the parliament of fowls. The ending is made up of a series of awakenings. First is that of the fairy queen:

Oberon. Now, my Titania; wake you, my
   sweet queen.
Titania. My Oberon! What visions have I
   seen!

(IV. i. 72-3)

The wonder of romance is conveyed in the awakening of the four lovers. 'Half sleep, half waking' (IV. i. 146) they tell Theseus that overnight their feelings have changed, and they cannot tell how or why. They are not sure whether they are in the land of the waking or the dreaming:

Demetrius. These things seem small and
   undistinguishable,
Like far-off mountains turned into clouds.
Hermia. Methinks I see these things with

> parted eye,
> When everything seems double.
>
> (IV. i. 184-7)

It is impossible to be sure grammatically what the repeated 'these things' refers to (the events of the night? the lovers' present condition? Theseus's retinue?), and in the lovers' dazed state of bewilderment, it is unfair to enquire too closely. The experiences of the night and the present happenings of the morning seem unreal, the one displaced and distorted by the perspective of the other. Gradually the lovers mark the limits of what they think to be dream and reality by mentally 'pinching themselves', checking and synchronising the respective versions of the latest fact, the arrival of the Duke. Demetrius concludes:

> Why, then, we are awake; let's follow him;
> And by the way let us recount our dreams.
>
> (IV. i. 195-6)

They are left not only with hazy recollections of a strange, dream-like ordeal, but with some proof of its occurrence, Demetrius's new-found love for Helena. This identifiable vestige of an intangible experience further confuses the boundary between being awake and being asleep. It should be stressed, however, that the lovers have not been dreaming. We have watched their doings when they were under the sway of fairy power, and we must accept the truth of the events, even if we want to interpret it more as a figurative than literal truth, showing the volatile, dream-like caprice of young love.

Bottom likens his time with the fairy queen in the woods to 'a dream past the wit of man to say what dream it was' (IV. i. 204), but in his inimitable way he extends the experience to the status of 'a most rare vision'. His is no idle, deceptive dream, but a vision full of religious significance, as his confusion of *Corinthians* I, 2, 9 shows:

> The eye of man hath not heard, the ear of man hath not seen, man's hand is not able to taste, his tongue to conceive, nor his heart to report, what my dream was!
>
> (IV. i. 208-11)

The biblical version ends not with 'my dream' but with 'the things which God hath prepared for them that love him'. Bottom's wondering, respectful awe shows that he accepts the episode as a God-given insight into truth. In many ways, his choice of allusion is appropriate in the context of romance. In the biblical version, Paul is justifying faith in the Spirit as a mystery, contrasted with things accessible to mortal reason, which he describes as 'the wisdom of man', and which he subordinates to faith. In echoing this doctrine, Bottom unwittingly casts light on the action of *A Midsummer Night's Dream* and on the spirit in which we should approach literary romance. 'The wisdom of man' as voiced by Theseus can make nothing of the strange happenings in the forest, and he sees them as 'antique fables' and 'fairy toys' told by infatuated lovers who are as deranged as poets and madmen:

> ... the natural man receiveth not the things of the Spirit of God: for they are foolishness unto him: neither can he know them, because they are spiritually discerned.
>
> (I *Corinthians*, ii, 14)

We, who have witnessed the deeds of Oberon and Puck, have more faith in the mystery. But even for us, there remains the impenetrable and talismanic secret of the magic flowers. The humble love-in-idleness, simultaneously the secret of love and the speckled pansy, challenges us to dismiss it as a 'weak and idle theme', dares us to be so childish as to believe in its magical properties. And love is such a sub-rational affair that we dismiss the flower at our peril. Irrational, improbable and artificial as the events of romance may be, the mode is capable of carrying a 'great constancy' apprehensible by those willing to awaken their faith. At the same time, *A Midsummer Night's Dream* is a 'self-conscious' romance, since the contrary view, Theseus's voice of reason, finds its place alongside the mysterious motifs of true romance. The ending gives us a 'goodnight' from both Theseus and Puck.

The interlude, 'Pyramus and Thisbe', another story from romance, serves the double function of relaxing the tone into that of a happy wedding feast, and it creates yet another recession into a fictional world. 'It is nothing, nothing in the world' (V. i. 78) protests Philostrate, and indeed the play is 'like a tangled chain; nothing impaired, but all disordered' (V. i. 124). For that matter, though, the whole of Shakespeare's play is 'nothing' in its elusive insubstantiality. The interlude has all the old romance features: 'A lover that kills himself most gallant for love' (I. ii. 19), a lion (which appears in the *Arcadia* and *Rosalynde*), and a lady loved by the hero, moonlight (paralleled in the *Arcadia*, Montemayor's *Diana*, Sannazaro's *Arcadia*, and many other romances), but it has nothing so incredible as fairies or the transformation of a man into an ass. The artistic effect that Peter Quince aims at is close to what the *Dream* as a whole achieves:

> Gentles, perchance you wonder at this show;
> But wonder on, till truth make all things plain.
>
> (V. i. 126-7)

The ending, though hinging upon remorseless death instead of Ovid's metamorphosis of the lovers into the dark red berry of the mulberry tree, retrieves something for the future. Pyramus's soul is in the sky, and in good *Romeo and Juliet* fashion, 'the wall is down that parted their fathers' (V. i. 342). The differences between 'Pyramus and Thisbe' and the *Dream* as a whole, lie not in the materials, but in the respective attitudes to artifice. Ignoring such aspects as plausibility of conduct, consistency of atmosphere, truth of human responses and so on, Quince concentrates on matters which Shakespeare leaves to our 'imaginary forces', like bringing the moonlight onto the stage. The artisans make the same mistake as Frolick in *The Old Wives' Tale* when, hearing about the 'King or a lord, or a Duke that had a fair daughter', he worries about 'who drest his dinner then?'[8] They show unawareness of art as an illusion capable of creating a self-sufficient and convincing world which 'grows to something of great constancy, But howsoever strange and admirable' (V. i. 26-7). Like Theseus, they ignore the call to faith and imagination necessitated by the romance mode, hinted at by Bottom and Saint Paul. Perhaps this is why Theseus enjoys the play, whereas the imaginative Hippolyta is irritated by it.

The courtiers' ridicule of the players is directed mainly at the literal-mindedness of the mechanicals' attempts to create verisimilitude, but they do not realise a quiet irony at their own expense. The play of 'Pyramus and Thisbe', seen as a romance whose dénouement depends on chance, accident, and an unseen force of 'Fate', resembles the events which the lovers have themselves encountered in the woods. When Hermia extends to Helena her wish that 'good luck grant thee thy Demetrius' (I. i. 221), she speaks prophetically: it *is* good luck, no more, no less. In romance the actual result, death or marriage, is sometimes arbitrary, and these lovers are fortunate that the deities placed in temporary control over their destiny (and the permanent deity, the dramatist), are benevolent, while the 'Fates' ruling the lives of Pyramus and Thisbe are less sympathetic. The lovers have no right to criticise the genre of dramatic romance, and if they had the distance and insight of a Feste, each would admit that 'I was one, sir, in this interlude'.[9] Even Theseus cannot complain of the seething brains and shaping fantasies of poets, for without them he would never have existed. Such thoughts are whimsical but, as well as illustrating Shakespeare's apparent lifelong obsession with the sin of ingratitude, they seem to be invited by the play itself. Its series of overlapping endings folds the play inwards in a series of receding artifices, until we wonder whether the life which the play relinquishes us to is yet another vision, 'No more yielding but a dream'.

The Merchant of Venice gives a different compromise between the comic ending and the romance desire for endlessness. It is again debateable what we call the ending, for there are two distinct dramatic climaxes, each followed by quieter, anti-climactic sections. The first climax is the scene in which Bassanio chooses the leaden casket and plights his troth to Portia (III. ii). The scene is ceremonial and hushed, full of rapt expressiveness of love and joy:

> O love, be moderate, allay thy ecstasy,
> In measure rain thy joy, scant this excess!
> I feel too much thy blessing. Make it less,
> For fear I surfeit.
>
> (III. ii. 111-4)

Bassanio likens his confusion to the effect in a crowd of a prince's speech,

> Where every something, being blent together,
> Turns to a wild of nothing, save of joy
> Express'd and not express'd.
>
> (III. ii. 182-4)

Nerissa happily cries 'Good joy, my lord and lady', and she immediately wins a husband in Gratiano. They begin to discuss the feast which will celebrate the two marriages, and they even joke about who will have the first child. If the prime issue were the marriage of Portia, the play is more or less over at this point, and there are all the trappings, the 'wonder', of the comic ending in the treatment of the scene. The rest of the play is about married love rather than courtship, and even in this context, the course of true love does not run smooth.

The action continues with the news of Antonio's financial ruin. From here on, we build towards the second climax, the confrontation of Portia and Shylock in the courtroom (IV. i). The development might be interpreted in different ways. As many critics have noted,[10] the play presents a running debate about value, measured by feelings or by finance. Even Portia is described in monetary terms as the golden fleece, 'nothing undervalu'd To Cato's daughter, Brutus' Portia' (I. i. 165-6), and many Jasons come in quest of her. Even Bassanio comes as a fortune-hunter. This makes the marriage less crucial than the resolution of the clash between conceptions of value based on money, epitomised most starkly in the actions of Shylock, and conceptions of value based on love and friendship, belonging to Portia in Belmont. Alternatively, we could place Portia herself even closer to the centre, and say that the play shows her developing in character from weary fatalism generated by the mercenary aims of her suitors and the lax, aristocratic boredom of one who cannot 'choose' her destiny ('so is the will of a living daughter curb'd by the will of a dead father' (I. ii. 18-22)), to the point where, after the 'lott'ry' has been settled, she takes her own future into her own hands. With adaptable independence, she takes on the barrister's role and dominates proceedings. It is she also who brings news to Antonio of the successes of his argosies, and as if she has herself become now a representative of powers of providence, she will not disclose 'by what strange accident' she chanced on the letter. (More cynically, however, we might suspect that she has paid the bill herself, with her massive wealth.) No matter what overall structure we choose to find in the play, it is a peculiar comedy in that it keeps going long after the celebration of marriage. Like the romances, it presents a vision of cycles moving from joy to disaster to joy, into the future.

The play keeps going even after the triumph in the courtroom. Act Five, so easily seen as a flat anticlimax after the tenseness of the struggle against Shylock, seems designed to retrieve the ethic of love after the severe challenge made to it, but even so, there are odd tonalities. The lyrical aria between Lorenzo and Jessica as they sit upon the bank watching the moonlight and recalling mythical lovers, strikes a note of idealism, but it thickens in a kind of cloying self-indulgence as the music plays. The poetry seems to mark time, to the point of stagnation, with a waiting expectancy, and 110 lines pass while all that happens is the setting of the moon. Normally, the tempo of a romance or comedy quickens after the climax, but here it moves with a deliberate slowness. There is even a touch of disease in the air. "This night methinks is but the daylight sick." (V. i. 124) Suddenly, however, as Portia is reunited with Bassanio, a cascade of puns on 'light' switches the play into a bantering tone that lasts until the end. Unfortunately, even this climax cannot be seen unequivocally as the joyful festivity of reconciliation, for the jokes hide barbs. The two pairs of lovers have their first quarrel when they discuss 'the rings', and even though we are confident that the women are simply playing a game, there seems to be an element of self-righteous power-domination, in the way they keep the men on edge for so long. Is this Shakespeare's sardonic prediction of the future of their marriages, in their bickering over trivia? For the women, there is an important point at stake, for they are seeking to establish the principle of fidelity in relationships. They indignantly harp on the 'false heart' that will give away a betrothal ring, as if its value is no more than mercenary: "I'll die for't but some woman had the ring." (V. i. 208) There plays about the rings themselves an ambiguity, for they are regarded by the men as mere trinkets, by the women as profoundly significant symbols. Bassanio with shamefaced exasperation splutters that they have given to the lawyers the rings given by Portia and Nerissa:

> Sweet Portia,
> If you did know to whom I gave the ring,
> If you did know for whom I gave the ring,
> And would conceive for what I gave the ring,
> And how unwillingly I left the ring,
> When nought would be accepted but the ring,
> You would abate the strength of your
>   displeasure.
>
>   (V. i. 192-8)

The interchange demonstrates anything but an easy, affectionate exercise of romantic forgiveness, considering that the ring is an ancient motif of recognition from romance. In this play of "struggle",[11] even reconciliation between lovers has its distresses. In this case the women, when they admit that they were the lawyers, use the rings to inform the men that they have all shared in the arduous and frightening trial in the courtroom, emphasising the mutuality of suffering in love. The loss of the rings also threatens momentarily the happiness of the two couples, and to this extent the women use the episode to symbolise the trust and fidelity necessary to the shared quality of love. By shaming the men, they also establish some dominance in the relationships. At the same time, Bassanio's refrain 'the ring' brings laughter to a theatre audience, and the laughter sounds a challenge to a convention in which tiny trinkets may somehow embody experiences and relationships. *Othello* takes the hint past harmless parody. The loss of a handkerchief, an even more mundane object, has disastrous consequences, because of the symbolical value accorded it by one character who pins his faith on the romantic vision of life. In the comic world, the potentially tragic chain of events is arrested by a timely disclosure, and a return to common sense, but there is a lurking suspicion that the happy state may not be permanent.

If *The Merchant of Venice* gives us an ending distinguished by its capacity to 'keep going' into and through incipient disaster, it also excludes one character from the *bonhomie* of festivity. Shylock is the clearest example of what Northrop Frye calls the 'scapegoat' figure, upon whose distress the comedy is secured. Compassionate actors and critics have seen Shylock's fate as too harsh for a comedy, but in the moral stresses of the play it is defensible. Shakespeare, by the very direction of his comedy, has played advocate on behalf of love and forgiveness, though he has tested them both thoroughly, and he has placed himself against a devil who respects only the 'compulsion' of the law without recognising any concept of mercy:

> My deeds upon my head! I crave the law,
> The penalty and forfeit of my bond.
>   (IV. i. 201-2)

The brazen world of legality and money is directly challenging the ethics of the golden world of feelings. The integrity of the writer forces him to provide a genuine resolution, like Sidney in the *Old Arcadia,* without evading the terms of the struggle. Portia must attack and defeat Shylock with legalistic arguments, for he respects no others. The Jew has placed himself outside a society based on human values, and he resists all appeals to sympathy and forgiveness:

> By my soul I swear
> There is no power in the tongue of man
> To alter me.
>   (IV. i. 235-17)

His implacable ruthlessness is condemned even by the judge, who feels that at law he must uphold the Jew's claim. Having defeated Shylock with his own form of reasoning, by logic-chopping and mercenary legalism, it is not only just but imperative that Portia, on behalf of the forces of love, must extract the full penalty. In fact, Antonio extends to Shylock the 'mercy' of allowing him to live, and giving him the use of half his goods during his lifetime. The deeper irony, of course, is that the defendants themselves are not entirely innocent of Shylock's offences. Portia's suitors have been mercenary, including Bassanio, and Antonio makes his living as a speculative merchant. The crowing rudeness of Gratiano in the courtroom is considerably less than generous. And Shylock himself has explained that his tactics are valid in a world where Jews are few and Christians are many:

> O father Abram, what these Christians are,
> Whose own hard dealings teaches them
>   suspect
> The thoughts of others!
>
> (I. iii. 155-7)

The tenuous answer is, that whereas Shylock is consistently mercenary and revengeful, the Christians are redeemable because of their basic ethics of human value. Bassanio, for all his faults, does learn from the *milieu* of Belmont, and chooses the leaden casket, instead of consistently seeing human worth in terms of monetary worth. Because of their implication in the Jew's guilt, however, the Christians cannot afford to be complacent. They should see his defeat as an event which exorcises an element in their own society. Shakespeare is trying to establish a principle or concept which is not represented wholly in any one character, and it is the absence of an embodiment of this principle which forces the dramatist to test with vigilance every action and assumption. As a consequence, Antonio is left alone at the end, a minor scapegoat. Because his trade is money, he is given a monetary reward for his generosity, but he must endure the loneliness of a man who does not base his life *fully* on an ethic of love. The ending of the play must 'keep going' because the basic threats to its world are still at large, just as the Blatant Beast is at large after Book VI of *The Faerie Queene,* and more aptly, as Mammon is untouched by his encounter with Sir Guyon.

After the three previous comedies which present variations on the 'endless ending', *As You Like It* returns to a straightforward celebratory ending in the fashion of Robert Greene and *Henry the Fifth.* Even the play's closely followed source, Lodge's *Rosalynde,* is not so weightily concluded as the play. The dramatist slows down the tempo of the last action, expanding what was a rushed and relieved summary in the prose work, into a slow, ceremonial occasion, noticeable after the chatty conversationalism and pace of the rest. The two or three pages at the end of *Rosalynde,* where the interest shifts from love to the national welfare as the Duke triumphantly leads his men back to overthrow the tyrant, are eliminated in the play and replaced by a miraculous conversion of the bad Duke when he enters the skirts of the forest. Even he is brought into the fold, and poses no future threat. There are some anticipations of trouble. Jaques bequeaths to Touchstone 'wrangling; for thy loving voyage Is but for two months victuall'd' (V. iv. 185), recalling for a moment Rosalind's advice that maids are May when they woo, but the sky changes when they are wives. Jaques himself, remembering Euphues, serenely leaves the wedding feast for sober contemplation. His retreat is the 'tremor in the balance' described by Anne Barton, but it is not allowed to cause us distress.[12] Nothing really threatens the moment of 'true delights', and the aesthetic finality is as marked as the emotional:

> First, in this forest let us do these ends
> That here were well begun and well begot.
>
> (V. iv. 164-5)

Shakespeare even pulls the trick of introducing a new character, Hymen, to establish the mystical nature of the marriages. He has no need of this supernatural introduction. In Lodge's work, the capable resourcefulness of 'the amorous Girle-boy'[13] holds the situation in firm control after she reaches the forest, and she carefully prepares and effects the *coup de théatre* in which all she need do is display her true identity, to bring about the happy ending. No supernatural influence is needed. Earlier in the story, the disguised Rosalynde comforts her lover by saying that she has a friend 'that is deeply experienst in Negromancy and Magicke, what art can do shall be acted for thine aduantage',[14] but this is simply a reassuring fiction without significance for the plot. Shakespeare is taking up Lodge's hint of magic and he makes the ending *seem* like a spell. Rosalind decides the time has come to draw the couples to the ark in marriage, after Celia and Oliver have vowed their love. Orlando is showing impatience with the charade, and needs more tangible reassurance:

> *Rosalind.* Why, then, to-morrow I cannot
>   serve your turn for
> Rosalind?
> *Orlando.* I can live no longer by thinking.
> *Rosalind.* I will weary you, then, no longer
>   with idle talking . . .
>
> (V. ii. 46-8)

This is a curiously intense moment, for both recognise—Orlando with irritation, Rosalind with disappointed pique—that they are no longer playing games of words and disguises, but playing in earnest with their future lives. With businesslike briskness, Ganimede promises to bring together Rosalind and Orlando,

Phebe and Silvius, on the morrow when Celia and Oliver are to be married. The claim is that magical power is involved:

> Believe then, if you please, that I can do strange things. I have, since I was three year old, convers'd with a magician, most profound in his art and yet not damnable.
>
> (V. ii. 57-60)

The claim is emphasised by repetition:

> *Orlando.* Speak'st thou in sober meanings?
> *Rosalind.* By my life, I do; which I tender dearly, though I say I am a magician.
>
> (V. ii. 64-6)

Although sceptical, Orlando is inclined to believe the story:

> I sometimes do believe and sometimes not.
>
> . . . . .
>
> But, my good lord, this boy is forest-born,
> And hath been tutor'd in the rudiments
> Of many desperate studies by his uncle,
> Whom he reports to be a great magician,
> Obscured in the circle of this forest.
>
> (V. iv. 3 and V. iv. 30-4)

The repeated emphasis on the supposed magical powers of Ganimede establishes a sense of romance mystery, even if we detect a Puckish joke by Shakespeare that it is he, as dramatist, who is Rosalind's tutor, who can bring about whatever ending he wishes. The several sets of phrases that suddenly break out, take on the force of incantations, as if all the characters are spell-bound: 'And so am I for . . .'; 'I will marry/satisfy/content you . . . to-morrow'; 'You say that you'll . . .'; 'Keep you your word . . .' (V. ii. 75-101). Rosalind breaks the spell, for it is too early: 'Pray you, no more of this; 'Tis like the howling of Irish wolves against the moon' (V. ii. 103-4). But the spell-like tone is re-established in the final scene. The formality with which Rosalind and Celia are presented in their own persons by Hymen, a divine figure mysteriously produced and accompanied by 'still music', takes us into yet another mode, reminiscent not so much of the magic spell as the neoplatonic axioms of marriage as an earthly analogue of divine harmony:

> Then is there mirth in heaven,
>   When earthly things made even
>   Atone together.
>
> (V. iv. 102-4)

After the heightened, ceremonial song of Hymen in praise of marriage, there is hushed economy in the interchange, as Rosalind is recognised, and reconciled with her father and lover. The patterned, rocking repetitions are noticeable after the flexible speech rhythms of the dialogue before this final scene:

> *Rosalind.* [*To Duke*] To you I give myself, for I am yours.
> [*To Orlando*] To you I give myself, for I am yours.
> *Duke Senior.* If there be truth in sight, you are my daughter.
> *Orlando.* If there be truth in sight, you are my Rosalind.
> *Phebe.* If sight and shape be true,
> Why then my love adieu!
> *Rosalind.* I'll have no father, if you be not he;
> I'll have no husband, if you be not he;
> Nor ne'er wed woman, if you be not she.
>
> (V. iv. 110-18)

Only Phebe's plaintive wail (the shift in tone indicated by the different metre), hints that the identity of 'Ganimede', understood by the audience throughout, is now clear also to the characters. The masque-like stasis of the wooing tableau is broken on the entrance of Jaques de Boys, to report the situation outside the woods, and an air of busy activity is resumed with rustic revelry.

Unlike Viola at the end of *Twelfth Night*, Rosalind retires, takes off her disguise and returns, before the betrothals. Whereas in the prose account, the narrator can simply tell us this, and bring her back without more ado, the dramatist must fill a vacuum while Rosalind changes, and attention falls on the chatter of Touchstone. When she returns, the tone has altered. She is now a limited character, Rosalind the court-dweller, and no longer the forest-born magician. This is one reason why Hymen takes over the role of controlling deity, imposing upon the woman a limited place in the human pattern of betrothals, after her period of freedom in disguise. In fact, she does not say a word after the wedding song sung by Hymen, until the epilogue. The case reverses that of Viola. Rosalind has been liberated by her masculine disguise, able to speak her mind and exuberantly act out her impulses, and when she takes off the disguise, there is inevitably a narrowing of the range of emotions and activities expected from her. Rosalind is literally brought down to earth, and the exercise of destiny which she has held in the forest, must now be yielded up to a more coercive form of providence—social conventions, as represented in the conservatism of the comic ending.

The figure of Hymen may have been suggested to Shakespeare by Lyly's gods, but the dramatic function is different. Hymen does not adjudicate but presides; the character does not influence the plot but indicates the existence of a mystical hierarchy above the human courtship. The marriage is in this case no compromise but an inevitable outcome of expectation. Hymen does not belong to any characterised society like the fairies in the *Dream* and the gods in Lyly. The best comparison for the scene, I think, is Spenser's *Epithalamion*. Both are intended as offerings to the socially sanctioned deity of married love, in order to elevate the occasion above individual common experience:

> And thou great Iuno, which with awful might
> The lawes of wedlock still dost patronize,
> And the religion of the faith first plight
> With sacred rites hast taught to solemnize:
> And eeke for comfort often called art
> Of women in their smart,
> Eternally bind thou this louely band,
> And all thy blessings vnto vs impart.
>
> . . . . .
>
> And thou fayre Hebe, and thou Hymen free,
> Grant that it may so be.
> Til which we cease your further prayse to sing,
> Ne any woods shal answer, nor your Echo ring.[15]

Spenser's poem, of course, is written throughout in this reverential, unhurried way, whereas Shakespeare has to make a radical shift of tone in order to achieve such a plateau in this play. He creates in a new way the sense of endlessness demanded by romance, by lifting the events of the betrothal from the temporal flux into the realm of stable social harmony. The pains of courtship, its bullying, its strategical, testing lies (signalled by Rosalind's disguise), its moments of animal rapacity and its sharp distresses, are all gathered into a moment when the *significance* of the event is celebrated. For a short time, the ending of *As You Like It* is an endless monument to the capacity of betrothal to clarify, surpass and consummate a period of time by establishing a form of stability.

Rosalind's epilogue snatches back for a moment the abrasiveness of prose after the ceremoniousness of poetry, as a reminder of what has led up to the betrothals. She speaks now not as a representative of fortune, nor in the figure of Ganimede who had been liberated by disguise to speak about women from the outside. She speaks for the dramatist who has been playing games of invention upon us: 'My way is to conjure you'. As if to emphasise the mischievous element of feigning throughout the play, Rosalind suddenly speaks as a boy-actor: 'If I were a woman . . .' 'If' is the language of hypothesis, summing up the conjectured likelihoods of the golden world which are pressed upon us by the conjuring of the dramatist.[16]

By making us now aware of the strategy he has been employing, Shakespeare takes us a step away from the magical delights of the marriage scene and from the jubilant pastime in the forest of Arden, and allows us to slip back into the world without close.

In *Much Ado About Nothing* Shakespeare presents yet another variation on the comic/romance ending. The nature of the experiment might be summed up by saying that he manages to fuse two different kinds of material which are potentially discrepant, and he does so by giving equal attention to two sets of relationships. The "love" between Claudio and Hero comes from the world of romance, although in essence the presentation threatens our belief in romantic sentiment. The love between Beatrice and Benedick mingles aspects of the rough and tumble English comic tradition (*Gammer Gurton's Needle* and *the Taming of a Shrew*, supplemented by Shakespeare's own *The Shrew*) with something we might call a more realistic social observation. Paradoxically, just as the romance plot comes to challenge romance itself, so the "realistic" plot represents a far more solid and trustworthy basis for romantic love between man and woman. The paradoxes emerge partly out of the blend itself, for we are encouraged to compare and contrast the behavior and feelings of the two sets of lovers. The ending introduces new complexities.

Partly it is the strong definition of a total society in Messina which allows Shakespeare to encapsulate the two kinds of material in a single focus. In this little society, with its constant gossiping, eavesdropping, "noting", and suspicion,[17] no relationship goes unnoticed. Such prying vigilance eventually exposes weaknesses in the literary, romantic ethic of love based on appearances, while fostering a strong-minded wariness about the precariousness of relationships in the mature, open-eyed lovers. But eventually the tides merge with each other at least for one moment in the flow of "wonder" which marks the prototypical romance ending, followed by the ebb of circumstantial explanation to be delivered after the play is over:

> FRIAR: All this amazement can I qualify,
> When, after that the holy rites are ended,
> I'll tell you of fair Hero's death.
> Meantime let wonder seem familiar,
> And to the chapel let us presently.
>
> (V.iv.67-71)

The formula hardly varies from play to play, although the tone of the ending is profoundly different. In this play, for example, we should not underestimate the effect of the social ethos, created partly even by the purely comic characters, Dogberry and his little group of Keystone cops. They, the official "watchers", prefer to sleep while the other characters are scrutinizing each other closely, and yet they inadvertently reveal a truth which nobody else sees. They mangle words while their courtly betters are speaking so elegantly and wittily, and yet they are able to communicate in far more honest and straightforward terms than others are capable of.

The Hero-Claudio plot has almost purely romantic sources, ranging from the ancient Greek erotic romance, *Chaereas and Callirhoe*, to the sixteenth century *Orlando Furioso* by Ariosto, and stories by Bandello, together with contemporary Italian plays.[18] It is identified by the most time-honored conventions of romance such as love at first sight, the bed trick, the false death, and the apparent resurrection. We find the characteristic blend of tones (expressed in poetic rhetoric whereas the rest is in prose), ranging from the language of sentimental love to the somber dirge, artificial in expression but full of tragic feeling:

> Pardon, goddess of the night,
> Those that slew thy virgin knight;
> For the which, with songs of woe,
> Round about her tomb they go.
>   Midnight, assist our moan;
>   Help us to sigh and groan,
>   Heavily, heavily.
> Graves, yawn, and yield your dead,
>
>   Till death be uttered,
>   Heavily, heavily.
>   (V.iii.12-21)

We would expect such a chivalric, romantic plot to be full of the generous, optimistic, and amorous vision which we associate with the mode. But by this time Shakespeare is beginning more than just to hint at a retreat from romance conviction, and there is much to make us suspicious. Claudio is a soldier, and conducts his love affair somewhat like one, plotting, campaigning, and eventually bullying his lover. He loses faith in her fidelity almost instantaneously on the basis of a rumor without even bothering to investigate, and refusing to believe in her chastity. His language at this point is rejective and self-centered:

> But fare thee well, most foul, most fair!
>   Farewell,
> Thou pure impiety and impious purity!
> Tor thee I'll lock up all the gates of love,
> And on my eyelids shall conjecture hang,
> To turn all beauty into thoughts of harm,
> And never shall it more be gracious.
>   (IV.i.102-7)

Something has gone very sour when romance sentiment can so rapidly become untrusting and ungenerous, and we begin to glimpse the origins of a Troilus and an Othello, both so romantic in their affection, so vituperative in their mistrust of female sexuality.

Even the ending does not retrieve the purity of wonder, because Claudio seems ready again to fall in love with the appearance of Hero, without really showing that he has learned much about himself or about the woman. "Which is the lady I must seize upon" (V.iv.53) and "Why, then she's mine" (V.iv.55) are hardly reassuring statements in their content, and far from wondering in tone.

Beatrice and Benedick, presumably older and more experienced, appear to have abandoned romantic expectations. Each advises the younger person of the same sex against commitment to love:

> CLAUDIO: Can the world buy such a jewel?
> BENEDICK: Yea, and a case to put it into. But speak you this with a sad brow, or do you play the flouting Jack to tell us Cupid is a good hare-finder, and Vulcan a rare carpenter? Come, in what key shall a man take you to go in the song?
>
> CLAUDIO: In mine eye she is the sweetest lady that ever I look'd on.
> BENEDICK: I can see yet without spectacles, and I can see no such matter.
>   (I.i.155-62)

Benedick's mockery of conventions from romance literature is matched by Beatrice's debunking tone when she advises the younger woman:

> For, hear me, Hero: wooing, wedding, and repenting, is as a Scotch jig, a measure, and a cinquepace; the first suit is hot and hasty, like a Scotch jig, and full as fantastical; the wedding, mannerly modest, as a measure, full of state and ancientry; and then comes repentance, and, with his bad legs, falls into the cinquepace faster and faster, till he sink into his grave.
>   (II.i.60-7)

We rapidly gather, however, that these two are using the tone of superior world-wisdom to conceal (even from themselves) their own feelings, and by dwelling upon their mutual determination *not* to marry, they reveal ironically to all around that they are preoccupied with each other with a strength of subliminal feeling that must culminate in marriage. This is precisely what happens, after Don Pedro and his accomplices plot to pull down the defenses of wit a wariness so cleverly built up by the characters themselves. There is a clear parallel in the way that one brother, the taciturn Don John, destroys a relationship through subterfuge, while Don Pedro, through equal manipulativeness, "creates" a love-affair, as if they represent respectively he malignant and benign operations of a single social strategy which controls and determines personal relationships. Indeed, one might even see them a personifications of Fortune and Providence in the romance world. Another mark of the society is a strict segregation of the men and the women into different camps, and communication between the two must be conducted at a distance, either through conventions, through aggressive wit, or sometimes through deviously coded messages (employed most subtly between Beatrice and Don Pedro). The destructive potential is such a state of sexual apartheid is unleashed over the affair of Hero's alleged unchastity, and the men and the women retreat into belligerent positions of separate loyalties. The situation is of great importance to Beatrice and Benedick since their new-found access to a mutual and direct communication is at stake. It should already be clear that the play is neither affirming nor challenging romance conventions alone. It is a play about social conventions themselves, in which courtly manners and literary conceptions of love are included but are not the totality. Under such complex conditions, the ending of the comedy cannot possible be a simple one.

In attempting to break the deadlock between men and women that exists after the broken marriage, Beatrice proposes something which challenges romance conventions and the comic ending. She asks Benedick to cross the picket lines and join the women, and she does so in a chilling manner. When she requires him to prove his love for her and to "Kill Claudio!" (IV.i.287), she is laying down a condition which will ensure her own future confidence in Benedick, but she is also threatening the fabric of the comic ending. It is a challenge to the playwright to recognize his options, a potential invitation to be consistent to the moral vision of a play which has presented Claudio as reprehensibly untrusting, untrustworthy, and undeserving of the woman's love. The moment had come in *Love's Labour's Lost* and almost in *The Two Gentlemen of Verona,* and again it is not allowed to destroy the comic vitality. We are presented with a much safer and more comfortable resolution with the "resurrection" of Hero from her grave. But just for an instance we are dared to contemplate directly the potential dishonesty involved in manipulating the comic ending, the element of arbitrariness involved, all in the context of a play which throws a somewhat sardonic light on the manipulative, coercive tendencies of society itself. However, as the chasm yawns, it is equally quickly covered over by the timely willingness of Benedick to assist in the comic compromise, and all is well. By a hair's breadth, romance wins its battle against social realism. The moment hardly exists outside the time it takes to says the lines, for it stands so far from the providential benevolence of the romance fictions which create the plot and which lead us to expect a happy ending. The momentary tremor, however, does rapidly open a vein which we will find running through *Twelfth Night,* a suspicion that the comic, romance world is fragile, impermanent, and vulnerable.

Much Ado, a play full of wonderfully functional parallels and contrasts in the structure, turns upon an unexpectedly archetypal distinction between night and day, for as the malevolent deeds are done by darkness, the benevolent ones are done under the sun-ripened honeysuckle. The point of change, marking the delicate balance, comes at a significant moment after the "burial" of Hero:

> DON PEDRO: Good morrow, masters; put your torches out;
> The wolves have prey'd; and look, the gentle day,
> Before the wheels of Phoebus, round about
> Dapples the drowsy east with spots of grey.
> (V.ii.24-7)

In *Twelfth Night,* Shakespeare returns to the formula for ending *The Comedy of Errors,* coincidence. No one character has the special knowledge needed to end the confusions, and it must be left to the whirligig of time to bring its own revenges. All that is needed is the physical proximity of the twins, and it is simply a matter of time before this happens. The wonder of recognition in the romance world fills the spectators, who at first 'throw a strange regard' (V. i. 204) upon Sebastian and Viola. Duke Orsino exclaims in amazement:

> One face, one voice, one habit, and two persons!
> A natural perspective, that is and is not.
> (V. i. 208-9)

Olivia's response is 'Most wonderful' (V. i. 217). As the truth dawns, there is the feeling of awakening from a dream, for each character is at one and the same time, an outsider and a participant, seeing double, as through a 'natural perspective'.

The source for *Twelfth Night,* Rich's short, Italianate romance, 'Of Apolonius and Silla', does not climax with such eloquent simplicity. The Viola-figure tears off her clothes to the waist and reveals her sex—a gesture which might happen in a prose work but hardly on the stage. The responses of Julina (Olivia in the play), who is pregnant by the person she thought was Silvio, is one of Rich's wry touches, as she 'did now thinke her selfe to be in a worse case than euer she was before, for now she knewe not whom to chalenge to be the father of her childe',[19] and she departs full of grief. It is only later that the real Silvio appears and in remorse returns to Julina. Meanwhile, the Duke's response to Silla's disrobing is first of all an emotional one—he is 'amased'—and then he becomes aware of the moral implications of the situation, recognising that Silla is 'the branche of all vertue', that he has wronged her, and that her 'liberalitie . . . can neuer bee sufficiently rewarded'. Impressed by the love she has exhibited towards him, he 'rewards' her patience by marrying her. The marriage is a result of Apolonius's perception into Silla's true worth. By displaying her womanhood, she has forced him to notice it. The news of the marriage, which 'seemed so wonderfull and strange', spreads through Greece, and when Julina and Silvio are reunited, the former is 'so rauished with ioye, that she knewe not whether she were awake, or in some dreame'. A final sentence sums up the formal completion of the story:

> And thus, Silvio hauing attained a noble wife and Silla, his sister, her desired husband, thei passed the residue of their daies with such delight as those that haue accomplished the perfection of their felicities.[20]

The differences between the two accounts are important. Rich seems more interested in the intricacy of unravelling the knot, squeezing each incident dry for homely and ironic detail. The brisk narration of the ending shows that it is of less interest to Rich than the complicated manoeuvring during the courtship. Shakespeare's scene is built upon a simpler formula, but it is presented with much more lingering and patient attention, before relaxing. His climax is also more richly amplified in its range of emotional responses, as each character sees the moment as a product of the past. There is Sebastian's poignant glimpse of the past:

> I had a sister
> Whom the blind waves and surges have
>   devour'd:
>   (V. i. 220-1)

while Viola fears her brother is a spirit, 'come to fright us' (V. i. 227-8), and she anxiously tries to corroborate the story by the physical evidence of moles and mathematical calculations. There is a third vital difference. Rich leaves no loose ends. His people are married for good reasons and live happily ever after. Viola in the play, however, projects the formal close into the future when she shall put on woman's clothing:

> If nothing lets to make us happy both
> But this my masculine usurp'd attire,
> Do not embrace me till each circumstance
> Of place, time, fortune, do cohere and jump
> That I am Viola.
>   (V. i. 241-5)

The Duke briefly acts as spokesman for the moral point of view when he says of Sebastian, 'right noble is his blood', but then he frames his proposal to Viola, not in the rigorously moral terms of Rich's Duke, but in a more or less aesthetic desire to 'have share in this most happy wreck' (V. i. 258). He does not profess present love for her, only a desire to see her in woman's weeds, when presumably he will love her.

His final speech again draws attention to a problem evaded by the prose writer, that Viola cannot truly be Orsino's lover, or even a woman, until she don a woman's clothes:

> Cesario, come;
> For so you shall be while you are a man;
> But when in other habits you are seen,
> Orsino's mistress, and his fancy's queen.
>   (V. i. 371-4)

Perhaps there is an implication here that Orsino has at last learned to restrain his self-indulgent feelings so that he can see the truth with an accurate eye (or does 'his *fancy's* queen' spell danger?); or perhaps the point is the formal one, that the comedy will not properly end until the solemn combination shall be made, a quiet hint that the future is not so closed off and womb-like as Rich has made it sound.[21] It is a dramatic necessity for Viola to wait until after the play has finished to change her clothes and 'become' a woman, but Shakespeare emphasises the point in such a way that it reinforces the idea of a woman trapped inside disguise and a social identity. Rosalind escapes by going offstage and changing her clothes, before joining the new social pattern in a more limited role. Viola remains at the end, as throughout, trapped by the situation. One wonders momentarily about the position of Maria at the end, in the light of the opportunism and off-handedness of Sir Toby's drunken proposition, 'Come by and by to my chamber' (IV. ii. 69). We learn that he has married her 'in recompence' for devising the joke on Malvolio (V. i. 351), a sardonic reflection on the 'reward' in the source. This betrothal seems to be based either on a drunken whim or upon a joke played on somebody else, neither of which seems a good basis, especially after Toby has already tried to make a match between Maria and Sir Andrew.

A further disquieting note is struck by Malvolio's parting snarl, 'I'll be reveng'd on the whole pack of you' (V. i. 364), throwing into relief the fact that part of the comic effect ('loude laughter' rather than 'soft smiling' or delight) has been built upon the darkness of his imprisonment and his painful awareness, that either he is mad, or the world is. For a moment, the sympathy of Olivia turns upon the audience a strong hint that its glee at Malvolio's predicament has been as nasty as the trick itself:

> Alas, poor fool, how have they baffl'd thee!
>
> . . . . .
>
> He hath been most notoriously abus'd.
>   (V. i. 356 and 365)

Our complicity in the practical joking is reflected in the uneasy reaction of Sir Toby's entourage who, quite safely detached in their capacity as onlookers, begin to acquire a conscience about Malvolio's suffering, as the drunkenness of night turns into the hangover of the morning after. Toby begins to wish he 'were well rid of this knavery' and he, with Maria and Andrew, are absent from the final moments, perhaps in penitent hiding. Fabian tries to excuse his cronies by pleading the general happiness of the occasion:

> Good madam, hear me speak,
> And let no quarrel nor no brawl to come
> Taint the condition of this present hour,
> Which I have wond'red at.
>
>   (v. i. 342-5)

None the less, Malvolio's threat has already forecast a 'brawl to come' that is inescapable. As is the case with the major characters, Fabian is trying to evade the consequences that the brazen world holds, and he prefers to live in the old tales told by knitters in the sun. With slight uneasiness he explains the trick played against Malvolio:

> How with a sportful malice it was follow'd
> May rather pluck on laughter than revenge,
> If that the injuries be justly weigh'd,
> That have on both sides pass'd.
>
>   (v. i. 353-5)

He suggests that Malvolio's pride alone has been hurt, and that his puritanical austerity, a threat to the 'cakes and ale' of the comic world, deserved its fate. But Malvolio's parting cry lingers, and it refers to the future rather than the 'justly weigh'd' moral deserts of the past.

Feste's song at the end is fragmentary in sense, and equivocal in tone. The final verse cheerfully sums up the idea that the golden, fictional world is now closed, and that more unpleasant facts, held at bay during the play, await us:

> A great while ago the world begun,
>   With hey, ho, the wind and the rain;
> But that's all one, our play is done,
>   And we'll strive to please you every day.

As in the songs at the end of *Love's Labour's Lost,* we are tempted to see a disengagement from art leading the audience back to the reality outside the theatre. But there is a weary shrug in 'But that's all one', as if the speaker hardly has the energy or the desire to draw into any rational relationship the vast distances of time outside the play and the limited existence of its characters. The disengagement in the *Dream* is much more gradual and gentle, equally generous to both worlds. In the first four verses of the song there is a sardonic and depressing progression from the foolishness of childhood's illusory delights, the suspiciousness of early manhood, post-marital *ennui,* and finally the drunken, vacuous head of middle-age. To underline the wearily fatalistic outlook comes the refrain, 'For the rain it raineth every day'. It is impossible to pin a particular significance or meaning upon the song, but its atmosphere is one of disconsolate melancholy. It picks up a tone struck particularly in the jaded, spiritless and post-drunken, satiated weariness of Sir Toby Belch at the end of the night of debauchery:[22] I would we were well rid of this knavery . . . Come by and by to my chamber." It reminds us that the 'going-on power of life' can be as depressing and meaningless as death itself, and that this is a devastating answer to the willed illusion of an 'improbable fiction' (III. iv. 122). Golden lads and lasses must, like chimney-sweepers, come to dust.

Notes

[1] Almost all modern critics stress the significance of this moment, but see especially Bobbyan Roesen, who demonstrates how the denouement is carefully prepared for by muted reference to death: "*Love's Labour's Lost*", *Shakespeare Quarterly*, iv (1953), pp. 411-26. More generally on the play, I should like to say I have found the following accounts helpful: Ralph Berry, "The Words of Mercury", *Shakespeare Survey,* xxii (1969), pp. 69-77; J. L. Calderwood, "*Love's Labour's Lost:* a wantoning with words", *Studies in English Literature,* v (1965), pp. 317-32; J. V. Cunningham, "With That Facility: false starts and revisions in *Love's Labour's Lost*" in *Essays on Shakespeare* (Princeton, 1965); Philip Edwards, *Shakespeare and the Confines of Art* (London, 1968); Inga-Stina Ewbank, " 'These Pretty Devices': a study of masques in plays" in *A Book of Masques,* ed. T. J. B. Spencer (Cambridge, 1967).

[2] Leggatt: "The enclosed world of courtship is attacked from two sides at once. A new life begins in Jaquenetta's belly, and an old life ends somewhere in France: courtship is only a moment in a larger cycle." *Shakespeare's Comedy of Love,* p. 83.

[3] Malory, *Le Morte d'Arthur,* Book IV, Chapter 19.

[4] *The Parliament of Fowls,* lines 660-1.

[5] *The Faerie Queene,* I.xii.41.

[6] Barber, p. 117: "The only syntax that matters is 'When...Then...' " There is considerable literature on the Songs, but see especially Cyrus Hoy, *The Hyacinth Room* (London, 1964), pp. 36-8: C. M. McClay, "The Dialogues of Spring and Winter: a key to the unity of *Love's Labour's Lost,*" *Shakespeare Quarterly,* xviii (1967), pp. 119-27.

[7] Aristotle, *op. cit.* At this point I might mention that my understanding of *The Dream* has been enhanced

by the following critical accounts: J. L. Calderwood, "*A Midsummer Night's Dream* and the Illusion of Drama", *Modern Language Quarterly*, xxvi (1965), pp. 506-22; G. K. Hunter, *Shakespeare: The Later Comedies,* Writers and Their Works, p. 143 (London, 1962); P. A. Olson, "*A Midsummer Night's Dream* and the meaning of Court Marriage". *English Literary History,* xxxiv (1957), pp. 95-119; Norman Rabkin, *Shakespeare and the Common Understanding* (New York, 1967); M. Taylor, "The Darker Purpose of *A Midsummer Night's Dream*", *Studies in English Literature,* ix (1969), pp. 259-73 and (especially) D. P. Young, *Something of Great Constancy: the art of 'A Midsummer Night's Dream'* (New Haven, 1966).

[8] *The Old Wives' Tale,* sig. B2 v. Northrop Frye uses the quotation in his discussion of conventions of comedy and romance in *A Natural Perspective* (New York, 1965), p.13.

[9] *Twelfth Night,* v. i. 360.

[10] See for example, Sigurd Burckhardt, *Shakespearean Meanings* (New Jersey, 1968), and J. R. Brown, *Shakespeare and His Comedies* (London, 1962), as well as the balance account of these issues in Leggatt.

[11] James Smith, *Shakepearian and Other Essays* (Cambridge, 1974), pp.43-68 *passim.* I find all of Smith's essays on the comedies very impressive, since they show that we do not *need* to follow Frye in order to rigorous!

[12] Anne Barton, '*As You Like It* and *Twelfth Night:* Shakespeare's Sense of an Ending', in *Shakespearean Comedy,* Stratford-upon-Avon Studies, xiv (1972). As the title implies, I am indebted to this essay, as well as to D. P. Young, *The Heart's Forest: a study of Shakespeare's pastoral plays* (New Haven, 1972); R. P. Draper, "Shakespeare's Pastoral Comedy," *Etudes Anglaises,* xi (1958), pp. 1-17; S. Barnet, " 'Strange Events': improbability in *As You Like It*", *Shakespeare Survey,* viii (1955), pp. 40-51; M. Mincoff, "What Shakespeare did to Rosalynde", *Shakespeare Jarhbuch,* xcvi (1960), pp. 78-89; John Shaw, "Fortune and Nature in *As You Like It*", *Shakespeare Quarterly,* vi (1955), pp. 49-50.

[13] Lodge, *Rosalynde* (1592), Scolar Press facsimile, sig. M3 r.

[14] *Ibid.* sig. 03 r.

[15] Spenser, *Epithalamion,* 11.389-408.

[16] See Young, *The Heart's Forest,* pp. 46-50 and M. S. Kuhn, "Much Virtue in *If,*" *Shakespeare Quarterly,* xviii (1977), pp. 40-50. Kuhn compares the practice of Sidney, and concludes that "*As You Like It* is a series of inspired improvisations in the key of *If.*"

[17] Barbara Everett, "*Much Ado About Nothing*", *Critical Quarterly,* iii (1961), pp. 319-35, perhaps the best piece on the play. See also the fine essays by James Smith (above) and A. P. Rossiter, *Angel With Horns* (London, 1961).

[18] See Bullough, *Narrative and Dramatic Sources of Shakespeare* II; C. T. Prouty, *The sources of "Much Ado About Nothing"* (New Haven, 1950) and L. G. Salingar, *Shakespeare and the Traditions of Comedy* (Cambridge, 1974), pp. 298-325 *passim.*

[19] Rich, *Farewell,* sig. L4 r.

[20] Sig. M1 r.

[21] I have found the following pieces full of insight on *Twelfth Night:* Hunter, *The Later Comedies;* Harold Jenkins, "Shakespeare's *Twelfth Night*", *Rice Institute Pamphlets,* xlv (1959); Clifford Leech, *Twelfth Night and the Design of Shakespearian Comedy* (Toronto, 1968); L. G. Salingar, "The Design of *Twelfth Night*", *Shakespeare Quarterly,* ix (1958), pp. 117-39.

[22] I am reassured to find my harsh criticism of Sir Toby supported independently by Ralph Berry in "*Twelfth Night:* the experience of the audience", *Shakespeare Survey* 34 (1981), pp. 111-20.

Richard A. Levin (essay date 1985)

SOURCE: Introduction to *Love and Society in Shakespearean Comedy: A Study of Dramatic Form and Content,* University of Delaware Press, 1985, pp. 13-29.

[*In the following essay, Levin contends that in his romantic comedies, Shakespeare explores the conflict between romantic and antiromantic values, such as the opposition between love and the desire for fortune. Levin stresses that this conflict was apparent in Elizabethan society and in other literature of the time, and that in part the tension deals with the perceived failure of Elizabethan society to live up to the values extolled in medieval romance.*]

> The Stage is more beholding to *Love,* then the Life of Man.
>
> Francis Bacon, *Essays*

> Love gives . . . counsel
> To inquire for him 'mongst unambitious shepherds,
> Where dowries were not talk'd of: and sometimes
> 'Mongst quiet kindred, that had nothing left
> By their dead parents.
>
> John Webster, *The Duchess of Malfi*

Along with *As You . . . Like It,* these plays [*The Merchant of Venice, Much Ado About Nothing,* and *Twelfth Night*] represent Shakespeare's maturest and perhaps best work in romantic comedy. Although critics occasionally stress the differences among the comedies, a great deal can be gained by trying to understand what the plays have in common—that is, by attempting to discuss them as expressions of a single theory of comedy.[1] In an effort to interpret the plays in light of such a theory, I limit myself to the three comedies that are most alike, and mention only in passing *As You Like It,* which is distinguished from the others by extensive use of pastoral.

The subject matter of Shakespearean comedy is society or, more precisely, man and woman in their social relationships. The dramatic focus is certainly no narrower, for although the young in these plays fall in love, woo, and marry, much of the action is only tangentially related to courtship. Leo Salingar makes this point while defining what he takes to be the attitude towards society expressed in the plays. Shakespeare's comedies, he writes,

> are essentially celebrations of marriage . . . which [Shakespeare] presents in a social as well as a personal aspect. Not content with a single love story, he usually contrives to bring several couples together for common rejoicing in the final scene. . . . Again, the marriage plot in his comedies is often entangled in social or moral considerations affecting society at large, but in such a way that by the end of the comedy marriage appears as the resolution of the broader tensions, as the type or focus of harmony in society as a whole.[2]

Salingar avoids specialized approaches to the comedies caught in such adjectives as "romantic" and "festive," while isolating essential features that they share; and he speaks for what has until recently been the twentieth-century mainstream when he says that the marriage celebrations symbolize achieved social "harmony." There have always been dissenters, however, and today many critics question whether the comedies characteristically resolve social "tensions."

One way of summing up the current discontent with romantic-festive criticism is to observe that such criticism relies too exclusively on the melodramatic contours of the plays; this is Ralph Berry's point when he laconically observes: "To overstate the matter crudely, the comedy is supposed to move from Bad to Good; and the social situation at the end of the play is the victory of Us over Them."[3] Melodrama may at first seem like the wrong word, for not many critics emphasize the dependence of these plays on medieval and Renaissance romances, which often made important use of melodrama. Nevertheless, mainstream twentieth-century accounts have tended both to divide the characters along clear moral lines and to establish sympathies with a virtuous group, which (as in melodrama) prevails. For example, in *Shakespeare's Festive Comedy,* the most influential modern book on the comedies, C. L. Barber praises for their social virtues the characters who marry; in *Twelfth Night,* Viola possesses "perfect courtesy" and exhibits "undaunted, aristocratic mastery of adversity," while Sir Toby is "gentlemanly liberty incarnate" and Maria has "perfectly selfless tact." Malvolio, on the other hand, is "self-absorbed" and vain.[4] Barber regards the faults of the "good" characters as only venial, indeed, as mere festive excesses; hence, he refers to a "communion embracing the merrymakers in the play and the audience, who have gone on holiday in going to a comedy" (pp. 8-9). This melodramatic element in festive criticism, though subtly handled, has nevertheless come to seem problematic in two related ways.

In the first place, Shakespeare's rich portrayal of character and society tends to break down clear-cut moral distinctions between one character and another and between socially ostracized or marginal characters and the predominant society. Second, this moral blurring tends to render ambiguous the affective structure of the comedies. The outsiders are far more than killjoy spirits; at times, at least, they attract interest and sympathy, and seem "notoriously abus'd," to use Olivia's description of Malvolio at the end of *Twelfth Night.* The audience feels that these characters are not merely absent from the celebrations, but are excluded, and perhaps unfairly; the situations are complicated and elicit conflicting emotions.

The revisionist tendency in comedy criticism has been somewhat slower to assert itself than have related innovations in the study of Shakespeare's history plays and tragedies. The reason, I think, is that of all the dramatic genres, comedy seems best approached by employing the assumptions of earlier twentieth-century scholarship. Elmer Stoll and his successors rejected what they saw as the confusion between life and literature in nineteenth-century "character analysis," and they argued, instead, that Shakespeare wrote for the popular theater and made his meaning unambiguous by drawing upon character types and a variety of other dramatic conventions: "By the comments of good characters, by the methods pursued in the disposition of scenes, and by the downright avowal of soliloquy, [Shakespeare] constantly sets us right."[5] A contemporary exponent of these views asserts that Shakespeare's meaning is generally evident from the "basic form or structure" of his plays, and he warns against subverting clearly rendered judgments of character and action.[6] As far as comedy goes, these critics do seem to believe that good wins and bad loses.

In view of the confident assertion that such interpretations are supported "by the overwhelming majority of viewers and readers down to the present,"[7] it is worth noticing that in fact the newer trend in criticism has significant historical precedents. I want to review some of this record, beginning first with claims about Shakespeare's freedom from convention in presenting character, and turning then to his interest in the point of view of outsiders. Because nineteenth-century examples of such criticism are the best known, I turn to still earlier illustrations.

In 1609 *Troilus and Cressida* appeared in a Quarto edition with a first and second issue, and to the latter was added an anonymous preface.[8] The writer, who regards *Troilus* as a comedy, introduces it by referring to Shakespeare's earlier comedies, which, he says, are not to be styled "vanities"; quite the contrary, the public should "flock to them for the maine grace of their gravities." They are "so fram'd to the life," he proclaims, "that they serve for the most common Commentaries, of all the actions of our lives."

This defense of Shakespeare's verisimilitude echoes traditional arguments about the nature and purpose of comedy. Later in the century, Shakespeare's characterization gets more distinctive praise. In 1664, Margaret Cavendish published a letter defending Shakespeare from an attack casting aspersions on his lowlife characters. No ordinary knockabouts these, she replies; Shakespeare can "Express Properly, Rightly, Usually, and Naturally, a Clown's, or Fool's Humour, Expressions, Phrases, Garbs, Manners, Actions, Words, and Course of Life."[9] Cavendish elaborates by saying that Shakespeare is distinguished by his ability to portray the broad spectrum of society: he has "so Well . . . Express'd in his Playes all Sorts [classes] of Persons, as one would think he had been Transformed into every one of those Persons he hath Described." She then lists some of Shakespeare's successful characters and includes many from the comedies. Hers is a remarkable tribute to the Shakespeare many writers have undoubtedly responded to over the generations; perhaps only Coleridge is as eloquent when he says that Shakespeare "darts himself forth, and passes into all the forms of human character and passion."

The rise of neoclassicism did not do much for Shakespeare's reputation. As Brian Vickers remarks, "the canons of criticism were tested against him, and he was found wanting."[10] Nevertheless, his grasp of life is occasionally praised inadvertently, as when Rymer rebukes him by saying that "history and *fact* in particular cases . . . are no warrant or direction for a Poet," and goes on to fault Shakespeare for showing the world as it is and not as it ought to be. Other critics do mention Shakespeare's ability to portray manners and thus to distinguish one individual sharply from another, but in general one must wait for the dean of neoclassical critics, Dr. Johnson, to find Shakespeare measured for his command of nature, not literary rules. "His drama is the mirrour of life," Johnson declares, and embellishes the thought with striking imagery: from Shakespeare "a hermit may estimate the transactions of the world, and a confessor predict the progress of the passions."[11]

Johnson explains Shakespeare's ability to break down the barrier between life and art by observing that Elizabethan plays did not often conform to strict definitions of genre. Shakespeare's plays, Johnson writes,

> are not in the rigorous and critical sense either tragedies or comedies, but compositions of a distinct kind; exhibiting the real state of sublunary nature, which partakes of good and evil, joy and sorrow, mingled with endless variety of proportion and innumerable modes of combination; and expressing the course of the world, in which the loss of one is the gain of another; in which, at the same time, the reveller is hasting to his wine, and the mourner burying his friend; in which the malignity of one is sometimes defeated by the frolick of another; and many mischiefs and many benefits are done and hindered without design. (P. 66)

Interpreting this remark as it affects comedy, one can say that while a play superficially conforms to comic practice (ending happily for the "reveller"), a full response will actually collapse melodrama along two fronts. First, "good and evil" are "mingled," or, as Johnson puts it later in the *Preface,* Shakespeare is not "always careful to shew in the virtuous a disapprobation of the wicked; he carries his persons indifferently through right and wrong" (p. 71). Second—and here Johnson contributes to an understanding of the affective structure of the comedies—neither one's attraction nor sympathy belongs exclusively to the reveller; one is impartial towards the winner and the loser.

Concerning this second question of audience response, the historical record is inevitably less clear, since early critics did not often pause to make finer discriminations. Yet these writers occasionally noted the plight of outsiders and marginal characters.

The Merchant of Venice was first entered in the Stationers' Register in 1598 with the title: "A booke of the Merchaunt of Venyce, or otherwise called the Jewe of Venyce."[12] A subsequent entry, along with the two Quartos of 1600 and 1619, call the play "the booke of the merchant of Venyce" or "The most excellent Historie of the Merchant of Venice," and they sometimes add a running title that mentions the "extreame crueltie of Shylocke the Jewe towards the sayd Merchant" and "the obtayning of Portia by the choyse of three chests." Whether Shakespeare's or not, these titles are of interest. Antonio, the merchant, is the title character, though he has only a subordinate role in the main plot and never weds. Many of the conventions of comedy function to throw attention on the romantic plot; the title helps to make Antonio a competing center of attention. The alternative title provided by the Stationers' Register entry introduces still another possible focus, Shylock, who is physically absent from the celebration, having left the stage in act 4 distraught and unwell. The title suggests that even original productions may have given Shylock some of the importance he subsequently received.

In his copy of the Second Folio, King Charles I wrote in titles for three comedies: he called *Much Ado,* "Beatrice and Benedick"; *Twelfth Night,* "Malvolio"; and *All's Well That Ends Well,* "Parolles." Early court records also refer to "Beatrice and Benedick" and "Malvolio," but whether or not the king knowingly followed precedent, one can still wonder whether he assigned the titles frivolously or, with literary tact, realized the names would help bring the plays into focus.

Curiously, Leonard Digges, a poet and translator (and perhaps Shakespeare's acquaintance), seems also to draw attention to unexpected characters when in 1640 he contrasts Jonson's failure to draw crowds as successfully as Shakespeare:

> Let but *Falstaff* come,
> *Hal, Poins,* the rest you scarce shall have a roome
> All is so pester'd: let but *Beatrice*
> And *Benedick* be seen, loe in a trice
> The Cockpit Galleries, Boxes, all are full
> To heare *Malvolio* that crosse garter'd Gull.[13]

Shakespeare's characters steal the show. The characters Digges names here all belong to the subplot or are engaged in subplot action. Is Digges also saying that these characters, even Malvolio, gain the audience's affection, perhaps at the expense of main plot characters? It is impossible to pin down precisely how Digges responded to the play as a whole.

The most intriguing early discussion of Shakespeare's intentions in comedy comes in a single paragraph in Rowe's 1709 preface to *The Works of Mr. William Shakespeare.*[14] All but three of the comedies, he starts out by saying, should really be classed as "tragi-comedy." The best indication of what Rowe means comes with his mention of *The Merchant*:

> Though we have seen that play received and acted as a comedy, and the part of the Jew performed by an excellent comedian, yet I cannot but think it was designed tragically by the author. (P. 453)

For Rowe, Shylock's "deadly spirit of revenge" "cannot agree either with the style or characters of comedy." Rowe believes that Shakespeare intentionally disturbed the comic mood, for he calls *The Merchant* "one of the most finished of any of Shakespeare's" plays. How Rowe interprets Shylock's effect on the play is hard to determine, but it is interesting to note that he also observes that "there is something in the friendship of Antonio to Bassanio very great, generous, and tender." Rowe seems to have anticipated subsequent interest in the "outsider" in Shakespeare.

Though the focus of Rowe's long paragraph is somewhat blurred, he keeps returning to characters who are what he calls "diverting"—such as Malvolio, Jaques, and Parolles. Whether they elicit sympathy as well he does not say. Only with regard to Falstaff, discussed as one of Shakespeare's great comic creations, does Rowe anticipate Maurice Morgann's general approach as well as his specific conclusions about the *Henry IV* plays:

> I do not know whether some people have not, in remembrance of the diversion [Falstaff] had formerly afforded them, been sorry to see his friend Hal use him so scurvily when he comes to the crown. (P. 452)

Rowe questioned whether *Henry IV, Part 1* and *2,* had clear dramatic "emphasis," to use Stoll's term. He perhaps had the same doubt about *Much Ado,* because he mentions the attractiveness of Beatrice and Benedick and he includes in his edition Charles Gildon's comment on the play, with its damaging assessment of Claudio. Since the *Preface* was reprinted in editions of Shakespeare all through the eighteenth century, Rowe has been called "the most disseminated Shakespeare critic before Johnson" (Vickers, *Critical Heritage,* 2:9); it is therefore plausible to think that well before Morgann readers were considering the problematic tone and structure of the comedies and other plays.

Any sketch of early remarks on the emotional structure of Shakespeare's plays should indeed turn to Morgann's "An Essay on the Dramatic Character of Sir John Falstaff."[15] Though Morgann never discusses the comedies, they were written in the same years as were the two parts of *King Henry IV,* making his argument pertinent. While asserting the apparent paradox that Falstaff is no coward, Morgann raises a profound question about audience response to Shakespearean drama.[16] One response, he alleges, is a product of the rational mind or "the *Understanding,*" while another depends on subtler *"Impressions,"* many of which are unconscious (p. 146). In real life, Morgann claims, we make the latter judgments all the time—and trust them—and we do the same with Shakespeare because of the way in which he creates character. Alone among dramatists, Shakespeare not only gives prominence to certain features in order to comply with the needs of dramatic form; he also creates "a certain roundness and integrity" in the characters (p. 167n). Hence, if criticism is to convey audience response accurately, it must sometimes be willing to consider his characters "rather as Historic than Dramatic beings," and, "when occasion requires, to account for their conduct from the *whole* of character, from general principles, from latent motives, and from policies not avowed" (p. 169n).[17] Finally, the result of such a response may be to disturb the ostensible structure of the plays; though Falstaff has his faults—Morgann's is not a sentimental account—when Hal rejects him at the end of *2 Henry IV,* "we can scarcely forgive the ingratitude of the Prince in the new-born virtue of the King" (p. 149).

More than a century after Morgann's essay, A. C. Bradley says of it that "there is no better piece of Shakespeare criticism in the world," and draws on Morgann in his own discussion of "The Rejection of Falstaff." Moreover, all through the nineteenth century, critics, often working under Morgann's direct influence, focused on Shakespeare's characterization and the point of view of such outsiders as Shylock, Malvolio, and Jaques, who were often praised at the expense of an intolerant conventional society.

What lessons can be drawn from the existence of polarized attitudes in comedy criticism from the earliest times to the present? Some critics imply an answer by seeking to integrate the countervailing tendencies in a single syncretic approach, treating one alternative as dominant while giving the other a subordinate and qualifying role. For example, a tempered romantic-festive theory draws upon the notion that Shakespeare's plays are often self-reflexive. The action of the comedies, it is alleged, evolves only under highly artificial circumstances; while the comedies work their way to a satisfying conclusion, we are to notice comic form holding at bay more threatening forces, reminiscent of the "real" world. Such a theory, offered by Anne Barton and Alexander Leggatt, among others, gives a fairly prominent place to the darker forces in the plays, and yet, in my opinion, ultimately mutes them by removing the festive celebration from all adverse scrutiny.[18] This celebration becomes an image of art and is unrelated to life.

Scholars who suggest that Shakespeare often builds into his plays divergent and even incompatible points of view offer another possible approach to the comedies. Norman Rabkin, for example, adopts from modern physics the term *complementarity* to describe the phenomenon whereby Shakespeare allows for two "equally valid, equally desirable" alternatives that yet seem to contradict one another.[19] Likewise, Raymond Powell sees in many of the plays either "complex" effects that enrich initially simple responses or "contradictory" signals that simply cannot be reconciled with one another. Both critics find Shakespeare truer-to-life because he includes these ambiguities, and again, both critics, taking *The Merchant of Venice* as their sample romantic comedy, find competing visions that conform to the two conflicting critical traditions that I have described.

While I am in general agreement with these critics, my strategy is in certain ways distinctive. I develop only the antiromantic alternative for each of the plays I discuss. I have little to add to current romantic-festive accounts, whereas I think the full integrity and coherence of the antiromantic outlook in the plays has not been appreciated.[20] The antiromantic point of view does not appear only fitfully—for example, when Shylock confronts his enemies, or when Malvolio suffers in a dark cell. Rather, every element of these plays contributes to an antiromantic interpretation. To see that this is so, and to realize, also, the possibility of far more heartening glosses of the action, is to become newly alert to the range of meanings these plays contain.

My readings therefore take for granted the fact that conventional signposts, if followed, would lead to a romantic-festive interpretation. But I respond instead to the accumulation of psychological and social detail that guides us past the conventions until the melodramatic contours of the plays become blurred. All the characters, insider and outsider alike, are found to be part of *one* world; they shed light on one another, and the influence they exert on each other tends to suggest how much they all have in common.

According to the festive-romantic account, the celebration at the end of the comedies commemorates the emergence of an ideal society. The alternative I am suggesting is that the plot of the comedies traces the struggle for inclusion into society and that the celebration merely establishes the identity of the winners. In this interpretation, success depends on such considerations as birth, wealth, good looks, intelligence, cunning, and on occasion the willingness to *forsake* ideals—not to *adhere* to them. Failure does not necessarily depend on one's evil nature, but on such things as the disadvantages of birth, the prejudices of society, lack of cunning, and one's unwillingness or inability to adapt to the prevailing winds. The plots define, in the language of *Lear,* "who loses and who wins; who's in, who's out," and as the king's handy-dandy rhythms suggest, it is no easy matter distributing moral debits and credits among the winners and losers.

This interpretation relates to certain changes that have taken place in the understanding of Renaissance England. A few decades back, literary scholars (historians were more cautious) presented the Elizabethan age as a conservative one in which Tudor orthodoxies won wide acceptance. The disruptions and dissent of the period were isolated and idiosyncratic phenomena. The intellectual ferment on the continent was said not to affect England until the seventeenth century; likewise, the social and political tensions that eventually led to civil war in England were judged not to have been significant until early Stuart times. And, finally, Shakespeare appeared as almost an apologist for the Tudor regime, a traditionalist who either ignored the ferment that grew up around him or else stood against it.

Contemporary scholarship, on the other hand, has followed the advice that Herbert Howarth offers in his chapter title, "Put Away the World-Picture,"[21] finding in the period greater detachment from, as well as more opposition to, Tudor pieties. No secure status quo put to rest questions about economic or social or political or religious matters; balancing optimistic endorsements of Tudor life are contrary tendencies, expressed, for example, in harsh strains of satire, in philosophical scepticism, and in a tendency to contrast sharply the ideals people espouse with the reality that they live.

Positing such a milieu helps us to understand the comedies. We should note especially that the darker portrayal of people and society was sometimes presented in the period as a failure to live up to the values applauded in medieval romance. Are men and women able to serve selflessly a cause higher than themselves, or are they unable to put self-interest aside? For example, Michael Drayton, in *Piers Gaveston* (1593), defines contemporary times through a series of negative comparisons with the Middle Ages when "Machivels were loth'd as filthie toades" and "true gentilitie" flourished.[22] Such a contrast between medieval and Renaissance times is also implied in *The Spanish Tragedy,* where the villain, a Machiavellian schemer, has murdered Horatio, a courtly lover and chivalrous knight. And in *The Jew of Malta,* another play from around 1590, Marlowe curtly dismisses the notion that ideals are anything more than camouflage. Taking aim at the hypocritical claims of constituted authority, the Machiavel declares in the prologue: "Many will talk of title to a crown; / What right had Caesar to the empire? / Might first made kings." An unvarnished view of events, Marlowe alleges, will always show a competition for power.

Though one expects Shakespeare to portray people and society more subtly than Marlowe, he is just as blunt in *King John,* probably written just prior to *The Merchant,* the earliest of the three comedies I am considering. With Marlovian vigor, *King John* depicts a world where self-interest rules in politics, a self-interest so strong that it must always be cloaked in professions of generosity, morality, or honesty.[23] In the Bastard's soliloquy exalting "commodity" (2.1.561-98), Shakespeare shows how fully he had absorbed the antiromantic point of view.

Apparently for reasons of conscience, the King of France has supported Arthur's attempt to seize the English throne from King John. As the English and French armies ready for battle, both lay siege to Angiers, demanding the town's surrender. A citizen comes forth with the proposal that the two kings should make peace by marrying John's niece, Blanch, to the French Dolphin. The speaker colors his real motive, which is of course to save himself with the city, by describing Blanch and the Dolphin as romantically matched: "If zealous love should go in search of virtue, / Where should he find it purer than in Blanch?" (2.1.428-29). The strategy works. To rid himself of Arthur's threat, John offers lands to go with Blanch; the French king quickly agrees, thus betraying Arthur. In the soliloquy that follows, the Bastard, adopting a pose of the contemporary satirist, "rails" against the kings, who have embraced "commodity" or "advantage"—that is, self-interest. The Bastard develops a comprehensive indictment—from the top of society to the bottom, everyone is susceptible. He imagines "commodity" as "that sly devil" who tempts man to forsake noble enterprises and betray the promptings of conscience. His speech gets to the heart of antiromantic thought in the nineties: dedication to self-interest replaces dedication to society; everyone boasts of ideals while seeking personal advancement.

The conflict between romantic and antiromantic values is fully developed in the Renaissance literary *topos* that debates the relative strength of *love* and *fortune*. Both terms are elusive. *Fortune* refers, first of all, to change in the external world as it affects the well-being of an individual. However, because a social structure provides advantages and also stands as a bulwark against adverse fortune, *fortune* frequently meant social position or privileged social position. *Fortune* receives further definition when used in conjunction with *love,* while *love* itself is frequently defined in terms of *fortune,* as Shakespeare's Sonnet 116 testifies: "Love is not love / Which alters when it alteration finds." The opening of *Lear* repeatedly defines *love* and *fortune* as opposites: Albany, rebuking the Duke of Burgundy's interest in Cordelia's dowry, says, "Love's not love / When it is mingled with regards that stands / Aloof from th' entire point" (1.1.238-39). And Cordelia echoes him by sneering at Burgundy "since that respects of fortune are his love" (248). Love and fortune are conflicting motives, one selfless, one selfish; by the end of the sixteenth century, the prevailing view makes fortune's hand by far the stronger.

Such is the Player King's assessment in *Hamlet,* when in the *locus classicus* for this theme in the Renaissance, he anticipates his wife's remarriage after his death:

> 'tis not strange
> That even our loves should with our fortunes change:
> For 'tis a question left us yet to prove,
> Whether love lead fortune, or else fortune love.
> The great man down, you mark his favorite flies,
> The poor advanc'd makes friends of enemies.

And hitherto doth love on fortune tend,
For who not needs shall never lack a friend,
And who in want a hollow friend doth try,
Directly seasons him his enemy.

(3.2.200-209)

The Player King maintains that fortune dominates all relationships: between husband and wife, king and subject, friend and friend. Actions that at first appear haphazard have a clear pattern, as soon as it is evident in which direction fortune lies; the world moves as one, abandoning ideal commitments and flocking after fortune.

The Player King's speech defines the antiromantic plot of the comedies. All the characters seek to take an advantageous place in society. In spite of their ideals, the world proves too tempting; hence, the journey is one that involves moral compromise. Shakespeare reflects contemporary custom in making marriage the main symbol of social cohesion; Elizabethan attitudes towards marriage also shape the choice characters make in these plays.

Most of the marriages portrayed in the comedies take place near the top of the social scale. In Elizabethan life, such marriages were heavily influenced by considerations of fortune—by the desire, that is, to effect "the economic or social or political consolidation or aggrandizement of the family."[24] Lawrence Stone identifies three other "personal" motives for marriage during the period. One, the desire for a compatible mate, becomes important, but not until the end of the seventeenth century. And he minimizes the role of sexual attraction and love: "Bacon was right when he said that 'the stage is more beholding to love than the life of man.'" Though Stone probably underestimates the influence of love and attraction on marriage arrangements, a substantial conflict no doubt existed between life and romantic literature, which, true to medieval courtly traditions, idealized love over all mundane interests. If, then, Shakespeare wished to bridge the gap between literature and life, he would show fortune playing an unexpectedly large role.

The sonnets help to clarify how Shakespeare's mature comedies draw on the theme of love and fortune. In these poems, most of which Shakespeare probably wrote in the same years as the comedies, the speaker is closely involved with two people, the so-called dark lady and a handsome, well-born young man.[25] The speaker's attitude towards the woman is anything but courtly; G. Wilson Knight describes his feelings for her as "finer than lust and cruder than love." The young man, on the other hand, is the "master mistress" of the speaker's "passion"—he, and not the woman, is idealized in this sonnet sequence, and theirs is the relationship that violates social conventions. The nature of this violation is elusive, though the men are certainly of markedly disparate social rank and the speaker's conduct has somehow exposed him to scandal, which he fears will taint the friend. In any event, the speaker responds with a soaring affirmation: love is tested by hostile fortune, and true love not only survives, it grows and becomes purified. The sonnets contrast such an attachment with relationships formed under fortune's influence and therefore subject to erosion.[26]

In the three comedies under discussion, and in *As You Like It* also, one character loves—or at least tries to love—with the purity described in the sonnets: the two Antonios of *The Merchant* and *Twelfth Night,* Don Pedro of *Much Ado,* and Celia in *As You Like It.* In each instance, the beloved disengages himself or herself, sometimes quite crudely. It is hard to avoid the impression, for example, that Bassanio taps a rich friend for money so he can court a woman "richly left." In *Much Ado* Claudio asks Don Pedro, his friend and patron, not merely about Hero's dowry, but rather, about her inheritance, meanwhile avoiding the prince's hint that it will pain him to help Claudio to a wife. Rosalind, a princess in exile, does not concern herself with Orlando's status, though before expressing love for him she learns he is a son of a man who in his lifetime had been her father's ally. The friends who detach themselves all marry, whereas with one exception, Celia, the friends making the sacrifice remain single. The implication would seem to be that marriage represents a betrayal of affection for self-interest.

E. K. Chambers noticed these parallels between the sonnets and one of the plays, *The Merchant,* but he concluded that they were inadvertent and that a personal note had intruded.[27] While many readers probably do feel a distinctive poignancy in Shakespeare's handling of such instances of friendship, I believe the main theme of which they are a variation—namely, the conflict between love and fortune—is fully integrated into the comedies. Fortune is a constant temptation.

Most of these marriages would readily appear to an Elizabethan audience as the sort which permits the aggrandizement or consolidation of fortune. Sometimes, as we have seen, money is expressly mentioned. However, since Renaissance society was "even more obsessed with status than with money," it is generally necessary to weigh wealth and status together in a complicated equation;[28] thus Count Claudio marries somewhat beneath him and in exchange gets a wife who brings a dowry and an eventual inheritance. When a marriage does bridge a social gap and no money is involved, it is usually because one of the partners is situated at the pinnacle of society and can afford to be self-indulgent. Orsino is one such partner and Olivia another, although the latter is not above making rudimentary inquiries about Cesario's birth before falling in love with "him."

Those seeking wealth and status are usually conscious that they do so. Their friends and families can help to make them aware by treating the nuptial more or less as a business arrangement. Claudio and Hero's courtship is an example. On the other hand, Gratiano makes an opportunity for himself by tagging along when Bassanio sails for Belmont.

Sometimes more elaborate subterfuges are undertaken, and in *Twelfth Night* they affect the basic development of the plot. Three characters maneuver for advantageous marriages. The steward Malvolio makes an amateurish effort to win Olivia's favor and become "Count Malvolio." Maria, Olivia's lady-in-waiting, hopes to marry Sir Toby, Olivia's uncle. Since Malvolio and Sir Toby are antagonists and the rise of one would mean the fall of the other, as part of Maria's campaign to win Sir Toby she sets out to destroy his rival. Recognizing Malvolio's ambition because it parallels her own, she skillfully exposes it and humiliates him. Meanwhile Viola (as I hope to show) schemes to win the bachelor duke, and like Maria, she is willing to sacrifice a third party, in this case Olivia (a potential rival for Orsino) to get what she wants. If I am right about Viola, an important result follows: the detection of hidden scheming contributes to the collapse of the "melodramatic play"—even the "romantic heroine" shares antiromantic motives with other characters.

The foregoing examples probably underestimate the desire of human beings to believe that they act for laudable motives; Claudio and Bassanio seem to forget fortune as they warm to the language of love; they thus anticipate the results of a worldly Renaissance proverb, "Marry first and Love will come after."[29]

Shakespeare's appraisal of the motives for marriage extends far beyond the obvious pursuit of wealth and status. He offers subtler motives that arise from social pressures and that always remain unconscious to some degree. Beatrice, in *Much Ado*, makes the most resolute attempt to understand these pressures—and to resist them.

When at war's end the soldiers approach Messina, conversation in the household of Beatrice's uncle turns to marriage, and Beatrice implies that although her cousin might marry, she herself will not marry any man until he proves himself worthy of her. However, no sooner is her cousin's betrothal announced than Beatrice candidly confesses to altered feelings:

> Good Lord, for alliance! Thus goes every one to the world but I, and I am sunburnt. I may sit in a corner and cry "Heigh-ho for a husband!"
> (2.1.318-20)

Beatrice wants to marry and take a place in society. Not to marry puts one at a disadvantage; Beatrice calls herself "sunburnt" not because she is unattractive—Benedick boasts of her "beauty"—but because, according to a Renaissance proverb, to suffer adverse fortune is to become exposed to the sun.[30] Beatrice's "alliance" describes a marriage that essentially fits Stone's first category: an arrangement that allows for the consolidation of social position. Nevertheless, her desire for such a marriage has little to do with crude ambition for wealth or status. She expresses a subtler feeling: that marriage is the *sine qua non* of social acceptance. In effect, society spreads its protective umbrella for those who marry; those who do not marry are left like wallflowers at a dance, to be stared at by others. Beatrice identifies a key fear in the comedies, the fear of exclusion and ostracism.

To all outward appearances, Beatrice is comfortably situated. Far from being neglected, this amusing and clever young woman is commonly the center of attention. And only her cousin is about to marry, not, as Beatrice says, "every one." Her sense of alarm therefore calls for an explanation. It is partly the product of social pressure; others constantly remind the independent-minded Beatrice that she is "odd, and from all fashions" (3.1.72). The voice of society, though strong, has tremendous influence only because of a primitive fear of isolation in the human soul; social disapproval seems to forbode a severing of the ties that bind the individual to the community.

These emotions probably vary in intensity over the centuries. Today, the primitive fear is presumably unchanged, but society does not speak with as strong a voice. In Shakespeare's England, society had a firm structure, and it enforced rules of conduct; as a result, inclusion and exclusion were decisive events. Furthermore, since in that hierarchical society only a few privileged positions existed, the possibility of exclusion and the fear of exclusion were correspondingly greater than they are now.

As a result, Shakespeare's audience would have been extremely well prepared to notice the influence of irrational forces as characters seek a place in society. In each play, the plot is shaped by two chain reactions, the first of which may be termed the "ripple effect": as soon as one courtship is announced, others get underway. Jaques comments on the phenomenon when, in the fifth act of *As You Like It,* Touchstone and Audrey enter to join others in a multiple marriage ceremony: "There is sure another flood toward, and these couples are coming to the ark." Beatrice herself is an example: within a "sevennight," she joins her cousin in a double wedding. In *The Merchant*, after Bassanio discloses his plan to woo, Lorenzo promptly elopes with Jessica, and Gratiano tells Bassanio that he "must" accompany him to Belmont.

A fear strong enough to send characters scurrying towards the altar has other consequences as well. The fear is in part experienced as the thought that some deficiency warranting exclusion will be discovered in oneself. To protect against this self-doubt, characters employ an unconscious defense: they locate a critical lack in another person; he should be excluded, and not they themselves. It might be thought that the target of attack would be a social equal or superior with whom one competes for inclusion; however, because social pressure discourages such behavior, the hostile feelings are deflected onto a person society agrees to leave at least partially unprotected.

Aggression against the precariously situated character intensifies his fears, and he consequently projects and finds reasons why someone else should be excluded. The pressure exhibited by the ripple effect thereby elicits a reverse movement as well—so delicate is the social mechanism, in Shakespeare's view. Whereas the ripple effect shows one character after another exerting an influence that leads all of them towards marriage and social inclusion, the reverse effect portrays a desperate attempt to avoid exclusion by pushing another character out.

The ripple effect is primarily represented by several children of privilege, all without serious impediments to success; the reverse effect focuses on two characters—both made vulnerable by social attitudes, but one far more so. In *Twelfth Night,* for example, Sir Toby's hand is stronger; though an unruly drunk, as uncle to the Countess Olivia, he is likely to remain a hanger-on in her household. On the other hand, the steward Malvolio, though occupying a responsible position in the same household, is not "to the manner born," and social prejudices, for the time being covert, may be activated, especially if he is seen to be ambitious. In *The Merchant,* the opponents are Antonio and the Jewish usurer Shylock, and in *Much Ado,* Don Pedro, a prince, and Don John, his bastard brother. The desire of Antonio and Don Pedro to keep their male friends and not court women makes them vulnerable in society.

Invariably, the better-connected character gains the upper hand and makes the other "odd man out." The excluded character promptly strikes back at his immediate adversary and the society protecting him. This attack can take the form of attempted revenge or an appeal for justice or both. In responding, the social "insiders" sometimes consider punishing the marginal character, but as his life is too closely intertwined with theirs, they keep guilt at a safe distance by rejecting the outsider's claim and blaming him both for his own suffering and the difficulties he has caused them.

At the celebration, the one or two characters who know more about the antiromantic forces that have been at work keep a discreet silence; the rest remain unconscious of their complicity and assuage their consciences by interpreting life as if it resembled a romantic comedy where the rewarded are the virtuous and the punished are the evil.

Shakespeare unsentimentally portrays the ostracized man as a bitter man. Nevertheless, through adversity he arrives at a measure of understanding; stripped of his own hypocritical pretensions, he penetrates society's as well, thus suggesting to the audience crucial questions about the plays.

The epigraph to this book alludes of course to Lear's mad but illumined ravings on the heath (4.6.150-72). Handy-dandy is a game, named after a formula spoken when a child presents to another two closed hands, one containing a hidden object and the other empty. The object may "change places" (153) so confusingly that it becomes impossible to identify the correct hand, except by chance. Similarly, Lear suggests, only a blind man, who cannot see and therefore cannot be misled by appearances, knows how impossible it is to identify who in reality is the "justice," who the "thief." Lear finds moral equality between "the great image of authority" and the beggar or outcast, an equality often obscured because "thorough tatter'd clothes small vices do appear; / Robes and furr'd gowns hide all." Lear alleges that only the act of condemnation provides telltale evidence of guilt; the justice who with bloody hand whips the whore, "hotly lusts to use her in that kind" for which he whips her.[31] Similarly, in the comedies, society's condemnation of the outsider suggests that they have concealed likenesses. Through both deliberate and unconscious acts, blame passes to the outsider. Though his transgressions have been the most serious, he was exposed to the greatest pressures, and other characters have succumbed to similar temptations with far less excuse. The point, of course, is not that an absolute moral equality exists between the outsider and society; were this the case, the collapse of one "melodramatic" play would give rise to another. Instead, the audience learns to avoid complacency and to consider both the romantic and the antiromantic aspects of experience.

Notes

[1] For rejections of an attempt to develop a consistent interpretation of the comedies as a group, see Ralph Berry, *Shakespeare's Comedies* (Princeton: Princeton University Press, 1972), 3-4, and Alexander Leggatt, *Shakespeare's Comedy of Love* (London: Methuen & Co., 1974), xi-xii.

[2] Leo Salingar, *Shakespeare and the Traditions of Comedy* (Cambridge: At the University Press, 1974), 17.

[3] Ralph Berry, "Shakespearean Comedy and Northrop Frye," *Essays in Criticism* 22 (1972): 39.

[4] C. L. Barber, *Shakespeare's Festive Comedy* (Princeton: Princeton University Press, 1959), 248-52.

[5] Elmer Edgar Stoll, *Shakespeare Studies,* 2d ed. (1942; reprint, New York: Frederick Ungar Publishing Co., 1960), 263. For Stoll's influence on Barber, see Barber, *Shakespeare's Festive Comedy,* 169, 178, 198. Stoll also is an influence on Northrop Frye, who develops a theory of comedy comparable with Barber's; see especially *A Natural Perspective* (New York: Columbia University Press, 1965), chap. 1, where, for example, Frye (p. 26) echoes Stoll's warning that Shakespeare is a "score to be played" and not "a book to be read" (*Studies,* 408).

[6] Richard L. Levin, *New Readings vs. Old Plays* (Chicago: University of Chicago Press, 1979), 199. Related views are expressed by Harriet Hawkins, "'Conjectures and Refutations': The Positive Uses of Negative Feedback in Criticism and Performance," in *Shakespeare, Man of the Theater,* ed. Kenneth Muir, Jay L. Halio, and D. J. Palmer (Newark: University of Delaware Press, 1983), 105-13.

[7] Levin, *New Readings,* 199.

[8] The "Preface" is reprinted by E. K. Chambers, *William Shakespeare: A Study of Facts and Problems* (Oxford: At the Clarendon Press, 1930), 2:216-17. A recent critic perhaps alludes to this preface when rejecting its approach to the comedies: A. P. Riemer writes that the plays "refuse to relate to the world of mundane reality in a direct manner; they are incapable of being treated as explicit commentaries on or critiques of life" (*Antic Fables* [New York: St. Martin's Press, 1980], 11).

[9] Margaret Cavendish, Letter 113, from *CCXI Sociable Letters;* reprinted in *Shakespeare: The Critical Heritage,* ed. Brian Vickers (London: Routledge & Kegan Paul, 1974-75), 1:42-44. I quote below from Coleridge's *Biographia Literaria* (1817); reprinted in *The Collected Works of Samuel Taylor Coleridge,* vol. 7, *Biographia Literaria or Biographical Sketches of My Literary Life and Opinions,* (2 vols.), ed. James Engell and W. Jackson Bate (Princeton: Princeton University Press, 1983), 2:27.

[10] Vickers, *Critical Heritage,* 2:1. Thomas Rymer's *A Short View of Tragedy* (1693) is reprinted in abridged form by Vickers, *Critical Heritage,* 2:25-85, and I quote below from p. 53.

[11] Dr. Johnson's *Preface to Shakespeare* (1765); reprinted in *The Yale Edition of the Works of Samuel Johnson,* vol. 7, *Johnson on Shakespeare,* ed. Arthur Sherbo (New Haven, Conn.: Yale University Press, 1968), 7:65.

[12] The entry in the Stationers' Register and the quarto and Folio titles for *The Merchant* are reprinted in Chambers, *Facts and Problems,* 1:368-69.

[13] Leonard Digges, "Upon Master William Shakespeare, the Deceased Authour, and his Poems" (1640), ll. 55-60; reprinted in Vickers, *Critical Heritage,* 1:28.

[14] Nicholas Rowe's "Life of Shakespeare," reprinted in *The Plays and Poems of William Shakespeare,* ed. James Boswell (London, 1821), 1:450-54.

[15] The essay is reprinted, with Morgann's manuscript corrections, in *Maurice Morgann: Shakespearian Criticism,* ed. Daniel A. Fineman (Oxford: At the Clarendon Press, 1972), 141-215.

[16] Though critics reacting against nineteenth-century character analysis made Morgann notorious for his failure to consider the plays as theater, he in fact attempts to define audience reaction. This aspect of Morgann is noted by E. A. J. Honigmann, *Shakespeare: Seven Tragedies: The Dramatist's Manipulation of Response* (London: Macmillan & Co., 1976); see especially chap. 2, "Impressions of 'Character.'"

[17] Morgann's passage is discussed by J. I. M. Stewart, *Character and Motive in Shakespeare* (1949; reprint, New York: Barnes & Noble, 1965), 117-22, esp. 118, and by L. C. Knights, *Explorations* (London: Chatto & Windus, 1946), 12. A. C. Bradley's praise for Morgann, mentioned below, and cited by Knights, p. 13, is from *The Scottish Historical Review* 1 (1903): 291; "The Rejection of Falstaff" is in Bradley's *Oxford Lectures on Poetry* (London: Macmillan & Co., 1920), 247-75.

[18] See Anne Barton's introductions to the comedies under discussion in *The Riverside Shakespeare,* gen. ed. G. Blakemore Evans (Boston: Houghton Mifflin, 1974); also Leggatt, *Shakespeare's Comedy of Love.* Anne Barton's *Shakespeare and the Idea of the Play* (London: Chatto & Windus, 1962), published under the name Anne Righter, has influenced most discussions of Shakespeare's plays as self-conscious "artifice."

[19] Norman Rabkin, *Shakespeare and the Common Understanding* (New York: Free Press, 1967), 12. Rabkin develops his thesis further in *Shakespeare and the Problem of Meaning* (Chicago: University of Chicago Press, 1981). Below I mention Raymond Powell, *Shakespeare and the Critics' Debate* (Totowa, N.J.: Rowman & Littlefield, 1980), 7-8. Two other recent writers who have explored how Renaissance interest in paradox and debate affects the literary forms of the period are Joel B. Altman, *The Tudor Play of Mind* (Berkeley and Los Angeles: University of California Press, 1978), and Robert Grudin, *Mighty*

Opposites: Shakespeare and Renaissance Contrariety (Berkeley and Los Angeles: University of California Press, 1979).

[20] The fullest antiromantic reading of the comedies is Elliot Krieger, *A Marxist Study of Shakespeare's Comedies* (London: Macmillan Press, 1979).

[21] Herbert Howarth, *The Tiger's Heart* (London: Chatto & Windus, 1970), chap. 8.

[22] In Patrick Crutwell, *The Shakespearean Moment* (New York: Random House, 1960), 33.

[23] I develop these ideas further in "*King John*'s Bastard," *The Upstart Crow* 3 (1980): 29-41.

[24] Lawrence Stone, *The Family, Sex and Marriage: In England 1500-1800* (New York: Harper & Row, 1977), 271. Stone's conclusions about Elizabethan motives for marriage have been modified by, for example, Keith Wrightson, *English Society: 1580-1680* (New Brunswick, N.J.: Rutgers University Press, 1982), 66-88.

[25] The assertions in this sentence are about disputed matters. The sonnets have never been satisfactorily dated; an important effort to establish verbal and thematic links between these poems and Shakespeare's plays of the mid- to late-nineties is made by Molly M. Mahood, "Love's Confin'd Doom," *Shakespeare Survey* 15 (1962): 50-61. Critics also disagree about whether the speaker has more than one male friend and on the social status of the friend addressed most frequently; in his edition of the sonnets (Boston: Ginn & Co., 1904), H. C. Beeching argues that this friend was "of good birth and fortune" but not necessarily of the nobility (p. xxi). Below I quote G. Wilson Knight, *The Mutual Flame* (London: Methuen & Co., 1955), 15.

[26] This paragraph puts the relationship between the friends in the positive light in which the speaker desires to see it. Events nevertheless force the speaker to question his and his friend's conduct. The two of them are certainly swayed by fortune. In Sonnet 62, the speaker holds up for antiromantic analysis his reasons for desiring the relationship in the first place. Is it "sin of self-love," he asks, which explains his desire to bask in the reflected glory of the friend?

[27] E. K. Chambers, *Shakespeare: A Survey* (London: Sedgwick & Jackson, 1925), 117.

[28] The quote is from Lawrence Stone, *The Crisis of the Aristocracy: 1558-1641* (Oxford: At the University Press, 1965), 223.

[29] Tilley, L534. Quoted by G. R. Hibbard, "Love, Marriage, and Money in Shakespeare's Theatre and Shakespeare's England," in *The Elizabethan Theatre VI*, ed. Hibbard (Hamden, Conn.: Shoe String Press, n.d.), 139.

[30] In a note on this passage, Dr. Johnson (p. 366) points out that in *All's Well*, 1.3.18, "to go to the world" means "to marry." Although Johnson finds the passage in *Much Ado* somewhat obscure and suggests an emendation, he at one point provides the metaphoric reading I give to "sunburnt": "I am left exposed to wind and 'sun.'" Modern scholarship has discussed the proverbial association of exposure to the sun with adverse fortune; see P. L. Carver, "'Out of Heaven's Benediction to the Warm Sun,'" *Modern Language Review* 25 (1930): 478-81, and John Dover Wilson, *What Happens in "Hamlet"* (Cambridge: At the University Press, 1935), 32-33. Shakespeare uses the proverb in *Lear*, 2.2.163 and, in the opinion of both Carver and Wilson, in *Hamlet*, 1.2.67.

[31] With the thought here, compare *Tim.* 5.1.39: "Wilt thou whip thine own faults in other men?"; and *MV* 1.3.160-62: "O father Abram, what these Christians are, / Whose own hard dealings teaches them suspect / The thoughts of others!"

LOVE TRAGEDY

Evelyn Gajowski (essay date 1992)

SOURCE: "Human Affiliation and the Wedge of Gender," in *The Art of Loving: Female Subjectivity and Male Discursive Traditions in Shakespeare's Tragedies,* University of Delaware Press, 1992, pp. 120-26.

[*In the following essay, Gajowski argues that in Shakespeare's love tragedies, Shakespeare emphasizes the humanity common among male and female characters, despite culturally enforced conceptions of gender roles. Gajowski focuses on the characteristics of the female protagonists in these plays and the nature of their love for the male protagonists.*]

    Only connect . . .
        —E. M. Forster, *Howards End*

The love tragedies offer Shakespeare the opportunity to explore in gender relationships the paradox of men and women as distinct from one another in their masculinity and femininity, yet connected to one another in their common humanity. And he insists on the common humanity connecting the sexes despite the wedge driven between them by cultural constructions of gender. "The problem appears to be one of construction," as psychoanalyst Carol Gilligan puts it, "an issue of judgment rather than truth" (1982, 171). To be a full human being, Shakespeare intimates, is to be a relational, rather than an autonomous being; yet he gives unblinking attention to the excruciating vulnerability involved in doing so. When he narrows the focus in tragedy to the single, particular heterosexual relationship, rather than the multiple relationships or the general social milieu of comedy, he intensifies his scrutiny of cultural constructions of the masculine and the feminine. The love relationship is the crucible in which Shakespeare tests and examines constructions of masculinity and femininity and discloses the common humanity that eludes and defies those constructions. The emphasis in the tragedies is on the human uniqueness underlying the cultural constructions of gender and, consequently, the disparity—even conflict—between the two.[1]

Shakespeare represents as honorable, heroic, and noble not martial but marital matters, not conventional adventure and conquest, but venturing and questing in matters of the heart. Love depends upon the ability and willingness to give of oneself to another despite the vulnerability of doing so, recalling the message on the lead casket in *The Merchant of Venice:* "Who chooseth me must give and hazard all he hath" (*The Merchant of Venice,* 2.7.9). This emphasis on active generosity in love characterizes the female protagonists of the comedies:

> *Rosalind.* To you I give myself, for I am yours.
> (*As You Like It,* 5.4.117)

> *Olivia.* Love sought is good, but given unsought is better.
> (*Twelfth Night,* 3.1.156)

> *Helena.* I dare not say I take you, but I give
> Me and my service, ever whilst I live,
> Into your guiding power.
> (*All's Well That Ends Well,* 2.3.102-4)

In the love tragedies, active generosity is made explicit in Juliet's quintessential expression of her love for Romeo (*Romeo and Juliet,* 2.2.133-35). Juliet, Desdemona, and Cleopatra all generously commit themselves in love; they "give" freely of themselves without hesitation and without qualification. Generosity in love, if we agree with E. M. Forster, is held in a delicate balance with its opposite, expectation: "when human beings love they try to get something. They also try to give something, and this double aim makes love more complicated [than other experiences]. It is selfish and altruistic at the same time," he says; "it is this emotional communion, this desire to give and to get, this mixture of generosity and expectation, that distinguishes love" ([1927] 1985, 50-51). Yet Juliet, Desdemona, and Cleopatra are remarkable in neither expecting nor demanding any "measure for measure" of emotional commitment from their lovers in return. Nor do they weigh and judge any defects or faults of character in the balance. Juliet refuses to blame her husband for killing her cousin, even as Cleopatra refuses to berate Antony for his repeated acts of disloyalty and mistrust. Desdemona's submission to Othello's mistreatment despite her awareness that she is undeserving of it makes the generosity of her forgiveness approach the absoluteness of charity.[2] All three female protagonists love the whole of the other person for that person's sake; they love for the intrinsic value of loving, rather than for any instrumental value.

If love depends upon the ability and willingness to give of oneself to another despite the vulnerability of doing so, Juliet, Desdemona, and Cleopatra "hazard" as well as "give" in love without hesitation and without qualification. The emphasis falls on their confidence in the choice of husband or lover, whether that choice occurs invisibly within the dramatic action, as is true of Juliet,[3] or before the action of the play begins, as is true of Desdemona and Cleopatra. Human beings value and try to balance the competing claims of stability and risk. This balance is never a "tension-free harmony," as political and moral philosopher Martha Nussbaum puts it; it is, rather, "a tension-laden holding-in-focus" (1986, 372). Shakespeare's female protagonists sacrifice stability and balance and embody the willingness to hazard, wager, and risk all: "That I did love the Moor to live with him, / My downright violence, and storm of fortunes, / May trumpet to the world" (*Othello,* 1.3.248-50). The risk they take in love constitutes in part the value of that love.

The fragility of the love between two people lies in its peculiar vulnerability to happenings in the world. Because the odds against intimacy are so great, we wonder that it flourishes at all—in our world as well as in the dramatic worlds of Shakespeare's tragedies. The female protagonists in *Antony and Cleopatra, Othello,* and *Romeo and Juliet* share with the speaker in Shakespeare's sonnets the courage to love despite awareness of the vicissitudes of human existence. Desdemona's confidence in her love allows her to rejoice at the prospect of its deepening: "The heavens forbid / But that our loves and comforts should increase, / Even as our days do grow!" (*Othello,* 2.1.195-97). Although she is free of the doubts that haunt Othello, she understands that his expressions of absoluteness of affection, are, perhaps, attempts to protect his love from the unknown that the passage of time brings:

> If it were now to die,
> 'Twere now to be most happy; for I fear
> My soul hath her content so absolute
> That not another comfort like to this
> Succeeds in unknown fate.
> (*Othello,* 2.1.189-93)

Whereas Othello, like so many of Shakespeare's male protagonists—and like the speaker in John Donne's *Songs and Sonnets*—is capable of trusting only in the immutable and the stable, Desdemona, like so many of his female protagonists, is capable of the far more difficult thing, trusting in the mutable and the unstable. Her confidence in the face of mutability, as we have seen, is somewhat akin to that of the speaker in Shakespeare's sonnets.[4] Juliet and Cleopatra share this confidence. Cleopatra, further, shares with the speaker in Shakespeare's sonnets the confidence that what she loves will stand against death. In Sonnet 18, for example, the speaker expresses confidence that his love will stand against the ravages of time, although with a deliberateness and self-consciousness about his poetic artistry that is absent in Cleopatra's tribute:

> Shall I compare thee to a summer's day?
> Thou art more lovely and more temperate:
> Rough winds do shake the darling buds of May,
> And summer's lease hath all too short a date;
> Sometime too hot the eye of heaven shines,
> And often is his gold complexion dimm'd,
> And every fair from fair sometime declines,
> By chance or nature's changing course untrimm'd:
> But thy eternal summer shall not fade,
> Nor lose possession of that fair thou ow'st,
> Nor shall Death brag thou wand'rest in his shade,
> When in eternal lines to time thou grow'st.
>   So long as men can breathe or eyes can see,
>   So long lives this, and this gives life to thee.

It is not coincidental that Antony takes on mythological proportions—"His legs bestrid the ocean; his rear'd arm / Crested the world, his voice was propertied / As all the tuned spheres" (*Antony and Cleopatra*, 5.2.82-84)—when Cleopatra's poetic artistry immortalizes him. Nor is it coincidental that Shakespeare's dramatic artistry includes both death and the confidence in the human capacity for love that stands against death. Cleopatra's poetic imagination, like Shakespeare's dramatic artistry, creates art; art, in turn, shapes future imaginative and cultural impressions. In a very real way, our contemporary sense of who Antony is is the result of Cleopatra's making. In a very real way, our contemporary understanding of the ability to love in the face of human mutability and mortality is that of Shakespeare's making. Literature does more, of course, than mimetically "reflect a context outside itself," as Jean Howard observes; it also constitutes a means of production, or "one of the creative forces of history." Literature is accorded real power when we acknowledge that, rather than "passively reflecting an external reality," it actively participates in "constructing a culture's sense of itself" (1986, 26, 25).

In *Othello*, more so than in any other work, Shakespeare rigorously interrogates the unilateral standards of female chastity and male honor—and the dependency of the latter upon the former—and finds them wanting. The single sonnet which offers an image of ideal love assumes that it depends upon a constancy that is mutual. The opening lines of Sonnet 116 insist that the love that does not "admit impediments" is a "marriage" of "true" minds:

> Let me not to the marriage of true minds
> Admit impediments; love is not love
> Which alters when it alteration finds,
> Or bends with the remover to remove.

The sexual relationships in the love tragedies suggest that love likewise depends for its existence upon a constancy that is mutual. As the dramatic action of the romantic comedies and the early action of the love tragedies discloses, two lovers must be able to establish trust in one another. They must be able to receive one another's love without suspicion, jealousy, or fear. The foundation of the love and the continuing trust in that foundation, as the dramatic action of *Othello* most painfully discloses, must remain constant or the love will be undermined. Because *Othello* dramatizes the disintegration of the male protagonist, the emphasis falls on mutual constancy that is destroyed. Because *Romeo and Juliet* and *Antony and Cleopatra* dramatize the ennoblement of the male protagonist, the emphasis falls on mutual constancy that is produced or reproduced.

The ravages of human love, which so often "with base infection" meet, never reach the "star" of absolute constancy. Absolute constancy exists instead as an ideal, "an ever-fixed mark" by which to gauge the tempests of sexual relations:

> O no, it is an ever-fixed mark
> That looks on tempests and is never shaken;
> It is the star to every wand'ring bark,
> Whose worth's unknown, although his highth be taken.

That is not to say that the female protagonists in the love tragedies are heroic in the depth and totality of their emotional commitment, and the male protagonists are less than heroic in their lack of a like commitment. Shakespeare depicts both constancy and inconstancy in the romantic comedies, the sonnets, and the romances, but nowhere more so than in the love tragedies, I think, does he force upon us the disparity between the two.

Love and friendship are distinct from other human traits or virtues in their being not states of being or activities, but in their very nature, relationships between separate individuals.[5] Being loving or being

Act V. Scene iii. In a tomb belonging to the Capulets. Juliet reaches out to Friar Lawrence as Romeo and Paris lie dead before her. Painted by James Northcote, R. A. University of Michigan Library.

friendly is not a state of character, such as the state of being courageous, for example, awaiting an appropriate opportunity, such as the battlefield, to reveal itself. Just as generosity involves another person, who must be there to receive, love involves another person, who must be there to be loved. The other person is significant, moreover, not merely as an object who receives the activity of giving or love, but as "an intrinsic part of love itself," as Nussbaum puts it, who actively gives or loves in return. Love and friendship are deeply relational—and therefore more vulnerable—because the particular nature of the other "enters more deeply" into defining the particular nature of the relationship (1986, 344).

Mutuality in affection depends not only upon connectedness but also separateness and a mutual respect for that separateness. The other needs to be recognized not as a possession, an extension, or a projection of the self, but as a separate, independent human being whose separateness and independence are valued for their own sakes—for their intrinsic rather than their instrumental value (Nussbaum 1986, 355). The uniqueness of Shakespeare's representation of sexual relationships is his creation of females who are independent, yet relational, human beings. Juliet, Desdemona, and Cleopatra are all endowed with a self-estimation that is independent of the estimations of the men in their dramatic worlds; perhaps it is this singular characteristic—their theatrical subjectivity—that accounts for the fascination that they, and Shakespeare's other female protagonists, hold for audiences and readers over a period of four hundred years. Shakespeare takes pains to convey this sense of independence in the opening action of each play. Yet, having established them as independent rather than clinging figures, he further endows them with a relational, affiliative capacity that the male protagonists often lack.[6] One of the many remarkable things about Cleopatra is that she is a political being, Queen of Egypt, yet, at the same time, devoted to Antony. Men, of course, have "deep yearnings for affiliation," as Miller points out. These needs exist in men as well as women, "deep *under the surface* of social appearance," or cultural constructions of gender. Men, like women, long for "an affiliative mode of living," of course, but have deprived themselves of it for so long that they have made themselves unable to believe in it ([1976] 1986, 87-88). Shakespeare's females, like the contemporary women in Carol Gilligan's study, "replace the bias of men toward separation with a representation of the interdependence of self and other." Also, like the women in Gilligan's study, their sense of integrity is interpenetrated with "an ethic of care"—to see themselves as women is "to see themselves in a relationship of connection" (1982, 170, 171).

Shakespeare's comprehension of human complexity is equaled by his artistry, by his ability to transmute this understanding into the richness and diversity of particular characters in action. This understanding represents as supreme not structures of cultural, religious, military, or political power, but the emotional commitment of personal relationships among family, friends, and lovers. Even as we come to understand this implicit truth manifest in work after work across all genres, so we come to appreciate an artistry that simultaneously uses and breaks literary tradition, that exploits and criticizes in tragedy as in comedy cultural constructions of masculinity and femininity. It presents romantic and antiromantic discursive practices only to expose their inadequacy and to frame an authentic emotional commitment that is rooted in psychological reality. Romeo sheds chivalric roles in his deepening connection to Juliet; Othello falls prey to Iago's misogyny despite his connection to Desdemona; Antony oscillates between Petrarchist, Ovidian, and Orientalist constructions of Cleopatra in his incipient understanding of her "infinite variety."

Shakespeare's female protagonists are remarkable for their totality of being that eludes and defies, disrupts and subverts male constructions of the female. This is nowhere more evident in the canon or, perhaps, in all of western tradition, than in his characterization of Cleopatra. Yet as early as a crossdressed Viola, Shakespeare stresses not patriarchal constructions of femininity but, rather, human traits—sturdiness, sweetness, wittiness, melancholy, resilience—that surpass constructions of either gender. When Shakespeare does decide to endow his females with stereotypically feminine traits—the obedience of Juliet and Desdemona; the chastity of Desdemona; the fear of Juliet and Cleopatra; the devotion of all three female protagonists—it is to evaluate not them, but rather, men and the constructions of woman that operate so powerfully in the dramatic worlds of the plays. Juliet, Desdemona, and Cleopatra recognize and appreciate their lovers' totality of being; this recognition and appreciation, as the dramatic action of play after play discloses, demands reciprocity. For the value of all of Shakespeare's protagonists lies in their human traits, the capacity for love—its generosity, its confidence, its constancy, and its mutuality—supreme among them. Our own understanding of the comprehensiveness of Shakespeare's view of humanity depends upon our understanding of the complexity of his females, as of his males.

Notes

[1] I agree with Kate McLuskie's claim that an important part of the feminist project is "to insist that the alternative to the patriarchal family and heterosexual love is not chaos but the possibility of new forms of social organization and affective relationships" (1985, 106). The difference between McLuskie and myself is her refusal to acknowledge the contribution of the artist to such a project. The assumption that the dramatic text mimetically reflects the patriarchal culture in which it is produced seems overly deterministic to me. The assumption that artists participate in the consolidation of the dominant ideology rather than any subversion of it renders them, of course, mere factotums of that order—all exposure, critique, or condemnation of the inequities in the dominant order drained from their texts. See Louis Montrose for a discussion of "the inevitably reductive tendency" toward an "overcompensatory positing of subject as wholly determined by structure" (1986, 9).

[2] I am aware of the difficulty of considering the generosity of Shakespeare's female characters as an admirable trait. Because it is a stereotypically feminine trait, some assume it is, therefore, not admirable. This view, again, reveals the intervention of materialist/historicist thought upon feminist thought. In psychotherapy, it is true that, as Jean Baker Miller notes, "women often spend a great deal more time talking about giving than men do." By contrast, the question of whether a man is a giver or giving enough does not enter into his self-image; he is concerned more about doing than giving ([1976] 1986, 50).

[3] By invisible I mean that we cannot point to a specific moment in the dramatic action of *Romeo and Juliet*, whether the feast scene or the orchard scene, and say, "Here, Juliet makes her choice." Rather, her nature is imbued, in the way Fromm describes, with a readiness for emotional commitment that governs all her interactions with Romeo: "Faith is a character trait pervading the whole personality, rather than a specific belief" (1956, 121).

[4] See Sonnet 115, chap. 3, n. 8.

[5] For the understanding of mutuality in this and the following paragraph, I am indebted to the views of Nussbaum. She is discussing Aristotle's notion of *philia*, which she translates as *love* rather than *friendship* (1986, 354). See her chap. 12, on relational goods and the vulnerability of the good human life (1986, 343-372).

[6] The attribution of relational capacities or affiliative modes of living to Shakespeare's female characters leads some critics to conclude that Shakespeare is a "patriarchal bard" (McLuskie 1985; but see also McLuskie 1989, 224-30). The assumption is that his attribution of those human traits which are culturally labeled *feminine* to female characters constitutes his active, if not deliberate, participation in the reproduction of patriarchy. This view, again, reveals the enormous impact of materialist/historicist thought upon feminist thought. Peter Stallybrass, however, concludes a recent interrogation of the problems of connecting analyses of gender to analyses of class with a useful suggestion: "it is important to work with both feminism and marxism," he maintains, "without trying to 'marry' them" (1989). Acting to create female-defined values is a more fruitful endeavor, I believe, then reacting to those of male-dominated approaches. Shaping female-defined discursive practices is, in other words, a more valuable strategy than aping male-dominated discursive practices.

COURTSHIP AND MARRIAGE

B. J. Pendlebury (essay date 1975)

SOURCE: "Happy Ever After: Some Aspects of Marriage in Shakespeare's Plays," in *Contemporary Review,* Vol. 227, No. 1319, December, 1975, pp. 324-28.

[*In the following essay, Pendlebury examines the development of Shakespeare's treatment of marriage in his plays, noting that in the early comedies, the prospect of marriage is of primary significance and is represented in an optimistic manner, whereas in the later plays, Shakespeare's tone regarding marriage shifts to a more pessimistic one.*]

Many a good hanging prevents a bad marriage! So says Feste in *Twelfth Night.* Now, clearly we must not attribute to Shakespeare himself the view expressed in a flippant remark by a professional jester. Indeed, we cannot safely assume that Shakespeare personally endorsed the judgments of any one of his characters. However carefully we scrutinise particular plays, we can never say with confidence: 'This is what Shakespeare thought about marriage'. Nevertheless, it is interesting to examine those plays that are particularly concerned with marriage and to try to see what assumptions underlie both speeches and actions.

If we consider first the early comedies, we cannot help noticing that the prospect of marriage is frequently of central importance. *Two Gentlemen of Verona, A Midsummer Night's Dream, Twelfth Night, Much Ado About Nothing,* have this in common: each of them illustrates the saying that 'the course of true love never did run smooth', and the action is mainly concerned with the efforts of the lovers to overcome all obstacles to their union. In the end, misunderstandings are cleared up, external opposition is overcome, the lovers are paired off, and we are to suppose that they live 'happy ever after'. There is a strong presumption that marriage is the ultimate good. Indeed, so much emphasis is placed on marriage as the natural happy ending that Shakespeare will often strain probability to bring it about, as when, in *As You Like It,* he provides Celia with a mate by the sudden conversion of the villainous Oliver into a man of honour. But, however the pairing is managed, the implication is always the same: 'Journey's end in lovers' meeting', and everybody rejoices in the prospect of a wedding.

It is noteworthy that the society presented in these early plays is not what is nowadays called 'permissive'. Romantic love is meant to end in marriage; and marriage is taken seriously as a sacrament. In *Twelfth Night,* for example, the marriage of Olivia and Sebastian is described as 'A contract of eternal bond of love'. And this is typical of the tone adopted by Shakespeare's characters whenever they refer seriously to marriage. Even Benedick, in *Much Ado,* though given to making cynical jokes about married men, speaks differently when he asks Leonato's consent to his own union with Beatrice:

> But for my will, my will is, your good will
> May stand with ours, this day to be conjoin'd
> In the state of honourable marriage.

This same play shows very clearly that unchastity is not lightly regarded. There is indeed 'much ado' when Claudio is deceived into thinking that Hero is 'an approved wanton'. His furious indignation is shared by his friend the Prince, who speaks of Hero as 'a rotten orange', an unworthy gift to be offered to an honourable man. There is, indeed, a hint of a more modern attitude to 'pre-marital sex' in Leonato's attempt to make excuses for his daughter. As he says to Claudio:

> Dear my lord, if you in your own proof
> Have vanquish'd the resistance of her youth,
> And made defeat of her virginity,—

And Claudio takes the point:

> I know what you would say: if I have known her,
> You will say she did embrace me as a husband,
> And so extenuate the forehand sin.

It is significant that, though the anticipation of the wedding by betrothed lovers might be thought venial,

Claudio refers to it as 'the forehand *sin*'. It would appear that Shakespeare's audience was ready to applaud a high moral tone on the subject of feminine chastity. This impression is reinforced in the later plays.

An aspect of marriage that we might call the social relationship between husband and wife receives comparatively little direct mention in most of the comedies. It seems to be assumed that the husband will be the dominant partner and the master of the household. In the few comedies where we see the principal characters actually married, it is the husband who does as he chooses and the wife who is expected to be submissive, though she may sometimes show her displeasure by nagging. In the *Comedy of Errors*, when Antipholus is late coming home to dinner, and his wife, Adriana, complains to her sister, Luciana counsels patience and submission. A man, she says, is master of his liberty, but equal liberty is not given to woman. To Adriana's assertion that only asses submit to a bridle, she replies:

> Why, headstrong liberty is lash'd with woe.
>
> . . . . .
>
> The beasts, the fishes, and the winged fowls
> Are their males' subjects and at their
>   controls:
> Men more divine, the masters of all these,
> Lords of the wide world and wild watery
>   seas,
> Are masters to their females, and their lords:
> Then let your will attend on their accords.

The notion of wifely submissiveness as a necessary ingredient of married bliss is, of course, the main topic in *The Taming of the Shrew*. In the early scenes, Katharina appears as a shrew indeed, wilful, violent, and unlikely to promise much happiness to a prospective bridegroom. The play, however, shows us the taming of Katharina by Petruchio, a wooer 'as peremptory as she is proud-minded'. The shrew is systematically bullied until she can be shown as a model of obedience. She is so changed that she lectures her sister on her wifely duties, arguing that a husband's care for his wife deserves in return 'But love, fair looks, and true obedience'. And she concludes:

> Such duty as the subject owes the prince
> Even such a woman oweth to her husband;
> And when she is forward, peevish, sullen,
>   sour,
> And not obedient to his honest will,
> What is she but a foul contending rebel,
> And graceless traitor to her loving lord?

This conversion of the high-spirited Katharina into a patient Griselda is surely somewhat repugnant to a modern reader, unless he is indeed a 'male chauvinist pig'. One cannot help suspecting that *The Taming of the Shrew* is an example of wish-fulfilment, a fantasy designed to appeal to a hen-pecked husband. Perhaps enough has been said to show that, though in the early comedies it is generally assumed that successful wooing leads to married bliss, there are some hints that it is not always undisturbed. Nevertheless, in the early plays, most of the references to marriage are decidedly optimistic.

When we come to consider the later plays, we find that the tone has changed. In many of them, the question of marriage is not crucial; but, where it is, there is a decided note of pessimism. There is a masculine obsession with the danger of being deceived by an unfaithful wife; and the reactions of a husband who believes he has been deceived provide the central motive for more than one play.

Of these, *Othello* is the outstanding example. The story is to some extent anticipated in *Much Ado*, for in both plays we see a villain who contrives to represent an innocent woman as an 'approved wanton'. In *Othello*, the villain's spite is directed against the hero, and the interest is concentrated on the intensity of the Moor's feelings for Desdemona. Othello is not merely indignant at an affront to his honour: he suffers the most violent emotional disturbance imaginable short of actual madness. He is indeed aware that he may be an object of ridicule,

> A fixed figure for the time of scorn
> To point his slow unmoving finger at,

but this notion is subordinate to the sense of ruined happiness. It is subordinate also to a sense of righteousness in his intention to kill Desdemona. 'Yet she must die', he says, 'else she'll betray more men'; and later in the same speech:

> Ah, balmy breath, that dost almost persuade
> Justice to break her sword.

And after Desdemona's death, Othello describes himself as

> An honourable murderer, if you will:
> For nought did I in hate, but all in honour.

The modern reader finds it difficult to accept this notion that a husband has the right to punish unchastity with death. At best, it may be regarded as what Orsino calls 'A savage jealousy, That sometimes savours nobly'.

What one might call the 'cuckoo-theme' is pursued with less fearful consequences in more than one of the later plays. In *Cymbeline*, we have basically the same situation as in *Othello,* the innocent heroine being slandered by a villain. But there are important differences. The husband, Posthumus Leonatus, goes far to bring his troubles on himself. He has been exiled from Britain by the king, Cymbeline, the father of Imogen, to whom Posthumus is secretly married. In idle conversation in Rome, Posthumus boasts of his wife's virtue and is provoked by the cynical Iachimo into betting on it. Iachimo is confident of winning:

> I will lay you ten thousand ducats to your ring, that, commend me to the court where your lady is, with no more advantage than a second conference, and I will bring from thence that honour of hers which you imagine so reserved.

The acceptance of this wager does not endear Posthumus to us. It would seem that he thought of Imogen as a possession, valued indeed at a high price, yet valued in terms of ducats, like a horse or a hound. Imogen, of course, justifies her husband's trust by repelling Iachimo; but the resourceful villain contrives to be carried in a trunk into Imogen's bedchamber; then, when Imogen is asleep, he is able to observe a mole on her breast and also to steal her bracelet. Back in Rome, he convinces Posthumus that he has won his bet, and so provokes an outburst of rage from the supposedly wronged husband. 'O that I had her here, to tear her limb-meal', exclaims Posthumus. Seeking a vengeance that by no means 'savours nobly', he writes to his henchman Pisanio, commanding him to kill Imogen. He seems confident that the charge of adultery will be sufficient to induce Pisanio to obey his command. Pisanio, however, refuses either to believe the accusation or to carry out the order. In fact, he helps Imogen to set out on a series of extraordinary adventures which, most improbably, lead to a happy reunion with Posthumus.

This obsession with the risk of being a cuckold is to be found also in *The Winter's Tale,* where Leontes, King of Sicily, unjustly suspects his queen, Hermione, of adultery with his friend Polixenes. No slandering villain is involved, the jealous nature of Leontes being solely responsible for the situation. Leontes, it seems, is mainly troubled by the fear of being an object of scorn. After encouraging Hermione to entertain Polixenes in the garden, he addresses his young son thus:

> Go, play, boy, play; thy mother plays, and I
> Play too; but so disgraced a part, whose issue
> Will hiss me to my grave: contempt and
>   clamour
> Will be my knell.

Like Posthumus, he suffers a sense of outrage and is driven to seek vengeance. As in *Cymbeline,* the plot miscarries, and chance leads to a complex of strange happenings, ending twelve years later with an improbable reconciliation. Though the play includes elements of comedy and romance, it is the jealousy of Leontes that provides the chief motive power for the action, and it is the scenes displaying this jealousy that seem most firmly set in the world of reality.

When we consider the stories of *Othello, Cymbeline,* and *The Winter's Tale,* we cannot fail to be struck by the frequency with which Shakespeare returns to this theme of the deceived husband. Moreover, one feels that resentment carried to a murderous conclusion is implicitly condoned, if not actually justified. Those characters who condemn the supposed cuckold's bloodthirsty intentions do so in the complete conviction of the wife's innocence. There is no suggestion that Desdemona and Imogen would not have deserved to die, had they really been guilty of adultery.

It will doubtless occur to the feminist that the offences considered by Shakespeare are all on one side. 'Frailty, thy name is woman!' says Hamlet, but the frailty of man in his relations with woman is viewed more leniently. When Mark Antony deserts his wife for Cleopatra, there are no outbursts of indignation and resentment from Octavia, such as we have when Leontes or Posthumus thinks himself betrayed. In this matter, Shakespeare evidently accepts different standards of conduct for men and women.

In the histories, the tragedies, and the tragi-comedies, we find few pictures of a happy marriage. Hotspur and his Lady are shown to be affectionate, but Hotspur is too much absorbed in political affairs to have much time for his wife. The case of Brutus is similar. He loves and respects Portia; but he too is absorbed in a conspiracy, and it is only after a scene of reproaches that he confides in her.

For a marriage that is something like an equal partnership, one must turn to *Macbeth*. The wicked thane and his Lady are united in their ambitions. When Macbeth is prompted by the witches to indulge in the hope of making himself king, he writes to his wife:

> This have I thought good to deliver thee, *my dearest partner of greatness,* that thou mightst not lose the dues of rejoicing by being ignorant of what greatness is promised thee.

Macbeth knows that he can count on encouragement and support from his wife. She may upbraid him when he wavers, but in times of crisis she gives him the help he needs. Almost without exception, Macbeth and his Lady express affection and esteem in the way they speak to one another. At their meeting in Act I, Lady Macbeth greets her husband as 'Great Glamis! Worthy Cawdor!', and he addresses her as 'My dearest love'. Later in the play, each of them shows affectionate concern for the other. When Macbeth sees the ghost of Banquo, Lady Macbeth stands by him staunchly, ever ready to help, and troubled about his health and state of mind. And when his 'dearest chuck', as he calls her, loses her reason, Macbeth in his turn is solicitous for her well-being. Altogether, one sees in *Macbeth* the best picture of a genuine partnership in marriage that Shakespeare has given us. That this partnership should be that of a 'butcher and his fiend-like queen' is an ironic comment on the chances of a perfect marriage.

Though it is impossible to generalise with any confidence on Shakespeare's views on marriage, we may reasonably assert that, as Shakespeare grew older, he took a more gloomy view of the possibility of a happy marriage. His exploration of the darker side of human nature is not, of course, exclusively concerned with marriage; yet anyone reviewing the work of his later years cannot help noticing the prominence given to stories of marital infidelity. It may be argued that the tragi-comedies end in reconciliations; but it is difficult to feel that there is any conviction in their contrived and improbable endings. We may well conclude that in his later years Shakespeare became embittered on the subject of marriage: it is only his early comedies that embody the assumption of the fairy stories that 'the prince and the princess were married and lived happy ever after'.

Carol Thomas Neely (essay date 1985)

SOURCE: "Introduction: Wooing, Wedding, and Repenting," in *Broken Nuptials in Shakespeare's Plays*, Yale University Press, 1985, pp. 1-23.

[*In the following essay, Neely examines the way in which marriage—achieved and postponed or destroyed—influences the structure and themes of Shakespeare's plays. Neely maintains that marriage becomes the focal point for relationships, both social and emotional, for men and women in the plays.*]

Marriage in Shakespeare's plays is a crucial dramatic action and a focus for tensions and reconciliations between the sexes. Movements toward marriage constitute the subject of the comedies; disrupted marriages are prominent in many of the tragedies; the establishment or reestablishment of marriage in one or two generations is the symbol of harmony in the late romances. The plays' marriages are counterpointed by what I call broken nuptials, extending Leo Salingar's use of the term.[1] These are parodic or irregular wedding ceremonies, premature or postponed consummations, estrangements, mock deaths, and real deaths—anything that disrupts the process of wooing, betrothal, wedding, marriage. These broken nuptials express the anxieties, desires, and conflicts of the couples who enter into marital unions as well as the external pressures placed on these unions by parents, rulers, the community. My study will examine how marriage, achieved or broken, influences the themes and structure of the plays and serves as the focus for the social and emotional relations of the sexes.

My emphasis on marriage is the result of my desire to explore women's roles in Shakespeare's plays. This exploration led me, as it has led feminist scholars in many disciplines, to examine the contexts in which women are defined, a project precisely articulated by the late Michelle Rosaldo in her reflections on the nature of feminist anthropology:

> It now appears to me that woman's place in human social life is not in any direct sense a product of the things she does (or even less a function of what, biologically, she is) but of the meaning her activities acquire through concrete social interactions. And the significances women assign to the activities of their lives are things that we can only grasp through an analysis of the relationships women forge, the social contexts they (along with men) create—and within which they are defined.[2]

Marriage is the social context that centrally defines the female characters in Shakespeare's plays; with few exceptions their conflicts, crises, and character development occur in connection with wooing, wedding, and marriage. Their roles and status are determined by their place in the paradigm of marriage—maiden/wife/widow—which likewise governed the lives of Renaissance women.[3] The introduction to a Jacobean women's legal handbook starkly notes the inevitability and restrictiveness of this paradigm for women: "all of them are understood either married or to be married and their desires [are] subject to their husband. I know no remedy though some women can shift it well enough."[4] Even exceptional historical women like Queen Elizabeth or extraordinary characters like Cleopatra do not escape definition in terms of the paradigm: Elizabeth made strategic use of the conventional roles she eschewed, manipulating her marriageability to gain political advantage and presenting herself as wife to England and as mother to her people,[5] while Cleopatra creates for herself a symbolic marriage to Antony at the end of Shakespeare's play. Examining women characters in the context of marriage facilitates a balanced evaluation of the power and limits of their roles.

There is a long tradition of criticism that scrutinizes the roles of women in Shakespeare; recently such criticism has proliferated and become increasingly self-conscious about its methodology and its goals. This criticism, in both its current and earlier versions, has assessed the place of the women characters in somewhat contradictory ways. One strand concerns itself with analyzing the strength, influence, and complexity of the women in the plays, compensating for their past neglect, misreading, and stereotyping. Nineteenth-century forerunners of this approach, like the historians who studied exemplary women, isolated and extolled prominent female characters, admiring their strength, wit, intelligence, power—and also their charm and beauty.[6] Recent critics, more self-conscious about their goals and more sophisticated in their methods, document the ways in which Shakespeare's women have been misread and stereotyped by critics, editors, and producers.[7] They read Kate's role of shrew and even her speech of subordination positively, make Cleopatra the hero of her play, emphasize Desdemona's sexual assertiveness.[8] They analyze the implications of female conversations and friendships, of female doubling, of women's commentary.[9]

Another strand of criticism stresses instead the constrictions placed on the female characters by the patriarchal structures within the plays and by the male-authored text in which they exist. Such critics show that Shakespeare's female characters inevitably are defined and define themselves in relation to men. They demonstrate that even strong, central women like Lady Macbeth and Cleopatra are socially and sexually contained by the structures of patriarchy, that the assertive comic heroines are restricted by the marriages which conclude their stories.[10] They analyze how these marriages achieve social and political harmony for the patriarchy as well as providing emotional union for the couple.[11] They reveal how the tragic heroes' fantasies of women cripple men and destroy female characters, illuminating the way in which the men's development of their own identity depends on and exploits women.[12]

Some very recent studies, drawing on and benefiting from both strands of criticism, analyze the relationship between the commanding heroines and the confining culture, between the idealization and degradation of women, and trace changes in gender relations through different genres. Linda Bamber explores how women conceived of as the other, as the representatives of external reality, assume different functions in comedy, history, tragedy, and romance.[13] Peter Erickson examines how men and women take on each other's qualities and roles, and how women are granted power or deprived of it in different plays.[14] Marianne Novy weighs the varying interactions between mutuality and patriarchy, between reason and emotion, and their effects on women's roles.[15]

My book grows out of and has been nourished by all this work, extending earlier explorations by focusing on the relations of the sexes in marriage. I examine the plays primarily as dramatic structures without reference to their determinants in Shakespeare's psyche. I explore the social relations of the sexes within the plays but do not draw extensively on social history (an analogous body of texts, as I show later in the Introduction) to interpret these relations. My concern is with the ways in which the plays are influenced by other literary texts: by the conventions of drama, by the effects of their disparate sources, by generic expectations. I focus particularly on the ways in which gender relations are shaped by and shape the different genres in which Shakespeare wrote: the comedies of the 1590s, the problem comedies and tragedies (1600-08), and the romances that end his career. As Shakespeare responds to the demands of a variety of genres, recasting them in response to the overall development of his own art, the role of women, the nature of relations between the sexes, and the place of marriage alter. In exploring these transformations, each of the book's five chapters offers a sustained interpretation of a single play, which places it in the context of contemporaneous plays to provide a broad reading of a key phase of Shakespeare's development.

The five plays I reinterpret—*Much Ado About Nothing, All's Well That Ends Well, Othello, Antony and Cleopatra*, and *The Winter's Tale*—share a number of concerns and motifs. All have marriage as a central issue and each contains more than one courtship or marriage. Taken together, these plays encompass the whole process of wooing, wedding, and repenting. *Much Ado* begins with the beginning of courtship. The wedding ceremony and delayed consummation occur in acts 2 and 4 of *All's Well*. The opening of *Othello* is coterminous with Othello's and Desdemona's elopement. *Antony and Cleopatra* employ the rituals of courtship long after their affair is established and do not complete their union until after the rupture of Antony's actual marriages. In *The Winter's Tale* the long-standing marriage of Hermione and Leontes is disrupted early in the play and is restored only after the betrothal of their daughter, Perdita.

All of these plays embody the conflicts attendant on marriage by the incorporation of broken nuptials; these range from Claudio's denunciation of Hero during their wedding ceremony in *Much Ado* to Polixenes's interruption of Perdita's and Florizel's betrothal in *The Winter's Tale*. The mending of these ruptured nuptials is achieved primarily through the women's apparent or actual deaths. The strategic mock deaths of Hero, Cleopatra, and Hermione, accomplished with the assistance of other women, Helen's pretended death on a pilgrimage, and the real death of Desdemona engender—however problematically—their lovers' repentance and the rejuvenation of the unions. Although bonds between males are in conflict with courtship and marriage, prominent female characters, female friendships, and female doubles further heterosexual relations. Love relationships and marriages are also impeded by social and political tensions: patriarchal rivalry and friendship in *Much Ado*, class distinctions in *All's Well*, racial divisions in *Othello*, imperial war between Rome and Egypt in *Antony and Cleopatra*, estrangement between court and country, fathers and sons in *The Winter's Tale*.

I explore the pressures that make the transition from wooing to wedding so difficult and examine its effects on relations between the sexes, and especially on the status of the female characters. One way to start thinking about this transition as it is experienced by the women and men in the plays is to examine certain of the ideologies that shape it—to look at the functions, interactions, and implications of the conventions of courtly love, which is associated with courtship, and of cuckoldry, which is associated with marriage. These conventions coexist in all the plays examined here.[16] The men idealize their beloveds, and the women deny, mock, and qualify their lovers' protestations of commonplaces of what I will call Petrarchan love, the attenuated, formulaic Renaissance version of medieval courtly love relegated here to the period of courtship. Through this mockery the women enhance, but ultimately threaten, their status. By debunking Petrarchanism, they expose the emptiness of male idealization and the unreliability of male vows of undying love. They are able to seize control of courtship, to insist on the reality of female sexuality and shrewishness, and to affirm for themselves and other women a complex identity beyond the Petrarchan stereotypes. Apparently freer in courtship than most upper-class Renaissance daughters were, these heroines typically defy their fathers, choose their own marriage partners, and woo them aggressively. In the bedtricks of *All's Well* and *Measure for Measure,* women even coerce their husbands to consummate their marriages. But by attaining verbal superiority, and taking themselves off the pedestal, by asserting their desires and acting on them, Shakespeare's maids are moving toward and necessitating their subordination as wives—their domestication by silence, by removal of disguise, and by giving themselves, their possessions, and their sexuality to the husbands.

Deidealization, as it prepares the way for marital sexual union, activates the misogyny that coexists with idealization. Having dismantled the conventions of Petrarchan love, Shakespeare's maids, when they become wives or are about to, ignite the comic—or tragic—conventions of cuckoldry. Cuckoldry derives from misogyny and is the inverse of both medieval and Renaissance courtly love; it subordinates women in a variety of ways. Both conventions express anxiety about or hostility toward marital sexuality. Courtly love does so, in its medieval form, by encouraging adulterous love and, in its Renaissance form, by idealizing unattainable women and denying their sexuality. Cuckoldry does so by emphasizing women's dangerous sexuality and promiscuity and the precariousness of their possession by their husbands. On the other hand, courtly love implies some mutuality, either in a physically adulterous or sublimated relationship or in a mutually chaste courtship, whereas cuckoldry assumes asymmetry: the motif concerns itself only with female infidelity; women cannot be cuckolded. In this way, cuckoldry subordinates as well as denigrates women. The woman is the focus of courtly love conventions, however attenuated her presentation or self-absorbed her lover; the central image of courtly love is the woman's eyes, symbol of her ennobling influence over her lover. In contrast, the focus of cuckoldry is entirely on cuckold and cuckolder; in fact, there is not even a term comparable to *adulteress* to designate the woman's role in the cuckoldry triangle; nor is there a special term for her if she is the victim of infidelity. Cuckoldry's central emblem is, of course, the cuckold's horns, symbol of the sexual potency that has been appropriated by his rival.[17] The convention acknowledges the power of women's sexuality but represses this knowledge. Instead, male sexuality is emphasized, and wives are treated as property that serves to validate husbands' manhood, honor, and status.

The effect of the motif in Shakespeare's plays is complicated by the fact that usually the men are only imaginary cuckolds; the women are almost invariably chaste and faithful. Though they are vilified in misogynist commonplaces, they are eventually vindicated, and the plays prove them superior to the men in their fidelity, love, strength, endurance, while the men are made to look foolish or murderous and to experience guilt, punishment, repentance, forgiveness. So women's poswer is enhanced and confirmed by the men's slander, but only at the price of confinement in the most restrictive of stereotypes—only if they remain chaste, loving, obedient, and long-suffering, only if they are willing to die for love (or to pretend to die for love), to return after marriage to something resembling the chaste immobility of the Petrarchan beloved. In the plays as in the period, women's sexuality is a source of potential power and considerable anxiety.

Marriage especially may be the locus of sexual anxiety in the plays because it was the focus of multiple pressures in the culture in which Shakespeare lived and worked. Traditionally, the state, the church, the family, the local community, and the marriageable couple had powerful and conflicting designs on the institution of marriage. In Shakespeare's England these conflicts were particularly acute because of the political tensions which accompanied the establishment of an independent Protestant state, the religious changes which attended the Reformation and the creation of the Anglican church, the influential programs of the humanist reformers, and the extensive theoretical controversy about the nature of women, possibly generated by unsettling changes in their social roles. Attitudes toward the place of women, the nature of sexuality, and the function of marriage were contradictory and in flux in the Elizabethan period as they are in the plays, so that reading the social representations of women is as complicated a business as reading the literary ones. But those representations in the prescriptive literature provide a useful backdrop and an illuminating analogue to the literary representations that are the focus of this book.

Just as literary critics have arrived at various assessments of the role of female characters in the plays, so historians propound conflicting views on the status of women in the period. Traditionally, historians have assumed that ferment over women, sexuality, and marriage generated improvements in the status of women as well as that of men. They cite as evidence the presence of exemplary women who achieved political power or exhibited impressive intellectual accomplishments (Mary Tudor, Queen Elizabeth I, Margaret Roper, Lady Jane Grey, the Howard sisters, the Countess of Pembroke),[18] the humanists' advocacy of education for women, and Protestantism's new ideology of companionate marriage.[19] But most contemporary scholars of women, marriage, and the family argue that the status of women relative to that of men and to that of women in earlier periods diminished and emphasize their new restrictions. They discover that the remarkable accomplishments of exemplary women were anomalous, manifested asymmetries, and generated anxieties;[20] they argue that education for women was less available, less serious, more problematic than that offered men;[21] they show that women's economic freedom and potential declined;[22] they argue that companionate marriage in a patriarchal society demanded the increased subordination of women.[23] The evidence and arguments supporting the two assessments, taken together, reveal the paradoxical mixture of gains and losses that was the lot of Renaissance women.

In the period as in the plays, the ideology of marriage brings into sharp focus the contradictory attitudes toward women and the complicated blend of power and subordination which characterized their status. The Reformation had begun to transform the old ideology without altering the prescribed form of marriage, its traditional functions, or the attitudes that accompanied them. To the two conventional functions of the institution—the accomplishment of legitimate procreation and the avoidance of fornication—the state-and-church sponsored homilie on marriage joined a new one, the loving amity of the couple. Marriage "is instituted of GOD, to the intent that man and woman should live lawfully in a perpetuall friendship, to bring foorth fruite, and to avoid fornication."[24] Advocacy of companionate marriage—the loving sexual partnership of husband and wife—went hand in hand with other changes in attitude that had potentially positive implications for women. Love, once denounced as a dangerous disrupter of marriage, was now decreed essential to it. Celibacy having been demoted by the Reformation, marital sexuality was no longer viewed as a necessary evil but as a positive good—and not only by Protestants. Erasmus, for example, in his *Epistle in laude and praise of matrimonie*, extravagantly extolled copulation as a law of God and nature (even trees and rocks do it).[25] He implied that sexuality provides not just progeny (the main argument of the epistle) but intrinsic fair pleasure: "I here nat hym whiche wyll saye unto me that that foule pchynge and pryckes of carnall lust have come nat of nature, but of syn. . . . And as touchyng the fowlnes surely we make that by our imaginacion to be fowle, which of the selfe nature is fayre and holy" (sig. B8). He points out that men who fail to till their fields are punished and asks "what punyshment is he worthy whyche refuseth to tylle that ground which tylled beareth men? And in tyllage of the erthe is requyred a longe and paynefull labour, here the short tyllage is also entysed with a pleasure as it wer a reward prepared therefore" (sig. C6ᵛ). Since a harmonious sexual companionship requires the consent and compatibility of the couple, enforced marriage and the custom of wardship were increasingly condemned; and since sexual satisfaction was to be found in marriage by husband as well as wife, adultery was condemned for both and the double standard denounced,[26] as it is in Shakespeare's plays; directly by Emilia in *Othello* and indirectly by the paucity of either wayward wives or philandering husbands throughout the canon.

There are, however, a number of external and internal impediments to the success of companionate marriage. The new demand for the couple's mutual affection and sexual satisfaction was inevitably in conflict with the desire of parents to control their childrens' marriages for family advancement or consolidation, a conflict that is central to many of the plays. Although children were theoretically able to negotiate their own marriages, parents, especially upper-class parents, continued to regulate spousals in order to achieve or maintain status, cement alliances, gain economic advantage, and ensure continuity of family and property. Indeed, parental pressures may have been especially strong in the period (as they certainly are in the plays) due to economic and demographic factors that tender to increase competition for suitable matches. Since aristocratic fortunes were in decline, heirs from the peerage needed to marry lower-born brides from the expanding mercantile class, whose large dowries would restore depleted family reserves. At the same time, because the population (and hence the number of marriageable daughters) was increasing and the number of male heirs in the peerage was not, the competition to marry these daughters into the aristocracy was fierce. This competition is reflected in the doubling of the average size of dowries in the period from 1570-1590 (with still greater increases later) and in the increase in the ratio of dowry to jointure, the husband's provision for the wife after his death.[27] Hence fathers continued to betroth their children before they reached the age of consent (twelve) and to control their children's marriage prospects even after their deaths, through wills more restrictive and less imaginative than that of Portia's father in *The Merchant of*

Venice. Although legal marriage required only the consent of the couple, economic arrangements could not be accomplished without a ceremony and parental contracts;[28] therefore parental consent was often essential. Children who were wards (like Bertram and Helen) were under still more severe restraints, as their marriages could be auctioned off to the highest bidder and they had no appeal to parental affection.

Even when the couple's choice met the requirements of their parents and their society, they themselves (like Claudio and Hero) might find negotiating an amicable relationship difficult. These difficulties were exacerbated by the contradictory attitudes of the period toward women, sexuality, and male-female relations. In spite of the mutuality and companionship urged, in fact the woman had unequal status at every point in the process of wooing and wedding. She gave up more, she had to endure more, and she bore greater responsibility for the success—or failure—of the marriage. The very assumption of her emotional and sexual equality in the context of a male-dominated social order seems to have had the consequence of creating restrictions on her.

The prescriptive literature, while urging men to marry and providing them with detailed instructions on the choice of wives, rarely provides assistance for women beyond a vague admonition to choose a spouse wisely. This lack of helpful advice implies that women had no choice other than marriage, that their marriages were controlled by their parents even more than men's, and that men took the initiative in courtship—as they probably usually did in the period, if not always in Shakespeare's plays. Women, moreover, like Iago's "deserving woman" are warned to be wary of their wooers: "See suitors following, and not look behind" (*Oth*, II.i.157). Both the conservative Catholic Vives, in *Instruction of a Christian Woman*, written at the beginning of the fifteenth century, and the progressive anonymous compiler of *The Lawes Resolution of Womens Rights*, written at the beginning of the seventeenth century, sternly warn women to guard against the inevitable deceits of their wooers:

> Give none ear unto the lover, no more than thou wouldst do unto an enchanter or sorcerer. For he cometh pleasantly and flattering, first praising the maid, showing her how he is taken with the love of her beauty, and that he must be dead for her love, for these lovers know well enough the vainglorious minds of many, which have a great delight in their own praises, wherewith they be caught like as the birder beguileth the birds,[29]—

and against the violence which furthers these deceits:

> But to what purpose is it for women to make vowes, when men have so many millions of wayes to make them break them? And when sweet words, faire promises, tempting, flattering, swearing, lying will not serve to beguile the poore soule: then with rough handling, violence, and plaine strength of armes, they are, or have beene heretofore, rather made prisoners to lusts theeves, than wives and companions to faithfull honest lovers: So drunken are men with their owne lusts, and the poysen of Ovids false precept, *Vim licet appellant, vis est ea grata puellis:* That if the rampier of Lawes were not betwixt women and their harmes, I verily thinke none of them, being above twelve yeares of age, and under an hundred, being either faire or rich, should be able to escape ravishing. [p. 377]

Having survived the perils of courtship, the woman, at marriage, became in the apt term, a *femme couverte*, losing all her possessions along with her legal and economic rights: *That which the Wife hath is her Husbands.* "For thus it is, If before Marriage the Woman were possessed of Horses, Neate, Sheepe, Corne, Wool, Money, Plate, and Jewels, all manner of moveable substance is presently by conjunction the Husbands, to sell, keepe or bequeath if he die."[30]

Once married, the wife suffered more severely than the husband the consequences of the injunction to procrete; she endured the dangers of repeated pregnancies and childbirths (a poignant theme in the romances) and the difficulties of nursing and weaning (she is advised to nurse her children herself) and of child raising. Even the homilie on marriage acknowledges women's heavier burden: "Trueth it is, that they must specially feele the griefe and paines of their Matrimonie, in that they relinquish the liberty of their owne rule, in the paine of their travailing, in the bringing up of their children. In which offices they be in great perils, and be grieved with great afflictions, which they might be without if they lived out of Matrimonie" (p. 243). A similar but more radical acknowledgment occurs in *Lawes Resolutions* when, at the beginning of its chapter on laws pertaining to widows, they are counseled to rejoice rather than grieve at their husband's death: "Why mourne you so, you that be widowes? Consider how long you have beene in subjection under the predominance of parents, of your husbands, now you be free in libertie, '*fróe proprii juris,*' at your owne Law, . . . the vow of a widow, or of a woman divorced no man had power to disallow of, for her estate was free from controlment" (p. 232). As the passage suggests, the death of her husband was the wife's only escape from the afflictions of marriage. Although judicial separation, *divortium a mensa et thoro* (which did not legally dissolve the marriage or allow remarriage), was available to the wife in the case of the husband's adultery, brutality, or desertion, and although remarriage in the case of a husband's adultery was tolerated, most wives could not practically avail themselves of this option, since they had no money, property, or legal power.[31]

Even those parts of the ideology of marriage that might have been expected to alter and enhance women's status engendered demands for their subordination. The assumptions that sexuality was superior to celibacy and that sexual satisfaction was to be achieved in marriage by both men and women placed the wife's sexuality in a new light; she was no longer merely a necessary vessel for procreation but an active sexual partner. But sexuality, and in particular female sexuality, continued to be associated with sin and Eve's fall, and lasciviousness, inconstancy, and frailty were attributed especially to women.[32] The enhancement of women's sexual role made female incontinence more threatening. Hence chastity became the primary duty required of women throughout life in the forms of virginity, marital fidelity, widows' abstinence. Not only did the wife have to remain faithful but, unlike the husband, she had to prove her faithfulness by exhibiting the peculiarly Renaissance virtue of shamefastness and by avoiding all appearances of immodesty or wantonness. Elaborate restrictions on dress and behavior grew out of this emphasis on chastity and shamefastness. The liberal Tilney's advice to wives on how to protect their reputations is identical with if less elaborate than the counsel the conservative Vives gave to maids: stay at home. Going abroad was dangerous, Vives argues, because

> if a slander once take hold in a maid's name by folks' opinion, it is in a manner everlasting, nor cannot be washed away without great tokens and shows of chastity and wisdom. If thou talk little in company folks think thou canst but little good; if thou speak much they reckon thee light. If thou speak uncunningly, they count thee dull witted; if thou speak cunningly thou shalt be counted but a shrew. If thou answer not quickly thou shalt be called proud or ill brought up; if thou answer [readily] they shall say thou wilt be soon overcome. If thou sit with demure countenance, thou art called a dissembler. If thou make much moving, they will call thee foolish. If thou look on any side, then will they say, thy mind is there. If thou laugh when any man laugheth, though thou do it not of purpose, straight they will say thou hast a fantasy unto the man and his sayings, and that it were no great mastery to win thee. Whereto should I tell, how much occasion of vice and naughtiness is abroad.[33]

The woman's militant chastity was essential to counteract both her own "frailty" and men's deceit and aggression. While Shakespeare's women do not always stay at home, they do protect their chastity assiduously.

As the emphasis on sexual partnership in marriage resulted in more stringent demands for female chastity, likewise the call for a loving partnership between men and women resulted in or was accompanied by a contradictory insistence on rigid hierarchy. The husband's and the wife's contributions to marital amity were distinct and asymmetrical. The husband's duty was to govern his wife lovingly, firmly—untyrannically but absolutely. Tolerating the frailties of the "weaker vessel," he was to ignore small faults and correct large ones, not brutally but subtly, a strategy recommended as being effective as well as humane: "And therefore considering all her frailties she is to be rather spared. By this meanes thou shalt not onely nourish concord: but shalt have her heart in thy power and will. For honest natures will sooner be reteined to do their duties, rather by gentle wordes than by stripes."[34] Tilney's dialogue argues that the wife's sexuality could be similarly controlled: "In this long and troublesome journey of matrimonie, the wise man maye not be contented onely with his Spouses virginitie, but by little and little must gently procure that he maye also steale away her private will and appetite, so that of two bodies there may be made one onelye hart, which she will sonne doe, if love raigne in hir" (sig. B6). Many Shakespearean husbands, among them Petruchio, Benedick, Othello, and Leontes, manifest the desire to control their wife's will and appetite.

The wife's love, in contrast to the husband's, was to be expressed through the obedience promised by her (but not by her husband) in the Anglican marriage ceremony and enjoined on her by all the prescriptive literature and by the homilie on marriage: "But as for their husbands, them must they obey, and cease from commanding, and performe subjection. For this surely doth nourish concord very much when the wife is ready at hand at her husbands commandement, when she will apply her selfe to his will, when shee endehoureth her selfe to seek his contentation, and to doe him pleasure, when shee will eschewe all things that might offend him" (p. 242). If husbands should have faults, wives are to admonish them gently and tactfully, preferably in bed.[35] Women are urged to love and "endeavor to please" even vile, vicious, or vice-ridden husbands: "howe much more the husbande bee evill, and out of order, so much more is the woman's prayse, if shee love him" (Tilney, sig. D5). Hero, Helena, Desdemona, and Hermione all deserve such praise. Writings on marriage assume that conflict is inevitable but offer men and women complementary strategies of control and obedience for alleviating it.

The relative status of men and women when relations of the sexes were at their most friendly and civilized, the competing forces that interacted in companionate marriage, and the surface equality that masked and upheld male authority are not only expounded in Edmund Tilney's *The Flower of Friendshippe,* they are also embodied in its frame and its dramatic interplay. This pleasing work by a future master of the revels is a combination of instructive marriage treatise and witty dialogue with roots in Castiglione's *Courtier,* Pedro de Luján's *Coloquios Matrimoniales,* and Erasmus's marriage colloques.[36] Superficially, the dialogue represents dramatically the equality for men and women in marriage which it advocates. The pastime is first undertaken in preference to various sports rejected because the women in the company cannot participate. The husband's duties, delineated by Don Pedro, guest and game leader, and the wife's, expounded by Madame Julia, the hostess, are parallel and reciprocal. Husband and wife are urged to love and care for each other, to tolerate the spouse's weaknesses, to avoid various faults including adultery, to be discreet, perform their duties, raise the children. The dramatic interplay concerns sexual politics and is carefully balanced. Isabella, Julia's "feminist" daughter attacks women's subordination and defends their rights, like her prototype, Lord Julian, in *The Courtier* and like her successors in Shakespeare, Adriana and Emilia. Opposing her, Gualter mounts commonplace attacks on women's shrewishness and desire for mastery. His name, the same as that of Griselda's husband, marks him as a conventionally witty misogynist with many counterparts in dialogues, colloquies, the women controversy, and the drama, including Berowne, Benedick, and Iago.[37]

But in spite of its attention to balance and equality, the dialogue responds to the anxieties Gualter voices about female domination and unruliness by implicitly and explicitly affirming male authority. The frame arrangements, which apparently promote shared authority, are in fact controlled by Pedro, who proposes the pastime and, even as he delegates to Julia the garland of sovereignty for the first day, determines the topic. Her immediate return of the garland, ceding him the right to speak first, is inevitable; her token authority gives her no actual control over either topic or speaker. On the second day, Julia passes the garland to her friend and contemporary Aloisa, and when it is predictably returned to her, she willingly but obediently accepts the role of speaker: "For disobedience is a fault in all persons, but the greatest vice in a woman" (sig. D3). The duties enjoined are also not quite parallel. While both husband and wife are forbidden to commit adultery, only the wife is counseled to maintain a perfectly chaste reputation. Considerably more forbearance is urged for the wife than for the husband. An extreme case of wifely forbearance is represented in Pedro's example, which is welcomed by Julia as an apt conclusion to *her* lecture on the wife's duties. He tells of a wife who cures her husband's adultery by enhancing it for him: she brings a fine bed and hangings to make the bare surroundings in which he carries on his affair with a poor woman more pleasant, and in this way wins him back to her love (and more attractive bedchamber). "He should . . . have had a bed of nettles, or thornes, had it bene to mee" (sig. E6), retorts Aloisa, unmoved by the exemplary tale.

The tensions underlying equality and the mode of their resolution are clearest in the contrasting treatments of Gualter and Isabella. Gualter's misogynistic generalizations about the evils of women are not taken entirely seriously or adopted by Pedro, but they are never denied. Gualter's interpolations reiterate that, even at their best, women pose problems for husbands—that, for example, rich, fair, noble, and virtuous women all make bad wives because these advantages can turn a husband into a "slave" or a "bondman" (sigs. B5^v, B5), and that, at their worst, "they be shrewes all, and if you give the simplest of them leave to treade upon your foote, tomorrowe she will tread upon thy head" (sig. C7^v). Although the women persistently (but playfully) demand that Gualter be banished or silenced for his digressive and intrusive "prattle," Pedro tolerates him, significantly arguing that "he increaseth our sporte, and we cannot well want him" (sig. B7). Isabella, with equal persistence, inserts her own witty interpolations on behalf of women, disagreeing with Pedro's claim that marital equality is achieved by joining an older man to a younger woman, arguing that wives cannot be expected to love adulterous husbands, and asking sarcastically whether the wives should accommodate themselves to husbands who are mad or drunk. Julia and Aloisa similarly remark women's oppression and mock at excesses of male authority. But in contrast to the tolerance afforded Gualter's witty misogyny, Isabella's earnest arguments for equality between women and men in marriage are vigorously refuted.

No one supports Isabella in her direct challenge to the key doctrines of the wife's obedience. Isabella argues that this obedience should be reciprocated: "but as meete is it, that the husbande obey the wife, as the wife the husband, or at the least that there be no superioritye betweene them, as the aunciemt philosophers have defended. For women have soules as wel as men, they have wit as wel as men, and more apte for procreation of children, than men. What reason is it then, that they should be bound, whom nature hath made free" (sig. D8). She extends her case with an example from the Achaians in which gender roles are reversed, with the women ruling and the men doing the housework. Her argument is authoritatively attacked by the whole company. Gualter expresses the dangers in such role reversal when he responds to her utopian example by asking mockingly of such a wife's treatment of her husband, "and might she beat him too?" Julia for the first time in the dialogue asserts her maternal authority over Isabella, condescendingly urging her not to believe everything she hears and dismissing another sort of potential "equality"—that of separate spheres with men ruling outdoors and women in the home. This, she claims, is a barbarian and dangerous custom because it gives women a sphere, if only a limited one, for potential disobedience. She is immediately seconded by "father Erasmus" who has spoken only once before in the dialogue and whose succinct, unqualified assertion—the last word on the topic—is lent weight by his age, his reputation, and his appeal to religion: "both divine, & humaine lawes, in our religion giveth the man absolute authoritie, over the woman in all places" (E1). Julia then provides a rational, secular, psychological justification for Erasmus's declaration, arguing that men are naturally suited for sovereignty and women only rarely so.[38] Through this exchange the tensions that emerge from female demands for equality in marriage are decisively resolved.

But this resolution is temporary and fictional. The continuing dialectic between women's small gains in power and status and the restrictions urged in response to them characterizes the period and makes conclusive assessments of the woman's part difficult. These assessments, historians now emphasize, will differ according to which women are examined—women of what century, what country, what class, what marital status; according to which sources are used—diaries, letters, court depositions, demographic data, prescriptive or ideological texts, literature or drama; and according to what criteria are employed, which features isolated for analysis. Gualter's attacks on women may be extracted from Tilney's dialogue to emphasize the period's pervasive misogyny or Isabella's spirited and sensible arguments may be cited as evidence of its enlightened awareness of women's authority and inequality. When the complex, witty interplay of the prescriptive dialogue as a whole is taken into account, its relationship to actual marriages in the period becomes even harder to explicate. Do its form and symmetry and the presence of women as active eloquent participants reflect or condone new liberties gained by women? Does its final unequivocal support for male authority reflect or advocate increased restrictions for women? Or is it merely a playful fiction unrelated to women's lives?

Precisely the same questions can be asked about Shakespeare's plays, whose strong female characters are often silenced at the conclusions; they can be answered only with difficulty. Unless there were real women whose power and activities seemed threatening, it is hard to account for the numerous works like Tilney's devoted to the regulation of female behavior. But neither the fact of ideological ferment about women and marriage nor the presence of some exceptionally powerful women is proof of significant changes in the lives of most women, in the Renaissance or today. Most historians of women, marriage, and the family in the period would answer Joan Kelly's provocative question, "Did women have a Renaissance?" as she did—with an unqualified no.[39] But as these historians marshal evidence for the negative, they nonetheless make heretofore invisible women visible, devote sustained and subtle attention to them, and reweave their lives into the texture of history, redefining it. It is, ironically, as if today's historians were creating for those long dead women the Renaissance they never enjoyed.[40]

The contradictory assessments of women's place made possible by the complex evidence the period provides are neatly summed up in Juliet Dusinberre's *Shakespeare and the Nature of Women* (1976) and Lisa Jardine's *Still Harping on Daughters: Women and Drama in the Age of Shakespeare* (1983),[41] books which extend these assessments to encompass fictional women. Both books examine attitudes toward women in the drama by examining attitudes toward women in the period; both look at the effects of Protestantism and puritanism, virginity and chastity, humanist education, cross-dressing in drama and social life, the roles of exemplary historical women, and the influence of powerful female stereotypes. Employing similar material with similar aims, they construct precisely contradictory theses encompassing the period, the drama, and Shakespeare.[42] Dusinberre argues that the "feminism" (p. 1) of the period is reflected in drama which is "feminist in sympathy" and that Shakespeare questioned received stereotypes about women, "saw men and women as equal" (p. 308), and created strong, complex female characters who reflect the period's elevation of women's status. Jardine reads the drama as a reaction to, not a reflection of, social realities, a misogynist response to "the patriarchy's unexpressed worry about the great social changes which characterize the period" (p. 6). Strong, passionate women like Kate in *Taming of the Shrew*, the Duchess of Malfi, or Moll Cutpurse in Middleton's *Roaring Girl* (chap. 3 passim; chap. 4 passim; pp. 159-61) are not exemplary or liberating but are satiric creations or cautionary warnings. Such women are invariably contained or chastised by the drama; like Isabella in Tilney's dialogue, they are set up to be suppressed. Shakespeare's plays reflect this misogyny; his treatment of strong women reflects patriarchal anxieties, and his admirable heroines fit the "saving stereotypes" which the period created of patient, chaste, long-suffering, self-martyring women (pp. 184-93). Although these two books are in sharp contradiction to each other, each reflects, I think, one side of the complex truth about the representations of women both in the period and in the drama. Although Shakespeare certainly did not speak as a woman or in defense of women, he did represent them fully, absorbing and recreating in another dimension all of the contradictions that surround women's status. His created male and female characters articulate tensions in relations between men and women as clearly, and sometimes perhaps more clearly, than does the historical record, with its persistent tendency to erase female voices.

My study examines the complex ways in which women's roles are represented in Shakespeare's plays. The status of the female characters varies according to their place in the maiden/wife/widow paradigm. It varies, too, from genre to genre, from play to play, and from moment to moment in individual plays. In the comedies (and—

with more strain—in the problem comedies) the women are maidens who "can shift it well enough." Their assertions of verbal, social, and sexual power enable them to evade or manipulate financial pressures, fathers' commands, the intricacies of marriage contracts, and the stereotyping of themselves by romantic or misogynist lovers. They do so by using the resources of disguise, wit, greenworld escapes, parodic or postponed nuptials, salutary mock deaths, generative bedtricks. But at the conclusions of the comedies, the maidens' approaching subordination as wives is manifested dramatically not only in Kate's speech advocating obedience, but in the women's sudden silence, their removal of disguise, their return from the green world, their forgiveness of husbands "molded out of faults" (*MM*, V.i.441). Yet Portia maintains her power even *after,* her extravagant giving away of herself; she manifests it through her ability in the final scene to use her sexuality positively, to keep control of cuckoldry jokes (usually the male prerogative on the eve of consummation), and to engineer the commitment she desires from Bassanio and Antonio.

In the tragedies, maidens become wives and must often "relinquish the liberty of their owne rule." Their released sexuality is now execrated, their disobedience is experienced by the men as threatening, their subordination is demanded. Many of the women characters in the tragedies, however passionately loving or brutally strong-willed, move at the end of the plays toward isolation, passivity, madness, or suicide. Almost all die as a result of their love of men—Juliet, Portia, Ophelia and Gertrude, Desdemona and Emilia, Goneril, Regan, and Cordelia, Lady Macbeth and Lady Macduff. But Cleopatra's suicide is not obedient, not a punishment, not enacted just for love. In the romances, these tragic paradigms are averted by the splitting of female characters into mothers and daughters. the wife/mothers—good or bad—die or appear to die and can be idealized or scapegoated. The daughters, though they do not stay at home, remain impeccably pure maidens; their loving chastity regenerates (literally or symbolically) the virtues of their mothers and reconciles their fathers (who have mitigated their tyranny) with their suitors (who have tempered their desires). But Paulina is anomalous; neither a daughter nor a mother (we know she has three daughters, but she is never put in any dramatic relation to them), when "free in libertie," she makes use of her widow's role to sustain the long friendships with Hermione and Leontes which enable her to serve as catalyst to their reunion.

The rich characterization, dramatic development, and symbolic implications of the women's roles in the plays are, of course, far more difficult to interpret than this summary can begin to suggest. In this study I will explore the intricately interwoven contexts that define the meaning of women's actions in Shakespeare's plays: the relationships they forge with men and with each other; the dramatic and psychological significance of the institution of marriage and of the motif of broken nuptials; the structures of particular plays and their interactions with their sources; the nature of genres; and the development of the canon. It is not only that these contexts define women's actions. Making women newly visible in them transforms the meaning of marriage and broken nuptials, the texture of the plays, the shape of the genres, and the configurations of Shakespearean development.

Notes

[1] Leo Salingar, *Shakespeare and the Traditions of Comedy* (Cambridge: Cambridge University Press, 1974), pp. 302-05.

[2] Michelle Rosaldo, "The Use and Abuse of Anthropology: Reflections on Feminism and Cross-Cultural Understanding," *Signs* 5 (1980): 400.

[3] Ian Maclean, *The Renaissance Notion of Women* (Cambridge: Cambridge University Press, 1980), emphasizes the profoundly conservative effect of the dominant paradigm of marriage on Renaissance thinking about women. This paradigm, he argues (as well as vested interest in preserving it) is crucially responsible for the maintenance of unchanged views of women's inferiority throughout the period in the disciplines of theology (pp. 25-27), ethics and politics (pp. 65-67), and law (pp. 80-81); only in the area of medicine is there conceptual change, because there the absence of the paradigm of marriage "acts as a liberating force". (p. 45). "Marriage is an immovable obstacle to any improvement in the theoretical or real status of women in law, in theology, in moral and political philosophy" (p. 85).

[4] T. E., *The Lawes Resolutions of Womens Rights; or The Lawes Provision for Women. A Methodicall Collection of such Statutes and Customes, with the Cases, Opinions, Arguments and points of Learning in the Law, as do properly conceirne Women* (London: John Grove, 1632), p. 6.

[5] Allison Heisch, "Queen Elizabeth I and the Persistence of Patriarchy," *Feminist Review* 4 (1980): 45-56.

[6] Anna Jameson, *Characteristics of Women*, 2 vols. (London: Saunders & Otley, 1832); Mary Cowden Clarke, *The Girlhood of Shakespeare's Heroines*, 3 vols. (London: W. H. Smith and Son, 1850-55); Helena Faucit Martin, *On Some of Shakespeare's Female Characters* (London: Blackwood, 1885).

[7] Irene Dash, *Wooing, Wedding, and Power: The Women in Shakespeare's Plays* (New York: Columbia University Press, 1981).

[8] Coppélia Kahn, "*The Taming of the Shrew:* Shakespeare's Mirror of Marriage," in *The Authority of Experience,* ed. Arlyn Diamond and Lee Edwards (Amherst: University of Massachusetts Press, 1977), pp. 84-100; L. T. Fitz, "Egyptian Queens and Male Reviewers: Sexist Attitudes in *Antony and Cleopatra* Criticism," *Shakespeare Quarterly* 28 (1977): 297-316; S. N. Garner, "Shakespeare's Desdemona," *Shakespeare Studies* 9 (1976): 233-52.

[9] Carole McKewin, "Counsels of Gall and Grace: Intimate Conversations between Women in Shakespeare's Plays," in *The Woman's Part: Feminist Criticism of Shakespeare,* ed. Carolyn Ruth Swift Lenz, Gayle Greene, and Carol Thomas Neely (Urbana: University of Illinois Press, 1980), pp. 117-32; Marilyn Williamson, "Doubling, Women's Anger, and Genre," *Women's Studies* 9 (1982): pp. 107-20; Madonne Miner, "Neither mother, wife, nor England's queene: The Roles of Women in *Richard III,*" in Lenz et al., *Woman's Part,* pp. 35-55.

[10] Joan Klein, "Lady Macbeth: 'Infirm of Purpose,'" in Lenz et al., pp. 240-55; Clara Claiborne Park, "As We Like It: How a Girl Can Be Smart and Still Popular," in ibid., pp. 100-16

[11] Louis Adrian Montrose, "'The Place of a Brother': Social Process and Comic Form in *As You Like It,*" *Shakespeare Quarterly* 32 (1982): 28-54

[12] Madelon Gohlke, "'I wooed thee with my sword': Shakespeare's Tragic Paradigms," in Lenz et al., pp. 150-70; "'All that is spoke is marred': Language and Consciousness in *Othello,*" *Women's Studies* 9 (1982): 157-76; "'And When I Love Thee Not': Women and the Psychic Integrity of the Tragic Hero," *The Hebrew University Studies in Literature* 8 (1980), 44-65. Coppélia Kahn, *Man's Estate: Masculine Identity in Shakespeare* (Berkeley: University of California Press, 1981).

[13] Linda Bamber, *Comic Women, Tragic Men: A Study of Gender and Genre in Shakespeare* (Stanford: Stanford University Press, 1982).

[14] Peter Erickson, *Patriarchal Structures in Shakespeare's Drama* (Berkeley: University of California Press, 1985).

[15] Marianne Novy, *Love's Argument: Gender Relations in Shakespeare* (Chapel Hill: University of North Carolina Press, 1985).

[16] In *All's Well That Ends Well* the conventions are less central, and they are inverted. The woman idealizes her beloved, and the man actually participates (by virtue of the bedtrick) in what he imagines to be infidelity.

[17] Kahn, *Man's Estate,* discusses the significance of the horns and delineates cuckoldry's connections with misogyny, the double standard, and patriarchal marriage (pp. 119-22). She notes that while *cuckquean* is defined by the *OED* as a female cuckold, the word does not appear in Shakespeare (p. 120, n. 2).

[18] Pearl Hogrefe, *Tudor Women: Commoners and Queens* (Ames: Iowa State University Press, 1975), and *Women of Action in Tudor England: Nine Biographical Sketches* (Ames: Iowa State University Press, 1977).

[19] Juliet Dusinberre, *Shakespeare and the Nature of Women* (New York: Barnes and Noble, 1975), emphasizes the importance of these factors.

[20] Carole Levin, "Queens and Claimants: Political Insecurity in Sixteenth-Century England," paper delivered to Newberry Library Conference, Changing Perspectives on Women in the Renaissance, May 1983, and Louis Adrian Montrose, "'Shaping Fantasies': Figurations of Gender and Power in Elizabethan Culture," *Representations* 2 (Spring 1983): 61-94, explore some social and literary responses to the anxieties of having a woman on the throne. See also Heisch, "Queen Elizabeth I and the Persistence of Patriarchy."

[21] Margaret King, "Thwarted Ambitions: Six Learned Women of the Early Italian Renaissance," *Soundings* 76 (1976): 280-300; "The Religious Retreat of Isotta Nogarola (1418-1466)," *Signs* 3 (1978): 807-22; "Book-Lined Cells: Women and Humanism in the Early Italian Renaissance," in *Beyond Their Sex: Learned Women of the European Past,* ed. Patricia H. Labalme (New York: New York University Press, 1980), and other essays in this volume.

[22] Kathleen Casey, "The Cheshire Cat: Reconstructing the Experience of Medieval Women," in *Liberating Women's History,* ed. Berenice A. Carroll (Urbana: University of Illinois Press, 1976). pp. 224-49.

[23] Lawrence Stone, "The Rise of the Nuclear Family in Early Modern England," in *The Family in History,* ed. Charles E. Rosenberg (Philadelphia: University of Pennsylvania Press, 1975), pp. 13-57; *The Family, Sex and Marriage in England 1500-1800* (New York: Harper & Row, 1977), pp. 123-218. Stone discusses the period from 1530 to 1660 as the patriarchal stage in the evolution of the nuclear family.

[24] *Certaine Sermons or Homilies,* facsimile reproduction of 1623 edition, ed. Mary Ellen Rickey and Thomas B. Stroup (Gainesville, Fla.: Scholars' Facsimiles & Reprints, 1968), p. 239.

[25] Desiderius Erasmus, *A ryght frutefull Epystle in laude and prayse of matrymony,* trans. Richard Tavernour (London: R. Redman, 1530?), sigs. B3-B4^v.

[26] Although attacks on the double standard were commonplace, it did not, of course, disappear, as Keith Thomas incisively demonstrates in "The Double Standard," *Journal of the History of Ideas* 20 (1959): 195-216.

[27] Lawrence Stone, *Crisis of the Aristocracy 1558-1641* (Oxford: Clarendon Press, 1965), pp. 637-39, 643-45.

[28] George Elliot Howard, *A History of Matrimonial Institutions* (Chicago: University of Chicago Press, 1904), 1:377-80. Cf. Henry Swinburne, *A treatise of Spousals* written in the reign of Elizabeth I and first published in 1686, p. 15 (quoted in Howard, p. 377-78).

[29] Juan Luis Vives, *Instruction of a Christian Woman,* (1523) trans. Richard Hyrd (London: Thomas Berthelet, 1540), excerpted in *Vives and the Renascence Education of Women,* ed. Foster Watson (New York: Longmans, Green & Co., 1912), pp. 105-06.

[30] *Lawes Resolutions,* p. 130.

[31] Howard, *Institutions,* 2:71-85, and Thomas, "The Double Standard," 200-01.

[32] Maclean, *Notion,* p. 15-19. Stephen Greenblatt, *Renaissance Self-Fashioning from More to Shakespeare* (Chicago: University of Chicago Press, 1980), pp. 246-50, discusses Renaissance anxieties about sexuality even within marriage and their implications for Othello's relationship with Desdemona and his belief in her infidelity.

[33] Watson, *Vives,* pp. 94-95. Cf. Edmund Tilney, *A brief and pleasant discourse of duties in Mariage, called the Flower of Friendshippe* (London: Henrie Denham, 1568), sigs. E3ᵛ-E4ᵛ.

[34] Rickey and Stroup, *Homilies,* p. 241.

[35] Tilney, *Flower of Friendshippe,* sig. E7ᵛ.

[36] J. Moncado, "The Spanish Source of Edmund Tilney's 'Flower of of Friendshippe,'" *Modern Language Review* 65 (1970): 241-47, and Linda Woodbridge, *Women and the English Renaissance: Literature and the Nature of Womankind, 1540-1620* (Urbana: University of Illinois Press, 1984), pp. 59-60. I am especially grateful to Valerie Wayne, who is currently preparing an edition of Tilney's *Flower of Friendshippe,* for allowing me to read a draft of her introduction that illuminated the dialogue and its contexts.

[37] Woodbridge, *Women and the English Renaissance,* discusses the stock misogynist characters in the dialogues of the formal controversy on women (see her index), and includes a chapter on "The Stage Misogynist" (pp. 275-95).

[38] ". . . reason doth confirme the same, the man being as he is, most apt for the soveraignetie being in government, not onely skill, and experience to be required, but also capacity to comprehende, wisdome to understand, strength to execute, solicitude to prosecute, pacience to suffer, meanes to sustaine, and above all a great courage to accomplishe, all which are commonly in a man, but in a woman verye rare" (sig. C1).

[39] *Becoming Visible: Women in European History,* ed. Renate Bridenthal and Claudia Koonz (Boston: Houghton Mifflin, 1977), pp. 137-64.

[40] I was especially struck by this phenomenon at the Newberry Library Conference, Changing Perspectives on Women in the Renaissance, May 1983. During papers, brief presentations of works in progress, and lengthy discussion periods, participants, agreeing that women did not have a Renaissance, emphasized the numerous restrictions placed on them; at the same time, their presentations created a rich and complex existence for Renaissance women. This effect was apparent, for example, in Janel Mueller's analysis of *The Book of Margery Kempe,* Carole Levin's explorations of the insecurities created by Queen Elizabeth's reign, Mary Lamb's exploding of the myth of the Countess of Pembroke's patronage and her explorations of the functions of this myth, John Hill's report on the evidence for an extensive body of songs written by Francesca Caccini, Elissa Weaver's analysis of the nature of Italian sixteenth-century convent theatre, Jane Schulenburg's examination of the conditions for female sainthood, and Tilde Sankovitch's discussion of Madelaine and Catherine Des Roches's awareness of the special problems of female authorship and the female-centered myths they created in response to them.

[41] Lisa Jardine, *Still Harping on Daughters: Women and Drama in the Age of Shakespeare* (Totowa, N.J.: Barnes and Noble, 1983).

[42] Although neither book deals with Shakespeare as extensively as their titles might suggest, both wish to make him a central example of their respective theses about the period. Jardine begins by declaring that her book was generated by irritation at feminist criticism of Shakespeare, Dusinberre devotes a brief final chapter to him, and both books contain numerous remarks about particular moments in the plays. Both authors, however, are often at their least persuasive when analyzing these moments, perhaps because their piecemeal discussions of isolated characters, speeches, and scenes fail to do justice to the rich and complicated meanings these acquire as part of a complex whole. Jardine's book is a better one than Dusinberre's, but this is at least in part because she has had the benefit of much research that Dusinberre did not have available to her, including the feminist criticism which she finds inadequate, but which, like Dusinberre's book itself, has raised the issues she addresses.

Ann Jennalie Cook (essay date 1991)

SOURCE: "Secret Promises and Elopements, Broken Contracts and Divorces," in *Making a Match: Courtship in Shakespeare and His Society,* Princeton University Press, 1991, pp. 185-233.

[*In the following essay, Cook discusses many of the particulars of Elizabethan marriage laws and customs and then explores the way in which Shakespeare's plays address or correspond to real-life contemporary matrimonial issues. Cook concludes that Shakespeare represents courtship and marriage in a variety of positive and negative ways and that there is no easy way to determine what his own views on the subject were.*]

> Errour, condition, parentage, and vow,
> Adultery (the law will not allow
> Disparitie in divine worship) and
> Violence or force, or where we understand;
> In priesthood, there's profaneness, or else where,
> False faiths profest, wee likewise must forebeare,
> When there is precontract, for honesty,
> Affinitie, and disability:
> These twelve from present marriage us disswade,
> Or can retract from wedlock when 'tis made.
> —Thomas Heywood, *A Curtaine Lecture*

> Quoth she, "Before you tumbled me,
> You promised me to wed."
> So would I 'a' done by yonder sun,
> An thou hadst not come to my bed.
> —*Ham.*, IV.v.62-65

Though the conventional steps leading to an indissoluble marriage seemed clear enough to English subjects, there were also shortcuts, detours, and journeys abandoned altogether. In some cases, lovers made private rather than public promises to marry. And whatever the nature of their espousals, couples could and did consummate unions without waiting for a religious ceremony. Legally binding contracts, whether *de futuro* or *de praesenti,* might be set aside if any of several impediments existed. Elopements and secret weddings sometimes occurred. Under certain circumstances marriages were annulled, and on a few grounds even a form of divorce was possible. But because such situations represented a departure from prescribed behavior, a plethora of opinion, advice, legal restrictions, social stigma, and economic punishments converged upon those who strayed from the more conventional ways of making a match.

Of particular concern was the danger of clandestine meetings between an unmarried man and woman lest they lead to sexual intercourse. The Elizabethans' great fear of seduction derived from the ensuing stain on the female's reputation, the likelihood of pregnancy, and the possibility of her subsequent abandonment. At every level, the social structure required a child to be supported by his parents so he would not become a charge on the general public. Hence, church courts prosecuted with vigor cases of bastardy, fornication, prenuptial pregnancy, and adultery.[1] The homily *Against Whoredom and Uncleanness* was read in every parish, there were legal penalties for harboring unwed mothers, pregnancy meant dismissal for unwed servants, and midwives were instructed to use extreme means during labor for determining the fathers of illegitimate children. After 1610 "Euery lewd woman which shall haue any bastard which may be chargeable to the parish" was to be committed "to the house of correction, to be punished and set on work, during the term of one whole year."[2] Not surprisingly, the records show a low incidence of illegitimacy—about 3 percent or less, though a small upsurge around the turn of the century has not been fully explained.[3]

Aside from the activities of prostitutes and habitually wanton women, casual illicit sex seems to have been relatively common among the poor and the obscure.[4] Social historians account for differences in behavior between the upper and lower ranks in a variety of ways. They point to the opportunities for interaction provided by fairs or village festivities, by the movements of seasonal laborers, and by the employment of unmarried young adults as household servants.[5] Under such circumstances, a great deal more promiscuity might have occurred had it not been for strict formal and informal controls, particularly in the village or neighborhood, where all actions were matters of common knowledge. Yet advice routinely given to masters, together with the proceedings of the church's so-called bawdy courts and the tenor of much popular literature, confirms the existence of premarital and extramarital sexual activity. Philip Stubbes doubtless exaggerates in his complaint against festivals that "of fourtie, threescore, or a hundred Maides, going to the wood ouernight, there haue scarcely the third part of them returned home againe undefiled."[6] Nonetheless, illicit encounters did occur. In a suit for defamation it was alleged that one Isobel Lombye

> appoynted one Lancelot Osward her father's man a place wheare he shold come and have his pleasure of her and occupye her and seide further that he the saide Lancelot came and his prick would not stand and so came the second and third time to th'appoynted place and afforsaide and saide that yt . . . would not stand, and that the fourth tyme had his pleasure of her and occupyed her meanyng that the saide Lancelot Osward had carnell knowledge of the body of the said Isobel Lombye and that she was a whore.[7]

Understandably, a clever couplet counsels: "And for thy seruants let no *Belly* swell, / A baudy house is but an earthlie hell."[8]

This is not to suggest that seduction, or even bastardy, never occurred among the elite. Mary Fitton got pregnant by William Earl of Pembroke, while Penelope Rich bore five illegitimate offspring to her lover, Lord Mountjoy.[9] But these scandals did not typify the behavior of the privileged. Quite the opposite. Grace Mildmay recalls careful warnings from her governess: "Also, she advised me to avoyd such companye by all means possible, and to take heede of whom I received gifts, as a book wherein might be some fine words whereby I might betray myself unawares, or gloves or apples or such like, for that wicked companions would ever presente treacherous attempts."[10] All the advice books affirm Lady Grace's upbringing and caution against clandestine encounters. The household master declares, "I must take special heed of any secret meetings, messages, or more than ordinary liking between the men and women of my family. I must see that the men have no haunt of women to their chambers, lest lewdness becloaked under some other pretense."[11] As for the fine declarations of lovers, "Their fawning is but flattery: their faith falshoode: their faire wordes allurements to destruction: and their large promises tokens of death, or of euils worse then death."[12]

For a woman, sexual seduction was the evil worse than death. Among ordinary folk, chastity might or might not matter, but the importance of guaranteeing correct lines of inheritance and descent increased the significance of virginity for wealthy and titled females.[13] Stern are the warnings against even the appearance of impropriety: "She ought also to be more circumspect and to take better heed that she give no occasion to be yll reported of, and so to beehave her selfe, that she be not onlye not spotted wyth anye fault, but not so much as with suspicion."[14] The maidenhead is regarded as "brittle ware, which vnlesse your care be the greater for the preseruation, may get a cracke that no Art of man can make whole againe, and a blow, that no herbe is of sufficient efficacy to cure."[15] Writers graphically portray the techniques of unscrupulous wooers:

> They know the flexible disposition of Women and the sooner to ouerreach them, some will pretend they are so plunged in loue that except they obtaine their desire they will seeme to drown'd, hang, stab, poyson, or banish themselues from friends and countrie.... Some will pretend marriage, another offer continuall maintenance, but when they haue obtained their purpose, what shall a woman finde, iust that which is her euerlasting shame and griefe.[16]

Those who lose their virginity are denounced as "Monsters," "more vile then filthy channell durt fit to be swept out of the heart and suburbes of your Countrey."[17]

Because seduction could so easily masquerade as an intention to marry, secret betrothals came under particular criticism and suspicion. As part of their regular duties, parish priests were to report "Whether you know any to have made privy contracts of Matrimony, not calling two or more witnesses thereunto, nor having thereto the consent of their Parents."[18] These "privy contracts" were thought to derive from "knauery, falshood, and deceite.... wherby yong ignoraunt people are vtterly begiled and destroied."[19] Although a private handfasting or "besponsation" roughly followed the form of a public spousal, with *de futuro* or *de praesenti* vows, the clasp of hands, the kiss, and usually a ring or other token, its validity was difficult to prove.[20] Indeed, "it is so little esteemed of, (vnlesse it be very manifest) that another promise publique made after it, shall be preferred and preuaile against it."[21] Not even a ring could unequivocally demonstrate a betrothal, especially if it were made of rush or some other perishable substance.[22] Unless acknowledged by both parties or by witnesses, a private pledge had no legal standing, and it could be set aside if either partner were a minor.[23] Still, some lovers did make clandestine commitments. The dangerous consequences of believing a secret promise to marry appear in this contemporary report of a duel:

> My Lo. of Dunkelly fought in the feilde withe Sr Calistines Brooke vppon Wednesday last and ... thrust him quight throughe the hande vp into the arme. The cause breifly was Sr Cal: had promysed hys syster mariage, and gott her withe chylde and then refusing her my Lo. her Brother vndertooke her iust quarrell, whiche god iustly reuenged.[24]

With less peril than a duel might pose, an abandoned partner could sue for fulfillment of vows. Records of such suits appear in every ecclesiastical court, where the parties and those vouching for them sought to establish the credit of their testimony. For judges, as for society, factors of status or reputation or family influence heavily affected the verdicts.[25]

With either secret or public spousals, matters grew still more complicated if a couple indulged in sexual intercourse before being married *in facie ecclesiae*. This act translated the espoused condition into a binding union. Regardless of whether or not parents had consented, whether either partner had been forced into betrothal, whether contractual conditions had been fulfilled, whether fornication with someone else had previously occurred, or whether "the Man were constrained, through *fear of death* to know the woman," nonetheless "Spousals do become Matrimony by carnal knowledge."[26] There is some disagreement about a man's right to compel his intended bride to have intercourse, but even forcible rape could become matrimony if the woman wished.[27] The transformation of spousals into wedlock provided special protection for the female involved because it prevented her partner from breaking a contract on the grounds of unchastity. Such a manipulation of betrothal in order to seduce would otherwise have left the man free to marry while damaging the woman's chances for a respectable mate. Any difficulty in enforcing a permanent match centered solely on the problem of proving that a valid promise had actually existed. Unfortunately, while premarital consummation joined an espoused couple for life, it conveyed none of the legal benefits that accrued to properly wedded husbands and wives. According to one authority, "they which dare play man and wife onely in view of heauen, and closet of Conscience, let them be aduised . . . for on earth if the Priest see no celebrated Marriage, the Judge saith no legitimate issue, nor the Law any reasonable or constituted Dower."[28] Besides risking her property rights and the legitimacy of her children, the woman also risked prosecution by the church courts if she became pregnant and could not persuade her partner to marry her, while both offenders could be required to do public penance if found guilty of incontinence.[29]

Despite these serious consequences, some took betrothal as a license for sexual intimacy, equating it with matrimony itself. "Many make it a very mariage, and thereupon haue a greater solemnitie at their contract, then at their mariage: yea many take libertie after a contract to know their spouse, as if they were maried: an unwarrantable and dishonest practice."[30] Though moralists denounced "hādfasted persons brought and layd together: yea, certaine weekes afore they go to the church" for their "wicked lust,"[31] the existing evidence shows a good deal of premarital intercourse between engaged couples, mostly at the lower social levels.[32] According to one proverb, "Courting and wooing bring dallying and doing."[33] In some parishes as many as a third of the brides were, like Anne Hathaway, pregnant at their weddings.[34] But when a pregnancy did not lead to a wedding, the ensuing stigma was so great that some women invented promises of marriage, while some men either bribed a partner's silence or paid someone else to marry her.[35] Frequently, however, the ecclesiastical court records show that an unmarried mother was truly espoused to her baby's father. For instance, Grace Burles told the religious officials in 1602 that Edward Shipman "myndeth shortlye to marye her" but "was prest for a soldier in the last presse." And in fact, upon Edward's return six months after their child was born, he and Grace became husband and wife.[36]

As with seduction, however, sexual consummation of public or private spousals only infrequently characterized the behavior of the privileged. Unchaperoned encounters came more easily to ordinary individuals than to the daughters of elite families. Dalliances certainly occurred, but they were both scandalous and risky.[37] For example, Lady Sheffield tried for years to prove that she and the Earl of Leicester had made a secret contract in 1571 that was ratified one winter night in 1574 before the birth of their son in August. Though the child eventually sued for legitimization and his father's title, the case was first dismissed, then permanently estopped.[38] In desperate circumstances, lovers could resort to an elopement or a secret wedding, but such behavior invariably fueled gossip and criticism.[39] Everyone at court was shocked when Sir Thomas Perrot and Dorothy Devereux broke into a church and were married by a strange clergyman over the strenuous protests of the local parish priest, an action that provoked a Privy Council inquiry.[40] Denying the validity of his daughter Elizabeth's elopement with William Lord Compton, Sir John Spencer locked her up, beat her, and had to be imprisoned before the newlyweds could live together.[41] To ensure the legality of an irregular ceremony, a public wedding sometimes followed a covert one. Thus, when the widowed Lady Essex secretly wed the Earl of Leicester in 1578, her father later held a service attended by other nobles.[42] Similarly, Elizabeth Cecil and Edward Coke, married in 1598 without banns, with no special license, at night, and in a private house, repeated their vows at St. Andrew's Church after they were called before the archbishop.[43]

In instances of surreptitious ceremonies, officiating clerics were subject to censure and offenders to punishment by the church courts.[44] Moreover, the parties involved risked forfeiting the financial support guaranteed by spousal contracts, not to mention incurring parental wrath. Predictably, there was severe disapproval for "clandestine mariages," in part because they led to *Alienation of parents affection from their children, Disinheriting Heires, Enmity betwixt the friends of each party so married, Litigious suits in Law, Ruine of families.*"[45] A stature of 1597, designed to redress abductions of heiresses as a means of forcing marriages, sentenced offenders to death without a priest in attendance.[46] In virtually all quarters, an elopement represented a serious breach of propriety. Nonetheless, some couples did manage to wed in an irregular fashion, and certain members of the clergy connived at the rules.[47] In London such ceremonies were performed at several churches, including the Tower, Holy Trinity (Minories), St. James (Duke Place), and the chapels at the Mint and Newgate prison.[48] Whether private matrimony represented religious dissent, an evasion of impediments, or the assertion of personal choice, it was regarded as a subversion of the protocols surrounding more conventional marriage.

In contrast with impetuous lovers who copulated prematurely or married covertly, other espoused couples found reasons to break off their engagements. Certain penalties fell upon a fiancé who willfully reneged on his promise of marriage.

> By the Civil Law, whosoever having contracted Spousals *de futuro,* doth, without just Cause, refuse to deduce the same Spousals into Matrimony, doth not only lose the token (which is commonly a Ring) given to the other Party in pledge, and earnest of the Contract . . . together, with all other gifts whatsoever simply bestowed in hope of future Marriage . . . ; but is bound to make two-fold Restitution for the tokens and pledges received in Confirmation of the said Contract . . . whether they be Rings, Braceletts, Jewels, or other things.[49]

But there were legitimate grounds for dissolution. As discussed in chapter 2, those contracted in childhood could dissent when they came to years of discretion and thus cancel a parental agreement. However, to be valid, the dissent had to be made before a bishop, his chancellor, or a priest and other witnesses.[50] Betrothed partners could also dissolve their commitment by mutual consent, provided no sexual consummation had taken place, though a penance or reprimand was imposed for breaking a *de praesenti* vow.[51] Not living up to the stated conditions of the spousal contract also invalidated it—unless the conditions were manifestly impossible to fulfill, in which case the contract had been void all along. For example, if the agreement called for a wedding within a certain length of time or payment of sums of money or approval of another party, then the failure to meet such prerequisites provided grounds for ending the engagement.[52] The primary requirement for those under twenty-one, of course, was parental consent, as clerics were repeatedly warned.[53] Yet, for espoused minors, as with any betrothed pair, sexual intercourse canceled all contractual conditions and established an indissoluble union.[54]

Theoretically, more complicated causes for nullifying spousal agreements were supposed to emerge during the time it took to read the banns. These included the existence of a prior contract or marriage, a pending marital suit in an ecclesiastical court, fornication with another party, a foul disease or notable mutilation, consanguinity, extreme cruelty, notorious reputation, criminality, impotence, mistaken identity, holy orders, false religious faith, violence, threats, fraud, infancy, judicial dissolution, or "whensoever there is just and reasonable Cause."[55] Hence, authorities urged that during their espousal "both parties should disclose the one to the other, such imperfections, infirmities, and wants, in either of their bodies, as also the mediocritie & meannesse of their goods and substance, as in trueth it is: yea though it should be with the perill and losse one of the other."[56] Otherwise, the belated revelation of impediments could lead to embarrassing or intolerable situations, many of which are documented in the ecclesiastical court records.[57] If impediments were alleged during the wedding ceremony, the rite had to be deferred until the truth or falsity of the charges could be determined.[58]

Distinctions existed even among impediments. Some (prohibitive) prevailed only before a church wedding and/or consummation, while others (diriment) rendered the marriage invalid from its inception, abrogating both dower rights and legitimacy of offspring.[59] A state of annulment existed, for instance, when partners wed within the interdicted degrees of kinship, which after 1603 were posted in every parish church.[60] These comprised not only in-laws, such as the brother or sister of a deceased spouse, but also godparents and adopted relatives.[61] When anybody killed a spouse in order to marry someone else or made a promise of matrimony contingent upon the death of a spouse, the ensuing union was considered void. So were bigamous marriages (felonious after 1604) or those that followed a prior *de praesenti* promise to another party or those that could not be consummated.[62] Other grounds for nullification included an absence of two years (three years if outside England) with no consummation, as well as compulsion (again not involving sexual intercourse): "Matrimonie holdeth not when it is extorted by force, or by such a feare as may *cadere in constantem virum; quia matrimonia debent esse libera* [befall a strong man, because marriages ought to be uncompelled]."[63] Besides these limited conditions for annulment, a few situations could justify separation, or divorce *a mensa et thoro* (from bed and board), though such circumstances were rare indeed.[64] Adultery, heresy, idolatry, extreme cruelty, or an absence of five years with the presumption of death all provided grounds for a hearing before an ecclesiastical judge.[65] But even if the plaintiff won, a subsequent marriage was almost always prohibited.[66] Not only did all divorce petitions have to be substantiated by the testimony of independent witnesses in open court, but none would be granted without the oath of husband and wife not to wed again during their spouse's lifetime.[67]

Unfortunately, however irregular the circumstances of trothplight or matrimony, marriage was for life. Legal grounds for annulment or divorce from bed and board so seldom existed that the impatient were sternly warned not to expect rescue from the folly of a precipitate liaison:

> Whether therefore thou be married already, or art hereafter to enter into it, keepe vnitie now, and make thy choice so well as thou canst: and I, for my part, would never wish thee to conceiue any hope at all, that whonce that knot is rightly knit, thou canst afterward haue any vndoubted or certaine warrant, that for the adultery of thy wife (if it should fall out, that thy case should bee so hard) thou maist be at liberty to marry againe.[68]

Echoing that awareness, John Harington offers in verse a wry acknowledgment of the indissolubility of marriage.

A fond yong couple, making haste to marry,
Without their parents will, or friends consent,
After one month their marriage did repent,
And su'd vnto the Bishops Ordinary
That this their act so vndiscreetly done,
Might by his more discretion be vndone.
Vpon which motion he awhile did pause:
At length, he for their comforts to them said,
It had beene better (friends) that you had staid:
But now you are so hampered in the Lawes,
That I this knot may not vntye (my sonne)
Yet I will grant you both shall be vndone.[69]

Even in the most influential social circles, the law afforded little escape.[70] Marriage was "*Dura Servitus*, a hard Servitude, because it is for ever indisoluble . . . , how hard soever the Match be; whereas every other Servitude, may at any time be dissolved, the Lord or Master being pleased."[71]

A far higher proportion of defective courtships appear in Shakespeare's plays than seem to have occurred in his society, for the problems attendant upon unsanctioned love—then as now—form the very stuff of dramatic action. Yet in even the most improbable plots, signals as to the implications of irregular behavior appear. With characters of lowly status, such irregularity generally takes the form of sexual promiscuity, sometimes winked at, sometimes punished, sometimes insultingly referred to as "country matters" (*Ham.*, III.ii.111) or "country forms" (*Oth.*, III.iii.242). Such behavior unites elements as diverse as the profligacy of Joan la Pucelle, the fickleness of Lavatch, the attempted rape by Caliban, and the boast of Jack Cade: "There shall not a maid be married but she shall pay to me her maidenhead" (*2H6*, IV.vii.118-120).[72]

The Old Shepherd in *The Winter's Tale* laments that young swains are concerned with nothing "but getting wenches with child, wronging the ancientry, stealing, fighting" (III.iii.60-62). When he stumbles on an abandoned baby, he assumes there must be some "'waiting-gentlewoman' in the scape. This has been some stair-work, some trunk-work, some behind-door-work. They were warmer that got this than the poor thing is here" (71-74). The infant's supposed bastardy does not prevent the old man from taking it in "for pity" (73) even before he discovers its fardel of gold, any more than his grumbling about youthful liberty affects his kindly tolerance of it at the sheepshearing—at least until the dance of hairy men becomes obscene. Similarly, so long as Polixenes and Camillo presume Prince Florizel is merely amusing himself with a shepherdess, they admire her poised beauty. But when the pair begin moving through the stages of a formal betrothal, the mood changes. A public declaration of love, joined hands, the promise of dowry, the approval of the girl's father, everything but consent of Florizel's father, who "must not / Mark our contract" (IV.iv.416-417), push the couple right to the edge of a binding spousal before the outraged Polixenes declares, "Mark your divorce, young sir" (417).[73] Only at the point where dalliance threatens to become alliance, lawful and enforceable, does the violence of royal displeasure intervene. The king's view of Perdita's sexual hold over his son appears in the assumption that she might "These rural latches to his entrance open, / Or hoop his body more with thy embraces" (438-439). Though casual coupling can be expected from country folk, matrimony with their betters seems out of the question.

Thus in *The Merchant of Venice*, Jessica charges Lancelot Gobbo with "the getting up of the Negro's belly. The Moor is with child by you, Lancelot" (III.v.36-37).[74] The servant's retort that "if she be less than an honest woman, she is indeed more than I took her for" (39-40) implies the pair's mutual looseness, but this backstairs peccadillo is never even mentioned again, much less ratified by a wedding. A good deal more is made of carnality in *Love's Labour's Lost*. Navarre imposes stiff penalties for fornication: "a year's imprisonment to be taken with a wench" (I.i.276-277). Don Armado's apprehension and custody of Costard for toying with Jaquenetta—his sentence reduced to "fast a week with bran and water" (288-289)—provide comic sport. So does the Spanish knight's infatuation with this wench, this "hobbyhorse," this "hackney" (III.i.28-31), who has "sorted and consorted" (I.i.251) with him too. In the final shambles of the Pageant of Nine Worthies, Costard announces, "She's quick. The child brags in her belly already. 'Tis yours" (V.ii.670-671). Though which man has gotten the girl pregnant remains in doubt,[75] Don Armado completes the deflation of his own gentlemanly pretensions by confessing, "I have vowed to Jaquenetta to hold the plow for her sweet love three year" (870-871). Underscored by the obscene double entendre of his pledge, their sexuality and what may be a limited term of commitment counterpoint the chaster pursuits of the courtly figures, whose declarations and penances are also imperfectly or ambiguously observed. Rather consistently, however, in Shakespeare it is characters of low social status who fornicate with scant regard for the nicer restrictions of betrothal or marriage.

Though all acknowledged the existence of fleshly desires and many pursued them, such liberty seemed particularly threatening to those most bound by the protocols of courtship. Secret wooings and betrothals thus garner special attention because they can so easily disguise an intent to satisfy lust rather than to marry. Such circumstances appear in *Hamlet*, where Laertes and Polonius fear for Ophelia's virtue.[76] After all, the prince has "very oft of late / Given private time to you, and you yourself / Have of your audience been most free and bounteous" (I.iii.91-93). Though Hamlet has made no formal request to court her, "he hath importuned me with love" (110). Laertes advises Ophelia to regard the prince's interest as "The perfume and suppliance of a minute. / No more" (9-10), warning,

> Then weigh what loss your honour may sustain
> If with too credent ear you list his songs,
> Or lose your heart, or your chaste treasure open
> To his unmastered importunity.
> (29-32)

Polonius calls Hamlet's vows "mere imploratators of unholy suits, / Breathing like sanctified and pious bawds, / The better to beguile" (129-131). Obediently, Ophelia breaks off all further contact with the prince. No matter how much one may dislike Polonius, he is not simply thwarting a bona fide courtship here but, given the customs of the period, has good reason to fear seduction. In retrospect, he admits, "I feared he did but trifle / And meant to wreck thee," for "it is common for the younger sort / To lack discretion" (II.i.113-114, 117-118).[77]

Though, as will be noted in chapter 9, Hamlet's rank makes his conduct especially open to suspicion, a certain stigma attaches to any unsanctioned courtship. Seeing Bianca's shameless flirtation with her presumed tutor, Tranio and Hortensio abruptly reject the young "haggard" for "her lightness." "Fie on her, see how beastly she doth court him" (*Shr.*, IV.ii.39, 24, 34).

> See how they kiss and court. Signor Lucentio,
> Here is my hand, and here I firmly vow
> Never to woo her more, but do forswear her
> As one unworthy all the former favors
> That I have fondly flattered her withal.
> (27-31)

While Hortensio's criticism may represent the sour grapes of an unsuccessful suitor, Bianca still violates the rules of discreet feminine conduct, a further indication of her subsequent unruliness as a wife. And certainly the bawdy innuendo of Margaret in *Much Ado* marks her as a careless young woman fully capable of receiving her lover, Borachio, at Hero's chamber window. Though excused by Leonato—"I believe [she] was packed in all this wrong, / Hired to it by your brother" (V.i.291-292)—the waiting woman's behavior contrasts sharply with that of the modest Hero and the forthright Beatrice.[78]

Sometimes a secret wooing leads to a secret betrothal. However, without proof, this kind of pledge can always be broken. For example, in *A Midsummer Night's Dream*, Lysander charges, "Demetrius—I'll avouch it to his head—/ Made love to Nedar's daughter, Helena, / And won her soul" (I.i.106-108). According to her, he "hailed down oaths that he was only mine"

(243). Even Theseus admits, "I have heard so much, / And with Demetrius thought to have spoke thereof" (111-112). After his night in the woods, this lover confesses, "To her, my lord, / Was I betrothed ere I see Hermia" (IV.i.170-171). His acknowledgment, along with Theseus's earlier negligence and the fact that the pair have spent a night together unchaperoned, helps to explain why the duke overrules the wishes of Hermia's father.[79] Demetrius is precontracted to Helena, as Hermia is to Lysander, when Egeus demands that his child "here before your grace / Consent to marry with Demetrius" (I.i.39-40). However, when Theseus asks, "What say you, Hermia?" (46), she cleverly avoids any direct answer, which would constitute a public espousal, thus preserving her prior vow to Lysander intact, in contrast with the forsworn Demetrius. During the first part of *Two Gentlemen of Verona*, Proteus also enters into a secret spousal, complete with the offer of "my hand for my true constancy," "a holy kiss" to "seal the bargain," and an exchange of rings (II.ii.8, 7).[80] When Julia produces not one but two rings given by her faithless suitor, such replicative nonsense provides yet another instance of that mockery of courtship conventions which typifies this comedy. As a practical matter rings commonly demonstrate the validity of a private betrothal. However, even with such a token, even when clandestine vows are honored, a certain uneasiness attends most concealed wooings because of an uncertainty as to the motives and the morality involved. And the uneasiness derives in part from the cultural ambiguity attached to an activity both forbidden and indulged in.

Of no play is this so true as *Othello*. Though Desdemona does not even appear until some 450 lines into the action, her elopement with the Moor provides the chief subject for discussion during all the opening dialogue. Has she been bewitched, as her distraught father claims, or is she a willing partner in "making the beast with two backs" (I.i.118-119)? While explaining their courtship before the Venetian senate council, Othello—wittingly or unwittingly—reveals considerable impropriety of behavior. A frequent visitor to Brabanzio's home, the Moor has taken "a plaint hour," without her father's knowledge or permission, "and found good means / To draw from her a prayer of earnest heart / That I would all my pilgrimage dilate" (I.iii. 150-152). Their subsequent conversations, kept secret from Brabanzio, take on a questionable nature, especially in view of Desdemona's response to Othello's stories. The Quarto text says, "She gave me for my pains a world of sighs," but the Folio specifies a far more shameless "world of kisses" (158). After that,

> She wished she had not heard it, yet she wished
> That heaven had made her such a man. She thankèd me,
> And bade me, if I had a friend that loved her,

I should but teach him how to tell my story,
And that would woo her. Upon this hint I
  spake.

(161-165)

Now the alien Othello may not recognize any misconduct here, but a contemporary audience almost certainly would have.[81] Brabanzio himself declares, "If she confess that she was half the wooer, / Destruction light on my head if my bad blame / Light on the man!" (175-177), not because he approves of the match but because his daughter would be at fault to encourage Othello so blatantly. Moreover, Desdemona's subsequent actions heighten the initial suspicion regarding her character. She keeps her betrothal hidden from her father yet continues to see Othello privately and, as the play later reveals, to receive Cassio frequently as a go-between.[82] To elope, she slips away from her home by night, "Transported, with no worse nor better guard / But with a knave of common hire, a gondolier" (I.i.126-127).

Even after the stress of an elopement, the abrupt departure of her new husband from the Sagittary inn, and her predawn summons before the senate council, Desdemona speaks with remarkable composure to her distraught father and the other males assembled. Eliding altogether the fact that she has concealed Othello's courtship from Brabanzio, she facetiously compares herself to her mother in setting the obedience due a husband above that due a father. Rhetorically she sounds correct, but she falsely equates her mother's marriage with her own, which lacks either parental knowledge or approval.[83] With no alternative, since his daughter has confirmed Othello's claims, Brabanzio abandons his charges, bitterly presiding over a postnuptial betrothal: "Come hither, Moor. / I here do give thee that with all my heart / Which, but thou hast already, with all my heart / I would keep from thee" (I.iii. 191-194). However, he offers no dowry and refuses Desdemona houseroom during Othello's impending absence. In response, she defends "My downright violence and storm of fortunes" (249), frankly asking to accompany her husband to war, else "The rites for why I love him are bereft me" (257).[84] Where is the young woman her father describes as "A maiden never bold, / Of spirit so still and quiet that her motion / Blushed at herself" (94-96)? The question of whether she is "a super-subtle Venetian" (355) or the "virtuous Desdemona" (III.i.33) lies at the heart of Othello's agony. But long before the hero's doubts are ever raised, the play thrusts its viewers into a similar doubt regarding this irregular courtship. What kind of young woman would behave as Desdemona does, violating all the proprieties? Is she chaste or prodigal? Is she inherently deceitful or just unconventionally independent? Is her love a lust for the bizarre or a noble spiritual union? At the midpoint of the dramatic action, uncertainties regarding the heroine's morality begin to be resolved for the audience precisely when they are raised for Othello. Yet to see the courtship solely in modern terms, missing entirely its questionable aspects, results in a simplistic view of both Desdemona and Othello.[85]

While this tragedy opens after a secret wooing and an elopement have already occurred, other plots turn on the attempts to sanction a clandestine relationship with matrimony. In some cases, practical problems such as finding a priest to perform the ceremony without the necessary banns or parental consent are either minimized or ignored, with a corresponding emphasis on the means of eloping. Lysander and Hermia simply plan to decamp to another venue where "the sharp Athenian law / Cannot pursue us" (*MND*, I.i. 162-163). Other lovers are similarly vague about the marriage ceremony but full of elaborate plans for getting away. When asked if Silvia loves him, Valentine admits,

Ay, and we are betrothed. Nay more, our
  marriage hour,
With all the cunning manner of our flight,
Determined of: how I must climb her
  window,
The ladder made of cords, and all the
  means
Plotted and 'greed on for my happiness.

(*TGV*, II.iv. 177-181)

No fewer than three priests wait secretly to marry Anne Page—one at the deanery for Dr. Caius, one at Eton for Slender, and one at the church for Fenton. All the ceremonies would be considered irregular since they are performed at night "'twixt twelve and one" (*Wiv.*, IV.vi.48), but the marriage to Fenton would be "so sure that nothing can dissolve" it because he and Anne are "long since contracted" (V.v.215-216). A similar irregularity attaches to the secret wedding of Lucentio and Bianca, which also takes place at night. Biondello has arranged a clandestine wedding that will satisfy any legal requirement: "The old priest at Saint Luke's church is at your command at all hours. . . . Take you assurance of her, *cum privilegio ad imprimendum solum*—to th' church take the priest, clerk, and some sufficient honest witnesses" (Iv.v. 15-16, 19-21). The precise nature of the information in *The Taming of the Shrew* and *The Merry Wives of Windsor* is of course consistent with the realistic details provided for the entire courtship process by these comedies. However, in a society where eligible women of privilege were chaperoned with some care, stratagems for carrying off their stage counterparts may have attracted particular interest. Not only did seemingly gratuitous descriptions of corded ladders and pliant priests answer practical questions, but they appealed to the imagination of anyone who might wish, however fruitlessly, to pursue a similar course.

In quite a different vein Shakespeare is especially careful about what he does and does not present in *Romeo and Juliet*. With two minors whose parents would violently oppose any alliance, it is essential to show how and why the young couple are truly married. Hence, the spectator sees, step by step, the movement from the lovers' first encounter to their indissoluble union. In the balcony scene, Juliet repeatedly urges Romeo (and the audience) not to misjudge her morality: "In truth, fair Montague, I am too fond, / And therefore thou mayst think my 'havior light." "Therefore pardon me, / And not impute this yielding to light love" (II.i.140-141, 146-147). She assumes that with their mutual declarations of love, Romeo has made a private promise to marry her. Despite the physical impossibility of a handfasting, she even uses the correct legal term for their vows: "I have no joy of this *contract* tonight. / It is too rash, too unadvised, too sudden" (159-160; italics mine). By voicing the same misgivings that prudent adults might feel concerning her relationship with Romeo, Juliet establishes her purity as well as her passion. Though the only satisfaction Romeo asks that night is "Th'exchange of thy love's faithful vow for mine" (169), she proposes that he prove his sincerity in the only ethical way possible:

> If that thy bent of love be honourable,
> Thy purpose marriage, send me word tomorrow,
> By one that I'll procure to come to thee,
> Where and what time thou wilt perform the rite,
> And all my fortunes at thy foot I'll lay,
> And follow thee, my lord, throughout the world.
>
> (185-190)

Yet she can still see the alternative interpretation of her wooer's behavior: "But if thou mean'st not well, / I do beseech thee. . . . / To cease thy strife and leave me to my grief" (192-193, 196). In no other play do we get so clear a delineation of honorable intent in an unsanctioned courtship, for the dynamics of *Romeo and Juliet* require a firm belief in the lovers' integrity from first to last.

Further difficulties surround the wedding itself. First, a plausible explanation must be offered for any priest's willingness to officiate in such obviously irregular circumstances. Though chiding young Romeo for his impetuous commitment, Friar Laurence consents on reasonable grounds: "I'll thy assistant be; / For this alliance may so happy prove / To turn your households' rancour to pure love" (II.ii.90-92). A second problem, common to most elopements, arises from the restricted movements of unmarried girls beyond their own households. Since Romeo has no direct access to Juliet such as Lucentio has to Bianca, the Nurse becomes the essential agent between the lovers. She utters the usual warning against seduction in the guise of courtship: "If ye should lead her in a fool's paradise, as they say, it were a very gross kind of behaviour, . . . truly it were an ill thing to be offered to any gentlewoman" (II.iii.155-159). However, what the hero has in mind is a lawful marriage. In sending the following message to Juliet via the Nurse, he clarifies the strategy that will effect an almost impossible union and its consummation.

> Bid her devise
> Some means to come to shrift this afternoon,
> And there she shall at Friar Laurence' cell
> Be shrived and married. . . . [86]
>
> . . . . .
>
> Within this hour my man shall be with thee
> And bring thee cords made like a tackled stair,

Act V, scene iii. A melancholy cherub contemplates the deaths of Romeo and Juliet. Painted by R. Smirke, R. A. University of Michigan Library.

> Which to the high topgallant of my joy
> Must be my convoy in the secret night.
>
> (169-172, 177-180)

The excuse of going to confession is especially clever, for it offers Juliet a plausible reason to leave the Capulet house, it reasserts the lovers' virtue, and it satisfies the requirement for absolution before marriage. During the brief scene at Friar Laurence's cell, the same insistence upon the sanctity of the union appears, with Romeo's request to "close our hands with holy words" (II.v.6) and the friar's directive, "Come, come with me, and we will make short work, / For, by your leaves, you shall not stay alone / Till Holy Church incorporate two in one" (35-37).

Here is no transitory dalliance or secret promise of love, rashly consummated, but rather a religious consecration of private vows between a virgin and her betrothed husband. Nor is it a questionable nighttime affair but rather one inaugurated in the broad light of day, though not before the canonical deadline of noon. While the union might still be annulled at this point, especially in view of Romeo's subsequent killing of Tybalt, Juliet reconfirms her commitment, vowing to "die maiden-widowèd" (III.ii.135) if necessary and sending her bridegroom a ring as token of her fidelity. "O, find him! Give this ring to my true knight, / And bid him come to take his last farewell" (142-143). That same night a sexual consummation makes Romeo and Juliet husband and wife forever. In a final touch of pathos, their fathers tender belated offers of dower and dowry over the bodies of two dead children.[87]

> CAPULET. O brother Montague, give me thy hand.
>   This is my daughter's jointure, for no more
>   Can I demand.
> MONTAGUE. But I can give thee more,
>   For I will raise her statue in pure gold.
>
> . . . . .
>
> CAPULET. As rich shall Romeo's by his lady's lie,
>   Poor sacrifices of our enmity.
>
> (V.iii.295-298, 302-303)

With equal offers and clasped hands, the parents enact the spousal agreement between families that should have preceded the marriage of the young lovers, were it not for the feud. As the momentarily widowed wife of Romeo, Juliet will have from the Montagues a golden jointure equal to the golden dowry she brings from the Capulets.

The secret wedding in the tragedy raises other generally unrecognized issues concerning Paris's courtship of Juliet. Though in the play's immediate source he does not appear until after Romeo's banishment, from the first act Shakespeare shows this suitor following the route of conventional wooing. However, when Capulet agrees to the match, he abrogates the requirement for obtaining his daughter's consent, not even allowing a perfunctory interview between the couple. Juliet protests the breach of custom: "I wonder at this haste, that I must wed / Ere he that should be husband comes to woo" (III.v.118-119). During the following scene, Friar Laurence expresses reservations to Paris about the girl's free assent, observing, "You say you do not know the lady's mind? / Uneven is the course. I like it not" (IV.i.4-5). Juliet's possible coercion, which would constitute an impediment to the marriage, is precisely the problem Paris addresses when she arrives at the friar's cell. Before a clerical witness, he tries to elicit her consent.

> PARIS. Happily met, my lady and my wife.
> JULIET. That may be, sir, when I may be a wife.
> PARIS. That "may be" must be, love, on Thursday next.
> JULIET. What must be shall be.
> FRIAR LAURENCE. That's a certain text.
> PARIS. Come you to make confession to this father?
> JULIET. To answer that, I should confess to you.
> PARIS. Do not deny to him that you love me.
> JULIET. I will confess to you that I love him.
> PARIS. So will ye, I am sure, that you love me.
>
> . . . . .
>
> Juliet, on Thursday early will I rouse ye.
> (*Kissing her*) Till then, adieu, and keep this holy kiss.[88]
>
> (18-26, 42-43)

Though she has deftly parried each statement, Juliet's parting kiss means, to Paris, an acceptance of their betrothal. Instead, as both she and Friar Laurence well know, the spousal is not valid because of her prior marriage to Romeo. The Nurse may rationalize, "Your first is dead, or 'twere as good he were / As living hence and you no use of him," and advise, "I think it best you married with the County" (III.v.224-225, 217). But any such union would be bigamy. This dilemma, which provokes Juliet's desperate solution, stems from the fact that Shakespeare has taken care to delineate a secret marriage satisfying religious and civil law in every respect.

However, the playwright is equally capable of presenting situations that spell out the ugliest dangers implicit in irregular courtship, as he does in *Measure for Measure*. In the most reprehensible case, a gentleman has debauched one Kate Keepdown, who in turn has brought charges before the Duke that Lucio fathered her child. Privately he admits the deed, but publicly "I was fain to forswear it. They would else have married me to the rotten medlar" (IV.iii.166-167). According to Mistress Overdone, who has cared for the infant and its mother, Lucio "promised her marriage" (III.i.459-460). However, without evidence, that promise is impossible to prove, so the woman can be casually discarded, the bastard left to the charity of a bawd. A similar taint mars the relationship between Claudio and the pregnant Juliet.[89] Though he readily admits to a secret handfasting, this young man has been unwilling to wait for its public ratification before consummation: "Upon a true contract, / I got possession of Julietta's bed" (I.ii.133-134).[90] In neither of these situations, both involving private vows, does Shakespeare provide the scenes of unsullied wooing that lend such sympathy to the plight of Romeo and Juliet. Instead, the women here are treated like criminal bearers of bastards, Kate denied marriage by her despoiler, Juliet by the pious hypocrite Angelo, who decrees that the "fornicatress" merely "have needful but not lavish means" (II.ii.23, 24) for her imminent delivery.[91] Rather than legitimize the union and thus the unborn infant, Angelo focuses solely upon the sexual sin and thereby creates, as surely as Lucio does, a nameless child with no means of support. Both women are finally wed to their seducers at the public command of the Duke. His directive, "She, Claudio, that you wronged, look you restore" (V.i.524), meets with silent acquiescence, but Lucio fruitlessly protests, "I beseech your highness, do not marry me to a whore" (513-514).

Yet these are not the only instances of sexual abuse or aborted matrimony. When the loss of Mariana's dowry at sea leads Angelo to break their *de futuro* spousal agreement, he is squarely within his legal rights to refuse a bride when the provisions of the prenuptial contract have not been fulfilled.[92] But he also invents a charge of unchastity as grounds for deserting her[93] and adds to his offense by repeating the lie in public before the Duke.

> My lord, I must confess I know this woman;
> And five years since there was some speech
>   of marriage
> Betwixt myself and her, which was broke off,
> Partly for that her promisèd proportions
> Came short of composition, but in chief
> For that her reputation was disvalued
> In levity.
>   (214-220)

Amid all the critical focus upon *de praesenti* versus *de futuro* spousals in relation to the bed trick,[94] it is easy to lose sight of the ironic justice by which Angelo's carnal desire to "disvalue" Isabella "in levity" makes him the instrument for fulfilling his earlier slander against Mariana—and at the same time his act will "fulfill an old contracting" (III.i.538).

> This is the hand which, with a vowed
>   contract,
> Was fast belocked in thine. This is the body
> That took away the match from Isabel,
> And did supply thee at thy garden-house
> In her imagined person.
>
> . . . . .
>
> I am affianced this man's wife, as strongly
> As words could make up vows. And, my
>   good lord,
> But Tuesday night last gone, in's garden-
>   house
> He knew me as a wife.[95]
>   (205-209, 225-228)

Now kin to Claudio as seducer and to Lucio as both seducer and liar, Angelo is swiftly ordered by the Duke to their same marital fate—and for the same reason: "I thought your marriage fit," because the bride's unchastity might "choke your good to come" (417, 419).[96] A hard look at the period's legal penalties for bearing bastards, as well as the social stigma on debauched women, explains why this tough sentence is imposed, no matter how unpalatable it appears in today's very different world.

The matrimonial impediment of sexual dishonor finds its fullest and falsest expression in *Much Ado about Nothing*. There poor Hero is the victim of Don John's plot to make her appear unchaste, to poison the happiness of his brother's friend Claudio, and to embarrass Don Pedro for arranging the match. The enormity of the fault looms even before it is proven.[97]

> Don John. . . . Go but with me tonight, you shall see her chamber window entered, even the night before her wedding day. If you love her then, tomorrow wed her. But it would better fit your honour to change your mind.
>
> . . . . .
>
> Claudio. If I see anything tonight why I should not marry her, tomorrow, in the congregation where I should wed, there will I shame her.
>
> Don Pedro. And as I wooed for thee to obtain her, I will join with thee to disgrace her.
>   (III.ii.102-106, 113-116)

Much sentimental protest has been expressed against the heartlessness of Claudio's public accusation, but at this level of society, a charge of so serious a transgression must be made openly and affirmed by witnesses.[98] A private conversation with Hero's father might prevent the wedding but would not prevent speculation that perhaps Claudio, not Hero, is at fault—nor would it prevent Hero's being affianced to some other unsuspecting suitor. Equally important, the high drama of the accusation sustains the play's energy at this point.

The scene begins with an enactment of the nuptial ceremony that, except for a mock ritual in *As You Like It,* is the only such Christian ceremony to appear onstage in Shakespeare.[99] Impatient, Leonato calls for an abridged version of the rites—"Only to the plain form of marriage, and you shall recount their particular duties afterwards" (IV.i.1-3). Amid interruptions, evasions, and promptings from Claudio and Leonato, the priest asks for the couple's required reaffirmation of spousal vows, the anticipated denial of impediments to the marriage, and the father's consent to the match. And then Claudio commences his denunciation, vowing "Not to be married, / Not to knit my soul to an approvèd wanton" (43-44). At first her father raises a logical question as to whether the groom has deflowered Hero, an unethical but understandable act that would have translated their spousals into matrimony.

> I know what you would say. If I have known her,
> You will say she did embrace me as a husband,
> And so extenuate the forehand sin.
> No, Leonato,
> I never tempted her with word too large,
> But as a brother to his sister showed
> Bashful sincerity and comely love.
>
> (48-54)

After general charges of unchastity, confirmed by Don John and Don Pedro, Claudio faces Hero with the damning question: "What man was he talked with you yesternight / Out at your window betwixt twelve and one?" (83-84). Though the bewildered bride denies having talked with any man at such a time, the prince himself steps forward with eyewitness testimony. Moreover, he cites the admission of the "ruffian" to "the vile encounters they have had / A thousand times in secret" (92, 94-95). Amid the theatrics of these interrupted rites, it should not be forgotten that the angry bridegroom has, he thinks, the best of all possible reasons for backing out of marriage to a "rotten orange" who "knows the heat of a luxurious bed" (32, 41), especially since "she was charged with nothing / But what was true, and very full of proof" (V.i.106-107). The thrust of sympathy for Hero and the condemnation of Claudio arise not from the legal justification for his action but from the audience's awareness that the charge is false. However, the seriousness of the fault, at least by the standards of the time, is intensified by the dramatic buildup to the accusation, by the groom's outrage, by the bride's swoon, and by her father's sense of shame. No matter how much one criticizes Hero's accusers, it is unfair to attack them for being horrified at wantonness masquerading as innocence. To say that Claudio and Leonato, like Beatrice or Friar Francis, should have more faith in the virtue of one they love is not to condone sexual liberality.[100] Throughout *Much Ado,* Shakespeare explores the understandable responses of those who proceed sincerely upon incorrect assumptions just as skillfully as he explores their responses when the assumptions are correct. But if the dynamics of perception are being questioned, the desirability of virginity is not.

Though fornication is certainly the most spectacular ground for breaking a spousal agreement, other conditions can also nullify a contract or even a marriage in Shakespeare. By marrying Pistol, Nell Quickly reneges on her engagement to Nim, "and certainly she did you wrong, for you were troth-plight to her" (*H5,* II.i.17-18). When Bassianus seizes Lavinia because she is his "lawful promised love," his "true betrothèd love" (*Tit.,* I.i.294, 403), their prior spousal negates the one Titus Andronicus makes with Saturninus.[101] Legally, the emperor cannot marry Lavinia. Nor can Jessica marry Lorenzo without agreeing to "Become a Christian and thy loving wife" (*MV,* II.iii.21), for any union with a non-Christian would be considered invalid. So would the bigamous marriage proposed for Innogen and Cloten. If King Cymbeline and his queen do not recognize the princess as Posthumus's spouse, the courtiers declare, "She's wedded, / Her husband banished" (*Cym.,* I.i.7-8), and she herself calls her stepbrother "A foolish suitor to a wedded lady" (I.vi.2).[102] Although the couple have been separated, perhaps a step toward annulment, and although Cloten claims theirs "is no contract, none" (II.iii.112), this husband has consummated his marriage, for he has intimate knowledge of his wife's body and bedchamber. Like Juliet, Innogen would commit bigamy were she to marry again.

For very different reasons the alliances between Gertrude and her husband's brother, Claudius, as well as the one Richard III proposes to enter with his niece, Elizabeth, are also invalid. In both cases, the unions violate the interdicted degrees of kinship between spouses. The Ghost in *Hamlet* thus specifically refers to Claudius as "that incestuous, that adulterate beast" and charges, "Let not the royal bed of Denmark be / A couch for luxury and damnèd incest" (I.v.42, 82-83).[103] Similarly, in *Richard III,* Princess Elizabeth's mother poses the moral and legal objections to Richard's suit when she asks,

> What were I best to say? Her father's brother
> Would be her lord? Or shall I say her uncle?
> Or he that slew her brothers and her uncles?
> Under what title shall I woo for thee,

That God, the law, my honour, and her love
Can make seem pleasing to her tender years?
(*R3*, lines 50-55 after IV.iv.273; see p. 251)

Besides the sin of incest, Queen Elizabeth alludes to another nullifying impediment, criminality, which also applies to the Gertrude-Claudius marriage. Richard must make "quick conveyance with her good aunt Anne" (269), his wife, in order to marry the York princess. In describing his second courtship, the villain himself says that "sin will pluck on sin" (IV.ii.66). Since English law invalidated any matrimony achieved by the murder of a living spouse—or even a contract to wed upon a spouse's demise—the proposal to Elizabeth takes on a particularly sinister aura. Ironically, the same aura surrounds his grotesque wooing over the casket of Henry VI, when Richard swears he has killed Anne's husband and father-in-law to win her love.[104] Though he is lying about his motives for those killings, the audacious confession of so heinous an impediment adds to the macabre effect of Anne's entertaining his suit. In *Hamlet,* the audience is led to believe that, while Claudius obviously knows of the criminality nullifying his marriage, Gertrude may not. When Hamlet spells out their sin to her with "A bloody deed—almost as bad, good mother, / As kill a king and marry with his brother," she seems baffled: "As kill a king?" (III.iv.27-29). The prince expresses the legal implications of her condition in near-technical terms. This invalid union "makes marriage vows / As false as dicers' oaths" and is "such a deed / As from the body of contraction plucks / The very soul, and sweet religion makes / A rhapsody of words" (43-47). The matrimonial contract, the vows, the religious ceremony are all rendered empty words, devoid of authority. Hence, Hamlet later speaks of "a mother stain'd" (IV.iv.48; p. 777) and says Claudius "whored my mother" (V.ii.65). Quite aside from all the psychological and aesthetic reasons for Hamlet's plea that Gertrude not return to his uncle's bed, he recognizes the unlawfulness of the union.[105] To continue a sexual relationship is indeed "to live / In the rank sweat of an enseamèd bed, / Stewed in corruption, honeying and making love / Over the nasty sty" (III.iv.81-84). However offensively exaggerated his language,[106] Hamlet's position regarding an illicit liaison passing for matrimony echoes Elizabethan views.

To a certain extent, Edmund's relationships with Goneril and Regan present an even more interesting twist on the issue of criminality, since the impediment of a prior contract also affects his commitments to the sister queens. Though married to Albany, Goneril offers herself to Edmund, awards him a favor—"Wear this"—and gives him "This kiss," to which he responds, "Yours in the ranks of death" (Q sc. 16 and F IV.ii.21, 22, 25). The proceeding is an ominous enactment of private spousals, duly witnessed by Oswald. Spelling out the crime that lies between their pledges and a marriage, Goneril sends a letter to her lover on the battlefield:

"Let our reciprocal vows be remembered. You have many opportunities to cut him off.... There is nothing if he return the conqueror; then am I the prisoner, and his bed my jail, from the loathed warmth whereof, deliver me, and supply the place for your labour.

Your—wife, so I would say,—affectionate servant, and for you her own for venture, Goneril."
(Q sc. 20, 254-263; F IV.v.262-270)

Having in the meantime also promised himself to the widowed Regan, Edmund acknowledges his dilemma, "To both these sisters have I sworn my love," and he cynically decides,

"Let her who would be rid of him devise / His speedy taking off"
(Q sc. 22, 59, 68-69; F V.i.46, 55-56).

Unfortunately for his ambitious interest in both sisters' thrones, Edmund and Regan are arrested for treason by Albany, who delineates the illegalities nullifying the bastard's pledges.[107] Addressing Regan, he says,

For your claim, fair sister,
I bar it in the interest of my wife.
'Tis she is subcontracted to this lord,
And I, her husband, contradict your banns.
If you will marry, make your loves to me.
My lady is bespoke.
(Q sc. 24, 82-87; F V.iii.77-82)

All the terms of courtship—"subcontracted" (precontracted), "banns," "bespoke" (betrothed)—culminate in the bitterly logical conclusion that if Regan wishes to subsume her independent identity into Edmund's as his wife, then because he was first pledged to Goneril and she in turn is subsumed into her husband as his wife, both plaintiffs must make suit to Albany in order to marry. As the dying bastard concludes of his relationship to the now-dead sisters, "I was contracted to them both; all three / Now marry in an instant" (Q 223-224; F 203-204). It hardly seems necessary to point out how even these minor details of *Lear* mirror the larger issues of rightful and wrongful claims, familial fragmentation and incorporation, love sought and denied and granted, marital alliances proffered and retracted.

Elsewhere in Shakespeare, the attention shifts from impediments to improperly performed ceremonies. *As You Like It* is replete with absurdly mangled rites of various kinds, perhaps reminders not to take any of the improbable matches or events too seriously. In one defective ritual Touchstone brings Audrey before Sir Oliver Martext, his very name indicative of the curate's incompetence. Though her wooer would gladly avoid matrimony altogether, this country wench stoutly insists that she is "not a slut" (III.iii.33). "Sluttishness may come hereafter" (36), observes Touchstone dryly. Initially, the jester-bridegroom suggests the possibility of an irregular wedding outdoors: "Will you dispatch us here under this tree, or shall we go with you to your chapel?" (59-60). Even a bumbler like Sir Oliver seizes on another irregularity with "Is there none here to give the woman? . . . Truly she must be given, or the marriage is not lawful" (61, 63-64). Jaques says, "I'll give her" (65), but then he lectures Touchstone on the impropriety of a beggar wedding performed by a hedge priest.

> And will you, being a man of your breeding, be married under a bush, like a beggar? Get you to church, and have a good priest that can tell you what marriage is. This fellow will but join you together as they join wainscot; then one of you will prove a shrunk panel and, like green timber, warp, warp.
>
> (75-80)

Touchstone agrees with Jaques's final conclusion, but for his own reasons: "I am not in the mind but I were better to be married of him than of another, for he is not like to marry me well, and not being well married, it will be a good excuse for me hereafter to leave my wife" (81-84). When the misyoked pair, who "must be married, or . . . live in bawdry" (87) join "the rest of the country copulatives, to swear, and to forswear, according as marriage binds and blood breaks" (V.iv.55-57), Jaques predicts their "loving voyage / Is but for two months victualled" (189-190). The carnality underlying this precarious union tends to characterize lesser social ranks, as discussed elsewhere.

Though in Rosalind and Orlando carnal motivations are more sublimated, they too go through ceremonies that parody both marriages and betrothals. Reversing the usual order, Rosalind commands a mock wedding before there has been any spousal.[108]

> ROSALIND. Come, sister, you shall be the priest and marry us.—Give me your hand, Orlando.—What do you say, sister?
> ORLANDO. (*to Celia*) Pray thee, marry us.
> CELIA. I cannot say the words.
> ROSALIND. You must begin, "Will you, Orlando"—
> CELIA. Go to. Will you, Orlando, have to wife this Rosalind?
> ORLANDO. I will.
> ROSALIND. Ay, but when?
> ORLANDO. Why now, as fast as she can marry us.
> ROSALIND. Then you must say, "I take thee, Rosalind, for wife."
> ORLANDO. I take thee, Rosalind, for wife.
> ROSALIND. I might ask you for your commission; but I do take thee, Orlando, for my husband.
>
> (IV.i.116-131)

While this interchange comes perilously close to the prayer book's form, it cannot constitute a valid marriage because Celia, a woman, is even less qualified to be a priest than Sir Oliver Martext. Moreover, the impediment of mistaken identity might apply, since Orlando thinks his bride is Ganymede, although he calls her Rosalind.[109] By asking for his commission, as if he were an agent for another, she underscores the proxy nature of the ceremony, in which both Celia and herself appear as substitutes.

Before the actual wedding occurs, Silvius leads Phoebe, Orlando, and Rosalind through another ritual in act V, scene ii, where the litany mocks a recital of the catechism required before a nuptial. The shepherd intones each quality of a true lover, which the other characters affirm in turn. For example,

> SILVIUS. It is to be all made of faith and service. And so am I for Phoebe.
> PHOEBE. And I for Ganymede.
> ORLANDO. And I for Rosalind.
> ROSALIND. And I for no woman.
>
> (84-88)

Situated between the earlier parody of the prayer book rite and Hymen's rite yet to come, substituting for Christian theology a theology of love duly subscribed to by all the parties, this scene prepares spectators for the wholly pagan ceremony at the play's conclusion. At the same time, these preliminary vows, neither truly private nor truly public, converge with another quasi-spousal contrapuntal litany involving accusations of blame and conditional promises of fulfillment—"If this be so, why blame you me to love you?" and "I will marry you if ever I marry woman, and I'll be married tomorrow" (98ff., 107-109ff.). Next, before the duke and his court as witnesses, Rosalind obtains her father's required consent to marriage, and then the lovers publicly repeat their *de futuro* pledges. At last, with Hymen presiding, the only wedding Shakespeare ever completes onstage marks the apex of unreality, as far removed from the world of betrothal contracts, impediments, and the like as possible.[110] The skewed nature of all the rituals, none of which follows the prescribed forms, intensifies the nature of the final ceremony toward which all the action inevitably leads.

In a radically different fashion, the deformation of solemn rites—and the subsequent violation of those rites—appears in *Troilus and Cressida*. When Pandarus, like some perverse combination of the Nurse and Friar Laurence, a pimp-parent-priest, brings Troilus to Cressida's chambers, the lovers' wooing leads not to the altar but to bed. Though they kiss and promise to be ever true in love, such crucial words as "contract" and "marriage" are missing. Ironically, in the council chamber, Troilus's arguments to continue the war liken the Trojan military commitment to a husband's marital commitment: "How may I avoid—/ Although my will distaste what it elected—/ The wife I chose?" (II.ii.64-66). Yet he enters no such binding union with Cressida (although his appetite will soon enough "distaste what it elected"). Instead, Pandarus presides over them thus:

> PANDARUS. Go to, a bargain made. Seal it, seal it. I'll be the witness. Here I hold your hand; here, my cousin's. If ever you prove false one to another, since I have taken such pain to bring you together, let all pitiful goers-between be called to the world's end after my name: call them all panders. Let all constant men be Troiluses, all false women Cressids, and all brokers-between panders! Say "Amen."
>
> TROILUS. Amen.
>
> CRESSIDA. Amen.
>
> PANDARUS. Amen. Whereupon I will show you a chamber with a bed—which bed, because it shall not speak of your pretty encounters, press it to death. Away!
>
> (III.ii.193-205)

Here is a butchered form of both the betrothal and the wedding ceremonies.[111] The couple's living fathers neither know of nor confirm their secret bargain, no financial provision is made for the future, and no more sanctity attaches to their coupling than to the adulterous affair between Paris and Helen. It is not even clear from these lines that Pandarus actually joins Cressida's hand with Troilus's; in any case, this "bargain" he witnesses is no handfasting, the "pretty encounters" he blesses no consummation of marriage. Fittingly, Troilus gives as token of his love, not a ring or any other symbol of permanence and perfection, but a sleeve—external, perishable, decorative, a remnant of chivalric ritual. Unlike Juliet, Cressida is legally, if not morally, free to enter into another match at her father's bidding, though the second relationship with Diomedes will be just as degradingly sensual as the first one with Troilus. It is even symbolized by the same sleeve, passed like Cressida from one partner to another when she reenacts the earlier pledging rites and violates her prior "contract."

Shakespeare handles his other great union between unmarried partners quite differently. With Antony and Cleopatra there is no courtship, no betrothal, no wedding, but rather a state of flagrant adultery. At the play's opening, Antony is married to Fulvia and shortly thereafter to Octavia. During his brief term as widower, no one ever mentions a marriage to Cleopatra. Yet their relationship, always conducted on a heroic public scale quite unlike the cheap bedroom stealth of Troilus and Cressida, is appropriately solemnized at the play's end. At his suicide, Antony declares, "I will be / A bridegroom in my death, and run into't / As to a lover's bed" (IV.xv.99-101). When Cleopatra resolves to join him in death, she adorns herself not just as a queen but also as a bride: "Give me my robe. Put on my crown. I have / Immortal longings in me" (V.ii.275-276). For the first time she calls Antony "husband," making explicit the fact that her death ceremony is also their nuptial rite: "Husband, I come. / Now to that name my courage prove my title" (282-283).[112] When Iras dies, Cleopatra refers to the kiss that the groom traditionally bestows upon his bride: "If she first meet the curlèd Antony, / He'll make demand of her, and spend that kiss / Which is my heaven to have" (296-298)—the word "demand" perhaps an oblique allusion to marriage vows. Seeming to hear the groom's wedding promise, she responds with her last words, "O Antony! Nay. I will take thee too" (307), and thus echoes the *de futuro* pledges in the prayer book.[113] Their union, never conventional, never consistent with ordinary forms of spousals and weddings, is nonetheless officially ratified by Octavius when he decrees, "She shall be buried by her Antony. / No grave upon the earth shall clip in it / A pair so famous" (352-354). Customarily, only as husband and wife would they be interred in the same tomb.

Though history allows Shakespeare not to marry Antony and Cleopatra in any legal way,[114] history dictates that the dramatist unmarry Henry VIII in an entirely legal way. The only divorce or, more properly, dissolution of marriage in the canon threads its way through a labyrinth of political, religious, and aesthetic issues. This union is no casual promise to be lightly repudiated, no secret ceremony of questionable validity. Instead, the play must deal with matrimony of many years' standing. While the action makes restrained use of the ironies involved—Henry's meeting Anne before he considers divorce, his desperate need for a male heir, the juxtaposition of Anne's coronation against Katherine's death, that death making the subsequent birth of Elizabeth legitimate—the text also sets forth the legal grounds for Henry's action in great detail. Dramaturgically, it is important that the audience accept the validity of the annulment, despite the ambiguities of the king's motives and the sympathy Katherine elicits for her plight. According to Henry, questions as to "Whether our daughter were legitimate, / Respecting this our marriage with the dowager, / Sometimes our brother's wife," gave his conscience "a tenderness, / Scruple, and prick" (II.iv.176-178, 167-168). Katherine protests that her father and Henry's "gathered a wise council to them / Of every realm, that did debate this business, / Who deemed our marriage lawful" (49-51). The crucial point, historically, whether Katherine consummated her earlier union with Henry's brother, is never mentioned. Such evasion makes it seem easier for the marriage to be annulled, at least by English judges, who override the queen's refusal to accept any jurisdiction save the pope's. According to their decree, "for non-appearance, and / The King's late scruple, by the main assent / Of all these learnèd men, she was divorced, / And the late marriage made of none effect" (IV.i.30-33). Though vowing, "My lord, I dare not make myself so guilty / To give up willingly that noble title / Your master wed me to" (III.i.138-140), she is nevertheless set aside. "Katherine no more / Shall be called 'Queen,' but 'Princess Dowager,' / And 'widow to Prince Arthur'" (III.ii.69-71). For an audience more accustomed to marital unions than to the rare marital dissolution, Shakespeare does a masterful job of presenting the technical grounds for England's most famous divorce decree—without really touching on the disputed consummation or the disputed authority of the English courts in this matter.

Virtually all the problems associated with secret promises, illicit unions, broken betrothals, and even annulments of marriage appear in *All's Well That Ends Well,* a counterpart, in its way, to the farcical presentation of conventional courtship in *The Taming of the Shrew*.[115] As Margaret Ranald has shown, when the King of France enforces a marriage between Helen and the reluctant Bertram, the young man immediately sets up several bases for voiding the match: disparagement, coercion, nonconsummation, lengthy separation, and failure to comply with a conditional contract.[116] The first two grounds he can but glance at in the king's presence, especially when threatened with permanent royal displeasure. He yields with "Pardon, my gracious lord, for I submit / My fancy to your eyes" (II.iii.168-169). However, when commanded, "Take her by the hand / And tell her she is thine" (174-175), he replies merely, "I take her hand" (177), but does not say Helen will be his, thus not fully agreeing to what the king declares a "contract" (179). Later in private he is more definite about his enforced condition, wailing, "O my Paroles, *they have married me!*" (269; italics mine). As for consummating this marriage and thus making it permanently binding, Bertram immediately pledges, "Although before the solemn priest I have sworn, / I will not bed her" (266-267). He writes to his mother, "'I have wedded her, not bedded her, and sworn to make the "not" eternal'" (III.ii.21-22). Determined to avoid his bride, the young count vows, "I'll to the Tuscan wars and never bed her" (II.iii.270), callously financing his flight with Helen's dowry. Besides reversing the king's denial of his earlier wish to serve in Florence, this expedition sets up a separation that, if sufficiently prolonged, provides another ground for nullifying the marriage.

In a message Paroles delivers to Helen, Bertram expresses his intent, though in ambiguous terms:

> Madam, my lord will go away tonight.
> A very serious business calls on him.
> The great prerogative and rite of love,
> Which as your due time claims, he does acknowledge,
> But puts it off to a compelled restraint.
> (II.iv.39-43)

The phrases "compelled restraint," "rite of love," and "time claims" at least hint at the technical impediments involved in this situation—enforcement, nonconsummation, lengthy separation. Moreover, the terms "madam" and "my lord" avoid acknowledging the two as husband and wife. The final hurdle Bertram spells out in a letter to Helen: "'When thou canst get the ring upon my finger, which never shall come off, and show me a child begotten of thy body that I am father to, then call me husband; but in such a "then" I write a "never"'" (III.ii.57-60). Though difficult, the condition is not patently impossible to fulfill and thus forms yet another legitimate basis for annulment. That a dissolution of this marriage is his firm intent appears in the final words of Bertram's letter: "'Till I have no wife, I have nothing in France'" (74). It is at least worth noting that Helen's schemes to legitimize the union, which have made her appear unattractively aggressive to some critics, are equaled by Bertram's stratagems to invalidate the union. As a first response to his intention, she gives him "no wife . . . in France." By leaving, she can also avoid any legal prosecution so long as her whereabouts remain unknown.

Through the bed trick, of course, Helen fulfills Bertram's requirements and at last receives his unforced, unconditional consent to their marriage. Significantly, he accepts her immediately, with no proof at all. When she finally appears, claiming, "'Tis but the shadow of a wife you see, / The name and not the thing," Bertram instantly repeals her anomalous status with "Both, both. O, pardon!" (V.iii.309-310). Though this statement, uttered before witnesses, fully legitimizes her marital position, unreservedly ratifies their bond, and wholly acknowledges his faults, Helen goes on to show that she has also met all her husband's specific requirements.

> HELEN.   There is your ring.
> And, look you, here's your letter. This it says:
> "When from my finger you can get this ring,
> And are by me with child," et cetera. This is done.
> Will you be mine, now you are doubly won?
> BERTRAM. (*to the King*) If she, my liege, can make me know this clearly
> I'll love her dearly, ever ever dearly.

HELEN. If it appear not plain and prove
   untrue,
  Deadly divorce step between me and you.
                                    (312-320)

With a play whose action centers on the satisfaction of legal technicalities, it is appropriate that the principals' final speeches begin with "if" clauses demanding proof.[117] Ironically, each now offers to fulfill what has hitherto been the deepest wish of the other's heart: Bertram to love Helen "dearly, ever ever dearly" and she to grant him "deadly divorce."[118] A modern audience may not like the conditionality of these pledges, but they fit the mode of the play. The double acknowledgment of the match, both in Bertram's first instinctive outburst and in the formal presentation of irrefutable evidence, unites the passionate desire and the legal rationality that underlie not only the dramatic action but, ideally, marriage itself.

That passionate desire, so obvious and yet so restrained in Helen, shows up more grossly in a variety of ways. Lavatch's lusty pursuit of "Isbel the woman" (see chapter 4), combined with Paroles's discourse against virginity in the very first scene, emphasize the sexuality permeating the play. There is more than a hint of physical decadence in the king's "fistula" and its miraculous cure by the virgin he then favors so extravagantly. Debasing to their lowest levels both degree and desire, the central dramatic concerns, Paroles slanders the aristocratic Captain Dumaine by claiming that he "was a botcher's prentice in Paris, from whence he was whipped for getting the sheriff's fool with child—a dumb innocent that could not say him nay" and that "for rapes and ravishments he parallels Nessus" (IV.iii. 190-193, 255-256). Such intermingling of mean with noble characterizes the language, action, and structure of *All's Well*. Chief in this regard is Bertram's wooing of Diana. While Helen's behavior is a licit way to bed Bertram, his behavior is an illicit way to bed Diana. Here protestations of love mask little more than lust, as Mariana warns in the familiar terms of Elizabethan advice literature: "Beware of them, Diana; their promises, enticements, oaths, tokens, and all their engines of lust, are not the things they go under. Many a maid hath been seduced by them" (III.v. 18-21).

In this courtship, the antithesis of the lawful marriage to which Bertram was compelled, two points are repeatedly stressed: first, that Diana in no way encourages or reciprocates his passion, and second, that the count does indeed enter into a betrothal contract with her. Again, desire both combines and collides with legality. "Derivèd from the ancient Capilet" (V.iii. 161) and rightly named for the goddess of chastity, this young woman is "wondrous cold" when Bertram first speaks with her, and all his "Tokens and letters . . . she did re-send" (III.vi. 114, 116). Diana terms her virginity "the jewel of our house, / Bequeathèd down from many ancestors, / Which were the greatest obloquy i'th' world / In me to lose" (IV.ii.48-51). Moreover, she declares, "Marry that will; I live and die a maid" (76). In order to assault such icy resistance, as he thinks successfully, Bertram will promise anything. Helen accurately predicts the course of his "wanton siege":[119] "This ring he holds / In most rich choice; yet in his idle fire / To buy his will it would not seem too dear, / Howe'er repented after" (III.vii. 18, 25-28). When oaths fail to assure Diana of his steadfastness, Bertram concedes, "Here, take my ring. / My house, mine honour, yea my life be thine, / And I'll be bid by thee" (IV.ii.53-55). Ironically, the ring will in fact go to one rightly responsible for safeguarding his house, his honor, his very life, to one with a right to bid him obey—to his wife, Helen.

While Shakespeare emphasizes the perversion of using such a symbol to satisfy Bertram's "sick desires" (37), the ring's practical function is to provide undeniable testimony about the kind of relationship he has entered into. Thus, when he slanders Diana as "a common gamester to the camp," the token witnesses, "This is his wife. / That ring's a thousand proofs" (V.iii. 191, 201-202). He has indeed promised marriage, with exchange of his own ancestral signet for his bed partner's ring the outward symbol of this promise. In receiving it, Diana riddles, "You have won / A wife of me" (IV.ii.66-67). Though the officers say Bertram merely "fleshes his will in the spoil of her honour" (IV.iii. 17), Paroles testifies more damningly: "I knew of their going to bed and of other motions, as promising her marriage" (V.iii.265-267). Potentially, there are two impediments to a match with Diana—Bertram's prior contract with Helen and his pledge, "He had sworn to marry me / When his wife's dead" (IV.ii.73-74), which is nullified by criminality—the premise of a living spouse's death. However, because the count receives word of Helen's demise before he deflowers the presumed Diana, he knows that apparently these barriers to matrimony no longer exist. Were his wife truly dead, as Bertram supposes, then he has made a secret *de futuro* contract of marriage which, when consummated, becomes wedlock, precisely as Diana claims.

Yet the shameful seduction of Diana and the despised match with Helen are not the only knots in this tangled marital skein. Even before Bertram returns from Florence to France, Lafeu and the king plan another alliance, which is presented to the Countess of Roussillon for her approval.[120]

LAFEU. . . . I moved the King my master to speak
  in the behalf of my daughter; which, in the minority
  of them both, his majesty out of a self-gracious
  remembrance did first propose. His highness hath
  promised me to do it; and to stop up the displeasure
  he hath conceived against your son, there is no
  fitter matter. How does your ladyship like it?

COUNTESS. With very much content, my lord, and I wish it happily effected.

(IV.v.70-79)

When the last scene opens, Bertram, presumably a widower, stands ready to marry Maudlin (whom the audience never sees). Quite conventionally, the king, still acting as Bertram's guardian, ascertains each party's assent and decrees, "Then shall we have a match" (V.iii.30). Thus the young count will wed, not the "poor maid" (148) he has seduced nor the physician's daughter he has scorned, but the heiress of a nobleman, his first "choice" (46)—and his social equal.[121]

Yet in a comedy where no courtship proceeds in quite the usual way, this one too goes awry. First the "amorous token" (69) he produces for betrothal to Maudlin turns out to be Helen's gift from the king, arousing suspicion that Bertram might have murdered his unwanted wife. And then Diana appears, charging him with both seduction and a prior contract. In the face of these formidable impediments, Lafeu breaks off negotiations, declaring contemptuously, "Your reputation comes too short for my daughter, you are no husband for her" (178-179). Just at the point when it seems Bertram must acknowledge as spouse a woman with no fortune, with status inferior to Helen's and with a presumed stain on her virginity, Helen herself appears to rescue him. The final disposition of Diana comes at the king's hands: "If thou be'st yet a fresh uncroppèd flower, / Choose thou thy husband and I'll pay thy dower" (328-329). Ironically, once again royal beneficence is expressed in allowing an impoverished gentlewoman free choice of her mate, together with a generous portion. The action has come full circle. Yet within its orb Shakespeare has packed virtually every irregularity that might attend upon courtship—enforced marriage, nonconsummation, desertion, seduction, secret betrothal, a bed trick, and such impediments as duress, disparagement, unfulfilled conditions, criminality, and precontract. While many plays touch on aspects of irregular unions, *All's Well That Ends Well* explores these difficult, sensitive problems at length, making dramatic capital out of the loopholes in the fabric of matrimonial regulations.

Irregular or invalid courtship allows Shakespeare his fullest opportunity to explore the rules governing "nuptial breaches" (*Lr.*, Q sc. 2, 143) in the culture that he shared with his audiences. Crossing the boundaries between the licit and the illicit, he can both damn and justify premarital intercourse in *Measure for Measure*, ennoble a secret love in *Romeo and Juliet*, surround it with ambiguity in *Othello*, debase it in *Troilus and Cressida*. The frank sexuality of common folk can rebuke the perversions of a Sicilian king, lead to foolish unions in Arden or Navarre, amuse at Belmont, meet reproof in Roussillon. The whole panoply of impediments to marriage find their way into dramatic action: bigamy, consanguinity, criminality, precontract, false identity, unchastity, disparagement, compulsion, religious disparity. From blatant seduction to royal annulments, the canon treats the complexities of heterosexual commitments with great subtlety. No easy answers emerge, no facile generalizations apply, whether it be to genre or to gender, to rank or to race. Instead, there is at work a sophisticated detachment, which interlaces the requirements of source, character, and action with the technicalities determining one's precise marital status. And the ensuing judgments, whether aesthetic or ethical, can be manipulated into almost any configuration, depending upon each play's structure and textual signals. It finally becomes impossible to say whether Shakespearean drama affirms secret betrothals, runaway lovers, fornication, or any other irregular courtship practice. Instead, the fascination lies in the artistry with which the language, rituals, and symbols related to deviant matrimonial possibilities align themselves against the more conventional route to marriage.

Notes

[1] In addition to evidence in the works cited below, see Susan Dwyer Amussen, "Féminin/masculin: le genre dans l'Angleterre de l'epoque moderne," *Annales Économies, Sociétés, Civilisations* 40 (1985): 271-276; E.R.C. Brinkworth, ed., *The Archdeacon's Court*, Oxfordshire Record Society 23 (1942): passim; R. H. Helmholz, *Canon Law and the Law of England* (London: Hambledon Press, 1987), pp. 184-185. I am also indebted to unpublished work on London by R. Mark Benbow.

[2] Alan Macfarlane, "Illegitimacy and Illegitimates in English History," in *Bastardy and Its Comparative History*, ed. Peter Laslett, Karla Oosterveen, and Richard M. Smith (Cambridge: Harvard University Press, 1980), p. 73. See also Susan Dwyer Amussen, "Gender, Family and the Social Order, 1560-1725," in *Order and Disorder in Early Modern England*, ed. Anthony Fletcher and John Stevenson (Cambridge: Cambridge University Press, 1985), pp. 200, 207; E.R.C. Brinkworth, *Shakespeare and the Bawdy Court of Stratford* (London: Phillimore, 1972), pp. 73, 80-91; F. G. Emmison, *Elizabethan Life: Morals and the Church Courts* (Chelmsford: Essex County Council, 1973), pp. 25-30; Martin Ingram, *Church Courts, Sex, and Marriage in England, 1570-1640* (Cambridge: Cambridge University Press, 1987), pp. 237, 282, 285-291. Walter J. King, "Punishment for Bastardy in Early Seventeenth-Century England," *Albion* 10 (1978): 151, thinks that women were punished more harshly because removing males from productivity would have damaged the economy. However, since the mother could scarcely avoid detection and was also victimized by the lower status of her gender, a masculine system of justice inevitably placed the greater onus on

her. See, e.g., Susan Dwyer Amussen, *An Ordered Society: Gender and Class in Early Modern England* (New York: Basil Blackwell, 1988), pp. 111-117.

[3] Peter Laslett, "Introduction: Comparing Illegitimacy over Time and between Cultures," in *Bastardy*, pp. 14, 22; David Levine and Keith Wrightson, "The Social Context of Illegitimacy in Early Modern England," in *Bastardy*, pp. 159, 164, 170-171; Karla Oosterveen and Richard M. Smith, "Bastardy and the Family Reconstitution Studies of Colyton, Aldenham, Alcester and Hawkshead," in *Bastardy*, pp. 100-101; G. R. Quaife, *Wanton Wenches and Wayward Wives: Peasants and Illicit Sex in Early Seventeenth Century England* (New Brunswick, NJ: Rutgers University Press, 1979), pp. 225-242; Edward Shorter, *The Making of the Modern Family* (New York: Basic Books, 1975), pp. 80-85; Keith Wrightson and David Levine, *Poverty and Piety in an English Village: Terling, 1525-1700* (New York: Academic Press, 1979), pp. 126-127, 132.

[4] Emmison, *Elizabethan Life*, pp. 20-24; Ingram, *Church Courts*, pp. 158-163, 269-273; Laslett, "Introduction," pp. 54-59; idem, "The Bastardy Prone Sub-Society," in *Bastardy*, pp. 217-246; Levine and Wrightson, "Social Context," 164, 166, 168-171; Quaife, *Wanton Wenches*, pp. 229-230; J. A. Sharpe, *Crime in Early Modern England 1550-1750* (London: Longman, 1984), pp. 100, 110; Keith Wrightson, *English Society, 1580-1680* (London: Hutchinson, 1982), pp. 84-86; Wrightson and Levine, *Poverty*, pp. 128, 131-132.

[5] John R. Gillis, *For Better, for Worse: British Marriages, 1600 to the Present* (Oxford: Oxford University Press, 1985), pp. 23ff.; Ralph A. Houlbrooke, *Church Courts and the People during the English Reformation, 1520-1570* (Oxford: Oxford University Press, 1979), p. 58; Ingram, *Church Courts*, pp. 156-157, 225-226, 240-241; Ann Kussmaul, *Servants in Husbandry in Early Modern England* (Cambridge: Cambridge University Press, 1981), pp. 79-83; Alan Macfarlane, *Marriage and Love in England: Modes of Reproduction 1300-1840* (Oxford: Basil Blackwell, 1986), p. 296; David Underdown, *Revel, Riot, and Rebellion: Popular Politics and Culture in England 1603-1660* (Oxford: Clarendon Press, 1985), pp. 46, 49-52, 59-63; Wrightson, *English Society*, pp. 74-79.

[6] Phillip Stubbes, *The Anatomie of Abuses* (London, 1595), p. 109; see also pp. 57-58, 64.

[7] J. A. Sharpe, *Defamation and Sexual Slander in Early Modern England: The Church Courts at York*, Borthwick Papers 58 (1980): 21. For other examples see, e.g., Amussen, *Ordered Society*, pp. 71, 159, 167; Brinkworth, *Shakespeare and the Bawdy Court*, p. 75; Christopher Hill, "The Spiritualization of the Household," in *Society and Puritanism in Pre-Revolutionary England* (New York: Schocken Books, 1964), p. 448; A. L. Rowse, *Sex and Society in Shakespeare's Age: Simon Forman the Astrologer* (New York: Charles Scribner's Sons, 1974), pp. 52, 78-82; Alan G. R. Smith, *Servant of the Cecils: The Life of Sir Michael Hickes, 1543-1612* (Totowa, NJ: Rowman and Littlefield, 1977), pp. 165-166; Ashmolean MSS 306.349-349^v and 206.426 (references supplied by Barbara Traister in private correspondence).

[8] *The Uncasing of Machivils Instructions to his Sonne* (London, 1613), F3^v. See also Sir John Harington, *Nugae Antiquae*, ed. Henry Harington (London: Vernor and Hood, 1804), 1:107; idem, *The Letters and Epigrams of Sir John Harington*, ed. Norman Egbert McClure (Philadelphia: University of Pennsylvania Press, 1930), p. 269.

[9] Robert V. Schnucker, "Elizabethan Birth Control and Puritan Attitudes," *Journal of Interdisciplinary History* 5 (1975): 655; Katherine Usher Henderson and Barbara F. McManus, eds., *Half Humankind: Contexts and Texts of the Controversy about Women in England, 1540-1640* (Urbana: University of Illinois Press, 1985), p. 74. See also Lawrence Stone, *The Crisis of the Aristocracy, 1558-1641* (Oxford: Clarendon Press, 1965), pp. 609-610, 663-668.

[10] Rachel Weigall, ed., "The Journal of Lady Mildmay, circa 1570-1617," *The Quarterly Review* 215 (1911): 121.

[11] Robert Southwell, S.J., *Two Letters and Short Rules of a Good Life*, ed. Nancy Pollard Brown (Charlottesville: University Press of Virginia, 1973), p. 49.

[12] *Jane Anger, her Protection for Women* (London, 1589), C3^v. See also *A Lyttle Treatyse Called ye Image of Idlenesse* (London, 1574), B6; Isabella Whitney, *The Copy of a Letter . . . to her Unconstant Lover* (London, ca. 1567).

[13] See, e.g., Dorothy Leigh, *The Mother's Blessing* (London, 1616), pp. 33-43; Lu Emily Pearson, *Elizabethans at Home* (Stanford, CA: Stanford University Press, 1957), p. 282; Mary Beth Rose, "Moral Conceptions of Sexual Love in Elizabethan Comedy," *Renaissance Drama*, n.s., 15 (1984): 6-7; Keith Thomas, "The Double Standard," *Journal of the History of Ideas* 20 (1959): 195-216. Quaife, *Wanton Wenches*, pp. 244-249, argues that chastity was not particularly important to most people.

[14] Baldassare Castiglione, *The Courtier*, trans. Sir Thomas Hoby (London: David Nutt, 1900), p. 215. See also Giovanni M. Bruto, *The Necessarie, Fit, and Convenient Education of a Yong Gentlewoman*, trans. W. P. (London, 1598), 16ff.; Heinrich Bullinger, *The Christian State of Matrimony*, trans. Miles Coverdale (London, 1575), 91^v-92; Jacques DuBosc, *The Compleat Woman* (London, 1639), pp. 49, 62;

Thomas Gainsford, *The Rich Cabinet Furnished with Varieties of Excellent Descriptions* (London, 1616), p. 163ᵛ; Henry Willoby, *Willobie his Avisa, or the True Picture of a Modest Maid, and a Chast and Constant Wife* (London, 1594), pp. 5-9.

[15] Nicholas Breton, *A Poste with a Packet of Mad Letters* (London, 1633), p. 2.

[16] Ester Sowernam, *Ester Hath Hang'd Haman* (London, 1617), p. 45. See also Roger Ascham, *The Scholemaster* (London, 1570), pp. 29ᵛ-30; Thomas Dekker, "The Batchelors Banquet," in *The Non-Dramatic Works*, ed. Alexander B. Grosart (1884; reprint, New York: Russell and Russell, 1963), 1:245-246; John Downame, *Foure Treatises* (London, 1609), pp. 177ff.; Richard Jones, *The Passionate Morrice*, ed. F. J. Furnivall, New Shakspere Society, ser. 6, no. 2 (London: N. Trübner, 1876): 95-96; *The Lawes Resolutions of Womens Rights* (London, 1632), p. 377; Samuel Rowlands, *The Bride* (London, 1617), D3; Willoby, *Willobie his Avisa*, pp. 12, 21; Linda Woodbridge, *Women and the English Renaissance: Literature and the Nature of Womankind, 1540-1620* (Urbana: University of Illinois Press, 1984), p. 84.

[17] DuBosc, *Compleat Woman*, p. 64; Joseph Swetnam, *The Araignment of Lewde, Idle, Froward, and Unconstant Women* (London, 1615), p. 27. See also *The Mothers Counsell* (London, 1631), p. 3; Sowernam, *Ester*, p. 25.

[18] *A Collection of Articles, Injunctions, Canons, Orders, ordinances, and Canons Ecclesiastical* (London: Stevens and Co., 1846), p. 4. See also Emmison, *Elizabethan Life*, p. 144; Pearson, *Elizabethans*, p. 24.

[19] Bullinger, *Christian State*, 11ᵛ-12, 13ᵛ. See also Robert Cleaver, *A Godly Form of Householde Government* (London, 1598), p. 136; Thomas Dekker, "The Seven Deadly Sinnes of London," in *The Non-Dramatic Works*, ed. Alexander B. Grosart (1885; reprint, New York: Russell and Russell, 1963), pp. 46-47; Downame, *Foure Treatises*, pp. 177ff.; William Gouge, *Of Domesticall Duties* (London, 1622), p. 632; Juan Luis Vives, *The Office and Duetie of an Husband*, trans. Thomas Paynell (London, 1553), D5.

[20] *Lawes*, p. 54; Martin Ingram, "Spousals Litigation in the English Ecclesiastical Courts c.1350-c. 1640," in *Marriage and Society: Studies in the Social History of Marriage*, ed. R. B. Outhwaite (New York: St. Martin's Press, 1981), pp. 46-47; idem, *Church Courts*, pp. 196-198, 208-209; Chilton Latham Powell, *English Domestic Relations, 1487-1653* (New York: Columbia University Press, 1917), p. 17.

[21] *Lawes*, pp. 53-54. See also Matthew Griffith, *Bethel, or A Forme for Families* (London, 1633), p. 272; William Harrington, *The Comendacions of Matrymony* (London, 1528), A4-A4ᵛ; Henry Swinburne, *A Treatise of Spousals, or Matrimonial Contracts* (London, 1686), pp. 193-202.

[22] Pearson, *Elizabethans*, p. 333.

[23] Swinburne, *Treatise*, pp. 193-202.

[24] Philip Gawdy, *Letters of Philip Gawdy*, ed. Isaac Herbert Jeayes (London: J. B. Nichols and Sons, 1906), p. 103.

[25] Amussen, *Ordered Society*, pp. 106-107, 152-155; Emmison, *Elizabethan Life*, pp. 144-153; Houlbrooke, *Church Courts*, pp. 60-62; Ingram, *Church Courts*, pp. 191-218.

[26] Swinburne, *Treatise*, p. 226; see also pp. 30, 73, 150, 218, 224, 225. Further references include Jean Bodin, *The Six Bookes of a Commonweale*, trans. Richard Knolles (London, 1606), p. 15; *Lawes*, p. 54; William Perkins, *Christian Oeconomie*, trans. Thomas Pickering (London, 1609), pp. 23, 55.

[27] Bodin, *Six Bookes*, p. 15; *Lawes*, p. 60.

[28] *Lawes*, p. 117; see also p. 69. Other authorities are Henricus Cornelius Agrippa, *The Commendation of Matrimony* (London, 1540), B3; Harrington, *Comendacions*, A4, A6; Swinburne, *Treatise*, pp. 233ff.

[29] See, e.g., Brinkworth, *Shakespeare and the Bawdy Court*, pp. 14-18, 75, 80, 87.

[30] Gouge, *Domesticall Duties*, p. 202.

[31] Bullinger, *Christian State*, p. 57. See also Downame, *Foure Treatises*, pp. 177ff.; Richard Greenham, *Works* (London, 1599), p. 299; Robert Snawsel, *A Looking Glasse for Maried Folkes* (London, 1610), E3ᵛ.

[32] See n. 4 above.

[33] Morris P. Tilley, *A Dictionary of the Proverbs in England in the Sixteenth and Seventeenth Centuries* (Ann Arbor: University of Michigan Press, 1950), C739.

[34] Richard L. Greaves, *Society and Religion in Elizabethan England* (Minneapolis: University of Minnesota Press, 1981), pp. 204-213; P.E.H. Hair, "Bridal Pregnancy in Rural England in Earlier Centuries," *Population Studies* 20 (1966): 233-237; idem, "Bridal Pregnancy in Early Modern England Further Examined," *Population Studies* 24 (1970): 61, 65; Ingram, *Church Courts*, p. 220; Laslett, "Introduction," pp. 53-54; David Levine, *Family Formation in an Age of Nascent Capitalism* (New York: Academic Press, 1977), pp. 127-145; Levine and Wrightson, "Social

Context," p. 161; Oosterveen and Smith, "Bastardy," p. 109; Keith Wrightson, "The Nadir of English Illegitimacy in the Seventeenth Century," in *Bastardy*, p. 189; Wrightson and Levine, *Poverty*, p. 131.

[35] Amussen, *Ordered Society*, pp. 71, 112-115, 159, 167; Ingram, *Church Courts*, pp. 199, 282-283. For fictional treatments of these situations, see Edward Gosynhyll, *Here Begynneth the Schole House of Women* (London, 1560), A3-A3ᵛ; Dekker, "Batchelors Banquet," pp. 244-254; Thomas Heywood, *A Curtaine Lecture* (London, 1637), pp. 235-236.

[36] Wrightson and Levine, *Poverty*, pp. 128, 130. See also Emmison, *Elizabethan Life*, p. 3; Houlbrooke, *Church Courts*, pp. 60, 65; Ingram, *Church Courts*, pp. 267-268; Sharpe, *Crime*, pp. 81-82.

[37] Stone, *Crisis*, pp. 606, 663-666.

[38] Elizabeth Jenkins, *Elizabeth and Leicester* (New York: Coward-McCann, 1962), pp. 186-187.

[39] The word *elopement* is here used in its modern sense, but in the Elizabethan period it also meant leaving one's spouse to live with another partner, an offense for which a woman forfeited her dower rights. See *Lawes*, p. 144.

[40] Pearson, *Elizabethans*, pp. 321-322; Greaves, *Society*, p. 133; Kathy Lynn Emerson, *Wives and Daughters: The Women of Sixteenth-Century England* (Troy, NY: Whitston Publishing Company, 1984), p. 69.

[41] Greaves, *Society*, p. 133.

[42] Pearson, *Elizabethans*, p. 341.

[43] Catherine Drinker Bowen, *The Lion and the Throne: The Life and Times of Sir Edward Coke (1552-1634)* (Boston: Little, Brown, 1957), pp. 123-125; Emerson, *Wives*, p. 47; Pearson, *Elizabethans*, pp. 321-322.

[44] *Constitutions and Canons Ecclesiastical 1604* (Oxford: Clarendon Press, 1923), L3-L4; Emmison, *Elizabethan Life*, pp. 155-158; Gillis, *For Better*, p. 90; Greaves, *Society*, p. 181.

[45] Gouge, *Domesticall Duties*, pp. 205, 452; see also pp. 452-453, 212-213. Other authorities include Cleaver, *Godly Form*, p. 136; John Stockwood, *A Bartholomew Fairing for Parentes* (London, 1589), pp. 76-77; John Wing, *The Crowne Conjugall or, The Spouse Royall* (Middleburgh, 1620), pp. 125-126.

[46] 39 Eliz. c. 9; Thomas, "Double Standard," p. 211. Roger Fulwood was arraigned on this charge in 1637 after abducting Sara Cox, but the marriage was annulled, Sara declared a virgin, and Roger pardoned; see Antonia Fraser, *The Weaker Vessel* (New York: Alfred A. Knopf, 1984), pp. 22-25.

[47] Brinkworth, *Shakespeare and the Bawdy Court*, p. 108; Paul Hair, ed., *Before the Bawdy Court* (London: Paul Elek books, 1972), nos. 250, 449; Ralph A. Houlbrooke, *The English Family, 1450-1700* (London: Longman, 1984), pp. 311-312; G. E. Howard, *A History of Matrimonial Institutions* (Chicago: University of Chicago Press, 1904), 1:415; Ingram, *Church Courts*, pp. 214-218; Lawrence Manley, ed., *London in the Age of Shakespeare* (Philadelphia: Pennsylvania State University Press, 1986), pp. 272-273.

[48] Gillis, *For Better*, pp. 92-96; Edward J. Wood, *The Wedding Day in All Ages and Countries* (New York: Harper's, 1869), 2:235.

[49] Swinburne, *Treatise*, p. 229; see also p. 231. Refer as well to Houlbrooke, *Church Courts*, p. 61; *Lawes*, p. 72.

[50] Swinburne, *Treatise*, pp. 18-28, 43-44, 237. Ingram, *Church Courts*, pp. 173-174, found such dissents extremely rare.

[51] Swinburne, *Treatise*, pp. 165, 213-216, 236; William Whately, *A Care-Cloth, or a Treatise of the Cumbers and Troubles of Marriage* (London, 1624), p. 31; Pearson, *Elizabethans*, p. 319.

[52] Swinburne, *Treatise*, pp. 109-153, 223; *Lawes*, p. 54; Houlbrooke, *Church Courts*, pp. 56-67.

[53] See chaps. 2 and 4; Cleaver, *Godly Form*, p. 129; *Collection*, p. 4; *Constitutions*, L3ᵛ-L4, Q3ᵛ, Q4ᵛ; Stockwood, *Bartholomew Fairing*, p. 18.

[54] See above, n. 26.

[55] Swinburne, *Treatise*, p. 239, and pp. 5-7, 16, 223-224, 236-240. See also William Ames, *Conscience, with the Power and Cases Thereof* (London, 1639), pp. 198-202, 204; Bullinger, *Christian State*, 17ᵛ; Cleaver, *Godly Form*, pp. 96, 127; *Constitutions*, Q3ᵛ-Q4; Gouge, *Domesticall Duties*, pp. 181-186; Griffith, *Bethel*, pp. 270, 272; Harrington, *Comendacions*, B1-D2; *Lawes*, pp. 57-62; Pearson, *Elizabethans*, pp. 299-301; Perkins, *Christian Oeconomie*, pp. 24ff., 48ff.; Daniel Rogers, *Matrimoniall Honour* (London, 1642), pp. 96-120; Whately, *Care-Cloth*, pp. 30-31. *Epicoene*, in *Ben Jonson*, ed. C. H. Herford and Percy Simpson (Oxford: Clarendon Press, 1937), 5:264-268, ends with an amusing but technically accurate analysis of the legal grounds that nullify Morose's marriage.

[56] Cleaver, *Godly Form*, p. 95. See also Bullinger, *Christian State*, p. 56.

⁵⁷ See, e.g., Emmison, *Elizabethan Life*, p. 152. Ingram, *Church Courts*, pp. 174-211, 218, indicates that suits instituted on technical grounds were never numerous.

⁵⁸ Edmund Gibson, *Codex Juris Ecclesiastici Anglicani* (Oxford: Clarendon Press, 1761), 1:431.

⁵⁹ *Constitutions*, Q3-R1ᵛ; Gellert Spencer Alleman, *Matrimonial Law and the Materials of Restoration Comedy* (Philadelphia: University of Pennsylvania Press, 1942), pp. 125-126; Harrington, *Comendacions*, A2, C4ᵛ-D1; Houlbrooke, *Church Courts*, pp. 71-75; Ingram, *Church Courts*, p. 145; *Lawes*, pp. 65-66; Pearson, *Elizabethans*, pp. 300, 308, 325; Powell, *English Domestic Relations*, pp. 8-10; Margaret Loftus Ranald, *Shakespeare and His Social Context* (New York: AMS Press, 1987), p. 6; Alexander W. Renton and George G. Phillimore, *The Comparative Law of Marriage and Divorce*, in *Burge's Commentaries on Colonial and Foreign Laws* (London: Bradbury, Agnew, 1910), 3:19-24, 136-137; Swinburne, *Treatise*, pp. 223-228; Whately, *Care-Cloth*, p. 30.

⁶⁰ "Kindred and Affinity," *Time* (19 August 1940), p. 52; Naseeb Shaheen, "The Incest Theme in *Hamlet*," *Notes and Queries*, n.s., 32 (1985): 51; Oscar D. Watkins, *Holy Matrimony: A Treatise on the Divine Laws of Marriage* (New York: Macmillan, 1895), pp. 646, 708.

⁶¹ *Constitutions*, Q3; William Clerke, *The Triall of Bastardie* (London, 1594), M3-O3ᵛ and passim; Jean Louis Flandrin, *Families in Former Times: Kinship, Household and Sexuality*, trans. Richard Southern (Cambridge: Cambridge University Press, 1979), pp. 19, 24; Gibson, *Codex*, 1:412-415; Harrington, *Comendacions*, B1ᵛff.; *Lawes*, pp. 58, 61, 71; Pearson, *Elizabethans*, p. 300; *Depositions and Other Ecclesiastical Proceedings from the Courts of Durham*, Publications of the Surtees Society 21 (1845): 59; Swinburne, *Treatise*, p. 228. One correspondent of the period reports: "The marriage of Sir G. Allington is pronounced voyde in the High Commission and he fined 10,000ˡⁱ for his incestuous match [with his niece] and bound in 20,000ˡⁱ never heear[a]fter to accompany her againe; an excellent example"; Arthur Searle, ed., *Barrington Family Letters, 1628-1632*, Camden Society Publications, 4th ser., 28 (1983): 190.

⁶² Harrington, *Comendacions*, C2ᵛ; *Lawes*, p. 59; Renton and Phillimore, *Comparative Law*, p. 23. In cases of bigamy, desertion was often involved, with the abandoned spouse sincerely convinced of the missing partner's death; see, e.g., Amussen, *Ordered Society*, pp. 124-126; Ingram, *Church Courts*, pp. 177-180. The most notorious example of annulment based on inability to consummate was that of the Earl of Essex and Frances Howard; see chap. 2, n. 20.

⁶³ *Lawes*, p. 59; Perkins, *Christian Oeconomie*, p. 69.

⁶⁴ Alleman, *Matrimonial Law*, pp. 107, 113-114; Emmison, *Elizabethan Life*, pp. 164-170; Reginald Haw, *The State of Matrimony* (London: S.P.C.K., 1952), pp. 91-95; Houlbrooke, *Church Courts*, p. 68; Watkins, *Holy Matrimony*, pp. 9, 427-429.

⁶⁵ Gibson, *Codex*, 1:444-447; *Lawes*, pp. 64-67.

⁶⁶ William Vaughan, *The Golden-grove* (London, 1600), N6-N6ᵛ. For Lady Rich's experience when she fruitlessly tried to marry Lord Mountjoy after her divorce, see Fraser, *Weaker Vessel*, p. 295; Pearl Hogrefe, *Tudor Women: Commoners and Queens* (Ames: Iowa State University, 1975), pp. 88-89.

⁶⁷ Thomas Carter, *Carters Christian Commonwealth: Domesticall Dutyes Deciphered* (London, 1627), pp. 29-30; *Constitutions*, R1ᵛ-R2ᵛ. Some theologians argued that the innocent party should be allowed to remarry. See Ames, *Conscience*, pp. 210-211; Gouge, *Domesticall Duties*, p. 215; William Perkins, *Workes* (Cambridge, 1618), 3:69-71; John Rainolds, *A Defence of the Judgement of the Reformed Churches* (London, 1609); William Whately, *A Bride-Bush, or a Wedding Sermon* (London, 1617), p. 5. After being called before the Court of High Commission (see Fraser, *Weaker Vessel*, p. 295), Whately recanted his earlier position in *Care-Cloth*, "Advertisement," p. 80. Edmund Bunny's *Of Divorce for Adulterie, and Marrying Againe* (Oxford, 1610) is the best known polemic against remarriage of divorced persons. See also Catherine Belsey, "Alice Arden's Crime," *Renaissance Drama* 13 (1983): 83-102.

⁶⁸ Bunny, *Of Divorce*, p. 2. See also Bartholomaeus Batty, *The Christian Man's Closet*, trans. William Lowth (London, 1581), p. 101; Harington, *Letters*, p. 200; Samuel Rowlands, *Tis Merrie When Gossips Meete* (London, 1602), D3ᵛ.

⁶⁹ Harington, *Letters*, p. 284. For a couple forced to remain married despite the best efforts of the groom's family to have their union annulled, see Allison D. Wall, *Two Elizabethan Women: Correspondence of Joan and Maria Thynne, 1575-1611*, Wiltshire Record Society 38 (1982): xxvi, 8-12.

⁷⁰ Lawrence Stone, "Marriage among the English Nobility in the 16th and 17th Centuries," *Comparative Studies in Society and History* 3 (1960-1961): 202-203; idem, *Crisis*, pp. 660-662. Though Stone finds forty-nine instances of annulment or separation among the peerage between 1570 and 1659, he includes "notorious marital quarrels" in that figure instead of restricting it to legally sanctioned estrangements.

⁷¹ Swinburne, *Treatise*, pp. 184-185; *Lawes*, p. 69.

[72] See chap. 4, n. 103.

[73] See also David Bevington, *Action Is Eloquence: Shakespeare's Language of Gesture* (Cambridge: Harvard University Press, 1984), pp. 140-141; Pearson, *Elizabethans*, pp. 336-337. Confused about what constitutes valid matrimony (which would be indissoluble), Alan Powers believes that Florizel and Perdita "are really married for a minute or so—the shortest marriage in the opus. After all, Polixenes ends with, 'Mark your divorce, young sir.'" See "'Meaner Parties': Spousal Conventions and Oral Culture in *Measure for Measure* and *All's Well That Ends Well*," *The Upstart Crow* 8 (1988): 38.

[74] Horst Breuer presumes a sexual liberality in Shakespeare's time but does not discriminate along class lines in his analysis, "Shakespeares Mädchen und Frauen in Familiengeschichtlichen Kontext," *Anglia* 105 (1987): 69-93.

[75] Robert Ornstein, e.g., *Shakespeare's Comedies: From Roman Farce to Romantic Mystery* (Newark: University of Delaware Press, 1986), p. 39, thinks the baby is Costard's.

[76] Kenneth Muir, *Shakespeare's Tragic Sequence* (New York: Barnes and Noble, 1979), p. 75, feels their suspicion "is a better index to their own minds than it is to Hamlet's intentions or to Ophelia's frailty." Mark Taylor, *Shakespeare's Darker Purpose: A Question of Incest* (New York: AMS Press, 1982), p. 114, concurs. Angela Pitt, *Shakespeare's Women* (London: David and Charles, 1981), p. 53, is one of the few who note that Ophelia has seen Hamlet "unchaperoned and without her father's approval."

[77] Diane Elizabeth Dreher, *Domination and Defiance: Fathers and Daughters in Shakespeare* (Lexington: University Press of Kentucky, 1986), p. 78, believes Ophelia is sacrificed to "that static and oppressive female virtue: chastity," and, p. 52, she objects to Polonius's "blatant disregard for their [his children's] privacy," both wholly modern judgments. Lisa Jardine, *Still Harping on Daughters: Women and Drama in the Age of Shakespeare* (Totowa, NJ: Barnes and Noble, 1983), p. 72, and William G. Meader, *Courtship in Shakespeare; Its Relation to the Tradition of Courtly Love* (New York: Columbia University, King's Crown Press, 1954), p. 207, claim that Ophelia's return of Hamlet's gifts represents a broken engagement, but the text shows no promise of marriage.

[78] See, e.g., Allen H. Gilbert, "Two Margarets: The Composition of *Much Ado About Nothing*," *Philological Quarterly* 41 (1962): 61-71; Richard A. Levin, *Love and Society in Shakespearean Comedy* (Newark: University of Delaware Press, 1985), pp. 113-115.

[79] Laurence Lerner, *Love and Marriage: Literature and Its Social Context* (New York: St. Martin's Press, 1979), p. 20, is among those who find the duke's decision totally capricious. However, Leonard Tennenhouse, *Power on Display: The Politics of Shakespeare's Genres* (London: Methuen, 1986), p. 74, thinks Theseus ready "to generously forgive where Egeus . . . would be penurious and harsh." Shirley Nelson Garner, "*A Midsummer Night's Dream*: 'Jack shall have Jill; / Nought shall go ill,'" *Women's Studies* 9 (1981): 55, recognizes the betrothal but does not connect it with Theseus's decision.

[80] Powers, "'Meaner Patries,'" pp. 30, 32, calls this a *de futuro* contract but reveals an imperfect understanding of the status of spousals in law.

[81] Marianne Novy, *Love's Argument: Gender Relations in Shakespeare* (Chapel Hill: University of North Carolina Press, 1984), p. 85, disagrees, claiming that Desdemona "resourcefully finds a way to initiate courtship while seeming to him to be merely hinting." However, Peter Stallybrass, "Patriarchal Territories: The Body Enclosed," in *Rewriting the Renaissance,* ed. Margaret W. Ferguson, Maureen Quilligan, Nancy J. Vickers (Chicago: University of Chicago Press, 1986), p. 136, feels that the "untamed" Desdemona is indeed "half the wooer." More typically, A. J. Smith, *Literary Love: The Role of Passion in English Poems and Plays of the Seventeenth Century* (London: Edward Arnold, 1983), p. 38, claims, "Othello's tale of how he wooed her comes as an idyll in the midst of tumult."

[82] Wayne Holmes, "Othello: Is't Possible?" *The Upstart Crow* 1 (1978): 1-23, argues that Cassio and Desdemona have become lovers before Othello marries her. Stanley Cavell, *Disowning Knowledge: In Six Plays of Shakespeare* (New York: Cambridge University Press, 1987), pp. 131-132, is uncertain about the marriage's consummation. T.G.A. Nelson and Charles Haines, "Othello's Unconsummated Marriage," *Essays in Criticism* 33 (1983): 1-18, say Desdemona dies a virgin. Lynda E. Boose, "Othello's Handkerchief: 'The Recognizance and Pledge of Love,'" *English Literary Renaissance* 5 (1975): 362-363, sees the handkerchief with its strawberries (emblem of purity) as a miniature of blood-stained wedding sheets, suggesting that those sheets may be either a test or a proof of her virginity. Karl P. Wentersdorf, "The Time Problem in *Othello*: A Reconsideration," *Jahrbuch, Deutsche Shakespeare-Gesellschaft West* (1985): 73-74, speculates about premarital intercourse between Othello and Desdemona, a sexual union she then may have violated with Cassio. The text provides no evidence for any of these notions.

[83] Novy, *Love's Argument,* p. 128, claims that Desdemona "is trying to reassure Brabantio by putting her marriage into an orderly continuity of marriages, trying to remind him that his marriage too was won at the cost of a separation from a father," but Novy ig-

nores the irregular circumstances under which the daughter's match is made. Others who support the orthodoxy of Desdemona's response include Dreher, *Domination,* p. 44-45; Juliet Dusinberre, *Shakespeare and the Nature of Women* (New York: Barnes and Noble, 1975), p. 97; Marjorie Garber, *Coming of Age in Shakespeare* (New York: Methuen, 1981), p. 43; Gayle Greene, "'This That You Call Love': Sexual and Social Tragedy in *Othello,*" *Journal of Women's Studies in Literature* 1 (1979): 26.

[84] Stephen Greenblatt, *Renaissance Self-Fashioning: From More to Shakespeare* (Chicago: University of Chicago Press, 1980), p. 250, says it is this frank declaration that "awakens the deep current of sexual anxiety in Othello." Among those defending Desdemona's statement are Irene G. Dash, *Wooing, Wedding and Power: Women in Shakespeare's Plays* (New York: Columbia University Press, 1981), p. 108; Arthur Kirsch, *Shakespeare and the Experience of Love* (Cambridge: Cambridge University Press, 1981), p. 15. When other characters, like Juliet, express a desire for consummation, the circumstances are never so public as a senate council.

[85] The list of contemporary critics who either rebuke or idealize Desdemona is far too long to include here. Some few, like Stallybrass, "Patriarchal Territories," p. 141, see two Desdemonas—the "maiden never bold" and the woman of "downright violence." As I have argued in "The Design of Desdemona: Doubt Raised and Resolved," *Shakespeare Studies* 13 (1980): 187-196, the apparent contradictions in this character are a matter of external perception, for both the audience and Othello, rather than of internal inconsistency.

[86] Garber, *Coming of Age,* p. 120, mistakenly says the marriage was at 9:30 A.M.; however, Juliet goes to confession in the afternoon. Germaine Greer, "Juliet's Wedding," *Listener* (7 December 1978): 751, casts doubt on the validity of the ceremony because the audience does not see it, yet except for Hymen's rites in *AYL* and the aborted rites in *Ado,* no wedding occurs onstage. Certainly all the principals—Romeo, Juliet, and Friar Laurence—accept its validity, as eventually the parents do.

[87] Bevington, *Action,* p. 145, to some extent devalues this interchange by saying Capulet is reduced to "bargaining with Montague over a bridal portion for the young woman who is now married to her deathbed." So does Northrop Frye, *Northrop Frye on Shakespeare* (New Haven: Yale University Press, 1986), pp. 31-32, charging that the offer of statues indicates that "two miserable, defeated old men who have lost everything . . . simply cannot look their own responsibility for what they have done straight in the face."

[88] Novy, *Love's Argument,* p. 108, contrasts the stiff stichomythia of this interchange with the spontaneously lyrical poetry between Juliet and Romeo.

[89] Leo Salingar, *Shakespeare and the Traditions of Comedy* (Cambridge: Cambridge University Press, 1974), p. 319, observes Shakespeare's borrowing of names from earlier plays—"a second Juliet, secretly married, appears, and a second Claudio, whose 'headstrong' conduct in marrying without a dowry or a church ceremony . . . makes him the exact opposite of the suspicious, conventional Claudio in *Much Ado.*"

[90] See Marc Eccles, ed., *A New Variorum Edition of "Measure for Measure"* (New York: Modern Language Association of America, 1980), p. 35, for notes on "true contract." Marc Shell, *The End of Kinship: "Measure for Measure," Incest, and the Ideal of Universal Siblinghood* (Stanford, CA: Stanford University Press, 1988), p. 110, erroneously equates this contract with the private unions of Romeo and Juliet, Henry VIII and Anne Boleyn, perhaps even Shakespeare and Anne Hathaway, even though Claudio's spousal is not lawfully solemnized as are the other marriages.

[91] E. Pearlman, "Historical Demography for Shakespeareans," *Shakespearean Research Opportunities* 7-8 (1972-1974): 71, thinks that, with one-fifth of Elizabethan brides pregnant, "the utter ordinariness of the situation renders Angelo's response additionally fierce and puritanical." However, the women Pearlman refers to not only marry before the child is born but are rarely gentlewomen like Juliet.

[92] Meader, *Courtship,* p. 215, is wrong in claiming that an abrogation of the contract requires mutual consent. Without the dowry, its terms remain unfulfilled, but so long as no other contract intervenes, the spousal can be translated into matrimony by sexual intercourse.

[93] Carol Thomas Neely, *Broken Nuptials in Shakespeare's Plays* (Yale University Press, 1985), p. 93, mentions the slander in her analysis of this play but ignores the legitimate ground of the dowry's loss. Among others who discuss the technical aspects of this contract are J. Birje-Patil, "Marriage Contracts in *Measure for Measure,*" *Shakespeare Studies* 5 (1969): 111; W. W. Lawrence, *Shakespeare's Problem Comedies,* 2d ed. (1931; reprint, New York: Frederick Ungar, 1960), pp. 95-97; Margaret Loftus Ranald, "'As Marriage Binds and Blood Breaks': English Marriage and Shakespeare," *Shakespeare Quarterly* 30 (1979): 77-79.

[94] Ernest Schanzer, "The Marriage Contracts in *Measure for Measure,*" *Shakespeare Survey* 13 (1960): 81-89, says the Angelo-Mariana spousal was *de futuro,* the Claudio-Juliet spousal *de praesenti.* S. Nagarajan, "*Measure for Measure* and Elizabethan Betrothals," *Shakespeare Quarterly* 14 (1963): 115-119, thinks they were the reverse. Harriet Hawkins, "What Kind of Precontract Had Angelo? A Note on Some Non-problems in Elizabethan Drama," *College English* 36 (1974): 173-179, considers the whole matter irrelevant. Pow-

ers, "'Meaner Parties,'" minimizes the entire affair, speculating that "Shakespeare himself and Anne may have—and Claudio and Juliet definitely had—lived together as if married without witnesses" and thus "were married all along, that the only lack was a matter of form," pp. 33, 35. I cannot concur with his suppositions.

[95] Darryl J. Gless, *"Measure for Measure," the Law, and the Convent* (Princeton: Princeton University Press, 1979), p. 201, points out Mariana's use of specific references to a betrothal ceremony in her public accusation—"This is the hand which, with a vowed contract, / Was fast belocked in thine." He might also have mentioned "swor'st," "match," "affianced," "vows," "wife."

[96] Leah Marcus, *Puzzling Shakespeare: Local Reading and Its Discontents* (Berkeley: University of California Press, 1988), pp. 179-183, 194-195, sees the Duke's command entwined with a complicated set of historical associations, including abrogation of the requirement for an episcopal license, abuse of sexual standards through the unlawful bed tricks, coercive marriage, and aversion to special waivers such as papal indulgences. Neely, *Broken Nuptials*, p. 98, incorrectly calls the Claudio-Juliet wedding a "restored marriage." Moreover, she claims, p. 99, that women "have the potential to confer social respectability on men by marrying them and bearing their children, as Juliet and Kate Keepdown do." In the play's action, however, it would seem to be men who bestow respectability on women by marrying them and legitimizing their children.

[97] For another full discussion of the marital technicalities in *Ado*, see Ranald, "'As Marriage Binds,'" pp. 73-77, and idem, *Shakespeare and His Social Context*, pp. 11-32. Marilyn French, *Shakespeare's Division of Experience* (New York: Summit Books, 1981), p. 130, feels that Hero "is already suspect" because she has "been wooed and won by a great nobleman prior to this betrothal." However, the proxy wooing never figures into the accusation at the wedding, though Claudio's false suspicion of Don Pedro obviously presages his false suspicion of Hero.

[98] Among those objecting to Claudio's conduct are Levin, *Love and Society*, p. 86; Ornstein, *Shakespeare's Comedies*, p. 132; John Traugott, "Creating a Rational Rinaldo: A Study in the Mixture of the Genres of Comedy and Romance in *Much Ado about Nothing*," *Genre* 15 (1982): 157. Significantly, Shakespeare's source has the groom send a message instead of denouncing the bride at the wedding; see Geoffrey Bullough, *The Narrative and Dramatic Sources of Shakespeare* (London: Routledge and Kegan Paul, 1958), 2:118.

[99] Bevington, *Action*, p. 142, suggests that government policies against abuse of the prayer book may account for the absence of these rites onstage, as may their inherent lack of theatricality. This particular scene he terms "a central visual picture of inverted order," p. 144.

[100] Robert G. Hunter, *Shakespeare and the Comedy of Forgiveness* (New York: Columbia University Press, 1965), pp. 100-101, points out that Claudio's outburst stems not only from his sense that the proprieties have been violated but also from deep feelings of love for Hero. See also Janice Hays, "Those 'soft and delicate desires': *Much Ado* and the Distrust of Women," in *The Woman's Part: Feminist Criticism of Shakespeare*, ed. Carolyn Lenz, Gayle Greene, Carol Thomas Neely (Urbana: University of Illinois Press, 1980), p. 87. By contrast, Ornstein, *Shakespeare's Comedies*, p. 119, says this scene "discloses something about conventional attitudes that we would prefer never to have known." But Nadine Page, "The Public Repudiation of Hero," *PMLA* 50 (1935): 739-744, long ago insisted that audiences would have demanded public humiliation as a matter of justice.

[101] David M. Sundelson, *Shakespeare's Restorations of the Father* (New Brunswick, NJ: Rutgers University Press, 1983), p. 122, misses the betrothed status of Lavinia and Bassianus, calling him her "lover." Eugene M. Waith, *Patterns and Perspectives in English Renaissance Drama* (Newark: University of Delaware Press, 1988), p. 141, says that Bassianus "seizes his brother's bride."

[102] Dreher, *Domination*, pp. 47-48, first acknowledges this match as bigamy and yet seems to brush aside that insuperable barrier: "Neglecting her welfare, he [Cymbeline] matches her with a man she cannot love, simply to please his queen," p. 46. David Bergeron, *Shakespeare's Romances and the Royal Family* (Lawrence: University Press of Kansas, 1985), p. 145, claims that Cloten does not recognize the validity of Innogen's contract because of Posthumus's lesser rank. But even in his rage Cymbeline seems to acknowledge a marriage: "Thou took'st a beggar, wouldst have made my throne / A seat for baseness" (I.i.142-143).

[103] The definitive analyses of this marriage as incest are those of Roland Mushat Frye, *The Renaissance Hamlet* (Princeton: Princeton University Press, 1984), pp. 76-82; Jason P. Rosenblatt, "Aspects of the Incest Problem in *Hamlet*," *Shakespeare Quarterly* 29 (1978): 349-364; Lawrence Rosinger, "Hamlet and the Homilies," *Shakespeare Quarterly* 26 (1975):299-301; John Dover Wilson, *What Happens in Hamlet?* (Cambridge: Cambridge University Press, 1935), pp. 39-44. Shaheen, "Incest," p. 51, points out that the incest derives from *Hamlet*'s sources. Tennenhouse, *Power*, p. 89, deems the murder itself "incestuous in that it allows one member of the king's family to marry another."

[104] Richard P. Wheeler, "History, Character and Conscience in *Richard III*," *Comparative Drama* 5 (1971-1972): 316, notes Richard's awareness of the sin involved in wooing Princess Elizabeth but does not specify the nature of the sin.

[105] Neely, *Broken Nuptials,* p. 63, says that "Hamlet urges abstinence upon Gertrude even in marriage." Similarly, Tennenhouse, *Power,* p. 114, says the prince "insists upon shifting the crime from the fact of regicide to the act of 'incest,' namely the sexual relations between Claudius and his brother's wife which Hamlet *considers* illicit" (italics mine). Neither seems aware that, besides consanguinity, criminality invalidates the union. Ranald, "'As Marriage Binds,'" p. 73, and *Shakespeare and His Social Context,* p. 7, is virtually the only one who mentions this impediment. In *Historiae Danicae* the queen knows she has married her husband's murderer, a circumstance Shakespeare alters; see Bullough, *Narrative and Dramatic Sources,* vol. 7 (1973), 62.

[106] On this point see, e.g., C. L. Barber and Richard P. Wheeler, *The Whole Journey: Shakespeare's Power of Development* (Berkeley: University of California Press, 1986), pp. 277-280; Kay Stockholder, *Dream Works: Lovers and Families in Shakespeare's Plays* (Toronto: University of Toronto Press, 1987), p. 55.

[107] Garber, *Coming of Age,* p. 118, is one of the few who even notice the complexity of this situation.

[108] Peter Erickson, *Patriarchal Structures in Shakespeare's Drama* (Berkeley: University of California Press, 1985), p. 23, calls this a "wedding rehearsal"; Meader, *Courtship,* p. 205, calls it a "spousal." It is neither.

[109] Germaine Greer, "Love and the Law," in *Politics, Power, and Shakespeare,* ed. Frances McNeely Leonard (Arlington: Texas Humanities Resource Center, 1981), p. 124, says that Rosalind here corrects Celia in order to change the vows to present tense. However, the prayer book also begins with a repetition of the betrothal vows in the future tense before shifting to matrimonial vows in the present tense, just as in this mock ceremony; see chap. 7. Agnes Latham, ed., *As You Like It,* Arden Shakespeare (London: Methuen, 1975), pp. 134-135, thinks this a valid espousal, with Ganymede the surrogate for Rosalind (who in fact speaks in her own person). Yet in their bargain Orlando accepts Ganymede as a curative substitute, not an officially designated agent; see chap. 5.

[110] Alexander Leggatt, *Shakespeare's Comedy of Love* (London: Methuen, 1974), pp. 190-191, notes the contrast between Sir Oliver Martext and Hymen as wedding officiants. He alsoobserves, p. 212, that "the litany of the four lovers in V.ii. marks the transition" to "Hymen's entrance . . . the high point of miracle in the play," p. 213.

[111] Meader, *Courtship,* p. 225, says that this rite parodies the spousal in everything but confirmation of dowry; he appears to be unaware of the many points at which the ceremony is defective.

[112] Martha Tuck Rozett, "The Comic Structures of Tragic Endings: The Suicide Scenes in *Romeo and Juliet* and *Antony and Cleopatra,*" *Shakespeare Quarterly* 36 (1985): 162, acknowledges here a fusion of marriage, consummation, and maternity. Cavell, *Disowning Knowledge,* p. 18, also sees in the conclusion of *Ant.,* as in *WT,* "a new ceremony (or new sacrament) of marriage." Yet when he describes the ceremony, p. 28, he does not seem to recognize the signals to Jacobean audiences that would identify it as a wedding, rather than a "hallucinated, . . . more than half mad" rite. See also Howard Felperin, *Shakespearean Romance* (Princeton: Princeton University Press, 1972), p. 139; Alexander Leggatt, *Shakespeare's Political Drama: The History Plays and the Roman Plays* (London: Routledge, 1988), p. 187; Stockholder, *Dream Works,* p. 226.

[113] Most editors, including the Oxford editors, interpolate here a stage direction for Cleopatra to apply another asp, despite the absence of such a direction in the Folio text and the other indications that only a single serpent is used. I am indebted to a paper read by Edward Snow at the 1989 meeting of the Shakespeare Association of America for pointing out this misleading editorial practice.

[114] For a historical account of Antony's five marriages, see Eleanor Huzar, "Mark Antony: Marriages vs. Careers," *Classical Journal* 81 (1986): 97-111. In Egypt, Cleopatra and Antony did go through a marriage ceremony, but the union was not recognized in Rome, where Octavia was still his wife, p. 107. Nevertheless, as in Shakespeare, the couple were buried together in Egypt in a royal tomb, p. 110. Neely, *Broken Nuptials,* p. 243n. 13, notes that this pair are often married in other versions of the story. However, she does not see the last scene as a wedding rite, except in symbolic terms, pp. 161-162.

[115] Susan Bassnett-McGuire, "An Ill Marriage," *Shakespeare Jahrbuch Weimar* 120 (1984): 102, calls *AWW* an "analysis of the complexities of post-Reformation views of the marriage contract and . . . a warning to a class that has grown too complacent in its demands for absolute power."

[116] Margaret Loftus Ranald, "The Betrothals of *All's Well That Ends Well,*" *Huntington Library Quarterly* 26 (1963): 179-192, and *Shakespeare and His Social Context,* pp. 33-49. Powers, "'Meaner Parties,'" p. 37, notes coercion as a grounds for annulment but mistakenly claims that the bed trick would not have betokened consent. See also Joel Hurstfield, *The Queen's*

Wards: Wardship and Marriage under Elizabeth I, 2d ed. (London: Frank Cass, 1973), pp. 139-141, for a discussion of disparagement. For other analyses of the nature of the contract, see G. K. Hunter, ed., *All's Well That Ends Well,* Arden Shakespeare (London: Methuen, 1959), pp. 53, 60.

[117] Neely, *Broken Nuptials,* p. 87, interprets the "if" anaphora as an indication of the conditional nature of all human relationships.

[118] Bassnett-McGuire, "Ill Marriage," bases her analysis of this play on the ambiguity surrounding the concept of divorce as stated in Canon 107 of 1604, which codified the ban on remarriage of divorced persons. However, such a ban had long existed, and in any case Helen here acknowledges death as the only condition that will now divorce her from Bertram. Peggy Muñoz Simonds, "Sacred and Sexual Motifs in *All's Well That Ends Well,*" *Renaissance Quarterly* 42 (1989): 58, trivializes Helen's statement by asserting that she "mischievously threatens him with 'deadly divorce.'"

[119] This term reinforces R. B. Parker's contention, "War and Sex in *All's Well That Ends Well,*" *Shakespeare Survey* 37 (1984): 102, 105, that in this play sex is a spoil of war and war an evasion of sexuality.

[120] Neely, *Broken Nuptials,* p. 85, compares this arrangement to Octavia's in *Ant.* and Claudio's second match in *Ado.*

[121] Ornstein, *Shakespeare's Comedies,* p. 174, attributes Bertram's willingness to marry Maudlin solely to the fact that the alliance "will redeem him in the eyes of the King, his mother, and Lafew." He calls Bertram's "avowed love of the fair Maudlin" "a rehearsed artificiality," pp. 189-190. Neely, *Broken Nuptials,* pp. 82, 84, agrees. However, the king and Lafeu have thought this match fitting before Helen ever comes to court and may be responding to Bertram's earlier interest in the girl.

FURTHER READING

Cheatham, George. "Imagination, Madness, and Magic: *The Taming of the Shrew* as Romantic Comedy." *Iowa State Journal of Research* 59, No. 3 (February 1985): 221-32.

Argues that *The Taming of the Shrew* resembles Shakespeare's later comedies, like *A Midsummer Night's Dream,* in that it employs the metaphors of role-playing, madness, and magic to examine the transformative power of love.

Kahn, Coppélia. "'The Savage Yoke': Cuckoldry and Marriage." In *Man's Estate: Masculine Identity in Shakespeare,* pp. 119-50. University of California Press, 1981.

Analyzes the theme of the married man as cuckold in Shakespeare's plays. Kahn first reviews the motifs associated with cuckoldry in Shakespeare's work and then studies cuckoldry as a "male fantasy of female betrayal" in many of the plays.

Leggatt, Alexander. *Shakespeare's Comedy of Love.* London: Methuen, 1974, 272 p.

Studies the "internal variety" in Shakespeare's romantic comedies (*The Comedy of Errors, The Two Gentlemen of Verona, The Taming of the Shrew, Love's Labour's Lost, A Midsummer Night's Dream, The Merchant of Venice, Much Ado About Nothing, As You Like It, Twelfth Night*), focusing on the tension within each play between variances of style or dramatic idiom. Maintains that while certain plot devices and themes such as romantic love appear in each of the plays, they are never treated in the same manner.

Lindenbaum, Peter. "Time, Sexual Love, and the Uses of Pastoral in *The Winter's Tale.*" *Modern Language Quarterly* 33, No. 1 (March 1972): 3-22.

Examines the pastoral elements of the play, noting how pastoral life in Bohemia offers a sharp contrast to the world of the Sicilian court. Lindenbaum argues that although Perdita is presented as an idealized figure of the pastoral world and its values, the pastoral world itself is not romanticized. Lindenbaum maintains that Shakespeare presents a view of time as destructive, but through his depiction of pastoral life and Perdita's attitude toward life the audience is able to accept such a view of time in a calm, perhaps even an enthusiastic manner.

MacCary, W. Thomas. *Friends and Lovers: The Phenomenology of Desire in Shakespearean Comedy.* New York: Columbia University Press, 1985, 264 p.

Studies ten of Shakespeare's comedies (*The Comedy of Errors, The Two Gentlemen of Verona, Love's Labour's Lost, The Taming of the Shrew, A Midsummer Night's Dream, Much Ado About Nothing, the Merchant of Venice, As You Like It, Twelfth Night, The Winter's Tale*) and maintains that in them, Shakespeare offers an examination of "the orientation of desire and its constitution of individual identity." As such an exploration, MacCary argues, these plays may be compared to Plato's dialogues and Freud's metapsychological essays.

Ranald, Margaret Loftus. "'As Marriage Binds, and Blood Breaks': English Marriage and Shakespeare." *Shakespeare Quarterly* 30, No. 1 (Winter 1979): 68-81.

Stresses that knowledge of the matrimonial laws in Shakespeare's England can aid in one's understanding of the action of many of his plays. Ranald examines several plays that deal with particular facets of matrimonial legalities and demonstrates the significance of marriage in Shakespeare's comedies, poems, and tragedies.

Summers, Joseph H. *Dreams of Love and Power: On Shakespeare's Plays*. Oxford: Clarendon Press, 1984, 161 p.

Maintains that the plays analyzed (*A Midsummer Night's Dream, The Winter's Tale, Hamlet, Measure for Measure, King Lear, Antony and Cleopatra, The Tempest*), share a common trait: the emphasis on the dreams (hopes, fears, desires) of the characters, and that as audience members, we become involved in the dramas in our perception of the relationship between those dreams and our own. The chapters on *A Midsummer Night's Dream, The Winter's Tale* and *Antony and Cleopatra* focus in particular on the characters' dreams of love.

VanDenBerg, Kent. "Theatrical Fiction and the Reality of Love in *As You Like It*." *PMLA* 90, No. 5 (October 1975): 885-93.

Extends the critical approach to the play as self-reflective by arguing that Shakespeare's emphasis of the artificial nature of theatrical fiction is intended to make that artifice "a comprehensive metaphor of love." *As You Like It*, VanDenBerg explains, reflects itself in order to symbolize a reality that extends beyond itself.

Pericles

For further information on the critical and stage history of *Pericles*, see *SC*, Volumes 2, 15, and 36.

INTRODUCTION

Pericles has enjoyed a revival in scholarly interest during the twentieth century. Once ridiculed as so poorly written and disjointed that its authorship was questionable, the drama is now garnering more attention and praise as a transitional piece in Shakespeare's career. Most scholars now ascribe *Pericles* as the first of Shakespeare's romances, a genre in which the woes and troubles of the protagonist are miraculously reversed during the play's conclusion. Although critics note that the play is less complex and realistic than Shakespeare's earlier works, they argue that the playwright employs a dreamlike state and exotic setting purposefully to distance the audience from the distressing subjects of incest and prostitution. The majority of scholars agree now that Shakespeare did write the third, fourth, and fifth acts while an unknown author, possibly George Wilkins, is responsible for writing the lesser quality first and second acts.

In his study of Shakespeare's romance plays, John Dean argues that *Pericles*, like the other plays in this genre, centers upon the nature of love and on the juxtaposition between fidelity and moral love versus evil, self-serving love. Dean states that *Pericles* is about contrasts between good and immoral characters and about the cost of love. He states: "Like the use of the sea in his romances, the power of love is used to establish the marvelously fluid atmosphere which helps to keep the diverse ingredients of his romance plays in balance." Other criticism dealing with issues of love and romance focus on the varying nature and symbolic roles of the three couples at the center of the drama. In her comparison of *Pericles*, *Hamlet*, and *King Lear*, Kay Stockholder illustrates the similarities in sexual ideals in these plays, contrasting Pericles's struggles with incest with Hamlet's contentious relationship with Ophelia. Although *Pericles* ends in triumph, Stockholder argues that its fairytale structure "casts doubts on its possibility, a doubt that also attaches to the emotional veracity of the envisioned restoration of love and family." The issue of adultery has sparked considerable critical attention. Elizabeth Archibald, for instance, notes the contrasts between the true, romantic love shared by Pericles and Thaisa versus the unnatural and monstrous adultery between Antiochus and his daughter. Archibald states that in contrast to earlier versions of the story, Marina is not condemned, despite her purity, to a martyr's death for her exposure to brothel life, but rather Shakespeare redeems her through marriage. However, Archibald points out that Marina never expresses any opinion about her marriage nor her intended, and thus, there is no evidence that she loves Lysimachus, the prince whom she reforms. Other scholarship focuses on the pure and chaste nature of Marina, suspected to provide counter balance to the darkness of the incest theme and her role in the restoration of her father. Although much of the scholarship on *Pericles* deals with other issues, Hermann Ulrici argues that the play is centered around and unified by the triumph of love.

LOVE AND ROMANCE

John Dean (essay date 1979)

SOURCE: "The Theme of Love in Shakespeare's Romances," in *Elizabethan and Renaissance Studies*, Vol. 86: *Restless Wanderers: Shakespeare and the Pattern of Romance*, edited by Dr. James Hogg, Institut Für Anglistik Und Amerikanistik der Universitat Salzburg, 1979, pp. 264-77.

[*In the excerpt below, Dean argues that Shakespeare contrasts healthy and immoral forms of love in* Pericles.]

> "Hear my soul speak."
> *The Tempest*

1 *Love in the Literature of Romance*

Throughout all of Shakespeare's romances there is a strain of *théâtre à thèse*, that type of theatre which in an earlier form had all but destroyed the dramatic feasibility of *Timon of Athens*. The thesis which Shakespeare develops in each one of his romances is a variation on the theme of how love may be found, lost, and recovered. Each of Shakespeare's romances builds language and situation, character and tension to highlight a strong moral position, especially sexual conservatism, and to advance an argument in defense of fidelity. Whether or not Shakespeare held the views argued out by character and plot development in his romances is uncertain; it is clear, however, that certain ideas about love and human beings are the animating force in *Pericles, Cymbeline, The Winter's Tale* and *The Tempest*. Like the use of the sea in his romances, the power of love is used to establish the marvellously fluid atmosphere which helps to keep the diverse ingredients of his romance plays in balance.

Reading these four romances both as a set and individually one finds Shakespeare concentrating on the masculine and feminine expression of love as two distinguishable forms of love, on love as the most powerful shaping force in the lives of human beings, the need for reciprocity and a moral attitude with regards to love, the decay and degeneration of human love as a precursor to death, a distinction between the love of youth and the love of maturity, love as a private and a social bond, and love as an element which extends beyond mortal bounds.

Love has always been a dominant strain in the literature of romance. For Homer in the *Odyssey* love was important first of all as a family emotion, that special circle of affection shared by Odysseus, Penelope, Telemachus, Laertes, and Antikleia. The word for this form of love in Homer is *phílos*, by which Homer meant "that unalterable relation, far deeper than fondness and compatible with all changes of mood, which unites a normal man to his wife, his home, or his own body - the tie of a mutual 'belonging' which is there even when he dislikes them."[1] It is this force of *phílos* which keeps Odysseus directed back towards Ithaca, which makes him long for his wife and home even when he shares the delicious sea cave of the goddess Calypso. It is also the emotion which Penelope feels for Odysseus and which helps her to stay faithful to him, an emotion which Telemachus feels for his father, and the power with which Odysseus' mother Antikleia reaches out to him in Hades. A love of sexual passion, *éros*, is also an important part of the love theme in the *Odyssey*. But Homer regards it as a far more ambiguous sentiment, one with many negative overtones. *Éros* is the name given to the destructive love which the suitors feel for Penelope (*Od.* xviii, 212), and their longing to express this kind of love with Penelope ultimately results in their death.

Love is a unifying and moral sentiment in the Hellenistic romances when expressed by the hero and heroine—especially when expressed by the heroine. It gives the wanderers the strength to endure their sufferings and carries them onwards even when they lack an immediate goal. The same basic distinction is made between *phílos* and *éros* in the Hellenistic romances; all the heroines preserve their virginity and in the *Aethiopica, Daphnis & Chloe*, and *Apollonius of Tyre* the heroes preserve their virginity as well. The one exception is Clitophon in *Clitophon & Leucippe* who breaks the narrative tension established by the virginity theme by having sexual intercourse with the supposed widow Melitte at the end of the fifth book.[2] The one female exception with regard to chastity is the heroine Chloe in *Daphnis & Chloe*, who, although she does not lose her virginity, still indulges in the deathbed embrace of Dorcon.[3]

The temper of the love expressed between the hero and the heroine in the Hellenistic romances is strictly adolescent. *Apollonius of Tyre* almost provides an exception here, but when the love between Apollonius and his wife matures the focus of the story shifts to his daughter's adolescent love. Also the love scenes between the hero and heroine in the Hellenistic romances are imbued with a tone of sweetness, or *glukt s*, as the narrative slowly builds up a mood of expectation for their eventual marriage and discovery of their true identity. As noted earlier, in contrast to this strain of young, sweet, idealistic love in the Hellenistic romances there is also a strain of seasoned, sensual pleasures—a contrast of emotional sensibility which was suggested in the *Odyssey* only in Nausicaa's delicately expressed affection for Odysseus.

In marked distinction to both Homer's and Shakespeare's use of love is the lack of a sense of love as a family affection in the Hellenistic romances. With the exception of the second half of *Apollonius of Tyre* love is a sentiment expressed solely between two young lovers isolated from their families in the course of the narrative. In most cases their expressions of love are a kind of vernal *phílos*, a true love experienced by adolescents which is not expressed in family terms until the final reunion scene.

In Malory's *Le Morte D'Arthur* the theme of love matures throughout the long course of the narrative. At first it is strongly reminiscent of the adolescent affection one finds in Hellenistic romances, tempered by a more realistic approach to sensuality. But by the time the Sangrail narrative begins in Book XVII, and especially by the time of the "le Chevalier du Chariot" episode in Book XIX, the theme of love is treated in an extremely mature fashion.

Love in Malory is not normal family love, rather it is the ambiguous experience of mature passion between independent men and women. Guenever and Launcelot know what they are risking as long as they maintain their love, and they accept this risk as one of the attributes which makes their love rare and valued above all others. They act as if their love stands above human law, and the irony of Arthur's subsequent enforcement of human law is that it ends their love in as world-shattering and intense a fashion as such a rare love deserved.

The greatest sorrow of the love theme in *Le Morte D'Arthur* is that love does not lead the parted back together again. Until the appearance of the Sangrail and the quarrel over Guenever and Launcelot's adultery the force of love appeared to bind the Round Table fellowship. But then the Sangrail appears and offers the knights a higher, more-than-earthly love. The final exposure of Guenever and Launcelot irreparably divides the Round Table fellowship over the reality of mortal, imperfect love.

In Ariosto's *Orlando Furioso* love drives all human actions. Ariosto attaches love to every desire which a man or a woman may have, from a love of chastity and honour to a love of God and war. More particularly, love is important in the plot of *Orlando Furioso* because the rejection of Orlando's love by Angelica and her totally unreasonable preference for Medor drives Orlando temporarily insane. And thus the whole poem is built around "Orlando's acts . . . / Who fell bestraught with love, a hap most rare, / To one that erst was counted wise and stayd" (C.1, st. 1). All facets of human love are examined by Ariosto and love is rarely examined from one angle. Ariosto is careful to frame this driving motion through his distanced observations as narrator and then to return to the point of view of the individual character who is undergoing the experience of love. At times this narrative method will devalue the love which is being spoken of (as with Rodomont, Isabel, and Doralice, *O.F.* C.XXIX, st. 1.f.), or these comments may intensify the love (as with Ariosto's comments on Bradamant's experience of jealousy, *O.F.*, C.XXXI, st. 1.f.). At the end of the whole work the many diverse forms of love are bound in the atmosphere of good will established by the love between Ruggiero and Bradamant, while the last great enemy of love, the pagan knight Rodomont, King of Algiers, is killed.

The experience of love is a very mixed brew in pre-Shakespearean romance plays. In the three romance plays which we examined at an earlier point in this study the theme of love was presented quite differently in each play. Thomas Hughes portrays love in *The Misfortunes of Arthur* either as an ill, sexual passion, as with the interpretation of Guenever's love for Mordred (*T.M.O.A.*, I.ii., p. 267), or as a self-sacrificing power which great heroes can show for their country, as with Arthur's love for Britain (esp. in Arthur's death scene, *T.M.O.A.*, V.i.). *The Misfortunes of Arthur* manufactures sharp theatrical dichotomies between good and evil forms of love and prefigures the same technique of sharp divisions as that used by Shakespeare in a far more sophisticated fashion in *Pericles*. Robert Green's portrayal of love in *The History of Orlando Furioso* is very reminiscent in spirit of Ariosto's depiction of love in the *Orlando Furioso*: once love has touched a person they are all heat and fire, suddenly quite altered from a previous state of calm self-control into a state of daemonic possession. Because Orlando takes leave of his sense in *The History of Orlando Furioso* it is not a faith in love which leads him back to his sanity and his beloved Angelica, but rather the workings of chance and fortune. In John Day's *The Isle of Gulls* the love theme is an incongruous mixture of bawdry and high sentiment, often expressed by the same characters at the same time.[4] The play treats love as a robust game for courtiers and gallants, as a subject which is essentially lighthearted and offers little cause for pain.

Shakespeare's personal expression of the force of love which he showed in his sonnets portrays love as a guiding power in a changing world. As Shakespeare noted about the *philos* kind of love in Sonnet 116, it is not a love:

Which alters when it alteration finds,
Or bends with the remover to remove.
O no! it is an ever-fixed mark,
That looks on tempests and is never-shaken;
It is the star to every wand'ring bark,
Whose worth's unknown, although his height
  be taken.
                                    (St. 116, 2-8)

Whereas the *éros* kind of love leads to:

Th'expense of spirit in a waste of shame

. . . . .

Mad in pursuit, and in possession so;
Had, having, and in quest to have, extreme;
A bliss in proof, and prov'd, a very woe;
Before, a joy propos'd; behind, a dream.
                                    (St. 129, 9-12)

Although Shakespeare probably wrote his Sonnets earlier than his romances,[5] the ideas about love which he crystallized in the Sonnets quoted above are to be found again in the ordering principle of love which he used in his dramatic romances. In addition to what Shakespeare may have learned from earlier dramatic romances and his own ideas of love expressed in Sonnets 116 and 129, an argument for the superiority and permanence of *philos* love as contrasted to *éros* love is developed by John Gower throughout his *poème à thèse*, the *Confessio Amantis* —which served as the finest source work for *Pericles*. Finally in *Pericles* itself, which we shall now turn to, the dramatic progression is marked by a series of illustrations of the good and evil forms of love, with the plot tracing out a thematic pattern concerned with the protagonists' victimization or aid by different expressions of love.

2 Stable Pieces In A Shifting Tableau: Pericles

Pericles begins with a storm of passion as the adventurous and cocksure young prince confronts the primordial crime of incest. Shakespeare underlines

Pericles' state of sexual excitement and confusion, as the young prince is portrayed as being deeply in love with the incestuous daughter of King Antiochus before he knows of her crime, while after he learns of it he regrets the loss of a love which he felt could have lasted forever (see esp. *Per.* I.i.76-77). Pericles notes how the Daughter of Antiochus' face is the "book of praises, where is read / Nothing but curious pleasures" (*Per.* I.i.15-16) and how he would give "my unspotted fire of love to you" (*Per.* I.i.53).

Yet while his sexual ardour is in this initial inflamed stage, his first bite into the apple of his desire shows him that it is pitted with worms. His wanderings then begin in reaction to this discovery, and because of an earnest desire to prevent Antiochus' "tempest" of war from falling on his own people of Tyre (*Per.* I.ii.90-100). Love hurts in *Pericles*, and it is not until Pericles discovers Thaisa in Act two, scene three that his love, either his sexual ardour or his love for his own people, causes him anything but painful wanderings.

Having established one part of his argument about the pain of love and the destructiveness of unbridled sexual passion, Shakespeare then develops a thematic counterbalance with the court of Pentapolis and the healthy sensuality of King Simonides and his daughter. Directly before he goes to Pentapolis Pericles experiences false love in the court of Cleon and Dionyza of Tharsus, where he came seeking "not . . . for reverence, but for love" (*Per.* I.iv.97), not for the high respect for his office as Prince of Tyre, but a feeling which is naturally more genuine and kindly disposed. In retrospect the audience knows Pericles does not receive a genuine, lasting love until Pentapolis. In Pentapolis, however, he must first prove his worth in order to receive this love—a theme which Shakespeare will develop throughout the romances.

King Simonides and his daughter Thaisa stand out in sharp contrast to the loathsome sensuality of King Antiochus and his daughter. Directly after the banquet scene in Pentapolis in which Simonides tries to cheer up Pericles by flattering him with the appraisal that he has "heard you knights of Tyre / Are excellent in making ladies trip" (*Per.* II.iii.102-103), the focus switches to Helicanus telling Escanes about Antiochus and his daughter's punishment for their "heinous capital offence . . . [of] incest" (*Per.* II.iv.5, 2). The love argument expands as Shakespeare weaves in a full complement of light and dark threads in side-by-side contrast; by mid-play the evil lovers are being punished and the virtuous lovers appear to be receiving their just reward.

The next step in Shakespeare's dramatic argument is to exhibit Helicanus' love for Pericles by putting Helicanus through the test of being offered the leadership of Tyre. In Act one, scene two Helicanus was presented as the honest old counsellor, the only man in his court whom Pericles really trusted. But in Act two, scene four his heartfelt allegiance to Pericles is fully ascertained when he is *not* tempted to accept the offer of the permanent rulership of Tyre. What Pericles' "ancient substitute" (*Per.* V.iii.52) cares about most is staying true to Pericles. "Day serves not light more faithful than I'll be [to Pericles]" says Helicanus (*Per.* I.ii.110) and while Pericles is absent from Tyre he manifests this love by knitting together the Lords of Tyre in a tight bond of reverence and love for their prince.

With his marriage to Thaisa in the centre of the play (between Acts two and three), Pericles finds the "purchase of a glorious beauty / From whence an issue might . . . propagate" (*Per.* I.ii.72-73). Although the play has by this point established a balance between the unhealthy love of Antiochus' family, the healthy love of Pentapolis, and the fine guardianship of Helicanus—in romance the mood of fortune changes quickly and favourable circumstances rarely last. Gower's promise that the play would "make men glorious" (*Per.* Prol. 9) is not fulfilled easily; the cost of glory in romance is repeated suffering and loss. Pericles first underwent the loss of private desires, then the loss of his country, and now he must undergo the loss of his wife on the high seas of fortune. The last blow will be the removal of his one consolation in life, the "poor infant [Marina], this fresh-new seafarer" (*Per.* III.i.41). But as Shakespeare states in his next romance: "Some falls are means the happier to rise" (*Cym.* IV.ii.406). Pericles' life will seem splendid once he rises from this emotional depth.

Removing Pericles from stage center by the beginning of Act four allows Shakespeare to develop other examples of love: a Diana-like chastity and constancy in Marina which is prefigured in her mother's actions soon after her rebirth at the hands of Lord Cerimon (*Per.* III. iv), the self-less charity of Lord Cerimon, a man who cannot rest when others need his help (*Per.* III.ii.26 f.; V.iii, 60 f.), and an example of reformed licentiousness with Lysimachus, the governor of Mytilene (*Per.* IV.v.19 f.). In dark contrast to these people there are two examples of fraudulent emotion, as Shakespeare develops the love of Pandar, Bawd, and Boult for money, a love tempered by necessity (see esp. *Per.* V.i.168-171), and the conscience-denying, Lady Macbeth-like love which Dionyza shows for her daughter Philoten (*Per.* IV.i.1-13; IV.iii). Both the brothel keepers and Dionyza exemplify a type of affection in which he "who makes the fairest show means most deceit" (*Per.* I.iv.75).

This development of the ways of human emotions is accomplished at the risk of the audience losing sight of Pericles. Yet without this extensive development of the love theme there would be no plot to *Pericles*. Pericles' static, passive character is not a subject of profound dramatic exploration. Shakespeare builds up his romance drama of *Pericles* by exhibiting different facets of love; virtually each incident in the play (with the exception of the pirate crew of the great pirate Valdes) shows a different kind of love without developing or altering a major character's personality. "Pericles . . . hast a heart / That ever cracks for woe" (*Per.* III.ii.81-82) because of his adverse love experiences, and each member of his family likewise undergoes a great strain upon their life and love. But they move in the play like stable pieces in a shifting tableau. Only one character develops significantly in his loving in *Pericles*, Lysimachus, and Shakespeare keeps him in the dramatic background.

When one is dealing with an extremely emotional play like *Pericles*, indeed a play which "makes sense" at times because of emotional and not logical complementarity (as in the link between Act one, scene two and Act one, scene three)—it may seem odd to note a certain depersonalization of the characters. But the virtue of the protagonists in *Pericles*, both morally and aesthetically, lies in their emotional stability. Compared to characters like Hamlet or Lear, Pericles does not have much to offer an audience as a unique human being; but this is not the dramatic point of Pericles. Pericles, as well as Marina, Thaisa, Cerimon, and Helicanus are offered as exemplary figures; the "purchase is to make men glorious" (*Per.* Prol. 9). Shakespeare is stabilizing his romance diversity by building his play upon remarkably constant individuals whom we should enjoy as constant figures in contrast to an unstable world.

By the end of the play Pericles is hardened down by his adverse experiences to a silent, grieving man one step away from madness and death. Marina has been so hardened by her experiences that she reads her father's initial astonishment upon discovering her as cynicism and scorn (*Per.* V.i.164). Their reunion in Act five, scene one is not a sugar-sweet recovery scene. They have each endured long stretches of mirthless times and their mutual recovery does not explain the mystery of fortune. This scene expands upon the mystery of fortune by allowing them to recover those whom they had given up hope of ever finding. Life becomes like a "rarest dream . . . [of] wild . . . beholding . . . [filled with] the music of the spheres!" (*Per.* V.i.160, 220, 228). This is the "rapture of the sea" (*Per.* II.i.153) at work, the fitful tossing, blustering and shifting of people and events which luckily sometimes lead the wanderers home—a "home" for the wanderers' spirits which keeps its original value as long as the wanderers have kept their hearts' allegiance.

G. Wilson Knight has noted that the "most insistent impressionistic recurrence throughout *Pericles*, except for sea voyages, concerns the balancing of true and false virtues."[6] In *Pericles* this balance is an equilibrium of human affection which Shakespeare phrases as the forces of Diana confronting the forces of Priapus. In *Pericles* both Marina and Thaisa are identified with Diana (*Per.* II.iv.10; III.ii.110; IV.ii.149; IV.Prol.29), Pericles has a guiding vision of Diana (*Per.* V.i.238-249), and the play ends as a glorious triumph for her powers in the temple of Diana (*Per.* V.iii).

The powers of the goddess Diana suggest a certain cold distance, a reserve of purity, and most of all a moral constancy. In contrast, the force of Priapus suggests a lack of sexual control, an excessive, almost grotesque preoccupation with things sexual and sensual. The bawd sees Marina as a direct threat to the powers of Priapus, saying to her: "Fie, fie upon her! She's able to freeze the god Priapus, and undo a whole generation" (*Per.* IV.vi.3-5). When Marina prays to Diana to protect her virginity the Bawd mocks her prayers with, "What have we to do with Diana?" (*Per.* IV.ii.150).

Diana represents the spiritual force of love guiding the family of Pericles, while the forces of Priapus and other forms of reckless love (such as Dionyza's[7] love for Philoten) represent their spiritual adversaries. The world of Priapus in *Pericles* is diseased, while the people who have given in to this force, such as King Antiochus, his daughter, and the brothel keepers, have reverted to the moral level of troglodytes.

Pericles ends as a triumphant conclusion for the powers of Diana as opposed to the unruliness of Priapus. Shakespeare uses this ancient goddess and god not to suggest that they have a separate metaphysical reality for mankind, but as a concrete metaphor for the psychological and moral forces at work in *Pericles*. The gods of Greece protect Pericles' family (as the chorus wishes, *Per.*I.iv.97)[8] and they help to guide them all safely back to port. The greater power which aids Pericles' family, as personified by Diana, is a metaphor for their own constancy to love in a world where man is a "ball . . . play upon" (*Per.* II.i.58-61). Thus *Pericles* establishes an argument about the value of conservative love versus wasteful forms of love which will be repeated and developed in each succeeding romance by Shakespeare. . . .

Notes

[1] This definition of *phílos* is by C. S. Lewis in his *Preface to Paradise Lost* (Oxford: University Press, 1942), p. 23, A prominent example of *phílos* in the *Odyssey* would be *Od.* xiii, 40.

[2] But then *Clitophon & Leucippe* is also the most sexually pungent of the four Hellenistic romances popular in the age of Shakespeare, containing among other elements the longest digressions on pederasty.

[3] See: *Daphnis & Chloe, The Elizabethan Version from Amyot's Translation by Angell Daye* (London: David

Nutt in the Strand, 1890), rpt. from the original and ed. by Joseph Jacobs, pp. 43-44, Book I.

[4] Most notably by the two princesses Hipolita and Violetta in Act two, scene four, in which they talk about the promises of their forthcoming marriage. See: John Day, *The Isle of Gulls, op. cit.,* pp. 253-257.

[5] The dates of the Sonnets are usually assigned to 1592-1595, although they were first printed by Thomas Thorpe in 1609. *Pericles* was written about 1608-1609 and entered in the Stationer's Register on May 20, 1608. *Cymbeline* was written about 1609-1610, in which time Simon Forman records having attended a performance. *The Winter's Tale* was written about 1610-1611, and Simon Forman saw it on May 15, 1611. *The Tempest* was written in 1611, and presented on November 1, 1611 at court. For more on the dating of Shakespeare's Sonnets and plays see: Hyder E. Rollins, ed., *Shakespeare's Sonnets* (Philadelphia: J. B. Lippincott, 1944), New Variorum Edition; E. K. Chambers, *William Shakespeare: A Study of Facts and Problems,* 2 Vols., *op. cit.;*

[6] G. Wilson Knight, *The Crown of Life, op. cit.,* p. 48.

Dionyza's name derives from the Greek god of sensual recklessness, Dionysus. Shakespeare chose to keep her name as it is in the sources, where it is alternately spelled "Dionyse" (Gower) and "Dionisiades" (Twine) - while he altered other names in his adaptation. See: *N&DSOS,* Vol. 6, *op. cit.* pp. 383, 433.

Bibliography

Achilleus Tatius of Alexandria: The Adventures of Leucippe and Clitophon. ed. and trans. Stephen Gaselee. 1917.

Achilleus Tatius. *The Loves of Clitophon and Leucippe,* trans. William Burton, ed. Stephen Gaselee and H. F. B. Brett-Smith. Oxford, 1923.

———. "*Leucippe and Clitophon,*" ed. Ebbe Vilborg. Stockholm, 1955.

Aeschylus. *Agamemnon,* trans. Richmond Lattimore in *Aeschylus I.* Chicago, 1953. The University of Chicago Complete Greek Tragedies Vol. I.

Apollonii Regis Tyri, Historia, Latin text ed. Alexander Riese. Leipzig, 1893. A collation of manuscripts "A" and "P".

Apollonius of Tyre, The Old English, ed. Peter Goolden. Oxford, 1958.

Apollonius of Tyre. Early and Middle English Text, ed. Josef Raith. München, 1956.

Apuleius, Lucius. *The Golden Ass,* trans. William Adlington. 1566; rpt. 1893 in the Tudor Translation Series, no. 4.

Ariosto, Ludovico. *Tutte le opere di Ludovico Ariosto,* ed. Cesare Segre. Milan, 1964.

———. *Orlando Furioso,* trans. Sir John Harington. 1591; rpt. 1631.

———. *Orlando Furioso,* trans. Guido Waldman. 1974.

Beaumont, F. & Fletcher, J. *Philaster or Love Lies a-Bleeding.* 1969, in The Revels Plays series.

———. *In Two Volumes,* ed. J. St. Loe Strachey. 1950.

Boccaccio, Giovanni. *The Decameron . . . Translated into English anno 1620,* ed. Edward Hutton, 2 Vols. New York, 1940.

Borges, Jorges Luis. *A Personal Anthology.* 1972.

Callisthenes of Olynthus. *Historia Alexandri Magni,* ed. W. Kroll. Berlin, 1926. The "A" version.

———. *Der griech. Alexander roman Rezension B,* ed. Leif Bergson. Stockholm, 1965. The "B" version.

———. *Beiträge zur klassischen Philologie,* Heft 4 ed., U. von Lauenstein, Heft 12, ed. H. Englemann. Meisenheim am Glan, 1932. The "G" version.

———. *The Alexander Romance,* trans. and ed. E. H. Haight. New York, 1955.

Chariton. *Chaereas and Callirhoe,* trans. Warren E. Blake. Ann Arbor, Michigan, 1939.

Clyomon and Clamydes, ed. Betty J. Littleton. Paris, 1968.

Common Conditions. In *Five Anonymous Plays,* ed. J. S. Farmer. 1908.

Common Conditions, ed. Tucker Brooke. New Haven, 1908. An Elizabethan Club Reprint, no. 1.

DaVinci, Leonardo. *The Drawings of.* 2nd revised edition, ed. Kenneth Clark. 1968-1969.

John Day. *The Ile of Guls.* As it hath been often Acted in the Black Fryers, by the Children of the Revels. 1633. B.M. no. 644.d.76.

———. *The Isle of Gulls.* 1831. Part xviii for the Old English Drama Series.

———. *The Works of John Day,* ed. A. H. Bullen, with introd. by R. Jeffs. 1881; rpt. 1963.

———. *The Ile of Guls.* 1936, ed. with an introd. by G. B. Harrison.

Euripides. *Elene - Euripides' Helen*, ed. A. M. Dale. Oxford, 1967.

———. *Euripides' Helen*, trans. R. Lattimore. Chicago, 1956.

Gascoigne, G. and Kinwelmershe, F. *Giocasta - Jocasta: A Tragedie written in Greeke by Euripides, translated and digested into Acte by.* 1566; rpt. 1906.

Gower, John. *Confessio Amantis*, ed. R. A. Peck. New York, 1968.

Greene, Robert. *The Plays and Poems of*, ed. J. Churton Collins, Vols. I and II. Oxford, 1905, 1908.

———. *Friar Bacon and Friar Bungay*, ed. J. A. Lavin. 1969.

———. *Greene's "Pandosto" or "Dorastus and Fawnia" Being the Original of Shakespeare's "Winter's Tale"*, ed. P. G. Thomas. 1907.

———. *Pandosto The Triumph of Time.* In *Elizabethan Prose Fiction*, ed. M. Lawlis. New York, 1967, pp. 226-277.

Greene, Robert. *The Historie of Orlando Furioso One of The Twelve Pieres of France.* 1594. B.M. no. C.34. c. 38.

———. *The Scottish History of James the Fourth*, ed. N. Sanders. 1970.

———. *A Disputation in Cony Catchers and Bawdy Baskets*, ed. G. Salgado. 1972.

Hall, Joseph. *The Collected Poems*, ed. A. Davenport. 1949.

———. *The Life and Works*, ed. T. E. Kinloch. 1951.

———. *Virgidemiarum.* 1602.

Harington, Sir John, trans. *Orlando Furioso In English Heroical Verse.* 3rd ed., 1634.

Hawthorne, Nathaniel. *The House of The Seven Gables.* 1907; rpt. 1916.

Hazlitt, W. Carew, ed. *A Select Collection of Old English Plays.* 1874.

———. *The English Drama and Stage.* 1869.

Heliodorus. *HLIODOROY AITHIOPOKON - Les Éthiopiques (Théagene et Chariclée)*, ed. R. M. Rattenbury and Rev. T. W. Lumb. Paris, 1960, 2nd ed.

———. *An Aethiopian History Written in Greek by Heliodorus, Englished by Thomas Underdowne.* c. 1569; rpt., 1895. The Tudor Translation Series, no. 5.

———. *Heliodorus' Ethiopian Story*, trans. with an intr. by Sir Walter Lamb. 1961.

Hemingway, Ernest. *Death in the Afternoon.* 1932; rpt. 1966.

Herodotus. *HRODOTOY ISTORIA, Herodotus*, ed. A. D. Godley, 4 Vols. New York, 1921-1938; rpt. 1963.

———. *The Famous Hystory of Herodotus . . . translated into English by B.R.* 1584; rpt. 1924. The Tudor Translation Series, no. 6.

Herodotus. *Herodotus: The Histories*, trans. Aubrey de Sélincourt. 1972; rpt. 1975.

Holinshed, Raphel. *Shakespeare's Holinshed: An Edition of Holinshed's Chronicles, 1587*, ed. R. Housley. 1968.

———. *Holinshed's Chronicle as Used in Shakespeare's Plays*, ed. Allardyce and J. Nicoll. New York, 19 5.

Homer. *OMEROU ODYSSEIA, The Odyssey of Homer*, ed. W. B. Stanford. Vol. I, 1959; rpt.1974. Vol. II 1958; rpt. 1965.

———. *The Odyssey of Homer*, trans. R. Lattimore. New York, 1965; rpt. 1967.

———. *The Iliad of Homer*, trans. R. Lattimore. Chicago, 1951; rpt. 1967.

Hugo, François-Victor, trans. *Oeuvres Completes de William Shakespeare.* Paris, 1859.

Jonson, Ben. *The Complete Works*, ed. C. H. Herford and P. Simpson. Oxford, 1925.

Kazantzakis, Nikos. *The Odyssey - A Modern Sequel*, trans. K. Friar. 1959.

Longus. *DAPNIN KAI XLOHE - Daphnis and Chloe*, ed. with trans. by G. Thornley and J. M. Edmonds. 1916.

———. *Daphnis and Chloe, The Elizabethan Translation from Amyot's Translation* by Angell Daye, ed. J. Jacobs. 1890.

———. "Daphnis and Chloe by Longus." In *Three Greek Romances*, trans. Moses Hadas. New York, 1953, pp. 17-98.

Lucian. *Complete Works*, Vol. I, ed. A. M. Harmon, Vol. VIII, ed. M. D. Macleod. Cambridge, Mass., 1913-1967, 8 Vols.

———. *True History and Lucius or the Ass,* trans. Paul Turner. 1958.

Lyly, John. *The Complete Works,* ed. R. Warwick Bond.

———. *Campaspe.* In *Five Elizabethan Camedies,* ed. A. K. McIlwraith. 1934; rpt. 1945.

Lyly, John. *Gallathea and Midas,* ed. A. B. Lancashire. 1969.

Malory, Sir Thomas. *The Works,* 3 Vols., ed. Eugène Vinaver. Oxford 1947.

———. *Le Morte D'Arthur,* ed. J. Cowen 1969; rpt. 1976.

———. *The storye of the most noble and worthy Kynge Arthur,* Thomas East edition. 1585.

———. *The Most Ancient and Famous History of the Renowned Prince Arthur,* W. Stansby for J. Bloome, 1634.

Mann, Thomas. *Die Geschichten Jaakobs.* Berlin, 1933.

———. "The Tales of Jacob." In *Joseph and His Brothers,* Vol. I, trans. H. T. Lowe Porter. 1934.

Melville, Herman. *Moby Dick.* New York, 1967.

———. *Mardi.* New Haven. 1973.

———. *The Confidence Man.* New York, 1955.

Menander. *MENANDROY SAMIA. The Samia of Menander,* ed. C. Dedoussi, Athens, 1965.

———. *MENANDROY DYSKOLOS. Menander's Dyskolos* ed. W. E. Blake New York, 1960.

———. *A Commentary,* ed. A. W. Gomme, and F. H. Sandback. Oxford, 1973.

———. *Plays and Fragments,* trans. P. Vellacott. 1967.

Middleton, Thomas. *Works,* ed. A. H. Bullen. 1885-1886.

Montaigne, M. *The essays of . . . Done into English by John Glorio, anno 1615,* ed. J. Saintsbury. 1892-1893.

———. *Works,* trans. J. M. Cohen. 1958. rpt. 1966.

———. *Essais,* ed. Maurice Rat, 2 Vols. Paris, 1962.

Montemayor, Jorge de. *Diana,* trans. B. Yong. 1598. B.M. no. C. 59.i.19.

Monmouth, Geoffrey of. *The History of the Kings of Britain,* ed. L. Thorpe. 1966.

Mucedorus, ed. James Winny in *Three Elizabethan Plays: Edward III, Mucedorus, Midas.* 1959.

———. *The Comedy of,* ed. K. Warnke and Ludwig Proescholdt. Halle, 1878.

Ninus Romance, The. In *The Love Romances of Parthenius and Other Fragments,* trans. and ed. S. Gaselee. Cambridge, Mass., 1935, pp. 382-397.

Ovid. *Metamorphoses, Shakespeare's,* trans. A. Golding, ed. W. H. D. Rouse, 1904; rpt. 1961.

———. trans. R. Humphries. Bloomington, Indiana, 1958.

Peele, George. *The Works of,* under the general editorship of C. T. Prouty, New Haven, 1951 -.

Petronius. *The Satyricon,* trans. W. Arrowsmith. Ann Arbor, Mich., 1959.

———. trans. J. P. Sullivan. 1965; rpt. 1972.

Richardson, Samuel. *Pamela.* "Everyman" ed., n.d. Vol. II.

Shakespeare, W. *The Complete Works,* ed. Peter Alexander. 1951.

———. ed. W. A. Neilsen. Boston, 1906.

———. ed. Sylvan Barnet. New York, 1972.

———. *The First Folio of 1623,* ed. H. Staunton. 1866.

———. *The Comedy of Errors,* ed. R. A. Foakes. New Arden, 1962.

———. *Cymbeline,* ed. Edward Dowden. Arden, 1903.

———. ed. J. M. Nosworthy. New Arden, 1955.

———. ed. R. Hosley. Signet, 1968.

———. *Love's Labour's Lost,* ed. Richard David. New Arden, 1951.

Shakespeare, W. *A Midsummer's Night's Dream,* ed. J. D. Wilson. Camb., 1924.

———. *Pericles,* the 1609 text, ed. A. Morgan. New York, 1891.

———. ed. J. C. Maxwell. Cambridge, 1956.

———. ed. F. D. Hoeniger. New Arden, 1963.

———. ed. E. Schanzer. Signet, 1965.

———. and Fletcher, John. *The Two Noble Kinsmen*, ed. C. Leech. Signet, 1966.

———. *Sonnets*, ed. H. E. Rollins. New Variorum ed., 1944.

———. *The Tempest*, ed. F. Kermode. New Arden, 1954.

———. ed. R. Langbaum. Signet, 1964.

———. ed. Anne Righter. Penguin, 1968.

———. *The Winter's Tale*, ed. J. H. P. Pafford. New Arden, 1964.

———. ed. F. Kermode. Signet, 1963.

———. ed. Ernest Schanzer. Penguin, 1969.

Sidney, Sir Philip. *The Countess of Pembrokes Arcadia.* (The New Arcadia) ed. Albert Feuillerat. Cambridge, 1912; rpt. 1963.

———. *The Countess of Pembrokes Arcadia* (The Old Arcadia), Oxford, 1973.

The Misfortunes of Arthur, ed. H. C. Grumbine. Berlin, 1900.

———. ed. W. Carew Hazlitt. In *Old English Plays*, Vol. IV, 1874.

The Rare Triumphs of Love and Fortune, ed. W. Carew Hazlitt. In *Old English Plays*, Vol. VI, 1874.

———. ed. W. W. Greg. 1931. The Malone Society.

Virgil. *The Aeneid*, trans. C. Day Lewis. 1952.

Wolf, Virginia. *Orlando*. 1942.

Xenophon. *The Cyropaedia of Xenophon*, 2 Vols., trans. and ed. W. Miller, 1916.

GENRE

R. S. White (essay date 1985)

SOURCE: "Shakespeare's Romances: *Pericles*," in *'Let Wonder Seem Familiar': Endings in Shakespeare's Romance Vision*, Humanities Press, 1985, pp. 115-130.

[*In the following excerpt, White defends* Pericles *as the most perfect example of the romance genre among Shakespeare's plays.*]

Pericles

Pericles is the one and only pure romance in the Shakespearean canon, and viewed as such it has a strange and moving beauty of its own. The courtly wit of the early comedies is replaced by a hushed honesty of poetic statement, and a sense of reverent awe, as a man finds himself at the mercy of the elements and the gods. As the play moves through its recurrent rhythms of turbulence and stillness, grief and joy, the central figure can adopt only humble patience as his basic point of view, fully aware that he is involved in living a life which lies at the discretion of destiny:

> We cannot but obey
> The powers above us. Could I rage and roar
> As doth the sea she lies in, yet the end
> Must be as 'tis.
> (III. iii. 9-12)

A sense of miracle and mystery informs the movement of the story, and hangs in the air around the most astonishing mystery of all, the human capacity to remember, so that the past becomes a part of the present.

Shakespeare returns in *Pericles* to the oldest form of narrative romance—not only to its source in Apollonius of Tyre but also to Heliodorus, Achilles Tatius and the *Odyssey*—and he creates out of these romances of the sea perhaps the one wholly successful dramatised version in English of this essentially episodic and narrative form. Like Spenser, Shakespeare realises that the sea itself is the element which can bind such stories to an eternal rhythm, and the journey carries Fortune's message, instead of simply creating a neat situation for further developments on land, as in plays like *The Comedy of Errors*, *Twelfth Night* and *The Tempest*. Man is placed at the centre, but within an immeasurably large universe of time and destiny, surrounded by all the dangers of the mariner in a storm:

> As Pilot well expert in perilous waue,
> That to a stedfast starre his course hath bent,
> When foggy mistes, or cloudy tempests haue
> The faithfull light of that faire lampe yblent,
> And couer'd heauen with hideous dreriment,
> Vpon his card and compas firmes his eye,
> The maisters of his long experiment,
> And to them does the steddy helme apply,
> Bidding his winged vessell fairely forward fly.
> (*Faerie Queene*, II, vii, 1)

so does Pericles, helplessly but studiously, navigate his life.

To see *Pericles* as anything less than a near-perfect dramatic romance is to judge its accomplishment by the wrong standards. It is a straightforward revival of a mode extremely popular in the 1580s, and a revival which succeeds where they failed. Eye-witness accounts of narrative romance placed on the stage during the earlier period are unsympathetic, and the reason seems to be that the plays lacked the true heartbeat of feeling and inwardness with romance as a way of looking at the world, which *Pericles* achieves so triumphantly. Sidney's description of the staged romances which he had seen, asserts that romantic drama is inferior to Italian comedy as a dramatic form, if indeed romance is a form at all. He condemns the plays for not obeying the Aristotelian unities, and for requiring us to make impossible assumptions about the time and places represented on the stage, 'which, how absurd it is in sense, even sense may imagine, and art hath taught, and all ancient examples justified—and at this day, the ordinary players in Italy will not err in'.[1] His dismissive description of a typical play implies that the early plays took over wholesale the plots of romance—travel to far-flung regions, desultory battles, life-stories of knights, their ladies and children—but without a convincing and central point of view. George Whetstone launched a similar attack, condemning the English playwright because he 'groundes his works on impossibilities',[2] flouting credibility and ignoring the dramatic unities. His description suggests, but does not condone, a positive kind of drama, based on love, separation, travel, quests, reversals of fortune, and spectacle, but the plays fail for lack of quality ('indiscrete workinge') and lack of theatrical effectiveness. Stephen Gosson attacks the romantic plays chiefly on the ground that they are not concerned with teaching virtue. 'What learne you by that?'[3] he demands, after describing the kind of rambling narrative mentioned by Sidney and Whetstone. With this inauspicious pedigree, Shakespeare saw fit, at the time of his greatest maturity, to turn back to dramatic romance. Without the elegant self-sufficiency of the love-plot in a romantic comedy, and without the hints of self-parody of *Cymbeline,* and without the complex mixture of modes adopted in *The Winter's Tale* and *The Tempest, Pericles* is pure dramatised romance, and as such should be evaluated and understood in its own terms. However disputed is the question of particular sources,[4] there is no doubt that they lie in the region of narrative romance pure and simple, without irony or allegory, and for this reason also, the play should be judged in terms of the genre itself, and the limits which it sets for itself. The Greek and medieval story of Apollonius of Tyre, and the conventional bed of adventures encountered by Sidney's Pyrocles, come from an ancient and solemn stock going right back to the *Odyssey,* a mode that presents time and eternity, men and gods, birth and death, along a single line of consciousness. Whetstone's rhetorical question, 'What learne you by that?' can be answered after the experience of *Pericles:* we learn the largest lessons, that patience in adversity is a supreme virtue, that despair is a sin, and that, using the human capacities for memory and hope, time and nature will arrange eventually for good to assert itself over the forces of evil and of fortuitous calamity. The moral categories of romance are large, but that is because eternity is large. The triumph of romance morality is the triumph of endless time, over circumstance and over endings.

Commentators agree, with some minor quibbles, that Shakespeare took over another dramatist's play at the beginning of Act III.[5] By common consent, what he immediately begins to add to the play is dramatic poetry of an immeasurably higher quality. He may find different centres of interest—in particular, familial relationships rather than courtly intrigue—but he does not radically alter the direction of generic expectations. The play has already asserted itself as a romance, with its anonymous, virtuous knight confronting forces of evil, its pageantry, its large scale of time and space, its rudimentary moral categories, and its narrative basis, resting on reconciliation and separation. If the play had continued at the same tempo and the same measure of poetic relaxation, it would have been little better, and no worse, than the dramatised romances deplored by earlier critics—plays such as *Clyomon and Clamydes* and *Common Conditions*. Of course, the sudden shift of gear in poetic concentration and intensity is part of the process of lifting the play into a higher realm, but in addition, and perhaps more important, Shakespeare begins to *generalise* the experience. He immediately declares himself to be in control of the medium, rather than at its mercy, consciously working in the furrows of ancient romance but genuinely adapting it to a new mode of drama, rather than simply assuming that the narrative itself will work its effect as it does in the ample, sprawling works of prose romance. He knows he is painting a very large picture on a small canvas, and accordingly he adapts his materials and his instruments. He does this in two ways. First, the scene where he picks up the story is deliberately placed on a scale and a plane that takes the narrative itself into vast reaches of time, space and morality, to declare its largest significance. Secondly, he uses the figure of Gower, who has probably been given to him by the innovatory craftsmanship of his collaborator, to achieve more ambitious ends than simply those of a narrator in a prose work, who can tide us over inessential parts of the plot.

III. i spans the spectrum of artistic representation from an intense realisation of the sounds and sights of the stormy night at sea, through to the rarest of mystical experiences, an apprehension of how inseparably involved are the processes of being born, of living, and of dying. The scene begins with an invocation of gods who determine not only the moral life, but the elements:

Act III, scene i. Pericles, Thaisa, and baby Marina. University of Michigan Library.

> Thou god of this great vast, rebuke these
>   surges,
> Which wash both heaven and hell; and thou
>   that hast
> Upon the winds command, bind them in brass,
> Having call'd them from the deep! O, still
> Thy deaf'ning, dreadful thunders; gently
>   quench
> Thy nimble sulphurous flashes!
>
> (III. i. 1-6)

Images are both specific and numinous, describing noise, and at the same time placing humanity in an insignificant corner of the universe:

> The seaman's whistle
> Is as a whisper in the ears of death,
> Unheard.
>
> (III. i. 8-10)

At this moment, the child is placed in the hands of Pericles, a 'piece' of his dead queen, and born at the moment of her death, out of the very shudder and pangs of the heaving storm:

> Now, mild may be thy life!
> For a more blusterous birth had never babe;
> Quiet and gentle thy conditions! for
> Thou art the rudeliest welcome to this world
> That ever was prince's child. Happy what
>   follows!
> Thou hast as chiding a nativity
> As fire, air, water, earth, and heaven, can
>   make,
> To herald thee from the womb.
>
> (III. i. 26-34)

Superstition may express a symbolic truth, and the sailors insist that in order to still the storm, the body of the wife must be given to the sea, for nature cannot tolerate the non-living. She will go, however, to the stillness at the centre of existence which dimly we intuit to be the genesis as well as the exodus of creation:

> A terrible childbed hast thou had, my dear;
> No light, no fire. Th'unfriendly elements
> Forgot thee utterly; nor have I time
> To give thee hallow'd to thy grave, but
>   straight
> Must cast thee, scarcely coffin'd, in the ooze;
> Where, for a monument upon thy bones,
> And aye-remaining lamps, the belching whale
> And humming water must o'erwhelm thy
>   corpse,
> Lying with simple shells.
>
> (III. i. 56-64)

In this one scene, Shakespeare has spanned extremes of time and imagination that are essential to the romance experience, especially at the time of the endless ending at its most permanent level, where death rolls into birth, grief into action, storm into serenity, for time without ending. When placed within the large scope of the gods and the elements, human life is as insignificant and unheard as a whisper, as precarious as a duck in a storm (III. Chorus, 1. 49). But when apprehended from within, as the fact of creation itself, the same human life has a warm miraculousness and sanctity that shadows and overshadows all the rest of the tangible world and the remote gods. The immensity of the sea, identified with destiny and history, is juxtaposed with the warm, tiny baby. Up to this scene, the story has been little better than a good yarn, full of incident and suspense. Now it is suddenly something much larger. The scene is elemental, a storm at sea. The situation is human: a man is confronted with the simplest and most mysterious occurrences of death and birth simultaneously. In this scene, after his many experiments with the human dimensions of romance, Shakespeare has reached its *raison d'etre*, and has opened up the philosophy that experience may be apprehended through both ends of a telescope at the same time.

The device of Gower as presenter of the action may be Shakespeare's idea, but it is simpler to assume that it was introduced by the collaborator. It is, in fact, a cleverly functional way of getting around the more obvious problems in adapting a story well-known in prose romance to the foreshortening medium of the drama. Gower replaces the narrator in the prose work, the person who can explain the action, fill in long gaps in time, provide an occasional moral comment on the goodness or wickedness of the characters, establish a friendly, trusting relationship with the audience, and ultimately, by judicious framing of events, allow the episodes of action to speak for themselves. Time and again he insists, like the Chorus in *Henry V*, that the audience must exercise its imagination, in order to accept the changes of time and scene:

> Be attent,
> And time that is so briefly spent
> With your fine fancies quaintly eche:
> (III. Chorus. 11-3)

> In your imagination hold
> This stage the ship, upon whose deck
> The sea-toss'd Pericles appears to speak.
> (III. Chorus. 58-60)

> Imagine Pericles arriv'd at Tyre,
> Welcom'd and settled to his own desire.
> (IV. Chorus. 1-2)

> The unborn event
> I do commend to your content;
> Only I carried winged time
> Post on the lame feet of my rhyme;
> Which never could I so convey,
> Unless your thoughts went on my way.
> (IV. Chorus. 45-50)

His intimate tone with the audience creates a moment of friendly sociability at the end, when he thanks the audience for their attentiveness, patience, and co-operativeness. Gower is created as the storyteller in Sidney's mode, keeping children from play and old men from the chimney corner with the simplicity and enchantment of his telling. Technically speaking, he turns what could have been a rambling, barely connected sequence of events into a series of tightly constructed and dramatically intense episodes. In his attitude to the story itself, Gower is the narrator well-known in romance, continually referring back to his book, his historical record which he is simply re-telling, and he establishes the agelessness of the tale:

> To sing a song that old was sung,
> From ashes ancient Gower is come,
> Assuming man's infirmities,
> To glad your ear, and please your eyes.
> It hath been sung at festivals,
> On ember eves and holy-ales;
> And lords and ladies in their lives
> Have read it for restoratives.
> (I. Chorus. 1-8)

By being 'ancient' Gower, and self-confessedly 'an old man', he places himself in our own world of mortality and ageing—the world in which we see Pericles grow old— whilst pushing the story itself back into an age before time itself, a world transcending time. In his scene-setting, he is on the one hand bald and rudimentary in speaking of the story, but precise and evocative in suggesting that we are simultaneously witnessing a scene, and also ourselves *part* of a different scene, hearing his tale, and at times the two dimensions meet:

> The cat, with eyne of burning coal,
> Now couches 'fore the mouse's hole;
> And crickets sing at the oven's mouth
> Aye the blither for their drouth.
> (III. Chorus. 5-8)

That word 'now' has a reference backwards into an historical present, and a more immediate sense for us, as we sit at the feet of the storyteller. Finally, by mentioning twice the skill of Marina in creating some work of art, such as music or needlework, Gower uses Sidney's device from the *Arcadia*, in reference to Pamela,[6] in order to sharpen the distinctions still further between artifice and reality, time and timelessness, in such a way that each of the dimensions is eternally present in the experience of a living audience witnessing an event which, however fictional and ancient, is living before our eyes. With a disarming simplicity, the presence of Gower as a narrator takes the dramatist much of the way toward convincing us that the dénouement contains the true romance sensation of a timeless event which is being enacted in time. The combination of stilted artifice in the lines of Gower, and the tonal familiarity in his relationship with the audience, causes the story itself, the action, to spill out of its boundaries of convention and improbability, into a set of animated and lifelike events, more or less as the time-bound contours of the play eventually swell into an experience of timeless significance.

At the beginning of the final Act, Pericles and Marina, father and daughter, are both revealed static as art. Pericles has immobilised himself, having not spoken for three months, and he is 'discovered', presumably behind a curtain, like a statue. Marina, with her 'sweet harmony', likened often to a goddess, exists at this moment also as a cameo, framed in a leafy shelter on the edge of the island. Her physic is music, an art that moves through time and yet plays on stillness, and she has the equal permanence and impermeability of an allegory of a living statue:

> for thou lookest
> Modest as Justice, and thou seem'st a palace
> For the crown'd Truth to dwell in.
>
> . . . . .
>
> Yet thou dost look
> Like Patience gazing on kings' graves, and
>   smiling
> Extremity out of act.
>
> (V. i. 119-39 *passim*)

It is extraordinarily apt and moving that in this image Shakespeare is harking back some eight years in his own creative life to Viola, who sat like patience on a monument, for the immobilising element at work in these two characters is the sad loss of a past which must now lovingly be retrieved and re-connected.[7] Pericles' story is 'too tedious to repeat', and it springs from the loss of a beloved daughter and a wife, an estrangement from the only tangible relics that could prove the existence of his own long and stressful existence on earth. Equally, Marina was once high-born, but nothing remains of her past:

> My derivation was from ancestors
> Who stood equivalent with mighty kings;
> But time hath rooted out my parentage,
> And to the world and awkward casualties
> Bound me in servitude.
>
> (V. i. 89-93)

She confesses her own discarded past, a present truth which can always be told of things that are no more:

> If I should tell my history, it would seem
> Like lies, disdain'd in the reporting.
>
> (V. i. 117-8)

The managerial fussiness, the executive prying, of the petty people around, who have no past themselves of consequence to this event, enhances, and does not distract from the stillness between two people who slowly, like sleepwalkers, realise that filaments to the truth of a personal past are beginning to glow. For Lysimachus, there is 'sacred physic' (V. i. 73) in the reconciliation, and for Pericles, as he lovingly runs the fingers of his mind around the beauty of Marina, and around the loosely bound, re-found relationship with his daughter, the event is the sign that sleeping existence has joined the waking so fluently that his own past is his present, and there is no rift of separateness:

> O, stop there a little!
> This is the rarest dream that e'er dull sleep
> Did mock sad fools withal. This cannot be:
> My daughter's buried. Well, where were you
>   bred?
> I'll hear you more, to th' bottom of your
>   story,
> And never interrupt you.
>
> (V. i. 159-64)

Surely the greatest mystery is how the things that are no more, that we call simply 'memory' or stories, are still now, and still with us as a part of what the present is. Now the hero of the play may declare his identity, and be liberated into present existence, his history validated and re-integrated:

> I am Pericles of Tyre; but tell me now
> My drown'd queen's name, as in the rest you
>   said
> Thou hast been godlike perfect,
> The heir of kingdoms and another life
> To Pericles thy father.
>
> (V. i. 203-7)

And Marina can slip in the final detail to prove that she is no goddess but a human being with her own past that connects with the existence of others:

> Is it no more to be your daughter than
> To say my mother's name was Thaisa?
> Thaisa was my mother, who did end
> The minute I began.
>
> (V. i. 208-10)

The genius of Shakespeare lies in his capacity to give the simplest words to the strangest capillaries of the flowing blood of living people in the extremity of feeling. With the music of the spheres, he goes on to remind us that the moment is a sacred awakening, whose occurrence coaxes us to believe in miracles, and in the existence of gods. And at this moment there is indeed a goddess on hand to remind Pericles that he must draw the sleeping and the waking parts of his mind into a clear conjunction, or else he will be condemned to a split between his own past and his future. Diana appears, and speaks:

> Reveal how thou at sea didst lose thy wife.
> To mourn thy crosses, with thy daughter's,
>   call,
> And give them repetition to the life.
> Or perform my bidding or thou liv'st in woe;
> Do it, and happy - by my silver bow!
> Awake, and tell thy dream.
>
> (V. i. 242-7)

The play has awakened a deity at this moment specifically in order to prove that gods and goddesses do not exist, except for human uses. The supernatural is an explanation, a justification, a reminder, of the most moving and significant human recognitions, people reunited with their individual pasts and with the collective, fragmented pasts of others.

All within this scene has been within human comprehension, a wonderful but not impossible accident of meeting, whose significance is to re-join not only a father and a daughter but two personal versions of the past to a verifiable present. What remains, in the short, final scene, is to complete the story in a fictively satisfying manner, to reconcile Pericles and his daughter with the most notionally important person of all, a wife and a mother. Perhaps it is fictional only, and improbable when judged by the narrowest standards of probability, that Thaisa lives as Diana's nun, and can be reconciled with her husband and daughter. But since we have witnessed, within the sphere of the possible, events that may easily be ascribed to the supernatural, Shakespeare is prepared here to take the gamble, and trust that our faith here has been so awakened to the *potential* beauty of the rhythms that life has given us - separation and reunion - that we may be convinced of this, final device of his plot. Once we accept the miracles of history, and of the way the timeless memory may occasionally determine events within time, then little lies in our way to project our imaginations into the hypothetical wonder of living a life and yet knowing that every moment is a moment of full existence, in which everything from the past may unexpectedly be called into being as a part of the living present.

It is necessary to make a narrow but significant distinction concerning the kind of reconciliation effected at the end of *Pericles*. It is not so important, as it is at the end of *The Winter's Tale*, that a *family* has been brought together again. It is more accurate to say that each individual has been brought into living relationship again with his or her own past, and that in a strangely haunting way, this leaves each still in some sense alone, and separate. Each individual has had to live in full, again, the traces of his or her past: such a redefinition of personal identity, such a refocussing of 'now', brings on absorbed reflections in self. A space for solitude still surrounds each character, even in community. After all, Pericles, Marina and Thaisa have never really had time to know each other, even in pairs. The feeling that permeates the ending is significantly different in *The Winter's Tale*, where the dramatic attention is placed upon the reconciliation between a husband and wife who had, before the rupture, lived closely with each other for several years. Perdita is somewhat an outsider to this warm and joyous event, and her presence at court has more of a symbolic value in providing the occasion for a true family reconciliation. *Pericles* dwells more on the notion of continuity re-established in the personal history of separate individuals. For Pericles, Marina *is* Thaisa as she was when his young wife, whilst for Leontes, Hermione is herself, and has lived for as long as he has. Leontes picks up the threads in the present, within time: Pericles is allowed to go back in time and pick up the threads from the occasion of the storm. At the endings of both plays, there is a sense of regret at *temps perdu*, but the feeling operates in different ways.[8]

It is worth adding that, although Shakespeare may have taken over the writing of *Pericles* from an inferior dramatist, he manages to make the play into a unity by concentrating upon the substance of the fragment he uses. The idea that the play represents a man retrieving his personal past is built into even the first two Acts. Pericles is specific on the point that he is losing touch with his own past, as he goes from country to country, shedding relationships, status and even identity, until he becomes simply an anonymous knight from the romance world. When he is washed up on the shore of Pentapolis, he says to the courteous and generous Fishermen:

> What I have been I have forgot to know;
> But what I am want teaches me to think on:
> A man thronged up with cold.
>
> (II. i. 71-3)

Then, when he meets the kind old king Simonides, the father of his future wife, he is stirred to recall something of the past he has lost, and to reflect upon the occurrence:

> You king's to me like to my father's picture,
> Which tells me in that glory once he was;
> Had princes sit like stars, about his throne,
> And he the sun, for them to reverence;
>
> . . . . .
>
> Where now his son's like a glowworm in the night,
> The which hath fire in darkness, none in light.
> Whereby I see that Time's the king of men;
> He's both their parent, and he is their grave,
> And gives them what he will, not what they crave.
>
> (II. iii. 36-48)

Shakespeare raises such casual asides to the status of large statements on human existence, by building into his fable the notion of a person, through familial reconciliation, discovering something of his own lost past. Even the most sensational incident, the initial incest between the King of Antioch and his daughter, is curiously reversed and seen through a glass darkly by Shakespeare, when he draws the greatest warmth out of the reconciliation of Pericles and his own daughter:

> I am great with woe, and shall deliver weeping.
> My dearest wife was like this maid, and such a one

My daughter might have been.
(V. i. 105-7)

With a trembling tenderness that could never be demeaned by the use of the word 'incest', Pericles shows how human and reasonable it may be for an elderly man to see in his daughter the image of a wife whom he loved as a young woman, and whom he lost whilst she was still young:

> My queen's square brows;
> Her stature to an inch; as wand-like straight;
> As silver-voic'd; her eyes as jewel-like,
> And cas'd as richly; in pace another Juno;
> Who starves the ears she feeds, and makes
>   them hungry
> The more she gives them speech.
> (V. i. 107-12)

His daughter at this moment is cased as richly as a work of art, yet she is warmly human, 'mortally brought forth', and her presence is like a memory which is re-created in the present. Of course, Shakespeare is doing nothing so crudely schematic as to suggest a repetition of the feelings of the King of Antioch: but in the early *datum* of the play he has found a significance that can be brought back unobtrusively, so that the play's own past may be mirrored, with profound differences, and the present may be seen as repetition, but dressed with the glow of an eternal present. Living memory is the fulcrum around which the play turns, and the deepest remembrance of all is that of the storm at the centre, which even the grown-up Marina, in some curious way (IV. i. 54ff.), can remember in detail, having been told so often by her nurse. The sea which takes away and destroys, also acts as a magical preservative, and can bring back in its tides, until it seems like the capacity for human memory itself.

In an unobtrusive moment, Marina, too, is reconciled with her own past, for she is given in marriage to Lysimachus, the main customer at the brothel in which she had stayed, and a man whom she had converted to a purer way of life. In this liaison, we might be tempted to see Shakespeare's characteristically sardonic or perfunctory teaming-up of available partners, in order to manipulate a wholly neat ending. However, here there seems to be a more intrinsic aptness. Whereas Pericles had initially run away from the apprehension of evil in the court of Antioch, feeling slightly tainted himself by its presence, Marina in the brothel was as militantly virtuous and evangelical as Britomart, Spenser's figure of chastity. Refusing to run away or to compromise, Marina has stoically refused to recognise any personal implication in the evil around her, but instead has sought to convert it into virtue. She cannot hope to succeed with the professionals in the brothel since, as the Bawd pertinently and rather touchingly points out, society will not allow them the luxury of being respectable - they must shift for themselves as best they may, or else undertake even more degrading and potentially damaging occupations, such as going into the army, in order to lose a leg (like Ralph in *The Shoemaker's Holiday*). With Lysimachus, it is otherwise. Nobly-born, he has a full choice over whether to conduct a life of good or evil, and under Marina's influence he chooses good. It would not be appropriate for Pericles to be reminded of the court of Antioch, since he himself had willingly chosen to forsake this part of his own personal history (and we discover, accordingly, that the King of Antioch is dead). But for Marina, if she is to be re-united with her own past, it is essential that the brothel interlude be recalled and absorbed into her life in the present, since she had not flinched from it, and at the time she had accepted responsibility for changing it. We should not make too much of her betrothal at the end, since primarily it is a convenience to round off the story, but there is certainly a deeper appropriateness in it than immediately strikes the eye, and the episode fits into the vision of the play as a whole.

Pericles is a play that majestically invites complete dismissal by the mind which strives to work in a purely rational way, by its own utter submission to a naked sense of the wonder of life lived through time. Because it is so loftily uncompromising to scepticism and niggling doubts, it is not only a true romance, but it is also not particularly popular,[9] since we always presume that Shakespeare is, if nothing else, rational. I hope to have shown that the fault lies in us, not in the play. There are enough hints in the worldly-wise words of Gower to reassure us that Shakespeare is still himself, cautiously guarding himself against the most ungenerous and mean-minded of 'rationalists' by conceding that his story is merely a story, and nothing else. He had done the same many years earlier in the words of a self-proclaimed fairy, Puck, at the end of *The Midsummer Night's Dream,* and there still seems enough in that play to enchant and disturb audiences. 'The truest poetry is the most feigning' said one of his most corrosively cynical creations, Touchstone, and although Shakespeare is the most elusive of writers, hedging himself with the intelligent camouflage of rationalism, it may be true that occasionally we can take his words straight, as an expression of a born storyteller, who is also trying to tell the truth. . . .

Notes

[1] *A Defence of Poetry, Miscellaneous Prose of Sir Philip Sidney,* ed. Katherine Duncan-Jones and Jan van Dorsten (Oxford, 1973), p.113.

[2] Whetstone, Dedication to *Promos and Cassandra* (1578).

[3] Gosson, *Plays Confuted* (above), sig. C6 r.

[4] As for all the plays, the most thorough presentation of sources and analogues for *Pericles* comes in Geoffrey Bullough's monumental *Narrative and Dramatic Sources of Shakespeare,* vi (1966). See also the scholarly introductions to the Arden and New Cambridge editions, edited by F. D. Hoeniger and J. C. Maxwell respectively. Also generally relevant to the material in this chapter are the treatments by Hallett Smith in *Shakespeare and the Greek Romances: A study of origins* (Kentucky, 1970), and Felperin. Because my concentration is upon romance itself, it is not necessary here to attend to Felperin's interesting argument about medieval, morality traditions behind *Pericles* in "Shakespeare's Miracle Play", *Shakespeare Quarterly* 18 (1967), pp. 363-74.

[5] See the discussions in Bullough, Hoeniger and Maxwell.

[6] Sidney, *New Arcadia,* p.483.

[7] Wilson Knight points out the echo of *Twelfth Night,* in *The Crown of Life,* p.65. It is interesting to note in this context the similarities between *Pericles* and Chaucer's 'Man of Law's Tale', a connection mentioned, but not developed, by Ann Thompson in *Shakespeare's Chaucer* (Liverpool, 1978), pp. 83-4. They cannot be explained merely as the result of a shared source.

[8] General reference could be made here to D. W. Harding, 'Shakespeare's Final View of Women', *Times Literary Supplement* (1979), pp. 59-61; and C. L. Barber, "'Thou that beget'st him that did thee beget': Transformation in *Pericles* and *The Winter's Tale*", *Shakespeare Survey,* 22 (1969), pp. 59-67.

[9] But it was highly popular in its own day. The vogue of such a "mouldy tale" is what seems to have irked Ben Jonson. Judging from recent performances in England by the Prospect Theatre Company and the Royal Shakespeare Company, there is no reason why *Pericles* cannot be popular again with some audiences. Perhaps it is really the critics who are unsympathetic, with some exceptions such as John Arthos, "*Pericles, Prince of Tyre:* A Study in the Dramatice Use of Romantic Narrative", *Shakespeare Quarterly,* iv (1953), and of course Wilson Knight, whose essays in *The Crown of Life* on all these plays have a vibrant respect.

LANGUAGE AND STRUCTURE

Maurice Hunt (essay date 1990)

SOURCE: "*Pericles, Prince of Tyre,*" in *Shakespeare's Romance of the Word,* Bucknell University Presses, 1990, pp. 18-40.

[*In the excerpt below, Hunt examines the language, dialogue, and speech patterns in* Pericles.]

I shall approach my thesis about the importance of the word in *Pericles* by way of the play's most farcical dialogue. In *Shakespeare and the Confines of Art,* Philip Edwards remarks that "the uncouth fishermen who succour the shipwrecked Pericles are in the play only to show the warmth of kindness as a contrast to the previous coldness of both humanity and the elements."[1] While the low characters undoubtedly produce this dramatic impression, they play a more complex role in the play's design than the part suggested by Edwards. It has been widely noted that Shakespeare often comically distorts serious dramatic themes or values in order to call attention to them.[2] For example, after hearing the Porter at the gate, who can be unaware of Macbeth's tendency to equivocate damnably? The dramatist—Shakespeare presumably—employs this familiar technique early in *Pericles*.[3] One of the most amusing scenes of the play, the Prince's encounter with three rustic fishermen, burlesques and hence accentuates a motif central to several episodes and speeches that critics, for the most part, have ignored. In fact, Pericles' notorious passivity cannot be truly understood without reference to the motif, which concerns a bold verbal protest against evil.[4] The first tempest that Pericles endures washes him ashore in Simonides' Greece, where he overhears Pilch, Patchbreech, and their master describing the evils of their world.

> *3. Fish.* Faith, master, I am thinking of the pour men that were cast away before us even now.
> *1. Fish.* Alas, poor souls, it griev'd my heart to hear what pitiful cries they made to us to help them, when, well-a-day, we could scarce help ourselves.
> *3. Fish.* Nay, master, said not I as much when I saw the porpoise, how he bounc'd and tumbled? they say they're half fish, half flesh; a plague on them, they ne'er come but I look to be wash'd! Master, I marvel how the fishes live in the sea.
> *1. Fish.* Why, as men do a-land: the great ones eat up the little ones. I can compare our rich misers to nothing so fitly as to a whale: a' plays and tumbles, driving the poor fry before him, and at last devours them all at a mouthful. Such whales have I heard on a' th' land, who never leave gaping till they swallow'd the whole parish, church, steeple, bells, and all.

(2.1.18-34)

Such homespun philosophizing possesses a certain appeal. The fishermen's fanciful speeches attract the audience that has just heard Pericles' unspectacular poetry and the mainly limpid expression of act 1.[5] Pericles might realize that the fisherman's little allegory could apply to his own affairs. He has experienced great Antiochus's treachery and the feelings of helplessness attending it. Like great fish, tyrannical men ruled by appetite can and do eat up less powerful mortals, even when the latter are princes. That fact, after all, moved Pericles, once he was safe in Tyre, to tell Helicanus about Antiochus's vice and the sinful king's possible attack upon their city. Nonetheless, Patch-breech, not Pericles, completes the allegory and draws a moral:

> 3. Fish. But, master, if I had been the sexton, I would have been that day in the belfry.
> 2. Fish. Why, man?
> 3. Fish. Because he should have swallow'd me too; and when I had been in his belly, I would have kept such a jangling of the bells, that he should never have left till he cast bell, steeple, church, and parish up again.
>
> (2.1.36-43)

The fishermen's talk of whales, sin, and the swallowing and disgorging of a man, interwoven with mention of religious restoration, echoes the biblical story of Jonah. For Jacobeans, Jonah was the most memorable figure swallowed by a whale. According to Norman Nathan, features of the Jonah story apparently impressed Shakespeare during the writing of *Pericles*.[6] Since the moral of the story illuminates the play, a brief summary will be helpful. Jonah found himself in the whale's belly because terrified sailors threw him overboard in order to appease divine wrath, which had taken the form of a tempest battering their ship.[7] Jonah freely became the sacrificial victim when he confessed that he was attempting to flee God's presence. His guilty flight derived from his refusal to obey God's commandment that he publicly proclaim ("cry against") the evil of Nineveh's citizens. Jonah's error involved his failure to believe in Providence; he lacked faith that God would somehow use a public protest, which from a mortal viewpoint appeared dangerous, to bring forth good not only for the sinners but for the proclaimer himself. Resurrected from the beast, Jonah bravely enters the wicked city and, in an act of personal salvation, cries, "Yet forty days, and Nineveh shall be overthrown!" (Jonah 3:1-10). Immediately the Ninevites reform, proclaiming a fast, donning sackcloth and averting ruin. Jonah's words, faithfully uttered, possess redemptive power.

In *Pericles,* Patch-breech's method for obtaining salvation whimsically recalls the moral of the Jonah story. By jangling the church bells, Patch-breech, if swallowed by leviathan, would work a personal and social resurrection. Despite the comic warping, the thematic connotations of his remark are clear. A vigorous jangling of church bells, a spiritual stirring, defeats a great villain and the evil associated with him. The nonverbal nature of the fisherman's protest does not detract from its verbal implications. Like Jonah, Patch-breech gains his salvation from the symbolic whale, from hellmouth, because he makes a bold spiritual protest against evil.[8] Within the generally serious context of romance, Shakespeare's viewer momentarily enjoys a comic rendering of a familiar truth.[9]

What importance can this truth have for Pericles? Hamlet before the Gravedigger demonstrates that Shakespeare on occasion conveys significant truths to the audience through homely speech to which a somewhat patronizing protagonist is ironically deaf.[10] Taken by the fishermen's colorful method, Pericles simply exclaims:

> How from the finny subject of the sea
> These fishers tell the infirmities of men;
> And from their wat'ry empire recollect
> All that may men approve or men detect!—
>
> (2.1.48-51)

At this dramatic moment, Pericles plays the role of the submissive hero.[11] Studied pathos informs his self-portrayal. In his own words, he is

> A man whom both the waters and the wind,
> In that vast tennis-court, hath made the ball
> For them to play upon, entreats you pity him;
> He asks of you, that never us'd to beg.
>
> (2.1.59-62)

It is not surprising that Pericles, given his view of himself as acted upon rather than acting, overlooks Patch-breech's message about the redemptive effect of personal stirring. Stirring is generally preferable to passivity, and the Prince at this instant represents the less attractive quality. Regarding an energetic assertion of self, the fishermen have a comic advantage over Pericles in this scene. Instead of being foils who heighten the Prince's nobility, they are mainly spokesmen for pragmatic viewpoints that the hero cannot fully appreciate (2.1.63-65, 85-88). In its various forms, stir is an important value in *Pericles*.[12] By making Pericles passive, and by making him the butt of the fishermen's jokes, Shakespeare causes the viewer to value the energetic rustics' insights.[13] Pericles in Antiochus's court argued at length against the efficacy of a verbal protest against evil. In rejecting the linguistic form of virtuous stirring, he denies the value of the motif recommended by one of the play's major comic scenes.

Pericles' negative argument in Antioch results from the failure of certain extraordinary words to warn him of a lethal threat. At the play's outset, the Prince perceives the face of Antiochus's daughter as "the book of praises,"

> where is read
> Nothing but curious pleasures, as from thence

> Sorrow were ever raz'd, and testy wrath
> Could never be her mild companion.
>
> (1.1.16-19)

In a Renaissance conceit described as conventional by Ernst Curtius, Pericles reads words in the text of his beloved's face.[14] Such words however are false; the beautiful, apparently innocent Daughter has been committing incest with her father for some time. Antiochus tries to drive Pericles away by pointing out the skulls of unsuccessful suitors and invoking another kind of visible language:

> Yon sometimes famous princes, like thyself,
> Drawn by report, advent'rous by desire,
> Tell thee, with speechless tongues and
>   semblance pale,
> That without covering save yon field of stars,
> Here they stand martyrs slain in Cupid's
>   wars;
> And with dead cheeks advise thee to desist
> For going on death's net, whom none resist.
>
> (1.1.35-41)

While the treacherous words of a facial book entice Pericles, the significantly speechless language of Antiochus's macabre text fails to inform him of the danger in which he stands. Thus the Prince recklessly offers to read the riddle whose solution confers the Daughter as a bride upon the solver. From the riddle, Pericles learns that the Daughter whom he has been courting feeds incestuously upon her father's flesh. In the words of Northrop Frye, "if Pericles fails to slove the riddle, he must die; if he succeeds in solving it, he must die. The logic is that of the Arabian Nights."[15] The first consequence constitutes the gruesome penalty for failing to interpret Antiochus's enigma; the second reflects Antiochus's vicious resolve to keep his discovered vice secret. In either case, the word in the form of a riddle proves savagely destructive. Aware of the riddle's message, Pericles struggles to avoid both consequences. When pressed by suspicious Antiochus to expound the conundrum, the Prince, despite his horror, answers politicly:

> Great king,
> Few love to hear the sins they love to act;
> 'Twould braid yourself too near for me to tell
>   it.
> Who has a book of all that monarchs do,
> He's more secure to keep it shut than shown;
> For vice repeated is like the wand'ring wind,
> Blows dust in others' eyes, to spread itself;
> And yet the end of all is bought thus dear,
> The breath is gone, and the sore eyes see clear
> To stop the air would hurt them. The blind
>   mole casts
> Copp'd hills towards heaven, to tell the earth
>   is throng'd
> By man's oppression; and the poor worm
>   doth die for't.
> Kings are earth's gods; in vice their law's
>   their will;
> And if Jove stray, who dares say Jove doth
>   ill?
> It is enough you know; and it is fit,
> What being more known grows worse, to
>   smother it.
> All love the womb that their first being bred,
> Then give my tongue like leave to love my
>   head.
>
> (1.1.92-109)

Pericles risks death either by misinterpreting the riddle or by directly telling the King that he knows of the incest. This entrapping dilemma causes him to answer in obscure words. "To spread itself" (be widely broadcast), "vice repeated," in Pericles' opinion, must be like a "wand'ring wind" that blows dust in sinners' eyes. For his story's success and his own safety, the teller of a vicious tale must blind powerful sinners, his subjects, to the true application and meaning of his narrative.[16] But the sinners' delusion, their blinding, is only momentary. Pericles believes that the "breath" will be "gone": the special narration will eventually fail. The Prince implies that were he to broadcast Antiochus's incest, the tyrant's "sore" eyes would "see through" his veiled story, discovering a way to silence permanently the narrator. Thus Pericles vows that he will not be like the blind (unperceptive) mole whose protests against evil—its "Copp'd hills"—identify it and bring about its untimely death. He believes that evil "grows worse" when made more known; when sin is declared, not only the teller but innocent people associated with him are also sometimes vengefully struck down. Difficult poetry does not conceal Pericles' assurance that he will remain silent concerning incest. In terms of Pericles' complex metaphor, the vicious word blinds the faculty of sight; in due time, however, the pained eyes see their way to extinguish the word. Evil, whose knowledge is gained through the riddle, sets speaking, seeing, and hearing at odds with one another and restricts the faculties. Such a war among the faculties occurred when sin at the Fall originally impaired the act of knowing.[17] Shakespeare projects the Prince's present desire to be mute and deaf into the last act. Sitting in darkness, refusing to speak, and not crediting what he hears, the protagonist aboard his ship presents a powerful image of despair, acting out his earlier antiverbal attitude in a painful way that he could never have imagined.

Pericles remains true to the logic of his tortuous reply; he conceals Antiochus's incest once he has fled to Tyre. Melancholy, however, results from his harboring of the secret. Evil known but closely kept can fester, incapacitating the knower as much as evil contemplated does. In the negative silence wrought by

Antiochus's riddle, Shakespeare builds into the design of *Pericles* a linguistic obstacle to the word's triumph. Elizabethans lacked a conceptual basis for the destructive verbal complement of the creative Johannine and Augustinian Word. The nearest they came were characterizations of the Devil as the grand equivocator, the father of lies, and of mankind's language as the confused product of Babel. Yet neither of these ideas amounts to the anticreative word, the terrible obverse of both John's Word (John 1:1-4) from which the world was made and Augustine's notion of human speech, fully expressive of thought because based on the analogy of the Word (Christ) that delivers God without diminishment.[18] For illustrations of the linguistic obverse, we must turn to Renaissance literature. Lear's "Never, never, never, never, never," undoubtedly the most nihilistic verse of trochaic poetry in world literature, approximates this prototypic anticreative (or decreative) word for which the Elizabethans had no metaphysical explanation.

The decreative force of Antiochus's riddle is clarified by speech-act theory developed during the past few decades.[19] J. L. Austin defines speech acts as either explicit or implicit illocutions of varying perlocutionary force. According to this linguistic philosopher, an illocution is "the performance of an act in saying something."[20] Thus when a minister declares, "I baptize this child in the name of . . . ," the utterance is properly an act done in speech (that of baptizing). According to speech act theorists, "the speaking of language is not merely the conveying of some conceptual content . . . but is primarily a mode of doing in its own right, namely the performing of acts 'such as making statements, giving commands, asking questions, making promises, and so on.'"[21] Austin characterizes the perlocutionary force of an utterance as "what we bring about or achieve *by* saying something, such as convincing, persuading, deterring, and even, say, surprising or misleading."[22] Unlike the categories of traditional grammar, Austin's concepts help us understand more clearly that Antiochus's riddle represents the antithesis of the creative word.

Classified grammatically, the riddle makes up a declarative statement metaphorically communicating not only Antiochus and the Daughter's incest but the unnatural intensity of their familial intimacy as well:

> I am no viper, yet I feed
> On mother's flesh which did me breed.
> I sought a husband, in which labour
> I found that kindness in a father.
> He's father, son, and husband mild;
> I mother, wife, and yet his child:
> How they may be, and yet in two,
> As you will live, resolve it you.
>
> (1.1.65-72)

Regarded as a declarative statement ending in a command, the riddle is the Daughter's utterance—the "I's" of the enigma all refer to her. And yet Pericles reads rather than hears the riddle, an act reminding the informed auditor that the riddle is in fact Antiochus's. Regarded as Antiochus's speech act, the riddle constitutes neither a declarative statement nor a command. Considered as the performance of an act in speech (an illocution), it commits Antiochus to killing listening venturers (since solving the riddle will result in death as surely as misinterpreting it will). As a decreative word, the riddle undoes life as effectively as the Christian Word infuses it. Its perlocutionary force (what it brings about or achieves) devitalizes Pericles, muting him, forcing him to deny the moral promptings of his conscience, eventually draining the life from his cheeks and very being as melancholic stupor predominates. Vestiges of the belief that the royal word could create reality *ex nihilo* still surfaced during Jacobean times; as God's deputy, the ruler participated in the Johannine creativity of the divine word. In Antiochus's riddle and its destructive effect upon the Prince of Tyre, Shakespeare at the beginning of *Pericles* dramatizes a horrific parody of the nurturing word, a parody that initiates a tyrannical silence and broken life for Pericles. What creative word, we wonder, can match this decreative riddle, rectifying the chaos brought into being by it.

Still, it would be a mistake to imply that Pericles becomes victimized by decreative words. He *chooses* to pledge silence. By his commitment to silence, he virtuously desires to protect his subjects from Antiochus's retaliation. Pericles stated that "Kings are earth's gods; in vice their law's their will; / And if Jove stray, who dares say Jove doth ill?" As a rule, this saying might indict the speaker of a certain lack of courage, of a moral weakness blamable, for example, in the wavering Cleon who accedes to Dionyza's depraved plot against Marina. Applied to Pericles' predicament in Antioch, it can be appreciated, however, as ethical flattery by which a good ruler protects his people and himself from death. Regarded from one viewpoint, Pericles' attempt to convince Antiochus that he will not publish the crime deserves credit. Moreover, only a fool would berate a tyrant in his own court. In act 1, Pericles' situation contrasts with that of Jonah in one important respect: a deity does not order Shakespeare's character to "cry against" vice. Nevertheless, Shakespeare does evoke the tale of Jonah in the subsequent fisherman episode and does suggest that a declaration can defeat evil and restore good. While Antiochus has forced Pericles to deny this truth, Shakespeare thrusts it upon the viewer in scene after scene of the play. The theater audience thus wonders when Pericles can embrace and act out a truth whose worth, by act 5, has been repeatedly staged. Will Pericles be able to speak stirring words that characterize him as a redemptive hero instead of a helpless victim of the gods?[23]

In the play's early scenes, Shakespeare recasts his primary sources, focusing upon the good resulting from a verbal declaration of a special kind—that involving fault or evil. Ironically Pericles had to use words to tell Antiochus that he would not verbalize the tyrant's secret. Despite their oblique, clouded nature, these words betray Pericles by convincing Antiochus that the Prince is aware of his sin. Resolved to exterminate Pericles even in his own country, Antiochus conscripts an assassin, Thaliard. Thaliard at first unconsciously echoes the Prince's belief that the relating of a monarch's faults can only be harmful. Antiochus's confiding in a servant has created a reluctant henchman. Thaliard judges that

> he was a wise fellow and had good discretion that, being bid to ask what he would of the king, desir'd he might know none of his secrets: now do I see he had some reason for't, for if a king bid a man be a villain, he's bound by the indenture of his oath to be one.
>
> (1.3.3-8)

The remainder of this short scene reveals, however, the benefits of proclaiming a monarch's misdeeds. The "seal'd commission" (1.3.13), which Helicanus has slyly devised, does not "speak sufficiently" to the anxious citizens concerning Pericles' vanishing. They do not believe that their ruler is absent traveling. Consequently, Helicanus creates another white lie while Thaliard, undetected, eavesdrops. Helicanus declares that, because Antiochus was angry with Pericles for an unknown reason, the Prince penitently is toiling as a common sailor. In terms of the central passage in scene 1, the white lie represents a dramatic virtue. As *Hamlet* reveals, the divulging of a monarch's fault—the breaking of a seal on a commission—can be providential. Swayed by Helicanus's declaration, Thaliard decides that he will leave Pericles to the sea's anger and give up his murderous pursuit.[24] The playwright's poetry and prose may be flat; nevertheless, the scene helps shape a redemptive design.

The next scene of the play also refutes Pericles' ideas about the relationship between speech and evil. Suffering from severe hunger, Cleon, King of Tharsus, asks his queen, Dionyza,

> . . . shall we rest us here,
> And by relating tales of others' griefs,
> See if 'twill teach us to forget our own?
>
> (1.4.1-3)

Sad narratives, however, are counterproductive in Dionyza's opinion:

> That were to blow at fire in hope to quench it;
> For who digs hills because they do aspire
> Throws down one mountain to cast up a higher.
> O my distressed lord, even such our griefs are;
> Here they are but felt, and seen with mischief's eyes,
> But like to groves, being topp'd, they higher rise.
>
> (1.4.4-9)

Cleon, at any rate, decides to tell the story of Tharsus's "superfluous riots" in order to awaken divine comforters. By introducing his tale with the words, "This Tharsus, o'er which I have the government" (1.4.21), Cleon makes his story of his city's decline a mirror for magistrates in which the body politic's misrule of itself is reflected in the distraught King. The pathetic conclusion of his tale forms a moral for mankind:

> O, let those cities that of plenty's cup
> And her prosperities so largely taste,
> With their superfluous riots, hear these tears!
> The misery of Tharsus may be theirs.
>
> (1.4.52-55)

Cleon implies that the ruin of his city partly results from a monarch's fault—his own. His final plea coincides with the arrival of Pericles' fleet of ships. Cleon believes that a savage nation, aware of the vulnerability of Tharsus, expects an easy conquest of starving men. Pericles, admitting that "we have heard your miseries as far as Tyre" (1.4.88), informs him, however, that the ships bring the means for life. Cleon's onstage story resembles a tale reflecting a king's failure, one that appears to produce a comforter—a prince with a saving gift of grain. The dramatic sequence thus quickly refutes Dionyza's belief about the futility of telling certain stories. Uttered words prove providential. Furthermore, Pericles would never have set sail for any shore if he had followed his advice to Antiochus. Faced with Helicanus's criticism for hiding the root of his sadness, Pericles stated, "[H]eaven forbid / That kings should let their ears hear their faults hid!" (1.2.61-62). In keeping with this sentiment, the Prince then told Helicanus about the evil threatening them. This admission prompted the advice that Pericles travel for a while, words that prove fruitful for Cleon and his hungry subjects as well as for Pericles. In this instance, the Prince's unexpected admission is private. Only near the end of the play does Pericles experience the good resulting from a public declaration of royal evil.

In the second act, Shakespeare continues to focus upon the efficacy of protest—in this case a stirring verbal protest. Even though Pericles, his armor recovered, wins the offstage tourney and thus Thaisa's hand in marriage, as a "mean" knight he must demonstrate his worth to Simonides. Unfortunately, Pericles' passivity reaches new extremes in Simonides' hall of state. The Prince claims that his victory comes more by fortune than by merit (2.3.12); he avoids the seat of honor, stating that a lesser place is far more fit for him (2.3.23); he laments time's tyranny and his forlorn life (2.3.37-47); and he denies any skill in dancing (2.3.104). Later, he rejects Simonides' praise of his musical abilities, claiming that he is "the worst of all her scholars" (2.5.29-31). Moreover, when Simonides proposes that the stranger become Thaisa's tutor, Pericles declines: "I am unworthy for her schoolmaster" (2.5.40). Finally, when the King shows him Thaisa's love letter, Pericles fearfully exclaims,

> 'Tis the king's subtlety to have my life.—
> (Kneels.) O, seek not to entrap me, gracious lord,
> A stranger and distressed gentleman,
> That never aim'd so high to love your daughter,
> But bent all offices to honour her.
>
> (2.5.44-48)

Such pithless sentiments convince neither the audience nor Simonides that Pericles deserves Thaisa. The hero balks at assuming any role requiring mastery, whether it be one of lover, schoolmaster, or son-in-law to a king. Clearly, Pericles' experience of venturing for Antiochus's daughter, which he finds reflected in a seemingly similar contest for the beautiful Thaisa, has intellectually crippled him. Brooding upon Antiochus's manners, Pericles concluded:

> How courtesy would seem to cover sin,
> When what is done is like an hypocrite,
> The which is good in nothing but in sight!
>
> (1.1.122-24)

The more courteous that Simonides appears, the more Pericles imagines that he is as inwardly devilish as the earlier fair-speaking giver of a lovely daughter through a trial. For the marriage to occur, Simonides must jar Pericles from his dogmatic opinion about appearance and reality. Critics have often noted that Simonides succeeds by playing the role of the heavy father in the manner that Prospero later does vis-à-vis Ferdinand. While his worthiness must also be proved, Ferdinand, unlike Pericles, does not need to be freed from an imprisoning idea. Nevertheless, Pericles, like Ferdinand, strongly reacts to the apparently hostile father's claims that the young man represents a traitor. In both plays, the reaction is a stirring protest:

> Sim. Traitor, thou liest.
> Per.   Traitor?
> Sim.   Ay, traitor.
> Per. Even in his throat—unless it be the king—
> That calls me traitor, I return the lie.

> Sim. (Aside.) Now, by the gods, I do applaud his courage.
> Per. My actions are as noble as my thoughts,
> That never relish'd of a base descent,
> I came unto your court for honour's cause,
> And not to be a rebel to her state;
> And he that otherwise accounts of me,
> This sword shall prove he's honour's enemy.
>
> (2.5.54-63)

By this vigorous verbal protest, Pericles redeems himself not only in Simonides' eyes but in those of the theater audience also. Dramatically, this speech—not the tourney—wins Thaisa. No longer passive, Pericles learns that Simonides' role was assumed and that one assumption will not cover superficially similar cases.[25] The swiftness of the change in Pericles' stated regard for Thaisa amounts to regrettable drama. Promising, in only one line of blank verse, to love Thaisa as much as life does the blood fostering it, Pericles does not permit much character analysis. In light of Shakespeare's linguistic thesis, however, his bold telling a king of his error amounts to a special triumph.

Despite this personal victory, Pericles, in the middle scenes of the play, reveals a mistaken idea of the word's power, mainly because he confuses the proper responses to metaphysical and moral evil. In Shakespeare's last plays, what appears to be metaphysical evil usually deserves silence. Because he lacks the knowledge of Diana's providence, Pericles bewails every woe. Having lost the material evidence of his heritage in the first tempest endured, the Prince laments,

> Yet cease your ire, you angry stars of heaven!
> Wind, rain, and thunder, remember, earthly man
> Is but a substance that must yield to you;
> And I, as fits my nature, do obey you.
> Alas, the seas hath cast me on the rocks,
> Wash'd me from shore to shore, and left me breath
> Nothing to think on but ensuing death.
> Let it suffice the greatness of your powers
> To have bereft a prince of all his fortunes;
> And having thrown him from your wat'ry grave,
> Here to have death in peace is all he'll crave.
>
> (2.1.1-11)

What begins as an angry command quickly becomes a somewhat spiritless complaint. According to John F. Danby, we hear in this speech "the cliché of resignation instead of the vast moment of spiritual forces that turns on 'patience.'"[26] Appearing at the beginning of the fisherman episode, Pericles' complaint contrasts with the rustics' comparatively stirring speech and with their lesson concerning the value of stir.

In his study of *Pericles,* Danby distinguishes between Stoic patience, which he equates with apathy, and active Christian patience *(patiens),* which he describes as a "release of charity."[27] While Pericles is often charitable, Danby judges that, in complaints like the speech quoted above, the protagonist expresses an imperfect attitude. In the play's most famous passage (3.1.56-64), Pericles imagines Thaisa's body, "scarcely coffin'd," plummeting through the sea to the ooze, where "the belching whale" and "humming water" overwhelm her corpse, "lying with simple shells." Expressed in remarkable poetry, these images cannot obscure Pericles' mistaken belief that the gods are indifferent to human value. In Danby's analysis of the arresting speech, Pericles "fully realizes death's final 'apathie'—away from the storm, on the sea's floor, 'lying with simple shells': an apathy which is the opposite of patience as death is the opposite of life."[28] In the Prince's vision, the whale's belching suggests a bestial indifference to human redemption; the image evokes Jonah's experience only to deny its truth. Pericles' poetry finally becomes stirred, imaginatively original; yet its faithless content paradoxically concerns stasis—the gradual ceasing of all movement and loss of human value.

Like Posthumus and Leontes, Pericles does not understand that the gods inflict suffering upon elected men and women in order to refine their souls and develop spiritual states of mind. The hero of late Shakespearean romance learns that metaphysical evil is not evil after all. Rather, it consists of "crosses" that a ruling god or goddess lays upon him in order to make his final joys more delightful for having been delayed. Pericles complains pointlessly to Neptune and Aeolus, for example, measuring the gods by mortal wishes:

> The god of this great vast, rebuke these surges,
> Which wash both heaven and hell; and thou that hast
> Upon the winds command, bind them in brass,
> Having call'd them from the deep! O, still
> The deaf'ning, dreadful thunders; gently quench
> Thy nimble sulphurous flashes!
>
> (3.1.1-6)

Regarded in light of the play's verbal dramaturgy, the word "rebuke" deserves special consideration in this passage. Pericles urges Neptune to speak against the unruly waves. But like Jupiter in *Cymbeline* and Apollo in *The Winter's Tale,* Diana does not make Pericles capable of receiving spiritual truths by "gently quenching" rough forces of suffering, the necessary school-

Frontispiece to the 1714 edition of Rowe's Shakespeare's Works. *Act III, scene ii. Lord Cerimon and two gentlemen lift Thaisa alive from her coffin. University of Michigan Library.*

masters of the soul. By stilling the raging sounds of the sea, wind, and atmosphere, Neptune and Aeolus, in Pericles' conception, would work the stasis that the Prince usually desires but from which he does not develop character. Finally, when Thaisa appears to die during childbirth, Pericles indicts all the Olympian deities:

> O you gods!
> Why do you make us love your goodly gifts,
> And snatch them straight away? We here below
> Recall not what we give, and therein may
> Use honour with you.
>
> (3.1.22-26)

Lychorida's reaction to these words—"Patience, good sir" (3.1.26)—unequivocally indicates that Shakespeare, at least, did not intend them to reflect a refined virtue. Even though Pericles' imaginatively existential vision of the gods' indifference to human worth proves mistaken in the complete context of *Pericles*, his immediate reaction to his philosophical discovery helps preserve comatose, apparently dead Thaisa. Her physical salvation hinges upon the salvatory word. Immediately after his vision of Thaisa's sinking body, Pericles exclaims,

> O Lychorida,
> Bid Nestor bring me spices, ink and paper,
> My casket and my jewels; and bid Nicander
> Bring me the satin coffer.
>
> (3.1.64-67)

If Pericles believes that neither Nature nor the gods will save Thaisa, then he has reason to impress a human signature upon his wife's loss. The word written by pen and ink—not the reward of jewels—works Thaisa's preservation. Cerimon labors to revive Thaisa mainly because Pericles' words inform him that she is a queen. She thus survives because the King affectionately includes her "passport" with her senseless body.

After Thaisa's sea "burial," Pericles' complaints cease; apparently he grasps the futility of addressing the gods about metaphysical evils. When Dionyza later hypocritically laments Thaisa's loss, Pericles admits that

> We cannot but obey
> The powers above us. Could I rage and roar
> As doth the sea she lies in, yet the end
> Must be as 'tis.
>
> (3.3.9-12)

With these words Pericles expresses the proper attitude toward metaphysical evil in the world of the last romances—faithful silence.[29] Yet as happens so often in the play, his triumph is shortlived; Marina's "death" shatters Pericles' spirit and he sinks into the absolute apathy of despair.

Moral evil, on the other hand, warrants verbal rebuke, a point left to Marina to demonstrate during her trials in the Mytilene brothel. Like Pericles in Antiochus's court, Marina would hear no evil. For example, she stops her ears when the Bawd tells her that she shall "taste gentlemen of all fashions . . ." and "have the difference of all complexions" (4.2.74-76). Marina also resembles her father in petitioning the gods to end her suffering:

> For me,
> That am a maid, though most ungentle
>   fortune
> Have plac'd me in this sty, where, since I
>   came,
> Diseases have been sold dearer than physic—
> That the gods
> Would set me free from this unhallow'd
>   place,
> Though they did change me to the meanest
>   bird
> That flies i' th' purer air!
>
> (4.4.94-101)

Like Pericles, Marina does not realize that her painful bondage to the fallen world amounts to a phase in a divine plan. Both Marina and Pericles lack Thaisa's ability to endure adversity patiently by trusting the gods, especially Diana, to bring events to their own divine end. Nonetheless, an important difference between the characters emerges. Marina complains to the gods; however she never makes Pericles' mistake of blindly indicting them. More important, Marina knows that moral evil deserves vigorous chastisement. No one, Pericles stated, dares to tell an earthly Jove that he acts wrongly. Marina, on the contrary, courageously risks telling the erring Governor of Mytilene that he dishonors himself by visiting the stews. While critics have often compared Marina's youthful innocence to that of Miranda, Marina's name does not signify a passive character, as the Latin gerund does in the case of Prospero's daughter. At first Lysimachus thinks that Marina's whorish dwelling place "proclaims" her to be "a creature of sale" (4.6.76-77). But her brave declaration that a virtuous man would never enter a sty gives Lysimachus a good opinion of her:

> *Mar.* Do you know this house to be a place
>   of such resort, and will
>   come into't? I hear say you're of
>   honourable parts and are the
>   governor of this place.
>
> . . . . .
>
> If you were born to honour, show it now;
> If put upon you, make the judgement good
> That thought you worthy of it.
> *Lys.* How's this? how's this? Some more; be
>   sage.
>
> (4.6.78-80, 91-94)

Marina's biting, fearless criticism of a ruler's faults prompts (not retards) good understanding:

> *Lys.*   I did not think
>   Thou couldst have spoke so well; ne'er
>   dreamt thou couldst.
>   Had I brought hither a corrupted mind,
>   Thy speech had alter'd it.
>
> (4.6.101-4)

Despite his disclaimer, Lysimachus has brought a degraded mind to the brothel and Marina's sharp words have altered it. After hearing her, he guiltily denies his lust:

> For me, be you thoughten
> That I came with no ill intent; for to me
> The very doors and windows savour vilely.
>
> (4.6.108-10)

Marina's stirring verbal protest proves redemptive for Lysimachus and those patrons subjected to it.[30] Her role provides a corrective commentary upon Pericles' idea about the futility of speaking out against evil. Shakespeare earlier hinted at the transformational power of Marina's speech. It has often been noted that Marina incarnates the moment of her birth at sea through a symbolic voice capturing the storm and its sounds. She verbally recreates for Leonine Pericles' and the sailors' brave industry during the tempest accompanying her birth, even assuming the voices of different men amid the imagined roar (4.1.49-64). By recreating an originally terrifying moment through charmingly innocent speech, Marina stylistically suggests that the unhappy events of that moment are finally innocent—as they in fact are within the scheme of Diana's providence. Equally important, she reveals her special gift for verbally metamorphosing disaster into something less threatening. Lysimachus's comic turn-around in his imaginative valuing of the doors and windows of the brothel stresses how thoroughly her fearless speech revolutionizes sight into a moral faculty.[31] In act 5, however, the change occurs in the opposite fashion. There, Pericles' visions of Marina as Justice and Patience cause him to revalue her speech.

At the beginning of the last act, melancholy Pericles remains concealed behind a curtain on board his ship, withdrawn from the gods who seemingly reclaim their gifts just as mysteriously as they give them. Helicanus then presents him as a dismal spectacle that stresses the vanity of speech and sight. "May we not see him?" Lysimachus asks. Helicanus replies:

> You may;
> But bootless is your sight; he will not speak
> To any.
> Lys.   Yet let me obtain my wish.
> Hel. Behold him. *(Pericles discovered.)*
>   This was a goodly person,
>   Till the disaster that, one mortal night,
>   Drove him to this.
> Lys. Sir king, all hail! the gods preserve you!
>   Hail, royal sir!
> Hel. It is in vain; he will not speak to you.
>
> (5.1.32-40)

In this episode, Pericles profoundly dramatizes his original reaction to sin; seeing and hearing no evil was his professed wish after learning of vice. His isolation ironically reflects this desire, not mankind's solitude in a cruel world. A challenger of her father's dramatic spectacle, Marina confronts it, finally shattering it and introducing her father to the restorative virtues of a story retold.

At first, Lysimachus believes that Marina's "sweet harmony" and "other chosen attractions" will "allure, / And make a batt'ry" through Pericles' "deafen'd ports" (5.1.44-46). Marina's song, however, makes no impact by itself; her physic will be her woeful story:

> . . . she speaks,
> My lord, that, may be, hath endur'd a grief
> Might equal yours, if both were justly weigh'd.
> Though wayward fortune did malign my state,
> My derivation was from ancestors
> Who stood equivalent with mighty kings. . . .
>
> (5.1.86-91)

Hearing these words, Pericles sees the unknown maiden in a new light:

> . . . my queen's square brows;
> Her stature to an inch; as wand-like straight;
> As silver-voic'd; her eyes as jewel-like
> And cas'd as richly; in pace another Juno;
> Who starves the ears she feeds, and makes them hungry
> The more she gives them speech.
>
> (5.1.108-13)

A beautiful sufferer, Marina forces Pericles to revise his conviction that grief should look grievous. Transcendental imagination occurs when terrible suffering abates somewhat; Pericles, by a psychological reflex, adopts a view as brilliant as his painful vision was dark. After his great denial of speech, the word rings with a silver tone in his ears, and he fully enjoys its simple reality. Marina fears that her story of suffering will "seem / Like lies, disdain'd in the reporting" (5.1.118-19). Pericles, however, insists that his supreme vision will guarantee the truth of any words she speaks:

> Prithee, speak;
> Falseness cannot come from thee, for thou look'st
> Modest as Justice, and thou seem'st a palace
> For the crown'd Truth to dwell in. I will believe thee,
> And make my senses credit thy relation
> To points that seem impossible . . .
>
> (5.1.119-24)

In Pericles' eyes, Marina's heavenly beauty makes her speech resound truthfully in his ears, and her musical words intensify his rare view. Word and vision wonderfully complement each other, making possible a familiar Platonic coincidence.[32]

> Tell thy story;
> If thine consider'd prove the thousandth part

Act 5, scene 1. Marina, accompanied by her maid, sings to Pericles. By W. Hilton. The University of Michigan Library.

Of my endurance, thou art a man, and I
Have suffer'd like a girl; yet thou dost look
Like Patience gazing on kings' graves, and
   smiling
Extremity out of act. What were thy friends?
How lost thou them? Thy name, my most
   kind virgin?
Recount, I do beseech you. Come, sit by me.
                                    (5.1.134-41)

Trusted "by the syllable" (5.1.167), Marina's narration of Cleon's and Dionyza's treachery, bloodthirsty Leonine's attack, and the pirates' mercenary rescue positively identifies Pericles' lost daughter. Marina opens the book of monarchs' faults. Her words of evils suffered have a homeopathic effect when one grief drives out another and Pericles is fully revived.[33] Cerimon's recovery of Thaisa depended upon "still and woeful music" (3.2.90) whereby one bitterness expelled another. Marina invites her listeners to remember her trials and imagine her martyr-like faith, comparing these images with personal woes whenever the latter seem extreme. Pericles does say that if Marina's story proves the thousandth part of his misfortunes, he has not suffered manfully.

Marina's invitation extends to the theater audience as well as to Pericles. Pericles' advice that every book of monarchs' acts be kept closed contrasts with Shakespeare's decision to open Gower's and Twine's volumes and stage (publicly proclaim) the chief deeds of Pericles' life. According to Gower, lords and ladies have read the saga of Pericles "for restoratives" (Chorus 1.7-8). Shakespeare's sorrowful play can revitalize its viewer by presenting images of griefs greater than any suffered or imagined possible. Marina's brief tale is such an image. It is the composite—in fact, the miniature—of the play in its cathartic working. Just as her tale of suffering displaces Pericles' grief, promoting his recovery and making possible the formal ending of romance, so the larger tale of Pericles works upon the viewer's woes, placing them in perspective. The word proves to be restorative metadramatically as well as dramatically. A tale involving a monarch's faults can redeem not only a king but a society as well.[34]

Gower's periodic dumb shows and his commentaries upon them have predisposed the viewer of *Pericles* to believe by act 5 that the spoken word and vision acquire a special virtue when they interact for complete understanding. In the Chorus to act 2, for example, Gower first tells the viewer that Pericles is safe and honored in Tharsus; then he announces, "tidings to the contrary / Are brought your eyes; what need speak I?" (Chorus 2.15-16). Onstage this pantomime occurs:

> *Enter, at one door,* Pericles *talking with* Cleon; *all the train with them. Enter, at another door, a* Gentleman, *with a letter to* Pericles; Pericles *shows the letter to* Cleon; Pericles *gives the Messenger a reward, and knights him. Exit* Pericles *at one door, and* Cleon *at another.*

If performed spiritedly, the spectacle exemplifies the epistemology originally formulated in *The Rape of Lucrece:*

> To see sad sights moves more than hear them
>   told,
> For then the eye interprets to the ear
> The heavy motion that it doth behold,
> When every part a part of woe doth bear.
>   (1324-27)

While the dumb show under consideration possesses this affective merit, the theater audience remains perplexed about the meaning of the distressing emotions portrayed. The viewer requires Gower's resumed speech to know that the letter in the dumb show comes from Helicanus, the faithful counselor governing Tyre, who notifies Pericles that the assassin Thaliard has stopped there in his pursuit of him. When Gower explains that Helicanus advises further flight, the viewer grasps the meaning of the rushed exits at the dumb show's close. Eye and ear thus explicitly complement each other for knowledge; directly speaking of a monarch's faults has clarified understanding. Gower prefaces the initially ambiguous dumb show of act 3, complete with another messenger, a new letter, and the same quick departures of Pericles and Thaisa—exits that are in this case joyous—with the assurance "What's dumb in show I'll plain with speech" (Chorus 3.14). Rather than acquiring negative connotations, Gower's "plain" signifies "explains"—a welcomed activity. Thus the viewer hears that Helicanus has told Pericles that Antiochus and the Daughter are dead and that Tyre's lords will deprive the Prince of rule unless he returns immediately. By act 4, Shakespeare's instruction for harmonizing the eye and ear has become emphatic. Regarding the actors in the dumb show of Marina's tomb, Gower requests that the viewer "like motes and shadows see them move awhile." Then he promises, "Your ears unto your eyes I'll reconcile" (4.4.22).[35] The more enigmatic the dumb show's spectacle, the more the viewer appreciates the enlightenment given by the spoken word; the more plain the poetic word as choral narrative, the more he or she values the power of the vision. In summary, through the choral technique of *Pericles,* Shakespeare highlights the interaction of faculties crucial to the protagonist's final recovery, pointedly underscoring the word's clarifying power.[36]

Pericles' dream-vision of Diana is part of the linguistic design under discussion. The deity who visited the seventeenth-century stage often bodied forth a Neo-Platonic virtue proper to itself.[37] Were their rare pageant not dissolved, Ceres and Juno, for example, would have chastely taught Ferdinand and Miranda the Idea of Married Fertility by joining them in symbolic dance with April's nymphs and August's reapers.[38] Given the dramatic context and Diana's symbolic meaning, Shakespeare's informed playgoer awaits Pericles' sudden knowledge of Chastity.[39] However, instead of the intuition of Chastity, Pericles receives from Diana the command to travel to Ephesus, offer sacrifice upon her altar there, and give both his and Marina's trials "repetition to the life" before the assembled worshippers. In this instance, giving a tale repetition to the life does not entail describing events exactly as they happened; rather, the goddess directs Pericles to narrate a story of suffering in such stirring words that it lives in listeners' minds. His fulfillment of Diana's bidding is letter-perfect:

> Hail, Dian! to perform thy just command,
> I here confess myself the king of Tyre;
> Who, frighted from my country, did wed
> At Pentapolis the fair Thaisa.

> At sea in childbed died she, but brought forth
> A maid-child call'd Marina; who, O goddess,
> Wears yet thy silver livery. She at Tharsus
> Was nurs'd with Cleon, who at fourteen years
> He sought to murder; but her better stars
> Brought her to Mytilene; 'gainst whose shore
> Riding, her fortunes brought the maid aboard us,
> Where, by her own most clear remembrance, she
> Made known herself my daughter.
> (5.3.1-13)

Pericles obeys a deity's command to tell a story involving evil (the evil of a king) even as his counterpart Jonah finally divulged the wickedness of Nineveh in an act pleasing to God and assuring salvation. Pericles' faithfully told story is restorative; his public narration makes his identity known to the nun Thaisa, who faints upon hearing this revelation. Revived a second time by Cerimon, she threatens to recreate the play's original conflict:

> O, let me look!
> If he be none of mine, my sanctity
> Will to my sense bend no licentious ear,
> But curb it, spite of seeing.
> (5.3.28-31)

Now, however, no radical conflict in knowing presents itself. The viewer realizes that the problem has been resolved; all the faculties cooperate in revealing husband and wife to each other. Thaisa's eyes and ears record the truth; Pericles is a "Great sir" (5.3.26). Gower predicted that Pericles would prove awful both in deed and word. Antiochus's greatness was merely totalitarian force; the King of Tyre, on the other hand, inspires awe because he humbly submits to divine edict. Great in this sense, he practices an active faith far different from his passive obedience to what he supposed was the gods' will. Thaisa's vision of her husband opens her ears to his bizarre yet true narrative of the family's preservation. The efficacious working of words has recreated the sanctity of the family as only the theater audience can fully appreciate.

After the royal family's reunion, Gower speaks the Epilogue. He explains that Fame conveyed Cleon and Dionyza's plot against Marina to the ears of Tharsus's citizens. Outraged, they burned the rulers in their palace: "The gods for murder seemed so content / To punish; although not done, but meant" (Epilogue. 15-16). After supposedly murdering Marina, Dionyza taunted her conscience-stricken husband:

> Be one of those that thinks
> The petty wrens of Tharsus will fly hence,
> And open this to Pericles.
> (4.3.21-23)

While birds do not miraculously "open" the fault to Pericles' ears, an earthly power—fame—inevitably does disclose the crime to Cleon and Dionyza's subjects. Instead of a god's lightning bolt, the common telling of a story of monarchs' faults brings about the tyrants' ruin. That dramatic point, however, is hardly necessary for the viewer aware of a verbal truth in *Pericles*.[40]

David Solway (essay date 1997)

SOURCE: "The State of Letters: *Pericles* as Dream," in *Sewanee Review*, Vol. CV, No. 1, Winter, 1997, pp. 91-5.

[*In the following essay, Solway argues that the dream nature of the play unifies it and explains any incongruities.*]

> Some to the Lute, some to the Viol went,
> And others chose the Cornet eloquent.
> These practising the Wind, and those the Wire,
> To sing Mens Triumphs, or in Heavens quire.
> —Andrew Marvell, *Musicks Empire*

Pericles, despite its earlier composition and disputed status, best sums up, of all the late plays, the character of Shakespearean romance. Its schematic form, its "gaps" and archaisms, its unadorned outlines and loose texture enable the spectator to observe with minimal distraction the tragicomic Muse at work. Its subject then appears not as any peculiar or local set of circumstances—misunderstandings, departures, reconciliations—but as nothing less than the universal dream of retrieval and atonement. The romance may be regarded as a dream not only in its unrealistic or improbable character—the comedies would answer to this description too—but in its particular *themes* of the recovery of self and the domestication of time as well as in the curious structure which it exhibits.

If we consider *Pericles* sympathetically, resisting the temptation to dismiss it as partially spurious or inferior, we see that it resembles a kind of "thought experiment" or imaginary voyage through time to an atemporal destination. The voyage, pursued in two directions at once—forward to a redeemed and glorious future and backward to an ideal, lost condition—blends anticipation and memory, thought and dream, into a single mythic consummation. In the prologue to act 3 Gower poses the rhetorical question "Who dreamt, who thought of such a thing?"; and Lysimachus, in expressing his wonder and delight with Marina, uses similar language: "I did not think/Thou woulds't have spoke so well; ne'er dreamt thou coulds't." The play is intended "to take [delight] our imagination," but only if we empathize with the hero and consent to "think his pilot thought" as we navigate in the straits between experience and dream.

Marilyn French in *Shakespeare's Division of Experience* tells us that the romances "are shot through with dream devices like projection, surrogation, and transformation," but she is content to let the matter rest on this level of analytic abstraction. It may be more helpful in considering the dream structure of *Pericles* to recall in greater detail what Freud has to say about the architectonic of the dream. Here we find that the "dream work" (the shaping of the dream out of the "dream thoughts") is governed by the four functional principles of condensation, displacement, representability, and secondary elaboration.

By condensation is meant something like overdetermination—that is, each dream image is determined by several dream thoughts that contribute to the psychic density of that image. Such condensation is perhaps most evident in the charged latency of the pun, over which the romance enjoys no privileged monopoly but which nevertheless finds a most welcoming reception therein. For example, early in act 1 Pericles compares Antiochus' incestuous daughter to a viol played before her time and links the image with the concept of law in the locution *lawful music.* The suggestion is that a law has been *violated,* and an ear attuned to semantic concentricities may recall this earlier turbulence in Marina's "Never was waves nor wind more violent," uttered some acts later. A similar fusion of image and thought occurs when Pericles, comparing himself to a treetop that protects its subject and nourishing roots, confesses to a royal apprehensiveness that makes his body "pine." And Cerimon, the magus or dream-figure to whom we all appeal, clearly stands for the magical *ceremony* that controls, harmonizes, and redeems the elemental ferocity of Nature. Name, function, person, and idea dovetail into single presence.

Images can also be overloaded with contradictory meanings and associations. Fire is one of the "unfriendly elements" and is responsible with the other three for Marina's "chiding . . . nativity"; yet Thaisa is revived to music and fire, so that her "fire of life kindle[s] again." Similarly the "fair viol" that was played before its time is then played, so to speak, after its time in Cerimon's command—"The viol once more." From the standpoint of Nature the music to which Thaisa is revived is also not a lawful music. But where, earlier, social law had been violated, here it is natural law that is transcended by Asclepian sanction.

The image of the sea is equally susceptible of antithetic density: the destructive element, devouring ships and men with insatiable indifference, becomes "this great sea of joys" that is lethal only through its superabundance of sweetness.

Sometimes the paronomasia is not only to be found in the spry amalgamation of contraries, but in the incremental heightening of effect, as, for example, "He bears/A tempest which his mortal vessel *tears*" (italics mine). Here the related ideas of dismemberment and sorrow are brought close together—along with the complementary association of salt waters, uniting the violence of the sea with the bitter helplessness of its victims.

Displacement implies that the dream appears as "elsewhere centered," requiring the dreamer to discount the manifest content of his dream in favor of its latent content, its raison d'être or substratum of meaning. The manifest content of our play is the story of tribulation and suffering through which we trace Pericles' coming of age, his passing through life's manifold stages of adolescent fancy, tragic bereavement, and mature reconciliation—helped along, albeit, by several lottery-like windfalls. The latent content is not any particular series of crises or adventures but the storm of life itself, whirring us from our friends, in which we detect the perennial search for a divine father, a Cerimon whose "blest infusions" redeem us from our disenfranchisement. The pressure of the reality principle is unremitting and is explicitly acknowledged by Pericles: "We cannot but obey/The powers above us," he admits with resignation. Yet the pleasure principle continues to operate, modestly triumphant in the numinous figure of Cerimon whom Pericles addresses: "Reverend sir,/The gods can have no mortal officer/More like a god than you."

We need not dwell unduly upon either of the two remaining structural rules since they are largely self-evident. The dream cannot tolerate abstraction but must be representable in visual and aural terms. Consequently *any* play resembles a dream in its sensuous manifestation, but the romance with its visions, hieratic choreography, and musical interludes would satisfy the dream criterion more vividly and appositely. As for secondary elaboration—the papering over of lacunae to give a semblance of logic or coherence—we have in *Pericles* the choric device of Gower to explain or explain away illogicalities, asking pardon for using "one language in each several clime" (for convenience) and declaring that he stands "i' th' gaps" in order to inform or "teach" his audience.

We note as well the preponderance of other recognizable dream features: time elasticities (see the beginning of act 4 in both *Pericles* and *The Winter's Tale*), sudden changes of place, unwarranted knowledge (Diana's revelation—or Jupiter's "book" in *Cymbeline*), magical retributions, and the like. But these are not, properly speaking, principles of organization. Here it suffices to say there can be little doubt that the four basic structural principles adumbrated by Freud—condensation, displacement, representability, and secondary elaboration—can be distinctly observed leavening the dream thought (or the play thought) into the finished product itself.

Admittedly these principles of organization may also apply to literature in general and to poetic drama in particular, but they are most robust and ubiquitous in the romance play with its patently thaumaturgic elements, its unabashed reliance on miracle and revelation, and its congenial atmosphere of transcendent intercessions.

Dreams, we are told, are circuitous and intricate ways of expressing fundamental conflicts in the human soul. Occasionally a solution is offered, waiting upon decipherment; more often, perhaps, the dream presents an impossible resolution that can be experienced only at one remove from reality, in the *locus amoenus* of a region without geotemporal coordinates (second star to the right and straight on till morning). The conflict in the dream that is *Pericles* is the eternal one going on between the destructive and capricious realm of Nature, the elemental world indifferent to human desires (signified by the tempest, the realm of the "masked Neptune"), and the world of spirit or imagination, of human longing for harmony and election (signified by music and vision).

The spectator responds to the play in precisely the same way as Pericles reacts to Marina's narrative: "This is the rarest dream that e'er dull sleep/Did mock sad fools withal." We recognize a world in which dreams, bearing their "goddess argentine," are visionary and evangelical and "wishes fall out as they're willed." But, if Pericles thinks he is dreaming Marina and the events she recounts, as in some sense he surely is, we may then ask: Who is dreaming the play? The author in his creative fit, we may reply; but we might also decide that the play is dreaming itself and that the characters are dreaming one another—or at least that both play and characters seem intended to give that impression. The play may be said to be dreaming itself in so far as it is a dream whose content is another dream—the dream of resolution, restoration, happiness, accompanied by celestial music. Further, if we are not *consciously* accountable for our dreams, there exists a very real sense in which our actual dreams may be conceived as dreaming themselves, that is, they proceed without the intervention of the controlling sensibility.

But the dreamer and the dream, the dancer and the dance, subsist in a web of complex intersections that cannot be so readily sundered, as Augustine had hoped when he thanked his God that he was not responsible for his dreams. So the play, as is more or less the case with every pastoral romance, represents the collective dream of desiring, impoverished humanity. *Ultimately it is the spectator who is dreaming the play.* Time becomes the medium of reunification: obstacles are overcome and discontinuities annealed. Illogicalities are explained away, suffering is redeemed, death conquered, envy and resentment transmuted by the dream alchemy into reconciliation and requited love.

The riddle with which the play opens, alluding to Antiochus' incestuous daughter as both a mother and a wife, finds its resolution toward the end in the (similar yet different) magnanimous contradiction of a daughter giving birth to a father: "Thou . . . beget'st him that did thee beget." Marina is restored to her father, restoring him in the act of restoration, and preparing for the climactic reunion with the mother and wife who is Thaisa. It is here that the *authentic riddle*—the riddle of time, loss, and separation—is solved in the dream of a sublime atonement. Thus the cherubim at the gate put down their flaming swords and receive the exile, "led on by heaven and crowned with joy," into his lost inheritance.

When the curtain falls, the dreamer awakens to find himself once again banished into the world of conflict and bereavement. But the memory persists of a magical compensatory realm in which Lord Cerimon, "this man/Through whom the gods have shown their power," may once again, as we dream the dream at two removes, "from first to last resolve" us.

Notes

* G. Wilson Knight (*The Crown of Life*) suggests that the play can be seen as providing "a panorama of life from adolescent fantasy and a consequent fall, through good works to a sensible and fruitful marriage, and thence into tragedy, with a reemergence beyond mortal appearances into some higher recognition and rehabilitation." Derek Traversi (*Shakespeare: The Last Phase*) thinks the play records "a symbolic pilgrimage in search of an ideal expressed in terms of devotion to chivalrous love." (Although as Traversi also thinks that Marina is betrothed to Cerimon rather than Lysimachus, one is a little disposed, perhaps, to question his authority.)

David Skeele (essay date 1998)

SOURCE: "*Pericles* Deconstructed," in *Thwarting the Wayward Seas: A Critical and Theatrical History of Shakespeare's Pericles in the Nineteenth and Twentieth Centuries*, University of Delaware Press, 1998, pp. 126-45.

[*In the following excerpt, Skeele discusses textual unity in* Pericles *in the context of postmodern theories.*]

"I do not fear the flaw."

(act III, scene i)

One of the more pervasive images in current popular culture is that of the "channel surfer." In this image, a person (for some reason, usually a male)[1] sits in the dark, staring glassily at a flickering television screen, while his hand clutches a remote control. As his finger presses down on the channel button, rhythmically, every two or three seconds, he is confronted by a quick succession of disconnected snapshots: "gangster-rap" video, wildlife documentary, sexy beer commercial, "real-life" police drama, Barney the Dinosaur, Australian-rules football—the world as a bewildering array of incongruous images.[2] Though it lies outside the bounds of the cliché, it would not be difficult to imagine our hypothetical channel surfer wearying of this electronic collage and attempting to focus on one program for a length of time. However, on a number of these programs—fashion shows, music videos, advertisements—he would find the same rapid-fire barrage of images being consciously employed. He would find that his restless search for instant, momentary gratification had actually become an *aesthetic*.

To expand the boundaries even further, let us follow our attention-deficient subject into the realm of the extremely unlikely. Let us imagine that he decided, in a fit of self-improvement, to escape the mind-numbing influence of his television by attending a live performance: a live performance scripted, of course, by the world's most recognizable icon of high culture, William Shakespeare. To his surprise, when he enters the theater, he finds that the jumbled scrap heap of images and associations that he thought he had left safely in his den has followed him into the Renaissance. Anachronistic bits of costuming and setting blend in bizarre combinations. Different scenes are played in completely different styles, as though they belonged in separate plays. Scenes are transposed, cut into smaller fragments, and scattered throughout the play. Abstract, metaphorical visual images take precedence over (and even displace) the coherence of the words and the continuity of the plot.

Now let us become truly ridiculous and suppose that our channel surfer, enraged at this perceived degradation of his aesthetic experience, consults a stack of the latest criticism in order to find the "true" meaning of the play he has just seen—to find the coherent and unified pattern that has just been so egregiously violated. What does he find instead? In one book, he finds that Shakespeare's texts consist merely of the "free play of language," isolated word fragments floating in random configurations through the void. In another, he finds that all previously discovered patterns of meaning were simply tools of a patriarchal, elitist ruling body: "cultural constructions" which must now be "deconstructed" and replaced with alternative political agendas. Thumbing through the rest of the pile, he encounters a maze of related ideas, all of which seem to come down to one basic idea: there is no pattern, there is no central meaning. Shakespeare's plays, finally, consist of jumbles of dissociated ideas and images. With a sigh, he turns on the T.V.

This account is, of course, somewhat absurd, yet it does indeed seem that our present age is characterized by a feeling of fragmentation and that this feeling permeates everything from popular culture to the most complex levels of Shakespeare interpretation. This is not to suggest, however, that fragmentation is unique to current Shakespeare study and performance—it has been lurking in the Western psyche for a long time. Early in the century, modernist interpreters of Shakespeare were clearly aware of a growing sense of dislocation, yet their response was to fight against it by continuing to search for new unifying patterns. Many contemporary Shakespeareans, on the other hand, show a contrasting tendency to embrace the fragmentation and (while not entirely free from the anxiety that attends being adrift in a void) to revel in the freedom of being more disconnected than ever before from old biases and assumptions. It is this particular paradigm shift, perhaps more than any other, that has convinced many cultural commentators that we have entered a new age: the age of postmodernism.

With the newfound dominance of this paradigm of fragmentation, the present would seem to be a propitious time indeed for the most fractured of Shakespeare's plays. One could reasonably expect that this chapter might form the happy ending to this narrative, in which *Pericles* suddenly vaults to the forefront of the canon: the once "miserable" fragment now reigning supreme in a postmodern kingdom of fragments. While such a drastic change of status is still possible for *Pericles*—one could at least say that the idea is less ridiculous now than at any other point in the play's history—the actual situation is far more ambiguous. This ambiguity is due in part to the very contemporaneity of postmodernism. Because the present is always in a state of transition, of flux, it is impossible to know whether an essay on or production of *Pericles* (or any other play) represents the fruits of a coherent movement or is simply a wobbly indicator of some future trend. In the case of *Pericles,* the situation is complicated by the fact that few critics and directors who might be considered postmodern have yet to turn their full attention to the play. Consequently, this chapter offers hints, not certainties; not a resolution, but the suggestion of a postmodern *Pericles* in progress.

Literary criticism has been particularly neglectful of *Pericles,* though the critic's attack on textual unity significantly predated the director's. The main wellspring of the new attitude toward fragmentation is a critical philosophy, introduced by Jacques Derrida, that was unveiled in America as early as the late 1960s. Known as "deconstruction," this philosophy was originally presented as a critique of the limitations of structuralism—in fact, deconstruction is considered the first "post-structuralist" movement. Though any attempt to describe deconstruction within a space appropriate to this study will inevitably result in gross oversimplification, it is possible to elucidate several of the ways in which Derrida stretched or transcended these limitations. One of Derrida's main objections to the structuralists' method was that in attempting to fit the text into their predetermined structures, they were not really dealing with the works in their totality. Parts of the text that did not fit the model—flaws, gaps, ruptures—were being glossed over, mended, or pushed into the margins. It is precisely these flaws, Derrida suggested, that should be the focus of critical analysis, for they are the keys to the text's disunity, the refusal of its language to conform to any externally imposed framework of meaning. It was this rejection of meaning that formed the centerpiece of Derrida's argument. For while he applauded the work of structuralists in helping to destroy the myth of realizable authorial intention, he felt that they were far too timid in their liberation of the text. By replacing the imposed unity of the author with the imposed unity of "structure," he maintained, they were simply trading in one set of chains for another. Rather, he argued that one must eradicate the notion of a "presence" of *any* kind behind the words. One must embrace the "absolute danger"[3] of breaking free from the idea of inherited meaning altogether and celebrate in its place the "free play of language."

What, then, does deconstructive criticism seek to reveal in a particular text, if it is not some inherent meaning? Answer: it usually seeks simply to reflect itself. In other words, in always seeking to prove its basic credo—that no text has inherent meaning—deconstructive criticism, at least in its purest form, ends up being primarily *about* deconstructive criticism.

By completely freeing texts from the authority of inherited meaning and dismissing the need for unified structure, deconstruction opened up new vistas of possibility for Shakespearean criticism. Yet, as Hugh Grady points out, the *direct* impact of deconstruction proper on Shakespeare studies has been minimal. For several reasons, the theorists whom Howard Felperin calls "textual" deconstructionists[4]—those who use the text primarily as a proving ground for deconstruction—have mostly (though not completely) avoided Shakespeare.[5] Of the "textual" critics that have chosen to deconstruct Shakespeare, virtually none have evinced interest in *Pericles.*

There are a couple of possible reasons for this neglect. Deconstruction is essentially a subversive act, one that takes a certain glee in dissecting the sacred cows of Western Civilization. While critical opinion of *Pericles* has certainly improved over the years, there is little shock value to be gained in dismantling it, as it is still one of the least sacred cows in the Shakespearean pasture. Also, a major tactic of deconstructive criticism is to attack the idea of textual unity. Here again, *Pericles* makes a rather unattractive target: the unity established for it by modernist critics is still so fresh, so fragile, so debatable, that the play would be a straw man to even a novice deconstructionist. Compared to a tightly structured work like *Othello*, whose unity has remained beyond reproach for centuries, *Pericles* seems to deconstruct itself.

Deconstruction's greatest impact on Shakespeare interpretation has been indirect, as its influence has rippled outward into several schools of criticism that were already deeply involved in the study of Shakespeare. Such schools, represented most notably by feminism and new historicism/ cultural materialism, have adopted the critical license afforded by deconstruction without necessarily accepting the extremity of its assault on meaning or its ideological barrenness. The critics allied with these schools have been referred to by Felperin as "contextual" deconstructionists, meaning that their interpretations, no matter how radically liberated from the constraints of inherited meaning, are not left floating in a moral void but are placed within the context of a particular ideology.

Still, while *contextual* poststructuralists have had a profound effect on the state of Shakespeare studies, even they have yet to contribute much to the interpretation of *Pericles*. In fact, Steven Mullaney's cultural materialist reading—in *The Place of the Stage* (1988)[6]—constitutes one of the few significant poststructuralist considerations of the play. Cultural materialism and new historicism are highly contextual—both of them being based to one degree or another in Marxist analysis of the mechanics of cultural dominance and subjugation—and their relationship to deconstruction is somewhat complex. If most poststructuralist literary criticism can be said to have sprung in part from the writings of Derrida, historically inflected poststructuralism owes more of a debt to Michel Foucault. Where Derrida had held up the literary text as the site of discontinuity and disjuncture, Foucault, in such works as *Discipline and Punish* (1975) and *The History of Sexuality* (1978),[7] did the same for the great "text" of history. Foucault thoroughly attacked the notion that the denizens of a historical period can be characterized by some unified worldview or central cultural attitude—a notion championed by such "old" historicists as E. M. W. Tillyard in his *The Elizabethan World Picture*. Foucault looked for the contradictions, the cracks in the world picture, the margins surrounding the center, and rather than seeing a single dominant outlook shaping a given culture, he found a multiplicity of voices, a babble of discourses fighting for political and cultural dominance.

New historicist and cultural materialist critics of Shakespeare examine Elizabethan England through the same fractured lens, and in doing so, they do not so much shatter textual unity as render the whole question quite irrelevant. For these critics, the Shakespeare text is not a self-contained structure; it is not an isolated body that can be "privileged" over other written material of the period. Rather, it is simply one text among many historical "texts" competing for pride of place with diaries, theological tracts, royal proclamations, and writs of deed. In other words, a play like *Pericles* should not be analyzed as a self-contained soliloquy but as part of a dialogue: a text in conversation with other texts. As Mullaney writes:

> I have sought . . . to view the popular stage not only or primarily as a literary phenomenon, but as one of a diverse body of cultural practices. . . . In *The Place of the Stage*, literary analysis is conceived not as an end in itself but as a vehicle, a means of gaining access to tensions and contradictions.[8]

The particular tensions and contradictions he identified with regard to *Pericles* were those endemic to an age moving rapidly into capitalism. He begins his argument by citing Frederic Jameson's theory that the genre of Shakespearean romance is a nostalgic, Utopian response to the growing power of the marketplace, as Shakespeare "opposes the phantasmagoria of imagination to the bustling commercial activity at work all around it."[9] After noting one major contradiction inherent in the theory—that the play which exhibits this "phantasmagoria" is itself part of the "bustling commercial activity"—Mullaney found several scenes in which Shakespeare, nonetheless, seems in his text to demonstrate anxiety over the capitalistic implications of parts of his story. For his first example, Mullaney used one of the least remarked-upon scenes in the play: act I, scene iv, in which Pericles brings grain to relieve the starving citizenry of Tharsus. As Mullaney noted, in one of Shakespeare's prime sources, Lawrence Twine's *Pattern of Painfull Adventures* (1579), the hero Apollonius (Twine's version of Pericles) displays a Machiavellian side that Shakespeare takes great pains to suppress. Unloading his wheat in the Tharsian marketplace, Apollonius demands that the Tharsians pay "eight peeces of brasse for every bushel." Though he quickly decides to return the money, this only serves to redouble the populace's debt to him. As Mullaney observes, "a gift marks the beginning of a coercive system of exchange, one that comes into play . . . in cultural situations where more overt systems of obligation or domination are unavailable" (139). In significant contrast to this display of mercantile greed and cunning, the scene penned by Shakespeare (Mullaney was not concerned with questions of authorship) takes place not in a marketplace, but in a neutral area somewhere near the harbor, and his

Pericles simply asks for "love" and "harbourage" in return for his gift.

Mullaney's observation that Shakespeare seems to have cleaned up the less spiritual aspects of his story is even more interesting when applied to one of the play's most notorious gaps in logic: the scene in which Pericles inexplicably decides to leave his infant daughter in the care of Cleon and Dionyza for fourteen years. This is a plot twist that has proven resistant even to most myth-criticism (which relies little on realistic logic), and though Mullaney did not attempt to fill in the gap, he did give it significance. In Twine's version, Apollonius "leaves his daughter to embark on a voyage around the Mediterranean, 'meaning . . . to exercise the trade of merchandize'" (139).

Next, Mullaney tackled the brothel scenes. After pointing out that these scenes represent the only time in the play in which Shakespeare allows the marketplace onto the stage (perhaps because of the unflattering picture of commerce that they paint), Mullaney again used discrepancies between Twine and Shakespeare to suggest the latter's anxiety over a changing cultural climate. Twine's daughter-figure, here named Tharsia, escapes degradation and ruin through a markedly different strategy than her Shakespearean counterpart: she repeatedly enthralls would-be customers so much with her tale of woe that they forget about sex and agree to pay merely for the privilege of listening. As Mullaney observed, what Tharsia does is essentially to create a theater within the brothel. Because sexual assignations were rumored to be frequent amid the anonymity of the theater-crowd and because "Shakespeare's audience was lured into the theatre at least in part by the promise of illicit liaisons," this is a combination that would have made great sense to an Elizabethan audience. However, where Tharsia's actions baldly affirm the economic interdependency of playhouse and whorehouse, Marina's proselytizing revealed Shakespeare practicing "an evasion of the economic and cultural roots of the popular stage" (145).

Clinching Mullaney's argument was the figure of Gower. By bringing the "moral Gower" onstage to narrate the play, Shakespeare is essentially championing one source over the other, using Gower's powerful authorial, authoritative presence to "obscure the discomfiting significance of Twine's *Painfull Adventures*." Because Gower is a distinctly medieval presence, he is able to "introduce *Pericles* as a tale of universal significance, ancient but unaging, forever timely and uncontaminated by historical and cultural contexts" (148). Because Mullaney regarded the use of such an onstage authorial voice to be an unprecedented theatrical innovation, *Pericles* achieves a new importance, representing the Elizabethan-Jacobean theater's first "radical effort to dissociate the popular stage from its cultural contexts." It was a harbinger of the tradition—

Act 4, scene 4. Gower stands before Marina's monument, dumb show in the background. University of Michigan Library.

eventually practiced by generations of playwrights (and, it is implicit, literary critics)—of imagining "that popular drama could be a purely aesthetic phenomenon, free from history and historical determination" (147).

Mullaney's criticism aside, it is interesting to note that the postmodern *stage* seems to have provided a slightly more hospitable home for the disunified *Pericles* than has the poststructuralist publication. Though in the modernist era, new interpretations of the play tended to appear on the page decades before they found their way to the stage, it seems clear that deconstructive, postmodern productions of *Pericles* have preceded poststructuralist critiques: that it is the director who has seized the initiative.

Peter Sellars has frequently been referred to as a "deconstructionist," and perhaps no director has worn the mantle so deservedly. Since his first professional productions in the early 1980s (such as *Pericles* in 1983), he has brought to bear an interpretive method that flies in the face of orthodox directorial objectives, such as unity of concept, clarity of plot, and historical consistency. Loosely paralleling the doctrines of Derrida and Foucault, Sellars's is a methodology that favors multiplicity over unity, the excitement of the individual moment over the cogency of the whole, the clash of competing discourses over the search for a central meaning. He has declared that "we live in a world that is about simultaneity and contradiction,"[10] and the jarring juxtaposition of disparate elements is apparent in virtually every aspect of his production work.

For instance, his productions almost invariably contain a mixed bag of often contradictory historical references, as he tries to incorporate into them a "deliberate notion that time is circular, which we lost in the early nineteenth century with the invention of photography."[11] Acting styles may differ radically from character to character. The production's tone may fluctuate wildly. Moments of high drama are undercut by juvenile humor, and comedy often contains deep pain. Sellars even fragments the audience's viewpoint. In an attempt to keep the audience from merely sitting and absorbing "predigested culture,"[12] Sellars often intentionally fashions visual imagery that clashes with the action or environment of the play. He calls this "visual counterpoint,"[13] and uses it to call the audience's attention to the choices he is making, to encourage them "to shift focus between the simultaneous worlds of the author and the director"[14] (a clear echo of the self-referentiality of deconstructive criticism—the production is not simply about the text, but about the *production* of the text).

In his interpretation of Shakespeare, Sellars reveals another strong affinity with deconstruction: a special fascination with the flaws in the pattern, the places where unified understanding begins to unravel. As he says:

> My recipe is . . . [to] go through and find the repetitions and obscure passages . . . I also find where Shakespeare has taken a detour . . . I isolate those repetitions, the obscure passages and the detours—and I make *these* the base of the production because these are the things I first resisted.[15]

Because *Pericles* is still generally held to be one of Shakespeare's main repositories of repetitions, obscure passages, and detours, it is not entirely surprising that Sellars gravitated toward it, nor even that he chose it to be the inaugural production of his reign as artistic director of Boston Shakespeare Company. Not only did *Pericles* seem promisingly flawed, but it epitomized Sellars's view of contemporary life as an "image glut, a series of rapid, moving images from every period of civilization."[16] Noting that *Pericles* consists of a conglomeration of diverse influences and styles, Sellars compared the play to a wonderfully eclectic piece of architecture:

> Architecture is one living link we have with a play like *Pericles*, which contains classical, Christian and Egyptian references. Down where I live, near Wall Street, there is a hilarious . . . building with classical, Christian and early Egyptian elements. We're surrounded by this incredible web of references that we never notice.[17]

In his characteristically anachronistic production of *Pericles*, Sellars managed to incorporate all of these references. For instance, he brought a trace of Egypt (or at least the African continent) into the production by casting black actor Ben Halley, Jr. as Pericles and having him played as a "richly-clad African."[18] In the set design (a collaboration between Sellars and Michael Nishball), the play's classical references were reinforced through a series of perspective drawings from Serlio's *Five Books of Architecture* that were projected on the walls (a device which also served to give the already-impressive stage space a startling sense of depth). Perhaps the most important historical reference was the one he seems to downplay in his description of the building: Wall Street itself.

Sellars is not merely a "textual" deconstructionist. Like Mullaney, he is intensely interested in the workings of class and power—specifically in the parallels between the seats of economic power in the play or opera text and the "oppressive class structure that . . . is alive and well . . . in the United States of America."[19] In *Figaro*, he made the parallel clear by placing the Count's abode in the Trump Tower, in *Job* he flanked God with corporate sponsors Mickey Mouse and Donald Duck, and in *Pericles* he made use of the same kinds of analogies. The court of Tyre became a stuffy board of directors (making Pericles' lust for travel and adventure that much more understandable), Simonides was a tuxedoed clown, and the Knights at Pentapolis translated into demonic businessmen. When Pericles suffers his greatest fall from fortune, it too was communicated in present-day economic terms. Upon learning of Marina's supposed death, he signified his catatonic despair by "becom[ing] a kind of imperial wino, snoozing his misery away under a cardboard carton."[20]

It was not only the historical references that clashed. The acting showed similar signs of deliberate fragmentation. Terry Hands had made the observation that the minor characters are sketched in broad strokes and that "Shakespeare's method appears to avoid peripheral involvement in order to focus on Pericles himself." Sellars apparently agreed, using a distinct and separate acting style to highlight Pericles' difference from the people surrounding him. Ben Halley, Jr. was a hugely romantic, almost bombastic figure, sharply contrasting his powerfully resonant voice and razor-sharp articulation to the more prosaic comic mannerisms of most of the other characters. The resulting impression, as Elizabeth Hageman elegantly phrased it, was of Pericles as "a man of glorious rhetoric in a landscape of unreason, of triviality."[21]

Costuming increased the gulf between Pericles and these characters, particularly the device (drawn, perhaps, from Sellars's experience in puppetry and Asian theater) of outfitting all of the evildoers in a variety of plastic masks ranging from the comic to the frighteningly grotesque.

The journey through the "landscape of unreason" began in the court of Antioch (Sellars kept the order of scenes largely intact), and here masks and costuming combined to create an atmosphere at once sinister and sensual. Antiochus, naked except for a series of studded leather bands (and studded leather jockstrap), wore a bearded, bald-headed mask which froze his expression into a perpetual snarl. Played by Henry Woronicz, he stalked the stage aggressively, brandishing a giant sword. His daughter, though unmasked, was in a similar state of undress, wearing only a skimpy white bikini. Jack Kroll of *Newsweek* remarked on the eerie sexuality of the scene, as well as on its connections to contemporary pop culture: "The daughter in her skivvies is as sexy as a Hustler layout; the father looks like Conan the Barbarian. The scene is truly erotic."[22]

From barbarian Antioch, Pericles traveled (equipped with a modern suitcase) to Tharsus, where Tom Foley and Sindri Anderson played a Cleon and Dionyza who were chillingly indifferent to their starving populace. Wearing cartoonish old-age masks, the royal couple "discussed the famine raging in their midst while eating small wedges of food from their forks."[23]

On the shores of Pentapolis, Pericles encountered clownish Fishermen. Wearing colorful ragtag outfits, funny hats, and Pinocchio noses, they ice fished into a trap in the stage and counseled Pericles in broad Gloucester accents. In the court of Simonides, however, the roles were reversed. Though Simonides wore a comic rubber nose to go with his elegant evening wear (a surreal coming-out party was the intended look),[24] in this aristocratic household it was "the mean Knight" Pericles who was the clown. For this scene, costume designer Craig Sonnenberg placed Pericles in a bushy, preposterous crown of laurels and made his "rusty armor" into a torso-length fat-suit (suggesting, perhaps, that he has inherited his father's middle-aged gut?). Dressed in this manner, clutching his emblematic twig, he made a touchingly pathetic suitor, particularly in contrast to the svelte, business-suited Knights. The Knights were both comic and threatening. Wearing red hockey masks and moving in herky-jerky unison, they presented a bizarre picture of deadly corporate conformity. The tournament was staged as a dance contest, with the stiffly stylized disco movements of the Knights eventually giving way before the superior skills of Pericles, who swept Thaisa off her feet with an energetic jitterbugging number. As described by Kevin Kelly, the end of the tournament played "like a sharp satire on chivalry" as "the Knights run offstage in disgrace and are heard hotfooting it through the basement."[25]

The play's most disturbing scenes—as well as its funniest—were probably those set in Mytilene. Here the corporate world once again reared its ugly head, as the major set piece indicating the brothel was a large onstage television set to which its employees sat glued, its flickering light a constant reminder that white slavery was a logical extreme in a world so crassly commercial. The constumes were also disturbing. Pandar sported tennis shoes, schoolboy shorts and blazer, and a pig mask. Boult looked like a syphilitic Dickens villain, dressed in a long frock coat and a pockmarked mask that elongated his nose and twisted his mouth into an evil sneer. The Bawd's faintly ravaged plastic face (fringed by a cheap blond wig) was the most "realistic" in the play, which made it the most chilling, creating the look of a woman whose demeanor had been paralyzed by one too many bad facelifts. Lysimachus journeyed to the brothel in a business suit, funny glasses, and a bulbous red nose. Webster A. Stone of the *Harvard Crimson,* who had mixed feelings about Sellars's masks, felt that in this scene they helped solve one of the trickiest moments in the play: "When Lysimachus removes his mask repenting of his past ways, the easy gimmick becomes a tour-de-force."[26]

Stone (along with most of the other critics) was less positive about the production in general. One of the main problem areas cited by critics was the acting. Coming into Boston Shakespeare, Sellars inherited what was essentially a semiprofessional pick-up company, with a few veteran performers sprinkled among a corps largely made up of Harvard undergraduates and recent graduates. Unable to afford very many guest actors of Halley's caliber, Sellars was guaranteed an uneven level of performance—undoubtedly the one type of fragmentation he did *not* intend. Sandra Shipley's "lovely"[27] Thaisa emerged unscathed, and Halley was generally admired—though Stone called him "a stiff, operatic James Earl Jones" whose "manner is too rigidly classical and neither dramatic nor human." From there it generally went downhill. Sellars had the inspired notion of casting Boston street performer Brother Blue in the role of Gower, but the result was, in the words of Kevin Kelly, "a good idea gone slightly awry." "Brother Blue speaks the lines in his own disjointed manner, and with gestures of a certain arthritic grace," Kelly wrote, "unfortunately, he garbles most of his speeches." An even bigger problem, it seems, was Jeannie Affelder's Marina. Hageman attributed the production's failure (in her eyes) to Affelder's "wooden" performance, while Stone wrote that she "moves and speaks with soulless uniformity."

It was not only the acting that turned off some of the critics—a general distrust of Sellars's methods was apparent in the reviews. "Postmodern" was barely in the vocabulary of the average reviewer in 1983, and at least two critics viewed Sellars's fragmentation of the play as the result of simple lack of vision or avant-garde pretentiousness rather than as something that might possibly be a valid aesthetic in its own right. Hageman felt that "[the play's] lack of success should be attributed to Sellars's failure to pattern the moods of the play." Stone wrote that "though this production has some innovation, drama and wit, more often it is confused, contrived, disjointed and dull." Only Kroll fully appreciated Sellars's efforts, writing that "the lesser-known Shakespeare plays are a Pandora's box crammed full of surprises. Sellars dives into this box like a child discovering all sorts of treasures." Citing the great diversity of the Elizabethan audience[28] (consisting at once of "'groundlings' having fun" and "more 'refined' types being turned on the deepest profundities of art"), Kroll astutely ascribed the director's eclecticism to a desire to make the play accessible on different levels simultaneously. Kroll found this "double-dip Shakespearean power" in evidence throughout the production: the scene at Antioch "mixes melodrama and poetry in just the right fizzing proportions"; the brothel scenes "mix bawdiness and chastity in a blend of Mel Brooks vulgarity and John Keats romanticism"; "from the skid-row imagery" of Pericles' despair "Sellars moves with tremendous emotional force to the great reunion scene."

For Kroll, then, this fragmented, disunified *Pericles* was not ultimately incoherent. Sellars, like many critics influenced by deconstruction, does not follow a Derridean party line, eschewing the possibility of meaning altogether. Rather, he aims at a clash of multiple meanings, at what Amy S. Green calls postmodernism's "new model of coherence, a coherence based on tensions, oppositions and flux,"[29] and Kroll's reaction suggests that he may have achieved it.

Of course, not everyone found coherence in this *Pericles*, but it is a testament to Sellars's skill in blending elements of humor into the production (and perhaps to the relative sophistication of his jokes) that there was little misreading of his efforts as mere pandering to the masses or simple parody of the play. Kevin Kelly remarked that "this just may be the funniest *Pericles* of all time," but he never saw fit to question Sellars's seriousness of intent.

Michael Greif, who directed *Pericles* at the New York Shakespeare Festival in 1991, was not quite so fortunate. Sellars may have benefitted somewhat from the respect and tolerance that a small city could be expected to bestow on a resident nascent hero of the avant-garde. The New York critics, on the other hand, showed no such reticence, having already sharpened their teeth on postmodern Shakespeare by the time of Greif's production. In 1989, the Festival had produced *Cymbeline*, staged by new artistic director JoAnne Akalaitis as a "Romantic fantasy set in Victorian England" and presented as a collage of discordant images and viewpoints drawn from the vivid, overheated nineteenth-century imagination. This production has become almost legendary for the loud and vicious media shouting match it incited between most of the city's newspaper reviewers, who excoriated it, and a group of scholars, who rallied to its defense in the pages of *American Theatre*.[30] To the critics, the show's fractured, anachronistic perspective marked it as pure cartoon parody, a director indulging in a series of what Frank Rich called "sniggling music-hall gags at the play's expense."[31] Clive Barnes labeled it a "misreading so ignorant as to be effectively beneath consideration,"[32] and John Simon called it "staggeringly, unremittingly, unconscionably absurd."[33] In return, scholar Elinor Fuchs ridiculed the New York press at length for their own ignorance of this new aesthetic of fragmentation, one which consciously sought to give the audience "a multiple and decentered way of understanding the world and our own subjectivity . . . [and to] demand that [they] respond to many 'texts' at once."[34] In the same issue, James Leverett mocked the critics for their devotion to the "shrine of unity," which he defined as "the narrow set of aesthetic criteria that ultimately serve to mask the pernicious operations of social power and privelege."[35]

Not quite the same firestorm was ignited by Greif's *Pericles*. Yet in its wildly anachronistic settings and costumes and its violent changes of mood and tone, it was a production every bit as fragmented and decentered as Akalaitis' *Cymbeline*. In some ways, his visual framework was even more eclectic than Akalaitis's, blending historical references drawn from a period spanning over a thousand years. Greif did, however, pattern his history slightly more formally than did Akalaitis her crazy quilt Victoriana. If there was any ruling visual concept for Greif, it was the idea of Pericles' journey as a trip through time as well as space. Beginning in a primitive Antioch (circa 200 B.C.), he moved the story through the ages in a not-quite-linear fashion until he reached a Mytilene, which closely resembled contemporary Miami Beach. Mirroring this progression even as he guided the audience through it was Gower, who began the night draped in a robe-like piece of canvas and ended it looking like a "suave, sport-jacketed Harry von Zell."[36]

Throughout all of these radical shifts place and time, the stage space remained remarkably simple. Giving the play a seashore motif, designer John Arnone placed the action in a pit of sand backed by a series of sliding screens, which could be changed to indicate each new setting. It was, however, a distinctly artificial seashore, for like Sellars, Greif lost no opportunity to call attention to his artistic process, to expose the theatrical under-pinnings. The offstage characters sat on folding chairs, clearly visible to the audience ("in hallowed avantgarde cliché fashion,"[37] sneered John Simon). Stagehands moved props and scenery in clear view, even openly operating a thunder sheet and sprinkler during the storm scene.

Within this spare theatrical frame, however, the combination of Arnone's assorted properties and backdrops and the "style-jumping flair"[38] of costume designer Gabriel Berry made each setting thoroughly unique. In Antioch, the characters were "swathed in Roman era cloths and drapings,"[39] as hooded corpses hung behind them and an ominous jet of flame periodically blasted out of the floor. Tharsus appeared to be a French North African protectorate, with Steve Mellor's Cleon in a fez and black actress Saundra MacLain sporting a leopard-skin leotard (a combination that simultaneously managed to suggest a contemporary American Shriner and his tacky suburban wife). Pentapolis was played in the broadest comic fashion. It featured a medieval "jousting tournament à la Monty Python,"[40] hosted by a goofball Simonides in a blonde Prince Valiant wig. The six knights were represented by a cardboard cut-out (with one actor sticking his head through different neckholes to play the different characters), which knocked over furniture and other actors as it was clumsily manipulated by stagehands. The brothel was peopled with "seedy beach rats" with Brooklyn accents and decorated with a sign announcing "We welcome only guests using condoms." Like Sellars, Greif supplied his brothel with a television, but the statement it made was somewhat less subtle, as it continually broadcast the Clarence Thomas hearings.

In general, the critical response to Greif's postmodern treatment was harsh. Interestingly, it was not quite as caustic as the venom to which Akalaitis had been subjected. Perhaps the critics who had pilloried *Cymbeline* had been chastened by the unexpected counterattack in *American Theatre*, but more likely a "travesty" of *Pericles* seemed less of a call to arms (Frank Rich opened his review by saying: "People may not hold their noses at the mere mention of . . . *Pericles,* but at the very least they shrug their shoulders"[41]). Otherwise, much of the critical reaction was nearly identical: a somewhat muted version of the same antipostmodern rhetoric. The primary objects of scorn, predictably, were the production's apparent lack of coherence and its apparent lack of seriousness, two qualities that seemed to the critics to go hand in hand. As Rich wrote:

> Since *Pericles* is a hodgepodge, there is nothing wrong in principle with Greif's own leapfrogging, or if you will, post-modern approach. But the . . . constant about-faces in tone tell the audience early on that there is no blazing passion underlying the director's conceits, no personal vision that might weave the loose threads into a magical, dreamy tapestry.

John Simon also made the facile equation that anachronism and change of tone equal parody (he called the former "the easiest theatrical jape") and complained that "you do not save a romantic yet serious play, flawed as it may be, by camping it up." Howard Kissel, whose *New York Post* review was entitled "More Parody Than *Pericles*," attacked both director and audience by declaring that Greif's discordant style "is probably a logical choice for the T.V. generation, for whom coherence is not a priority. Accustomed to the disjointed style of sitcom, they are contented to settle for a few yocks and not worry too much about how it all fits together."[42] Even some of the show's supporters proceeded on the assumption that Greif's approach was intentionally tongue in cheek. Michael Feingold, after spending several paragraphs mocking the kind of academic solemnity that could have produced the *Pericles* of Terry Hands, congratulated Greif for taking "this overladen tale in the playful spirit in which it was intended." David Sheward opined that "director Michael Greif has wisely decided that the only way to go with material like this is to stage it as a joke, since it is impossible to perform with a straight face."[43]

Greif, who felt he was taking the play very seriously, was surprised by the charges that he had directed a parody. And he was equally puzzled by the notion that he had intentionally rendered *Pericles* incoherent. In a recent interview, he said, "I didn't set out to create a 'postmodern' *Pericles*. I was simply trying to bring out what I saw in the play."[44] What he saw in the play, deep down, was something vaguely approaching unity: "My approach was to take each scene at its own face value and play it for all it was worth, but at the same time the whole play represents the journey of Pericles. It is an *oblique* journey—it doesn't move in a straight line—but there is a mythic journey which runs through all of the scenes." Greif's invocation of the word "myth" is surprising, but his preparatory reading included large doses of Carl Jung and Joseph Campbell, and several of the conclusions he reached regarding the play were not much different than those of his modernist predecessors. For instance, Greif saw woven into the play the same counterpoint of contrasting characters that Daniels had identified, and like him, he chose to accentuate this pattern with the use of thematic doubling. Greif had followed Daniels in casting the same actress (Martha Plimpton) as both Marina and the Daughter of Antiochus, but he even came up with some interesting new combinations, with Bobo Lewis playing both the Lychorida and the Bawd, and Byron Nelson doubling as Antiochus and Simonides.

This last contrast was especially important to Greif. Like a number of structuralist critics, he saw the "bad father" Antiochus and the "good father" Simonides as perfect reverse reflections of each other, polar opposite guideposts on Pericles' journey, and he tried to emphasize that both in his casting and his staging. It was perhaps the slapstick "tomfoolery"[45] at Pentapolis that had been seized on most frequently by detractors, but Greif argued that the broad comedy of the scene was not intended as diversion but was in fact thematically essential. It is not uncommon to hold up Pentapolis as the counter-reflection of Antioch. In this scene, both Hands and Daniels played up the sense of chivalry, honor, and human kindness that were so noticeably absent in the opening scene. But Greif went much farther. Taking the idea that the tournament the audience sees could be one that is totally colored by Pericles' imagination, Greif presented it as an *idealized* vision of the tournament. In other words, in order to banish the shadows of the first scene, his Pericles conjured up "an adolescent cartoon fantasy,"[46] a Pentapolis which in its total buffoonery, its complete lack of seriousness, existed as the ultimate remedy for the gloom of Antioch.

In Greif's judgment, however, this concept was only partially successful. Just as many people had a hard time adjusting to the multiple viewpoints and subjectivity of Akaliatis's Victorian kaleidoscope, many of the audience and critics of *Pericles* were thrown by the farcical treatment of the scene. "I don't think the audience really got the connection [to the earlier scene]," admitted Greif. Part of the problem, he felt, was the fact that Antioch had not been made nearly sinister enough to justify the extremity of its antidote—its menace was no competition for the delirious comedy that followed a few scenes later. The other problem was that the scene at Pentapolis was "*too* funny—it kind of overwhelmed the production. The audience though they'd caught the tone of the whole production, and they just *expected* to laugh after that scene." Such a reaction from the audience then made it difficult to lure them back into the scenes that he wished to treat more seriously. Rich agreed with Greif's assessment, blaming the "unmoving" reconciliation scene on "the jokey tone of the sequences preceding this reunion," which "make it impossible for the actors to raise the production's emotional temperature at that late juncture, no matter how hard they try."

Greif's use of film clips during the latter portions of the play also provoked controversy. During Marina's kidnapping, an old black-and-white movie showing pirates swarming onto a galleon was projected onto the back wall, and the dumb show in which Pericles reacts to the news of his daughter's death was treated as a silent film, with an overly made-up Campbell Scott (the actor who played Pericles) shown soundlessly wailing and tearing his hair. Greif conceded that the first clip was unnecessary and "gimmicky" but defended the dumb show as an integral part of another throughline in the production. Like Sellars, Greif endowed his production with a certain postmodern self-referentiality, asserting that "*Pericles* is a story that is partly about the act of storytelling, and I was interested in looking at the different ways we have of doing that." To that end, he had Don R. McManus, as Gower, explore a variety of different styles of delivery as he moved through the ages. "When we got to this particular dumb show," said Greif, "we realized that we were at the point in history—early Hollywood—where we really *had* dumb-shows. [The silent movie] was one of the most important ways we told stories."

Though some of Greif's throughlines remained obscure—either through audience misperception of his ideas or uncertain execution of them—for many the journey of Pericles did seem to chart a coherent course through the rapidly changing styles, settings, and periods, thanks largely to the performance of Campbell Scott. Scott (the son of George C. Scott and Colleen Dewhurst) brought a combination of gentle intelligence and boyish charm that was admired by nearly all the reviewers. For Feingold, he was the production's "constant still center of virtue and integrity." Robert Simonson wrote that "Scott's steady-as-he-goes performance provides the center that holds this capricious dramatic universe together."[47] David Richards echoed these sentiments, noting that "without Mr. Scott's solid and reliable performance, the production would be doomed by its determination to go off in a dozen different directions."[48]

Not all of the actors fared as well with the critics, most of whom found the general performance level to be as diverse as the rest of the production. Richards declared that "in keeping with Pericles' peregrinations, the acting is all over the place," while Clive Barnes complained that the performances "veered narrowly between the painlessly mediocre and the painfully inadequate."[49] The most intense criticism was saved for the Marina of Martha Plimpton. Greif consciously chose "to defy the cliché that says she is a passive, demure creature." Instead, he and Plimpton strove to find the edge to Marina, "the anger and spirit of an adolescent who has just been deprived of the closest thing to a parent she has ever known."[50] The choice was a risky one, and not many critics were pleased to lose the traditional angel of innocence. Jan Stuart noted that "the bullish Plimpton tends to browbeat others into virtuosity [sic] rather than win them over to it," though she did, he added, "save the character from blandness."[51] Richards called her "a frightful scold, for a creature whose purity is supposed to speak for itself," while Feingold was harsher still: "Martha Plimpton's Marina is nothing but a shrill, streetwise tramp—unfortunate, since the script spends so much time praising her demure behavior and silver-voiced musicality." Plimpton did have at least two defenders in John Michael Koroly, who felt that her "gutsy, fiercely confident interpretation of her character saves it from becoming just another virtuous maiden,"[52] and Mimi Kramer, who welcomed the idea of "a beautifully pissed-off Marina."[53]

Kramer was one the production's few wholehearted advocates, one of the few who fully approved of both the play and Greif's treatment of it. Fascinatingly, she identified this *Pericles* as a rare example of *unobtrusive* directorial handling. In Kramer's view, it was the director of *unified* Shakespeare who was guilty of the "sledgehammer" approach, as he tried to straitjacket all the parts of a play into a "self-serving conceit." Contrastingly, Greif's "idea seems to have been to direct each scene in whatever style or with whatever conceit would serve it best." For Kramer, Greif had managed to create a *Pericles* that was anachronistic yet serious, fragmented yet ultimately coherent:

> The current production swings between broad comedy and wild histrionics without ever descending into . . . camp . . . Mr. Greif, who clearly knows what's poignant, what's witty, what's melodramatic, keeps us entertained while never letting us forget the darker strands of the play's fabric.

Gerald Weales of *Commonweal* was equally enthusiastic. Having attended the play with *Theatre Week* critic Elizabeth Osborn, Weales wrote that "the production confirmed both Osborn's faith in the play's essential coherence and my sense of its grand incoherence, and at the same time delighted both of us . . . with no mandatory tone to violate, it vacillates between excessive broadness and touching lyricism."[54] After making note of the thread provided by the play's father/daughter theme (a theme pointed up for Weales by Greif's casting), he closed his review by saying, "Thematic coherence, after all, but that seems of much less importance than the theatrical vigor that Shakespeare and Greif gave to scene after scene."

In the eyes of a few commentators, at least, Greif's postmodern *Pericles,* like that of Sellars, achieved a "coherence of tensions, oppositions and flux."[55] Though the success attained by both directors was mixed, their productions heralded the arrival of a new kind of *Pericles:* one that values the fragmentation of the text, not just as a problem to be "fixed" but as something that is interesting and exciting in itself.

It is, of course, difficult to predict the future of the postmodern *Pericles,* or the poststructural one. It seems fairly safe to say, however, that we have not seen the last of this kind of approach to the play, both on the page and on the stage. The various methodologies that comprise poststructuralism continue to thrive in the academy, and it is almost inevitable that more of its critics will eventually turn their attention to *Pericles*—perhaps when there are no more dominant traditions left to subvert or central plays left to decenter. The road is somewhat harder for postmodern Shakespeare performance. In the theater—particularly the *classical* theater—the grip of tradition tends to unclench more slowly. However, as the information age continues to exacerbate our sense of a fragmented world and as talented young postmodern directors continue to unveil their unique visions of that world, it is not hard to imagine that fractured, fragmented Shakespeare productions will proliferate, and even that fractured, fragmented *Pericles* will continue to assume a more prominent place among them.

Even though it is unclear what lies immediately over the horizon for *Pericles,* the distance it has traveled since the nineteenth century and the perils it has navigated along the way provide an intriguing narrative. It is a voyage filled with fierce battles, with wildly fluctuating fortunes, and at the beginning, even a bit of suspense. The late eighteenth century, where it reemerged into the public consciousness after over a hundred years of neglect, proved an unfortunate launching point, running the play immediately afoul of the influential George Steevens. During its tumultuous passage through the nineteenth century, where it was generally blasted for its refusal to conform to either Victorian morality or the realist aesthetic, it looked as though it might founder and sink before its journey had truly begun. Fortunately, in the closing years of the century, a hasty inclusion among Shakespeare's "Romances" provided *Pericles* with the hint of a reprieve, as did the miraculously successful stage production of Samuel Phelps.

In the twentieth century, however, the sailing has been considerably smoother, as *Pericles* has seen a remarkable reversal of earlier judgments. In the modern age, with the rise of a new breed of professional, "problem-solving" Shakespeareans capable of unifying absolutely anything (and resultingly, a new critical paradigm which stressed unity at all costs), the most challenging of Shakespeare's "problems" began to take on a new value. Eventually, the stage director (who has always been a problem-solving critic), inspired in part by critical reappraisals, began to fashion powerful and innovative productions that heightened profoundly the esteem of the play.

In recent years, the paradigm of unity and seamless construction has weakened its hold, usurped to an extent by a new interest in fragmentation and deconstruction. Whether this trend holds great promise for *Pericles* is still uncertain. Critical consideration of the play has temporarily (one can only assume) slowed to a trickle, though a couple of recent productions have suggested that a deliberately fragmented approach can be a fruitful one. And alongside these "postmodern" stagings, more traditional productions continue to proliferate. During the winter of 1991-92, no less than four American regional theaters were offering nearly simultaneous productions of the play (Greif's was one), prompting Maggie Kramm of *American Theatre* to write an article on the phenomenon. "This convergence of *Pericleses* isn't really a coincidence," she ventured, "*Pericles* is seemingly a play whose time has come round."[56] Whether this is true remains to be seen, but it is clear that the play has reached a level of importance and esteem that would have once been unthinkable. Not a bad achievement for a miserable fragment.

Notes

[1] Channel surfing is one of the favorite time-wasting activities of MTV's Beavis and Butthead. Female comedians regularly lampoon the adult male's obsessive attachment to the television remote. I am unaware of any popular references to female channel surfers, although there is probably very little basis for ascribing the trait exclusively to males.

[2] Channel surfing as a metaphor for and influence on postmodernism is, of course, not an entirely original concept. For instance, Raymond Williams makes a similar point in *Television, Technology and Cultural Form* (New York: Schocken Books, 1975), 87. Cited in Amy S. Green, *The Revisionist Stage: American Directors Reinvent the Classics* (Cambridge: Cambridge University Press, 1994), 174.

[3] Jacques Derrida, *Of Grammatology,* trans. Gayatri Chakravorty Spivak (Baltimore: Johns Hopkins University Press, 1976), 5. Quoted in Vincent B. Leitch, *Deconstructive Criticism: An Advanced Introduction* (New York: Columbia University Press, 1983), 24.

[4] Howard Felperin, *Beyond Deconstruction: The Uses and Abuses of Literary Theory* (Oxford: Oxford University Press, 1985). Cited in Grady, *The Modernist Shakespeare,* (Oxford: Oxford University Press, 1991) 214.

[5] As Hugh Grady writes, " . . . because Derrida has directed his primary attention to philosophical texts and issues, and because the Yale deconstructors had begun their careers as specialists in the nineteenth century who had early been concerned with reversing New Criticism's valorization of the Renaissance over Romanticism, deconstructive close readings of Shakespeare are among the most prominent texts of neither deconstruction in general nor of contemporary Shakespeare criticism." In Grady, *The Modernist Shakespeare,* 214.

[6] Mullaney prefers the term "cultural materialist" to "new historicist" (xi), and I am not one to question his preference. Grady, in *Modernist Shakespeare*, makes a reasonable distinction between the two schools, stating that new historicism, as typified by the work of Stephen Greenblatt, tends to be fairly apolitical, while cultural materialism is more Marxist inflected. Mullaney's work does seem to focus more on economic power structures than the more generic patterns of "subversion and containment" which characterize new historicism.

[7] Dates given are those of English editions.

[8] Steven Mullaney, *The Place of the Stage* (Chicago and London: University of Chicago Press, 1988), x.

[9] Frederic Jameson, *The Political Unconscious: Narrative as a Socially Symbolic Act* (Ithaca: Cornell University Press, 1981), 148. Cited in Mullaney, *The Place of the Stage*, 140.

[10] In Richard Trousdell, "Peter Sellars Rehearses *Figaro,*" *The Drama Review* 35, no. 1 (Spring 1991): 83.

[11] In Arthur Bartow, *The Director's Voice* (New York: TCG, 1988), 279.

[12] Bartow, *Director's Voice,* 284.

[13] Peter Sellars, quoted in Don Shewey, "'I Hate Decoration Onstage': Peter Sellars Talks About Design," *Theatre Crafts* (January 1984): 24.

[14] Amy S. Green, *The Revisionist Stage: American Directors Reinvent the Classics* (Cambridge: Cambridge University Press, 1994), 149.

[15] Bartow, *Director's Voice,* 277.

[16] Shewey, "I Hate Decoration," 27.

[17] Shewey, "I Hate Decoration," 27.

[18] Elizabeth Hageman, "Shakespeare in Massachusetts, 1983" *Shakespeare Quarterly* 35 (1984): 224.

[19] Quoted in Green, *Revisionist Stage,* 154.

[20] Jack Kroll, "Daring to be Different," *Newsweek,* 14 November 1983, 83.

[21] Hageman, "Shakespeare in Massachusetts, 1983," 224.

[22] Kroll, "Daring to be Different," 83.

[23] Kevin Kelly, "*Pericles* with Great Feeling," *Boston Globe,* 13 October 1983.

[24] According to Sandra Shipley, the actress who played Thaisa, in telephone interview, 22 June 1995.

[25] Kelly, "Great Feeling."

[26] Webster A. Stone, "Beyond Interpretation," *Harvard Crimson*, 21 October 1983.

[27] Kelly, "*Pericles* with Great Feeling."

[28] *Pericles* is, of course, Jacobean, if the most commonly held date of composition (1608) is correct, but it was performed in an "Elizabethan" manner: publicly, at the Globe.

[29] Amy S. Green, *The Revisionist Stage: American Directors Reinvent the Classics* (Cambridge: Cambridge University Press, 1994), 177.

[30] December 1989. The response came in the form of two full-length articles—Elinor Fuchs's "Misunderstanding Postmodernism" (pp. 24-31) and James Leverett's, "Why the Critics Turned Savage" (pp. 25, 63-65)—and two shorter commentaries—David Norbrook's "The Cold WarRevisited" (27) and Nancy Graves's "Did Frank Rich Really Look?" (29).

[31] *New York Times*, cited in Fuchs, "Misunderstanding Postmodernism," 28.

[32] Clive Barnes, *New York Post*, cited in Fuchs, "Misunderstanding Postmodernism," 28.

[33] John Simon, *New York*, cited in Fuchs, "Misunderstanding Postmodernism," 28.

[34] Fuchs, "Misunderstanding Postmodernism," 25.

[35] Leverett, "Why the Critics Turned Savage," 63.

[36] Michael Feingold, "By Fire and Water," *Village Voice*, 3 December 1991.

[37] John Simon, "Prince of Tiresome," *New York*, 9 December 1991.

[38] Feingold, "Fire and Water."

[39] Ibid.

[40] L. C. Cole, "The Prince and the Snooper," *New York Native*, 16 December 1991.

[41] Frank Rich, "*Pericles* Hints at Shakespearean Things to Come," *New York Times*, 25 November 1991.

[42] Howard Kissel, "More Parody Than *Pericles*," *New York Post*, 25 November 1991.

[43] David Sheward, "*Pericles*," *Back Stage*, 29 November 1991.

[44] Telephone interview, 19 June 1995.

[45] Simon, "Prince of Tiresome."

[46] Telephone interview, 19 June 1995.

[47] Robert Simonson, "*Pericles, Prince of Tyre*," *Theatre Week*, 30 December 1991.

[48] David Richards, "The Perils of Pericles, a Serial Adventure," *New York Times*, 1 December 1991.

[49] Clive Barnes, "The Perils of the Public's *Pericles*," *New York Post*, 25 November 1991.

[50] Telephone interview, 19 June 1995.

[51] Jan Stuart, "*Pericles* with Postmodern Spice," *New York Newsday*, 25 November 1991.

[52] John Michael Koroly, "*Pericles, Prince of Tyre*," radio review for WRSU-FM, New Brunswick, New Jersey, aired 15-21 December 1991. Transcripts in the archives of the Public Theater.

[53] Mimi Kramer, "Mirabile Dictu," *New Yorker*, 9 December 1991.

[54] Gerald Weales, "The Bard Lives: *Pericles & Night's Dream*," *Commonweal*, 14 February 1992.

[55] Green, *The Revisionist Stage*, 177.

[56] Maggie Kramm, "The Hero Nobody Knows: Five Actors Playing Pericles," *American Theatre*, (June 1992): 10-17.

SEXUALITY AND TRADITION

Kay Stockholder (essay date 1985)

SOURCE: "Sex and Authority in *Hamlet, King Lear* and *Pericles*," in *Mosaic*, Vol. XVIII, No. 3, Summer, 1985, pp. 17-29.

[*In the essay below, Stockholder reveals the thematic ties between* Pericles, Hamlet, *and* King Lear, *arguing that the plays reflect Shakespeare's views on gender roles, sex, and power.*]

The central importance of the family to Shakespeare's plays has been discussed recently by many critics, notably by C. L. Barber who sees religious issues replacing domestic ones as the focus of meaning for Shakespeare's time. He argues that the consequent emotional pressure on the family and particularly on women gave rise to the conflicts that shaped the tragedies. Though his understanding of the problems needing resolution differs from more traditional readings, he agrees with both traditional and with feminist and psychoanalytic critics that the last plays portray resolutions to the conflicts that torment Shakespeare's tragic protagonists.[1] In this essay I will argue through a detailed comparison of *Pericles* to *Hamlet* and *King Lear* that the last plays do not resolve, but rather conceal the conflicts that shape the tragedies, and that the relations among these plays decisively indicate that Shakespeare was entrapped in the attitudes toward sexuality and women with which his protagonists struggle. I hope to show that Shakespeare not only struggled within, rather than cooly portrayed, the ideas and attitudes toward sexuality and women that he inherited from his time, but that these attitudes were also central to his portrayal of issues pertinent to the problems of rule and authority in the commonwealth.[2] The four last plays have many characteristics in common, but I choose to concentrate on *Pericles* both because its parallels to *Hamlet* and *King Lear* are particularly striking, and because its very flaws and unevenness make more visible the impulses that generate the characteristics shared with the more polished *Cymbeline*, *Winter's Tale* and *Tempest*. Also, *Hamlet* and *King Lear*, pinnacles of Shakespeare's early and later achievement, mark stages in a progress from the naturalistic character portrayal of the earlier play through the mixture of naturalism and Manichean symbolism of the later, to the symbolic mode of the late plays that give only devious expression to the passions that shaped the tragedies.

Parallels between the relatively naturalistic worlds of the two tragedies and the highly symbolic world of *Pericles* make it possible to see the three plays as marking stages of a single emotional and intellectual trajectory. That trajectory extended from the tragedies in which wicked women increasingly came to represent evil and corruption, and good women came to represent a redemptive virtue which alone could make possible viable human relations in family, polity and cosmos. The polarized symbolic ladening of female figures stressed the naturalistic framework and psychology of the tragedies until Shakespeare abandoned them in favor of the highly symbolic plots, and relatively single-dimensional characters and remote affect of the late romances. These plays rely on quasi-magical events to achieve a vision of love, family and polity redeemed by a radiantly pure woman coupled with a man of proven worthiness. However, the symbolic action and single-dimensional characters reveal Shakespeare's retreat rather than his release from the associations of sexual corruption and cruelty that cling to images of women. These associations, further, find their primary expression in either overt or covert incest. As this warping of sexuality invades the heart of Shakespeare's portrayals of families it also turns the family, for him the model and source of psychic, political and divine hierarchical harmony, into a nightmare vision in which humanity "preys upon itself like monsters of the deep."

This triangulated reading of the parallels in *Pericles* to *Hamlet* on the one hand and to *King Lear* on the other will function in two directions. Reading *Pericles* in the light of *Hamlet* and *King Lear* allows the light that such a reading emits to play back on features of the earlier plays that otherwise remain in the shadows. Both *Hamlet* and *King Lear* are predominantly naturalistic plays in the sense that the events comprising them do not violate our ordinary sense of causality. The probability with which events flow from the initiating circumstances or "givens" of the works can obscure the emotional or ideological significance of both the events and the initiating circumstances. The dream-like atmosphere of *Pericles* encourages us to interpret the quasimagical events as symbolic of mental, spiritual or emotional states. Therefore the clearly symbolic events of the later play which parallel the seemingly naturalistic events in earlier plays reveal the emotional and ideological significance of the tragedies. Conversely, this approach allows us to see in the probable plots of the tragedies the emotional forces lying hidden in the improbable events and Neo-platonic ideology of *Pericles*.

The situation in which Pericles initially finds himself has strong parallels to that which Hamlet confronts. The ghost calls upon Hamlet to cleanse Denmark of the pollution spreading from his mother's incestuous bed, while Pericles, having discovered the incest between Antiochus and his daughter, finds his country endangered by Antiochus' wrath. Though Hamlet confronts incest more immediately than does Pericles, both react with fear and melancholy, and both must leave their respective countries to fulfill their mission. As well, we encounter both figures as princes rather than as kings. Hamlet's filial status does not overtly signify unwillingness to assume his own maturity. Rather, the circumstances that have deprived him of his throne—Claudius' murder of King Hamlet, his marriage to Gertrude and election to the throne—appear as plot givens. But these broad parallels suggest that the external circumstance also expresses Hamlet's character, a suggestion borne out as well by some structural relations within the play itself. One such relation is the parallel between Fortinbras and Hamlet, both sons of warrior fathers. Fortinbras is also a prince rather than a king, though no reason accounts for his uncle sitting on Norway's throne. The unexplained parallel emphasizes the contrast between Hamlet's and Fortinbras' attitudes toward their fathers' martial values. Fortinbras, who espouses his father's values, acquires full authority at more or less the same time as Claudius' death, which would have empowered Hamlet had he lived. Unlike both Fortinbras and Laertes, Hamlet never makes a bid for power by leading an army to Denmark. Both Fortinbras and Laertes are openly ambitious, while Hamlet's ambition, which he half acknowledges to Rosencrantz and Guildenstern, is obscured by the attention he focuses on avenging, or on failing to avenge, his father's death.

The contrast emphasized by the parallel between Fortinbras and Hamlet relates Hamlet's ambivalent desire to be king to his ambivalence about the martial values his father represents. Though without as much emphasis, Hamlet is as sharply contrasted to Fortinbras as is Prince Hal, on the one hand, and Falstaff on the other, to Hotspur. Whereas Hal wins Hotspur's honors from him before transcending the Feudal ethos on which they are based as he becomes King, Hamlet values the scholar Horatio for having so well "comingled" his "blood and judgment." And as Falstaff, as he contemplates the honorable but dead Hotspur, congratulates himself for remaining alive, Hamlet, though in a different tone, pits the value of honor against the life lost in its pursuit, when he wonders at Fortinbras' thoughtless risk of his own and others' lives "even for an eggshell" (IV.iv.53).[3] While he calls himself a coward in comparison to Fortinbras, he also reflects that "Sure he that made us with such large discourse, / Looking before and after, gave us not / That capability and godlike reason / To rust in us unus'd" (IV.iv.36-39). The combination of Hamlet's intellectual distance from his father's values, and his initial eagerness to "sweep to [his] revenge" shows him as a man divided: on the one hand he judges himself by his father's standards, while on the other he undermines his self-esteem by questioning the standard on which that judgement is based.

The circumstances that Hamlet confronts, and the play's total structure, make military honor the proof of worthiness to rise from filial to paternal status, and from subject to monarch. Hamlet's refusal of martial values therefore renders him in his own eyes unworthy of the crown he seeks. He resolves that conflict only when, despite having had the opportunity, which Claudius previously denied him, to raise an army while out of the country, he declares himself as "Hamlet the Dane," come "naked" (V.i.251) to the kingdom. Having rendered himself defenseless, his definition of himself as the Dane ironically anticipates his death rather than his coronation. Rather than assume authority, he asserts his regal rights only in the dying words by which he gives Denmark's throne to Norway under Fortinbras. Thereby he not only undoes Claudius' diplomacy; he also reverses his father's previous victory over Norway. In a doubly ironic twist Hamlet revenges himself on an idealized father (whose ghost would presumably forever squeak and gibber in the streets of a Denmark rules by a Norwegian king) by conferring the kingdom upon the son of his father's enemy. The irony is pointed when Hamlet receives posthumously from Fortinbras the "solder's music and the rite of war" against which he defined himself.[4]

However, it is Ophelia's grave beside which Hamlet resolves the conflicts among his sense of unworthiness, his animosity toward his father that generates it, and his ambition by simultaneously declaring his sovereignty and his powerlessness. By claiming Ophelia in the grave to which his nakedness will shortly bring him, he intertwines assuming political sovereignty and personal maturity with assuming husband- and fatherhood. The strong parallels between *Hamlet* and *Pericles* will further suggest that Hamlet's dual ambivalence, that can be resolved only by dying, joins to his unacknowledged hatred of his father, his unacknowledged disgust with his own and women's sexuality.

At the beginning of his play Pericles, like Hamlet, is also a prince rather than a king, despite his father having had that title. The omission of any external circumstance to account for his not having fully succeeded his father, along with the generally mythological aura of the play, more directly than *Hamlet* suggests that Pericles' princely status represents his inner unreadiness to assume full maturity. Furthermore, the play's action overtly brings into a single symbolic unit the roles, only tangentially related for Hamlet, of king, father and husband. Until Pericles has found a bride and fathered a child he does not assume authority.

In the first stage of his journey Pericles encounters in Antiochus and his daughter an externalized and distanced version of the "damned" incest that suffuses Hamlet's world with pestilent vapors. Confronting their riddle, Pericles is in the double-bind that for Freud characterizes the human condition—either guilty of incest, or if not, then plagued with guilty desire. Pericles will die if he cannot solve the riddle of Antiochus' incest, but by solving it he first incurs a Hamlet-like melancholy, and then Antiochus' murderous wrath. The combination of his initially mysterious melancholy and the danger he confronts from Antiochus by which he later explains it, suggests in a schematic way Hamlet's melancholy and Claudius' threat to his life.

Hamlet differs from Pericles in that he experiences himself closer to and implicated in the disease of his world. He fears that his imagination might be "as foul as Vulcan's stithy" (III.ii.84), while Pericles' figure remains separate from the evil he confronts. Pericles' quest for a bride, which fills the first half of his play, highlights Hamlet's relation to Ophelia, which, though pervasive, is obscured by the political events that shape the plot. The significance of the seemingly fortuitous connection between Hamlet's loss of Ophelia and of a kingdom emerges in the retrospective light of Pericles' story. Conversely, Hamlet's possibly foul imagination, his fascinated loathing of his mother's sexuality and disgust with Ophelia's, and his doubts about his courage are overt, while Pericles, defining himself as courageous and pure, confronts more unambiguously evil figures. But the parallels between the more naturalistic action of *Hamlet* and the symbolic action of *Pericles* indicate that Antiochus represents both Pericles' association of sexuality with incest and with fear of paternal reprisal. The suffering he undergoes, apparently through misfortune, then, as for Leontes' in the *Winter's Tale,* constitutes a penance for unacknowledged crimes, designed to render him worthy of wife, child and kingdom.[5]

Having encountered an externalized form of his incestuous longings in Antiochus and his daughter, Pericles next encounters an externalized image of the emotional consequences of having associated sexuality with incest. It is as though Hamlet's inner wasteland, that momentarily afflicted Pericles, generates the blighted city of Tarsus. Pericles evades his emotional dilemma by casting himself as princely benefactor who restores the wasteland, as Hamlet was to have cleansed Denmark. But the emotional inadequacy of symbolic action appears in the shipwreck he suffers on leaving Tarsus, which casts him on the shores of Pentapolis divested of his princely garments. Arriving "naked," like Hamlet on his return to Denmark, he receives from the sea his father's rusty armor, which permits him successfully to compete in the tourney for Thaisa's hand. The juxtaposition of events shows him, like Hamlet, associating martial prowess with the paternal approval that allows him to win a bride.

The significance of the parallels as well as the differences between the two plays appears in the analogy between the scene in which Pericles regains his father's armor and the grave-digger scene in *Hamlet*. Pericles encounters on the shores of Pentapolis three fishermen lamenting the shipwreck they have just witnessed. Like the gravediggers in Hamlet, though less wittily, they moralize on the human condition through the imagery of their trade. In further analogy to the gravediggers who unearth skulls, they, casting their net into the sea, retrieve Pericles' father's rusty armor, and, as the grave diggers acquaint Hamlet with Ophelia's death, so Pericles learns of the tourney from the fishermen, the prize for which is the king's daughter. As Pericles dons the armor he emphasizes its symbolic significance when he says that his

> dead father did bequeath to me
> With this strict charge, even as he left his
>   life,
> 'Keep it, my Pericles, it hath been a shield
> 'Twixt me and death'
>
> (II.i.123-26)

Though nothing overtly indicates that Pericles was estranged from his father, the rusty armor suggests a loss more remote than the wreck Pericles has just survived. The dream-like quality of the entire configuration represents the restoration of a damaged relationship. That restoration joins in a single image Pericles' martial and marital success, which becomes the precondition for his intended return to the throne of Tyre. Pericles' marriage to Thaisa therefore results from his implied reconciliation to his father. That connection is made almost overt when Pericles is reminded of his own father by Simonides' regal bearing as he blesses their union. In the sequence Pericles, by reconciling himself to his father's values as represented in the armor, ceases to be the Hamlet-like figure whose association of sexuality with incest renders him impotent to wrest Antiochus' daughter from her father. In becoming instead the conquering hero he proves himself worthy of the king's daughter.[6]

As Pericles overhears and comments on the fishermen's wisdom, so Hamlet also overhears the gravediggers, comments on their acumen, and like Pericles from the fishermen, Hamlet too receives from the gravediggers a memento of his father, but one that symbolizes his rejection of rather than reconciliation to him. The clown establishes the significant connection between Yorick's skull, Hamlet's past, and King Hamlet's honor in war, when just prior to recovering Yorick's skull, he says that he has been a grave-maker from the day that "King Hamlet oe'r came Fortinbras," which was "that very day that young Hamlet was born" (V.i.140, 142). Rather than his father's armor, Hamlet receives the skull of his father's jester, a role much closer than warrior to that which Hamlet plays. His jester's role, and the brooding mind it conceals, make him the antithesis to what we know of King Hamlet, the "valiant Hamlet/ (For so this side of our known world esteem'd him,)" (I.i.87-88). Because Hamlet rejects his father's values the gravedigger scene presages a different future for him than does the fisherman scene for Pericles. Instead of armor cast up by the sea to presage his martial victory, Hamlet receives as an omen of his own death the jester's skull; instead of winning a bride through proof of his valor he vies with Laertes for priority in grief for Ophelia's death, and sends the jester's skull "to my lady's chamber" (V.i.187). The fisherman scene in *Pericles* makes interdependent Pericles' escape from death, his achievement of husband- and fatherhood, and of a kingdom. The parallels between the two scenes reveal the integral relationship between Hamlet's failure to win a wife (except in the tomb), his failure to win a kingdom, his refusal of martial values, and his meditations upon and movement toward death.

These parallels invite a closer examination of the role of women in *Hamlet,* who at first glance seem to have little in common with the polarized female figures in *Pericles*. Gertrude and Ophelia, despite Hamlet's vision of them, are Shakespeare's most ordinary women.

Though Hamlet surrounds them both with images of sexual foulness and corruption, their actions are those of persons who are trivial or frightened. They are so lightly drawn as to leave in question the state of their consciousness, but Gertrude at worst seems "frail," and the most severe reading of Ophelia leaves us with a girl who in confusion and fear betrays Hamlet's trust, and in further confused fear tries to redeem herself for that betrayal by secretly offering herself to him. However, though they are and feel themselves to be powerless, their sexuality is made to represent the something rotten in Denmark that pervades Hamlet's world and imagination. Though no shades either of mocking cruelty or of divine redemption, of hell or heaven, symbolically extend the resonance of their characters, they become emblematic of duplicity and depravity when Polonius and Claudius, having posed Ophelia with a prayer book to entrap Hamlet, moralize on the vignette. For Polonius she illustrates the way in which "devotion's visage" can conceal "the devil himself," and for Claudius she shows the "plastering art" that in concealing the "harlot's cheek" represents his soul. The play leaves a gap between their relatively trivial characters and the association of women's sexuality with betrayal, decay and death.[7]

That gap, along with the parallel circumstances, points to a similarity beneath the obvious differences between the women who populate the protagonists' worlds. Hamlet's mother's incestuous love of Claudius colors his view of all sexuality, necessarily including his own. He most closely approaches a sexual relationship when, disobeying the Ghost's command to leave Gertrude to heaven, he evokes verbally the "rank sweat" of Gertrude and Claudius' "enseamed bed" (III.iv.92) and their "reechy kisses" (II.iv.186). In urging Gertrude to be chaste he tries to cleanse his imagination of sexuality, since he can envision only an incestuous sexuality or sterile sexlessness. But unable to accept a sterile life, and unable to disassociate sexuality from incest, decay and death, he draws Ophelia into the "unweeded garden" of his incestuous imagination and claims her after she, decked in wild flowers, has found a "muddy death."

Pericles' confrontation with incest is at once clearer, and totally externalized. The murky vapors that surround and obscure *Hamlet* and invade its protagonist have solidified into the fairy-tale-like figures of Antiochus and his daughter, leaving to the figure of Pericles an untarnished virtuous heroism. But both figures, to begin their journeys toward maturity, must disentangle sexuality from incest. Hamlet's discovery of an incestuously polluted bed at the center of a sordid world is rendered with emotional probability. In *Pericles* the two components are separated into distinct episodes. Pericles, by solving Antiochus' not too difficult riddle and bringing upon himself the wrath of the competing father, flees his country in order to protect it, only to encounter the mysteriously blighted country of Tarsus. However, the symbolic meaning of that mystery later emerges when Dionyza plans to murder Pericles' daughter, Marina. As the evil woman whose inner corruption emanates blight and corruption, she functions similarly to the more naturalistic figure of Gertrude and to the blacker, more symbolic figures of Goneril and Regan—as well as, to look further down the road, to the more fairy-tale-like figures of Cymbeline's queen and Sycorax.

One detail in particular brings the women in the two plays, so differently characterized, into meaningful imaginative configuration. When Ophelia has refused to see Hamlet and returned his letters, she has betrayed Hamlet's love to the interests of Polonius's political strategies. Hamlet knows that much by the time he encounters Ophelia reading her prayer book, whether or not he also knows that she at that moment is a willing decoy. And whether or not such knowledge would justify his harshness, she, having allowed her attractions to be prostituted to political ends, makes appropriate Hamlet's demand that she get to a nunnery. That phrase, emphasized by repetition, contains the polarized extremities in which Hamlet sees Gertrude's sexuality. Its literal level couples sexual purity with a sterile life, while its colloquial meaning couples sexuality with the corruption and decay that occur when the sun "being a god kissing carrion" breeds "maggots in a dead dog" (II.ii.180-83). Those extremes define Hamlet's sexual imagination, making Gertrude's description of the "dead men's fingers" that "liberal shephards give a grosser name" (IV.vii.169-70) and that clung to the drowning Ophelia, an appropriate token of Hamlet's relation to his sexuality. He cannot conceive of a middle-ground whereon sexuality can be both loving and healthily generative.[8] It is therefore appropriate to Hamlet's character that his version of Pericles' tourney for Thaisa is his combat with Laertes at Ophelia's grave, and that his trajectory ends at a point that corresponds to Pericles' loss of Thaisa at sea.

In *Pericles* the opposing images contained in Hamlet's single phrase separately expand into fully developed action. Thaisa, in order to avoid being married to any knight but Pericles, has previously vowed to become a priestess of Diana. As though her words must be fulfilled, she apparently dies in childbirth during a tempest, is thrown into the waves which wash her up on the shores of Ephesus, where for fourteen years she becomes a priestess, living as chastely as Hamlet desired that Gertrude should. In the absence of an explanation for her failure even to think of rejoining Pericles, the literal nunnery acquires symbolic resonance. Meanwhile Marina, having been rescued from Dionyza by pirates who sell her to a bawdy house in Mitylene, gets herself to a nunnery in its colloquial sense. However, her virtue glows so radiantly that, rather than being besmirched, it cleanses the brothel. All of the final restorative action, including the destruction of Cleon and Dionyza's corrupt kingdom, pivots on her purity, the radiance of which alone can purify men's imagination of their own and women's sexuality. Reading this expansion of Hamlet's image back into *Hamlet* shows that Hamlet's world and mind can be cleansed only by female virtue so transcendentally pure that it can be imagined only in a world governed by something other than ordinary causality. Ordinary women in probable worlds can never suffice, and therefore no Hamlet can acquire a wife and become king of an ordinarily healthy and fertile kingdom.

The echo of Hamlet's words in the action of *Pericles* relates the women in *Hamlet* to those in *Pericles*. But the female figures that populate *Pericles* have more in common with those in *King Lear* though they are even less probable and more radically polarized between good and evil. Marina clearly corresponds to Cordelia. Like Cordelia she is separated from her father, and like her she "redeems nature from the general curse/ which twain have brought her to" (IV.vi.207-08). Though the evil women, Antiochus' daughter and Dionyza, are not kin to Marina, Dionyza's threat to Marina's life parallels Goneril and Regan's hatred of Cordelia and their contribution to her death.

The parallels between the women in *Pericles* and those in *King Lear* show that the associations of women with cruelty, obvious in the action and imagery of *King Lear,* are present, though submerged, in the later play. Pericles' visit to the blighted Tarsus, presided over by Dionyza, generates echoes of the cannibalistic horrors associated with sexuality and family in *King Lear.* As Pericles approaches Tarsus, Cleon says that "Those mothers who, to nuzzle up their babes, / Thought nought too curious, are ready now / To eat those little darlings whom they lov'd" (I.iv.41-44), an image that recalls Antiochus' riddle, "I am no viper, yet I feed / On mother's flesh which did me breed" (I.i.64-65). In his rage at Cordelia, Lear says that she will be as welcome to his bosom as "The barbarous Scythian, / Or he that makes his generation messes / To gorge his appetite" (I.i.116-18). The confused generational reversal of the whole play, reflected in the ambiguity of this line, aligns that image with those of Goneril and Regan as pelicans, wolves and foxes. Both plays associate the family with cannibalistic images of children devouring parents and of parents devouring children.

The incestuous elements of *King Lear* are more submerged than they are in *Pericles*. The "kind nursery" (II.i.123) that Lear anticipated with Cordelia is more suggestive of pre-oedipal infantile feelings. However, the overt incest of *Pericles* casts into relief the eroticism of *King Lear*, which in view of the fact that Lear confronts only daughters-*cum*-mothers can not be other than incestuous. Lear's abdication is associated with Cordelia's marriage by both events composing a single occasion. Lear emphasizes the connection between the two events by describing the ways in which the "vines of France and milk of Burgundy" (I.i.84) strive for Cordelia's hand, as he asks for her declaration of love. Some incestuous suggestion appears when, despite declaring herself inarticulate, Cordelia echoes the marriage ceremony in saying that she will "obey you, love you, and most honour you" (I.i.98). The implied incestuous feeling becomes more overt when Lear says that he will go to Cordelia "like a smug bridegroom" (IV.vi.200). Cordelia's figure in this way acquires tinges of incestuous sexuality, but her exile from the stage preserves her halo. The association of corrupt sexuality and sadistic cruelty with incest, as well as with illegitimately exercised authority, appears instead in the configuration formed by Goneril and Regan's abuse of power and their convoluted sexual relationship to Edmund.

The incest underlying Lear's vision of both sexuality and corrupt authority appears when Lear, on the heath, enjoins the gods to discover and punish the various crimes of their enemies. The play makes overt all the crimes, save only the incestuous "simular of virtue" (III.ii.54). Lear's abrupt mention of incest explains the gap in logic between his invocation of social evils and his self-justifying declaration that he is "more sinn'd against than sinning" (III.ii.59). The dramatic context, in which the storm is both an image of his rage and the consequence of his failings as King, makes his own the "pent-up" guilts that he says have generated the punishing storm. As though in horrified recoil from the pit of shame opened by his catalog of sins, instead of confessing his sins, he proclaims his relative innocence. The evil in himself, the knowledge of which he here avoids, is related to the dominant images of evil in the play, the figures of Goneril and Regan, whose sexuality is equated with the devil: "But to the girdle do the gods inherit, / Beneath is all the fiend's" (IV.vi.128-29). But as it was Lear's flesh that "begot these pelican daughters," so Lear's psyche is reflected in the clustered association of cruelty, misused authority and illicit sexuality which comprises their figures.[9] After having acknowledged his abuse of authority and penetrated the foul smells of his own birth through the "sulphurous pit" beneath women's girdles, he demands an "ounce of civet" to "sweeten" his imagination (IV.vi.133-34). The imagery suggests that he exiled Cordelia to keep her uncontaminated by his imagination which, like Hamlet's, is as "foul as Vulcan's stithy." Proximity to him would befoul her image, and rob nature of the ideal feminine purity that alone can redeem both male sexuality and authority.[10] The parallels of *Pericles* to *King Lear* show that the tempests, shipwrecks and betrayals by which Pericles loses both Thaisa and Marina—so soon after acquiring them— conceal and express his continuing incapacity to remain close to them without sullying the associated image of redeeming purity. The symbolic step he made toward women and authority when he accepted his father's armor and won Thaisa's hand has failed to excise from his vision of women and family hidden associations with incest and its correlate infusion of all sexuality with the odor of disease and crime.

The later action of *Pericles* parallels that in *King Lear* as the early action parallels that in *Hamlet*. The transition occurs when Simonides pretends displeasure with Thaisa for being so "absolute" in her choice of Pericles, and for "Not minding whether I dislike or no" (II.v.19-20). Daughter and father each pretend to frustrate the other's desire in a playful and somewhat flirtatious version of Cordelia's catastrophic disobedience. Simonides' mock-tyranny is a pale version of Lear's rage at Cordelia for giving him only "half [her] love." Having lost Cordelia to another king, Lear embarks on an inner journey through desolate isolation and victimization. Instead of dying, like Hamlet, when he loses his women, Pericles passes in an instant from the threshold of a mature sovereignty and fatherhood to a Lear-like simulacrum of old age and impotence. Having been with Thaisa only long enough for her to bear a child, he loses her to a tempest, and he loses his daughter Marina, who will become a double of Thaisa, by giving her away to Dionyza and Cleon. Having left Marina at Tarsus, he declares that "Till she be married, madam, / By bright Diana, whom we honour all / Unscissor'd shall this hair of mine remain, / Though I show ill in't" (III.iii.27-30). The images that describe Pericles when he visits what he believes to be Marina's tomb in Tarsus, though they lack the deep resonance of those in *King Lear,* recall Lear's travail on the health. Gower tells us that Pericles swears "Never to wash his face, nor cut his hairs. / He puts on sackcloth, and to sea. He bears / A tempest, which his mortal vessel tears, / And yet he rides it out" (IV.iv.27-31). The disproportion between the seemingly casual way in which he decides to leave Marina at Tarsus and the depths of feeling suggested by his symbolic entry into old age suggests that the action represents otherwise unexpressed emotion. Lear's fierce ambivalence toward Cordelia, his quick reversal from a warm vision of himself in her care, to one of himself as the "Barbarous Scythian," has been reduced to Pericles' minor uncertainty about whether to press on to Tyre or to leave Marina at Tarsus, and Lear's victimization by his cruel daughters has similarly been reduced to Pericles' self-imposed disfiguration. The events too are softened, but remain parallel. Cordelia's death corresponds both to Thaisa's seeming death and to Marina's near death at Dionyza's hands.

While Pericles for a second time wanders the seas, to be brought by good fortune or secret fate to the shores of Mitylene, Marina has demonstrated in the brothel her fierce Cordelia-like integrity that threatens to put bawdy-houses out of business. She wins the admiration of the governor Lysimachus by being able, like Miranda, to make men "as cold as a snowball" (IV.vi.140). The ambiguity that surrounds Simonides in relation to his daughter also surrounds Lysimachus in relation to Marina, for though he declares that no low intention brought him to the brothel, it is not clear what else might have done so. However, only after Marina's shimmering purity has proven its power to transform men does Pericles arrive at Mitylene to be discovered in prostrate catatonia by Lysimachus and other lords. Their discovery of him parallels the soldier's discovery of Lear decked in wild flowers, and just as Cordelia rains on Lear the medicinal drops of her compassionate tears, so Marina's beatific virtue that cleanses men's low sexuality is to Pericles the "sacred physic" that heals both body and soul. Both scenes are suffused with the aura of transformation and regeneration. Pericles asks Marina, "But are you flesh and blood?" (V.i.152) as Lear wonders if he is already in heaven, and both figures are prepared in fresh garments for regenerative sleep amidst healing music.

Lear challenges guilt and approaches, for a blissful moment before her death, a lover-like union with Cordelia, thereby disassociating sexuality, for that moment, from guilt and punitive cruelty. That union hints at the restored youth that will be bestowed on Pericles when Lear says "I kill'd the slave that was a-hanging thee," and "I have seen the day, with my good biting falchion / I would have made them skip" (V.iii.274, 276-77). But whereas Lear dies dreaming that Cordelia lives, Pericles wakes to the "rarest dream" of Marina's actual life, and is restored to youth when he washes, shaves and is reunited, guided in a dream-vision by the chaste Diana to Thaisa, Marina's double as well as her mother. Symbolically their reunion restores both inner and outer wastelands by rescuing sexuality and fertility from the corruption of the brothel, and purity from the sterility of the nunnery. But only amidst psychologically improbable characters and fantastic events can Pericles have a wife. A trace of the same feelings that in a probable world would associate women with incest and corrupt authority appears when Pericles decides not to return with Thaisa to Tyre as King and Queen. Instead Marina and Lysimachus will reign there while he and Thaisa will rule in Pentapolis. Like many other events of the play—the many years during which Pericles leaves Marina in Tarsus, Thaisa's long sojourn in the nunnery—this one also lacks a naturalistic explanation. That gap, when filled with the motivations suggested by the parallels among the plays, allows us to see Pericles as one who secretly is identified with the evil figures who appear to be external to him. He cannot return to his own kingdom and assume his rightful power because ideological solutions do not resolve psychic dilemmas.

The foregoing discussion of the psychological dynamics of these plays has not assumed authorial intention. But parallels among the motifs that are clearly within Shakespeare's conscious intentions support this comparative reading. Hamlet, in his probable world, describes his father, and by implication himself, as a moderately good man trying to survive amidst corruption and duplicity. Only at the end does he place his trust in a divine providence that seems to assist him in accomplishing his mission. Both *King Lear* and *Pericles* shape their protagonists' fate around the question of whether the world makes manifest divine justice. The gothic chambers of Lear's relatively probable world, in which an extraordinarily good Cordelia can be defeated by the extraordinarily evil Goneril and Regan, echo with that question. Pericles' improbable world, at the center of which is Marina's power to sweeten the male imagination, leaves no question of the gods' justice. As Antiochus and his daughter received the "due and just reward" for their "monstrous lust" (Epilogue), when struck by lightning, so Cleon and Dionyza's outraged subjects burn them in their palace. But the very improbability of the events which assert divine justice casts doubt on its possibility, a doubt that also attaches to the emotional veracity of the envisioned restoration of love and family.

Both on the abstract level of authority and justice, and on the more immediate one of sexuality and familial feeling, the visionary conclusion conceals the conflicts that shaped the tragedies. It reveals that for Shakespeare nature itself was the price of redeemed nature. Pericles conceals the aura of sex-loathing in the flattened and fairy-tale figures, but the parallels in character, action and language to that in the more emotionally immediate tragedies reveal that only the most strenuous control prevents the vision of radiant female perfection from betraying its origin in its own opposite. However, it implies no denigration to say that Shakespeare failed to give restored and transcendent life to the golden statues that emerged from Romeo and Juliet's tomb, for not even the greatest authors can stand outside of their history. Rather, I think that Shakespeare's struggle with the ideas and values of his time was deeper than that of ordinary mortals, and was transformed in his art into depictions, specifically, of the emotional cost for men of making women into symbols of good and evil, and, generally, of how humanity struggles in the toils of its own ideas and values.

Notes

[1] C. L. Barber, "'Though that begetst him that did thee beget': Transformation in *Pericles* and *The Winter's Tale*," *Shakespeare Survey*, 22 (1969), 59-68, and "The Family in Shakespeare's Development: Tragedy and Sacredness," in *Representing Shakespeare: New Psychoanalytic Essays*, ed., Murray M. Schwartz and Coppélia Kahn (Baltimore, 1980), pp. 188-202.

[2] Arthur Kirsch, *Shakespeare and the Experience of Love* (Cambridge, 1981), argues that for Shakespeare "erotic disorder is disorder in the kingdom" (p. 148).

[3] All quotations are from the Arden Editions of Shakespeare's works.

[4] K. R. Eissler, in *Discourse on Hamlet and "Hamlet"* (New York, 1971), p. 113, thinks Hamlet's success in reaching maturity is represented by Fortinbras' accession to the crown.

[5] Coppélia Kahn, *Man's Estate: Masculine Identity in Shakespeare* (Berkeley, 1981), p. 212, sees the father-daughter incest as a projection of mother-son incestuous impulses, and sees Pericles as a guilty son punished by a providential tempest for sins not dramatized as his.

[6] Leslie Fiedler, *The Stranger in Shakespeare* (New York, 1972), p. 217, argues as I do that in Thaisa and her father Pericles encounters a second version of Antiochus and his daughter.

[7] Linda Bamber in *Comic Women, Tragic Men: A Study of Gender and Genre in Shakespeare* (Stanford, 1982), p. 78, also finds the gap between Gertrude's and Ophelia's portrayal and Hamlet's language significant of Hamlet's sexual hatred. She, however, sees his projections as signs of a disintegrating manhood.

[8] Many critics, drawing on the work of D. W. Winnicott, *Playing and Reality* (New York, 1971) and others, see Hamlet's difficulty residing primarily in his failure to reconcile himself to women and to accept the feminine side of himself. See David Leverenz, "The Women in *Hamlet*: An Interpersonal View," *Signs,* 4 (Winter 1978), 291-308; Theodore Lidz, *Hamlet's Enemy: Madness and Myth in Hamlet* (New York, 1975), p. 82; Bamber, p. 90.

[9] The incestuous component of *King Lear* has been noted, in different ways, by many critics. See Myra Glazer Schotz, "The Great Unwritten Story: Mothers and Daughters in Shakespeare," in *The Lost Tradition: Mothers and Daughters in Literature,* ed. Cathy N. Davidson and E. M. Boner (New York, 1980), p. 47; Meredith Skura, "Interpreting Posthumus' Dream from Above and Below: Psychoanalysts and Literary Critics, "in *Representing Shakespeare*, p. 205.

[10] Lorie Jerrell Leininger, in "The Miranda Trap; Sexism and Racism in Shakespeare's *Tempest*," in *The Woman's Part, Feminist Criticism of Shakespeare,* ed. Carolyn R. Lenz, Gayle Greene and Carol Thomas Neely (Urbana, 1980), pp. 285-94, is critical of the symbolic freighting of chastity and lust to represent all virtue and vice in *The Tempest*.

Lorraine Helms (essay date 1990)

SOURCE: "The Saint in the Brothel: Or, Eloquence Rewarded," in *Shakespeare Quarterly,* Vol. 41, No. 3, Fall, 1990, pp. 319-32.

[*In the following essay, Helms traces the literary precedence of* Pericles*'s Marina, discussing subtle differences in attitudes towards the commodification and patriarchal control of a woman's sexuality.*]

The fifty-third declamation in Lazarus Piot's 1596 translation of Alexander Silvayn's *The Orator* tells a tale "of her who having killed a man being in the stewes, claimed for her chastity and innocencie to be an Abbesse." The narrative is prefaced by an imperative statement in the guise of a law: "The order of the religious women is such, as they must be pure, chast, and free from all crime, but the Abbesse must be the chastest of all the rest." The declamation that follows subjects this fictive law to a narrative that challenges its implicit definitions of chastity and purity: "It chanced that a certaine yoong Nunne of Naples was to saile into Sicilie to be an Abbesse there"; but en route she was captured by pirates, who sold her to a brothel. When clients were brought to her, she persuaded them to give her "the accustomed reward" while leaving her a virgin. A soldier who could not be so persuaded tried to rape her. She killed him with his own sword. She stood trial for murder and was acquitted. Then she sailed on to Sicily, where she "claimed for her chastity and innocencie to be an Abbesse."

Piot's declamation, printed as an analogue to Shakespeare's *Pericles* in Bullough's *Narrative and Dramatic Sources of Shakespeare,* emerges from a nexus of legal, religious, literary, and rhetorical contexts that form the prehistory of the brothel scenes in *Pericles*.[1] The declamation was originally gathered among those of Seneca the Elder as the *controversia* of the *Sacerdos Prostituta*. Like the would-be abbess of Piot's declamation, the Senecan character of the Prostitute Priestess has been abducted by pirates, sold to a pimp, and held captive in a brothel. She has defended herself against rape, first through eloquence and then through homicide, killing the soldier who assaults her. Seneca's *controversia* ends inconclusively, for no court determines whether the Prostitute Priestess is fit for the order of the vestal virgins.[2]

The Senecan motif of the Prostitute Priestess reemerges in Greek romance, Christian hagiography, and Shakespearean drama. In exploring its history, I do not wish to study sources for the brothel scenes of *Pericles,* nor to place the motif within an unvarying discursive tradition. Rather, I intend to explore the relation between the cultural contexts and the structural transformations of the varied texts and performances in which the Prostitute Priestess appears. The Senecan declamation is part of the prehistory of tales of saints and princesses imprisoned in brothels; it reveals an ancient rhetoric of rape in the subtext of romance, legend, and drama. As the motif moves from the quasi-theatrical rhetorical setting of Roman declamation through a textual history in hagiography and romance to its theatrical representation on the Shakespearean stage, generic conventions transform the cultural work of the Prostitute Priestess. In the Senecan *controversia* the declaimers, having created a conflict between a law of religious chastity and a narrative of abduction, attempted rape, and homicide, then test their rhetorical skill by improvising arguments for or against the candidacy of the Prostitute Priestess. Their improvisations forestall narrative closure, continually renegotiating the ideological meaning of the rhetoric of rape. In the narratives of hagiography and romance, authorial closure almost effaces this open-ended rhetoric. The case of the Prostitute Priestess is closed. In *Pericles,* where a performance text again configures the resolution of the narrative, the case is altered. Marina reanimates the figure of the Prostitute Priestess, as the Shakespearean playtext reenacts the Senecan rhetoric of rape.

THE SENECAN RHETORIC OF RAPE

The Roman schools of declamation, originally instituted to train advocates in deliberative and forensic rhetoric, had, under the Empire, become a venue for private performances before an elite audience of aficionados. The forensic oration became a fictional *controversia,* notorious for its artificial style and sensationalized themes; the rhetorical agon became a quasi-theatrical debate in which the declaimers sometimes spoke *ethicos,* in the character of the plaintiff or defendant in a case.[3]

The *controversiae* consisted of a real or fictional law, such as the pontifical rule about the priestess's chastity, and a *narratio,* a sketch of the facts in the case. The narrative is designed to expose conflicts and contradictions in the statute. Seeking their arguments in the gaps and seams of judicial discourse, the declaimers choose one side of the case to argue and then invent rhetorical *colores,* glosses that specify motive and circumstance. In hypothesizing an internal structure for external events, *colores* enable a judge to reach a just—or at least justifiable—decision. Unconstrained by the exigencies of actual cases, the declaimers devised sensationalized themes to test the coherence of real and fictive laws, competing for the most extravagant *colores* and the most ingenious *sententiae.*

Seneca the Elder transcribed the *controversiae* for his nephew, Seneca the Younger, who assimilated their *sententiae* and *colores* into his tragedies. Quintilian, Tacitus, Pliny, Petronius, and Juvenal all condemn the discourse of the declaimers for its self-indulgent delight in ornament and its wanton disregard of realism. "The declamations," Quintilian complains, "which we used to employ as foils wherewith to practise for the duels of the forum, have long since departed from the true form of pleading and, owing to the fact that they are composed solely with the design of giving pleasure, have become flaccid and nerveless: indeed, declaimers are guilty of exactly the same offence as slave-dealers who castrate boys in order to increase the attractions of their beauty."[4]

Senecan declamation emerges from the relentlessly patriarchal contexts of Roman rhetorical culture. Its practitioners as well as its critics structure their discourses through metaphors of gender and violence. The *controversiae* are misogynistic tales of terror that take place in a rhetorical heterocosm peopled by pirates, kidnappers, rapists, cruel stepmothers, and poisoners. Yet the improvisational theatricality of Senecan declamation complicates and to some extent compromises its reproduction of social and legal ideologies. Composed, as Quintilian complains, "solely with the design of giving pleasure," the ludic agon fragments forensic argument and denies juridical closure. In the *controversia* of the *Sacerdos Prostituta,* the narrative premise that interrogates the fictive statute exposes ideological gaps in the representational structure of the declamation itself. The statute reads: "A priestess must be chaste and of chaste [parents], pure and of pure [parents]." The accompanying narrative states:

> A virgin was captured by pirates and sold; she was bought by a pimp and made a prostitute. When men came to her, she asked for alms. When she failed to get alms from a soldier who came to her, he struggled with her and tried to use force; she killed him. She was accused, acquitted and sent back to her family. She seeks a priesthood.

(1.2)

By asking whether there are any circumstances in which an enslaved prostitute can legally become a holy virgin, the declaimers disturb the cultural significations of female chastity and purity; they undermine the patriarchal distinction between virgin and whore by constructing a narrative that deliberately blurs it.

At the center of this declamation lies the question of sexual pollution. In Seneca's transcription of the speech of Cestius Pius, the declaimer insists that the Prostitute Priestess has incurred *stuprum,* the defilement of illicit sexuality. Even if she has retained her virginity, her experience has irrevocably defiled her:

> You offered yourself, a girl in a brothel. Even if nobody outraged you, the place itself did so [*locus ipse violavit*]. You offered yourself with harlots, beautified to please the populace, dressed in the clothes the pimp had provided. Your name hung at the door; you received the wages of sin [*pretia stupri*] . . . the hand that aspired to sacrifice to the gods took immoral gains.

(1.2.7)

For the prosecutors, *stuprum* is a material pollution transmitted through "the place itself." "Pollution rules," writes Mary Douglas, "by contrast with moral rules are unequivocal. They do not depend on intention or a nice balancing of rights and duties. The only material question is whether a forbidden contact has taken place or not."[5]

Pollution rules create sharp boundaries between the pure and the defiled body, boundaries that no question of motive and intention can penetrate. Another declaimer, Publius Asprenas, quarantines the polluted body of the Prostitute Priestess by policing the boundaries between the sacred space of the temple and the profane space of the brothel: "Once you enter a brothel, all temples are closed to you" (1.2.10). Publius Vinicius, also speaking against her, alludes to her motives only to dismiss their significance: "Do you regard yourself as chaste just because you are an unwilling whore?" (1.2.3).

The advocates of the Prostitute Priestess, however, posit an internal purity that eludes *stuprum:* "I guarantee," swears Pompeius Silo,

> a priestess whom no bad fortune can make unchaste. Some women can be forced to it by slavery: she served barbarians and pirates, remaining inviolate in their hands. Some women can be depraved by the evil habits of a decadent age . . . she will remain chaste to the end. You may put her in a brothel: even through this she managed to carry her chastity away untouched.

(1.2.20)

While those who argue against her equate the woman's defilement with the material circumstances of her imprisonment, her advocates stress the discrepancy between her invincible chastity and the physical conditions of the brothel. By insisting on internal purity, they create a precondition for an argument based on rules of morality.[6]

In the arguments of those who speak against her, sexual defilement carries with it all other forms of pollution. Interpreting her act of homicide, Publius Asprenas argues: "You consorted with men who were murderers, smeared with human blood: hence, of course, your ability to kill a man" (1.2.9). Rather than survive by killing, a woman so defiled "could," as Publius Vinicius puts it, "do nothing more upright [*nihil honestius*] than to die" (1.2.3). If death demonstrates chastity, then the ability of the Prostitute Priestess to survive implies the *audacia* of sexual license, and her act of homicide convicts her of unchastity. The rapist then is innocent, and his intended victim becomes the criminal: "*Was she justified in killing an innocent man who wanted to employ the body of a prostitute?*" asks Latro. Although she was acquitted of homicide, her trial "showed not that she was pure but that the law could not touch her" (1.2.14).

Again, her advocates distinguish between her internal purity and the material circumstances of her captivity. Albucius presents the homicide in these *colores:*

> There came a man of fierce and violent temperament, sent, I believe, by the gods themselves to put on display the chastity of one destined to be priestess, not to violate it. She told him to keep his hands off her holy body: "You must not dare to harm chastity that men preserve and gods look forward to." When he came rushing to his doom, she said: "Look, your weapon—you do not realise that it is in the cause of chastity that you carry it." And seizing the sword she drove it into her attacker's breast. Those same immortal gods took care that this deed of hers should not go unnoticed; an accuser turned up to bear witness to her chastity in the courts. No-one could believe a man had been killed by a woman, a youth by a girl, one armed by one unarmed. It was too great a feat for it to be supposed to have taken place without the aid of the immortal gods.
>
> (1.2.18)

The Prostitute Priestess acts forcefully by seizing the soldier's weapon. With it she appropriates the phallic power to penetrate another's body. To minimize the risk of this appropriation, Albucius' *color* denies her agency. To credit the gods with the defense of her chastity validates the survival of the Prostitute Priestess without questioning the vulnerability of ordinary women.

Albucius' *color* closes the ideological gap that the figure of the Prostitute Priestess opens; but when the declamation was performed, it was only one among many rhetorical *colores*. The purpose of declamation was not to hold the mirror up to nature but to argue *in utramque partem*. In order to construct a narrative that pushes the legal dilemma to its most sensationalized extreme, the declaimers forgo patriarchal criteria for the realistic representation of women. They endow the Prostitute Priestess with the abilities to speak eloquently and kill ruthlessly. Eloquence and courage, arts and arms, Mercury and Mars: the Prostitute Priestess challenges the male monopoly of these qualities, endeavors, and symbols, and it is for this that she stands trial. The declaimers may call her speech either divine eloquence or meretricious wheedling, her martial skill either miraculous or murderous, and her survival either a triumph or a transgression. Yet the open structure of the declamation subversively suggests that a woman can survive and even triumph in the worst circumstances that the male imagination can devise for her. Consigned to the brothel, she may reinterpret prostitution; elected to the priesthood, she may reinterpret religion. The declaimers cannot debate their conflicting interpretations of their character's status without inadvertently raising the question of her self-interpretation.

THE CASE IS CLOSED

The motif of the Prostitute Priestess has proved as resilient as the character herself, outlasting the legal and religious institutions in which the declamation originated. It endures in two major forms, each with many variants. One is the figure of the virgin martyr from Christian hagiography; the other is the kidnapped princess of Greek romance. As the hagiographers and romance writers adapt the theatricalized agon of rhetorical performance to narrative structures, they jettison the declamatory *argumentum in utramque partem*. Saints' lives and Greek romances present only one side of the argument, exerting narrative authority to close the case of the Prostitute Priestess.

The virgin martyrs, all beautiful and wellborn, are enslaved in brothels for refusing to worship pagan idols or for rejecting pagan suitors. *The Golden Legend* tells the tale of Agnes, who, at the age of thirteen, was sought in marriage by the son of the prefect of Rome. She refused the offer. She was, as punishment, sent to a brothel. But an angel surrounded her with a bright light. When men entered the brothel and perceived this radiance, they offered her reverence. The son of the prefect, like the soldier in the declamations, came to the brothel and tried to rape her. He dropped dead at the edge of the holy light. Although Agnes, through her prayers, successfully resuscitated her would-be rapist, the pagan priests insisted she be burned as a sorceress. But the fire would not burn her, for she prayed; and as she prayed, the flames lost their heat. Finally a lieutenant commanded that she be stabbed with a sword, and thus Agnes achieved her martyrdom.[7]

The saints' lives depart from the story of the Prostitute Priestess most obviously by replacing her act of homicide with martyrdom. Yet the hagiographers have incorporated the advocates' arguments into their narrative premises. Like Pompeius Silo, the hagiographers find that physical contact with the brothel and its inhabitants need not constitute loss of chastity. They also take up Albucius' hint that the Prostitute Priestess escapes miraculously, elaborating on the divine aid that enables a captive to avoid rape.

The hagiographers do not grant complete victory to the advocates, however. In one crucial particular they appear to have taken the prosecutor Publius Vinicius at his word: when placed in a brothel, a woman can do nothing more upright than to die. When this premise is incorporated into the narrative structure, the mortification of the virgin in the brothel becomes the foundation for her sanctification, implicitly challenging the Augustinian argument against the suicide of rape victims. In *The City of God* Augustine condemns Lucretia for choosing suicide after she has been raped by Tarquin. He argues that, though she chose suicide to prove that she had not consented to Tarquin's lust, Christian victims of rape need not die, for they "have within themselves the glory of chastity, the witness of their conscience. They have it also in the presence of their God and need nothing more."[8] But the hagiographers must demonstrate the chastity of their subjects not for the witness of conscience, not before God, but in narratives that will persuade male readers. The survival of the saint would not give her legend an adequate principle of closure, for "the witness of conscience" remains radically inconclusive when the conscience is a woman's and the narrative is a man's. The chastity of the living Prostitute Priestess raises a legal debate; that of the dead saint resolves a narrative dilemma.

When the Prostitute Priestess's aggressive self-defense has been transformed into the Christian virtue of passive endurance, the narrative need no longer ask whether killing one's would-be rapist is justifiable. The Christian martyrs lack the martial skills that made the homicide possible. They lack these skills, at any rate, in the medieval saints' lives. But there is at least a partial exception among the earliest legends. Thecla, whose history appears in the apocryphal *Acts of Paul*, is the prototype of the androgynous saint who exchanges a woman's status for spirituality.

To follow Paul, Thecla cut her hair. She abandoned her family and her fiancé. In the course of her wanderings, she was imprisoned and tortured. She was condemned to be burned in the theatre at Iconium and threatened with wild beasts in the arena at Antioch. When an official of Antioch attempted to embrace Thecla in the marketplace, she "ripped his cloak, took off the crown from his head, and made him a laughingstock." Unlike other virgin martyrs, Thecla went on from Antioch to a full career of preaching in Seleucia, at last ending her life in "a noble sleep."[9]

The unorthodox legend of Thecla, John Anson notes, "possesses at least the verisimilitude of what might be described as a historical fiction," while the legends that emerged from a later monastic culture take place in "a world of pure erotic romance."[10] Unlike the "erotic romance" of orthodox hagiography, the apocryphal history of Thecla (for which its author, a presbyter of the second century, was expelled from the church) remains on the margins of Christian narrative. Like the Prostitute Priestess, a saint who inhabits those margins need not die to defend herself against rape. Thecla's legend incorporates the subversive survival of the Prostitute Priestess into its fictive premises. Like later hagiographies, however, its textual strategies occlude the rhetorical agon of the Senecan advocates and prosecutors. To recover the open interrogation of that agon, the story of the saint in the brothel must be enacted rather than narrated.

"Marina Thus the Brothel 'Scapes"

Death concludes the history of the virgin martyr. In the romance sources and analogues of Shakespeare's *Pericles*, from *Historia Apollonii Regis Tyri* to the *Gesta Romanorum*, Gower's fourteenth-century *Confessio Amantis*, and Twine's *The Patterne of Painefull Adventures*, marriage provides closure for the story of the eloquent virgin imprisoned in the brothel. In all these romances a virgin princess is kidnapped by pirates and sold to a pimp who places her in a brothel. Like the Prostitute Priestess, she persuades the clients to give her alms. The narrators, like the advocates of the Prostitute Priestess, praise her eloquence as miraculous. Her oratory not only preserves her virginity; it reunites her with her royal father and gains her a husband as well.

These narrative romances, like the saints' lives, take up only one side of the argument the declamation raises, recounting the negotiations between the prisoner and her clients rather than disputing their significance. As a virgin in a brothel, the heroine is a woman displaced downward. The royal marriage of the princess, like the martyrdom of the saint, restores order by ceremonially reintegrating her into her proper social status: marriage is the structural equivalent of the martyrs' sanctification.[11]

The tradition of the *Historia Apollonii Regis Tyri*, however, takes the brothel scenes from juridical contexts of violence and death to economic contexts of money and marriage. The princess Tharsia, like the Prostitute Priestess and the saints, is forcibly abducted and held in a brothel against her will, but the violence that underwrites the exchange of women in the declamation and the saints' legends is partly obscured by an emphasis on commercial exchange. Physical force merges with symbolic violence; sexual domination becomes a strategy for economic exploitation.[12]

Like the romances and saints' lives, *Pericles* presents only one side of the declaimers' argument, theatrically representing a valiant virgin whose eloquence and courage are rightly rewarded. Following the romance tradition, the opening lines of *Pericles*'s brothel scenes emphasize not the violation but the commodification of the female body:

> *Pand.* We lost too much money this mart by being too wenchless.
> *Bawd.* We were never so much out of creatures.

We have but poor three, and they can do no more
than they can do; and they with continual action
are even as good as rotten.

(4.2.4-9[13])

A few lines later, the Pander and the Bawd specify the means by which Marina too will be commodified. Her body will be verbally anatomized for a pornographic advertisement:

> *Bawd.* Boult, take you the marks of her, the color
> of her hair, complexion, height, her age, with
> warrant of her virginity, and cry, "He that will give
> most shall have her first." Such a maidenhead were
> no cheap thing, if men were as they have been.
>
> (ll. 57-61)

Further violence lies in the subtext of this threatened fragmentation. The "continual action" in which the three whores engage is like military action; in the brothels of Mytilene, sexuality has become a war of attrition, for action has made the prostitutes "rotten":

> *Bawd.* The stuff we have, a strong wind will blow
> it to pieces, they are so pitifully sodden.
> *Pand.* Thou sayest true, there's two unwholesome,
> a' conscience. The poor Transylvanian is dead that
> lay with the little baggage.
> *Boult.* Ay, she quickly poop'd him, she made him
> roast-meat for worms.
>
> (ll. 18-25)

The bawds' metaphoric configuration of military action and venereal disease resonates with the historical conditions of the sixteenth-century syphilis epidemic. Syphilis, a disease of early modern naval exploration and military conquest, reanimated the ancient fear of physical pollution that underlies the Roman idea of *stuprum.* The fact of syphilis transferred the corporeal pollution of illicit sexuality from the realm of ritual dread into the world of early modern medical discourse. In times of plague, *stuprum* regains its primitive material foundation; contagion supersedes Augustinian shamefastness.

Fear of contagion could be exploited ideologically to renew traditional social hierarchies. Syphilis, explains the London physician William Clowes, arose from "the licentious and beastly disorder of a great number of rogues and vagabonds, the filthy life of many lewd and idle persons, men and women." Although, as Clowes admits, "some other of better disposition are many times infected," the syphilitic became an underworld figure, for the primary carriers of the disease, prostitutes and discharged soldiers, were socially vulnerable and readily marginalized.[14]

Since venereal infection and social marginalization are reciprocal, the bawds' threat suggests a terrorist tactic of germ warfare: to threaten a princess with the occupational hazards of prostitution is to exploit the hierarchy of gender in rebelling against the hierarchy of class. Prostitution will destroy the dynastic value of the fetishized hymen. Then, in the diseased flesh of the syphilitic whore, the fragments of the pornographic image will be grotesquely reunited, as Marina becomes yet another "little baggage."

Like the Prostitute Priestess, Marina converts her clients through the power of eloquence: "Come," says one who has heard her sermon in the stews, "I am for no more bawdy houses. Shall's go hear the vestals sing?" (4.5.6-7). The gentlemen of Mytilene move between the brothel and the temple. These *loci,* which homologously represent the bodies of the prostitute and the priestess, are landmarks in the symbolic geography of what Peter Stallybrass calls "patriarchal territories."[15] Marina's eloquence, like that of the Prostitute Priestess, reconfigures those territories, exposing the motives of those who draw the boundaries. When Lysimachus, the governor of Mytilene, arrives at the brothel, Marina confronts local authority:

> *Mar.* Do you know this house to be a place of such
> resort, and will come into't? I hear say you're of
> honorable parts, and are the governor of this place.
> *Lys.* . . . O, you have heard something of my power,
> and so stand aloof for more serious wooing. But I
> protest to thee, pretty one, my authority shall not
> see thee, or else look friendly upon thee. . . .
>
> (4.6.79-81, 86-90)[16]

Despite Marina's similarities with the Prostitute Priestess, the narrative structure *Pericles* inherited from romance does foreclose dramatic possibilities to which the rhetorical *narratio* remains open. Marina and her predecessor Tharsia are above all marriageable; the homicidal martial art of the Prostitute Priestess does not reemerge to diminish that quality. Verbal suggestions of the character's androgynous power, however, do remain. Although Marina never uses physical force to repel an attacker, the "sweet harmony" of her eloquence "make[s] a batt'ry through [Pericles'] deafen'd parts" (5.1.47), and he tells her "thou art a man, and I / Have suffered like a girl" (ll. 136-37). For Bawd and Pander, Marina's rhetorical victory over her would-be clients is "virginal fencing" (4.4.57). When they send their servant Boult to rape her and break her to the trade, she responds with ferocity:

> Thou hold'st a place for which the pained'st fiend
> Of hell would not in reputation change.
> Thou art the damned door-keeper to every
> Custrel that comes inquiring for his Tib.
> To the choleric fisting of every rogue
> Thy ear is liable; thy food is such
> As hath been belch'd on by infected lungs.
>
> (4.6.163-69)

Marina's pugnacious oration is a vestige of the martial skill of the Prostitute Priestess, but it is not in itself sufficient to convert Boult. For those employed in the whorehouses of Mytilene, economic need is impervious to the persuasive powers of a moralizing rhetoric:

> What would you have me do? Go to the wars, would you? Where a man may serve seven years for the loss of a leg, and have not money enough in the end to buy him a wooden one?
>
> (ll. 170-73)

Marina's eloquent response is of limited practical value:

> Do any thing but this thou doest. Empty
> Old receptacles, or common shores, of filth,
> Serve by indenture to the common hangman:
> Any of these ways are yet better than this...
>
> (ll. 174-77)

At last, confined rhetorically to the economic marketplace, she strikes a bargain with him:

> If that thy master would gain by me,
> Proclaim that I can sing, weave, sew, and
>   dance,
> With other virtues, which I'll keep from
>   boast,
> And will undertake all these to teach.
> I doubt not but this populous city will
> Yield many scholars.
>
> (ll. 182-87)

The art of eloquence, extended into music, weaving, and riddle lore, purchases Marina's freedom from the brothel. Unlike the Prostitute Priestess and the saints, she need neither kill nor die to avoid prostitution; eloquence preserves her chastity without bloodshed. Her most characteristic combat occurs in a feminized form more appropriate for preparing a trousseau than repelling a rapist. In embroidering, Shakespeare's Gower tells us, Marina "would with sharp needle wound / The cambric, which she made more sound / By hurting it" (4.Chorus.23).

The practice of embroidery requires costly leisure, and Marina's proficiency testifies to her meticulous education. Unlike the Prostitute Priestess's martial skill, it is a traditionally feminine accomplishment. It is, the 1596 preface to *A Booke of Curious and Strange Inventions* argues, suitable for women who are either "of a high degree" or who hope to elevate themselves socially: "For many maidens but of base degree... / With noble ladies oft companions be / Sometimes they teach the daughter of a king."[17] This advice for displaying or acquiring status is doubly significant for a princess imprisoned in the material circumstances of a prostitute. Marina's ability to rise above these circumstances comes from joining entrepreneurial ability to the skills her noble birth and training have given her. Although a princess, like a prostitute, may be a commodity, the princess's price includes the charges of her birth and breeding, a higher rate than pimps and bawds can pay.

Since Marina's escape does not depend on martial prowess, the textual echoes of androgyny need not be theatrically reinforced by verbal or visual cues that suggest that Marina could defend herself physically against Boult's attempted rape. She does not challenge the male monopoly on violence as the Prostitute Priestess does. Marina's eventual triumph allows her to return to her rightful place in a patriarchal world where fathers and husbands are a woman's best protection against pirates and pimps.

The metaphoric androgyny of Marina's "virginal fencing" does resonate with the theatrical convention of the boy actor, but this resonance does not necessarily question representational strategies for naturalizing beliefs about women's vulnerability. In the dramatic fiction Marina's eloquence conquers the brothel's customers, but in the theatrical *mise-en-scène* physical contrasts between the adult who plays Boult and the feminized boy who plays Marina may reinforce patriarchal hierarchies predicated on violence. As the rhetorical convention of speaking *ethicos* creates the Prostitute Priestess from the declaimers' discourse, the theatrical convention of the boy actor encodes Shakespeare's Marina as a vulnerable and hence feminine presence. On the Shakespearean stage the figure of Marina fuses the rhetorical fiction of the androgynous Prostitute Priestess with the historical reality of the sexually ambiguous boy actor; his problematic status as theatricalized demimondaine underscores the economic value of Marina's sexual vulnerability.[18]

There was historically no female presence to challenge androcentrism in the schools of declamation. Nor did women, though present as spectators in the playhouse, appear on the Shakespearean stage.[19] Yet in both venues the dynamics of performance may have operated in some measure to subvert the androcentrism inscribed in the representational strategies of the narrative tradition. Despite Gower's active attempts to "stand i' th' gaps" of the story (4.4.8), the theatrical structure of *Pericles* remains open. Gower cannot defeat theatrical indeterminacy through his narrative strategies because it is not Gower, the representative of ancient authority, but the actor playing Gower who will "stand i' th' gaps," and no actor can control the performance when he is not onstage.

When the theatrical dynamics of the performance text underscore conflicts and contradictions in the fictive premises of the play text, they render Gower's commentary ineffective. Like the declaimers whose *argumenta in utramque partem* reveal gaps in statutory law, the characters of the brothel scenes offer antithetical interpretations of the events in the brothel. The bawds and Marina each articulate one premise in the patriarchal ideology of rape; each is an inadequate response to the dramatic situation. Taken together, however, they expose the conflicts that singly they would occlude.

The bawds, like the accusers of the Prostitute Priestess, trivialize rape and prostitution. Both rape and prostitution, they assume, occur only with the implied consent of lascivious and greedy women. The Shakespearean theatricalization of this attitude produces a comic *mise-en-scène* for the brothel at Mytilene. But when Marina is introduced into this comic setting, her repugnance belies the bawds' assumptions, exposing their economic motives. Marina's reaction, however, ironically heightens the bawds' theatrical vitality, thus keeping their perspective before the audience. Though Marina may cherish her maidenhead as a pearl beyond price, the bawds remain onstage to appraise its market value. The theatrically grotesque effect of this dual perspective problematizes audience response: while the bawds' opportunism mocks the horror with which patriarchy acknowledges the violation of aristocratic virginity, Marina's rage embarrasses the prurient laughter that greets the sexual exploitation of the unprotected. The case, argued *in utramque partem,* is altered.

Yet *Pericles* does not explicitly reopen the case of the Prostitute Priestess. Pericles, restored to political and domestic authority as king and father, ratifies the marriage of Marina and Lysimachus: "This prince, the fair betrothed of your daughter," he announces to Thaisa, "Shall marry her at Pentapolis" (5.3.71-72). But eloquent Marina, like Isabella, the eloquent virgin of *Measure for Measure,* responds with silence to the announcement of her marriage. Because her silence, like Isabella's, must be negotiated theatrically, it resonates more deeply with the theatrical ellipses of the Senecan declamation than with the narrative closure of the romance.[20]

The Senecan rhetoric of rape, originating in the semi-improvisational contexts of the Roman schools of declamation, returns via the scripted silences and antagonistic perspectives of the Shakespearean play text to trouble the narrative closure that hagiography and romance had imposed on the motif of the Prostitute Priestess. The destiny of the Prostitute Priestess must be renegotiated with each performance of the declamation, and as it is renegotiated, debate over the source, extent, and legitimacy of female resistance to male violence is renewed. In the rhetorical play of advocates and prosecutors, no formal resolution can achieve more than a temporary victory of one contestant over another in the continual agones that establish patriarchal hierarchy; no judicial decision can authoritatively categorize the Prostitute Priestess as virgin or whore.

The narrative tradition reinscribes the transgressive Prostitute Priestess into a fixed status within patriarchal structures. This reinscription, as the legend of Thecla reveals, is vulnerable to slight variations of plot and characterization, yet the textual strategies of legend and romance work to efface that vulnerability. Whether the story of the eloquent virgin ends with the death of a saint or the marriage of a princess, narrative resolution evades the dilemma of the declamation, insisting that patriarchal categories adequately represent women's sexuality. When the hagiographers and the writers of romance grant their authority to a woman's tale of abduction and attempted rape, the closure of their narratives also closes the case of the Prostitute Priestess. The declaimers' judicial inquiry into the veracity of the victim is replaced with an authoritative representation of her imprisonment, painted in the rhetorical *colores* of her advocates.

From this narrative tradition, *Pericles* derives a dramatic plot that permits Marina to escape the brothel but not to evade the marriage that reinserts her into the patriarchal structures of Mytilene. In the transformation of that narrative for theatrical representation, however, its ideological closure is disturbed—a disturbance to which Gower's ineffectively authorial presence testifies. Gower's speech, like Marina's silence, and like the antagonistic perspectives of the brothel scenes, must be performed, and the contingencies of performance, mediating between the resolution of the playtext and the spectator's response, may intervene to expose the improvisational (and hence provisional) quality of that resolution. The politics of actors' or directors' choices for line readings and stage images, the extra dramatic relation that a strong performer may establish with the audience, even the danger of a missed cue or a bumbled exit may, in various ways, problematize dramatic closure, evoking instead the open-ended *controversia.* The Prostitute Priestess is not only Marina's literary precursor, passing through classical and medieval discourses of gender and violence en route to the Shakespearean playtext. She is the survivor of a dramatic agon through which the rhetoric of rape may still be contested.

Notes

Earlier versions of this essay have been presented at the Department of Classics, Stanford University; at the Center for Renaissance Studies at SUNY, Binghamton; and at the 1988 meeting of the Philological Association of the Pacific Coast. I am especially grateful for the generosity of Christopher Faraone, Jay Fliegelman, Judy Evans-Grubbs, Kathy Gaca, Phyllis Gorfain, and John J. Winkler, who have read and criticized various drafts of this essay.

[1] *Narrative and Dramatic Sources of Shakespeare*, 8 vols. (London: Routledge and Kegan Paul, 1957-1975), Vol. 6, 546-48. For discussions of declamation as a literary source for Renaissance drama, see Eugene M. Waith, "John Fletcher and the Art of Declamation," *PMLA*, 66 (1951), 226-34; "*Controversia* in the English Drama: Medwall and Massinger," *PMLA*, 68 (1953), 286-303; *The Pattern of Tragicomedy in Beaumont and Fletcher*, Yale Studies in English, no. 120 (1952), 86-98; and Joel B. Atlman, *The Tudor Play of Mind: Rhetorical Inquiry and the Development of Elizabethan Drama* (Berkeley: Univ. of California Press, 1978). Suzanne Gossett challenges Waith's view that the influence of declamation results only in rhetorical virtuosity, arguing that Beaumont and Fletcher create a strong emotional effect by manipulating the standard rape plot of earlier drama. See "'Best Men are Molded out of Faults': Marrying the Rapist in Jacobean Drama," *English Literary Renaissance*, 14 (1984), 305-27.

[2] *Controversiae*, 1.2. Quotations from Seneca are from the Loeb edition, trans. Michael Winterbottom (Cambridge, Mass.: Harvard Univ. Press, 1974). Further references to this edition will appear in the text.

[3] For discussions of the social and literary history of Roman declamation, see S. F. Bonner, *Roman Declamation in the Late Republic and Early Empire* (Liverpool: Univ. Press of Liverpool, 1949); Harry Caplan, "The Decay of Eloquence at Rome in the First Century" in *Of Eloquence: Studies in Ancient and Mediaeval Rhetoric*, Anne King and Helen North, eds. (Ithaca, N.Y.: Cornell Univ. Press, 1970), pp. 160-95; and Wesley Trimpi, *Muses of One Mind: The Literary Analysis of Experience and Its Continuity* (Princeton, N.J.: Princeton Univ. Press, 1983), pp. 306-27.

[4] *Institutes*, 5.12.17. Quotations from Quintilian are from the Loeb edition, trans. H. E. Butler (London: Heinemann, 1921), p. 307.

[5] *Purity and Danger: An Analysis of Concepts of Pollution and Taboo* (London: Routledge & Kegan Paul, 1966), p. 130.

[6] For an economical and provocative discussion of "the paradoxes that govern the laws of rape" when based on rules of morality, see Frances Ferguson, "Rape and the Rise of the Novel" in *Misogyny, Misandry, and Misanthropy*, R. Howard Bloch and Frances Ferguson, eds. (Berkeley: Univ. of California Press, 1989), pp. 88-113.

[7] Jacobus de Voragine, *Here begynneth the legende named in latyn legenda aurea that is to say in englyshe the golden legende* . . . (Westminster: Caxton, 1483), fols. lxxvii^r-lxxviii^v. See also the lives of Theodore, Eugenne, and Pelagyen in *The Golden Legende*. For discussions of the virgin martyr, see John Anson, "The Female Transvestite in Early Monasticism: The Origin and Development of A Motif," *Viator*, 5 (1974), 1-32; and Jane Tibbetts Schulenburg, "The Heroics of Virginity: *Brides of Christ and Sacrificial Mutilation*" in *Women in the Middle Ages and the Renaissance*, Mary Beth Rose, ed. (Syracuse, N.Y.: Syracuse Univ. Press, 1986), pp. 29-72. For discussions of the complicated history linking "valor and virginity," see Nancy Huston, "The Matrix of War: Mothers and Heroes" in *The Female Body in Western Culture: contemporary perspectives*, Susan Rubin Suleiman, ed. (Cambridge, Mass.: Harvard Univ. Press, 1986), pp. 119-36; Jo Ann McNamara, *A New Song: Celibate Women in the First Three Christian Centuries* (New York: Harrington Park, 1985); Marina Warner, "Virgins and Martyrs" in *Alone of All Her Sex: The Myth and the Cult of the Virgin Mary* (New York: Knopf, 1976), pp. 68-78; and Lisa Jardine, *Still Harping on Daughters: Women and Drama in the Age of Shakespeare* (Brighton: Harvester Press, 1983), pp. 169-95.

[8] *The City of God*, 1.19. Quotations from Augustine are from the Loeb edition, trans. George E. McCracken (London: Heinemann, 1957), p. 91.

[9] "The Acts of Paul and Thecla," trans. Wilhelm Schneemelcher, in *The Other Bible*, ed. Willis Barnstone (San Francisco: Harper and Row, 1984), pp. 447-53, esp. pp. 451, 453.

[10] "The Female Transvestite," p. 11 (cited in n. 7, above).

[11] The deployment of marriage and death as homologous narrative resolutions extends from pre-classical Greece to modern novels. See Helene P. Foley, *Ritual Irony: Poetry and Sacrifice in Euripides* (Ithaca, N.Y.: Cornell Univ. Press, 1985), pp. 84-92; Eva C. Keuls, *The Reign of the Phallus: Sexual Politics in Ancient Athens* (New York: Harper and Row, 1985), pp. 130-52; and Margaret Higonnet, "Speaking Silences: Women's Suicide" in *The Female Body*, pp. 68-83 (cited in n. 7, above).

[12] In one romance, however, Xenophon of Ephesus' *Ephesiaca*, the imprisoned heroine, Antheia, does kill a guard who tries to rape her. See Arthur Heiserman, *The Novel before the Novel* (Chicago: Univ. of Chicago Press, 1977), pp. 51-52; and Thomas Hägg, *The Novel in Antiquity* (Berkeley: Univ. of California Press, 1983), pp. 31-32. For a discussion of *Pericles*'s assimilation of the economic subtexts of romance from a different perspective, see Steven Mullaney, *The Place of the Stage: License, Play, and Power in Renaissance England* (Chicago: Univ. of Chicago Press, 1988), pp. 137-42; and for a suggestive study of "the peculiar sensibility that made [Greek romance] available to Shakespeare," see Terry Comito, "Exile and

Return in the Greek Romances," *Arion*, 2 (1975), 58-80, esp. p. 61.

[13] Quotations from *Pericles* are from *The Riverside Shakespeare*, G. Blakemore Evans, ed. (Boston: Houghton Mifflin, 1974); to avoid confusion with my own interpolations, Evans's brackets have been silently deleted.

[14] *A Short and Profitable Treatise Touching the Cure of the Disease Called (Morbus Gallicus) by Unctions* (1579; rpt. New York: Scholars' Facsimile, 1945), p. 149. Studies of the sixteenth-century syphilis epidemic include Charles Dennie, *A History of Syphilis* (Springfield, Ill.: Charles C. Thomas, 1962); R. S. Morton, *Venereal Diseases* (Baltimore: Penguin, 1966); and William Pusey, *The History and Epidemiology of Syphilis* (Springfield, Ill.: Charles C. Thomas, 1933). In *Harlots, Whores, & Hookers: A History of Prostitution* (New York: Taplinger, 1979) Hilary Evans notes the effect of the epidemic on prostitution: "From this time on, the problem of the prostitute could never be dissociated from that of disease; henceforward she represented a sanitary as well as a moral problem" (p. 64). See also E. J. Burford, *Bawds and Lodgings: A History of the London Bankside Brothels c. 100-1675* (London: Peter Owen, 1976), pp. 113-15 and passim; and Ruth Mazo Karras, "The Regulation of Brothels in Later Medieval England," *Signs*, 14 (1989), 399-433. Andrew Welsh also notes *Pericles*'s emphasis on venereal disease in "Heritage in *Pericles*" in *Shakespeare's Late Plays: Essays in Honor of Charles Crow*, Richard C. Tobias and Paul G. Zolbrod, eds. (Athens: Ohio Univ. Press, 1974), pp. 89-113, esp. pp. 103-5.

[15] "Patriarchal Territories: The Body Enclosed" in *Rewriting the Renaissance: The Discourses of Sexual Difference in Early Modern Europe*, Margaret W. Ferguson, Maureen Quilligan, and Nancy J. Vickers, eds. (Chicago: Univ. of Chicago Press, 1986), pp. 123-42.

[16] On the related motif of the judge and the nun, see Leo Salingar, *Shakespeare and the Traditions of Comedy* (Cambridge: Cambridge Univ. Press, 1974), pp. 298-321.

[17] Giovanni Battista Ciotti, *The First Part of Needleworks: Or, A Booke of Curious and Strange Inventions* (London, 1596). I quote this English translation of Ciotti from a microfilm copy at the Huntington Library. On the "elevated class associations" and the feminizing functions of embroidery as a component of sixteenth- and seventeenth-century women's educations, see Rozsika Parker, *The Subversive Stitch: Embroidery and the Making of the Feminine* (London: The Women's Press, 1986), pp. 60-81. Jane Schneider describes some of the economic foundations and symbolic associations of women's needlework in "Trousseau as Treasure: Some Contradictions of Late Nineteenth-Century Change in Sicily" in *The Marriage Bargain: Women and Dowries in European History*, Marion A. Kaplan, ed. (New York: Haworth Press, 1985), pp. 81-119. Weaving and spinning are, Schneider notes, associated with dowries throughout European tradition. Penelope and St. Agatha, "the Christianized Penelope," could postpone marriage by claiming that the work of their looms was incomplete.

[18] On the status of apprentices at the public theatres, see Gerald Eades Bentley, *The Profession of Player in Shakespeare's Time, 1590-1642* (Princeton, N.J.: Princeton Univ. Press, 1984), pp. 113-46. For the legal records concerning boys' impressment and apprenticeship at the private playhouses, see Harold Hillebrand, *The Child Actors* (1926; rpt. New York: Russell and Russell, 1964), pp. 160-63 and 197-99. In *Homosexuality in Renaissance England* ([London: Gay Men's Press, 1982], pp. 54-56) Alan Bray describes homosexual prostitution in the London theatrical milieu; Stephen Orgel pursues the implications of Bray's work in "Nobody's Perfect: Or Why Didthe English Stage Take Boys for Women?" *South Atlantic Quarterly*, 88 (1989), 7-29.

[19] For discussions of female spectators in the Elizabethan and Jacobean playhouses, see Katharine Eisaman Maus, "Horns of Dilemma: Jealousy, Gender, and Spectatorship in English Renaissance Drama," *English Literary History*, 54 (1987), 561-83; and Jean E. Howard, "Scripts and/versus Playhouses: Ideological Production and the Renaissance Public Stage," *Renaissance Drama*, 20 (1989), 31-49.

[20] I do not know of a production of *Pericles* that has problematized Marina's silence as recent productions of *Measure for Measure* have problematized Isabella's. On the ideology of Isabella's performance choices, see Paola Dionisotti's and Juliet Stevenson's remarks on the 1978 and 1983 Royal Shakespeare Company productions in *Clamorous Voices: Shakespeare's Women Today*, Carol Rutter, ed. (London: The Women's Press, 1988), pp. 26-52. On the ways performance texts of other plays have used scripted silences, see Philip C. McGuire, *Speechless Dialect: Shakespeare's Open Silences* (Berkeley: Univ. of California Press, 1985).

Maria Teresa Micaela Prendergast (essay date 1996)

SOURCE: "Engendering *Pericles*," in *Literature and Psychology*, Vol. XXXXII, No. 4, 1996, pp. 53-75.

[*In the essay below, Prendergast traces the influence of the Oedipus story in* Pericles, *revealing elements of the play which Shakespeare is unable to resolve.*]

Because it derives from a "bad" quarto and because it may not be solely by Shakespeare, the ambiguous, even illegitimate status of *Pericles* has long been the most discussed aspect of the play.[1] Given this ongoing preoccupation with the play's illegitimacy, it is curious how few scholars have noted the extent to which *Pericles* itself is about legitimate and illegitimate textuality. From the beginning of the play, Shakespeare raises the question of whether he can, in fact, be considered the sole author of the play. Not only does he introduce us to Gower as the authoritative progenitor of *Pericles,* but he then has Gower refer to a long tradition of telling the Pericles story, a tradition that appears to stretch back to the earliest days of storytelling itself.[2] If, by questioning his sole authority over his text, Shakespeare echoes critical concerns about the legitimate authorship of *Pericles,* this interrogation of exclusive authorship, in the play, is presented as an ideal to strive for, not as an unfortunate textual problem; in fact, for Shakespeare, the acknowledgement of one's literary predecessors promises a kind of immortality: just as Gower is brought back to life every time a younger author (like Shakespeare) retells the story of *Pericles,* so, it appears, Shakespeare will be brought back to life each time a later author, or audience, takes up this story.

Yet despite the premise that an author gains literary immortality when he dispossesses himself of his text, the play's initial conflict between the ideal of accepting one's authorial lineage and the temptation to deny one's literary predecessors spills over into the body of the text; here it is recast as a conflict between possessive, infertile endogamy and the ideal of exogamy—in which the father dispossesses himself of his progeny in order to ensure the immortality of his lineage. But the parallels between literary and familial lineage are more than mere analogies in the play; in fact, one is often confused with the other. Just as Gower, at times, appears as a sort of father figure to Shakespeare, so the father figures in this play often describe their progeny as texts. I would argue that Shakespeare sets forth this complex interaction between familial and textual lineages in order to accentuate an ideal of "dispossession"—an ideal set forth in the paradox that one can only gain literary and familial immortality by denying one's own text and progeny.

In *Pericles,* I will argue, this ideal of dispossession has strong Oedipal resonances; as Shoshana Felman tells us, the Oedipus story appears, at first, to be the myth of a possession (of a kingdom, of a woman, of the solution to a riddle, of one's story). But, as it turns out, "Oedipus is not the myth of the possession of a story, but the myth, precisely, of the dispossession by the story—the dispossession of the possessor of the story (1046)."[3] Like the Oedipus plays, *Pericles* is about a young man who attempts to gain possession of a kingdom by claiming the king's daughter—a woman whose identity is closely wrapped up in a riddle. More significantly, *Pericles* is also about the tension between possession and dispossession of woman or text. Both frame and central drama set forth man's desire to possess an object—whether it be one's story or one's child; both frame and tale, however, enact the paradox that it is only by dispossessing oneself of story and child that one can gain immortality. Thus, if fathers, in this play, must let go of their children to the suitors who claim them, so, Shakespeare suggests, established authors must let go of their texts to younger writers who would inherit them. This ideal of textual and filial dispossession, epitomized by Gower and Pericles, is opposed in the play by the possessive father, Antiochus, whose desire to hold on to his daughter (a daughter whom he presents as a kind of text) threatens not only the young men who would become his sons-in-law, but the very existence of Antiochus's lineage itself.[4]

But if the play and its framing drama are about the repressive / redemptive relations between fathers and sons, the play is also about relations between fathers and daughters—between Antiochus and his daughter, between Pericles and Marina, and between Cleon and his daughter. Imitating the chronology of the play, I will discuss, first, how Shakespeare sets forth his ideal of dispossession (and the temptation of possessiveness) by contrasting Gower with Antiochus, then examine Pericles's status as would-be father and artist before exploring why Shakespeare finally changes focus from his hero Pericles to his heroine Marina. This change, I believe, affirms his ideal of dispossession (one that, I will argue later, Shakespeare himself was only partially able to realize), as I suggest that, for Shakespeare, the ultimate act of dispossession is the movement from a male to a female lineage.[5]

Shakespeare's presentation of Gower as a genial and unthreatening literary progenitor would at first seem to support Harold Bloom's thesis that Shakespeare never experienced the sort of Oedipal anxieties that strong poets after Milton have had to face: according to Bloom, Shakespeare simply did not have a predecessor commanding enough to touch off such primal fears (11). Yet the structural pattern of *Pericles*—its rhythmic development from father to father—suggests that the play is in fact about Oedipal fears and fantasies. Specifically, it is about Shakespeare's triumph over paternity by his deformation of the Freudian Oedipal scene; for if the classic Oedipal moment develops out of the father's competition with his son over the possession of the mother, *Pericles* is, instead, about a father / son conflict over possession of the daughter. The play, then, authorizes the son's Oedipal desires by dramatizing the son's right to possess the woman that he would claim from the father, while displaying the father's continued possession of the daughter as an unnatural act. If, then, the Freudian

Oedipal scene is resolved when the son surrenders his claim to his mother, here it can only be resolved when the father dispossesses himself of his daughter, yielding her to the younger generation that claims her.[6] That Shakespeare would ally himself with the son's Oedipal fantasy is not, perhaps, surprising; Shakespeare was, after all, a literary "son," who inherited most of his plots—including the story of Apollonius of Tyre *(Pericles)*—from previous authors. Shakespeare's "filial" status as a writer would, it appears, encourage him to view the Apollonius story as belonging not to his literary father, Gower, but rather to younger authors, like himself, who would claim the text as their own.[7]

That Shakespeare entered into some sort of competitive relationship with his *auctor* Gower raises the question of how important it would be for a Renaissance writer to claim a text as his own—how important, in other words, the modern concept of originality would be for someone like Shakespeare. Clearly an author who bases his plays on well-known, even well-worn, tales would not be concerned with claiming that his plots were solely of his own invention; but it is true that, during the sixteenth century, many authors came to believe that a significant text should, to some extent, depart from the ideas and structures of its predecessors. This increasing concern with originality has been charted by David Quint, who traces how authors like Ariosto, Ronsard, and Rabelais exploit the notion of a literary vernacular to claim that they are originating a vital literary tradition in their own language.[8]

But if this gradual emphasis on asserting one's independence from one's *auctor* allowed Renaissance writers greater freedom to create fictional spaces that they could claim as their own, it also gave birth to some anxiety: for if a text's significance inheres in its author's ability to outdo previous authors, then this author, in turn, makes himself vulnerable to being effaced by younger authors who invent new versions of his text.[9] Shakespeare, I believe, attempts to resolve this dilemma by presenting his ideal of dispossession: each older author willingly gives up his text to the next generation of writers, a sacrifice for which he is rewarded when he is acknowledged as an enabling source; his immortality is, then, ensured by each generation of writers that is inspired by the text.[10] The ideal of dispossession is a strategy that Shakespeare employs when he acknowledges his story's origins in Gower's *Confessio Amantis,* without diminishing his own, original, perspective on this "mouldy tale."[11]

It is, above all, Shakespeare's portrayal of Gower that allows him to set forth this ideal of dispossession, for Gower's first action in the play is to relinquish his claim to the Apollonius story: he opens the play by telling us that the story is not, originally, his-that it is part of an older tradition (I.Cho.1); and he ends his prologue by surrendering his text to its readers (I.Cho.41-2).[12] Between these two remarks, he openly describes himself as a sacrificial figure who willingly gives up his text to its audience: "I life would wish, and that I might/Waste it for you like taper-light" (I.Cho.15-16). By freely dispossessing himself of his text, Gower follows the logic of the Oedipal paradigm as it is expressed in *Pericles:* the text, though his progeny, belongs to a younger generation, not to the father who created it. This perpetual transmission of the Apollonius story from literary father to son represents a notion of textuality as fluid and open-ended—constantly revised and revived by each new generation that receives it.[13]

If Gower is presented to us as the ideal, self-sacrificing father, he is immediately followed by Antiochus, who is both an oppressive father and a repressive artist. Rather than freely dispossess himself of his progeny, he transforms her into a sort of art object that he can claim as his absolute possession. Antiochus's daughter appears as an instrument (a "fair viol") that is "played upon" by her father (I.i.82) and as the "book of praises" (I.i.16) authored by her father and presented to be viewed—but not touched—by the suitors for her hand. Antiochus, then, is an artist/father who retains absolute possession of that which he creates: he is, in fact, a nightmare version of the petrarchan lover—an artist who attempts to possess his beloved by transforming her from an alien, enigmatic woman into an idolatrous fetishized text, a text to which only he has the key.[14]

What distinguishes Antiochus from Gower, above all, is Antiochus's inability to recognize "otherness"—the existence of any person or experience that is not the mirror image of the self and that, therefore, cannot be absolutely controlled or possessed by the self.[15] It is this instinct to repress otherness—whether otherness is experienced as one's uncontrollable unconscious, the annihilating experience of death, the threat of sexuality (which Lacan and Freud compare to death), or the alien presence of woman—that leads Antiochus to transform his daughter from complex subject into a reassuring, narcissistic image of himself; he does so by imposing an incestuous relationship upon her.[16]

Antiochus's refusal to recognize his daughter as a subject in her own right is echoed in the riddle that he creates to prevent the suitors from gaining access to her:

> Which to prevent he made a law,
> To keep her *still,* and men in awe;
> That whoso ask'd her for his wife,
> His riddle told not, lost his life.
> (my italics; I. Cho. 35-9)

In Antiochus's shaping hands the riddle appears not as an enigma, but rather as an extension of the father's absolute law. The emphasis on "law" reminds us that Antiochus, as father and king, embodies patriarchal culture at its most pervasive and repressive. For Antiochus, law is censorship—a law the tyrant invokes to silence both his daughter and the suitors for her hand.[17] The repressive connotations of this law are expressed in the word "still": the term not only reminds us of Antiochus's repressive hold over his daughter, but it also signifies his stilling of his daughter's voice in choosing a future husband. And by refusing to let go of his daughter, Antiochus keeps her static ("still"), as his "glorious casket" (I.i.78)—the unnamed object of her father's passion. Where Shakespeare's puns normally open up into a proliferation of possible meanings, these *double entendres* compel the reader to return to the obsessive and narrow significance which Antiochus would impose on his daughter.

As the play moves from Gower to Antiochus, then, it regresses from a vision of literary and sanguineous paternity as fluid and open-ended to a concept of text and progeny as static, idolatrous objects to be possessed and mastered by the father.[18] Shakespeare's portrayal of Antiochus's victims dramatizes this latter vision, for they appear to us as "heads displayed at the entrance" (I.s.d.) of Antiochus's palace—heads which are left to "tell thee, with speechless tongue and semblance pale, / That . . . / Here they stand martyrs slain in Cupid's wars" (I.i.35-7).[19] Deprived of speech, the suitors, like Antiochus's daughter, have been transformed from complex subjects in their own rights into silent emblems of Antiochus's castrating power.[20]

The contrast between the opposing notions of authorship embodied in Gower and Antiochus inheres, then, in the paradox of otherness. Antiochus hopes to retain control over his life by repressing otherness—by transforming subjective woman, enigmatic text, and threatening sexuality into a static projection of the self; ironically, this instinct for self-possession leads to the loss of self—to the death of his lineage. In contrast, Gower is an author who faces death (dispossession of his text) by recognizing the unstable, dynamic, and elusive polyphony of his text; this process actually ensures his immortality: he is brought back to life each time he allows the Apollonius/Pericles story to be rewrought by a new author. The play, after all, begins with the resurrection of Gower: "To sing a song that old was sung, / From ashes ancient Gower is come" (I.Cho.1-2). Shakespeare's Gower, then, presents an alternative to Antiochus, who stands for the Lacanian notion that the Father is absolute truth. This rigid notion of fatherhood (embodied in Antiochus) may be displaced by Gower, who represents a more liquid, communal and risky notion of truth.

If the play opens with a strong focus on father figures, it soon yields place to Pericles, who must, in reading the riddle, choose between two notions of paternity: if he mis-reads the riddle, he identifies himself with Antiochus, and, thus, allows himself to be turned into another petrified image of Antiochus's power; but if he reads past the notion of riddle-as-law and into the deeper layers of the text, he moves away from the temptation of fixation that is epitomized by Antiochus and into a more fluid and dynamic notion of artistry represented by Gower and by the generous father figures that follow him—Pericles's father and Simonides. By turning from the tyrannical Antiochus and towards the generous Simonides (the image of Pericles's true father), Pericles acts out the sort of process which Shakespeare himself may have undergone. In adapting Gower's popular version of the Apollonius story, Shakespeare does not envision Gower as an Antiochus-like father figure whose tyrannical hold on his story blocks the creativity of younger authors; rather, he envisions Gower as an *auctor* who freely dispossesses himself of the Apollonius story to younger authors who would rename and revise this traditional tale (much as Simonides generously gives his daughter up to Pericles).

The apparent analogy between Shakespeare's position as younger author and Pericles's position as a young suitor is strengthened by the constant references to Antiochus as both tyrannical father and a blocking author/artist whose influence Pericles must learn to reject. This eventual rejection results from Pericles's reading of both Antiochus's riddle and the *imago* of the daughter. Satisfied, at first, with the external appearance of the daughter, Pericles does not seek to inquire beyond the superficial image that Antiochus presents to him: he first reads her as "the book of praises, where is read / Nothing but curious pleasures" (I.i.16-17);[21] but when Pericles turns from Antiochus's daughter-as-text to the text of the riddle itself (with which Antiochus's daughter is identified), he learns to look beyond the daughter's enticing facade: "Fair glass of light, I lov'd you, and could still, / Were not this glorious casket stor'd with ill" (I.i.77-8). The images of transparency that dominate this couplet reveal what Pericles has learned as he looks beyond the exterior of the "fair" princess: the princess is not, as she appears to be, the subjective Other that Pericles must risk encountering; rather, she is an idolatrous image wrought by her father—a beautiful vessel that encloses her father's primal sin.[22]

What separates Pericles from the other suitors—what allows him to understand the meaning of the riddle—seems to be his gift of self-recognition; thus, looking up at the suitors' heads, he comments:

> Antiochus, I thank thee, who hath taught
> My frail mortality to know itself,
> And by those fearful objects to prepare
> This body, like to them, to what I must,

> For death remember'd should be like a mirror,
> Who tells us life's but breath, to trust it error.
>
> (I.i.42-7)

Where Antiochus's repression of his daughter's subjectivity and his execution of her suitors reveals his obsession with holding on to absolute power, Pericles is, from the beginning, represented as willing to recognize man's ultimate powerlessness in the face of death. It is this characteristic ability to recognize what others repress that allows Pericles to look beyond the riddle's superficial appearance as Antiochus's absolute "law" and perceive the deeper, repressed layers of meaning hidden within it. By recognizing his mortality, then, Pericles frees himself from the paralysis of repression and fixation that characterizes Antiochus and those who fall under his influence.[23]

It is at this moment that *Pericles* most strongly recalls *Oedipus Rex*. Both works, as I noted earlier, involve a riddle, incest, and a contest with a father; but Shakespeare presents the Oedipal experience in such a way as to distance his work from the tragic implications of *Oedipus Rex*. For where Oedipus solves the riddle of man's birth and mortality only to fall blindly into incest, Pericles discerns incest itself in the relationship between Antiochus and his daughter; thus, in solving the riddle, he is able to turn away from the temptation of incest; in the process, he avoids possessiveness—a trait that, in this play, is closely associated with incest.

The difference between these two hero-rulers is expressed, as well, in their opposing reactions to the riddle.[24] Where Oedipus rashly believes that, in solving the Sphinx's riddle, he has gained mastery over his life and destiny, Pericles never reveals any hubristic sense of self-mastery: in fact, he never articulates the apparent answer to the riddle.[25] If, then, the story of Oedipus is, as Shoshana Felman puts it, about "misrecognition" of "one's history," the story of Pericles represents the hero's ability to avoid the staticity and idolatry that is associated with a hubristic confidence in absolute meanings, as he recognizes, instead, the enigma of his mortality (1025).[26]

The logic of *Pericles*, then, is paradoxical: Antiochus, who holds on to life by clinging to his daughter while demonstrating his absolute power over her suitors, soon dies a terrible death, leaving no progeny to continue his lineage; in contrast, Pericles, who keeps his mortality in mind, and who recognizes how little control he has over his fate, is immortalized as he recognizes that he is part of a past, present, and future lineage.[27]

This process of recognition begins as Pericles looks past the false model of fatherhood—Antiochus—to recognize his own father, who, unlike Antiochus, freely bequeaths his heritage to his progeny (much as Gower and Shakespeare recognize the ancient lineage of the Apollonius story):[28]

> An armour, friends! I pray you, let me see it.
> Thanks, Fortune, yet, that after all thy crosses
> Thou giv'st me somewhat to repair myself;
> And though it was mine own, part of mine heritage,
> Which my dead father did bequeath to me, With
> this strict charge, even as he left his life:
> "Keep it, my Pericles; it hath been a shield
> "'Twixt me and death".
>
> (II.i.119-26)

The pun on "repair" ("re-père") reinforces the link between the "rusty armour" (II.i.118) of Pericles's father and Pericles's recognition of his lineage (which will soon be fulfilled, as Pericles himself becomes a father). As such the armor might well recall Gower's "Apollonius of Tyre"—a rather rusty piece that Gower's literary son nonetheless recognizes as a vital source of his creativity. Significantly, it is after he takes on his father's armor that Pericles is first referred to as an artist (II.v.25-8); he becomes an artist not only by acknowledging his father, but also by taking on a wife, with whom he creates Marina.[29]

It is after recognizing his heritage that Pericles is freed to move from the problematic Antiochus to the more constructive father figure Simonides, whom Pericles calls "my father's picture" (II.iii.37); for Simonides (in contrast to Antiochus) is a king who allows his daughter both free speech and the freedom to choose a husband. The chiasmic relationship between Antiochus and Simonides is expressed in their speech and actions as well. Where Antiochus appears as a welcoming father-in-law, who "seem'd not to strike, but smooth" (I.ii.78) while secretly plotting to have Pericles killed, Simonides severely tests Pericles's love for Thaisa, but says, secretly, "Now, by the gods, I do approve his [Pericles's] courage" (II.v.57). Significantly, Thaisa appears as the opposite of Antiochus's daughter: not only does she speak for herself, but both women are compared in antipodal ways to caskets: where Antiochus's daughter is a "glorious casket" who is, psychically, dead, Thaisa later appears in a casket, seeming to be dead, while she is, in fact, alive.[30]

If, then, the incestuous kingdom of Antiochus is characterized by castration, censorship, and superficial appearance, the kingdom of Simonides inspires the fertile continuity of a lineage—a lineage that grows out of the union of Pericles's and Thaisa's families; their progeny is Marina, whose birth inverts Pericles's threatened death at the hands of Antiochus. About Marina's birth Gower states, "Hymen hath brought the bride to bed, / Where by the loss of maidenhead / A babe is molded" (III. Cho. 9-11). This bed / maidenhead rhyme inverts the rhymes of Antiochus's rather grisly couplet: "Till Pericles be dead / My heart can lend no succour to my head" (I.ib.170-71).

Yet it is also true that the specter of death hangs over Pericles's family—whether it be Antiochus's attempt to assassinate Pericles, Thaisa's "death" in childbirth, or Marina's threatened death at the hands of Dionyza's henchman. The threat of death may in part be due to contamination—specifically to Pericles's contamination by the incestuous affair between Antiochus and his daughter.[31] Pericles himself notes that "vice repeated is like the wand'ring wind, / Blows dust in others' eyes, to spread itself" (I.i.93-5). This potential regression into narcissism and incest is, then, experienced as a kind of plague that endangers the existence of Pericles, Thaisa and Marina.[32]

Even more problematic is how the separate members of Pericles's family threaten each other. Marina's innocent birth threatens her mother with death, while Thaisa and Marina displace Pericles, who is absent through most of Acts III-IV: woman and child, it appears, simply by being Other, threaten to efface the identity and autonomy of man and parent.[33] Yet there is clearly a difference between the threat evoked by Thaisa and Marina and that evoked by Antiochus and Dionyza. Antiochus and Dionyza both represent parental figures who repress all symptoms of subjectivity in others; Thaisa and Marina, in contrast, represent the risk of otherness itself—the risk that each person must undertake in order for the family lineage to be maintained: the play, then, repeats its essential paradox—to cling to life and power (as do Antiochus and Dionyza) is to die; to risk death (to recognize the Other) is the only means by which one may recover one's self and lineage. This is why, if Pericles, Thaisa, and Marina are threatened with death and censorship, they are, finally, reunited. This recovery occurs, as Richard Hillman tells us, when Marina remembers her father—when father, daughter, and mother recognize at once each other and themselves (431).[34]

But what does it mean that the text presents woman as the fulfillment of a patriarchal lineage? It does not necessarily mean that women represent an alternative to the tyrannical power of the father, for Dionyza and Bawd are, like Antiochus, autocratic parental figures. But by representing the continuation of a lineage through the daughter, rather than the son (the image of his father), Shakespeare does suggest the importance of recognizing otherness—a recognition enabled when the father rejects the glamour of incest to affirm, instead, the daughter's rights to her subjective existence; this recognition takes place when Pericles frees Marina to marry Lysimachus, much as Simonides freed Thaisa to marry Pericles.

Dispossession in the play, then, is expressed as the movement from incest to exogamy—the movement that, according to Claude Lévi-Strauss, is the founding moment of culture, when man no longer keeps his woman to himself, but rather surrenders her to other men in order to forge alliances with other tribes. Such an alliance appears to take place near the end of the play, as Lysimachus tells Pericles: "I have another suit," and Pericles answers: "You shall prevail, / Were it to woo my daughter" (V.i.259-60): the marriage between Lysimachus and Marina in fact binds the kingdoms of Tyre and Mytilene to each other. But the way in which this alliance is achieved problematizes the notion that exogamy fully promotes a recognition of otherness; for, in the process, Marina's power and presence seem to be occluded. Although the alliance between the two men takes place in the presence of Marina, she is uncommonly silent during the scene: it is as if the pact between Lysimachus and Pericles has turned Marina into an object of exchange, no longer a subject in her own right.

Feminist critics, of course, have long claimed that exogamy marginalizes women; most notably, Gayle Rubin has pointed out that woman is at once the crucial element in the process of exogamy and the person least empowered by this process:[35]

> The exchange of women does not necessarily imply that women are objectified, in the modern sense, since objects in the primitive world are imbued with highly personal qualities. But it does imply a distinction between gift and giver. If women are the gifts, then it is men who are the exchange partners. And it is the partners, not the presents, upon whom reciprocal exchange confers its quasi-mystical power of social linkage. The relations of such a system are such that women are in no position to realize the benefits of their own circulation. (174)

This, in fact, seems to be what happens to Marina: so long as she is a virgin—unclaimed by any man—she develops into a powerful artist, an artist who essentially shapes the recovery of Pericles; but once Pericles agrees to give Marina in marriage to Lysimachus, her role diminishes dramatically: in fact she speaks only one more line in the play.[36] Shakespeare's ideal of dispossession, in other words, remains determined by the conventional Renaissance construction of woman as subordinate to man.[37] The silencing of Marina suggests that Shakespeare is, finally, unable to sustain the notion of woman as much more than an object, despite his condemnation of Antiochus for turning his daughter into a textual object.[38]

But what is, finally, significant about Shakespeare's portrayal of Marina is not so much her diminishment via the process of exogamy—this process, after all, is conventional to Renaissance culture; rather, it is the extended space that Shakespeare dedicates to representing Marina as a consummate artist and subject in her own right. For, in the interval between Marina's separation from Pericles and her eventual absorption into the institution of marriage, Shakespeare dedicates almost two of his acts to Marina's development into an artist whose rhetorical power eclipses not only the speeches given by Gower but also the artistry of Pericles himself. Thus if Marina's alter ego, Antiochus's daughter, appears as an *object d'art*—a musical instrument to be manipulated by her author (I.i.82-6)—Marina is, from the beginning, presented as a powerful artist and musician (IV.Cho.7-8); she is, in fact, a variety of artists—weaver, embroiderer, lute player, singer, and writer (IV. Cho. 21-28). As the play develops, her artistic talent becomes increasingly mythologized, until she appears to be the exemplary Orpheus, who, with her "sweet harmony / And other chosen attractions, would allure, / And make a batt'ry through his [Pericles's] deafen'd ports" (V.i.44-6).[39]

It is not surprising, then, that Marina is able to resist characters who would turn her from subject to object. She evades Dionyza's Antiochus-like attempts to turn her into a static art object—a frozen "monument" inscribed with "glitt'ring golden characters" (IV.iii.42-5): her absence from the tomb that would contain her dramatizes the difficulty of transforming her into a mere *imago* of the artist. Marina is similarly threatened by Boult, who says of her: "She has a good face, speaks well, and has excellent good clothes; there's no farther necessity of qualities can make her be refus'd"; soon after, he adds, "I have drawn her picture" (IV.ii.44-6,91). Another autocratic artist, Boult—encouraged by his mistress Bawd—expects to turn Marina from complex artist into a static, mastered art object, by "castrating" her virginity, much as Antiochus cut off the heads of the suitors: "I must have your maidenhead taken off, or the common hangman shall execute it" (IV.iv.128-30). But unlike the silent suitors and princess, Marina avails herself of speech to free herself from those who would suppress her.[40]

Shakespeare's presentation of Marina thus seems to embody two opposing concepts at once: on the one hand, he presents her as a subjective artist in her own right, a character who, like her father, generously dispossesses herself to the next generation, which, in turn, will renew her as part of a dynamic family lineage. In this sense, the diminishment of Marina's character may be seen as part of an overarching pattern of constructive dispossession that includes male as well as female characters: just as we saw that Gower gives way to Shakespeare, so Pericles's father gives way to Pericles, who in turn is effaced by Marina, just as she, once married, will apparently give way to her future progeny. On the other hand, Marina's silent absorption into marriage—a silence which contrasts with Pericles's active affirmation of his love for Thaisa—suggests that Shakespeare was, finally, unable to transcend the conceptual limits of Renaissance thought; for this reason he does not represent Marina as an active participant in the system of exogamy.

A similar pattern underlies Shakespeare's presentation of his literary lineage. Despite his generous recognition of his *auctor,* Shakespeare presents Gower in somewhat self-serving terms: the fact that he takes his story from the work of an author who, he suggests, was never enthralling to begin with, allows him to sidestep the challenge of mastering a formidable literary predecessor; and although Shakespeare recognizes Gower's influence over him, he also marginalizes him—limiting his presence to the framing sections of the text.[41] His relationship to his literary successors is similarly self-protective, for he cannily presents his successors as audience rather than as potentially threatening authors who are more likely to outdo him as artist by creating their own, more powerful versions of Pericles.[42]

Yet both of these arguments have another face to them; if Gower is marginalized by Shakespeare, he is also amplified by him:[43] Shakespeare revitalizes his predecessor's work by creating a marginalia of it—by adding to it subtlety and complexity, just as Gower elaborated on the Latin "Apollonius of Tyre."[44] And if Shakespeare takes the easy way out by representing his successors as audience, this evasion nonetheless leaves us free to amplify our own version of the play—as authors, readers, or critics;[45] for the play develops by teaching us not just what moral bits we should digest but also how to read past the text's surface. We are encouraged to engage in this activity when we witness Pericles looking past the glossy surface of Antiochus's daughter, or when we hear Simonides comment that "Opinion's but a fool, that makes us scan / The outward habit by the inward man" (II.ii.55-6).[46]

The text, then, alternates between an ideal of recognition and moments of repression, between possession and dispossession. This complicated plot is underscored by the play's most famous weakness. The play, as we have it, is illegitimate—a bad quarto that may be only partially by Shakespeare. The corrupt state of the text accidentally reinforces Shakespeare's aesthetics of dispossession. In its present state we cannot worship it as an idolatrous object of Shakespeare's genius, much as Antiochus transforms his daughter into an image to be worshipped; rather its marred surface reinforces the challenge that Gower and Shakespeare leave as an ideal to the readers of Pericles—to remember and "re-père" the text by recognizing the problematic relation between the text as we have it and its absent ideal, much as the play itself moves back and forth between the author's instincts for control and the ideal of an open-ended relationship between writer and reader.

Notes

[1] I wish to thank Mihoko Suzuki and the members of her Shakespeare Association seminar on Shakespeare's romances, who first read and commented on the paper from which this article derives. Careful commentary from Gordon Braden, Jay Dobrutsky, Clare Kinney, Dan Kinney, and Tom Prendergast were also invaluable in helping me transform the paper into an article.

[2] Most critics who focus on Gower are more interested in his role as mediator between text and audience; this is particularly true of the commentaries by Eggers, Hillman, Hoeniger (both in his article and in the introduction to his edition of *Pericles*), Knowles, Marshall, Nevo, and Peterson.

[3] Felman goes on to add that, "Any kingdom or possession coming out of the psychoanalytic riddle-solving is, in fact, incestuous, and, as such, is bound to bring about a Plague" (1046, her italics). Similarly, *Pericles* begins with Antiochus—a tyrannical ruler of his kingdom and possessive father—who engages in an incestuous relationship with his daughter; as a result, he dies of plague-like symptoms. For a reading of how this link between tyranny and plague runs through medieval Western literature, see Wallace, 189-90.

[4] I discuss the daughter's status as text later in this article.

[5] I will not address the problems of textual integrity that have dominated discussions of this play. Rather than speculate on what the play was "originally" like, I prefer to work on the play as we have it, following Derek Traversi's contention that "the existence in *Pericles* of a definite unity of purpose can be detected even in the early scenes" (an opinion that can be traced back to Knight, 33) (20). The blood father-daughter lineage that I will also be examining has, of course, been charted by such critics as Frye, Hoy, Knight, Peterson, and Traversi, but they have not developed the analogy between literary and blood lineage in this play.

[6] Given this fantasy, it is interesting that none of the mothers in this play is portrayed as sexually desirable, except Thaisa—who is first presented to us as a daughter.

[7] In fact, the text—like Antiochus's daughter and Marina—may be viewed as an object over which father and son (Gower and Shakespeare) compete to prove their status as creators and procreators. I discuss this paradigm below.

[8] On this concept of originality in the Renaissance, see also the works by Barkan, Guillory, Hathaway, and Weinberg listed in the *Works Cited*. The question of whether sixteenth-century writers were actually more original than their predecessors is not an area that I will explore in the article; more germane to my argument is the extent to which the *idea* of being more original came into its own in this century.

[9] That this problem is a concern for Renaissance writers is particularly central to Quint's discussion of *Don Quixote*. On this problem in other Renaissance authors, see Ferguson on Boccaccio, and Guillory and Kerrigan on Milton.

[10] This abstract contract may, of course, be violated by younger authors who refuse to acknowledge their literary progenitors. As I will argue at the end of the article, the evasion of such issues reveals the extent to which Shakespeare was, finally, unable to fulfill the ideal of dispossession that he sets forth in his play.

[11] This phrase derives from Ben Jonson's famous satire of the play, "On *The New Inn*, Ode: To Himself."

[12] For a different reading of these lines, see Knowles; unlike most critics, Knowles believes that the antecedent to "who" in this quotation is Gower, not the audience of *Pericles*. It would, then, be Gower, not his audience, "who best can justify." If Knowles is right, however, then the phrase sets up a contradiction between the "judgement" of the audience and the "justifying" of Gower.

[13] For a more skeptical reading of Gower's self-sacrificial tendencies, see Dickey, 552. We may find an analogy to this aesthetics of dispossession in Shoshana Felman's assertion that the passing of a text from one generation to the next—an Oedipal text in particular—diminishes the temptation to possess a text absolutely (1025).

[14] On this concept of Petrarchism, see Braden, Freccero, and Vickers. Antiochus, of course, differs from the classic petrarchan lover by actually sleeping with the object of his affection.

[15] For Lacan's definition of otherness see *The Four Fundamental Concepts*, 188 *et passim*. Lacan traces the construction of a unified self to the "mirror stage," in which the child creates a unified concept of himself out of the varied fragments that constitute his psyche (*Ecrits* 1-7). Although Lacan's theories help us to think about *Pericles* in interesting ways, I am not arguing that the text is relentlessly Lacanian: if Lacanian thought illuminates many areas of the text, it does not predict all of them. For a more insistently Lacanian reading of *Pericles*, see Nevo.

[16] For Lacan, the notion of otherness arises from the Oedipal experience: "the ways of what one must do as man or as woman are entirely abandoned to the drama,

[17] Lacan discusses the notion of the father-as-Law in *The Four Fundamental Concepts:* "The father, the Name-of-the-father, sustains the structure of desire with the structure of law" (34). The concept that the father masters desire by means of his absolute law is illustrated in Antiochus's sexual mastery of his daughter and his mastery of her suitors by means of his riddle-as-law. On the close relationship between Antiochus as incestuous father and as tyrannical ruler, see also Jordan, "Eating the Mother," 337-40 and Relihan, 286-7.

[18] I use "idolatry" in the Augustinian sense—the sense that an idol is a reductive *imago* of the deity which gives the worshipper the illusion that he can control, manipulate, and fix his elusive deity, or beloved. For an extended discussion of this notion of idolatry, see Freccero. This perspective suggests that Shakespeare has been reading not only Gower but also Ovid, with whom Shakespeare shares an ongoing interest in incest, family, and metamorphoses. As Leonard Barkan has shown in his reading of the Metamorphoses, Ovid, too, equates incest with idolatrous, static, mastered art objects; and just as exogamy, for Ovid, represents a release from obsession, incest, and narcissism, so the written word represents a release from static, self-interested image-making (9).

[19] The stage directions come from the First Quarto of *Pericles.*

[20] On this aspect of the play, see also Nevo, 37-9, and Stockholder, 18.

[21] G. Wilson Knight expresses this moment as: "the result more of fascination, almost lust, than love" (37).

[22] I have followed the practice of most critics in capitalizing the noun "Other," to differentiate it from the adjective "other."

[23] This paradoxical perspective on mortality is dramatized by Knight, who notes that, in the play, death is a delusion (16)—it is only the denial of death that leads to mortality. The ability to face his mortality is a motif that characterizes Pericles. See also I.i.5; II.i.6-10, 71-6; II.iii.75-6 *et passim.*

[24] My reading of Oedipus here is strongly influenced by Harold Alderman's essay on the hermeneutics of Oedipus.

[25] Nor is Pericles ever presented as an absolute ruler of his kingdom. Even when we see him acting as a ruler, he does not appear as absolute master of his realm: when we first see him in Tyre, he is allowing Helicanus to lecture to him about how he should follow the advice of his counselors (I.ii.35-124). It is interesting, then, that the play ends as Pericles willingly dispossesses himself of Tyre to his daughter and her husband.

[26] Pericles points to this failure of self-recognition in Antiochus when he tells him: "Few love to hear the sins they love to act; / 'Twould braid yourself too near for me to tell it, (I.i.93-4).

[27] On the importance of family lineage in this play, see also Peterson, chapter one.

[28] For a reading of this scene that overlaps with mine, see Stockholder, 22. Dickey, 556-66; Hunt; 3-11, and Relihan, 287-94 present a more skeptical reading of Pericles's tendency toward dispossession.

[29] On Pericles as artist, see also II.iii.15-17.

[30] The contrast between Antiochus's daughter and Thaisa is heightened by the presentation of the suitors in the two kingdoms. Unlike the speechless suitors at Antioch, who are turned into frozen images of Antiochus's castrating power, the young suitors in Pentapolis, wearing emblems that represent their love-lorn states, appear as walking ekphrases—as words expressed as flesh.

[31] On contamination, see Freud, *Totem and Taboo,* chapter two, or Douglas, *Purity and Danger,* chapters seven and eight. On contamination and romance, see Frye, 137. This perspective on Pericles seems to have been first articulated by Knight: "He has not actively sinned, except in giving way to a lustful and cheating fantasy, but the result is immersion into an experience of evil with accompanying disgust and danger" (38). For a religious interpretation of contamination as the Fall of Man, see Marshall's article. Such associations between incest and plague recall, of course, the story of Oedipus.

[32] For Pericles, the threat of incest is clearly bound up with that of censorship. Pericles finds himself stifled by the Law of Antioch: "The great Antiochus, / 'Gainst whom I am too little to contend, / . . . Will think me speaking, though I swear to silence" (I.ii.17-20). See Cyrus Hoy's essay for an insightful exploration of the father-daughter incest threat as it affects Pericles as well as Antiochus.

[33] On this concept, see Lewis, 160. Benson and Jordan, *Renaissance Feminism,* discuss this problem as a general preoccupation of Renaissance literature by men.

[34] On this point, see also Adams; 48, Lewis, 160; and Nevo, 47.

[35] For further developments of this theory, see also Irigaray and Sedgwick.

[36] It is true, however, that this line affirms Marina's newfound identity as her mother's daughter, rather than as a wife-to-be: "My heart/Leaps to be gone into my mother's bosom" (V.iii.44-5).

[37] See also Helms, 330, on Marina's final absorption into patriarchy. On Renaissance constructions of women as subordinate to men, see especially Kelso, Maclean, and Henderson and McManus.

[38] This continual equation of woman with texts (rather than with authors) is compared to exogamy by Levi-Strauss, who tells us that, "the emergence of symbolic thought must have required that women, like words, would be objects that were exchanged" (469). Marina's appearance as an object of exchange between men is, then, analogous to the text of *Pericles* itself—the text that Gower gives up to Shakespeare, thus forging a close alliance between the two male artists.

[39] Marina's eloquence and artistry have been commented on by a number of critics. See, for instance, Archibald, 294-99; Dickey, 563; Helms, 328-30; and Kiefer, 217.

[40] That the text, finally, moves past this presentation of Marina as an all-powerful and generous artist to focus instead on the vision of a reunited family, reinforces the notion that Shakespeare, in this play, gives more importance to the idea of a fertile and continuous lineage than he does to the fulfillment of any one individual's desire.

[41] That Shakespeare wishes us to view Gower's text as not entirely interesting is suggested in the first lines of *Pericles*. It is interesting, from this perspective, that he represses the influence of the far more influential Ovid in his text, despite his obvious debts to this literary father.

[42] This emphasis on the audience's inheritance of the text runs from the beginning of the text, where Gower asks us to "accept my rimes" (I.i.16), to the end, where he pleads for us to be "evermore attending" (Epilogue.17).

[43] On Gower's role as an active author of and within the play, see especially the articles by Hillman and Marshall.

[44] For a chart of amplifications of the riddle, see Adams, 26.

[45] For a fuller discussion of the audience's role in *Pericles*, see Peterson, chapter one.

[46] Shakespeare again calls attention to this process when he has Cleon remark, "who makes the fairest show means most deceit" (I.iv.75), or when he presents Cerimon reading life in the apparently dead Thaisa. This pedagogy of "close reading" is itself a risk for Shakespeare; not only does it give us (his audience) a means by which we may usurp his authorial power by coming up with our own conclusions about the work, but we may learn to be attentive to the places where Shakespeare is, finally, unable to give up his text to the next generation that claims it—when he, for example, gives Marina up to Lysimachus, rather than affirms her continuing subjectivity.

Works Cited

Adams, Robert. *Shakespeare: The Four Romances*. New York: W.W. Norton and Company, 1989.

Alderman, Harold. "*Oedipus the King:* A Hermeneutic Tragedy." *Philosophy and Literature* 5 (1981): 176-85.

Archibald, Elizabeth. "'Deep Clerks She Dumbs': The Learned Heroine in *Apollonius of Tyre* and *Pericles*." *Comparative Drama* 22 (1988-89): 289-303.

Barkan, Leonard. *The Gods Made Flesh: Metamorphosis and the Pursuit of Paganism*. New Haven: Yale UP, 1986.

Benson, Pamela Joseph. *The Invention of the Renaissance Woman: The Challenge of Female Independence in the Literature and Thought of Italy and England*. University Park: The Pennsylvania State UP, 1992.

Bloom, Harold. *The Anxiety of Influence*. London: Oxford UP, 1966.

Braden, Gordon. "Beyond Frustration: Petrarchan Laurels in the Seventeenth Century." *Studies in English Literature, 1500-1800* 26 (1986): 5-23.

Dickey, Stephen. "Language and Role in *Pericles*." *English Literary Renaissance* 16 (1986): 550-56.

Douglas, Mary. *Purity and Danger: An Analysis of the Concepts of Pollution and Taboo*. London: Ark Paperbacks, 1966.

Eggers, Walter F. Jr. "Shakespeare's Gower and the Role of the Authorial Presenter." *Philological Quarterly* 54 (1975): 434-43.

Felman, Shoshana. "Beyond Oedipus: The Specimen Story of Psychoanalysis." *Lacan and Narration: The Psychoanalytic Difference in Narrative Theory*. Ed. Robert Con Davis. Baltimore: The Johns Hopkins Press, 1983.

Ferguson, Margaret. *Trials of Desire: Renaissance Defenses of Poetry.* New Haven: Yale UP, 1983.

Freccero, John. "The Fig Tree and the Laurel: Petrarch's Poetics." *Diacritics* 5 (1975): 34-9.

Freud, Sigmund. *Totem and Taboo: Resemblances between the Psychic Lives of Savages and Neurotics.* New York: W. W. Norton and Co., 1950.

Frye, Northrop. *The Secular Scripture: A Study of the Structure of Romance.* Cambridge: Harvard UP, 1982.

Guillory, John. *Poetic Authority: Spenser, Milton, and Literary History.* New York: Columbia UP, 1983.

Hathaway, Baxter. *The Age of Criticism: The Late Renaissance in Italy.* Ithaca: Cornell UP, 1962.

Helms, Lorraine. "The Saint in the Brothel: Or Eloquence Rewarded." *Shakespeare Quarterly* 41 (1990): 319-32.

Henderson, Katherine W. and McManus, Barbara F. *Half Humankind: Contexts and Texts of the Controversy about Women in England, 1540-1640.* Urbana: University of Illinois Press, 1985.

Hillman, Richard. "Shakespeare's Gower and Gower's Shakespeare: The Larger Debt of *Pericles.*" *Shakespeare Quarterly* 36 (1985): 427-37.

Hoeniger, David F. "Gower and Shakespeare in *Pericles.*" *Shakespeare Quarterly* 33 (1982): 461-79.

———.Ed. and Intro. *Pericles.* London: Methuen, 1963.

Hoy, Cyrus. "Fathers and Daughters in Shakespeare's Romances." *Shakespeare's Romances Reconsidered.* Ed. Carol Kay McGinnis and Henry E. Jacobs. Lincoln: University of Nebraska Press, 1978.

Hunt, Maurice. "A Looking Glass for Pericles." *Essays in Literature* 13 (1986): 3-11.

Irigaray, Luce. *This Sex Which is Not One.* Trans. Catherine Porter with Carolyn Burke. Ithaca: Cornell UP, 1985.

Jonson, Ben. *The Complete Poems.* Ed. George Parfitt. New Haven: Yale UP, 1982.

Jordan, Constance. "Eating the Mother': Property and Propriety in *Pericles.*" *New Essays on Renaissance Literature in Honor of Thomas M. Greene.* Ed. David Quint, Margaret Ferguson, G. W. Pigman, III, Wayne A. Rebhorn. Binghamton: Medieval and Renaissance Texts and Studies, 1992.

———. *Renaissance Feminism: Literary Texts and Political Models.* Ithaca: Cornell UP, 1990.

Kelso, Ruth. *Doctrine for a Lady of the Renaissance.* Urbana: University of Illinois Press, 1956.

Kerrigan, William. *The Sacred Complex: on the Psychogenesis of Paradise Lost.* Cambridge: Harvard UP, 1983.

Kiefer, Frederick. "Art, Nature, and The Written Word in *Pericles.*" *University of Toronto Quarterly* 61 (1991-1992): 207-25.

Knight, G. Wilson. *The Crown of Life: Essays in Interpretation of Shakespeare's Final Plays.* London: Oxford UP, 1947.

Knowles, Richard Paul. "'Wishes Fall Out as They're Will'd:' Artist, Audience, and Pericles's Gower." *English Studies in Canada* 9 (1983): 14-24.

Lacan, Jacques. *Ecrits: A Selection.* Trans. Alan Sheridan. New York: W.W. Norton & Co., 1977.

———. *The Four Fundamental Concepts of Psycho-Analysis.* Ed. Jacques Alain Miller. Trans. Alan Sheridan. New York: W.W. Norton and Co., 1981.

Lévi-Strauss, Claude. *The Elementary Structures of Kinship.* Trans. James Harle Bell and John Richard von Sturmer. Ed. Rodney Needham. Boston: Beacon Press, 1969.

Lewis, Anthony J. "'I Feed on Mother's Flesh;' Incest and Eating in *Pericles.*" *Essays in Literature* 15 (1988): 147-63.

Maclean, Ian. *The Renaissance Notion of Woman.* Cambridge: Cambridge UP, 1980.

Marshall, Cynthia. "The Seven Ages of *Pericles.*" *Journal of the Rocky Mountain Medieval and Renaissance Association* 8 (1987): 147-62.

Nevo, Ruth. *Shakespeare's Other Language.* New York: Methuen, 1987.

Peterson, Douglas L. *Time, Tide, and Tempest: A Study of Shakespeare's Romances.* San Marino: The Huntington Library, 1973.

Quint, David. *Origin and Originality in Renaissance Literature: Versions of the Source.* New Haven: Yale UP, 1983.

Relihan, Constance. "Liminal Geography: *Pericles* and the Politics of Place." *Philological Quarterly* 71 (1992): 281-99.

Rubin, Gayle. "The Traffic in Women: Notes on the 'Political Economy' of Sex." *Toward an Anthropology of Women*. Ed. Rayna R. Reiter. New York: Monthly Review Press, 1975.

Sedgwick, Eve Kosofsky. *Between Men: English Literature and Male Homosocial Desire*. New York: Columbia UP, 1985.

Shakespeare, William. *Pericles*. Ed. D. F. Hoeniger. New York: Methuen, 1963.

Stockholder, Kay. "Sex and Authority in *Hamlet, King Lear*, and *Pericles*." *Mosaic* 18 (1985): 17-29.

Traversi, Derek. *Shakespeare: The Last Plays*. New York: Harcourt, Brace, and Co., 1955.

Vickers, Nancy J. "Diana Described: Scattered Woman and Scattered Rhyme." *Critical Inquiry* 8 (1981): 265-79.

Wallace, David. "'Whan She Translated Was': A Chaucerian Critique of the Petrarchan Academy." *Literary Practice and Social Change in Britain, 1380-1530*. Ed. Lee Patterson. Berkeley: University of California Press, 1990.

Weinberg, Bernard. *A History of Literary Criticism in the Italian Renaissance*. Chicago: The University of Chicago Press, 1961.

FURTHER READING

Archibald, Elizabeth. "'Deep clerks she dumbs': The Learned Heroine in *Apollonius of Tyre* and *Pericles*." *Comparative Drama* 22, No. 4 (Winter 1988-89): 289-303.

    Compares the treatment of Marina's liberal arts education and high level of intellect in *Pericles* to earlier sources of the story, arguing that they are de-emphasized in Shakespeare's *Pericles*.

Bishop, T. G. "*Pericles*; or, the Past as Fate and Miracle." In *Shakespeare and the Theatre of Wonder*, pp. 93-124. Cambridge, England: Cambridge University Press, 1996.

    Examines the literary structure of *Pericles* and the role of storytelling.

Cutts, John P. "*Pericles*." In *Rich and Strange: A Study of Shakespeare's Last Plays*, pp. 4-22. Washington State University Press, 1968.

    Refutes F. D. Hoeniger's arguments concerning the Job-like nature of Pericles.

Fawkner, H. W. "Miracle." In *Shakespeare's Miracle Plays: "Pericles," "Cymbeline," and "The Winter's Tale,"* pp. 13-56. Cranbury, NJ: Associated University Presses, 1992.

    Discusses *Pericles* as a transition in Shakespeare's writing.

Hunt, Maurice. "A Looking Glass for *Pericles*." *Essays in Literature* XIII, No. 1 (Spring 1986): 3-11

    Compares *Pericles* with Thomas Lodge and Robert Greene's *A Looking Glass for London and England* to provide precedent for the reputed novel concepts of Shakespeare's play.

Mincoff, Marco. "Pericles, Prince of Tyre." In *Things Supernatural and Causeless: Shakespearean Romance*, pp. 27-41. University of Delaware Press, 1992.

    Provides an overview of *Pericles*, examining Shakespeare's alterations for his version from earlier texts and the structural and stylistic devices he employs.

Mullaney, Steven. "'All That Monarchs Do': The Obscured Stages of Authority in *Pericles*." In *The Place of the Stage: License, Play, and Power in Renaissance England*, pp. 135-51. Chicago: The University of Chicago Press, 1988.

    Considers the cultural context for the emergence of the romance plays, specifically *Pericles*.

Relihan, Constance C. "Liminal Geography: *Pericles* and the Politics of Place." *Philological Quarterly* 71, No. 3 (Summer 1992): 281-99.

    Examines the relationship between *Pericles*'s foreign setting and Shakespeare's intended message concerning James I's politics.

Thomas, Sidney. "The Problem of *Pericles*." *Shakespeare Quarterly* 34, No. 4 (Winter 1983): 448-50.

    Refutes F. David Hoeniger's theory that Shakespeare wrote the first two acts of *Pericles* in a deliberately inferior quality for effect.

Womack, Peter. "Shakespeare and the Sea of Stories." *The Journal of Medieval and Early Modern Studies* 29, No. 1 (Winter 1999): 169-87.

    Compares *Pericles* with the fifteenth-century East Anglican play *Mary Magdalen*, arguing that both plays emerge from a common tradition of the miracle play.

Young, Alan R. "A Note on the Tournament Impresas in *Pericles*." *Shakespeare Quarterly* 36, No. 4 (Winter 1985): 453-56.

    Postulates on the sources of Shakespeare's knowledge of impresas as indicated in *Pericles*.

The Phoenix and Turtle

For further information on the critical history of *The Phoenix and Turtle*, see *SC*, Volumes 10 and 38.

INTRODUCTION

Shakespeare's *The Phoenix and Turtle* is a short poem originally published as part of the collection *Love's Martyr*, compiled by Robert Chester in 1601. The 67-line poem remained untitled until an American edition in 1807 took the name from the two birds whose funeral is described. The central paradoxes of the poem for many scholars are the portrayal of a funeral for the phoenix, whose supernatural character lies in its regenerative power, and the suggestion that the funeral also marks the death of truth and beauty, which has provoked intense speculation on the poem's metaphysical and neo-Platonic influences. Long considered one of Shakespeare's strangest poetic productions and frequently overlooked in favor of the his dramatic works, *The Phoenix and Turtle* has recently come under scrutiny for its evocation of themes and ideals that animate Shakespeare's plays.

The Phoenix and Turtle portrays the union of two lovers, the phoenix and the turtle-dove, who have died. The Neoplatonic suggestion in the Threnos that truth and beauty are themselves the elements of this union has caused such scholars as Heinrich Straumann (1977) to claim that the poem is at once a celebration of such a union and a statement of its impermanence, a theme he also identifies in *Hamlet*, *Cymbeline*, and *Romeo and Juliet*. The union of the two birds has been interpreted by Brian Green (1979) as using alchemical fusion as an allegory for spiritually pure love. Scholars have disputed the sexual nature of this love-union, and the gender of the birds has remained particularly contested, as G. Wilson Knights details (1955). Dennis Kay (1998) argues that the "self-consuming uniqueness" of this love "implies a rarefied turning away from carnality," while Murray Copland (1965) identifies the metaphysical implications of the poem as merely fashionable trappings of a depiction, in unison with Shakespeare's dramatic works, of a deeply human problem. Using a psychoanalytic approach, Philip K. Bock (1993) reads the poem as an expression of the essential human longing for individuation within unity, a theme that appears most strikingly in *Hamlet*.

The concern with difference within unity in the poem has attuned interpreters to its Christian elements: particularly its evocation of the Trinity, neo-Platonic love, and its stylistic resemblances to burial services from *The Book of Common Prayer*, as Richard C. McCoy argues (1997). The mortality of the phoenix, and the fact that there is no offspring of its union with the turtle dove, signifies the continued union of truth and beauty, the poem suggests to many critics, but the irrecoverable loss for human beings of such an ideal. Vincent Petronella (1975) has described *The Phoenix and Turtle* as a "vision of an overwhelming disaster—the destruction of those values linked with the Phoenix and the Turtle-Dove": constancy and self-sacrifice. He reads the poem as a depiction of "defunctive" mystic ecstasy: it is not the spiritual ecstasy which distances the soul from the body, but that "body and soul are consumed together."

The ideality of the relationship between the phoenix and turtle does not lend itself to the reading that the poem describes the relationship between Queen Elizabeth and the Earl of Essex, the political background that many critics speculate served as the inspiration for the work. Murray Copland insists that "behind the birds an eminently desirable human possibility is being mooted." The poem itself, critics argue, enacts a problematic mediation between the transcendent and the mortal, and emphasizes the unattainability of ideal values in the mortal sphere. Scholarly interest has been rejuvenated in the poem as a complex if condensed expression of metaphysical reflections on love as well as an articulation of the problem of mortality, themes elaborated in many of Shakespeare's major works.

OVERVIEW

Dennis Kay (essay date 1998)

SOURCE: "Miscellaneous Poems: 'The Phoenix and Turtle.'" in *William Shakespeare: Sonnets and Poems*, Twayne Publishers, 1998, pp. 81-88.

[*In the essay that follows, Kay provides a general introductory discussion of the poem, with particular attention to its textual history and critical reception.*]

The Phoenix and Turtle is Shakespeare's contribution to *Loves Martyr: or, Rosalins Complaint, Allegorically shadowing the Truth of Love, in the constant Fate of the Phoenix and Turtle* (1601), a volume of poems associated with Sir John Salusbury and compiled by Robert Chester. Appended to this work are "Some new compositions, of severall modern writers whose names are subscribed to their several workes, upon the first subject: viz., the Phoenix and Turtle." These modern writers are "Ignoto" (possibly John Donne), Shake—speare, John Marston, George Chapman, and Ben Jon—son. Shakespeare's poem appears without a title.

Chester's *Love's Martyr* is an allegorical poem (treating the myth of the phoenix's rebirth from its own ashes) whose occasion and meaning remain obscure. Chester was a member of the household of Sir John Salusbury of Lleweni in Denbigh, North Wales.[2] Salusbury was distantly related to Queen Elizabeth. In 1586, he married Ursula, the illegitimate daughter of the fourth earl of Derby; and in 1601, the year Chester's poem was published, he was knighted by the queen. In 1586, just three months before the wedding, Sir John's brother Thomas was executed for treason. One possible reading of Chester's poem and its publication, then, is that it was composed as private consolation at the time of the execution and the marriage in 1586, and then published—with a dazzling group of authors lending their luster to the occasion—at the time of Salusbury's knighthood and the family's rehabilitation in 1601. It is relatively easy to see why the younger poets—each of whom was in need of patronage—might have been drawn to write for Chester's volume in praise of the Salusburys and the queen.

Given the importance of the phoenix in Queen Elizabeth's cult, connections with her have been proposed: many scholars have claimed to find an allegory of her relationship with the earl of Essex, executed in 1601.[3] Most commentators support the connection between Chester's poem and the circumstances of Salusbury's wedding in 1586 and suggest that Shakespeare's piece was written at the same time as the other "modern" poems, some time before 1601.[4] Nevertheless, such a connection by no means rules out the possibility that the poem was written, or perhaps revised, in the context of the Essex rebellion and the queen's conduct during and after it. Marie Axton's subtle suggestion—that the relationship at the core of the poem involves the queen and her subjects—indicates that a profitable area of study would be the continued exploration of the connections between the poem and the cult of Elizabeth.[5]

In a radical assault upon received wisdom, E. A. J. Honigmann goes further and argues, as part of his "early-start" view of Shakespeare's writing career, that his poem is much earlier than 1601 and that it should be seen as contemporary with the Salusbury nuptials.[6] He makes this argument as part of his attempt to revive and justify the speculation that William Shakespeare was the same person as a William

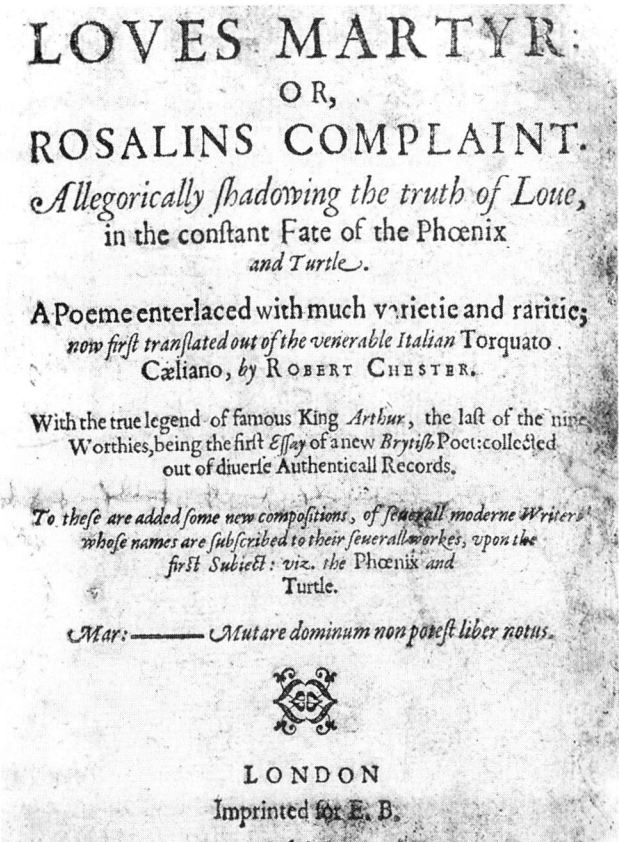

A title page to Love's Martyr or, Rosalin's Complaint, *which contains Shakespeare's* The Phoenix and Turtle.

Shakeshafte, who was a retainer of a gentry household at Hoghton Tower in Lancashire in the 1580s—at a time when the historical record for William Shakespeare is essentially blank.

The Hoghtons of Hoghton Tower were connected with the Stanley earls of Derby. Ursula, who married Salusbury, was the sister of Ferdinando Stanley, also known as Lord Strange, who was later, and briefly, earl of Derby. Lord Strange had a company of players, including at various times Richard Burbage, Edward Alleyn, and, as Honigmann argues, William Shakespeare. Among other pieces of evidence, the presence of compliments to ancestors of the Stanley family in Shakespeare's early history plays may not be accidental.[7]

From what we know about Shakespeare's early life, Honigmann's theory must remain speculation, but he may have opened up a vein of research that will prove fruitful. Even if Shakespeare's "early start" is not accepted, Honigmann's fuller demonstration of his connection with the Stanley family plausibly connects Shakespeare to the Chester volume. It might also be noted that in 1601 Shakespeare's own relation to the patronage system was clouded in ambiguity. His patron Southampton was sentenced to death in February 1601 in the aftermath of the Essex rebellion and, although reprieved, was to remain in prison for several years. Also in 1601, Shakespeare's father died (buried on 8 September), and shortly afterwards his right to bear the coat of arms that had been granted in 1596 was challenged (albeit unsuccessfully) by the York Herald.[8]

My following remarks, pending the discovery of further evidence to support Honigmann's claim, assume a later date for *The Phoenix and Turtle.* Shakespeare's poem owes something to the Eighth Song ("In a grove most rich of shade") in Sidney's *Astrophil and Stella* and seems to be related in setting and subject to Matthew Roydon's *Elegie* on Sidney, published in *The Phoenix Nest* (1593). In themselves these possible connections do not necessarily contradict Honigmann, since Sidney had died in 1586, and Roydon's poem was clearly written quite soon afterwards.[9]

Shakespeare's poem is brief, a mere 67 short lines disposed in 17 stanzas. The formal components of the piece are immediately apparent. The first of two marked sections consists of 13 four-line stanzas rhymed *abba*. It is followed by the Threnos, consisting of 5 three-line stanzas. The first section is further divided into two parts, namely an invocation of 5 stanzas followed by the explicit announcement "Here the anthem doth commence" (21). There are some obvious symmetries about this arrangement—5 stanzas of Prologue, 8 of Anthem, 5 of Threnos. Furthermore, the numerical center of the poem is occupied by a stanza expressive of stasis, a still point in defiance of time:

> So between them love did shine,
> That the Turtle saw his right
> Flaming in the Phoenix' sight;
> Either was the other's mine.
>
> (33-36)

Such features may (or may not) indicate the presence of architectural or numerological structural principles in the poem, just as the line total may (or may not) relate to Queen Elizabeth's age (she turned 68 in September of 1601). The poem also seems to imply some form of ceremonial actuality beyond the imagined procession, with its reference to the "tragic scene" (52), to "this urn" (65), which is "Here" (55).

Shakespeare's poem connects with the end of Chester's piece—which he had evidently read attentively—where from the funeral pyre of the phoenix and turtle rises up a new phoenix in whose heart lives "a perpetual love / Sprong from the bosom of the turtle dove." In other words, before Shakespeare's poem begins, we are to imagine the funeral pyre and the placement of the ashes in the urn.

The beginning invocation, in the tradition of poems (such as Skelton's *Philip Sparrow* and the rhyme "Who Killed Cock Robin?") purporting to be funeral masses for dead birds, summons to the burial service the "bird of loudest lay," the swan, the crow, and the presiding eagle, and banishes the screech owl, as well as "Every fowl of tyrant wing." At the head of the procession is the "death-divining swan" in the office of the priest, accompanied by the proverbially long-lived crow, whose breath engenders its offspring. There is a perhaps a suggestion of comprehensiveness in this anthology of birds, with the four elements implied by the crow (the earth), the swan (water), the eagle (the air), and the phoenix (fire) (Roe, 51). Such compendiousness is a common elegiac topos, which was held to be both panegyric and implicitly consolatory. The "bird of loudest lay" ought, of course, to be the phoenix, having risen again; but since we learn that the Phoenix and Turtle left "no posterity" (59), some scholars have argued that it cannot be and is in fact the nightingale, or the crane, or cockerel. Others, with equal confidence, have argued that it must be the phoenix.[10]

The congregation sings its anthem on the lovers' unity in diversity:

> So they loved as love in twain
> Had the essence but in one,
> Two distincts, division none:
> Number there in love was slain.
>
> (25-28)

Shakespeare uses the languages of academic logic and philosophy paradoxically in the service of metaphor and ambiguity—"How true a twain / Seemeth this concordant one!" (45-46). The implication that love can be so powerful as to overwhelm logic and reason is a Shakespearean commonplace, although hardly unique to him. For example, one of the lovers in John Donne's *Songs and Sonnets* speaks thus to his mistress of the riddle of the phoenix—"We two being one, are it" ("The Canonization").

Much of the interpretive difficulty, as well as much of the richness and strange beauty of the poem, is generated by Shakespeare's attempt to express the mysteries associated with the idea of union. As with many Renaissance writers, he approaches this challenge through the medium of paradox—whereby he conveys through words a meaning that highlights the limitations of words to convey meaning. Commenting on such lines as

> Hearts remote, yet not asunder;
> Distance, and no space was seen
> 'Twixt this Turtle and his queen:
> But in them it were a wonder.
>
> (29-32)

and

> Single nature's double name

> Neither two nor one was called.
> (39-40)

Maurice Evans writes, "This love is something which at once preserves and destroys incompatibility, which simultaneously negates and maintains distinction" (Evans, 55). Many commentators have remarked upon the abstract language—love, constancy, essence, reason, property, and so on. Such terminology, as well as the use of paradox in these stanzas, has given rise to many Neoplatonic readings of the poem.

Shakespeare is vague about the identity of the speakers of the first two sections. The opening set of instructions, with its imperative tone—"Let the bird of loudest lay . . . Let the priest in surplice white"—is followed by an announcement from another unidentified speaker—"Here the anthem doth commence," after which a third speaker, with a more philosophical tone of abstraction and paradox, takes over.

The union of the Phoenix and Turtle is celebrated and defined as a moment in which Reason is" in itself confounded." Reason's response is twofold. First it proclaims, rounding off the anthem with the rhymes that had begun it,

> "How true a twain
> Seemeth this concordant one!
> Love hath reason, Reason none,
> If what parts, can so remain."
> (45-48)

Reason is then allocated the role of "chorus" to the "tragic scene" of the dead lovers and responds with the final Threnos, in which an attempt is made to interpret the miraculous events that have gone before. The passage perhaps recalls Hymen's injunction at the end of *As You Like It* to "Feed yourself with questioning; / That reason wonder may diminish" (5.4.138-39). At this point in the poem, 52 lines have elapsed, which may be expressive of the completion of an annual cycle as a consoling metaphor for death and continuity.

The core of Reason's second speech, in a style markedly different from its exclamation in the immediate aftermath of the Anthem, is the understanding that the unique union of the Phoenix and Turtle—the logic-defying conjunction of "two distincts," beauty and truth—has left the world. In other words, the Phoenix and Turtle are dead and gone:

> Beauty, Truth, and Rarity,
> Grace in all simplicity,
> Here enclosed in cinders lie.
> (53-55)

The self-consuming uniqueness leading to the final, issueless incineration of the Phoenix and Turtle is summed up in the vaguely Neoplatonic phrase "married chastity," which implies a rarefied turning away from carnality. There is an analogous, though less renunciatory, passage in Spenser's *Prothalamion* (1596), where the poet imagines a blessing being pronounced over the two betrothed couples—

> And let your bed with pleasures chast
>   abound,
> That fruitfull issue may to you afford,
> Which may your foes confound,
> And make your joyes redound. . . .
> (103-6: *Shorter Poems*, ed. Oram, 766)

—a wish that yokes married chastity and abundance. In fact the Chesters' married chastity was closer to the Spenserian than to the Shakespearean model celebrated in the poem. They were far from childless and indeed by 1601 had ten children, one of whom was 14 years old. This fecundity was a point John Marston was quick to make in his own poem that followed on the heels of Shakespeare's:

> O twas a moving *Epicedium!*
> Can Fire? can Time? can blackest Fate consume
> So rare creation? No, tis thwart to sense,
> Corruption quakes to touch such excellence,
> Nature exclaimes for Justice, Justice fate,
> Ought unto Nought can never remigrate.
> Then looke; for see what glorious issue
>   (brighter
> Then clearest fire, and beyond faith farre whiter
> Than Dians tier) now springs from yonder
>   flame?
> (Cited by Roe, 46)

Shakespeare's strange and haunting poem was published, as we have seen, in 1601. There was a reissue in 1611. And there seems little reason to doubt the accuracy of the attribution to Shakespeare, unusual though the poem is. None of the other authors whose work was included raised any objection. Since Malone, and despite a period in the nineteenth century when some doubts were raised, its place in the canon is now established. F. T. Prince (xlii) calls it "a priceless addition to Shakespeare's lyrics," and it has inspired some remarkable critical responses over the last 60 or 70 years.

There has been little agreement, however, among commentators about the tone of the conclusion:

> Truth may seem, but cannot be,
> Beauty brag, but 'tis not she,
> Truth and Beauty buried be
> To this urn let those repair
> That are either true or fair;
> For these dead birds sigh a prayer.
> (62-67)

Some critics have argued that the Phoenix and Turtle have bequeathed to mortals an image of ideal love to which they can aspire.[11] Others view the conclusion as tragic, as a recognition of the gulf separating mortal comprehension (which sees only "dead birds") from the essential nature of the creatures and their union. Still others try to hold both views: Roe, for example, claims that the poem "views its Platonism from the perspective of a tragic denouement and regards its subject as a melancholy one. And yet its tone is buoyant" (54).

The academic criticism of the poem is of recent origin, really beginning in the mid-twentieth century, when its inclusion in Helen Gardner's *The Metaphysical Poets* (1957) stimulated interest. Since then it has continued to enjoy rarefied acclaim.[12] The separate tradition of biographical/historical reading has continued and remains vigorous. But there was for many years—outside and inside the academy—a vogue for treating the poem as almost abstract "pure poetry" ("the magic of sound and cadence," in the words of Robert Ellrodt, "making comment unnecessary"). Here are some of the other comments the poem has nonetheless elicited:

> [The poem] floats high above the plane of intellectual apprehension . . . There is surely no more astonishing description of the highest attainable by human love . . . an immediate intuition into the nature of things. It is inevitable that such poetry should be obscure, mystical, and strictly unintelligible . . . it necessarily hovers between the condition of being the highest poetry of all and not being poetry at all.[13]

> . . . in celebration of a mystical love-union beyond sex, as we understand it, and all biological categories. . . .[14]

> . . . the beauty of the poem consists in a marriage between intense emotion and almost unintelligible fantasy. It is inexhaustible because it is inexplicable; and it is inexplicable because it is deliberately unreasonable, beyond and contrary to both reason and nature. (Prince, xliv)

> As an anonymous work it would command our highest admiration. The oracular, which of all styles is the most contemptible when it fails, is here completely successful; the illusion that we have been in another world and heard the voices of gods is achieved.[15]

The Phoenix and Turtle has inspired many such remarks. Taking the scholarship as a whole, it is clear that the poem has generated less unease or embarrassment than the longer narrative poems. Critics repelled by Venus or made impatient by Lucrece seem to be reduced to wordless awe by *The Phoenix and Turtle*. The comparative rarity of comment on the piece by female scholars and critics is also notable.[16]

Notes

[2] Carleton Brown, ed., *Poems by Sir John Salusbury and Robert Chester*, EETS ES 113 (1914).

[3] William H. Matchett, *"The Phoenix and the Turtle": Shakespeare's Poem and Chester's "Loues Martyr"* (The Hague: Mouton 1965).

[4] John Buxton, "Two Dead Birds," in *English Renaissance Studies Presented to Dame Helen Gardner*, ed. John Carey (Oxford: Oxford University Press, 1981), 44-55.

[5] Marie Axton, *The Queen's Two Bodies: Drama and the Elizabethan Succession* (London: Royal Historical Society, 1978), 118-20. See also Anthea Hume, "*Love's Martyr*, 'The Phoenix and the Turtle', and the Aftermath of the Essex Rebellion," *Review of English Studies*, n.s., 40 (1989), 48-71.

[6] E. A. J. Honigmann, *Shakespeare: The "Lost" Years* (Manchester: Manchester University Press, 1985), 90-113.

[7] See the concise summary in Andrew Gurr, *The Shakespearean Playing Companies* (Oxford: Clarendon Press, 1996), 257-62.

[8] For the coat of arms, see Schoenbaum, 228-32.

[9] Dennis Kay, *Melodious Tears: The English Funeral Elegy from Spenser to Milton* (Oxford: Oxford University Press, 1990), 64-66.

[10] Baldwin, *Literary Genetics*, 368; Peter Dronke, "The Phoenix and the Turtle," *Orbis Litterarium* 23 (1968), esp. 208.

[11] See Dronke and Robert Ellrodt, "An Anatomy of *The Phoenix and the Turtle*," *Shakespeare Survey* 15 (1962), 99-110.

[12] For example, William Empson, "The Phoenix and the Turtle," *Essays in Criticism* 16 (1966), 147-53.

[13] J. Middleton Murry, *Discoveries* (1924), cited in Rollins, *Poems*, 565-66.

[14] G. Wilson Knight, *The Mutual Flame: On Shakespeare's Sonnets and "The Phoenix and the Turtle"* (London: 1955).

[15] C. S. Lewis (1954), 509.

[16] An exception is Marjorie Garber, "Two Birds With One Stone: Lapidary Re-Inscription in *The Phoenix and Turtle*," *The Upstart Crow* 5 (1984), 5-19.

S. M. Bonaventure (essay date 1964)

SOURCE: "The Phoenix Renewed," *Ball State Teachers College Forum,* Vol. V, No. 3, Autumn, 1964, pp. 72-76.

[*In the following essay, Bonaventure considers the diverse interpretive approaches to the poem and defends a metaphysical reading.*]

There is a suggestion of poetic justice in some of the phenomena which prefaced the fourth centenary of Shakespeare's birth. Witness his Phoenix attesting its immortality by rising with new life and brilliance from the ashes of dry discussions on authenticity and sources to wave in its plumes, in Robert Ellrodt's borrowed image, "various light in different eyes."[1]

In view of such renewal, special interest attaches to surveys such as those of R. Ellrodt and of J. W. Lever,[2] from which we can deduce how long a road separates the modern reader of Shakespeare from the eighteenth-century scholar. The latter, in his search for "beauty, truth andrarity" in Shakespeare, ignored without apology the brief "poeticall Essaie" on the Phoenix and the Turtle appended over Shakespeare's signature to Robert Chester's allegorical *Love's Martyr* (1601). Remonstrance, if any, was no doubt met with the authority of George Steven's Preface to his edition of the plays (1793), which denied any significance to Shakespeare's lyric poems; or in America, with Emerson's damning praise of them as poets' poems.[3] But the scholar of the mid-twentieth century, whatever his locus, cannot ignore the flash of light which *The Phoenix and the Turtle* throws on Shakespeare's relation to seventeenth-century poetic development. However, he must be prepared to find a Phoenix that has not only risen from its ashes by the power of the modern metaphysical afflatus, but has also been refracted, atomized, and even divinized. The wide range of modern response to the various dimensions of the poem is to be hailed as both negatively and positively advantageous. It can prove an astringent for the "creative" reader and at the same time lead towards further clarification and new synthesis. The present study is an attempt to focus the chief points of divergence in studies of the last decade and perhaps carry the current Phoenix dialogue one step farther in its logical progression.

In the last decade little argument has been raised over earlier explorations of *The Phoenix and the Turtle* for personal allegory and biographical significance. There have been heard no concerted denials that the poem provides a fascinating mirror in which the reader may catch reflections of the concepts and the idiom of Shakespeare's plays and sonnets: the "marriage of true minds"; the "pair of loving turtledoves / That could not live assunder. . . ." in *1 Henry VI;* Helena and Hermia living as though in one body in the romantic world of *A Midsummer Night's Dream.* Nor has there been incentive to challenge the clear parallels between the sonnets and the verses of the Phoenix lyric,[4] which have convinced readers that the doctrine of *The Phoenix and the Turtle* "consummates that of the *Sonnets.*"[5] Some scientific formal interest has been generated by the focusing of *The Phoenix and the Turtle* as "a copybook example of technique"[6] in its tripartite progression from Invocation to Anthem and finally to a climactic Threnos, in a symmetrical stanzaic pattern of 5-8-5; in the corresponding modulation from pictorial presentation to purely abstract generalization; and the equally significant change from quatrains in truncated trochaics to triplets built on only three rhymes.

A higher degree of rejuvenating scholarship has flowered in detailed examinations of literary influence—classical, medieval, Elizabethan—as Shakespeare's assemblage of symbolical birds of mourning has been traced to Ovid's *Amores,* poems of Lactantius and Claudianus, Pliny, Petrarch, and to Chaucer's *Parlement of Foules.* But the fervor of all such studies has been inevitably cooled by the realization that Shakespeare had only to reach for one of the most popular Elizabethan poetical miscellanies, *The Phoenix Nest* (1593), and read Matthew Roydon's "Elegy for Astrophil" to find a model for his memorial tribute: the eagle, the swan, the turtle-dove, and the phoenix introduced in fitting order. The Arabian setting is here, too, and the death-dealing flame.

More recently, however, it is the logical, metaphysical, and theological dimensions of *The Phoenix and the Turtle* which have been the prime discoveries, attaching to the poem new significance and heightened value. For it is in these dimensions that it is most feasible to attempt delineation of Shakespeare's individual response to his subject, his medium, and his milieu. Yet it is precisely in these same dimensions that further clarification is needed. On these levels, scholarly arguments have reached a variety of opposed positions. For Cleanth Brooks, *The Phoenix and the Turtle* illustrates not only the Donnean metaphysical conceit but with equal clarity the paradoxical nature of all poetic experience. It is his considered opinion that "A history of poetry from Dryden's time to our own might bear as its subtitle 'The Half-Hearted Phoenix.'"[7] Yet a direct antithesis is reached by Alvarez in his clearly articulated study, in which by close analysis of the language—the "terms" of the poem—he structures the conclusion that "Shakespeare, in this poem at least, is the more honest logician and not at all the Metaphysical poet."[8]

To pass from ideas and idiom to the tone of the poem is not to enter an area of unanimous response, but rather to hear echoes of symbolic, metaphysical, or rhetorical reading. Does the funereal setting and the final urn of the ashes distill a somber, melancholy atmosphere? Is the tone of *The Phoenix and the Turtle* that of a disillusioned Hamlet in his responses to Queen Gertrude and Ophelia? Need it be identified as the voice of satire setting an ancient ideal equation of truth and beauty against a Renaissance world in which beauty can stand no test of reason or time, and truth must always be unpalatable: truth and beauty are never to be found in one and the same individual? Is the Phoenix lyric to be read as a road sign pointing backwards to the author of the *Sonnets*, of *As You Like It* and *A Midsummer Night's Dream*, but already forecasting the bitter world of *King Lear* and of the Problem Comedies? The influence of Heinrich Straumann's reading of *The Phoenix and the Turtle* as a turning-point towards a tragic view of life[9] may well have disposed other readers to hear the Threnos of the poem as a bleak assertion of tragic paradox.

It is clear that the arguments posed in modern re-examination of Shakespeare's Phoenix are not to be resolved in the light of literary tradition and conventions. Such knowledge cannot suffice to illuminate poetic communication which to one reader presents "a paradigm of the Trinity in the theological connotations of essence—distincts, divisions, and number";[10] to another, "nowhere suggests an allegory of religious mysteries or even of divine love";[11] and to a theologian remains a "metaphor of metaphor" attempting to express in a physical image the metaphysical relation of abstractions.[12]

The intellectual challenge is not met in the poem at the outset. In the opening Invocation, Shakespeare walks smoothly in the narrative and pictorial tradition of the bird-elegy. In the Anthem there is one final sensuous communication in terms of the doctrine of transmission of spirits in love:

> So between them love did shine,
> That the turtle saw his right
> Flaming in the phoenix' sight;
> Either was the other's mine.
>
> (11.33-36)

The eyes of each are for the other the source of the consuming flame. Then follows the development of the phoenix image that makes evident Shakespeare's originality of treatment and his power in weaving the texture of paradox. One is drawn to echo F. P. Wilson's judgment that Shakespeare, had he turned from dramatic verse to nondramatic at the end of the century, might have been the greatest of the metaphysical poets.[13] For here the rhetorical and symbolic conventions are lifted from the level of the sensuous imagination, refined to the language of pure mathematical abstraction, and organized within the frame of rational argument.

> So they lov'd, as love in twain
> Had the essence but in one;
> Two distincts, division none
> Number there in love was slain.
>
> (11.25-28)

The mathematical terms, *twain, none, one,* are placed in emphatic rhyme position and repeated in this position within the Anthem to set the paradox in sharper focus.

> That it cried, 'How true a twain
> Seemeth this concordant one!
> Love hath reason, Reason none,
> If what parts can so remain.'
>
> (11.45-48)

Here Shakespeare's terse handling and compression of grammatical pattern suggest Donne's intellectual effect, but they do not rest on this level.

It is the central quatrain of the Anthem that reveals most clearly the essential character of Shakespeare's metaphysical mode.

> Property was thus appaled,
> That the self was not the same;
> Single nature's double name
> Neither two nor one was called.
>
> (11.37-40)

Here we find the double negation, the Scylla and Charybdis upon which modern interpretation breaks up into contradictory splinters. In the poem Shakespeare has followed Petrarch in identifying the Phoenix with only one sex, as the Turtle's queen. He has moved toward Donne in the paradox of unity in duality. But the unity of Shakespeare's vision is not the metaphor of one Phoenix, echoing the traditional idea of the bird's bisexuality; it is a unity that transcends Neo-Platonic philosophy of love with its psychological paradox of lovers who die to self and yet live, each in the beloved. The Phoenix and the Turtle are united—fused—by one mutual flame which transforms them, raises them to a new level of being to which the terms of human individuality and unity do not apply. Or if they are made to apply, it can only be analogically, and hence can be expressed only by negation of logical meaning. The negation remains ontologically logical within the Christian concept of grace fundamental in Elizabethan thought. Through grace (the union with Christ by Divine Charity) man is reborn to a new life, a supernatural life in which he is "one with Christ" yet retains his individuality of soul. Shakespeare's negation echoes that of St. Paul: "*I* live now not I, but Christ liveth in me."[14] Shakespeare uses here the later technique of Donne's "Canonization" in applying to concepts of human love the language of theology, but his purpose and vision rise above Donne's fusion of intellect and passion and reach a level of universal truth that remains uniquely his.

There remains the climax of Shakespeare's Phoenix song, the soaring Threnos with its contemplation of the transcendentals. The first triplet, in its enumeration of qualities, echoes tersely the idea of number—multiplicity—reduced to *simplicity:*

> Beauty, Truth, and Rarity,
> Grace in all simplicity,
> Here enclos'd, in cinders lie.
>
> (11.53-55)

The closing line of the third triplet provides another atomic paradox: "married chastity." Chester's expansive companion poem may be trusted as a basis for reading here "chaste love" such as he emphasizes, a love identified with fidelity or constancy. The traditional image of the Turtle as a bird dedicated to Venus but chaste in its one mating for life combines here with the Phoenix to suggest the concept of absolute constancy in married life. To what degree Shakespeare's phrasing may have been prompted by the biblical thought that in the resurrection "they shall neither marry nor be married" remains conjecture. In the metaphysical vein the phrase would permit of translation in terms of such love as that celebrated by Donne in his "Valediction," love so completely and purely a union of minds and souls that it rests not in physical union, which is the essence of "sublunary love." In this sense the term presents no paradox, only a literal statement of fact.

The Threnos closes with an exhortation which, on surface reading, may suggest paradox. "Truth and Beauty buried be." Yet Reason calls on those "That are either true or fair. . . ." to approach their tomb. The intellectual idiom and rational structure are set into double negation, drawing the reader's attention to transcendent values. Here the communication may appear anti-rational and even self-contradictory. But within the consistent context of Christian philosophy and theology there is no difficulty here in following Shakespeare to a consideration of absolute values in their transcendent relation, on an analogical but rational plane. If the reader remains on the level of the absolutes focused in the preceding stanzas, he will not fail to distinguish easily between the ideal or transcendent Truth and Beauty that has been achieved by the Phoenix and the Turtle and the human level of those who approach their tomb. In such resolution of the paradox there is heard, not the presage of bleak tragedy, nor merely brave undertones. It is rather a harmony of solemn rhetoric and inspired idealism rising to a note of triumph and universal hope. The communication is made in Shakespeare's unique metaphysical mode by which he penetrates the world of vision—of universal truth—and leads after him those whose ears are attuned to the true accent of his voice and language. For the modern mind that finds the traditional realm of exegesis and analogy an alien world, the metaphysical voice of Shakespeare may be lost in "unintelligible mystery" or drowned out by the babel of commentary.

Notes

[1] "An Anatomy of 'The Phoenix and the Turtle,'" *Shakespeare Survey,* XV (1962), 99.

[2] "The Poems," *ibid.,* 25-30.

[3] R. W. Emerson, Preface to *Parnassus,* as quoted by A. Alvarez, "The Phoenix and the Turtle," in *Interpretations,* ed. by John Wain (London, 1955), p. 4.

[4] The most obvious parallels can be noted in Sonnets 14, 36, 101, 136.

[5] C. S. Lewis, *English Literature in the Sixteenth Century* (Oxford, 1954), p. 508.

[6] A. Alvarez, "The Phoenix and the Turtle," in *Interpretations,* ed. by John Wain, p. 4.

[7] *The Well Wrought Urn* (New York, 1947), p. 18.

[8] *Op. cit.,* p. 11.

[9] Heinrich Straumann, *Phönix und Taube* (Zurich, 1953).

[10] J. V. Cunningham, "'Essence' and *The Phoenix and the Turtle,*" *ELH,* XIX (1952), 273-75.

[11] Ellrodt, *op. cit.,* p. 105.

[12] W. Ong, S. J., "Metaphor and the Twinned Vision," *Sewanee Review,* LXIII (1955), 199-200.

[13] *Seventeenth Century Prose,* The Ewing Lectures (U. of California, 1960), p. 12.

[14] Galatians 2:20.

LOVE AND ROMANCE

G. Wilson Knight (essay date 1955)

SOURCE: "Shakespeare's Poem," in *The Mutual Flame: On Shakespeare's Sonnets and* The Phoenix and the Turtle, Methuen and Co. Ltd., 1955, pp. 193-204.

[*In the following essay, Knight relates the imagery and the paradoxically tragic regeneration of the Phoe-*

nix to the creative process, but rejects a narrow biographical interpretation of the poem.]

This, then, is the context in which we must study Shakespeare's contribution. *The Phoenix and the Turtle* has received a sensitive handling. John Masefield accorded it high praise in his *William Shakespeare* (1911). In *Discoveries* (1924) J. Middleton Murry wrote that 'it gives us the highest experience which it is possible for poetry to give, and it gives it without intermission'. It was the subject of an interesting monograph by 'Ranjee' (Ranjee G. Shahani) in *Towards the Stars* (which I reviewed in *The Criterion*, April, 1931). I have myself written of it in *The Shakespearian Tempest* (1932; App. A, 320-5) and *The Christian Renaissance* (1933; XII, 327-9). It was an important step in the general argument of Kenneth Muir and Sean O'Loughlin in *The Voyage to Illyria* (1937). Cleanth Brooks has touched it in *The Well-Wrought Urn* (1947); Bonamy Dobrée has broadcast an appreciation of its music (1948); and we now have Heinrich Straumann's monograph (p. 149). But these are only a few examples of the interpretations that have from time to time been offered, many of which are crisply summarised in the *New Variorum* (1938) edition of Shakespeare's *Poems* by Hyder Edward Rollins. Among these was an interesting essay by Alfred von Mauntz in 1893 (*Shakespeare Jahrbuch*, XXVIII, 308-10), seeing the poem, rather as did *The Voyage to Illyria* later, as a symbolic representation of Shakespeare's estrangement from Southampton, regarded as the friend of the Sonnets; and a significant contribution by Charles Downing (*The Shrine;* May, 1902; 34-7), reading the various poems of our collection in terms of ideal and idealist, suggesting the equation of Shakespeare's Phoenix with the Fair Youth of the Sonnets, and regarding his dramatic work as a development from this central inspiration. To these we may add the discussion of Shakespeare's source, or background, material in T. W. Baldwin's *On the Literary Genetics of Shakespeare's Poems and Sonnets* (1950).

We need commit ourselves to no biographical details. Shakespeare may have had more than one ardent love, and *The Phoenix and the Turtle* need be referred to no particular person or event. Even so, we shall, I think, be right in allowing it to include, to gather up and transmute, the experience of the Sonnets, in its own particular fashion. It is quite different in tone. 'Its very concinnity and restraint', wrote Grosart, 'compared with the fecundity of *Venus and Adonis* and *Lucrece*, differentiate it from all other of Shakespeare's writings. I discern a sense of personal heart-ache and loss in these sifted and attuned stanzas, unutterably precious' (Int., xlv). Ranjee compared it to 'the mystic fire in the heart of the opal' (60); and in reviewing his essay I found it natural to define the quality of Shakespeare's poem by quoting Donne's line from *A Valediction* 'like gold to airy thinness beat'. Its quality is well characterised by one of Michelangelo's finest sonnets:

> So friendly is the fire to flinty stone,
> That, struck therefrom and kindled to a blaze,
> It burns the stone, and from the ash doth raise
> What lives thenceforward binding stones in one.
>
> Kiln-hardened this resists both frost and sun,
> Acquiring higher worth for endless days—
> As the purged soul from hell returns with praise,
> Amid the heavenly host to take her throne.
>
> E'en so the fire struck from my soul, that lay
> Close-hidden in my heart, may temper me,
> Till burned and slaked to better life I rise.
>
> If, made mere smoke and dust, I live today,
> Fire-hardened I shall live eternally;
> Such gold, not iron, my spirit strikes and tries.
>
> (34)

Such is the hard, resistant, tempered quality of the poetry in *The Phoenix and the Turtle*.

It is not obviously optimistic. If Marston's contribution is the most ecstatic and Jonson's the most moral, Shakespeare's may be called, as Carleton Brown observed, the most tragic. Such love as the love of the Sonnets is, as we have seen (p. 69), naturally tragic, and we may profitably compare *The Phoenix and the Turtle* with Marvell's *A Definition of Love*. Of the poem's paradoxes I have elsewhere (see p. 200 below) written. Much of it, in substance, if not in form, recalls the Sonnets. We have 'truth' and 'beauty' together as in the Sonnets (p. 45), and a similar, and greater, stress on chastity.

Carleton Brown finds the birds' failure to leave 'any posterity' a stumbling-block. 'This last stanza', he writes, 'is especially remarkable, for it flatly contradicts Marston and Chester, both of whom, as we have seen, give account of a fair creature which issued from the ashes of the Phoenix' (*Poems by Salusbury and Chester*, Int., lxxiii). His comment well illustrates the inadequacy of the biographical approach. The new Phoenix is as surely present within Shakespeare's poem as in the lyric ecstasy of Marston which *follows;* the sequence is vital. Besides, as we shall see, the 'bird of loudest lay' is itself a likely candidate.

We have already (pp. 48, 185) equated the Turtle, or Turtle-Dove, with the female element in the Shakespearian bisexuality which loved the Fair Youth and

A second title page for Love's Martyr or, Rosalin's Complaint, *which contains Shakespeare's* The Phoenix and Turtle.

composed the plays. The Turtle-Dove is a normal Shakespearian symbol of love-constancy, as at *1 Henry VI,* II, ii, 30-1. The dove is Venus' bird: her car is drawn by 'two strengthless doves' at *Venus and Adonis,* 153; the association recurs elsewhere (e.g. *The Rape of Lucrece,* 58; *Romeo and Juliet,* II, V, 7); and in *The Tempest* (IV, i, 94) Venus' dove is associated directly with her island, Paphos, as in *Love's Martyr.* We should normally in Shakespeare expect a single Turtle-Dove to be female, as in Paulina's lines:

> I, an old turtle,
> Will wing me to some wither'd bough, and there
> My mate, that's never to be found again,
> Lament till I am lost.
> *(The Winter's Tale,* v, iii, 132)

The bird itself is female even when compared with a male, as when Troilus insists that he is as true 'as turtle to *her* mate' (*Troilus and Cressida,* III, ii, 185). But here, on the pattern of our other poems, the Turtle is the male partner. That this is not quite natural within Shakespeare's world may be seen from the equation of the dove with gentleness underlying Juliet's agonised, 'Dove-feather'd raven! wolvish-ravening lamb!' (*Romeo and Juliet,* III, ii, 76); and, still more, by the series of paradoxes developed by Helena in *A Midsummer Night's Dream* when, with a significant grouping of effects, she compares herself ironically to Daphne chasing Apollo, the dove pursuing a griffin, or a 'mild hind' the tiger (II, i, 231-3). We do not *expect* our Turtle to be, in any obvious sense, a typical male: that is certain.

As for the Phoenix, it is always, and necessarily, baffling. It occurs in the Sonnets:

> Devouring time, blunt thou the lion's paws,
> And make the earth devour her own sweet brood;
> Pluck the keen teeth from the fierce tiger's jaws,
> And burn the long-liv'd Phoenix in her blood . . .
> (19)

Lion and tiger are natural associations, and we must never forget that it is itself a kind of eagle. It is preeminently royal and golden, whereas the Dove is 'silver' (*Venus and Adonis;* 366, 1190; and see p. 153, references). In *A Lover's Complaint,* the 'beauteous' and 'maiden-tongued' (99-100) youth, who so resembles the young man of the Sonnets, is given a phoenix-comparison:

> Small show of man was yet upon his chin;
> His phoenix down began but to appear
> Like unshorn velvet on that termless skin,
> Whose bare out-bragg'd the web it seem'd to wear;
> Yet show'd his visage by that cost more dear,
> And nice affections wavering stood in doubt
> If best were as it was, or best without.
> (92)

The Phoenix is used here the more naturally for the border-line, and so in a sense bisexual, age of the youth, set between boyhood and manhood, and we may observe how precisely this border-line state of 'down' is, as in the Sonnets, shown as the secret of the attraction, and how exactly it is related to the Phoenix. But the Phoenix may also be a creature of militant virility, as in *3 Henry VI:*

> YORK: My ashes, as the Phoenix, may bring forth
> A bird that will revenge upon you all,
> And in that hope I throw mine eyes to heaven
> Scorning whate'er you can afflict me with.
> Why come you not? what! multitudes, and fear?
> CLIFFORD: So cowards fight when they can fly

>   no further;
> So doves do peck the falcon's piercing talons;
> So desperate thieves, all hopeless of their
>   lives,
> Breathe out invectives 'gainst the officers.
>
>   (I, iv, 35)

Compare Enobarbus', 'In that mood, the dove will peck the estridge' (*Antony and Cleopatra*, III, xi, 195). The Phoenix is associated with strong action, backed by 'heaven'; the Dove with female weakness, in contrast to the falcon's 'talons'. Traditionally the Phoenix is represented as an eagle-like bird, with just such talons of its own.

In *Richard III* the Phoenix' 'nest of spicery' is once compared by Richard to natural procreation, with the womb as both the grave of old bitterness and the nurture-ground of comfort (IV, iv, 424). The context is dramatically ironical.

Shakespeare's two most resplendent male lovers, Timon and Antony, are compared with it. Timon, who 'flashes now a Phoenix' (II, i, 32), enjoys the comparison the more appropriately in that his love and personality are abnormal: he has, indeed, precisely those magical qualities, that blend of sweetness with virility, that lonely completion, which the bird symbolises. The comparison of Antony to 'thou Arabian Bird' (*Antony and Cleopatra*, III, ii, 12), humorously reported as coming from Lepidus, is relevant, though less important.

Female and royal persons of chastity and virtue may also receive the comparison. Imogen, with her 'mind so rare', is 'alone the Arabian bird' (*Cymbeline*, I, vi, 17); and in Cranmer's prophecy at the conclusion to *Henry VIII*, Queen Elizabeth is compared to 'the bird of wonder' or 'maiden Phoenix', from 'the sacred ashes' of whose 'honour'—it is a *spiritual* propagation—a new sovereign is to rise in 'star-like' majesty (*Henry VIII*, v, v, 40-8).

The bird can be crisply defined as a creature of highest virtue, in both the old and the modern senses of the word. It holds magical properties; power must be contained; and it is significant that our two female candidates are royal. Its presence in *The Tempest* is natural:

>   Now I will believe.
> That there are unicorns; that in Arabia
> There is one tree, the Phoenix' throne, one
>   Phoenix
> At this hour reigning there.
>
>   (III, iii, 21)

Observe the 'throne': it is a royal bird, a kind of super-eagle.

The Phoenix and the Turtle itself gives us some help. The Phoenix, though female, comes first, as the leading partner; but the Dove's 'loyal breast' (57) also suggests the female sex. The Phoenix is the Turtle's 'queen' (31), royalty being preserved. The poem, too, opens with a list of mourners, and these are important. One, the crow, is called 'treble-dated', which means unusually long-lived. It is sexually abnormal:

> That thy sable gender mak'st
> With the breath thou giv'st and tak'st . . .
>
>   (18)

This has been interpreted in three ways: that the bird, crow or raven, (i) changes its sex at will, which Grosart (242) recorded as still a popular belief concerning the crow; (ii) conceives not 'by conjunction of male and female', but by 'a kind of billing at the mouth' (Swan's *Speculum Mundi*, 1635; 397); (iii) conceives and lays its eggs at the bill (*Hortus Sanitatis*, III, 34). The first reading involves a dubiously correct translation of 'gender', and Grosart apparently, according to Hyder Edward Rollins, changed his mind; the other two may be grouped together. The various references are given in Rollins' *New Variorum* notes, to which I must refer the reader.[1]

We accordingly have an interesting sequence. The mourners of the opening stanzas hold exact significances. Our first stanza emphasises chastity ('chaste wings'); the second banishes evil and death (the owl); the third, after rejecting tyranny ('tyrant wing'), preserves royalty in the eagle; the fourth sounds the music of immortality in the 'death-divining' swan; and the crow signifies long life and sexual abnormality (bisexuality, propagation by *kisses* only,[2] or propagation without any sexual partner). Our positive values are: chastity, royalty, immortality, and some form of non-sexual or bisexual unity and propagation, *related, as in poetry, to both music and breath*. These, being the primary constituents of the Phoenix itself, are correctly represented in our ceremonial.

All our many sexual confusions and abnormalities are component to the poem's central purpose in celebration of a mystical love-union beyond sex, as we understand it, and all normal biological categories. I cannot then agree with Ranjee that 'the very title suggests the sex duality', nor that it is 'a sex poem, albeit in a very special sense' (36), unless we mean that it is sexually paradoxical, and that that paradox is the heart of it. Here are our central stanzas:

> Here the anthem doth commence:
> Love and constancy is dead;
> Phoenix and the Turtle fled
> In a mutual flame from hence.
>
> So they lov'd, as love in twain
> Had the essence but in one;

> Two distincts, division none:
> Number there in love was slain.
>
> Hearts remote, yet not asunder;
> Distance, and no space was seen
> 'Twixt the Turtle and his queen:
> But in them it were a wonder.
>
> So between them love did shine,
> That the Turtle saw his right
> Flaming in the Phoenix' sight;
> Either was the other's mine.
>
> Property was thus appall'd
> That the self was not the same;
> Single nature's double name
> Neither two nor one was call'd.
>
> (21)

These lines should by now need little comment. Ranjee (42-5) well discusses the words 'essence', 'distincts', 'division' and 'property' in terms of scholastic thought. The general conclusion of the whole poem is, as I put it in *The Shakespearian Tempest* (App. A, 324), that 'the very death of truth and beauty creates a third unknown immortality'. But, though to this extent optimistic, the experience is firmly *objectified,* and the frame-work correspondingly tragic. The lovers are *seen* to disappear, having fled this dimension in a 'mutual flame'. The transcending of numerical distinction is our central thought. Ranjee (40) says, 'it is not two who have gone—it is *one*'; and yet there is really more in it than the simple resolution of duality in unity. In *The Christian Renaissance,* during a comparison of the poem with Christian symbolism (the Trinity, the Incarnation, Dante's Gryphon, etc.)—Ranjee (42) also made a cross-reference to Trinitarian doctrine— I wrote: 'Here we see not merely a transcending of duality: rather the duality-unity dualism is itself transcended' ('The Eternal Triangle', XII, 329). This is what our stanzas are trying to define. For 'distance, and no space was seen', we might compare T. S. Eliot's more distant than stars and nearer than the eye' in *Marina*.[3]

We have already (pp. 42, 61) compared the love shining 'between' them to Sonnet 24 and Donne's 'great Prince' of *The Ecstasy*. It is a 'flaming' reality born from the union of eyes, the Turtle's 'right' (i.e. perhaps, what is properly its own) being seen by the Turtle burning within the Phoenix' 'sight', or act of seeing, as in Sonnet 24 (p. 40).[4] Such lovers see themselves not merely reflected in the other's eyes, but in the other's sight. With 'either was the other's mine' we can compare 'thou mine, I thine' of Sonnet 108. On 'Property . . . appall'd' Ranjee comments: 'Existence in its metaphysical aspect was scandalised at this impossible condition' (44).

So the paradoxes go on. For 'if what parts can so remain' (48) we may compare Shelley's definition of love in *Epipsychidion* as a reality where 'to divide is not to take away' (161). Within all this there is really only the one paradox, and for its elucidation we may again turn to Michelangelo:

> If love be chaste, if virtue conquer ill,
> If fortune bind both lovers in one bond,
> If either at the other's grief despond,
> If both be governed by one life, one will;
>
> If in two bodies one soul triumph still,
> Raising the twain from earth to heaven beyond,
> If Love with one blow and one golden wand
> Have power both smitten breasts to pierce and thrill;
>
> If each the other love, himself forgoing,
> With such delight, such savour, and so well,
> That both to one sole end their wills combine;
>
> If thousands of these thoughts, all thought outgoing,
> Fail the least part of their firm love to tell,
> Say, can mere angry spite this knot untwine?
>
> (32)

Here, instead of paradox, we have, in the fifth line, the transcendental word 'soul'. Once agree that each person has, or is related to, some higher soul-self holding its being in another dimension, and all becomes clear. Donne regularly thinks in these terms; as in *A Valediction* and throughout *The Ecstasy*. Lovelace, in *To Lucasta, Going beyond the Seas,* says that Faith and Troth, 'like separated souls', can yet meet, beyond space, 'above the highest sphere', greeting each other as angels, even though 'unknown' (i.e. to the earthly consciousness). We may suppose that true lovers are attuned, through love, to this dimension; in each other's eyes, to use Shakespeare's imagery, they see the dimension in which exist both souls in unison and unity. The two personalities remain distinct, until in death they attain each their greater selves, which are one: hence our various unity-affirmations, as in 'The world one Phoenix, till another burns' (p. 182, with accompanying references). Something of this massive unity can be glimpsed before death, and that is the meaning of Michelangelo's 'one life', 'one will', 'one soul'; but the 'smitten breasts' remain two.

In such terms you can also see why the lover's love of the loved one is *simultaneously self-union and integration* (pp. 35-7) *within his own total self*.

The concluding *Threnos,* spoken by Reason, maintains a strict objectivity and pathos, peculiarly evident in 'cinders' (55) and 'buried' (64). 'Eternity' (58) comes in naturally, with whatever assurance it can give. 'Chastity' (61) recurs. the lack of 'posterity' (59) fitting well enough the story of the Sonnets. 'Truth' and 'Beauty' (64) refer respectively to Dove and Phoenix, and, though a reference to Keats' *Grecian Urn* is natural, we must here read 'truth' in terms of loyalty as well as metaphysical insight. Truth 'cannot be', because in temporal terms loyalty, as the Sonnets suggest, will inevitably weaken; though this is not to say that the more metaphysical meaning is not also contained. The 'prayer' (67) points on to Prospero's epilogue in *The Tempest*. With a fine reserve the poet leaves us, as does Pope in *Eloisa to Abelard,* with a tragic conclusion, but we get the essence of neither poem by remaining content with that, and here, should we wish to know more, we may concentrate on the lines

> Phoenix and the Turtle fled
> In a mutual flame from hence.
>
> (23)

These suggest, as indeed many earlier phrases in *Love's Martyr* have suggested (e.g. 163-4, 178), that the flame of the Phoenix' burning is also the flame of mutual, but sexually separated, love, corresponding to the 'joy's bonfire' in Donne's image of 'one fire of four inflaming eyes, and of two loving hearts' (*Epithalamion,* XI); always fleeing 'from hence', and piercing dimensions beyond earthly computation.

A question arises concerning the 'bird of loudest lay' who introduces the poem and summons the various mourners. Grosart suggests the nightingale, and he was followed by Ranjee. Sir Osbert Sitwell offers the Peacock (see *T.L.S.,* 1941, 199, 203, 352, 359, 364). In my 'additional note' to Appendix A of the 1953 re-issue of *The Shakespearian Tempest,* I returned to the older view, supported by the use of 'sole Arabian tree' (2), so exactly corresponding as it does to the bird's description in *The Tempest* (p. 198), that this bird is *the Phoenix itself.* T. W. Baldwin notes that the Phoenix is a songbird in Lactantius' *Carmen de Phoenice* (*T.L.S.,* 1941, 287; and see his relation of Shakespeare's 'trumpet' to Ovid in his *Literary Genetics,* XVI, 363-4 and 368). In the old English poem based on Lactantius it is certainly credited with wondrous vocal powers:

> As soon as the Sun o'er the salty streams,
> On high doth soar, the haughty bird
> Joyfully leaves his lofty perch,
> Darting upward on dauntless wing,
> And singing exultant, seeks the light.
> Glorious the greeting he giveth the Sun,
> His spirit athrill with rapture of bliss;
> Warbling melodies wondrous sweet,
> With various art and voice more clear
> Than ever men heard the heavens beneath,
> Since the King of Glory, the great Creator,
> Established the world. More winsome far
> Than any music that men may make;
> And sweeter than any earthly strain,
> This trancing song. No sound of trump
> Or horn or harp, or harmonies clear
> Of organ-pipes, or purest tones
> Of mortal voice, or music of the swan,
> Or aught that God hath given to cheer
> Earth's heavy toil, may touch this song.
> He carols and sings in unceasing delight
> Till the Sun descends in the southern sky;
> Then sinketh his song and silent falls,
> The beautiful bird then bows his head
> And listening alert lifteth his wings
> Beating them thrice, then bideth at rest.
>
> (120; trans, J. Duncan Spaeth[1])

The references to the trumpet and swan's music are interesting, since we find them in Shakespeare's poem.

If this reading be accepted, we find the Phoenix celebrating the obsequies of itself and the Turtle. For a bird accustomed to rise from its own ashes, this need not be considered a task beyond its power. Besides, the process neatly balances the process found later (first, I think, observed by Middleton Murry in *Discoveries;* 1924), when Reason 'in itself confounded' (41) sings in the concluding 'theme' (49) the triumph-song of its own death-knell. It is primarily to these two mechanisms that we owe our sense, resembling that given by Blake's *Mental Traveller,* of self-regeneration and revolving movement.

But surely, within the poem, the establishing of a living Phoenix rather weakens the point and pathos of the close? In so far, however, as we are prepared to agree with those (pp. 105-7, 147-8, 193) who see Shakespeare's dramas as flowering from whatever love experience, or experiences, lie behind the Sonnets and *The Phoenix and the Turtle,* there is a possible answer. The 'bird of loudest lay' becomes Shakespeare's greater poetry, rising from the ashes of the love from which it draws its inspiration. Many years ago I suggested, in *The Shakespearian Tempest* (App. A, 323-4), that stanzas 2 to 6, being made of leading Shakespearian themes and symbols, might be said to constitute a brief summing up of Shakespeare's total work. Since this work must be supposed to represent a fall from the perfection which prompts and inspires it—for it is Beatrice, not Vergil, who guides Dante through Paradise—we can indeed call it one vast threnody on the wondrous thing—love, vision, divine insight, names do not matter—which, once, twice, or perhaps more often still, came, stayed for a while, and was gone.

But that is not the whole truth. In *Timon of Athens* and *Antony and Cleopatra* we feel as, later, in Byron's *Sardanapalus*, 'the mutual flame' itself; we are within its warmth, its sphere of radiation; and in the Final Plays, concluding with *Cymbeline, The Tempest* and *Henry VIII*, we are aware of some new Phoenix, some new, earthly and yet unearthly, perfection, rising from the flame. Each of these five plays just mentioned contains one of our few Phoenix references.

Notes

[1] See too *Shakespeare's Poems* in The Yale Shakespeare, ed. Albert Feuillerat, 1927;165-6; T. W. Baldwin and D'Arcy W. Thompson in *The Times Literary Supplement*, 1941, 287 and 397; and [T.W.] Baldwin's [on the] *Literary Genetics*, [*of Shakespeare's Poems and Sonnets* (Urbana: University of Illinois Press: 1950)] XVI, 372.

[2] For kisses as a legitimate form of soul-contact in what might be called the Phoenix' field of moral valuation see Baldwin's *Literary Genetics,* XVI, 372 and 375. Compare, too, our references to kisses in the Cantos, pp. 163-4, 178 above; also p. 89, note.

[3] Walter Whiter concluded his *A Specimen of a Commentary on Shakespeare* (1794) with a note on *The Phoenix and the Turtle* as a reflection of Christian dogma. For the poem's scholastic affinities, see also J. V. Cunningham in *E.L.H.,* XIX; 4; Dec., 1952; 265-76.

[4] T. W. Baldwin notes here that 'the Phoenix, as bird of the Sun, had flaming eyes' (*Literary Genetics,* XVI, 374). According to Ranjee, the Turtle saw his 'justification for existence in the appreciation with which the Phoenix regarded him' (43).

[1] Princeton University Press, 1921.

Heinrich Straumann (essay date 1977)

SOURCE: "'The Phoenix and the Turtle' in its Dramatic Context," *English Studies,* Vol. 58, No. 6, December, 1977, pp. 494-500.

[*In the following essay, Straumann argues that* The Phoenix and Turtle *reflects a shift in Shakespeare's expression and concept of "the possible union of beauty and truth" towards an emphasis on the fleetingness of such a union.*]

Scholars and critics seem, on the whole, agreed on the opinion that at the turn of the 16th to the 17th century Shakespeare must have undergone some vital changes, if not a crisis, in his views about man and the basic values he had accepted before that time. And even those who are sceptical of interpretations along such lines will readily admit that the tone of his works is clearly no longer the same after 1601. Whatever conflicting views on 'The Phoenix and the Turtle' may exist, there can be no doubt about the poem being published just at the time when that change had taken place or was still taking place. Incidentally Professor Kenneth Muir was one of the first to point out that aspect.[1] The difficulties begin with the interpretation of its basic meaning and its possible significance for the understanding of that change. It is perhaps well to remember that the poem consists of three parts, namely first the description of a funeral attended by various birds, then a highly complex anthem on the singular union of the phoenix and the turtle, and finally the Threnos, that is the lament uttered by Reason on the death of the two birds, and especially relevant in our context:

> Beauty, truth and rarity,
> Grace in all simplicity,
> Here enclos'd, in cinders lie.
>
> Death is now the Phoenix' nest,
> And the Turtle's loyal breast
> To eternity doth rest;
>
> Leaving no posterity:
> 'Twas not their infirmity,
> It was married chastity.
>
> Truth may seem, but cannot be;
> Beauty brag, but 'tis not she;
> Truth and beauty buried be.
> To this urn let those repair
> That are either true or fair:
> For these dead birds sigh a prayer.

I can only briefly—as a sort of reminder—refer to some of the main aspects of the well over one hundred different viewpoints, theories and interpretations that have been set forth in the last fifty years or so before we get to the main point, that is the significance of the poem in the context of the plays.[2]

One can roughly distinguish three different trends in the various approaches. First there are those who are above all interested in what they consider to be the personal allegory of the poem. They start from the fact that the poem was published in a collection entitled *Loves Martyr or Rosalins Complaint* with two subtitles containing references to the Phoenix and the Turtle. The collection was edited by Robert Chester and dedicated to Sir John Salusbury, an Esquire at the court of Queen Elizabeth and the husband of Ursula Stanley, with whom he had ten children. In view of this fact it is difficult to understand the expression 'married chastity' and 'leaving no posterity' which Shakespeare uses for the union of the phoenix with the turtle if one assumes that the whole collection was meant to be a eulogy of the Salusbury marriage, unless one resorts to the idea that Shakespeare composed the whole poem as it were tongue in cheek[3]—but to me at least the tone of the whole seems to make this well nigh impossible. Thus a number of other candidates have been suggested, for instance Essex and Queen Elizabeth,[4] Salusbury and Elizabeth, the Earl of Bedford and his famous wife Lucy, Shakespeare himself and the Earl of Southampton as well as other less plausible public figures of the time. But there is no direct evidence for any of these assumptions—except of course that the poem *can* be seen as a celebration of the fulfillment and a lament over the end of a friendship or a love relationship.

The second group of interpreters try to approach the poem by putting it in the context of the traditions and conventions of that genre. In this light a great number of different elements have been suggested, for instance the court of love tradition of French origin, Chaucer's *'Parlement of Foules'*, the medieval bestiaries with their allegorical implications, the *Elegy* on the death of Sir Philip Sidney in the collection *The Phoenix Nest* with similar birds as in Shakespeare's poems, the literature of emblems with many references to the characteristics traditionally attributed to the different birds, e.g. the turtle as a symbol of conjugal faithfulness, the phoenix with its associations of singularity, immortality, chastity, hope, constancy—or with persons of outstanding fame. Added to all this there is a touch of the platonic conceptions fashionable at the time, especially since Lyly's *Euphues,* that is the equation of beauty, truth and goodness, the concept of non-sensual love, and the problem of the existence or non-existence of an idea beyond the concrete world: 'Truth may seem but cannot be', and finally the question of scholastic philosophy, especially the problem of 'essence'.[5]

The belief of these critics seems to be based on the assumption that Shakespeare when confronted with the task of writing the prescribed eulogy simply toyed with all those traditional and fashionable devices in order to prove that he could do this as easily and effectively as anyone: in other words that there is a considerable measure of irony in the whole.

Finally there is a third group of critics whom for lack of a better term we may refer to as idealists. The idealists stress the intellectual and thematic aspect of the poem, i.e. for them the theme of the poem is the miracle of fulfilled love, the fusion of the feminine and the masculine principles in bisexual love, the union of two different entities beyond the world of human realities, beyond life and death and therefore beyond any rational understanding, partly in the sense of scholastic philosophy (especially according to J. V. Cunningham). In this way one has further arrived at the idea that the poem is meant to be a concentrated paradox ultimately expressing Shakespeare's self-conscious understanding of poetry and the poetic process: 'Form wedded to imagination but dying when the poem is finished' (R. A. Underwood).[6] The poem could then be seen as a kind of forerunner of the metaphysical style. In view of all the possibilities represented by the three groups of interpretations one may well have one's doubts about any definite solution of the problem. But I think there *is* a way out—as I tried to show as early as 1953[7]—and this lies in the principle of interleaved levels of meaning, i.e. in the fact that the poem was composed with an inherent multiple appeal, so that it could be read first as a personal allegory (now lost), secondly as a brilliant display of a number of literary conventions and fashionable topics, and thirdly as the expression of a highly complex idea about the union of two values fatally exposed to destruction and yet continuing in their existence. To this may be added a hidden quasi magical element[8] appearing in the use of trochaic tetrameters otherwise rather rare in Shakespeare but used by the poet for songs approaching that character in the plays, e.g.

> Much Ado: 'Pardon, goddess of the night . . .
> (V, 3, 12)

> Merry Wives: 'Fie on sinful fantasy . . .'
> (V, 5, 99)

> Lear: 'Be thy mouth or black or white . . .'
> (III, 6, 68)

Whatever part the scholastic element in the poem may have played at that time—one thing is certain and it must have struck the contemporary reader as well as it strikes the modern one: the couple of the phoenix and the turtle dove are referred to by Shakespeare as 'co-supremes and stars of love', that is as two ultimate values associated with beauty and truth and further connected with qualities such as grace, simplicity, rarity, loyalty, and love.

Now beauty and truth are united in love—but this union is not permanent: the two co-supremes disappear in a mutual flame, they are enclosed in the cinders of an urn and do not, together, exist any more in reality. Real truth and real beauty have gone from this world, because as realities they only exist in a union through love, and love and constancy are dead. Or, in a more abstract paraphrase: a synthesis of a highest aesthetic value with a highest moral value is only possible as an idea—but not as a real thing, or at the utmost as a very short-lived phenomenon. And yet the last three lines of the poem seem to contradict this:

> To this urn let those repair
> That are either true or fair
> For these dead birds sigh a prayer.

This can only mean that there *are* still true and fair human beings—but one is *either* true *or* fair, i.e., one cannot be both at the same time, and with reference to the other three lines immediately preceding them and expressing the idea that there is only apparent truth and apparent beauty, one may add that even those who may be considered as bearers of these attributes do not really possess them—because the attributes can only be real in the aforementioned short-lived union through love. We may pray for the synthesis but we cannot achieve it as a permanent entity.[9]

Now the question is: does this concept occur elsewhere in Shakespeare, and if so in what context? There is no other passage in which the phoenix and the turtle dove appear together directly in a combined metaphor. On the other hand there are a number of passages where at least attitudes similar to the one expressed in our poem can be found—especially the sonnets, where the question of truth or constancy and beauty existing together in one person is repeatedly brought up, for instance in sonnets 14, 53, 105. In the latter the final couplet clearly says that the attributes 'fair, kind and true' have so far never existed in one person together:

> Fair, kind and true, have often lived alone
> Which three till now never kept seat in one.

In the plays, too, the theme plays its special part. In the present context I shall refer to the *existential* aspect of the problem exclusively, that is to characters and their demeanour directly connected with the problem and not to further reaching implications such as the questions of human identity[10]—I wish to avoid any speculations beyond what the text really yields.

A well known example is the passage in *Cymbeline*, where Iachimo on first meeting Imogen begins to doubt whether he will win his wager about the faithlessness of woman and of Imogen especially:

> If she be furnished with a mind so rare
> She is alone the *Arabian* bird
>
> (I, 6, 17)

Iachimo does not believe in the miracle of the absolute constancy of a beautiful woman's love, and he tries everything to prove his point, but the miracle though seriously threatened with destruction continues to the end. Beauty and truth, love and constancy remain victorious.

Cymbeline is a late play, and it is obvious that in the plays of our period (that is shortly before and after 1601) the situation is different. In the following plays normally considered to have been composed before 1600 the question of truth and beauty appearing together in one and the same person is clearly put: in *The Two Gentlemen of Verona* it is the girls Julia and Silvia whose constancy in love and belief in their lovers is put to a test which they pass successfully though not without difficulties. Similarly Helena and Hermia in *A Midsummer Night's Dream*, although their love and their lovers are threatened with deception finally manage to get through their trials and hardships unscathed.

In *Romeo and Juliet* love and constancy triumph but it is a short-lived triumph and yet the catastrophy that overtakes the lovers makes them as Capulet says:

> Poor sacrifices of our enmity
>
> (V, 3, 304)

That is through their death they create goodwill and peace between the hitherto hostile families, not forgetting Montague's final word about ' . . . true and faithful Juliet', as he says.

A remarkable though not yet vital change in this syndrome of values is to be found with the women characters in *The Merchant of Venice, Much Ado About Nothing, Twelfth Night* and *As You Like It,* that is the four plays which according to Chambers were produced between 1597 and 1600, or if one prefers to follow Peter Alexander somewhat earlier, but definitely before 1600. The change in no way affects the attractiveness of the women characters—on the contrary critics generally seem to agree that they are definitely more mature, more differentiated and therefore more human and more 'real' than the earlier ones; they are equally devoted in their love and constancy—but in order to get united with their lovers they are willing or obliged to resort to all sorts of tactics, ruses and mystifications to achieve their ends. Portia cheats a little when arranging the test of the caskets for Bassanio; Nerissa joins Portia in feigning disbelief about her ring; Jessica on eloping with Lorenzo takes part of Shylock's treasure with her. Viola cleverly conceals her identity and yet manages to express her true feelings in her cryptic remarks to Orsino. Rosalind risks, or pretends to risk making fun of the sonneteering Orlando although or rather because she loves him deeply. In all these plays the union of love, constancy and beauty remains intact, but truth has to be kept secret—at least temporarily.

This theme borders on the tragic in *Much Ado About Nothing* where through a diabolical intrigue the 'maiden truth' of the heroine seems to be so utterly defiled that her lover can only speak of her in the contradictory terms of 'most foul, most fair' and will henceforth 'turn all beauty into thoughts of harm' (IV, 1, 108)—i.e. even there the negative statement is enhanced by its juxtaposition with the principle of beauty. Here, too, truth and the person embodying both truth and beauty have to be carefully hidden in order to survive until the veils and the masks can be dropped and love be restored. This, on a level of wit and bantering also applies to Beatrice and Benedick. Whatever the impediments, the trinity of love, beauty and truth in these plays finally remains undisputed.

All these plays were written before the publication of our poem. In the plays composed after 1601 the situation is entirely different. In *Hamlet* the physical beauty of Ophelia is repeatedly referred to and never questioned but in her dependence on her father she betrays her qualities of honesty and truth towards her lover. In the nunnery scene Hamlet himself puts the problem in a nutshell:

> . . . the power of beauty will sooner transform honesty from what it is to a bawd than the force of honesty can translate beauty into his likeness: this was sometime a paradox, but now the time gives it proof. I did love thee once.
>
> (III, 1, 112)

That is: Hamlet once believed in the union of beauty and honesty in human beings, especially in Ophelia and possibly also in his mother—but through what has happened at court and particularly through Ophelia's conduct at this moment his belief in that union has totally collapsed. Ophelia perishes.

In *Troilus and Cressida* the theme of the infidelity of an attractive woman was and has remained a classic. In *All's Well That Ends Well* Helena is forced to take refuge in deceit in order to achieve her end. In *Measure for Measure* the problem is somewhat different, but here, too, Isabella's virtue can only be saved at the price of the bed trick, i.e. through carefully prepared deceit.

In Desdemona we see absolute truth, devotion, love and constancy united—but she becomes a victim of the terrible blindness and delusion of her husband and is killed. For Cordelia, to whom the term 'grace in all simplicity' seems to be specially applicable truthfulness towards her father and her devotion for him assume absolute priority—she is not allowed to live. In *Antony and Cleopatra* Shakespeare chose a subject that corresponded exactly to the new concept: the race towards catastrophe of a couple ensnared in uncontrolled passion but unable to believe in mutual loyalty except in a moment of violent death. In short the attributes of beauty, truth, love, constancy etc. still appear in all these plays, but their union in one and the same person does not occur anymore or if it does, it will be destroyed by hostile forces—bodily strangled as in the case of Desdemona and Cordelia.

Only in the very last plays, the romances, is the existence of a woman character embodying both beauty and truth and finding fulfillment in love again made possible—but Imogen and Hermione, as well as Perdita and Miranda owe this to almost incredible luck or else to magic.

From all this I for one can only draw one conclusion. As in no other work and in the smallest possible space the *Phoenix and the Turtle* represents a clearly defined turning point both in poetic expression and in the abstract of Shakespeare's existential concept of the possible union of beauty and truth i.e. of two highest values, through love in a woman character. Before 1601 this union is seen as possible and it can even be permanent. After 1601 the union, if it occurs at all, is only very short-lived and is bound to end in death through violence. Only in the last plays can the union be found again—but by then it is nothing short of a miracle.

Notes

[1] Kenneth Muir and Sean O'Loughlin, *The Voyage to Illyria* (London, 1937). It is however only fair to mention that Kenneth Muir seems to dissociate himself now from much of what is said in this book.

[2] The most complete and detailed summary of the different interpretations of the poem is given by R. A. Underwood in his book *Shakespeare's 'The Phoenix and the Turtle': A Survey of Scholarship*, Salzburg Studies in English Literature (Salzburg, 1974).

[3] See Georges Bonnard, 'Shakespeare's Contribution to Robert Chester's *Love's Martyr*', *English Studies*, XIX (1937), 66-9.

[4] See William H. Matchett, *'The Phoenix and the Turtle': Shakespeare's Poem and 'Love's Martyr'* (The Hague, 1965).

[5] See J. V. Cunningham, ' "Essence" and the "Phoenix and the Turtle" ', *ELH. A Journal of English Literary History*, 19 (1952), 265-76.

[6] R. A. Underwood, *op.cit.*, pp. 299 and 353, and especially K. T. S. Campbell, ' "The Phoenix and the Turtle" as a Signpost of Shakespeare's Development', *British Journal of Archeology*, X (1970), 169-79.

[7] See Heinrich Straumann, *Phoenix und Taube: Zur Interpretation von Shakespeares Gedankenwelt* (Zürich, 1953), especially pp. 28-35.

[8] See R. A. Underwood, *op.cit.*, pp. 287-9.

[9] In this respect I fundamentally differ from Peter Dronke's otherwise highly illuminating *essay* 'The Phoenix and the Turtle', *Orbis Litterarum*, XXIII (1968), 199-220. Dronke, who argues that 'the bird of loudest lay' must be the phoenix itself, does not sufficiently account for the expression 'either-or' in the last but

second line of the poem. He therefore concludes that 'the vestiges of perfection are made possible in time' (p. 211).—On the other hand Robert Ellrodt in his equally instructive essay 'An Anatomy of the "Phoenix and the Turtle" ', *Shakespeare Survey*, 15, 1962 (pp. 99-108), believes that in the apparent contradiction of the final lines of the Threnos 'lies the deeper meaning of the poem' and that Shakespeare does not refer to 'true lovers and beautiful creatures' but to 'Love and Constancy, Truth and Beauty' as such.

[10] See Daniel Seltzer, ' "Their Tragic Scene": "The Phoenix and the Turtle" and Shakespeare's Love Tragedies', *Shakespeare Quarterly*, XII (1961), 91-101.

Philip K. Bock (essay date 1993)

SOURCE: "'Neither Two Nor One': Dual Unity in 'The Phoenix and Turtle,'" in *The Undiscover'd Country: New Essays on Psychoanalysis and Shakespeare*, edited by B. J. Sokol, Free Association Books, 1993, pp. 39-56.

[*In the essay that follows, Bock contends that* The Phoenix and Turtle, *like* Hamlet, *explores a form of unity within which each element retains its identity.*]

Written at about the same time as *Hamlet*, Shakespeare's brief poem, *The Phoenix and Turtle*, bears little superficial resemblance to his longest play.[1] Yet condensed into its 67 lines one finds a number of dynamic elements that may have been displaced from the author's awareness while he was writing the tragedy. *The Phoenix and Turtle* depicts a paradoxical dual unity that, I shall argue, can best be understood as representing the early 'normal symbiosis' between mother and child. This developmental phase is nostalgically commemorated (it has been lost), and it is represented as 'chaste' (devoid of genital sexuality and its attendant anxieties). The poem thus mediates contradictions (found clearly in *Hamlet*) between reality and appearance and between good and bad mother images, though at the great cost of dissolving the ego and negating procreation.

The main focus of this paper is on the text of the poem and its developmental resonances, but a larger cultural problem is also addressed. This has to do with the responses of audiences since Elizabethan times to the treatment of dual unity in the poem. Unlike *Hamlet* which is probably Shakespeare's best known work, *The Phoenix and Turtle* has suffered a virtual cultural repression, neglected by critics and anthologists, at times even denied a place in the canon. To understand this treatment we must first grasp what the poem is saying about the process of individuation and death.

I believe that Shakespeare has managed to represent the dynamics of early (pre-oedipal) experience, especially our unconscious desire to merge with the maternal imago. This representation is so threatening that we will systematically misread the poem until we are prepared to wrestle with its deep ambiguity. Western civilization has denied the paradoxical nature of the experience out of which the human capacity for culture develops; but we now suspect that the separation of mother from child is what first constitutes the opposition of culture to nature, and that the 'transitional object' (Winnicott, 1971), created in the widening space between mother and child, is the first genuine artefact.

Shakespeare used the formal resources of Elizabethan verse together with the multivocal avian symbols of his tradition to embody his (and our) nostalgia for a lost unity. His vision, I believe, has validity across cultures: the 'dead birds' of the poem's final line are exactly analogous to the *Dead Birds* that, in Robert Marshall's classic ethnographic film, symbolize human mortality to the Dani People of New Guinea. Let us now examine the crucial text.

THE PHOENIX AND TURTLE

Let the bird of loudest lay,
On the sole Arabian tree,
Herald sad and trumpet be,
To whose sound chaste wings obey.

But thou shriking harbinger,
Foul precurrer of the fiend,
Augur of the fever's end,
To this troop come thou not near.

From this session interdict
Every fowl of tyrant wing,
Save the eagle, feath'red king;
Keep the obsequy so strict.
Let the priest in surplice white,
That defunctive music can,
Be the death-divining swan,
Lest the requiem lack his right.

And thou treble-dated crow,
That thy sable gender mak'st
With the breath thou giv'st and tak'st,
'Mongst our mourners shalt thou go.

Here the anthem doth commence:
Love and Constancy is dead,
Phoenix and the Turtle fled
In a mutual flame from hence.

So they loved as love in twain
Had the essence but in one,
Two distincts, division none:

Number there in love was slain.

Hearts remote, yet not asunder;
Distance and no space was seen
'Twixt this Turtle and his queen:
But in them it were a wonder.

So between them love did shine,
That the Turtle saw his right
Flaming in the Phoenix' sight;
Either was the other's mine.

Property was thus appalled,
That the self was not the same;
Single nature's double name
Neither two nor one was called.

Reason, in itself confounded,
Saw division grow together,
To themselves yet either neither,
Simple were so well compounded:

That it cried, 'How true a twain
Seemeth this concordant one!
Love hath reason, Reason none,
If what parts, can so remain.'

Whereupon it made this threne
To the Phoenix and the Dove,
Co-supremes and stars of love,
As chorus to their tragic scene.

THRENOS

Beauty, Truth, and Rarity,
Grace in all simplicity,
Here enclos'd, in cinders lie.

Death is now the Phoenix' nest,
And the Turtle's loyal breast
To eternity doth rest.
Leaving no posterity,
'Twas not their infirmity,
It was married chastity.

Truth may seem, but cannot be,
Beauty brag, but 'tis not she,
Truth and Beauty buried be.

To this urn let those repair
That are either true or fair;
For these dead birds sigh a prayer.

The Structure of the Poem

The Phoenix and Turtle falls into three apparently clear sections: the opening five stanzas that I shall call the invocation, an eight stanza anthem and a closing threnody of five stanzas that is attributed to 'Reason'.

The general tone of the poem is nostalgic: someone is looking back on unique events that cannot recur. As William Matchett (1965) notes, the diction is legalistic and the syntax highly compressed; there is also a high incidence of scholastic and logical terminology (Alvarez, 1955). The avian symbols employed are conventional with one crucial exception: in Shakespeare's poem, the Phoenix seems finally dead, never to be reborn, though an alternative reading of even this point seems to be possible (Wilson Knight, 1955; Axton, 1977).

All of the birds mentioned have traditional connotations: the screech owl foretells death; the eagle is King of the birds and must therefore be invited to the ceremony although other 'fowl of tyrant wing' (birds of prey) are excluded. The 'death-divining' white swan and the long-lived black crow are named as priest and mourner, respectively. The Phoenix is unique and beautiful, while the Turtle (-dove) represents constancy in love (cf. *Troilus and Cressida,* III, ii, 178, a work of the same period). Nevertheless, the invocation is quite indirect. The identity of the narrator is uncertain. The 'bird of loudest lay' who is to call the others to assemble is not further identified, and the owl is not directly named; rather, a 'shriking harbinger' is cautioned to 'come not near'. Order is imposed by the narrator so that the 'obsequy' will be 'strict', with all due ceremony observed (unlike the 'maimed' rites of Polonius and Ophelia in *Hamlet*).

The anthem begins in stanza six and only then do we learn the identity of the dead birds. The cause of their immolation is not given; instead, we move to a description of their unique relationship:

> Hearts remote, yet not assunder;
> Distance and no space was seen
> 'Twixt this Turtle and his queen.

The opposition between unity and duality was overcome in their love: 'Number there in love was slain' for 'Either was the other's mine'. Reason itself is 'confounded' by the perfect union of this 'twain' and declares that

> Love hath reason, Reason none,
> If what parts, can so remain.

The threnody follows and we are informed that, hereafter, 'Truth may seem, but cannot be' for 'Truth and Beauty buried be' with the ashes of the two rare birds. They left 'no posterity', but this was not due to any 'infirmity', rather, 'It was married chastity'. Their burial urn is presented as a shrine for latter-day lovers who are urged to 'sigh a prayer' for the departed.

Although the sections of the poem appear to be clearly marked, a curious *embedding* actually takes place. The lines, 'Here the anthem doth commence' and 'Whereupon it made this threne' belong neither to the anthem (which they seem to begin and end, respectively) nor to the other sections. Throughout the poem, categorical boundaries are established only to be immediately violated. Birds of 'tyrant wing' (predators) are forbidden to attend the ritual, but the royal eagle is made an exception. The owl is excluded because of its association with death, yet the 'death-divining' swan is invited to serve as priest. The crow, a scavenger, is admitted among the mourners due to its black color, with an allusion to the folk belief that crows conceived orally. No simple criterion is allowed to stand: both structural and conceptual category boundaries are deliberately obliterated. Even the rhyme scheme (*abba*) involves embedding.

These 'overlapping frames' give additional depth to the poem—a literary technique that Robert M. Adams (1953), borrowing from the visual arts, called *trompe-l'oeil*. In *The Phoenix and Turtle* there is a similar deepening of perspective as we move from the invocation to the threnody, and beyond.

The anthem, like many Metaphysical lyrics, dwells upon a paradox, using figures drawn from diverse fields of knowledge including law, logic and mathematics. In John Donne's (1965) poem 'The Canonization' (written after 1602), the dual unity of a much more sensual love is celebrated in a series of similes. Curiously, Donne refers to three of the birds that appear in Shakespeare's poem:

> Call us what you will, we're made such by
>   love;
> Call her one, me another fly,
> We're tapers too, and at our own cost die,
> And we in us find the Eagle and the Dove;
> The Phoenix riddle hath more wit
> By us; we two, being one, are it,
> So, to one neutral thing both sexes fit.
> We die and rise the same, and prove
> Mysterious by this love.
>
> (19-27)

Here, too, the lovers' ashes are consigned to 'a well-wrought urn' (33), and others are urged to invoke the 'pattern' of their ideal love—a love that also dies in flames and that is 'Mysterious' (i.e., beyond reason).

The Paradox of 'Dual Unity'

The Phoenix and Turtle were one, yet they did not merge their separate identities: 'Two distincts, division none', and yet 'between them love did shine'. This paradox appalls 'Property' and confounds 'Reason':

> Single nature's double name
> Neither two nor one was called.

Alvarez (1955) is certainly right to see here a systematic attack on Reason, using her own logical devices; however, I choose to follow Joel Fineman (1977, pp. 409-10) who sees in this and other instances of dual unity a 'delicate paradox at the center of Shakespeare's erotic imagination', a theme that he traces through several 'branching pairs of siblings' in the plays.

From the perspective of modern Freudian theories of psychic development, the anthem may be interpreted as a veiled account of early childhood experience (see Faber, 1985, p. 71). During the second through fifth months of life, the child is gradually differentiated out of the symbiotic matrix of the maternal environment and begins the transition to individual ego organization. As summarized by Mahler, Pine and Bergman (1975), the 'normal symbiotic phase' constitutes

> a vague dual unity that forms the primal soil from which all subsequent human relationships form . . . Vestiges of this phase remain with us throughout the entire life cycle . . . Here the world becomes increasingly cathected, especially in the person of the mother, but as one dual unity with the not yet clearly demarcated, bordered-off, and experienced self.
>
> (1975, p. 48)

D. W. Winnicott (1971) has emphasized that human individuation is a paradoxical process, for an initial 'perfect' adaptation of the mother to her infant's needs must 'fail' so that the new self can be born. Mothering must be 'good enough' to ensure the child's survival; but if it is too good it may prevent the 'psychological birth' of the child, creating an overwhelming nostalgia for dual unity. Particularly important in the early months is the *mirroring* by the mother of the child's face and experience (Lacan, 1968; Robson, 1967). I detect this type of reflection in the ninth stanza:

> So between them love did shine,
> That the Turtle saw his right
> Flaming in the Phoenix' sight;
> Either was the other's mine.

That is, the Turtle sees his own self mirrored in the eyes of the Phoenix. But this exceptionally intense, 'flaming', mutual gaze is also dangerous, for as Otto Fenichel wrote, 'In the unconscious, to look at an object may mean . . . to devour the object looked at, to grow like it [or] to force it to grow like oneself (1937, p. 9).

In most Renaissance works, the unique phoenix is depicted as genderless or as vaguely masculine. Shakespeare's rare bird is female, but this is also the case throughout Robert Chester's compilation, Love's Martyr (see Grosart, 1878), where the poem first appeared. Shakespeare may simply have adopted the convention of the larger work in which the dove is male and the phoenix is the turtle's 'queen' (Grosart, 1878). In twelve other places in Shakespeare the gender of the bird is unstated, reference being made primarily to its beauty, rarity, long life or resurrection, while in two plays the phoenix is merely the emblem of a house or of a ship. Two passages, however, clearly indicate that Shakespeare's phoenix can be female. The phrase 'her blood' in Sonnet 19 refers to a phoenix, and in Henry VIII, Cranmer prophesies the spiritual rebirth of Princess Elizabeth, 'the maiden phoenix', as Queen (V,iv.40). Political interpretations of The Phoenix and Turtle (Grosart, 1878; Matchett, 1965; and Axton, 1977) will be discussed below.

The Phoenix of our poem is, I feel, more maternal than 'maiden'. She relates to her constant lover through an intense mutual gaze that dissolves boundaries. G. Wilson Knight called the poem a 'celebration of a mystical love-union beyond sex' (1955, p. 199), and there is something quite magical about this perfect relationship. In a totally different context, Hans Loewald wrote of 'the original oneness, most obvious in the mother-infant dual unity, which shines through or is sensed as remaining the innermost core in later family relations . . . an intimate unity that is anterior to what is commonly called sexuality' (1980, p. 396). This is the magical innocence that pervades the great Medieval paintings of Virgin and Child. But Loewald suggests that our vision 'tends to be blurred by a nostalgic longing for such a state', and he reminds us that this relationship 'may be experienced by the child . . . as a threatening, overpowering force' (1980, p. 19, emphasis added; cf. Holland, 1975, pp. 35-8). (As a first surviving son, Shakespeare may well have experienced maternal over-protection during the eighteen months before his younger brother was born.)

The developing child must move away from the 'vague dual unity' of normal symbiosis to construct an ego that will embody the reality principle and deal reasonably with the external world. Oedipal struggles follow and build upon this achievement. The Phoenix and Turtle, however, seem locked into a static dual unity. Reason (an ego function) is unable to resolve the paradox: 'How true a twain,/ Seemeth this concordant one,' it cries. In admiration of this irrational state, Reason creates the Threnos in which those who are 'either true or fair' are invited to pray at the shrine of ideal Truth and Beauty; for with the death of our protagonists,

> Truth may seem but cannot be,
> Beauty brag, but 'tis not she,
> Truth and Beauty buried be.

Connections With Hamlet

The echo in the penultimate stanza (quoted just above) of Hamlet's repeated references to 'seeming' versus 'being' first stimulated me to investigate the relationship between the poem and the play. Contradictions between reality and appearance are, of course, widespread in Shakespeare's plays, and it is possible that these works are no more closely related than any two works from the same pen; however, careful examination reveals some striking parallels.

Let us begin with the birds referred to in the poem. The owl is explicitly mentioned only once in Hamlet, when the mad Ophelia says, 'the owl was a baker's daughter' (IV,v,42). King Claudius calls this a 'conceit' on her dead father, although later in the same scene Ophelia refers to her father as 'my dove' (168). Some critics have suggested that Ophelia's words allude to a legend in which a baker's daughter was turned into an owl when she refused to give bread to Jesus. Perhaps we may use this information to interpret the second stanza of our poem. The owl would then symbolize the 'bad mother' who withholds nourishment and comfort from her child, and who is therefore excluded from the memorial service. On the other hand, the idealized female Phoenix of the poem would represent the 'good mother'. The eagle could then be interpreted as a negative father image: although feared as a 'tyrant', he cannot be excluded from the domestic scene any more than Claudius can be excluded from the Danish court.

The eleventh stanza of our poem is marked by an extra syllable in each line. Here the central paradox is restated in slightly different terms:

> Reason in itself confounded,
> Saw division grow together,
> To themselves yet either neither,
> Simple were so well compounded.

Reason is unable to comprehend the dual unity in which simple elements are 'compounded' yet retain their essential identity. (Note the enactment of the paradox in the singular subject and plural verb of the last line. The plural subject and singular verb of line 22 was pointed out to me by Andrea Good.) Likewise, 'Property' was 'appalled,/ That the self was not the same'. The words 'confound' and 'appall' appear together in only two other places in Shakespeare's works. The earliest is in Venus and Adonis (line 882). The goddess (whose emblem is the dove) is startled by the sudden yelping of hounds which 'Appalls her senses and her spirit confounds'. This line follows a passage in which Venus is likened to a doe with 'swelling dugs' who hurries to nurse her fawn—clearly a 'good mother'.

The only other co-occurrence of these terms is in Act II of Hamlet. The first Player has just given the Prince a 'taste' of his quality—a passionate speech about the death of Priam and the grief of Hecuba, during which he seems to weep. Left alone, Hamlet reflects on the irony that this actor, 'in a fiction', could express such deep emotions while he, with far truer motives, can do (and perhaps can feel) nothing. What if the Player had a genuine 'cue for passion'? He might then weep and scream in ways that would

> Make mad the guilty, and appall the free,
> Confound the ignorant, and amaze indeed
> The very faculties of eyes and ears.
> (II,ii,564-6)

I read this passage as an ironic reflection on how strong emotions can be represented on the stage and the effects of such 'playing' on different parts of an audience. (Cf. Adams 1953, p. 240, on this scene.) It leads logically to Hamlet's decision to *use* the players to test the conscience of the King (i.e., to 'Make mad the guilty'), although the scheme ultimately falls on its inventor's head.

The words 'confound' and 'appall', then, appear in both poems and the play in contexts that involve conflict between appearance and reality. The maternal concern of Venus for her reluctant young lover corresponds to the relationship of the Phoenix to the Turtle and also to Gertrude's attitude toward Hamlet. Indeed, Gertrude later compares her son to a dove (V,i,286)! I shall argue below that the Phoenix, though not named, is also present in *Hamlet*. Now, however, let us consider one other pair of words.

In the second stanza of *The Phoenix and Turtle*, the owl is referred to as a 'harbinger' and a 'precurrer' of death. As noted by F. T. Prince (1960, p. 176, n.6), a similar pair of words occurs in the very first scene of *Hamlet* when Horatio describes the spiritual and astronomical omens that foretold the murder of Julius Caesar, adding:

> And even the like precurse of fear'd events,
> As harbingers preceding still the fates
> And prologue to the omen coming on,
> Have heaven and earth together demonstrated
> Unto our climatures and countrymen.
> (I,i,121-5)

The Ghost enters immediately, enhancing the *trompe-l'oeil* effect, for Horatio's words refer both to Caesar and to the play, *Julius Caesar*, which Shakespeare's audience may have seen the previous year on the same stage, perhaps with the same actors. Also, 'our countrymen' are both Danes and Englishmen, for Horatio's mention of a Roman lunar eclipse is usually taken as an allusion to the celestial events of 1598, when one solar and two lunar eclipses were visible in England. At some level of symbolism, the Phoenix and Turtle may also be the sun and moon, with their mutual annihilation representing an eclipse, for there is ample evidence to link the Phoenix with the sun god, Hyperion, and thus with Hamlet.

Symbolism Of The Phoenix

In Egyptian religion the phoenix (*bennu*) was associated with the sun gods, especially with Osiris when he was represented as the morning star. This glorious bird (probably a heron), spent the night in a sacred tree near the temple of the sun. Its morning flight from its nest in a high palm or sycamore through which shone the rays of the rising sun may be the source of legends about its periodic rebirth from the ashes of a fiery death (Muller, 1918). Herodotus recorded parts of the legend, including the association of the phoenix with the temple at Heliopolis.

I agree with William Matchett (1965, p. 19) that not every element of the phoenix legend need be used to interpret Shakespeare's poem; however, it is far from self-evident just which parts of the legend *are* relevant. For example, the Chinese phoenix (*fêng-huang*) is one of four spiritual animals, the others being the unicorn, the tortoise and the dragon. It appears to belong to a sign system that is entirely different from that of Shakespeare's animals. However, when one reads that it too is associated with the sun, that other birds 'assemble to pay it homage', and that 'when it goes away the country is visited with calamities' (Ferguson, 1928, p. 99), one hesitates to dismiss this information.

Shakespeare's knowledge of the phoenix myth was most likely derived from Ovid's *Metamorphoses*. Neither in the original nor in Arthur Golding's translation of 1567 (Rouse, 1904) is there any mention of the flames in which the bird expires, but this element could have been known to him from other sources. (Dryden added the flames to Ovid's poem in his translation a century later.) The Latin version, which Shakespeare certainly knew, stresses the *filial piety of the phoenix* in transporting its genitor's ashes to the temple of the sun. In Miller's literal rendering, after he has built his nest of spices, the old phoenix 'ends his life amidst the odours. And from his father's body . . . a little phoenix springs.' When he is strong enough, the new phoenix 'bears his own cradle and his father's tomb through the thin air, until, having reached the city of the Sun, he lays the nest down before the sacred doors of the Sun's temple' (*ante fores sacras Hyperionis aede reponit*) (Miller, 1916, pp. 392-3).

In Golding's translation we find only a reference to *Phebus* (Book XV, 447); however, I believe the word 'Hyperion' in the original Latin is highly significant.[2] The name of the Titan links the phoenix legend with Hamlet's idealization of his dead father, for on two occasions the Prince compares his father to Hyperion

(I. ii, 140; III, iv, 56). There is a double irony in this identification, for in the myth, Hyperion married his sister, Theia, and passed his authority over the sun to his son, Helios. In the play it is Claudius who marries his 'sometime sister', Gertrude, while Hamlet is frustrated in his hope for succession.

A few lines later in Book XV of *Metamorphoses* we come to the story of Egeria, a queen who mourned continually for her dead husband. Her tears of grief were finally pitied by Diana (= Artemis = Phoebus' sister) who 'made of her body a cool spring and of her slender limbs unfailing streams' (Miller, 1916, p. 393). The contrast with Gertrude's hasty remarriage is striking; however, Shakespeare chose to use the more familiar figure of weeping Niobe, applying the image of dissolving flesh to Hamlet himself (I, ii, 129). Ovid stresses the purity of the phoenix, and Golding's translation mentions the bird's 'unsullied' beak and claws. Perhaps Hamlet's flesh was too 'sullied' by ambivalence to perform adequate mourning rites for his father. There are other hints in the *Metamorphoses* about the possible symbolic meanings of birds mentioned in *The Phoenix and Turtle*, but these would take us too far afield.[3]

Interpretation

Some critics connect the assembly of birds in *The Phoenix and Turtle* with the literary convention of the 'parlement of fowls', dating back at least to Chaucer, but I believe that we must seek a more dynamic interpretation. There is something dreamlike about the assembly. It has, for me, the quality of a screen memory representing and concealing the primal scene. If I let myself freely associate to the remembered poem, I find the following sequence: a phallic image of the 'sole Arabian tree', a loud cry (in the night), a silent approach to the 'tragic scene' in which a loving pair are witnessed in the frightening dual unity of coitus, confounding Reason and threatening the observing self by reactivating early memories of pleasure and danger. Reason (ego organization) now reasserts itself by denying what has been seen and insisting on 'married chastity' (or perhaps oral conception, as in the crow). It punishes the parents by wishing for their death, but makes restitution by idealization, projection of the parental imagos into 'eternity', and perhaps by a regressive fusion with the lost maternal object. If these associations seem more oedipal than symbiotic, we should recall Loewald's observation that the oedipal stage contains 'in its very core features of primary identification and symbiosis' (1980, p. 399; cf. Hamilton, 1969).

Let us review the poem once again. Although it uses the same vocabulary as the Sonnets that deal with dual unity (e.g., Sonnet 36), it does not have the *texture* of a Sonnet (cf. Wheeler, 1972, on Sonnets 88-96). Murray Schwartz (personal communication) has suggested that there is something highly depersonalized and austere about *The Phoenix and Turtle*. In the opening stanzas, a narrator issues commands, positioning other actors and assigning roles for the ritual to follow. The care with which this is done indicates that something of great importance is taking place and that the ritual can be dangerous if not properly conducted. At the very least, it provokes anxiety-laden memories.

Rosalie Colie wrote that 'paradox demands of its framers both total control over expression and thought, and the appearance of effortless manipulation of expression and thought' (1966, p. 34). The anthem section, however, is far from effortless; *obsessive* would be a better word. The mourners turn the paradox this way and that, as if to reassure themselves that dual unity is possible. Colie is correct that 'Love gives the illusion of solving, for a time at least, the fundamental metaphysical problem of the one and the many' (1966, p. 96), but the perfect love of the Phoenix and Turtle is too fantastical to produce this illusion. For me, at least, Anthony and Cleopatra are better examples of dual unity, as are the lovers in many of Donne's poems (see Faber, 1985; Donne, 1965). In *The Phoenix and Turtle*, Reason acknowledges and accepts the paradox, but does not resolve it. Indeed, the final response of Reason to dual unity is not logical but *aesthetic:* 'Whereupon it made this threne'.

The threnody (in tercets, each with a single rhyme) is more serene than the anthem and it employs an even higher level of abstraction. We have moved from the strong commands of the invocation through the repeated paradoxes of the anthem to a soft sigh of resignation. I envision the assembled mourners circling an urn in which the merged ashes of Phoenix and Turtle rest, solemnly chanting the first four stanzas of the *Threnos*. But the last stanza (like the disputed final lines of Keats's 'Ode on a Grecian Urn') seems to me to be in a different voice:

> To this urn let those repair,
> That are either true or fair,
> For these dead birds, sigh a prayer.

Who speaks these lines? As part of the threnody they should be chanted by the chorus of birds; however, I suspect that they are spoken by the voice of Reason (heard briefly before in stanza 12). Another possibility is that the narrator who began the poem, 'Let the bird of loudest lay', concludes it with a parallel command: 'To this urn let those repair . . .' In either case, the *trompe-l'oeil* technique places the threnody within yet another frame. As Adams observed, 'Shakespeare violates the aesthetic frame by calling attention to it in order to . . . create the effects of depth and distance' (1953, p. 242). We move back from the dream, or the memory, or the memory of the dream, into nostalgia for a dual unity that will never again be ours.

Conclusions

Can we have it both ways? Can *The Phoenix and Turtle* represent the symbiotic dual unity of mother and child during the early months of life and also express much later oedipal conflicts? And does this poem help us to understand Hamlet's 'awful dilemma'? I believe so.

We have Loewald's (1980, pp. 398-9) authority for recognizing the symbiotic core of the oedipal situation; he also summarizes the traditional psychoanalytic view of Hamlet as a play in which 'incestuous oedipal fantasies' dominate sexual life in adulthood. The oedipal situation is a drama of frustrated succession, and the Prince is trapped in a no-win position. Following Freud, Ernest Jones (1949) argued forcefully that Hamlet's unconscious identification with his uncle would not allow him to act out the revenge that was his duty. Behind this conflict, I suggest, lies an earlier, ambivalent identification with his mother: a desire to return to her womb coupled with an intense fear of personal annihilation (cf. Fineman, 1977). The only 'resolution' of this paradox that Shakespeare could then envision was the death of both parties.

Hamlet's ambivalence toward Ophelia involves the problems of reality and appearance, expressed in terms of truth and beauty ('Are you honest? . . . Are you fair?'). He fears the power that beauty has to corrupt honesty, and he concludes that truth and beauty can coexist only in a nunnery ('married chastity') or in death (III,i,101ff.; I am indebted to Marian Bock for this suggestion). But since their love was perfectly true and chaste, why must the Phoenix and Turtle die?

A number of scholars answer this question by denying that the phoenix is really dead. Grosart argued that all the poems in *Love's Martyr*, including Shakespeare's, constitute an elaborate political allegory in which 'the "Phoenix" was Elizabeth and the "Turtle Dove" Essex' (1878, p. xliv). Despite the forced reading that this imposes on many lines (and the embarrassing fact that Essex was dead and the Queen still alive in 1601 when Chester's book appeared), Matchett (1965) reluctantly concludes that Grosart may have been correct.

Marie Axton has also given qualified support to an allegorical interpretation. In her fascinating study of theological and legal doctrines related to the succession, she finds that 'the love between the Turtle and his Queen is described in language used by lawyers and poets for their phenomenon of the king's two bodies' (Axton, 1977, p. 128), and she concludes that 'The urn which encloses the cinders of Beautie, Truth and Raritie is, of course, the Phoenix . . . If the miracle occurs the birds who burned in mutual flame *are* the true and fair who come to the urn; there is never a moment when there is not a fire or a Phoenix' (1977, p. 129).

I cannot accept Axton's mystical interpretation. *Love's Martyr* contains political allegory, but I doubt that this helps us to understand Shakespeare's contribution. *The Phoenix and Turtle* is too brief (and too ambiguous) to make a final decision possible, but I believe that Shakespeare took the occasion of Chester's volume to write about the paradox of ideal love out of the depths of his personal experience, using several images that preoccupied him at the beginning of his great tragic period.

To summarize, I have not argued that Freudian theory explains the creation of this or any other work of art; but I do believe that consideration of early developmental experience can deepen our understanding of *The Phoenix and Turtle* and can illuminate its relationship to *Hamlet*. Similar echoes of dual unity are found in some of the other plays, but it is above all in Prince Hamlet that we sense, despite all his intelligence and wit, what Winnicott (1971, p. 83) called 'a crippled capacity to be'. More intensely than most people, Hamlet both longed and feared to lose his self. He yearned for the ideal; but perfect love, truth or beauty exist only within the mind. Thus, Shakespeare's urn—the final repository of Truth and Beauty—is one with Donne's 'well-wrought urn', with Keats's Grecian urn, and even with a certain plain gray jar upon a hill in Tennessee.[4]

Notes

[1] [All Shakespeare citations are from the Riverside Shakespeare, G. Blakemore Evans, ed., Boston, MA: Houghton Mifflin, 1974.] This edition differs from the original text of *The Phoenix and Turtle* only in its modernized spellings and in the word 'queen' which is capitalized in Robert Chester's book, *Love's Martyr* (Grosart, 1878). When the words 'phoenix' and 'turtle' are capitalized in this paper they refer to the birds in Shakespeare's poem only.

[2] In his notes on the source of *The Tempest*, Robert Langbaum comments that Shakespeare 'paraphrases a speech of the witch, Medea, in Ovid's *Metamorphoses*—using Arthur Golding's translation (1567), which he apparently checked against the Latin original' (Langbaum 1964, p. 126). Shakespeare seems to have used a similar procedure in relation to the phoenix legend.

[3] Bruno Bettelheim (1976, p. 213) reminds us that the owl, raven and dove visit the sleeping Princess in the

Brothers Grimm version of 'Snow White'; in that context, he interprets them as symbols of wisdom and maturity. See also Bock (1984, pp. 89-93). Shakespeare may have been aware of *The Phoenix Nest* (1953), a memorial to Sir Philip Sidney, who died in 1586, but I doubt that there is any connection between this work and his poem.

[4] See Wallace Stevens, 'Anecdote of the Jar'. For an unusual interpretation of *Othello* see Kirsch, who comments on the 'child-like wonder' in Othello's character and his investment of Desdemona with 'that sense of symbiotic exaltation which is the remembrance of childhood' (1978, p. 731). Barron (1960, p. 268) views Macbeth and Lady Macbeth as resembling 'a mother and son who have failed to achieve separate identities' (1960, p. 268). He argues that they are unable to procreate because they are too closely merged, and refers to the same theme in *The Phoenix and Turtle*. Felperin (1964) suggests that Keats's ode was directly influenced by Shakespeare's poem.

MORTALITY

Richard C. McCoy (essay date 1997)

SOURCE: "Love's Martyr's: Shakespeare's 'Phoenix and Turtle' and the Sacrificial Sonnets," in *Religion and Culture in Renaissance England,* edited by Claire McEachern and Debora Shuger, Cambridge University Press, 1997, pp. 188-208.

[*In the following essay, McCoy studies the combination sacred and earthly elements in* The Phoenix and Turtle *and suggests the term "relic" to describe the blending of mortality and continued spiritual power.*]

In its paradoxical intensity and cryptic brevity, "The Phoenix and Turtle" is one of Shakespeare's most enigmatic works. I. A. Richards calls it "the most mysterious poem in English," and, for him and many others, its mysteries are profoundly cosmic: "there is a religious quality in its movement, a feeling in it as though we were being related through it to something far beyond any individuals. This Phoenix and Turtle have a mythic scale to them, as though through them we were to become participants in something ultimate."[1] William H. Matchett and others find its riddles more worldly, discerning oblique allusions to the alarming events and apprehensions of Elizabeth's last days, specifically the revolt and death of the Earl of Essex as well as fears of an unsettled succession.[2] The latter approach has been more alluring to recent critics, including myself. Intimations of immortality are less dazzling nowadays than hints of topicality, and we are drawn more to the man of an age than the bard for all time.[3]

In approaching this poem and several related sonnets, I want to read them both ways, exploring the verse's topical implications without ignoring what Richards calls its "religious quality." Indeed, I want to show how both dimensions amplify one another and correct the false dichotomy between the religious and political, as well as between the transcendent and contingent, assumed in much recent criticism. This is part of a larger revisionist effort to rectify what Debora Shuger calls "the almost total neglect of society's religious aspects in favor of political ones . . . in recent literary scholarship."[4] I am also interested in addressing another omission noted by Jonathan Bate in a piece entitled "Love Locked Out: The Downgrading of the Affections in New Shakespeare Criticism" and want to reconsider the ambiguities of Shakespeare's conception of love.[5]

"The Phoenix and Turtle" is Shakespeare's contribution to a collection called *Love's Martyr,* and his poem grapples with the enigmas of both love and martyrdom, probing questions at the core of all his work. As John Keats recognized long ago, suffering in Shakespeare—as in life—yields few miracles, but, in trying to sketch out "a system of Salvation which does not affront our reason and humanity," Keats, like Shakespeare, still assigns suffering some kind of redemptive value.[6] Shakespeare's ideas of love are shaped by Christian beliefs in altruism and sacrifice, but love is hardly miraculous in "The Phoenix and Turtle" or many other love poems. As John Kerrigan points out in his edition of *The Sonnets and A Lover's Complaint,* love neither attains transcendent Platonic perfection nor absolute Christian communion. The sonnets may celebrate "Love as an absolute, but . . . Love's Growth is . . . bound up with the body, its sexuality and decay."[7] In the final sonnets to the young man, love's growth is firmly bound by decay and death. I call them sacrificial sonnets because they equate love and death by describing both as a form of rendering, but what is rendered remains ambiguous. By examining their account of human sacrifice and considering what the poems themselves render, I hope to clarify what we make of them and what we take from them.

Love's Martyr is a collection of "poeticall essaies" compiled by Robert Chester and published in 1601. Chester is the author of the long eponymous poem, "Love's Martyr, or Rosalin's Complaint," which was evidently the inspiration for shorter works by a more illustrious group. This includes, in addition to Shakespeare's "Phoenix and Turtle," poems by Ben Jonson, George Chapman, John Marston, and the anonymous "Ignoto." Each poet works variations on the theme of the phoenix, described in the dedication as "an Invention freer than the Times."[8] The phrase provocatively hints at topical implications and political constraints even as it claims to transcend them. As a symbol of chastity and immortality, the phoenix was frequently associated with Elizabeth, and its myth of death and resurrection may anticipate a hopeful if inscrutable resolution of the pending succession crisis. Afterwards, the commemorative medals marking her death and James's succession depict a phoenix on one side and her image on the other, while eulogies such as Henry Petowe's "Elizabetha Quasi Vivens" proclaim that a "Phoenix from her ashes doth arise."[9] Reviewing this material in his exhaustive study of *Love's Martyr*, William Matchett acknowledges that the figure is indeterminate but contends that "in the last decade or so before her death in 1603, Elizabeth would almost inevitably have come to mind as the 'long-liv'd' phoenix."[10]

The other member of this legendary couple is harder to identify. Matchett takes up A. B. Grosart's conjecture, first advanced in the latter's 1878 edition of *Love's Martyr*, that Essex is the devoted turtle dove and makes a convincing case.[11] This requires recognizing how the anthology's vagaries reflect the Earl's changing relationship to the Queen. F. T. Prince concludes in his edition of Shakespeare's poems that "Chester's fantastic compilation" seems "to have grown by a process of accumulation and accretion over a considerable period."[12] It was a period fraught with anxiety regarding the succession as well as tensions between Elizabeth and her troublesome favorite. *Love's Martyr* may have started as an effort to promote a more positive relationship between these two powerful figures, but, by its publication in 1601, putting the best face on the Earl's execution was the only recourse.

Chester's own long poem is the keystone of the collection, but its main plot is bizarre and even unseemly. A chaotic jumble of lover's complaint, Arthurian legend, herbal lore, and other incongruities, it begins with Nature complaining to Jove that a paragon of female virtue may die without issue: "This *Phoenix* I do feare me will decay,/ And from her ashes neuer will arise" a comparable successor (p. 15). The Phoenix herself subsequently laments her predicament but hopes that the lover promised by Jove "will blesse,/ And alter my halfe-rotten tottering state" (p. 32). Nature promises her a cozy love nest "in secrecies sweet Bower" (p. 28) and suggests various herbal remedies for barrenness, including a form of hormone therapy:

> The seede of this Horminum drunke with
>   wine,
> Doth stirre a procurations heate in vs,
> And to Libidenous lusts makes men incline,
> And mens vnable bodies doth refine:
> It brings increase by operation,
> And multiplies our generation.
>   (p. 95)

The poem's erotic atmosphere is, to say the least, weird, combining libidinous encouragement with anxiety about sexual incapacity. Chester is fixated on what he calls here and elsewhere the procreative "operation," and his Phoenix worries throughout that "such operation in me is not placed" (p. 24). If directed at the Queen, Chester's talk of the lady's "halfe-rotten tottering state" seems especially offensive, as does urging her to reproduce at the age of 68. Yet such incongruities were typical of the cult of Elizabeth, especially in its waning years. The strains imposed by a courtly style of compulsory, perennial seduction—the tendency to rhetorical excess, wishful thinking, and outright denial—are sometimes obvious, especially in a practitioner as inept as Chester.

Despite its provocative urgency, Chester's erotic narrative is probably a decorative pretext for another, more sober agenda. Behind the poem's apparently "aphrodisiacal intention," Matchett discerns a political rather than conjugal proposal, one no less presumptuous or unlikely.[13] According to Matchett, Chester is not actually encouraging a belated marriage between Elizabeth and Essex as a solution to the impending succession problem. Instead he tries to promote a "mutual understanding which would make Essex the Queen's copartner in governing the country and determining the succession."[14] Essex was eager to help broker the succession. He was one of the first of Elizabeth's courtiers to begin secretly corresponding with James VI, and he felt that his prominence as a privy counselor and Earl Marshal entitled him to assume such a role.[15] So did others, as Robert Parsons's dedication of *A Conference About the Next Succession to the Crown of England* to Essex in 1595 indicates: "No man is in more high & eminent place or dignitie at this day in our realme, then your selfe, whether we respect your nobilitie, or calling, or fauour with your prince, or high liking of the people, and consequently no man like to haue a greater part of sway in deciding of this great affaire."[16] Chester's version of the phoenix myth may be a less provocative promotion of such a role for Essex in its celebration of a legendary *discordia concors*.

Unfortunately, their actual relationship only grew more discordant. Elizabeth and Essex quarreled over Ireland in the Privy Council in 1598 until she boxed his ears and he reached for his sword. Essex was arrested the next year after returning from Ireland against orders and bursting in on her unannounced. *Love's Martyr* can be seen adjusting to these deteriorating circumstances as some poems acknowledge and apologize for an obscure offense. Chester's conclusion asks the beloved to "saue my poore life, and be not tyrannous" (p. 149). The lover laments being forsaken by his Phoenix (p. 151) and banished from her presence (p. 155), and he appeals for clemency:

> O tongue thou has blasphemed thy holy
>   Goddesse
> Let me do penance for offending thee,
> Me do thou blame for my forgetfulnesse:
> Heare my submission, thou wilt succour me.
>   (p. 156)

Such lines were apparently written when it was still possible to make amends and to save Essex from further punishment.

By the time *Love's Martyr* was published in 1601, the Earl's execution foreclosed any hope of forgiveness. By that point, the contributors to *Love's Martyr* could only present his death in the best light possible. In poems written by Shakespeare, Marston, and Chapman, the Turtle's devotion is proven by his death. Thus the Turtle who asks his beloved in Chester's verse to *"pittie me that dies for thee"* (p. 149) becomes the titular "love's martyr." For the Earl's admirers, Essex remained the Queen's most devoted servant rather than a traitor, and his execution made him "love's martyr" as well. Certainly he saw himself this way until the end. In a letter to Fulke Greville written before his departure for Ireland in 1599, he proclaimed that if his "death [would] either quench the great fire of rebellion in Ireland, or divert those dangers which from foreign enemies are threatened, I should joy to be such a sacrifice."[17] When he returned against orders the next year and was arrested and arraigned before a special commission of his peers, he professed "a loyall faithfull unspotted heart, unfained affection and desire, euer to doe her Majestie the best service he could, which rather then he would lose, he would if Christianity and Charity did permit, first teare out of his breast, with his owne hands."[18] Finally, at the trial following his failed coup in 1601, he calmly declared that "that he was not at all solicitous for life, which he had always wished above all things to lay down with an entire fidelity to GOD and his sovereign."[19] However, under pressure from his chaplain, this proud self-righteousness gave way to remorse, and, when his spiritual adviser "spoke to him of the constancie of Martyrs at their death ... the Earle, with passion, said that they dyed in a good cause, but he should dye in a BAD CAUSE."[20]

Nevertheless, despite the Earl's last-minute contrition and the government's effort to publicize it, the image of a saintly, martyred devotion persisted in popular songs and elegies. One ballad says that his "soule so sweet doth rest on high/ To liue with Christ eternally," and another imputes a powerful Christian humility to his last words:

"God's will be done!" quoth he;
   "Yet shall you strangely see
God's strong in me to be,
   though I am weake."[21]

Robert Prickett numbers Essex among the saints and, since his tribute was published a year after Elizabeth's death, his reproaches to the Queen are barely veiled:

Vnkinde his Country, that worthy bloud to
   craue,
Which was for her, and for her seruice bent

His mother *England* hauing slaine her sonne,
The world will saye it was vnkindly done.[22]

Recrimination is more muted in *Love's Martyr*, and its verses take a more affirmative view of devotion unto death, emphasizing the eternal rewards of love's martyrdom. In Chester's concluding cantos, the Phoenix and Turtle propose to die together "in a manner sacrificingly" (p. 136), and their union in death produces "a more perfect creature" (pp. 139-40). Jonson claims that true love attains perfection itself and preserves the social order:

That is an *Essence* most gentile, and fine.
Pure, perfect; nay divine:
It is a golden Chaine let down from
   Heauen, . . .
[Love] in a calme and God-like vnitie,
Preserues *Communitie*.
                                    (pp. 191-2)

Marston's exaltation of love's "deuinest *Essence*" also renders it immortal; as he says, "corruption quakes to touch such excellence" (p. 185). By contrast, Shakespeare takes a darker view of love's rewards, and the preservation of community becomes more precarious.

The political implications of Shakespeare's poem are particularly intriguing. Both the Phoenix and Turtle are already dead, and the first lines are a summons to a parliament of fowls.[23] There is considerable apprehension about maintaining legitimate authority after their death:

From this session interdict
Every fowl of tyrant wing,
Save the eagle, feather'd king
                                    (9-11)

The eagle is the legitimate successor, but the immediate authority behind these invitations and interdictions during the interregnum is explicitly heraldic: "Let the bird of loudest lay/ . . . Herald sad and trumpet be." Medieval treatises such as the *Modus Tenendi Parliamentum* gave the Earl Marshal and Constable, who jointly headed the College of Arms and Heralds, authority to preside over such transitions, not only officiating at royal funerals and coronations but also summoning parliament in the case of an unsettled succession.[24] This is why Essex eagerly sought these offices. Yet, with Essex now dead and the Earl Marshalcy vacant, the identity of "the bird of loudest lay" and the question of heraldic authority is uncertain. Like other contributors to *Love's Martyr*, Shakespeare may describe hopes and fears for an orderly succession, but he is characteristically circumspect about who is in charge. The poem's religious aspects are no less tantalizing, and there is just as much anxiety about maintaining liturgical protocol as political order:

> Keep the obsequy so strict.
> Let the priest in surplice white,
> That defunctive music can,
> Be the death-divining swan,
> Lest the requiem lack his right.
>
> (12-16)

Despite this concern about ceremonial propriety, Shakespeare's customary pun on right and rites does not make clear what either entails, and the political and ritual purpose of this assembly is never clearly established.

The provocatively Catholic term, "requiem," is especially confusing. Shakespeare uses the word only one other time, at a pivotal juncture in *Hamlet*. At Ophelia's funeral, the "churlish priest" (5.1.240) denies her the full service because he suspects her of committing suicide. The requiem mass is a crucial component of the Roman Catholic funeral service, "since only with the offering of the eucharistic sacrifice of the requiem mass does the act of the Church become an effectual intercession with God for the soul of the faithful."[25] It is often the first in a series of masses offered for the soul of the deceased, and such acts of intercession are essential to maintaining the communion of the saints or what Jacques Le Goff calls "the solidarity of the dead and the living."[26] However, the Reformation put an end to the belief in purgatory and the system of indulgences it sustained. The aim of the funeral service shifted, as Ralph Houlbrooke explains, from "intercession to commemoration" as the sermon, formal eulogy, and funeral monument acquired greater importance.[27] More radical Puritans rejected both functions, repudiating *The Book of Common Prayer*'s promise of a "sure and certain hope of the resurrection to eternal life" as too presumptuous while objecting to the vanity of commemorative tributes.[28] The result of such conflicts was a kind of liturgical irresolution. In Houlbrooke's account, "the English reformers, after pulling down the structure of inherited observances, failed (partly because of their own divisions) to create a generally accepted way of death thoroughly imbued with their spirit."[29] The Church of England of Shakespeare's time pursued a characteristically erratic *via media*. The burial service in *The Book of Common Prayer* is fairly Protestant, consisting only of psalms, lessons, and prayers for the dead. However, as Roland Mushat Frye explains, a requiem mass was retained in a separate Latin missal called the *Liber Precum Publicarum*, published in 1560.[30] As Frye points out, Ophelia's funeral is fraught with denominational confusion and scandalous obscurity, while her "maimed rites" are haunted by a sense of liturgical irresolution and inefficacy. A similar sense of inefficacy pervades the "maimed rites" of "The Phoenix and Turtle." Ceremonial roles are carefully assigned, but nothing happens. As John Arthos remarks, "the rite is never performed. All we have is a summons . . . followed by an anthem and lament."[31] Since the "Phoenix and the Turtle fled/ In a mutual flame from hence" (23-4), the anthem describes an event which already happened somewhere else:

> So they lov'd, as love in twain
> Had the essence but in one:
> Two distincts, division none;
> Number there in love was slain.
> Hearts remote, yet not asunder;
> Distance and no space was seen
> 'Twixt this Turtle and his queen:
> But in them it were a wonder.
>
> (25-32)

Their love *was* indeed a wonder, a blend of death and sexual consummation taking the form of a perfect communion, but it occurs entirely in the past tense. This approximation of a eucharistic sacrifice is over and done with at the moment of poetic vision, and it can only be elegiacally recalled in what Marston dismisses as a "mouing *Epicedium*" (p. 185). By evoking a requiem, "The Phoenix and Turtle" conjures up a faint hope of communion between the living and the dead, but, as in *Hamlet*, this ritual is replaced by a troubled, disappointed remembrance whose connection to the deceased is far more tenuous.

Shakespeare's lovers shared love's "essence but in one," but this proves less enduring than the essence described by Marston and Jonson. The poem ends on a note of transience and loss:

> Beauty, truth, and rarity,
> Grace in all simplicity,
> Here enclos'd, in cinders lie.
> Death is now the Phoenix' nest,
> And the Turtle's loyal breast
> To eternity doth rest;
> Leaving no posterity:
> 'Twas not their infirmity,
> It was married chastity.
>
> (53-60)

By insisting that their union leaves no posterity, Shakespeare denies the phoenix its traditional regenerative powers. The funeral pyre contains only "cinders" with none of the auguries of "a more perfect creature" (pp. 139-140) glimpsed elsewhere in *Love's Martyr*. Matchett reads the insistence on "no posterity" as criticism of Elizabeth's failure to produce an heir, noting that it is carefully hedged by praise for "married chastity."[32]

The poem's last stanza is especially downcast. Truth and beauty are dead and buried in the preceding lines, and, while some survivors may still partake of one of these qualities, they exist only in diminished form as separate alternatives:

> To this urn let those repair
> That are either true or fair:
> For these dead birds sigh a prayer.
>
> (65-7)

All that remains of the mythical Phoenix and Turtle are "these dead birds," and prayer is reduced to a wordless, helpless "sigh." Shakespeare's urn contains the ashes of "love's martyrs," but, unlike Ignoto's "rare-liue vrne" or "flame that . . . feedes the others life" (p. 181) or Donne's version of the "Phoenix ridle" and the "well wrought urne" in "The Canonization," Shakespeare's version offers little hope for a resurrection or pattern for emulation.[33]

For Donne, love's martyrdom insures canonization, however ironically, but the ambiguities of love and martyrdom in Shakespeare are more mysterious and confusing. Shakespeare's final sonnets to the young man, 124 through 126, also deal with the dynamics of martyrdom and sacrifice, and rendering is perceived first as love and then death. Rendering is alternately worldly and transcendent, sinister and edifying, and it is described as a calculating but futile exchange, a form of mutual redemption, and, finally, a cruel and oddly callous human sacrifice. We experience in these sonnets a weird slippage from the ridiculous to the sublime—"the fools of Time" turn out to be love's martyrs—as well as from perfect love to complete indifference—the lover who spoke tenderly of a "mutual render, only me for thee" in the penultimate sonnet coldly contemplates the "lovely boy's" ultimate rendering and rending by Nature and Time in the last poem.[34] To return to the original question, what is rendered by Shakespeare's version of human sacrifice?

Sonnet 124 insists that love is neither "the child of state," nor "fortune's bastard," nor "subject to time's love, or to time's hate." Love is detached from all contingency, far from the rise of "smiling pomp" and the fall of "thralled discontent." Moreover, love is immune to the fluctuations of "policy, that heretic" even as it "all alone stands hugely politic." That paradox along with repeated references to volatile if vague affairs of state makes this sonnet especially provocative. The Variorum is full of speculations about Jesuit spies and Catholic martyrs, Gunpowder plotters, and, of course, the Essex conspirators.[35] Like the claim to "an Invention freer than the Times" made in *Love's Martyr*, the sonnet's insistence on its own transcendence of "th'inviting time" only arouses suspicions of some contemporary implication, yet its deliberate vagueness prevents confirmation of the suspicions it arouses. Like love, the poem keeps a safe distance from current political conflicts by standing aside, "hugely politic." Its obscurities derive from a blend of deniability and what Annabel Patterson calls "functional ambiguity," a poetic strategy devised to "touch covertly" on sensitive topics.[36]

The poem's final couplet is notoriously baffling: "To this I witness call the fools of time,/ Which die for goodness, who have lived for crime." Who are these figures and what does their death mean? How does a life of crime culminate in a good death, and how does a criminal life make a credible witness? Amidst all these perplexities, "the fools of time" are presented as "love's martyrs." The original Greek meaning of martyr is witness, and they do bear witness to love's endurance through their death. In a final stunning contradiction, "the fools of time" prove by their deeds the truth of the words of sonnet 116: "Love's not time's fool." In making martyrs of "the fools of time," Shakespeare dramatizes the fundamental paradox of love and love's martyrdom. From one perspective, martyrdom guarantees transcendence and immortality achieving by a replication of Christ's passion what Peter Brown calls the "abolition of time" and attaining perpetual bliss in exchange for a willing submission to human mortality.[37] From another, more *politique* angle, there are few actions more vulnerably contingent or tragically absurd. As Miri Rubin shows, martyrdom is an inherently unstable category, raising "serious problems of perspective, empathy, judgement," and, though perceived as a categorical absolute, it is "intrinsically amenable to historical change."[38]

No period of English history was as vivid or volatile in its shifting perception of martyrdom as Shakespeare's lifetime. He was born a few years after the publication of Foxe's *Book of Martyrs*, the most powerful work of protestant hagiography ever published. Yet for all the fervor inspired by the courageous acts described, Reformation sectarianism also prompted uncertainty and a *politique* skepticism about martyrdom's validity: one person's martyr was another's rebel, heretic, or fanatic fool. Foxe himself denounces one of England's most renowned martyrs, Thomas à Becket, as "that olde Romishe traytor" for his stand against royal supremacy.[39] John Donne published *Pseudo-Martyr* in 1610 to denounce what he calls "an inordinate and corrupt affectation of martyrdome."[40] Yet, as St. Paul recognized in his first epistle to the Corinthians (4:9-10), such skepticism is inevitable: "God hath set forth us the apostles last, as it were appointed to death: for we are made a spectacle unto the world, and to angels, and to men. We are fools for Christ's sake, but ye are wise in Christ; we are weak, but ye are strong; ye are honourable, but we are despised." From a worldly perspective, martyrs are inevitably "the fools of time."

Shakespeare's own perspective on these ambiguities is profoundly *politique*. The poet turns to the "fools of time" for support, yet he remains cool and aloof. As for martyrdom's rewards, he is characteristically equivocal. In *Love's Martyr*, the other contributors take a providential perspective: Ben Jonson defines love as "a golden Chaine let down from Heauen" (p. 191), and John Marston calls it the "Soule of heauens labour'd *Quintessence*" (p. 185). Shakespeare's Phoenix and Turtle were once the living embodiments of ideal "Beauty, truth, and rarity" (line 53), but their earthly remains are now mere "cinders" (line 55). What remains of "the fools of time" and what their martyrdom accomplishes is still more obscure, but neither immortality nor transcendence are guaranteed.

The last two sonnets to the young man are no less equivocal about the results of love's martyrdom. Sonnet 125 begins by calling for a kind of emotional and existential cost-accounting:

> Were't ought to me I bore the canopy,
> With my extern the outward honoring,
> Or laid great bases for eternity,
> Which proves more short than waste or ruining?

In a broad sense, this is a question about the value of ceremonial homage, but it also raises the issue of what is owed or "ought to me." The event described sounds like a specific historical occasion, an actual procession which Shakespeare could have joined as a liveried retainer and member of the King's Men or protégé of an Earl. Yet this concrete detail is quickly swamped by the poet's disdain for "outward honoring." The honors paid to earthly greatness, seen *sub specie aeternitatis,* collapse into exercises in Ozymandian futility. In its proclaimed hostility to worldly honors, sonnet 125 is no less evasively "politic" than 124, including hints of the speaker's proximity to greatness while denying its importance to his true feelings.

At the same time, the images of ritual fealty and the language of political patronage are suffused with religious symbolism. While the canopy was held by favored servants in an aristocratic or royal progress, it was also carried above the host in Corpus Christi processionals. Eucharistic terminology pervades the poem, but here too there is nothing but scorn for those preoccupied with "outward honoring." Those "dwellers on form and favor" are dismissed as "pitiful thrivers, in their gazing spent," and Stephen Booth detects a reference to *The Book of Common Prayer* which enjoins believers not to "stand by as gazers and lookers on them that do Communicate."[41] Similarly, in his *Apology of the Church of England* (1564), John Jewel contends that those who abstain from receiving Communion should be excommunicated. Jewel contrasts the substance of the Communion service with the vanity of Corpus Christi processions by attacking the latter for bringing

> the sacraments of Christ to be used now as a stage play and a solemn sight; to the end that men's eyes should be fed with nothing else but with mad gazings and foolish gauds, in the selfsame matter wherein the death of Christ ought diligently to be beaten into our hearts, and wherein also the mysteries of our redemption ought with all holiness and reverence to be executed.[42]

Many reformers were intent on purging the Eucharist of the idolatrous trappings of spectacle such as the canopy, the elevation and display of the host, and the Communion rail.[43] This poem seems intent on moving past outward signs to a space in which the meaning of Communion can be "beaten into our hearts."

The poet stakes out this space in the last quatrain where the eucharistic imagery is strongest and the mood most intimately harmonious:

> No, let me be obsequious in thy heart,
> And, take thou my oblation, poor but free,
> Which is not mixed with seconds, knows no art,
> But mutual render, only me for thee.

Booth notes possible references to Leviticus, an Old Testament source for the liturgical protocols of the Communion service. The first is the description in chapter 1, verse 13 to "an oblation made by fire for a sweet savour unto with lord." The phrase "not mixed with seconds" coupled with a pun on "pure" suggests the unadulterated, refined flour reserved for communion wafers, a prescription based on Leviticus 2.1: "His offering shall be of fine flour."[44] The pun makes the "oblation" intensely ambiguous: is the self offered poor or pure? The desire to be "obsequious in thy heart" is also somewhat unsettling. The root meaning of obsequy is to follow as in a procession. By picking up the imagery of the first, the last quatrain moves the "outward honoring" of the progress inward while professing a more genuine, heart-felt devotion. Nevertheless, the pronoun is startling because, rather than moving within himself, the poet moves into the beloved, becoming "obsequious in *thy* heart," and his devotion is as invasive as it is intimate.[45] Finally, we may wonder at the degree of true reciprocity in their relationship of "mutual render," since the oblation goes all one way, offering "only me for thee."

The final couplet of sonnet 125 shatters this tentative mood of holy communion between lover and beloved by turning violently against an enemy who seems to materialize out of nowhere: "Hence, thou suborned informer! A true soul/ When most impeached stands least in thy control." Who is this intruder, and why this abrupt outburst of hostility at the end of a poem celebrating consummate harmony? Commentators offer several explanations, some suggesting that the anger may be directed at the "dwellers on form and favor" who could also be rivals for the beloved's affection. However, as Booth notes, by directly addressing the "suborned informer" as "thou" after asking the beloved to "take thou my oblation," the speaker may imply that his beloved has turned into the enemy just as he does in so many other sonnets. Here, the drama is heightened, and the expulsion of an enemy threatening "a true soul" acquires the force of excommunication or even exorcism.

The abrupt change in tone at the end of sonnet 125 prepares us for the otherwise incongruous emotions of the final poem to the young man as the mood shifts from intimate reciprocity to heated hostility to cold detachment. In sonnet 126, the poet begins by admiring his beloved's apparent triumph over time, marvelling that the "lovely boy . . . hast by waning grown, and therein show'st/ Thy lovers withering, as thy sweet self grow'st." The young man's blessings acquire a sinister, heartless edge since he apparently thrives at the expense of his lovers' "withering," but the poet emphasizes that this victory is only temporary. Nature who now preserves this youth will eventually sacrifice him because "Her audit, though delayed, answered must be,/ And her quietus is to render thee." The harmonious "mutual render" of the previous poem is here replaced by a rendering and rending of this "minion of her pleasure" by forces of destruction. The poem fairly gloats at the prospect of human sacrifice, evening the accounts of Nature's audit and reversing the temporary ascendancy of the "lovely boy." In this sense, sonnet 126 provides an answer, "though delayed," to the question posed in the previous sonnet about what is owed or "ought to me" in exchange for both the "outward honoring" and the inward "oblation." Here the rendering of "me for thee" is answered by the sacrifice of thee for me. As Joel Fineman says of the sonnet's memorializing impulses, "there is something necrophiliac in the way the young man's poet regularly looks forward to the time in which 'your monument shall be my gentle verse.'"[46] In sonnet 126, that impulse becomes almost ghoulish in its gleeful anticipation of a fatal "quietus." In the final sonnets to the young man, the volatile mixture of violence and the sacred, of cruelty and altruism, of annihilation and redemptive sacrifice that lurks just beneath the surface of their eucharistic imagery—and the eucharist itself—blows up in our faces. What do we make of this emotional explosion, and what do these sonnets finally render?

For some older critics, the answer is everything. The initial emphasis in sonnet 125 on the lovers' almost holy communion and "mutual render" strikes many as profoundly and positively religious. Through a combination of Christian and humanist eschatology and a belief in poetry's sacramental potency, the sonnets' echoes of Scripture prove truly redemptive. In the words of sonnet 16, "To give away yourself keeps yourself still," while "all losses are restored" as miraculously as they are in the conclusion of sonnet 30. C. S. Lewis proclaims this belief resolutely, arguing that the sonnets move "from extreme particularity . . . to the highest universality . . . the greatest of the sonnets are written from a region in which love abandons all claims and flowers into charity [sustaining a] . . . transference of the whole self into another self without the demand for a return."[47] This is the leap of critical faith astutely described by Murray Krieger in his study of the sonnets as a "resort to miracle," a leap he himself makes with both feet.[48] Krieger's argument is based on an explicitly sacramental conception of poetry as a medium "analogous to the Incarnation, the word made body."[49] To read the sonnets is to take communion, receiving a real, if poetic presence.[50]

For more recent critics, the sonnets render almost nothing. *Shakespeare's Perjured Eye* by Joel Fineman describes a fall from visionary poetics and "epideictic ontology" to mere rhetorical repetition and representation. The sonnets have become an "unhappy ineffectual simulacrum" which no longer evokes "mimetically or metaphorically, the things toward which it gestures."[51] They are ineffectual because they have no sacramental potency, having dwindled from a quasi-liturgical form of incantation to an enfeebled commemoration of an all too familiar absent presence.[52] In his subtle analysis of sonnets 125 and 126 entitled "Pitiful Thrivers: Failed Husbandry in the Sonnets," Thomas Greene finds the same unbridgeable gap between the human and divine. He wants to resist a merely "skeptical reading" which leads to an overwhelming sense of futility, and he sees the final poems to the young man and their "culminating moment" of "mutual render" as a possible solution to the sonnets' otherwise pervasive "sense of depletion" and fear of waste.[53] However, for Greene, redemption derives not from romantic affirmation or sacramental efficacy but from an absurd if gallant exertion in which "the reader can recognize the implausibility of the asserted constancy while regarding the struggle to hope, the conative pathos, with respect."[54] This gives us something more but not much. For Greene, the sonnets resemble a Beckettian monologue resounding in the abyss, and his praise of conating (an exercise beloved of Beckett's Malone) hardly counters a larger sense of isolation and failure.[55]

I think the sacrificial sonnets offer something more, something between the all or nothing polarity that Shakespeare's language frequently forces on us. Criticism which focuses largely on the self alone and its "conative pathos" misses the deeper, more anguished pathos of love and loss. Shakespeare's conception of love remains bound by Christian ideas of altruism, but suffering and sacrifice hardly assure salvation. His lovers are generally doomed to become "love's martyrs," caught in what Miri Rubin calls "the terrible logic of martyrdom" which enforces "the raw convergence of Love and Death [and] . . . the terrible claim that death is . . . the truest token of love."[56] Missing from this equation is the celestial reward promised by the Christian system of salvation.

There is finally no "sure and certain hope of the resurrection" for love's martyrs in Shakespeare. His vision of human sacrifice in both the love poetry and the sonnets has its eucharistic aspects, but neither "The Phoenix and Turtle" nor the sacrificial sonnets are truly sacramental. What we get instead of a real presence or holy communion are "dead birds" and "fools of time." Yet these poetic renderings remain sacred objects of a sort, not sacraments but relics. I take the term from Patricia Fumerton who takes it, in turn, from Walter Pater in order to advance her audacious argument for what she calls a "cultural aesthetics." Fumerton remains committed to the principles and practices of historicism, but she argues for a revisionist approach "whereby the subjective experience of the Renaissance 'spirit' continually revivifies an otherwise passed away or dead art."[57] The freshness of such an approach derives in part from her attention to the emotional aspects of material culture, those precious and enduring qualities which give its remnants life and value.

Nevertheless, these remnants are hardly traditional relics. The dust and bones of Christian martyrs and the implements of their torture and death are transfigured into tokens of immortality, and, as Peter Brown says, "every fragment is linked by a bond to the whole stretch of eternity."[58] Relics are signs of a spiritual victory over physical dismemberment and destruction, of blissful immortality over excruciating pain. As such, they become venerated as a means of miraculous healing. They also allow a sense of palpable contact with the sanctified dead whose spirit and power endures within them. In "The Phoenix and Turtle" and the sonnets, love's martyrs are more vulnerable to the ravages of time, but they believe that love is not time's fool and their devotion unto death makes their faith compelling. Their relics are not particularly propitious: the "cinders" of "dead birds" are a funereal dead end rather than a magical cure. They are like Yorick's skull, a disturbing *memento mori*. As Brown points out, true Christian relics are the antithesis of a *memento mori*, since all morbid associations are repressed by their detachment from the grave and encasement in splendor.[59] Yet Shakespeare's "chop-fallen" fragments arouse feelings of intense affection as well as revulsion and unease. It is finally the capacity of these figures and images to stimulate emotion that is the source of their power as relics. What Walter Pater found most valuable in the artistic relics of the past were their traces of "great passions [that] may give us this quickened sense of life," passions that encompass the "ecstasy and sorrow of love."[60] Shakespeare's love poetry gives us the relics of love's martyrs, and these relics, in turn, give a "quickened sense of life."

Notes

[1] I. A. Richards, *Poetics: Their Media and Ends*, ed. Trevor Eaton (The Hague, 1974), pp. 50, 58.

[2] William H. Matchett, *"The Phoenix and Turtle": Shakespeare's Poem and Chester's Love's Martyr* (The Hague, 1965). See also Marie Axton, *The Queen's Two Bodies* (London, 1977), pp. 116-30.

[3] See Leah S. Marcus's subtle discussion of topicality in her introduction to *Puzzling Shakespeare: Local Reading and Its Discontents* (Berkeley, 1988), pp. 1-50.

[4] Debora Shuger, *Habits of Thought in the English Renaissance: Religion, Politics and the Dominant Culture* (Berkeley, 1990), p. 5.

[5] *Times Literary Supplement* (24 December 1993), pp. 3-4. See also J. R. Mulryne on the devaluation of emotion in recent criticism in his introduction to *Theatre and Government under the Early Stuarts* (Cambridge, 1993), p. 4.

[6] John Keats, "To George and Georgiana Keats" (April, 1819), in Keats, *Letters*, ed. Maurice Buxton Forman (Oxford, 1952), p. 336.

[7] William Shakespeare, *The Sonnets and A Lover's Complaint*, ed. John Kerrigan (New York, 1986), p. 54.

[8] Robert Chester, *Love's Martyr*, ed. Alexander B. Grosart (London, 1878), p. 180. Hereafter cited in the text using Grosart's pagination (i.e., the numbers at the bottom of the page).

[9] Ernst Kantorowicz, *The King's Two Bodies: A Study in Medieval Political Theology* (Princeton, 1957), pp. 388-9 and 413, and Henry Petowe, *Elizabetha Quasi Vivens* (London, 1603), sig. B3v; see Shakespeare, *Henry VIII*, where Elizabeth is described as "the maiden phoenix/ . . . [whose] ashes new create another heir/ As great in admiration as herself" (5.3.40-2); all references to Shakespeare's plays are from *The Riverside Shakespeare*, ed. G. Blakemore Evans (Boston, 1974), hereafter cited in the text.

[10] Matchett, *"The Phoenix and Turtle,"* p. 27.

[11] Grosart, "Introduction" to Chester, *Love's Martyr*, pp. xxxv ff. See Matchett's review of the scholarly speculation and debate (*"The Phoenix and Turtle"*, p. 101). Walter Oakeshott agrees with Matchett's interpretation in *"Love's Martyr,"* *Huntington Library Quarterly*, 39 (1975), 29-49. While accepting the identification of the Phoenix with Elizabeth, Anthea Hume rejects the equation of the Turtle with Essex, arguing instead that the dove represents the Queen's more genuinely devoted subjects in "Love's Martyr, 'The Phoenix and Turtle,' and the Aftermath of the Essex

Rebellion," *Review of English Studies*, 40 (1989), 48-71. Axton sees the Phoenix as the Queen and the Turtle as her subjects, but adds that the latter also represents the Queen "in her capacity as a natural woman" (*The Queen's Two Bodies*, p. 119).

[12] See William Shakespeare, *The Poems*, ed. F. T. Prince, (London, 1960), p. xl.

[13] Matchett, *"The Phoenix and Turtle,"* p. 154.

[14] Ibid., p. 194.

[15] On negotiations between Essex and James, see D. Harris Willson, *King James VI and I* (London, 1956), pp. 149-53. On the Earl's potential role in managing the succession, see my *Rites of Knighthood: The Literature and Politics of Elizabethan Chivalry* (Berkeley, 1989), pp. 100-1.

[16] [Robert Parsons], *A Conference About the Next Succession to the Crowne of Ingland* ([?Antwerp], 1594), sig. A2v-3r.

[17] The Earl of Essex to Fulke Greville (1598-99,? January I), HMC, Salisbury, vol. IX, part ix, p. 4.

[18] Fynes Moryson, *An Itinerary* (Glasgow, 1908), vol. II, p. 317.

[19] Thomas Birch, *Memoirs of the Reign of Queen Elizabeth* (London, 1754), vol. II, p. 474.

[20] William Barlow, *A Sermon Preached at Paules Crosse, on the first Sunday in Lent; Martii 1, 1600. With a Short discourse of the late Earle of Essex his confession and penitence, before and at the time of his death* (London, 1601), sig. E2v.

[21] W. R. Morfill (ed.), *Ballads from Manuscripts* (Hertford, 1873), vol. II, p. 245 and *The Roxburghe Ballads*, ed. W. Chappell (Hertford, 1869-71), vol. I, p. 566.

[22] Robert Prickett, *Honors Fame in Triumph Riding* (1604), ed. A. B. Grosart (Manchester, 1881), pp. 31-2.

[23] William Shakespeare, "The Phoenix and Turtle" in Shakespeare, *The Poems*, ed. F. T. Prince (London, 1960), p. 179, line 1; hereafter cited in the text by line number.

[24] See my discussion of these ancient feudal offices in my *Rites of Knighthood*, pp. 34-5, 92-4, and 100-1.

[25] "Requiem," in Samuel Macauley Jackson (ed.), *The New Schaff-Herzog Encyclopedia of Religious Knowledge* (Grand Rapids, 1950).

[26] Jacques Le Goff, *The Birth of Purgatory*, trans. Arthur Goldhammer (Chicago, 1984), p. 5. See also Eamon Duffy, *The Stripping of the Altars: Traditional Religion in England, 1400-1580* (New Haven, 1992), pp. 348-9.

[27] Ralph Houlbrooke, *Death, Ritual and Bereavement* (London, 1989), p. 40.

[28] David E. Stannard, *The Puritan Way of Death: A Study of Religion, Culture and Social Change* (New York, 1971), pp. 73-4 and 100-2 and Patrick Collinson, *The Elizabethan Puritan Movement* (Berkeley, 1967), p. 370.

[29] Houlbrooke, *Death, Ritual and Bereavement*, pp. 41-2.

[30] Roland Mushat Frye, *Renaissance Hamlet: Issues and Responsibilities in 1600* (Princeton, 1984), p. 306. See also J. Dover Wilson's discussion of requiems in *Hamlet* and "The Phoenix and Turtle" in J. Dover Wilson, *What Happens in Hamlet* (Cambridge, 1967), pp. 298-9.

[31] John Arthos, *Shakespeare's Use of Dream and Vision* (London, 1977), p. 63.

[32] Matchett, *"The Phoenix and Turtle,"* p. 51 and pp. 194-202.

[33] John Donne, *The Complete Poetry*, ed. John T. Shawcross (Garden City, NY, 1967), lines 23 and 33; hereafter cited in the text. See Cleanth Brooks's more affirmative comparison of these two poems, which finds hints of resurrection in both, in *The Well Wrought Urn* (New York, 1947), pp. 16-21.

[34] All references to Shakespeare's sonnets are to Stephen Booth's edition, *Shakespeare's Sonnets* (New Haven, 1977).

[35] See Hyder Edward Rollins (ed.), *A New Variorum Edition of Shakespeare, The Sonnets* (Philadelphia, 1944), vol. I, pp. 311-15.

[36] Annabel Patterson, *Censorship and Interpretation: The Conditions of Writing and Reading in Early Modern England* (Madison, 1984), p. 18. Here and elsewhere, Patterson argues for authorial control and comprehension of these ambiguities, and I also think that Shakespeare knows exactly what he is doing in sonnet 124 even if we do not. However, for an alternative account emphasizing both the author's and the critic's confusion in the face of political conflicts, see Peter Erickson's discussion of "ideological ambivalence" in Erickson, *Rewriting Shakespeare, Rewriting Ourselves* (Berkeley, 1991), p. 15-17.

[37] Peter Brown, *The Cult of the Saints: Its Rise and Function in Latin Christianity* (Chicago, 1981), p. 78.

[38] Miri Rubin, "Choosing Death? Experiences of Martyrdom in Late Medieval Europe," in *Martyrs and Martyrologies: Papers Read at the 1992-93 Meetings of the Ecclesiastical Historical Society* (Oxford, 1993), p. 153.

[39] Cited in Helen C. White, *Tudor Books of Saints and Martyrs* (Madison, 1963), p. 175.

[40] John Donne, *Pseudo-Martyr,* ed. Anthony Raspa (Montreal, 1993), pp. 34 and 91. In France, the *politiques* were a group of moderates, including Montaigne and Bodin, who opposed religious zealotry and sectarian strife and favored patriotism and toleration; see Richard S. Dunn, *The Age of Religious Wars, 1559-1689* (New York, 1970), p. 29. Donne wrote *Pseudo-Martyr* in the same spirit to encourage Catholics to take the oath of allegiance. The term also acquired a pejorative sense of temporizing cynicism as in Nashe's description of Machiavelli as "a pollitick not much affected to any Religion" in *The Retvrne of Pasqvill* in Nashe, *Works,* ed. Ronald B. McKerrow (Oxford, 1958), vol. I, p. 79.

[41] Booth's discussion of the poem's eucharistic imagery is especially illuminating; see Booth (ed.), *Shakespeare's Sonnets,* pp. 429-30.

[42] John Jewel, *An Apology of the Church of England* (London, 1564), ed. J. E. Booty (Charlottesville, 1974), p. 32 and pp. 35-6.

[43] See Duffy *Stripping of the Altars* (pp. 95-102), on "seeing the host" as the literal high point of the traditional Mass a practice reformers sought to suppress.

[44] Booth, citing Hilton Landry, in Booth (ed.), *Shakespeare's Sonnets,* p. 428; see also Landry, *Interpretations in Shakespeare's Sonnets* (Berkeley, 1963), p. 126.

[45] See Desdemona who "saw Othello's visage in *his* mind" (1.3.252). Such devotion has been aptly described by Stephen Greenblatt as a kind of subversive submission in *Renaissance Self-Fashioning: From More to Shakespeare* (Chicago, 1979), pp. 240-54.

[46] Joel Fineman, *Shakespeare's Perjured Eye: The Invention of Poetic Subjectivity in the Sonnets* (Berkeley, 1986), p. 157.

[47] C. S. Lewis, *English Literature in the Sixteenth Century* (Oxford, 1954), p. 505.

[48] See "The Resort to 'Miracle' in Recent Poetics", chapter 1 in Krieger, *A Window to Criticism: Shakespeare's Sonnets and Modern Poetics* (Princeton, 1964), pp. 3-27. The same argument is renewed in Krieger, *Poetic Presence and Illusion: Essays in Critical History and Theory* (Baltimore, 1977), pp. 49-54. Krieger concedes that the miracles of art are really tricks and illusions but claims that their very impossibility proves them "nothing less than a miracle" (*Window to Criticism,* p. 213); see *Poetic Presence,* p. 50.

[49] Krieger, *Window to Criticism,* pp. 4-5.

[50] Krieger, *Poetic Presence,* pp. 49-50.

[51] Fineman, *Shakespeare's Perjured Eye,* p. 218.

[52] See Fineman's discussion of the young man as an "incarnated image of an absent presence" (*Shakespeare's Perjured Eye,* p. 271).

[53] Thomas M. Greene, "Pitiful Thrivers: Failed Husbandry in the Sonnets," in Patricia Parker and Geoffrey Hartmann (eds.), *Shakespeare and the Question of Theory* (London, 1985), pp. 241-2, 230, and 232.

[54] Ibid., pp. 239 and 240.

[55] Samuel Beckett, *Malone Dies,* translated by the author, in *Three Novels by Samuel Beckett* (New York, 1965), p. 218.

[56] Rubin, "Choosing Death?," p. 182.

[57] Patricia Fumerton, *Cultural Aesthetics: Renaissance Literature and the Practice of Social Ornament* (Chicago, 1991), p. 26.

[58] Brown, *The Cult of the Saints,* p. 278.

[59] Brown, *The Cult of the Saints,* pp. 75-8.

[60] Walter Pater, *The Renaissance: Studies in Art and Poetry* (1893), ed. Donald L. Hill (Berkeley, 1980), p. 190.

Vincent F. Petronella (essay date 1975)

"Shakespeare's 'The Phoenix and the Turtle' and the Defunctive Music of Ecstasy," *Shakespeare Studies: An Annual Gathering of Research, Criticism, and Reviews,* Vol. VIII, 1975, pp. 311-31.

[*In the essay that follows, Petronella discusses the structuring trope of ecstasy, which does not effect the separation of the immortal soul from the body, but the state of "love-in-death."*]

Twenty years after G. Wilson Knight declared that *The Phoenix and the Turtle* had been "unjustly" and "too long" neglected, Muriel Bradbrook observed that "very little has been written upon this poem."[1] Another twenty years passed. During that interim a different note was sounded when Robert Ellrodt announced that *The Phoenix and the Turtle* would have become smothered in "the dust of scholarly debate" if it were not for the clarifying commentary of scholars like Heinrich Straumann, A. Alvarez, G. Wilson Knight, F. T. Prince, and C. S. Lewis.[2] Although the poem has escaped suffocation (as if any great piece of literature can ever be deprived of life in this way) and has been elucidated in different ways, a critical debate still goes on as to what the poem means and, specifically, as to what the significance of the dead Phoenix is.

Several readings of the poem hinge on the way the Phoenix's role is interpreted. In order to simplify a discussion of the diverse commentary, we can label "orthodox" those critics who believe that Shakespeare is asking us to respond traditionally to the legendary Arabian bird and hence to see a revived Phoenix in the poem. The "unorthodox," on the other hand, are not ready to accept this characteristic of the Phoenix tradition given the context of Shakespeare's poem.

One of the orthodox critics is William Empson, who explains that although the poem "expresses the despair felt by the spectators (the 'chaste' or non-predatory birds who are the voice of Reason) . . . at last the magic works and a new Phoenix rises from the ashes"; another is J. V. Cunningham, who goes even further by claiming that "[Phoenix and Turtle-Dove] become one and yet neither is annihilated . . . they have only passed into the real life of Ideas from the unreal life of materiality."[3] For I. A. Richards, the Turtle-Dove "is consumed, burnt up on the pyre, in the flames of her [the Phoenix's] regeneration"; and for Sister Mary Bonaventure, the Phoenix and the Turtle are "united—fused—by one mutual flame which transforms them, raises them to a new level of being . . ."—a process that is suggestive of the grace through which "man is reborn to a new life."[4] All of the orthodox readings are not so obviously "Christian" as this last one, nor are they all necessarily explicit about the regeneration of the Phoenix. Alvarez, for example, speaks of the theme of *The Phoenix and the Turtle* in terms of the "transcendence of Reason by Love"; but he goes on to say that "the very difficulty of the anthem is that it will not rest in the power of faith to transcend Reason (and this makes me suspicious of a purely Christian interpretation)."[5] Behind many of the orthodox approaches is the seminal criticism of G. Wilson Knight. In *The Mutual Flame* he reasserts a point he had made in *The Shakespearian Tempest:* ". . . the very death of truth and beauty [Turtle-Dove and Phoenix] creates . . . immortality"; the "new Phoenix," therefore, is present in Shakespeare's poem.[6]

Antithetical to the orthodox view of the Phoenix image is that represented by critics like Robert Ellrodt, who are not at all convinced that Shakespeare's *The Phoenix and the Turtle* is a poem dealing with a revived Arabian bird. Shakespeare's "very subject," writes Ellrodt, "was a modification of the Phoenix myth which implied disbelief in, or at least disregard for, the time-honoured legend . . . Beauty, truth and rarity here enclosed in cinders lie, and any assurance, any hint of survival in a world beyond, is withheld. The rest is silence."[7] Murray Copland puts this even more strongly: "Shakespeare's most original and imaginative stroke in *The Phoenix and Turtle* is to assert that the unique, peerlessly beautiful bird is fully and finally *dead* . . . the Phoenix is . . . laid asleep for ever. Its bed is, simply and baldly, the final bed of death."[8] And Muriel Bradbrook, in a refutation of certain ornithological points made by Ronald Bates in his analysis of the poem, says nothing about a revived Phoenix, so that at least in this regard she apparently concurs with Bates, who, like Copland, does not accept the idea that a renewed Phoenix is part of the poem.[9] Daniel Seltzer, who in turn takes issue with Miss Bradbrook's literal understanding of the "married-chastity" stanza (ll. 59-61), makes helpful connections between *The Phoenix and the Turtle* and Shakespeare's tragedies by demonstrating how the absence of a revived Phoenix creates the "tragic scene" of the poem.[10] Similarly, Elias Schwartz discusses the relationship between poem and tragic drama; he notes that in the Threnos, Reason laments the "total extinction" of Phoenix and Turtle—the emphasis being "not on the immortality of the Phoenix . . . but on its death."[11] As do the orthodox critics, the unorthodox echo over the years an earlier study of the poem; if the orthodox have G. Wilson Knight, the unorthodox have A. H. R. Fairchild, who in 1904 wrote the following about the Threnos: "Since the death of the phoenix and turtle, absolute beauty, real truth, the world-rarity of their union, and grace, which were their unique characteristics, have passed away . . . real beauty and true wisdom are lost . . . the hope of restoration rests entirely in those 'that are either true or fair' . . ."[12]

As if one major controversy were not enough in critical analyses of so relatively brief a work by Shakespeare, a second area of contention has expanded along with the problem of the Phoenix image: the question whether Shakespeare's *The Phoenix and the Turtle* is a metaphysical poem in the technical, literary sense. If the first controversy compels us to grapple with the interpretation of a provocative symbol, the second one forces us to question the style of the poem, especially its tone of poetic voice. "Nothing could in fact be further from the methods of Donne's love-poetry than the method of this poem," writes F. T. Prince in the New Arden edition of *The Poems*.[13] Agreeing with this judgment are Alvarez, who tells us that Shakespeare in *The Phoenix and the Turtle* is "not at all the Metaphysical poet," and C. S. Lewis, who states that Shakespeare here "is not writing 'metaphysical poetry' in the technical sense critics give to that term, but he is writing in the true sense, a metaphysical poem."[14] Generally these are negative reactions to Cleanth Brooks's well-known essay dealing with Donne's *Canonization* and the language of paradox that links the great metaphysical poet with the style of *The Phoenix and the Turtle*.[15] Brooks does not tell us explicitly that Shakespeare's poem anticipates the metaphysicals; nevertheless, the implication is clear. Helen Gardner, although she does not include a reference to Brooks's essay in the select bibliography of her edition of *The Metaphysical Poets*, follows the lead of those who believe, as Brooks does, that *The Phoenix and the Turtle* is part of the metaphysical tradition.[16] Some scholars, in fact, go so far as to describe Shakespeare as either one who "might have been the greatest of the metaphysical poets" had he concentrated primarily on nondramatic poetry around 1600 or one who wrote at least one poem that is a metaphysical work par excellence.[17]

In addition to considering the problems of symbol and style, any serious student of *The Phoenix and the Turtle* must eventually address himself to the question of the poem's literary genetics. What are the relevant sources and analogues of this poem? In the words of at least one scholar, a thorough response to this kind of question would assume the dimensions of a study "as extensive and multifarious as *The Golden Bough*, so full is [*The Phoenix and the Turtle*] of esoteric classical and post-classical lore."[18] Indeed a thorough commentary on the symbolism, style, and genetics of any complex piece of literature implies the massing of volumes of scholarly and critical materials. The scope of my analysis does not permit this kind of extensive consideration of *The Phoenix and the Turtle*, fascinating as such an undertaking might be. And yet it is my purpose to explore the poem's literary genesis as well as its symbolic and stylistic elements in order to understand better what forces are at work beneath the marmoreal surface of Shakespeare's enigmatic elegy.[19] At the same time, I should make it clear at the outset that I believe this poem is not to be restricted to any one explanation. Its highly suggestive imagery and its sometimes intriguing genesis do not allow for rigid critiques of origin, meaning, and structure. Straumann's emphasis upon the principle of *Mehrdeutigkeit*, or "layers of meaning," as it concerns *The Phoenix and the Turtle* is a perfectly sound one, as is Muriel Bradbrook's reminder that "negative capability, or the power to refrain from specific associations is not out of place in the reading of poetry."[20] At the outset, then, I can say that my study of *The Phoenix and the Turtle* will be a critical conflation—hopefully, one that leads to a greater awareness and comprehension of the intricacies of the poem at hand—rather than strictly a refutation of what has already been said by others.

If we look first at Shakespeare's image of the unrevived Phoenix, we see before us a symbol of death—a symbol of a supposedly immortal force rendered mortal. The call is out for "defunctive music" for a defunctive pair of birds, one of which has in some mysterious way lost the legendary function of self-regeneration. This depiction of the Phoenix should not be loosely referred to as an original detail, for it is unlikely that the dead, unrevived Phoenix in Shakespeare's poem would have come as a shock to the well-read Renaissance Englishman, primarily because prior to the composition of *The Phoenix and the Turtle* three important writers had already dealt with the same idea. Petrarch, Marot, and Spenser are names that do not crop up often enough in discussions of sources and analogues for *The Phoenix and the Turtle*, and one wonders why this is so, for in Petrarch's *Canzoniere* 323 (*Standomi un giorno solo a la fenestra*) lurks the unrevived Phoenix that remains just as unrevived in Marot's *Des Visions de Petrarque* and Spenser's *Visions of Petrarch*.[21] Specifically, Petrarch tells us of a "strania fenice" that

> Volse in se stessa il becco,
> Quasi sdegnando, e 'n un punto disparse:
> Onde 'l cor di pietate, e d'amor m'arse.
> (58-60)[22]

"A solitary Phoenix," writes Petrarch, "turns its beak upon herself in disdain and vanishes aloft, causing the heart to burn with pity and love." In Marot's

> Comme en desdaing, de son bec s'est feru,
> Et des humains sur l'heure disparu:
> Dont de pitié et d'amour mon cueur ard.[23]

Spenser has two versions of the lyric from which the above comes, the earlier one appearing in *A Theatre for Worldings* (1569) as "Epigrams": the Phoenix alone in a wood strikes himself

> with his beake, as in disdaine,
> And so forthwith in great despite he dide.
> For pitie and loue my heart yet burnes in paine.
> (62-64)[24]

The later version occurs in *Complaints* (1591) as *The Visions of Petrarch*. Here Spenser expands his own earlier translation and produces a long lyric made up of seven fourteen-line sonnets, the fifth one of which is in the "Shakespearean" form:

> I saw a Phoenix in the wood alone,
> With purple wings, and crest of golden hewe;

> Strange bird he was, whereby I thought
>   anone,
> That of some heauenly wight I had the vewe;
>   Vntill he came vnto the broken tree,
> And to the spring, that late deuoured was.
> What say I more? each thing at last we see
> Doth passe away: the Phoenix there alas
>   Spying the tree destroid, the water dride,
> Himselfe smote with his beake, as in
>   disdaine,
> And so foorthwith in great despight he dide:
> That yet my heart burnes in exceeding paine,
>   For ruth and pitie of so haples plight.
>   O let mine eyes no more see such a sight.
>
>   (57-70)[25]

By adding two lines to the original twelve-line Petrarchan stanza, Spenser underscores the shock of seeing the Phoenix die by what becomes essentially an act of suicide. No miraculous resurrection follows the self-immolation. Spenser emphasizes a thematic line similar to that of Shakespeare's *The Phoenix and the Turtle*. This is, of course, not in any way absolute proof that Shakespeare knew either the original material of Petrarch or the versions of Marot and Spenser, but there is no question about the possibility of Shakespeare's having been familiar with one or all of the above. Clearly the idea of an unrevived Phoenix is not new with Shakespeare, nor is the idea of a female Phoenix, which appears in Chester's *Loves Martyr* as well as in Matthew Roydon's elegy on Sir Philip Sidney in *The Phoenix Nest* (1593).[26]

Shakespeare in *The Phoenix and the Turtle* uses not only the image of the unrevived Phoenix but also another ingredient found in the Petrarch-Marot-Spenser poems and referred to in Marot's and Spenser's titles: the wondrous visionary experience. To see the Phoenix is marvelous enough, but to see the Phoenix die and fail to regain its own life is a nightmare vision almost beyond words. Shakespeare's *The Phoenix and the Turtle* is similarly a vision of an overwhelming disaster—the destruction of those values linked with the Phoenix and the Turtle-Dove. Love—spiritual and erotic—is central to Shakespeare's poem but is dealt with as part of a mystical or magical perception of the obliteration of love and truth symbolized by the Turtle-Dove and the Phoenix. The poem is apocalyptic. It is a "Jacobean" insight into what could and what might indeed happen in the lives of individual men or in the world in general. What makes the poem's vision powerful is the pulsation of *energia* and *enargia* generated by an intense, ecstatic music. Or, to put it another way, *The Phoenix and the Turtle* is a work dealing with the music of ecstasy. But the ecstasy does not succeed in doing what it is traditionally supposed to do, although the poetry achieves a power of expression that compels our sensory faculties to respond fully. To put it still another way, we may say that the music and the ecstasy are "defunctive"—that is, no longer capable of functioning to bring about a hopeful and enduring vision of truth and love. In brief, *The Phoenix and the Turtle* is about "defunctive" ecstasy, mystical ecstasy that does not work.[27]

To understand why mystical ecstasy is ineffectual in *The Phoenix and the Turtle*, we should review briefly the tradition of ecstasy and the very close association between music and spiritual rapture, always bearing in mind that ecstasy and music are present in Shakespeare's poem not only as subjects but also as principles governing the poem's style. In recent years the nature of spiritual ecstasy has captured the interest of literary critics by way of John Donne's poetic analysis of the experience in *The Extasie*. Scholarly and critical emphasis upon *The Extasie* and related literary materials (English or otherwise) has not run its course. One of the reasons for this is that no one discussion of either the religious ecstasy itself or its incorporation into a literary setting solves the mystery of its supranatural qualities in the strictly religious context or its potency as an aesthetic value in a work of art. This is not the place to discuss at length Donne's poetry or the scholarship dealing with Donne and his contemporaries outside of Shakespeare. But we can at least take advantage of the time and effort contributed by others in establishing here a working definition of the ecstatic experience.

"Mystic ecstasy in the Christian sense," says the *Oxford Dictionary of the Christian Church*, "is one of the normal stages of the mystic life. . . . The chief characteristic of the ecstatic state is the alienation of the senses, caused by the violence of the Divine action on the soul." In his edition of Donne's poetry, John T. Shawcross tells us that Christian mystics used the term "ecstasy" to describe "a state of extreme and abnormal awareness"—an awareness "derived from the detachment of the soul from the body, the soul standing outside the body contemplating their [i.e., body's and soul's] unity and relationship." To these statements we may add Theodore Redpath's explanation that "ecstasy" is the "mystical state in which a soul, liberated from the body, contemplates divine truths."[28] If we let the one word *ecstasy* stand for a cluster of related words, Robert Petersson advises us, it refers to "the state in which man is farthest removed from his normal human condition, the state in which prayer perfectly attains its ideals"; it is a term inseparable from closely related experiences such as vision, trance, transport, rapture, and union itself.[29] Such is the nature of spiritual ecstasy. But what of sensual ecstasy? A commonplace similarity exists between spiritual ecstasy and sensual ecstasy despite the emphasis that the first places on the soul and the second on the body. It is not necessary to argue here about the similarity. Only the naïve or the strictly puritanical would fail to respond to the erotic element in St. Teresa's spiritual ecstasy and the spiritual power of the earthly lovers' experience in *The Extasie* of Donne. Love theorists from Plato through Ficino, Bruno and Leone Ebreo have said much about the role of "divine madness" (i.e., "frenzy," "furor," "enthusiasm," or "ecstasy") in the life of the lover.[30] In his *Commentary on Plato's "Symposium,"* Ficino writes: "... there are four kinds of divine madness. The first is the poetic madness, the second is that of the mysteries, the third is that of prophecy, and the fourth is that of love."[31] Ecstasy, we are to understand, occurs over a wide range of categories; it is not limited solely to a world of disembodied creatures.

The Phoenix and the Turtle reflects the Ficinian analysis of the *furores,* but whether Shakespeare was consciously using Ficino's work or that of any other Renaissance writer in composing this poem is impossible to determine finally. Standing within a rich intellectual tradition as it does, Shakespeare's poem is a reflector of developments in the history of thought. And the relationship between poetic text and the intellectual tradition strikes me as shedding more light on this poem than any theory of biographical or political associations. What I am suggesting is that the Neoplatonic discussions of "divine madness" (or what Shakespeare calls "fine frenzy" in *A Midsummer Night's Dream* [V.i.12]), with the religious mystical vestiges that the term carries, are deeply involved in the thematic and stylistic constitution of *The Phoenix and the Turtle.*

Consider first "poetic madness": this is heard and felt by virtue of the poem's heightened incantatory quality. The poetry is intense, marked sometimes by what apparently is a sense of total abandon. Its lyrical intensity is achieved by a hard-driving, basically trochaic, meter that energetically presses all sixty-seven lines of the poem to get somewhere without hesitation. No caesural rest-stops here—Shakespeare's libretto affords no timeless fermatas. To complement this rhythmical urgency, the poem is structured so that prior to the Threnos, several stanzas, although rhyming *abba,* very often become four lines ending not only in rhymed words but also in words related through assonance:

> Let the bird of loudest lay,
> ... tree,
> ... be,
> ... obey.
>
> (1-4)[32]

> Here the anthem doth commence;
> ... dead;
> ... fled
> ... hence.
>
> (21-24)

> So between them love did shine
> ... right
> ... sight:
> ... mine.
>
> (33-36)

Or the line endings may be related through consonance—assisted by one instance of a partial repetition of end words (stanzas 9 and 12):

> So they lov'd, as love in twain
> ... one;
> ... none:
> ... slain.
>
> (25-28)

> Hearts remote, yet not asunder;
> ... seen
> ... queen;
> ... wonder.
>
> (29-32)

> That it cried, How true a twain
> ... one!
> ... none,
> ... remain.
>
> (45-48)

And at least one stanza has a touch of both assonance and consonance:

> But thou shrieking harbinger,
> ... fiend,
> ... end,
> ... near.
>
> (5-8)

This handling of the line endings, together with the rhymed triplets of the Threnos and the quick-paced rhythm of the lines throughout the poem, creates a lyrical intensity that flickers occasionally to permit, as it were, an almost Skeltonic flippancy to flash through. But Shakespeare is not writing meaningless doggerel or a *jeu d'esprit*. The intense lyricism he develops is an attempt to capture a poetic ecstasy commensurate with the vision that the poem offers us. This is done neither with grim solemnity nor tongue-in-check; on the contrary, Shakespeare executes it with a metaphysical mixture of levity and seriousness.

Never mellifluous, yet melodic (even to a frenetic degree), the lyricism of *The Phoenix and the Turtle* is bolstered by several musical-aural images: "loudest lay," "trumpet," "sound," "shrieking," "defunctive music," "requiem," "anthem," "Threne," "Chorus." Several of the words in the poem have a double function, one of which is submerged musical metaphor: "treble," "division" (occurring twice, once at line 27 and again at line 42), "number," "concordant," "parts," and perhaps "confounded" (l. 41). In addition to the individual words and phrases with musical-aural values, the poem has as its conclusion a funeral song. That the poem becomes a piece of music is a result of the sound it makes combined with its many musical-aural references. In this way *The Phoenix and the Turtle* is poetic and musical at the same time that it speaks about poetry and music; and as the style is in keeping with the idea of "defunctive music," so the subject matter is defunction—the lack of function and the lack of effective power to prevent defunction. G. Wilson Knight maintains that in *The Phoenix and the Turtle* tempest (usually associated with tragedy) becomes music (symbolically linked with love and union in Shakespeare) and that "the tempest-music distinction is resolved."[33]

It is true that love and union do occur in *The Phoenix and the Turtle,* but what does not occur is the regeneration of love and union. The magic does not work. The music here would not succeed in reviving a broken Coriolanus. If the music of *The Phoenix and the Turtle* can in any way be thought of as a kind of Orphic incantation, with its traditionally magic power to influence the astrological powers above in order to achieve a revival of spirit, the incantation fails.[34]

Incantation, magic-song, ecstasy, furor are all terms that apply to the style and subject matter of *The Phoenix and the Turtle.* But if ecstasy is supposed to be the state in which a literal separation of soul from body takes place, then why talk of union of Phoenix (soul) and Turtle-Dove (body), as if this were the end toward which the poem's central characters are supposed ultimately to be headed?[35] Ideally the ecstatic state would find soul released from body. But in *The Phoenix and the Turtle* the ecstasy is never brought off, and this is the reason why Shakespeare speaks of "division none" and the "mutual flame" of death. The problem here is that body and soul are consumed together, mutually. Never does the soul become separated in order to enjoy observing the body from a distance as it would do if true spiritual ecstasy took place. If any separation were to occur (either explicitly or implicitly) in Shakespeare's poem, it would become the kind of separation of body and soul that is in fact death. But rather than dramatizing the soul's standing off from the body, the poem confronts us with the death of both body and soul. Immortality, then, is out of the picture, no less than ecstatic fulfillment. Tragic tempest does not become comic or unifying music here, as Knight argues; instead, the enthusiastic music of ecstasy falls on the deaf ears of stony mortality, which in turn means that music gives way to a brewing tempest, the tempest suggestive not of tragedy but of pathetic calamity. One's awareness of what Shakespeare is doing is greatly increased if one understands that the sound of music in *The Phoenix and the Turtle* is also the sound of ominous, far-off thunder.

The monitory and oracular quality of *The Phoenix and the Turtle* links it with those two other *furores* discussed in the Platonic tradition: the madness of prophecy and the madness of mystery (religious rite). The bird imagery of the poem asks us to recall the commonplace use of winged creatures in discerning omens or prophecies. Furthermore, the personification Reason singing the Threnos is symbolically apt in that it suggests the clear-mindedness and hence the clear-sightedness rather than simply the frenzy of prophecy. In this way Shakespeare concludes his poem. Earlier, Reason has been puzzled, stumped—its dilemma reinforcing the "madness" element in the poem:

> Reason, in itself confounded,
> Saw division grow together,
> To themselves yet either neither,
> Simple were so well compounded:
>
> That it cried, How true a twain
> Seemeth this concordant one!
> Love hath reason, reason none,
> If what parts, can so remain.
>
> *(41-48)*

At this point it appears that ecstasy or "enthusiasm" has prevailed, for Reason is at sixes and sevens.[36] But Reason has the last word in *The Phoenix and the Turtle,* and what Reason is talking about to us is death as the finality of being—what is described in *Macbeth* as "the be-all and the end-all—here" (I.vii.5).

Reason makes its recovery in the third section of the poem's tripartite structure. It is this framework that organizes the ritualistic movement, the first notable indication of which is the formal gathering of the different birds who are asked to "keep the obsequy so strict," particularly the swan, who will bring to the requiem his "right" (i.e., "his due" with a pun on "rite"). Prophecy and religious rite are traditionally interconnected, and in Shakespeare's poem the themes of prophecy and mystery-rite, although not presented in any clearly sectarian way, work together to heighten the ecstatic pulse of the poetry. Instead of working toward the level of divine understanding, however, *The Phoenix and the Turtle* takes us in the direction of a rational, rather than a nonrational or "enthusiastic," vision. Shakespeare is using ecstatic style and content for strictly terrestrial ends, as does Ben Jonson in *Ode enthousiastike,* one of his contributions to *Loves Martyr.* Speaking of the Phoenix-Lady in exalted terms, Jonson writes,

> Her breath for sweet exceeding
> The *Phoenix* place of breeding,
> But mixt with sound transcending
> All *Nature* of commending.[37]

Jonson's poem is not the enigmatic song that Shakespeare offers us, and whether he is following Shakespeare's lead or vice versa has not been finally determined; in any event, he attempts to do something similar to what Shakespeare is doing: make use of the ecstatic experience in a secular poem. One major way in which Shakespeare's poem differs from Johnson's, however, is in developing the kind of stylistic and thematic *energia* that recalls the Platonic interest in the divine madnesses of prophecy and religious rite. All of the *furores* involve emotional intensity and are in this way related to one another, but central to *The Phoenix and the Turtle* is the all-important love-madness, which, as Ficino tells us, turns the head of the charioteer in man's soul "toward the head of all things."[38] The poem's tripartite structure, a feature recognized by many of the commentators already referred to, acts as a vehicle for the theme of love-madness. Commentary on the poem's structure, however, has not touched upon the similarity between the stylistic mode of *The Phoenix and the Turtle* and that of the Orphic pastoral. A consideration of the similarity is illuminating. Richard Cody, commenting on the *Orfeo* of Poliziano as part of a discussion that eventually focuses on Shakespearean drama, analyzes the basic rhythm of Neoplatonic pastoral in terms of three phases: *Emanatio* (procession), *Raptio* (rapture or ecstasy), and *Remeatio* (return or recession).[39] Poliziano, like Pico della Mirandola and Ficino, envisions the Orpheus myth as an allegory of the death and the new life of the Rational Soul, "lost and found again in the flames of intellectual love"; the *Orfeo,* moreover, portrays the death of Orpheus as a gift of Love (Eros) to the Rational Soul.[40] This is not to say that Shakespeare's poem is about Orpheus or that it is a Neoplatonic pastoral. It does manifest, however, pastoral elements and a handling of the mystery of love-in-death. But *The Phoenix and the Turtle* is more than a quasi-pastoral depiction of birds in a forest or meadow, and it is more than a poem expressing Neoplatonic values. It is, in fact, a richly metaphorical portrait of an attitude, a frame of mind. And I contend that the intellectual attitude is made concrete not only by suggestive symbols but also by structural rhythm. The first twenty lines constitute the *Emanatio* of Shakespeare's poem: in comes a procession made up of "the bird of loudest lay," the "shrieking harbinger" (i.e., screech owl), the eagle, the swan, and the crow. We then move into the anthem and its attempt to analyze the mystery of love-madness and the love-death of Phoenix and Turtle-Dove; this is the poem's *Raptio,* and rapturous it is. Union is spiritual and physical for Phoenix and Turtle-Dove; their mutual consummation, given one of the meanings of dying in Shakespeare's time, is highly erotic as well as hopefully regenerative. But although the erotic ecstasy takes place, the spiritual ecstasy never reaches its special kind of climax. Reason, as I have already indicated, is perplexed at this point: only momentarily do Apollonian values surrender to Dionysian ones. It is as if the *furores* (poetry, prophecy, and religious rite) combine to drive the love-ecstasy into divine clarification, a clarification that hopefully will endure forever. But, alas, with the *Remeatio* (the Threnos in this case) the poem's movement recedes, and Reason leads the way. Phoenix and Turtle-Dove have not attained the divine level through ecstasy; instead, they become the subject of Reason's dirge on the grim fact that truth and beauty have been destroyed beyond the point of revival. If the poem is a frame of mind, it portrays the Jacobean intellectual landscape.

Poetry, ritual, prophecy, and love are the enticing ingredients in an artistic *olla podrida;* they blend and become the overall tone and meaning of *The Phoenix and the Turtle.* To say that the tone of *The Phoenix and the Turtle* is a mixture of seriousness and playfulness is to get closer to what the poem means. With its tripartite structure reflecting the *Emanatio-Raptio-Remeatio* triad of the Neoplatonists, *The Phoenix and the Turtle* to some extent partakes of the Orphic tradition of poetic theology, which always implies *serio ludere,* that is, jesting in earnest, playfulness combined with learned diligence.[41] This helps us to understand why the verse technique discussed earlier has a flippant air about it and why levity works hand in hand with seriousness. The poem exhibits a metaphysical wit as it deals with "serious" metaphysical issues. Seen this way, the poem is simultaneously a metaphysical poem (in the literary sense) and a metaphysical poem (in the philosophical sense).[42] We are asked to take its vision seriously, but we are also permitted to enjoy the wit and the irony of the vision. Ecstasy is ultimately defunctive in the world of *The Phoenix and the Turtle,* but ecstasy also governs the pulse of the poem until the voice of Reason enumerates the ontological details of life and especially those of death.

Notes

[1] See Knight's review of Ranjee G. Shahani's *Towards the Stars: being an appreciation of "The Phoenix and the Turtle"* (Rouen: n.p., 1931) in *The Criterion,* 10 (April 1931), 40; rpt. in Knight's *Shakespeare and Religion* (New York: Simon & Schuster, 1967), pp. 342-45. See also his *The Imperial Theme* (London: Oxford Univ. Press, 1931; 3rd ed. London: Methuen, 1951), p. 349; and *The Christian Renaissance* (New York: Norton, 1963), pp. 235-37. Knight's full reading of *The Phoenix and the Turtle* is found in *The Mutual Flame* (1955; rpt. London: Methuen, 1962), pp. 193-204. Miss Bradbrook's comment occurs in her *Shakespeare and Elizabethan Poetry* (London: Chatto & Windus, 1951), p. 247, n. 26.

[2] Ellrodt, "An Anatomy of 'The Phoenix and the Turtle,'" *ShS,* 15 (1962), 99. The works Ellrodt refers to at this point are as follows: Straumann, *Phönix und Taube* (Zurich: Artemis-Verlag, 1953); Alvarez in *Interpretations,* ed. John Wain (London: Routledge & Kegan Paul, 1955); Knight (see above); Prince, *The Poems,* New Arden Shakespeare (Cambridge, Mass.:

Harvard Univ. Press, 1960); and Lewis, *English Literature in the Sixteenth Century* (London: Oxford Univ. Press, 1954), pp. 508-9. In *Shakespeare: The Poems* (London: Longmans, Green, 1963), F. T. Prince can say with surety that the poem has arrived critically: "... in our time *The Phoenix and Turtle* has become one of the most admired of Shakespeare's poems, benefitting from the change of taste which has brought Metaphysical poetry back into favour" (p. 44).

[3] Empson, "The Phoenix and the Turtle," *EIC*, 16 (April 1966), 152. Some of the material in this essay Empson uses in his introduction to *Narrative Poems*, Signet Classic Shakespeare, ed. William Burto (New York: New American Library, 1968), pp. xxxvi-xlvii. Cunningham's statement is found in "'Essence' and *The Phoenix and Turtle*," *ELH*, 19 (Dec. 1952), 272; see also his "Idea as Structure: *The Phoenix and Turtle*" in *Tradition and Poetic Structure* (Denver: Alan Swallow, 1960), pp. 76-89.

[4] Richards, "The Sense of Poetry: Shakespeare's 'The Phoenix and the Turtle'" in *Symbolism in Religion and Literature*, ed. Rollo May (New York: Braziller, 1961), p. 206. The statement by Richards also appears in *Daedalus*, 87 (1958), 86-94; and S. M. Bonaventure, "The Phoenix Renewed," *Ball State Univ. Forum*, 5 (Autumn 1964), 75. Cf. W. J. Ong, "Metaphor and the Twinned Vision," *SR*, 63 (Spring 1955), 193-201.

[5] Alvarez, p. 8. See also K. T. S. Campbell's "The Phoenix and the Turtle as a Signpost of Shakespeare's Development," *British Journal of Aesthetics*, 10 (April 1970), 169-79. Campbell, who is not concerned with the religious or mystical elements in the poem, does not really come to grips with the Phoenix problem; but he does see Shakespeare's aesthetic in a strong, positive light: Shakespeare avoids the radical resolution of "the destructive crisis of identity" adopted by many of our present-day poets in "their fragmentation and destruction of the poetic symbol itself" (p. 178).

[6] Cited above, pp. 200, 195.

[7] "An Anatomy of 'The Phoenix and the Turtle,'" *ShS*, 15 (1962), 107-8.

[8] "The Dead Phoenix," *EIC*, 15 (July 1965), 285.

[9] Bradbrook, "'The Phoenix and the Turtle,'" *SQ*, 6 (Summer 1955), 356-58; Bates, "Shakespeare's 'The Phoenix and Turtle,'" *SQ*, 6 (Winter 1955), 19-30. Shakespeare, writes Bates, "contradicts Chester and the others [in *Loves Martyr*]" as far as the expectation of a new little Phoenix is concerned (p. 29). Monroe K. Spears, in his introduction to *Narrative Poetry*, The Laurel Shakespeare, ed. Charles J. Sisson (New York: Dell, 1968), also subscribes to the unorthodox view that "the unique Phoenix was consumed and not reborn (p. 39). One should consult, in addition, the forthright analysis of the poem by Edward Hubler in his edition of Shakespeare's *Songs and Poems* (New York: McGraw-Hill, 1959). The poem, writes Hubler, is "Shakespeare's allegory of love," in which the Phoenix is clearly not an emblem of Christian immortality (pp. xlvii and 318, gloss on line 23 of the poem).

[10] "'Their Tragic Scene': *The Phoenix and Turtle* and Shakespeare's Love Tragedies," *SQ*, 12 (Spring 1961), 96, 99-100. See Bradbrook in her essay, p. 357. Seltzer comments interestingly on the thematic similarities between *The Phoenix and the Turtle*, *Troilus and Cressida*, and *Antony and Cleopatra* in his Signet edition of *Troilus and Cressida* (New York: New American Library, 1963), pp. xxxiv-xxxvi.

[11] "Shakespeare's Dead Phoenix," *ELN*, 7 (Sept. 1969), 27-28.

[12] "*The Phoenix and Turtle:* A Critical and Historical Interpretation," *Englische Studien*, 33 (1904), 372-73.

[13] P. xliv. Reaching the same conclusion after a full study of scholarship on the poem is Richard A. Underwood in "Shakespeare's 'The Phoenix and Turtle,'" *DAI*, 31 (1970), 2357-A.

[14] Alvarez, p. 11; and Lewis, p. 509.

[15] *The Well-Wrought Urn* (New York: Harcourt, Brace & World, 1947), pp. 3-21, especially 19-21.

[16] (Baltimore: Penguin, 1957), pp. 23, 39-42, 316. Miss Gardner explains that Shakespeare created out of the Phoenix myth "a myth of his own" (p. 39, n. 1).

[17] F. P. Wilson, *Seventeenth Century Prose*, The Ewing Lectures (Berkeley: Univ. of California Press, 1960), p. 12; and Seltzer, pp. 96-97.

[18] James A. K. Thomson, *Shakespeare and the Classics* (London: George Allen & Unwin, 1952), p. 46.

[19] It is not my intention to worry the problem of the poem's occasion or its literary relationship to Robert Chester's *Loves Martyr*. Many reliable scholars have already offered us the results of patient searches for useful data in this regard. Essential to a thorough study of sources and analogues are the following: *Robert Chester's "Loves Martyr, or Rosalins Complaint,"* (1601), ed. Alexander B. Grosart, The New Shakespeare Society (London: N. Trübner, 1878); Carleton Brown, *Poems by Sir John Salusbury, Robert Chester, Etc.*, Early English Text Society (London: Oxford Univ. Press, 1913); *The Phoenix Nest* (1593), ed. Hyder Edward Rollins (Cambridge, Mass.: Harvard Univ. Press, 1931); especially the elegy (now usually attributed to Matthew Roydon) on Sir Philip

Sidney; G. Bonnard, "Shakespeare's Contribution to R. Chester's *Loves Martyr: The Phoenix and the Turtle*," *ES*, 19 (April 1937), 66-69; *The Phoenix and the Turtle*, ed. Bernard H. Newdigate (Oxford: Shakespeare Head Press, 1937), especially pp. xvi-xxiv; *The Poems*, New Variorum Shakespeare, ed. Hyder Edward Rollins (Philadelphia: Lippincott, 1938), pp. 323-31 and 559-83; Thomas W. Baldwin, *On the Literary Genetics of Shakespeare's Poems* (Urbana: Univ. of Illinois Press, 1950; Heinrich Straumann, *Phönix und Taube;* G. Wilson Knight, *The Mutual Flame*, pp. 156-224; *The Poems*, New Arden Shakespeare, ed. F. T. Prince, pp. xxxviii-xlvi, 179-83; J. W. Lever, "The Poems," *ShS*, 15 (1962), pp. 18-30, especially pp. 25-30; William H. Matchett, *"The Phoenix and the Turtle": Shakespeare's Poem and Chester's Loves Martyr* (The Hague: Mouton, 1965); *The Poems*, New Shakespeare, ed. J. C. Maxwell (London: Cambridge Univ. Press, 1966), pp. xxvi-xxxiii; *The Reader's Encyclopedia of Shakespeare*, ed. Oscar J. Campbell and Edward G. Quinn (New York: Crowell, 1966), pp. 476-77, 632-33; *Narrative Poems*, Signet Classic Shakespeare, ed. Burto, intro. Empson; and Richard Allan Underwood, "Shakespeare's 'The Phoenix and Turtle': A Survey of Scholarship." Unfortunately the first volume (*Early Comedies, Poems, "Romeo and Juliet"*) of Geoffrey Bullough's *Narrative and Dramatic Sources of Shakespeare* (New York: Columbia Univ. Press, 1957) does not include a section devoted to *The Phoenix and the Turtle*.

[20] Straumann, p. 37; Bradbrook, "'The Phoenix . . . ,'" p. 357. Also instructive with regard to the idea of multiple readings is Helen Gardner's use of the Gestalt-oriented approach to art in her *Religion and Literature* (New York: Oxford Univ. Press, 1971), pp. 34-35, where by means of an illustrative pattern of four linked equal rhomboids the point is made that "there is no 'right way' to read the image."

[21] William Matchett, in his study of Shakespeare's poem and Chester's *Loves Martyr*, is one of the few scholars who discusses in some detail the Petrarch-Marot-Spenser material in connection with *The Phoenix and the Turtle* (p. 24). See also Robert Ellrodt's essay in *ShS*, 15, pp. 101, 109 n. 14. Consideration of the earlier treatment of the Phoenix by Petrarch and then by Marot and Spenser in their translations would have made the articles by Murray Copland (especially p. 285) and Elias Schwartz (p. 25 and passim) more convincing. In the Variorum edition of *The Works of Edmund Spenser*, ed. Edwin Greenlaw et al, II (Baltimore: Johns Hopkins Press, 1947), Marot is mentioned in connection with *A Theatre for Worldlings* and then again in commentary on *The Visions of Petrarch*, but not in connection with the Phoenix (pp. 274-76, 611). In R. P. C. Mutter's edition of *Spenser's Minor Poems: A Selection* (London: Methuen, 1957) an entry is lacking for the Phoenix in the glossary, although *The Visions of Petrarch*, 5, is printed on page 53. References are made to Spenser's *Visions* in Muriel Bradbrook's *Shakespeare and Elizabethan Poetry*, pp. 24, 29, but never are these made in connection with her comments on *The Phoenix and the Turtle* (pp. 32-34, 145, 247 n. 26). W. B. C. Watkins, in *Shakespeare and Spenser* (Princeton: Princeton Univ. Press, 1950), considers Marot's translation of Petrarch but makes no specific reference to the Phoenix image in general or to *The Phoenix and the Turtle* in particular (p. 225). What is even more unusual, Alfred W. Satterthwaite's useful account of *Spenser, Ronsard, and DuBellay* (Princeton: Princeton Univ. Press, 1960) never mentions the name of Marot. The same thing is true of William Nelson's *The Poetry of Spenser* (New York: Columbia Univ. Press, 1963), see especially pp. 64-83. And in a full-length essay on "The Reputation of Clément Marot in Renaissance England," *SRen*, 18 (1971), pp. 173-202, Anne Lake Prescott presents a much-needed study but does not take note of either Marot's *Des Visions de Petrarque* or Spenser's *Visions of Petrarch*. The Marot-Spenser relationship as it regards the *Visions* does come into discussions by John Hollander, "Spenser and the Mingled Measure," *ELR*, 1 (Autumn 1971), 234-35 n. 13; and by Veselin Kosti , "Spenser's Sources in Italian Poetry," Diss. Univ. of Belgrade 1969, pp. 13-14. Kosti argues that there is a possibility that Petrarch's original *Canzoniere* 323, rather than Marot's version, influenced Spenser in the *Visions* (p. 14). Cf. Pauline M. Smith, *Clément Marot, Poet of the French Renaissance* (London: Athlone Press, 1970).

[22] *Petrarch: Sonnets and Songs*, trans. Anna Maria Armi (New York: Pantheon, 1968), pp. 446, 448. The loose translation following the quotation is mine.

[23] *Oeuvres Complètes de Clément Marot*, II, ed. B. Saint-Marc (Paris: Garnier, 1879), p. 131.

[24] *The Poetical Works of Edmund Spenser*, ed. J. C. Smith and E. De Selincourt (1912; rpt. London: Oxford Univ. Press, 1961), p. 606.

[25] Ibid., p. 526.

[26] See Matchett, pp. 21-29. In a brief but helpful statement on *The Phoenix and the Turtle*, Richard Wilbur makes one comment that may be misleading: Poets often made "*ad hoc* revisions of mythology or conventional symbolism . . . the phoenix is assigned the feminine gender . . ." (*The Complete Pelican Shakespeare* [Baltimore: Penguin, 1969], p. 1404). Wilbur seems to be implying that Shakespeare was original in assigning the feminine gender to the Phoenix. But as Matchett and others have shown, Shakespeare was not. For the use of a female Phoenix with conventional self-regenerative powers, see William Smith's *Chloris* (1596), Sonnet 23, in *The Poems*

of *William Smith*, ed. Lawrence A. Sasek (Baton Rouge: Louisiana State Univ. Press, 1970), p. 60. Matthew Roydon's elegy with its female Phoenix (along with a Turtle-Dove and other birds, ll. 41-42) was printed along with Spenser's *Astrophel* in 1595. For the view that the elegy beginning "As then, no winde at all there blew" is indeed Roydon's, see Lisle Cecil John, *The Elizabethan Sonnet Sequences* (New York: Columbia Univ. Press, 1938), p. 181; Hallett Smith, *Elizabethan Poetry* (Cambridge, Mass.: Harvard Univ. Press, 1952), p. 58; *A Literary History of England*, ed. Albert C. Baugh, 2nd ed. (New York: Appleton-Century-Crofts, 1967), pp. 384-86; and *The Renaissance in England*, ed. Hyder Edward Rollins and Herschel Baker (Boston: Heath, 1954), p. 231.

[27] Several commentators have used terms that are relevant to my discussion of *The Phoenix and the Turtle*, but generally the ecstatic element in the poem is not fully explored. G. Wilson Knight, in *The Mutual Flame*, speaks of the Phoenix symbol in light of "the flaming mysticism of a Crashaw" (p. 153) and calls Marston's contribution to Chester's *Loves Martyr* a poem possessing "lyric ecstasy," making it the "most ecstatic of the contributions" (pp. 194-95). "Music," "ecstasy," and "vision" are considered in Knight's chapter on Shakespeare's poem (pp. 203-4). In his New Arden edition of *The Poems*, F. T. Prince tells us that *The Phoenix and the Turtle* "shows unsurpassed musical imagination" and that Shakespeare creates "a kind of ethereal frenzy" (pp. xliii-xliv). Robert Ellrodt's discussion mentions "the soul rapt in contemplation" (p. 105); and C. S. Lewis states that the "oracular" style is in *The Phoenix and the Turtle* "completely successful" (p. 509). John Masefield, in *William Shakespeare* (London: Williams & Norgate, 1911), begins his brief discussion of *The Phoenix and the Turtle* by stating that "spiritual ecstasy is the only key to work of this kind" (p. 249). Regarding *defunctive*, the *OED* cites Shakespeare's *The Phoenix and the Turtle*, line 14, after indicating that the word pertains to "defunction or dying." *Defunctive* is a term not only for death but also for a state in which function is lost. The "defunctive music" of the swan is funereal music, the music of death, but it is also music bemoaning the loss of function, whether it be the life-function or function in general.

[28] *Oxford Dictionary of the Christian Church*, ed. F. L. Cross (London: Oxford Univ. Press, 1958), p. 437; *The Complete Poetry of John Donne*, ed. John T. Shawcross (New York: Doubleday, 1967), pp. 130 and 401; and *The Songs and Sonnets of John Donne*, ed. Theodore Redpath (London: Methuen, 1956), pp. 88-93. See also A. J. Smith, "The Metaphysic of Love," *RES*, NS 9 (Nov. 1958), 362-75; Frank A. Doggett, "Donne's Platonism," *SR*, 42 (July-Sept. 1934), 284-90; E. M. W. Tillyard, *The Metaphysicals and Milton* (London: Methuen, 1960), pp. 79-84; G. R. Potter, "Donne's *Extasie*, Contra Legouis," *PQ*, 15 (July 1936), 247-53; George Williamson, "The Convention of *The Extasie*," in *Seventeenth Century Contexts* (London: Faber & Faber, 1960), pp. 63-77; Louis L. Martz, *The Wit of Love* (Notre Dame, Ind.: Univ. of Notre Dame Press, 1969), pp. 48-50; Helen Gardner, "The Argument about 'The Ecstasy,'" in *Elizabethan and Jacobean Studies: Presented to Frank Percy Wilson*, ed. H. Davis and H. Gardner (Oxford: Clarendon Press, 1959), pp. 279-306; René Graziani, "John Donne's 'The Extasie' and Ecstasy," *RES*, NS 19 (May 1968), 121-36; Charles Mitchell, "Donne's 'The Extasie': Love's Subtle Knot," *SEL*, 8 (Winter 1968), 91-101; John E. Parish, "The Parley in 'The Extasie,'" *XUS*, 4 (1965), 188-92; and Elizabeth T. McLaughlin, "'The Extasie': Deceptive or Authentic?" *BuR*, 18 (1970), 55-78. G. Wilson Knight is fond of referring to Donne's *Extasie* in *The Mutual Flame*, passim.

[29] *The Art of Ecstasy: Teresa, Bernini, and Crashaw* (New York: Atheneum, 1970), p. 26. Any full discussion of spiritual ecstasy must eventually make reference to the episode of the seraph and the flaming arrow in St. Teresa's *Vida*. Here the mystery of ecstatic experience comes alive, as it also does in Bernini's magnificent sculpture at Santa Maria della Vittoria (Rome) and in Crashaw's passionate poem of *The Flaming Heart*. In connection with the last, see Mario Praz's fine essay in *The Flaming Heart* (New York: Doubleday, 1958), pp. 204-63.

[30] Plato's *Phaedrus* deals generally with the four madnesses; in his *Ion* he focuses on poetic "madness" and in the *Symposium* on amatory "madness." Marsilio Ficino acknowledges these Platonic sources in his own analysis of the four madnesses (the *furores*) in *Commentary on Plato's "Symposium,"* trans. Sears R. Jayne, University of Missouri Studies, 19 (1944), pp. 231-33. Leone Ebreo's consideration of love-ecstasy occurs his *Dialoghi d'Amore*, available in the translation by F. Friedberg-Seeley and Jean H. Barnes: *The Philosophy of Love* (London: Soncino Press, 1937), p. 176. Bruno's *De gli eroici furori* has been translated by Paul E. Memmo as *The Heroic Frenzies* (Chapel Hill: Univ. of North Carolina Press, 1964). The third dialogue of Part I of Bruno's work asserts that although there are many species of frenzies, all of these may be reduced to two sorts: " . . . blindness, stupidity, and an irrational impulse which tends to bestial folly" and " . . . a certain divine rapture which makes some become superior to ordinary men" (p. 107). In addition to the very useful translation, Memmo's edition offers a substantial introduction, part of which deals with the business of the *furores* as discussed by Plato, Ficino, and Bruno (pp. 17-20).

[31] Jayne's trans., p. 231.

[32] All references to *The Phoenix and the Turtle* are drawn from F. T. Prince's New Arden edition. The

question whether the title of the poem should include the second "the" before "Turtle" is quite important to Murray Copland (pp. 279-80). Frankly, I believe Copland is attempting to split hairs. For a counter-argument to Copland see Empson's introduction to the Signet Classic Shakespeare edition of *Narrative Poems* (p. xxxvi, note).

[33] *The Christian Renaissance* (New York: Norton, 1963), pp. 235-37.

[34] Cf. Castiglione's discussion of music, the spirit, and ecstasy in *The Book of the Courtier*, trans. Charles S. Singleton (New York: Doubleday, 1959), pp. 74-76, 104-6, 356. Very helpful studies dealing with music, magic, Orphic incantation, and ecstasy are D. P. Walker, *Spiritual and Demonic Magic from Ficino to Campanella* (London: The Warburg Institute, Univ. of London, 1958), esp. pp. 3-29; Walker, "Orpheus the Theologian and Renaissance Platonists," *JWCI*, 16 (1953), 100-20; F. W. Sternfeld, *Music in Shakespearean Tragedy* (London: Routledge & Kegan Paul, 1963), pp. 79-97; Edward J. Dent, "Music in Shakespeare," in *A Companion to Shakespeare Studies*, ed. H. Granville-Barker and G. B. Harrison (1932; rpt. New York: Doubleday, 1960), pp. 142-43 and 156-60; W. H. Auden, "Music in Shakespeare," in *The Dyer's Hand and Other Essays* (New York: Random House, 1968), pp. 507-11; John Hollander, *The Untuning of the Sky* (Princeton: Princeton Univ. Press, 1961), pp. 111, 199-201, 233-38, 353-54, and passim; Gretchen L. Finney, "Ecstasy and Music in Seventeenth-Century England," *JHI*, 8 (April 1947), 153-86; Finney, "'Organical Musick' and Ecstasy," *JHI*, 8 (1947), 273-92; F. W. Sternfeld, "Shakespeare and Music," in *A New Companion to Shakespeare Studies*, ed. Kenneth Muir and S. Schoenbaum (London: Cambridge Univ. Press, 1971), pp. 157-67; Catherine M. Dunn, "The Function of Music in Shakespeare's Romances," *SQ*, 20 (Autumn 1969), 391-405; Edgar Wind, *Pagan Mysteries in the Renaissance* (1958; rev. ed., London: Penguin, 1967), passim; and Michael Fixler, "The Orphic Technique of 'L'Allegro' and 'Il Penseroso,'" *ELR*, 1 (Spring 1971), 165-77. Jerome Mazzaro's *Transformations in the Renaissance English Lyric* (Ithaca, N.Y.: Cornell Univ. Press, 1970) considers at length the "shift from music and words to music and self-understanding and words and self-understanding . . ." (p. 185). In his Variorum edition of *The Poems*, Rollins tabulates information on "Musical Settings for the Poems" (pp. 610-21). What is quite surprising is that *The Phoenix and the Turtle* has never been set to music. It would make an excellent text for a choral group accompanied by an orchestra. Inga-Stina Ewbank refers to the poem as "incantation" and "song" in *A New Companion to Shakespeare Studies* (p. 105); and in the earlier *Companion to Shakespeare Studies*. George Rylands writes regarding *The Phoenix and the Turtle*: "Shakespeare's own adventure in the metaphysical style combines at once the quality of a proposition in Euclid and of a piece of music" (p. 111).

[35] For the Phoenix as soul and the Turtle-Dove as body, see Knight's *Mutual Flame*, pp. 164-65, 186. I agree with Knight in seeing these associations, although I think of them as only one possible set of associations as far as the two central symbols of the poem are concerned.

[36] For the relationship between ecstasy, enthusiasm (the "ravishing of the spirit"), and music, consult Hollander, *The Untuning of the Sky*, pp. 199-201, and Finney, p. 179 and passim.

[37] *The Complete Poetry of Ben Jonson*, ed. William B. Hunter, Jr. (New York: Doubleday, 1963), p. 334. For informative notes on Jonson's poems in *Loves Martyr* see also pp. 96-101, 333 of Hunter's edition. In commenting on Jonson's *Ode* in *The Mutual Flame*, G. Wilson Knight says nothing about the significance of the poem's title, but he does call John Marston's pieces in *Loves Martyr* the "most ecstatic" of the contributions (p. 194) and points to the first of these, "A Narration and Description of a Most Exact Wondrous Creature, Arising out of the Phoenix and Turtle-Dove's Ashes," as exhibiting "lyric ecstasy" (p. 195). It is clear that Marston's Phoenix does revive. J. B. Leishman has some pages on *The Phoenix and the Turtle*, Jonson's *Ode*, and Donne's *Extasie* in *The Monarch of Wit* (1951; rpt. New York: Harper, 1965), pp. 177, 225.

[38] *Commentary on Plato's "Symposium,"* p. 232.

[39] *The Landscape of the Mind* (Oxford: Clarendon Press, 1969), pp. 34-35. Edgar Wind, in *Pagan Mysteries in the Renaissance*, deals quite interestingly with the *Emanatio-Raptio-Remeatio* pattern in his discussion of Pico's closely related *Pulchritudo-Amor-Voluptas* triad (pp. 36-52, esp. 37 and 45-46). Ecstasy is also dealt with here.

[40] Cody, p. 29.

[41] Ibid., p. 76 and passim.

[42] Cf. C. S. Lewis, p. 509 (see note 14 above). Monroe Spears, in his introduction to the Laurel Shakespeare edition of the narrative poetry (cited earlier) calls *The Phoenix and the Turtle* an "ontological" poem that speaks of the impossibility of love (pp. 39, 42).

RELIGIOUS AND MYSTICAL ELEMENTS

H. Neville Davies (essay date 1995)

SOURCE: "'The Phoenix and Turtle': Requiem and

Rite." *The Review of English Studies*, Vol. XLVI, No. 184, November, 1995, pp. 525-29.

[*In the following essay, Davies examines the ritual imagery, specifically its Christian derivation, of* The Phoenix and Turtle.]

In Shakespeare's *The Phoenix and Turtle*, a swan is appointed to officiate as priest at the birds' funeral, 'Lest', as the poem explains, 'the requiem lack his right' (line 16).[1] Editors invariably adhere to the spelling of the first edition for the last of those quoted words, though a strong case could be made for replacing 'right' by 'rite' on the grounds that to do so would give a truer indication of the primary sense of the line. But whatever spelling may be preferred, F. T. Prince's responsive comment that 'the alternative meanings remain suspended in the words, and all add something to their tone and weight' needs to be borne in mind.[2] For one of the consequences of privileging 'right', by the retention of that form in our edited texts, seems to have been an unfortunate neglect of sustained allusion to religious ritual. This is specially damaging when one comes to the crow stanza, the stanza that immediately follows the swan stanza.

The general pattern established in connection with the swan-priest is repeated in connection with the crow-mourner, in each instance two reasons being given for assigning the particular role to that particular bird. Thus the swan is called upon to act as priest because, in the first place, his distinctive surplice-white plumage means that he naturally looks the part, while by a slightly more ingenious conceit the curious lore of the swan-song is exploited to suggest that this species of bird has unique expertise in 'defunctive music' (line 14), precisely the kind of music required for a funeral.[3] Then, in a more or less parallel stanza, the crow is similarly regarded as doubly qualified to participate in the ritual. His distinctive mourning-black plumage means that he is no less suitably attired than the swan, while, once again, bird-lore, this time about crows propagating by a strange process of heavy breathing, is wittily drawn upon, confirming that this is a bird ideally fitted to perform the function of mourner. Of course, modern readers familiar enough with the notion of the swan-song may well be entirely ignorant of the altogether more arcane business of the crow's supposed reproductive procedures, and consequently some explanatory intervention has become necessary. So, in slightly varying terms, annotators obligingly shed light on the obscure pneumatics of exhalation and inhalation involved in this corvine coupling; but, having supplied their helpful information, the annotators signally fail to reveal how the process they describe is relevant to the part the crow is called upon to play in the poem's obsequies.

The relevance must surely lie in an allusion to the Burial Service as set out in the Elizabethan Book of Common Prayer, for the crow's giving and taking of breath,

> That thy sable gender mak'st
> With the breath thou giv'st and tak'st,
>
> (ll. 19-20)

is expressed in words that recall the quotation from Job that supplies one of the 'sentences' with which the Anglican funeral rite begins: 'The Lord giveth, and the Lord taketh away'.[4] It is worth observing that the present tense of the quotation in its Elizabethan form (as opposed to the Authorized Version's past tense that was subsequently incorporated in the 1662 Prayer Book) matches the present tense in the poem. Furthermore, the words from Job that associate the crow's mating habits with the ritual of the Burial Service are reinforced in turn by the way they recall other biblical texts in which the breath of life is given or withdrawn by divine will, verses such as Genesis 2: 7, 'The Lord God also made the man of the dust of the ground, and breathed in his face breath of life; and the man was a liuing soule' (Geneva Bible), 'The Lorde God also dyd shape man, [euen] dust from of the grounde, & breathed into his nosethrylles the breath of lyfe, and man was a lyuyng soule' (Bishops' Bible), as well as Psalm 104: 29, 'if thou take away their breath, they dye and returne to their dust' (Geneva Bible), 'Thou takest away their breath, they die, and return again to their dust' (Common Prayer Psalter). Unlike his evasive predecessors, the latest editor of Shakespeare's poem does at least endeavour to explain the significance of Shakespeare's 'giv'st and tak'st', but by asserting that 'the phrase suggests an exchange of lovers' vows' he can only be said to have missed the point. The context supplied by the fanciful note is misleadingly wrong, the sombre ritual of a funeral inappropriately replaced by a notion that refers to the love and constancy of the birds when they were alive.[5]

Since the conduct of a funeral provides the basis for the early part of the poem, it naturally follows that, contrary to what might otherwise have been expected, the priest who officiates at the service is mentioned before the mourners who bring the dead birds to the church. And in this respect the sequence of stanzas 4-6 corresponds exactly to the ordering of the Elizabethan Burial Service. The introductory rubric that there introduces the Funeral Sentences explains how these texts are to be uttered as the body of the deceased is carried through the churchyard: 'The priest meeting the corpse at the church stile, shall say: Or else the priests and clerks shall sing, and so go either into the church, or towards the grave.' Accordingly, in the poem, after the summoning and gathering of the birds for the funeral, the appointment of the swan in stanza

4 puts the figure of the priest, who begins the ritual by the action of meeting the corpse 'at the church stile' (i.e. out at the lich-gate), in the appropriate position at the very start of the rite. The crow, who is associated with the funeral sentences and who is to walk ('go') as mourner in procession through the churchyard as the sentences are recited or sung, is therefore not introduced until stanza 5. Indeed, Shakespeare's 'shalt thou go' (line 20) in the poem's crow stanza corresponds directly to the instruction 'and so go' that is found in the Prayer Book rubric.

In the Elizabethan Anglican rite the psalms that in earlier and later periods formed a required part of the Order for the Burial of the Dead were excluded from the service. This meant that once the grave had been reached, and while the corpse was being prepared for interment, the processional sentences were simply followed by more set words that were either spoken by the priest or sung by the choir as an anthem. Once again the poem adheres to the liturgy of Shakespeare's time by reproducing this ritual sequence and adopting, as one would expect with birds, the musical option, for stanza 6 begins with the brusque, rubric-like announcement 'Here the anthem doth commence' (line 21). To describe this anthem, though, as a 'song of praise', as the recent New Cambridge edition does in a gloss that apparently recalls an unfortunate remark by I. A. Richards, is to disregard the nature of the ritual of which it forms a part.[6] Richards had unaccountably turned the funeral procession into a 'commemorative procession' during which an anthem was 'chanted', and in an influential account of the poem has described this processionally chanted anthem as 'a song of praise and gladness'. However, readers of the poem not only need to imagine the anthem as a liturgically performed choral setting of a religious text, but ought to think specifically in terms of an anthem that corresponds to the Funeral Anthem identified by the words duly prescribed in the Book of Common Prayer. Far from being a 'song of praise', the Prayer Book text begins with the sobering recognition that 'Man that is born of a woman hath but a short time to live, and is full of misery', continues with the melancholy observation that 'In the midst of life we be in death', and concludes with anxious pleading that we be spared 'the bitter pains of eternal death' and, 'at our last hour', not 'for any pains of death to fall from God'. Thomas Morley's graciously dignified four-part setting provides a late Elizabethan response to these sombre words that gives the right musical context for the poem's use of the word *anthem*.[7]

Yet it need not be supposed that whenever the words of the Prayer Book are recalled in Shakespeare's poem there has to be an allusion to the Burial Service. The range of allusion to religious ritual is wider and freer than that. So it is that when the crow is described as 'treble-dated' (line 17) in a way that calls attention to the venerability and endurance of a bird whose experience comprehends, in Yeats's words, 'what is past, or passing, or to come', and whom longevity makes a patient observer of the changes and chances of this fleeting world—presumably a mourner at many funerals—we may also respond to the concomitant invocation of the 'treble-dated' *Gloria patri*, 'As it was in the beginning, is now, and ever shall be: world without end', though the psalms to which this doxology is regularly appended had in fact been banished from the Elizabethan funeral liturgy. It is an invocation that coalesces naturally with the treble dating in Revelation 1: 8 where the antithesis of beginning and ending recalls the divine giving and taking of breath that the crow's reproductive behaviour emblematizes: 'I am Alpha and Omega, the beginning and the ending, saith the Lord, Which is, and Which was, and Which is to come, *euen* the Almightie' (Geneva Bible). The final line of the poem, 'For these dead birds sigh a prayer', even seems to hint at the pre-Reformation practice of intercession for the souls of the faithful departed. In the end, the imaginative ritual of this poem, founded though it is on deeply ingrained religious traditions, proves to be distinctively *sui generis*.

Notes

[1] Quoted throughout from *The Riverside Shakespeare*, ed. G. Blakemore Evans (Boston, 1974), 782.

[2] *The Poems*, ed. F. T. Prince, Arden Shakespeare (London, 1960), 180.

[3] Typically Shakespearian is the subsidiary word-play invested in the epithet 'death-divining' (line 15) which lends delicate support to the priestly appointment by incidentally activating the incorporated noun *divine* (i.e. a Doctor of Divinity) to supplement the main sense of the enveloping verb. The gentle implication (nothing more than that) is that the swan has some entitlement to be regarded as a serious theologian.

[4] *The Book of Common Prayer, 1559: The Elizabethan Prayer Book*, ed. J. E. Booty (Charlottesville, Va., 1976), 309-13 (p. 309).

[5] *The Poems*, ed. J. Roe, New Cambridge Shakespeare (Cambridge, 1992), 233.

[6] Later in the service, after the interment, there is a briefer second anthem in which lamentation and supplication give way to consolation, but even those words taken from Rev. 14: 13 cannot be described as a 'song of praise': 'I heard a voice from heaven saying unto me, Write, From henceforth blessed are the dead which die in the Lord. Even so saith the Spirit, that they may rest from their labors' (p. 310). Richards's 'The Sense of Poetry: Shakespeare's "The Phoenix and the Turtle" ',

originally broadcast as a talk in 1957-8, is here quoted from his *Poetries: Their Media and Ends*, ed. T. Easton (The Hague, 1974), 53. It was first printed in *Daedalus*, 87 (1958), but gained wide currency when it was included in G. Hammond (ed.), *Elizabethan Poetry: Lyrical and Narrative* (London, 1984), a volume in Macmillan's popular Casebook Series.

[7] Morley's settings of 'Man that is born of a woman', 'In the midst of life', and 'Thou knowest, Lord' (the three sections of the first anthem, referring successively to birth, living, and dying) and 'I heard a voice' (the second anthem) comprise, together with his music for the three introductory Burial Sentences, a full choral Service for the Burial of the Dead. See Appendix below.

Murray Copland (essay date 1965)

SOURCE: "The Dead Phoenix," *Essays in Criticism*, Vol. XV, No. 3, July, 1965, pp. 279-87.

[*In the essay that follows, Copland criticizes a mystical interpretive approach to the poem, given the "fashionable" status of metaphysical images in the Elizabethan age.*]

The Phoenix was a striking bird on three counts: (a) its beauty, (b) its uniqueness, and (c) its self-resurrecting habit.

In Shakespeare's poem *The Phoenix and Turtle* the attribute (a) is prominently present:

Truth and Beautie buried be.

Here Truth = the Turtle, and Beautie = the Phoenix.

As for (b), Robert Chester, whose *Love's Martyr* prescribed the bare postulates for the poem, had introduced a personal variation of a certain imaginative power. The usual Phoenix is complete in itself; Chester's requires a mate, and finds that mate in a true Turtle. This is not necessarily a muddling idea. If the Phoenix is seen as a poetic hyperbole for the summit of female attainment in beauty, accomplishment and virtue—the vision of a lady who might be complimented on such freedom from flaw as to seem virtually superhuman, so that one might expect her, by some divine dispensation, to be raised above the embarrassing necessities of normal human procreation—then the Turtle becomes, equally, a hyperbolical compliment to a man refined enough to deserve her. I do not claim that Chester's own intention was as simple as this; but it does seem to me that it is on much these straightforward terms that Shakespeare elects to understand Chester's brace of birds.

Countless writers, even Wilson Knight among them, have committed the howler—for surely it is that—of referring to Shakespeare's poem as 'The Phoenix and the Turtle'. If, in Platonic terms, the Phoenix represents the 'idea' of female beauty and the Turtle the 'idea' of fidelity, mated they have grown into a third 'idea' which by virtue of its ideality will necessarily have to include these two. This is, of course, the 'idea' of human love—human love in its barely imaginable perfection. Now I take it that an 'idea' cannot be a duality; it must be a unity. Shakespeare appears to have called his poem *The Phoenix and Turtle*. That is, the subject is *one* thing, not two.

In the line

Phoenix and the *Turtle* fled,

they *are* presented as separate creatures, but only in aid of the next antithetical line wherein they are all the more strikingly fused:

In a mutuall flame from hence.

Here *Phoenix* needs no article, precisely because of the bird's uniqueness: whereas *Turtle* needs its 'the' to establish (for this is the first mention of the dead protagonists) that this is not any old turtle (as, in fact, is the case in *Love's Martyr*) but itself a type, an ideal, and therefore unique, just as much as its mate.

It is immaterial whether Shakespeare had two actual dead lovers in mind. But I do not think the poem is being properly read if the reader does not realise that human love is under discussion; he should appreciate that behind the birds an eminently desirable human possibility is being mooted. If such a man and woman could exist and love like this, then *The Phoenix and Turtle* would be their fitting elegy.

It may be clear by now that I am against overmuch mystifying of this poem, which critics have tended to etherealise out of existence.

Is it so very crude to see in Shakespeare's acceptance of Chester's bright idea of a mated Phoenix a rather original, compellingly beautiful, but nonetheless natural and likely enough conceit to come upon in a late-Elizabethan Platonizing poem? Donne himself filched the idea for his own 'Parliament of Fowls' poem, the delightful St. Valentine's Day Epithalamion, where the application is wholly unmysterious and as 'human' as could be—an actual wedding:

Till now, Thou warmd'st with multiplying
  loves
Two larkes, two sparrows, or two Doves,
All that is nothing unto this,
For thou this day couplest two Phoenixes.

Phoenixes and dragons, painted in gold, adorn the exterior roof edge of the Temple of Heaven, Tian tan, Beijing, China.

But Donne is not here in a particularly 'Platonic' vein; that would scarcely suit his occasion:

> . . . one bed containes, through Thee,
> Two Phoenixes, whose joyned breasts
> Are unto one another mutuall nests,
> Where motion kindles such fires, as shall give
> Yong Phoenixes, and yet the old shall live.

The Elizabethans, sexually, must have been on the whole a happily proficient, promiscuous, and uninhibited race. We can assume this from the fascinated glee with which they pounced upon the newly unearthed Platonic version of love and made it all the fashionable rage. Lord Herbert of Cherbury's serious-minded Melander and Celinda are happily conscious of their limelighted position as, in Gilbert's phrase, 'most particularly pure' young people. It is their sense of the wild eccentricity of the notion which causes these poets to place such stress on the abstention from physical intercourse. The exaggerated contempt in which they place bodily pleasure has little to do with Plato, who notably conveys an appreciation of its charms.

The Shakespeare stanza about 'married Chastitie' comes as a shock because Shakespeare meant it to do so. Poems in the 'metaphysical' mode characteristically proceed by shock tactics, both of style and of thought. *The Phoenix and Turtle* is very obviously a single, somewhat haughtily restrained demonstration on Shakespeare's part that if 'everyone was doing it, doing it, doing it' he was very well competent to do it too; and, by a natural enough impulse under the circumstances, there is perhaps present a certain willingness to outdo all the others in sheer transcendence of transcendentalism.

Can it be doubted that this is, consciously, Shakespeare's contribution to the fashion of which Donne was the acknowledged leader—a fashion which I fancy the contemporary bright young men took with a certain seriousness as a discussion of the problem 'What should love be like'? Think how Lord Herbert's *Ode upon a Question moved, whether Love should continue for ever?* takes exception to Sidney's *In a Grove most rich of Shade* (in *Astrophil and Stella*) and Donne's *The Ecstasy* cocks a snook at both. Shakespeare's poem is clearly at home in this context. Place stanzas 7-12 of *The Phoenix and Turtle* beside stanzas 32-33 of Lord Herbert's *Ode* and stanzas 9-12 of *The Ecstasy* and the community of ambition to be brilliantly intellectual and ineffably Platonic shines out.

We need not be surprised that this section which celebrates the unity-out-of-duality which love may encompass is, in each of the three poems, one of the easiest parts to interpret. The metaphysical poets prided themselves on their intellectuality, just as their critics tend to do today. But, in spite of themselves, they were first and foremost poets. With the characteristic procedure of poets, they seized upon the most imaginatively captivating and emotionally disturbing of the thoughts which their genuinely intellectual contemporaries came up with, and thereafter, contented, applied themselves to exploiting to the full, by means of ever refined-upon expression, those imaginative and emotional potentialities which their artistic flair had sensed. There are, in fact, few 'thoughts' in most metaphysical poems; and those few tend to be bold, clear, and easily graspable. In the passages I have specified it would be a poor reader at any period who did not immediately see what the poet is 'on about'.

Fashions are tyrannical dictators, which accounts for the stylistic unfamiliarity we sense when we place *The Phoenix and Turtle* beside the bulk of the Shakespeare we fancy we know. Shakespeare does not habitually introduce images unprepared, undeveloped, unmodified, or unrelated to context. He does so here, however, with the very Donne-like pun in

> Either was the others mine.

where the image of quarry-seams of inexhaustible riches is flashed, as it were, for a moment upon the screen. Again, the Donne manner welcomes words of quite slangy modernity. In *The Ecstasy* occurs what we tend to think of as a twentieth-century usage of the word 'sex'. In Shakespeare's poem we have what must have been a flashily new usage of the word 'starres' to mean 'leading actors'—two centuries before the first recorded example in the *O.E.D.*, it is true, but I cannot see what other meaning can make full sense in this context. Like the Sidney and Lord Herbert poems, and *The Ecstasy*, most of the Shakespeare poem is cast in four-line stanzas, a helpful form if your aim is to be spare, compressed, aphoristic.

But there is no need to see Shakespeare as *merely* following a fashion. More than one critic has sensed that Shakespeare was aware of the quaintness and artificiality of the form he had chosen. Chester had landed him not only with 'metaphysics' but with birds. And not only the bird-obsequies idea, but also the curious Chinese-nest-of-boxes development whereby the birds gather to chant an anthem to the dead lovers in which Reason is alleged to have composed an elegy on the same dead lovers, seems to be Shakespeare's half-humorous, half-affectionate pastiche-tribute to the odd charm and elusive structure of the mediaeval dream-allegory form.

Moreover, my portrait of the lusty layabout Elizabethan is to a certain extent an oversimplification. England was still on its Protestant mettle and Pauline ethics must have lingered on, an uneasy feeling in the pit of the young man's stomach. This layabout was capable, at times, of a yearning (taken to extremes it becomes the Hamlet-disgust) which accounts for, among other things, the genuinely ecstatic close of Lord Herbert's *Ode*. There is no reason to suppose that Shakespeare was not himself in imaginative bondage to the idea of 'the white cold virgin Snow' upon the heart, admiring it, as most must, from a distance. It is because the modern world is so worried about its own potency (which atomic radiation further calls in question) that we tend to find such expressions not strangely alluring, but downright offensive. Critics have taken Prospero's reiterated warnings to the forgiven Ferdinand not to break Miranda's

> Virgin-knot, before
> All sanctimonious ceremonies may
> With full and holy right, be ministred

as something of a personal insult. The modern feeling is that restraint can only come from inadequacy.

To sum up so far: what for brevity's sake we may call the Chaucerian element in conceit and structure allows Shakespeare to wear his 'metaphysics' with a difference—as any dandy will want to bring his own touch to the prevailing fashion, to preserve his self-respect. Nonetheless, it *is* a modish poem; but that also entails making a perfectly sober contribution to the contemporary inter-poets debate which aimed at evaluating the new ideas of love that were in the air.

This brings me at last to the third of the Phoenix's traditional attributes, the most distinctive of all, its immortality.

Most commentators have assumed that, since the Phoenix was traditionally an immortal bird, Shakespeare's poem must be 'about' some kind of immortality. Some critics (for example, I. A. Richards in *Daedalus*, lxxxvii, Summer 1958) have even become so possessed by this assumption as to interpret Shakespeare's unspecified 'bird of lowdest lay' as the reborn Phoenix herself, summoning the other birds to weep at her own funeral. But this is degrading Shakespeare to the equal in tastelessness and unintentional comedy of Chester himself. Shakespeare has devoted seven stanzas to rapturous celebration of the absolute union and fusion of the lovers. Has he done so merely to separate them for ever in death? Richards would have it so:

> To the Phoenix, death is now a nest, a
> symbol of rebirth,
> but to the *Turtles* loyall brest,
> it is a place of final repose.

Yet we are told that they fled in a mutual flame from hence, and also that they left no posterity!

Can we at any rate command enough sense of humour to agree that 'the bird of lowdest lay' cannot possibly be the Phoenix? It is not widely recognised that the poem's fourth line

> To whose sound chaste wings obay

is a command. Overpunctuated in the style of Victorian editors it would read:

> To whose sound, chaste wings, obay!

This command is in strong antithesis to the prohibition introduced by the 'But' of the second stanza. 'The bird of lowdest lay' is not one with special magical virtue to compel its stainless compeers as maids can tame unicorns; it is simply whatever bird is noisiest—and there is no reason to suppose that Shakespeare had any very clear idea of which that was. It is told off to perch 'On the sole *Arabian* tree' for the obvious reason that this was the traditional scene of the Phoenix's tragedy, and therefore a suitable orchestra for the 'Chorus to their Tragique Scene': critics tend to forget that the funeral anthem is the twittering of a flock of birds settled on the branches of a tree—the movement of the mourners (the flying together) is over before the service commences. (We remember another occasion when Shakespeare notably likened the branches of trees to 'choirs'.)

I cannot, however, admit that the poem is about immortality in any sense whatsoever, unless perhaps it was conceived as an *attack on* the belief in immortality.

When a poet in the Donne vogue condescends to use a traditional image, he plumes himself on his ingenuity in giving it a new twist—see what Donne does with the Phoenix itself in the two quotations I have already given from his Epithalamion. Shakespeare's most original and imaginative stroke in *The Phoenix and Turtle* is to assert that the unique, peerlessly beautiful bird is fully and finally *dead*. Only this can account for the combination of such depth and gravity of mourning with a certain mischievousness brought in by the Cock Robin framework, of which, after so much ineffability, we are somewhat bluntly reminded in the last line:

> For *these dead Birds,* sigh a prayer.

In the words I have italicised pathetic simplicity is not incompatible with a certain smile.

The Dead Phoenix is *the* 'metaphysical' shock conceit on which the whole poem depends.

> Death is now the *Phoenix* nest

represents poetic inversion for the sake of emphasis. A nest is not only 'a symbol of rebirth', as Richards claims, but also a symbol of the home, the family, security, warmth, and snuggling down to sleep. Previous Phoenixes, homing to their welcoming *hearth* (sacrificial altar), folded their wings to sleep, only to wake the next 'day', to rise again. But the Phoenix is now laid asleep for ever. Its bed is, simply and baldly, the final bed of death.

> And the *Turtles* loyall brest,
> To eternitie doth rest.

The 'And' links, as it should, two equalities. Nothing else would be decent in a poem which has put the Phoenix and the Turtle so absolutely on the same level (co-supremes).

The muted ending of '*sigh* a prayer' (my italics) is analogous, although on a different scale, to the drained, stunned close of *King Lear*. And, indeed, need we be surprised that a poet should wish to shock us with a mortal Phoenix who also confronted us inexorably with a hanged Cordelia? *The Phoenix and Turtle* is genuinely a poem of mourning, a meditation on the hard fact of mortality. It is thus centrally, not peripherally, Shakespearian.

In the world of *King Lear* there is no revealed God, no saving Christ sent in from outside. If human beings want the amelioration of the Christ-function, they can have it only in so far as they are prepared to shoulder the burden themselves and *become* Christ to the extent that a human being is capable of doing this. Only human beings can 'show the heavens more just', by enacting heaven in their own behaviour. The saintly, Christlike imagery which clusters around Cordelia in the later part of the play indicates that she is the summit of human success in this direction. But she remains mortal for all that: no woman is so much of a Phoenix that she cannot be killed. All of Christ that the world can have can be murdered any day in the death of one person. This is why the death of one such person can reasonably affect us as if all the Christlike potentialities of the world had been snatched away from us for ever at one fell swoop. It is this emotional, but *not* wholly irrational, reaction which is the informing creative conception in Donne's *Anniversaries*:

> All have forgot all good,
> Forgetting her, the maine reserve of all.

William Empson (in *Some Versions of Pastoral*) has also noticed the community of ideas between *The Phoenix and Turtle* and Donne in this respect.

It is notable that the more inclined Shakespeare becomes to stress the necessity for positive, responsible endeavour on the part of human beings (as in *The Tempest*) the more firmly, although sadly, he insists on the illusoriness of consolations based on fulfilment anywhere but here, in this life, now. No play takes a more religious tone with moral obligation than *The Tempest;* yet its most famous, because most moving and memorable, speech is an almost unbearably wistful assertion of inevitable and total dissolution.

If *The Phoenix and Turtle* does not, after all, impress us as a work loomingly tragic in the manner of *King Lear,* that is partly because of the poem's most subtle paradox, slipped gently into the last two stanzas (in which I trust I may be allowed to assume that 'faire' is a straightforward synonym for 'beautiful'):

> Truth may seeme, but cannot be,
> Beautie bragge, but tis not she,
> Truth and Beautie buried be.
>
> To this urne let those repair,
> That are either true or faire,
> For these dead Birds, sigh a prayer.

If, as we are told, Truth and Beautie are irrecoverably buried, who are these surviving 'true and beautiful' mourners who are invited to sigh a prayer—'bragging', 'seeming' impostors? Obviously not. Human beings (or birds) may still be born who may be called true or beautiful, but we cannot believe, in this moment of particular grieving, that we shall ever want to revere them as the embodied 'ideas' of Truth and Beautie (notice where we do and do not find capital letters in these stanzas). I sense a touch of affectionate humour in 'dead Birds' in that Shakespeare is not, characteristically, concerned about the forms in the heavenly warehouse; the sigh is a wistful one; the poem is rather addressed (how Chaucerian this is!) to the uncapitalised 'yonge, fresshe folkes, he or she' of the penultimate line—it is an admonition to them, in view of their certain mortality, to be as true and beautiful (yes, and as *chaste*) as it lies in their power to be, but not to be too humourless about it. 'Ideas' are strange birds; and, poor birds, they're dead.

Humorous or not, the paradox of these last stanzas is paralleled in the paradoxical closing lines of *King Lear:*

> The oldest hath borne most, we that are yong,
> Shall never see so much, nor live so long.

Mystical readings of *The Phoenix and Turtle* debase it. The poem is as sad, searching, tender, human, and humane, as we should expect from the author of the tragedies.

Brian Green (essay date 1979)

SOURCE: "Shakespeare's Heroic Elixir: A New Context for 'The Phoenix and the Turtle,'" *Studia Neophilologica,* Vol. 51, No. 2, 1979, pp. 215-235.

[*In the following essay, Green interprets* The Phoenix and Turtle *as an "alchemical recipe" that is intended to enact a transformation of the reader's values and ideals"*]

Critics generally recognise the language of scholasticism as an important stylistic context for Shakespeare's *Phoenix and Turtle*[1] J. V. Cunningham, who formally proposed the context, refers the poem to the Thomist doctrine of the Holy Trinity, i.e., the relationship between the Phoenix and Turtle is continuous with that between the Persons of the Trinity.[2] The reciprocal relation between the Father and the Son derives from their mutual participation in the Holy Ghost, who both joins them together and in turn issues from their relation. *The Phoenix and Turtle,* then, symbolises the union between two real human lovers on the analogy of this unfathomable, transcendent relationship of Divine Love which unites the Father and the Son. For the most part, this interpretation should raise few objections. The principal, unitary idea in the doctrine of the Trinity is a commonplace in Elizabethan thought, so that Shakespeare's outlook could hardly have avoided being at least coloured by it. Nevertheless, certain areas of the interpretation are not entirely satisfactory.

To begin with, the poem simply does not contain any allusion to Divine Love itself. There is the danger, therefore, when filtering a poem through a reconstructed system of its embedded ideology, of losing the emphasis in the poet's original vision. Moreover, the doctrine of the Trinity is of a different order of experience: it requires an accommodation which is purely intellectual, whereas *The Phoenix and Turtle* achieves itself in a fusion of thought, feeling, perceptions, and sympathies. The reading of the Anthem is, it's true, systematic and highly ingenious, but it is incapable of saying how the poem works as a literary whole. For the diction of the poem has a vitality which the rather too theoretical "influence" does not do justice to. More damagingly, Cunningham claims to have identified the external source of Shakespeare's conception of this human relationship, and to have clarified the poem's controlling theme, but without saying what Shakespeare has done with that source. The poem's account of the central relationship pursues the full quality, meaning, and value of the physical and psychological *coming together* of the two birds, and Cunningham's interpretation does not tell us that. Scholasticism should be acknowledged as a possible context because it shows how strongly the diction refers us beyond the poem. But these objections are perhaps sufficient to indicate that the scholastic interpretation is far from irrefragable. I propose to read the poem in another context, the language of alchemy.

I

As a starting-point, I want to examine a stanza from the heart of the poem, stanza 9, which is readily intelligible, and yet not easy to grasp:

> So betweene them Loue did shine,
> That the *Turtle* saw his right,
> Flaming in the *Phoenix* sight;
> Either was the others mine.
>
> (33-36)[3]

The main point of interest in this stanza is that the word "mine" (36) is usually read as a possessive pronoun. The line is then taken to mean that the birds loved each other so deeply that they identified themselves with each other. This reading is open to serious question, however, for at least three reasons. First, the first-person reference is a startling irruption into an otherwise evenly-textured commentary, so that it is not immediately clear whose conscious self is being engaged. Second, to take the word as a pronoun is to make the line sound too much like a facetious conundrum. And third, there is a more concrete sense of the word, "An abundant source of supply" (*OED*, s.v. *Mine*, sb., 1.c). Rollins accepts this substantival meaning, as proposed by Schmidt, "a rich source of wealth", and by Feuillerat, "the source of inexhaustible treasure" (pp. 327, 328). Prince, on the other hand, feels that this image does not develop in the poem, and is un-Shakespearian. He offers in turn the meaning "self".[4] And yet, perhaps we do not need to make a straight choice between these two basically opposed readings of the word.

The word is obviously intended to be ambiguous, and it is possible to read it as a pun in which the sense of the noun, "source of wealth", predominates over that of the pronoun, "self".[5] What we have here is a far-fetched and artificial metaphor, whose physical accuracy may not be impressive but whose aptness is most certainly a striking one. In the metaphor, the poem emphasises splendour and wealth, thereby associating the value which the birds have for each other with the ultimate source of all earthly wealth, and the strength of their love with the security which the ownership of such a source guarantees. The union of the two birds suggests itself as an analogue of the maintenance of a public, political order. This meaning is obviously reconcilable with the immediate context and, in fact, in this sense, "mine" might be taken as a conceit for the depth and availability of the love existing "Twixt this *Turtle* and his Queene" (31). This metaphysical reading accords perfectly with the convention of intellectual wit. It rediscovers, exalts, and reinforces a relationship within the external universe. This, I think, is the simplest and most natural interpretation of the word, and must be taken as its primary meaning, even though the idea itself is not elaborated.

There is, however, another kind of ambiguity in our original stanza that we have yet to examine. So far, we have assumed that it is the radiance of the "shining" Love that enables the Dove to "see" what he is committing to the Phoenix; that "his right" derives its "flame" from Love. But it is equally possible to construe a causal syntactic link between "Flaming" and "mine". The moment one notices a further reference of the word "mine", viz., "mineral" or "ore" (*OED*, s.v. *Mine*, sb. 2), one is able to appreciate another attempt by the poem to depict the force of the love between the two birds; that is, a metaphorical description of the natural spontaneity of their desire in the presence of each other. It may well be more appropriate to take it that the "flames" issue from these combustible "minerals". For, if so, this makes it easier to connect the action of "shining" with the later image of the birds as "starres of Loue" (51).

Moreover, there happens to be another connotation of "mine" which supports the meaning "mineral", and throws more light on the poem than any of the meanings adduced so far. In his poem *Providence*, Herbert expresses a unitary notion of the external universe, and celebrates the harmonious merging of animate and inanimate bodies in the Great Chain of Being:

> Frogs marry fish and flesh; bats, bird and
>   beast;
> Sponges, non-sense and sense; mines, th'earth
>   & plants.
>
> (135-36)[6]

"Mines" are said to "marry" earth and plants because they were thought to grow in the womb of the earth, where they formed metals in a protracted evolution which the alchemist tried to optimise inside his own laboratory. To the alchemist, a mine was primal, undifferentiated, elemental matter, or what in the technical jargon was called "remote" matter.[7] The following passages from *The Alchemist* will illustrate what I mean—we have good reason to believe that Jonson's play is a reliable and accurate record of some of the ideas of Renaissance alchemy:

> *Surly.*   The egg's ordained by nature to that
>   end,
> And is a chicken *in potentia*.
> *Subtle.*   The same we say of lead and other
>   metals,
> Which would be gold if they had time.
> *Mammon.*   And

> that
> Our art doth further.
> *Subtle.* Ay, for 'twere absurd
> To think that nature in the earth bred gold
> Perfect, i' the instant. Something went before.
> There must be remote matter.
>
> . . . . .
>
> Nor can this remote matter suddenly
> Progress so from extreme unto extreme,
> As to grow gold, and leap o'er all the means.
> Nature doth first beget th' imperfect' then
> Proceeds She to the perfect.
>
> (II.iii.133-40, 155-59)[8]

The "remote matter" in Shakespeare's poem is the heart (29), and, growing together, the "Hearts" of the two birds produce a perfect love instantaneously, as the phrase "no space" (30) suggests (cf. *Lr.* V.iii.54 and *Ant.* II.i.31). This esoteric language serves as an index to the extraordinary intimacy which the birds feel. The Turtle sees his natural potentiality—what he can become—being realised in the Phoenix's acceptance of his sacrifice. Also, in order to assert the uniqueness of their union, the poem takes natural possibility beyond its "extreme" in the eulogising understatement "But in them it were a wonder" (32), i.e., only in these two alone is such a perfect relationship not too "absurd" or irrational. (Reason, of course, can make nothing of their "artful" union.)[9] This alchemical association of the word "mine" is by no means an isolated image in the poem, and we shall go on to see some illuminating correspondences between *The Phoenix and Turtle* and practical alchemy. Indeed, this alchemical connection clarifies the mode of love in the entire poem.[10]

II

The practical aims of the Great Work were twofold: to transmute base metals into gold by means of the Philosophers' Stone or Elixir, and to confect "a universal medicine for the treating of all maladies" (Ruland, p. 369), the Elixir of eternal life. All perfectly proportioned material bodies were not subject to decay, and the Elixir could establish the balance of the basic elements in the human body, viz., Sulphur, Mercury, and Salt. Sulphur is characterised by fire, Mercury by fumes, and Salt by ash. It was an alchemical conviction that illness resulted from the in equilibrium of these three principles. According to the tenets of Hermetic philosophy, these three hypostatical principles are not chemical elements, but simply abstractions of certain human qualities. In addition, Sulphur is identified with the soul (*anima*), Mercury with the spirit (*spiritus*), and Salt with the body (*corpus*)[11]

Turning to *The Phoenix and Turtle*, we notice that its tripartite format roughly matches this doctrine of the three primary "substances". The first section, the Summons (1-20), emphasises the ideas of spirit or breath, particularly in words like "bird", "Herauld", "trumpet", "fiend", "death-deuining", and "breath", but also through its mood of sombre formality and ritual, and its sense of sympathetic unison. The second section of the poem, the Anthem (21-52), refers explicitly to fire. The third section, the Threnos (53-67), does not merely refer directly to ash, it reiterates the cycle of birth-procreation-death. And, co-operating with the "strictness" with which the birds are selected, the logically systematic movements of the three sections—"Let" (and its concomitant imperatives), "Here the Antheme doth commence", "So" (25, 33), "thus" (37), "That" (45), "Whereupon" (49)—regulate the poem, as if by a procedure being correctly followed in order to obtain a desired result.

Understandably, alchemists recognised the value of secrecy, and went so far as to devise systems of cryptic symbols for describing their apparatus and recording formulae and procedures, "to wrap up their *Secrets* in *Fables*, and spin out their *Fancies* in *Vailes* and *shadows*" (Ashmole, p. 440). For instance, if the "proven" technique was correctly performed, the alchemist expected to see the mixture go through a series of gradual changes, identifiable by a corresponding sequence of coded colours. There were three main stages in the process of the Great Work: the black, the white, and the red. At the first stage of the operation, the natural colours of the mixture are all turned black by heating. When the sublimate, or solid residue, reaches the white stage through more heating, it is capable of transmuting base metals into silver. Finally, at the red stage, it can transmute metals into gold. Now, each of these stages has its own set of symbols, among which birds are common: "The colours of the Great Work were often represented by birds, such as the crow (black), swan (white), and phoenix (red). The formation of a white sublimate was sometimes expressed by depicting a swan or dove in upward flight" (Read, p. 17). The eagle also symbolised sublimation.[12]

In *The Phoenix and Turtle*, the funereal imagery in the Summons corresponds to the black stage (*separatio, divisio, putrefactio*) in the making of the Elixir. In the Anthem, the description of the Dove, which is usually silver in colour, and of the Phoenix, which is usually gold, corresponds to the change from the predominance of the white stage to that of the red. It is not possible to say precisely at what stage during the Great Work the Elixir actually comes into being, but the presence of both "birds", white and red, is required, so that each seems to metamorphose the other in the action of their union.[13] According to A. E. Waite, "The constituent forces of the Elixir are harmonised and united, so that they overcome divided substances, compelling them to assume its own nature and relinquish that which was theirs".[14] Both "birds", then, are represented by the same "essence" (26), or qualitative extract, i.e., by the perfect part of their composite nature (Ruland, p. 137). The Anthem enigmatically enacts the central concern of alchemy, the process of *coniunctio*, in which the male and female principles of the universe unite. The Rebis or hermaphrodite is often used as an emblem of this union, and "marriage" is the term most frequently used to describe it.[15] The two "birds" mingled so "equally" (as Donne puts it in *The Good Morrow*) that the Phoenix ultimately resisted physical corruption;[16] that is, the mixture was so pure that the Elixir was achieved without leaving behind any residue of impurities: "Leauing no posteritie, / Twas not their infirmitie, / It was married Chastitie" (59-61). Finally, if *The Phoenix and Turtle* does have an allegorical harmony, then this alchemical figuration should persist until the end. The important image in the closing stanza is "vrne", which is the "nest of the fowl" for all alchemists, or in our poem "the *Phoenix* nest" (56), in other words the vessel in which the Great Work is performed; at the same time, the vessel is a mystical idea, symbolising fire. Inside the vessel is the Elixir or the new, perfected, "exalted" Phoenix.[17]

Without attempting to seek a comprehensive and consistent extrapolation from the sequence of birds in the poem to the symbols of alchemy, we can see that there are some suggestive correlations. Admittedly, the peacock, whose rainbow-coloured tail marks an intermediary phase in the Great Work, is absent. Also, the sexes of the birds seem to be reversed; in alchemical recipes, normally, the queen is white and the king red.[18] But what confirms the language of alchemy as at least an *imaginative* context for *The Phoenix and Turtle*, and strongly recommends that we take seriously the interpretation it offers, is the poem's structure of thought, feeling, and action, i.e., the energetic intensification and amplification given by the overall movement of the poem, which parallels the mounting tension in the alchemical operation. For it was also a common belief among alchemists that by repeating a successful procedure they increased the efficacy of the Elixir. Traditionally, the phoenix is the symbol of resurrection and immortality, and that is part of the significance of the phoenix's appearance in the opening stanza of this poem. It no longer represents simply the red stage of the Great Work, but is the finished product. The phoenix was actually one of many symbols for the Elixir (Ruland, p. 249). This "new" phoenix, then, is proof of the perfect purity that must be maintained in the other substances if the whole operation is to proceed successfully again.[19]

Equally cogent is the insistence in the Summons on purity and piety. Strictly speaking, there were two kinds of alchemy. One was practical, which was concerned with money and longevity. The other was mystical, and its aim was spiritual perfection. Moral purity and piety were prerequisites for success, and an alchemist had to be "A pious, holy, and religious man, / One free from mortal sin, a very virgin" (*Alch.* II.ii.98-99). Conversely, the practical transmutation of base metals became merely an emblematic analogue of the spiritual regeneration of sinful human nature. Alchemy was a high calling, and the Great Work an application of cabbalistic wisdom, the secrets of Creation itself.[20] As we saw earlier, it was a tenet of alchemy that the alchemist improved Nature. Theophrastus's *Book of Nature* contains one of the earliest explications of this theory: "Nature never produces that which is perfect, or that which is complete in its condition, but man has to complete it. This completing art is called alchemical" (Ruland, p. 99). Man himself, of course, is the most excellent part of Creation, but he is in no less need of a little alchemical "art". As serious alchemists were fully aware, actually attaining the Elixir would be of far less value, psychologically and morally, than striving after it (Holmyard, pp. 15, 156-59; Shumaker, p. 170).

The interpretation of the word "mine" in *The Phoenix and Turtle* which this discussion has yielded so far is that the word suggests the creative, mysterious, and exalting dynamic of human love. All that remains now is to reach an interpretation of the alchemical imagery that will be appropriate to the treatment of love within the poem as a whole.

III

In searching for a coherent context for this alchemical interpretation of "mine", we may begin by noticing that, on a theoretical level, the poem itself is an alchemical recipe. On the artistic level, however, the poem is neither mere description nor prescription, but the Elixir itself. The poem is "rightly placed" (*Alch.* II.iii.174), arranged in a way that is meant to educe human beings to their highest state of perfection.

The subdued tone of the poem's closing injunction engages the reader's heart and mind directly in an act of pious commemoration at a sepulchral shrine, an act which is meant to transform the reader's state of mind. When we arrive at the final stanza, we "project" our private moral values onto the values out of which the poem has been framed, and our "base" notions of love are thereby "transmuted" into a more enriched and spiritual form of relationship, an "heroic" love.[21]

The purpose and function of the poem's allegory is to involve us in this metaphysical process, to make us participate in it and so complete its movement; or, as Goddard says of Shakespeare's characteristic technique, the allegory incarnates the poem's "own image within everyone who genuinely comes to grips with it".[22] The

Threnos, for instance, must become part of a dialectical process if it is to fulfil its function in the poem. For the "essence" of Shakespeare's Elixir is the paradox, which, by its nature—working through verbal contradiction and surprise—provokes a response from the reader.[23] Paradox defies paraphrase or summary, so Reason's version of the poem's central paradox—the union of chastity and beauty, let us say—remains plausible only so long as it is not met and resisted. The reader is forced to make his own assessment of the central paradox—as he sees it—in order to complete the processes of the poem. The basic mode, then, of the poem's presentation of love is kinetic—rhetorically cathartic—since it demands an answering dramatisation of the reader's own moral being.

Finally, considering the points of connection between the three sections of the poem in relation to its alchemical register, one sees that the terms used to depict the alchemical vessel, *nest* and *vrne*, assimilate the elegiac procession of birds in the first section of the poem. Clearly, if the imaginative organisation of the poem has this allegorical progression from *nest* to *vrne*, birth to death, then any reading of stanza 9 ought to recognise that theme. And the reading I would offer is: that each bird was, at once, the source and goal of the other; each was necessary to the other because each created the need in the other, and fulfilled it. This reading not only supplements the ideas of worth and power, intention and potentiality, but also reinforces the ceremonial pulse of the first two sections of the poem. The whole stanza might then be paraphrased as follows: "Their love was so sure and strong that it enabled the Turtle to appreciate fully the part he was playing *in the making of* the new Phoenix".

Here, I think, is an experience of the reality of sexual love that is continuous with the intellectual and emotional impact of the Great Work itself. It is an experience of self-knowledge coming in a moment of responsible self-sacrifice, and it is the function of the poem's alchemical language to bring this out. The poem takes it upon itself to fashion and perfect the reader's humanity, and in that sense is redemptive. For the cumulative action of the poem is a kind of initiation into "eternitie", giving us a sense of freedom and illumination.[24] After drawing us into the burial of the two "dead Birds", the poem makes us feel stronger and rejuvenated, by resurrecting our idea of their true love into the world of the new Phoenix. In all its small proportions and short measures, *The Phoenix and Turtle* is Shakespeare's *Magnum Opus*.[25]

Notes

[1] E.g., Hallett Smith, introd. to the poem, in *The Riverside Shakespeare*, ed. G. Blakemore Evans (Boston: Houghton Mifflin, 1974), p. 1795, and Frank Kermode, "Shakespeare's Learning", in his *Renaissance Essays: Shakespeare, Spenser, Donne* (1971; London: Fontana, 1973), pp. 196-97.

[2] "'Essence' and the *Phoenix and Turtle*", *ELH*, 19 (1952), 265-76.

[3] All quotations of *PhT* are taken from *The Poems*, ed. H. E. Rollins, A New Variorum Ed. of Shakespeare (Philadelphia: Lippincott, 1938), pp. 323-31.

[4] F. T. Prince, ed., *The Poems*, The Arden Shakespeare (London: Methuen, 1960), pp. 181-82.

[5] See J. C. Maxwell, ed., *The Poems*, The New Shakespeare (Cambridge: Cambridge Univ. Press, 1966), p. 221. Cf. P. Dronke, "The Phoenix and the Turtle", *Orbis Litterarum*, 23 (1968), 217, and W. H. Matchett, *The Phoenix and the Turtle: Shakespeare's Poem and Chester's* Loues Martyr, Studies in English Lit., 1 (The Hague: Mouton, 1965), p. 43.

[6] *The English Poems of George Herbert*, ed. C. A. Patrides, Everyman's Univ. Lib., No. 1040 (London: Dent, 1974), p. 133. "Mine" also has a specific legal usage: see Jeremy Taylor, "The Marriage Ring", Sermon XVII.5.

[7] Martin Ruland the Elder, *A Lexicon of Alchemy* (Frankfurt, 1612), trans. A. E. Waite (1893; rpt. London: Watkins, 1964), pp. 398, 386-90; hereafter cited as Ruland.

[8] Ed. A. B. Kernan, The Yale Ben Jonson (New Haven: Yale Univ. Press, 1974), pp. 74-75. See J. Read, *The Alchemist in Life, Literature and Art* (London: Nelson, 1947), p. 40, and E. H. Duncan, "Jonson's *Alchemist* and the Literature of Alchemy", *PMLA*, 61 (1946), 699-710.

[9]
  Arte then what *Nature* left in hand doth take,
  And out of *One* a *Twofold* worke doth make.
  A *Twofold* worke doth make, but such a worke
  As doth admitt *Division* none at all
  (See here wherein the *Secret* most doth lurke)
  Unlesse it be a *Mathematicall*.
    It must be *Two*, yet make it *One* and *One*
    And you do take the way to make it *None*.

W. [R]edman, *Ænigma Philosophicum* [sic], ll. 5-12, rpt. in *Theatrum Chemicum Brittanicum*, ed. Elias Ashmole (London: Nath. Brooke, 1652), p. 423; hereafter cited as Ashmole.

[10] I am hardly the first to notice this link between *PhT* and the language of alchemy, but no one to my knowledge has explored the connection in any detail. R. G. Shahani, "The Phoenix and the Turtle", *N & Q*, 191

(1946), 122, and A. Alvarez, "William Shakespeare: *The Phoenix and the Turtle*", in *Interpretations: Essays on Twelve English Poems*, ed. J. Wain, 2nd ed. (London: Routledge, 1972), p. 13, and Dronke (p. 218) give only momentary recognition to the alchemical ring of the words "Simple" and "compounded". As a gloss on these words, the following extract from Roger Bacon's *Radix Mundi* is particularly apposite: "This is a great and certain truth, that the Clean ought to be separated from the Unclean, for nothing can give that which it has not: Forthe pure substance is of one simple Essence, void of all Heterogeneity: But that which is impure and unclean, consists of Heterogene parts, is not simple, but compounded (to wit of pure and impure) and apt to putrifie and corrupt" (trans. W. Salmon, *Practical Physick*, London: T. Howkins & J. Harris, 1692, Bk. III, Ch. xxxix, p. 590). Interestingly enough, the patron god of alchemy is Hermes the Herald, and the *arbor philosophica* is a favourite symbol for the alchemical process as a whole. See C. G. Jung, *Psychology and Alchemy*, trans. R. F. C. Hull, 2nd ed., The Collected Works of C. G. Jung, XII (London: Routledge, 1968), 420.

[11] J. M. Stillman, *The Story of Alchemy and Early Chemistry* (1924; rpt. New York: Dover, 1960), pp. 319-22; E. J. Holmyard, *Alchemy* (Harmondsworth: Penguin, 1957), p. 174.

[12] J. D. Mylius, *Philosophia reformata* (Frankfurt, 1622), rpt. in Jung, p. 373, fig. 200.

[13] Cf. Chapman's *Hero and Leander*:

> This place was mine: *Leander* Now t'is thine;
> Thou being my selfe, then it is double mine:
> Mine, and *Leanders* mine, *Leanders* mine.
> O see what wealth it yeelds me, nay yeelds him:
> For I am in it, he for me doth swim.
> Rich, fruitful I love, that doubling selfe estates
> *Elixer*-like contracts, though separates.
>   (III.411-17)

The Complete Works of Christopher Marlowe, ed. F. Bowers (Cambridge: Cambridge Univ. Press, 1973), II, 468. The red stage is sometimes called the "Mine of Celestial Fire" (Ruland, p. 398).

[14] *The Secret Tradition in Alchemy: Its Development and Records* (1926; London: Stuart & Watkins, 1969), pp. 99-100.

[15] Ruland, p. 394; Thomas Norton, *The Ordinall of Alchimy*, Ch. v, rpt. in Ashmole, p. 90; C. G. Jung, *Mysterium Coniunctionis: An Inquiry into the Separation and Synthesis of Psychic Opposites in Alchemy*, trans. R. F. C. Hull, The Collected Works of C. G. Jung, XIV (London: Routledge, 1963), 457; W. Shumaker, *The Occult Sciences in the Renaissance: A Study in Intellectual Patterns* (London: Univ. of California Press, 1972), pp. 178, 183. Cf. the 7th emblem in Lambsprinck's *De Lapide Philosophico Libellus* (Frankfurt, 1625), which depicts the same bird in two states of being, as both flying up from and falling back into its nest. The accompanying motto reads: "Duæ aves in sylva nominantur; / Cum tamen saltem una intelligatur" ("Two birds are called by name in the wood / Although only one should be understood by it", H. M. E. de Jong, *Michael Maier's* Atlanta Fugiens: *Sources of an Alchemical Book of Emblems*, Janus Suppléments, 8, Leiden: Brill, 1969, p. 91).

[16] *John Donne: The Complete English Poems*, ed. A. J. Smith, Penguin English Poets (Harmondsworth: Penguin, 1971), p. 60, l. 19. Editors and critics take the word "right" as it occurs in *PhT* at l. 16 as a key to its usage at l. 34, and arbitrarily assume that its meaning is, if not static, at least abstract. But "right" can also mean "territory, estate, dominion" (*OED*, s.v. Right, sb.¹, II.11.b). This usage may be rare, but it provides the semantic weight I suspect is lacking from the way we usually read the word in the context of the Turtle and his "Queene". I would suggest that the word be taken to mean the physical body or "domain" of the "royal" Turtle.

[17] Ruland, pp. 402, 434; Jung, *Psychology and Alchemy*, pp. 236-39. The association of phoenix and dove in alchemical illustrations lends some support to this interpretation. For instance, the depiction of the transmutation of elements in the 18th-century *Sapientia veterum philosophorum . . . de summa et universalis medicina*, Paris Bibl. de l'Arsenal MS. 974, esp. fig. xxxviii, vividly clarifies what I take to be the poem's underlying structure of thought, feeling, and action. For a facsim. rpt. of the figs., see S. K. de Rola, *Alchemy: The Secret Art* (London: Thames & Hudson, 1973), pp. 108-17, esp. Pl. 50.

[18] There is no consistency in the literary tradition of the phoenix (Jung, *Psychology and Alchemy*, pp. 228-32; Shumaker, pp. 181, 196). See also G. Wilson Knight, *The Mutual Flame: On Shakespeare's Sonnets and* The Phoenix and the Turtle (London: Methuen, 1955), pp. 151-55, Matchett, pp. 21-29, and W. Empson, "The Phoenix and the Turtle", *Essays in Criticism*, 16 (1966), 153.

[19] The phoenix was thought to spring as pure and fresh as "a young virgin out of her ashes" (Jonson, *Mercury Vindicated from the Alchemists at Court*, ll. 86-87, in *The Complete Masques*, ed. S. Orgel, The Yale Ben Jonson, New Haven: Yale Univ. Press, 1969, p. 217).

[20] A. G. Debus, "Alchemy", *Dictionary of the History of Ideas: Studies of Selected Pivotal Ideas*, ed. P. P. Wiener (New York: Scribners, 1973), I, 31-32.

[21] I use "heroic" in Bruno's sense of the word, describing not only the nature of love's aspiration but also its nobility. See P. E. Memmo, Jr., trans., *Giordano Bruno's* The Heroic Frenzies: *A Translation*, Studies in Romance Lang. and Lit., 50 (Chapel Hill: Univ. of N. Carolina Press, 1964), pp. 17-18.

[22] H. C. Goddard, *The Meaning of Shakespeare* (London: Univ. of Chicago Press, 1951), II, 151. Cf. A. Fletcher, *Allegory: The Theory of a Symbolic Mode* (Ithaca: Cornell Univ. Press, 1964), pp. 73-74.

[23] See A. E. Malloch, "The Technique and Function of the Renaissance Paradox", *Studies in Philology*, 53 (1956), 191-203, esp. 195.

[24] C. J. Jung, "The Idea of Redemption in Alchemy", in his *The Integration of the Personality*, trans. S. Dell (London: Kegan Paul, Trench, Trubner, 1940), Ch. v, p. 251; M. Eliade, *The Forge and The Crucible*, trans. S. Corrin (London: Rider, 1962), pp. 151-52. Matchett remarks on the theological overtones of "Grace" being suggestive of sanctification (p. 50), but does not explicitly connect this idea with the concept of redemption.

[25] Warm thanks to Timothy Cribb, Churchill Coll., Cambridge, for stimulating comments and helpful criticism.

FURTHER READING

Buxton, John. "Two Dead Birds: A Note on *The Phoenix and Turtle*." In *English Renaissance Studies: Presented to Dame Helen Gardner in honour of her Seventieth Birthday*, ed. John Carey, pp. 44-55. Oxford: Clarendon Press, 1980.

Contends that the poem should be read as "an exhibition of pure poetry" rather than a comment on the political atmosphere of the day.

Hume, Anthea. "*Love's Martyr*, 'The Phoenix and The Turtle,' and the Aftermath of the Essex Rebellion." *Review of English Studies* XL, No. 157 (February 1989): 48-71.

Reads 'The Phoenix and Turtle' as a close retelling of the Elizabethan Essex Rebellion.

Romeo and Juliet

For further information on the critical and stage history of *Romeo and Juliet*, see *SC*, Volumes 5, 11, and 33.

INTRODUCTION

One of Shakespeare's most popular plays, *Romeo and Juliet* continues to attract the attention of scholars interested in the ill-fated romance of its two young lovers. Set in medieval Italy, the drama details the clandestine love of Romeo Montague and Juliet Capulet, members of two feuding Veronese families. Because of this feud and the dictates of the day, which gave Juliet's father the right to promise her in marriage to any man of his choosing, Romeo and Juliet's secret marriage culminates in tragedy for both the couple and their families. Historical commentary on the work has focused on a variety of stylistic and design issues, and particularly its status as a successful tragedy. More recent scholarship has carried on another principal line of inquiry by concentrating on the tragic love between Romeo and Juliet. Attempts have been made by critics of the latter half of the twentieth century to understand Shakespeare's representation of love in *Romeo and Juliet*, especially in its social contexts. The significant juxtaposition of sexual desire and death has also been studied by scholars, as have the roles of language and gender in constructing the love affair.

Contemporary critics have offered numerous approaches to the passionate romance of Romeo and Juliet, assessing this subject as the central element in the play. Geoffrey Hutchings (1977) considers love as a force beset by social predicaments, human foibles, and the vicissitudes of fortune. He emphasizes Romeo's role as a sensitive, at times ridiculous, lover whose shared passion with Juliet is thwarted by the lovers' isolation and leads to disaster. R. Stamm (1986) examines the pivotal scene of Romeo and Juliet's first meeting, which Shakespeare presents in the form of a love sonnet. In addition to considering the importance of the words spoken during this encounter, Stamm highlights Shakespeare's use of gesture and touch to reveal the magnitude of passion between Romeo and Juliet. Barbara L. Estrin (1981) portrays the young couple as dreamers whose love stands as an ideal vision that awakens the self and transcends death.

The related nature of death and desire has been further investigated by critics of *Romeo and Juliet* who maintain that the work is a dramatic depiction of the *Liebestod* myth—a juxtaposition of romantic passion and death. Contradicting the point of view of many recent commentators who consider the deaths of Romeo and Juliet ironic or somehow justly deserved, William C. Carroll (1981) contends that the ending of the play—in which golden statues of the now-dead lovers are erected by their apparently contrite families—reveals the triumph of their passionate love over death. Lloyd Davis (1996) considers the rhetoric and poetic discourse of desire in *Romeo and Juliet*. According to Davis, the idealized romance in this tale of desire unfulfilled reveals itself to be tragically fatal, furthering the Renaissance theme of sex and death as inextricably intertwined.

The relationship between the action of *Romeo and Juliet* and the social components of love, desire, gender, and romance also figures prominently in contemporary criticism of the work. Catherine Belsey (1993) offers a cultural perception of the drama, in which she views the inherent contradictions of desire represented in the play's tragic outcome. Carolyn E. Brown (1986) observes the imagery of falcon and falconer as indicative of a unique gender dynamic, with Juliet adopting the role of master and Romeo that of her trained servant. Robert Appelbaum (1997) examines a related subject, that of masculinity in *Romeo and Juliet*. Appelbaum envisions the family rivalries as a violent and masculine assertion of the patriarchal symbolic order, to which Romeo offers an alternative in the form of erotic desire, but from which he cannot escape. Susan Snyder (1996) also closely examines the feud between the Montagues and Capulets as a central concern. According to Snyder, this feud may be interpreted as a metaphor for ideology, which seems to pervade the drama of Romeo and Juliet's love.

LOVE AND ROMANCE

Geoffrey Hutchings (essay date 1977)

SOURCE: "Love and Grace in *Romeo and Juliet*," in *English Studies in Africa,* Vol. 20, No. 2, September, 1977, pp. 95-106.

[*In the following essay, Hutchings considers* Romeo and Juliet *"a study of love and passion" in a social context.*]

In the Prologue Shakespeare summarizes his plot; we know what to expect. He also tells us what sort of play he is writing: a story of love overthrown by misadventure in the context of social hatreds, and not an Aristotelian tragedy.[1]

Shakespeare was beginning to exploit the idea that lovers are essentially vulnerable in a wicked world. Paradoxically, just because love "beareth all things, believeth all things, hopeth all things, endureth all things", those who love are vulnerable. Indeed, if I may, in discussing so punning a play, make my own very serious word play, love *bareth* all things in both senses of the verb; and what is bare is vulnerable. In later plays, whether the outcome is comic or tragic or delicately ambivalent, this vulnerability accompanies love; and often true love itself is most vulnerable to the counterfeit emotions with which the unwary may confuse it—mere physical passion, lust for power, narcissistic self-indulgence. All of these counterfeits are powerfully presented in *Othello,* for example, or in the single character of Malvolio in *Twelfth Night.* And this is a theme running not only through Shakespeare but through all western literature, for, as Denis de Rougemont wisely observed, "Happy love has no history—in European literature."[2]

In *Romeo and Juliet* we have a study of love and passion. This love is essentially domestic and sexual. We do not have, as in *King Lear,* a profound examination of great theological issues. But the play does take love very seriously, and places it in a social context where first it offers hope, as Friar Laurence is quick to see; where it suffers isolation and death; and finally where it achieves, in death, a reconciliation, "a glooming peace". Friar Laurence's passionate rebuke to the grief-stricken Romeo conveys the seriousness:

> Why railest thou on thy birth, the heaven, and
>   earth?
> Since birth and heaven and earth, all three,
>   do meet
> In thee at once; which thou at once wouldst lose.
> Fie, fie, thou shamest thy shape, thy love, thy
>   wit,
> Which, like a usurer, aboundest in all,
> And usest none in that true use indeed
> Which should bedeck thy shape, thy love, thy wit.
> Thy noble shape is but a form of wax,
> Disgressing from the valour of a man;
> Thy dear love sworn but hollow perjury,
> Killing that love which thou hast vowed to
>   cherish;
> Thy wit, that ornament to shape and love,
> Misshapen in the conduct of them both,
> Like powder in a skilless soldier's flask
> Is set afire by thine own ignorance,
> And thou dismembered with thine own
>   defence.
> What, rouse thee, man! Thy Juliet is alive.
> (III.iii.119ff.)

This play is not simply a moving tale of *Liebestod;* it is based upon more than a romantic death-wish: to love is to be responsible.

I shall discuss the play as a dramatic account of the nature of love; love beset, as it must be, by social conventions, accidents, laughter, hatreds, hypocrisies, lies, lusts and prurience. The predicament and the very identities of the two "star-crossed lovers" must therefore be defined in the context of, and in contrast to their community and their friends. For a proper consideration of *character* in the theatre is a consideration of *dramatic function.* The didactic principle I am aiming at is that good analysis of the play is a synthesis of the characters, and analysis of character is a synthesis of the play.

Let us consider first the setting of the lovers' stage. They are brought together in that beautiful sonnet duologue in Act 1, Scene 5. How are we prepared for this? The prologue, to which I have already referred, is at once frame and summary. Appropriately its formality provides a link between the dramatist and his company on the one hand, and the spectators on the other: the plot is given in eight lines, the octave of the sonnet. The diction provides an indication of the thematic treatment we can expect. The repetition of *civil* in "civil blood makes civil hands unclean" underlines the socially significant setting and establishes an ironical contrast between the aspirations of polite, that is, civilized society and actual conduct. We might compare with this Capulet's generous promise to Paris that his will in the matter of his daughter's marriage will wait upon her consent (I:ii.17ff); and also Juliet's later promise to her mother of dutiful consent to her parents' wisdom of choice (I.iii.98ff.). But passion is to betray both Capulet's generosity and Juliet's duty.

"A pair of star-crossed lovers" they are called. They are to be hunted down by fate. The portents of that fate are numerous. At different times before the bloodshed starts we are warned by Tybalt, an unreliable witness; by Friar Laurence, a thoroughly reliable witness; and even by the lovers themselves of impending disaster. And that disaster will be achieved in misadventure; at a crucial moment a messenger is delayed by pestilence and cannot deliver his missive. As a dramatic device it would be feeble, at best melodramatic; but it is not a dramatic device. Unlike some film directors, Shakespeare does not even show this incident on stage. It is a small link in a chain of events; just as, when deep social discontent erupts into riot on the flimsiest excuse, it is not the excuse that matters but the discontent. These lovers "take their life" at the end as they took their life at the beginning: "From forth the fatal loins of these two foes". Theirs is the civil blood that pays the price of ancient grudge. The guilt for these piteous overthrows is social. Love and procreation is responsibility.

The sestet of the opening chorus then prepares the way from the mere story to the dramatic spectacle. I like Shakespeare's request to his audience for "patient ears" to match the toil of the players. Dramatic experience demands effort from players and spectators alike.

We are taken straight into a scene at once comic and brutal. The Capulet servants are obsessed with violence and bawdry; indeed the two are not distinguished. Loins, we see, are fatal in many respects. The impulse that "will push Montague's men from the wall" is the same as that that will "thrust his maids to the wall". At the sight of the Montague servants, Sampson boasts "My naked weapon is out." Despite appearances, it is neither good, nor clean, nor fun. Disturbingly, we find that the ancient grudge has become a servants' quarrel; Capulet and Montague are themselves too old to do more than rail. Among the younger gentlefolk, some, like Benvolio, are peace-makers, and some, like "the fiery Tybalt", are quarrellers. But the gentlefolk have little influence; it is the servants and the citizens who riot, to the exasperation of their governor, the Prince.

And only after the Prince's fury has curbed the riot is there any mention of Romeo. A mood, a scene has been set and yet Romeo is not completely part of it. Both the sense and the sound of his mother's rhyming couplet herald a shift of dramatic mood.

> O where is Romeo? Saw you him today?
> Right glad I am he was not at this fray.
> (I.i.116f.)

Benvolio, although he does not speak in rhyming couplets, completes this shift as he describes in delicate, ornate verse the artifice of his friend's passion:

> Madam, an hour before the worshipped sun
> Peered forth the golden window of the East,
> A troubled mind drave me to walk abroad;
> Where, underneath the grove of sycamore
> That westward rooteth from this city side,
> So early walking did I see your son.
> (I.i.118ff.)

How clever of Romeo to be found under a sycamore tree! He is identified with the popular Elizabethan song of unrequited love "A poor soul sat sighing by a sycamore tree". (Shakespeare was to use the song with great effect in *Othello*.) The artificiality of Benvolio's verse reflects the convention of Renaissance love poetry, for the term "artificial" carried far fewer pejorative overtones for the Elizabethans than it does for us. But Benvolio's lines are clearly marked in their artificiality by contrast with the direct power of the Prince's eloquence just heard:

> Three civil brawls, bred of an airy word
> By thee, old Capulet, and Montague,
> Have thrice disturbed the quiet of our streets
> And made Verona's ancient citizens
> Cast by their grave-bessiming ornaments
> To wield old partisans, in hands as old,
> Cankered with peace, to part your cankered hate.
> If ever you disturb our streets again,
> Your lives shall pay the forfeit of the peace.
> (I.i.89ff.)

Montague himself, commenting on his son's behaviour just before the entrance of Romeo, speaks feelingly and simply of his concern, but with portentous dramatic irony. Using an image deep in the mind of European art he talks of Romeo:

> As is the bud bit with an envious worm
> Ere he can spread his sweet leaves to the air
> Or dedicate his beauty to the sun.
> (I.i.151ff.)

Blake used a very similar image to suggest guilt and beauty in "O Rose, thou art sick", and garden imagery, with its echoes of Eden, runs through all our folk song, that most fundamental part of our literature. Caroline Spurgeon has said that Shakespeare "visualises human beings as plants and trees, choked with weeds, or well primed and trained and bearing ripe fruits, sweet smelling as a rose or noxious as a weed".[3] The image is important because it links back to the sort of concerns with rank disorder that have been established before Romeo's entrance, and forward to such scenes as Friar Laurence's culling herbs in his garden in the early morning after we have witnessed Romeo and Juliet declaring their love. Passion can wither the plant; it needs the orderly cultivation of a wise gardener to help it grow in love.

Romeo, when he enters, is ridiculous; a very conventional melancholic lover. His first long speech is an anthology of the conventional paradoxes of love poetry. The theatre audience knows that he will soon be thrust into a situation where such paradoxes as "brawling love" and "loving hate" have real point, but right now he is a poseur playing a word-game with well-known rules: "Feather of lead, bright smoke, cold fire, sick health" (I.i.180). Until either his own natural wit or a twitch of Benvolio's brings him close to his senses it might well be asked "Dost thou not laugh?" If a lover is to play his role thoroughly he might as well have the misunderstanding and even mockery of his friends. That, too, is in the script. Not surprisingly, Romeo breaks into couplets:

> Griefs of mine own lie heavy in my breast
> Which thou wilt propagate, to have it pressed
> With more of thine. This love that thou has shown
> Doth add more grief to too much of mine own.

> Love is a smoke made with the fume of
>   sighs;
> Being purged, a fire sparkling in lovers' eyes;
> Being vexed, a sea nourished with lovers' tears.
> What is it else?

He is running out of steam; or is his memory failing?

>   A madness most discreet,
> A choking gall and a preserving sweet.
> Farewell my coz.

Benvolio is swept into rhyme himself as he says,

>   Soft! I will go along.
> And if you leave me so, you do me wrong.

It is an elegant joke, for Benvolio is twitting Romeo in lover's lingo. But Romeo's next remark reveals an honesty and a deeper insight into his own condition:

>   Tut, I have left myself, I am not here.
>   This is not Romeo, he's some other where.
>   (I.i.186ff.)

This self-absorbed posturing is a counterfeit of love, and as a context, as a garden in which to cultivate love, no more promising than the violence and bawdry with which the scene opened.

The next scene, Act 1, Scene 2, contains the first mention of Juliet. Again it emerges that the feud is no longer actively fostered by Capulet as the head of his house. He, rather, is concerned with the dynastic side of his responsibilities. When Paris presses his suit, old Capulet is conscious that his daughter is a highly desirable match:

> Earth hath swallowed all my hopes but she;
> She's the hopeful lady of my earth.
>   (I.ii.14f.)

He anticipates a good match for her, but is in no hurry to arrange it, a view that changes later when Tybalt's death underlines the sudden brevity of life.

When Benvolio and Romeo again appear, Benvolio is trying to persuade Romeo to turn his attention elsewhere than to Juliet. His advice is practical, commonplace and cynical:

>   Tut, man, one fire burns out another's burning,
>   One pain is lessened by another's anguish.
>   Turn giddy, and be holp by backward turning.
>   One desperate grief cures with another's
>   languish.
>   Take thou some new infection to thy eye,
>   And the rank poison of the old will die.
>   (I.ii.45ff.)

This cynicism is only the other side of the coin to Romeo's infatuation and it became very common in early seventeenth-century poetry. In spirit it is very like Suckling:

>   Out upon it, I have lov'd
>   Three whole days together;
>   And am like to love three more,
>   If it prove fair weather.

Benvolio has slipped into one of the commonest verse-forms of the age, the six-line stanza consisting of a quatrain followed by a rhyming couplet. It was a form that admirably served the fashionable madrigalists of the day. Romeo rebuts the argument in the same coin:

> When the devout religion of mine eye
> Maintains such falsehood, then turn tears to
>   fires;
> And these, who, often drowned, could never
>   die
> Transparent heretics, be burnt for liars!
> One fairer than my love? The all-seeing
>   sun
> Ne'er saw her match since first the world
>   begun.
>   (I.ii.88ff.)

The next time Romeo talks about devout religion in love, is when he and Juliet are making their sonnet about holy palmers' kisses. It is admittedly less conventional, more moving verse, but partly so because at last we believe him. We have been led to that moment. No wonder Friar Laurence is concerned with the suddenness of Romeo's changes. No wonder he wants, for political reasons, and out of love for Romeo to confer on the passion of the lovers the grace and responsibility of matrimony.

But Juliet must be introduced to the audience before she can meet Romeo. The scene that introduces her, however, is dominated by the Nurse. Juliet emerges as affectionate and dutiful, but she is given no more than six lines in this scene (Act 1, Scene 3) before, two scenes later, she encounters Romeo. How is the quick-witted, passionate, rather knowing young girl whom we see later related to this scene? It is a challenge to the director and to the actress who plays Juliet; for, in this scene, Juliet must be depicted and defined by her reactions to those who surround her. And the Nurse is the dominating character. The Nurse also dominates Lady Capulet, that rather waspish character. This serves the useful dramatic purpose of establishing for Juliet a confidante who does not represent parental authority. Lady Capulet, it is clear, has delegated a good number of her parental responsibilities to the Nurse. Juliet has been wet-nursed and brought up by this garrulous old earth-mother, whose first utterance is to swear by her "maidenhead at twelve year old". Charac-

*Act I, scene v. A Hall in Capulet's House. Romeo, Juliet, Nurse, Guests and Maskers.
Painted by William Miller. University of Michigan Library.*

teristic. Juliet at nearly fourteen, it appears, is not as experienced as her Nurse had been. The Nurse, like the other servants, is bawdy. Her heartiness is no doubt preferable to their violence, but passion is no less appetite for her than for them, and no less obsessive. Her husband, "God be with his soul, A' was a merry man", seems to have had a pretty uncomplicated notion of educating women to fit their station in life. "Thou wilt fall backward when thou hast more wit", he had said to the infant Juliet, and the Nurse finds the child's grave "Ay" killingly funny. It is rather like a modern pantomime: the adults entertain themselves at the expense of the children by devising a bawdy entertainment that can be taken in what sense thou wilt. And now that Juliet is nearly fourteen she can share the joke with her Nurse. Juliet is isolated even here at the outset. To her, marriage is "an honour that I dream not of" (I.iii.67); to Lady Capulet it is a dynastic necessity, and to the Nurse it is bed and babies. I do not think Shakespeare is denying the force of the views of the two adults, but Juliet clearly expects more.

As Juliet has her Nurse, so Romeo has Mercutio. But in Mercutio we find a wit, a vitality and a charm that leave even the Nurse a pale character by comparison. They have their bawdy minds in common, but where the Nurse plods, Mercutio skips and romps and gallops. Mercutio is the young Renaissance gallant; he is thoroughly familiar with the conventions of polite society (even his fencing is a match for that of the fiery Tybalt) but he is also a sceptic, he sees through those conventions. And as the Nurse dominates her scene, so, even more powerfully, does Mercutio his. Romeo's own wit is but a foil to Mercutio's; chronic punster and quibbler that he is, Romeo seems at times content merely to tempt Mercutio to display his verbal virtuosity, as when he says:

> Is love a tender thing? It is too rough,
> Too rude, too boisterous, and it pricks like
>   thorn.

Mercutio, as he is meant to, picks up the suggestion.

> If love be rough with you, be rough with love.
> Prick love for pricking, and you beat love down.
>
> (I.iv.25ff.)

Moments later he is launched into his Queen Mab speech. It is inspired fooling, witty, superbly inventive and shows a marvellous control of language, again by its vigour and originality exposing Romeo's effete languishing. It is the speech of a sceptic: aldermen, lovers, lawyers, ladies, courtiers, parsons, soldiers, the very pillars of society, are all mocked skilfully. When Romeo interrupts, and accuses him, "Thou talkest of nothing" (I.iv.106), he consigns his speech to "vain fantasy, which is as thin of substance as the air". But there are many dimensions to the fantasy. Queen Mab and her fairies represent whim, frustration, misfortune, whatever mortals cannot account for either in rational understanding or in systematic belief. Morally they are ambivalent; there is certainly something arbitrarily malevolent about them, as we can see in *A Midsummer Night's Dream*. Awareness of this malevolence gives to Mercutio his aggressive edge. And there seems to be something deeply melancholic in Mercutio, for all his vigour. Unlike Romeo's it is not a contrived melancholy, but the melancholy of the sceptic, caught up in, and yet distrusting the institutions of society.

Romeo is sensitive to the tenseness of the situation, and just before the young men enter the enemy's ballroom he shows himself without affectation:

> . . . my mind misgives
> Some consequence, yet hanging in the stars,
> Shall bitterly begin his fearful date
> With this night's revels and expire the term
> Of a despisèd life, closed in my breast,
> By some vile forfeit of untimely death.
> But He that hath the steerage of my course
> Direct my sail! On, lusty gentlemen!
>
> (I.iv.106ff.)

A wonderful piece of theatre, this. We have dancers, weaving in and out of the light, men and women engaged in normal social intercourse, that "necessary conjunction which betokeneth concord" that Sir Thomas Elyot had commended in his *Governor* (and which his descendant T. S. Eliot quoted in *East Coker*). Romeo's language is elevated and ornate, but beginning now to shed the stilted phrasing of his earlier infatuation. He uses the imagery of light and dark which is Shakespeare's continuously repeated image in this play, his *leitmotiv*.

> It seems she hangs upon the cheek of night
> As a rich jewel in an Ethiop's ear.
>
> (I.v.45f.)

And as the dancers move and the lovers become aware of each other, Tybalt rages and sends for his rapier. Light and dark indeed. Old Capulet shows himself generous towards Romeo but at the same time extremely touchy about his authority. And seconds before the lovers meet to compose their sonnet of awakened love, Tybalt has stormed out on two portentous couplets:

> Patience perforce with wilful choler meeting
> Makes my flesh tremble in their different greeting.
> I will withdraw. But this intrusion shall,
> Now seeming sweet, convert to bitterest gall.
>
> (I.v.89ff.)

Thus he echoes Romeo's misgivings. The scene is set, the forces marshalled, and the drama now must run its course.

The moment of this meeting is now ritualized in a dramatic sonnet, Romeo offering a quatrain and Juliet a quatrain. Then their lines are mingled through to the final couplet which they share. The sonnet elegantly traces the progress and passion of their physical contact and—I repeat—ritualizes it. The ceremony is so enchanting that they start afresh, though this time they are interrupted by the Nurse at the end of a quatrain, Juliet having justly commented on the literary achievements of them both, "You kiss by the book."

My obvious interest in the verse-forms of *Romeo and Juliet* is not just a pedantic preoccupation with technical details; it is more importantly a concern for dramatic detail. An Elizabethan audience must have been responsive to these modulations, and since they take such obvious physical forms as rhyme-patterns, they should strike our ears too and set our minds alert for their importance. This importance I have tried to show wherever I have referred to the verse forms. We cannot divine the importance by the application of trite formulas, like rhyming couplets mean formality, and madrigal stanzas signal insincerity. The immediate context, rather, will supply us clues. My claim is simply that a modulation of verse form signals *something*, a modulation of mood or emphasis, for example. In this dramatic sonnet bedded in the dialogue of an important scene we can sense the ritual significance of a meeting. The protagonists are changed permanently by it. The sonnet makes a ceremony of the change, and formalizes it in ritual, directing the lovers' concomitant actions. It is dramatic justification of Yeats's great lines,

> How but in custom and in ceremony
> Are innocence and beauty born?

Once it is past, the play continues, accelerates in fact. It is surely significant that when the lovers start the ritual again, they are interrupted and the consequences of the ceremony begin to become apparent. Romeo and Juliet are quickly isolated. In revealing Juliet's identity to Romeo, the Nurse is true to bawdy form, and places in addition an unpleasant emphasis on Juliet's status as an heiress:

> I tell you, he that can lay hold of her
> Shall have the chinks.

Romeo underlines his isolation by taking the pecuniary image and developing it in his own sense:

> Is she a Capulet?
> O dear account! My life is my foe's debt.
> (I.v.116ff.)

The love now created between Romeo and Juliet is exposed to the howling storms of its social context. It is interesting to compare this play to *Othello,* where we witness the tragedy of a noble love, founded on domestic virtue, destroyed. John Danby has observed that the good in the relationship between Othello and Desdemona requires "a community of goodness in which to be permanent. It is vulnerable so long as there is anywhere around it the intention to wound."[4] This intention arises in what I see as a profound sense of sexual alienation in Iago. He is completely obsessed with sex as appetite, as self-gratification, and he destroys Othello by playing on this theme. The community on Cyprus is poisoned by barrack-room smut. Even a decent enough person like Cassio is infected, and discusses his whore in terms that degrade both her and himself. And Emilia, for all her fondness for Desdemona, cannot help because she too is infected by the alienation. Of men she says

> They are all but stomachs and we all but food;
> They eat us hungerly, and when they are full
> They belch us.
> (III.iv.108ff.)

Desdemona cannot communicate her sense of love to anyone on the island. The community cannot sustain it.

Do we have any such case in *Romeo and Juliet?* The violent smut of the servants in the opening scene could well fit into the garrison barracks on Cyprus, though it is less obsessive than Iago's. But we surely cannot identify the gay bawdry of Mercutio or of the Nurse with Iago's obsessions. Apart from anything else, Mercutio and the Nurse are very funny. This raises the old question of the distinction between bawdry and filth. I cannot account for it very well in the abstract, though I feel intuitively there ought to be a distinction. Here is Mercutio:

> The ape is dead, and I must conjure him.
> I conjure thee by Rosaline's bright eyes,
> By her high forehead and her scarlet lip,
> By her fine foot, straight leg, and quivering thigh,
> And the demesnes that there adjacent lie.
> (II.i.16ff.)

Romeo's mad humours have thoroughly deserved this mockery. Besides the phallic fantasies of Cupid's darts, and the flaccid cliché of conventional love-poetry, Mercutio's is honest realism—of a sort. And certainly there is no intent to wound, which would distinguish Mercutio from the Capulet servants. But is intention alone a valid criterion? Benvolio warns Mercutio, "An if he hear thee, thou wilt anger him" (22), to which Mercutio replies:

> This cannot anger him. 'Twould anger him
> To raise a spirit in his mistress' circle
> Of some strange nature, letting it there stand
> Till she had laid it and conjured it down.
> That were some spite.
> (II.i.23ff.)

And after more bawdry, they give up the search for Romeo, who enters the garden to find Juliet.

But why, we must ask, has Shakespeare given Romeo these friends, and why has he put this scene between the lovers' first meeting at the ball and their second in the garden? Modern audiences, in my experience, find the garden scene movingly comic, a reaction well exploited in the famous 1960 production by Franco Zeffirelli at the Old Vic. If the Romeo of the early scenes is a rather effete young man playing at love, Juliet has now released in him a more direct, lusty, impulsive energy. Zeffirelli had Romeo speak his lines with an urgent intensity, and shin lithely up and down the balcony half a dozen times to say his farewells. The audience was rocked with a gentle, wry, sympathetic laughter, a reaction, surely, to the lovers' vulnerability. A Romeo transformed, as his friends later recognize, is surely a reading of the character better warranted by the text and by dramatic necessity than languid romantic Romeos of the fashion earlier in this century. And so the juxtapositions of scene in Act 2 serve to contrast phallic comedy with romantic comedy, and these two sorts of comedy are in turn contrasted with the darker parts of the play. In fact, the most pungent comedy is never very far from tragedy, as we can see elsewhere in Shakespeare, in Chaucer, Chekhov, Dickens and the Mozart of the great operas.

What is achieved in all these contrasts? Perhaps, in a sense Mercutio is right. Bawdy talk cannot anger Romeo; he now loves and is beloved in earnest. The sort of de-personalized obsession with physical appetite that characterizes bawdy talk and that sometimes counteracts the insincerity of many common attitudes to love, is a different sort of emotion entirely from that now aroused in Romeo. Romeo is learning a new dimension to himself, skilfully guided by Juliet's instincts. In the balcony scene he is still tied to the rhetoric of love, and Juliet has to school him beyond the mere conventions. She well knows what she is doing and how far it exposes her:

> O gentle Romeo,
> If thou dost love, pronounce it faithfully.
> Or if thou thinkest I am too quickly won,
> I'll frown, and be perverse, and say thee nay,
> So thou wilt woo. But else, not for the world.
>
> (II.ii.93ff.)

Romeo's reply to this is passionate rhetoric:

> By yonder blessèd moon I vow . . .

But Juliet cuts him short—

> O, swear not by the moon, th' inconstant moon,
> That monthly changes in her circled orb,
> Lest that thy love prove likewise variable.
>
> . . . . .
>
> Do not swear at all
> Or if thou wilt, swear by thy gracious self,
> Which is the god of my idolatry,
> And I'll believe thee.
>
> (II.ii.109ff.)

Juliet's directness is magnificent. It is she who proposes marriage. But since she is neither brazen nor falsely modest, she has no need of bawdry, which is one of our defences against false modesty. Mercutio and his friends represent that defence, and remind us that the lovers exist in a society which needs such defences. Romeo and Juliet are learning a brighter existence. Teilhard de Chardin put it very beautifully:

> The only right love is that between couples whose passion leads them both, one through the other, to a higher possession of their being. The gravity of offences gainst love therefore is not that they outrage some modesty or virtue. It is that they fritter away, by neglect or lust, the universe's reserves of personalization.[5]

When Romeo returns to his friends he joins in with their high spirits and, after some verbal duels with Mercutio, evokes this compliment from Mercutio:

> Why is not this better now than groaning for love? Now thou art sociable. Now art thou Romeo. Now art thou what thou art, by art as well as by nature.
>
> (II.iv.86ff.)

This reminds us of Romeo's earlier observation, "This is not Romeo, he's some other where" (I.i.197). But being sociable has social consequences. Though Romeo does not confide his love to any friend but Friar Laurence, he is drawn into the web of hatred, obligations, honour and revenge that a corrupt society has spun for him. The tragedy begins. Romeo is isolated inspirit and then physically banished by society. With Mercutio's death, and the plague he bestows on both houses in the feud, the young gallants part company. Even good, sane Benvolio disappears.

Juliet too is isolated, even from her Nurse. For all the Nurse's human warmth, she fails Juliet in the crisis. For the Nurse has no resources beyond her earthy humour. And that humour serves well enough in ordinary circumstances but not in a crisis. Her upbringing has left Juliet a very direct person. But she expects more of life than does the Nurse. While the Nurse is bawdy, Juliet is truly sensual, passionate, and even so she is properly modest. In love she attains that higher possession of her being that Teilhard spoke of:

> Spread thy close curtain, love-performing night,
> That runaway's eyes may wink, and Romeo
> Leap to these arms, untalked of and unseen.
> Lovers can see to do their amorous rites
> By their own beauties; or, if love be blind,
> It best agrees with night. Come, civil night,
> Thou sober-suited matron, all in black,
> And learn me how to lose a winning match,
> Played for a pair of stainless maidenhoods.
> Hood my unmanned blood, bating in my cheeks,
> With thy black mantle till strange love grow bold,
> Think true love acted simple modesty.
> Come, night. Come, Romeo. Come, thou day in night;
> For thou wilt lie upon the wings of night
> Whiter than new snow upon a raven's back.
> Come, gentle night.
>
> (III.ii.5ff.)

"Think true love acted simple modesty." But the social context will not bear such lovely, simple modesty. Even as Juliet speaks, the audience knows Mercutio and Tybalt are dead and Romeo banished. The Nurse is undiscriminating in her grief. Her habit of keeping Juliet in suspense for any news now leads her to burble on about "Tybalt, the best friend I had". Hyperbole is an ineradicable quality of her mind.

But look where her garrulousness leads her:

> There's no trust,
> No faith, no honesty in men; all perjured,
> All forsworn, all naught, all dissemblers.

> Ah, where's my man? Give me some aqua
>   vitae.
> These griefs, these woes, these sorrows make
>   me old.
> Shame come to Romeo!

Is not this somewhere close to Emilia's rancour, "They are all but stomachs and we all but food"? Juliet swiftly rebukes the Nurse:

> Blistered be thy tongue
> For such a wish! He was not born to
>   shame.
> Upon his brow shame is ashamed to sit.
>   (III.ii.85ff.)

And in her grief she later utters the thought that will be echoed like a *motiv* by her father when she has died, and by Romeo when he sees her in the tomb:

> . . . I'll to my wedding-bed,
> And death, not Romeo, take my maidenhead.
>   (III.ii.136ff.)

Denis de Rougemont sees this as yet another chapter in the celebration of *Liebestod*—an identity of love and death—in European literature. But I think he is wrong. Romeo and Juliet are brought to passionate life in their love. Their marriage is consummated, and the consummation symbolized in the beautiful poetry of the scene in the wedding-bed. But that bed is turned by external pressures, by cankered hate in society, into a sacrificial altar.

Juliet is isolated further by the marriage her father would arrange with Paris, and by her Nurse's readiness to temporize:

> I think you are happy in this second match,
> For it excels your first.
>   (III.v.223f.)

When the reserves of personalization have been frittered away by neglect or mere lust, one man is very much like another. Did not Emilia say as much to Desdemona?

> And have we not affections,
> Desires for sport, and frailty, as men have?
>   (*Othello*, IV.iii.101f.)

The comedy is over. Juliet recognizes her Nurse's advice for what it is, and finds herself isolated:

> Ancient damnation! O most wicked fiend!
>   (III.v.236f.)

Friar Laurence's goodness fumbles, and is not enough to save her. The rest of the play deals with the consequences of her isolation, the exploitation of her vulnerability.

Notes

[1] This paper was first delivered as a lecture at the 1976 Grahamstown Shakespeare Conference.

[2] Denis de Rougemont, *Passion and Society* (London: Faber, 1956), p. 52.

[3] Caroline Spurgeon, *Shakespeare's Imagery and What It Tells Us* (Cambridge: Cambridge Univ. Press, 1966), p. 19.

[4] John F. Danby, *Shakespeare's Doctrine of Nature: a Study of King Lear* (London: Faber 1961), p. 164.

[5] Pierre Teilhard de Chardin, *Human Energy* (London: Collins, 1969), pp. 74-5.

Barbara L. Estrin (essay date 1981)

SOURCE: "*Romeo and Juliet* and the Art of Naming Love," in *Ariel: A Review of International English Literature,* Vol. 12, No. 2, April, 1981, pp. 31-49.

[*In the following essay, Estrin probes Romeo and Juliet's vision of love and their efforts to realize this vision.*]

In Act II of *Romeo and Juliet,* Mercutio defines the successful man, incorrectly assuming that Romeo's recovered wit signals the decline of his infatuation for Rosaline:

> Why is this better now than groaning for love? now
> art thou sociable, now art thou Romeo; now art thou
> what thou art, by art as well as by nature: For this
> drivelling love is like a great natural that runs lolling
> up and down to hide his bauble in a hole.[1]

To be Romeo at his best is to have acquired distance from the amorous situation and to have "separate[d]" himself, as Pyrocles admonishes Musidorus in the *Arcadia,* "a little from himself," so that his "own mind may look upon [his] own proceedings."[2] The capacity for reason distinguishes man from the beasts, raising him above all other creatures. Groaning, drivelling and lolling are mannerisms of a "natural," one who feels victimized by, rather than master of, his situation. Sociability, as a manifestation of reason, signals for Mercutio the measure of manhood. Conversely, love marks a retreat from the art of forming, and so becoming, fully what man was destined to be. To "hide" is to fail to evince the jewel of the complete, and hence fully alive, self.

When, in Act III, he affirms the gravity of his wound as he slips into the death hole from which he tried to extract Romeo, Mercutio makes the figure of his speech literal by facing the very fate he feared:

> Ask for me tomorrow, and you shall find me a grave man. I am peppered, I warrant, for this world. A plague a both your houses! Zounds, a dog, a rat, a mouse, a cat, to scratch a man to death!
>
> (III.i.98-105)

"Peppered," "sped" (III.i.92) "scratched" by death, as he claimed Romeo had been "stabbed . . . run through" (II.iv.15) and cleft (II.iv.16) by love, Mercutio is badgered into the grave, rendered solemn instead of witty, made the steward ("grave," *N.E.D.* IV, p. 374), instead of the owner of his being. His presence in the play demands that the flatness of nature be enriched by the fulness of art. His injury reduces him to the animal—dog, rat, mouse, cat—he hoped to overcome.

For Mercutio, art is the opposite of death because it stabilizes the self, confirming man's formulative presence in the universe. Art makes the whole self visible by completing nature. At the opposite extreme is the dream which begins by depleting nature to foster the invisible. In the "Queen Mab" speech, Mercutio describes the expansion of airy nothing into a something of fancy. Queen Mab is "no bigger than an agate stone / On the forefinger of an alderman / Drawn with a team of little atomies" (I.iv.55-57). The list of diminutives grows as Mercutio expounds on the inflationary process of fancy.

The fallacy of the dreamer is that he makes the small disproportionately large; the strength of the artist is that he preserves things as they are, neither denying the self, like the lover Mercutio disdains, nor exaggerating the self, like the dreamer Mercutio deflates. If wit raises man by pushing nature into its destined fulness, the dream distorts him, distending the little that is. In Mercutio's sphere, the hero maintains the balance between the merely bestial and the wholly vacuous by developing what he might, most abundantly, be. The *raisonneur* of the play, Mercutio defends the jewel of the self which the lover, as he defines him in II.iv, seems anxious to hide.[3] If the dreamer expands the microscopic, distorting it to defy the test of the real, the artist encompasses the actual, using it to soften the impact of the fates. The dreamer dissolves into an empty vista; the artist evolves out of the natural world.

Romeo and Juliet begin as dreamers, testifying to the immensity of their love. But they succeed for a while as artists containing, as Mercutio would wish them to do, the natural impulses initially igniting them. The life they form bridges, however briefly, the moonshine beams drawing them together and the graveside truth pulling them apart. They create, in the moments they share, an art of love, described even by the chorus of Act II as a configuration of a full body out of the raw material of life:

> Passion lends them power, time means, to meet
> Temp'ring extremities with extreme sweet.
>
> (Prologue, II, 13-14)

The subject of temper is at once the power in the lovers (passion) and the circumstances without them (time). Thus they cast the shape of their love (extreme sweet) from the situations (extremities) in which they are caught, freeing themselves both from descents of nature and flights of emptiness.

In his praise of Romeo, Mercutio begins with nature and ends with art. In their paeans to each other, Romeo and Juliet start with art (extreme sweet) so that they might enjoy their nature (extremities). For Mercutio, wit is the culmination of human experience; for Romeo and Juliet it is the means whereby they can touch and so return to the element they mutually desire. Romeo is clever when he meets Mercutio in II.iv because he has learned by then the satisfying consummation of language and because he knows, by then, the overwhelming need of love. The words he shared with Juliet to discover his nature are now the tools he uses against the world to protect his secret.

During the opening sequences, the lovers approach Mercutio's ideal. The introductory sonnet (I.v.95-109) and the balcony scene (II.ii) manifest their wish to share an art which at first recognizes, and then builds upon, the solidly present cycle of nature. They use the reason Mercutio so avidly espouses to ensure the union they so physically desire, their wit determining the course of their bodies. The happiness in the early scenes stems from a belief found first in the lovers' creative capacity, evidenced in the echoes of Genesis in II.ii.37-47, and the second in the earth's created endowment, manifested in the references to nature of II.ii.133-35. Romeo and Juliet exult in the strength they impress upon each other and in the support they derive from the world, fixing the metaphors for their love on the certainty of the constellations (II.ii.184-85) and the reality of the senses (II.ii.165-66). They move from moments of self doubt to periods of self-confidence (II.ii.28-34; II.ii.139-41) when they confirm their feelings in a natural setting. In the first half of the play the lovers cement their union with what they think is a firm physical bond. Their effort through the second half is to salvage what they made despite the inexorable retreat of the structure underlying their hope. In the *aubade* (III.v.1-35), they begin to see nature's unavoidable indifference to their plight. Just before she takes the Friar's potion (IV.iii.15-59), Juliet envisions her physical end as a mental collapse, the animal in her destroying the reason earlier directing it. The edifice of love topples when she imagines her uncontrolled body "dashing" (IV.iv.54)—as Mercutio had seen the brutes "scratching" (III.i.102)—her defenceless brains. Nature oblit-

Leonardo DiCaprio as Romeo and Claire Danes as Juliet in the masque scene from the 1996 film directed by Baz Luhrmann.

erates in that scene the art which it had once sustained. The tragedy in the final acts is defined while the lovers witness the erosion of the foundation binding their union. Nature withdraws, leaving an empty art—hollow statues instead of supple bodies. Yet, if Mercutio saw, in his gravity, the levelling power of the bestial, Romeo and Juliet remember in the vault the soaring strength of the creative. What remains in the enveloping gloom at the end is the recollected light of the beginning, the lovers determined to secure the golden vision originally inspiring them. Thus Romeo seeks to preserve with a kiss (V.iii.120), and Juliet to restore with an embrace (V.iii.166), the image of the life they named together.

That sense of co-operation is apparent from their first encounter where the ingredients of fairy tale romance become the properties of actual experience. Their love begins with the Pygmalion formula, the melting of art into life—a formula which allows them, in turn, to live that life as art:

Romeo. If I profane with my unworthiest hand
This holy shrine, the gentle sin is this,
My lips, two blushing pilgrims, ready stand
To smooth that rough touch with a tender kiss.
Juliet. Good pilgrim, you do wrong your hand too much,
Which mannerly devotion shows in this;
For saints have hands that pilgrims' hands do touch,
And palm to palm is holy palmers' kiss.
Romeo. Have not saints lips, and holy palmers too?
Juliet. Ay, pilgrim, lips that they must use in prayer.
Romeo. O, then, dear saint, let lips do what hands so;
They pray, grant thou, lest faith turn to despair.
Juliet. Saints do not move, though grant for prayers' sake.
Romeo. Then move not, while my prayer's effect I take.

(I.v.95-109)

When Romeo calls Juliet a shrine, he makes her both the container of the saint and the thing contained, exalting and embodying her. Unlike the conventional sonneteer, he can touch the Petrarchan idealized woman and yet not die of her. When Juliet takes his hand, she raises him to the level he has praised her, allowing him to join her on the same plane. The gratification is immediate. Through the submerged metaphor of a ladder, Juliet's indulgence emboldens Romeo to climb even one rung higher:

> Have not saints lips and holy palmers too?

Is it Juliet who maintains his equilibrium, keeping Romeo from toppling over with audacity or tripping out of dizziness. Like Rosalind with Orlando, she puts him "to entreaty," refusing him momentarily so that they can have more "matter" to discuss, letting him take the reins by giving him something to do. The lovers alternatingly provide tasks for each other, extending the arena of the possible to the height of the exhilarating. Demanding prayer, Juliet keeps Romeo looking up. Begging Juliet to join him in the name of balance, Romeo reminds her of the possibility, always near, of despair. If she falters now, things may reverse themselves. Romeo might slip into the void. Similarly, Juliet suggests the need for equanimity when she argues for continual vigilance. If Romeo stops praying to her, he becomes inconstant, himself subject to change. Thus, in concert, they find a solution:

> *Juliet.* Saints do not move, though grant for prayer's sake.
> *Romeo.* Then move not while my prayer's effect I take.

Permitting the kiss, Juliet bestows herself on Romeo, acknowledging her feelings by consenting, but encouraging his suit by permitting it "for prayer's sake." Such a constant coming-to-be and fulfillment is the promise of the sonnet, a mutual exchange to keep from changing. The gentleness (granting) of nature preserves the stillness (or permanence) of art.

The banter about movement anticipates Florizel's speech to Perdita in *The Winter's Tale:*

> When you do dance, I wish you
> A wave o' th' sea, that you might ever do
> Nothing but that, move still, still so,
> And own no other function.
> (IV.iv.140-43)

Florizel's play on moving and stillness in the seemingly contradictory line "move still, still so" suggests at once the peace (stillness) he has found in her motions and the inexhaustibility ("still," in the Renaissance, meaning always) of her sexuality. Not only does Perdita dance but she "moves" (inspires) Florizel to contemplate eternity (stillness). Granting without moving, Juliet maintains the opposite eternity of Perdita. In the late play, Shakespeare's sympathies are clearly with the reproductive powers Florizel compares to the sea. Thus, Perdita progresses towards a maternal fulfillment to be achieved in future "stillness." In *Romeo and Juliet,* the young lovers attempt a permanence through the art of their current lives. By allowing Romeo to imbibe the kiss, Juliet breathes life into him, becoming the muse of the prayers he formulates to get more. The give and take of the kiss in this initial scene permits both lovers to realize a fulness not (as in *The Winter's Tale*) in anticipation of some promised and remote generation but as an actualization of a present and willing nature. The lovers in this play find a state which is at once solidly unchangeable ("saints do not move") and softly yielding ("grant for prayer's sake"). They provide thereby the conditions—Juliet by imploring Romeo to pray afresh, Romeo by urging Juliet to kiss again—which foster both immediate gratification and persistent desire. They stimulate each other by coming to life, simultaneously as they guarantee each other by surfacing as art, in an abiding vehicle for love.

The continuity of speaking becomes the incentive for expansiveness as the lovers meet again in the Capulet garden. When Juliet sighs, Romeo exults. Yet, as he praises her, he places himself in the exigency of the moment prior to the initial sonnet. In the garden, separate from Juliet, he seems to have fallen off the imaginary ladder. It is only through the process of the balcony scene that Romeo finds the courage to climb to, and enjoy, the heights of their first encounter. Overhearing Juliet, he is overcome by the wonder he perceives:

> O, speak again, bright angel! for thou art
> As glorious to this night, being o'er my head,
> As is a winged messenger of heaven
> Unto the white-upturned wond'ring eyes
> Of mortals that fall back to gaze on him
> When he bestrides the lazy pacing clouds
> And sails upon the bosom of the air.
> (II.ii.28-34)

Like the saint of the initiating sonnet, Juliet is a bright angel. But unlike the woman contained in the earlier metaphor, this Juliet is unreachable—a "winged messenger of heaven." She moves majestically in the spheres above, while Romeo, in typical Petrarchan fashion, falls back into the ground below. Passive and bereft of energy, Romeo is overtaken, his eyes fixed on the soaring and powerful eagle of his image.

It is Juliet who returns him to himself by recreating him, not out of the vacuous clouds in the sky, but out of the solid substance of the earth. In her garden, Juliet becomes a kind of Adam in reverse, unnaming the universe, decomposing—in order to recompose—the world. By moving backwards in time and recreating the experience of Genesis, she moves upwards in space, revitalizing the sense of Adam's dream:

> And the Lord God said, *It is* not good that man should be alone; I will make him a help meet for him.
>
> And out of the ground, the LORD God formed every beast of the field, and every fowl of the air; and brought *them* unto Adam to see what he would call them: and whatsoever Adam called every living creature, that was the name thereof.
>
> And Adam gave names to all cattle, and to the fowl of the air, and to every beast of the field; but for Adam there was not found a help meet for him.
>
> And the LORD God caused a deep sleep to fall upon Adam, and he slept; and he took one of his ribs, and closed up the flesh instead thereof.
>
> And the rib, which the LORD God had taken from man, made he a woman, and brought her unto the man.
>
> And Adam said, This *is* now bone of my bones, and flesh of my flesh: she shall be called Woman, because she was taken out of man.
>
> Therefore shall a man leave his father and his mother, and shall cleave unto his wife: and they shall be one flesh.
>
> (*Genesis* 2.18-24)

The process of Eve's emergence is curious. First God forms every beast of the ground for Adam to name, so that he becomes the arbitrary and wholly conscious word maker. But the woman—the companion—was taken, not out of the earth, but from Adam's rib; he was made less in order to be made more. Further, the moment of Adam's greatest creativity occurs during a trance, the height of his powers realized during the depths of his sleep.

In the joy of Adam's awakening the two negative components—the usurping of the body, the surrender of the mind—do not detract from the pleasure of discovering the wholly made being. Adam still names the woman, as he had all the other creatures, but he names her after himself, as she had been taken out of him. He feels a double triumph, returning to himself the namer, discovering himself—the maker. The joy is immediate (now) but it bears with it a sense of the past (now, in view of these accumulated facts) and the future (now, in light of these forthcoming events). The exultation is temporary, preceded as it was by Adam's absence in the conditions necessary for creation, and foreshadowing, as it does, a future leavetaking in the circumstances governing marriage. History surrounds the now with anterior and ensuing diminution but it can never retract the joy of believed-in power.

In the balcony scene, Juliet allows Romeo to experience Adam's moment of happiness by giving to him, however fleetingly, a belief in his own capacity for making and a consequential faith in his own resources for giving. The scene in the Capulet gardens parallels the scene in Eden. At first Romeo is, through his own hyperbole, rendered as passive as Adam, while Juliet finds the means to bring him to himself. She begins by defining her terms:

> Tis but thy name that is my enemy;
> Thou art thyself, though not a Montague.
> What's Montague? it is nor hand, nor foot,
> Nor arm, nor face, nor any other part
> Belonging to a man. O, be some other name!—
> What's in a name? that which we call a rose
> By any other name would smell as sweet;
> So Romeo would, were he not Romeo call'd,
> Retain that dear perfection which he owes
> Without that title.—Romeo, doff thy name,
> And for thy name, which is no part of thee,
> Take all myself.
>
> (II.ii.37-47)

Juliet is in sequence God, then Adam, then Eve until Romeo awakens, newly baptized, ready to act and name and be Adam to the Eve she has become. The exchange of roles continues throughout the scene as one enters the other and as each revels in the self the other made and found. At first Juliet reforms Romeo by unnaming him, starting with hand and foot, returning him, part by part, to the nature of his origin and directing him, name by name, towards the art of his aspiration.[4] In the recreative moment she seems like the God of Genesis. But, in the next line, she descends to the place of Adam:

> What's in a name? that which we call a rose
> By any other name would smell as sweet;
>
> (II.ii.43-44)

By equating Romeo to the rose, Juliet renders him part of the found universe which she, like Adam, merely names. The more she speaks the further she retreats, enlarging Romeo's promise as she diminishes her role. He is next the "dear perfection" (II.ii.45), at once the precious ("dear") beginning and the ultimate ("perfection") consummation of her life. When she asks him to substitute herself for his name, Juliet crawls into Romeo, emerging the nascent Eve of Genesis. She becomes, in that act, flesh of the flesh, bone of the bone which is their mutual compound. With the command, "take all myself," she makes Romeo simultaneously the God who "took" Eve from man's rib and the Adam who named her because she was so taken. Through the giving of herself Juliet converts Romeo into the begetter of her life—"all." The mutuality of the exchange continues as the lovers toss each other compliments testifying to their power to rework the world.

Romeo in turn makes Juliet his Adam and his God:

> I take thee at thy word:
> Call me but love, and I'll be new baptized;
> Henceforth I never will be Romeo.
>
> (II.ii.49-51)

By "taking" Juliet at her word, Romeo credits her as mortal and believes in her as "saint" (II.ii.55), perceiving that she is, as he was to her, his origin and his destiny. If she renames him, he will be reborn, no longer the old Romeo but the "new baptized" self. Such a rebirth is premised on a creative mutuality which neither is ashamed to call love. The Romeo who earlier lay gazing in passivity is now active in appreciation, ready to "tear" the word (II.ii.57) Juliet cannot bear and prepared to dare the world (II.ii.68) which tries to stop him.

Recovered, Romeo reveals how he entered Juliet's enclave. He compares himself retrospectively to the bird he called Juliet, flying in backward glances to the now attained heights:

> With love's light wings did I o'er-perch these walls,
> For stony limits cannot hold love out,
> And what love can do that dares love attempt;
> Therefore thy kinsmen are no let to me.
>
> (II.ii.66-69)

And Juliet, too, speaks in excess:

> My bounty is as boundless as the sea,
> My love as deep; the more I give to thee,
> The more I have, for both are infinite.
>
> (II.ii.133-35)

Both lovers emerge limitless, their happiness based on the illusion of strength (paralleling the moment after Adam's trance) inspired by the renaming process. Juliet's goodness (bounty) equals her generosity and that equals her boundlessness. Like the sea returning to the shore, she crests with still more to give, expressing, in the reference to the ocean, the circular completion of Romeo's earlier metaphor of the bestriding bird in the heaven's range. The extension builds on nature, stretching its limits to a vision of grandeur and moving outwards from a fixed centre towards a limitless circularity. Juliet's concluding expansion downwards in the sea corresponds to Romeo's initial praise upwards in the skies, rounding the universe *now*.

Having defined her fulness not by her ability to take but by her capacity to give, Juliet casts herself as the maker Mercutio praised. When she calls Romeo the "god" of her "idolatry" (II.ii.113), she summarizes the progress of the scene where Romeo moves from passive worshipper, to active Adam to idealized god. As god, Romeo is the object of her adoration; as idol he is the image she carved. The illusion of creativity satisfies their craving, forming a temporary frame of love around the core of nature. In the course of time, reality will break through with the dark truth of its unyielding presence but for the moment, at least, the lovers seem to be able to bend the lines of the world to the encircling purposes of their art.

They are able to so shape their vision because they find in nature a pattern of certainty where they can hinge their imagined flights. The process by which they fix their beliefs is like the process by which they proclaim their love—a movement towards resolution from a position of uncertainty. Immediately following the mutual discovery of power Romeo, left alone, fears for its loss:

> O blessed blessed night! I am afeard,
> Being in night, all this is but a dream,
> Too flattering—sweet to be substantial.
>
> (II.ii.139-41)

Repeating Mercutio's admonition about dreams, Romeo tests his own expanded expectation against the inflationary process of wish-fulfillment. All this is "too flattering-sweet," he whines, worried that, inspired on insufficient grounds, he has been flattered into believing himself the hero of his own life. During that moment alone, Romeo loses faith in art because he has lost touch with nature. The sweetness of the night is unsubstantial. It cannot be seen or smelled or heard.

It is only in the reawakening of his senses that Romeo is able to rekindle his faith. When Juliet calls him back, he combines sight and sound by comparing her voice to music:

> How silver-sweet sound lovers' tongues by night,
> Like softest music to attending ears!
>
> (II.ii.165-66)

Juliet's voice provides a light that awakens touch ("soft") sound ("music") sight ("silver") and taste ("sweet") to the nature of the world. With the word "attending," Romeo pushes his present listening into a projected act. The sweetness promises more than a "now." It anticipates a "then," leading him to expect fulfillment because of an instantly realized substance.

Similarly, Juliet prolongs the word of departure so that it becomes the signal for return:

> Good night, good night! parting is such sweet
> sorrow
> That I shall say good night till it be morrow.
>
> (II.ii.184-85)

Sound restores Juliet's faith here just as it earlier bolstered Romeo's. If she continues calling it will, as surely as day follows night, be morrow. By centring her prolongation of the "now" on a permanently recurring cycle, Juliet attempts to guarantee her word. Her art is linked to nature, the sorrow of the parting "sweet" because the repetition of the sound will make Romeo return to her when the sun completes its journey in the sky. While the lovers rejoice in their own creative capacity, they hinge that potential on what they assume to be the firm foundation of nature's reserve. If they began the balcony scene with an imagined dream of love, they close it with a felt experience of life, reiterating with the sweetness, a solid sight and sound and smell. That sweetness recalls Juliet's rose which appeared as a promise of what nature, signalling its immutable "bounty," might give.

In the opening acts, the lovers feel confident that the shrine they build has the strength of a sympathetic cosmos at its centre. But their early belief is fleeting. What they discover subsequently is that the centre does not hold. The foundation keeps slipping out from under them. The last acts "scratch" away the illusion of art, leaving only—what Mercutio found—the indifference of nature.[5] In the first half of the play Romeo and Juliet turn figurative flights of fancy into uplifting possibilities of hope. The birds of their immediate imagination signified the high level of their ultimate aspiration. They gave to each other, when they exchanged vows, the capacity to realize a creative life. The more they touched, the more they sparked the universe with their desire, converting external objects into manifestations of their inner state. They named the world out of the selves they promoted in each other. But in the final acts, the bird-songs of their early expansive similes are replaced by the death-knells of reductive actuality.

The *aubade* begins with Juliet's attempt to transform the lark into the nightingale she covets just as, in the balcony scene, she had reconstructed Romeo into the lover she desired:[6]

> Wilt thou be gone? it is not yet near day:
> It was the nightingale, and not the lark
> That pierced the fearful hollow of thine ear;
> Nightly she sings on yond pomegranate tree.
> Believe me, love, it was the nightingale.
>
> (III.v.1-5)

. . . . .

> Yond light is not daylight. I know it, I:
> It is some meteor that the sun exhales,
> To be to thee this night a torch-bearer,
> And light thee on thy way to Mantua:
> Therefore stay yet; thou need'st not be gone.
>
> (III.v.12-16)

Romeo's perception, she claims, is shaped by the pressure of a reality he fears, the hollow in his ear pierced by his failure to believe in love. Sensing the vacancy, Juliet tries, as she so successfully earlier had tried, to fill it with the bird of her imagination. In her efforts to prolong Romeo's stay, she asserts the logic of her calculations, rendering the light Romeo paints an exhalation of the sun, a torch left as a remainder from the day before instead of a signal sent as a herald of the morn ensuing. Such a wish to reverse time is based, not as her sweet sorrow speech was, on the certainly seen and solidly stable cycle of the fixed star, but on the dubious gift and sudden miracle of the variable meteor. With the redundant, "I know it I," she desperately recalls the strength of her earlier intuitions about nature and her previous assertions of being, both of which empowered Romeo to find his way with her. Juliet clings to the assumptions of self and the vision of nature inaugurating her reformation of the world.

It is Romeo this time who reminds Juliet that reality nullifies her expectations:

> Night's candles are burnt out, and jocund day
> Stands tiptoe on the misty mountain tops:
> I must be gone and live, or stay and die.
>
> (III.v.9-11)

On the one hand, day flattens Juliet's heightened expectations, reducing her hopes to the mist of dreams. On the other, day stands ready, poised like a dancer, to begin the journey across the sky launching (from tiptoe) the inevitable succession of the spheres and manifesting (with the jocund) the utter indifference of the planet. Romeo's counter to Juliet here forces her to face not the sound of her fancy but the role of reality. The *aubade* contrasts with the balcony scene, the lovers issuing to each other the responsibility for dealing with nature, the necessity of parting from their dreams.

Romeo commands Juliet to say what he has already seen; she orders him, in turn, to do what he himself has proposed:

> It is, it is: hie hence, be gone, away!
> It is the lark that sings so out of tune,
> Straining harsh discords and unpleasing
> sharps.
> Some say the lark makes sweet division;
> This doth not so, for she divideth us:
> Some say the lark and loathed toad change
> eyes;

> O, now I would they had changed voices
>   too!
> Since arm from arm that voice doth us affray
> Hunting thee hence with hunts-up to the day.
> (III.v.26-35)

In Act II, the sound of voices had signalled an awakening of the lovers' faith; now the rousing echo of nature initiates the destruction of hope. With the line "arm from arm that voice doth us affray," Juliet acknowledges the defeat of the body through the devastation of the mind. Romeo and Juliet are torn apart (physically frayed) by the voice that makes them psychologically fearful. Left armless (defenceless) they are bereft of the power to enclose nature within the sphere of their desire. As light now approaches, they remain in the darkness of distress (woe as grief). Further, the sight of day increases the sound of their lamentation (woe as exclamation), leaving them, as Mercutio had found Romeo in the beginning, subjugated by sound, overwhelmed by sight, the very forces they had, in Act II, so well mastered. Their eyes are now turned downwards towards the grave as they feel themselves betrayed by, rather than formulating, reality:

> *Juliet.* O God! I have an ill-divining soul:
> Methinks I see thee, now thou are below,
> As one dead in the bottom of a tomb:
> Either my eyesight fails, or thou look'st pale.
> *Romeo.* And trust me, love, in my eye so do
>   you:
> Dry sorrow drinks our blood.
> (III.v.54-59)

Parting this time, Juliet envisions Romeo not as the enshrined saint she might bring to life but as the contained body nature has already cast in marble. In the balcony scene, the lovers instilled liquid life into each other; here dry sorrow drinks their blood, sucking the life they had formed, sapping the expectations they had raised. Early, Romeo and Juliet, the creative artists, felt themselves infinitely ready to give; now nature, the controlling force, manifests itself as inexorably destined to take.[7]

While "dry sorrow" attacks from without in Act III, "cold fear" circulates from within in Act IV. When she imagines her death there, Juliet extends the fear of the *aubade* until it reaches every part of her body, moving from the torn arms to the frozen marrow of her being:

> I have a faint cold fear thrills through my
>   veins,
> That almost freezes up the heat of life:
> (IV.iii.15-16)

The fear is active, penetrating Juliet's body, controlling her totally. In the potion-taking moment, Juliet reverses the process of the balcony scene where she used her mind to construct the Romeo she desired:

> Alack, alack, is it not like that I,
> So early waking, what with loathsome smells
> And shrieks like mandrakes torn out of the
>   earth,
> That living mortals, hearing them, run mad:
> O, if I wake, shall I not be distraught,
> Environed with all these hideous fears?
> And madly play with my forefathers'
>   joints?
> And pluck the mangled Tybalt from his
>   shroud?
> And, in this rage, with some great kinsman's
>   bone,
> As with a club, dash out my desperate
>   brains?
> O, look, methinks I see my cousin's ghost
> Seeking out Romeo, that did spit his body
> Upon a rapier's point:—stay, Tybalt, stay!—
> Romeo, I come! This do I drink to thee.
> (IV.iii.45-58)

Here, death becomes all physical. It "smells" and "shrieks" and "environs" her until she sees herself madly playing with her forefathers' joints and in a rage "dashing" out her "desperate" brains. While she speaks, Juliet turns the faith for which Romeo prayed in the initial sonnet into the despair he feared. The corpses closing in on her smash and depress her spirit. Having begun with a brain hopeful enough to create a body, she ends here with bodies powerful enough to unmake her mind. Death for Juliet, as it was for Mercutio, is "madness"—the dashing—the confounding of reason. Already in the throes of her anticipated derangement, Juliet imagines Tybalt's ghost avenging Romeo. As she drinks the potion, she bids Tybalt "stay," seeking to keep from her lover—in order to prevent him from feeling—the despair that has overtaken her. Similarly, Romeo will "stay" with Juliet to stop "death's pale flag" (V.iii.16) from advancing on her cheek. Faced with the onslaught of unavoidable fate, both lovers attempt somehow to pre-empt it, to overtake it before it unmakes them. Thus, they die in an effort to revive the image of the heroic selves they once made possible.

If, in Act IV, Juliet contemplates the body quelling the mind, Romeo remembers, in Act V, the mind infusing the body. His famous dream speaks of the power they had together found:

> I dreamt my lady came and found me dead—
> Strange dream, that gives a dead man leave to
>   think!—
> And breathed such life with kisses in my lips
> That I revived, and was an emperor.
> (V.i.6-10)

Once more, Romeo turns Juliet into the goddess inspiring him to strength. She breathes "such life" into him that he feels, as Adam did for the moment of naming, the maker of the world. He gives her the ability to give him a life of creative power. In *Antony and Cleopatra,* Cleopatra dreams there was an emperor Antony who, after his death, becomes the energetic source of her final act. But in this play, the dreamer is the emperor, having already been granted the energy to control his life. This mutual bringing to strength by memory (he dreaming her reviving him, she imagining him restoring her) counterbalances the encroaching levelling to weakness by destiny.

If Juliet sought to protect Romeo from Tybalt, so Romeo takes on death, finding in the tomb the same monster that Juliet saw. But if Juliet with the potion envisions a future based on dissolution, Romeo in the vault seeks to preserve a past premised on consolidation. Act IV ends with Juliet feeling only the darkness. Act V ends with each lover recovering light. In the vault Romeo vows to act:

> Ah, dear Juliet,
> Why art thou yet so fair? shall I believe
> That unsubstantial Death is amorous,
> And that the lean abhorred monster keeps
> Thee here in dark to be his paramour?
> For fear of that I still will stay with thee,
> And never from this palace of dim night
> Depart again: here, here will I remain
> With worms that are thy chambermaids; O, here
> Will I set up my everlasting rest,
> And shake the yoke of inauspicious stars
> From this world-wearied flesh.—Eyes, look your last!
> Arms, take your last embrace! and lips, O you,
> The doors of breath, seal with a righteous kiss
> A dateless bargain to engrossing death!
> Come, bitter conduct, come, unsavoury guide!
> Thou desperate pilot, now at once run on
> The dashing rocks thy sea-sick weary bark!
> Here's to my love! O true apothecary!
> Thy drugs are quick.—Thus with a kiss I die.
> (V.iii.103-20)

Romeo does not passively await or groan or sigh, he actively "stays," "remains," "shakes" and "run[s] on." Finally, with "a kiss," he "dies" reversing the process by which he came to life in the early sonnet. There, the lovers kissed, advancing from stillness to movement. Here, Romeo retains—with a kiss—the beauty originally prompting him to move. Similarly, Juliet dies with a "restorative" seeing the kiss as a means for revitalizing the shrine of the self Romeo worshipped:

> I will kiss thy lips;
> Haply some poison yet doth hang on them,
> To make me die a restorative.
> Thy lips are warm!
> (V.iv.164-66)

In actively stalking Death, the lovers consciously revive the golden images inspiring their union.[8] The statues the Montagues erect are merely symbols of the conscious artifice their children—following Mercutio's philosophy—struggled to make of their lives. Doing their own undoing, Romeo and Juliet retain the vision that enabled them, however briefly, to achieve a fulness of being, an awakening of self, in the naming of love.

Notes

[1] *Romeo and Juliet,* ed. Brian Gibbons (London: Methuen, 1980), II.iv.90-95. All references are from this edition and will be cited in my text.

[2] *The Countess of Pembroke's Arcadia,* ed. Jean Robertson (Oxford: Clarendon Press, 1973), p. 19.

[3] Critics who see Mercutio as merely vulgar assign him the role of foil to Romeo. But such dismissals misconstrue the importance of his defence of reason and underestimate his role as spokesman for art. Among those who cite his carnality are Harold C. Goddard, *The Meaning of Shakespeare, Vol. I* (Chicago: University of Chicago Press, 1951), pp. 120-23; Harley Granville-Barker, *Prefaces to Shakespeare, Vol. II* (Princeton: Princeton University Press, 1947), pp. 335-38; and J. Dover Wilson, "The Elizabethan Shakespeare," *Proceedings of the English Academy* (London: Oxford University Press, 1929), 123.

[4] Harry Levin makes a similar distinction between art and nature when he argues that "Juliet calls into question not merely Romeo's name but, by implication,—all names, forms, conventions, sophistications, and arbitrary dictates of society as opposed to the appeal of instinct directly conveyed in the odor of a rose." See "Form and Formality in *Romeo and Juliet,*" *Shakespeare Quarterly,* XI (1960), p. 4.

[5] On nature's callousness, Frederick Turner writes: "The lovers call their love infinite, but in the world of time there can be nothing infinite. Time itself turns against the lovers, and blindly ejects them from its system as incompatible with its texture and tissue. The lovers treat time subjectively . . . and time revenges itself blindly for such temerity." See *Shakespeare and the Nature of Time* (Oxford: Clarendon Press, 1971), p. 126.

[6] Comparing the balcony scene to the aubade, Mark Rose writes: " . . . the segments of the early scene are arranged to give the effect of the dream dominating "reality," the lovers overwhelming the "outsiders" as the short initial segment yields to the long lyric episode. The [aubade] suggests "the dream" dissolving

into "day," the magical world of the lovers literally overwhelmed before our eyes." See *Shakespearean Design* (Cambridge, Mass.: Harvard University Press, 1972), p. 72. Similarly, James Black counterpoints the two scenes: "The fact that in each of these scenes the setting is the same and the stage picture reduplicated lends emphasis to the pathetic alteration in the speakers' tones and circumstances. The parallels emphasize the differences: things look the same but are painfully altered. Thus the audience is looking at what it saw before, but is being forced to see more intensely." See "The Visual Artistry of Romeo and Juliet," *Studies in English Literature* 15 (1975), 247.

[7] Commenting on the way nature retracts its support, Donald Stauffer maintains: "In no other play does Shakespeare envisage a general moral order operating with such inhuman, mechanical severity." See *Shakespeare's World of Images* (Bloomington: Indiana University Press, 1973), p. 55.

[8] M. H. Mahood writes that "Romeo and Juliet 'cease to die, by dying'." See *Shakespeare's Word Play* (London: Methuen, 1957), p. 72.

R. Stamm (essay date 1986)

SOURCE: "The First Meeting of the Lovers in Shakespeare's *Romeo and Juliet*," in *English Studies,* Vol. 67, No. 1, February, 1986, pp. 2-13.

[*In the following essay, Stamm analyzes the suggestive words and gestures of Romeo and Juliet's first meeting, which he sees as "an unique combination of formality and spontaneity, of elegance and intensity, of wit and passion."*]

No observer of Shakespeare's tragedy can fail to notice the importance of the first meeting of the lovers. It constitutes the climax prepared by the preceding scenes of Act I, and, in the structure of the whole play, it is—like Romeo's fateful duel with Tybalt and the death scene—one of the turning points. It is the event that changes Romeo's and Juliet's lives, bringing them intense happiness at first and suffering and death in consequence. Shakespeare used all the resources of his rapidly developing art to provide this decisive encounter with a very special kind of dramatic life, moulding the first exchange of his young lovers into the form of a sonnet, of which he knew himself a master. To go with it he chose imagery also derived from the Petrarchan tradition with its tendency to express love in religious terms. And he saw to it that this poetic inset did not remain a literary exercise by integrating it in a dramatic event with its specific movements and gestures. As a result he achieved an unique combination of formality and spontaneity, of elegance and intensity, of wit and passion. Its impact is felt by every reader, performer or spectator, but to analyse and explain it has proved a difficult task for the critics. In their discussions they have often been struck by one or the other of its qualities only and overlooked or played down other aspects.

A great deal of attention has been paid to the sonnet form by which the encounter is set off against the surrounding speeches in prose and blank verse, and in consequence of this it was often studied as a mainly oral event, a tendency that has not died out in spite of the contributions of Harley Granville-Barker. Bertrand Evans, for instance, sees the meeting as a 'conversation'. He says of the lovers: 'In the seventeen lines of their initial conversation, the force of their sudden love, intense as religious devotion, is figured forth by the motif of their exchange: "profane . . .holy shrine . . . pilgrims . . . pilgrim . . . devotion . . . saints . . . pilgrims . . . holy palmers' . . . saints . . . holy palmers . . . pilgrim . . . prayer . . . saint . . . pray . . . faith . . . Saints . . . prayers' . . . prayer's . . . sin . . . sin . . . Sin . . . trespass . . . sin". Such is the predominent vocabulary of their exchange, the very sound of which marks the brief encounter as being a moment of transcendent passion; and these lines are made even more potent by the special setting in which, because of the Prologue, we hear them: by its very intensity this sudden love bids us remember that the lovers are doomed, and the sounds echo as in a tomb.'[1] This exclusively aural reaction ignores everything that is happening in the scene.

Nicholas Brooke's approach is less one-sided as his primary interest in verse and music is balanced by his perception of a performed ritual and an appeal to the test of the theatre: 'Seeing the Act in its fullness, with its functional contrasts of prose and several kinds of verse, we can see this climax in a very elaborate verse becomes musically almost inevitable. And the sense of ritual is dramatically right: what, out of context, would be empty courtliness, in its context is solemn celebration. In psychological terms, this sonnet represents the spell of mutual recognition; but thus formalized, the psychological moment is carried forward into full betrothal—the implication of such recognition. To grasp the best of *Romeo and Juliet,* we have to grasp that this does work on the stage.'[2] This is well said, and we would like to know how exactly this works on the stage.

In such an inquiry we expect to derive help from Harley Granville-Barker's *Preface* to the play. What we find there, however, seems strangely uneven. When he comes to our scene he invites us: 'One must picture them there. The dance is over, the guests and the maskers are in a little chattering, receding crowd, and the two find themselves alone. Juliet would be for joining the others; but Romeo, his mask doffed, moves towards her, as a pilgrim towards a shrine.

If I profane with my unworthiest hand . . .

It is hard to see what better first encounter could have been devised. To have lit mutual passion in them at once would have been commonplace; the cheapest of love tragedies might begin like that. But there is something sacramental in this ceremony, something shy and grave and sweet; it is a marriage made already. And she is such a child; touched to earnestness by his trembling earnestness, but breaking into fun at last (her defence when the granted kiss lights passion in him) as the last quatrain's metre breaks for its ending into

You kiss by the book.'³

The producer critic begins with a few practical remarks on the introductory grouping on stage, but then he becomes as vague and impressionistic as any normal literary critic, repeating Shakespeare's very words instead of suggesting their scenic equivalents. After a glance at the beginning of 'the cheapest of love tragedies', which seems rather otiose to the present-day reader, he offers a fine sentence on the effect and the meaning of the ceremony enacted by the young couple, but again we look in vain for a word on the way how it is enacted. And what is then said of the behaviour of the child Juliet is hardly more than a personal projection from Granville-Barker's sensitive and imaginative mind.

For a more specific remark on the sonnet's gestic implications we can turn to J. L. Styan, whose attempt to read it as a theatrical score is as follows: 'In *Romeo and Juliet,* Shakespeare even borrows the formal sonnet, rich in its own amorous allusions, and makes it serviceable to the actors:

> If I profane with my unworthiest hand
> This holy shrine, the gentle pain is this:
> My lips, two blushing pilgrims, ready stand
> To smooth that rough touch with a tender
>   kiss.
>   (I.v. 93-6)

This sonnet not only conveys a tone suitable to an idealized encounter, but also precise indications of gesture and attitude. In Juliet's reply,

> Good pilgrim, you do wrong your hand too
>   much,
> Which mannerly devotion shows in this:
> For saints have hands that pilgrims' hands do
>   touch,
> And palm to palm is holy palmers' kiss . . .
>   (97-100)

Shakespeare contrives to signal the withdrawal of her hand from his lips and indicate her modesty as she perhaps turns aside with the cadence of the last lines.'⁴ The hint concerning the withdrawal of Juliet's hand is useful, but it does not lead to a coherent account of the integration of speech and action. When Styan returned to the passage in a later book, he read a radical contrast between speech and action into the text, a procedure that may have recommended itself to some of the modern producers of the play: 'The imagery of saints and pilgrims falls within the literary mode of courtly love, but it is an error to accept it on this level. On the stage the eye belies the idealism of the words, since the same words describe a pattern of gesture and behaviour that scarcely fits either saint or pilgrim: in the acting the sonnet seems more like a series of cues for a flirtation. Not only does Romeo take Juliet by the hand and lead her out of the dance, but he kisses it and then her lips, and these not once but twice. Juliet, for her part, is no shy virgin, and on

> Saints do not move, though grant for prayers'
>   sake

she actually takes the initiative while denying her power to initiate: in all this her wit is equal to Romeo's. The whole rhythm of gesture in this piece, while exactly planned for performance, also makes a mockery of the Petrarchan convention, eyes contradicting ears.'⁵

Here we are far away, indeed, from ceremony and ritual as well as from Granville-Barker's child lovers: A clever young couple knows how to overcome the awkwardness of a first meeting by the fun of undercutting traditional imagery by flirtatious acting.
Two important German studies arrive at different views of the interplay of speech and gesture in the sonnet-scene. According to them the two elements are complementary, two aspects of one and the same event, in which a spiritual and an erotic experience become united. Inge Leimberg concludes: 'Die Motivreihe "devout religion of mine eye" (I.2.Z.91), "touching hers, make blesséd my rude hand" (I.5.Z.51) erreicht einen Höhepunkt an dieser Stelle, wo die Wirklichkeit taktil-sinnlicher Erfahrung sich spannungsvoll mit dem Motiv der Geliebten als der angebeteten Heiligen begegnet. Die höchste Wertsphäre trifft zusammen mit realer Gegenwart und konkretem Erleben, das ideelle Streben mit dem erotischen Verlangen, der Ernst des einen Motivs mit dem spielerischen Charakter des andern, . . . '⁶

A remarkable development of Inge Leimberg's line of thought can be studied in the unusual and unusually well written article devoted exclusively to our theme by Wolfgang Baumgart.⁷ He finds the climax of the scene and the centre from which speech and imagery are derived in the lovers' first touch of each other's hand. He thinks that Juliet refers to it in her line 'And palm to palm is holy palmers' kiss'. For him the meeting of the palms of the two young hands is the perfect expression of the birth of love, mute and yet more eloquent than all the elaborate speeches that have sprung from it. He insists that this first touch had nothing in common with anything resembling a conventional handshake: 'Kein Händedruck ist es, was die Liebenden in erster körperlicher Berührung zusammenführt. Vielmehr übertragen die empfindlichen Hautflächen der inneren Hand, vom Handteller bis zum Innern der Finger und der Fingerspitzen, aneinandergelegt, Inneres an Inneres, *palm to palm,* das erste wechselseitige Fühlen lebendiger Begegnung der Körper.'[8] In that searching first touch Baumgart discovers a metaphor of the kiss desired by Romeo and, perhaps less consciously at first, by Juliet, pointing the way to the fulfilment of the two kisses that follow. And he is careful to explain how this crucial meeting of palm and palm can come about. When her former partner leaves her, Juliet, he thinks, remains immobile at the end of the last dance figure, one hand half raised, until Romeo comes up to her and places one of his palms against it. The significance of her gesture appears almost inexhaustible to Baumgart. He connects it with the religious imagery in the sonnet and stresses the resemblance between it and a hand raised in the act of benediction.

One would like to agree wholeheartedly with an article remarkable for its insight into the possibilities of gestic as against oral expression, but there is an inescapable objection against Baumgart's reading of the text. The idea that Juliet is referring to the manner how Romeo's and her own hand have just met when she says 'And palm to palm is holy palmers' kiss' has no support in it. What she intends is a far more general remark, and her choice of words is conditioned by the desire for rhetorical variation. She replaces 'pilgrim' by 'palmer' and 'hand' by 'palm' in order to avoid excessive repetition and because she discovers an opportunity for a pun. This consideration renders Baumgart's argument rather dubious.

His method should also warn us against the danger of isolating one particular event in the tragedy too much. We therefore begin our own study of the meeting by recalling what we have learnt concerning the destined lovers in the preceding scenes. We have become better acquainted with Romeo than with Juliet. From the beginning he appears different from his cheerful friends, absorbed as he is by his Petrarchistic cult of an ideal and ideally inaccessible mistress. In fact, he avoids the contacts with reality and with other people as much as possible, and what we hear from Benvolio and old Montague of his tearful morning walks to the sycamore grove and the self-sought confinement in his darkened room reminds us of a figure in a tapestry representing scenes from the *Roman de la Rose.* His absence from the first street brawl shows how far he has withdrawn from the normal life of his friends. When he makes his entry we are struck by the abundance of his fanciful love rhetoric and his poverty of significant gestures. His references to his actual surroundings are weak and merely *pro forma.* He registers the departure of his father with a useless question, which reveals how deeply he is lost in himself:

> Was that my father that went hence so fast?
> (I.i.160)[9]

The same goes for the two unrhymed lines by which he unexpectedly interrupts his rhymed tirade on love:

> Where shall we dine? O me! What fray was here?
> Yet tell me not, for I have heard it all.
> (171f.)

The first is a routine question. He does not wait for an answer as this could lead to purposeful action, but pretends for a moment an interest in the disorderly scene which has left its marks in the street. Again he prevents an answer by a not very plausible evasion. A little later he makes an attempt to get rid of the company of Benvolio ('Farewell, my coz.' [193]); when his friend refuses to take the hint, he tolerates the presence of a partner, who, with his objections and his good advice, keeps playing the balls into his hands that he knows how to use very skilfully in his display of verbal acrobatics. Even when they meet Capulet's thickwitted servant in need of reading help, Romeo finds it hard to break away from his self-absorption; he tries to obtain water for the mill of his love complaints when he replies 'Ay, mine own fortune in my misery' to the simple question 'I pray, sir, can you read?' (I.ii.57f.) Then, however, he feels obliged to accept the practical situation and to read out the list of the invited guests. As the name of Rosaline, the goddess he worships, is on it, he allows Benvolio to persuade him that he should visit Capulet's ball.

Also in Scene I.iv, in which Romeo and the rest of the uninvited guests are getting ready for this visit, he does his best to secure a passive role for himself. Benvolio is looking forward to the pleasure of dancing, but not Romeo:

> *Romeo.* Give me a torch, I am not for this ambling.
> Being but heavy I will bear the light.
> *Mer.* Nay, gentle Romeo, we must have you dance.
> *Romeo.* Not I, believe me. You have dancing shoes
> With nimble soles, I have a soul of lead
> So stakes me to the ground I cannot move.
> (I.iv.11-16)

And he repeats his refusal:

> *Ben.* Come, knock and enter, and no sooner in
> But every man betake him to his legs.

> *Romeo.* A torch for me. Let wantons light of heart
> Tickle the senseless rushes with their heels,
> For I am proverb'd with a grandsire phrase—
> I'll be a candle-holder and look on.
> (33-8)

As in the earlier scene, Romeo's love melancholy prevents him from joining his friends in their physical activities only; he shares their delight in punning and combats of wit. But while they are all enjoying their outrageous wordplay, a new quality makes itself felt in his depression:

> *Romeo.* And we mean well in going to this masque,
> But 'tis no wit to go.
> *Mer.* Why, may one ask?
> *Romeo.* I dreamt a dream tonight.
> (48-50)

The carefully cultivated pose of the languishing lover is being undermined by a premonition rooted in deeper layers of his consciousness. Mercutio senses the change behind his friend's words and tries to overcome it by his Queen Mab phantasy. Romeo cannot tell his dream, but listens, fascinated like everybody else, by Mercutio's extraordinary performance. Finally, however, he finds it too much of a good thing and defends himself against it—his plight recalling that of Juliet for a moment, when she is confronted by her nurse's eloquence:

> *Romeo.* Peace, peace, Mercutio, peace.
> Thou talk'st of nothing.
> (95f.)

The marvellous talker seems to have achieved his purpose of convincing his friend that dreams are nothing. But he cannot keep him from returning to his premonition and finding very precise words for it. It is remarkable that this first uncertain contact with his fate does not paralyse Romeo like his yearning for the unattainable Rosaline. The unfamiliar energy in his encouragement 'On, lusty gentlemen' (113) suggests that the dreamer has come close to his waking hour.

When the ball begins Juliet has remained a less clearly defined figure than Romeo. Still, she has been characterized by a few telling strokes that we should keep in mind. She has been the subject of a short discussion between her father and Count Paris. We learn from it that 'She hath not seen the change of fourteen years' (I.ii.9) and that Capulet considers his only child to be almost too young for marriage. When she appears herself in Scene I.iii, she cannot say much since the nurse and her mother do most of the talking. When Lady Capulet wants to know her thoughts about marriage and then, quite specifically, about Count Paris as a suitor, her answers are obedient, but also quite

Leonard Whiting as Romeo and Olivia Hussey as Juliet in a scene from the 1968 film directed by Franco Zeffirelli.

noncommittal. In fact, her reply to her mother's brusque main question shows that she can easily compete with the young gentlemen out of doors in the arts of ornate speech and punning and that she is mistress of the diplomatic if sentence:

> I'll look to like, if looking liking move,
> But no more deep will I endart mine eye
> Than your consent gives strength to make it fly.
> (I.iii.97-9)

Another hint that she is by no means a naive child but a young lady with her wits about her is given where she manages to stop the nurse's overwhelming flow of words by capping her repeated 'it stinted, and said "Ay"' by an energetic: 'And stint thou too, I pray thee, Nurse, say I.' (58) In consequence of this clever punning intervention the nurse's tongue actually comes to a standstill—after a few more spurts of speech, of course—a result Lady Capulet's direct order 'Enough of this, I pray thee, hold thy peace' (49) failed to produce. That Juliet has all sorts of social stratagems at her command appears quite clearly immediately after the meeting scene when, in order to get the name of her new lover out of the nurse without betraying her feelings to the old chatterbox, she has recourse to Cressida's trick,[10] pretending interest in more than one of the departing guests.

In the ball scene Juliet enters with the rest of the Capulets and obeys her father's urgent invitation to dance. Romeo, one of the young masquers welcomed by Capulet, disregards this invitation, sticking to his decision to stand aside and watch. He sees Juliet and is struck by her beauty:

> What lady's that which doth enrich the hand
> Of yonder knight?
>
> (I.v.41f.)

His as yet half-conscious desire to touch her hand himself manifests itself in a discreet demonstrative gesture and in the metaphor 'enrich her hand'. Too busy to listen properly the servant addressed gets rid of the untimely questioner by a bare 'I know not, sir'. Romeo does not insist since he is getting more and more absorbed by the vision before him. As he tries to find words for his reaction, he seems balanced between his new passionate and his former rhetorical self. The first three of his lines surprise by that brilliance and spontaneity which will be his in the balcony scene:

> O, she doth teach the torches to burn bright.
> It seems she hangs upon the cheek of night
> As a rich jewel in an Ethiop's ear—

What follows fails to keep to the same level, recalling, by its antithetical elaboration and trite image, Romeo's earlier love oratory:

> Beauty too rich for use, for earth too dear.
> So shows a snowy dove trooping with crows
> As yonder lady o'er her fellows shows.
>
> (43-8)

More important than this relative relapse is the effect of the new, powerful emotion on his mood. He overcomes his old coddled depression and, with it, his passivity for good. His energy is set free, and he wants to contrive a way of moving from the admiring and praising of the beautiful creature before him to the meeting her and the touching of her hand:

> The measure done, I'll watch her place of stand,
> And touching hers, make blessed my rude hand.
>
> (49f.)

Now the dancers disappear and the fascinated observer follows them, making room for the wild scene of the taming of Tybalt by old Capulet. When it is ended Juliet returns and, 'The measure done', is conducted back to her 'place of stand' and left there by her partner.

Romeo approaches, doffs his masque, kneels before Juliet, touches and gently raises her hand offering to kiss it. The effects of this first tender touch, described by Baumgart with so much empathy, make themselves felt. A wave of delight overcomes him, but it cannot render the hero of an early play by Shakespeare speechless. He speaks before the intended kiss and, in order to tame his emotions, he chooses the demanding form of a cross-rhymed quatrain for his first address:

> If I profane with my unworthiest hand
> This holy shrine, the gentle sin is this:
> My lips, two blushing pilgrims, ready stand
> To smooth that rough touch with a tender kiss.
>
> (92-5)

It is difficult for him to find words and images for the message which has passed from hand to hand with the most convincing urgency. His perturbation is great, and the playwright has seen to it that it leaves its marks on his deceptively smooth lines. Two of them are outstanding. The first is the half-line 'the gentle sin is this', a fragment of a thought, not directly connected with the properly organized sentence that precedes and follows it. Romeo cannot be fully coherent at this moment, breathless and passionate as he is. The dramatic significance of this loose bit of speech has escaped too many editors and critics. Their blindness to it has sent them on a vain chase after emendations or fine-spun explanations trying to make sense of what is not meant to make sense. Another sign of Romeo's turmoil appears in the awkwardness of the imagery in the second part of his quatrain. For a moment the old self-absorbed acolyte of the artificial cult of love asserts himself again in the narcissistic and almost grotesque comparison of his lips to two blushing pilgrims.

We now approach the most decisive and moving moment in this love encounter. So much depends upon Juliet's reaction to Romeo's appeal. With spontaneous empathy she senses his predicament, but she notices his blunders, too. What she says in a quatrain of her own is beyond anything he could have hoped for:

> Good pilgrim, you do wrong your hand too much,
> Which mannerly devotion shows in this;
> For saints have hands that pilgrims' hands do touch,
> And palm to palm is holy palmers' kiss.
>
> (96-9)

It is difficult to do justice to everything she achieves in these words with great ease and naturalness. She enters into the imaginative scene that Romeo has begun to enact—not quite successfully in consequence of his excitement. She corrects his mistakes and distributes the roles in it properly: For the part of the pilgrim she casts, not the lips of the lover kneeling in front of her, but himself, and for herself she accepts the role, not of an impersonal shrine, but of a personal saint. She quickly withdraws her hand from his, thus refusing the kiss he intended to place on it. This is not done from coyness or shyness, but because her own emotions tell her that a kiss on her hand is no longer enough. So she induces a different development of the playlet in which they are now both passionately engaged. To speak here of scheming and calculation would betray a poorish way of seeing things. The fact is that the girl proves herself more mature than the boy; she takes control of the situation and is able not only to mend Romeo's speech, but to perfect the love that has sprung up in both of them.

In order to understand what is happening to the lovers now we should remember John Keats's version of the Romeo and Juliet theme. At the critical moment in *The Eve of St. Agnes*, Porphyro is able to enter into Madeline's dream of love,[11] a consummation so absolute that the couple cease being human and mortal as they glide by all the obstacles in their way out of the castle into another world of myth and legend. Juliet's perfect response to Romeo's appeal corresponds to Porphyro's passing into Madeline's dream. What happens after the decisive event takes a few minutes in the poem and a few days in the play, but Shakespeare's lovers cannot simply glide away from reality and life; their sufferings and their deaths become as real as their ecstatic happiness.

On hearing Juliet's reply Romeo does not misinterpret the withdrawal of her hand. He feels how completely she is with him, and therefore his bewilderment leaves him at once. He jumps to his feet and boldly asks: 'Have not saints lips, and holy palmers too?' As he tries to embrace her they allow free play to their passionate wit and are carried by it to the immense satisfaction of their first kiss:

> *Juliet.* Ay, pilgrim, lips that they must use in prayer.
> *Romeo.* O then, dear saint, let lips do what hands do:
> They pray: grant thou, lest faith turn to despair.
> *Juliet.* Saints do not move, though grant for prayer's sake.
> *Romeo.* Then move not, while my prayer's effect I take.
> (100-5)

As the kiss unites the lovers, the sonnet, the form they have chosen for their coming together, is complete. They should stop now, but their youthful vehemence and desire for another kiss drive them on through an excessive quatrain:

> *Romeo.* Thus from my lips, by thine, my sin is purg'd.
> *Juliet.* Then have my lips the sin that they have took.
> *Romeo.* Sin from my lips? O trespass sweetly urg'd.
> Give me my sin again.
> *Juliet.*   You kiss by th' book.
> (106-9)

The delight they take in each other betrays them into this anticlimax. As they expand the sonnet their wit becomes more quibbling than before, and Juliet herself is critical of it in her final remark. Behind the fun of going on beyond the limits of the sonnet and of wringing further effect out of its imagery the hint is lurking that this new-born love is too violent to respect forms and conventions and that the excess in it might prove dangerous. Before embarking on the third quatrain the couple may well be lightly touched by the consciousness of this and hesitate a moment, and the words 'Thus from my lips, by thine, my sin is purg'd' may come somewhat hesitatingly from Romeo's lips. It cannot be more than the passing of a white cloud announcing the darker ones which crowd in upon the lovers when they seek and obtain information concerning each other's name and family at the end of the scene. The recognition of what has happened to them makes Romeo cry out:

>   Is she a Capulet?
> O dear account. My life is my foe's debt.
> (116f.)

Soon this will be echoed by Juliet's

> My only love sprung from my only hate.
> Too early seen unknown, and known too late.
> Prodigious birth of love it is to me
> That I must love a loathed enemy.
> (137-40)

When the curious nurse wants to know what she is talking about Juliet's sly answer is subtly balanced between banter and wistfulness:

>   A rhyme I learn'd even now
> Of one I danc'd withal.
> (141f.)

Again her *savoir faire* reminds us of that early maturity which stood her in such good stead when she had to cope with Romeo's first blundering address.

It has been our aim in this essay to show how intimately the sonnet is connected with the gestic events of the meeting scene and how much the importance of its dramatic functions outweighs the decorative ones. By way of conclusion we propose a comparison with the love encounter of Horatio and Belvidera in *The Spanish Tragedy* by Thomas Kyd, a play with which Shakespeare was certainly acquainted. It may have given him the idea of using a poetic pattern for the purpose of coordinating gestures and words in an intensely emotional scene:

> *Bel.* If I be Venus thou must needs be Mars,
> And where Mars reigneth there must needs be wars.
> *Hor.* Then thus begin our wars: put forth thy hand,
> That it may combat with my ruder hand.
> *Bel.* Set forth thy foot to try the push of mine.
> *Hor.* But first my looks shall combat against thine.
> *Bel.* Then ward thyself, I dart this kiss at thee.
> *Hor.* Thus I retort the dart thou threw'st at me.
> *Bel.* Nay then, to gain the glory of the field,
> My twining arms shall yoke and make thee yield.
> *Hor.* Nay then, my arms are large and strong withal:
> Thus elms by vines are compass'd till they fall.
> *Bel.* O let me go, for in my troubled eyes
> Now may'st thou read that life in passion dies.
> *Hor.* O stay awhile and I will die with thee,
> So shalt thou yield and yet have conquer'd me.[12]

Kyd produces an extraordinary slow-motion effect by providing a verbal stimulus for every significant gesture in Horatio's and Belvidera's approach to the physical consummation of their love. Some of these provocations to action are ingeniously combined with war imagery, but imagery gives way to direct expression as the scene becomes more passionate. Dialogue and gestures are strictly patterned by a combination of rhymed couplets with stichomythia, so strictly that the movements which are named and executed, either simultaneously or successively, can recall those of mechanical puppets. The whole scene is dominated by the double meaning of the word 'dying', and the playwright makes the most of the terrifying irony in the situation of the couple, who, unlike the audience, do not know that the consummation towards which they are striving will be death for Horatio and catastrophe for Belvidera. A sensational effect is achieved, but the scene adds hardly anything to the delineation of the two figures, mainly because of Kyd's radical concentration on the physical, generic side of their love-making.

Shakespeare accepts the principle of coordinating speech and gesture in a poetic form for the meeting of his lovers. His theme, however, is different. His young lovers, too, are not far from the brink of an abyss, but to begin with he leads them, not towards sexual satisfaction, but to that first experience when love is immense and full of delightful promises, not for the senses alone, but the imagination and the mind as well. In order to achieve this he frees himself of Kyd's pedantic way of relating word and gesture, and he replaces the imagery of war by the images of the saint and the pilgrim. The generic reactions of Horatio and Belvidera are abandoned in favour of personal ones, that permit us to see Romeo and Juliet as individuals. Shakespeare's score for the give and take between the poetic form, speech, imagery, and gesture is written with a light hand, suggestive much rather than coercive, so discreet that its subtleties have often gone unobserved. We hope to have drawn attention to some of them, to the hints especially that Romeo is not suddenly turned into a new man by love at first sight, but moves gradually from his former to his new self, that he is bewildered when he speaks the first quatrain of the sonnet, that it is Juliet's perfect reaction in the second quatrain which gives him confidence and the boldness that carries the couple through the wit combat of the sestet to their first kiss, and that the additional quatrain signals a possibly ominous excess in their love.

Notes

[1] Bertrand Evans, *Shakespeare's Tragic Practice* (Oxford, 1979), p. 27.

[2] Nicholas Brooke, *Shakespeare's Early Tragedies* (London, 1968), p. 95.

[3] Harley Granville-Barker, *Prefaces to Shakespeare,* Second Series (London, 1930), p. 8.

[4] J. L. Styan, *Shakespeare's Stagecraft* (Cambridge, 1967), p. 57.

[5] J. L. Styan, *Drama, Stage and Audience* (Cambridge, 1975), pp. 56f.

[6] Inge Leimberg, *Shakespeares 'Romeo und Julia'* (München, 1968), p. 149.

[7] Wolfgang Baumgart, 'Romeo begegnet Julia' in *Archiv für das Studium der neueren Sprachen und Literaturen,* vol. 206, 1970, pp. 81-95.

[8] Baumgart, *ibid.,* p. 87.

[9] Quotations are taken from the *Arden Edition* of the play by Brian Gibbons.

[10] Cf. *Troilus and Cressida,* I.ii.

[11] Cf. *The Eve of St. Agnes,* Stanza XXXVI.

[12] Thomas Kyd, *The Spanish Tragedy*, ed. by Philip Edwards (London, 1959), II.iv.34-49.

DEATH AND DESIRE

William C. Carroll (essay date 1981)

SOURCE: "'We Were Born to Die': *Romeo and Juliet*," in *Comparative Drama*, Vol. 15, No. 1, Spring 1981, pp. 54-71.

[*In the following essay, Carroll explores the juxtaposition of love and death in* Romeo and Juliet, *viewing the ending of the play as "positive" in that it eternalizes the title characters' love rather than ironically presenting their demise.*]

While Romeo and Juliet consummate their marriage offstage, their one night in the sheets of love is shaded by the ghostly presence of winding sheets. Tybalt's death hangs over Verona, as old Capulet says to Paris:

> Look you, she lov'd her kinsman Tybalt
>   dearly,
> And so did I. Well, we were born to die.
> 'Tis very late, she'll not come down to-night.[1]
> (III.iv.3-5)

Indeed she won't, for she is dying sexually above even as her father pronounces his platitudes and arranges her hasty marriage to Paris. Juliet governs her own comings and dyings to the end.

Capulet's sententious wisdom, bracketed between a bow to a dead loved one and transactions with a new suitor, reminds us of *Romeo and Juliet*'s constant association of birth, love, and death, from the Nurse's proleptic obituary of Juliet's parallel, Susan (I.iii.18), through the image clusters of wombs, tombs, sex, and death, to the brittle beauty of Liebestod in the final scene. The ending of the play represents the consummation, in all senses, of Romeo and Juliet's love, and its inescapable location in the tomb powerfully focuses our attention on their claustrophobic isolation and triumph. The only "problem" the ending seems to have caused modern readers is whether or not it is "ironic" and, if so, to what extent. Perhaps the most extreme prosecutorial revision of the ending was quoted in Richard Levin's *New Readings vs. Old Plays*, in which the unnamed critic reported that his background reading left him "with one overriding impression: that the average audience of *Romeo and Juliet* would have regarded the behavior of the young lovers as deserving everything they got,"[2] including, presumably, a double suicide. Other ironic readings focus on the alleged inadequacy or "materialism" of the golden statues raised by the dead lovers' parents. In general, though, the ending of *Romeo and Juliet* has not provoked the kind of controversy that marks the ending of *King Lear*, for example. It seems, from one point of view, to be perfectly conventional and appropriate, and so it is, but I do not think we have yet fully understood why it is so.

I return for a moment to Capulet's commonplace that "we were born to die." Similar sentiments are to be heard in other of the tragedies, but in *Romeo and Juliet* Shakespeare goes to great lengths to stress the inevitability of Capulet's vision. Specifically, as many readers have pointed out, *Romeo and Juliet* contains allusions to, even as it embodies, a journey.[3] Feste's song assures us that "journeys end in lovers meeting" (*TN*, II.iii.4), as they certainly do for Romeo and Juliet (with the suggestive pun *meeting = mating*), yet we are never allowed to forget that all journeys must *end*, and that the ending, both goal and foreclosure, determines the shape of the journey itself. In *Romeo and Juliet*, Shakespeare investigates this teleological puzzle in which the lovers' foreknown end colors the nature of their journey, continually darkening our belief in their potential and actual happiness.

The very existence of the Prologue begins the shadowing, especially with its look toward a "fearful passage" (1. 9) and the eerie double grammar in which the "pair of star-cross'd lovers take their life" (1. 6), the journey and the suicide collapsed into the simultaneously transitive/intransitive verb. Nowhere but in Shakespeare could we find the journey and its end so economically and chillingly packaged. Romeo, as has often been pointed out, senses this fatality and frequently expresses it in similar terms:

> . . . my mind misgives
> Some consequence yet hanging in the stars
> Shall bitterly begin his fearful date
> With this night's revels, and expire the term
> Of a despised life clos'd in my breast,
> By some vile forfeit of untimely death.
> But He that hath the steerage of my course
> Direct my sail! On, lusty gentlemen!
> (I.iv.106-13)

Thus the end or "consequence" ironically begins with the beginning (which is why it is "bitter"), the first breath initiating the expiration of the last. Romeo bravely urges on the sea-journey of his fate, asking only that someone ("He") at least direct his course, but he has yet to learn that there is no such thing as an "untimely death."

Throughout the play we will be reminded of journeys and endings. Romeo will tell Juliet that "love" prompted his journey to her, a journey dangerous but potentially rewarding—like Drake's, for example:

> I am no pilot, yet, wert thou as far
> As that vast shore wash'd with the farthest sea,
> I should adventure for such merchandise.
>
> (II.ii.82-84)

The actual journey Romeo makes—to "sojourn in Mantua" (III.iii.169)—is not as far as the farthest sea, but might as well be, since he will never see Juliet alive (or awake) again. In a conceit as tedious as its speaker, Capulet takes Juliet's tears as the occasion on which to launch her metaphorical journey:

> In one little body
> Thou counterfeits a bark, a sea, a wind:
> For still thy eyes, which I may call the sea,
> Do ebb and flow with tears; the bark thy body is,
> Sailing in this salt flood; the winds, thy sighs,
> Who, raging with thy tears, and they with them,
> Without a sudden calm, will overset
> Thy tempest-tossed body.
>
> (III.v.130-37)

The irony of Capulet's fatuous prophecy becomes more evident when Juliet launches herself on an even riskier course of action by taking both the Friar's advice and his potion, intending to join Romeo later in Mantua. When Juliet's "dead" body is discovered, her mother's lament borrows a now familiar trope: "Most miserable hour that e'er time saw/ In lasting labor of his pilgrimage!" (IV.v.44-45). The pilgrimage of time ought never to be a surprise, but it always is. Capulet recapitulates the play's paradox of beginnings and endings when he tells Paris that Death has "lain with thy wife. There she lies,/ Flower as she was, deflowered by him" (IV.v.36-37). Youth, defloration, death: they turn out to be the same thing, even verbally, as a single pun compresses the beginning, fulfillment, and end of life into a single sour irony. Perhaps the lovers are not entirely pretending when, after their one night together, they cannot agree on whether it is day or night, nightingale or lark, "more light and light" or "more dark and dark" (III.v.36). In fact, the play continually suggests that such distinctions are really identities.

"In lasting labor of his pilgrimage"—Lady Capulet's allusion—deepens the idea of the journey by suggesting the longest journey, the pilgrimage of earthly life. Shakespeare has hinted at this more resonant metaphor earlier, in the famous sonnet of Romeo and Juliet's first meeting:

> *Romeo.* If I profane with my unworthiest hand
> This holy shrine, the gentle sin is this,
> My lips, two blushing pilgrims, ready stand
> To smooth that rough touch with a tender kiss.
> *Juliet.* Good pilgrim, you do wrong your hand too much,
> Which mannerly devotion shows in this:
> For saints have hands that pilgrims' hands do touch,
> And palm to palm is holy palmers' kiss.
>
> (I.v.93-100)

This is kissing by the book, to be sure, but even the audience can scarcely anticipate the rough touch of death these young pilgrims will finally experience in the ultimate shrine of love. However innocently the pilgrimage is invoked here, Shakespeare clearly knew the word's root and medieval meaning.[4]

Something more than image-clusters and iterated verbal signs points to a pilgrimage in *Romeo and Juliet*, however. In their brief moment on the stage, Romeo and Juliet recapitulate the emblematic moments of all human life—beginning, middle, and end—making the structure and movement of the play seem to follow the main lines of the ultimate pilgrimage plot, *Everyman*, or even more to the point, *Lusty Juventus*. I am not suggesting that Shakespeare was consciously imitating either of these plays, though the evidence for his knowledge of the Morality tradition has long been documented, and several other plays have been shown to have a "deep structure" derived from the typical Morality plot.[5] What I want to suggest here, instead, is that *Romeo and Juliet* becomes far more powerful when we recognize the deepest analogy it offers.

Romeo and Juliet are rarely alone on the stage, as many readers have noted. They are almost always entangled in family webs of one sort or another, the feud being the largest one, surrounded by well-meaning but interfering authority figures who guide and misguide their lives. On three well-chosen occasions, however, Shakespeare isolates his lovers to focus our understanding of their life. The first of these moments, in the balcony scene, locates us in familiar emblematic geography—in the *hortus conclusus* of Capulet's walled orchard.[6] As Rosalie Colie has noted about this moment, "The virgin is, and is in, a walled garden: the walls of that garden are to be breached by a true lover, as Romeo leaps into the orchard."[7] As is usual for the lovers, though, the outside world intrudes soon enough, this time in the form of the Nurse's persistent voice offstage. Their physical positions on the stage are also significant: Romeo below, Juliet above.

The second scene of isolation is predictable—the bedroom, or the balcony just outside it, after the night of consummation. Moreover, in contrast to his source Arthur Brooke, Shakespeare gives the lovers only this single night together, heightening the pathos and incidentally isolating the moment even further. Physically, this seems to be the same "upper station" at which Juliet appeared earlier.[8] But even this lovely aubade is darkened by death, and Romeo leaves with the kind of line that he might speak in the final scene in the tomb: "Farewell, farewell! One kiss, and I'll descend" (III.v.42). The lovers' physical positions—first both above, then one descending—seem emblematic again. Juliet follows Romeo's descent in a fearful imagining:

> O God, I have an ill-divining soul!
> Methinks I see thee now, thou art so low,
> As one dead in the bottom of a tomb.
>
> (III.v.54-56)

Romeo later relates an ironic inversion of this vision, just before he hears of Juliet's "death":

> . . . all this day an unaccustom'd spirit
> Lifts me above the ground with cheerful
>   thoughts.
> I dreamt my lady came and found me dead—
> Strange dream, that gives a dead man leave to
>   think!—
> And breath'd such life with kisses in my lips
> That I reviv'd and was an emperor.
>
> (V.i.4-9)

This romance fantasy of exaltation and rebirth is not only youthful wishing but also the fairy-tale fulfillment which the play is designed to counteract. The audience should know, even if Romeo does not, that what goes up must come down. Romeo's descent from the momentary elevation of Act III, Scene v is permanent. Once again, too, it is the Nurse who has interrupted the lovers' idyll.

The third moment in which Romeo and Juliet are alone together on stage is of course the final scene in the tomb. Much has been written about this scene as the inevitable completion of the tomb-womb theme, the logical result of the blood feud in Verona, and as a powerfully dramatic moment in its own right. I will examine the scene in more detail shortly. I would like now to observe its place in a line of images: from garden through bedroom to tomb, from courtship through sexual completion to death. These are the Three Ages of Man, as it were, the major emblematic moments in the pilgrimage of earthly life. Even the stage blocking reflects this movement: the lovers separated, one below and one above; the lovers united above, till one descends; and the lovers united below, forever.

These three moments provide a linear and irreversible chronological sequence, finally emblematic of the earthly pilgrimage. They are also all the *same* moment. Each scene takes place at night, each contains similar language and double-entendres, each emphasizes the isolation of the lovers. Moreover, each scene represents a dream displacement of female sexuality, from the walled garden and the actual marital bed to Romeo's explicit references at the tomb to the "womb of death" (V.iii.45) and the "palace of dim night" (V.iii.107) where "Death is amorous" (V.iii.103) and has become Romeo's rival. For once, the lovers will not be interrupted before they can complete their making of love and death: *Romeo:* "Thus with a kiss I die" (V.iii.120); and *Juliet:* "O happy dagger,/ This is thy sheath; there rust, and let me die" (V.iii.170).

Several other incidents in the final act increase this momentum towards mortality. In "The Tragicall Historye of Romeus and Juliet," Brooke alludes to an apothecary, for example, from whom Romeus can buy poison, but Shakespeare gives his apothecary a most unusual appearance and inventory:[9]

> meagre were his looks,
> Sharp misery had worn him to the bones;
> And in his needy shop a tortoise hung,
> An alligator stuff'd, and other skins
> Of ill-shap'd fishes, and about his shelves
> A beggarly account of empty boxes,
> Green earthen pots, bladders, and musty
>   seeds,
> Remnants of packthread, and old cakes of
>   roses
> Were thinly scattered, to make up a show.
>
> (V.i.40-48)

Clearly the agent of dismemberment and death, the cadaverous apothecary anticipates later merchants of mortality like the gravedigger in *Hamlet* or the country clown in *Antony and Cleopatra*.[10] The random assortment of corpses, skins, and musty seeds reminds us also of the tomb itself, both as Juliet imagines it (in IV.iii) and as Romeo finds it (in V.iii). Thus the cause and effect of death are linked together, as they also are in the Apothecary's report to Romeo that the penalty of selling death is in fact death (ll. 66-67).

In this speech, the iconography of death is heard but not seen. As we move toward the death-embrace in the tomb, Shakespeare similarly works to displace the visual, to remove part of the play from a strictly dramatic focus, and direct us towards other kinds of understanding. This process withdraws Romeo and Juliet from the temporal confinement of the drama proper and lifts the lovers toward other realms. Romeo's description of the Apothecary and his shop, not present in Brooke, begins the process. The stuffed animals, finally, also anticipate the lovers' memorialization in the form of statues.

Shakespeare also deletes from Brooke the few intimations of Romeo's vanity, as when he fantasizes "that if nere unto her he offered up his breath,/ That then an hundred thousand parts more glorious were his death" (ll. 2553-54), or when he admires his own actions:

> What Epitaph more worth, or halfe so excellent,
> To consecrate my memorye, could any man invente,
> As this, our mutuell, and our piteous sacrifice
> Of lyfe, set light for love.
>
> (ll. 2649-52)

Shakespeare has none of this, but dramatizes instead a singleminded drive in Romeo to rejoin Juliet with a minimum of meditation, just as Antony seeks Cleopatra once he has heard of her "death." Romeo's rhetoric itself changes with the anticipation of death: he expects that the poison will work so "that the life-weary taker may fall dead" (V.i.62). This phrasal *tmesis*, of the weary life-taker, shows that the taker of the poison knows the sort of gap he will soon have to leap. The poison, he continues, will work as quickly as "hasty powder fir'd" hurries from the "fatal cannon's womb" (ll. 64, 65). All three phrases once again compress cause and effect, beginning and ending. Everything in the play, it seems, works to isolate the lovers in both love and death.

The abandonment at the edge of death makes the suicides almost unbearably pathetic. But the loss of all worldly advisors at the lip of the grave ought also to seem a familiar dramatic moment. Just as Everyman, for example, is abandoned by Fellowship, Kindred, Goods, Beauty, Discretion, and so on, and accompanied into the grave only by Good-Deeds, so Romeo and Juliet are progressively and cruelly abandoned by their worldly advisors, those meddling adults who tell them how to live but cannot help them die. These young lovers' lives may end in tragedy unless they receive proper *counsel*, as Montague says about Romeo's initial melancholy: "Black and portendous must this humor prove,/ Unless good counsel may the cause remove" (I.i.141-42). For now, he continues, Romeo is "his own affections' counsellor" (I.i.147), but his affections cannot be easily governed, as we see. Both Romeo and Juliet seek desperately for counsel throughout the play, for a worldly guide on the vast pilgrimage.[11] Mother, father, friends, nurse, priest—all will fail and abandon them.

The play makes us believe a contradiction, that the lovers are self-sufficient but that they also need guidance and advice. The self-sufficiency is suggested in those few scenes where they exist alone on the stage and together seem all in all, their own affections' counselors. In the balcony scene, Juliet wonders who has spoken to her: "What man art thou that thus bescreen'd in night/ So stumblest on my counsel?" (II.ii.52-53). Her counsel is with herself now, though she will soon seek the aid of the Friar, ironically already present in the verb "stumblest." As the lovers thrill to their first discoveries of love, their rhetoric suggests the fulfillment of a fragile fantasy. Romeo has arrived in the walled garden, he tells us: "With love's light wings did I o'erperch these walls,/ For stony limits cannot hold love out" (II.ii.66-67). Still, the stony limits of the world, not to mention the tomb, soon require them to find worldly advice. For now, hermetically sealed off, they guide their own destinies:

> *Juliet.* By whose direction foundst thou out this place?
> *Romeo.* By love, that first did prompt me to inquire;
> He lent me counsel, and I lent him eyes.
> I am no pilot, yet, wert thou as far
> As that vast shore wash'd with the farthest sea,
> I should adventure for such merchandise.
>
> (II.ii.79-84)

Every parent eventually seems a *senex iratus*, no doubt. Certainly the Capulets and Montagues vary little from the stereotypical blocking figures of New Comedy. The young lovers turn instead to the equally sexless but more sympathetic Nurse and Friar for help. Even Lady Capulet bids the Nurse stay and "hear our counsel" (I.iii.9). These usages of the word merely prepare for the far more urgent and dangerous counsel required after Tybalt's death. When the Friar proposes that Romeo journey to Mantua, the Nurse is thrilled, in a speech hedged with irony: "O Lord, I could have stay'd here all the night/ To hear good counsel. O, what learning is!" (III.iii.159-60). But the Nurse fails signally when Juliet asks her how she can avoid the calamity of marrying Paris: "Comfort me, counsel me! . . . Some comfort, nurse" (III.v.208, 212). Worldly Wisdom, as it usually does, errs badly, for the Nurse recommends that Juliet marry Paris, incidentally committing bigamy, because all is lost and besides "Romeo's a dishclout to him" (III.v.219). Juliet is stunned, as we all are—"Speak'st thou from thy heart?" (l. 226)—and sarcastically thanks her: "Well, thou hast comforted me marvelous much" (l. 230). Morally, the Nurse has abandoned Juliet, and they can never be intimate again. As the Nurse leaves the stage, Juliet emotionally turns from her forever:

> Ancient damnation! O most wicked fiend!
> Is it more sin to wish me thus forsworn,
> Or to dispraise my lord with that same tongue
> Which she hath prais'd him with above compare
> So many thousand times? Go, counselor,
> Thou and my bosom henceforth shall be twain.
> I'll to the friar to know his remedy;
> If all else fail, myself have power to die.
>
> (III.v.235-42)

Turning from the Nurse's too-worldly wisdom to the Friar's religious perspective will not make any ultimate difference, but the lovers are too young to go it alone. We hear in the ominous rhyme remedy-die the logical outcome of worldly counsel in this play, and we hear again the paradox of circular identity in which beginnings are endings and solutions are dissolutions.

Juliet will find in the Friar guidance more moral but also more dangerous. The terminology of Juliet's supplication remains the same:

> Therefore, out of thy long-experienc'd time,
> Give me some present counsel, or, behold,
> 'Twixt my extremes and me this bloody knife
> Shall play the umpeer. . . .
>
> (IV.i.60-63)

Her petition ends with the ominously recurrent pun, "I long to die,/ If what thou speak'st speak not of remedy" (IV.i.66-67). The Friar's advice is well-meant but desperate, "a thing like death" (IV.i.74). Juliet must begin to enact her fate alone, for with Romeo banished, she sends her mother and the Nurse away before she drinks the potion—"Farewell! God knows when we shall meet again" (IV.iii.14)—though she once tries to call the Nurse back "to comfort me" (l. 17). But "My dismal scene I needs must act alone" (l. 19). Among the most terrible things she imagines, as she takes the potion, is her isolation in the womb of death, "stifled in the vault," before Romeo comes "to redeem me" (l. 32). Redemption from the tomb represents everyone's deepest desire, but it won't come to pass here. As with Everyman, the imagination of death constitutes the final isolation.

The portents and emblems around the final scene, then, are inevitable and severe. All earthly life has been an ironic rehearsal of this moment. The lovers, it seems, have always slept in "this palace of dim night." The message sent to Romeo has failed because of the plague; Romeo has killed his rival and sent away his servant; Friar Lawrence stumbles over graves. What more could happen? It is the end of the road, the consummation of the pilgrimage, and Romeo knows it:

> O, here
> Will I set up my everlasting rest,
> And shake the yoke of inauspicious stars
> From this world-wearied flesh.
>
> (V.iii.109-12)

Romeo lives a lifetime in a few days. Like a beast of burden after a long day, this abandoned child, who has presciently told us "I am no pilot" (II.ii.82), now crosses the bar and brings his journey to an end:

> Come, bitter conduct, come, unsavory guide!
> Thou desperate pilot, now at once run on
> The dashing rocks thy seasick weary bark!
> Here's to my love! [Drinks.]
>
> (V.iii.116-19)

The bravery these children reveal as they seal "a dateless bargain to engrossing death" (l. 115) thrills even the most jaded among us, in part because Shakespeare contrives to isolate them so completely. At the very last moment, the scene spectrally illuminating "grubs and eyeless skulls" (l. 126), Juliet awakens, still looking towards the "comfortable friar" (l. 148) for counsel and help. But this last worldly advisor, after offering to "dispose" of Juliet in a nunnery, inexplicably abandons her ("I dare no longer stay"—l. 159), and Juliet's dismissal of him echoes her earlier farewell to the Nurse: "Go get thee hence, for I will not away" (l. 160). Now they are alone, together, forever. Death is a relief.

The sense of closure at the end of *Romeo and Juliet* overwhelms us. Everything—theme, image, and structure—has led to this point in the tomb. Moreover, because the play has insisted on the identity of beginnings and endings, we are under a severe obligation to attend to the play's own ending as closely as possible. Here I particularly want to invoke the ways in which Shakespeare's ending deviates from that of Brooke's poem, for the deviations become quite frequent and significant in the final act. We have already seen Shakespeare's addition to the apothecary; even more strikingly, Brooke's Paris does not appear to be killed in the final scene, as he does in Shakespeare. But most significantly, Shakespeare rejects Brooke's religious orthodoxy altogether. This is most surprising, considering the language Brooke employs. Of course, Shakespeare frequently seems to avoid explicit religious declarations, while Brooke's Romeus, when he feels the poison working, makes a speech that seems perfectly in keeping with the iterative imagery of womb-tomb and descent-ascent we have seen in *Romeo and Juliet*:

> Lord Christ, that so to raunsome me
>   descendedst long agoe
> Out of thy fathers bosome, and in the virgins
>   wombe
> Didst put on flesh, Oh let my plaint out of
>   this hollow toombe,
> Perce through the ayre. . . .
>
> (ll. 2674-77)

This spiritual analogy, with its intimations of redemption, suggests the survival of Romeus in another time. But Shakespeare prefers to work for pathos in the final scene, and wants to emphasize loss rather than redemption. Therefore he does not reach for the spiritual analogy, just as he also passes up another clenching image in Juliet's last words:

> O welcome death (quoth she) end of
>   unhappines,

That also art beginning of assured happines;

. . . . .

. . . our parted sprites, from light that we see here,
In place of endlesse light and blisse, may ever live yfere.

(ll. 2773-74, 2787-88)

The end that is a beginning that is in fact endless—the play insists on this point elsewhere, but Shakespeare here rejects the too-easy final connection, the promise of a spiritual "endlesse light," and he makes his young lovers (by contrast with Brooke's) unreflective. Indeed, Juliet has no time to think, while Romeo's speech is studded with images of linear completion and closure: the "doors of breath" will be sealed, the journey completed (or shipwrecked), the everlasting rest achieved. No beginnings here, no final emblem of hope.

No final emblem of hope, in fact, is necessary or even possible. As we have seen, the play everywhere demonstrates that this last stage has always been present, that the love of Romeo and Juliet already contains its own beginning and end. Since death is a necessary part of their love, then it is an end that is endless. The lovers do not need any final hope, and the audience is denied a visibly convincing one—not out of a cynical or ironic motive, I think, but because Shakespeare is working towards something far more difficult, something literally un-thinkable: Romeo and Juliet are absolutely dead, but they have achieved the endless end.

The Friar's speech of self-defense is longer in Brooke (77 lines, with yet further paraphrases) than in Shakespeare (40 lines), but the real difference is in *where* the speech is delivered. In Shakespeare, the Friar and the corpses remain in the tomb for the rest of the play. But in Brooke,

The prince did straight ordaine, the corses that wer founde
Should be set forth upon a stage, hye raysed from the grounde,
Right in the selfe same fourme, (shewde forth to all mens sight)
That in the hollow valt they had been found that other night.

(ll. 2817-20)

The Friar must join them, and justify himself:

The holy fryer now, and reverent by his age,
In great reproche set to the shew upon the open stage,
(A thing that ill beseemde a man of silver heares).

(ll. 2825-27)

"Upon a stage"? How could Shakespeare have resisted it, especially when we see the heroes and heroines of later tragedies so frequently associated with a stage? The theatrical metaphor, as many readers have noted, almost comes to be expected at or near the end of the tragedies: Hamlet speaks to the "audience to this act" (V.ii.335) and his corpse is to be borne "like a soldier to the stage" (V.ii.396); and rather than allowing rude mechanicals to stage her story, Cleopatra acts her own death—"perform'd the dreaded act" (V.ii.331), as Dolabella says. The theatrical metaphor is not inevitable, of course, but it is so *available* here. Why not use it?

The staging of Brooke's ending would have become openly emblematic, moreover, as the lovers *ascend* once more, and to a stage at that. But this seems to be precisely why Shakespeare did not adopt the idea, for he wants to keep the lovers in the tomb. There is no escape, not through pious orthodoxy, not through some convenient eternizing self-consciousness, and certainly not through a play. In fact, the play becomes steadily less "dramatic," less obviously a play. Perhaps the most important thing about the Friar's speech is not what it says, for we have all seen what it recounts, but the fact that it is spoken at all. It translates the dramatic action of the play into another form—into narrative, into oratory.[12] The speech is conspicuously unnecessary in terms of the plot; though the Friar must exonerate himself, he is under much greater suspicion in Brooke. No, Shakespeare turns down the clenching allusions to new beginnings and the inevitable stage metaphor so that there may be no hint, no suggestion of a rebirth, religious or dramatic. He insists on the lovers' end. And Shakespeare further removes us from the lovers by retaining the Friar's long speech. Yet even here, Shakespeare deviates radically from Brooke. Brooke's Friar is unremittingly pious, marking his own guilt, looking forward to his own end, invoking the pilgrimage motif, anticipating his "great accompt, which no man else for me shall undertake . . . before the judgement seate of everlasting powre" (ll. 2852, 2854). Naturally, Brooke's Friar invokes Christ and his pity as well, while Shakespeare's Friar makes none of these gestures. Instead, he tells us the plot again, a "tedious tale" (V.iii.230) for the audience if not the characters. To tell us what we have seen is not only necessarily to misrepresent what we have seen, but to alter its very nature. Shakespeare eliminates the piety of Brooke's Friar, eliminates the more elaborate self-justification, takes him off the stage, and simply makes him tell the *plot*. Since we have seen the play, we can judge how well the Friar tells it, and we find his story accurate but not the truth. His version of this story is no doubt more faithful to fact than Horatio's condensation of Hamlet's story, but it fails in all sorts of ways. Shakespeare's Friar removes the story of Romeo and Juliet from the life of drama, in short, but we remain in the tomb, with Romeo and Juliet, their bodies lying before us in an embrace. The lovers are being transfigured, all right, but from drama into myth, from action into stasis. We shall finally see their petrifaction, as statues, to complete the movement.

The presence of an "inquest" after the protagonists' death recurs in many of the tragedies—the explanation of Cleopatra's suicide, the entrance and declaration of Fortinbras. The process of explanation begins to "withdraw" us from the tragic world. We meet the surviving figure of "order," and we sense the inadequacy of the world that survives.[13] In *Romeo and Juliet,* the inquest begins very early in the final scene, and has somewhat different aims, I think. We withdraw not only from the lovers, but from drama itself. Shakespeare's final deviation from Brooke reemphasizes this point. Brooke's narrator, not the characters, reports the memorialization of the lovers:

> And lest that length of time might from our myndes remove
> The memory of so perfect, sound, and so approved love,
> The bodies dead removed from vaulte where they did dye,
> In stately tombe, on pillers great, of marble rayse they hye.
> On every syde above, were set and eke beneath,
> Great store of cunning Epitaphes, in honor of theyr death.
>
> (ll. 3011-16)

Thus the *actual* bodies are elevated and memorialized, and written inscriptions offered, while in Shakespeare a far more controversial proposal is made:

> *Montague.* But I can give thee more,
> For I will raise her statue in pure gold,
> That whiles Verona by that name is known,
> There shall no figure at such rate be set
> As that of true and faithful Juliet.
> *Capulet.* As rich shall Romeo's by his lady's lie,
> Poor sacrifices of our enmity!
>
> (V.iii.298-304)

Of the actual bodies, which still lie before us on the stage (along with those of Paris and Tybalt), there is no mention. They have already ceased to exist, dramatically speaking, because they cannot move. They have become icons, a complex emblematic tableau which is being framed and distanced by the minute. Their story has been transmuted into an incomplete and passionless narrative, their bodies ignored while representations of their bodies are measured and discussed. This ending shows Shakespeare uncannily aware of the possibilities and limitations of representation itself.

Rosalie Colie argues that in the statues the "lovers are preserved in a nearly Ovidian way, not as plants, but in an *ecphrasis,* as memorial statues exemplifying a specific lesson to future generations."[14] This is a useful observation, but it elides the real difference: in Ovid's version of Pyramus and Thisby, the plants live on, forever, stained with and therefore bearing the lovers' blood. But statues cannot breathe, not until *The Winter's Tale* in any case. Shakespeare insists on the *gap* between bodies and statues, rather than an Ovidian continuity. James L. Calderwood offers by far the most elaborate explanation of the statues. For him, they embody the play's chief values, public and private:

> If the lovers' nominalistic conception of speech implies a verbal purity bordering on nonspeech, here in the silence of the statues is that stillness; and if their love has aspired to a lyric stasis, here too in the fixity of plastic form is that stillness. But by being publicly available—representing the lovers and their value but representing them for the Veronese audience—the statues surpass the aspirations and expressive aims of the lovers. The communicative gap between the private secret love and the social order oblivious to the existence of that love is bridged—and this seems the major significance of the statues—by *artistic form.*[15]

This is very good, but perhaps it is too good. It expands upon a slender reference and pictures something we don't even see. The statue scene in *The Winter's Tale,* or even the songs at the end of *Love's Labour's Lost,* sum up their plays more convincingly. Nor am I certain that "stillness" and "stasis" are virtues quite so unmixed.

Both Colie and Calderwood strain for a "positive" reading of the end, which is in fact a welcome gesture after so many recent ironic readings.[16] I also find in the statues, and especially their golden nature, an eternizing gesture. But what do the statues actually eternize? Certainly not the *love* of Romeo and Juliet. Colie sees the statues representing "a specific lesson to future generations," though it is hard to imagine what that "lesson" could be; and Calderwood believes that some "communicative gap" between the secret love and the social order will be bridged. But this is exactly what will not happen: the gap is in fact established by the statues. The characters in the play offer their own "positive" ending, and for them, it is sufficient, or as much as they can manage: an eternal memory to the resolution of their feud and to the deaths of Romeo and Juliet, but not to their love. One can move beyond this "positive" reading of the end without embracing an entirely "ironic" revisionist reading. For *nothing* could memorialize their love. It achieves its own perfection. While the others talk and statues are promised, the lovers' bodies continue to lie before us on the stage, locked in an embrace of permanence. The bodies render everything else unnecessary, and impossible.

In the final scenes of *Romeo and Juliet,* Shakespeare alters the very nature of the theatrical experience to produce quite a different kind of experience. The reference to the statues comes at the end of a sequence of representations, and therefore withdrawals—moments in which the lovers' vital nature fades away as they are transfigured and slowly petrified. From life to death, from drama to icon, from flesh to metal—the ending of the play not only confirms Capulet's maxim that "we were born to die," but also suggests that no representation of their love, other than drama, could satisfy. The statues can represent the lovers not as a single identity—their love—but only as separate entities—their bodies, hence their deaths. The play ends with the bodies still before us, the sun refusing to rise (for the final descent has been final), the drama of their love left even further behind; they end as they began, the subjects of a rhyming epigram, a final closed representation of their "story," a last attempt to represent the endless end: "For never was a story of more woe/ Than this of Juliet and her Romeo."

Notes

[1] All quotations from Shakespeare are from *The Riverside Shakespeare,* ed. G. B. Evans (Boston: Houghton Miffin, 1974). Hereafter cited in the text.

[2] Richard Levin, *New Readings vs. Old Plays* (Chicago: Univ. of Chicago Press, 1979), p. 152. In *The Music of the Close* (Lexington: Univ. Press of Kentucky, 1978), Walter C. Foreman, Jr., says very little about the end of *Romeo and Juliet.*

[3] The motif of the journey has frequently been discussed, beginning I believe with Moody Prior, *The Language of Tragedy* (1947; rpt. Bloomington: Indiana Univ. Press, 1966), pp. 69-70. See also the remarks of James L. Calderwood, *Shakespearean Metadrama* (Minneapolis: Univ. of Minnesota Press, 1971), pp. 109-10. The best comment on the journey as an element of tragic structure is by Maynard Mack, "The Jacobean Shakespeare," *Jacobean Theater,* ed. John Russell Brown and Bernard Harris (1960; rpt. New York: Capricorn Books, 1967), pp. 35-38.

[4] Cf. *AYL:* "how brief the life of man/ Runs his erring pilgrimage" (III.ii.129-30); *Lr:* "and from first to last/ Told him our pilgrimage" (V.iii.196-97); and *1H4:* "pilgrims going to Canterbury with rich offerings" (I.ii.126).

[5] For a famous example, see Bernard Spivack, *Shakespeare and the Allegory of Evil* (New York: Columbia Univ. Press, 1958); also Edmund Creeth, *Mankynde in Shakespeare* (Athens: Univ. of Georgia Press, 1976). Alan C. Dessen has recently reviewed the issue in "Homilies and Anomalies: The Legacy of the Morality Play to the Age of Shakespeare," *Shakespeare Studies,* 11 (1978), 243-58. For a recent dissenting view, see John Wasson, "The Morality Play: Ancestor of Elizabethan Drama?" *Comparative Drama,* 13 (1979), 210-21. Wasson argues that folk plays and miracle plays are more likely ancestors.

[6] In *Prefaces to Shakespeare* (Princeton: Princeton Univ. Press, 1947), Harley Granville-Barker describes the probable staging of this scene (II, 306).

[7] Rosalie L. Colie, *Shakespeare's Living Art* (Princeton: Princeton Univ. Press, 1974), p. 145.

[8] In "The Use of the Upper Stage in *Romeo and Juliet,*" *Shakespeare Quarterly,* 5 (1954), Richard Hosley describes these moments. He shows as well that only those scenes require the upper station; thus the final tomb scene would have been below, on the main stage with perhaps some use of the discovery space.

[9] In *Narrative and Dramatic Sources of Shakespeare,* I (New York: Columbia Univ. Press, 1966), 278-83, Geoffrey Bullough summarizes the major points of comparison. Quotations from Brooke, hereafter cited in the text, are from this edition.

[10] Perhaps Dickens was recalling the apothecary in his description of Mr. Venus' shop in *Our Mutual Friend,* ed. Stephen Gill (Baltimore: Penguin, 1971), where we find "human warious" as well as "Cats. Articulated English baby. Dogs. Ducks. Glass eyes, warious. Mummied bird" (I, vii).

[11] As one of its definitions of "counsel," the *OED* records: "One of the Advisory declarations of Christ and the apostles, in mediaeval theology reckoned as twelve, which are considered not to be universally binding, but to be given as a means of attaining greater moral perfection." The word recurs through many Morality plays, especially *The Interlude of Youth and Tide Tarrieth No Man.* In *Enough Is as Good as a Feast,* Worldly Man admits, "By my truth, me thinks I begin to war sick./ In sending away my counsellor I was somewhat too quick" (ll. 1219-20) (*English Morality Plays and Moral Interludes,* ed. Edgar T. Schell and J. D. Shuchter [New York: Holt, Rinehart, and Winston, 1969]). In several plays, such as *Horestes* and *Cambises,* one of the allegorical figures is actually named Counsel. In *Lusty Juventus,* the central figure of virtue is Good Counsaill, and the prologue explains "in this interlude by youth you shall see plain,/ From his lust by Good Counsel brought to godly conversation" (*The Dramatic Writings of Richard Wever and Thomas Ingelend,* ed. John S. Farmer [1905; rpt. New York: Barnes and Noble, 1966], p. 3.)

[12] Granville-Barker justifies the Friar's story "because the play's true end is less in the death of the star-crossed lovers than in the burying of their parents'

strife" (II, 323), a reading which seems to me quite wrong. Clifford Leech, however, says that the speech "is surely an indication of an ultimate withdrawal from the tragic: the speech is too much like a preacher's resumé of the events on which a moral lesson will be based," in "The Moral Tragedy of *Romeo and Juliet*," *English Renaissance Drama*, ed. Standish Henning *et al.* (Carbondale: Southern Illinois Univ. Press, 1976), p. 70.

[13] Cf. Mack and Foreman, *passim*.

[14] Colie, p. 146.

[15] Calderwood, p. 117.

[16] Leech finds it "difficult for us to get interested in these statues, or to take much joy in the feud's ending" (p. 71), and also points out the "curious ambivalence in the fact that the statues are golden" (p. 172, n. 15), since Romeo equates gold with poison earlier (V.i.80). I am greatly indebted to my colleague Stuart H. Johnson for helping me with this final section.

Catherine Belsey (essay date 1993)

SOURCE: "The Name of the Rose in *Romeo and Juliet*," in *The Yearbook of English Studies*, Vol. 23, 1993, pp. 126-42.

[*In the following essay, Belsey observes that* Romeo and Juliet *is a play about desire, and examines the ways in which culture and language construct erotic longing.*]

I

Is the human body inside or outside culture? Is it an organism, subject only to nature and independent of history? Or alternatively is it an effect of the signifier, no more than an ensemble of the meanings ascribed to it in different cultures, and thus historically discontinuous? Or, a third possibility, is this question itself reductive, a product of our wish to assign unambiguous causes and straightforward explanations?

When it comes to sexual desire, our culture is dominated by two distinct and largely contradictory models, both metaphysical in their assumption that we can identify what is fundamental in human nature. One metaphysic proposes that sex is a matter of the body, originating in the flesh and motivated by it, however people might deceive themselves with fantasies about romance. The other holds that love is a marriage of true minds, and that sex is (or ought to be) the bodily expression of this ideal relationship. Both models take for granted a dualist account of what it is to be a person, a mind on the one hand, and a body on the other, one of them privileged, the two either in harmony or in conflict. This dualism is associated with the Enlightenment and the moment of its crystallization is the Cartesian *cogito*.[1]

But in practice desire deconstructs the opposition between mind and body. Evidently it exists at the level of the signifier, as it imagines, fantasizes, idealizes. Desire generates songs and poetry and stories. Talking about it is pleasurable. At the same time, however, desire palpably inhabits the flesh, and seeks satisfaction there. Desire undoes the dualism common sense seems so often to take for granted.

The human body, we might want to argue in the light of our postmodernity, is subject to the imperatives of nature, but at the same time it does not exist outside culture. It owes to the differentiating symbol its existence as a single unit, with edges, limits. Psychoanalysis adds the presence of the symptom, evident on the body, the mark not of organic disease but of disorder at the level of the signifier, and psychoanalysis identifies the 'talking cure' as the disorder's remedy.[2] Desire, it urges, is an effect of difference, in excess of the reproductive drive. Furthermore, it knows itself as desire to the degree that it reads both the signifying practices of the body and the cultural forms in which desire *makes sense*. It is not possible to isolate the human body as natural organism, even methodologically: such a body would precisely not be human.

Romeo and Juliet is a play about desire. It is also a text poised on the brink of the Enlightenment, and it can be read, I want to suggest, as engaging with some of these issues, putting forward for examination in the process paradoxes that, for all the historical difference, a postmodern moment can find sympathetic. The bodies of the lovers are inscribed and, crucially, tragically, named. Their own account of love, while it displays a longing to escape the constraints of the symbolic order, reveals in practice precisely the degree to which it is culture that enables love to make sense. In *Romeo and Juliet* desire imagines a metaphysical body that cannot be realized.

II

Though there can be no doubt that Renaissance culture was profoundly and distinctively patriarchal, one sphere in which Shakespeare's women are perfectly equal to men is their capacity for experiencing sexual desire. Venus, Cleopatra, Portia in *The Merchant of Venice*,[3] and, of course, Juliet, are presented as sharing with their near-contemporaries, Alice Arden, the Duchess of Malfi, Beatrice-Joanna and Ford's Annabella, for example, an intensity of passion which is not evidently exceeded by that attributed to the men they love. These women are shown as subjects and agents of their own desire, able to speak of it and to act on the basis of it.

Meanwhile, Thomas Laqueur's *Making Sex* assembles persuasive documentation from the Greeks to the Renaissance of similar assumptions among European analysts of physiology and anatomy. Laqueur finds in this distinct sphere of knowledge, which is also, of course, a distinct discursive genre, what he calls the 'one-sex' model of the human body. The one-sex understanding of the body prevailed, he argues, until modern science redefined women and men as *opposite* and antithetical sexes. In the one-sex body the sexual organs are understood to be similarly distributed among men and women, though externally visible in men and internal in women. Thus the vagina commonly corresponds to the penis, the uterus to the scrotum, and so on. Laqueur is clear about the implications of this account for the understanding of erotic impulses themselves: both sexes were capable of intense sexual pleasure; both sexes experienced desire. Indeed, it was widely held that female pleasure was necessary to conception, and this was consequently seen as an important project of male sexual activity. Desire was not in any sense a masculine prerogative. On the contrary,

> The process of generation might differ in its nuances as the vital heats, the seeds, and the physical qualities of the substances being ejaculated differed between the sexes—but libido, as we might call it, had no sex.[4]

Some Renaissance physicians would have gone even further. Jacques Ferrand, for example, whose second treatise on lovesickness was published in Paris in 1623, argues that, being less rational than men, women are correspondingly more subject to violent erotic desires, and less able to resist their own impulses. A woman, according to Ferrand, 'is in her Loves more Passionate, and more furious in her follies, then a man is'.[5]

Laqueur does not, of course, imply that the one-sex body was the product of a less patriarchal culture. On the contrary, the male body represented the ideal of perfection; the female body, meanwhile, differed from it because women possessed less of the vital heat which pushed the sexual organs outwards. But the difference was one of degree, Laqueur insists, not kind. Women, less perfect than men, were in consequence less entitled to power and prestige. But they were not men's opposite, passive and passionless where men were active and desiring. That antithesis belongs to a later epoch.

Renaissance medical knowledge is neither a source of the plays nor a guarantee of their meanings. It is too easily supposed that we can read off the true meaning of fictional texts from the other knowledges of the period, as if the culture somehow shared a single, homogeneous account of the world, and was in that respect simpler, less diverse than our own.[6] We should not now expect popular romance to depict the world in the same way as psychoanalysis, and even current pornography frequently takes precious little account of elementary anatomy. I invoke Laqueur's extremely valuable work here simply as additional evidence that it was possible in the sixteenth and seventeenth centuries to imagine female desire, and even to take it seriously.

But there are also significant generic differences between Renaissance anatomy and Renaissance fiction. In the medical treatises libido had no necessary moral implications: this was a knowledge which set out to record the world it found in the authorities and in experience. The drama, however, makes no attempt at value-free analysis. It cannot avoid showing the implications of the passions it depicts, and consequently it tends, whether incidentally or as its main project, to offer an assessment and evaluation of female desire. But the judgements it makes are by no means univocal or monolithic. As my examples suggest, desire may lead women into bad ways (*Arden of Faversham, The Changeling*); it may be radically misdirected (*'Tis Pity She's a Whore*), or innocent in itself but unfortunate in its consequences (*The Duchess of Malfi*); its moral status may be profoundly ambiguous (*Antony and Cleopatra*); it may be seen as lyrical but at the same time absurd (*Venus and Adonis*). But alternatively, desire reciprocated may be the foundation of conjugal marriage and (we are invited to assume) the nuclear family, as it is in Shakespeare's comedies. It was the Enlightenment, according to Laqueur, which insisted on the two-sex model of male and female bodies, the woman's lacking what defined the man's. And it was also the Englightenment which tended to polarize male erotic activity and female passivity. Not until the nineteenth century was it established as a fact of nature that good women had no sexual feelings at all. The oppositional stereotypes of sexless virgin and voracious whore are not helpful in making sense of the work of Shakespeare and his contemporaries.

III

There was of course a convention, not that women should feel nothing, but that they should appear aloof in order to intensify male desire. This is the convention that Juliet unwittingly breaks when she declares her love at her window, only to be overhead by Romeo. It is quite late in their discussion, however, that she alludes, perhaps rather perfunctorily, to the proprieties of female behaviour: 'Fain would I dwell on form, fain, fain deny   What I have spoke, but farewell compliment!' (*Romeo and Juliet*, II.2.88-89). The moment for observing the conventions has clearly passed, and propriety itself soon becomes matter for a teasing romantic overture on her part: 'If thou thinkest I am too quickly won,   I'll frown and be perverse, and say thee nay,   So thou wilt woo, but else not for the world' (II.2.95-97).

At the heart of the play it is Juliet who speaks most eloquently and urgently to define, perhaps on behalf of both lovers, the desire experienced in the secret life of the body:

> Gallop apace, you fiery-footed steeds,
> Towards Phoebus' lodging; such a waggoner
> As Phaeton would whip you to the west,
> And bring in cloudy night immediately.
>
> (III.2.1)

The opening imperative, in conjunction with the image of the pounding, burning hooves, suggests the speeding pulses and the impatient ardour of desire, as well as its barely controlled power, and the allusion to Phaeton which follows evokes the boy's failure to manage Apollo's unruly horses, and so implies a surrender of what remains of restraint. Juliet's speech is entirely explicit in its invocation of love performed, acted, possessed and enjoyed. Their wedding night will be 'a winning match Play'd' between a symmetrically and reciprocally desiring couple 'for a pair of stainless maidenheads' (ll. 12-13). This necessarily clandestine love—perhaps the more thrilling because it is clandestine, because the fear of discovery intensifies the danger and the excitement[7]—is to be enacted in secret, in total darkness, and in silence:

> Spread thy close curtain, love-performing night,
> That [th'] runaways's eyes may wink, and Romeo
> Leap to these arms untalk'd of and unseen!
> Lovers can see to do their amorous rites
> By their own beauties.
>
> (l.5)

Act II, scene v. Juliet and Nurse in a room in Capulet's house. Painted by Robert Smirke. University of Michigan Library.

The (bed-)curtain of the dark is to exclude all outsiders, and the runaway god of love himself will close his eyes,[8] so that no one sees their union, not even the lovers. If 'see' is a metaphor (l.8), they are to be guided in the performance of their amorous rites by the beauty of each other's bodies. Love, the conceit implies, has no need of light, since its mode of 'seeing' is tactile, sensational. And the syntax here might lead us to suppose that if the lovers are 'unseen' by themselves as well as other people, so too, perhaps, the act is 'untalk'd of' by the lovers, since speech is also superfluous. Indeed, night is invited to obscure even the signifying practices of the virgin body: 'Hood my unmann'd blood, bating [fluttering] in my cheeks, With thy black mantle' (ll.14-15). It is as if Juliet imagines the presence of the desiring bodies as pure sensation, sightless, speechless organisms in conjunction, flesh on flesh, independent of the signifier. A rose by any other name, she had earlier supposed, would smell as sweet (II.2.43-44): the same gases, emanating from the same petals, striking the same nostrils, its physical being separable from the word that names it. The name, the signifier, and the symbolic order in its entirety are to be relegated to a secondary position, the place of the merely expressive and instrumental.

But these isolated, unnamed bodies (and roses) are only imaginary. The human body is already inscribed: it has no existence as pure organism, independent of the symbolic order in which desire makes sense In the sixteenth-century text Juliet's imagined act of love is paradoxically defined in a densely metaphoric and tightly structured instance of signifying practice. The speech depends on invocations repeated with a difference ('Come civil night [. . .] Come night, come Romeo [. . .] Come gentle night, (ll. 10, 17, 20)), framing an elaborate conceit in which the love-performing darkness both is and is not synonymous with Romeo himself, the lover who is ultimately to be perpetuated in little stars (l.22). The text specifies a wish in a tissue of formally ordered allusions, comparisons and puns, which constitute a poem, the zenith of signification, self-conscious, artful, witty. In order to bring before us its imagined bodies, the play here invokes a long poetic and rhetorical tradition, and in the process the lyricism which conjures up the act of love necessarily supplants it too. Moreover, this is a set piece, an epithalamion, though it is spoken, ironically, not by the assembled wedding guests, but by the bride herself, and in solitude.[9] What is enacted within it is desire imagining its fulfilment, and not the event itself, nor even any possible event. Love is inevitably performed within culture, within, indeed, a specific culture: bodies do not exist outside the cultural moment which defines them, and experience cannot be identified beyond the meanings a cultural tradition makes intelligible. What we call a rose might take any other name, but if it were name*less*, outside difference, who is to say that its smell would be 'sweet'? Here too a whole cultural tradition underlies the recognition (re-cognition) of this sweetness—and its association with love.

Romeo and Juliet is about desire. It is also one of Shakespeare's most evidently formal, conventional texts. As Rosalie Colie points out, the play draws on the traditions of Roman comedy, with its young woman and two suitors, one of them approved by her father. The garrulous nurse belongs to the same genre. Meanwhile, the Prologues to Acts I and II are sonnets, and the lovers converse in Petrarchan imagery. Mercutio, on the other hand, is an Ovidian figure. When the lovers are together they perform in joint and reciprocal set pieces: first a sonnet (I.5.93-106) and then an *aubade* (III.5.1-36). But there is no necessary contradiction, Colie proposes, between convention and desire: on the contrary, the effect in the text is precisely to naturalize the familiar forms. 'One of the most pleasurable, for me, of Shakespeare's many talents, is his "unmetaphoring" of literary devices, his sinking of the conventions back into what, he somehow persuades us, is "reality"'. The Petrarchan convention of love at first sight, she goes on to argue, 'is here made to seem entirely natural [. . .] its conventionality forgotten as it is unmetaphored by action.'[10]

In this respect, Colie might have added, Shakespeare's text is no more than a superlative instance of culture in general, which works precisely by unmetaphoring the device and naturalizing inherited forms. There is no unmediated experience located entirely outside the existing semiotic repertoire, though there are, as the play demonstrates, unexpected deviations, juxtapositions, turns, and resistances. In the play Ovid disrupts Petrarch; comic form leads to tragic denouement; choric narrative appropriates the lyric voice of the sonnet. Culture imagines the symbol as truth, and 'proves' its case by novelty, demonstrating that it is constantly possible to formulate something new, surprising or unexpected.

In a brilliant discussion of the formality of *Romeo and Juliet* Gayle Whittier argues that the play shows how the inherited word declines 'from lyric freedom to tragic fact.'[11] She points out that the poetic mode in which Romeo falls in love precedes him, and that he longs to be the author of the lover he becomes. But in Whittier's account the narrative mode of drama displaces the abstract and timeless paradoxes of Petrarchan poetry. It endows the word with flesh, and in the process necessarily subjects it to time and death. Poetry, Whittier argues, is transcendent: love is referential. The bodies of the lovers exist in time, and confront death: the poetry which precedes them also survives them.

The argument is extremely convincing, and it is eloquently presented. If in the end I put a slightly different case, the distinction between us is perhaps no more than a matter of emphasis. I want to stress the degree to which the letter invades the flesh, and the body necessarily inhabits the symbolic. This above all is the source of the tragedy of *Romeo and Juliet*. Petrarch, their names and the word of the Prince ('banished') are all decisive for the protagonists, but the symbolic order is not external to their identities: on the contrary, it is exactly the element in which they subsist. On the other hand, they exceed it too. The body which it defines is not contained by the symbol, and desire seeks to overflow the limits imposed by the differential signifier.

IV

In recognizing that the name of the rose is arbitrary, Juliet shows herself a Saussurean *avant la lettre,* but in drawing the inference that Romeo can arbitrarily cease to be a Montague, she simply affirms what her own desire dictates.

> O Romeo, Romeo, wherefore art thou Romeo?
> Deny thy father and refuse thy name;
> Or, if thou wilt not, be but sworn my love,
> And I'll no longer be a Capulet [. . .]
> 'Tis but thy name that is my enemy;
> Thou art thyself, though not a Montague.
> What's Montague? It is nor hand nor foot,
> Nor arm nor face, [nor any other part]
> Belonging to a man. O, be some other name!
> What's in a name? That which we call a rose
> By any other word would smell as sweet;
> So Romeo would, were he not Romeo call'd,
> Retain that dear perfection which he owes
> Without that title. Romeo, doff thy name,
> And for thy name, which is no part of thee,
> Take all myself.
>
> (II.2.33-49)

Identity, the speech acknowledges, exists in the symbolic as the Name of the Father. Juliet imagines a succession of (im)possibilities: that Romeo should repudiate his father's name, or she hers; that he should be named differently; and finally that he should simply remove his name, as if it were extrinsic, separable from identity. In place of Romeo's name Juliet offers her 'self', implying that beyond their names, as beyond the name of the rose, the lovers could exist as unnamed selves. This move to transcend the signifier, however, the play at once makes clear, is precisely a contradiction. In offering to take what she urges *literally*, Romeo can only propose punningly to assume another *name*, to adopt a different location in the symbolic:

> I'll take thee at thy word
> Call me but love, and I'll be new baptiz'd;
> Henceforth I never will be Romeo.
>
> (1.49)

But the signifier, however arbitrary, is not at the disposal of the subject. Romeo's name precedes him, makes him a subject, locates him in the community of Verona. It is not optional. Later Romeo will offer to excise his murderous name, but he cannot do so without killing himself:

> O, tell me, friar, tell me,
> In what vile part of this anatomy
> Doth my name lodge? Tell me, that I may sack
> The hateful mansion.
>
> (III.3.105)

Unlike hand or foot, Romeo's name is not something that he can lose and retain his identity, continuing to be the specific, differentiated Romeo that Juliet loves.

Lovers are prone to perceive the imaginary essence of the object of desire, to identify a 'self', a presence which subsists beyond the symbolic order, the 'dear perfection' of the loved one independent of the public and external name. This is the evidence of their idealizing passion. A lover who might be expected to know better, the author of Jacques Derrida's sequence of postcards, also affirms something of this kind:

> you will never be your name, you never have been, even when, and especially when you have answered to it. The name is made to do without the life of the bearer, and is therefore always somewhat the name of someone dead. One could not live, be there, except by protesting against one's name, by protesting one's non-identity with one's proper name.[12]

Here too, the letter kills, we are invited to suppose, but desire gives life. The name is a trapping, inessential, inherited or given, a reminder that the individual's autonomy is always imaginary, the effect of a place allotted by others, by the family, by a whole culture.

But Derrida's amorous-philosophical text is not naïve (of course!). The name is dead because it is ancestral; it is dead because in differentiating the person that it names, it constitutes a reminder of all the other possible objects of desire, and the arbitrariness that singles out *this* one; and it is dead finally because it stands in for the person it names, and thus supplants the being who elicits so much intensity, intervening between the lover and the loved one. But there is no suggestion that it is possible to do more than protest against the imposed identity, to insist on non-identity with *that*, to refuse the imposition. Though it imagines it in an oxymoron ('I am calling you [. . .] beyond your name, beyond all names',[13] the text does not in the end suppose that the person could exist independently, a free-floating essence beyond nomenclature, which is to say beyond difference.

Nor, indeed, is Shakespeare's text naïve. The name of Montague, imposed, ancestral, *is* Juliet's enemy, the text as a whole makes clear. If Romeo's non-identity with his name legitimates their love, the repudiated name returns, nevertheless, to ensure their tragedy. Even though his name is no part of the man Juliet loves, the play at once draws attention to the impossibility of discarding the name which differentiates him. Hearing in the darkness a voice reply to her musings, the shocked Juliet demands, 'What man art thou?' (l. 52), and how else can Romeo indicate who he is but by reference to a name which precisely cannot be specified without identifying an opponent of all Capulets:

> By a name
> I know not how to tell thee who I am.
> My name, dear saint, is hateful to myself,
> Because it is an enemy to thee.
>
> (II.2.53)

In the event, Juliet recognizes his voice, a property of the lover like hand or foot, or any other part, and promptly puts her recognition to the test—by naming him:

> My ears have not yet drunk a hundred words
> Of thy tongue's uttering, yet I know the sound.
> Art thou not Romeo, and a Montague
>
> (l. 58)

The question of names recurs at intervals throughout Derrida's 'Envois' to *The Post Card*. The text is at least in part an engagement with Oxford philosophy and its distinction between 'use' and 'mention' ('Fido is my dog'; ' "Fido" is a possible name for a dog'). But this issue is part of a larger debate in Western philosophy concerning the question whether proper names have meaning. The answer to this question has implications for our understanding of the relationship between language and the world,[14] and this in turn is the problem Derrida has addressed throughout his work. Proper names imply that words may be no more than substitutes for things, labels for the objects they refer to, without meaning in themselves. What, after all, does 'Smith' mean? If names have no meaning, however, but only reference, what are we to say when the name is Medusa, and the referent does not exist? And is 'Homer' meaningless? Or does 'Homer' precisely *mean* the anonymous author(s) of the *Iliad* and the *Odyssey,* who must have existed, but probably not as Homer? If so, is meaning independent of what goes on in the world, a matter of shared, inherited knowledge, which may be false? Who does Homer's name belong to? To an individual? Or to a culture? What *gives* it its meaning?[15]

The 'Envois' to *The Post Card* consists of a series of love letters to an unnamed person, addressed poste restante 'because of all the families' (p. 45). The epistolary form throws into relief the problems of 'communication', and the story of a passionate clandestine love makes evident how much is at stake in the process of writing. The secret love letter is a paradigm case of the urgency and the impossibility of meaning as immediate, transparent, individual, exclusive *presence*. All language is subject to what Derrida calls 'the Postal Principle as differantial relay' (p. 54). The message is always differed and deferred (differantiated), since the intervals and the distance, the delays and relays, separate the people it was designed to unite. Much of Derrida's love story concerns a critical, definitive, 'true' letter which fails to arrive. Instead it is eventually returned unopened, and remains for ever unread by the addressee, unopened by the sender, though it goes on to haunt the relationship, since its existence cannot be forgotten. This 'dead letter' is at once outside the living love affair and formative for it. In response to Lacan's account of *The Purloined Letter,* Derrida's text insists that the letter never arrives at its destination.

At the same time, *The Post Card* proposes, the letter can never ensure its own secrecy. However cryptic it is, however coded, designed exclusively for the recipient, if the message is intelligible, it is always able to be intercepted, read, misread, reproduced. Since it is necessarily legible for another, who does the letter belong to? To the sender, the addressee, or an apparently irrelevant unspecified third party, representative of the symbolic order in all its (dead) otherness? Their secret love does not belong exclusively to Romeo and Juliet. To the degree that it inhabits the symbolic, to the extent that it is relayed in messages and letters, even when the messages in question are those of the signifying body itself, love is tragically not theirs to control.

Derrida's text refuses to name its object of desire, the secret addressee of the love letters, though it plays with a succession of possible names (Esther, Judith, Bettina (pp. 71-73, 231)). It names others, however, who feature in the itinerary of the lover (Neil Hertz, Hillis, Paul, Jonathan, and Cynthia, and a woman who seems tantalizingly, comically, to be called Metaphysics (p. 197)). It thus keeps the reader guessing, about the identity of the beloved, and about whether the named and apparently non-fictional figures can be ruled out (p. 223). It names the writer, but only (punningly?) as acquiescent, as *j'accepte* ('this will be my signature henceforth [. . .] it is my name, that *j'accepte*' (p. 26)), leaving in doubt whether the whole story is fictional, or in some disguised and elusive way referential, 'true', and problematizing in the process those terms themselves. But though it withholds the name of the loved one, it substitutes a pronoun, 'you': a shifter, certainly, but no less differential for that. The amorous project is to locate the living object of desire beyond the inherited, dead signifier, to invest it with a transcendent existence outside mortality. At the same time, of course, *The Post Card* recognizes this impulse as imaginary, 'metaphysical', and perhaps in the process offers another clue—or possibly a red herring—which might lead us to identify the object itself:

> You have always been 'my' metaphysics, the metaphysics of my life, the 'verso' of everything I write (my desire, speech, presence, proximity, law, my heart and soul, everything that I love and that you know before me). (p. 197)

The beloved is not named, but is not nameless either, for the lover or the world:

> I have not named you while showing you to others, I have never shown you to others with the name they know you by and that I consider only the homonym of the one that I give you, no, I have called you, yourself. (p. 219)

'Yourself' is not an unmediated self. it is not a name, but at the same time it is not independent of the signifier. And as a shifter, it patently does not belong to the unnamed object of desire.

Romeo and Juliet are not reducible to their proper names, but they are not beyond them either, though in their idealizing, transfiguring imagery they repeatedly locate each other outside mortality, in the heavens, among the inauspicious stars, not at their mercy (II. 2. 2; 15-22; III. 2. 22-25). And their names are not their property: they do not belong to them in the same way as hand or foot, or any other part. As subjects, the lovers aspire both to love and to immortality only by virtue of the differentiating, inherited signifier, which subjects them, in the event, to death itself.

V

What is at issue in the *aubade* is the name of the lark.

> Wilt thou be gone? it is not yet near day.
> It was the nightingale, and not the lark,
> That pierc'd the fearful hollow of thine ear.
> (III. 5. 1)

The referential truth is available here, but it is not what matters. The debate is about the significance of the birdsong that the lovers hear, its meaning: not ornithology, but the time of day. The same bird known by any other name would make the same sound, but it would be of no interest unless a culture had already invested the song with the meaning of dawn. It is the lark: Romeo proves it on the evidence of other signifiers:

> Look, love, what envious streaks
> Do lace the severing clouds in yonder east.
> Night's candles are burnt out
>
> (l. 7)

The lark is already inscribed as 'the herald of the morn' (l. 6), and while the time of day is also referential, a matter of fact, it too is in question here in its meaning, as the signifier of the moment when Romeo's banishment takes effect, separating, because of their names, the desiring bodies of the lovers. The world of nature, of birdsong and morning, is already invaded by culture, even though it also exceeds it, and the knowledge that it purveys is necessarily at the level of signification.

Juliet's epithalamion is uttered, ironically, in the direct shadow of the Prince's sentence, immediately after it is pronounced (III. 1. 186-97), but thanks to the Postal Principle she does not yet know it. When the message that Romeo is banished is finally delivered by the Nurse, her account initially obscures the truth, and Juliet believes that Romeo is dead (III. 2. 36-70). Juliet's premature lament for Romeo here finds a parallel in the family's lamentations for her apparent death (IV. 5). Both are displaced, inappropriate, and yet not wholly irrelevant, since they anticipate the events of the play, as if the signifier lived a life of its own, partly but not entirely independent of the referent. Meanwhile, Friar Lawrence's letter fails to reach its destination and Romeo, in possession of another narrative, the public account relayed by Balthasar, tragically returns to act on Juliet's supposed death.

The Prince speaks the sentence of banishment, but it is to be carried out on Romeo's body, causing either his absence or his death. Romeo's absence is a kind of death for Juliet too, she affirms:

> Some word there was, worser than Tybalt's
>   death,
>   That murder'd me; I would forget it fain,
>   But O, it presses to my memory
>   Like damned guilty deeds to sinners' minds:
> 'Tybalt is dead, and Romeo banished.'
>
> (III.2.108)

The insistent signifier is determining for the bodies of the lovers, and yet at the same time it is not definitive, in the sense that its implications are not contained by its meaning. ' "Romeo is banished": to speak that word, Is father, mother, Tybalt, Romeo, Juliet, All slain, all dead.' (ll. 122-24). The signifier, which differentiates, specifies limits and imposes boundaries, also evokes an unspeakable residue, boundless and unlimited: 'There is no end, no limit, measure, bound, In that word's death, no words can that woe sound' (ll. 125-26). The woe exceeds the word because no word can make it present. Supplanted by the signifier, it exists as an absence hollowed out within the utterance—just as it does within the corresponding signifying practice of the body, the weeping which is to follow (ll. 130-31).

In the same way, the signifier cannot exhaust desire, since desire inhabits the residue that exceeds what can be said. Challenged to 'unfold' in speech the happiness of her marriage, Juliet replies:

> Conceit, more rich in matter than in words,
> Brags of his substance, not of ornament;
> They are but beggars that can count their
>   worth,
> But my true love is grown to such excess
> I cannot sum up sum of half my wealth.
>
> (II.6.30)

Love, Juliet claims, like the unnamed rose or the untalked of act, is more substantial than mere words. For this reason, she continues, its substance cannot be counted, cannot be summed up in words. And she makes the affirmation in an ornamental metaphor, an analogy between love and wealth familiar to us from the *Sonnets* and from Theseus's opening speech in *A Midsummer Night's Dream*. The comparison, which brings the intensity of the love before us, simultaneously has the effect of supplanting it, replacing it by the signifier, so that the speech demonstrates precisely the impossibility it affirms of putting love into words. This excess of love over the signifier is what invests desire with metaphysics, and at the same time, if Derrida is to be believed, the metaphysical with desire. As speaking subjects, we long for the unattainable verso of signifying practice—proximity, certainty, presence, the thing itself. Lovers long to make present the unspeakable residue which constitutes desire.

VI

Shakespeare's play ends with death, the golden statues—and names again. At the beginning of the final scene Paris decorously strews Juliet's tomb with flowers and sweet water, in a gesture appropriate to a man who would have been her bridegroom. He is interrupted by her actual bridegroom, whose intentions, in contrast, are excessive, in every sense of the word: 'savage-wild, More fierce and more inexorable far Than empty tigers or the roaring sea' (v.3.37-39). Alan Dessen makes the point that modern productions commonly include a structure which represents the tomb. This, he argues persuasively, is not necessarily how the scene would have been staged in the 1590s. On the contrary, the tomb might well have been no more than a stage door or a trap door in the stage, and Juliet's body might have been thrust out on a bier at the point when the scene shifts to the inside of the tomb. Including the tomb, as they do, Dessen says, modern productions often leave out Romeo's mattock and crowbar. In consequence, they fail to do full justice to the emblematic contrast the scene sets up between Romeo and Paris, the one sprinkling scented water on the grave, and the other violating the tomb with an iron bar, forcing open what he himself calls this 'womb of death' (l.45).[16] When Romeo, who is beside himself with passion, offers to *strew* the churchyard with the interloper's limbs, the contrast is surely complete.

Explaining his purpose, Romeo 'lies' to Balthasar:

> Why I descend into this bed of death
> Is partly to behold my lady's face,
> But chiefly to take thence from her dead
>   finger
> A precious ring . . .
>
>   (1.28)

The lie is also intelligible as a coded truth, a cryptic declaration of a real purpose, not intended to be legible to Balthasar, of re-enacting his clandestine marriage by a second exchange of rings. In the grotesque parody of the wedding night that follows, Romeo seeks a repetition in the tomb of the original darkness, silence and secrecy invoked so eloquently in Juliet's epithalamion, though once again these amorous rites are to be lit by beauty, as Juliet, who once taught the torches to burn bright (I.5.44), now 'makes This vault a feasting presence full of light' (v.3.85-86).

This time, too, the body signifies. There is blood in Juliet's face once more, to the point where Romeo seems almost to read the message it puts out:

> O my love, my wife,
> Death, that hath suck'd the honey of thy
>   breath,
> Hath had no power yet upon thy beauty:
> Thou art not conquer'd, beauty's ensign yet
> Is crimson in thy lips and in thy cheeks,
> And death's pale flag is not advanced there.
>
>   (1.91)

But because his understanding at this moment is constructed in accordance with another narrative, he cannot read the story of Juliet's living body. Again he turns to her, this time with a question: 'Ah, dear Juliet, Why art thou yet so fair?' (ll. 101-02). The audience could have told him the answer (and perhaps did in early productions?). But Romeo, in the light of what he thinks he knows, produces another hypothesis:

> Shall I believe
> That unsubstantial Death is amorous,
> And that the lean abhorred monster keeps
> Thee here in dark to be his paramour?
>
>   (1.102)

(It is tempting, especially in the context of Georges Bataille's current popularity, to find an erotics of death in this conceit, but it is worth bearing in mind that from the point of view of the audience, the account is ironic, since it represents precisely the wrong answer.)[17] The re-enacting of the wedding night remains in consequence imaginary. They die, as Juliet performed their epithalamion, separately. 'These lovers of the night remain', as Kristeva puts it, 'solitary beings.'[18]

Their grave is not, however, a private place. On the contrary, it is the family vault of the Capulets, a memorial, precisely, to the name, which is all that remains of their ancestors, but which lives on to shadow the present so tragically. Moreover, no sooner has he established the close-curtained secrecy of this second wedding night, than Romeo interrupts his address to Juliet to recognize the dead body of Tybalt in its bloody sheet (l.97). Once again Tybalt, who insisted on the importance of Romeo's name and the 'stock and honor' of his own kin (I.5.54, 58, 61), and who for that reason fatally sustained the feud, intervenes between the lovers, as an emblematic third party, representative of the inherited symbolic order in all its dead—and deadly— otherness. Finally, the whole community crowds in, the community which is ultimately responsible for the arbitrary and pointless ancestral quarrel, and which is powerless to reverse the effects of a violence carried on in the names of Montague and Capulet, and enacted on the bodies of the new generation.

VII

Romeo and Juliet are immortalized as signifiers. The promised golden statues are, of course, a metamorphosis, effigies of their bodies, beautiful, precious, and lifeless. Metamorphosis enacts something of the project of desire, arresting, and stabilizing the object, fixing it as possession—and supplanting it in the process. Like metaphor, metamorphosis offers an image in place of the thing itself, but the image is precisely *not the same*. Venus is able to hold the flower that Adonis becomes, but the flower is no longer Adonis. The reconciling golden statues appear too late to interrupt the fatal invasion of the signifier into the living organism. Verona will recognize the effigies of Romeo and Juliet, but the effigies will signify concord, not desire.

And yet finally, as is to be expected of signifiers, the lovers are incorporated into a love story, foretold by the Prince, dramatized by Shakespeare. The play closes, appropriately, with their names, which are not synonymous with the lovers themselves, but which are not independent of them either. The play, and the legend of love that the play has become, have been astonishingly popular from the Restoration period on. The text has been performed, adapted, cut, reinterpreted, rewritten as a musical, filmed,[19] and now produced as a movie starring cats. Even in death, therefore, the record of the lovers' desiring, inscribed bodies is preserved in the archive, filed, appropriately enough, under their names:

> For never was a story of more woe
> Than this of Juliet and her Romeo.
>
> (v.3.309)

Evidently it was possible, before the dualism of the Enlightenment separated us all neatly into minds and bodies, to identify another relationship between the organism and the culture in which it becomes a human being. *Romeo and Juliet* dramatizes the sexual desire which is produced at the level of the signifier and inscribes the body of the lover. The play also acknowledges the slippage between the signifier and the world it defines and differentiates. But above all, it puts on display the hopeless longing to escape the confines of the signifier, to encounter directly, im-mediately, the rose that exists beyond its name. And to this extent *Romeo and Juliet* suggests the degree to which the named, differentiated lover is always only a stand-in for something which cannot be embraced, a reminder, as Plato proposes, of 'an ideal that is out of sight, but present in the memory.'[20]

Does the continued popularity of the play, even in a predominantly Enlightenment culture, perhaps suggest a dissatisfaction with the neat Cartesian categories by which we have so diligently struggled to live?

Notes

I am grateful to Alan Dessen and Cynthia Dessen for their incisive comments on an earlier version of this essay.

[1] The dualism of the Enlightenment differs from Plato's and Augustine's. Both Platonic and medieval souls are immortal and their affiliations are divine. But the Cartesian mind is predominantly secular and human. Nor is its relation to the body always one of superiority. Enlightenment science, paradoxically, had the eventual effect of reversing Descartes's hierarchy.

[2] Charles Shepherdson, 'Biology and History: Some Psychoanalytic Aspects of the Writing of Luce Irigaray', *Textual Practice*, 6 (1992), 47-86. I owe to the clarity of that essay the theoretical framework of my argument here.

[3] *The Merchant of Venice*, III. 2. 108-14. Shakespeare references are to *The Riverside Shakespeare*, ed. by G. Blakemore Evans and others (Boston: Houghton Mifflin, 1974).

[4] Thomas Laqueur, *Making Sex: The Body and Gender from the Greeks to Freud* (Cambridge, MA: Harvard University Press, 1990), p. 43.

[5] Jacques Ferrand, *Erotomania*, trans. by Edmund Chilmead (Oxford, 1640), p. 214. Female desire was widely taken for granted in the Middle Ages, and natural philosophy commonly presented women as more libidinous than men (Mary Frances Wack, *Lovesickness in the Middle Ages: The 'Viaticum' and its Commentaries* (Philadelphia: University of Pennsylvania Press, 1990), pp. 110-25.

[6] The New Historicism sets out to break with this version of the Elizabethan world picture by insisting on the single anecdote which is not offered as 'representative'. But though it produces acute insights, the New Historicist juxtaposition of fiction with quite different knowledges, as if it could be taken for granted that they illuminate each other, risks repeating Tillyard's unifying and simplifying gesture. In 'Fiction and Friction', for example, after a number of disclaimers Stephen Greenblatt goes on to identify Renaissance England as 'a culture that knows, as a widely accepted physical truth, that women have occulted, inward penises' (*Shakespearean Negotiations: The Circulation of Social Energy in Renaissance England* (Oxford: Clarendon Press, 1988), pp. 66-93, p. 87). He then uses this medical knowledge to explain the transvestite theatre, female cross-dressing in Shakespeare's comedies, and homoerotic desire in the period. All this is suggestive, inventive, and challenging, but it fails to take account of the counter-knowledge, evident in the bawdy jokes of the theatrical tradition itself, that women lacked what men possessed. Greenblatt himself cites Viola's 'a little thing would make me tell them how much I lack of a man' (*Twelfth Night*, III.4.302-03). Gratiano's 'would he were gelt that had it' is comic if Nerissa is understood to be 'gelded' (*The Merchant of Venice*, V.I.144). See also: '"That's a fair thought to lie between a maid's legs." "What is?" "Nothing." ' (*Hamlet*, III.2.118-21), and David Wilbern, 'Shakespeare's Nothing', in *Representing Shakespeare: New Psychoanalytic Essays*, ed. by Murray Schwarz and Coppélia Kahn (Baltimore: Johns Hopkins University Press, 1980), pp. 244-63.

[7] Julia Kristeva, *Tales of Love*, trans. by Leon S. Roudiez (New York: Columbia University Press, 1987), p. 211.

[8] Gary M. McCown, ' "Runnawayes Eyes" and Juliet's Epithalamium', *Shakespeare Quarterly*, 27 (1976), 150-70, pp. 156-65.

[9] McCown, ' "Runnawayes Eyes" ', p. 165.

[10] Rosalie Colie, *Shakespeare's 'Living Art'* (Princeton, NJ: Princeton University Press, 1974), pp. 135-67, p. 145.

[11] Gayle Whittier, 'The Sonnet's Body and the Body Sonnetized in *Romeo and Juliet*', *Shakespeare Quarterly,* 40 (1989), 27-41, p. 27.

[12] Jacques Derrida, *The Post Card: From Socrates to Freud and Beyond,* trans. by Alan Bass (Chicago: University of Chicago Press, 1987), p. 39.

[13] Derrida, *The Post Card,* p. 130. Compare: 'But it is you I still love, the living one. Beyond everything, beyond your name, your name beyond your name' (p. 144).

[14] See J. R. Searle, 'Proper Names and Descriptions', *The Encyclopaedia of Philosophy,* ed. by Paul Edwards, 8 vols (London: Collier Macmillan, 1967), VI, 487-91.

[15] I am grateful to Andrew Belsey for a discussion of the problem of proper names.

[16] Alan C. Dessen, 'Much Virtue in "As" ' in *Shakespeare and the Sense of Performance: Essays in the Tradition of Performance Criticism in Honor of Bernard Beckerman,* ed. by Marvin and Ruth Thompson (Newark, NJ: University of Delaware Press, 1989), pp. 132-38.

[17] See Georges Bataille, *Erotism: Death and Sensuality,* trans. by Mary Dalwood (San Francisco: City Lights Books, 1986); and *The Tears of Eros,* trans. by Peter Connor (San Francisco: City Lights Books, 1989).

[18] Kristeva, *Tales of Love,* p. 216.

[19] See Jill L. Levenson, *Romeo and Juliet,* Shakespeare in Performance (Manchester: Manchester University Press, 1987).

[20] Kristeva, *Tales of Love,* p. 269.

Lloyd Davis (essay date 1996)

SOURCE: "'Death-Marked Love': Desire and Presence in *Romeo and Juliet*," in *Shakespeare Survey: An Annual Survey of Shakespeare Studies and Production,* Vol. 49, 1996, pp. 57-67.

[*In the following essay, Davis searches the poetics of desire in* Romeo and Juliet, *maintaining that the drama links desire, death, selfhood and the forces of time.*]

I

The action of *Romeo and Juliet* occurs between two speeches proclaiming the lovers' deaths—the prologue's forecast of events and the prince's closing summary. The vicissitudes of desire take place in this unusual period, after life yet before death. It is a kind of liminal phase in which social and personal pressures build to intense pitch before they are settled. Such liminal tension, as Victor Turner suggests, is the very stuff of which social dramas are made.[1] It figures a mounting crisis that envelops those observing and taking part in the unfolding action. At the same time, this temporal setting has a range of interpretative implications.

With the lovers' deaths announced from the start, audience attention is directed to the events' fateful course. The question is less what happens than how it happens. By framing the action in this way, the prologue triggers various generic and narrative effects. First, it establishes the play as 'a tragedy of fate' similar to Kyd's *The Spanish Tragedy,* which gives 'the audience a superior knowledge of the story from the outset, reducing the hero's role to bring into prominence the complex patterns of action'.[2] In turn, this generic marker initiates a compelling narrative, poised between prolepsis and analepsis, as opening portents of death are played off against background details and further intimations in the following scenes.[3] The tension between these hints and flashbacks fills the narrative with foreboding. The breakneck speed of events (in contrast to the extended time frame of Arthur Brooke's version, a few days as opposed to nine months)[4] sees the ordained end bear relentlessly on the lovers. They are caught between a determining past and future.

The narrative has a further generic analogue. Gayle Whittier suggests that the play develops through a contrast between sonnet lyricism and tragedy that is finally reconciled in death: 'the "spoken lines" of the Prologue predestine the plot of the play to be tragic from without, even as the spirit of Petrarchan poetry spoken by Romeo to Juliet finally necessitates their tragic deaths from within'.[5] What first appears as thematic conflict between two of the period's key literary modes makes way for a troubling similarity. The spirit of Petrarchism is revealed as tragically fatal and idealized romance collapses.

In this view, *Romeo and Juliet* stages the outcome of unfulfillable desire. Although it appears to reverse the erotic story told in the Sonnets, the dramatic narrative ends up paralleling the failing course of identity and desire which can be traced through those poems. There the poet reluctantly finds his desire shifting from the self-gratifying potential figured by the youth to the disarming dark lady, who offers instead 'a desire that her very presence at the same time will frustrate'.[6] This pattern initially seems to be inverted in the play— Romeo willingly renounces self-centred longing for Rosaline, Juliet tests and proves her self-reliance, both find true love in each other. However, their love ends in reciprocal death, with the Petrarchan images fatally embodied and materialized. The links between love and death unveil a dark scepticism about desire, despite bursts of romantic idealism. They convey a sense of futility and ironic fate which Romeo momentarily feels but is able to forget for a time, 'my mind misgives / Some consequence yet hanging in the stars / Shall bitterly begin his fearful date / With this night's revels' (I.4.106-9).

Such scepticism appears in many subsequent literary and psychoanalytic conceptions, where possibilities of romantic union are queried.[7] These questions carry implications about selfhood and desire and about ways of representing them. In theories and stories of divorce or isolation, selfhood is not effaced but conceived as incomplete; as Barbara Freedman puts it, 'The denial of self-presence doesn't negate presence but redefines it as a distancing or spacing we always seek but fail to close'.[8] Characters cannot attain their goals, and the inability to claim satisfaction affects desire as much as selfhood. Proceeding from an uncertain source, desire remains 'predicated on lack, and even its apparent fulfilment is also a moment of loss'.[9] In this view, desire and presence are forever intertwined: 'Differantiated [sic] presence, which is always and inevitably differed and deferred, and which in consequence exceeds the alternatives of presence and absence, is the condition of desire'.[10] They forestall each other's wholeness yet continue to provide the self with images of consummation, contentment and victory—the curtsies, kisses, suits, livings and battles which Mercutio's dreamers envisage but cannot clasp, 'Begot of nothing but vain fantasy, / Which is as thin of substance as the air, / And more inconstant than the wind' (I.4.98-100).

The recurrence of this viewpoint in fiction and theory suggests that *Romeo and Juliet* stages a paradigmatic conflict between ways of representing and interpreting desire. The play affects these possibilities by placing idealized and tragic conceptions of desire and selfhood in intense dialogue with each other. This dialogue continues to be played out in literary and theoretical texts since, as Alan Sinfield notes, notions of sexuality and gender are 'major sites of ideological production upon which meanings of very diverse kinds are established and contested'.[11] *Romeo and Juliet* informs and illustrates a cultural history of desire in which images of romantic fulfilment or failure carry great importance.

As well as being part of this history, Shakespeare's play has two other distinctive temporal features. First, as noted above, it unfolds over a charged time span. Time allows desire to be acted out but also threatens its fulfilment, by either running out or not stopping. This equivocal link affects desire's tragic course in *Romeo and Juliet,* 'as the time and place / Doth make against' the characters (5.3.223-4).

Secondly, its depiction of desire reverberates with erotic tropes from earlier traditions—Platonic, Ovidian, Petrarchan, as well as popular sayings. These tropes are used by the characters to talk and think about relationships, but they are also challenged for not allowing the gap between self and other to be bridged. They are unfulfilling since it feels as if they belong to someone else; as Astrophil puts it, 'others' feet still seemed but strangers in my way'.[12] The lovers are often dissatisfied with or unsure about the words of others. Their discontent grows from early dismissals such as Romeo's 'Yet tell me not, for I have heard it all' (1.1.171) and 'Thou talk'st of nothing' (1.4.96), or Juliet's 'And stint thou, too, I pray thee, Nurse' (1.3.60), to deeper disquiet over the inability of this language to match their experience: 'Thou canst not speak of that thou dost not feel' (3.3.64); 'Some say the lark makes sweet division; / This doth not so, for she divideth us' (3.5.29-30). The corollary of their frustration with the language of others and of the past is the value they put on their own: 'She speaks. / O, speak again, bright angel' (2.1.67-8); 'every tongue that speaks / But Romeo's name speaks heavenly eloquence' (3.2.32-3).

Like the lovers, the play also seeks to revise existing rhetorical conventions. It reworks these tropes into personal, tragic terms which underlie later literary and psychological conceptions. Hence, in addition to exemplifying Stephen Greenblatt's point that 'psychoanalysis is the historical outcome of certain characteristic Renaissance strategies',[13] *Romeo and Juliet* shows that these strategies develop in response to earlier discourses. The play's pivotal role in later depictions of desire stems from the way it juxtaposes historical and emergent conceptions.

These complex temporal and rhetorical effects are hinted at in the Prologue, which repeatedly sets past, present and future against each other. 'Our scene' is initially laid in a kind of continuous present, yet one that remains hanging between 'ancient grudge' and 'new mutiny'. Likewise, the 'star-crossed lovers take their life' in a present whose intimations of living and loving are circumscribed by 'the fatal loins' of 'their parents' strife'. As the birth-suicide pun on 'take their life' hints, sexuality is already marked by violence and death, its future determined by the past's impact on the present. The Prologue ends by anchoring the staging of 'death-marked love' in the here and now of the audience, who attend 'the two-hours' traffic of our stage'. It anticipates a successful theatrical conclusion, with the play's performance 'striv[ing] to mend' what the lovers 'shall miss'—a kind of closure that their desire cannot realize. In contrast to the simple linear Chorus to Act 2, which culminates in the lovers' union, the rebounding moments of the Prologue displace consummation with death.[14]

Galina Ulanova as Juliet and B. Bulgakov in Sergei Prokofiev's ballet of "Romeo and Juliet."

A complicity between sex and death is well known in Renaissance texts. Its function in *Romeo and Juliet* is, however, distinguished by temporal shifts which define the characters' relations. While the lovers in a poem such as Donne's 'The Canonization' exceed worldly time and place, and their post-coital condition is eternally celebrated, in Shakespeare's play the links between past and present, social and personal, cannot be transcended. The intense oneness felt by the lovers appears to signify mutual presence, but such intersubjective moments are overlaid with social and historical pressures. The drama alternates between instants of passion, when time seems to stand still, and inevitable returns to the ongoing rush of events. This contrast is manifested not only in the characterization and plot but in the interplay of underlying traditions, sources and tropes. The play reiterates and revises these conventions, confirming a conception of desire that speeds not to its goal but its end. In this conception personal presence can exist only as a transient, illusory sign of desire.

II

One of the main influences *Romeo and Juliet* has had on later depictions of love lies in its celebration of personal desire. The force of this celebration comes partly from its dramatic mode, staging the lovers' experiences for a 'live' audience. In the decades after the play was first performed, poetry (till then, the key romantic discourse) was changing from oral to written modes. Until the rise of the novel, drama remained the pre-eminent form for presenting love stories, and stage performance could give these tales the confessional tones which earlier forms of poetic recitation doubtless achieved. The Prologue enacts this shift by relocating the love sonnet in the drama, a move again underlined by the verse which the lovers will soon share in Act I, scene 5.

On stage, the impact of the 'personal' can come across in different ways—through physical, verbal, even interpersonal performance. In *Romeo and Juliet* these forms of presence concentrate in the protagonists' unshakeable love. It seems to assume an essential quality which captures the 'diachronic unity of the subject'.[15] This unity underwrites numerous adaptations of and responses to the play, from elaborate stage productions, operas and ballets, to more popular versions such as the American musical *West-Side Story* or the Australian narrative verse of C. J. Dennis's *A Sentimental Bloke,* whose colloquial tones add to the impression of true romance. For many audience groups, each of these transformations once again discovers the play's 'spirit', which surpasses local differences to reveal truths about desire and 'ourselves'.

The director's programme notes to a recently well-received production in Australia illustrate this kind of response. The mixed tones of confession and authority sway the audience to accept his views:

> My fascination with this play continues. Considerable research over the years has taken me twice to Verona and Mantua, but the conflict in Bosnia has brought the work urgently closer. I first considered a Muslim-Christian setting several months before the tragedy of Bosko and Admira . . . A study of the text supplies no religious, class, nor race barriers between the 'two households' and this makes Shakespeare's vision all the more powerful. When differences are minimal, ancient grudges seem the more difficult to understand. Yet they remain with us today, passed on by our parents. It seems the one thing we teach the next generation is how to maintain rage and other forms of prejudices. Thus this work is as much about young people in the Brisbane Mall today as it is about the hot days in medieval Verona . . . The human spirit, as portrayed by the 31 year old playwright, is a thing of wonder to be nurtured and treasured.[16]

Act III, scene v. In Juliet's chamber overlooking Capulet's orchard, Romeo and Juliet embrace as Nurse looks on. Painted by John Francis Rigaud. University of Michigan Library.

The paradoxical effects of citing 'real' personal and political situations are first to detach the drama from its own historical concerns and then to efface the ideological grounds of the current crisis. The revelation of 'human spirit' triumphs over any tragic significance. Indeed, the play's freedom from material contexts testifies to its, its author's, and our affirming 'vision'. This viewpoint recalls Coleridge's claim that Shakespeare is 'out of time', his characters 'at once true to nature, and fragments of the divine mind that drew them'.[17]

Because it hides sexual, class and ethnic factors behind archetypal human experience, this sort of perception of Shakespeare's work becomes a target of materialist criticism:

> Idealised and romanticised out of all dialectical relationship with society, it [Shakespeare's work] takes on the seductive glamour of aestheticism, the sinister and self-destructive beauty of decadent romance . . . this 'Shakespeare myth' functions in contemporary culture as an ideological framework for containing consensus and for sustaining myths of unity, integration and harmony in the cultural superstructures of a divided and fractured society.[18]

In relation to sexual issues, universal images of the personal in *Romeo and Juliet* can be seen as helping to naturalize notions of desire which reinforce an 'ideology of romantic love' in terms of 'heterosexualizing idealization' and the 'canonization of heterosexuality'.[19] Personal romance and desire are revealed as authoritative codes which conceal and impose official sexuality.

The kinds of ideological impacts that the 'personal' registers may be intensified *or* interrogated by the generic effects of 'Excellent conceited Tragedie', as the Quarto titles announce. The combination of personal experience and tragic consequence can turn *Romeo and Juliet* into an account of contradictory notions of desire and identity, in line with Jonathan Dollimore's recognition that, notwithstanding traditions of celebration 'in terms of man's defeated potential', tragedy questions ideological norms.[20] The genre's ambiguous drift to 'radical' or cathartic ends sees the play assume a kind of meta-textual disinterestedness, distanced from final interpretations as it seems to reflect on how desire may be conceived and staged. This distance can be observed in the play's citing and reworking of tropes and conventions from existing discourses of love and romance. The intertextual traces reveal continuities and changes in the depiction of desire, keyed to social and historical notions of the personal and interpersonal.

Platonism is traditionally seen as offering a set of tropes that affirm selfhood and desire as forms of true being despite possibilities of loss.[21] In the *Symposium*, for instance, Socrates defines love as desire for what one lacks, either a specific quality or a lost or missing element of the self. Aristophanes goes so far as to image love as a 'longing for and following after [a] primeval wholeness . . . the healing of our dissevered nature'. The *Symposium* deals with this incipiently tragic situation by redirecting desire to the heavens; in a comedic resolution, love's lack is fulfilled by catching sight of 'the very soul of beauty . . . beauty's very self'.[22] Such vision provides the model for Renaissance Petrarchism.

This model is famously reproduced in Pietro Bembo's Neoplatonic paean to divine love at the close of Castiglione's *The Courtier*. He recounts 'a most happie end for our desires', as the courtier forsakes sensual desire for a wiser love that guides the soul: 'through the particular beautie of one bodie hee guideth her to the universall beautie of all bodies . . . Thus the soule kindled in the most holy fire of true heavenly love, fleeth to couple her self with the nature of Angels'. This 'most holy love' is 'derived of the unitie of the heavenly beautie, goodnesse and wisedom', and in narrating its course Bembo himself undergoes an ecstatic loss of identity. He speaks as if 'ravished and beside himselfe', and emphasizes that 'I have spoken what the holy furie of love hath (unsought for) indited to me'.[23] Speaking and experiencing true desire are related forms of self-transcendence, and Bembo can rejoice in the loss of selfhood.

Similar experience underpins the double structure of Edmund Spenser's *Fowre Hymnes*, first published in 1596, around the time *Romeo and Juliet* was written. The hymn in honour of earthly love characterizes the lover as Tantalus, feeding 'his hungrie fantasy, / Still full, yet neuer satisfyde . . . For nought may quench his infinite desyre'. This figure is recast in the corresponding hymn of heavenly love, where the poet renounces his earlier poems—'lewd layes' which showed love as a 'mad fit'—for a lover linked to 'high eternall powre'.[24] In these instances, the lack or absence which motivates love is conceived positively, part of a spiritual response which lifts the lover beyond temporal identity. Through its philosophic or poetic utterance, the self is not destroyed but surpassed.

However, the link between lack and love can also affect selfhood less positively, even fatally. Classical texts again offer tropes and characters to Renaissance authors. Ovid depicts less drastic versions of desire and self-loss in the changes that Jove makes to pursue various nymphs. These can be read in varying ways—on the one hand, a carnivalesque switching of sexual roles for the sake of pleasure; on the other, a sequence of illusory identities that offers no final fulfilment. Though Jove's transformations bring different degrees of satisfaction, none is tragically oriented (at least for himself). In contrast, the tale of Narcissus sets desire and selfhood in irresolvable conflict. In Arthur Golding's 1567 translation of the *Metamorphoses*, Narcissus gazes into the pond to find that 'He knowes not what it was he sawe. And yet the foolishe elfe / Doth burn in ardent love thereof. The verie selfe same thing / That doeth bewitch and blinde his eyes, encreaseth all his sting'.[25] His desire cannot be satisfied, and the attempt to do so pains and then destroys selfhood.

Opposing notions of genre, time and character underlie these figures of ecstasy and loss. Platonic and Neoplatonic transcendence is marked by timelessness and selflessness. It brings narration and character to an end, as the self enjoys eternal fusion with the other. In comparison, Ovidian images of disguised or deluded self-loss entail conflict within or between characters. These interactions rely on distinct, often opposed, figures who respond to each other through time. Their fates frequently impose eternities of lonely, unfulfilled selfhood.

Platonic images of true desire and identity are invoked in Shakespeare's comedies during the 1590s; but even there, as characters move to romantic union, they are usually questioned. The disguises, confusions and mistakes through which love's destiny is reached may suggest random or enforced effects that unsettle 'nature's bias'. In a less equivocal way, Shakespeare's use of Ovidian images of desire and selfhood tends to limit or foreclose positive readings, especially where narcissistic traces are discerned. This tendency takes place in both comic and tragic genres: 'Like Ovid's tales, Shakespeare's comedies never lose sight of the painfulness and the potential for the grotesque or for disaster wrought by love's changes . . . If part of the Ovidianism of the comedies is their potential for violence and tragedy, it would seem logical to expect that Ovidianism to be developed in the tragedies'.[26] In *Venus and Adonis*, for example, the humour of the goddess's overweening desire and her beloved's petulance changes to grim consequence. 'The field's chief flower' (line 8) is mournfully plucked, recalling Narcissus's end, 'A purple flower sprung up, chequered with white, / Resembling well his pale cheeks, and the blood / Which in round drops upon their whiteness stood' (lines 1168-70). The characters have shared an ironic desire whose deathly goal was unwittingly imaged by Venus, 'Narcissus so himself himself forsook, / And died to kiss his shadow in the brook' (lines 161-2). As noted earlier, comparable effects occur throughout *Romeo and Juliet*, where moments of romantic union are disrupted by ongoing events that undercut their idealism. The mixed genres in these tales represent desire as a hybrid of the comic, tragic and ironic.[27]

Related images of threatening or incomplete desire and self-transformation are repeated through many sixteenth- and seventeenth-century texts, from the angst of sonneteers to Montaigne's musings in the *Apologie of Raymond Sebond* on 'The lustfull longing which allures us to the acquaintance of women, [and] seekes but to expell that paine, which an earnest and burning desire doth possesse-us-with, and desireth but to allay it thereby to come to rest, and be exempted from this fever'.[28] As most of these references suggest, this notion of erotic jeopardy is almost always tied to masculine conceptions of desire and selfhood. The pains of desire are indulged if not celebrated, and they may convert to misogyny, as in Hamlet's tirade against Ophelia or Romeo's charge that Juliet's beauty 'hath made me effeminate' (3.1.114).

This attitude echoes through Romeo's early laments about Rosaline. As Coleridge noted, he is 'introduced already love-bewildered':[29] 'I have lost myself. I am not here. / This is not Romeo; he's some other where' (1.1.194-5). Amid these tones of despair a self-satisfied note can be heard. The early Romeo is a 'virtual stereotype of the romantic lover',[30] whose role-playing brings a kind of egotistic reassurance. The lament for self-loss becomes proof of self-presence, a 'boastful positiveness',[31] with Romeo still to know the unsettling force of desire.

From this point, the play proceeds by exploring the limits of the Platonic, Ovidian and Petrarchan tropes. The seriousness of narcissistic absorption is questioned (underlined by Mercutio's quips at romantic indulgence);[32] yet the full consequence of desire is not realized in Platonic union but deferred to its aftermath. None of the conventional models can quite convey what is at stake in the lovers' story, and the discourse of desire must be revised.

III

Clearly, then, *Romeo and Juliet* invents neither tragic nor personal notions of desire. Both are strongly at work in Shakespeare's direct source, Brooke's *The Tragicall Historye of Romeus and Juliet* (1562): the threats to selfhood caused by love; the workings of 'False Fortune' and 'wavering Fortunes whele'; an intense desire that can be quenched 'onely [by] death and both theyr bloods'; time as tragic and ironic, first intimated in woe at Juliet's 'untimely death' and then gaining full significance as Romeus's man tells him 'too soone' of her end.[33]

While it reiterates these ideas, Shakespeare's play also develops and sharpens the connections among desire, the personal and the tragic. The lovers create new images of individuality and of togetherness in order to leave their worldly selves behind. Yet their efforts remain circumscribed by social forces. The ironic result is that the ideal identities the lovers fashion in order to realize their desire become the key to its tragic loss. Self-transcendence can be experienced but not as a kind of timeless ecstasy; instead it becomes entwined with unfulfilled desire.

The play personalizes desire in ways which constantly alternate between idealism and failure. As Kay Stockholder notes, threats to desire are 'externalized' and the lovers consciously create 'a radiant world apart by attributing all inimical forces to surrounding circumstance'.[34] In this reordering of reality, desire becomes part or even constitutive of private, individual identity. Romeo and Juliet's love is secret from others and transgresses the roles imposed by their families. In *The Petite Pallace of Pettie his Pleasure* (1576), George Pettie considered this opposition the key to the story: 'such presiness of parents brought Pyramus and Thisbe to a woful end, Romeo and Julietta to untimely death'.[35] In *A Midsummer Night's Dream* and *Romeo and Juliet,* resisting or contesting patriarchal authority allows a temporary move towards selfhood.

Through this contest, love appears to be one's own, yet both plays show the impossibility of holding onto it. The personal is as elusive as it is idealized, destined to slip back into constraining and distorting social forms. In retrospect, we may see this elusiveness prefigured in the lovers' first meeting, an intense bonding that occurs amid an elaborate ritual of masks and misrecognition. The symbolic means through which love must be expressed will prevent its consummation.[36] For the moment, however, love beholds a single object of desire, whose truth authenticates the lover and recreates both their identities: 'Deny thy father and refuse thy name, / Or if thou wilt not, be but sworn my love, / And I'll no longer be a Capulet . . . Call me but love and I'll be new baptized. / Henceforth I never will be Romeo' (2.1.76-93).

The nexus between identity and desire is strengthened by the need for secrecy. Hidden and equivocated as the lovers move between private and public realms, secret desire endows selfhood with interiority and intention. It grants a depth of character, and even if its longings are not fulfilled inner experience is confirmed. Juliet's cryptic replies to her mother's attack on Romeo reveal private pleasure couched in pain: 'O, how my heart abhors / To hear him named and cannot come to him / To wreak the love I bore my cousin / Upon his body that hath slaughtered him!' (3.5.99-102). Like secret desire, the obstacles to fulfilment sharpen internal experience and give it a kind of sensuous reality: 'runaways' eyes may wink, and Romeo / Leap to these arms untalked of and unseen. / Lovers can see to do their amorous rites / By their own beauties' (3.2.6-9).

This deep desire and selfhood develop in terms of intentionality—desire *for* someone, effected through imagination, speech and action. Desire marks the self as agent, and tragic desire portrays the onus of agency. It is felt sharply by Juliet before she takes the friar's potion, 'My dismal scene I needs must act alone' (4.3.19), and by Romeo as he enters the Capulet tomb 'armed against myself' (5.3.65). In this sense, the play's depiction of desire is linked to representations of subjectivity that emerge during the sixteenth century. It reflects the important role that tropes such as the secret, with its social and personal disguises, have in discourses which are starting to inscribe both an inner self and the individual as agent.

Even as it invests in such notions of selfhood, at its most intense desire in *Romeo and Juliet* surpasses individual experience and realizes an intersubjective union. The lovers re-characterize each other as much as themselves: 'Romeo, doff thy name, / And for thy name— which is no part of thee—/ Take all myself' (2.1.89-91). Again this effect has generic analogues, as we see the lovers' discourse moving beyond single-voiced Petrarchism. They share exchanges which reveal 'not only the other's confirming response, but also how we find ourselves in that response'.[37] Unlike contemporary sonnet sequences, which portray the poet by stifling the woman's voice (just as Romeo invokes and silences Rosaline), the play is marked by the lovers' dialogues. This reciprocity is epitomized by the sonnet they co-construct and seal with a kiss at their first meeting (1.5.92-105).[38] It is a highly suggestive moment, capturing the separateness of the lovers' world and speech from others, and also rewriting the dominant 1590s genre for representing desire. The sonnet is re-envoiced as dialogue, its meanings embodied in the climactic kiss. At the same time, the heightened artifice of the scene intimates its transience. The lovers start another sonnet but are interrupted by Juliet's garrulous nurse, who foreshadows the dire interventions of others. A further irony is also implied—as noted earlier, their union will be ended by events that literalize poetic tropes of love and death: Romeo really does die 'with a kiss' (5.3.120), and Juliet falls in eternal sexual embrace, 'O happy dagger, / This is thy sheath! There rust, and let me die' (5.3.168-9).[39]

The deaths verify the Prologue's vision of inescapable ties between sex and violence. Not only can the lovers not escape the eternal feud that frames them, they even play parts in it, responding impulsively, at the threshold of nature and nurture, to news of Mercutio's and Tybalt's deaths. For a moment their union bows under its violent heritage as each impugns the other: 'O sweet Juliet, / Thy beauty hath made me effeminate, / And in my temper softened valour's steel' (3.1.113-15); 'did Romeo's hand shed Tybalt's blood? . . . O serpent heart, hid with a flow'ring face!' (3.2.71-3)

Other characters also link sex and violence, suggesting that the connection has become naturalized and accepted. The Capulet servants joke aggressively about raping and killing the Montague women (1.1.22-4). The friar parallels birth and death, 'The earth, that's nature's mother, is her tomb. / What is her burying grave, that is her womb' (2.3.9-10), and is later echoed by Romeo, who calls the Capulet crypt a 'womb of death' (5.3.45). The friar also connects 'violent delights' to 'violent ends' (2.5.9), and the lovers' suicides suggest a final fusing of love and death. Yet as different interpretations maintain, this fusion's meaning may be tragic, romantic, or both. The lovers are 'consumed and destroyed by the feud' and seem to rise above it, 'united in death'.[40]

The final scene thus accentuates the connections among selfhood, death and desire. It caps off the discourse of tragic desire announced by the Prologue—a tradition of failed love known through numerous European novellas, the second volume of *The Palace of Pleasure* (1567), and two editions of Brooke's *Tragicall Historye* (1562, 1587). The action has thus had a doubly repetitive stamp, not only replaying this oft-told tale but restaging what the Prologue has stated. Foreknowledge of the outcome plays off against moments of romantic and tragic intensity, and triggers a kind of anxious curiosity that waits to see the details of the deaths—the near misses of delayed messages, misread signs, plans gone awry.

Through this repetitive structure, the play affirms precedents and conditions for its own reproduction as if anticipating future responses. Before ending, it even shows these possibilities being realized. The grieving fathers decide to build statues of the lovers, and the prince's final lines look forward to 'more talk of these sad things', in an effort to establish once and for all what desire's tragic end might mean (5.3.306). As Dympna Callaghan observes, the play not only 'perpetuates an already well-known tale', but its closure is predicated on 'the possibility of endless retellings of the story—displacing the lovers' desire onto a perpetual narrative of love'.[41]

Patterns of repetition weave through the play as well as framing it. Characters constantly restate what has previously been staged—in the first scene Benvolio explains how the opening brawl started, and later he recounts details of Mercutio's and Tybalt's deaths and

Romeo's involvement; the Chorus to the second act reiterates the lovers' meeting; the Nurse tells Juliet of Tybalt's death; the Capulets and Paris echo each other's lamentations over Juliet's apparent death;[42] and lastly the Friar recaps the whole plot to the other characters after the bodies are found. These instances are part of the effort to explain the violent meaning of events, but as the prince's closing words suggest, something extra needs to be told, 'never was a story of more woe / Than this of Juliet and her Romeo' (5.3.308-9). There is a sense that 'this' version of the story exceeds earlier ones. For all its repetition of tropes and narratives, in closing the play recognizes and stresses a difference from precursors.

Other repetitive designs through the play are used to underline the tension between desire and death. Four meetings and kisses shared by Romeo and Juliet structure the romance plot. They are in counterpoint to four violent or potentially violent eruptions that occur between the male characters, especially involving Tybalt. A muted fifth interruption is provided by the presence of Tybalt's corpse in the Capulet crypt where Juliet and Romeo finally meet and miss each other. These turbulent scenes frame the romantic ones, unsettling the lyric and erotic essence which they seem to capture.

The repetitions and retellings connect with the representation of time in the play, imposing a destructive pressure between the weight of social and family history and personal longings. Social and personal time are opposed, and desire is caught between these conflicting time frames. Social time is frequently indexed through the play, in general terms such as the 'ancient grudge' and through the scheduling of specific events such as Capulet's banquet and Juliet's wedding to Paris. Against this scheme, the lovers' meetings seem to dissolve time, making it speed up or, more powerfully, stop and stand still, as the present is transformed into 'the time of love'.[43] The lovers seek to disregard time and death in their union, 'Then love-devouring death do what he dare—It is enough I may but call her mine' (2.5.7-8). Yet this passionate energy also drives the drama to its finale, and Romeo's words link their union and separation with death. The time of love confronts the passing of its own presence.

In various ways, then, *Romeo and Juliet* renovates tragic desire for the Elizabethans and for subsequent periods. In early scenes it evokes a narcissistic poetics of desire as self-loss and death but moves beyond that to stage a dialogic reciprocal presence. The reappearance of death then inscribes ineluctable external influences—the determinations of time and history which frame desire—and the impossible idealization of self and other which passion seeks but fails to find. In this sense, Shakespeare's play marks a complex intersection between historical and emergent discourses of desire. First, in a period when modern institutions of family, marriage and romance are starting to appear, it translates Platonic, Ovidian and Petrarchan tropes of ecstasy and love into personal notions of desire. Next, it conceives desire as the interplay between passion, selfhood and death. And thirdly, its equivocal staging of love's death anticipates the tension between romantic and sceptical visions of desire that runs through many later literary and theoretical works.

It could be said that the play's symbolic bequest to these works is a notion of desire as lost presence. Though love continues to be celebrated as present or absent or present-in-absence in many texts (in different ways, Herbert's poetry and Brontë's *Wuthering Heights* come to mind), a significant line of literary works explores the interplay among desire, death and selfhood. Like *Romeo and Juliet*, these texts place desire in conflict with time, recounting moments of ideal presence whose future reveals they could never have been. This revision of desire begins with Shakespeare's later tragedies—*Hamlet, Othello, Macbeth* and *Antony and Cleopatra*—where one lover survives, though briefly, to feel the other's loss. It runs from the fallen lovers of *Paradise Lost* ('we are one, / One flesh; to lose thee were to lose myself' [9.958-9]), to the equivocal pairings at the end of Dickens's great novels or the images of foreclosed desire in Henry James's major phase. Its most poignant statement comes at the close of Scott Fitzgerald's *The Great Gatsby:*

> the green light, the orgiastic future that year by year recedes before us. It eluded us then, but that's no matter—to-morrow we will run faster, stretch out our arms farther . . . And one fine morning— So we beat on, boats against the current, borne back ceaselessly into the past.

If *Romeo and Juliet* helps to initiate this tradition, it does so as the last tragedy of desire. For in these later texts the note is of melancholic rather than tragic loss: what hurts is not that desire ends in death but that it ends before death. The present then becomes a time for recounting lost desire, and the self's task is to try to hold the story together. 'The subject's centre of gravity is this present synthesis of the past which we call history', writes Lacan.[44] Like Romeo's last letter, this history reveals the 'course of love' (5.3-286) to those who remain.

Notes

[1] *Drama, Fields, and Metaphors: Symbolic Action in Human Society* (Ithaca, 1974), pp. 40-1 and *passim*.

[2] Brian Gibbons, Introduction, in *Romeo and Juliet* (London, 1980), p. 37.

[3] On analepsis and prolepsis, see Shlomith Rimmon-Kenan, *Narrative Fiction: Contemporary Poetics* (London, 1983), pp. 46ff.

[4] Gibbons, Introduction, p. 54.

[5] Gayle Whittier, 'The Sonnet's Body and the Body Sonnetized in *Romeo and Juliet*', *Shakespeare Quarterly*, 40 (1989), 27-41; p. 40.

[6] Joel Fineman, *Shakespeare's Perjured Eye: The Invention of Poetic Subjectivity in the Sonnets* (Berkeley, 1986), p. 24.

[7] Two of the primary psychoanalytic texts are *Civilization and Its Discontents*, and *Beyond the Pleasure Principle*. A clear reading of this direction in Freud is offered by Jean Laplanche, *Life and Death in Psychoanalysis*, trans. Jeffrey Mehlman (Baltimore, 1976): 'the death drive is the very soul, the constitutive principle of libidinal circulation' (p. 124). Related scepticism underlies Lacan's view of the link between desire and demand. Desire is dependent on demand, but demand, 'by being articulated in signifiers, leaves a metonymic remainder that runs under it . . . an element that is called desire': desire leads only to desire. See *The Four Fundamental Concepts of Psycho-Analysis*, trans. Alan Sheridan (New York, 1981), p. 154; compare Catherine Belsey's gloss of Lacan's view—'desire subsists in what eludes both vision and representation, in what exceeds demand, including the demand for love'—in *Desire: Love Stories in Western Culture* (Oxford, 1994), p. 139.

[8] *Staging the Gaze: Postmodernism, Psychoanalysis, and Shakespearean Comedy* (Ithaca, 1991), p. 110.

[9] Belsey, *Desire*, pp. 38-9.

[10] Ibid., p. 70.

[11] *Faultlines: Cultural Materialism and the Politics of Dissident Reading* (Oxford, 1992), p. 128.

[12] *Sir Philip Sidney: Selected Poems*, ed. Katherine Duncan-Jones (Oxford, 1973), p. 117. As discussed below, this first sonnet's turn to a seemingly authentic self is also made in *Romeo and Juliet*.

[13] Stephen Greenblatt, 'Psychoanalysis and Renaissance Culture', in *Literary Theory / Renaissance Texts*, ed. Patricia Parker and David Quint (Baltimore, 1986), 210-24; p. 224.

[14] 'But passion lends them power, time means, to meet, / Tempering extremities with extreme sweet' (2 Chor. 13-14). The Chorus, not included in first Quarto, is reprinted in the Arden edition (see n. 2).

[15] Catherine Belsey, *The Subject of Tragedy: Identity and Difference in Renaissance Drama* (London, 1985), p. 34.

[16] Aubrey Mellor, 'From the Artistic Director', in Queensland Theatre Company Program for *Romeo and Juliet* (Brisbane, 1993), p. 3.

[17] Samuel Taylor Coleridge, *Lectures on Shakespeare and Other Poets and Dramatists*, Everyman's Library (London: Dent, 1914), p. 410.

[18] Graham Holderness, Preface: 'All this', in *The Shakespeare Myth*, ed. Graham Holderness (Manchester, 1988), pp. xii-xiii.

[19] See Dympna Callaghan, 'The Ideology of Romantic Love: The Case of *Romeo and Juliet*', in Dympna Callaghan, Lorraine Helms and Jyotsna Singh, *The Weyward Sisters: Shakespeare and Feminist Politics* (Oxford, 1994), pp. 59-101; Jonathan Goldberg, '*Romeo and Juliet*'s Open Rs', in *Queering the Renaissance*, ed. Jonathan Goldberg (Durham, 1994), 218-35; p. 227; and Joseph A. Porter, 'Marlowe, Shakespeare, and the Canonization of Heterosexuality', *South Atlantic Quarterly*, 88 (1989), 127-47.

[20] *Radical Tragedy: Religion, Ideology and Power in the Age of Shakespeare and His Contemporaries* (Chicago, 1984), p. 49.

[21] Cf. Michel Foucault, *The Use of Pleasure*, vol. 2 of *The History of Sexuality*, trans. Robert Hurley (New York, 1990), p. 5 and *passim*.

[22] *Symposium*, in *The Collected Dialogues of Plato*, ed. Edith Hamilton and Huntington Cairns (Princeton, 1985), 193a-c, 211d-e.

[23] Baldassare Castiglione, *The Book of the Courtier*, trans. Sir Thomas Hoby (London, 1948), pp. 319-22.

[24] *Fowre Hymnes*, 'A Hymne in Honovr of Love' (lines 197-203) and 'A Hymne in Honovr of Heavenly Love' (lines 8-28), in *Spenser: Poetical Works*, ed. J. C. Smith and E. de Selincourt (Oxford, 1979).

[25] *Shakespeare's Ovid: Being Arthur Golding's Translation of the 'Metamorphoses'*, ed. W. H. D. Rouse (Carbondale, 1961), book 3: lines 540-2.

[26] Jonathan Bate, *Shakespeare and Ovid* (Oxford, 1993), p. 173. Bate emphasizes Actaeon as another figure of self-consuming desire (p. 19 and *passim*).

[27] Cf. George Bataille's conceptions of eros as 'laughable', tragic and 'arousing irony', and of 'The complicity of the tragic—which is the basis of death—with sexual pleasure and laughter': *The Tears of Eros*, trans. Peter Connor (San Francisco, 1990), pp. 53 and 66.

[28] Michel de Montaigne, *Essays*, trans. John Florio (London, 1980), vol. 2, pp. 192-3.

[29] Coleridge, *Lectures*, p. 103.

[30] Harry Levin, 'Form and Formality in *Romeo and Juliet*', in *Twentieth-Century Interpretations of 'Romeo and Juliet': A Collection of Critical Essays*, ed. Douglas Cole (Englewood Cliffs, N.J., 1970), 85-95; p. 86.

[31] Coleridge, *Lectures*, p. 103.

[32] Joseph A. Porter emphasizes that Mercutio's opposition is to romantic love not to sex: *Shakespeare's Mercutio: His History and Drama* (Chapel Hill, 1988), p. 103.

[33] Geoffrey Bullough, *Narrative and Dramatic Sources of Shakespeare*, vol. 1 (London, 1966), lines 114, 210, 935, 2420 and 2532.

[34] Kay Stockholder, *Dream Works: Lovers and Families in Shakespeare's Plays* (Toronto, 1987), p. 30. In *Love's Argument: Gender Relations in Shakespeare* (Chapel Hill, 1984), Marianne Novy sees that the lovers' private world crystallizes in the aubade of Act 2, scene 1 (p. 108).

[35] Bullough, *Sources*, vol. 1, p. 374.

[36] On the interplay among misrecognition, desire and the symbolic, see Catherine Belsey, 'The Name of the Rose in *Romeo and Juliet*', *Yearbook of English Studies*, 23 (1993), 126-42; on the significance of the lovers being masked from each other, see Barbara L. Parker, *A Precious Seeing: Love and Reason in Shakespeare's Plays* (New York, 1987), p. 142.

[37] Jessica Benjamin, *The Bonds of Love: Psychoanalysis, Feminism, and the Problem of Domination* (New York, 1988), p. 21.

[38] Edward Snow suggests that the sonnet registers 'an intersubjective privacy' that subdues 'sexual difference and social opposition': 'Language and Sexual Difference in *Romeo and Juliet*', in *Shakespeare's 'Rough magic': Renaissance Essays in Honor of C. L. Barber*, ed. Peter Erickson and Coppélia Kahn (Newark, 1985), pp. 168-92; p. 168; Novy contrasts this scene with the sticho-mythic exchange between Juliet and Paris at 4.1.18-38 (*Love's Argument*, p. 108).

[39] On the love-death oxymoron, cf. Whittier, 'Sonnet's Body', p. 32.

[40] Coppélia Kahn, 'Coming of Age in Verona', in *The Woman's Part: Feminist Criticism of Shakespeare*, ed. Carolyn Ruth Swift Lenz, Gayle Greene and Carol Thomas Neely (Urbana, 1980), pp. 171-93; p. 186. Marilyn Williamson regards the deaths as alienating rather than uniting, 'Romeo's suicide fulfills a pattern to which Juliet is both necessary and accidental': 'Romeo and Death', *Shakespeare Studies*, 14 (1981), 129-37; p. 132.

[41] Callaghan, 'Ideology', p. 61.

[42] See Thomas Moisan, 'Rhetoric and the Rehearsal of Death: the "Lamentations" Scene in *Romeo and Juliet*', *Shakespeare Quarterly*, 34 (1983), 389-404.

[43] Julia Kristeva, *Tales of Love*, trans. Leon S. Roudiez (New York, 1987), p. 213.

[44] *The Seminar of Jacques Lacan*, Book 1, *Freud's Papers on Technique 1953-1954*, trans. John Forrester (New York, 1991), p. 36. On literature and psychoanalysis as twin discourses of mourning and melancholia, see Julia Reinhard Lupton and Kenneth Reinhard, *After Oedipus: Shakespeare in Psychoanalysis* (Ithaca, 1993), esp. pp. 32-3.

GENDER AND SOCIETY

Susan Snyder (essay date 1996)

SOURCE: "Ideology and Feud in *Romeo and Juliet*," in *Shakespeare Survey: An Annual Survey of Shakespeare Studies and Production*, Vol. 49, 1996, pp. 87-96.

[*In the following essay, Snyder contends that the feud between the Montagues and the Capulets in* Romeo and Juliet *is a metaphor for ideology, arguing that social "norms themselves bring about the tragedy" of the play.*]

Romeo and Juliet are very young. They are young to be married, and also young to be protagonists in a tragedy. Shakespeare made a special point of Juliet's extreme youth, first subtracting two years from the already tender age of Arthur Brooke's heroine (instead of sixteen, just under fourteen), and then having the characters disagree more than once over whether she is old enough to marry.[1] Romeo, presumably somewhat older than Juliet, is nevertheless not yet grown up: still in the family home, fussed over by his parents, free to roam about with his friends but apparently not seen as ready for adult responsibility.

Why did Shakespeare insist on his tragic lovers as adolescents? To be sure, their youthfulness accentuates the generational conflict implicit in the story, the tragic disjunction that Franco Zeffirelli exploited so well in his compelling film version. But the extreme youth of Romeo and Juliet opens up a possibility beyond the traditional clashes of young and old. The very embeddedness in family that signals their tender years may itself be the point. It is surely significant that each of the two protagonists is introduced to us first as the object of parental concern. In the opening scene the Montagues worry about Romeo's solitary moping, fearing that some secret sorrow may blight their promising son before he ever arrives at maturity.[2] In the scene directly following, Capulet is busy providing for his daughter's future by negotiating her marriage with Paris. It is important that each of these parental discussions takes place before we even meet the young person being discussed. Our initial view is of Romeo as a son, Juliet as a daughter.

Juliet as daughter of the house continues a prominent emphasis. Even her love scenes with Romeo are played out inside the Capulet enclave, with one family member or another always threatening to intrude. Romeo is seen in the streets rather than enclosed in Montague domesticity, in the company of his friends rather than his parents. This reflects, of course, the relative freedom accorded to young males as opposed to young females. But the difference in terms of family embeddedness may be more apparent than real. Romeo's peer group is not separate from kinship structure but a kind of extension of it, in that his habitual companions are Montague allies.

All of us are always being shaped into our ways of being and knowing by extensive social processing, but the lives of the young make this process especially visible. Romeo and Juliet do not necessarily have less autonomy than adults who have undergone the full ideological conditioning afforded by society's institutions. Yet their subordinate situation as children, acted on (cajoled, lectured, ordered, modelled) by the parents who in effect own them, makes that lack of autonomy more apparent. And the major constituting force that operates in their society is the feud between Montagues and Capulets.

At first glance this would seem too comprehensive a claim for the feud's reach and impact. The quarrel involves only two families, and it is not always taken seriously even by Montagues and Capulets. H. B. Charlton finds the family feud unsatisfactory as Fate's instrument in *Romeo and Juliet*, 'unsubstantial', because it is sometimes treated comically and does not consistently inform the feelings and actions of most characters. In any case, thinks Charlton, such barbaric mores are not realistic in the civilized Verona the play depicts.[3] (On this last point, one wonders how a study published soon after World War II could ignore such abundant evidence in the recent history of civilized Western Europe of resurgent group hatreds and the barbaric behaviour they generated.) Critics in their own time have less trouble seeing the destructive dimensions in Veronese civility. Marilyn Williamson, for example, points to the violent atmosphere of the play's society.[4] For Coppélia Kahn, the feud is 'an extreme and peculiar expression of patriarchal society'.[5] I agree that informing social institutions are the play's major tragic force, though I would quarrel with Kahn's term 'peculiar' if it is meant to characterize the feud as uncommon, individual rather than general. The dramatic *expression* of dynastic hostility may seem extreme and eccentric, but the feud in its operations acts like any ideology, indeed offers a model of how ideology works.

Like ideology in Althusser's classic formulation, the feud has no obvious genesis that can be discerned, no history. It pervades everything, not as a set of specific ideas but as repeatedpractices. The feud-system is not in fact predicated on any substantive difference between Montagues and Capulets. A Jerusalem production which presented Montagues as Arabic-speaking Palestinians and Capulets as Hebrew-speaking Jews had its own political point to make about the clash of rival cultures.[6] Shakespeare, though, with his 'two households both alike in dignity', seems to be creating a different sort of division, one that is obviously arbitrary and artificial. The members of his rival houses belong to the same culture, use the same verbal and behavioural languages. When Montagues intrude on the Capulet festivities, only their faces have to be covered; nothing else in their bearing or manners marks them as outsiders. What's in a name? Everything, it would seem. One thinks of Lacan's two identical doors with *Ladies* over one and *Gentlemen* over the other.

Shakespeare also emphasizes the artificial nature of the feud by suppressing the account of its origins given in this source. Brooke explains that it was their very equality of station that gave rise to enmity between the two families, breeding envy and hatred which in time became 'rooted'.[7] Shakespeare says only that the quarrel is 'ancient'.[8] The first scene subtly enacts this 'always already' quality of the feud, when a question of origins is raised only to fall short of an answer. The elder Montague asks Benvolio what started the latest round of hostilities—asks, we should note, only *after* both of them have automatically taken part in the fighting. Benvolio can't give a good explanation because the clash was already under way when he entered. The audience has been on the scene longer than he has, but any answer spectators can give to 'how did this start?' is no more definitive than Benvolio's. We have seen the Capulet servants come on already primed to fight, as if they need contrary Montagues to define their manhood. Or rather, this has been Sampson's stance, while Gregory twits him and plays generally with words. But the feud, like ideology, flattens out personal differences, slotting individuals into predetermined roles; after some actual Montagues arrive on the scene, Gregory quickly falls into line with Sampson's pugnacity—just as Benvolio, whose natural bent is to peacemaking and who a few minutes later tries to stop the servants' scrap, must nevertheless slide into his appointed slot to cross swords with Tybalt. The dominance of an 'assigned form of subjectivity'[9] over individual temperament or initiative is evident in the exaggerated symmetry of the whole sequence: servants matched by opposing servants, nephew of one house paired off against nephew of the other, Capulet patriarch answered by Montague patriarch, all entering as if on cue and doing the same thing.

The Montague-Capulet feud may be like ideology in having no apparent beginning, but is it not different in coming to a publicly announced end in the last moments of the play? I shall delay addressing this somewhat problematic issue till the end of my essay, and consider here another question that has probably occurred to more than one reader already. Is it legitimate to see the feud as shaped by Shakespeare enacting the workings of ideology as conceived by modern theorists? Where we may accept without difficulty readings that discern in his plays and poems the features of specific ideological systems, explore their contradictions, and trace their transmutations, the assumption in these cases is that Shakespeare need have made no conscious effort to delineate these systems, which rather inscribe themselves through us without our awareness or cooperation. But doesn't taking the feud as a metaphor for ideology in general imply some conscious intent on Shakespeare's part?

Yes, it does, and the assumption is not unwarranted. Without precognizing Althusser, Shakespeare nevertheless displays in *Romeo and Juliet* a very conscious concern with society's impact on the individual, especially in the characters' meditations on names and their power. Names define us as individuals, announce who we are. Yet no name is unique to one person. It has been attached to others in the society, blood kin in the case of the surname, saints or leaders or forebears in the case of the given name. Names are imposed on infants before they are individuals, by society and its central unit the family. The considerable dynastic and cultural freight they carry begins the child's constitution as a subject. 'Romeo Montague' inscribes the young man who is called that into a particular subject-position. (We tend to see this dimension mainly in the family name, but Juliet laments over the given name as well: 'Deny thy father and refuse thy name' is preceded by 'Wherefore art thou Romeo?' And her lover, invited to doff his offending name, responds 'Henceforth I never will be Romeo.')

Juliet's familiar 'what's in a name?' meditation shows up the power of ideology by signally underestimating its force. She and Romeo have met unlabelled, as it were, a faceless youth and an anonymous girl at a party. They have not encountered each other before in the usual contextual way because of the enmity between their families. Each asks for the name of the other, and discovers conflict:

ROMEO   Is she a Capulet?
O dear account! My life is my foe's debt . . .
JULIET My only love sprung from my only hate!
Too early seen unknown, and known too late![10]

In soliloquy later, Juliet convinces herself that *seeing*, responding to individual looks and attitudes, can blot out *knowing*, which acknowledges the social context. She tries to separate her lover's name from his essential properties.

'Tis but thy name that is my enemy.
Thou art thyself, though not a Montague.
What's Montague? It is nor hand, nor foot,
Nor arm, nor face, nor any part
Belonging to a man.
                                        (2.1.80-4)

Name and self are not so easily divisible, though. While Romeo immediately disavows his name, Juliet even here goes on calling him 'Romeo' and 'Montague', and worries about the danger of his staying with her, 'considering who thou art' (2.1.106). A name may not be a body part, but Romeo will soon feel it to be just as intrinsic. Fearing that Juliet hates him for killing her cousin Tybalt, he attributes the act to 'that name's cursed hand'. The contorted phrase makes manifest the social construction of his agency. Contradicting Juliet's earlier optimism, he feels 'Romeo' as something so enmeshed with his being that it needs to be forcibly ripped out of his body (3.3.101-7). What has happened to change his perception from 'Henceforth I never will be Romeo' to 'In what vile part of this anatomy / Doth my name lodge?' is the reactivation of the feud: the need to avenge Mercutio, who died taking Romeo's own place against Tybalt, by killing in turn the enemy Capulet. Romeo's name has turned out to be a part of his self after all, directing his actions and defining his responses.

Juliet's hopeful separation of essence from what seems to her an external label—'Thou art thyself, though not a Montague'—is soon shown to be wrong, then. Even the supporting argument that she uses at the time is suspect. 'That which we call a rose / By any other word would smell as sweet' (2.1.85-6) sounds self-evidently true. But would that flower really retain its full sweetness in our subjective judgement if we were not conditioned to think of the rose as the best, the most worthy? The blossom itself retains its natural properties under any name, but our use and valuation of it must alter. The name 'rose' carries with it considerable cultural baggage, suggesting surpassing beauty combined with difficulty of access (surrounded by thorns), hence something supremely precious, as well as the paragon, the ideal. What Ophelia means when she calls Hamlet 'th' expectancy and rose of the fair state' (*Hamlet*

3.1.155) would be significantly altered if she talked of 'th' expectancy and lilac', even though lilacs smell sweet too—especially since the 'fair state' of the audience for whom Shakespeare wrote this line had a rose as its familiar symbol.

Shakespeare did not need Althusser's analysis in order to grasp the workings of interpellation or to feel the force of the dual meaning of *subject,* the 'autonomous' agent who is formed by and in a social formation to which he is subjected. Jonathan Dollimore approaches the same question through parallels between Montaigne's 'custom' and Althusser's 'ideology', concluding that 'the Renaissance possessed a sophisticated concept of ideology if not the word'.[11] The preoccupation with names in *Romeo and Juliet* points directly to the most basic function of ideology, central also to the feud: identifying, hailing or interpellating into predetermined subject-positions. The feud operates in the classic way of language, and of ideology: it creates meaning by differentiating. Terry Eagleton, following Jameson, finds the opposition between self/familiar/good on the one hand and non-self/alien/bad on the other 'the fundamental gesture of all ideology'.[12] Capulets define who they are against Montagues, Montagues against Capulets. 'This' can only be distinguished when set against 'that', however arbitrary such distinctions are in language and other social constructions.[13] The feud is not a matter of contrary ideas, not a matter of ideas at all, but of repeated, habitual actions that keep reasserting the defining distinctions between 'us' and 'them'.

Ideology is what constructs our consciousness and makes sense of our world. It is pervasive, working everywhere. Can this be said of the feud? After all, not everyone in Verona is a Montague or a Capulet. We get fleeting glimpses of some nameless citizens, and various members of another family come in for more extended attention as individual characters: Prince Escalus, and especially his two kinsmen Mercutio and Paris. But on scrutiny the Montague-Capulet hostility can be seen to gather in and organize these third parties as well as the two central clans. The feud exemplifies the workings of any ideology, of Ideology itself, but the specifics of its enactment express their historical moment.[14] The Veronese discourse of family division thus embraces some important social imperatives of early modern élite culture in Western Europe: the obligation to maintain one's honour by avenging insults, the obligation to contract a suitable marriage and adapt appropriately to the married state.

To some extent these were gendered. It was men who were bound in this way by the code of honour. Marriage, though expected of both sexes, was more central and defining for women, since a wife took on the loyalties as well as the status of her new family along with its name. In *Romeo and Juliet* Lady Capulet not only makes the case for marriage to her young daughter but also demonstrates her own thorough conditioning as a wife. Presumably not a Capulet by birth, she nevertheless has committed herself totally and fervently to the family feud. Her husband, born into the anti-Montague faith, can be easygoing about it at times, as when he accepts Romeo's presence at the party. His wife, a typical convert, is possessed by her acquired faith. She is not on hand to comment on this first occasion, but after Romeo has killed Tybalt she fills the air with cries of grief and demands for revenge. Indeed, it is presumably her role as chief mourner for Tybalt in 3.1, as contrasted with her husband's silence, that led Malone and subsequent editors to list Tybalt in the Dramatis Personae as the nephew of *Lady* Capulet, not Capulet himself.[15] But family titles like *nephew* and *brother* routinely included in-laws as well as blood relatives,[16] and Tybalt's own deep investment in Capulet family values, not to speak of his interment in the family tomb, strongly suggests that he is a Capulet born. While a woman's transfer of loyalties to her husband's kin was fitting, a man's proper adherence was to his own clan. Lady Capulet's extreme sorrow for Tybalt, then, and her murderous designs on his slayer convey not special concern for her own family of birth but complete interpellation as a Capulet by marriage.[17] To Juliet as a prospective bride she lays out the same course, inviting her to be the decorative cover to the book that is Paris—in other words, to take her meaning from her husband. 'So shall you share in all he doth possess / By having him, making yourself no less' (1.3.81-96). Paris himself, like Juliet initially, gives docile heed to the imperative of suitable alliance; indeed, this is his sole motive for action in the play. The marriage of Paris and Juliet never takes place, but it is his moves towards that union that involve him fatally in the bloodshed of the feud.

Like his kinsman Paris, Mercutio gets entangled in the feud and dies in consequence. By his intervention in the fight to uphold Romeo's masculine good name when Romeo himself refuses to rise to Tybalt's insulting provocations, Mercutio brings out the other specific historical face of ideology in this play, the masculine code of honour. Mercutio presents himself as a scorner of codes and conventions. He shows no sign of negotiating like Paris for a bride, he delights in recasting Romeo's Petrarchan metaphors of adoration for Rosaline into leering physicality. He mocks standard beliefs like the power of dreams to prognosticate, and standard practices like the formulas of fencing. Yet Mercutio is as deeply implicated in ideology as anyone else. His reduction of woman to a set of sexual parts to be attacked is not really his own, but derives from another ideological strain, as extreme as Petrarchan adoration and even hoarier as a cultural tradition. And for all his disdain of the *duello,* he hurls himself with no question at all into the duel proposed by Tybalt. His response is as mechanical as any we have witnessed in the opening Montague-Capulet brawl. Mercutio himself attributes his death to the family feud, obsessively repeating through his last moments 'A plague o' both your houses . . . A plague o' both your houses! . . . A plague o' both your houses . . . Your houses!' (3.1.91-108).

When these specific ideological ramifications thus draw in the two chief 'outsiders' in the play, and the third 'outsider' finally reads his own implication in theirs ('And I, for winking at your discords, too / Have lost a brace of kinsmen', 5.3.293-4), the feud does appear all-pervasive. No part of society that we see can escape from its influence.[18] Romeo and Juliet themselves are deeply conditioned by it, although they also, necessarily, transcend the family division. I call this movement beyond the feud necessary not only because it allows their love for each other to begin and develop, but also because their venture outside the circumscribing feud-ideology makes that ideology visible, as it would never be if everyone continued to operate inside its unspoken premises.

Transcendence is perhaps a misleading term for the lovers' attempted isolation of themselves from the feud. Enclosed by Veronese social formations, they do not rise above so much as withdraw inward. Romeo and Juliet have no space of their own. Their love scenes are all played out inside the Capulet establishment, constantly impinged upon by Tybalt, or the Nurse, or Lady Capulet. The closest the lovers come to a shared private space is Friar Laurence's cell, where they met in 2.5 to be married. But that encounter is brief and driven (Friar Laurence feels it necessary to 'make short work' of the marriage ceremony, line 34). Moreover, this respite from the feud is granted not by escape from ideology but by the temporary ascendancy of a rival one, the Friar's Christian agenda of reconciling the two warring houses. Nor does a freer space seem to be imaginable for Romeo and Juliet somewhere else. A milieu less insistently enclosing might make visually possible the option of leaving the city together and finding a new life somewhere else. Instead, the play's physical dimensions only confirm that 'there is no world without Verona walls' (3.3.17). Verona, constituted by the feud, asserts itself like any ideology as the only reality there is.[19] Even as they die, another Capulet enclave surrounds the young pair, the family tomb.

Hemmed in as they are, how can Romeo and Juliet constitute even an inner space in terms different from the all-powerful norm? As is suggested by Friar Laurence's transgression of the feud's dictates to sanction their love, opportunity arises through the presence of rival ideologies coexisting with and sometimes challenging the dominant one. For example, Romeo and Juliet can initially meet and talk as they do not only because they are momentarily free of family-name labels but because Juliet's father is for once tolerating the presence of a Montague. He restrains the angry Tybalt, swayed by imperatives other than the feud:

> Content thee, gentle coz, let him alone.
> A bears him like a portly gentleman,
> And, to say truth, Verona brags of him
> To be a virtuous and well-governed youth.
> I would not for the wealth of all this town
> Here in my house do him disparagement.
> (1.5.64-9)

Such indulgence at first glance seems to support Charlton's dismissal of the feud as too light-weight to sustain its role in the tragic structure, let alone to express the central shaping force of any culture. If the family enmity can be so easily set aside by the leader of one faction, how can it nevertheless represent the all-powerful operations of ideology? But one can see in Capulet's attitude not a casual shedding of the feud but an internal disruption in the social ideology, as the dominant discourse is crossed by other, locally influential ones. Montagues are to be spurned, yet good cheer must be fostered at social gatherings, especially by the host. Categorically, a Montague is an enemy, yet a particular young man's good behaviour and reputation make it hard to treat him rudely. For convivial Capulet, whose favourite activity is preparing and presenting feasts, the primary value at this moment of cross-purposes is surely hospitality. '*Here in my house*', whatever you do, don't spoil the party.

Normally kept apart by the reigning ideology, Romeo and Juliet can thus come together in a kind of aporia created by ideological contestation, which in turn enables them to find in their sonnet-exchange discourses that they can share, of romantic courtship and religion. Religion will continue as a common discourse embodied in Friar Laurence. The commonality has in fact preceded this first meeting: it is another sign of crossed ideologies that these two young people so firmly separated by the feud can nevertheless share without any special dispensation the same confessor. His cell is another aporia, or a version of the first, the (only) place where hereditary enemies can meet and formally unite.

The discourse of romantic courtship presents a more complicated picture. The first exchange between Romeo and Juliet is in some ways highly conventional, grounded in a familiar cultural master-script. Their dialogue falls neatly into the standard sonnet's three quatrains and a couplet, and in typical sonnet fashion elaborates a conceit, the lover as pilgrim. In showing so clearly the impress of literary tradition, this wooing passage may remind us of Romeo a few scenes before, expounding his hopeless love for Rosaline in Petrarchan clichés. If that earlier love-talk nevertheless feels more artificial, it is partly because the speaker's diligence in piling up the conceits and oxymora suggests a scholar's zeal rather than a lover's;[20] but partly because, with the other party to the courtship not even present, Romeo's one-sided romance acquires the flavour of rhetorical exercise. The passage between Romeo and Juliet at the Capulet party moves more naturally: proposition, response, adjustment and further proposition, new response. Here Romeo's speech has a real purpose, pleading for a kiss. And they do kiss, twice. Juliet breaks off the second sonnet begun by Romeo with 'You kiss by th' book' (1.5.109). While the latter part of her teasing complaint underlines how the impersonal discourse of literary love has written itself through their exchange, the first part nevertheless acknowledges real physical contact between them. The later love-speech of Romeo and Juliet uses rhyme much less and highly wrought form not at all. Their language cannot of course completely escape tradition—no language can. But in subsequent dialogue between the lovers convention is not prominent as such, and familiar materials are reworked to flow, with the verse, more freely.[21]

This often-noted evolution, from romantic discourse shaped by convention to a more direct lyricism that seems to override form, enacts through language the withdrawal of Romeo and Juliet from the defining difference imposed on them by the feud, into immediate, fervent engagement with each other. Perhaps their very youthfulness, which on the one hand highlights the social processing they are undergoing, on the other hand makes that withdrawal more possible in that the processing is not complete. They are less fixed by constant conditioning than their elders, less habituated to their social roles as Montague and Capulet. Even so, the grip of ideology is tenacious, and apt to tighten in moments of emotional crisis. Both lovers offer examples of this tenacity, and both temporary re-conformings are accentuated by a lapse into 'speaking by the book'. Trying to deal with Tybalt's rage right after his marriage to Juliet, Romeo has been unconventional in both action and speech: 'I do protest I never injured thee, / But love thee better than thou canst devise . . . good Capulet—which name I tender / As dearly as mine own—be satisfied' (3.1.67-71). But when Mercutio takes up Tybalt's challenge on Romeo's behalf and is mortally wounded as a result, conventional reactions and conventional language suddenly reclaim Romeo. Now, not before, he worries about his 'reputation stained / With Tybalt's slander' (lines 111-12). The news that Mercutio is dead completes Romeo's total absorption into the avenger-role prescribed for him in the code of honour, the role from which he had earlier distanced himself so carefully.

> He gad in triumph, and Mercutio slain?
> Away to heaven, respective lenity,
> And fire-eyed fury be my conduct now.
> Now, Tybalt, take the 'villain' back again
> That late thou gav'st me.
>
> (lines 122-6)

The style of his speech as well as its substance belongs to revenge tragedy. In the scene following, Juliet in her turn is repossessed by ideology. She has begun this sequence in soliloquy, wishing impatiently for night and her bridegroom, her speech hastening along with her desire and overflowing the artificial pentameter bounds. Now the Nurse tells her that Tybalt her cousin is dead by the hand of that same bridegroom.

> O serpent heart, hid with a flow'ring face!
> Did ever dragon keep so fair a cave?
> Beautiful tyrant, fiend angelical!
> Dove-feathered raven, wolvish-ravening lamb!
> Despisèd substance of divinest show!
> Just opposite to what thou justly seem'st—
> A damnèd saint, an honourable villain.
>
> (3.2.73-9)

When Juliet lapses into her feud-assigned form of subjectivity as outraged Capulet, her speech changes. All at once, she is speaking in hackneyed images and formally balanced end-stopped lines. Her shock at suddenly having to superimpose Romeo the murderer on Romeo the lover is certainly real, but its articulation through neat oxymora (reminiscent of Romeo's own conventional language of emotion before his meeting with Juliet) makes clear that she is speaking as a generic Capulet.[22] As Orwell might say, feudthink generates bookspeak.

Yet if the language of Romeo and Juliet, apart from these lapses, hints at a journey beyond the prevailing ideology, the constraints implicit in the play's action leave them with nowhere to go, nothing to do except die. For individuals who try to advance beyond their ideology but cannot undo its constitutive influence, there is no feasible way to live. The deaths of Romeo and Juliet can be seen as the final expression of a process of excommunication that was adumbrated earlier when Romeo was banished from Verona. Exclusion, as Goran Therborn reminds us, is the main form of sanction invoked by ideology against those who transgress its barriers and definitions.[23] The crime that cut Romeo off from his social existence came about through acts of ideological rebellion: crossing over the feud-barrier to love an 'enemy', refusing (as a result) a challenge in violation of the code of honour. The lovers' deaths look avoidable on the plot level, a matter of misunderstanding and bad timing, but from this perspective that tragic finale inside the family tomb (a setting that visibly manifests the weight of past practices) is all too inevitable. Laurence Stone thinks that an Elizabethan audience would have understood the tragedy of Romeo and Juliet as self-inflicted: their destruction came about because, by placing personal passion before obedience to family imperatives, they violated the norms of their society.[24] I have been arguing that, on the contrary, the norms themselves bring about the tragedy. One could go further and propose that the tragic predicament—possibilities for human development narrowed down and cut off—is built into the operations of ideology. That which is necessary to give us a stable identity and a consistent view of the world is by the same token what limits and distorts us. The suicides of Romeo and Juliet represent one version of ideology's destructive power. An alternative outcome to the action, less dramatic but just as tragic in its own way, would portray the two young people as recaptured for good by their social conditioning. Romeo would become the Tybalt of the Montagues, challenging Capulets on cue and advancing his manly reputation. Juliet would have an elaborate church wedding and afterward live comfortably in her different sphere as the rich and decorative cover to Paris's book.

Does the destruction of this young pair do anything to transform the feud and ideological force it represents? Certainly Capulet and Montague join hands in their mutual grief at the very end of the play, initiating what the Prince calls 'a glooming peace'. Taking the hopeful view, we might conclude that the union of Romeo and Juliet, born in the contradictions of ideology that open up possibilities for change and development, signals even in their death the end of the old system and the beginning of a new phase. But the hopeful view has to ignore or discount the ironies that hedge that reconciliation of the patriarchs. The fathers propose to seal their peace by erecting gold statues to their children, an image that not only suggests vulgar show but also resonates disturbingly with Romeo's recent diatribe against gold as a poison, a murderer (5.1.81-5). Memorializing the feud's victims in a medium that is synonymous with corruption and death makes at best an inauspicious beginning for a new era of peace. What is more, as many readers have observed, the proposals of Montague and Capulet suggest in their form renewed competition rather than cooperation.

> CAPULET O brother Montague, give me thy hand.
> This is my daughter's jointure, for no more
> Can I demand.
> MONTAGUE But I can give thee more,
> For I will raise her statue in pure gold,
> That whiles Verona by that name is known,
> There shall no figure at such rate be set
> As that of true and faithful Juliet.
> CAPULET As rich shall Romeo's by his lady lie . . .
>
> (5.3.295-302)

Both fathers speak the language of commercial rivalry as they strive not to be outdone in conspicuous display. If mercantile competition played a part in their feud, it has never been so noticeable as in this moment of supposed reconciliation.[25]

Traditional productions of *Romeo and Juliet,* while often cutting or omitting entirely Friar Laurence's lengthy explanations in the last scene, usually present the reconciliation to be taken at face value. Directors more inclined to social criticism interrogate it. Viewers of Michael Bogdanov's 1986-7 RSC production, for example, could have little assurance of a brave new world in Verona when they witnessed the actual unveiling of those golden statues, staged as an empty public relations event with the Prince speaking from cue cards and *papparazzi* photographing all the surviving principals in appropriate poses. The handshake of Capulet and Montague became a photo op.[26] In any case, even the most optimistic reading or staging of the final exchange between Capulet and Montague as marking a definitive social change leaves unaltered the larger tragic script of ideology. If this particular instrument of forming subjectivities becomes outmoded, a new system of distinctions and codes will replace it as the 'ancient' order of things that divides and excludes in order to define.

Notes

[1] Arthur Brooke, *The Tragicall Historye of Romeus and Juliet* (1562), fol. G4. Her mother says that most of the girl's friends are already married. In Painter's version Juliet is almost eighteen: *The Palace of Pleasure* (1567), Nnn2r.

[2] Montague likens him to 'the bud bit with an envious worm / Ere he can spread his sweet leaves to the air / Or dedicate his beauty to the sun' (I.I.148-50).

[3] H. B. Charlton, *Shakespearian Tragedy* (Cambridge, 1948), pp. 59-60.

[4] Marilyn Williamson, 'Romeo and Death', *Shakespeare Studies,* 14 (New York, 1981), 129-37; pp. 135-6. Her main point is Romeo's bent to self-destruction, which she sees as expressing his society's pervasive violence.

[5] Coppélia Kahn, 'Coming of Age in Verona', *Modern Language Studies,* 8 (1978), repr. *'Romeo and Juliet': Critical Essays,* ed. John F. Andrews, Garland Shakespearean Criticism Series, 10 (New York, 1993), 337-58; p. 337.

[6] Reported on *All Things Considered,* National Public Radio, 27 July 1994.

[7] *Romeus and Juliet,* A2r.

[8] Prol. 3; I.I.101. G. K. Hunter points to the lack of content in the enmity between Capulets and Montagues when he observes that the feud has 'little political reality' and exists to put pressure on the love of Romeo and Juliet: 'Shakespeare's Earliest Tragedies: *Titus*

Andronicus and *Romeo and Juliet*', *Shakespeare Survey* 27 (Cambridge, 1974), pp. 1-9; p. 5.

[9] This term, preferred by Goran Therborn over role (*The Ideology of Power and the Power of Ideology* [London, 1981]), better emphasizes inward conditioning along with the behaviour it generates.

[10] 1.5.116-38. For the formality of the lovers' rhymed couplets here as an expression of the feud mentality, see below, pp. 94-5.

[11] Jonathan Dollimore, *Radical Tragedy: Religion, Ideology and Power in the Drama of Shakespeare and his Contemporaries*, 2nd edn (Durham, N.C., 1993), pp. 17-18; the idea is developed in ch. 10.

[12] Terry Eagleton, *Ideology: An Introduction* (London and New York, 1991), p. 126; cf. Fredric Jameson, *The Political Unconscious* (Ithaca, N.Y., 1981), pp. 114-15. Althusser came close, in his essays on Freud and Lenin and in *Lenin and Philosophy*, to equating language and the symbolic order with ideology as agents constructing the subject. Catherine Belsey completes the connection in *Critical Practice* (London and New York, 1980), ch. 3.

[13] The lack of real difference between Montagues and Capulets (see above, p. 88) illustrates Saussure's central dictum that language is a system of differences with no positive terms, a system which creates meaning rather than discovers a pre-existing one. For the inextricable relation of language and ideology, see Rosalind Coward and John Ellis, *Language and Materialism: Developments in Semiology and the Theory of the Subject* (London, 1977). Erik Erikson in *Identity and the Youth Cycle* (New York, 1980) discusses (pp. 97-8) the function of group identification and exclusion in the adolescent years, the founding of identity on difference.

[14] 'Existential ideologies always exist in concrete historical forms, but are never reducible to them': Therborn, *The Ideology of Power*, p. 44.

[15] Eighteenth-century editions before Malone's of 1790 list Tybalt as Capulet's kinsman.

[16] Both Capulet and Lady Capulet refer to Tybalt as the son of 'my brother' (3.5.127; 3.1.146).

[17] Lady Capulet demonstrates that one of Juliet's propositions about names is not naive wish but fact. Her assertion that in union with Romeo she would 'no longer be a Capulet' (2.1.78) has the whole weight of contemporary theory and practice of marriage to support it.

[18] The feud is an example of Althusser's ideology of the ruling class, as that class is embodied in the three élite clans on view. The potentially opposing interests of the lower classes are not thematized: Capulet and Montague servants are instead shown as interpellated by their masters' feud, identified with the interests of the houses they serve. Althusser's formulation is not completely appropriate here, however, since the *cui bono* question—whose interests are served by the constituting force?—is not relevant to the feud as presented by Shakespeare. Ideology in *Romeo and Juliet* is not analysed structurally but experienced from the subject's point of view; its origins and purposes are not visible.

[19] Here again Shakespeare departs significantly from earlier versions of the story, in which Juliet begs to accompany her lover into exile, either openly as his wife or in disguise. Brooke has Romeus refuse for fear that Capulet will pursue and harm them, but in the world Shakespeare has created, to leave the city together is not even conceived as possible.

[20]
Feather of lead, bright smoke, cold fire, sick health,
Still-waking sleep, that is not what it is! . . .
Love is a smoke made with the fume of sighs,
Being purged, a fire sparkling in lovers' eyes,
Being vexed, a sea nourished with lovers' tears.

(1.1.177-89)

[21] Several critical studies chart the lovers' shift out of conventional speech: perhaps the best known of these is Harry Levin, 'Form and Formality in *Romeo and Juliet*', *Shakespeare Quarterly*, 11 (1960), 3-11. Kiernan Ryan applies Romeo's line 'Love goes toward love as schoolboys from their books' (2.1.201) to this movement beyond the 'prescribed texts': '*Romeo and Juliet*: The Language of Tragedy', *The Taming of the Text: Explorations in Language, Literature, and Culture*, ed. Willie van Peer (London and New York, 1988), pp. 106-21; p. 116.

[22] W. H. Auden notes the radical disparity between this conventional speech and the one that opened the scene, without suggesting any function for the difference: 'Commentary on the Poetry and Tragedy of *Romeo and Juliet*', *Romeo and Juliet*, Laurel edn (New York, 1988), p. 26.

[23] The victim of this process 'is excluded from further meaningful discourse as being insane, depraved, traitorous, alien, and so on. The excommunicated person is condemned, temporarily or forever, to ideological nonexistence . . . Usually ideological excommunication is connected with the material sanctions of expulsion, confinement, or death' (Therborn, *The Ideology of Power*, p. 83).

[24] Lawrence Stone, *The Family, Sex, and Marriage 1500-1800* (New York, 1977), p. 87.

[25] Among critics who have found irony in the final rapprochement of Capulet and Montague, see Clifford Leech, 'The Moral Tragedy of *Romeo and Juliet*', *English Renaissance Drama*, ed. Standish Henning et al. (Carbondale, Ill., 1976), pp. 59-75, p. 70; on the competitive nature of their speeches, Nathaniel Wallace, 'Cultural Tropology in *Romeo and Juliet*', *Studies in Philology*, 88 (1991), 329-44; p. 342; Thomas Moisan, '"O Any Thing, of Nothing First Create!": Gender and Patriarchy in the Tragedy of *Romeo and Juliet*', *In Another Country: Feminist Perspectives on Renaissance Drama*, ed. Dorothea Kehler and Susan Baker (Metuchen, N.J., and London, 1991), pp. 113-36; p. 125; Greg Bentley, 'Poetics of Power: Money as Sign and Substance in *Romeo and Juliet*', *Explorations in Renaissance Culture*, 17 (1991), 145-66; pp. 163-4.

[26] For an account of several stagings of the final scene, see Barbara Hodgdon, 'Absent Bodies, Present Voices: Performance Work and the Close of Romeo and Juliet's Golden Story', *Theatre Journal*, 41.3 (October, 1989), repr. Andrews, pp. 243-65. Bogdanov's is discussed pp. 252-4.

Robert Appelbaum (essay date 1997)

SOURCE: "'Standing to the Wall': The Pressures of Masculinity in *Romeo and Juliet*," in *Shakespeare Quarterly*, Vol. 48, No. 3, Fall, 1997, pp. 251-72.

[*In the following essay, Appelbaum investigates the tragic limitations of masculinity in* Romeo and Juliet, *discussing its socially-constituted relationship to symbolic order and rejection of the female.*]

What is masculinity? In a brief essay that rings true for me with respect to my own experience as a man, Homi K. Bhabha warns us not to speak of "masculinity in general, sui generis." What we are talking about when we talk about masculinity, Bhabha writes, is a certain "prosthetic reality—a 'prefixing' of the rules of gender and sexuality" that is somehow removed from the subject, that "is strangely separating from me, turning into my shadow," even as it "supplements and suspends" the male subject, suspends the "lack-in-being" that constitutes male subjectivity. This "'prefixing' of the rules" will obviously vary from situation to situation, from culture to culture, and from period to period, if not from individual to individual. It is not to be confused with an essence or a substance. But it is also something that a man can't dispense with. It is "the 'taking up' of an enunciative position" without which the male subject cannot articulate himself as a man in his masculinity.[1] When he was a boy, Bhabha's father used to challenge him with the playful question "Are you a man or a mouse?"—implying that there is no choosing between the two. And in an important sense there isn't any choosing. The system is already in place; in virtually any given situation a regime of masculinity will be already hegemonic, wearing a mask of coercive but universal normativity. If a man is to articulate himself as a man, the rule for doing so is already in place; and if a man is to articulate himself at all, he is already under compulsion, in most situations, to do so *as* a man. And yet the regime itself—as Bhabha knows it, as most of us today have known it, and as it seems for the most part to have been known in Shakespeare's time as well—is fundamentally unstable. It is the regime of a lack, operating as if it were the regime of a being, and its goals are always elusive and unsatisfiable, even if they are also the conditions that "supplement and suspend" the male subject while regulating his behavior.

This dilemma of masculinity is rehearsed in the oftencited masculinist patter that opens *Romeo and Juliet* and leads to a renewal of violence in the world of the play. "To move is to stir, and to be valiant is to stand," the Capulet servant Gregory argues, preparing to incite a brawl. But what is a man, then, really to do? To stir or to stand? The assertive masculinity that Gregory is trying to grasp immediately slips out of his hands and out of his words, since to stand, as his companion, Sampson, rejoins, is to "take the wall," and yet "the weakest goes to the wall"; the wall is a place for women (1.1.9-14).[2] To be a man is to move, to stir, to push, to thrust ("I will push Montague's men from the wall, and thrust his maids to the wall" [ll. 16-17]); but it is also to stand, to show oneself standing, "to show [oneself] a tyrant," and attempt to exact tribute to one's masculinity, to secure ratification that one is standing: "My naked weapon is out"; "I will frown as I pass by, and let them take it as they list" (ll. 21,34,41). On the one hand, the man wants to take up the position that is already waiting for him, the position of his own lack; he wants to stir and occupy it, displacing his rivals, abusing their women. On the other hand, the man wants to wear the mask of having the position occupied; he wants to show himself not stirring toward it but already standing there in possession of his masculinity. Valiantly standing, he is confirmed, at last, in his manhood. Or is he?

It is clear from its context that the rivalry between the Capulets and the Montagues is also, for the men, the impetus for an inward rivalry, an inward pressure to masculine self-assertion that cannot be appeased or concluded. Both Gregory and Sampson find themselves called upon (from where is unclear) to initiate an incident of masculine aggression—to stir or to stand and, either way, by being embroiled in a fight, to attain to the realization of a normative value. But what is lacking from the regime of aggression that they are trying to observe is a genuine endpoint, a normativity that, once attained, can bring their masculinist goals of aggression to a final resolution: a mask of adequacy.

Here as elsewhere in Shakespeare the regime of masculinity seems to have a doubleness that is all but insoluble. If masculinity is a prefixing of the rules, those rules are invested in systems of power about which the Shakespearean canon is already ambivalent, and which the canon commonly depicts as unstable and insufficient. Moreover, if the regime of masculinity demands that its unsatisfiable goals be followed to the end, and subjects such as Sampson and Gregory, or, for that matter, Tybalt and Mercutio, are compelled to try to complete themselves in ways that can only result in their death, the Shakespearean canon often dramatizes what appears to be a desire to escape from the regime, to overcome or run away from the snares it sets. *Romeo and Juliet* is not a play particularly marked by what might be taken to be signs of psychological complexity; on the contrary, it seems bent on schematizing its psychologies and laying its schematizations bare. But for just this reason, it provides, I believe, an especially interesting test case of this insoluble double bind: the ambivalent prosthetics of masculinity.[3] Against its opening and recurring spectacle of masculine aggression, the play juxtaposes a pair of alternatives: civil peace, apparently embodied in the person and decrees of its Prince; and civil love, sponsored by the affair between its eponymous hero and heroine and the regime of heterosexual love they try to observe. But it is fair to wonder what kinds of alternatives, if any, civil peace and civil love really supply. My position is that they do not supply genuine alternatives: in the world of *Romeo and Juliet,* the regime of masculinity is constituted as a system from which there is no escape, but in keeping with which there is no experience of masculine satisfaction either, although the drama played out by Romeo may seduce us into thinking that there is both one and the other.

One might continue this line of inquiry by looking into the nature of the alternatives themselves. What would it mean for a male *not* to be a man in the world of *Romeo and Juliet,* to be a male subject without being a captive of the masculinist regime? Or, if any male were inevitably its captive, the system being both prosthetic and mandatory, what would it mean to find fulfillment in the system, as if, in being its captive, one were also expressing one's freedom and transcending the system's constraints?

Both the fixity of the gender system in *Romeo and Juliet* and the illusions of transcendence the system apparently fosters have recently been attacked by Jonathan Goldberg. The focus of Goldberg's critique is the play's conventional reception as a celebration of what amounts to compulsory heterosexuality.[4] In *Romeo and Juliet* the hard realities of life in Verona are apparently healed by the fervid, heterosexual love of the two main characters. Romeo's manliness is put in the service of a woman ("For stony limits cannot hold love out" [2.2.68]), and Juliet's femininity is put in the service of her man ("all my fortunes at thy foot I'll lay, / And follow thee my lord throughout the world" [ll. 147-48]). Of course, their love is doomed, but that seems to be because, as the prince tells their fathers, Capulet and Montague, "a scourage is laid upon your hate" (5.3.292). Love, heterosexual love, would thus seem to be the predominant value of the play, and the regimes of masculinity and femininity required by such a value would seem therefore to be equally predominant, equally necessary to the world of the play.

But Goldberg deconstructs the circulation of desires in the play, exposing the "open Rs," as Goldberg and Mercutio and Juliet's Nurse all put it, toward which sexual desire in the play is frequently headed. Goldberg shows how desire frequently inclines in unexpected homosocial and homosexual directions; and he underscores how, if desire is ever structured in the course of the play as a celebration of a heterosexist ethos, it is only by way of a certain kind of *performance* of gender identities and gender relations, more or less deliberately and openly engaged in. Given the ease with which the fixity of gender relations and desire can be deconstructed, Goldberg shows us, it is a mistake to conclude that the play really exalts heterosexual love in quite the way popular audiences and high-school teachers imagine that it does. It is more plausible to conclude that the exaltation of the heterosexist ethos is a construction imposed on the play by readers and performers as they pursue their own ideological agendas, including the often-unconscious agenda of compulsory heterosexuality.

But although Goldberg himself doesn't develop the point, one thing remains clear: whether or not the play exalts heterosexual love as it is popularly held to do, the play dramatizes an *attempt* to exalt it, an attempt to overcome patterns of violence and aggression through an engagement with what the two main characters take to be the joyful "bounty," as Juliet puts it, of their mutual desire. And this attempt, too, involves a kind of performance of gender.[5] The main characters understand immediately that what is happening between them entails the embrace of an economy of desire that fixes them in a bipolar gender relationship. If their economy of desire requires them to embrace what seems to be an alternative system of values ("Deny thy father" [2.2.234]), in embracing that system, they nevertheless reduplicate, on a highly individualized, sublimated level, a normative structure of gender. However urgently their desire for each other seems to summon them toward escape and transgression, in other words, it also envelops them in a structure that requires them to perform and re-perform their relation as a dialogue of gender—to perform it, essentially, *as* a performance. The impulses toward escape and transgression that their desire entails can thus be interpreted not as drives toward departing from the regime of gender performance but as individualized expressions of the regime's authority. Impulses toward escape and transgression, placed in the service of an attempt to exalt the power of heterosexual love and heterosexist identities, are in fact manifestations of the regime of gender and the inescapable power of masculinist prosthetics.

Certainly Romeo and Juliet believe that they can bypass the boundaries of this system—leaping over walls; standing "proof" against the "enmity" of their families; Juliet vowing to lay at Romeo's feet a fortune that is not in her power to bequeath or, when threatened by her official engagement to County Paris, to "leap . . . / From off the battlements of any tower" (4.1.77-78). But their belief in escape is, again, an expression of the system that determines them. The system itself is complex, and those very endpoints of value toward which one might incline in order to bypass the limits of masculinist aggression—civil peace and heterosexual love—are among the system's constitutive normative elements. The *mise-en-abyme* of masculinist aggression that individuals such as Sampson, Gregory, and Tybalt are determined to embrace is part of the same system that permits Prince Escalus, speaking from a position of unquestioned authority, to condemn them for their "pernicious rage" (1.1.84). And it is part of the same system that leads Romeo—with the oxymoronic acceleration that characterizes his affair with Juliet—to "stand on sudden haste" (2.2.94) and pursue his passion to his death. If the regime of masculinity in *Romeo and Juliet,* as elsewhere in the Shakespearean canon, prefixes the rules, the rules are multivalent, offering what appear to be options. But the options themselves are contained within and intrinsic to the overall structure of masculinity; they are part of what fixes it, enforces it, and makes it compelling. When men experience themselves—when they experience themselves *in* their masculinity—they find themselves in a condition of unresolvability. But they also find themselves under compulsion, precisely, to resolve themselves, to struggle toward a condition of masculine fulfillment as if their masculinity were a single, stable, normative goal. This is the rule; that is the pressure of masculinity in the world of the play. And if endless cycles of violence are expressions of the regime of masculinity, so is the promulgation of the law, a law of peace, which itself has the right to resort to violence ("*On pain of torture,* from those bloody hands / Throw your mistempered weapons to the ground" [1.1.86-87, emphasis added]). So, too, is the promulgation of the idea of an alternative, the idea of standing apart from the masculinist regime in practices of heterosexual love.

In saying this, I am agreeing with some of the phenomenological aspects of masculinity noted in Coppélia Kahn's important 1980 essay "Coming of Age in Verona," which argues that *Romeo and Juliet* is a play about the achievement of mature masculine and feminine "identities."[6] But I am disagreeing with her conceptual apparatus, beginning with the ideas of identity and integration which control her concepts of gender and dramatic action. Kahn argues that "*Romeo and Juliet* plays out a conflict between manhood as violence on behalf of the fathers and manhood as separation from the fathers and sexual union with women."[7] This argument sees Romeo as having two obvious choices; he can make war on behalf of the father or make love, in effect, on behalf of himself. Circumstances (but not "fate," Kahn insists) cause him to choose both, to experience the conflict of choosing both, and to suffer the consequences. I agree that such a conflict is experienced in the play. But I disagree with Kahn's explanation and with her strategy of privileging that experience as the play's central psychological dilemma. Kahn understands masculinity as the condition of an identity, a condition, specifically, of the ego as understood in ego and object-relations psychology—a condition of integration at which the ego *arrives* precisely when it "comes of age." But it is notable that none of the young men in the play ever really arrives at this condition of masculine integration; and I believe it can be shown that none of them was ever really headed that way.

Another way of putting this is to say that the young men in *Romeo and Juliet* are not, as men, *in control of themselves;* they are not in control of the project of masculine autonomy to which they understand themselves to be pledged. Autonomy, to be sure, along with the circumstances under which it can be imagined or asserted, is a problem with which Shakespearean characters are often confronted.[8] But the idea of an explicitly masculine autonomy is especially troublesome for Shakespearean characters. Masculinity is not a single thing they can get a hold of, although they are constantly under pressure to do so. Masculinity is rather a regime, triangular in structure; the triangle is constituted by a pair of masked positions of incommensurate sites, in pursuit of which the subject, operating from the third position, the position of the subject-self, is doomed to vacillate. When men in *Romeo and Juliet* experience themselves in their masculinity, they experience an indefinite inadequacy in the face of an aggressive pressure to drive forward in two different directions and yet also to stay in place, to sustain themselves apart from the objectives they are being pressured to pursue. They have to go forward, they have to stir, now as aggressor, now as the one confirmed in his title to aggress; but they also have to remain in that third position, from which they embark in pursuit of their objectives, the self. "I have lost myself," Romeo complains in his opening scene; "I am not here" (1.1.197). "This wind you talk of," Benvolio complains to Mercutio—dreams, fantasy, desire, which Mercutio has shown himself capable of finding anywhere, in anyone, since desire itself, "Queen Mab," has its own autonomy—"blows us from ourselves"

(1.4.104). The men want to achieve the endpoints of their masculinist system, but that system proves to be one of male inadequacy and incompletion, a system blowing masculine selves from their selves.[9]

Of course, abandoning Kahn's position has its costs, since her idea of a mature masculine identity at least provides us with a model of masculinity as a positive value. One of the problems faced by members of the critical community today when talking about the subject of masculinity grows out of what might be thought of as the critical community's ideological moment. There is today a predisposition toward the idea that masculinity—not particular men, who may be one thing or another as the case may be, but masculinity itself—is always first of all *at fault*. Masculinity isn't innocent. It is a structure, a regime, a dominant system that is held to account; and what it is held to account for is the violence and oppression that seems to be the corollary of its hegemony. Whatever else it may be, masculinity is the gender of destructive aggression on the one hand and of homosocial domination on the other. And so, if we forgo the idea that there might nevertheless be a *healthy* masculinity, a universally normative condition of masculine identity to which young men can aspire—whether in Shakespeare's time or in our own—we are in danger of being unable to assert anything at all about masculinity except so far as it is a phenomenon which must be refused, denied, pathologized, subverted, or otherwise abjected.

The problem entailed is worth pausing over briefly. For what our ideological moment seems to militate against is our ability to sustain our interest in the idea of the tragic subject himself—a subject now increasingly isolated from critical discourse, relegated to the province of the merely masculine, the merely dominant.[10] But what we find ourselves experiencing when we attend a good performance of a Shakespeare tragedy—including that performance which we attend in our heads when we read or reflect on the playscripts—may be incommensurate with our vocabulary for describing it or our concepts for assessing it. But it is surely insensitive, if not despotic, to dismiss the claims of students of Shakespeare when they tell us that the tragic subject in Shakespeare, all but invariably a masculine subject, doesn't engage them, doesn't command their attention anymore.[11] Nor will it do simply to avoid the theoretical quandaries that critical thinking about masculinity has produced and talk instead about Shakespeare's tragic subjects as if they weren't predominantly male and weren't predominantly invested in perpetuating structures of masculinist hegemony. Precisely because of their investment in masculinist hegemony, Shakespeare's tragic subjects no longer command the universal respect that was once thought to be a corollary of the liberal humanist worldview.[12] Precisely because of our current difficulty in discussing the structure of masculinity without putting it on trial and pronouncing it guilty, our experience of tragic subjectivity in Shakespeare has been unable to find a suitable critical vocabulary. Those of us for whom masculinist tragedy is still in some way engaging and still in some sense *of value* are being called to craft a language for describing masculine tragic subjectivity in Shakespeare which neither dodges our current critical awareness of the repercussions of masculinist hegemony nor rejects out of hand the experience and reality of masculine subjectivity. We need to find a way of talking about tragic masculine subjects in Shakespeare which allows us, at the very least, to continue to *see* them.

The way to this reconceptualization, however, is not always clear. The concept of healthy masculinity—a masculinity worth achieving, worth performing—is extremely difficult to sustain given the current terms of critical theory. The topic of masculinity leads immediately to the dual problem of domination and deceit, of hegemony and the false consciousness that sustains it; "healthy masculinity" in these circumstances is oxymoronic. Even the openly sympathetic readings of contemporary psychoanalytic critics seem to require a condescending pathologization of the tragic subject, an equation of the psychology of tragic (male) experience with illness: dissociation, psychic alienation and numbing, anxiety, melancholia.[13] In a tradition that begins with Freud himself, even where male subjectivity is taken as a norm, tragic male subjectivity is also already an emblem of neurosis. The problem, therefore, is not only that much of the English-speaking world is no longer confident about what it should mean to be a man;[14] the problem is also that, as members of the critical community, we are heirs to a critical language which takes for granted that masculinity as such is suspect, already marked as pathological, even if it is also assumed to be normative, inescapable, and indispensable.

Among the factors contributing to our current critical quandary is the apparent polarity in the very concept of gender. "'Masculinity' does not exist," a contemporary sociologist of gender insists, "except in contrast with 'femininity.'"[15] And therefore, in any situation in which women can be seen to be oppressed in relation to men, the men are already complicit in a system of domination and for the most part unable to do anything about it. Since to be a man is to not be a woman, and therefore to not be one of those weaklings who in Shakespeare's time are caused perforce to "go to the wall," a man, *as a man,* is always already hegemonic. "Art thou a man?" the friar complains to Romeo, underscoring at once the relational and the hegemonic character of masculine performance. Then why are you crying? Why are you being weak? Why are you not asserting your manly strength? "Thy tears are womanish. . . . Unseemly woman in a seeming man" (3.3.109-12).

Even allowing for differences between the gender systems of Shakespeare's time and that of our own—such as the "one-sex" theory and an easier environment for the expression of love between men—recent Shakespeare criticism frequently repeats the censuring gestures of contemporary sociology, making masculinity into something that has to account for itself as the gender that is almost always *at fault*.[16] Consider, for example, Alan Sinfield's treatment of *Henry V*, in which Sinfield is concerned to see the play as a terrain of "warring ideologies," one of which is the ethos of masculinity in the England of *Henry V*.[17] Sinfield argues that "sexualities, genders and the norms proposed for them are principal constructs through which ideologies are organized."[18] He notes that in the societies of Shakespeare's plays masculinity is constructed as a norm, the greatest threat to which is that "disastrous slide back into the female" which Shakespeare's characters call "effeminacy."[19] In the England of *Henry V*, as in early modern society generally, Sinfield argues, order is identified with "the dominance of masculine attributes." *Henry V* dramatizes a struggle for the assertion of a normative masculinity both in the conflict between a supposedly masculine England and an effeminate France and, at the conclusion of the play, in Henry's anxious sexual conquest over Katherine. Of course, masculinity *requires* femininity. England requires the France it will dominate; Henry requires Katherine, needing her not only for her sexual surrender but also for the children she is supposed to bear. But that is just the point. "The dominant," Sinfield concludes, ". . . takes from its others what it can incorporate, leaving the remainder more decisively repudiated."[20]

Under the weight of critical analyses like this, it is hard to see how to talk about healthy masculinity—indeed, it is hard to see how to talk about masculinity as anything at all but a phenomenon that ought to be repudiated. A deep reason for this problem, one as vested in our own ideological situation as it is in Shakespeare's, has been discussed among Lacanian feminists. "Our dominant fiction," Kaja Silverman writes, "calls upon the male subject to see himself, and the female subject to recognize and desire him, only through the mediation of images of an unimpaired masculinity. It urges both the male and the female subject, that is, to deny all knowledge of male castration by believing in the commensurability of penis and phallus, actual and symbolic father."[21] Our dominant fiction prevents us from acknowledging the fallibility of masculine subjectivity; it seduces us into identifying masculinity as that which, precisely, cannot fail us. Failure in itself is emasculating; or rather, failure *is* emasculation, and emasculation is the one thing our dominant fiction will never concede to male subjects. Hence, if a man is to find himself in any position other than one of impossibly unimpaired potency, he shall have to find himself, as Silverman puts it, "at the margins"; he shall have to find himself in a masculine subjectivity that has somehow escaped the system of our dominant fiction. But the status of that escape is, again, highly problematic—especially if being a man means primarily not being a woman, and not being a woman means being a subject complicit in the domination of women.

Laurence Harvey as Romeo and Susan Shentall as Juliet in a scene from the 1954 film directed by Renato Castellani.

A number of situations in Shakespeare in fact dramatize this dominant fiction. It is especially prominent, as Sinfield suggests, in the history plays, which stand in relationship to *Romeo and Juliet* in a way that may require reassessment. In the opening scene of *1 Henry VI*, for example, where the leading men of England gather at the funeral of Henry V, Gloucester eulogizes Henry by focusing on the specifically masculine quality of violent aggression through which Henry asserted his kingliness: "England ne'er had a king until his time: / Virtue he had, deserving to command. . . . / He ne'er lift up his hand but conquered" (1.1.8-9, 16). At issue here is a whole set of fears about the future of England, which had been held together, on this account, precisely by Henry's masculine power, his "virtue," his ability by right to conquer and command. What the leaders of England are apparently faced with now, left with an infant Henry VI to occupy the place of a king, is a vacuum, an absence of commanding, conquering masculine virtue. "In stead of gold," Bedford laments,

>   we'll offer up our arms,
> Since arms avail not now that Henry's dead.
> Posterity, await for wretched years,
> When at their mothers' moist'ned eyes babes
>   shall suck,
> Our isle be made a nourish of salt tears,
> And none but women left to wail the dead.
> Henry the Fift, thy ghost I invocate:
> Prosper this realm, keep it from civil broils. . . .
>
>   (ll. 46-53)

What Bedford's speech bewails is that England is about to despoil itself of its own men and ultimately of manhood itself; what it invokes as cure is the maintenance of that commanding, conquering virtue which only Henry V had been able to embody; what it requires is a prosperity founded on the power of masculinity to control the effects of inadequacy and to prevent civil broils from resulting in total emasculation, the isle left "a nourish," and "none but women left to wail the dead." On all these accounts, then, once we abandon the idea of healthy masculinity, a mature and normative condition of masculine identity, we become unable to talk about men except as agents of legitimized oppression. We might find a different kind of masculine subjectivity "at the margins" now and then; but it would have to be rare, a masculinity without masculinity, an inadequate masculinity—even though it is just such a condition, *1 Henry VI* seems to argue, that leads us into civil disorder and decay and the end of both manhood and men.

The problem is further complicated when we turn to a second major characteristic of the masculinist fiction in Shakespeare and elsewhere. If masculine experience is relational, such that its very difference from the feminine oppresses feminine experience, a chief strategy of its ideology is the effacement of relationality itself. "Any theory of the subject has always been appropriated by the 'masculine,'" Irigaray famously complained.[22] Triumphant virtue in Shakespeare frequently defines itself as a kind of self-relational, supra-gender entity. Hamlet's "What a piece of work is a man" is a primary example of this. Although the speech degenerates in the end to bawdy banter, where Hamlet is required to add that, as he doesn't like "man," he doesn't like "woman" either, the "man" whom Hamlet would celebrate if he could is situated less on a male-female axis than on an animal-human/human-divine axis of representation.[23] To be "a man" here is to be a subject whose manliness stands in for humanness, and whose humanness represents man-to-man capacity, "express and admirable . . ." (*Hamlet*, 2.2.303-10).

So the problem in talking about masculinity in Shakespeare's plays, as in many other contexts, stems not from the oppressive relationality of masculine performance but from its overcoming of relationality altogether. If masculinity is a quality or family of qualities that acquires its meaning from relationality with respect to femininity, it is also a relational condition that aspires to efface its relationality, to raise itself to a condition of self-adequacy, where the category of femininity is moot. It is not for nothing that, in chiding Romeo, Friar Lawrence argues against both Romeo's womanly grief and his beastly rage: "thy wild acts," the friar adds, "denote / The unreasonable fury of a beast" (3.3.110-11). The manliness the friar wants Romeo to exemplify is a condition of self-directedness and self-control: it is not only a way of not being a woman; it is also a way of not being a lower animal. When it succeeds in being what it is, masculine subjectivity, it appears, is destined to require nothing but itself and to attain to a condition of self-related self-control. Unfortunately, this second version of the commensurability of penis and phallus, this elevation of a particular anatomical-cultural condition to a universal value, can be just as oppressive as the first version. Even the apparently healthy masculinity toward which the friar encourages Romeo to aspire may have to be rejected as the work of an oppressive ideology, the instrument and product of a dangerous dominant fiction from which there is no escape but in gender performance at the margins or in the "fatal strategies" that Baudrillard, hailing the death of the subject, characterizes as the "crystal revenge" of "the object and its destiny."[24]

Psychoanalytic criticism of Shakespeare, it is true, has often remained focused on the internal condition of the subject and has been able to locate both relationality and its effacement within the developmental dynamics of the male psyche. In the work of Janet Adelman, for example, we encounter the men in Shakespeare as men, aware of their manhood, conscious or semiconscious of the difference between themselves and women as the outcome or analogue of internal demands, intrinsic to their inward drives and experiences of selfhood.[25] Being a man in Shakespearean drama, in Adelman's reading, involves a project of identity-generating differentiation, a project of refusing feminine identifications and especially what Adelman calls the "maternal matrix"; yet the project is mainly a matter of ego formation and is therefore constitutive of personal identity. If being a man means having a self of a certain kind, not being a man could amount to not having a self at all. Indeed, it is just this threat of not having a self, of being engulfed by the maternal other, that impels men to engage in rituals of rejecting and oppressing femininity. The formation of masculine and therefore sexually hegemonic selves is ultimately an outcome of the logic of ego formation; and in Adelman's reading, Shakespeare's tragic male subjects are thus constitutively tragic in keeping with the same structure by which they are constitutively men with selves. In other words, tragic male subjectivity is born out of what in Shakespeare becomes an inevitable confrontation with the structure of masculine autonomy and its inherent pre-oedipal aversion to femininity.

However, even if one grants Adelman's hermeneutic premises—that Shakespeare's complex characters can be read as representations of deeply psychological beings with egos and unconscious motives, and that these beings themselves reflect the "development" of Shakespeare's career as a student of the self—one is still left with an idea of the masculine as a negative value. It is a negative value for Adelman because in the first place masculinity is an identity at which one arrives only by repudiating femininity. Without doubting that male subjects in Shakespeare frequently betray a desire to identify with father figures as well as a drive to avoid being smothered by antipathetic maternal figures, one may wonder whether such a psycho ontological structure can entirely account for the dilemmas of masculinity that Shakespeare's characters regularly face. There are grounds for worrying that, in making fear of the mother into the primary motive of tragic subjectivity, Adelman solves the problem of the bipolarity of gender simply by turning the problem on its head and making maternal femininity into a positive ideal whose negation is the condition of masculinity. Once again, being a man means not being a woman, for the most part out of a fear of woman; it means evading the maternal matrix by taking up an ego-ideal inseparable from a whole system for sustaining the dominant fiction of the male phallus and for perpetuating the oppression of women. This theory may help to account for certain kinds of character formation common to male subjects and especially male subjects in Shakespearean tragedy. But it both enshrines the ego as the motor force of subjectivity and interprets male ego formation as a pathology. As a result, it cannot account for the project either of the masculine ethos in the plays or of the mode of tragedy through which Shakespeare so energetically puts that ethos into play. It cannot account for the drives of masculinity or for the positive values of its complex regime; it can explain only the reactive drives that may negatively bolster masculinist behavior. The theory still leaves us with masculinity as illness.

It may be possible, however, to bypass both the repudiating and the pathologizing of masculinity as we find it in Shakespeare and to grant that men in plays such as *Romeo and Juliet,* invested in the regime of masculinity though they are, seldom if ever attain to the goal of normative masculinity which serves as the ideological justification for the oppression of women. It may be possible to see them as *failing subjects,* whose failure is *also* a part of the regime of masculinity and its ideological norms, but whose failure is precisely what makes them into subjects of tragedy, comedy, and history—into the subjects whose ethical dilemmas and psychic dramas are of interest to us. The difference may be subtle. But it may enable us to return to the idea of masculinity as an inescapable and positive if perplexing and dangerous structure. In this way we may be able to embrace, if not the ethos of Shakespeare's world or the conventional masculinity it often seems to promote, at least our sense of Shakespearean drama as in large part the tragic, comic, and historic drama *of men:* of men called on to take part, inadequately, in the perpetuation of an inadequate world.

The dominant fiction of the commensurability of penis and phallus, for example, is not a fiction that the Shakespearean canon consistently sustains or unproblematically promotes. If the plays of the Henriad celebrate the moment of Henry V's final triumphs, they also cast a cold eye upon it. What Henry V had accomplished, the Henriad makes clear, was a personal incarnation of masculinist ideology; but it wasn't only through ideology that he accomplished it. Power exercised in the register of the real—real force, real conquest—was required for the ideology as such to succeed in reproducing itself; the ideology itself was otherwise vulnerable to attack and decay. Moreover, for all the talk about Henry V's virtue, the talk is frequently retrospective. In the *Henry VI* plays, the adequacy of Henry V's masculinity, its fullness with respect both to the demands of ideology and the demands of the real, is only a memory. That it is already missing recalls a point often made by Freud and Lacan alike that the *symbolic* father, whose function is to determine the system of subjectivity that everyone is forced to operate under, is always already dead; Lacan calls him "the dead Father."[26]

In fact, the Shakespeare canon commonly represents full masculinity as a historical problem, associated with the problem of national sovereignty and what Francis Barker calls the historical "tremos of the land."[27] The problem is historicity itself: all subjects are subjects of history and therefore of historical conflict and the insufficiencies of the politico-historical project. The dominant fiction of masculine adequacy is vulnerable to the tremors of historical depredation; thus the fiction usually works only on the level of memory, the memory of the dead father. Rather than urging the fiction of the commensurability of penis and phallus, in fine, the Shakespeare canon commonly urges their incommensurability. The male subjects in Shakespeare can't sustain it—not even Tybalt, Mercutio, or Romeo. *Pace* Kahn's argument to the contrary, the historical process that characters in the plays commonly call "fate" overtakes them.

Moreover, if we turn to specimens of nonbelligerent behavior among the men in Shakespeare's plays, we will find not a demand placed on the fiction of adequacy but the overt rehearsal of a fiction of inadequacy. This fiction is also a *masculine* performance; it is not at all innocent of collusion in the oppression of women, and it finds ways of masking the inadequacy it embraces. But it is nevertheless the performance of a lack. When Romeo complains "I have lost myself," comic though his behavior might be in the early going, he at least puts his finger on the choice of misguidedness which is governing his behavior, his choice of *himself* in having lost his self, his choice of what Barthes once called the persisting "precious remainder" or "supplement" of personal identity.[28] He is "not here." But he is in a condition of desire, and of desire for desire, embracing the lack that impels him. What he is lacking is a woman—or so at least he thinks. But his insistence on fixity in the identity of the person he lacks, and his own fixity on himself as the one who is lacking, indicate that fixation itself may be his final aim. "[F]orget to think of her," Benvolio says with regard to the unrequiting Rosaline; "Examine other beauties." "O," Romeo responds, "teach me how I should forget to think" (1.1.225-28). Bare self-consciousness—Descartes's *cogito*—is the final term in the argument here, the supplement that turns absence into presence, lack into identity: since I cannot not think, you cannot dissuade me from my fixation; you cannot have me "Examine other beauties"; I cannot help but think, and if I think, I cannot help but think of what I am lacking, of her who causes me to perceive and to embrace my lack.

> He that is strooken blind cannot forget
> The precious treasure of his eyesight lost.
> Show me a mistress that is passing fair,
> What doth her beauty serve but as a note
> Where I may read who pass'd that passing
>   fair?
> Farewell, thou canst not teach me to forget.
>   (ll. 232-37)

Of course, as soon as he meets Juliet, Romeo's desire finds and fixes on another object to different effect. If the Shakespeare canon commonly expresses, as Barber and Wheeler put it, a "concern to realize and live in the identity of another," it is also quick to differentiate between the reality of erotic cathexis and the false consciousness of rhetorical, pseudo-Petrarchan posturing.[29] But the first object lesson to be drawn here is that, although Romeo has held himself aloof from the kind of masculine aggression that most of the characters in the opening scene have been drawn into, we are nevertheless encountering in him a strategy of masculine performance.[30] For all its rhetorical flourishes and false consciousness, this is a strategy that tries to find masculinity in relation to the female not as the object of thrusting but as the one which (whom) one lacks, and in whom one finds, precisely, a fixed reflection of one's lack. Petrarchanism provides Romeo with a strategy for performing a gender role that both insists on gender difference and allows him to remain aloof from the psychic requirement of thrusting or standing *against* an other.

But to return to my initial point. Masculinity may often seem like a value asserted by Shakespeare's men for the purpose of homosocial hegemony and, by the same token, for the rejection of the female and the oppression of women. And among many of Shakespeare's men this is exactly how the regime of masculinity works. But that is because it is at once multivalent and unsatisfiable, requiring a man to articulate himself in both one way and another, now in aggression, now in a retreat from aggression; now in thrusting, now in standing; now in an impossible attempt to annihilate one's lack, now in an equally impossible attempt to embrace it. Such men are caught in a struggle to resolve themselves in a system where resolution is impossible, a system where resolution is a legacy of the dead rather than an accomplishment of the living, and men propel themselves to resolve themselves by not being resolved.

Irresolution, however, is at best an uncertain value. The shadow of the dead father hangs over the world of the plays not only as a ghostly presence, as in *Hamlet*, but also operationally, as in the history plays. And the dead father stands for both symbolic and ideological order, operating as the guarantor of all social life, especially for men in their masculine identities within the context of a patriarchal system.

In *Romeo and Juliet*, in spite of all the disorderly conduct that constitutes the main action of the play, the context of masculinist patriarchy is particularly well marked. The symbolic role of the dead father is supplied by the living Prince Escalus, who in practice is an absolute monarch. "If ever you disturb our streets again," he says to the street fighters, "Your lives shall pay the forfeit of the peace" (1.1.96-97). Strong words, and not the words that a relatively restricted monarch such as the sovereign prince of England would be entitled to pronounce.[31] Escalus is represented as being at once the principle of law and order in his society and its principal enforcer, holding in his person judicial, legislative, and executive powers all at once. He is what James I, referring to himself, trying to obviate the limitations of the English constitution, called a "speaking law."[32] And although the people may at times disobey or skirt the law he represents, they never violate the principle of law itself (as for example the rebels and factions of the history plays frequently do); nor do they challenge the authority of Escalus to decide and enforce it. Patriarchy and the system of legal sanctions and mechanisms that express and legitimate it, concentrated in the person of the prince, stands over the reality of life in Verona as it stands over the memory of life in the earlier history plays, in *Julius Caesar*, in *Troilus and Cressida*, and in *Hamlet*. Shakespeare evidently endorses this aspect of Verona; certainly he takes care to follow his sources, situating the action of the play within the context of a historically invulnerable patriarchy. His main source,

Arthur Brooke's *Tragicall Historye,* opens with a celebration of the town's political and economic stability, depicting it as a somewhat isolated polity whose "renown" is based on its imperviousness to historical depredation.[33] And Shakespeare seems to adopt Brooke's attitude toward Verona and its social order. If the town is subject to the contagion of what the Prologue calls an "ancient grudge" (l. 3), a contagion clearly calling for purgative elimination, it is nonetheless invulnerable to decay from without; and it has never experienced an outbreak of disorder such as to threaten legal and social stability. Indeed, it is precisely because the symbolic order of the law is historically invulnerable that the "ancient grudge" can be resolved by a purgative cleansing—the sacrifice of Romeo and Juliet on the altar of civic life—rather than by warfare. The prince may have his hands full maintaining order between the Capulets and the Montagues, but he doesn't need to worry about maintaining legality between his subjects and himself. The primary *symbolic* order of Verona is safe because the "dead Father" of Verona is also alive and, as Henry V was (and as James I would soon claim to be), capable of enforcing the law by the exercise of violence.

Against the sovereign masculinity of Prince Escalus, however, the play juxtaposes the compromised masculinity and sovereignty of its "Rebellious subjects, enemies to peace," as Escalus calls them (1.1.81)—the other men of the play, clinging to their varied, unresolved, and inadequate masculinities. Among them are the other father figures of the play: Capulet, Montague, and Friar Laurence, none of whom can succeed in establishing himself as a "speaking law." Capulet is temperamental and capricious, at times indulgent, at times an impatient martinet, and wholly ineffectual. Sometimes we find him asserting his patriarchal prerogatives benevolently, or at least pretending to do so, as when he insists on allowing Juliet some freedom in her choice of spouse (1.2.17-19), or on allowing Romeo to be a guest at his party (1.5.65-74). In these cases we find him expressing a kind of normative paternalism, well within the range of Tudor stage values.[34] He knows the reach of his powers and the social good they are supposed to serve. "It is my will," he says to Tybalt, telling him to indulge Romeo's presence in his house (l. 72). He also knows his limits, his place within the larger social order of Verona. "Montague is bound as well as I," he tells Paris, "In penalty alike, and 'tis not hard, I think, / For men so old as we to keep the peace" (1.2.1-3). Yet, when his power is challenged, Capulet is unable to exercise it without giving in to what amounts to ineffectual hysteria; he cannot manipulate the system of deference and courtesy through which he has otherwise pledged himself to manage his social and familial affairs. "Hang thee, young baggage! disobedient wretch!" (3.5.160), he complains to Juliet when she tries to assert the autonomy he had earlier granted her and has now inexplicably determined to withhold. "Speak not, reply not, do not answer me! / My fingers itch" (ll. 163-64). Capulet is an exemplar of paternalism on trial; but as the action proceeds, his paternalism continually fails, his authority undermined by turns of events he cannot control, his composure shattered at the shattering of his expectations. There is little if any conquering virtue in him, although Capulet certainly wants to act as if there were, and as if his experience of social life were equal to his symbolic, legal position in it.

Montague is even less firm in his patriarchal standing. Diminished in his virility in part through old age, uxorious to a fault (the play implies), he is shown to be incapable of stirring—either as the young men do, in search of his foe, or as a paternal figure might aspire to do, in search of exacting tribute to his dignity. "Hold me not, let me go," he complains to his wife as he first appears onstage. "Thou shalt not stir one foot to seek a foe," his wife decrees (1.1.79-80). This diminished figure is shown, moreover, to have little influence on his son, Romeo, who keeps himself, as Montague indulgently complains, "so secret and so close" (l. 149). Romeo never once considers his father's wishes when engaging in his affair with Juliet. He never pauses before the law of his father.

As for Friar Laurence, to whom Romeo regularly turns instead: although the friar endeavors to promote a kind of order in the world of Verona, similar in virtue to the prince's, his methods are indirect, and both his position and his character, his inner virtue, are obviously suspect. He is a priest and an herbalist and a self-appointed supplement to Prince Escalus in his aim to bolster the social order as well as to minister to it. But the friar is in many respects the play's most salient example of a man who *gets it wrong,* who *fails* to achieve his objectives, although he ultimately finds that his one objective of reuniting the Capulets and the Montagues has been achieved *for* him, partly as a consequence of his own mistakes. There is no better index of the friar's compromised paternalism and his inadequate masculinity than one of his final lines, when he abandones Juliet to her fate. "Come go," he says to her, using a common idiom, but using it here, I think, symptomatically as well, inadvertently betraying his paralyzing dilemma. Which is it? To come or to go? For his part, it doesn't matter. "I dare no longer stay" (5.3.159). Romeo might well have realized that, when one needs a *father,* it is asking for trouble to turn to a *friar.* For all his supplementary skills in dispensing medicine and platitudes, for all his ability to hold before Romeo the ideal of healthy and mature masculinity, he is nevertheless marginalized by his position as a priest—a celibate and cloistered man, attached to political power but also divided from it, maneuvering for power by indirect and even devious means. "Take heed, take heed," he advises Romeo, while commanding him to act like a man (3.3.145). Just as the friar will run away from the Capulet tomb, and thus fail to prevent the double suicide of his charges, so he advises Romeo to act manly by submitting to banishment, by being patient and staying in Mantua—in effect by doing nothing but running away.

The masculine order of Verona is thus represented as dispersed among a number of imperfect masculinities, tied together in a fundamentally stable structure, whose absolute legality is embodied in the person of the prince. At the top of this structure the prince guarantees the symbolic order of the law. Beneath him, we are given to understand, a number of "citizens" are available to rise to the occasion of guaranteeing the law as well. The citizens appear on the scene whenever violence breaks out and, along with the prince, restore the peace. But neither the prince nor his citizens familiarize us with their internal experience—we experience them from afar, as the Capulets and Montagues experience them; we experience them as completed beings, whose authority is both irresistible and subject to resistance; we experience them as if they were dead fathers. The men whose internal experience we come to be acquainted with, on the other hand, are all of them incapable of realizing the hyper-adequacy that the prince and the citizens of this exceptional town seem to sustain without difficulty. The fathers are ineffectual; the sons (and the sonlike servants) are self-destructive. The fathers cannot enforce their own laws; the sons can neither enforce those laws on behalf of their fathers nor discover adequate forms of self-assertion.

What is crucial, it seems to me, is that against the norms represented by the prince and the citizens—the adequate masculine legality that determines Verona's condition as a world at least temporarily apart from the depredations of history and sovereignty-challenging war—the play juxtaposes the inward experience of failed normativity and represents this failure as the structure of life among its tragic men. The men whom we come to know as men are under pressure, in effect, to *perform*. But the fathers cannot perform as fathers; the sons cannot perform as sons either for the sake of their fathers or for themselves. Against the backdrop of an assured masculine order, guaranteed by the life of a dead father, they experience their own pressures to perform as imperatives to achieve the impossible, to end a cycle of repetition by means of repetition. The fathers cannot enforce the law so long as they themselves are living in a self-imposed condition of "mutiny" or "rebellion," which subjects them to the same kind of conflicting impulses and degenerative forces that the kingless nobles discover among themselves at the beginning of *1 Henry VI*. Insofar as they attempt to enforce the law for their fathers, the sons are in effect acting in the interest of a false law in order to assume the position of a false father, caught between the symbolic alternatives of stirring and standing. Even the well-wishing Benvolio is caught in this trap: "I drew to part them" (1.1.108). Instead of exacting tribute to the law of peace, which he thinks he can represent, Benvolio ends up fighting like the others. All of the men, so far as they are involved in their unresolvable feud, are caught up in structures of repetition underwritten by the equality of each side (both "alike in dignity") and the falsehoods through which each side tries to differentiate itself as an autonomous patriarchal entity.

The alternative of erotic desire and the pacifism that may accompany it, represented by Romeo and, to a lesser extent, by Benvolio and Mercutio, is also compromised by the inadequate masculinity of the feuding fathers. Clearly the alternative of erotic desire establishes obstructions, blocking a natural pathway to the intermarriage that Shakespeare elsewhere values so highly as a mode of sustaining social integration among the ruling classes.[35] But it should be recalled that the erotic drive is also a fundamental condition of the performance of masculinity, which the young men take up not in relation to paternal authority but entirely in relation to themselves. If the enforcement of the law, whether the true law or a false one, may be seen as a primary objective of men in their capacity as agents of masculine hegemony, then deviation from the law in the direction of erotic satisfaction is equally fundamental to masculinity as men experience it, equally constitutive of them as men and, commonly, as subjects who aren't women.

But the erotic drive also seems to place the man in a condition of indeterminate dissatisfaction; or, rather, the erotic drive as Romeo engages with it becomes a site of indeterminate dissatisfaction. Even after he has transferred his affections to Juliet, Romeo endeavors to hold himself aloof from both his object and his aim in order to sustain himself in a condition of isolation. As Edward Snow has shown, Romeo's language throughout the play is distancing, controlling, structuring, as if practicing an erotics of estrangement.[36] "Eyes, look your last!" Romeo cries out as he begins to die, in the end separating even sensual experience from his willful subjectivity (5.3.112).[37] After Romeo has repudiated his Petrarchan posturing, he tries to use his imagination as a "structuring" device, a faculty for isolating himself in the circumstances of his desire.[38] While Juliet makes her first entrance announcing "I am here" and all but concludes by saying "I do remember well where I should be, / And there I am" (1.3.5; 5.3.149-50), Romeo is always elsewhere and endeavoring to keep himself there. It is in his straying, after all, that he is able to engage in his endless embrace of the absent.

When he encounters Juliet, Romeo nevertheless experiences a transformation of his separateness. To him Juliet is not only an object of desire; she is also, as Lacan has said with respect to Hamlet's relation to Ophelia, an object *in desire*.[39] "I pray thee chide me not," Romeo says to the friar. "Her I love now / Doth grace for grace and love for love allow; / The other did not so" (2.3.85-87). It is Juliet's reciprocity that now controls Romeo's language and affections. He is in a situation where he finds not an answer to his demands but a completion to his desiring, an awakening to the divagations of its aims and claims upon him. When he first meets her, the sonnet he speaks with her has the character of a discovery, where the stale and oxymoronic figures with which he attempts to court her unfold into rolling conceits of negotiation and joint seduction. When he first espies her at her window, his language works around the emotion of adoration and the desire for satisfaction; he tries to fit himself into the orbit of his object so as to incorporate himself within her and yet avoid penetration ("O that I were a glove upon that hand, / That I might touch . . ." [2.2.24-25]). But he also calls upon her to speak; and once she speaks, the transaction between a self and an other becomes transformed into the relation of two selves in the course of a systemic desire, an economy of desiring and being desired: "grace for grace." The effect of this on Romeo frequently threatens to disrupt the possibility of speech altogether, to break apart the conditions under which Romeo has performatively separated himself into his masculine identity. "What shall I swear by?" "Do not swear at all" (ll. 112); "In what vile part of this anatomy / Doth my name lodge? Tell me, that I may sack / The hateful mansion" (3.3.106-8).

At this point it could be said that Romeo is being drawn into a destruction of his own symbolic order—a destruction already identified with something like a death drive and later signified in Juliet's epithalamion, where Romeo is to be "cut . . . out in little stars" (3.2.22). "Would I were sleep and peace," he says leaving her the first time, "so sweet to rest" (2.2.187). This affair obviously evokes in both not only an estrangement from the rules of sociality, which empowers them to defy the rules, but also the invention of an alternative system of performance, where the economy of a systemic desire is felt to take the place of every other economy. They are left with nothing but the desire itself: without it they "stand on haste" to die: without it they have no alternative *but* to die. And yet Juliet, seconded by the nurse and the friar, tries to turn desire in a conventional marital direction; and Romeo tries to deploy desire's conventionality as a pretext not for escaping the imperatives of masculine aggression, as he earlier tried to do, but for turning them into the imperatives of the symbolic order itself, imperatives that among other things demand the resolution of the family feud and all the masculine inadequacies that have sustained it. "[F]arewell," he says in response to Tybalt's challenge to fight; "I see thou knowest me not" (3.1.65). Intermarriage has worked. Indeed, as if this is where the economy of his desires has been leading him all along, Romeo now finds it possible not only to hold himself aloof from the pressures of masculine aggression experienced by the other young men, but to engage his masculinity from a superior position as a representative of the dead father:

> Draw, Benvolio, beat down their weapons.
> Gentlemen, for shame, forbear this outrage!
> Tybalt, Mercutio, the Prince expressly hath
> Forbid this bandying in Verona streets.
>
> (ll. 86-89)

But there is something pitiful about Romeo's intervention, not only in its fatal consequences but in its fundamental assumption that, merely by invoking the law, Romeo can cause it to be observed. To enforce the law by invoking it, one must be in possession of a sovereign authority that only the prince is capable of possessing, a sovereignty that the Capulets and the Montagues continually take themselves to represent but that none of them can have or really stand for, thrown, as they are, into the shame of their ultimate inadequacy.

Romeo, for his part, seduced into thinking that he can escape the system altogether by sublimating aggression into law, has instead been transformed into a more perfect representative of the regime of masculinity and its masks. He no longer leans upon the *cogito,* no longer retreats into the solitude of his own lack. Instead he insists on abolishing the lack; on having his object and entering into desire with her, while at the same time arrogating the power of symbolic order to his own person. In this last respect he tries to assume the power not of a man in relation to a woman but of a dead father over the social order as a whole. He insists, in effect, on achieving the impossible self-relatedness of a whole system of power. This is not the goal of an ego searching for integration, although an ideology of integration, presided over by the good dead father, is always available as an imaginary justification of what Romeo is insisting on. The goal is rather of an ego seeking its dis-integration, its cancellation, which the system itself seems to have laid out for any man who is not the imaginary prince, or the imaginary citizens harmoniously toiling under the prince's law, invulnerable to history.

When he hears that Juliet lies dead in her family's tomb, Romeo immediately understands his position, sees how Juliet has been inspiring him to aim toward his own cancellation, and enthusiastically embraces the prospect. "Well, Juliet, I will lie with thee to-night" (5.1.34). He will finally break the back of the language that has been determining him. He will not swear. But he will *lie* and thus culminate his desire while ending his life. In that way, of course, he will confirm the truth of the social order which makes the completion of his progress beyond it into a lie. Up against the wall, he'll find the solution to the dilemma of masculinity by refusing either to stand or to stir; he'll fulfill his masculinist calling by lying down, sacrificing himself. And, as the play makes clear, the social order will be much the better for it.

As a male subject in a Shakespearean tragic universe, Romeo can only oscillate, now thrusting himself forward, now standing aloof, awaiting a ratification he cannot receive. Without that ratification he is headed toward death. It is in that death he fulfills the highest ideals of the social order and its law-of-the-father, civil love and civil peace. But he doesn't accomplish those ideals for his *self*. Living as a man in Shakespeare's world, in the flow of history, even within a town where history seems to have temporarily come to an end, Romeo discovers that the regime of masculine performance laid down for him has always been strangely separating from him, even though he cannot do without it. If ending that separation seems to be the goal and reward of erotic love, it is possible only in death.

This discussion of the masculinist regime may not help anyone become more engaged with Shakespeare's male tragic hero. And after all, as tragic heroes go, Romeo is of a lesser order than characters such as Hamlet and Lear—in part, perhaps, precisely because as a young man with illusions, Romeo is bent on escaping the dilemmas of the system that contains him, of finding a way out of his conflict rather than (tragically) confronting them. But "helping" readers may not be the point. Readers will do with the plays what they will. It may be enough simply to have pointed out that as Shakespearean tragedy is commonly the tragedy of men, it is the tragedy, then, of masculine performance—which is to say, all ideological prejudices to the contrary, that it is the tragedy of inevitable inadequacies, inadequacies that nevertheless determine the drama of social and political order in the Shakespearean world. The full masculinity that few, if any, can attain—unimpaired legality and force—is a principle of order to which men like Romeo are pledged even when they are trying to escape its consequences. It is a principle of order they cannot do without. How else can civil order be sustained? And without civil order—without the *premise* of civil order—how else are they to try to escape it and make themselves into subjects trying to be men?

Notes

[1] Homi K. Bhabha, "Are You a Man or a Mouse?" in *Constructing Masculinity*, Maurice Berger, Brian Wallis, and Simon Watson, eds. (New York and London: Routledge, 1995), 57-65, esp. 57-58.

[2] All quotations from Shakespeare follow *The Riverside Shakespeare*, ed. G. Blakemore Evans (Boston: Houghton Mifflin, 1974); Evans's square brackets have been silently elided to avoid confusion with my own interpolations.

[3] On the idea of psychological complexity in Shakespearean theater, see, among others, Francis Barker, *The Tremulous Private Body: Essays on subjection* (London and New York: Methuen, 1984); Catherine Belsey, *The Subject of Tragedy: Identity and Difference in Renaissance Drama* (London and New York: Methuen, 1985); Stephen Greenblatt, "Psychoanalysis and Renaissance Culture" in *Literary Theory/Renaissance Texts*, Patricia Parker and David Quint, eds. (Baltimore: Johns Hopkins UP, 1986), 210-24; Joseph A. Porter, "Character and Ideology in Shakespeare" in *Shakespeare Left and Right* Ivo Kamps, ed. (London: Routledge, 1991), 131-46; Bert O. States, Hamlet *and the Concept of Character* (Baltimore and London: Johns Hopkins UP, 1992); Katharine Eisaman Maus, *Inwardness and Theater in the English Renaissance* (Chicago and London: U of Chicago P, 1995). It is probably safe to say that the jury is still out on this issue.

[4] Jonathan Goldberg, "*Romeo and Juliet*'s Open Rs" in *Queering the Renaissance*, Jonathan Goldberg, ed. (Durham, NC: Duke UP, 1994), 218-35.

[5] One inevitably owes one's vocabulary concerning gender "performance" to Judith Butler, *Gender Trouble: Feminism and the Subversion of Identity* (New York and London: Routledge, 1990); and *Bodies That Matter: On the Discursive Limits of "Sex"* (New York and London: Routledge, 1993). In the first book, Butler defines gender as "an enactment that performatively constitutes the appearance of its own interior fixity" (*Gender Trouble*, 70). She later qualifies this with the statement that she is referring to a group of gender-producing "acts, gestures, enactments" (sometimes adding "desire" to her list of terms) that are "*performative* in the sense that the essence of identity that they otherwise purport to express are *fabrications* manufactured and sustained through corporeal signs and other discursive means" (*Gender Trouble*, 136). In the second book, Butler assimilates her account of performativity to Derrida's notion of citationality or iterability: "The norm of sex takes hold to the extent that it is 'cited' as such a norm, but it also derives its power through the citations it compels" (*Bodies That Matter*, 13). The provisionality of Butler's theory may be indicative of both its weaknesses and its usefulness. In any case, without desiring to commit myself to Butler's entire theoretical apparatus, I shall be trying here to understand the "performance of masculinity" as precisely the stylized but nevertheless largely compulsory "citation of norms" that Butler refers to. The strength of Butler's concept is, I think, that it allows us to conceive of gender as a contingent and provisional form of behavior which is nevertheless neither arbitrary nor optional.

It is also important to note the adaptation of the idea of masculine performance put forward in Laura Levine,

[6] *Men in women's clothing: Anti-theatricality and effeminization, 1579-1642* (Cambridge: Cambridge UP, 1994); and in Cynthia Marshall, "Man of Steel Done Got the Blues: Melancholic Subversion of Presence in *Antony and Cleopatra*," *Shakespeare Quarterly* 44 (1993): 385-408.

[6] Coppélia Kahn, "Coming of Age in Verona" in *The Woman's Part: Feminist Criticism of Shakespeare*, Carolyn Ruth Swift Lenz, Gayle Greene, and Carol Thomas Neely, eds. (Urbana: U of Illinois P, 1980), 171-93. For a full appreciation of Kahn's position, one must consult her *Man's Estate: Masculine Identity in Shakespeare* (Berkeley: U of California P, 1981), where the same essay appears in abbreviated form, but where Kahn's ideas about masculinity and identity are given fuller scope.

[7] Kahn, 173.

[8] "The cause is in my will," says Julius Caesar just before his assassination, asserting a license of autonomy which is both self-consuming and ill-fated; "I will not come" (*Julius Caesar*, 2.2.71).

[9] Compare Antony's remarks in *Antony and Cleopatra*: "I have fled myself. . . . "; "O, whither hast thou led me, Egypt?" (3.11.7, 51). Remarks like this appear with some frequency in Shakespeare's canon. As Greenblatt notes, "In Renaissance drama . . . the traditional linkages between body, property, and name are called into question; looking back upon the theatrical and judicial spectacle, one can glimpse the early stages of the slow, momentous transformation of the middle term from 'property' to 'psyche'" (221). On this reading, the experience of erotic longing and especially of men longing for women would be one among a number of dramatic instances where the problem of identity is being queried and elaborated, and *Romeo and Juliet* would be a pretty clear example of bodies, properties, and names and the relations among them ("What's in a name?" [2.2.43]) being processed through storytelling. A play such as *Romeo and Juliet*, however, like many of Shakespeare's romantic dramas, inevitably adds a story of gender performance to its story about bodies, properties, and names and inevitably begins to construct gender performance (and the problems attendant on it) as yet another element in the struggle toward the construction of a psyche.

[10] See Madelon Sprengnether, "Introduction: The Gendered Subject of Shakespearean Tragedy," and Gayle Greene, "Leaving Shakespeare," both in *Shakespearean Tragedy and Gender*, Shirley Nelson Garner and Madelon Sprengnether, eds. (Bloomington: Indiana UP, 1996), 1-27 and 307-16. In an ironic allusive subheading—"The World We Have Lost"—Madelon Sprengnether refers to the difference between Shakespeare study today and Shakespeare study in the time of Maynard Mack's *King Lear in Our Time* (1965).

[11] On this topic, see Sprengnether's account of the "Feminist Thematics" controversy, 9-12. Also in Garner and Sprengnether, eds., see Shirley Nelson Garner, "Shakespeare in My Time and Place," 287-306.

[12] For a concise restatement of this issue, see Terence Hawkes, *Alternative Shakespeares, Volume 2*, Terence Hawkes, ed. (London: Routledge, 1996), 1-16.

[13] See my remarks on Janet Adelman and psychoanalytic criticism below (p. 261ff).

[14] On this subject, see two related studies: Paul Smith, *Clint Eastwood: A Cultural Production* (Minneapolis: U of Minnesota P, 1993); and Dennis Bingham, *Acting Male: Masculinities in the Films of James Stewart, Jack Nicholson, and Clint Eastwood* (New Brunswick, NJ: Rutgers UP, 1994). Smith suggests that the problem of accepting a form of nonpathological masculinity has become increasingly inherent in our prevailing conditions of cultural production, where ideal masculinity is always already a form of "hysterical masculinity." Bingham sees a kind of wounded masculinity functioning as norm in most of the movies starring icons of Hollywood manhood.

[15] R. W. Connell, *Masculinities* (Berkeley and Los Angeles: U of California P, 1995), 68.

[16] On the idea of the "one-sex" theory, see "Fiction and Friction" in Stephen Greenblatt, *Shakespearean Negotiations: The Circulation of Social Energy in Renaissance England* (Berkeley and Los Angeles: U of California P, 1988), 66-93; and Thomas Laqueur, *Making Sex: Body and Gender from the Greeks to Freud* (Cambridge, MA, and London: Harvard UP, 1990). A recent essay that helpfully explores the implications of the theory for the generation of male writers just before Shakespeare, and for Renaissance criticism in general, is Mary Ellen Lamb, "Apologizing for Pleasure in Sidney's *Apology for Poetry*: The Nurse of Abuse Meets the Tudor Grammar School," *Criticism* 36 (1994): 499-520. On homoerotic bonding, see Bruce Smith, *Homosexual Desire in Shakespeare's England: A Cultural Poetics* (Chicago: U of Chicago P, 1991).

[17] Alan Sinfield, *Faultlines: Cultural Materialism and the Politics of Dissident Reading* (Berkeley: U of California P, 1992), 109-43.

[18] Sinfield, 128.

[19] Sinfield, 134.

[20] Sinfield, 142. An argument similar to Sinfield's, which makes the additional move of tying the oppression of women to the ideological erotics of male bonding and the "one-sex" theory, can be found in Phyllis

Rackin, "Foreign Country: The Place of Women and Sexuality in Shakespeare's Historical World" in *Enclosure Acts: Sexuality, Property, and Culture in Early Modern England*, Richard Burt and John Michael Archer, eds. (Ithaca, NY, and London: Cornell UP, 1994), 68-95.

[21] Kaja Silverman, *Male Subjectivity at the Margins* (New York and London: Routledge, 1992), 42.

[22] Luce Irigaray, *Speculum of the Other Woman*, trans. Gillian C. Gill (Ithaca, NY: Cornell UP, 1985), 133.

[23] See Terence Hawkes, *Shakespeare's Talking Animals: Language and drama in society* (London: Edward Arnold, 1973), 131; Hawkes is responding to Robert B. Heilman's "Manliness in the Tragedies: Dramatic Variations" in *Shakespeare 1564-1964: A Collection of Modern Essays by Various Hands*, Edward A. Bloom, ed. (Providence, RI: Brown UP, 1964), 19-37.

[24] Jean Baudrillard, *Fatal Strategies*, trans. Philip Beitchman and W. G. J. Niesluchowski, ed. Jim Fleming (New York: Semiotext(e), 1990).

[25] See Janet Adelman, *Suffocating Mothers: Fantasies of Maternal Origin in Shakespeare's Plays, Hamlet to The Tempest* (New York: Routledge, 1992). A theoretical parallel of Adelman's interpretive readings is developed in Nancy Chodorow, *Feminism and Psychoanalytic Theory* (New Haven, CT: Yale UP, 1989); and Chodorow, *Femininities, Masculinities, Sexualities: Freud and Beyond* (Lexington: UP of Kentucky, 1994).

[26] Jacques Lacan, *Écrits: A Selection*, trans. Alan Sheridan (New York and London: W. W. Norton, 1977), 199; cf. Elizabeth Grosz, *Jacques Lacan: A feminist introduction* (London and New York: Routledge, 1990), 68-69.

[27] Francis Barker, *The Culture of Violence: Tragedy and History* (Chicago: U of Chicago P, 1993).

[28] Roland Barthes, *S/Z*, trans. Richard Miller (New York: Hill and Wang, 1974), 190-92. See also Joel Fineman, "Fratricide and Cuckoldry: Shakespeare's Doubles" in *Representing Shakespeare: New Psychoanalytic Essays*, Murray M. Schwartz and Coppélia Kahn, eds. (Baltimore: Johns Hopkins UP, 1980), 70-109; Fineman argues that for the Shakespearean male there is always "a psychological need to build a distance between himself and his desire, lest he lapse into the psychotic discovery of No Difference between self and object, between his self-regard and his imagination of his mother, between his identity and the context of his identity" (103). I am of course making a different claim. Like Barthes, I am accounting for identity as a form of supplementarity, and I am allowing for an embrace of one's desire which maintains a separation from the object of one's desire. I am allowing for an embrace of desire, in other words, whose purpose is precisely the maintenance of difference and separation.

[29] C. L. Barber and Richard P. Wheeler, *The Whole Journey: Shakespeare's Power of Development* (Berkeley: U of California P, 1986), 169.

[30] Here I am taking exception to Marianne Novy's argument in "Violence, Love, and Gender in *Romeo and Juliet* and *Troilus and Cressida*" (in Novy, *Love's Argument: Gender Relation in Shakespeare* [Chapel Hill: U of North Carolina P, 1984], 99-124). Novy holds that Romeo is here equating sexuality with violence, just as characters such as Sampson, Gregory, and Mercutio are apt to do. Novy also holds that Romeo shares a belief in "the manhood of violence" (107), and that what happens as Romeo tries not to be violent and tries to unite himself with Juliet is that Romeo (along with Juliet) is managing to "transcend the aggressions and stereotypes of the outside in their secret world" (108). This kind of argument about transcendence, however, is precisely the object of Goldberg's critique in "*Romeo and Juliet*'s Open Rs." While it is true that Romeo's language goes through a metamorphosis when he meets Juliet, a phenomenon I will be commenting on below, it is tendentious to claim that, since some of Romeo's metaphors for love before he meets Juliet contain figures of violence, Romeo at this time is, in Novy's word, "equating" love (or sexuality) with violence. For what it is worth, Romeo's aloofness from aggression—his "effeminacy" in this respect—has been a commonplace of performances for some time; Zeffirelli's film version gives this aloofness particular emphasis by framing Romeo apart from the other men in the play both visually and aurally. (Cf. Jill, Levenson, *Shakespeare in Performance: Romeo and Juliet* [Manchester, UK: Manchester UP, 1987].) Still another interpretation of issues involved here, one that I am not pursuing, inclining toward a reading of male-female and aggression-passivity oppositions in the play as elements of a carnivalesque subversion of opposition, will be found in François Laroque, "Tradition and Subversion in *Romeo and Juliet*" in *Shakespeare's "Romeo and Juliet": Texts, Contexts, and Interpretation*, Jay L. Halio, ed. (Newark: U of Delaware P, 1995), 18-36. Laroque's reading is perhaps not unrelated to the revisionism of Baz Luhrmann's popular film *William Shakespeare's Romeo and Juliet*, which is destined to have a major impact on our reception of the gender relations in the play, but which was released after most of this essay was written.

[31] For a discussion of constitutional constraints on the English monarch, see David Lindsay Keir, *The Constitutional History of Modern Britain, 1485-1937*, 3rd ed. (London: Adam and Charles Black, 1946); and J. P. Sommerville, *Politics and Ideology in England, 1603-1640* (London and New York: Longman, 1986).

[32] James VI and I, *The Trew Law of Free Monarchies* in *The Political Works of James I,* ed. Charles Howard McIlwain (Cambridge, MA: Harvard UP, 1918), 53-70, esp. 63.

[33] Arthur Brooke, *The Tragicall Historye of Romeus and Juliet* (1562), quoted here from *Narrative and Dramatic Sources of Shakespeare,* ed. Geoffrey Bullough, 8 vols. (New York: Columbia UP, 1957-75), 1:286.

[34] On the ethic of "paternalism." see Leonard Tennenhouse, *Power on Display: The politics of Shakespeare's genres* (Methuen: New York and London, 1986).

[35] For an extended treatment of this subject, see David M. Bergeron, *Royal Family, Royal Lovers: King James of England and Scotland* (Columbia and London: U of Missouri P, 1991).

[36] Edward Snow, "Language and Sexual Difference in *Romeo and Juliet*" in *Shakespeare's "Rough Magic": Renaissance Essays in Honor of C. L. Barber,* Peter Erickson and Coppélia Kahn, eds. (Newark: U of Delaware P; London: Associated University Presses, 1985), 168-92.

[37] See Snow, 175.

[38] Snow, 174. By calling Juliet's sensibility "Blakean," Snow obviously tries to avoid the suggestion that her sensibility is fundamentally "feminine"; but the suggestion is there all the same. The problem, of course, is that Juliet is traditionally seen as one of Shakespeare's strong, and hence in some sense "masculine," women.

[39] Jacques Lacan, "Desire and the Interpretation of Desire in *Hamlet,*" trans. James Hulbert, in *Literature and Psychoanalysis: The Question of Reading: Otherwise,* Shoshana Felman, ed. (Baltimore and London: Johns Hopkins UP, 1982), 11-52.

FURTHER READING

Brown, Carolyn E. "Juliet's Training of Romeo," in *Studies in English Literature 1500-1900,* 36, No. 2 (Spring 1996): 333-55.

    Brown discusses the element of power in the love relationship of Romeo and Juliet, examining imagery of Juliet as a falconer and Romeo as her well-trained falcon.

Cox, Marjorie Kolb. "Adolescent Processes in *Romeo and Juliet.*" *The Psychoanalytic Review* 63, No. 3 (Fall 1976): 379-92.

    Argues that the tragic outcome of *Romeo and Juliet* derives from difficulties its characters have in dealing with the problems of adolescence.

Franson, J. Karl. "'Too soon marr'd': Juliet's Age as Symbol in *Romeo and Juliet.*" *Papers on Language and Literature* 32, No. 3 (Summer 1996): 244-62.

    Considers the theme of premature marriage in *Romeo and Juliet.*

Goldstein, Martin. "The Tragedy of Old Capulet: A Patriarchal Reading of *Romeo and Juliet.*" *English Studies* 77, No. 3 (May 1996): 227-39.

    Contends that an internal disagreement between the patriarchal Capulet and Lady Capulet, rather than the public feud between the Capulets and the Montagues, provides the "driving force of the play."

Hays, Peter L. "The Dance of Love and Dance of Death in *Romeo and Juliet.*" *The Dalhousie Review* 51, No. 4 (Winter 1971-72): 532-38.

    Explores festive dancing and its antithesis, the duel or dance of death, in *Romeo and Juliet.*

Kaiser, Gerhard W. "*Romeo and Juliet.*" In *The Substance of Greek and Shakespearean Tragedy Under Special Consideration of Shakespeare's 'King Lear,' 'Macbeth,' 'Othello' and 'Romeo and Juliet,'* pp. 179-208. Salzburg: Institut für Sprache und Literatur, 1977.

    Interpretation of *Romeo and Juliet* that focuses on the play's tragic elements caused by "the rashness of the lovers' passion."

Kiliõski, Janusz. "Elements of Neo-Platonism in William Shakespeare's *Romeo and Juliet.*" *Studia Anglica Posnaniensia* 17 (1984): 271-77.

    Sees the love between Romeo and Juliet as a form of Neo-Platonic divine love.

Knowles, Ronald. "Carnival and Death in *Romeo and Juliet*: A Bakhtinian Reading." *Shakespeare Survey* 49 (1996): 69-85.

    Discusses *Romeo and Juliet* in view of Mikhail Bakhtin's notion of the carnivaleque, which parodies and inverts dominant social ideologies and dogmas.

Kozikowski, Stanley J. "Fortune and Men's Eyes in *Romeo and Juliet.*" *Concerning Poetry* 10, No. 1 (Spring 1977): 45-49.

    Examines the motif of false or mutable fortune in *Romeo and Juliet.*

Levenson, Jill L. "Shakespeare's *Romeo and Juliet*: The Places of Invention." *Shakespeare Survey* 49 (1996): 45-55.

    Observes Shakespeare's stylistic transformation of his source work for *Romeo and Juliet,* featured in the dramatist's use of rhetoric.

Mason, H. A. "Love and Death in *Romeo and Juliet.*" In *Shakespeare's Tragedies of Love: An Examination of the Possibility of Common Readings of 'Romeo and Juliet,' 'Othello,' 'King Lear,' and 'Antony and Cleopatra,'* pp. 42-55. London: Chatto & Windus, 1970.

Briefly surveys critical regard of the balcony scene in *Romeo and Juliet*, and considers the link between love and death in the play.

Novy, Marianne. "Violence, Love, and Gender in *Romeo and Juliet* and *Troilus and Cressida*." In *Love's Argument: Gender Relations in Shakespeare*, pp. 99-123. Chapel Hill: University of North Carolina Press, 1984.

Highlights the private world of *Romeo and Juliet* in which the lovers achieve "mutuality" and differing genders are not polarized.

Porter, Joseph A. *Shakespeare's Mercutio: His History and Drama*. Chapel Hill: University of North Carolina Press, 1988, 281 p.

Extensive study of Shakespeare's complex representation of Mercutio and of this character's sources.

Riess, Amy J. and George Walton Williams. "'Tragical Mirth': From *Romeo* to *Dream*." *Shakespeare Quarterly* 43, No. 2 (Summer 1992): 214-18.

Proposes that *Romeo and Juliet* was written earlier than *A Midsummer Night's Dream*, and that elements from the preceding tragedy were used to create humor in the later comedy.

Snyder, Susan. "Beyond Comedy: *Romeo and Juliet* and *Othello*." In *The Comic Matrix of Shakespeare's Tragedies: 'Romeo and Juliet,' 'Hamlet,' 'Othello,' and 'King Lear,'* pp. 56-90. Princeton, N. J.: Princeton University Press, 1979.

Maintains that *Romeo and Juliet* uses the structure of romantic comedy in order to create a tragedy brought about by mischance.

Wells, Robin Headlam. "Neo-Petrarchan Kitsch in *Romeo and Juliet*." *The Modern Language Review* 93, No. 4 (October 1998): 913-33.

Probes Shakespeare's satire of Petrarchan "male erotic fantasy" in *Romeo and Juliet*.

Young, Bruce W. "Haste, Consent, and Age at Marriage: Some Implications of Social History for *Romeo and Juliet*." *Iowa State Journal of Research* 62, No. 3 (February 1988): 459-74.

Questions the critical assumption that early marriages were common in Renaissance England, contending that *Romeo and Juliet* expresses concern with the young age at which Juliet is forced to marry.

Sonnets

For further information on the critical history of the Sonnets, see *SC*, Volumes 10 and 40.

INTRODUCTION

Shakespeare's sonnets have been studied for possible biographical elements and for their placement within the sonnet-writing tradition in Europe. Scholars have examined Shakespeare's frequent use of paradox and punning in his sonnets and have debated over his employment of natural, and sometimes ambiguous, imagery to convey his themes. Ultimately, much of the interest for general readers as well as for critics revolves around the sonnets's conventional theme of love with its focus on the poet-lover himself and the objects of his affection.

After observing that Shakespeare's sonnets "regularly outsell everything else he wrote," Anthony Hecht (1996) explains why they are so appealing. The sonnets, Hecht remarks, successfully communicate in fourteen brief lines not only a lover's feelings "of perfect happiness, but also submission, self-abnegation, jealousy, fear, desperation, and self-hatred." The object of love in the sonnets is "the Friend," or fair young man, who appears in the early poems of the sonnet sequence. The poet's love for the Friend has been described by some critics as homosexual and by others as asexual and idyllic. John Dover Wilson (1964) characterizes it as the "affectionate admiration . . . of a man of mature years for another man much younger than himself." Wilson asserts that the older man's affection includes an altruistic concern for the younger man's well-being. According to Wilson, this romantic, idealized love turns into tragedy when the younger man steals the poet's mistress (the "Dark Lady" of the sonnets), thereby revealing himself to be shallow and unworthy of the poet's admiration.

An assessment of the Dark Lady and her role in Shakespeare's theme of love and romance can be found in Robert W. Witt's 1979 discussion of sonnets 127-52. The Dark Lady, Witt observes, is the focus of the poet's lust rather than of his love and is characterized in terms of her sexual attractions. Witt notes that the Dark Lady "disdains" the poet and that, therefore, any love he might feel for her "can lead only to despair." Witt contrasts this negative, false love of the poet's with his "reasonable" and therefore genuine love for the young Friend. According to Witt, the Friend's sexual liaison with the Dark Lady represents a "test" of the poet's devotion to his friend; ultimately, the poet passes this test of love by forgiving the "truly repentant" young man.

David K. Weiser (1987) shares Wilson's opinion that the young Friend does not live up to the poet's idealized view of him. However, Weiser argues that the Dark Lady's behavior proves even more disappointing to the poet and that his sonnets to her reveal a "single, nearly obsessive train of thought" aimed not simply at her but at his own needs and the faultiness of his perceptions.

The poet's self-absorption is an issue for several other commentators, who describe it in terms of narcissism, or self-love. Jane Hedley (1994) and Elizabeth Harris Sagaser (1994) both suggest that the poet's love for the Friend folds back onto itself until the poet's own thoughts and words become the source of his preoccupation. Hedley notes that the poet manipulates words and indulges in puns and double meaning expressly to fulfill his desire to turn the object of his affection into an idealized, mirror image of himself. Sagaser puts a positive light on the poet's self-absorption. She remarks that while "the celebration of cerebral experience" was a common practice in Renaissance poetry, most of the love lyrics of the period concentrated on the tormenting effect of love on the mind. Sagaser asserts that by contrast, Shakespeare's sonnets—despite their focus on the brevity of life and the fleeting nature of love—convey a degree of pleasure or melancholy joy. Sagaser contends that this joyful meditation on death is positive because it prepares the poet in advance for the day when he will lose the object of his affection.

Like Sagaser, Philip Martin (1972) believes that there are positive aspects to the poet's narcissism. Martin rejects a commonly held assessment of the poet as submissive and self-abnegating and argues instead that the poet's apparently negative self-image is in fact "an unusual mingling of irony with acknowledgement of limitations." Martin concludes that, far from idealizing the Friend, the poet shows his awareness of the young man's imperfections and finally, an acceptance of himself.

Hallett Smith (1981) and John Klause (1983) look at the ways in which the poet is characterized in the sonnets. Smith discusses the self-absorbed or "meditative" quality of the poet's voice. Klause describes the poet as a "protagonist" who demonstrates his humanity through his contradictory assertions about love. Like Martin, Klause does not regard the poet as humble or submissive; Klause suggests that the poet is too inconsistent in his behavior to be considered humble. Instead, Klause asserts, the poet saves face by pretending to be something other than he is when confronted with the Friend's betrayal and the Dark Lady's cruelty.

OVERVIEW

Anthony Hecht (essay date 1996)

SOURCE: Introduction to *The Sonnets,* edited by G. Blakemore Evans, Cambridge University Press, 1996, pp. 1- 28.

[*In the following essay, Hecht examines the types of love which are expressed in Shakespeare's sonnets. He also compares the poetical imagery in the sonnets with that found in Shakespeare's plays. Throughout his essay, Hecht traces scholarly assessment of the sonnets and how this assessment has changed over the centuries.*]

It may be that the single most important fact about Shakespeare's Sonnets—at least statistically—is that they regularly outsell everything else he wrote. The plays are taught in schools and universities, and a large annual sale is thereby guaranteed for *Hamlet, Macbeth, Romeo and Juliet,* and *A Midsummer Night's Dream.* But the Sonnets are still more widely read. There are several diverse factions among their readership, many of which are not scholarly. Some people are eager for a glimpse into what they suppose is Shakespeare's private life; they hope for scandal. There are those who treat the Sonnets as biographical fiction; they yearn to decode the poems and reveal a narrative of exciting, intimate relationships. And there are readers whose overriding preoccupation with sexual politics makes them determined that no one shall view the Sonnets in any way that differs from their own.

In all likelihood, however, the largest group within this readership is made up of young lovers, for whom these sonnets compose a compact and attractive *vade mecum.* The poems speak directly to their condition, being rich and emotionally complex, and they describe states of perfect happiness, but also submission, self-abnegation, jealousy, fear, desperation, and self-hatred.

It is possible to argue that there exists no work of comparable brevity and excellence that digests such intimate emotional experience. What is more, the Sonnets are written with an astonishing self-consciousness, a deep sense that love opens enormous vistas of novel reflection, not all of it flattering. Loving another human being, we find that our motives are no longer disinterested; everything we do or feel is no longer purely a personal matter, but is strangely compromised by our relationship with this other person; our hopes and fears are not only generated by another, but by how we wish to be thought of and how we have come to feel about ourselves. Initially, when we fall in love, this does not appear as any sort of danger, or indeed as anything to be deplored. Our own happiness seems enormously enlarged by being both shared with and caused by another. That is only the beginning of what, for a thoughtful person, becomes an increasingly complicated state of mind, with almost infinite permutations, most of them unforeseeable. How do we react, for example, when the person we love commits a transgression that really wounds us? If the relationship is not immediately halted, it is necessary to palliate the fault, first and foremost to ourselves, and then to the beloved. The simple first step is to fall back upon reassuring proverbial wisdom ('To err is human' or 'No one is perfect'), and, while acknowledging our pain, to temper our feelings with the suspicion that, in our idolatry of the beloved, we may have imagined an impossible perfection which it would be ludicrous to expect anyone to live up to, and which may itself have put an insupportable burden on the person we love. We begin to blame ourselves for what may have been unrealistic expectations. And if we are deeply enamoured, we wish to spare the beloved any additional anguish of guilt that would be entailed by our explicit blame. Yet this kind of generous thinking can end in the danger of our viewing ourselves as supine and servile, and lead to an active form of self-hatred. So to guard against that danger and against any tendency to blame the beloved, we may find ourselves determined to assert our unconditional love—which is, after all, as we desperately tell ourselves, what love ought to be—and to rebuke any third party who might criticise the beloved, a rebuke designed as much to confirm our own commitment as to silence the critic. I have known both heterosexual and homosexual instances of this kind of devotion which, to an outsider, is likely to seem perverse, obstinate, and full of misery. Consider, for example, the following:

> No more be grieved at that which thou hast done:
> Roses have thorns, and silver fountains mud,
> Clouds and eclipses stain both moon and sun,
> And loathsome canker lives in sweetest bud.   4
> All men make faults, and even I in this,
> Authòrising thy trespass with compare,
> Myself corrupting salving thy amiss,
> Excusing thy sins more than their sins are;[1]   8
> For to thy sensual fault I bring in sense—
> Thy adverse party is thy advocate—

>   And 'gainst myself a lawful plea commence:
>   Such civil war is in my love and hate   12
>   That I an accessary needs must be
>   To that sweet thief which sourly robs from me.
>
>   (Sonnet 35)

The first line presupposes a penitent attitude on the part of the beloved. Whatever the offence that is referred to as 'thy sensual fault', it is clearly something that would cause a deeper sense of guilt than could be cleared away with a simple apology. What was done is serious enough for the speaker to think of himself as offering absolution—an absolution based on the universal imperfection of all sublunary, terrestrial things that figure in the catalogue of the following three lines. It should be noted that the moon and sun, beyond the orbit of imperfection, are not themselves contaminated, but are viewed through imperfections nearer at hand. These imperfections are traditionally explained as a consequence of the fall from grace in the Garden of Eden and of man's first disobedience. (Milton himself was to write of that paradise, 'Flow'rs of all hue, and without thorn the rose'.[2]) This fallen world is thus a kind of paradox, where 'loathsome canker lives in sweetest bud'. What is being said here is complex. 'Loathsome canker' is strong language, potentially wounding to the beloved: will it seem vengeful? The speaker may hope that its tone of indictment will be sufficiently mitigated by the description 'sweetest bud'. The fifth line is more tactful, and finds fault first of all with the speaker himself for so much as venturing to excuse the beloved, and for doing so by means of metaphorical examples. There is good reason for him to apologise. The instances that he cites from nature are consequences of our fallen state and are now unalterable. To describe the faults of the beloved in the same terms is to risk saying something like: 'There's no point in your apologising, because you can't *help* doing what you do'—which makes the beloved a primitive or perverse creature and completely invalidates the sincerity of the grief mentioned in the first line. The speaker goes on, in the seventh and eighth lines, to balance any offence he may have given by proclaiming himself the worse sinner of the two, both for making too much of the trespass in the first place, and then for taking upon himself the role of the priest offering absolution, as if he himself were without taint.

The ninth line is pivotal and richly suggestive. William Empson has described it as containing at least three possible lines of thought: (1) 'I bring in reason, arguments to justify [your sensual fault]'; (2) 'I bring in feelings about it, feel it more important than it really was (and thereforeexcuse it more than it needs)'; (3) 'I bring extra sensuality to it; I enjoy thinking about it and making arguments to defend it, so that my sensuality sympathizes with yours.'[3] It can also bear this further meaning: 'To the sensuality of your fault I bring in (to my regret) my own sensuality, which may well, alas, have been the initial cause of your arousal, though now it is not directed at me—in other words, I am myself the unwitting author of your newfound promiscuity.'

Lines 10 and 11 are a very ingenious paradox:

> Thy adverse party is thy advocate—
> And 'gainst myself a lawful plea commence.

They may be a way of lessening slightly the gravity of the moral predicament in which both parties are now deeply enmeshed. But in addition, the paradox turns the whole focus of complaint and indictment against the speaker himself, leaving the beloved out of the picture to such a degree that with the twelfth line the love and hate are not merely balanced; we are entitled to feel that the *hatred* is as much self-directed as it is directed at the sensual fault of the beloved, and the *love* is that which is not only directed towards the beloved but generates the requisite (and, to the speaker, degrading) absolution. This 'civil war' is, in Marlowe's words, an 'intestine broil',[4] and it is highly complex. (1) Love and hate are at war. (2) The speaker is at war with himself, as well as with the beloved. (3) He is furthermore at war with the impulses of war and the impulses of hate. This warfare may end in total disaster. It seems almost, in fact, on its way to that very end in the concluding couplet, which, among other things, seems to say that the very distraction of the speaker may be driving his beloved from him; or that his generous willingness to forgive transgressions has encouraged the beloved to feel that no harm has been done; and either alternative would be a highly undesirable state of affairs. These two possibilities are mutually exclusive, and this leaves the speaker in an agonising and insoluble predicament. What is finally so effective about this poem is its stunning dramatic power. It hovers among alternatives, all of them anguishing, delicate in its manoeuvring, tense in its anxiety not to place too much blame on the beloved, but unable to conceal the torment from which the poem sprang. The 'sweet' and 'sour' of the last line echo the mixed imperfections that began the poem, in which the loathsome canker must find out and infect the sweetest bud.[5] The bitterness here is not wholly veiled by the cosmic explanation that *everything* is corrupt. The human drama is based on the terrible truth that thinking about and imagining infidelity is at least as poisonous as any proof of it, and as sickening to the contemplator. *Othello* and *The Winter's Tale* are extended illustrations of this, if any confirmation were needed. Moreover, the speaker's drama in Sonnet 35 is enhanced by the fact that we are allowed—indeed, virtually invited—to feel that he is discovering the complexity of his situation as the poem develops. The first line is grammatically and syntactically independent. It can be conceived as spoken in the uncomplicated spirit of charity, sympathy, and good will.

The illustrative examples of imperfection in the lines that immediately follow are fairly conventional, and might initially seem to confirm the permissiveness and generosity of the first line, did they not almost unwittingly introduce the appalling note of universal corruption. And from there on we move into increasing darkness and unending corridors of guilt.

It seems to me impossible not to find deeply moving and compelling the complicated and tormenting emotions latent in this poem, though it may be added that such riches are, or might be, implicit in any love poetry that is searching enough. In England in the 1590s there was a vogue of sonnet-writing in which poets admonished themselves, in the words of Philip Sidney, to look in their hearts and write.[6] Such introspection and honesty are not easy in any age, and it is the general consensus that, of all the sonneteers, Shakespeare was beyond question the most penetrating. He was also the one who seemed most perfectly to adapt the form itself to his analytic or diagnostic and deeply dramatic purposes.

It may be as well at this point to say something about the sonnet as a literary form; this is not so simple a matter as commentators have supposed. In the 1870s Walter Pater argued that some parts of the early play *Love's Labour's Lost* resembled the Sonnets: 'This connexion of *Love's Labours Lost* with Shakespere's poems is further enforced by the actual insertion in it of three sonnets and a faultless song.'[7] The song, of course, is the one that ends the play: 'When daisies pied and violets blue'. But as to the three sonnets, only two of them count as such by our modern and conventional definition; the third is a poem in tetrameter couplets twenty lines long. So it should be said here that there are at least two distinct definitions of the sonnet. One of them is not formally precise; it is given by the *Oxford English Dictionary* as simply 'A short poem or piece of verse'—in early use especially, one 'of a lyrical and amatory character'. Though *OED* calls this loose definition rare and indeed obsolete, it was current in English between 1563 and 1820, and it is worth remembering that Donne's *Songs and Sonets* (1633) contained not a single poem composed in the conventional fourteen-line form. Giroux (see n. 7 above) nevertheless continues to refer to *Love's Labour's Lost* as 'the sonnet play'. He would have done much better to have cited *Romeo and Juliet,* which employs far more sonnets, as well as sonnet fragments.[8] Indeed, Shakespeare seems in that play to have counted upon his audience's familiarity with some aspects of the sonnet form, and with that form's association with amatory verse.

Under the formal modern definition, the sonnet is a fourteen-line poem, usually written in pentameter verse, though Sidney, for example, sometimes used hexameters, and there have been other variations. The fourteen-line sonnet can be divided into two sorts, the Italian or Petrarchan on the one hand, and the Shakespearean on the other. The Italian poet Petrarch (1304-74) did not invent the Petrarchan form; it was used earlier by Dante (1265-1321) and his circle, but Petrarch's use of this form of sonnet to celebrate his beloved Laura made it widely known, and it was much imitated, notably in France by Ronsard (1524-85) and Du Bellay (*c*. 1522-60). The Petrarchan sonnet is composed of an octave—an initial passage of eight lines, rhyming ABBAABBA—followed by a sestet—six lines requiring only that each line have a rhyming mate. In addition to the separation of octave from sestet by rhyme-scheme, there is almost invariably a subtle but dramatic shift, a change of tone or point of view, introduced by the sestet and bringing to the poem a sort of 're-vision' or revelation. The severe restriction placed on the rhyming words in the octave—only two rhyme sounds for eight lines—is not difficult to overcome in Italian, which has an abundance of rhyming words; despite the fact that it is very much more difficult to deal with in English, the Petrarchan sonnet has become the preferred form, used by Milton, Wordsworth, and many more recent poets.

The Shakespearean sonnet, too, is named after its most famous practitioner, but as a form it was already firmly established, and was used by Shakespeare's predecessors and contemporaries, including Spenser, Surrey, Sidney, Giles Fletcher, Samuel Daniel, Michael Drayton, Thomas Lodge, Richard Lynche, William Smith, and Bartholomew Griffin. It consists of three quatrains rhyming ABAB, CDCD, EFEF, and concluding with a rhymed couplet, GG. This form is particularly easy to 'catch by ear' and identify when spoken aloud. The final six lines of a sonnet, even though written in Shakespearean form, can become its sestet, and Shakespeare often seemed to think of his sonnets in terms of the Italian division, including the dramatic or rhetorical relationship of octave to sestet. This is clearly the case in Sonnet 35, discussed above, and Shakespeare enjoyed the rather luxurious advantage of being able to write his sonnets in the spirit of either the form named after him or the Petrarchan fashion,[9] as can be shown by comparing Sonnet 73 and Sonnet 18:

> That time of year thou mayst in me behold
> When yellow leaves, or none, or few, do hang
> Upon those boughs which shake against the cold,
> Bare ruined choirs, where late the sweet birds sang.   4
> In me thou seest the twilight of such day
> As after sunset fadeth in the west,
> Which by and by black night doth take away,
> Death's second self, that seals up all in rest.   8
> In me thou seest the glowing of such fire

Shakespeare's contemporaries. Clockwise from top: Ben Jonson, Fletcher, Drayton, Shirley, Massinger, Beaumont, (center) Spenser. University of Michigan Library.

> That on the ashes of his youth doth lie,
> As the death-bed whereon it must expire,
> Consumed with that which it was nourished
>   by.   12
> This thou perceiv'st, which makes thy love
>   more strong,
> To love that well which thou must leave ere
>   long.
>
> (Sonnet 73)

This sonnet is a perfect example of the Shakespearean form. Three quatrains, each with its own governing figure of decline, serve as incremental parts of a discourse; each parallels and reinforces the others with beauty and delicacy of detail, and describes the inexorable truth of the natural world's mutability. William Empson's imaginative account of the fourth line is famous:

> there is no pun, double syntax, or dubiety of feeling, in
>
> Bare ruined choirs, where late the sweet birds sang,
>
> but the comparison holds for many reasons; because ruined monastery choirs are places in which to sing, because they involve sitting in a row, because they are made of wood, are carved into knots and so forth, because they used to be surrounded by a sheltering building crystallised out of the likeness of a forest, and coloured with stained glass and painting like flowers and leaves, because they are now abandoned by all but the grey walls coloured like the skies of winter, because the cold and Narcissistic charm suggested by choir-boys suits well with Shakespeare's feeling for the object of the Sonnets, and for various sociological and historical reasons (the protestant destruction of monasteries; fear of puritanism), which it would be hard now to trace out in their proportions; these reasons, and many more relating the simile to its place in the Sonnet, must all combine to give the line its beauty, and there is a sort of ambiguity in not knowing which of them to hold most clearly in mind.[10]

But these boughs are either themselves (by metaphoric transmutation) the bare ruined choirs, which shake against the 'cold', used as a noun; or else 'cold' is an adjective modifying bare ruined choirs themselves. This is not merely grammatical quibbling. Empson places a certain weight on the physical presence of a ruined church, cathedral, or monastery, and derives from these stones a good deal of religious controversy and historical ferment, to say nothing of the putative narcissism of the beloved—an imputation expounded at greater length in 'They that have power', an essay on Sonnet 94 in *Some Versions of Pastoral*.[11]

The decline of the year, of the day, of the fire, involving the repetition of autumnal, russet and golden colours, even in the fire, is also graduated in brevity, gaining force thereby. The second quatrain is emotionally more ambiguous than the first, since death is explicitly mentioned, but its terrors are tempered by the soothing comparison with sleep, and more especially a sleep that 'seals up all in rest'. This note of tranquillity is close to Macbeth's 'Come, seeling night, / Scarf up the tender eye of pitiful day' (3.2.46-7).[12] The four lines progress from twilight to dark, and we are permitted to regard that conclusion as either a consummation devoutly to be wished or else as the end of all the pleasures, beauties and joys of this mortal world. But the final quatrain is dramatically and emotionally the most dense and meaningful. The fire, once brilliant, has dimmed; its ashes now serve to extinguish the very flame that, when those ashes were wood, they fed. What is implied, of course, is that the vigour and liberties of our youth are precisely what serve to bring us, by the excess of that youthful folly and energy, to our demise. We are thus self-executed. This is not altogether remote from the notion (to be found in Donne's 'Farewell to Love') that every sexual experience abbreviates our lives by one day. This sense that youth, injudiciously or wantonly expended, brings about its own forfeiture, is restated in other terms in Sonnet 94, where Shakespeare writes of those who 'rightly do inherit heaven's graces / And husband nature's riches from expense'. These are people who maintain their youth and beauty seemingly for ever because they are by temperament 'Unmovèd, cold, and to temptation slow'.

And then we come to the deeply unnerving couplet. A number of critics have observed that 'To love that well' means either to treasure your own youth, or to love the poem's speaker, whose old age and imagined death have been the subject of this poem. Either alternative presents problems of emotional complexity. If the beloved is being instructed to husband his own youth and beauty, there is the double pathos of his being instructed by the decay of the poet before him, and of the poet's making himself into a seemingly disinterested object lesson. In addition, this act of husbandry is cruelly doomed, since youth is something 'thou must leave ere long'. If, on the other hand, the beloved is being praised for the nobility of loving someone whom he is destined soon to lose, the poignancy is greatly increased, and the continued love, especially in the face of a ravaged lover, is quietly heroic. Something of the deep risk of all mortal attachments is expressed, and we once again realise that to avoid such attachments may be the safer and more prudent course, but it is not to live life to its fullest, whereas to love means to expose oneself to every possible kind of grief. On being told his newly married wife is dead, Pericles exclaims:

> O you gods!
> Why do you make us love your goodly gifts
> And snatch them straight away?
>
> *(Per.* 3.1.22-4)

Something of Ben Jonson's anguished cry upon the death of his first son—'O, could I lose all father, now'—haunts the ending of the poem.

Sonnet 18 offers a direct contrast to Sonnet 73 in form and structure.

> Shall I compare thee to a summer's day?
> Thou art more lovely and more temperate:
> Rough winds do shake the darling buds of May,
> And summer's lease hath all too short a date;   4
> Sometime too hot the eye of heaven shines,
> And often is his gold complexion dimmed;
> And every fair from fair sometime declines,
> By chance or nature's changing course untrimmed: 8
> But thy eternal summer shall not fade,
> Nor lose possession of that fair thou ow'st,
> Nor shall Death brag thou wand'rest in his shade,
> When in eternal lines to time thou grow'st.   12
>   So long as men can breathe or eyes can see,
>   So long lives this, and this gives life to thee.
>
> (Sonnet 18)

This sonnet is decisively Petrarchan, notwithstanding its Shakespearean rhyme-scheme. To begin with, it is rhetorically divided into octave and sestet, the change between the two parts balanced on the fulcrum of the word 'But' at the beginning of the ninth line. The poem is widely and deservedly admired. Great riches of implication are packed into the interrogatory first line, which is a single sentence. A summer's day is itself full of meanings both lovely and ominous. It represents the season of growth, fertility, flowers, juvenescence, love, when days are not only luxurious in themselves but at their longest of all the seasons of the year. But that fact itself reminds us of a single day's brevity, no matter how long it lasts by count of daylight hours. We are already made conscious of the portents of decline and imperfection that are inevitably to follow. And how may it be said that some human being is 'like' a summer's day? This person is declared to be superior to any of them, since even the best of them have their faults. There is, I think, a danger, in reading the octave, of forgetting that the descriptive terms drawn from the world of nature are in fact metaphors for human imperfection and mutability. The third line, for example, is filled with the most delicate and tender solicitude for the fragility of beauty—and not just the beauty of buds. We are disposed to think of Hamlet's description of his father as 'so loving to my mother / That he might not beteem the winds of heaven / Visit her face too roughly' (*Ham.* 1.2.140-2). Even the most seemingly benign forces of nature, the 'eye of heaven', can induce drought and parch the skin; in Sonnet 62 Shakespeare describes himself as 'Beated and chopped with tanned antiquity'. The octave concludes with a vital distinction between 'chance' and 'nature's changing course'. Of these two forces, the latter is predictable, the former not; both are perilous. The sequential progress of the seasons is inexorable, and that it should present itself as a law of nature in the last line of the octave was implicit in the first line. But chance is another matter. In medieval times it was personified, notably by Boethius and Dante, as the pagan goddess Fortuna. Her vagaries and fickleness were proverbial, but a belief in her power provided a wonderful solution to an otherwise vexing theological problem. How could a beneficent and omnipotent God visit calamity or misfortune upon the meek, the pious, and the innocent? Speculation along these lines invited all the perils of heresy and atheism. But

Fortuna, with her authority strictly confined to mundane and earthly matters, could be as capricious as she liked, and thereby exculpate God from any charge of negligence or malignity. This solution can, however, be viewed in many ways, not all of them comforting. The licensed rule of chance, undiscriminating as death itself, was reassuring to those in unfavourable circumstances, as a guarantee that if things get bad enough they could only take a turn for the better. Kent reassures himself in this way—not altogether justifiably—when he is put in the stocks: 'Fortune, good night; smile once more; turn thy wheel' (*Lear* 2.2.173). That turning of the wheel of chance also assured men that no temporal greatness was durable, and that the mighty would surely fall. If this was a consolation to the powerless, it was a serious admonition to the powerful, urging clemency and charity upon them in that season when they were in a position to confer such favours. But when chance turns to havoc, as it does in Donne's *The First Anniversarie,* very little in the way of consolation or admonition is offered:

> 'Tis all in pieces, all coherence gone;
> All just supply, and all Relation:
> Prince, Subject, Father, Sonne, are things
>   forgot,
> For every man alone thinkes he hath got
> To be a Phoenix, and that there can bee
> None of that kinde, of which he is, but hee.[13]

King Lear abounds in this sort of apocalyptic chaos of vanity and disorder, and it is this chaos that is quietly implied in Sonnet 18 by the word 'chance'.

Then comes the brilliantly defiant sestet, in which the poet promises to immortalise his beloved in deathless verse. It needs immediately to be said that this is not personal vanity, nor even a shrewd intuition on Shakespeare's part, but a poetic convention that can be traced back to classical antiquity. It can be found in Homer and Virgil, and J. B. Leishman noted that 'passages on the immortalizing power of poetry are very frequent in Pindar's Odes'.[14] This tradition was so strong among the Pléiade—the group of poets who acclimatised the sonnet form in France—that Ronsard in one of his sonnets threatened to withhold immortality from one particular unnamed lady unless she acceded to his decidedly carnal desire. The convention is to be found in Spenser's 'Epithalamion':

> Song made in lieu of many ornaments,
> With which my love should duly have bene
>   dect . . .
> Be unto her a goodly ornament,
> And for short time an endlesse moniment[15]

and in Shakespeare's own Sonnet 55:

> Not marble nor the gilded monuments
> Of princes shall outlive this pow'rful rhyme.

If Shakespeare is undoubtedly invoking an ancient convention in asserting the poet's capacity to confer immortality, it is not the only convention he employs in his sonnets. We commonly assume that, whatever else love may be, it is at the very least a spontaneous and undeniable impulse, but it was not always thought to be so, and in the Renaissance, views about it were much more complicated. One modern critic has declared flatly: 'L'amour? une invention du douzième siècle.'[16] What could seem more pedantically offensive to our habits of feeling and thought? But the fact is that in classical literature, love is almost invariably regarded as an aberration, a dangerous taking leave of one's senses, most likely to lead to catastrophe and generally to be deplored. Many of the greatest Greek tragedies—*Oedipus Rex, Medea, Hippolytus, The Bacchae*—treat love as a tragic madness; so does Virgil in the episode of Dido in the *Aeneid*. The whole calamity of the Trojan war was brought about by a surrender to this insane impulse, which is treated in the *Iliad* as altogether unworthy and trifling in comparison with grave matters of war and heroism. The hero Odysseus, in the *Odyssey*, rejects all manner of solicitations from Calypso, Circe, and the Sirens; all these kinds of love are dangerous and to be avoided. Romantic love was historically a late development, and first manifested itself in Provence during the age of medieval feudalism, to which it bears a kind of metaphoric resemblance.

In the poetry developed by the troubadours and poets of Languedoc, the poet-lover always humbles himself in a submissive relationship to his beloved, a posture that duplicates the relation of a vassal towards his feudal lord. Indeed, as C. S. Lewis has pointed out, the lover addresses his beloved as *midons,* 'which etymologically represents not "my lady" but "my lord" '. Lewis notes that 'The lover is always abject. Obedience to his lady's lightest wish, however whimsical, and silent acquiescence in her rebukes, however unjust, are the only virtues he dares to claim.'[17] He goes on to assert that 'an unmistakable continuity connects the Provençal love song with the love poetry of the later Middle Ages, and thence, through Petrarch and many others, with that of the present day'.[18] Anyone reading Shakespeare's Sonnet 57—'Being your slave, what should I do but tend / Upon the hours and times of your desire?'—would do well to remember the strength and antiquity of this tradition. It is a tradition virtually insisted upon in the final couplet of that sonnet:

> So true a fool is love that in your will
> (Though you do any thing) he thinks no ill.

This is more than merely abject; 'true' in these lines means not only genuinely and certifiably a fool but also 'faithful'. The implication is that fidelity not merely exposes one to folly but requires it.

These matters of tradition and convention lead us directly to the insoluble question of just what in the Sonnets may be said to be (as Wordsworth claimed they were)[19] a key with which Shakespeare unlocked his heart, and what may instead be attributed to a traditional posture belonging to the kind of fourteen-line love poem that he inherited. Are we to regard these poems as anything other than the surviving pages of an intimate diary, transcribing the poet's exact and authentic feelings on every topic he addresses? There are always readers who seek, not art, but something documentary and unassailably factual; when these two categories seem mysteriously intermingled, they will always prize the second over the first. Susan Sontag has said that

> Between two fantasy alternatives, that Holbein the Younger had lived long enough to have painted Shakespeare or that a prototype of the camera had been invented early enough to have photographed him, most Bardolators would choose the photograph. This is not just because it would presumably show what Shakespeare really looked like, for even if the hypothetical photograph were faded, barely legible, a brownish shadow, we should probably still prefer it to another glorious Holbein. Having a photograph of Shakespeare would be like having a nail from the True Cross.[20]

Those who cherish the Sonnets for their documentary value are inclined to dismiss as irrelevant, if not actually wrong, T. S. Eliot's pronouncement in 'Tradition and the Individual Talent':

> the poet has, not a 'personality' to express, but a particular medium, which is only a medium and not a personality, in which impressions and experiences combine in peculiar and unexpected ways. Impressions and experiences which are important for the man may take no place in the poetry, and those which become important in the poetry may play quite a negligible part in the man, the personality . . . One error, in fact, of eccentricity in poetry is to seek for new human emotions to express; and in this search for novelty in the wrong place it discovers the perverse. The business of the poet is not to find new emotions, but to use the ordinary ones and, in working them up into poetry, to express feelings which are not in actual emotions at all. *And emotions which he has never experienced will serve his turn as well as those familiar to him.* [My italics][21]

Those who reject this view in so far as it applies to the Sonnets most often declare thatEliot's formula is based on the nervous self-protection of an unusually fastidious and evasive man. But such an explanation fails to take into account the fact that Eliot has done very little more than reformulate some observations of Coleridge in *Biographia Literaria* (XV, 2), so this view is not quite so idiosyncratic as has sometimes been asserted. Indeed, though the Sonnets were not published until much later, already in 1598 Francis Meres, in *Palladis Tamia: Wit's Treasury,* referred to the circulation of Shakespeare's 'sugred Sonnets among his private friends',[22] and it is reasonable to suppose that the poet would only have countenanced this kind of intimate distribution of his work if he felt it to be within the bounds of good taste. This is a question to which I shall return.

A word or two should perhaps be said here about metre and diction as they apply to these poems. Iambic pentameter—'When I do count the clock that tells the time' is the most familiar metrical pattern in English verse. It is employed by Chaucer in *The Canterbury Tales,* by Shakespeare and Marlowe in their plays, by Milton, by Wordsworth, by the Victorians Tennyson and Browning, by Frost, Stevens, and the poets of today. It is the metre of most of the sonnets in English from Sir Thomas Wyatt to Richard Wilbur. Each line is composed of five feet, and each foot is composed, generally speaking, of two syllables, with the strong accent on the second of these, as in the naturally iambic words 'today' or 'because'. Any moderate acquaintance with the body of English poetry will so habituate a reader to this metre that it will become something that can be recognised involuntarily, as a dancer will recognise the rhythms of a waltz, a foxtrot, or a tango, each with its identifiable idiom and pattern. In the same way, a reader of poetry will in due course become habituated to the sound and weight of a line of five iambic feet, though knowing that any given line will probably deviate in some regard from complete regularity. Such deviations are licensed by convention, and conventions change with the passing of time. Deviations of stress are useful and attractive for a number of reasons. They supply the rhythmical variety that is essential in a long poem or a five-act play. They make possible a flexibility of syntax and a directness of colloquial speech that a strictly regular metre would distort. They serve as a kind of counterpoint or syncopation, if the 'ideal' pattern of the regular iambic line is kept in mind, varying from that ideal in the way a jazz musician will improvise riffs on an established harmony and measure, or the way Elizabethan composers wrote what were called 'Divisions upon a Ground'. As readers, we welcome the introduction of non-iambic feet into a poem nominally iambic in character because we can hear in such poems the authentic sound of a human voice speaking in an idiom we can regard as reasonably 'natural'. There are many degrees and styles of such naturalness, and these too vary from period to period. But metrical flexibility allows a poet to avoid inverted word order and other peculiarities, and permits the words of a poem to speak with a true sense of emotional urgency, whether of anger, rapture, grief, or devotion.

It must be said that Shakespeare's Sonnets are in general metrically regular, especially by comparison with the great liberties he took with metre in the later plays. He often uses feminine endings (an extra, unaccented eleventh syllable at the end of a line), and twelve of the fourteen lines of Sonnet 87 ('Farewell, thou art too dear for my possessing') end in this way, most of these endings being composed of the participial *-ing*.

Clearly, matters of metre are intimately connected with questions of diction, and the diction of Shakespeare's Sonnets is worth noticing for its comparative spareness and simplicity—a sometimes deceptive simplicity. It is as far from the harsh brass choirs of Donne's Holy Sonnets, on the one hand, as it is from the stately elegance and learning of sonnets by Spenser and Sidney on the other. Just as Shakespeare made use of classical mythology only in the most chary and tentative way, so he employed a diction that not only distinguishes his work from that of his fellow sonneteers but from the language of his own work as a dramatist, both early and late. Drama presents human beings speaking to one another in something approximating the manner of ordinary human discourse, whereas we often think of poetry as violating the normal modes of speech. Furthermore, one would suppose that when, in the course of his plays, Shakespeare turns to 'heightened' forms of speech, he would reserve such heightening for the chief utterances of his major characters, as when Macbeth says:

> No; this my hand will rather
> The multitudinous seas incarnadine,
> Making the green one red.
> (*Mac.* 2.2.58-60)

But it is merely a nameless Second Gentleman, never to reappear, who observes at the beginning of the second act of *Othello*:

> I never did like molestation view
> On the enchafèd flood.
> (*Oth.* 2.1.16-17)

The fact that Shakespeare can allot language like this to persons of no dramatic consequence whatever means that he is not attempting, by such musical flourishes, to convey character, but is simply treating with exuberant and exploratory relish the resources of the English language.

The solid facts about the Sonnets that can be called undisputed are few. In 1599 William Jaggard published two of the Sonnets (138 and 144) in a collection of poems called *The Passionate Pilgrim,* in which a number of other poems, some of them now firmly identified as being by other hands, were also attributed to Shakespeare. The 1590s were the time of the great vogue for sonnets in England, but Shakespeare's Sonnets did not appear until 1609, when they were published by Thomas Thorpe in a volume usually believed to have been unauthorised by Shakespeare. Thorpe possibly hoped to cash in, belatedly, on what was by then a waning interest in the form. His edition was mysteriously and indeed notoriously dedicated to 'THE.ONLIE.BEGETTER.OF.THESE.INSUING.SONNETS.M\ :sup:`R`.W.H.', and there has been a great deal of argument over this man's identity ... . There has been at least as much conjecture about the order of the poems as about the dedication, some critics proposing that they should be linked by rhyme, or by words that connect one sonnet with another. Some of the sonnets are clearly linked in rhetorical structure as part of a developed argument; several in Thorpe'ssequence are clustered round a specific theme. This order, fretted over and argued about, has not yet been superseded by any other that wins wide consent, and it has some elements of design and logic to recommend it. It is generally assumed that the first 126 sonnets are addressed to a young man; the remainder concern a woman. Both involve poems of unusual intimacy, sometimes openly bawdy and erotic in character, though the humour is similar to that of the off-colour jokes that can be found in many of the plays. The poems concerned with the man are, for the most part, more respectful than those about the woman, but even the first group takes liberties that would be admissible between friends in the plays, but are less likely between a poet and his titled patron—if indeed they are to be taken as addressed to the Earl of Southampton. Shakespeare had dedicated other poems to Southampton in words of conventional servility, though it has been correctly noted that the language Shakespeare used in his prose dedication of *The Rape of Lucrece* to Southampton is very closely echoed in Sonnet 26. Southampton, of course, is one of the leading candidates for the 'young man'—along with William Herbert, Earl of Pembroke—among those who wish to decode the sequence into a personal narrative.

The question of the historical identity of the man is interestingly linked to another question. A group of the earliest sonnets in the sequence is concerned to urge the young man to marry and beget children who will perpetuate his beauty. 'What man in the whole world', asks C. S. Lewis, 'except a father or potential father-in-law, cares whether any other man gets married?' He regards this repeated recommendation of marriage as 'inconsistent . . . with a real homosexual passion. It is not even very obviously consistent with normal friendship. It is indeed hard to think of any real situation in which it would be natural.'[23] Lewis's remarks here seem amusingly suspicious of the benefits of marriage, since he finds it improbable that one friend should recommend it to another; but far more important is his comment that it is hard to think of a 'real situation' in which such a recommendation would be natural. *Are* we to imagine a real situation behind the poems? Is Shakespeare always writing *in propria persona?* Some critics have proposed that these 'marital' sonnets were commissioned to be passed on to the young nobleman as if coming from his mother.

The problem is not confined simply to the question of the young man's identity, or that of the so-called Dark Lady who is the subject of the later sonnets. Some critics with a strong narrative bent have come up with a detailed plot of sexual betrayal and infidelity which supposes that Shakespeare is simultaneously attached both to the young man and to the woman, and makes the fatal mistake of introducing them to each other, which leads, as in a third-rate film script, to their instant infatuation with each other, their abandonment of the playwright, and their exclusive erotic interest in each other. Followers of this line of argument suggest that Shakespeare acknowledged the double desertion in Sonnet 40—'Take all my loves, my love, yea, take them all'—and Samuel Butler adds the excruciating twist, perhaps suggested to him by Rostand's *Cyrano,* that some of the sonnets addressed to the Dark Lady were written by Shakespeare for the young man to pass on as his own.

There is at least one further major puzzle that seems beyond the reach of any solution. This has to do with the sexual orientation of the poet, and the quality and degree of his intimacy with the young man. (The quality and degree of his intimacy with the woman is unambiguous.) About these matters almost no one feels neutral. Many of Shakespeare's plays have been construed to demonstrate an explicit or implicit homosexual bias on the playwright's part. The relationship between Horatio and Hamlet, between Antonio and Bassanio, and between Iago and Othello—to say nothing of Orsino's erotic interest in Viola disguised as a boy and played by a boy actor, as well as Olivia's interest in Viola, who she thinks really is the boy she pretends to be, or the relationship between Falstaff and Hal[24]—all these seem homoerotic to some readers. And these arguments are invariably advanced by appealing to the 'evidence' of the Sonnets.

There was an established tradition in Europe that placed a higher value on the love relationship between men than on love between the sexes. Towards the end of the *Morte D'Arthur* (Book XX, ch. 9), Malory has King Arthur speak in a mood close to despair:

> 'And therefore,' said the king, 'wit you well my heart was never so heavy as it is now, and much more am I sorrier for my good knights' loss than for the loss of my fair queen; for queens I might have enow, but such a fellowship of good knights shall never be together in no company.'[25]

Montaigne, in his essay 'On Friendship' (by which he means the friendship between men), says something not dissimilar:

> To compare the affection toward women unto it [i.e. friendship], although it proceed from our own free choice [as distinguished from the bonds of child and parent], a man cannot; nor may it be placed in this rank. [Venus's] fire, I confess it . . . to be more active, more fervent, and more sharp. But it is a rash and wavering fire, waving and divers, the fire of an ague subject to fits and stints, and that hath but slender hold-fast [i.e. grasp] of us. In true friendship is a general and universal heat, all pleasure and smoothness, that hath no pricking or stinging in it, which the more it is in lustful love, the more is it but a ranging and mad desire in following that which flies us.[26]

'The exaltation of friendship over love was a widespread Neoplatonic commonplace . . . popularized in the writings of John Lyly'[27]—and not in Lyly's works alone, or in Montaigne's. There was the biblical story of David and Jonathan; the Homeric account of Achilles and Patroclus; the classical legend of Damon and Pythias; and, if more authority were needed, Aristotle's argument that relations between men who are friends must of necessity be closer than any possible relationship between men and women because men bear a closer resemblance to one another—an argument advanced in *The Merchant of Venice* by Portia herself in speaking of the 'love' between Bassanio, her 'lord', and his friend, Antonio. There is, moreover, a theological basis for the devotion of Antonio and Bassanio to each other. The play pointedly confronts the Old Testament (Law) with the New Testament (Love), and the latter is figuratively dramatised as an enactment of John 15.13: 'Greater love than this hath no man, when any man bestoweth his life for his friends' (Geneva Bible). Such love is expressly 'greater' than connubial love, and *The Merchant of Venice* exhibits much wit in giving each a due and proportionate place in its dramatic fable.

Since it was at times a part of Shakespeare's poetic strategy to invert, parody or burlesque sonnets in the conventional Petrarchan tradition—see, for instance, Sonnet 130: 'My mistress' eyes are nothing like the sun'—it may be useful to illustrate this device by citing just such a model along with Shakespeare's irreverent treatment of the same conventions. The following sonnet by Sir Thomas Wyatt is in fact a translation of Petrarch's sonnet, *In vita* CIX, 'Amor, che nel penser mio vive e regna':

> The longe love, that in my thought doeth harbar
>   And in myn hert doeth kepe his residence,
>   Into my face preseth with bolde pretence,
>   And therin campeth, spreding his baner.   4
> She that me lerneth to love and suffre,
>   And willes that my trust and lustes negligence

> Be rayned by reason, shame and reverence,
> With his hardines taketh displeasure.   8
> Wherewithall, unto the hertes forrest he fleith,
> Leving his enterprise with payn and cry;
> And ther him hideth, and not appereth.
> What may I do when my maiser fereth   12
> But in the feld with him to lyve and dye?
> For goode is the liff, ending faithfully.[28]

This remarkable poem draws its central metaphoric structure from a tradition that reaches back to the *Roman de la Rose,* which had been partly translated into English by Chaucer. The image is that of a faithful knight dedicated to the service of love, and obedient to the rebuke and correction of a sternly chaste but beautiful mistress, and thus destined to love and suffer simultaneously. But the image of knight-errantry, with all its military embellishments, goes back to the classical identification of love and war, the love of Venus and Mars, the proverbial association that links these forces in the expression, 'All's fair in love and war.' Wyatt's translation of Petrarch is lovingly compounded of a double allegiance: to Love, the involuntary passion that shows itself like a banner in the flushed face of the lover in the first quatrain—and to the beloved, to whom the lover submits in meek obedience, shame, and contrition in the second quatrain. It then becomes the complex duty of the lover to be faithful both to his passion and to his mistress; his loyalty to the former is expressed as a vassal's fidelity to his sovereign lord, and a resignation to accept death itself if that should be called for.

This very set of metaphors—military in character, involving notions of fidelity to the point of death, loyalty, treason, betrayal, and triumph—figures, with deliberate allowance made for the irony of its deployment, in what is probably Shakespeare's most outrageously libidinous sonnet:

> Love is too young to know what conscience is,
> Yet who knows not conscience is born of love?
> Then, gentle cheater, urge not my amiss,
> Lest guilty of my faults thy sweet self prove.   4
> For thou betraying me, I do betray
> My nobler part to my gross body's treason:
> My soul doth tell my body that he may
> Triumph in love; flesh stays no farther reason,   8
> But rising at thy name doth point out thee
> As his triumphant prize. Proud of this pride,
> He is contented thy poor drudge to be,
> To stand in thy affairs, fall by thy side.   12
>   No want of conscience hold it that I call
>   Her 'love' for whose dear love I rise and fall.
>
>   (Sonnet 151)

It does not take a long acquaintance with this poem to realise that it is laden with puns, most of them leeringly sexual. Critics have ransacked the *OED* and precedents from Elizabethan literature in tracing the various meanings buried in this wordplay, but there has been very little agreement about whether this is to be regarded as a poem to be admired or simply a crude and embarrassing piece of youthful sexual raillery. Moreover, not only has the quality of the poem been left in doubt, but its meaning as well. For while the puns have been glossed, it is often left unclear which meanings apply to particular words as they make their multiple appearances from line to line. In addition, there has been little if any discussion of the rhetorical structure and premise of the poem.

It posits a dramatic context, an anterior situation, known to the person addressed, the beloved, and to be inferred by us, the readers. It is a defence against a prior accusation, a self-exculpation, a *tu quoque* argument, but presented in a spirit of bawdy good humour, and free from any sense of guilt or of wounded feelings. Indeed, our whole task as readers is to determine the nature of the charge against which the poem has been composed as if it were a legal brief for the defence. The brief wittily employs all the ancient metaphors of vassalage and faithful military service, of warfare, treason, and triumph that had been part of the Petrarchan conventions, but which are here adapted to carnal purposes where before they had served the most discarnate and spiritual ends.

The first two lines both contain the words 'love' and 'conscience'. To make any sense of them whatever requires a recognition that a different meaning applies to those words in each of the lines. 'Love' in the opening line is Cupid, too young to know or care about the damage he inflicts with his weapons of bow and arrow (the military imagery of weapons is implied right at the start), too young to feel the pang of sexual arousal himself, and thus unaware of the pain he causes others—hence, without conscience. But in the second line 'conscience' as carnal knowledge is begotten by the passion of love (the root meaning here is *con scire,* 'to know together', in the biblical sense: 'And Adam knew Heva his wife, who conceiving, bare Cain' (Gen. 4.1 in the Bishops Bible)). For reasons that I hope presently to make clear, I am at variance with critics who regard the phrase 'gentle cheater' as an oxymoron, especially when they argue that 'cheater' implies fraud, deceit or infidelity. The *OED* cites these very lines to illustrate its first definition of 'cheater': 'The officer appointed to look after the king's escheats; an escheator' (though this meaning became obsolete after the seventeenth century, when the modern sense implying 'fraud' replaced it). An escheater was 'an officer appointed yearly by the Lord Treasurer to take notice of the escheats in the county to which he is appointed, and to certify them into the Exchequer';

the office is therefore one concerned to demand forfeits from those who have defaulted from their obligations, usually financial. In the present case, the 'gentle cheater' is an 'assessor' of some sexual malfeasance, which the sonnet will shortly make somewhat clearer; and the epithet seems to be used without complication in an affectionate and jocular spirit.

The phrase 'urge not my amiss' is densely compressed and probably cannot be construed in isolation from the line that follows: 'Lest guilty of my faults thy sweet self prove'. I would claim in defence of my reading of 'gentle cheater' that it chimes harmoniously with 'sweet self', as any suggestion of sexual treason would not. The third and fourth lines, taken together, are a central crux of the poem, and can plausibly be interpreted in contradictory and mutually exclusive ways. If 'urge' is understood as 'incite', we may read the lines as meaning: 'Do not incite me to some known but unspecified offence (1) lest you be to blame for my fault by inciting me, or (2) lest you turn out upon further inquiry to be guilty of the very same fault yourself.' If, on the other hand, 'urge' means 'accuse' or 'allege', the lines mean: 'Do not charge me with this unspecified fault, lest in some way you turn out to be responsible for it.' There is a further possible complication. In the seventeenth-century orthography of Thorpe's edition, the fourth line is printed: 'Least guilty of my faults thy sweet selfe proue'. And if 'Least' is taken in the modern sense, as distinct from a legitimate spelling of 'Lest', the line would mean: 'Distance yourself as emphatically as possible from my ways and errors.' But this meaning cannot be fitted intelligibly into the rest of the sonnet.

All this leaves us tantalisingly uncertain about what the fault may be, though the entire remainder of the poem is devoted to it, in the form of a legal defence and exculpation, commencing with the first word of the fifth line—'For'—as the beginning of a demonstration and proof of innocence in regard to the charge. From the evidence of the argument for the defence, the charge appears ambiguously to be that the lover has either made sexual demands of too great and burdensome a kind, or else is sexually backward, shy, and indifferent in performance.

The fifth line, with its punning use of 'betray' and 'betraying', is not without its own complexities and puzzles. It has been proposed by some critics that 'betraying' means an overt act of infidelity, and that what is being claimed is something like: 'Every time you are unfaithful to me, I become sexually aroused.' This seems to me at best unlikely, though it is of course possible. Far more plausible is the suggestion that 'betraying' is used here to mean 'seducing', as when Cleopatra says:

> I will betray
> Tawny-finn'd fishes; my bended hook shall pierce
> Their slimy jaws; and as I draw them up,
> I'll think them every one an Antony,
> And say, 'Ah, ha! y'are caught.'
> (*Ant.* 2.5.11-15)

In contrast to 'betraying', 'betray' here means the treasonable conveyance of the soul ('my nobler part') to the gross and carnal powers of the body. The body itself commits treason by subverting the soul from its chief goal and purpose. The 'I' in the fifth line betrays his own soul by subjecting it to the base authority of his body, so much corrupting the soul that it grants permission to the body to pursue its own lewd ends. And having gained this permission from the soul, the body seeks no further check upon its lusts (such checks as might be offered either by the soul or by outside authority), 'But rising at thy name doth point out thee / As his triumphant prize'. It should be noted here that the 'I' who has been advancing the whole argument of the poem has, rather interestingly, disappeared in this description of the warfare between soul and body. This familiar convention of spiritual and bodily conflict dates back at least as far as St Paul's Epistle to the Galatians 5.17: 'For the flesh lusteth against the Spirit, and the Spirit against the flesh: and these are contrary one to the other' (Geneva Bible). This conflict was played out in such poems as Andrew Marvell's 'A Dialogue between the Soul and the Body' and 'A Dialogue, between the Resolved Soul and Created Pleasure',[29] and may be found in other poems as well. In the present case, however, the conflict is circumvented or simply avoided by the total capitulation of soul to body.

The 'rising' of the ninth line and the 'pride' of the tenth refer to the tumescence of male sexual arousal; flesh is said to be 'proud' when it swells. The wit here lies in the fact that this truth pertains equally to body and to spirit: a man swollen with pride is guilty of spiritual sin. But these acknowledgements of vigorous sexual reaction are now excused—and indeed glorified—as a testament to the obedience and duty of a vassal to his *midons,* his absolute sovereign, the disposer of his fortunes good and bad, his very life and death. It is 'flesh' which is the subject of lines 8-14, and by flesh is meant the male sexual organ, which is personified as faithful even unto death, rising and falling at the behest of the beloved. For this reason it seems to me highly unlikely that the word 'cheater' in the third line can contain any overtones of perfidy on the part of the beloved—a meaning which would involve the notion that the speaker is sexually aroused only by the infidelity of his beloved. This is, as I acknowledged, possible, though it raises the whole ludicrous puzzle of frequency. For a man to say of himself that he is instantly aroused by a woman's beauty is at least understandable. To defend his reputation by saying he is aroused only by infidelity on the part of the woman he loves must mean he is aroused at far less frequent intervals, as well as in more curious circumstances, and it becomes thereby a somewhat feebler defence.

There is much more to this sonnet than has been here too briefly summarised, but we must return to the nature of the 'amiss' mentioned in the third line. Has the speaker been accused of sexual negligence, indifference, or impotence? Or of making too insistent carnal demands upon the beloved? The poem can, astonishingly, be read both ways, and in both cases the same argument for the defence works. If she has said to him that he has failed to gratify her sexual appetite, his response is that her 'betrayal' or seductive looks instantly result in sexual arousal on his part, so he is blameless. If, on the other hand, she has accused him of being too insistent upon satisfying his own carnal appetites, his response is that she herself must be blamed for his behaviour by the initial betrayal (i.e. seduction) that leads him to the further betrayal of his soul to his body. No doubt all this is forensic jesting, and the sort of banter not uncommon between lovers. Those who feel the point is overworked should consider once again how much in the way of traditional Petrarchan devices, metaphors of war and treason, images of vassalage and fidelity, are, as I think, brilliantly crowded into a mere fourteen lines. This may not be one of Shakespeare's greatest sonnets, but it is surely one of his wittiest.[30]

Sonnet 151, though full of puns and complicated wordplay, is still a comparatively simple poem in terms of its tone, and it probably intends a simple and comparatively straightforward meaning, if only we were so situated as to know the nature of the 'amiss' with which it is concerned. Far more complicated in terms both of tone and meaning is Sonnet 87:

> Farewell, thou art too dear for my possessing,
> And like enough thou know'st thy estimate:
> The charter of thy worth gives thee releasing;
> My bonds in thee are all determinate.   4
> For how do I hold thee but by thy granting,
> And for that riches where is my deserving?
> The cause of this fair gift in me is wanting,
> And so my patent back again is swerving.   8
> Thy self thou gav'st, thy own worth then not
>   knowing,
> Or me, to whom thou gav'st it, else
>   mistaking;
> So thy great gift, upon misprision growing,
> Comes home again, on better judgement
>   making.   12
>   Thus have I had thee as a dream doth
>   flatter,
>   In sleep a king, but waking no such matter.

The genius of this poem consists in its absolute command of tonal complexity throughout, by which it is left brilliantly ambiguous—through tact and diplomacy, with bitterness and irony, or with matter-of-fact worldliness—just which of the two parties involved is to be blamed for the impasse and end of what had once been a deeply binding relationship. The pretext of the poem is one of self-mortification characteristic of the traditional early love sonnets discussed above .... The lover insists upon his own unworthiness, particularly as regards the exalted, unapproachable condition of the beloved. Although there is a pun on the word 'dear' in the first line—a pun made the more explicit by the possibly commercial language of the second line—puns are not the building blocks of this poem as they are of others. The lover begins in what seems initially to be a spirit of generous renunciation: the line can mean both (1) 'I am prepared to give you up' and (2) 'I appear not to have much choice in the matter, so I am giving you up.' Taken in conjunction with the first line, however, the second line of the poem seems to include or suggest the following possible meanings:

(1) You know how much I love you.
(2) You know how much you deserve to be loved.
(3) You have a very high opinion of yourself.
(4) You know how much others love you.
(5) You know the value of the opinions of
  (a) me
  (b) yourself
  (c) others
  (d) all of us.

The poem continues to manoeuvre between these modes of worldliness and unworldliness in a way that, by its skill, speaks of two different kinds of pain, and at the same time makes the pain almost tolerable by the sheer act of lively intelligence that went into the making of the poem, which is clearly no raw, unmediated transcription of experience. By the time we reach the end of the second line, the poem has begun to seethe with implied hostility, governed nevertheless by conventions of propriety and the decorum of charity. We cannot fail to notice the pervasive language of law and commerce, those two ledger-keeping modes of coming to terms with the world; and we cannot fail to feel the irony of the application of those modes to questions of love.

The speaker here seems to be giving the beloved a writ of freedom to depart, and justifying that departure by several different kinds of 'reason', generally practical and intended as plausible. The words 'estimate', 'charter', 'bonds', 'riches', 'gift', 'patent', 'misprision', and 'judgment' all speak, as might a shrewd auctioneer, from a market-place perspective. Beneath the surface of supposedly self-abnegating relinquishment, we detect a flavour of bitterness and scarcely repressed resentment. This may be most openly expressed, and at the same time best concealed, by the lines

> For how do I hold thee but by thy granting,
> And for that riches where is my deserving?

We do not love anyone on the basis of merit, or rank, or wealth, or for other worldly advantages. Love mixed with or tainted by calculation is highly suspect—is indeed not love at all. It follows then that if the beloved is willing to accept as a legitimate excuse for withdrawing from the relationship any of the various 'worldly' and practical excuses proposed by the lover, then the lover cannot but conclude that the love has not been mutual, whatever he may have thought it to begin with; that the beloved, surveying the prospect or prospects, has both reason and right to seek elsewhere, since no real love seems to be involved. The very word 'misprision' means both a misunderstanding or mistake, and also a clerical error of the ledger-keeping sort. The final irony of the poem lies in the fact that both parties were deeply deceived—the beloved by either underestimating himself or overestimating the lover, and the lover by having believed that he was loved.

This mutual deception and self-deception are re-examined by Shakespeare in Sonnet 138:

> When my love swears that she is made of truth,
> I do believe her, though I know she lies,
> That she might think me some untutored youth,
> Unlearnèd in the world's false subtleties.   4
> Thus vainly thinking that she thinks me young,
> Although she knows my days are past the best,
> Simply I credit her false-speaking tongue:
> On both sides thus is simple truth suppressed.   8
> But wherefore says she not she is unjust?
> And wherefore say not I that I am old?
> O love's best habit is in seeming trust,
> And age in love loves not t'have years told.   12
>   Therefore I lie with her, and she with me,
>   And in our faults by lies we flattered be.

Sonnet 93 deals with the subject even more directly—'So shall I live, supposing thou art true, / Like a deceivèd husband . . . ' Sonnet 138 is a private meditation, with no express addressee, and may perhaps exhibit a certain candour of insight that direct address might forbid in the name of tact. But each is concerned with love as illusion, as self-deception, as bitterly unreal—in ways that remind us that the world of *A Midsummer Night's Dream* is not altogether as taintless as it might at first appear.

This capacity for illusion and self-deception concerns not only matters of love but our very sense of ourselves, of our worth—our self-image and self-respect. This issue raises its head in the sonnets about the 'rival poet'. These are usually regarded as a group made up of Sonnets 78-80 and 82-86. But even in so 'early' a sonnet as the celebrated 29—'When in disgrace with Fortune and men's eyes'—we find the quatrain:

> Wishing me like to one more rich in hope,
> Featured like him, like him with friends possessed,
> Desiring this man's art, and that man's scope,
> With what I most enjoy contented least . . .

Such vulnerability, modesty, uncertainty, are touching in their own right, and a small solace to lesser poets in their moods of tormenting self-doubt.

I have earlier raised the topic of how literally and precisely we should allow ourselves to read these poems as documentary transcriptions of personal events. This calls for a few further words. A number of philosophers, beginning perhaps with Plato, have argued on a variety of grounds that poetry is a tissue of lies. This was Stephen Gosson's view in *The School of Abuse* (1579), and John Skelton, maintaining that religious poetry is 'true', touches upon the same conventional topic when he asks:

> Why have ye then disdain
> At poets, and complain
> How poets do but feign?[31]

This view, that poets are only feigning, did not differ greatly from ideas that were forcibly advanced during the period of the Enlightenment, when the domain of truth was confined more and more strictly to what could be known with scientific precision. It is a view still voiced in certain quarters to this day. But we may approach the question in another way—one that centres on the nature of poetic form and the demands it makes on the materials it must employ and put into artistic order. The raw materials of poetry can be recalcitrant; the demands of form can be severe. How are these conflicting elements to be reconciled? Here is W.H. Auden's especially persuasive answer to that question:

> In the process of composition, as every poet knows, the relation between experience and language is always dialectical, but in the finished product it must always appear to the reader to be a one-way relationship. In serious poetry thought, emotion, event, must always appear to dictate the diction, meter, and rhyme in which they are embodied; vice versa, in comic poetry it is the words, meter, rhyme,

which must appear to create the thoughts, emotions, and events they require.[32]

If what Auden says is right (and it seems to me almost indisputable), then the question of the documentary nature of the Sonnets is largely irrelevant. This will no doubt leave some readers feeling cheated. But the Sonnets are, first and last, poems, and it should be our task to read, evaluate, and enjoy them as such. Devoted attention to each of them in its own right will yield striking discoveries. They are not all equally inventive or moving. Some are little more than conventional; others are wonderfully original and ingenious. Scarcely any lacks true merit, many of them are beyond compare, and in bulk they are without question the finest single group of sonnets in the language. They contain puzzles which will probably never be wholly answered, and this may be a part of their enigmatic charm. But most of all they speak with powerful, rich, and complex emotion of a very dramatic kind, and we cannot fail to hear in them a voice of passion and intelligence.

Notes

[1] For this reading of the line, as against the more familiar 'Excusing thy sins more than thy sins are', see the Commentary, p. 147 ... .

[2] Milton, *Paradise Lost*, IV, 256.

[3] William Empson, *The Structure of Complex Words*, 1951, pp. 272-3.

[4] Christopher Marlowe, *Hero and Leander*, 1, 251, in *Works*, II, 438.

[5] Compare Sonnet 94: 'For sweetest things turn sourest by their deeds.'

[6] See the first sonnet in Sidney's *Astrophil and Stella*.

[7] Walter Pater, *Appreciations*, 1889, p. 167. A similar identification is made more recently by Robert Giroux, *The Book Known as Q* 1982, pp. 140-1, citing Pater and referring to *Love's Labour's Lost* as 'the sonnet play'.

[8] See Prologue to Act 1; 1.2.45-50; 1.2.88-93; 1.5.93-110; Prologue to Act 2; 5.3.12-17; 5.3.305-10.

[9] It should be added that while these two canonical varieties of the sonnet predominate among Shakespeare's ventures in the form, there are individual sonnets that deviate from both; for rhetorical purposes, or under the pressure of overwhelming feelings, the 'divisions' of some sonnets are at odds with both the Petrarchan and the Shakespearean convention. See, for example, Sonnets 66, 145, and 154.

[10] William Empson, *Seven Types of Ambiguity*, 2nd edn, 1947, pp. 2-3.

[11] William Empson, *Some Versions of Pastoral*, 1935, pp. 89-115.

[12] This is pointed out by Stephen Booth (ed.), *Shakespeare's Sonnets*, rev. edn, 1978, p. 259.

[13] John Donne, *The First Anniversarie*, lines 213-18, in *The Epithalamions, Anniversaries and Epicedes*, ed. W. Milgate, 1978, p. 28.

[14] J. B. Leishman, *Themes and Variations in Shakespeare's Sonnets*, 1961, p. 27.

[15] Edmund Spenser, *Epithalamion*, lines 427-32, in *Works, Minor Poems*, II, 252.

[16] Charles Seignobos, quoted by Maurice Valency, *In Praise of Love*, 1958, p. 1. Much the same claim is made by C. S. Lewis, *The Allegory of Love*, 1936, p. 2: 'Every one has heard of courtly love, and every one knows that it appears quite suddenly at the end of the eleventh century in Languedoc.'

[17] Lewis, *Allegory of Love*, p. 2.

[18] *Ibid.*, p. 3.

[19] William Wordsworth, 'Scorn not the Sonnet', a sonnet published in 1827.

[20] Susan Sontag, *On Photography*, 1977, p. 154.

[21] T. S. Eliot, *Selected Essays 1917-32*, 1932, pp. 9-10.

[22] E. K. Chambers, *William Shakespeare: A Study of Facts and Problems*, 2 vols., 1930, II, 194.

[23] C. S. Lewis, *English Literature in the Sixteenth Century Excluding Drama*, 1954, p. 503.

[24] See W. H. Auden, 'The Prince's Dog', in *The Dyer's Hand and Other Essays*, 1962, pp. 182-208.

[25] Sir Thomas Malory, *Le Morte D'Arthur*, ed. Janet Cowen, 2 vols., 1969, II, 473.

[26] *The Essays of Michael, Lord of Montaigne*, trans. John Florio (1603), 3 vols., 1928, I, 195-209.

[27] See David Bevington (ed.), *The Complete Works of Shakespeare*, 1980, p. 1582.

[28] R. A. Rebholz (ed.), *The Complete Poems of Sir Thomas Wyatt*, 1978, pp. 76-7.

[29] Elizabeth Story Donno (ed.), *Andrew Marvell: The Complete Poems*, 1972, pp. 25-8 and 103-4.

[30] Anyone who wants to see how carefully constructed, how densely packed, a sonnet of Shakespeare's can be, and who would also like to see how a sensitive and painstaking reader with responsible critical intelligence can unpack those meanings and reveal that design, cannot do better than read Roman Jakobson on Shakespeare's Sonnet 129, in Roman Jakobson and Lawrence G. Jones, *Shakespeare's Verbal Art in 'Th'expense of spirit'*, The Hague, 1970.

[31] John Skelton, 'A Replication Against Certain Young Scholars Abjured of Late', in John Scattergood (ed.), *John Skelton: The Complete English Poems*, 1983, p. 384.

[32] W.H. Auden (ed.), *Selected Poetry and Prose of Byron*, 1966, p. xix.

LOVE AND ROMANCE

John Dover Wilson (essay date 1964)

SOURCE: "The Friend and the Poet," in *An Introduction to the Sonnets of Shakespeare for the Use of Historians and Others*, Cambridge University Press, 1964, pp. 31-44.

[*In the following excerpt, Wilson examines the sonnets which describe the love that the "Poet," or Shakespeare, feels for his young male "Friend." After asserting that the relationship between the two men was not homosexual, Wilson speculates about the Friend's social rank and his personality, and suggests that when a poet as great as Shakespeare was settles his affections on one so apparently "commonplace" and uncomprehending as was his Friend, the consequences can be "tragic."*]

The nature of the friendship and the character of the Friend

We can now leave Thomas Thorpe for the time and pass on to consider the two leading characters in his copy. We know the name of one already, and the sonnets to the Friend when seen in the sunlight tell us much for certain about the other, though assuredly without the help of C. S. Lewis we could not otherwise have guessed so much; while the sonnets to the Dark Woman leave questions in our mind about him that will have to be faced at a later stage. But at the outset the Friend's name and personality are among the shadows of the cave, and if we would learn about them, all we have are those scattered hints which the Poet's love has given us.

The 'love' in question is of course the affectionate admiration—perhaps adoration would at times not be too strong a term—of a man of mature years for another man much younger than himself, in this case perhaps fifteen to seventeen years younger. Such affection, though not unusual, especially with men of an imaginative or poetical temperament, may seem strange or even repellent to most ordinary people. And as many readers nowadays, when all matters of sex are openly debated, will be ready to assume without question that Shakespeare was writing about homosexuality, something had better be said about that at once. Though a brief reference to it by C. S. Lewis has already been quoted, and I agree with him, I do so on rather more explicit grounds.

Whatever, then, psychologists may postulate about the love that inspires these sonnets, it is certain that Shakespeare was not a conscious paederast, and for two good reasons. First of all in sonnet 20, which is perhaps the most intimate of the series, he expressly dissociates his passionate admiration from sexual desire, and does so with a frankness characteristically Elizabethan, in such terms as to suggest that the sonnet was written partly in order to make this point unmistakably clear. That the love was passionate on both sides can hardly be denied by anyone who had read the reference to 'hungry eyes' in sonnet 56 or the couplet of 110. And the second reason is even more cogent, namely that a major theme of the sonnets is the Poet's infatuation for a woman which holds him in its grip and with which he not infrequently contrasts the humble and selfless adoration he feels for his young friend. The affection is so absolute that he is ready to forgive his adored anything except such actions as injure the adored himself. And there is much to forgive, for it becomes evident as the sonnets go forward that the young man is amusing himself by making love to the Poet's mistress; behaviour that, as the Poet is really deeply in love with the woman, causes him such distress, at times agony, as to introduce a note of tragedy into the series, compared with which the supplications for pity and the lamentations that are the stock-in-trade of the conventional sonneteers sound very hollow and insincere.

A genuine friendship such as that celebrated by Shakespeare is nearly always based upon reciprocal admiration, together with a readiness to make allowances on the part of the elder for the younger. When Samuel Johnson, as he often did, declared to James Boswell that he loved him, there was much to admire on both sides, but the great doctor must have known that there were aspects of Bos's character he could not admire. The relationship between the poet Gray and his young Swiss friend Bonstetten seems to have been of much the same character. And Beeching,[1] who cites it as a striking parallel to the friendship revealed in the *Sonnets,* gives extracts from Gray's letters which express Shakespeare's attitude with truly astonishing similarity. For example, 'It is impossible with me to dissemble with you; such as I am I expose my heart to your view, nor wish to conceal a single thought from your penetrating eyes.' And when in absence he writes, 'My life now is but a conversation with your shadow,' he persuades us that Shakespeare spoke the simple truth when he wrote the letter we label Sonnet 43.

But the young Friend had his faults, and the fault that gave most trouble to the Poet was wantonness; a fault to which young men are prone, as Boswell certainly was and Bonstetten also, to judge from Gray's warning against the temptations his good looks laid him open to. But a young gentleman at the time of Elizabeth and James was conscious of fewer inhibitions than a Swiss Protestant, or a Scot having to behave more or less respectably in Georgian England (whatever he might do in Edinburgh). And the word 'lascivious' is twice used of the Friend in the *Sonnets,* while the trouble it led Shakespeare into will have to be considered later when we come to deal with the problem of the Dark Woman.

But had the boy not been admirable in other respects, Shakespeare could not have continued to praise him in 126 sonnets. Nor is it likely the Friend would have accepted this iteration of praise had he not enjoyed receiving it.

> Being fond on praise, which makes your
> praises worse

says the Poet at 84. 14, reproaching him for enjoying the flattery of others. That he gave his Poet a portrait of himself is sufficient indication that he was fond. Is it not probable, also, if not certain, that he was proud to claim the friendship of a leading poet and dramatist of the day? The whole tenour of the *Sonnets* goes to prove that, at any rate for most of the period they cover, they celebrate 'the marriage of true [i.e. mutually affectionate] minds'.

Yet there are two features in this particular friendship which differentiate it from the parallels just cited. In the first place both partners to it were Elizabethans. Perhaps the best thing said upon this aspect comes from the most learned of eighteenth-century editors of Shakespeare, Edmund Malone, who in reply to a stupid note by Steevens upon sonnet 20 wrote:

> Such addresses to men, however indelicate, were customary in our author's time and neither imported criminality, nor were esteemed indecorous. To regulate our judgement of Shakespeare's poems by the modes of modern times, is surely as unreasonable as to try his plays by the rules of Aristotle.

That leaves nothing more to be said on this topic, certainly not by a modern critic less learned in Elizabethan manners than Malone.

The other feature which distinguishes this pair of friends from any other known to history is the extent of the gap between their personalities. I am not thinking at the moment of differences of rank or of the difference, spoken of in chapter 2, between the pebble and the clod, so much as of the gulf that divides one of the greatest of human imaginations from his young Friend who, whatever intellectual gifts he possessed, must have been intellectually and emotionally quite commonplace in comparison. How much did his adored Bonstetten understand or enter into the mind of the poet Gray? Still less could the Friend have fathomed the far greater spirit that brooded over him. Such spiritual disparities are often fraught with tragic issues. The love which a Shakespeare or a Beethoven lavishes upon the object of his devotion is accepted by the beloved as a matter of course, as a tribute due to the value of his personality, though that value is largely if not wholly the creation of the worshipper's imagination. And tragedy comes when the youth gets tired of adulation, or finds another adorer, or—as happened, I believe, in this case at the end—just grows up while the worshipper grows old.

Turn now for a time from the relations between Poet and Friend to what we can otherwise glean about the personality and status of the latter. First of all he was, of course, very handsome; it is a theme upon which the Poet plays a hundred variations, without however giving us many particulars, so that there is little to get hold of if one is seeking to identify him. From sonnet 20 we learn that his beauty was of a feminine cast and elsewhere that, in keeping with this, he was endowed with a delicate complexion. This is specially insisted upon in 99 which compares his breath also to the scent first of violets and then of roses. That same sonnet has, too, the line

> And buds of marjoram had stol'n thy hair.

This is generally understood as a reference to colour, and Beeching with a bunch of half-opened marjoram blooms before him defines the colour as that of the pigment 'brown madder'. But, as l. 14 of the sonnet makes clear, it is scent ('sweet') as well as colour that Shakespeare has in mind throughout, and since marjoram is noted especially as an aromatic herb, used in the making of scents of various kinds, H. C. Hart was surely right in thinking that Shakespeare was speaking of perfume. Yet he may well have been thinking of colour, too. If, for example, the boy was William

Herbert, he may have resembled his uncle Sir Philip Sidney whom Aubrey describes as 'extremely beautifull' with hair 'a dark ambor colour'.[2] Finally, 'buds', while an apt description of the close curls shown in all the representations of Herbert we possess, seems ill-suited to the long ringlets of Southampton. Beyond these hints there is little else to help us in the way of personal description.

More can, I think, be gathered about the youth's rank or social status. That he belonged to a much higher class than the Poet's can hardly be reasonably denied, though many critics have denied it. The importance attached to the young man's perpetuating his stock by begetting an heir is almost enough by itself to indicate high rank. And when Shakespeare writes

> Be as thy presence is gracious and kind

he is assuredly speaking of a nobleman. We do not normally describe the bearing of a commoner as 'gracious' or refer to his company as his 'presence', a word particularly associated with persons who hold court and are besieged by suitors.

Sonnets 36 and 37 again cannot be rightly understood unless we assume a considerable difference in rank between the two persons concerned. In 36 the Poet confesses to some fault, possibly a piece of gaucherie,[3] which he feels will make it awkward for the young man to admit acquaintance with him publicly. He therefore humbly suggests that they shall part company for a while, and pretend not to know each other if they chance to meet:

> I may not ever more [any longer]
>   acknowledge thee,
> Lest my bewailéd guilt should do thee shame;
> Nor thou with public kindness honour me,
> Unless thou take that honour from thy name.

And in the next sonnet he takes comfort in the thought that, even if separated from his Friend, the love they bear each other, or at least he bears him, enables him to imagine himself sharing in the Friend's 'glory':

> For whether beauty, birth, or wealth, or wit,
> Or any of these all, or all, or more,
> Entitled in thy parts do crownéd sit,
> I make my love engrafted to this store,
> So then I am not lame, poor, nor despis'd.

The sense of social inferiority, general throughout the *Sonnets,* is here very evident; and beauty, birth, wealth, and wit[4] make an almost complete catalogue of the advantages of being born a handsome young nobleman.

A number of other terms or references point in the same direction. Sonnet 96, for instance, warning the young man against his besetting sin, exclaims:

> How many gazers mightst thou lead away
>   [i.e. seduce]
> If thou wouldst use the strength of all thy
>   state!

Sonnet 101, again, claims that the Poet's praise will 'much outlive a gilded tomb', which I take to be an allusion to the painted monuments beneath which Elizabethans of distinguished families lay after death. And from 16 and 47 we learn, as already noted, that the young man had had his portrait painted to give away to his friend as persons of fashion were wont, as young Sir Philip Sidney had his painted by Paul Veronese to give away to Hubert Languet. Incidentally, Languet's ecstasies over the portrait were very much in the manner of Shakespeare's in sonnet 46.[5] Then there is the Rival Poet who was clearly courting the Friend not as a lover but as a client for his patronage. Who this other poet may have been and how far he seems to have succeededwill be discussed later. Enough at the moment to remark that it was only noblemen or persons of like distinction who were usually courted for patronage in Shakespeare's day.

When pouring forth these passionate addresses to a handsome young nobleman was Shakespeare, then, only fawning upon him in the hopes of patronage himself? Keats, the poet who is recognised as nearest to Shakespeare in spirit and of all poets understood him best, would have rejected such a notion with scorn, if not with laughter. And a charming book on the *Sonnets* by his friend Charles Armitage Brown[6] devotes a whole chapter to the persuasive thesis 'He was never a flatterer'. A. C. Bradley, again, Shakespeare's most penetrating modern critic, finds it quite impossible to take the language of many of the sonnets as that of interested flattery.[7] Equally positive on the other side was the official biographer of a generation ago who informs us that 'the sole biographical inference which is deducible with full confidence from the *Sonnets* is that at one time in his career Shakespeare like the majority of his craft disdained few weapons of flattery in an endeavour to monopolise the bountiful patronage of a young man of rank'.[8] To me it is a sufficient reply to Lee's aspersion to point out that a poet who rebukes, however gently, a young man for loose living (95, 96), for making himself cheap (69), for his love of flattery (84. 14), for self-satisfaction (67.2), for keeping the said poet up for hours waiting for an appointment he fails to observe (57, 58), is going a queer way about to curry his favour. And we are led to ask whether his biographer, for all his learning in the conceits and sources of these poems, had ever troubled to sit down and think out what Shakespeare was trying to say. For what an attentive reader hears is the voice not of a client craving patronage but of an ardently affectionate uncle or guardian who, while loving the young man for his beauty and grace, both in mind and person, keeps an eye open for his faults, while he has no hesitation in offering advice when he feels it serviceable to do so; much as the humanist Languet does in his affectionate letters to the young and beautiful Philip Sidney: as indeed in that age, when the government of nations rested upon the shoulders of princes and nobles, all men of learning and art who were admitted to their friendship felt it a public duty so to do.

But the friendship of Languet and Sidney differed in two important respects from that of Shakespeare and his young Friend. The humanist-diplomatist, well known in all the courts of Europe, was not likely to labour under any great sense of inferiority in company with a young English knight, even though he were the nephew of the Earl of Leicester. Shakespeare, on the other hand, was a common player, by statute classed with rogues and vagabonds, and it is impossible for us to imagine the social gulf that separated him from anyone of noble rank. A nobleman might honour a famous player with his acquaintance, or even his friendship. Burbadge was so honoured.[9] But neither party would or could ever forget that the one was conferring an honour upon the other; the difference of rank was so absolute that nothing could bridge it. One cannot read the *Sonnets* attentively without realising that the friendship between player and nobleman was nevertheless very real, came indeed to be very intimate. Yet Shakespeare is always aware of the social gulf and not infrequently bewails it, reminds himself of it or is even reminded of it by the Friend. One striking example has already been quoted from sonnets 36 and 37. Still more explicit are the following lines from 87:

> My bonds in thee are all determinate.
> For how do I hold thee but by thy granting?
> And for that riches where is my deserving?

But this consciousness, I feel sure, is what lies behind most of the passages in which the Poet dwells upon his condition: for example,

> Let those who are in favour with their stars
> Of public honour and proud titles boast,
> Whilst I, whom fortune of such triumph bars . . .
>   (25)

> When in disgrace with Fortune and men's
>   eyes
> I all alone beweep my outcast state . . .
>   (29)

> . . . made lame by Fortune's dearest spite . . .
>   (37.3)

> Some glory in their birth . . .
> But these particulars are not my measure . . .
>   [i.e. are not granted me by fortune]
>   (91)

> Alas, 'tis true I have gone here and there
> And made myself a motley to the view . . .
>   (110)

Beeching glosses 'motley to the view' as 'a public jester', and asserts 'there is no reference to the poet's profession' and that 'the sonnet gives the confession of a favourite of society'. He may be right, but he rather wilfully holds that Shakespeare never refers to himself as a player. Of the next line in the same sonnet Tucker writes: 'One does not by that profession [i.e. the profession of an actor] "gore his own thoughts", still less does he "make old offences of affection new".'[10] Yet Shakespeare was playwright as well as actor; may not these words tell us what a dramatist might confess to if he drew upon his own experiences or the characters of those about him in creating his plays? Surely, too, there cannot be any doubt about this, in the very next sonnet,

> O, for my sake do you with Fortune chide,
> The guilty goddess of my harmful deeds,
> That did not better for my life provide
> Than public means, which public manners
>   breeds.
> Thence comes it that my name receives a
>   brand.
>   (111)

Even Edmund Chambers, who finds attempts to interpret the *Sonnets* as 'largely interpreting the obscure by the obscurer still' takes 'brand' to be an allusion to the old tradition of 'the infamous *histrio* of the early Fathers'.[11] And this suggestion is supported by 112, which begins:

> Your love and pity doth th' impression fill
> Which vulgar scandal stamp'd upon my brow;

and so carries on the reference to 'brand' in 111.5.

C. S. Lewis[12] finds it 'hard to think of any real situation in which it [the love Shakespeare expresses] would be natural'. Could any situation render it more natural than this humble adoration of an Elizabethan player for a handsome boy of high rank? Yet even humbler assuredly than this situation demanded. One cannot imagine the boisterous Burbadge, for instance, assuming, still less genuinely possessing, that selflessness, self-abnegation, self-effacement, call it what you will,[13] which both Lever and Lewis find as the unique quality of Shakespeare's *Sonnets*. It was natural, not to the man, but to the poet, and to that particular kind of poet who has no identity apart from the objects he is continually informing and filling, objects that thus become the creatures of his imagination, one of them being in this case the young Friend. To use an expression too often debased as a cliché, he idealised him.[14]

Notes

1. Beeching, *The Sonnets of Shakespeare*, pp. xv, xvi.

2. Aubrey, *Brief Lives*, edited by O. Lawson Dick (1949), p. 278.

3. Cf. lll. 3-4: 'That did not better for my life provide/ Than public means which public manners breeds'—a confession, as I understand it, that a player does not know how to behave in society.

4. I.e. a trained intelligence, or (perhaps) culture.

5. See S. H. Pears, *Correspondence of Sir Philip Sidney and Hubert Languet*, pp. 21, 42, 77; and Dowden, *op. cit.* p. xxii.

6. *Shakespeare's Autobiographical Poems* (1838). Though published fifteen years after Keats's death we may assume it owes much to conversation with him.

7. A. C. Bradley, *Oxford Lectures on Poetry* (1909), p. 332. Cf. his reply to Lee, *ibid.* 312-14.

8. Sidney Lee, *The Life of Shakespeare* (1916), p. 23.

9. See E. K. Chambers, *The Elizabethan Stage* (1923), II, 308.

10. Tucker, *op. cit.* p. XXXV.

11. *Shakespearean Gleanings*, p. 49. See *Cambridge History of English Literature* VI, 'The Puritan Attack upon the Stage', on the practice by puritan writers of quotation from the early fathers when attacking the stage.

12. *English Literature in the Sixteenth Century*, p. 503.

13. Bradley (*op. cit.* p. 334) uses the term 'prostration' but rightly rejects 'humiliation'.

14. Cf. above p. 35 and Rupert Brooke on the Birmingham businessman contemplating whom 'when the mood was on' him, he found 'splendid and immortal and desirable' *(The Collected Poems of Rupert Brooke* (1918), p. liii).

Robert W. Witt (essay date 1979)

SOURCE: "Recognition of Beauty," in *Elizabethan and Renaissance Studies*, Vol. 77: *Of Comfort and Despair: Shakespeare's Sonnet Sequence*, edited by Dr. James Hogg, Institut Für Anglistik Und Amerikanistik der Universitat Salzburg, 1979, pp. 166-77.

[*In the following excerpt, Witt evaluates the sonnets which focus on the poet's "mistress," or "the Dark Lady," as opposed to the poems which center around the poet's male friend. Witt argues that while the earlier poems to "the Friend" demonstrate the ideals of "reasonable love," those to the Dark Lady represent the destructiveness of a lustful, "sensual," and therefore false love. This negative love, Witt asserts, eventually teaches the poet to appreciate all the more the "beauty" of the true love he has for his friend.*]

VIII. Recognition of Beauty (Sonnets 130, 127, 132, 128, 145)

Most commentators seem to agree that Sonnets 127-152 are concerned with the poet's mistress rather than the friend. Also, many agree that the Quarto order of these sonnets is not correct. In fact, more commentators seem to agree on this point regarding the sonnets in this group rather than the sonnets in the first series. The general reaction to these sonnets is that they should tell a story of attraction, disillusionment, and remorse. J. W. Lever thinks that the "lighter eulogies of the Mistress" should begin the series followed by the "Will" sonnets and then the sonnets of "remorse and atonement which seem the only possible ending to the story."[1] Edward Hubler maintains that "if the sonnets are arranged in the order of the events of an ill-starred amour (compliments, invitations to love, consummation, joy, weariness, rejection) it will be found that the sonnets fall nicely into place and that no poem is left over."[2] James Winny has the opinion that a case for rearrangement of the poems should have "the object of clarifying the development of the lover's self-awareness." The groups then would be determined by "the extent of the speaker's respect for the lady and the sharpness of his moral perception. . . ."[3]

Arranged in such a manner, the sonnets in this series would represent the opposite idea of those in the first series and thus would serve to depict the opposite of the reasonable love of the first series. Numerous commentators have seen at least something of this distinction between the two series and several maintain that to distinguish the two kinds of love is indeed Shakespeare's purpose in the two series. Rafael Koskimies, for instance, says that the sonnets to the dark lady "signify the other end of the scale—the phenomenon of love Platonists call 'sensual love.' "[4] The sonnets to the young man, of course, signify reasonable love. Northrop Frye sees the same distinction. To him the sonnets to the friend tell "a 'high' story of devotion, in the course of which the poet discovers that the reality of his love is the love itself rather than anything he receives from the beloved."[5] The two groups, furthermore, present "a contrast of two opposed attitudes to love . . . ," and the mistress is "an incarnation of desire rather than love. . . ."[6]

In stage four the poet apparently alluded to a false woman with whom he had been involved during a period of absence from the friend and with whom the friend also became involved. She represented a different kind of love from that which the poet shared with the friend, and in this experience the poet realized more fully the worth of the friend and of the love which the friend represents. The poet also realized that what he felt for the woman was but a madding fever. But the woman also became the trial or test of the poet's love for the friend in that stage when the friend apparently also became involved with her. The poet, of course, endured the trial successfully and never thought of renouncing the friendship but excused the friend and, ironically, was made more aware of the inward beauty of the friend because of the involvement. The friend was truly repentant which reveals the beauty of his soul and the depth of his love for the poet. The mistress, moreover, was the aggressor, not the friend; thus the poet exonerated the friend and saw him more clearly as the Ideal. Throughout this group of poems in the fourth stage the poet shows his awareness that the friendship or reasonable love is greater and of more worth than the kind of love represented by the woman.

In the second series then Shakespeare develops the episode more fully to make clearer the distinction between the two kinds of love, and the distinction is ultimately the difference between comfort and despair. The poet has been led in the first series upward achieving finally sovereign happiness through his love for the friend. Now Shakespeare dramatizes the poet's descent into despair because of sensual love. The first stage in both series is similar—recognition of beauty. But only the first stages are similar; thereafter the two series go in completely different directions. The first stage, of course, is crucial. The lover may through the exercise of reason ascend the ladder to the highest plane, or he may through following the appetite descend into frustration and despair. In the first series the poet recognizes the beauty of the friend but exercises reason in the first stage and thus becomes an example of Bembo's ideal older lover:

> . . . if they [older men] be inflamed with beautie, and to it bend their coveting, guided by reasonable choice, they bee not deceived, and possesse beautie perfectly, and therefore throughthe possessing of it, alwaies goodnesse ensueth to them: because beautie is good, and consequently the true love of it is most good and holy, and evermore bringeth forth good fruites in the soules of them, that with the bridle of reason restraine the ill disposition of sense. . . .
>
> (Bk. IV, p. 596)

In the second series, however, the poet is an example of one who is "inflamed with beautie" but who does not "with the bridle of reason restraine the ill disposition of sense. . . ."

At first the poet seems to be following Bembo's advice, and he enjoys the beauty of the woman much in the way Bembo suggests. In Book IV Bembo explains that the lover should enjoy the beauty of the beloved through the senses of sight and hearing because they are the ministers of reason:

> Let him lay aside therefore the blinde judgement of the sense, and enjoy with his eyes ye brightnesse, the comelinesse, the loving sparkels, laughters, gestures, and all the other pleasant furnitures of beautie: especially with hearing the sweetnesse of her voice, the tunablenesse of her wordes, the melody of her singing and playing on instruments. . . .
>
> (pp. 604-605)

In the poems of this first group the poet appears to be enjoying the beauty of the woman in just those ways.

Sonnet 130 seems an appropriate poem to begin this section because Shakespeare accomplishes at least two purposes with it. He shows that the poet is "inflamed" with the beauty of the woman, and he again makes clear that he is not writing a Petrarchan sequence. Many, of course, have observed that this sonnet satirizes the conventional description of the Petrarchan mistress. It may, in fact, be a direct response to the seventh poem in Watson's *Passionate Centurie of Love*.[7] If so, then Shakespeare no doubt regarded that poem as the epitome of the Petrarchan convention. But Shakespeare's primary purpose in satirizing the convention is perhaps to point up the idea that he is not writing a Petrarchan sequence. In the first series the poet was careful to point out that his beloved was not the false, painted beauty of the Petrarchan poets, and here he again makes clear that the beloved, this time a woman, is something other than the conventional beauty of the Petrarchan poets. The three quatrains all elaborate on this idea. The woman's eyes are not like the sun, nor are her lips red as coral. She is, furthermore, brunette rather than blonde, the conventional beauty. Some perfumes are more delightful than the woman's breath, and music is more pleasing than her voice. In short, she is a woman, not a goddess.

As in the first series, Shakespeare implies that such extravagant comparisons obscure rather than reveal the beauty of the subject. A woman so described appears false; thus the poet will describe his mistress realistically as a woman, not as something never seen on land or sea. As suggested, though, the (perhaps) main purpose in satirizing the convention is to make clear the distinction between the conventional Petrarchan sequence and the poems which are to follow in this series. In the first series the poet was concerned with reasonable love rather than the physical desire of the Petrarchan poets. In this series he is concerned with physical desire, but with a difference. The love of the Petrarchan poets was unrequited, and the despair which they express results from not possessing the mistress. Shakespeare does not intend to deal with unrequited love; he intends to dramatize the despair which results from possessing the mistress. In other words, he intends to represent the neo-Platonic opposite of reasonable love, sensual love.

The poet certainly establishes in this poem that he is attracted to the woman or, as Bembo says, inflamed with her beauty. He does not mean for the description to deprecate her. She is not unattractive, at least not as the poet sees her now, but she is human. The portrait is intended as a compliment, of course, as the poet insists throughout the sequence that extravagant praise tends to obscure the beauty of the subject. He tells us in the couplet that she is beautiful to him:

> And yet by heaven I think my love as rare
> As any she belied with false compare.

She is as beautiful as any woman misrepresented through extravagant, and hence false, comparisons.

In 127 the poet continues to praise the beauty of his mistress and to point up the difference between her and the conventional Petrarchan mistress. Formerly, he says, black was not thought beautiful or, if so, was not called beautiful. Now, however, black is the heir by succession of beauty, and what was formerly called beautiful (blonde beauty) is "slander'd with a bastard shame. . . ." He explains in the second quatrain why this has come to be:

> For since each hand hath put on Nature's power,
> Fairing the foul with Art's false borrow'd face,
> Sweet Beauty hath no name, no holy bower,
> But is profan'd, if not lives in disgrace.

Since everyone now through the use of cosmetics and other artificial means tries to appear fair (blonde) but succeeds only in looking false and artificial, true blonde beauty has fallen in disgrace and is no longer considered beautiful. Because there are so many false blondes, all are considered to be so. The poet ordinarily associates painting with eloquent or extravagant praise; he, thus, may be attacking the Petrarchan poets here also. Since the Petrarchan poets have represented their mistresses as blonde but have made them appear false and ridiculous by the use of extravagant comparisons, all blonde beauty has suffered and fallen into disrepute. The poet explains in the sestet that such is the reason he has chosen a dark mistress or the reason he pictures the mistress as dark. She is not false; she is not a Petrarchan mistress.

The sestet also emphasizes that the poet is quite taken with the beauty of the mistress:

> Therefore my mistress' eyes are raven black,
> Her brow so suited, and they mourners seem
> At such who not born fair no beauty lack,
> Slandering creation with a false esteem:
> Yet so they mourn becoming of their woe,
> That every tongue says beauty should look so.

The mistress's eyes and brow appear as mourners dressed in black. The poet then gives the idea another turn. They are mourning for those who were not born blonde but who have made themselves appear so and thus slander nature. Yet her black eyes and brow are so charming that everyone now says that she is the example of true beauty. She, in other words, is at least partly responsible that black is now "beauty's successive heir. . . ."

Perhaps Shakespeare chose to emphasize the eyes of the mistress in pointing out how she differs from the conventional beauty because Castiglione advocates black eyes. In Book III of *The Courtier* the Lord Julian explains that the eyes are "a guide in love, especially if they have a good grace and sweetnesse in them, blacke, of a cleare and sightly blackenesse" (p. 525). At any rate, in 132 the poet again concentrates on the eyes of the mistress and continues the mourner image of 127 but gives it yet another turn:

> Thine eyes I love, and they, as pitying me,—
> Knowing thy heart torment me with disdain—
> Have put on black, and loving mourners be,
> Looking with pretty ruth upon my pain.

The poet is attracted to the woman's eyes not only because they are beautiful but also because they look on him with pity knowing that the heart disdains him. This is the reason that they seem to be mourning. The poet suffers pain because at this point his love is unrequited. Perhaps the poet realizes that the look of pity in the woman's eyes may be an indication of hope for him. The Lord Julian explains in Book III of *The Courtier* that the eyes "oftentimes declare with more force what passi there is inwardly, than can the tongue, or letters, or messages," and later that through the eyes a person "may see as farre as the hart" (pp. 524, 525). Thus the poet may be encouraged by the woman's eyes even though her heart still, seemingly at least, does not admit him.

The woman's eyes, at any rate, are her most attractive feature as the poet says later in the poem. The morning sun does not become the grey skies of dawn better nor the evening star "Doth half that glory to the sober west" as the eyes become her face. It is, of course, the "mourning eyes" which so become her face, and the poet hopes that her heart will also mourn for him:

> Oh, let it then as well beseem thy heart
> To mourn for me, since mourning doth thee grace,
> And suit thy pity like in every part.

Since mourning causes your eyes to be beautiful (both that they are black and that they look with compassion on me), let your heart also have compassion and dress it appropriately so that you will be consistent in every part—you will be compassionate in every part and you will be beautiful in every part. The poet will then more firmly assert that black is now "beauty's successive heir":

> Then will I swear Beauty herself is black,
> And all they foul that thy complexion lack.

When the woman becomes beautiful not only in appearance but also in her heart, then the poet will swear rather than merely state that she represents the height of beauty and all who are not like her are ugly and detestable. Complexion implies both coloring and disposition;[8] thus she must be both beautiful in appearance and compassionate by nature. Others to be considered beautiful must be like her in both respects.

Thus far the poet has followed Bembo's advice and has admired the woman with his eyes. In 128 he seems to be following the advice even further and enjoys her beauty through the sense of hearing as she plays a musical instrument. She is his music, and his ear is confounded (amazed) when she plays music on "that blessèd wood. . . ." The poet's primary intention in this sonnet, though, is not merely to admire the woman as she plays the instrument but to ask for a kiss, and he neatly uses the situation as a basis for that plea. He envies the jacks "that nimble leap/ To kiss the tender inward of thy hand. . . ." His lips, though, should be given that privilege and would be most happy if they were:

> To be so tickled they would change their state
> And situation with those dancing chips
> O'er whom thy fingers walk with gentle gait,
> Making dead wood more blest than living lips.

His lips would willingly become like dead wood and literally would change positions with the keys if they could have the pleasure of kissing her fingers. In the couplet the poet uses logic to advance his plea:

> Since saucy jacks so happy are in this,
> Give them thy fingers, me thy lips to kiss.

Grant me a greater privilege than the keys enjoy—allow me to kiss your lips.

The neo-Platonists, of course, allowed kissing as Bembo explains in Book IV of *The Courtier*. In order to please her lover the woman, he says, "may also lawfully and without blame come to kissing. . . ." This is lawful because, he continues, "the reasonable lover woteth well, that although the mouth be a parcell of the bodie, yet is it an issue for the wordes, that be the interpreters of the soule, and for the inwarde breath, which is also called the soule." Thus "a kisse may be saide to be rather a coupling together of the soule, than of the body" (p. 607). So the poet may still be following the course of reasonable love in desiring a kiss from the woman. Kissing, however, is dangerous for the sensual lover as Bembo warns in the same passage: "For since a kisse is a knitting together both of bodie and soule, it is to bee feared, lest the sensuall lover will be more enclined to the part of the bodie, than of the soule" (p. 607). The poet in this poem may be inclining more toward sensual love than reasonable love. The poem seems at least to suggest that he is as he wishes to kiss the "tender inward" of her hand and that his lips would be "so tickled" as the keys. This is, after all, the crucial first stage in the relationship, the stage in which the lover can incline in either direction. The poet has thus far been attracted by the woman but has admired or enjoyed her beauty only through the sight and hearing, the proper ways for the lover who is guided by reason. In this poem, though, he seems to be inclining in the other direction and longing to possess her beauty as a sensual lover. The poem thus serves as a transition into the next section where the poet indeed becomes the sensual lover, forsaking reason altogether. The poem also begins to point up the difference between the two relationships. In the first stage of the friendship the poet greatly admired the beauty of the friend and enjoyed that beauty through the senses of sight and hearing (Music to hear), yet he never expressed any desire to touch the friend or to kiss his hand or lips. This poem then becomes the turning point in the relationship with the woman. The poet rather than exercising reason as he did in the relationship with the friend begins to incline toward sensual love and the subjugation of reason.

If 145 is by Shakespeare and if it is intended as a part of the sequence, it should be placed at this point. The poet continues to concentrate on the woman's lips as in the previous poem but here shifts his thought from kissing her lips to the words which her lips utter:

> Those lips that Love's own hand did make
> Breath'd forth the sound that said 'I hate'
> To me that languish'd for her sake. . . .

The woman has been portrayed in Sonnet 132 as disdaining the poet, and certainly he could be thought of as languishing as he asks her to have pity on him. For these reasons, at least, 145 is appropriate here, but it also represents a turning point. The woman in this poem does apparently show compassion for her lover:

> But when she saw my woeful state,
> Straight in her heart did mercy come
> Chiding that tongue that ever sweet
> Was us'd in giving gentle doom,
> And taught it thus anew to greet:
> 'I hate' she alter'd with an end
> That follow'd it as gentle day
> Doth follow night, who like a fiend
> From heaven to hell is flown away:
> 'I hate' from hate away she threw,
> And sav'd my life, saying—'Not you'.

The woman still disdaining the poet and on the verge of denying any feeling of love for him suddenly takes pity on him and changes her mind in mid-sentence. Her statement implies, of course, that she is now willing to give in to his pleas, and so the poem also serves as a transition to the next section.

The poet has admired the woman's beauty, but whether consciously or no has come to desire the physical possession of her beauty. She, moved by his suffering, has given in to his importunings and has indicated a willingness to return his love in the way that he wishes. This relationship, consequently, cannot ascend to a higher level. The poet after being "inflamed with beautie," does not "with the bridle of reason restraine the ill disposition of sense. . . ." No goodness then can ensue from this relationship; it can lead only to despair.

Notes

[1] *The Elizabethan Love Sonnet*, 2nd ed. (London: Methuen & Co., Ltd., 1966), p. 174.

[2] *The Sense of Shakespeare's Sonnets* (Princeton: Princeton University Press, 1952), p. 38.

[3] *The Master-Mistress: A Study of Shakespeare's Sonnets* (New York: Barnes & Noble, 1968), p. 92.

[4] "The Question of Platonism in Shakespeare's Sonnets," *Neuphilologische Mitteilungen*, 71 (1970), 268.

[5] "How True a Twain," *The Riddle of Shakespeare's Sonnets*, ed. Edward Hubler (New York: Basic Books, 1962), p. 38.

[6] *Ibid.*, pp. 51-52.

[7] Patrick Cruttwell, *The Shakespearian Moment: And Its Place in the Poetry of the 17th Century*, Modern Library Edition (New York: Random House, 1964), pp. 18-19.

[8] Ingram and Redpath, p. 304.

David K. Weiser (essay date 1987)

SOURCE: "Awareness Lost," in *The Mind in Character: Shakespeare's Speaker in the Sonnets*, University of Missouri Press, 1987, pp. 139-85.

[*In the following excerpt, Weiser briefly contrasts the idealized love of the sonnets in what he calls the "Fair Youth section" with the "destructive" and "distressing" sex of the "Dark Lady" section. Weiser then looks more closely at the relationship between the poet and the Dark Lady, and argues that initially at least, the Dark Lady sonnets reveal more about the poet's own selfish needs than about the lady herself.*]

To separate the last twenty-eight sonnets from all the others is a vulnerable but by no means arbitrary decision. It is impossible to prove that sonnets 127-54 do revolve on one sustained relation without obtaining a signed, notarized statement by the poet, yet the traditional view that these sonnets deal with a "Dark Lady," real or imaginary, has much to recommend it. Eight of these sonnets do explicitly address a woman, while many others refer to feminine features, and five mention her emblematic coloring. In the absence of contrary evidence, it is reasonable to assume that the other poems continue to address the same person. Sonnet 144 directly supports such an assumption: "Two loves I have of comfort and despair." And sonnets 133 and 134 draw the same love triangle. Therefore, the loves, the "man right fair" and the "woman coloured ill," may be regarded as the only auditors addressed by Shakespeare's speaker. They define two distinct areas of experience, creating two discrete bodies of poetry. As Hyder Rollins points out, the theme of time that has been so pervasive throughout the sequence does not appear after 126.[1] It should be added that two other themes, ideal love and poetic immortality, are also absent from sonnets 127-54. Just as the speaker never returns to the procreation theme after sonnet 17, he also drops the basic contrast of natural process against eternal love and poetry, establishing a thematic distinction that corresponds to the change in the quality of his dialogue.

The twenty-eight poems addressed to a woman maintain a single, nearly obsessive train of thought and in that respect resemble the opening group of sonnets 1-17. An exact contrast can be drawn here: Shakespeare's sonnets begin with an insistence on nature and fertility, but end by reiterating the opposite themes—sterility and frustration. The two smaller groups of the 1609 sequence thus define antithetical extremes. Just as continence is the speaker's main target in the Procreation group, promiscuity becomes his subject in the closing section. The difference, however, is more than thematic because he has by now abandoned sententious preaching and is concerned with the dramatic rendering of his own experience. Although his depiction of destructive sex might be said to confirm conventional morality, what most impresses us in these sonnets is the authenticity with which they represent one man's ordeal. This quality made the Dark Lady sonnets repugnant to Victorian taste, but questions of morality, however we respond to them, are not crucial to these poems. Our interest focuses on the speaker, his inner life, and the modes of self-expression that he develops out of a new, often distressing liaison. The ideal love that had evolved around the figure of the youth now disappears as completely as the ideal of procreation had vanished before.

The last group of sonnets is no less distinctive in tone than in its thematic range. Again, we observe a gradual development in which the speaker discovers and defines himself through interaction with the object of his love. Dividing these sonnets into soliloquies and dialogues, we find that only eighteen out of twenty-eight actually address the woman by using various forms of "thou" or "you." Dialogue has fallen to a lower proportion than in the Fair Youth section, suggesting that the decrease will be accompanied by a lessening in the intensity of dialogue. Even those sonnets that directly address the mistress fail to establish anything like the closely feltreciprocity of an "I/ thou" relation. She remains remote from the speaker, alien to what he considers his best self. Her alleged lack of integrity or moral "worth" may well reflect the speaker's own dissatisfaction with what he has become. Such a sense of personal limitation, if not failure, is most clearly defined in the ten soliloquies. Addressing himself, as well as personifications of love and of his soul, the speaker probes the familiar yet unresolved questions of identity and self-knowledge. In addressing the young man, as we have seen, he underwent a process of testing and reaffirming the personal values that hinge on ideal love. Now, with that form of love entirely excluded, he must pursue some other, equally stable basis on which to build his poetic structures of personal affirmation. A comparative reading of these sonnets will determine whether such an alternative has been found.

. . . . .

II. Initial Dialogues

It would be oversimplifying to call sonnets 1-126 a dialogue of comfort, as the idealized youth cannot sustain the image that is imposed upon him. But one need have little hesitation in viewing sonnets 127-54 as a dialogue of despair. If the youth has disappointed the speaker by resembling the festering lilies of 94, the woman who is seen as merely a "weed" offers less joy and a deeper sense of disillusion. Just as the soliloquies of this section show a reduced depth of introspection, the dialogues indicate that the essential process of interrelation is no longer viable. Like the soliloquies again, the dialogues addressed to a woman have a definite pattern of distribution. Sonnet 128 stands apart as an introduction, while the other dialogues fall into three consecutively numbered groups: 131-37, 139-43, and 146-52. Each of these clusters marks a phase in the overall pattern of the speaker's decline. The Dark Lady dialogues are even more emphatic than the soliloquies in their exposure of a gradual weakening. The speaker, having grown from a detached observer of nature to an active participant in the experience of ideal love, reaches an impasse in his continued attempt to define himself. His ability to sustain a relation of dialogue will be impaired, not by the partner he blames but by his own failure to achieve a satisfactory understanding of himself.

The opening of sonnet 128 is distinguished by its elaborately subordinated syntax. Lines 1-8 compose a suspended sentence that can be typographically arranged:

> How oft, when thou my music play'st
>   Upon that blessed wood
>   Whose motion sounds with thy sweet
> fingers
>   When thou gently sway'st the wiry concord
>   That my ear confounds,
> Do I envy those jacks
>   That nimbly leap
>   To kiss the tender inward of thy hand,
>   Whilst my poor lips,
>   Which should that harvest reap,
>   At the wood's boldness
>   By thee blushing stand.

This outline of parallel structure calls attention to the poem's extremely artificial language. Although such a style conforms to Elizabethan taste, the pattern seems rigid and monotonous for Shakespeare. Within eight lines we find three temporal clauses ("when" twice and "whilst") and four relative clauses that begin with "whose," "that" twice, and "which." The total effect is one of strained, mechanical ingenuity. Furthermore, the repeated couplings of adjective and noun reinforce the impression that the poet (perhaps imitating his lady at the keyboard) is plodding through a five-finger exercise; "blessed wood," "sweet fingers," "wiry concord," "tender inward," and "poor lips" all are placed within the octet. However well she may perform on the virginal, his verbal playing remains uninspired.

The opening line suggests this analogy and prepares us for the mannerism wit that follows: "Thou, my music, music play'st." At the center of the poem's conceit is the lady who is identified with the music she performs. She serves as the subject of the speaker's praise, "my music," and the object of her own performance. The "jacks" of the keyboard instrument provide another opportunity for facile punning, with the nursery-song echo of jacks being "nimble" contributing to a gamelike atmosphere. Personification is carried on relentlessly in the speaker's description of his envious lips, as well as the "dancing chips" or "saucy jacks" and the lady's fingers that "walk with gentle gait." But no sense of personality or of personal relation emerges from this series of compliments and conceits. The lady functions only as a stimulus to the speaker's hearing and his wit. Beneath his polite flattery lies a scarcely concealed concern for his own pleasures and an indifference to the other's experience. Thus in the couplet he proposes dividing her between himself and his wooden rivals: "Give them thy fingers, me thy lips to kiss." The division is facetious, just as the entire sonnet attempts to be. But it is precisely this evasion of serious contact that limits dialogue in the Dark Lady sequence. One has only to recall the last line of sonnet 20, where a comparable division appears: "Mine be thy love, and thy love's use their treasure." There the speaker had asked for no less than a full interchange of affection, with merely sexual "use" reserved for women. The refusal to grant women the same seriousness accorded to his friend underlies sonnet 128 and the dialogues it introduces.

Contrasting 128 with an analogous sonnet will further illustrate the new, more restricted relation. Sonnet 8 is the only other that absorbs music into its central theme: "music to hear, why hear'st thou music sadly?" The similarity is enhanced as both opening lines turn "music" into an epithet for the person addressed. The youth, however, is told to listen, enjoy, and understand what he hears. Although the music will modulate to yet another image of procreation, the speaker is still concerned with what the other person thinks and feels. Correspondingly, the youth can be said to establish his own presence in the text as a real, contradictory human being. That he is chastised for self-love, instead receiving empty compliments, only increases his worth in our eyes. We are led to share what the speaker discovers in music's "speechless song," the fear that "thou single wilt prove none." No such involvement is conveyed by the speaker's address to the "thou" of sonnet 128. The poem serves as an overture to all these dialogues by suggesting that the speaker's interest in the woman is confined to her influence on himself.

Sonnets 131-36, the first continuum of dialogue, set forth the initial phase of the speaker's relation to his mistress. Polite compliment still abounds here but does not conceal intermittent feelings of resentment. The tendency to avoid direct and intimate encounter manifests itself in the "triangle" situation that is elaborated in 133 and 134 as well as in the puns on "Will" in 135 and 136. Both pairs of sonnets allow a third party to intervene between the lovers; the youth and "Will" (who is not simply the poet) are impediments to a stable union of "I" and "thou." Even in sonnets 131 and 132, where the lovers are alone, the speaker shows exaggerated interest in the opinions of those who criticize his lady: "some say . . . / Thy face hath not the pow'r to make love groan." He can reply to the doubters only by swearing, but in 131 he swears "to myself alone," and in 132 he promises to refute them only on condition that the lady show him her favor: "Then will I swear beauty herself is black, / And all they foul that thy complexion lack." Such an urge to verify the lady's beauty by making a formal declaration is a peculiar feature of these dialogues. The speaker's aim is really to convince himself by means of a legally binding statement to others. He never considers what the "thou" feels and whether she requires such testimony. By the end of the sequence, in sonnet 152, he will confess to a lack of good faith in all his swearing: "For all my vows are oaths but to misuse thee." The absence of real affection can be traced throughout these poems in the very texture of their dialogue.

In sonnet 131 the speaker admits for the first time that he is dissatisfied with the beloved: "Thou art tyrannous, so as thou art." The opening line and its repetition of "thou art" set up the basic structure of the dialogue in which the speaker probes for the lady's essence, what she truly is. By calling her "tyrannous," he praises ambiguously: she has the cruelty that belongs to the courtly-love tradition but not the beauty that should go with it. She is set apart from those "whose beauties proudly make them cruel." The speaker then employs the formula "thou art" to justify his continued love for one who is neither fair nor kind: "to my dear doting heart / Thou art the fairest and most precious jewel." The lady is therefore one thing to the impartial world and another in the speaker's view. No attempt to ease the contradiction is made; nor is the overfamiliar jewel metaphor helpful in giving poetic force to the speaker's subjective feelings. Instead of pursuing his argument, he tells of an imaginary debate with his lady's detractors. For unspecified reasons, he dares not defy them openly and swears to himself "to say they err." He reinforces his case by invoking "a thousand groans but thinking on thy face." Since such a private demonstration will convince no one, its only function is to prove the speaker's faithfulness. Yet there is something suspicious about these quasi-legal proceedings in which he reiterates to himself what he cannot maintain in public. His referring twice to "thy face" suggests an unwillingness to accept the "thou" as a person rather than a collection of specific parts or attributes. Whatever the woman is, she should be more than a face. The other attributes mentioned in this sonnet, "thy black" and "thy deeds," only strengthen our suspicion that the speaker's attitude toward her is far less enthusiastic than he pretends. His personified groans are said to testify that "thy black is fairest in my judgment's place," but the compliment could reflect his own defective judgment rather than the lady's beauty. Any doubts as to the highly critical perspective in which he sees and judges her are finally dispelled by the couplet:

> In nothing art thou black save in thy deeds,
> And thence this slander as I think proceeds.

Using "black" here in its pejorative sense undercuts the speaker's previous defense of his lady's coloring. Again, since the significance of "thy deeds" outweighs that of "thy face," it is evident that all the compliments (if such they really were) have been nullified.

Sonnet 131, then, addresses the lady directly but does not truly function as a dialogue. The speaker seems to be thinking aloud about his mistress, evaluating her much as one would appraise the "precious jewel" to which she is likened. He is nearly oblivious to her living presence, and when he does acknowledge it the results are bitterly ironic. He resorts to the interjection "yet in good faith" to prepare her for the unpleasant things that supposedly "some say." But good faith is the very element missing in this interrelation. By choosing the phrase he attempts to compensate for what he senses to be a tangible lack of respect for the woman. The speaker thus protests too much, leaving the inescapable impression that the harsh opinions of others are also his own. When he inserts the ingenuous "as I think" in line 14, he is not refuting the "slander" but implicitly defending it. An obvious condescension is shown here, as if the lady were obtuse enough to accept so damning a defense. The dialogue situation could therefore be defined as one of "speaking through" the auditor; the speaker directs his words to her but not his ultimate meanings. The orientation is egocentric in a way the Fair Youth dialogues never were. As a result of the unrealized dialogue, the speaker's self-portrayal also becomes rather shallow. He is condemned to role playing as the conventional lover ruled by his "dear doting heart" and sighing no less than "a thousand groans." It may sound anachronistic to say that Shakespeare's speaker in this section has given us dialogues that are "inauthentic" in an existential sense, but we have already seen how the dialogues involving the youth, no less artificial in their format, achieve a dramatic interdepedence of two people, a "marriage of true minds." In Dark Lady dialogues like sonnet 131, the lovers are never together, although they are alone with each other.

Sonnet 132 continues from its predecessor by performing another anatomy of the "thou." Again, we find "thy face" as well as "eyes" and "complexion." To those purely physical features are added "thy heart" and "thy pity." Nothing is said about the speaker after line 1: "Thine eyes I love, and they, as pitying me." He is presented as merely a victim of the lady's disdain, so that the "I" reappears only in the couplet promising to swear "beauty herself is black." This reticence, combined with an entirely conventionalized representation of the "thou," creates a highly attenuated form of dialogue. It recalls the introductory sonnet 127 by using the conceit of her dark eyes as "mourners." But now the speaker's "pain" (not counterfeit beauty) has made her eyes "put on black, and loving mourners be." An inner division is projected onto the woman. For if her eyes are dark "as pitying me," her heart continues to "torment me with disdain." The main argument is thus a supplication; her heart should "mourn for me, since mourning doth thee grace." The speaker links "mourning" to "morning" by loose association rather than by a pun. At the center of the poem he devises an epic simile: just as the "morning sun" and evening star suitthe beauty of the sky, so "those two mourning eyes become thy face." It is not immediately clear what this "proud compare" has to do with the speaker's request for favor. He connects black (via mourning) with sympathy, so that the mistress whose eyes are charitable should now "suit thy pity like in every part." Not only is the reasoning convoluted, the imagery itself lacks energy:

> And truly not the morning sun of heav'n
> Better becomes the gray cheeks of the east,
> Nor that full star that ushers in the ev'n
> Doth half that glory to the sober west—
> As those two mourning eyes become thy face.

When compared to sonnet 33, "Full many a glorious morning have I seen," 132 reflects a substantial decline of imagination. The "heav'nly alchemy" seen in the earlier poem had an equivalent in the speaker's own tranformation of language through his art. In 132 his vision has subsided from metaphor to meek comparisons. There is but one slight metaphor in the five lines quoted above, "the grey cheeks of the east." The rest is merely the rhetoric of plain statement buttressed by padding modifiers: "The morning sun," "full star," and "sober west." The speaker is no longer an active part of the scene he describes. Instead of integrating nature into his own experience, he conveys an impersonal account of heavenly beauty. The picture is passively recorded, suggesting a familiar source of aesthetic pleasure without making it fully visual. Perhaps the weakness stems from a circularity in the images; no transformation can occur when we see two aspects of the same form, the "cheeks" and "face" of heaven compared to the woman's.

A general tendency has been illustrated here, for these poems are almost totally lacking in nature imagery. It should be remembered that the sonnets began with a vision of physical nature as background to the themes of procreation, ideal love, and poetic eternity. The last sonnet to convincingly invoke the workings of natural process was 104, with its retrospect of "three beauteous springs to yellow autumn turned." Subsequent sonnets anticipate the Dark Lady group by avoiding direct observation of the natural world. After 126, we note only a few images drawn from natural phenomena, and these are always subordinated to the dominant context of human relations. Sonnet 132 departs from this trend by attempting to revive the perspective of natural beauty. What emerges, however, is the type of hollow praise that was ridiculed in sonnets 21 and 130. This mistress's eyes are suddenly like "the morning sun," so that the speaker now resembles the muse "stirred by a painted beauty" to a similarly bombastic style. Perhaps an element of personal concern can be found in the closing injunctions to "let it . . . beseem thy heart" and "suit thy pity." But the couplet betrays the speaker's remote and calculating attitude. He will not swear to the lady's beauty unless she grants him favor; in other words, he will not unconditionally take the first step toward asserting her worth. Even the promised oath is weakened by abstraction and overstatement. Rather than defend the woman, he bypasses her entirely and arrives at the unnecessary generalization that "beauty herself is black." The closing line shies away from direct encounter with the mistress through a process of reversal: "And all they foul that thy complexion lack." Somewhere between the abstract "beauty herself" and the inclusive "all they," the person in question has been ignored. An authentic confrontation of "I" and "thou" has still not taken place.

The remaining sonnets in this first phase are no less disappointing if we look for depth of dialogue. What they do give us is a sketch of the speaker's unresolved attitudes expressing themselves through wit rather than feeling. Sonnets 133 and 134 deal primarily with a situation and only secondarily with the persons who compose it. The same love triangle, or at least a congruent one, had been set out in sonnets 40-42, chiding the friend for the speaker's double betrayal. Now in 133 it is the lady's turn to be blamed, with none of the forgiveness that was so quickly granted to the youth: "Beshrew that heart that makes my heart to groan." The plea of the preceding sonnet has apparently been denied, for there is now a consistency between the lady's heart and her "cruel eye." The first four lines, however, do not even mention her. They speak of "that heart" and "it" rather than "thy heart" and "thou." Impersonal diction also implies the absence of a personal subject in the rhetorical questions of lines 3-4:

> Is't not enough to torture me alone,
> But slave to slavery my sweet'st friend must
>   be?

The actions of torture and enslavement are carried out as if automatically because the speaker's concern lies not with the woman herself but with the consequences of the actions he imputes to her. In quatrain 2 he is forced finally to acknowledge her existence by "thy cruel eye" and then more directly: "And my next self thou harder hast engrossed." But the passive verbs that follow, "I am forsaken" and "thus to be crossed," still exemplify his tendency to avoid contact.

The speaker's central strategy for avoiding dialogue is to portray himself as the victim of a higher force. In grammatical terms, this often means functioning as object rather than as subject. The nominal "I" appears only twice, each time entrapped by passive constructions: "I being pent" as well as "I am forsaken." Such syntax corresponds to the conventional imagery that highlights his weakness and dependency. For example, the causative form "that makes my heart" is combined with the groaning that sonnet 131 had cited as the epitome of love's effects. The "tyrannous" behavior countenanced there is now demonstrated with no apology. Other familiar images that follow from this opening are concentrated in the first quatrain: "wound," "torture," and "slavery." Each prescribes a passive, helpless role for the speaker; it is the syndrome of Petrarchan love, from which the Fair Youth sonnets had been relatively free. All that prevents this dialogue, and several others, from becoming entirely stereotyped is the three-sided relationship. In dramatic terms, the speaker's emphasis has shifted from character to plot, since he, the woman, and the friend are not free to modify their roles. An ironic disparity thus arises, since his images of Petrarchan dependence are very much out of place. This woman's cruelty is not customary chastity but its exact opposite. The "slavery" she provokes is not courtly service but a humiliation shared by the speaker and his friend "whom thou harder hast engrossed."

Sonnet 133 sets the stage and introduces the people of this drama without showing how they will speak to each other, if at all. At its center, the speaker maps out his threefold loss of "myself," "my next self," and "thee." The only escape he can devise is a fantasy derived from poetic convention. He turns the interchange of lovers' hearts into a metaphor of mutual imprisonment:

> Prison my heart in thy steel bosom's ward,
> But then my friend's heart let my poor heart
>   bail.

The "thou" has been reduced to an allegorical symbol; her "steel bosom" differentiates her from the living hearts of the two men. In proposing an exchange, the speaker forgets that as a captive he cannot ransom his fellow prisoner. The unusual inversion in line 10, which is entirely monosyllabic, reflects his uncertainty as to the subject-object relation. We expect "my friend's heart" to perform an action but find it to be an object. Inevitably, there is some confusion; who is bailing out whom"? The second proposal made by the speaker is similarly obscure: "Whoe'er keeps me, let my heart be his guard." He uses "whoe'er" as a means of evading the lady once again. It implies that his love for her is neither lasting nor exclusive. Moreover, "his" could refer ambiguously to "whoe'er" or to the friend. In this confusing array of pronouns, the ostensible idea is that the speaker will function as an intermediary; he will be kept by the lady or "whoe'er" while he keeps his beloved friend. The pattern of possession here is one of three concentric circles, with the speaker's love for his friend as a cell within the larger jail of his own captivity. All his conceits attempt to control imaginatively what is uncontrollable, the lady's sovereignty over him: "Thou canst not then use rigor in my jail." Nevertheless, the couplet returns to inescapable reality:

> And yet thou wilt; for I being pent in thee,
> Perforce am thine, and all that is in me.

This closing stresses the speaker's role as object and victim. Yet it is he who defines the triangle from its focal point, determining what the lady can and cannot do. He takes refuge in his own articulateness, controlling not reality but its verbal representation. In that sense, he dominates the poem and the situation it describes. Not surprisingly, there are seventeen "I" pronouns as opposed to eight references to "thou." The imbalance in quantity suggests an egocentric orientation on the speaker's part. His closing words, "all that is in me," may therefore carry a secondary sense that qualifies their overt surrender of autonomy. All that the speaker has created in this sonnet, even his depiction of the lady's power, belongs to him.

Sonnet 134 opens with a direct link to the situation defined in the previous poem: "So now I have confessed that he is thine." The first-person verb here begins a series that reflects the speaker through the first three lines: "I have confessed," "I myself am mortgaged," "myself I'll forfeit." These verbs progress in their tenses from perfect to present to future, creating a sense of finality and completeness; the main possibilities for the timing of actions have been accounted for. It is virtually the same effect as that of the more compressed sequence in sonnet 129: "had, having, and in quest to have," although three different verbs now are used. The speaker tries to extricate himself from his present captivity by setting up an imaginary future. He will make a forfeit of his own self "so that other mine / Thou wilt restore." He soon realizes that character traits that determine the future make this projected escape impossible: "But thou wilt not . . . / For thou art covetous, and he is kind." The sonnet concludes with another patterned repetition of first-person verbs: "So him I lose . . . Him have I lost." Emphasis has been gained by using the same verb twice while the sequence of tenses has been reversed, moving from present to perfect and excluding the future. The triangular situation attains a timeless stasis when the simple present tense is finally reiterated: "Thou hast both him and me; / He pays the whole; and yet am I not free."

Although the speaker's attention still centers on the situation, he does consider the human factors that keep it in alignment. The underlying metaphor has changed from the jail of 133 to a courtroom in which the lady holds her "bond" or "statute" of beauty against both men. She is represented as a "usurer" rather than merely a "steel bosom," closely corresponding to Shylock in the trial scene of *The Merchant of Venice* when his character has devolved to a mythic stereotype. She, too, is attacked for taking needless advantages by putting forth "all to use." The specific reference here is to the friend, who like Antonio in the play "came debtor for my sake." However, the speaker's own debt to the usuress, and her exploitation of it, do not provoke his complaint. Those two corners of the triangle are presented as accomplished facts, while the friend's involvement is inveighed against. Worst of all, the youth's complicity deprives the speaker of his "comfort." So great is his self-centeredness he displays no more interest in his friend's feelings than in those of his mistress. He assumes that loving her must simply be a punishment for the youth, although he mentions her beauty explicitly. He sees the usury of love as an abuse, even thou this love convention is traditionally beneficent, as in sonnet 6:

> That use is not forbidden usury
> Which happies those that pay the willing loan.

We cannot determine whether the speaker is justified in making his "dark" assertions about the lady. But the formulaic, abstract quality of his thought cannot be denied. His tendency to reduce all three people to one-dimensional figures works against her, since she (however arbitrarily) is given the villain's role. No margin for judgmental error has been provided. The speaker rejects outright the possibility that the "thou" he addresses could be capable of change; nor does it occur to him that his own schematic view of things could be mistaken. Enjoying his narrow certainty, he tries to establish simple facts rather than coming to terms with complex, uncomfortable feelings. There are no questions in this sonnet and no commands; all the sentences are simply declarative. There is no appeal to the two lovers who have betrayed him, only an objective-sounding inventory of events and consequences. The language of the sonnet remains spare and "factual," containing a total of only four adjectives: "free" is repeated as a rhyme word; "kind," with "covetous" as its opposite, reappears in "unkind." Each person has been neatly labeled, the woman being "covetous," the youth "kind," and the speaker "not free." This last modifier, shared by both men, is highlighted by the parallel between the two end-stopped phrases "nor he will not be free" and "and yet am I not free." The lack of adjectives throughout this sonnet reflects the speaker's reluctance to qualify in any way his basic assumptions about the love triangle he has plotted. Although sonnet 134 does grant human motivations to all three people, it reduces them to stereotypes. In following out the ramifications of this scheme, the speaker's imagination is confined to an uncharacteristic rigidity. Figurative language has been harnessed completely to a single "conceit," so that four related terms—"will," "bond," "statute," and "use"—represent the relationship of both men to the lady. No room is left for spontaneous exercise of the imagination, for ornamental or sensuous metaphor. The friend has "surety-like" become the speaker's "debtor," while he is "mortgaged" and "forfeit." His mind is just as tightly "bound" to the scheme he has created, making him the victim not of others' actions but of his own desire to simplify human relations by means of self-fulfilling predictions about them.

In the two "Will" sonnets that continue this initial phase of dialogues, the speaker succeeds brilliantly in avoiding a direct confrontation with the woman. The higher force that he interposes between them is expressed in the various meanings of the word *Will*, until the speaker's identity fades behind a semantic screen. Unlike the pun on "lie" in sonnet 138, no suggestion exists here of any dissatisfaction beneath the surface of cleverness. "Will" is mentioned thirteen times in sonnet 135, six times in 136. Yet the constant equivocations go untouched by any feeling other than wit for wit's sake. Perhaps the imaginative germ for these poems lies in the phrase "mortgaged to thy will" in sonnet 134, where a pun had already combined the legal term with the psychological "will" (volition or power of choice), as well as its slang sense of "sexual organ." Another origin may be the use of "will" and "wilt" as auxiliary verbs in sonnet 133 ("and yet thou wilt") and 134 ("but thou wilt not, nor he will not"), anticipating "wilt thou" in 135. Whatever their immediate source, these two sonnets project the speaker's persistent tendency to escape the consequences of the erotic relationship. This getaway is flawless because its statements are polysemously perverse; they can be variously and endlessly deciphered while the grossly physical sense of "Will" is never far away. For example, sonnet 136 begins by assuaging the lady's conscience, "if thy soul check thee." Its argument depends on the pun "I was thy will / And will thy soul knows is admitted there." Although the primary movement is from the man named "Will" to "will" as a faculty of the soul, we are reminded of the underlying sexual symbolism by the verb "admitted." On other occasions, the physicality is explicit, as in the speaker's request in 135 "to hide my will in thine." Yet even here the secondary, spiritual sense should not be overlooked. The speaker indeed does hide or lose his will in the sense of an ability to make decisions for himself. His identity and the woman's have been submerged in the lowest and most common denominator, so conveniently a homonym for his name. Both sonnets exploit unlimited possibilities for punning, so that the speaker appears a most willing victim. The second sonnet is the weaker; "Will" appears less frequently and with less effect because the puns and equivocations have become familiar. A similar decline occurs in other pairs of sonnets, such as 29 and 30 or 113 and 114, where the second derives from and repeats an initial inspiration.

In this case, the central argument scarcely merits repetition because its implications are damaging to the speaker. In sonnet 135, quatrain 3 demonstrates by analogy that as the sea adds rain to its water, "so thou being rich in will, add to thy will / One will of mine." Although analogies between love and the sea (in terms of infinite extent) need not be derogative, this one is. The "thou" is reduced to elemental nature, after the opening line had already brought her down to the status of anonymous, generalized womanhood: "Whoever hath her wish, thou hast thy will." But the plea for indifference, rather than exclusive love, slights the speaker no less than the woman. In "making addition thus," he surrenders any claims he may have had to an individuality achieved through love. He is content to let her think "all but one, and me in that one will." The second version of this belittling argument is significantly more extreme. The nature imagery, however conventional, is replaced by the simple arithmetic of reduction. The analogy this time takes in lines 7-8 as well as the third quatrain:

> In things of great receipt with ease we prove,
> Among a number one is reckoned none.

The woman therefore corresponds to a thing "of great receipt" while the speaker is merely one "among a number." According to the axiom given here, his love for her adds nothing to her "store." Being "reckoned none," the speaker imputes a loss of value to himself and to the idea of love. When he asks to "pass untold" and pleads "for nothing hold me," his self-annihilation is complete. All that remains of him, at best, is "a something sweet to thee," while the couplet substitutes a name for his actual selfhood: "and then thou lov'st me for my name is Will." This reductive arithmetic needs to be taken seriously, despite the amusingly evasive action of the puns. Nowhere else in the sonnets can Hamlet's words be applied so tellingly: "reason panders will." The application of quantitative terms, together with the sterile imagery, precludes the emotional depth of an "I/thou" relation. Through both sonnets, imperatives abound as the speaker tells his beloved to "add," "think," "swear," and "love." He functions as the commanding subject whereas she, having a "blind soul," is no more than the object of his cajoling. Yet the mask of "Will" has a restrictive influence on the speaker too. He can no longer present himself through an inclusive "I" that organizes his experience directly. He has objectified part of himself as "Will" and is forced to speak in the third person about this new and partial image: "Will will fulfill the treasure of thy love." The triumphant wit of these two sonnets is literally self-defeating. They continue the first phase of dialogues, in which the speaker admits his dependence on the woman, by successfully ignoring all the unwelcome implications of that dependence.

Sonnet 137 ends this cluster of dialogues and marks the speaker's first attempt to define his experience in order to come to terms with it:

> Thou blind fool love, what dost thou to
> mine eyes,
> That they behold and see not what they see?

He has now become aware of the inner contradictions that were implied before. The alteration of beauty, reproved and then condoned in 127, has now begun to cause intense suffering since his eyes "know what beauty is, see where it lies, / Yet what the best is take the worst to be." Beauty, despite the speaker's previous claims, has not really changed; its constant qualities, he admits, have been distorted through his subjective error. Although this new awareness marks a dramatic growth, it is channeled into a highly restrictive scheme. The fault supposedly lies not in the speaker but in Cupid. In effect, using this outmoded personification provides a convenient label for what Jakobson and Jones termed "the malevolent culprit" by whom "the joy was proposed and the bait laid."[8] As in sonnet 129, knowing true love does notprevent one from choosing its counterfeit. As in Ralegh's "A Farewell to false Love," sonnet 137 contains "hooks" that trap the victim. Shakespeare's version, however, internalizes the image: "Why of eyes' falsehood hast thou forged hooks, / Whereto the judgement of my heart is tied?" The fatal link is located between the faculties of sight and judgment, rather than between the external world and himself.

Poetic convention is thus subverted by the speaker's self-anatomy; he presents himself as the object of a mythic, external force. Blaming the "blind fool" Cupid for his own faulty vision, he unwittingly points to the psychological origin of his decline. From the beginning of the sonnets, he had been a reliable observer sketching nature, the youth, and himself with unquestioned accuracy. Now, by calling his own perception into doubt, he undermines the basis on which his understanding of the world depends. The process of seeing, pondering, and making sense of things can no longer function effectively. Sonnet 137, with its repeated rhetorical questions, illustrates the static quality of uncertain perception:

> Why should my heart think that a several
> plot,
> Which my heart knows the wide world's
> common place?
> Or mine eyes, seeing this, say this is not,
> To put fair truth upon so foul a face?

When these questions are answered definitively in the couplet, the speaker has at last forgotten Cupid and forthrightly blames his own inconstancy:

> In things right true my heart and eyes have
> erred,
> And to this false plague are they now
> transferred.

The "things right true" may simply be ideal love and beauty, or perhaps the speaker's pursuit of those ideals in his friendship with the youth. The "plague," as in sonnet 151, is the mistress herself. Suffering at her hands comes as a deserved punishment, much as real plagues were religiously ascribed to God's wrath. A rigid morality operates here, one that resembles Edgar's view at the end of *King Lear:*

> The gods are just, and of our pleasant vices
> Make instruments to plague us:
> The dark and vicious place where thee he
> got
> Cost him his eyes.
>
> (5.3.171-74)

Cupid in sonnet 137 serves as the mere agent of an unnamed internal force by which the speaker's eyes "are transferred." Given the basic scheme of self-division in which sight and judgment are corrupted, it must be his rational soul that censures them. That soul, as sonnet 146 will stress, also owes its allegiance to a higher force. Sonnet 137 in this way anticipates the later, more powerful invocation: "Poor soul, the center of my sinful earth." It marks a breakthrough inthe speaker's introspective quest, although it fails to isolate in his own soul the actual causes of his error.

Notes

"It seems worth noting that the word *time* is used seventy-eight times in sonnets 1-126 and not once in the remaining ones. Rearrangers have not always observed this fact," *Variorum,* 1:52-3.

. . . . .

[8] Roman Jakobson and Laurence Jones. *Shakespeare's Verbal Art in Th'Expense of Spirit,* p. 18. The Hague: Mouton, 1970.

SELF-LOVE

Philip Martin (essay date 1972)

SOURCE: "Self-Love and Love Itself," in *Shakespeare's Sonnets: Self, Love and Art,* Cambridge University Press, 1972, pp. 64-99.

[*In the following excerpt, Martin discusses the manner in which the sonnets deal with positive self-love—a trait that he describes as "necessary, if the self is to survive and not disintegrate." Martin asserts that the poet of the sonnets is neither as "passive" nor as "slavish" as some critics have described him, but that instead, the poet reveals a healthy knowledge and irony about himself and the object of his affection.*]

A proper self-love

The Sonnets are concerned with two kinds of self-love; so far we have seen only the damaging kind. It is time to look at sonnets which show self-love as a virtue: where the emphasis shifts from self-love as harmful to self-love as necessary, if the self is to survive and not to disintegrate. Shakespeare's sense of the self—his own and that of others—persists even in the extreme self-renunciation of his love for the friend. With the mistress, too, despite the disruptive effect she has on his personality, he never quite loses a radical awareness of who and what he is.

'When I am worthy of myself', Wordsworth said; and even at his nadir the poet of the Sonnets strikes us as knowing what his worthier self requires. This needs to be said, because some readers have found him a passive, even a supine figure. Yvor Winters puts this view as strongly as anyone:

> In the first place there is in a large number of the poems an attitude of servile weakness on the part of the poet in the face of the person addressed; this attitude is commonly so marked as to render a sympathetic approach to the subject all but impossible, in spite of any fragmentarybrilliance which may be exhibited.[1]

And speaking of Sonnet 66 he says (p. 108): 'Shakespeare (like Arnold after him, in "Dover Beach") turns aside from the issues he has raised to a kind of despairing sentimentality, and the effect is one of weakness, poetic and personal.' Perhaps surprisingly, the answer to this comes from Bernard Shaw. Of a play about Shakespeare by Frank Harris he says:

> Shakespeare is presented with the most pathetic tenderness. He is tragic, bitter, pitiable, wretched and broken among a robust crowd of Jonsons and Elizabeths; but to me he is not Shakespeare because I miss the Shakespearean irony and the Shakespearean gaiety. Take these away and Shakespear is no longer Shakespear; all the bite, the impetus, the strength, the grim delight in his own power of looking terrible facts in the face with a chuckle, is gone; and you have nothing left but that most depressing of all things: a victim.[2]

That, of course, is just what Winters takes him to be, but then he gives no sign of being able to detect the Shakespearean irony. It is there all the same, and Shaw is right in his account of what it does for Shakespeare's stature. He is right, too, about something else which Winters appears to miss:

> the language of the sonnets addressed to [the aristocratic friend], extravagant as it now seems, is *the language of compliment and fashion,* transfigured no doubt by Shakespear's verbal magic, and *hyperbolical* . . . , but still unmistakeable for anything else than the expression of a friendship delicate enough to be wounded, and a manly loyalty deep enough to be outraged
>
> (pp. 765-6).

The words I have italicized remind us of things which cannot be forgotten without at times completely misreading the Sonnets. Often irony and fashionable hyperbole appear together, and in such a way that the first undercuts the second.

But before considering this, we might look at the kind of thing which seems most likely to provoke Winters' attack. We could take the group, Sonnets 33-5:

> Full many a glorious morning have I seene,
> Flatter the mountaine tops with soveraine eie,
> Kissing the golden face the meddowes greene;
> Guilding pale streames with heavenly alcumy:
> Anon permit the basest cloudes to ride,
> With ougly rack on his celestiall face,
> And from the for-lorne world his visage hide
> Stealing unseene to west with this disgrace:
> Even so my Sunne one early morne did shine,
> With all triumphant splendor on my brow,
> But out alack, he was but one houre mine,
> The region cloude hath mask'd him from me now.
>   Yet him for this, my love no whit disdaineth,
>   Suns of the world may staine, where heavens sun stainteth.
>
> Why didst thou promise such a beautious day,
> And make me travaile forth without my cloake,
> To let bace cludes ore-take me in my way,

Hiding thy brav'ry in their rotten smoke.
Tis not enough that through the cloude thou
    breake,
To dry the raine on my storme-beaten face,
For no man well of such a salve can speake,
That heales the wound, and cures not the
    disgrace:
Nor can thy shame give phisicke to my
    griefe,
Though thou repent, yet I have still the losse,
Th'offenders sorrow lends but weake reliefe
To him that beares the strong offenses losse.
    Ah but those teares are pearle which thy
        love sheeds,
    And they are ritch, and ransome all ill
        deeds.

No more bee greev'd at that which thou hast
    done,
Roses have thornes, and silver fountaines mud,
Cloudes and eclipses staine both Moone and
    Sunne,
And loathsome canker lives in sweetest bud.
All men make faults, and even I in this,
Authorizing thy trespas with compare,
My selfe corrupting salving thy amisse,
Excusing thy sins more then thy sins are:
For to thy sensuall fault I bring in sence,
Thy adverse party is thy Advocate,
And gainst my selfe a lawfull plea
    commence,
Such civill war is in my love and hate,
    That I an accessary needs must be,
    To that sweet theefe which sourely robs
        from me.

The first thing to notice is the progression of moods and attitudes through these three sonnets. The first consists largely of 'hyperbolical' praise of the friend ('my Sunne') followed by a profession of the poet's lowliness:

But out alack, he was but one houre mine,
The region cloude hath mask'd him from me
    now.

Yet even here the image is not quite so hyperbolical as it may seem: the sun *permit*[s] the basest cloudes' to obscure it, and so, it seems, does that other sun, the friend. And while 'disgrace' is applied to the actual sun, the word's implications tend to rub off on the metaphorical one: a word for the wise, perhaps. So far, no reproof; and the couplet recognizes, and seems to accept, that what happens in the heavens can also happen here: 'Suns of the world may staine, where heavens sun staineth.'

In the next sonnet, while the early imagery is the same, from the very first words the tone is quite different:

intimate, simple, reproachful. A lesser poet, a lesser man, might have pretended not to be hurt or angry, especially if he were a sycophant of the person addressed. But hurt and anger, being part of the experience, must be given expression: it is controlled, certainly, it is not an outburst, but it might well be something even harder for the friend to bear.

Why didst thou promise such a beautious
    day . . . ?
Tis not enough that through the cloude thou
    breake.

The control, besides giving weight and edge to the reproof, conveys the impression that whatever the friend has done, he should have realized what effect it would have on the poet. This sonnet is dramatic in a way that few of Shakespeare's are: it implies a scene, even a 'scene', with successive stages of expostulation and reply, the poet's demands on the youth's shame and loyalty growing increasingly harder to bear with equanimity, until, with the final couplet, the response is tears, and the poet half-regrets, perhaps, the pressure he has put on the youth, and so moves quickly and generously to forgiveness. 'Ah but those teares are pearle which thy love sheeds'. This impulse carries over into the next sonnet, in the desire to allay the friend's distress: 'No more bee greev'd at that which thou has done'. Yet this very generosity, as he sees almost at once, compromises him:

All men make faults, and even I in this,
Authorizing thy trespas with compare,
My selfe corrupting salving thy amisse,
Excusing thy sins more then thy sins are.

Beyond anything encountered so far, the central insight of this poem is a moral one: if you attempt to excuse the sin of those you love, you may yourself be guilty of sin; in taking their sin upon you, you take with it some of its corruption. And this insight is inseparable from others: that although selves may become involved with each other they remain separate identities separately answerable for their destinies, and that it may even be worse for a man to find excuse for a friend's fault than it was for the friend to commit it. The first fault is merely 'sensual' (performed at the bidding of the senses), the second a matter of 'sense' (that is, reason): a distinction resembling the traditional one between sins of the flesh and sins of the spirit. The imagery, as often in the Sonnets, could carry more than one set of implications: 'Roses have thornes, and silver fountaines mud'. The fault is thus 'authorized with compare' to the natural defects of purely sensory things, and so (despite the bluntness of that final word 'mud') it is made to seem less reprehensible. Yet the friend is not a rose or a fountain, he is a human and therefore a moral being, and this fact, lurking beneath the images, undermines their argument. Such 'compare', however much the poet would like it to be valid, is a falsification, as he recognizes.

These are not poems of 'servile weakness on the part of the poet'. To take the most doubtful case first: the third sonnet may be anything but muscular and aggressive but the poet here faces and forces into words a painful truth. This in itself is, as I said of Sonnet 94, a sign of moral strength. As for the two earlier sonnets: in the first the oblique firmness of the imagery leaves the friend in no doubt that he is under judgment, and in the second the tone of wounded love carries its own strong authority: 'Tis not enough . . . /Though thou repent, yet I have still the shame': the voice speaks with unanswerable justice.

If the poet's attitude seems at times a weak one, reflection will often show that it is nothing of the kind. Often he is simply telling the truth, though the truth may not be as simple as it appears. To give an obvious example, 'Farewell thou art too deare for my possessing'[3] may at first seem a beautifully sad and noble gesture of renunciation, but the next line, 'And like enough thou knowst thy *estimate*', will send the mind back to revalue 'possessing' and, still more carefully, 'deare'. The play of attitudes throughout this poem is subtle and delicate, the imagery suggesting that in the youth's sense of his value, there may be both calculation and justice, so that the poet, with a humility which seems realistic rather than servile, renounces his claims upon him. It is not weakness but a heart-rending honesty which sounds in the couplet:

> Thus have I had thee as a dreame doth flatter,
> In sleepe a King, but waking no such matter.

What we encounter, then, is an unusual mingling of irony with acknowledgement of limitations. These two features recur, singly or together, in sonnet after sonnet, and even where the irony is missing or played down, the complete openness, which in another man might well arouse our embarrassment, even our contempt, remains extraordinarily dignified. I am not sure how this can be explained. Perhaps the honesty itself is extraordinary both in kind and degree. There are no half-truths in it, no self-deceptions passing unrecognized; and it is the admixture of these which makes the lip curl when so many hearts are apparently laid bare. Half-truths and self-pity: and as a rule the Sonnets so fully comprehend this, when it is present, that the remaining objection drops away.

Of course, in discussing Sonnet 87, I may have underestimated the irony. In the Sonnets, its extent, as I have tried to show earlier, is often hard to gauge. Here, for instance, one cannot be sure whether the low estimate of the poet is his own or the youth's; whether, indeed, the whole account of their respective merits is not the youth's. (And the youth has the upper hand: 'For how do I hold thee but by thy granting?') To the poet, since he is sadly resigned to the situation and is withdrawing, it hardly matters whether the estimate of things is the friend's or that of others. It is clear that some irony is present, and along with it a completely dignified if bitter resignation.

In Sonnet 57, the irony is of such a kind that some readers miss it altogether: readers, especially, of Professor Winters' kind, who if they find a plain meaning will not look for another.

> Being your slave what should I doe but tend,
> Upon the houres, and times of your desire?
> I have no precious time at al to spend;
> Nor services to doe til you require.
> Nor dare I chide the world without end houre,
> Whilst I (my soveraine) watch the clock for you,
> Nor thinke the bitternesse of absence sowre,
> When you have bid your servant once adieue.
> Nor dare I question with my jealious thought,
> Where you may be, or your affaires suppose,
> But like a sad slave stay and thinke of nought
> Save where you are, how happy you make those.
>   So true a foole is love, that in your Will,
>   (Though you doe any thing) he thinkes no ill.

Here once more is the fashionable extravagance and hyperbole, the courtly and Petrarchan language of lowly devotion to the beloved. But isn't it, while very beautiful, just a little overdone? The movement of the first two lines, for example, is not merely graceful, it is mannered: perhaps the vassalage is being laid on a trifle heavily? And what precisely is the tone of 'I have no precious time at al to spend'? Or rather, the tones. For it seems to me that this line, and indeed the whole poem, can be read in one tone and then again in another. We can read it 'straight' and it will seem beautiful but a trifle fulsome. Or we can take the exaggerations as indicating irony: the rise of the voice in the third line, the greater swell required by the fifth ('Nor dare I chide the world without end houre'), the ritual phrases which are yet, one feels, deliberately too-conspicuous: 'my soveraine', 'your servant', 'like a sad slave'. Taking its bearings from these, the reading will make of the poem a sustained and subtly devastating protest against the treatment the poet has had to endure. Miss Mahood's comment on the end of the next sonnet could hardly be bettered for this one: what we hear, she says, 'may be the voice of a man prostrate with adoration or of one querulous with impatience—"You think this is what I am made for, do you?" '.[4] This catches the ambivalence exactly. But in suggesting this interpretation, we need not go to excess like Seymour-Smith (p. 141): a tone of 'heavily sarcastic bitterness', he comments, with no suggestion of anything else. And again, of lines 3 and 4: 'Forthright and even savage irony, reflected in the rhythm, rescues Shakespeare's state of subservience from utter pusillanimity'; lines 5 to 8 'establish without doubt the bitterly sarcastic tone'. Here is a reader at the opposite extreme from the one who finds no irony at all. Both are wrong; Seymour-Smith because he grossly magnifies the poem's quiet delicate voice and because he seems deaf to any other. But in fact there are two voices which can be heard speaking simultaneously. The friend is meant, I think, to take the poem first as an effusive and oh-so-sad compliment, and only later to do the double-take: 'Did he really mean that? I don't suppose he was being sarcastic?' Precisely because the sonnet is equivocal its protest is the more effective. But of course, the protest is largely qualified by the fact that what the poet says is quite literally true: he does hang about, watching the clock, waiting for the friend to come. Love *has* made him 'a sad slave', 'so true a foole'. There is in the poetry a kind of verbal shrugging of the shoulders and a rueful half-smile,especially in the couplet. It is the fact that the poet sees himself in these two ways at once that makes it possible and even essential to hear the two tones together throughout the poem.

There is, of course, real point in Seymour-Smith's remark about the saving irony. If the irony were not there, Shakespeare would indeed cut a pathetic figure. The irony is a great deal more than protest: it is not just a way of hitting back at the friend for humiliating him. It is at the same time a mode of self-knowledge and a kind of self-assertion: he can see himself from an extra point of view and can thus, to some extent, transcend his predicament. Since the irony operates against the friend as well as himself, each of them is seen with some measure of liberating detachment. The poet may be the youth's sad slave, which reflects no credit on the slave, but the friend's imperfections are seen as well: he may call forth a love 'this side idolatry' but he can behave badly just the same, and his lover can say so.

He does, again and again: not only in this sonnet but in others already discussed, and in many more. This brings me back to Shaw's stimulating and perceptive comments, and to the charges of weakness, pusillanimity, sycophancy.

> A sycophant does not tell his patron that his fame will survive, not in the renown of his own actions, but in the sonnets of his sycophant. A sycophant, when his patron cuts him out in a love affair, does not tell his patron exactly what he thinks of him. Above all, a sycophant does not write to his patron precisely as he feels on all occasions; and this rare kind of sincerity is all over the sonnets. Shakespear, we are told, was 'a very civil gentleman'. This must mean that his desire to please people and be liked by them, and his reluctance to hurt their feelings, led him into amiable flattery even when his feelings were not strongly stirred. If this be taken into accout . . . we shall see more civility and hyperbole than sycophancy even in the earlier and more coldblooded sonnets.[5]

If this, which seems to me apt, is taken together with the claim that Shakespeare is *not* 'that most depressing of all things: a victim', it constitutes a strong defence of the poet: he is neither victim of the Dark Lady nor sycophant of the Fair Friend. And in the poems examined so far it is abundantly clear that irony and a certain noble honesty are the chief marks of his freedom and independence. There is little that can be done to a man with these qualities, no matter how generous and therefore vulnerable his heart is. If a man sets himself at nought, as Shakespeare so frequently does, and yet so manifestly and fully exists, he has triumphed over his circumstances: he is to be seen 'as having nothing and possessing all things'.

Lastly, something might be said about those sonnets[6] in which the poet acknowledges a more than physical absence from the friend—'That I have frequent binne with unknown mindes' (117)—and yet ends (in 121 and 124 especially) by affirming a great deal besides guilt. For these are again poems of self-knowledge, and more, of self-acceptance: if the poet begins in contrition he ends in charity towards himself; which may sound more comfortable than it is. These sonnets are the counterpart of the three with which this chapter begins. Now it is the poet who has offended and the friend who must forgive. The beautifully cadenced protestations of 109 (whichopens the sequence) raise the main issues, yet may be felt to take them a little too easily:

> O never say that I was false of heart,
> Though absence seem'd my flame to quallifie,
> As easie might I from my selfe depart,
> As from my soule which in thy brest doth
>   lye:
> That is my home of love, if I have rang'd,
> Like him that travels I returne againe,
>
> . . . . .
>
> Never beleeve though in my nature raign'd,
> All frailties that besiege all kindes of blood,
> That it could so preposterouslie be stain'd,
> To leave for nothing all thy summe of good:

'Water' is needed for the poet's 'staine', but this he himself can provide. One is to suppose, I think, that the self-examination has not gone very deep so far.

In the next two sonnets, more painful admissions are made:

> Alas 'tis true, I have gone here and there,
> And made my self a motley to the view,
> Gor'd mine own thoughts, sold cheap what is most deare.

'Gor'd mine own thoughts' means much more, of course, than Seymour-Smith's anaemic gloss, 'been untrue to my deepest beliefs', which gets none of the physical associations of stabbing, piercing, covering with blood. This, more gravely confronted now, is what it means to be governed by 'all frailties that besiege all kindes of blood'. And yet sin is behovely:

> by all above,
> These blenches gave my heart an other youth,
> And worse essaies prov'd thee my best of love,
> Now all is done, have what shall have no end.

Even here, then, blessings flow from the fall, and in the next sonnet's image of a 'nature . . . subdu'd/To what it workes in, like the Dyers hand' we and the friend are prompted to a sense of inevitability. The poet is admitting his fault, asking pardon for it ('Pitty me then, and wish I were renu'de'), but also acknowledging his nature, which is not the same thing at all. If, in the words of Sonnet 117, he has 'hoysted saile to al the windes', then not only does he 'returne rebukt to [his] content' (119), but his final word on the episode, spoken in 121, is an acceptance of himself with all his faults and a dismissal of what the world may say of him, true or false.

> Tis better to be vile then vile esteemed,
> When not to be, receives reproach of being.

Immediately this seems to imply that others have spoken falsely of him, but while this may be the occasion of the reflections here, the effect of the poem is to set the self, with all its imperfections, against its calumniators:

> Noe, I am that I am, and they that levell
> At my abuses, reckon up their owne.

Here, says Wilson Knight, Shakespeare 'asserts a kind of beyond-good-and-evil claim for himself'.[7] Not quite; but the poem, in its context, certainly reads like a self-affirmation, and a balanced one at that: there is no note of apology, no 'servile weakness' before either the friend or the world. This, like the better-known Sonnet 146 ('Poore soule the center of my sinfull earth') is the 'song of a man who has come through'. And sonnet 124 is the song of a love that has come through.

Notes

[1] 'Poetic Style in Shakespeare's Sonnets' in Barbara Herrnstein (ed.), *Discussions of Shakespeare's Sonnets,* p. 107.

[2] George Bernard Shaw, Preface to *The Dark Lady of the Sonnets* in *Prefaces by Bernard Shaw* (London, 1938), pp. 763-4.

[3] Sonnet 87. A precise and admirable account of it is to be found in M. M. Mahood, *Shakespeare's Wordplay,* pp. 108-9.

[4] *Shakespeare's Wordplay,* p. 109.

[5] Preface to *The Dark Lady of the Sonnets,* p. 766.

[6] Sonnets 109-12, 117-21, 123-4. The first two of these sets are well discussed by C. L. Barber, pp. 29-30.

[7] G. Wilson Knight, *The Mutual Flame* (London, 1955), p. 14.

Jane Hedley (essay date 1994)

SOURCE: "Since First Your Eye I Eyed: Shakspeare's Sonnets and the Poetics of Narcissism," in *Style,* Vol. 28, No. 1, Spring, 1994, pp. 1-30.

[*In the following excerpt, Hedley contends that self-love or narcissism is pervasive in Shakespeare's sonnets. After observing that the sonnet genre in general can be perceived as one where the poet is "talking to himself," Hedley also remarks that Shakespeare's sonnets in particular convey narcissism through their use of puns and through the poet's clear desire to become one with his beloved.*]

The love that is celebrated in the first one hundred and twenty-six of Shakespeare's *Sonnets* is narcissistic, as several commentators have noticed[1]: "it is love by *identification*," as C. L. Barber explains (662).[2] Writing about the *Sonnets* in 1960, Barber preferred to try to understand the lover's posture in these poems "without resort to psychoanalytic formulations" (667); more recently, however, Joseph Pequigney has analyzed that posture in terms of Freud's account of "the inclination toward a narcissistic object choice" in homosexual men. The parallels are so close and so pervasive, Pequigney argues, that the *Sonnets* "could usefully be considered a proof-text" for Freud's account of homosexual object choice. Though Pequigney has resorted to psychoanalytic formulations, his discussion of narcissism in the *Sonnets* is no less thematically oriented than Barber's, and indeed every critic who has discussed the sequence in terms of narcissism (cf. also Stephen Spender, Philip Martin, and Paul Zweig) has been more preoccupied with narcissism as theme or content than with its formal or stylistic manifestations.

What I hope to demonstrate is that Shakespeare's *Sonnets* are narcissistic not only in the sense that they thematize love by identification, but also in the sense that they involve the poet in a distinctively narcissistic use of language and poetic form. Like dreams, Shakespeare's sonnets to the fair young man are doing a certain kind of psychic "work" that has a number of symptoms or hallmarks, including the semantic instability of their language. Wordplay is pervasive in the *Sonnets,* and whereas it sometimes enriches their arguments in ways that are pleasurable and satisfying for us as readers, at other times it interferes with their intelligibility and creates relationships between consecutive sonnets that are bewilderingly unstable. This kind of semantic instability is closely associated, as I will argue, with the narcissistic agenda of the sequence.

Obsessive repetition, contradiction, and non sequitur are also pervasive, and they too collaborate with the narcissistic agenda of the *Sonnets.* Thus the order in which they were published in the 1609 Quarto seems unsatisfactory not because it is not, but because it probably is, the order in which these poems were actually written. The sequence is informed by a repetitive, oscillating rhythm of identification and estrangement between the poet and the fair young man, whose "beauty's form," as he asserts in sonnet 24.1-2, "Mine eye hath . . . stelled . . . in table of my heart." In order to keep that image alive, he must be continually inventing and overcoming pretexts of estrangement or of difference between himself and it. At intervals throughout the sequence this narcissistic imperative subverts the linear, diachronic processes of exposition, argumentation, and story telling on behalf of a more primal imaginative tendency that is synchronistic and tautological. That tendency, which is also served by wordplay, cannot finally be accommodated within the Symbolic Order: it is at odds with language-as-communication and with the boundaries language establishes between self and not self, past and present, "mine" and "thine."

"Thou Art Thy Mother's Glass"

The Ovidian myth of Narcissus was a well-established reference point for the western tradition of literary love making long before Freud called attention to its saliency. In the *Roman de la Rose,* for example, the fountain in which the lover first catches sight of his "rose" carries the inscription "Here starf the fayre Narcissus."[3] In Petrarch's "Una candida cerva" the miraculous allegorical vision of Laura as a pure white doe is said to have lasted until "I fell into the water, and she disappeared."[4] Joel Fineman has recently argued that far from offering an alternative to the ostensibly heterosexual orientation of the "Petrarchan" poet-lover, Shakespeare's *Sonnets* bring out into the open "the homosexual truth subtending the poetics of admiration from Beatrice onwards" (17). What Fineman means, I take it, by "the homosexual truth" that "subtends" this tradition is that the Petrarchan poet-lover is ostensibly in love with a member of "the opposite sex," but really with a psychic projection that corresponds to an idealized image of himself, what Freud called the "ideal ego." If Fineman is right, then what is unusual in Shakespeare's sonnets to the fair young man is not the narcissistic posture of the lover, but his openness about it: narcissism is explicit in these poems both as an attribute of the beloved and as the matrix of the poet's love for him.

The first seventeen sonnets of the sequence, the so-called "procreation" sonnets, accuse the fair young man of narcissism and warn him that if he persists in "having traffic with thyself alone" he will suffer Narcissus's fate. Northrop Frye, in his influential essay on the *Sonnets,* made the erroneous assumption that by urging his friend to marry the poet was trying to cure him of narcissism: the purpose of sonnets 1-17, according to Frye, is "the awakening of Narcissus" (17). But as Stephen Spender more accurately points out, the poet is not recommending to the young man that he cease to be narcissistic: procreation is recommended in these sonnets as a way to give Narcissus's posture a new lease on life (Spender 120-21).[5] A child, the poet argues, would renew the image both he and the young man are in love with and thereby defeat the natural process of aging that threatens to destroy its beauty. Sonnet 3 thus begins with the invitation to "Look in thy glass, and tell the face thou viewest, / Now is the time that face should form another" (3.1-2).[6]

The fair young man is not, however, the only narcissist in the case. As Zweig points out, the poet's advice to him in sonnet 3 "is the advice he himself has followed in the course of his strange infatuation. If the poet loves the boy . . . it is because the boy's youth has become a rejuvenating mirror which enables him to roll back the years and conquer the worst enemy of Narcissus: time's encroaching ugliness" (105). In loving the young man he recovers an (idealized) image of himself, an image of which the aging process had bereft him. And thus after seventeen sonnets that urge the young man to beget a son, the poet begins to proffer his own imagination—and his poems—as a mirror in which the young man's beauty can outlive the face that wears it: "Yet do thy worst, old Time: despite thy wrong, / My love shall in my verse ever live young" (19.13-14). The language of his vow is here crucially ambiguous: "My love" means either "the one I love" or "my love for him" or both. What this ambiguity suggests is that the image he would preserve is a narcissistic projection, the figment of his own desire.[7]

Verbal ambiguity is pervasive in the *Sonnets,* and I will argue later that the pervasiveness of ambiguity and double entendre is itself an important aspect of "the poetics of narcissism." At this point, however, it is enough to point out that the poet seems never to tire of juggling in this way with possessives, especially in phrases and compounds like "my love," "my self," "your will[iam]" "your eye [I]," which can be doubly inflected by their syntactic context to mean both "you whom I love/am thinking about/am forced to obey" and "my feelings/thoughts/wishes/self." The proverbial notion that "a friend is another I," which Stephen Booth finds explicitly referred to in at least nine of the fair-young-man sonnets (cf. Booth, *Shakespeare's Sonnets* 192, 333), is thus hauntingly implicit in many others as well. With repetition, what passes at first for a lover's hyperbole or jeu d'esprit comes more and more to connote anxiety and, in poems that glance at the beloved's unfaithfulness or unworthiness, a pathetic defenselessness against the tendency toward narcissistic identification with him.

In his 1910 essay on Leonardo da Vinci, Freud explained "the inclination toward a narcissistic object-choice"[8] as the outcome of an intense erotic attachment to the mother that is repressed during the Oedipal crisis but resurfaces in adolescence to control the son's erotic life. Ovid's myth of Narcissus, as Freud had noticed, is the story of a boy whose mother loved him too much.[9] In adulthood, identifying with his mother, such a son "takes his own person as a model in whose likeness he chooses the new objects of his love" (100). His love objects are "revivals of himself in childhood"; he loves them in the way that his mother loved him:

> Thou art thy mother's glass, and she in thee
> Calls back the lovely April of her prime,
> So thou through windows of thine age shall see
> Despite of wrinkles, this thy golden time....
> (3.8-12)

Reviewing Pequigney's and Fineman's psychoanalytic studies of the *Sonnets* in 1987, W. Thomas MacCary suggests that this paradigm has a broader range of application than Freud himself was inclined to give it. MacCary argues that sonnet 3 and others recall an early childhood experience that is continually being reenacted by all of us in our most intimate relationships, not only those of us "who persist in making 'mirror object-choices'" (229).[10] In loving another we seek to recapture the experience of being loved that is associated with "the mirror stage," the point at which, even before the acquisition of language, the self first begins to be envisaged. At this stage of development, as it has been delineated by Jacques Lacan and elaborated by other theorists,[11] every child begins to conceive of itself as a distinct, separate person by "introjecting" a maternal image of itself (cf. Wilden 173-74; Muller and Richardson 29-30). Like the Oedipal crisis, a later stage of development that coincides with the acquisition of language and with entry into the Symbolic Order, the preverbal "mirror stage" involves an experience of loss as well as gain: what is lost is a primordial sense of oneness with the mother; what is gained is an "ideal ego," our self encountered first as the apple of her eye. When we fall in love the pre-Oedipal "mirror stage" reasserts itself to some degree: both the intensity of our emotion and the imaginary status of its object are signals or symptoms of this. And thus MacCary concurs with Fineman insuggesting that to make a "mirror object choice" in adulthood is simply to render explicit the narcissistic basis of all romantic love.

In sonnet 62, about halfway through the sequence, the poet explicitly acknowledges the narcissistic basis of his own infatuation. He begins the sonnet by accusing himself of "self-love": "Sin of self-love possesseth all mine eye / And all my soul and all my every part" (62.1-2). But after elaborating this self-accusation for two full quatrains, he abruptly withdraws and revises it in view of the image he actually sees whenever he looks in the mirror:

> But when my glass shows me myself indeed
> Beated and chopped with tanned antiquity,
> Mine own self-love quite contrary I read;
> Sin so self-loving were iniquity.
>
> 'Tis thee (my self) that for my self I praise,[12]
> Painting my age with beauty of thy days.
> (62.9-12)

"For my self" in this context means both "instead of myself" and "on my own behalf," calling attention once again to the intrapsychic status of the mirror relation. What the couplet thus confesses is that self-love has been rekindled in the experience of loving another: the "ideal ego" is lost but then found again in the "ego ideal" that mirrors it back.[13]

Sonnet 62 calls attention also to the strange economy of this transaction—whereby, as Freud explains, "the subject seems to yield up his whole personality in favor of an object-cathexis" ("On Narcissism" 76).[14] So ready is the poet of the *Sonnets* to do this that, as he explains to the friend in sonnet 88,

> When thou shalt be disposed to set me light,
> And place my merit in the eye of scorn,
> Upon thy side against myself I'll fight,
> And prove thee virtuous, though thou art forsworn.
> (88.1-4)

To be willing to give the young man's faithlessness the color of honor at the expense of his own reputation seems extravagantly self-abnegating, foolishly altruistic: but the poet goes on to explain that "I by this will be a gainer too,"

> For bending all my loving thoughts on thee,
> The injuries that to my self I do,
> Doing thee vantage, double vantage me.
> (88.9-12)

He too will be a gainer in this transaction insofar as he preserves the ego ideal in which he has a narcissistic investment.

If, however, the lover could and did "yield up his whole personality in favor of an object-cathexis," he would no longer have a standpoint from which to say, "I love you," or to write poems that say so: thus his inclination to identify with the beloved must finally be resisted or repressed. In sonnet 39 it seems that we can watch the poet work this out for himself. The sonnet begins with a rhetorical question—"Oh how thy worth with manners may I sing, / When thou art all the better part of me?"—a hyperbolical compliment to the beloved, which is then repeated with a greater sense of urgency in lines 3 and 4: "What can mine own praise to mine own self bring, / And what is't but mine own when I praise thee?" Reiterated thus, the question conveys that the poet finds his own posture unsettling and problematic; as he juggles with personal pronouns he both asserts and recoils from total identification with the beloved. In the second quatrain he argues, somewhat paradoxically, that for the sake of their love they must put some geographical distance between them: "Even for this, let us divided live, / And our dear love lose name of single one. . . ." Just as, in the Ovidian myth, Narcissus surprised himself with the wish "that what I love were absent from me!" (lines 467-68),[15] so in the last six lines of this poem absence is hailed as a bitter but necessary expedient:

> O absence, what a torment wouldst thou prove,
> Were it not thy sour leisure gave sweet leave
> To entertain the time with thoughts of love,
> Which time and thoughts so sweetly doth deceive,
> And that thou teachest how to make one twain,
> By praising him here who doth hence remain.
> (39.9-14)

Identification with the object of one's love is a regressive tendency that must finally be resisted, according to Freud, if the ego is to survive as a center of volition and consciousness. In sonnet 39 it seems that the poet knows this and is willing to "name" the condition of "oneness" he desires only in the context of insisting that it not be consummated. But the argument as he frames it is not about selfhood as a metaphysical or psychic abstraction; the topic of this sonnet is his poethood, his capacity to go on writing poems. The suggestion is that distance between himself and his beloved friend must be continually reinvented or recircumstanced in order for love poems to continue to be written.

There is only one poem to be written about perfect "at-onement" in love, a memorial poem whose lovers are beyond being able to use the pronouns *I* and *you*, and who were never human in any case: "The Phoenix and Turtle." The argument of that poem is that such a relationship confounds the linguistic and logical categories ("Number there in love was slain. . . . Property was thus appalled, . . . Reason in itself confounded") that must nevertheless be brought into play in any attempt to expound its truth. The phoenix and the turtle were miraculously two and yet one: this miracle took them out of the world as we know it into eternity. In the *Sonnets*, "love by identification" is able to be sustained as a human, subjective experience only imperfectly, only insofar as distance is continually reopened, difference continually reestablished, between the one who says "I" in these poems and his beloved "alter ego." No sooner has one pretext of estrangement been overcome, than another must present itself. This, I would suggest, is "the riddle of Shakespeare's *Sonnets*": it is necessary always for the poet to be "praising him here who doth hence remain."

. . . . .

". . . All My Best is Dressing Old Words New"

Wordplay or "punning" in the *Sonnets* is not only an occasional obstacle to the intelligibility of their arguments; it is Shakespeare's most inveterate stylistic habit, his signature trope. Sonnets are more hospitable to this trope than plays could possibly be, and therefore wordplay is both more prevalent and more openly associated with narcissism in the *Sonnets* than it is in Shakespeare's plays. In order for the relationship between narcissism and wordplay to emerge, it will be necessary to add to the psychic profile of narcissism that was quickly epitomized in the first section of this essay; to explain the sonnet form itself as a medium of representation whose limitations also create special opportunities for narcissistic fantasy work; and to discuss in psychoanalytic terms the trope known to Shakespeare and his contemporaries as "syllepsis."

After he had fallen in love with his own reflection, Narcissus thought at first that he had an ongoing relationship with another person, but he soon realized that he did not: their gestures toward each other were simultaneous and identical. What the Ovidian fable tells us in this way is that love by identification has a psychological bias that is powerfully synchronistic and tautological; that quality is its attraction and its limitation also. This is reemphasized by the fate of Echo, the nymph who loves Narcissus but is incapable of initiating dialogue and must always use his words to express her desires. The closest Echo can come to saying something of her own is by repeating (and thereby recontextualizing) Narcissus's words whenever he happens to say something she can use to speak of her love for him. When Narcissus rejects her, Echo pines away until she is just a voice. She is literally consumed by love, and the fable depicts this process as one of ever-closer identification with the beloved.

As Narcissus himself nears death, Echo undertakes, in a final act of loving selflessness, to repeat whatever he says to his reflected image so that it will seem to love and suffer with him in words as well as gestures that precisely match his own. When language is thus assimilated to the mirror relation, the limitations of that relation become apparent: the difference between echo and dialogue is a measure of Narcissus's fatal unwillingness to forego the pleasures of what Lacan calls "the Imaginary" on behalf of authentic intersubjectivity.[28] Ovid tells us that "even when he had been received into the infernal abodes, he kept on gazing on his image in the Stygian pool" (3:504-05): in death he becomes an emblem of self-willed exile from the Symbolic Order, the order of language-as-communication and also of history, becoming, and change.

The sonnet sequence is a genre that will afford the narcissist a relatively high degree of satisfaction both of his inclination to be talking to himself[29] and of his appetite for the recuperation of diachrony into synchrony. The sonnet form itself is synchronistic in the sense that its argument is converted by its metric structure and its rhyme scheme into a synchronic array of phrases and clauses that will hang together in the mind as a simultaneous unity. Along with his contemporaries Spenser and Daniel, Shakespeare clearly understood the sonnet form in this way. All of them learned from Petrarch and from the French poets of the *Pléiade* that sonnets in sequence are hospitable to the stance or project of being "all in war with Time for love of you" (15.13): time's passage need not be experienced as a dimension of the poems themselves, but can be allowed to take care of itself in the spaces between them. A sonnet sequence need not tell very much of a story: it will readily accommodate repetition and redundancy. So will its individual units; indeed the line of least resistance to the form of the sonnet is the kind of argument that progresses, as do many of Shakespeare's sonnets, by means of the reiterative reformulation of one idea.[30]

In sonnet 76 the poet of the *Sonnets* acknowledges, however, that his sequence is far more static and repetitious than most. "Why is my verse so barren of new pride?" (76.1) he asks, as if to forestall the criticisms of unsympathetic readers (including the friend himself, perhaps) by anticipating them. "Why write I still all one, ever the same, / And keep invention in a noted weed . . ." (76.5-6)? We could refer his self-accusation to the typically high redundancy of any one sonnet's argument ("still all one, ever the same"), to his propensity for mounting the same argument in sonnet after sonnet—sonnets 1-17 are a notorious case in point—or to his limited repertory of figurative and rhetorical strategies, a limitation to which he alludes in lines 3-4 by asking, "Why with the time do I not glance aside / To new-found methods, and to compounds strange?" Indeed he does seem never to tire of saying the same few things in the same way. Answering his own questions in the last six lines of the sonnet, he asserts that his feelings are such, their object such, that he can do no other: "O know, sweet love, I always write of you, / And you and love are still my argument" (76.9-10).[31]

He goes on to characterize his own use of language in a way that, interestingly enough, recalls the figure of Echo: "So all my best is dressing old words new, / Spending again what is already spent" (76.11-12). Often, as we have already noticed in working with sonnets 33 through 37 and 40 to 42, this is indeed how he gets from one topic or situation to another, both within and between sonnets: by generating new contexts for old words. "Dressing old words new" could also serve as a metaphorical definition of his most inveterate stylistic habit, the verbal device known to us as "punning" but to Shakespeare's contemporaries as "syllepsis."

The sixteenth-century rhetorician George Puttenham called syllepsis "the figure of double supply" (168): it occurs when a single word is doubly contextualized, usually by participation in more than one syntactic construction, and thereby has more than one of its possible meanings brought into play. Antanaclasis, a closely related figure, occurs when the same word is repeated in consecutive, coordinated clauses or phrases with a different meaning the second time (Todorov and Ducrot 278). Both figures exploit the haphazard polysemy of words and therebyconfront us with an element of arbitrariness and sheer contingency in the relation of signifier to signified within the verbal sign. They are akin to rhyme, and they can be used, along with rhyme and meter, to promote what Roman Jakobson calls the "poetic function" of language, whereby the sequential unfolding of the discourse is overtaken by relationships of similarity that fold the verbal medium back on itself to render it "self-focused" (Jakobson 69-70, 85-86).

The noun-verb "pun" did not appear in English until after the language had begun to be stabilized and institutionalized by dictionaries in the eighteenth century, and its appearance coincides with a shift in attitude toward syllepsis and kindred figures. In the sixteenth century these figures had not been reserved for joking or merely playful uses, but ever since the Age of Reason they have been regarded as unserious, even disreputable (Joseph 168; Easthope 112-17).[32] Freud takes this attitude for granted in *Jokes and the Unconscious,* where he explains that one of the ways in which puns give their author pleasure is by promoting the free play of the signifier, which is ordinarily repressed in the interest of transparent communication, of "saying one thing at a time" (119-20). Puns are enjoyable but also mysterious and a little unnerving, as Jonathan Culler suggests, because they "present the disquieting spectacle of a functioning of language where boundaries—between sounds, between sound and letter, between meanings—count for less than one might imagine, and where supposedly discrete meanings threaten to sink into fluid subterranean signifieds too undefinable to call concepts" (3).

Shakespeare's sonnets very often present such a spectacle. As Booth explains in his edition of *The Sonnets,* Shakespeare habitually and pervasively "uses more of the ideational potential in words than the logic [of a sonnet's argument] needs or can admit. He often uses words that have a common pertinence to a context other than the one in which he uses them; sometimes the words relate to one another through senses entirely foreign to the ones that relate to the assertions in which they appear" (*Shakespeare's Sonnets* 371). Shakespeare's use of this kind of wordplay goes far beyond any other poet of the Renaissance, and it is much more pervasive in the *Sonnets* than rhetorical terms like syllepsis and antanaclasis can properly suggest.

Where the *Sonnets* are at their most synchronistic and reiterative, this kind of wordplay assists them to double and redouble their simple arguments, blurring the semantic boundaries between consecutive statements to produce the haunting reverberation that has become Shakespeare's hallmark as a sonneteer.[33] This way of using language is especially effective in sonnets 1-17, where a series of different metaphors is used to make the same argument over and over again:

> From fairest creatures we desire increase
> That thereby beauty's rose might never die,
> But as the riper should by time decease,
> His tender heir might bear his memory;
> But thou, contracted to thine own bright eyes,
> Feed'st thy light's flame with self-substantial fuel,
> Making a famine where abundance lies.
>
> (1.1-7)

Here in sonnet 1, for example, the word "contracted" in line 5 means "betrothed" in the context of the legal language of lines 3 and 4 but may also mean "diminished," insofar as the rhetorical structure of the first quatrain sets up an opposition between the friend's posture and the "increase" we desire "from fairest creatures." Meanwhile the predominant meaning of "increase" in line 1 is not "growth" but "the begetting of offspring": it invokes the biblical injunction to increase and multiply, which the young man is accused of flouting. The relationship between "increase" and "contracted" is thus an instance of what Booth is talking about when he speaks of words being related by way of senses different from the ones that are relevant to the assertions in which they appear. In this instance the syllepsis does, however, make a meaningful contribution to the argument of the sonnet: it creates a nonce relationship between two different senses of "contracted" ("you are perversely self-betrothed, and thereby diminished") and, by extension, a relationship of mutual support between the two systems (legal and biblical-natural), whose norms and conventions the narcissistic young man is accused of frustrating.

Moving on to sonnet 2, whose argument is essentially the same, we find the young man being warned that "When forty winters shall beseige thy brow . . . / Thy youth's proud livery . . . will be a tottered weed of small worth held" (2.1-4). "Tottered weed" means "tattered garment" in the immediate context of the livery metaphor; but against the background of sonnet 1, where the young man's beauty and its fragility are metaphorically associated with the flowers of springtime, it acquires a second meaning: "withered plant." In sonnets 1-17 this kind of sylleptic linkage often obtains between neighboring sonnets, helping to synchronize many different metaphoric codes into a richly interactive network.

But, as soon as the *Sonnets* begin to address themselves to the vicissitudes of an ongoing relationship, the poet's propensity for "dressing old words new" begins to interfere with the intelligibility of consecutive sonnets' arguments: a word or phrase is "doubly supplied" to consecutive arguments or situations that take hold of it differently, and the sylleptic overlap renders each of these contexts semantically unstable and/or incomplete. The first line of a sonnet seems thus to mean one thing as a continuation of the previous sonnet's argument and then something quite different as a new situation crystalizes around it.[34] Interestingly enough, both of these instances of "double supply" seem often to occur at moments in the lover's discourse when the boundaries between subject and object also threaten to dissolve or "count for less than one might imagine," moments when he expresses both desire and fear at the prospect of an identification with the beloved so total that he would no longer be "himself."

Shakespeare's sylleptic wordplay is itself the work of desire:[35] by continually folding the language of the sonnets over on itself, it traduces the linear, diachronic processes of exposition, argumentation, and story telling on behalf of the narcissistic stasis of the mirror relation. Often, as in sonnets 1 through 17, this word play enhances the sonnet's capacity to work with language in a way that is more pleasurable for us as readers than ordinary speech and argumentative prose, which are in the business, mostly, of "saying one thing at a time." But at other times Shakespeare's propensity for "dressing old words new" is confusing: it keeps a coherent scenario or story line from forming and makes the arguments of consecutive sonnets hard to follow, evenas they seem to bear witness to an interpersonal crisis. This is what happens whenever the poet's need to be inventing pretexts of alienation from his beloved alter ego is at cross-purposes with the narcissistic pleasure he meanwhile obtains from "spending again what is already spent."

One instance of this difficulty that has greatly troubled editors and commentators is the antanaclasis that links the end of sonnet 93 with the beginning of 94 but thereby renders the argument of 94, which is difficult anyway, even harder to establish. In this part of the sequence, especially in sonnets 91 through 96,[36] there is thematic overlap and sometimes also syntactic run-on from one sonnet to the next. The possibility they all entertain, though it takes several different forms in quick succession, is that the friend's constancy in love does not match the poet's: perhaps he has already forsaken the poet unbenownst to him, perhaps he is simply incapable of constancy in love. Sonnets 91 and 92 are closely and unproblematically linked together by syntactic run-on, and so are 92 and 93: in the last line of 92, for example, the poet worries that "Thou mayst be false and yet I know it not," and then sonnet 93 begins, "So shall I live, supposing thou art true. . . ." "It seems at first," says Stirling, "that 94 proceeds as surely from 93 as 93 proceeds from 92" (Stirling 102), especially since the couplet rhyme of 93 is picked up in the first quatrain of 94 with a repetition of the thematically important word *show:*

> How like Eve's apple doth thy beauty grow,
> If thy sweet virtue answer not thy show!
>
> They that have pow'r to hurt and will do none,
> That do not do the thing they most do show,
> Who, moving others, are themselves as stone,
> Unmoved, cold, and to temptation slow;
> They rightly do inherit heaven's graces. . . .

The problem is that whereas in 93 "show" is a noun that refers to the friend's appearance of harmless sweetness, in 94 it is a verb that refers to "their" manifest "power to hurt."

Stirling plays out the response of a hypothetical reader of the sequence to this shift in the meaning of a repeated word. "A reader stops. He reexamines the end of 93 to see whether it says what he thinks it said. It does, and so does 94.1-2. He begins to muse on ambiguity, on paradox, on 'controlled dichotomy'" (Stirling 103). Stirling's reader begins, that is, to rationalize the shift from one meaning of "show" to another: their "power to hurt" becomes, "interestingly enough, a power to injure by sweetness and true love . . ." (Stirling 102). After playing out this rationalization Stirling rejects it because the rest of sonnet 94 does not construe "their" "power to hurt" in this way. "What we have here," he concludes, "is not ambiguity but quite unnecessary confusion that keeps a pleasurable ambiguity from arising. Either the Q text is faulty or Shakespeare mismanaged his lines" (Stirling 103). Stirling's solution to the problem is to separate the two sonnets in his revised version of the Shakespeare sonnet order.

But the sonnets in question belong to a series that takes off from, and returns to, a strongassertion of "at-onement." The argument of 91, which begins "Some glory in their birth, some in their skill," is that for the poet his friend's love is all that matters: "having thee, of all men's pride I boast." No sooner has he made this assertion of total narcissistic investment in the friend, than he begins to worry that he may not really "have him," after all: "thou mayst take / All this away, and me most wretched make." From this point on, one way of framing this suspicion gives way to another in quick succession, each presenting a slightly different challenge to the poet's constancy: the friend may forsake him (91.13-14), but in that case he will simply perish (92.1-12); worse yet, however, the friend may only be pretending to love him ("Thy looks with me, thy heart in other place" [93.4]); or the friend may be one of those who do not betray their lover because they themselves never feel anything much ("Who moving others are themselves as stone" [94.3]); or he may be one of those who are so beloved of everyone that even though they have sinned, other people cannot help but love and praise them anyway ("Naming thy name blesses an ill report" [95.8]). The series of "what if's" has run its course by the end of sonnet 96, where the poet begs the friend not to use his charisma to corrupt other people's judgments by "making faults graces": "But do not so; I love thee in such sort, / As, thou being mine, mine is thy good report" (96.13-14). This was also the couplet of sonnet 36, and here, as there, the poet's overt gesture of psychic identification with the friend signals a shift from a negative to a positive image of him and a reassertion of psychic "at-onement." Here, as there, however, that assertion is predicated on a geographical separation between them: "How like a winter hath my absence been / From thee, the pleasure of the fleeting year," sighs the poet with apparent non sequitur in the first two lines of sonnet 97.

Here again, semantic instability is produced by the poet's propensity for "dressing old words new," coupled with his need to be continually broaching and overcoming pretexts of difference between himself and his beloved alter ego. It seems apparent here, as well as in the series of sonnets from 33 through 42, that his poems have been generated by a process of psychic improvisation, rather than as a series of reactions to external events. It is a process that calls upon the poet to discredit himself just as often as he calls the friend's integrity into question, so that he can continue to oscillate between having and lack, sameness and difference, distance and closeness.

"Yet This Thy Praise Cannot Be So Thy Praise To Tie Up Envy. . . . "

In sonnet 69, the sequence forestalls the assertion that "my friend and I are one" in still another way by focusing on disparaging things that other people are saying about the friend or the poet or both. Sonnets 66 through 72 share a common preoccupation with gossip and with all the different ways that other people's language might alienate the lovers by co-opting one of them: absorbing his image, or devaluing it in the eyes of the other.[37] The World, quasi-personified, becomes involved in a series of shifting alliances that produce alternative configurations of two against one as the World, the poet, and the friend are each in turn disparaged. What is at stake throughout this series, once again, is the poet's wish to identify with his friend and thereby to preserve the ego ideal in which he has a narcissistic investment. In this series, however, the danger that threatens their relationship is associated with the Symbolic Order more obviously and insistently than before: the World is a many-tongued monster whose power to disseminate rumors is antithetical and threatening to the poet's way of using language.[38]

The arguments of these sonnets are sometimes explicitly linked: the opening lines of sonnet 67 presuppose the couplet of 66, and sonnet 68 is linked by its opening lines to the couplet of 67, whose argument it repeats and extends. At other points in the series, however, all that consecutive sonnets seem to have in common is the mood and topic of world-weariness: thus, for example, in sonnet 71 the poet abruptly ceases to worry about his friend's reputation and begins instead to worry about his own standing in the eyes of the World. Here, as in the other series we have looked at, narrative and discursive continuities are only fitfully present; again, however, embedded in this series of sonnets is a full set of permutations of an oppositional mirror game. The game has three players this time, instead of two.

The series begins with sonnet 66, in which the poet repudiates the World in a lengthy catalogue of generalized indictments, personifying its multiform corruption with a series of one-line topsy-turvies: "As, to behold desert a beggar born, / And needy nothing trimmed in jollity . . . / And captive good attending captain ill" (66.2-3, 12). Overwhelmed, as it seems, by all of these figments of the World's deformity, the poet lacks the energy to go on living: he "would be gone" from the world, "Save that to die, I leave my love alone" (66.13-14). Does he fear that his friend will not be able to withstand the World's corruption once he is gone, or is it simply that he cannot bear to be parted from him? It seems, in any case, that his death wish triggers an intense and painful awareness of his friend's young life. In sonnets 67 and 68 he struggles to remain closely identified with the friend, arguing that the world is no fit place for him either:

> Ah, wherefore with infection should he live
> And with his presence grace impiety,
> That sin by him advantage should achieve
> And lace itself with his society.
>
> (67.1-4)

The world is depicted here and in sonnet 68 as a place where sin and falsehood lie in wait to feast vampirically upon the friend's beauty.

In sonnet 69, the World claims the friend for its own in a way that is even more disquieting for the poet: the World calls the friend's virtue into question. This is the crisis point of the series; as such it will bear closer examination. In sonnet 70, however, the poet moves to rescue his friend and reestablish their alliance against the World by refusing to believe the slander that is being circulated about him. Then in 71 and 72 the World repudiates the poet, and it is a question of whether the friend will go along and identify with the World against him, as in 72 the poet disconsolately and self-abnegatingly urges him to do.

The threat the poet has most to fear is broached in sonnet 69, where the World's co-optation of the beloved is associated with a disparaging use of language that is insidiously disseminative and thereby undermines the narcissistic economy of the mirror relation. The World is imaged as a many-tongued multitude that confounds its own praise of the friend by circulating rumors that there is more to be discerned than meets the eye:

> Those parts of thee that the world's eye doth view
> Want nothing that the thought of hearts can mend;
> All tongues, the voice of souls, give thee that due,
> Utt'ring bare truth, even so as foes commend.
> Thy outward thus with outward praise is crowned,

But those same tongues that give thee so
   thine own
In other accents do this praise confound
By seeing farther than the eye hath shown.
They look into the beauty of thy mind,
And that in guess they measure by thy deeds;
Then, churls, their thoughts, although their
   eyes were kind,
To thy fair flower add the rank smell of
   weeds:

But why thy odor matcheth not thy show,
The soil is this, that thou dost common
   grow.

This sonnet is rhetorically uneasy and full of ambiguity, both situational and linguistic. It seems that the World both praises and blames the friend: "those same tongues that give thee so thine own / In other accents do this praise confound. . . ." Meanwhile the friend is on overfamiliar terms with a World that contemns him—"The soil is this, that thou dost common grow"—and the poet, although he despises the World, repeats these rumors to the friend as if there might be some truth to them.

In this context, several of the poem's key words and phrases become capable of meaning several different things at once. "Outward praise" is a case in point: as Booth points out, the phrase could mean "praise of your outward appearance" ("Thy outward thus with outward praise"), or it could mean "praise that is public" (with a homonymic pun on "outward" and "uttered"), or "praise that appears to be genuine but is not" (*Shakespeare's Sonnets* 253-54), and indeed all of these possible senses of "outward" blend together in this context in such a way that the praisers and the object of their praise seem to merge as well. In the case of the word *soil,* it seems that Shakespeare has made a noun out of a verb meaning "resolve, explain"; but because this usage is unconventional and hence slightly unstable, other meanings of *soil* come into play also: especially "to dirty" or "sully" and—in view of the flower metaphor—"earth" or "ground" (cf. Booth, *Shakespeare's Sonnets* 254-55). Thus the same word seems to mean "solution" or "reason" and "dirty rumor"; instead of clarifying the friend's situation, as solutions usually do, this one makes it even murkier and muddier.

Linguistic instability is the symptom or hallmark in sonnet 69 of an interpersonal situation that is not just complicated, but disconcertingly labile and ambiguous. In sonnet 70 all these ambiguities are resolved as the poet, by unequivocally refusing to believe the gossip about his friend, restores the boundaries between self, friend, and World that had become blurred and indistinct in sonnet 69. At this point, however, the series is not yet complete: as in the series 33 through 38 and 91 through 96, it has run its full course only when the poet has worked his way round to a position as close as possible to that of the impoverished ego in Freud's account of object cathexis. Thus sonnets 71 and 72 are preoccupied with his own unworthiness to be loved: the world may be "vile," but he is even more worthless. In the couplet of 72, his total lack of self-esteem extends to his poems as well: "For I am shamed," he tells his friend, "by that which I bring forth, / And so should you, to love things nothing worth" (72.13-14). Once he has touched bottom in this way his focus changes in immediately following sonnets: in 73-74 love's enemy is Time and the aging process, rather than the World. Sonnets 75-77 engage in metapoetic reflection, much as we found the poet doing in sonnets 39 and 40.

Sonnet 75 generalizes about what it is like to be in love with the young man in terms that acknowledge the oscillating rhythm of this and other stretches of the sequence and are strikingly compatible with the Freudian notion of reciprocity between ego and object libido:

And for the peace of you I hold such strife
As 'twixt a miser and his wealth is found:
Now proud as an enjoyer, and anon
Doubting the filching age will steal his
   treasure;
Now counting best to be with you alone,
Then bettered that the world may see my
   pleasure;
Sometime all full with feasting on your sight,
And by and by clean starved for a look. . . .
                                   (75.3-10)

After two more sonnets of metapoetic reflection, still another pretext for "starving and pining," estrangement and further sonnets, is brought into play in sonnet 78: "every alien pen," "others' works," "the full proud sail of his great verse," in short, a rival poet.

"*. . . When First Your Eye I Eyed*"

Again and again we have discovered in Shakespeare's sonnets to the fair young man an oscillating rhythm of identification and estrangement, fullness and emptiness, that is continually being recircumstanced. In relation to this psychological process, any particular sonnet is a work of secondary elaboration that compromises, not always successfully, with its inexorable dynamics. Meanwhile the language of the sonnets is itself compromised by the poet's narcissism, which is to say that his poems bear the imprint of an uneasy compromise with the Symbolic Order, on behalf of the Imaginary, for the sake of "love by identification." The sonnet in which the poet comes perhaps closest to saying this in his own way is 105, another of his sonnets of metapoetic reflection, which argues gnomically that because "my love"—by which he means both "he whom I love" and "my love for him"—is "still constant in a wondrous excellence,"

> Therefore my verse to constancy confined,
> One thing expressing, leaves out difference.

As we have seen, the poet could not really afford to "leave out difference": to do so would be to forego the opportunity of giving his love in both senses a discursive embodiment. And he has not succumbed to tautology; but he has used rhyme, repetition, and word-play to create a tissue of language that is antidiscursive to a quite unusual degree.

Shakespeare's *Sonnets* are thus closer than the sonnets of any other poet, and closer, certainly, than his plays and his narrative poems can afford to be, to the permeable boundary between the intersubjective realm of language-as-communication and an intrasubjective realm of "fluid subterranean signifieds," where selfhood is also unstable and fluid. This quality is what gives them their distinctive power to pleasure but also to haunt us, as they have not ceased to do.

Notes

1 Oddly enough, however, Louise Vinge, in her comprehensive history of *The Narcissus Theme in Western European Literature up to the Early Nineteenth Century*, claims that there are "no allusions to the myth in Shakespeare's sonnets" (377).

2 The essay I am citing is a distilled version of Barber's introduction to the Laurel edition of the *Sonnets*, published by Dell in the same year.

3 Cf. Zweig 99; the inscription, which Zweig quotes also, is from Chaucer's translation of the *Roman*.

4 This is the last line of *Rime sparse* 190, as translated by Robert M. Durling in *Petrarch's Lyric Poems* (336).

5 Frye's and Spender's essays were published in the same volume (Hubler): that Frye's reading of the "procreation" sonnets prevailed until very recently among critics and in college classrooms is a symptom of the heterosexist inflection of *Sonnets* criticism and scholarship during the 1960s and '70s. The tide began to turn with the publication of Pequigney's and Fineman's studies in 1985 and 1986, respectively.

6 All quotations from the *Sonnets* are based on Stephen Booth's 1977 edition.

7 Cf. Bruce Smith: "Is 'my love' in this line a name for the friend, or does it refer to the poet's feelings?" Smith points out that "'Love' and 'my love' emerge after sonnet 13 as the poet's favorite epithets for the young man" (249).

8 Freud's first published reference to narcissism was in a footnote added to the 1910 edition of *Three Essays on the Theory of Sexuality*. A more extended and more interesting discussion of "the inclination toward a narcissistic object-choice" appears in *Leonardo Da Vinci and a Memory of his Childhood* (1910), where Freud explicitly cites the Greek legend of Narcissus (98-101). Cf. also "On Narcissism: An Introduction" (1914) (73-102) and "Some Neurotic Mechanisms in Jealousy, Paranoia and Homosexuality" (1922) (esp. 230-32). Pequigney cites all of these Freudian texts extensively in chapter 5.

9 *Leonardo Da Vinci* 99; cf. Ovid, *Metamorphoses* (3.344-46).

10 This is a position to which Freud himself tended more and more: in a footnote added to *Leonardo Da Vinci* in 1919 he argues that "everyone, even the most normal person, is capable of making a homosexual object-choice" and is repressing this tendency in adulthood (99).

11 MacCary also cites Otto Kernberg and Heinz Kohut as influential post-Freudian theorists of narcissism. A theorist whose work is even more relevant to the concerns of this essay is Janine Chasseguet-Smirgel because of the attention she gives to art and language.

12 I have restored the Quarto's typography in this line, as furnished by Booth in his facing-page edition (*Sonnets* 57). Booth's changes mask the word play on "my self." Pequigney also highlights this sonnet as one in which the poet confesses to "narcissism in the Freudian sense" (84). I take the couplet to be a gesture of homage to the friend rather than, as Pequigney does, a confession that the poet desires to "use [him] exploitatively . . . by sexual possession" (85). The poem's confessional rhetoric comes across to me as mock serious, a means, as it were, of hiding the poet's narcissism out in the open.

13 As Pequigney points out, sonnet 22 is very similar in its argument to sonnet 62 (87). The arguments of 31, 53, 59, 106, and 108 are also closely related: in all of them, the poet casts the friend as his "ego ideal" by arguing that the friend's image subsumes for him every past or present, remembered or conceivable object of love.

14 In the essay "On Narcissism" this formulation occurs in the context of a generalization about "the state of being in love."

15 In their entirety, lines 466-68 read, in translation: "What I desire, I have; the very abundance of my

riches beggars me [*inopem me copia fecit*]. Oh, that I might be parted from my own body! and, strange prayer for a lover, I would that what I love were absent from me!" (All quotations from Ovid's myth of Narcissus are from the Loeb Classical Library's facing-page edition of the *Metamorphoses*.)

· · · · ·

[28] This account of Lacan's notion of the Imaginary and its relationship to the Symbolic Order is indebted to Anthony Wilden, who explains that "in spite of the fact that the Imaginary is present in all human relations, Lacan avers that intersubjectivity cannot be conceived within its limits. . . . [I]ntersubjectivity is viewed by Lacan as primarily a symbolic relationship," mediated by language (175-77).

[29] Cf. MacCary. "I would maintain that any edifying reading of the *Sonnets* must account for their universal appeal by stressing that, as T. S. Eliot puts it in 'The Three Voices of Poetry,' lyric is by definition 'the poet talking to himself'" (229). Cf. also Bruce Smith, who takes a Foucauldian approach to their "privacy" in his chapter on the *Sonnets*.

[30] I have discussed the "synchronicity" of the sonnet at greater length elsewhere (Hedley, ch. 5).

[31] Kerrigan points out that "tautologies of selfhood" are "both commonplace in Shakespeare and central," appearing frequently in the plays as well as the narrative poems and sonnets (26-27). In an interesting brief discussion of the relationship between tautology and metaphor in the sonnets, he argues that "repetition, that essential protracted tautology, became, for Shakespeare, perfect eloquence" (29).

[32] Antony Easthope argues that when, for example, Alexander Pope exploits a single word's capacity to signify doubly, he endeavors to arrest and contain "any play of meaning and slide of the signifier" by mastering it syntactically and giving it a definite rhetorical and thematic purpose (Easthope 114-15).

[33] In an important exchange with John Crowe Ransom in 1940, Arthur Mizener coined the phrase "soft focus" to describe the figurative style of Shakespeare's sonnets in contrast to the sharp or "perfect" focus of the metaphysical conceit (Mizener 733).

[34] Cf. also sonnets 116-17: Booth comments that sonnet 117 "is something like a pun on sonnet 116," insofar as it picks up some if its metaphors and its language but "uses them to entirely different effect" (*Shakespeare's Sonnets* 392).

[35] Pequigney, and more recently Smith (229 ff.), have argued for a dimension of genital innuendo and of references to physical lovemaking in the language of these sonnets that was largely ignored by earlier commentators, although not by Stephen Booth in his edition. I have neglected this dimension of Shakespeare's wordplay for two reasons: first, because it is not "there" for me as often as it is for Pequigney (a difference which can be ascribed to the way in which puns rely on their audience to activate second meanings); and second, because the narcissistic pleasure in language recrudescent in these poems belongs to a phase of psychic development that precedes the genital organization of bodily pleasure and is associated more immediately with language: pleasure in nonsense, in chiming and rhyming, in double entendre for its own sake. That some of the wordplay in the *Sonnets* is also subversive of cultural taboos—against, for example, referring to anal intercourse in a love poem—is not, however, precluded by my analysis.

[36] In order to keep my discussion of this stretch of the sequence relatively brief I have neglected the way in which sonnet 91 is related to the interlinked sonnets that precede it: they too are worried about the possibility of losing the young man's love. But whereas the emphasis for several sonnets up through 90 is on the poet's bankruptcy ("Then hate me when thou wilt, if ever, now, / Now while the world is bent my deeds to cross" [90.1-2]), in 91 it is on the riches he possesses ("having thee"); the generalizing force of 91's reiterated summary of all the things other men "glory in" contributes, moreover, to the impression of a fresh beginning here.

[37] The sonnets on both sides of this group are *Tempus edax rerum* sonnets, which express the fear that death will part the lovers. In view of their preoccupation not with Time but with "the World," sonnets 66-72 do thus form a distinct group or cluster, which shares with the sonnets on both sides of it a mood of weariness and disenchantment that tinges this part of the sequence from as far back, at least, as sonnet 57.

[38] Sonnet 70 alludes unmistakably to the Blattant Beast, archenemy of courtesy and of poetry in *The Faerie Queene*, book 6: "Yet this thy praise cannot be so thy praise, / To tie up envy, evermore enlarged" (70.11-12). The many-tongued beast of Spenser's poem is vanquished and tied up by the Knight of Courtesy but gets free at the end of book 6, never again to be successfully bound: allegorically, the suggestion is that slander is ineradicably part of contemporary social life. The beast is depicted by Spenser in *The Faerie Queene* (6.12.39-41) as having preyed upon his own poem to discredit it in the eyes of its royal dedicatee.

Works Cited

Barber, C. L. "Shakespeare in his Sonnets." *Massachusetts Review* 1 (1960): 648-72.

Booth, Stephen. *An Essay on Shakespeare's Sonnets.* New Haven: Yale UP, 1969.

———, ed. *Shakespeare's Sonnets.* New Haven: Yale UP, 1977.

Bush, Douglas, ed. *William Shakespeare: The Sonnets.* Baltimore: Pelican-Penguin, 1961.

Campbell, Robert Jean. *Psychiatric Dictionary.* 6th ed. New York: Oxford UP, 1989.

Campbell, S. C. *Only Begotten Sonnets.* Totowa: Rowman, 1978.

Chasseguet-Smirgel, Janine. *The Ego Ideal: A Psychoanalytic Essay on the Malady of the Ideal.* Trans. Paul Barrows. New York: Norton, 1985.

Crosman, Robert. "Making Love Out of Nothing At All: The Issue of Story in Shakespeare's Procreation Sonnets." *Shakespeare Quarterly* 41 (1990): 470-88.

Culler, Jonathan. "The Call of the Phoneme: Introduction." *On Puns: The Foundation of Letters.* Ed. Culler. Oxford: Blackwell, 1988. 1-16.

De Grazia, Margreta. "The Motive for Interiority: Shakespeare's *Sonnets* and *Hamlet.*" *Style* 23 (1989): 430-44.

Dubrow, Heather. *Friendly Fire: The Counterdiscourses of English Petrarchism.* Ithaca: Cornell UP, 1995 (forthcoming).

———. "Values of Contingency: Undemonstrated Assumptions in the Criticism of Shakespeare's *Sonnets.*" Paper delivered at the 106th Convention of the Modern Language Association, Chicago, December 1990.

Eagleton, Terry. *Literary Theory: An Introduction.* Minneapolis: U of Minnesota P, 1983.

Easthope, Antony. *Poetry as Discourse.* London: Methuen, 1983.

Fineman, Joel. *Shakespeare's Perjured Eye: The Invention of Poetic Subjectivity in the Sonnets.* Berkeley: U of California P, 1986.

Freud, Sigmund. "Formulations on the Two Principles of Mental Functioning." 1911. *The Standard Edition of the Complete Psychological Works of Sigmund Freud.* Trans. James Strachey, et. al. Vol. 12. London: Hogarth, 1958. 213-26. 24 vols. 1953-74.

———. *The Interpretation of Dreams.* 1900. London: Hogarth, 1955. Vols. 4 and 5 of *The Standard Edition.*

———. *Jokes and their Relation to the Unconscious.* 1905. London: Hogarth, 1960. Vol. 8 of *The Standard Edition.*

———. *Leonardo Da Vinci and a Memory of his Childhood.* 1910. London: Hogarth, 1957. 59-138. Vol. 11 of *The Standard Edition.*

———. "On Narcissism: An Introduction." 1914. *On the History of the Psychoanalytic Movement, Papers on Metapsychology, and Other Works.* London: Hogarth, 1957. 67-102. Vol. 14 of *The Standard Edition.*

———. "Some Neurotic Mechanisms in Jealousy, Paranoia and Homosexuality." 1922. *Beyond the Pleasure Principle, Group Psychology, and Other Works.* London: Hogarth, 1955. 221-32. Vol. 18 of *The Standard Edition.*

———. *Three Essays on the Theory of Sexuality.* 1910. *A Case of Hysteria, Three Essays on Sexuality, and Other Works.* London: Hogarth, 1953. 135-245. Vol. 7 of *The Standard Edition.*

Frye, Northrop. "How True a Twain." Hubler 23-54.

Hedley, Jane. *Power in Verse: Metaphor and Metonymy in the Renaissance Lyric.* University Park: Pennsylvania State UP, 1988.

Hubler, Edward, ed. *The Riddle of Shakespeare's Sonnets.* London: Basic, 1962.

———. *The Sense of Shakespeare's Sonnets.* Princeton: Princeton UP, 1952.

Jakobson, Roman. "Linguistics and Poetics." 1960. *Language in Literature.* Ed. Krystyna Pomorska and Stephen Rudy. Cambridge: Belknap, 1987. 62-94.

Joseph, Sister Miriam. *Shakespeare's Use of the Arts of Language.* New York: Columbia UP, 1947.

Kerrigan, John, ed. The Sonnets *and* A Lover's Complaint. New York: Viking-Penguin, 1986.

Lacan, Jacques. *Speech and Language in Psychoanalysis.* Trans. Anthony Wilden. Baltimore: Johns Hopkins UP, 1968.

Laplanche, Jean, and J.-B. Pontalis. *The Language of Psychoanalysis.* Trans. Donald Nicholson-Smith. New York: Norton, 1973.

Levine, Steven. "Monet, Fantasy, and Freud." *Psychoanalytic Perspectives on Art* 1 (1985): 29-55.

MacCary, W. Thomas. Rev. of *Shakespeare's Perjured Eye,* by Joel Fineman and *Such Is My Love,* by Joseph

Pequigney. *Journal of English and Germanic Philology* 86 (1987): 228-32.

Martin, Philip. *Shakespeare's Sonnets: Self, Love, and Art.* Cambridge: Cambridge UP, 1972.

Mizener, Arthur. "The Structure of Figurative Language in Shakespeare's *Sonnets.*" *Southern Review* 5 (1940): 730-47.

Muller, John P., and William J. Richardson. *Lacan and Language: A Reader's Guide to* Écrits. New York: International UP, 1982.

Ovid [Publius Ovidius Naso]. *Metamorphoses.* Trans. Frank Justus Miller. 2 vols. Loeb Classical Library. 1916. London: Heineman, 1951.

Pequigney, Joseph. *Such is My Love: A Study of Shakespeare's Sonnets.* Chicago: U of Chicago P, 1985.

Petrarca, Francesco. *Petrarch's Lyric Poems: The Rime Sparse and Other Lyrics.* Trans. and ed. Robert M. Durling. Cambridge: Harvard UP, 1976.

Puttenham, George. *The Arte of English Poesie.* Ed. Gladys Doidge Willcock and Alice Walker. Cambridge: Cambridge UP, 1936.

Rollins, Hyder Edward, ed. *A New Variorum Edition of Shakespeare: The Sonnets.* 2 vols. Philadelphia: Lippincott, 1944.

Rosmarin, Adena. "Hermeneutics: Shakespeare's *Sonnets* and Interpretive History." *PMLA* 100 (1985): 20-37.

Shakespeare, William. *Sonnets.* Ed. Stephen Booth. New Haven: Yale UP, 1977.

———. "The Phoenix and Turtle." *The Poems.* Ed. F. T. Prince. London: Methuen, 1960.

Smith, Bruce. *Homosexual Desire in Shakespeare's England: A Cultural Poetics.* Chicago: U of Chicago P, 1991.

Spender, Stephen. "The Alike and the Other." Hubler 91-128.

Spenser, Edmund. *Poetical Works.* Ed. J. C. Smith and Ernest De Selincourt. 1912. London: Oxford UP, 1970.

Stirling, Brents. *The Shakespeare Sonnet Order: Poems and Groups.* Berkeley: U of California P, 1968.

Todorov, Tzvetan, and Oswald Ducrot. *Encyclopedic Dictionary of the Sciences of Language.* Trans. Catherine Porter. Baltimore: Johns Hopkins UP, 1979.

Vinge, Louise. *The Narcissus Theme in Western European Literature up to the Early Nineteenth Century.* Lund: Gleerups, 1967.

Wilden, Anthony. "Lacan and the Discourse of the Other." Lacan 157-312.

Wilson, John Dover, ed. *The Sonnets.* By William Shakespeare. Cambridge: Cambridge UP, 1966.

Zweig, Paul. *The Heresy of Self-Love.* Princeton: Princeton UP, 1968.

VOICE

Hallett Smith (essay date 1981)

SOURCE: "The Voices and the Audience in Shakespeare's Sonnets," *The Tension of the Lyre: Poetry in Shakespeare's Sonnets,* Huntington Library, 1981, pp. 1-12.

[*In the following essay, Smith draws on the writings of T. S. Eliot to show how the voice heard in the sonnets is directed both toward itself—in the form of a soliloquy or meditation—and toward an audience—the Friend, for example, but also posterity.*]

T. S. Eliot maintained that there are three voices of poetry. "The first voice," he said, "is the voice of the poet talking to himself—or to nobody. The second is the voice of the poet addressing an audience, whether large or small. The third is the voice of the poet when he attempts to create a dramatic character speaking in verse."[1] With the third voice we have nothing to do in considering the sonnets, though of course it is primary in any study of the plays. With the first two voices we shall be much concerned. The first voice requires some explanation.

Poems in which the poet seems to be talking to himself, or to nobody, are commonly reflective poems, poems of meditation, if we use that term in its most general sense. Shakespeare shows us one such poem in the process of composition, at the end of *Richard II.* There the deposed king, in prison, is trying to compare his prison to the world. There is no audience; he is speaking to himself, or to nobody. He has trouble making the comparison, until he realizes that, just as the world is crowded with people, so his prison is inhabited by thoughts.

> And these same thoughts people this little world,
> In humors like the people of this world:
> For no thought is contented.
> (V, v, 9-11)[2]

His poem is full of contradictions, of opposites—king and beggar, music and discord, the man who wastes time and the man who is wasted by time. The music he hears drives him mad, though it is supposed to cure madness:

> This music mads me, let it sound no more,
> For though it have holp mad men to their
>   wits,
> In me it seems it will make wise men mad.
> Yet blessing on his heart that gives it me!
> For 'tis a sign of love; and love to Richard
> Is a strange brooch in this all-hating world.
>   (V, v, 61-66)

Shakespeare's Sonnet 94, a famous and difficult one, may be a meditation directed to himself or to nobody:

> They that have pow'r to hurt, and will do none,
> That do not do the thing they most do show,
> Who moving others, are themselves as stone,
> Unmoved, cold, and to temptation slow,
> They rightly do inherit heaven's graces,
> And husband nature's riches from expense;
> They are the lords and owners of their faces,
> Others but stewards of their excellence.
> The summer's flow'r is to the summer sweet,
> Though to itself it only live and die,
> But if that flow'r with base infection meet,
> The basest weed outbraves his dignity:
>   For sweetest things turn sourest by their
>   deeds;
>   Lilies that fester smell far worse than
>   weeds.

There may be several reminiscences of New Testament passages here, but one that is certain is Matt. 6:28-29, "And why take ye thought for raiment? Consider the lilies of the field, how they grow; they toil not, neither do they spin: And yet I say unto you, That even Solomon in all his glory was not arrayed like one of these." There may also be a recollection of a passage in John Gerard's preface to his *Herball* (1597) which speaks of "one King Salomon, excelling all the rest for wisdome, of greater royalty than they all (though the Lillies of the field outbraued him.)"

Older interpretations of the sonnet, such as Empson's and Ransom's,[3] are based on the notion that the sonnet is addressed to the Fair Friend, though there is no internal evidence that this is so. I believe Melchiori is right when he says, "Sonnet 94, like sonnets 121, 129, 146, is a soliloquy in so far as it has to *get away* from the *private* context of the surrounding poems, and to debate, before the sessions of the poet's silent thought, matters of general concern."[4]

Of course the soliloquy and its shorter form, the aside, belong to a convention naturally and inevitably used by Elizabethan playwrights. The aside most often serves the purpose of revealing to the audience, though not to the other characters on the stage, someone's true feelings. Cordelia's comments after her sisters' flattering speeches are an example: "What shall Cordelia speak? Love, and be silent" and "Then poor Cordelia! / And yet not so, since I am sure my love's / More ponderous than my tongue" (*King Lear* I, i, 62-63, 76-78). But the aside may reveal viciousness as well as virtue, as in Richard Duke of Gloucester's asides when his nephew, young Prince Edward, expresses pious thoughts: "So wise so young, they say do never live long" (*Richard III*, III, i, 79).

The soliloquy is sometimes used for the same purpose as the aside: to inform the audience that the character's actions, and perhaps even speech, are not to be taken at face value. The soliloquy serves, then, as an artificial means of conveying from the dramatist to the audience a message which the playwright cannot convey directly. The character delivers the message, even though at times it is inconsistent with his character or at least with those traits that have so far been established on the stage. A classical case is Prince Hal's soliloquy at the end of the first tavern scene in *1 Henry IV*:

> I know you all, and will a while uphold
> The unyok'd humor of your idleness,
> Yet herein will I imitate the sun,
> Who doth permit the base contagious clouds
> To smother up his beauty from the world,
> That when he please again to be himself,
> Being wanted, he may be more wond'red at
> By breaking through the foul and ugly mists
> Of vapors that did seem to strangle him.
>   (I, ii, 195-203)

He goes on to philosophize, generally, about the pleasures of surprise: "nothing pleaseth but rare accidents." The followers of the older view of convention in Shakespeare (as represented by E. E. Stoll) would say that this is merely a warning to the audience not to judge Hal by his previous words and actions, as spectators in the theater are accustomed to do, but to wait until he reveals his true self. We will accordingly be in a conspiracy with the hero and enjoy a feeling of comic superiority towards the other characters, particularly Falstaff and Hal's father. Other critics, more in the train of A. C. Bradley than of Stoll, will take this speech to be relevant to Hal's character; *everything* he says and does on the stage is relevant, they say, and a character cannot step out of character. At any rate, here Prince Hal is not talking to himself or nobody. Rhetorically, he is addressing his absent comrades; it is an *apostrophe*, an address to something or someone, present or absent, which interrupts the surrounding discourse. But functionally, of course, he is talking to the theater audience.

The soliloquist par excellence who talks to himself is obviously Hamlet. How subjective and internal his thoughts are is emphasized in the final two lines of his first soliloquy:

> It is not, nor it cannot come to good,
> But break my heart, for I must hold my tongue.
>
> (I, ii, 158-59)

He meditates on his own inaction, on being and non-being, on the nature of man. These latter themes are appropriate enough for sonnets, and this brings us to the consideration of the "audience" of the Shakespeare sonnets.

W. H. Auden thought that these are private poems, with no audience indicated or envisaged:

> Though Shakespeare may have shown the sonnets to one or two intimate literary friends,—it would appear that he must have—he wrote them, I am quite certain, as one writes a diary, for himself alone, with no thought of a public.[5]

That this view is untenable will appear, I think, when we consider the question of the stated or implied addressee of the sonnets in groups and the rhetorical strategy of individual poems. Father Walter J. Ong has shown, in a notable paper, that "The Writer's Audience is Always a Fiction." In it he maintains that in the extreme case, the diary, the writer is not so simply addressing himself as one might think:

> The audience of the diarist is even more encased in fictions. What is easier, one might argue, than addressing oneself? As those who first begin a diary often find out, a great many things are easier. The reasons why are not hard to unearth. First of all, we do not normally talk to ourselves—certainly not in long, involved sentences and paragraphs. Second, the diarist pretending to be talking to himself has also, since he is writing, to pretend he is somehow not there. And to what self is he talking? To the self he imagines he is? Or would like to be? Or really thinks he is? Or thinks other people think he is? To himself as he is now? Or as he will probably be or ideally be twenty years hence? If he addresses not himself but "Dear Diary," who in the world is "Dear Diary"? What role does this imply?[6]

If it is true that even the diarist is addressing a *persona*, it must be even more true of the sonneteer, the poet who composes love poems. The audience exists, fictional or not, but it is not simple and it is not obvious.

Let us consider an example of Eliot's second of the three voices, Sonnet 87, a poem which is clearly addressed to another person, not a solitary meditation or soliloquy, but a message, rhetorically addressed to a recipient:

> Farewell, thou art too dear for my possessing,
> And like enough thou know'st thy estimate;
> The charter of thy worth gives thee releasing;
> My bonds in thee are all determinate.
> For how do I hold thee but by thy granting,
> And for that riches where is my deserving?
> The cause of this fair gift in me is wanting,
> And so my patent back again is swerving.
> Thyself thou gav'st, thy own worth then not knowing,
> Or me, to whom thou gav'st it, else mistaking,
> So thy great gift, upon misprision growing,
> Comes home again, on better judgment making.
> Thus have I had thee as a dream doth flatter:
> In sleep a king, but waking no such matter.

This is one of two sonnets with a feminine ending at every line. Taken by itself Sonnet 87 might be considered a metrical experiment and consequently of no great importance in content, but the other feminine-ending sonnet, 20, is notoriously significant: "A woman's face with Nature's own hand painted."

Number 87, addressed to a recipient, is peppered with personal pronouns: *my* (four times) and *thy* (six times); the vocabulary is that of technical legal possession and cost: *dear* (expensive), *possessing, estimate* (value), *charter, worth, releasing, bonds, granting, riches, gift, patent, worth* (again), and *gift* (again). A title for the poem might be "A Gift Recalled"—a subject which could have been handled as a meditation, a direct expression of grief at the loss of something valuable, but the presence of the person addressed is insisted upon, even into the concluding couplet:

> Thus have I had *thee* as a dream doth flatter:
> In sleep a king, but waking no such matter.

G. K. Hunter has made a distinction between the lyrical character and the dramatic character of the sonnets:

> The power of these poems does not reside in lyrical utterance, the version they represent is an individual's, and to that extent like lyric, but in them the reader is not concerned with solitary imaginings presented as of universal significance (as in the odes of Keats and Shelley), but with the relation of one human heart to others. By setting up a system of tensions between forces presented as persons, Shakespeare's sonnets interest the reader in a manner akin to the dramatic.[7]

The sonnets which begin in the imperative mood obviously imply or evoke a listener, as in Sonnet 90:

> Then hate me when thou wilt, if ever, now,
> Now while the world is bent my deeds to cross,
> Join with the spite of fortune, make me bow, . . .

The vigor imparted by the imperative has evoked enthusiastic response from some critics. George Wyndham, for example, wrote, "I doubt if in all recorded speech such faultless perfection may be found, so sustained through fourteen consecutive lines."[8]

The first edition of the 154 sonnets, published by Thomas Thorpe in 1609, does not divide the poems into groups. Most modern critics do divide them; almost unanimously, they consider the first seventeen sonnets to be addressed to a young man, urging him to marry and beget children. Even editors who rearrange the order usually keep the first seventeen together. One of the most recent of the rearrangers, Brents Stirling, says, "There are no intrusions and no convincing signs of internal disarrangement. All sonnets of the group join to express a theme found nowhere else in the 1609 collection: the first fourteen urge a young man to father children that he may save his rare qualities from Time's ruin; the last three, 15-17, offer the poet's verse as a defense against Time only to question it as a means of preservation and to reassert fatherhood as Time's adversary."[9]

Nowhere else in Elizabethan sonneteering do we find this theme. In fact, urging a young man to marry and have offspring struck C. S. Lewis as an absurd pretext for writing the poems. "What man in the world," he asked, "except a father or a potential father-in-law, cares whether any other man gets married?"[10] The question, if meant seriously, shows a surprising ignorance of sixteenth-century attitudes. Erasmus wrote an elaborate epistle to persuade a young gentleman (neither his son nor his potential son-in-law) to marry. It is included in Thomas Wilson's *Arte of Rhetorique,* of which there were eight editions between 1553 and 1585. Sidney wrote a poem in which the old shepherd Geron advises the young shepherd Histor to marry.[11] In an emblem book, Otto van Veen's *Amorum Emblemata* (1608), dedicated to "the most noble and incomparable pair of brethren" who were later to share the dedication of Shakespeare's First Folio, there is a poem containing many of the same arguments used in the first seventeen Shakespeare sonnets.[12] As J. W. Lever put it, the doctrine of Increase allowed Shakespeare "to express in the sonnet medium one of the most vital and comprehensive doctrines of the age."[13]

One of the seventeen sonnets usually considered a masterpiece is Number 12:

> When I do count the clock that tells the time,
> And see the brave day sunk in hideous night;
> When I behold the violet past prime,
> And sable curls [all] silver'd o'er with white;
> When lofty trees I see barren of leaves,
> Which erst from heat did canopy the herd,
> And summer's green all girded up in sheaves
> Borne on the bier with white and bristly beard;
> Then of thy beauty do I question make
> That thou among the wastes of time must go,
> Since sweets and beauties do themselves forsake,
> And die as fast as they see others grow,
>   And nothing 'gainst Time's scythe can make defense
>   Save breed, to brave him when he takes thee hence.

In the octave it is a meditation, the poet summoning up instances of the regrettable passage of time, speaking to himself as in 106 ("When in the chronicle of wasted time") and 30 ("When to the sessions of sweet silent thought"). In the sestet the young man is addressed, but fleetingly; he must go among the wastes of Time, and there is only his champion, Breed, to brave Time when he takes him thence. Characteristic Shakespearean motifs make their appearance—the hours of the day, the seasons of the year,[14] flowers and trees and harvest. Phrases from others in this little group of seventeen also give hints of the greatness of sonnets farther along in the collection: "the world's fresh ornament / And only herald to the gaudy spring" (1); "Thou art thy mother's glass, and she in thee / Calls back the lovely April of her prime" (3); "For never-resting time leads summer on / To hideous winter and confounds him there, / Sap check'd with frost and lusty leaves quite gone, / Beauty o'er-snow'd and bareness everywhere" (5).

As one reads through the first seventeen sonnets, he becomes aware of a second theme emerging from the shadow of the first ("From fairest creatures we desire increase"). It is the immortality of verse, an ancient topic, treated most eminently by Ovid and Horace, but more recently by poets of the Pléiade. Being celebrated in poetry is a way to immortality, even though for the poet (perhaps remembering his assignment) there is "a mightier way" (16.1), namely to have children. But 15, however it is nudged aside by 16, is one of the great ones:

> When I consider every thing that grows
> Holds in perfection but a little moment;
> That this huge stage presenteth nought but shows
> Whereon the stars in secret influence comment;
> When I perceive that men as plants increase,
> Cheerëd and check'd even by the self-same sky,

> Vaunt in their youthful sap, at height
>   decrease,
> And wear their brave state out of memory:
> Then the conceit of this inconstant stay
> Sets you most rich in youth before my sight,
> Where wasteful Time debateth with Decay
> To change your day of youth to sullied night,
>   And all in war with Time for love of you,
>   As he takes from you, I ingraft you new.¹⁵

This sonnet begins as a reflective poem; it is not until line 10 that the young bachelor is addressed directly. So we overhear the meditation on "the conceit of this inconstant stay," but the dramatic turn in line 10 emphasizes the person addressed, with sounds chiming on the word *you: you, youth, your, youth, you, you, new.* The intrusion of the immortality of verse theme on the propagation theme is made more striking by the return of the latter in the next sonnet, which is firmly linked to it:

> But wherefore do you not a mightier way
> Make war upon this bloody tyrant Time?

So far I have spoken of the propagation theme as an "assignment," though without specifying from whom. For all I know Shakespeare gave himself the assignment, for reasons beyond conjecture, but the generally held view is well expressed by Dover Wilson, who refers to the first seventeen sonnets as "a series of lovely poetical exercises, probably composed to order."¹⁶ In a recent fascinating survey of the English sonnet sequences, however, Carol Thomas Neely has suggested that propagation is really a metaphor for writing poetry. She points out that Petrarch introduces the metaphor and that he is followed by Spenser when he writes "Unquiet thought, whom at the first I bred" in his second sonnet, and by Sidney in the first sonnet of *Astrophil and Stella*:

> Thus great with child to speak, and helpless
>   in my throes,
> Biting my truant pen, beating myself for
>   spite,
> "Fool," said my muse to me, "look in thy
>   heart and write!"

"Shakespeare's opening sonnets to the young man," Neely writes, "urging him to beget a child, make this metaphor explicit by making it literal."

> ... But as the sequence progresses, another kind of procreation comes to supersede the first. ... The verse is first seen as identical with, then superior to, the physical child. ... The poetic begetting, however, must also be achieved by a kind of parthenogenesis since there seems little indication that love is generated in the youth. Shakespeare's opening sonnets manifest the sequence's underlying drive to breed and the way in which it is thwarted. The poet must do it by himself; he, and not the beloved, is the true 'onlie begetter' of the dedication. ... In all of the sequences, as in Shakespeare's, parthenogenesis prevails; the poet-lover creates his desires, his beloved, his poetry, all out of his own head and comes to lament the barrenness of the enterprise.¹⁷

This suggestion is brilliant and stimulating to thought. I wish I could accept it. But I cannot, because I think Shakespeare keeps the child and the poetry separate, in the couplet to Sonnet 17, the conclusion to the series:

> But were some child of yours alive that time,
> You should live twice, in it, and in my
>   rhyme.

That Sonnet 17 is the conclusion to the series is not perfectly evident to everyone. Some critics can admit that there are no further references to begetting of offspring in the remaining 137 sonnets without drawing any inferences from that fact. They are swayed by the awareness that the offspring theme has already been associated with immortality through verse, particularly in 15 and 17. They conclude that the young man of 1-17 is identical with the Fair Friend of 18-126. Stephen Booth, in his recent elaborate edition of the sonnets, comments, "Since a reader cannot be expected to know either that Sonnet 17 was the last of the sonnets in support of procreation or that Shakespeare is about to claim an immortality for his verse that the two preceding sonnets specifically question, line 12 [of Sonnet 18: "When in eternal lines to time thou grow'st"] will probably appear to lead into another exhortation to marry. The imperceptibility of the dividing line between the procreation sonnets and sonnets 18-126 is a primary reason for assuming that 1-126 all concern the same relationship."¹⁸

The dividing line is perceptible enough to me. There is little evidence in the first seventeen sonnets that the speaker feels love for the person addressed, or that he meditates to himself on the subject of love and is overheard. Beauty, yes, and its transitoriness, but not love. There is nothing like the conclusion of 19:

> Yet do thy worst, old Time: despite thy
>   wrong,
> My love shall in my verse ever live young.

The concluding sonnet (as I take it) raises another question in its first line: "Who will believe my verse in time to come?". The question of the credibility of poetry is not an idle question. Sidney deals with it seriously in his *Defense of Poetry*. He thinks it is particularly important in love poetry:

> But truly many of such writings, as come under the banner of unresistable love, if I were a mistress would never persuade me they were in love, so

coldly they apply fiery speeches,—as men that had rather read lovers' writings and so caught up certain swelling phrases, which hang together, like a man which once told my father that the wind was at northwest and by south, because he would be sure to name winds enough—than that in truth they feel those passions which easily (as I think) may be bewrayed by that same forcibleness or *energia* (as the Greeks call it) of the writer.[19]

It is important, then, that we consider the audience of the poem, fictional though it probably is, and respond appropriately. It is in this way, not merely by "overhearing," that we are able to judge the *energia* or forcibleness of the poem. Some sonnets of course are reflective, and some parts of sonnets are meditations which shift to the dramatic situation of the speaker-listener. In the propagation series, leading as it does into the celebration of the immortality of verse, we have a variety. Here it is well to return to the conclusion Eliot reaches in his essay on the three voices of poetry:

> I think that in every poem, from the private meditation to the epic or drama, there is more than one voice to be heard. If the author never spoke to himself, the result would not be poetry, though it might be magnificent rhetoric; and part of our enjoyment of great poetry is the enjoyment of *overhearing* words which are not addressed to us. But if the poem were exclusively for the author, it would be a poem in a private and unknown language, and a poem which was a poem only for the author would not be a poem at all.[20]

Notes

[1] "The Three Voices of Poetry" (1953), in *On Poetry and Poets* (1957), p. 96.

[2] All Shakespeare quotations are from *The Riverside Shakespeare*, ed. G. Blakemore Evans *et. al.* (1974).

[3] See my *Elizabethan Poetry* (1952), p. 189.

[4] Georgio Melchiori, *Shakespeare's Dramatic Meditations: An Experiment in Criticism* (1976), p. 68. J. W. Lever reached a similar conclusion: *The Elizabethan Love Sonnet* (1956), pp. 216-17.

[5] *Signet Classic Shakespeare* edition (1964), p. xxxv. Stephen Spender agrees: "The sonnets arean intermittently-kept poetic diary covering a period, supposedly, of three years" (*The Riddle of Shakespeare's Sonnets* [1962], p. 95). But a few pages later (p. 100) he writes, "A thing that is often forgotten by writers about the sonnets is that they are not a monologue. They are one side of a dialogue, or a speech . . . or they are letters."

[6] *PMLA* 90 (1975): 20.

[7] "The Dramatic Technique of Shakespeare's Sonnets," *Essays in Criticism* 3 (1953): 154. Hunter is discussing Sonnets 89 and 86.

[8] *The Poems of Shakespeare* (1898), p. cxxxix.

[9] *The Shakespeare Sonnet Order: Poems and Groups* (1968), p. 45.

[10] *English Literature in the Sixteenth Century, Excluding Drama* (1959), p. 503.

[11] *Poems of Sir Philip Sidney*, ed. William Ringler (1962), p. 105, lines 70-81.

[12] Mario Praz, *Studies in Seventeenth Century Imagery* (1939), 1:104-07.

[13] *The Elizabethan Love Sonnet* (1956), p. 190.

[14] H. S. Donow's useful *Concordance to the Sonnet Sequences of Daniel, Drayton, Shakespeare, Sidney and Spenser* (1969) reveals the fact that Shakespeare refers to *Time, winter, summer, spring, autumn,* and *day* far more often than his fellow sonneteers. Sidney exceeds him in references to *night*.

[15] The sources of the imagery in the first eight lines have been traced to passages in La Primaudaye's *The French Academie* (1586) and to similar passages in Barnaby Googe's translation of Palingenius, *The Zodiake of Life* (1560 and later). The best discussion is in John Erskine Hankins, *Shakespeare's Derived Imagery* (1953), pp. 253-56.

[16] *The New Shakespeare: The Sonnets,* ed. J. Dover Wilson (1966), p. 115.

[17] "The Structure of English Sonnet Sequences," *English Literary History* 45 (1978):365-67.

[18] *Shakespeare's Sonnets* (1977), p. 162. The great weakness of Booth's edition, I think, is his total adherence to Empson's doctrine that *all* glosses are valid. See his edition, p. xiii.

[19] *Miscellaneous Prose of Sir Philip Sidney*, ed. Katherine Duncan-Jones and Jan Van Dorsten (1973), pp. 116-17.

[20] *On Poetry and Poets,* p. 109.

John Klause (essay date 1983)

SOURCE: "Shakespeare's *Sonnets*: Age in Love and the Goring of Thoughts," in *Studies in Philology,* Vol. 80, No. 3, Summer, 1983, pp. 300-24.

[*In the following essay, Klause closely examines the apparent inconsistencies in the poetic voice of the sonnets. While acknowledging that the aging "Poet" of the sonnets sounds "humble" and "submissive," Klause asserts that this tone is intentionally used by the poet as a persuasive device and that it is not in conflict with the sonnets' powerful imagery.*]

To call the man whose travail is recorded in Shakespeare's *Sonnets* a protagonist may seem to grant him a status beyond his desert. Of a protagonist we expect at least that he struggle for or against something and that in his exertions, even when he is inconsistent, he prove himself a coherent personality. Shakespeare's Poet, it has been suggested, does neither.

Yvor Winters once complained of a "servile weakness" in the Poet.[1] And indeed, one is tempted to underscore evidence of an emotional and moral supineness in a man who is everywhere full of self-denigration: "To leave poor me thou hast the strength of laws, / Since why to love I can allege no cause" (49.13-14),[2] who envisions himself a "sad slave" without personal prerogatives, existing to serve through his presence or absence the pleasure of a sovereign Friend and living vicariously through him (57; 37.1-4); who allows his Friend moral obliquity, which he will rationalize for his master even when he is himself its victim: "Suns of the world may stain, when heaven's sun staineth" (33.14); who professes to have no rights, not even to pardon the injury inflicted on him (58.9-14); who blesses the Friend who steals his mistress ("sweet thief," "gentle thief" [35.14; 40.9]), and will then find more blame in himself for excusing the crime than in his Friend for committing it (35); who stumbles after his Lady like a "babe" after its mother, "crying" for attention (143); who knowingly, helplessly acquiesces in the falsehood necessary to keep a wildly irrational love alive: "Therefore I lie with her, and she with me, / And in our faults by lies we flattered be!" (138.13-14). It is no wonder that critics have proceeded beyond the view that the Poet is sometimes "trapped" into inertia,[3] to the conviction that, in some poems at least, he exhibits "an almost masochistic humility" or a "masochistic generosity."[4]

But is the Poet ever consistent enough to be described as passive or prostrate? His art and his self-confidence are alternately feeble and potent: his rhyme is now "barren" (16.4), now "pow'rful" (55.2). He acknowledges that "nothing 'gainst Time's scythe can make defense / Save breed" (12.13-14); yet he promises his Friend:

But thy eternal summer shall not fade.

. . . . .

So long as men can breathe or eyes can see,
So long lives this, and this gives life to thee.
(18.9, 13-14)

The Poet humbly confesses his verse to be plain—even monotonous and unadventurous (76), a "worthless boat" beside his Rival's "tall building . . . of goodly pride" (80.11-12). He nonetheless takes pride in his "true plain words," which are free from the "strained touches rhetoric can lend" (82.12, 10).

So is it not with me as with that Muse
Stirr'd by a painted beauty to his verse,
Who heaven itself for ornament doth use,
And every fair with his fair doth rehearse,
Making a couplement of proud compare
With sun and moon, with earth and sea's rich gems,
With April's first-born flowers, and all things rare
That heaven's air in this huge rondure hems.
(21.1-8)

This from the same Poet who compares his love to "a summer's day" and the "eye of heaven" (18.1, 5); to "the lily's white," the "sweet" of the "violet," and "the deep vermilion in the rose" (98.9-10; 99.1-3); to Helen and to Adonis (53); and, by implication, to the triune God himself (105). The Poet's love seems self-abnegating in the extreme:

If you read this line, remember not
The hand that writ it, for I love you so,
That I in your sweet thoughts would be forgot,
If thinking on me then should make you woe.
(71.5-8)

But this love candidly pleads for "recompense" (23.11). It is generous in granting the beloved independence: "Thee have I not lock'd up in any chest" (48.9). Or perhaps it is not:

So am I as the rich whose blessed key
Can bring him to his sweet up-locked treasure,
The which he will not ev'ry hour survey.
(52.1-3; *cf.* 75.3-8)

The lover who proves that love must be forever changing, growing (115), then insists that "it is an ever-fixed mark" (116.5) and in the next breath admits his own inconstancy (117). A voice remorseful ("Alas, 'tis true, I have gone here and there" [110.1]), self-convicted of "transgression" (120.3), can suddenly turn defiantly proud of its essential righteousness:

On my frailties why are frailer spies,
Which in their wills count bad what I think good?
No, I am that I am, and they that level
At my abuses reckon up their own;

I may be straight though they themselves be bevel;
By their rank thoughts my deeds must not be shown.

(121.7-12)

These psychological somersaults may seem too spectacular and unconnected to be turned by a character in a dramatic *praxis* or action—hence the impulse of many critics to abandon story in favor of idea.[5]

Some, however, have tried to face squarely the problem of the protagonist. They have challenged the portrait of the supine lover in either of two ways: by appeals to irony or to an ethical code.

The Poet's profession of vassalage, it is said, should not always be understood naively:

Being your slave, what should I do but tend
Upon the hours and times of your desire?
I have no precious time at all to spend,
Nor services to do, till you require.

(57.1-4)

Here and elsewhere one may find the words heavy with equivocation, called upon to express simultaneously devotion and reproach. "I am utterly yours. 'So true a fool is love,' I have no needs but yours. Indeed!"[6] And where the expressions of "self-naughting" are ingenuous, they are not the whines of servile helplessness but, in an almost religious sense, the effects of an active heroism (what Milton was to call "the better fortitude / Of patience and heroic martyrdom" [*PL*, 9.31-2]). "I may not evermore acknowledge thee" (36.9), "No longer mourn" (71.1), and "Although thou steal thee all my poverty" (40.10) spring "from a region in which love abandons all claims and flowers into charity." C. S. Lewis's formulation of this view has become classic:

> The self-abnegation, the 'naughting', in the *Sonnets* never rings false. This patience, this anxiety (more like a parent's than a lover's) to find excuses for the beloved, this clear-sighted and wholly unembit-tered resignation, this transference of the whole self into another self, without the demand for a return, have hardly had a precedent in profane literature. In certain senses of the word 'love', Shakespeare is not so much our best as our only love poet.[7]

The question of the Poet's consistency is also addressed under two assumptions: either that the problem would dissolve if the true "order" of the Sonnets were known,[8] or that the contradictions, real enough in themselves, are precisely the kind we might expect of a complex human being in turbulent love affairs.[9] Thus a plausible story may be seen to lurk in the *Sonnets*, and a plausible protagonist; and both can be discovered if only art may be rearranged to suit the logic of life or the illogic of life allowed to invade the ritual of art.

There is merit in all of these views. But aside from the obvious fact that at some points one may be incompatible with another (the lover either abandons all claims or ironically does not, is consistent or is not), none of these solutions is sufficiently cogent or comprehensive to escape major objections. Irony is a quality of mind, not of character, and may be found in a spirit morally feckless. A lover's ironic protest against his friend's faithlessness hardly qualifies as an "action." We might remember Carlisle's admonition to Richard II:

My lord, wise men ne'er sit and wail their woes,
But presently prevent the ways to wail.

(*R2*, III.ii.178-9)

If the Poet's self-naughting is genuine (and we shall see that it is not as straightforward and radical as Lewis proposed), it may in the abstract be deemed heroic and wise. But the Poet's generosity towards this particular Friend is in some ways less charity than connivance. The freedom granted from "claims" (insofar as it *is* granted) is the opportunity to receive with ingratitude, to ignore, forget, steal, and betray with impunity. Rearrangement may bring the *Sonnets* closer to a plausible sequence; but there is no authority to guarantee that Shakespeare's is one of those "likely" stories that are all too rare in and out of fiction. Furthermore, true contradictions will not be resolved by shuffling. And if they are allowed to stand, either an explanation must be found for the Poet's inconsistency or he must be judged helplessly, pointlessly wayward.

Discovering a rationale for inconsistency is not, in fact, an impossible task. We may see that irony and ingenuousness coexist in a lover whose self-martyrdom is at once real and strategic, generous and self-interested, noble and tainted, variable and utterly single-minded. In order to do so, we must dwell upon the implications of two facts about the Poet, to which he calls attention and which are so obvious that we tend to take them for granted: he is old and he is a liar.

The Poet's age in Shakespeare's *Sonnets* is not merely a hackneyed, implausible convention. Petrarch's reference to his own "weary spirit," "wrinkled skin," "decaying wit and strength" (Sonnet 81) had indeed inspired many of his successors (like Samuel Daniel, Richard Barnfield, and Michael Drayton—the eldest of whom was thirty-one years old at his work's first printing) to pose as superannuated in all but "desire."[10] But the counterfeit silver hair and furrowed brows of most of these sonneteers could not disguise the youth of the passion which they portrayed. Theirs were "the propositions of hot blood and brains." Like many youthful suitors, their lovers were young enough in sensibility to look upon desire and its sublimation as the only important facts of life. Even where the lovers' attitudes were reflective, the reflection, though sometimes deep, was narrowly channeled—as it tends to be if a young person decides that the problems surrounding love must be addressed before the rest of life can be attended to. When Shakespeare's Poet speaks of his age, however, we sense no discrepancy between his psychology and his pose.

>   my glass shows me myself indeed,
> Beated and chopp'd with tann'd antiquity.
>
> In me thou seest the glowing of such fire
> That on the ashes of his youth doth lie.
>
>   she knows my days are past the best.
>
>   . . . . .
>
> And age in love loves not t' have years told.
>   (62.9-10; 73.9-10; 138.6, 12)

Whatever his chronological age (he regards "forty winters" as an "antiquity" [2.1]), the Poet everywhere speaks from the perspective of a man who has weathered life. The disparity in years between him and his "lovely boy" (126.1), between him and the lady before whom he tries to suppress the "simple truth" of his age (138.8), colors almost every motive and action in the relationships to which the *Sonnets* refer.

That an older man should speak in sonnets, with the benefit of experience, is not a situation we would expect after reading Shakespeare's plays, where sonnet-lovers, mostly young, are almost invariably treated with condescension. In *Two Gentlemen of Verona* "wailful sonnets" are by definition "serviceable," little more than devices for a young man to use who would "lay lime to tangle" a lady's "desires" (III.ii.68-70). The poetical flights of the wooers in *Love's Labour's Lost* are products of immature, insincere, uneducated sentiment, which must be chastened; its language made more "honest" (V.ii.413). Orlando's "odes" and "elegies" in the forest of Arden are harmless and touching enough; they are also ridiculous, and Rosalind is right to call the young poet a "fancy-monger" in need of "good counsel" (*AYL*, III.ii.361-4). The romantic intensity of Romeo and Juliet, who speak in a sonnet at their first meeting and kiss on the couplet (*Rom.*, I.v.93-106), is no less callow for being genuine; and use of "the numbers that Petrarch flowd in" (at which an overwise Mercutio sneers [II.iv.38-9]) marks the couple for trouble who take the sonneteers' hyperboles too seriously.[11] As a form, then, the sonnet does not promise Shakespeare much. He takes it away from the young, however, among whom it has been abused, doing so not simply to parody an institutionalized silliness,[12] but to give "age in love" its proper voice. This voice is both consistent, true to the character from whom it issues, and inconsistent, as it must be to achieve the character's ends.

If the Poet in Shakespeare's *Sonnets* "loves not t' have years told" (138.12), he is forever telling his age anyway—not only by calling attention to his physical decline ("That time of year thou mayst in me behold" [73]), but by consistently revealing in himself the attitudes and preoccupations of a man whose "days are past the best" (138.6). He lives with memories of "precious friends hid in death's dateless night" and can "weep afresh love's long since cancell'd woe" (30.6-7). He speaks with nostalgia of a past when standards were simpler but higher, nobler, than those of a sophisticated present. "In the old age," in "days long since, before these last so bad," when hours were "holy," beauty was unambiguously "fair" (67.14; 68.9; 127.1); "antique" pens were as eloquent as modern ones—for all their "new-found methods" and "compounds strange"—are inarticulate (106.7; 76.4). The "time-bettering days" of this age of progress (82.8) have amassed a rich harvest of "new-fangled ill" (91.3). The Poet also dwells much upon the future—that is to say, the little time he has left, the "twilight" (73.5) from which he can already contemplate his death (71) and wish for it (66). He often raises issues of time and eternity with his Friend, who seems too young to be seriously concerned about them (see 77, especially). The Poet's many exhortations to the Friend to achieve immortality through procreation and his offers to the youth of an immortality in verse spring more from his own obsessions than from attention to the other's frame of mind.

It is understandable that a man who feels his living substance devoured by time, or rather "transfix[ed]," "mow[n]," "beated," "chopp'd," "crush'd," "drain'd," and "consum'd" (19.1; 60.9, 12; 62.10; 63.2, 3; 73.12), is most sensitive to "accounts" owing and owed, honored and neglected. Tallies become extremely important when supplies run short. Seeing himself in the growing shadow of extinction, the Poet allows his imagination to be filled with commercial and legal metaphors, which, though on occasion used ironically to remind a lover that love should not be mercenary, are in general approved analogies. Having long grappled with the world and provided a life for himself by "public means" (of which, one must admit, he sometimes seems ashamed [111.4]), the Poet naturally looks to the courts and the marketplace for a vocabulary to express his sense of (his own or another's) threatened or waning personal treasures, his understanding of love's privileges, rights, obligations, audits, losses, expenses, and "use" (e.g., 4, 21, 30, 49, 67, 74, 79, 87, 120, 122, 126, 134, 142, 146). In this respect

Shakespeare's economic and judicial motifs are more functional than those of most of his predecessors and contemporaries among sixteenth-century love-poets.[13]

The Poet's social status requires his deference to the Friend as to a superior. The older man bears the "canopy" for the young person of eminence (125.1), relies on him for patronage in competition with a rival (76-86). Love, of course, demands its own kind of obsequiousness (125.9), and, with whatever ironic demurrals, the Poet becomes the loved one's "slave" (57, 58). But age gives the elder the inclination and the right to treat the youth as a son in need of a father's care. Thus, running counter to the voice of dependency in the *Sonnets* (with a wholly plausible inconsistency) is that of the preceptor, who tries to teach his charge the value of a family, the lessons of time, and definitions of love; of the patient, concerned parent, ever ready to "play the watchman" for his loved one's sake, even when his love is betraying him (61.12); of the doting parent, quick to make excuses for the youth's "pretty wrongs" (41.1); of the protector, who vows to bear his Friend's heart, keeping it "so chary / As tender nurse her babe from faring ill" (22.11-12), and who pleads with the Lady who has enslaved his "sweet'st friend":

> My friend's heart let my poor heart bail
> Whoe'er keeps me, let my heart be his guard.
> (133.4, 10-11)

Even when the Poet speaks in words of self-pity he does not relinquish the paternal mantle:

> As a decrepit father takes delight
> To see his active child do deeds of youth,
> So I, made lame by Fortune's dearest spite,
> Take all my comfort of thy worth and truth.
> (37.1-4)

In weakness he maintains his authority.

The Poet's affair with the Dark Lady, like Antony's with Cleopatra,[14] is rather a combat between powers who are equals if not in age (the Poet seems older) then in stature. Adults stepping out of earshot of the youth who plays a part in both their lives, they must settle the issue of his possession themselves, with their own kind of frankness (133-4). Indeed, although age in love may feel compelled to hide its years (138), it speaks for the most part with a cynical honesty about itself and its object. The Poet's bawdy jokes and insults at his mistress's expense are the humorously bitter quips of a man tired of the illusions used by romance to dignify lust.

> No want of conscience hold it that I call
> Her "love" for whose dear love I rise and
>   fall.

> Wilt thou, whose will is large and spacious,
> Not once vouchsafe to hide my will in thine?

> In nothing art thou black save in thy deeds,
> And thence this slander as I think proceeds.
> (151.13-14; 135.5-6; 131.13-14)

The Poet is old and wise enough to see clearly that he perjures his eye in forcing it to swear its object lovable (152.13). Age will sin no less than youth, but it may be doomed to suffer a livelier appreciation of the preposterousness of its evil and the vileness of its guilt.

> What merit do I in myself respect,
> That is so proud thy service to despise,
> When all my best doth worship thy defect,
> Commanded by the motion of thine eyes?
>   But, love, hate on, for now I know thy
>   mind:
>   Those that can see thou lov'st, and I am
>   blind.

> Th' expense of spirit in a waste of shame
> Is lust in action.
> (149.9-14; 129.1-2)

The very fact of the Poet's age, then, continually insisted upon, is the source of two of the great incongruities in the *Sonnets:* that an older man has become "vassal" to a youth much inferior to him in insight and (though the elder is no saint) moral character; that (as seems most likely) this same man lives in open-eyed thrall to a passion which, as the young Hamlet believed, is supposed to be conquered by time:

> Ha, have you eyes?
> You cannot call it love, for at your age
> The heyday in the blood is tame, it's humble,
> And waits upon the judgment, and what
>   judgment
> Would step from this to this?
> (*Ham.*, III.iv.67-71)

Since love in all its forms is rarely scrupulous in observing rules of logic, common sense, or common expectation, we must acknowledge the incongruities to be part of a constant truth about human nature.

Some of the inconsistencies in the *Sonnets,* however, are too refractory to be accounted for by the Poet's forthright revelation of his age. In order to see how he might consciously and therefore plausibly be responsible for many of them, we must understand how in age he has become mendacious.

The Poet's attitude towards the truth is a complicated one.[15] Defined as something more than the "correspondence" of thought and fact (148.2), truth has for him a moral dimension—as fidelity ("I will be true" [123.14]) and authenticity ("Without all ornament, itself and true" [68.10]). With goodness and beauty truth is a transcendental value, the goal of human striving, and when found in a person occasions the highest compliment (105). Departure from such truths is either madness or a criminal betrayal. Yet a certain kind of verity, the Poet believes, is no more than a bland literalness, which as his practice indicates may be improved by hyperbole. Historical "records" he knows to "lie"; not only may the writers of history be in error, but "what we see," the facts themselves (123.11). This is not the kind of truth that will win one to its service. And devotion to another may lead a lover to abandon the truth in forsaking himself:

> Speak of my lameness, and I straight will halt,
> Against thy reasons making no defense.
>
> (89.3-4)

The Poet thinks he has grounds for appealing to the "virtuous lie" against a truth that is "niggard" (72.5, 8).

Shakespeare's plays often portray with some approval an idealism that is not too saintly to compromise itself. Tricksters like Prince Hal and Duke Vincentio become morally ambiguous in their resort to deception; but their diminution is the price exacted by a wicked world, perverse in its paradoxes, for the achievement of good. The sanctity of absolutists like Isabella and Cordelia is always splendid but not in every respect benign. If the world would be spiritually poor without martyrdom, it would be poorer still if it lacked the flawed but elementary moral successes of a flexible soul like Helena, the heroine of *All's Well that Ends Well,* who is mundane enough to banter with the crass Parolles on his own terms, who can imagine that "virtue's steely bones" may look "bleak i'th' cold wind" (I.i.103-4), who deceives her way to justice and love.

There is, in fact, a strong kinship between Helena and the Poet of the *Sonnets* which ought not to go overlooked in favor of more obvious parallels between male characters from the plays and the sonneteer. The middle-aged Antonio of *The Merchant of Venice* hazards himself for the prodigal young Bassanio, as does the sea-captain Antonio for the young Sebastian in *Twelfth Night.*[16] But Helena, if not the same age or sex as the older male friends, is their equal in devotion and in other respects much more like the figure in the poems. Not old herself she yet has the older generation on her side—the King, the Countess, Lafew—and acts as a representative of a past whose nobility threatens to become attenuated in "these younger times" (I.ii.46). She is a poet, author of a sonnet in the Shakespearean form (III.iv.4-17), which sounds familiar notes of self-denigration and selfless love:

> He is too good and fair for death and me,
> Whom I myself embrace to set him free.

In Bertram Helena loves a man superior to herself in rank but who is, though of a "well-derived nature" (III.ii.88), so far beneath her in moral stature that she must strive mightily to overcome his iniquity and to make him, not only her lover, but an object worthy of her love. (Whether or not she succeeds, of course, is a "problem.") As a woman rendered "inferior" by social conventions (the Poet of the *Sonnets* suffers a lowliness dictated by other social codes) she must be active in secret to pursue her goals; and secrecy involves lying and deceit.

The lies of the Poet are not so spectacular as a fabricated death-notice or a bed-trick, but they are just as real and just as purposeful. They are of several kinds. One may deny the "simple truth" to another person: "I lie with her, and she with me" (138.8, 13). One may also try to deny it to oneself, to make, as Macbeth says, "The eye wink at the hand" (I.iv.52). The Poet has been accused of such attempts at self-deception,[17] and the charge seems substantiated in his own professed resolve:

> So shall I live, supposing thou art true,
> Like a deceived husband, so love's face
> May still seem love to me, though alter'd new.
>
> (93.1-3)

He would lie to himself about the extent of the Friend's devotion and innocence, rationalize the Friend's obvious treachery, perjure his own eyes to love a formidably worthless Lady. As Macbeth's case reminds us, however, an acute mind cannot easily un-know a momentous, insistent truth already in its possession. In acknowledging that he sees himself lying, the Poet proves that he has not escaped an inconvenient knowledge. He is a manipulator of lies, not their victim, for his prevarications are primarily rhetorical.

Reading most of the *Sonnets* as rhetoric rather than as drama or meditation (although rhetoric may of course grow out of meditation and play its part in a dramatic action) may drastically alter our approach to the poems.[18] Such a reading makes less crucial the search for a linear plot and helps to explain contradictions that would remain even in a definitively established sequence of events. It may also affect significantly our estimate of the Poet's character. A rhetorician's design upon an audience (here, the Friend or Lady), his concern to teach or to move, may lead him to suppress or falsify history, his own motives, or his own condition. There is no need to trace a developing awareness in the Poet if, as his age and experience suggest, he knows most of the truth from the beginning, allowing only as much or as little of it into each poem as will serve his ends.

His purpose in the poems to the Friend, like Helena's in her dealings with Bertram, is to win the love of a man who must be made lovable and taught how to love. In the very first sonnet of a group which is almost universally believed to pertain to the early stages of the relationship the Poet reveals something of his method:

> From fairest creatures we desire increase,
> That thereby beauty's rose might never die,
> But as the riper should by time decease,
> His tender heir might bear his memory:
> But thou, contracted to thine own bright eyes,
> Feed'st thy light's flame with self-substantial fuel,
> Making a famine where abundance lies,
> Thyself thy foe, to thy sweet self too cruel.
> Thou that art now the world's fresh ornament,
> And only herald to the gaudy spring,
> Within thine own bud buriest thy content,
> And, tender chorl, mak'st waste in niggarding:
>   Pity the world, or else this glutton be,
>   To eat the world's due, by the grave and thee.
>   (1)

No less aware of the friend's self-absorption here ("Within thine own bud buriest thy content") than he is later ("The summer's flowr is to the summer sweet, / Though to itself it only live and die" [94.9-10]), the Poet withholds an explicit condemnation (plainspeaking, it is clear, would do no good) and attempts to make use of this trait in his argument. "Don't violate the logic of your narcissism," he suggests. "Produce another *self.*" There is criticism in the subtle plea to the young man that he become a different kind of "glutton" than he already is, but the irony is too sugar-coated to alienate a vain sensibility ("to thy sweet self too cruel," "tender chorl"). The rhetorician's flattery is offered on the premise that the youth will be moved to go out of himself, and thus "give the world its due," only by an ignoble appeal to his pride. The world needs, has aright to the "fairest creatures."

This exhortation is hardly calculated to bring the youth immediately to a state of heroic virtue. But the Poet, proceeding with the tolerance or patience that his own long lifetime of imperfection has taught him, is willing to settle for the slightest improvement, even if purchased with debased currency, in his pupil's art of giving. And whether or not the Poet was commissioned by a concerned parent to write the sonnets advocating marriage and begetting, it is in his own interest to encourage the young man whom he loves, or will love, to learn self-surrender. In order to teach this, the Poet must persevere, as the illogic of love urges him to do, in his concern for a Friend who over time comes to wound him deeply ("Kill me with spites, yet we must not be foes" [40.14]) and must direct his pleas and arguments by expediency.

What is expedient will change from moment to moment in a relationship that spans three years or more (104) and suffers a number of significant reversals. Flattery will alternate or combine with, displace or yield to, rebuke as quickly as the Poet feels they must to suit his purpose. So will "strained rhetoric" to "true plain words." Thus in Sonnets 33-5 the Poet's initial reaction to an injury done him is to accept it, even to prettify the wrong, for to do otherwise would be to lose the malefactor:

> The region cloud hath mask'd him from me now.
> Yet him for this my love no whit disdaineth:
> Suns of the world may stain, when heaven's sun staineth.
>   (33.12-14)

The irony in "no whit" and in the outrageous analogy between the two suns cannot be doubted. Yet the criticism is muted until the Poet feels it opportune to ask plainly and in anger, "Why didst thou promise?" (34.1). "Base clouds" then lose their "brav'ry," becoming "rotten smoke" (34.3-4); the Poet speaks with a frankness and an authority not heard before:

> Though thou repent, yet I have still the loss,
> Th' offender's sorrow lends but weak relief
> To him that bears the strong offense's cross.
>   (34.10-12)

But of what use is this naked blade of truth if it severs the bonds that love would keep whole? The Poet allows "tears" to "ransom all ill deeds" (34.13-14) (or pretends that they do) not because the injured man has melted before the penitent's weeping, but because he would keep the possibility of love alive. Forgiveness, hollow-sounding as it is, will by fiat prevent a breach, while providing an example of selfless devotion and proving the forgiver worthy to be loved. The Poet goes so far as to take upon himself the "sin" of "excusing" his Friend's "amiss" (35), relinquishing the brief authority that injured innocence had given him; for the Friend probably could not abide an extended awareness of his moral inferiority.

In these poems, then, are two great violations of the truth: the lies required by forgiveness and the lies told in self-diminishment. The Poet resorts to them here and throughout the *Sonnets* because to utter them is the only way to render them unnecessary—or rather, the only means allowed by a love that will not abandon its object. The lies are told in an irregular pattern. Retreat from the truth is made for the sake of an ultimate advance toward it, and the forward pressure diminishes or increases as circumstances change.

The conflict is especially tense after the Friend has seduced or been seduced by the Poet's mistress. "Take all my loves, my love, yea, take them all" (40.1). Outrage is tempered even as it is voiced, directed at "my love." A specious casuistry absolves the thief: "All mine was thine, before thou hadst this more. . . . I cannot blame thee" (40.4, 6), then absolution is invalidated: "But yet be blam'd" (40.7); then reaffirmed: "I do forgive thy robb'ry, gentle thief" (40.9); and allowed to stand, with a reminder to the sinner that forgiveness is heroic:

> And yet love knows it is a greater grief
> To bear love's wrong than hate's known
>   injury.
>
> (40.11-12)

The pattern is repeated in Sonnets 41 and 42: extenuation of "pretty wrongs"; a change of mind expressed in a bitter sexual joke: "Ay me, but yet thou mightst my seat forbear"; renewed forgiveness: "Loving offenders, thus I will excuse ye," attached to a reminder that the injured party lies on a "cross" and that forgiveness is gratuitous, since its rational grounds are the feeblest of logic:

> But here's the joy, my friend and I are one;
> Sweet flattery! then she loves but me alone.
>
> (41.1, 9; 42.5, 12, 13-14)

The sign of a more thorough forgiveness would be a more complete forgetfulness, and this the Poet tries to demonstrate to the Friend. Some of the *Sonnets* have seemed to many readers to be out of place because the Poet speaks in them in apparent unawareness of events which previous poems have recounted. In Sonnet 48, for example, not long after suffering his Friend's infidelity, the Poet anticipates losing what has already been lost: "thou wilt be stol'n, I fear." In Sonnet 70 he speaks of the youth's "pure unstained prime":

> Thou hast pass'd by the ambush of young
>   days,
> Either not assail'd, or victor being charg'd.
>
> (70.9-10)

These poems may well be out of order. It is just as likely, however, given the Poet's practice elsewhere, that he is passing over the truth in forgiveness and compliment. The Friend may have strayed, but he was not definitively "stol'n"; he was indeed "assailed" (41.6), and if not a "victor" in every battle, triumphant in the campaign as a whole. In the Poet's eyes, the youngman's prime was "unstained," the scarlet of his sins made white as snow. The same fiction, after all, is used by the Poet when, after a period of separation (estrangement?) (97-8), love no longer "new" (102.5), he celebrates the Friend's "truth" (101.2; 105.9) as though he had never cause to question it, or had not questioned it in fact (41.14). Then, confessing a guilt of his own, hoping that the forgiven sinner has learned the lesson of such generous deceit, he pleads with the Friend for a similar favor: "o'er-green my bad" (112.4).

The lies of self-diminishment, more varied than those spoken in the name of forgiveness, are as undeviatingly aimed at creating, preserving, and educating love. The "sad slave" describes his vassalage as a reproach to the master who abuses him (57-8). In the altruist's self-naughting there is surely a plea for sympathy:

> No longer mourn for me when I am dead
> Than you shall hear the surly sullen bell
> Give warning to the world that I am fled
> From this vile world with vildest worms to
>   dwell;
> Nay, if you read this line, remember not
> The hand that writ it, for I love you so,
> That I in your sweet thoughts would be
>   forgot,
> If thinking on me then should make you woe.
> O, if (I say) you look upon this verse.
>
> (71.1-9)

If the Poet really wished to be "forgot," he would not write and keep reminding his Friend to read. Much of the Poet's self-criticism is offered in the hope that it will be protested. The author who boasts of his "pow'rful rhyme" (55.2) and prides himself on the honest humility of his verse (82) does not in competition with a rival intend to convince his Friend that his own Muse is "tongue-tied" (80.4; 85.1) or that his "numbers are decay'd" (79.3); he seeks affirmation.

> Thus wisdom wishes to appear most bright
> When it doth tax itself; as these black masks
> Proclaim an enshield beauty ten times louder
> Than beauty could, display'd.
>
> (*MM*, II.iv.78-81)

A young lover may try to win the admiration of a lady by parading his vigor, his potential, or his achievement, as Astrophil does in his forty-first sonnet after he "obtain'd the prize" at a tournament. An older man will have to be loved for different reasons: not for his prowess, but for his tenderness, understanding, constancy, generosity, what is called in *A Lover's Complaint* "the charity of age" (70),[19] and in spite of his growing infirmities. The Poet, far from attempting to hide his debility, is forever proclaiming it, for it cannot be hidden and can at least be turned to modest account in flattering the Friend's sense of his own potency or virtue:

> As a decrepit father takes delight
> To see his active child do deeds of youth,
> So I.

This thou perceiv'st, which makes thy love
    more strong,
To love that well, which thou must leave ere
    long.
                                (37.1-3; 73.13-14)

Weakness, however, is not of itself attractive. To prove that discrepancy in age does not matter, that love

Weighs not the dust and injury of age,
Nor gives to necessary wrinkles place,
But makes antiquity for aye his page,
                                (108.10-12)

the Poet distinguishes himself in selfless dedication. If he is "nothing worth" (72.14), his whole energy will go to promoting and proclaiming the worth of his Friend, whose interests supersede the poor lover's own:

Bending all my loving thoughts on thee,
The injuries that to myself I do,
Doing thee vantage, double-vantage me.
Such is my love, to thee I so belong,
That for thy right myself will bear all
    wrong.
                                (88.10-14)

Nevertheless, the Poet does not relish or thrive on self-diminishment. His admission that he can "allege no cause" for his Friend to love him can hardly be ingenuous. The *Sonnets*, the self-naughting ones especially, offer a multitude of causes and, at least indirectly, ask the beneficiary of so much giving for a return. The "slave" would be made an equal. The eulogist would have his own worth affirmed. The constant lover would be shown loyalty. The trespasser would have his own trespasses forgiven even as he has forgiven a deep betrayal. Sonnet 120 is an open attempt to teach reciprocity: "if you were by my unkindness shaken / As I by yours, y'have pass'd a hell of time" (as the memory of *my* agony tells me).

But that your trespass now becomes my fee,
Mine ransoms yours, and yours must ransom
    me.
                                (120.5-6, 13-14)

One cannot easily inspire gratuitous forgiveness except by granting it, and the Poet has already offered it in full measure.

Since the Poet has continued to love his Friend despite "love's wrong" (40.12), the recompense he seeks is for an action that, despite its place in rhetorical arguments, is essentially unfeigned. Forgiveness is itself genuine. But it involves lying; and so does moral education. We may suspect that in Sonnet 62 the self-incriminator plays with the truth in order to challenge a complacent egotism that rarely gives.

Sin of self-love possesseth all mine eye,
And all my soul, and all my every part.
                                (62.1-2)

Although the Poet is not immune to pride, his confession and repentance before a young man who seems distinguished for narcissism is probably an invitation to follow a salutary example. We may also wonder if the Poet's contritions after he has "rang'd" and "made old offenses of affections new" (109.5; 110.4) are purposely exaggerated. They follow a separation for which the Friend seems responsible (87-96); and when a man goes elsewhere after being rejected, he would hardly have cause to consider himself unfaithful. It is probable that the friendship can be repaired at this point only if the Poet assumes a guilt he never knew and allows himself to be forgiven. Only thus may virtue be "rewarded."

Other gambits are available to the resourceful lover, and the Poet makes use of them without regard for their consistency, which is far less important to him than results. In the midst of all his sophistries, he sometimes risks forthrightness—an undisguised sermon:

Oh how much more doth beauty beauteous
    seem
By that sweet ornament which truth doth
    give!
                                (54.1-2)

or a direct calling to account:

For thee watch I, whilst thou dost wake
    elsewhere,
From me far off, with others all too near;
                                (61.13-14)

or a less direct (because attributed to the "world") yet daring insult:

But why thy odor matcheth not thy show,
The soil is this, that thou dost common grow.
                                (69.13-14)

His avowals of selflessness are interrupted by a reference to his desperate *needs:* "So are you to my thoughts as food to life" (75.1). When overtures seem to fail, he utters a "Farewell" (87), but of course does not immediately depart. He mingles with pleas for sympathy an angry challenge:

Then hate me when thou wilt, if ever, now,
Now while the world is bent my deeds to
    cross.
                                (90.1-2)

All of these episodes are desultory steps in an experiment that fails. If the final sonnets addressed to the

Friend (97-126) are in anything close to chronological sequence, they suggest a story that ends in the preceptor-lover's acrimonious defeat. Sonnet 97 refers to an "absence" which may have resulted from the friendship's temporary collapse. The previous sonnet, following upon statements of candid reproach (93-5), seems to represent a climactic complaint and a breaking off. The Poet has sensed that his Friend is trying to "steal [him]self away" (92.1), is seeking ways to let the rejected lover down easily ("there can live no hatred in thine eye, / Therefore in that I cannot know thy change" [93.5-6]). Although the Poet determines to live like a "deceived husband," supposing his love to be "true" (93.1-2), he knows the truth of his abandonment and proclaims to the Friend, who has "pow'r to hurt, and will do none":

> The summer's flow'r is to the summer sweet,
> Though to itself it only live and die,
> But if that flow'r with base infection meet,
> The basest weed outbraves his dignity:
>   For sweetest things turn sourest by their
>   deeds;
>   Lilies that fester smell far worse than
>   weeds.
>
>   (94.1, 9-14)

That is, the Friend may soothe his conscience with the thought that his kind appearance will not reveal a treachery which will therefore do no harm. But such a grand deception is impossible. When lilies fester, they smell—all the more foully for being so fair. In Sonnet 95 there is a sardonic warning: "The hardest knife ill us'd doth lose his edge." And in Sonnet 96, where the Friend is close to becoming a "stern wolf," betraying innocent lambs, the Poet urges:

> But do not so, I love thee in such sort,
> As thou being mine, mine is thy good report.
>   (96.13-14)

This couplet repeats word for word that of Sonnet 36, where it had the meaning: "Do not honor me publicly, for by so doing you detract from your own reputation. For you to be honored is all that I need." In the later poem, the words have a different sense: "Do not lead innocents astray. Since my love has so closely identified me with you, I would share your dishonor." The repetition and reversal are an economical means both of reminding the Friend of a longstanding devotion and of asserting that love will no longer tolerate perfidy.

The Poet marks his return to the Friend after the "absence" by pouring forth extravagant compliments as though no breach had occurred (97-9). The Friend, apparently resentful of long inattention, is not easily soothed; and the Poet strains to apologize for his reticence or his silences and to prove that they are not irredeemable (100-3). He returns to some of the old eulogistic themes (104-7), now, however, manifesting an impatience with them. When previously he had spoken with the youth about the true (or the good) and the beautiful, it was often to remind him that beauty had to earn the honor of goodness (e.g., 54; 68-70). Now, faced with the Friend's insistent and inordinate appetite for praise, the eulogist offers him the kind of excessive tribute that ought to embarrass any recipient. The true, the good, and the beautiful,

> "Fair," "kind," and "true" have often liv'd
>   alone,
> Which three till now never kept seat in one.
>   (105.13-14)

A special significance has been given to what becomes the Friend's epithet, "a god in love" (110.12)—"hallowed" be his name (108.8). "What's new to speak, what now to register," after this (108.3)?

But the Friend's mind is not to be swayed from what he perceives to be the Poet's infidelity, however vague a crime it may be; and the young man whose majesty has been wounded must be reassured, confessed and apologized to, and flattered (109-14). He is given what he wants. A silly bit of sophistry (115), however, (like Donne's "Loves Growth") proving that love can be both full and growing, ends with a double-edged couplet that hints at the Poet's exasperation: "Love is a babe, then might I not say so, / To give full growth to that which still doth grow" (115.13-14)—one interpretation of which is: "I've had to lie in order to give our love a chance." Sonnet 116 ("Let me not to the marriage of true minds") advances closer to the truth, for it describes the objective ideal ("Love alters not") measured against which no love is perfect:

> If this be error and upon me proved,
> I never writ, nor no man ever loved.
>   (116.13-14)

"And if this be *not* error, no man has loved. At any rate, I have not, nor have you; for we both have strayed." Such is the implied coda if the poem is written (as the context suggests) in response to the Friend's charges of inconstancy. This frankness is returned to, with less indignation, in Sonnet 120, after three pieces of half-serious casuistry which set out a faulty "logic" of forgiveness; and thereafter the tone of pleading disappears. Sonnet 121 betokens a new era of truth-telling that will be short-lived, for it marks love's "doom and date."

> I am that I am, and they that level
> At my abuses reckon up their own.
>   (121.9-10)

The Poet will no longer denigrate or apologize for his imperfect love. He has thrown away the Friend's book, or "tables," and its "tallies," for he does not need them to remind him of his obligations (122.1, 10). His contrition has yielded to pride in his integrity: "No! Time, thou shalt not boast that I do change" (123-4). Love's law is "mutual render, only me for thee"; and he has given from his side all that he can (125.12). Since the Friend has not done and will not do so, despite all the Poet's efforts to teach and to move him, the only words that remain to be spoken are those of a sadly bitter twelve-line *envoi*, addressed to a "boy" who remains "lovely" and a boy, and who is left with a somewhat ungenerous reminder (there is no final forgiveness) of the important word whose higher meaning he has failed to learn:

> [Time's] audit (though delay'd) answer'd
>   must be,
> And her quietus is to *render* thee.
>   (126.1, 11-12, emphasis mine)

It is not clear that all of the poems which follow those addressed to the Friend are rhetorically directed to another person. "Th' expense of spirit in a waste of shame" and "Poor soul, the center of my sinful earth," are meditations that require no audience; and those sonnets in which the Poet speaks to the Lady (or ladies) do not reveal the same complex purposes as those in the larger group. "Lust in action" does not need the help of subtle or heroic lies; indeed, as we have already noted, except in the suppression of the "simple" truths of age and infidelity (138) this passion is better served by a witty, prurient, sometimes brutal honesty.

But candor may serve a rhetorical purpose, upon which we may reflect briefly. The Poet freely insults both the Lady and himself: she is only ambiguously beautiful (127, 130, 131, 137, 141, 147) and a slut ("the bay where all men ride" [137.6]); he, a fool, whose eyes and judgment desire has blinded (137, 148) and who loves his foolishness too much to become wise. These indignities yoke the two together in a corrupt complicity which, the argument goes, they might as well enjoy:

> *Will* will fulfill the treasure of thy love,
> Ay, fill it full with wills, and my will one.
>   (136.5-6)

Insults also serve either as threats or as compliments, to be presented as occasion demands. The dishonored Lady is pushed toward compliance by being reminded that she is not worth an extended effort (142). Or she is "flattered" by learning the extent of her power to degrade her lover's mind and conscience (149).

There are other kinds of appeal in these poems: to the Lady's pity (139), to her fear of detraction (140), to her sense of humor (143). In constructing a piece of Donne-like casuistry for her (151), the Poet compliments her wit. Not all is rhetorical game, however. The sonnets which pray for the Friend's release arise out of a pathetic helplessness in the Poet, which, he knows, no amount of pleading can remedy, for the Lady is "covetous" and the Friend only fictitiously "kind" (133.3-4; 134.3-6). The sufferer addresses only to himself the vulgar humor which this helplessness evokes in him:

> I guess one angel in another's hell.
>   Yet this shall I ne'er know, but live in
>   doubt
> Till my bad angel fire my good one out.
>   (144.12-14)

In his complaints to the woman whom he despises yet craves, his reproaches are on occasion scathing enough to undermine any ulterior purpose in the rhetoric: "the bay where all men ride"; "the very refuse of thy deeds" (151.6);

> Nor are mine ears with thy tongue's tune
>   delighted,
> Nor tender feeling to base touches prone,
> Nor taste, nor smell, desire to be invited
> To any sensual feast with thee alone.
>   (141.5-8)

And his reflections on lust (129) and mortality (146) stand self-contained, the former in its own fierce disgust, the latter in its longing for a transcendent purity.

There is no sign in the second group of sonnets that the Poet simply moves from rhetorical assault to introspective meditation. He is never unaware of the moral and psychological truths in his case, and he adverts to them as he will. Having spun no great lies to be unraveled, these poems come to no conclusion. They portray in a credible randomness conflicts which, as the platonism of one sonnet acknowledges, will not be resolved until "there's no more dying" (146.14).

The Poet once admits to his Friend that in public displays "I have . . . Gor'd mine own thoughts" (110.1-3). Whatever its meaning in context, the phrase may be seen as relevant to the speaker's private story as well, suggesting that he has "wounded" his thoughts in a denial of his knowledge; that he has made them parti-colored (as "gores," or wedges of cloth, turn motley a fool's breeches); and that he has dishonored them (a heraldic "gore" was "a shaped area interposed between two charges, and was used as a mark of cadency or abatement of honour").[20] This admission itself may, as has been suggested, involve a goring of thought, but its use as a tactic does not detract from its basic truth. To his Friend the Poet offered his mind in a pastiche. To his Lady he presented the oblation of a stabbed and bleeding conscience, still alive to see but too weak to move a Will to action. On each count he has suffered an "abatement of honour." He feels himself shamed by "Th' expense of spirit" to which the wounding of his moral judgment has led. And in the "virtuous" lies which he told for the noblest of causes, it is impossible to separate heroism from ignominy. His fatherly concern, loving affection, patience, forgiveness, and long-suffering were all real; yet these virtues had to be devious (age in love knew how to be) to express themselves. Altruism was sometimes put to "use," flattery dispensed, wrongs publicly countenanced, truth suppressed, as love sacrificed some of its integrity that it might exist. And the sacrifice was also real. Unlike Helena's character, which was much more protected by appearing in an adult fairy tale, this liar's "nature" was "subdu'd / To what it work[ed] in, like the dyer's hand" (111.6-7)—and in vain, for the end which required but could not justify the means was lost. One might say in condescension that the Poet was proud and foolish to believe that he could ever succeed in creating love almost *ex nihilo;* and in saying so, such is Shakespeare's achievement in portraying a human dilemma in its bewildering complexity, one would be both correct and ungenerous. It is simpler to insist on what should now be evident, that the character whose situation has been examined here was neither an abjectly submissive nor an implausible protagonist.

Notes

[1] "Poetic Styles Old and New" (1959), reproduced in *Forms of Discovery* (1967) and reprinted in Peter Jones, ed., *Shakespeare: The Sonnets, A Casebook* (London, 1977), p. 153.

[2] All quotations from Shakespeare's works are taken from the edition of G. B. Evans, *et al., The Riverside Shakespeare* (Boston, 1975).

[3] See Hilton Landry, *Interpretations in Shakespeare's Sonnets* (Berkeley and Los Angeles, 1963), p. 63; Heather Dubrow, "Shakespeare's Undramatic Monologues: Towards a Reading of the *Sonnets*," *SQ,* XXXII (1981), 67.

[4] Giorgio Melchiori, *Shakespeare's Dramatic Meditations* (Oxford, 1976), p. 20; R. P. Blackmur, "A Poetics for Infatuation," in Edward Hubler, ed., *The Riddle of Shakespeare's Sonnets* (New York, 1962), p. 146. A. C. Bradley, in his *Oxford Lectures on Poetry* (2nd ed.; London, 1909), found in the Poet an adoring "prostration" before the Friend, but did not consider it as sinister as the "humiliation" seen by Hallam (p. 334).

[5] See Melchiori's study, for example, which focuses on poems that seem to rise above "context" or "sequence" and can be read as meditations lacking any "immediate frame of reference" (p. 37). James Winny in *The Master-Mistress: A Study of Shakespeare's Sonnets* (London, 1968) interprets the *Sonnets* as a working out of ideas rather than a chronicling of events (p. 29). Stephen Booth has atomized the poetry in his primary concern with the experience, not of the author or his characters, but of "the reader" (*An Essay on Shakespeare's Sonnets* [New Haven and London, 1969] and *Shakespeare's Sonnets: Edited with Analytic Commentary* [New Haven and London, 1977]).

[6] See Philip Martin, *Shakespeare's Sonnets: Self, Love and Art* (Cambridge, 1972), pp. 64-77; Landry, *Interpretations,* pp. 20, 66; Martin Seymour-Smith, "Shakespeare's Sonnets 1-42: A Psychological Reading," in Hilton Landry, ed., *New Essays on Shakespeare's Sonnets* (New York, 1976), pp. 30-1; Blackmur, "Poetics," p. 139.

[7] *English Literature of the Sixteenth Century* (Oxford, 1954), p. 505.

[8] Brents Stirling's *The Shakespeare Sonnet Order* (Berkeley and Los Angeles, 1968) is the most significant of recent renumberings.

[9] Philip Edwards, *Shakespeare and the Confines of Art* (London, 1968), p. 31; Kenneth Muir, *Shakespeare's Sonnets* (London, 1979), p. 81.

[10] See Sidney Lee, *A Life of William Shakespeare* (London, 1898), pp. 85-6. Ronsard's *Sonnets pour Hélène* were written when he was about fifty years old; but age is not in these poems the pervasive issue that it is in Shakespeare's.

[11] For discussions of the relationships between Shakespeare's plays and the *Sonnets* see Katherine M. Wilson, *Shakespeare's Sugared Sonnets* (London, 1974), pp. 26-80; Muir, *Sonnets,* pp. 123-38.

[12] Katherine Wilson's view that the *Sonnets* are *primarily* parody is difficult to credit. See *Sugared Sonnets,* p. 83.

[13] See Raymond Southall, *Literature and the Rise of Capitalism* (London, 1973), pp. 21-70, for a survey of "Love Poetry in the Sixteenth Century" in relationship to economic motives. One might contrast Shakespeare's use of economic metaphors with Sidney's practice in *Astrophil and Stella,* 18, where the language of the marketplace is effective in the poem, but is not especially appropriate to the speaker's character.

[14] See Muir, *Sonnets,* p. 136.

[15] For a different approach to the problem of "truth" in the *Sonnets* see Winny, *Master-Mistress,* pp. 121-44.

[16] See Bradley, *Oxford Lectures*, p. 334; and M. M. Mahood, "Love's Confined Doom," *ShS*, XV (1962), 54-5.

[17] Dubrow, "Undramatic Monologues," 63-4.

[18] For an indication of how a reading of love-poetry as rhetoric can affect its interpretation, see Richard Lanham, "Astrophel and Stella: Pure and Impure Persuasion," in *ELR*, II (1972), 100-15.

[19] The (Shakespearean?) poem published along with the *Sonnets* in Thomas Thorpe's edition of 1609.

[20] See W. G. Ingram and Theodore Redpath, eds., *Shakespeare's Sonnets* (1964; rpt. New York, 1978), p. 254.

FURTHER READING

Bayley, John. "Who Was the 'Man Right Fair' of the Sonnets?" *TLS*, No. 3748 (January 4, 1974): 15.

Examines the theme, tone, and wordplay of sonnets 40-43, and puts them in context with the "Dark Lady" sonnets.

Burnham, Michelle. "'Dark Lady and Fair Man': The Love Triangle in Shakespeare's Sonnets and *Ulysses*." *Studies in the Novel* 22, No. 1 (Spring 1990): 43-56.

Traces the influence of Shakespeare's sonnets on James Joyce's characterization of Molly Bloom, Leopold Bloom, and Blazes Boylan in his novel *Ulysses*.

de Grazia, Margreta. "The Motive for Interiority: Shakespeare's *Sonnets* and *Hamlet*." *Style* 23, No. 3 (Fall 1989):430-444.

Argues that the identification of Shakespeare with the speaker in his sonnets and with his character, Hamlet, is a product of eighteenth-century critical and editorial traditions.

Dubrow, Heather. "'Conceit Deceitful': The Sonnets." In her *Captive Victors: Shakespeare's Narrative Poems and Sonnets*, pp. 169-257. Ithaca, NY: Cornell University Press, 1987.

Compares Shakespeare's sonnets with other Renaissance poetry concluding that Shakespeare's poems are unique because they are more subtle in their use of narrative and dramatic techniques.

Duncan-Jones, Katherine. "Deep-dyed Canker Blooms: Botanical Reference in Shakespeare's Sonnet 54." *Review of English Studies* XLVI, No. 184 (November 1995): 521-25.

Suggests that the negative reference to a rose in Sonnet 54 was in fact meant to signify a poppy.

Fineman, Joel. "Introduction." In his *Shakespeare's Perjured Eye: The Invention of Poetic Subjectivity in the Sonnets*, pp.1-48. Berkeley: University of California Press, 1986.

Discusses the importance of the Renaissance sense of self—and more particularly Shakespeare's sense of self—to the meaning of Shakespeare's sonnets.

Graziani, René. "The Numbering of Shakespeare's Sonnets: 12, 60, and 126." *Shakespeare Quarterly* 35, No. 1 (Spring 1984): 79-82.

Suggests that some of the numbers attached to certain sonnets reflect their specific use of numerical imagery.

Green, Martin. "The Cankered Rose." In his *The Labyrinth of Shakespeare's Sonnets:An Examination of Sexual Elements in Shakespeare's Language*, pp. 12-41. London: Charles Skilton Ltd., 1974.

Discusses the relationship between the Poet, the Friend, and the Dark Lady in Shakespeare's sonnets.

Harbage, Alfred. "Extricating the Sonnets." In his *Shakespeare without Words and Other Essays*, pp. 63-77. Cambridge, MA: Harvard University Press, 1972.

Suggests that it is impossible to number or to accurately date Shakespeare's *Sonnets*.

Innes, Paul. *Shakespeare and the English Renaissance Sonnet: Verses of Feigning Love*. New York: St. Martin's Press, Inc., 1997, 238 p.

Argues that Shakespeare and other Renaissance poets employed markedly different styles and themes from one another while reworking the medieval courtly love tradition in their sonnets.

Marotti, Arthur F. "'Love Is Not Love': Elizabethan Sonnet Sequences and the Social Order." *ELH* 49, No. 2 (Summer 1982): 396-428.

Contends that collections of love sonnets were popular in England during the reign of Elizabeth I because she encouraged her courtiers to express their political ambitions via the language of love, but that after her death and with the accession of the misogynistic James I, amorous sonnet sequences were no longer popular.

Rosmarin, Adena. "Hermeneutics versus Erotics: Shakespeare's *Sonnets* and Interpretive History." *PMLA* 100, No. 1 (January 1985): 20-37.

Discusses the contradictions inherent in Renaissance love sonnets—such as the fact that they are private love poems which are meant for wide publication, or the fact that they deal ambiguously with the issue of fidelity—and the ways in which Shakespeare attempts to solve these conflicts.

Sagaser, Elizabeth Harris."Shakespeare's Sweet Leaves: Mourning, Pleasure, and the Triumph of Thought in the

Renaissance Love Lyric," in *ELH* 61, No. 1 (Spring, 1994): 1-26.

> Defines self-love or narcissism in three of Shakespeare's sonnets (29, 30, and 122) as the preoccupation with one's own thoughts concerning one's beloved; Sagaser argues that in the sonnets, self-love is an act of self-preservation in which the "poet-lover" fixates on the possibility or the thought of losing his beloved and of being left alone in order to prepare himself for the actuality of one day being alone.

Schalkwyk, David. "'She Never Told Her Love': Embodiment, Textuality, and Silence in Shakespeare's Sonnets and Plays." *Shakespeare Quarterly* 45, No. 4 (Winter 1994): 381-407.

> Reevaluates the importance of the actual identities of the Friend (or the "noble young man") and the Dark Lady, and their relationship to the poet in Shakespeare's sonnets.

Snow, Edward A. "Loves of Comfort and Despair: A Reading of Shakespeare's Sonnet 138." *ELH* 47, No. 3 (Fall 1980): 462-83.

> Contends that Sonnet 138 functions as a turning point between the "disgust with sexuality" expressed in such plays as *Hamlet* and *Othello*, and the androgyny and "sexual relatedness" expressed in a play such as *Antony and Cleopatra*.

Stallybrass, Peter. "Editing as Cultural Formation: The Sexing of Shakespeare'sSonnets." *Modern Language Quarterly* 54, No. 1 (March 1983): 91-103.

> Argues that Shakespeare's sonnets as we read them today are no longer a product of their own time but that of the nineteenth-century and its attitudes toward sexuality and, specifically, homosexuality.

Vendler, Helen. "Reading, Stage by Stage: Shakespeare's Sonnets." In *Shakespeare Reread: The Texts in New Contexts*, edited by Russ McDonald, pp. 23-41. Ithaca, NY: Cornell University Press, 1994.

> Suggests that Shakespeare's sonnets should be read and appreciated for the ways in which they are different from one another rather than for any similarities between them or for any generalizations that can be made about their themes.

Wait, R. J. C. "'A Better Spirit Doth Use Your Name.'" In his *The Background to Shakespeare's Sonnets*, pp. 77-86. London: Chatto & Windus, 1972.

> Looks to Shakespeare's sonnets for evidence regarding his life and work and, more particularly, his relationships with patrons and other poets.

Whittier, Gayle. "The Sublime Androgyne Motif in Three Shakespearean Works." *The Journal of Medieval and Renaissance Studies* 19, No. 2 (Fall 1989): 185-210.

> Discusses Sonnet 20 in terms of its use of androgyny as a symbol of the unification of and ultimate harmony between the sexes.

Wilson, Katharine M. "The Dark Lady." In her *Shakespeare's Sugared Sonnets*, pp. 81-145. London: George Allen & Unwin Ltd., 1974.

> Asserts that in his Dark Lady sonnets, Shakespeare parodied the sonnets of Elizabethan poets Sir Fulke Greville and Sir Philip Sidney and also made fun of the conventional description of a beloved lady traditionally praised in sonnets.

Venus and Adonis

For further information on the critical history of *Venus and Adonis*, see *SC*, Volumes 10 and 33.

INTRODUCTION

Venus and Adonis, first published in 1593, was dedicated to the Earl of Southampton. In his dedication, Shakespeare describes the poem as "the first heire of my inuention," a statement that has lead some scholars to suggest that the poem was Shakespeare's first literary endeavor. Most modern critics, however, have interpreted the statement as meaning that the work was either Shakespeare's first nondramatic piece, or at least his first published work. Likely composed from Book X of Ovid's *Metamorphoses*, the erotic tale of a mythological goddess's lust for a beautiful hunter was immediately popular, as evidenced by as many as ten reprintings over the twenty-five years following its initial publication. A rather lengthy period of critical disparagement followed, in which the figures in the poem were frequently reduced to allegorical significance. In the twentieth century, *Venus and Adonis* has elicited favorable scholarly comment, with a number of contemporary critics studying the complex romantic relationship of its principal characters. Focusing on Venus's desire and Adonis's denial, commentators have explored Shakespeare's ambivalent formulation of the rhetoric of love in the poem.

The exploration of erotic themes figures centrally in recent critical study of *Venus and Adonis*, with many scholars approaching this subject by means of Shakespeare's rhetorical treatment of romance and desire. Goran V. Stanivukovic (1997) argues that the rhetorical strategies of the poem provide its meaning, and that the failure of Venus's passionate arguments to woo Adonis reflects the impropriety of her lust. A. D. Cousins (1996) evaluates the predominately Petrarchan rhetoric employed by Venus in her seduction of Adonis, which contrasts with his silent, Platonic rhetoric of rejection. Cousins also examines the unique and transgressive quality of Shakespeare's poem which makes a male figure the chaste object of sexual desire. Tita French Baumlin (1990) evaluates Shakespeare's transformation of his direct source for the work, Ovid's *Metamorphosis*. Noting Shakespeare's ostensible imitation of Ovid, Baumlin contends that *Venus and Adonis* departs from its source material, principally in its humanized portrayal of Venus through her failed rhetoric of passion.

Regard for the element of ambiguity in *Venus and Adonis* is another dominant feature of contemporary critical interest. While acknowledging that some allegorical assessments of the poem can be considered reductive, Robert P. Merrix (1997) proposes an approach that privileges complexity, but retains allegorical significance. Merrix aligns Venus with domestic sexuality, contrasting this with Adonis's thirst for adventure and the unknown—symbolized by the boar that brings about his death. Despite such interpretations, Merrix also notes that both Venus and Adonis undergo social and psychological transformations in the poem. James Schiffer (1997) also values Shakespeare's complex representation of erotic desire in *Venus and Adonis*. Employing Lacanian psychoanalysis, Schiffer views the work as an ironic and tragicomic display of Venus's unquenchable phallic lust that, ultimately, defers final interpretation. Recent thematic assessments of the work have likewise privileged ambiguity in *Venus and Adonis*. John Klaus (1998), considering the theme of forgiveness, observes the pluralistic quality of the poem, which is in turn comic, satiric, and tragic. Analyzing the characters of Venus and Adonis, Klaus finds them to be at once guilty and pitiable. Nona Fienberg (1989) perceives the figure of Venus as mutable and diverse in contrast to Adonis, who remains fixed. In attempting to provide a theoretical framework from which to assess the poem, Fienberg employs the metaphor of "the marketplace of value" to describe the dynamically shifting struggle for sexual power in *Venus and Adonis*.

OVERVIEW

Tita French Baumlin (essay date 1990)

SOURCE: "The Birth of the Bard: 'Venus and Adonis' and Poetic Apotheosis," in *Papers on Language and Literature*, Vol. 26, No. 2, Spring, 1990, pp. 191-211.

[*In the following essay, Baumlin evaluates Shakespeare's transformation of his Ovidian source material in* Venus and Adonis.]

Many readers, modern and Elizabethan alike, have delighted in the sensuous sophistication and humor of *Venus and Adonis,* but critics have been by no means univocal in their evaluations of the genre and effect of the entire poem. Some have questioned its genre, one critic calling *Venus and Adonis* an allegory on the Neoplatonic ascent, others describing it as a serious debate on the relative concepts of lust and chastity, either siding against Venus as a Goddess of lust who assails Adonis's maidenly virtue or attacking Adonis's so-called "villainous" rejection of the life-giving principle of the Venus Genetrix.[1] Hallett Smith places the poem in the genre of Ovidian mythological-erotic poetry, but finds fault with its execution, calling it "an Ovidian poem that does not fully succeed," due to the unfortunate "rhetorical tradition which caused Shakespeare to put a large part of the poem into extended discourses by Venus" (1704). Certainly, if the poem is offered in imitation of Ovid, it does not succeed: though the poem's lush, sensuous imagery and delightful, earthy humor may well exceed the age's expectations of the Ovidian poem, the character of Shakespeare's Venus herself is fraught with problems. Compared to Ovid's divine creature, Shakespeare's Venus is gracelessly verbose, largely a grotesque, all-too-humanly ineffectual character. Yet the poem is not consistent with this characterization, for at the close of Shakespeare's poem, Venus does behave as one expects of the Goddess of Love, in fullest possession of all those divine powers readers would expect of an Olympian. And while this discussion is not meant to deny any thematic considerations on lust that various readers have found in the poem, perhaps it is well to examine the ways our expectations are frustrated when we read this youthful work. How are we to read the curious inconsistencies of tone, characterization, and voice in *Venus and Adonis*, these apparent blemishes in what we would expect of an Ovidian mythological erotic poem or, indeed, of the poetry of Shakespeare?

Venus and Adonis essentially displays a Venus who, like her poet-creator in relationship to his own models, faces a long-standing literary tradition of how a goddess *ought* to act, how her seduction *ought* to proceed. In his dedication of the poem Shakespeare characterized this work as his first serious attempt at literary art, the "first heire of my inuention." Taken as such, does not the poem give us—among the varied readings of the poem as numerous as its readers themselves—the struggles of a young poet striving to make his entrance into the literary scene? Unlike her Ovidian ancestor, Shakespeare's Venus must learn how to use the language of divine seduction, how to be the goddess she is reputed to be; this process of apotheosis, of learning and growing into the full-fledged Goddess of Love, mirrors a similar struggle in the inventive process of the new poet. Like Venus, who utilizes and must ultimately reject each of her models' persuasive rhetorics, so must the poet ultimately reject his source materials if he is to fashion his own voice and authority.

In this reading of the poem, *Venus and Adonis* is paradoxically most successful in its failure as an Ovidian love poem, in its rejection of its model. Here, in the genre of Ovidian love poetry, Shakespeare discovers the art which will serve him so well in his dramatic career: the art of finding the places in his source material where he can engage in combat with his predecessor, annihilating the old text to generate a new one most fully and unmistakably his own. Several questions, then, follow this line of thinking. Is *Venus and Adonis* offered in imitation of Ovid or as a critique of the Ovidian-styled poetic metamorphosis? What if the departures from the model reflect not the failure of the imitative poet but the triumph of the new poet who builds his poem by subverting his model? Finally, is it the poet who makes the poem, or the poem that makes, in some sense, the poet? The following analysis of *Venus and Adonis* seeks at least tentative answers to such questions.

Shakespeare's principal source, Ovid's *Metamorphoses*, presents an Adonis fully responsive to Venus's wooing. There Venus is scratched by Cupid's arrow as he kisses his mother, and Venus is compelled to love Adonis. Her seduction of Adonis is both brief and successful: as Golding translates it, Ovid's Venus

> lovd Adonis more
> Than heaven. To him shee clinged ay, and
>   bare him companye.
> And in the shadowe woont she was too rest
>   continually,
> And for too set her beawtye out most seemely
>   to the eye
> By trimly decking of her self.
>   (10.614-18)

Emphasizing their shared concerns, Ovid's poem shows Venus hunting with Adonis; unafraid to depart from her "trimly decked" image of sedate divinity, she dresses like Diana and runs "Bare kneed with garment tucked up" (620). Finally, she invites him to rest with her:

> But now unwoonted toyle hath made
> Mee weerye: and beholde, in tyme this Poplar
>   with his shade
> Allureth, and the ground for cowch dooth
>   serve to rest uppon.
> I prey thee let us rest us heere. They sate
>   them downe anon,
> And lying upward with her head uppon his
>   lappe along,
> She thus began: and in her tale she bussed
>   him among.
>   (10.642-47)

And thus, with kisses to punctuate the tale, Venus tells the Tale of Atalanta who refused love until the race with Hippomenes, where she learned her own limitations and let love transform her. In Ovid's version, then, the goddess Venus is above all a poet, for it is with poetry, the tale of Atalanta, that she effects the seduction. Her poetry, however, is naive; it takes for granted precisely what it has to prove: its persuasive power. Ovid is, in fact, himself naive regarding the persuasive power of poetic language: for Ovid, such powers are automatic.

For Shakespeare's self-critical age, however, it is the very power of language which must be proven. Thus the essential difference between Shakespeare's and Ovid's text: the Renaissance poet cannot take such powers for granted but must find and fashion them in the act of composing. As poets find inspiration in their predecessors and yet struggle against them—what Harold Bloom has called the "anxiety of influence"—so does their poetry engage in combat with their sources, as Bloom points out: "The poet's conception of himself necessarily is his poem's conception of itself, in my reading, and central to this conception is the matter of the sources of the powers of poetry," for "the truest sources, again necessarily, are in the powers of poems *already written*" (3). This view of the nature of the poetic art is particularly applicable to the Renaissance poet, who deliberately adopts a pre-existing text as his inspiration but must also somehow fashion his own poetic voice in the process. Ben Jonson illustrates such "anxiety of influence" in the age of the English Renaissance:

> A requisite in our *Poet,* or Maker is *imitation,* to be able to convert the substance or Riches of another Poet to his owne use. To make choise of one excellent man above the rest, and so to follow him till he grow very *Hee,* or so like him as the Copie may be mistaken for the Principall. Not, as a Creature that swallowes what it takes in, crude, raw, or undigested, but that feedes with an Appetite, and hath a Stomacke to concoct, devide, and turne all to nourishment.
>
> (1: 53-54)

This metaphor—feeding upon the model text in order to turn its material through digestion literally into the body of another text—implies the violence and subversion which J. Hillis Miller finds essential to the composing process, wherein the "host" poem becomes "food, host in the sense of victim, sacrifice":

> The previous text is both the ground of the new one and something the new poem must annihilate by incorporating it, turning it into ghostly insubstantiality, so that the new poem may perform its possible-impossible task of becoming its own ground. The new poem both needs the old texts and must destroy them. It is both parasitical on them, feeding ungraciously on their substance, and at the same time it is the sinister host which unmans them by inviting them into its home.
>
> (225)

Thus, markedly different in Shakespeare's account of the wooing is Venus's total lack of success in winning Adonis for her paramour; the emphasis falls, instead, upon the poet's self-conscious attention to her language as she attempts, and fails, to seduce Adonis. Hallett Smith has noted—and lamented—the combative, argumentative nature of Venus's rhetoric, which is "unadapted to the genre" of Ovidian love poetry, for the reader is burdened with Venus's extended discourses—like the one beginning at line 95, where "for eighty lines she discusses Mars, her own charms, Narcissus, torches, jewels, herbs, and the laws of nature which require propagation . . . so that instead of realizing evoked physical beauty we are listening to a lecture" (1704). Venus's discourses are indeed the lectures of a pedant, deliberately, if the rhetoric is to reveal important facets of Venus's initially flawed, ineffective character. Of course, this Venus fails to seduce a reader like Hallett Smith, fails to evoke the image of beauty that would entice him to judge her worthy of the same name as the Ovidian Goddess of Love, that would lead him to judge the poem itself as a "successful" Ovidian love poem. Similarly, this Venus fails to seduce a reader like Gordon Williams, who finds that her character is too grotesque in this early portion of the poem to be taken seriously at all (771). Venus's failure to persuade and seduce modern readers thus mirrors her own failure to seduce Adonis—and ultimately, this failure leads us to question the nature and source of poetic inspiration: from what source—either for Venus or for the poet himself—comes the rhetorical power to seduce? Is it the model that creates, legitimizes, or confirms the new poet? Clearly, the poet's experience of human struggle *against* language as well as with language—the poet's experience of human failure with language—sets in motion the motivations which will occupy the true poet for a lifetime.

The narrative voice introduces Venus to us as "sick-thoughted" (5), and though she begins her address with harmless Petrarchan compliment—"'Thrice fairer than myself,' thus she began, / 'The field's chief flower, sweet above compare'" (7-8)—she quickly renders her opening comments ineffective by telling Adonis that if he will come and sit by her she will "'smother [him] with kisses'" (18), forceful words indeed to be spoken to a young, inexperienced, and fearful lad. With this unfortunate speech, she "seizeth on his sweating palm" (25) and "being so enrag'd, desire doth lend her force / Courageously to pluck him from his horse" (29-30). She tucks the "tender boy" (32) under one arm and hauls him into the nearest thicket, where she throws him "backward . . . as she would be thrust" (41). Such brute force is the only reference in this first half of the poem to any powers she might possess and, far from emphasizing her divinity here, such a physical display simply makes us laugh at her even as it repulses Adonis. Telling us that she "govern'd him in strength, though not in lust" (42), the narrative deliberately emphasizes the failure of this kind of seduction; clearly, if this is a Goddess of Love, she demonstrates no power whatsoever to arouse her Adonis, as the rest of the poem proves.

Venus tells Adonis that she is well-schooled in Olympian seduction:

> "I have been wooed, as I entreat thee now,
> Even by the stern and direful god of war,
>
> . . . . .
>
> [Who] begg'd for that which thou unask'd
>   shalt have."
>
> (97-102)

To readers well versed in the mythological tales of Mars's and Venus's comic love affair, this reversal of roles—Venus seeking to imitate the God of War in her attempts to woo a young boy—emerges as delightfully ironic. And yet, beyond the comedy, Venus seems curiously unaware of the ill effects of her claims as she continues to describe how Mars's wooing made him "'my captive and my slave, [a] prisoner in a red rose chain . . . [and] servile to my coy disdain'" (101-12). This tactic is surely not a wise rhetorical choice for arousing the young and naive Adonis. She essentially claims that although Mars wooed her, she "'foil'd the god of fight'" (114) and enslaved his identity in her own likeness, for he "'learn'd to sport and dance, / To toy, to wanton, dally, smile, and jest'" (105-06). Though she claims to be using Olympian arts of seduction, her behavior and language so far seem so full of blundering and blustering that we can hardly believe the truth of the claim.

In fact, it is not the Olympian arts of lovemaking, but the Elizabethan courtier's arts of literary rhetoric that she slavishly imitates here, such as George Puttenham describes in *The Arte of* English Poesie. The "vtterance" of "amorous affections" demands a rhetoric that is

> variable, inconstant, affected, curious, and most witty of any others, whereof the ioyes were to be vttered in one sorte, the sorrowes in an other, and, by the many formes of Poesie, the many moodes and pangs of louers throughly to be discouered; the poore soules sometimes praying, beseeching, sometime honouring, auancing, praising, an other while railing, reuilling, and cursing. (59-60)

Shakespeare's Venus, who seems to be at the mercy of the Elizabethan rhetorician's advice, performs exactly as Puttenham prescribes, taking upon herself all the goals and functions of the orator: praising, blaming, persuading, instructing her audience Adonis in the arts of love. Choosing a language and argument that do not suit her audience's interests, she demonstrates only the comic insufficiency of Petrarchan language to move love. Although we are told that "to a pretty ear she tunes her tale" (74), the fact is that she has not tuned her words to suit her young, naive, and "pretty" audience. She has broken the first rule of persuasion, that one must adapt one's speech to the character of one's audience, and so her words are doomed to fail.

Filled with imperatives and *sententiae,* her speech makes of her more a querulous, ill-natured parent to the young Adonis than an alluring lover:

> "What seest thou in the ground? hold up thy
>   head,
> Look in mine eyeballs, there thy beauty
>   Lies;
> Then why not lips on lips, since eyes in
>   eyes?
> Art thou asham'd to kiss?"
>
> (118-21)

Incredulous that Adonis does not respond to her physical beauty, she complains vigorously in a comically verbose usage of *accumulatio:*

> "Were I hard-favor'd, foul, or wrinkled old,
> Ill-nurtur'd, crooked, churlish, harsh in voice,
> O'erworn, despised, rheumatic, and cold,
> Thick-sighted, barren, lean, and lacking juice,
> Then mightst thou pause, for then I were not
>   for thee,
> But having no defects, why dost abhor me?"
>
> (133-38)

Her intended seduction also includes a lengthy lecture upon his apparently misidentified sexual role, for just as "'Torches are made to light, jewels to wear'" (163), so also, she exhorts him, "'beauty breedeth beauty; / Thou wast begot, to get it is thy duty / [For] by law of nature thou art bound to breed'" (167-71).

Adonis's body language indicates his reactions—he attends to her speeches "with a heavy, dark, disliking eye" (182)—and he even interrupts her to cry, "'Fie, no more of love!'" (185); yet she further condemns her own suit by attempting to rouse him with an insult: "'Thou art no man, though of a man's complexion, / For men will kiss even by their own direction'" (215-16). Again she fails to adapt her argument to the character of her audience, but here her failure indicates a marked inexperience not only in oratory but also in the art of courtly love. Within her experience, a "true" male would immediately respond to her beauty if only to prove his masculinity. She does not understand that Adonis is not the lover she knew in Mars; Adonis is yet a child, with a child's emotions. She also does not seem to comprehend that by now Adonis is not slavishly adhering to the rules of Petrarchan amorous discourse: he is not coyly feigning resistance to her advances; he is an adversary. However, having attempted "railing, reuilling, and cursing" (Puttenham 60), Venus for a moment can speak no more: "This said, impatience chokes her pleading tongue, / And swelling passion doth provoke a pause" (217-18).

As if she has not said enough, though, Venus launches into a second unfortunate tirade, this time resorting to erotic metaphor in an attempt to awaken Adonis's sexual appetite:

> "I'll be a park, and thou shalt be my deer;
> Feed where thou wilt, on mountain, or in dale;
> Graze on my lips, and if those hills be dry,
> Stray lower, where the pleasant fountains lie."
> (231-34)

She goes on to describe her "'sweet bottom grass'" (236) and "'round rising hillocks'" (238), all in an apparent attempt to create within Adonis's mind an image of the female body and thus arouse his passions. The erotic language—here couched in the metaphors of natural landscape, literalization of "earthy" language—proves to be more comic in its inappropriateness than powerful in its imagery, more humanly desperate than divinely seductive. Still not the irresistible Goddess of Love of classical mythology, Venus appears here awkward, ineffectual, laughable—a point which the narrator further emphasizes in comic lament: "Poor queen of love, in thine own law forlorn, / To love a cheek that smiles at thee in scorn!" (251-52).

Certainly, in terms of the entire poem's erotic language, continually an aspect of the poet's art which readers have often appreciated, there appears an attempt to equal and even exceed Ovid's own mastery of lush, sensuous language. Flesh is a central concern in the poem, particularly "its moistness, its texture, Adonis's sweating palm, his rose-cheeks, his panting breath upon Venus's skin" (Bradbrook, *Shakespeare* 63). One particular erotic image in Arthur Golding's translation of Ovid—"The beauty of the lad / Inflam'd her" (10.610-11)—becomes a full motif in Shakespeare's version, where the narration continually describes flesh and passion in the language of heat and flame. For example, Venus is "red and hot as coals of glowing fire" (35); she is equated with a thirsty "passenger in summer's heat" (91); she paradoxically "bathes in water [the tears of her plea for Adonis's love], yet her fire must burn" (94); "Her face doth reek and smoke, her blood doth boil" (555); her cheek "flash'd forth fire, as lightning from the sky" (348). The sensuous imagery and veiled eroticism may well have contributed to the poem's apparent hold on Shakespeare's fascinated audience. There were seventeen editions of the poem between 1593 and 1675 (*Facsimile* i); Gabriel Harvey remarked that while wiser readers sought out *The Rape of Lucrece*, *Venus and Adonis* continued to be the favorite among the "younger sort," and throughout the period there are "frequent allusions to its somewhat disreputable popularity" (Prince xxvi).[2]

The nature and intensity of the erotic imagery, however, deserves added emphasis; indeed, as Stephen Greenblatt has shown (73-86), the concept of bodily heat was crucial to the Renaissance culture's concepts of sexuality and procreation, and thus of seduction as well. Contemporary medical journals and marriage manuals adhered to the Galenic model of anatomy, the idea that both male and female "seed" are "co-present in every person" (Greenblatt 84). Along with this theory came the belief that physical body heat is the crucial element in all aspects of sexuality: seed [both male and female] is produced and emitted by the concoction, or cooking, of blood; this cooking is accomplished through erotic friction between men and women" (Greenblatt 85). As Greenblatt points out, "there are endless references in the erotic poetry of the period to this heat," including *Venus and Adonis,* which "is dominated by the language of heat" (182 n33). Clearly, heat was believed to be the crucial force which caused the male genitalia to emerge in the adolescent boy (for it was widely accepted that women's bodies were by nature cooler than men's), and which caused—under the right amorous "friction"—the inner female genitals to release the "seed" necessary to conceive (Greenblatt 88, 81). Hence "medical texts prescribe[d] extended foreplay"—including "lascivious words"—"as an integral part of sexual intercourse" to help the woman heat her naturally cooler body (Greenblatt 79). Ambrose Parey, for example, advocated that if a husband "perceive [his wife] to be slow, and more cold, he must cherish, embrace, and tickle her . . . by little and little intermixing more wanton kisses with wanton words and speeches . . . that she may take fire and bee enflamed to venery" (Parey 889, quoted by Greenblatt 180 n19).

That the sexual heat is present not in the male Adonis but in the female Venus may be one of the finest touches of irony in the erotic language of the poem. Adonis is red and burning, but not with the heat of masculine sexuality: he is "red for shame" (36) and "burns with bashful shame" (49). Indeed, Shakespeare's readers must have found delightful humor and irony in the puns contained in Venus's amorous railing against the "'flint-hearted boy'" (95)—"'Art thou obdurate, flinty, hard as steel?'" she asks later (199)—for surely flint is "hard" (wittily alluding, perhaps, to male sexual arousal), but it is not hot, though paradoxically it is capable of striking a flame, as it has done in Venus. Clearly, the coldness in Adonis reflects his immaturity, his youth. And perhaps this reversal of sexual roles and the language of heat connected with Venus herself presents an image contributing to a picture of her divinity, since a goddess is presumably capable of more heat and more passion than a human woman, making her into a virago in the Latinate sense of the word—a masculinized, heroic female.[3] And yet her situation and her complete ineffectiveness at seduction make for a comic reversal of the heroic and emphasize her humanized blundering, for Venus's own impotent "wanton words" cannot "enflame" her intended mate and she is left with "swelling passion" (218)—an erotic pun that indicates the comic, humanized frustration of this goddess-virago.

To emphasize further the all-too-human ineffectiveness of this Venus, the poem introduces another courtship, one that contrasts greatly with Venus's comic and impotent verbosity. From a nearby copse, a

> breeding jennet, lusty, young, and proud,
> Adonis' trampling courser doth espy;
> And forth she rushes, snorts, and neighs
>   aloud.
>
> (260-62)

Adonis's horse, in "hot courage" (276), "breaketh his rein and to her straight goes" (264) in reply to the mating rhetoric, the vocal and physical display, of this jennet. In a comic reversal of Venus's plight, the mare in season simply makes her instinctive call and the courser immediately responds, while poor Venus drives her intended mate further away with her every attempt at "mating rhetoric."

Venus now resorts to physical persuasion when "like a lowly lover down she kneels" (350) and with one "tender hand his fair cheek feels" (352). This now-silent courtship game continues, however, to be adversarial—a "beauteous combat" (365) and a "war of looks" (355)—and her tongue, the "heart's attorney" (335), flies once again into the fray as the "engine of her thoughts" (367) to assail Adonis's remoteness:

> "Who is so faint that dares not be so bold
> to touch the fire, the weather being cold?
>
> Let me excuse thy courser, gentle boy,
> And learn of him, I heartily beseech thee."
>
> (401-04)

His nonverbal refutation of Venus's continued verbal onslaught of multiple sententia is simply a look that would kill, sending Venus into her own silent sortie—a pretended faint. Fearfully, Adonis attempts to revive her with "chaff[ing]" (477)—surely a comic irony, since the last thing Venus seems to need is more "friction"—and with the Elizabethan equivalent of artificial resuscitation, but even now Venus cannot leave aside her lecturing; she breaks off kissing to chatter on again, to rail against his "'hard heart,'" which has taught his eyes such "'scornful tricks'" (500-01).

Venus and Adonis may indeed be seen as two essentially different attitudes toward rhetoric (Lanham 84), Venus apparently believing wholeheartedly in the ability of her rhetoric to persuade; after all, her discourse moves Venus herself, for as she talks, she becomes increasingly impassioned, heated, carried away by her own Petrarchan conceits and carpe diem arguments. Adonis's one lengthy speech shows his own antithetical stance, his deliberate refusal to make use of his own "mating rhetoric" and his willful abandonment of argument altogether: "'More I could tell, but more I dare not say, / The text is old, the orator too green'" (805-06). Shakespeare has obviously reversed the traditional Petrarchan situation—a male wooing a cold and haughty though beautiful woman. And he has reduced the divinity of the Goddess of Love: here, this Venus has no greater seductive powers than any mere mortal and, in fact, appears in many ways more grotesque and more comically blundering than most mortals. Further, she seems oblivious to her own verbal sabotage of her wooing, even though Adonis forthrightly tells her that he objects to her speech, her "'idle, over-handled theme'" (770): "'Your treatise,'" he says bluntly, "'makes me like you worse and worse'" (774). And ultimately Venus's rhetoric serves not only to alienate Adonis but to alienate those readers who expect to find in her a divinely powerful and compelling character, however much readers may delight in the ornate figurative language and the erotic humor of the narrative. Shakespeare's Venus, far from being the artful Ovidian Goddess of Love, proves to be merely a querulous pedant in the arts of poetic seduction. And yet, as comic as her unwieldy, ineffective rhetoric is, the result of Venus's futile wooing proves to be very serious and poignant indeed: in refusing her amorous argument, Adonis refuses her language altogether, thus rejecting also her warning about the deadly boar. Ovid's Adonis did not heed her warning because he was too manly to be frightened away from hunting—"his manhood by admonishment restreyned could not bee" (10.832) from the sport. But Shakespeare's young man, in contrast, exits because Venus drives him away with her ill-chosen rhetoric: for over one hundred lines she elaborates on how and where and why and what he should hunt instead of the boar (660-768), and Adonis finally interrupts her warning speech, saying he fears "'You will fallagain / Into your idle over-handled theme'" (770-71). It would appear that though Venus possesses the godlike knowledge of Adonis's impending doom—"'I prophesy thy death, my living sorrow, / If thou encounter with the boar to-morrow'" (671-72)—she lacks the rhetorical ability to speak convincingly enough to save him. Adonis reveals that her ill-chosen discourse itself has led him to mistrust her sincerity altogether: "'I hate not love, but your device in love'" (789).

Yet, when she gazes upon his torn body, the result of her impotent rhetoric, this previously verbose, blundering orator now experiences a moment of utter silence when "dumbly she passions . . . [and] her voice is stopp'd" (1059, 1062). When she does find her voice again, her rhetoric has strangely changed: as she sees the body blurred through her tears, she laments, "'My tongue cannot express my grief for one, / And yet . . . behold two Adons' dead!'" (1069-70). Far from the comic, grotesque, humanized Venus of the previous passages, this grieving Venus now commands sympathy, offering a sincere and heartfelt elegy to Adonis:

> "Alas, poor world, what treasure hast thou lost!
> What face remains alive that's worth the viewing?
> Whose tongue is music now? what canst thou boast
> Of things long since, or any thing ensuing?
> The flowers are sweet, their colors fresh and trim,
> But true sweet beauty liv'd and died with him.
>
> . . . . .
>
> But when Adonis liv'd, sun and sharp air
> Lurk'd like two thieves, to rob him of his fair.
> "And therefore would he put his bonnet on,
> Under whose brim the gaudy sun would peep;
> The wind would blow it off, and being gone,
> Play with his locks; then would Adonis weep;
> And straight, in pity of his tender years,
> They both would strive who first should dry his tears."
>
> (1075-92)

What began in erotic, ironic comedy now ends in funeral elegy; Venus has progressed from the state of ineffectual, imitative Petrarchan poet to that of the fully competent elegiac poet who now, with the sovereign eloquence of a true Olympian, laments nature's own loss of the beloved Adonis: "'To see his face the lion walk'd along'" (1093) and the tiger and wolf would both be tamed by his voice (1096-97); in Adonis's presence "'the birds such pleasure took, / That some would sing, some other in their bills / Would bring him mulberries and ripe-red cherries'" (1101-03). The elegy continues as Venus accounts for Adonis's death by the boar, a death that is no murder—since all of nature loved him so dearly—but is caused by the kiss of the "unaware" boar:

> "But this foul, grim, and urchin-snouted boar,
> Whose downward eye still looketh for a grave,
> Ne'er saw the beauteous livery that he wore—
> Witness the entertainment that he gave.
> If he did see his face, why then I know
> He sought to kiss him, and hath kill'd him so.
>
> "'Tis true, 'tis true, thus was Adonis slain:
> He ran upon the boar with his sharp spear,
> Who did not whet his teeth at him again,
> But by a kiss thought to persuade him there;
> And nousling in his flank, the loving swine
> Sheath'd unaware the tusk in his soft groin."
>
> (1105-16)

And, as nature was "unaware" of its harm to the boy, so does Venus show recognition of her own naivete in this passage marked by poetic beauty and poignant self-knowledge, nowhere more moving than her moment of insight into her previous ignorance which would have killed Adonis though she loved him:

> "Had I been tooth'd like him, I must confess,
> With kissing him I should have kill'd him first.
> But he is dead, and never did he bless
> My youth with his, the more am I accurs'd."
>
> (1117-20)

Thus what some critics have called a shift of tone could be read as the poem's narrative progress—from grotesque comedy to pathos—which parallels the transformation in Venus herself: from ignorance to knowledge, from inexperience to experience.[4] Surely this is a Venus who has learned, in the time frame of this poem, some hard lessons about choice, consequence, and self-knowledge. This maturation of Venus is most strikingly displayed in the transformation of her rhetoric into the language of divine power. Whereas her earlier speeches produced none of the intended results, her language now has the power to change the course of human love and to transform Adonis's flowing blood into an anemone:

> "Sith in his prime, Death doth my love destroy,
> They that love best, their loves shall not enjoy."
> By this the boy that by her side lay kill'd
> Was melted like a vapor from her sight,
> And in his blood that on the ground lay spill'd,
> A purple flow'r sprang up, check'red with white.
>
> (1163-69)

An emphasis on the new-found power of her language to change human events may be indicated when her words are shown capable of producing the flower, for it is "by *this*"—that is, by her speech—that "the boy that by her side lay kill'd / Was melted like a vapor from her sight."[5]

Ovid's goddess, too, produces the anemone flower from the blood, but she does not curse all love that is to follow thereafter, as does Shakespeare's Venus. Here we learn how love became so problematic for all humankind, including the Petrarchans who were yet to follow this ill-fated lover; it was the curse of the grieving Venus with her now-powerful, divine language which altered the course of love affairs, so that human beings would mimic continually her own doomed love for Adonis:

> "Sorrow on love hereafter shall attend;
> It shall be waited on with jealousy,
> Find sweet beginning, but unsavory end;

> . . . . .
>
> It shall be fickle, false, and full of fraud,
> Bud, and be blasted, in a breathing while,
> The bottom poison, and the top o'erstraw'd
> With sweets that shall the truest sight beguile;
> The strongest body shall it make most weak,
> Strike the wise dumb, and teach the fool to speak.
>
> . . . . .
>
> It shall be raging mad, and silly mild,
> Make the young old, the old become a child.
>
> It shall suspect where is no cause of fear,
> It shall not fear where it should most mistrust,
> It shall be merciful, and too severe,
> And most deceiving when it seems most just;
>
> . . . . .
>
> It shall be cause of war and dire events,
> And set dissension 'twixt the son and sire."
>
> (1136-60)

Still characteristically aggressive and wordy, Venus offers lengthy elegy and curse of love in highly ornate, figurative language. Rhetorical flourish—here, notably anaphora, oxymoron, alliteration, antithesis, paradox—and verbal excess are still her distinguishing features. She talks to Adonis's corpse as if he can hear and offers an address to the flower itself as she plucks it, since the "'unripe'" (524) Adonis in life had shunned being too "'early pluck'd'" (528). She is clearly, however, now the fully transformed Goddess of Love who speaks in poetic imagery of divine loveliness, addressing the flower of her own creation as she places it in her bosom—"'Lo in this hollow cradle take thy rest, / My throbbing heart shall rock thee day and night'" (1185-86)—and who afterward, like a true Olympian "weary of the world . . . yokes her silver doves" and flies off to Paphos "through the empty skies / In her light chariot" (1189-92). In masterful imagery of remote divinity, Shakespeare's final verse affirms that this Venus is now truly the "queen" and a full-fledged goddess "not to be seen" (1193, 1194) by mere mortals in this human realm.

Why should Shakespeare depart so markedly from a genre already well established by Ovid, and indeed from material already masterfully treated by his Roman source? Characteristically, this youthful Shakespeare takes a well-known model and provides a new focus which demonstrates his poetic virtuosity as well as his ability to reject slavish imitation of his predecessor. He transforms the material into his own unique piece, one which explores a paradoxical transformation in Venus, herself, wherein Venus—already a goddess, though throughly humanized and ineffectual—undergoes a second apotheosis, as it were, into the truly powerful Goddess of Love. Thus, in contrast to Ovid's single metamorphosis (the transformation of Adonis into the flower) Shakespeare's version manages a triple metamorphosis: in the apotheosis of Venus from the humanized into the divine, she transforms Adonis into the flower *and* changes all love that will thereafter occur, providing a fine extra Ovidian twist in giving us a kind of "creation story"—"how love became so disagreeable"—that had been a favorite device of Ovid himself. The new poet thus manages to outdo his poetic forefather, to "out-Ovid" Ovid, no mean accomplishment for a fledgling poet setting out to rival the likes of Marlowe and Lodge.[6] In this sense *Venus and Adonis* is quite a "masterpiece," at least in the usage of the word that Richard Lanham reminds us to bear in mind for the Elizabethan age: a piece made by the artisan "to prove he is a master" (82), a sort of final exam to provide graduation from the status of journeyman to master.

And along the way, Shakespeare has had the opportunity to experiment with devices that will prove useful to him in later works. The mixture of comedy and tragedy, for example, prefigures the romances of his later career. I would not suggest, as others have done, that Venus is fully a tragic heroine,[7] but in Adonis's death and in that final image of the fully realized goddess "weary of the world," who bears the price of her apotheosis (the flower) in her bosom, lurk tragic overtones that Shakespeare will later develop more skillfully into the likes of his Cleopatra, who opens her play with shallow, silly quantitativeness about love ("If it be love indeed, tell me how much" [1.1.14]) but grows into a fully realized and heroic queen who has understood too late the boundless bounty that unconditional love might have offered. On the comic side, Venus bears affinities with Helena, the comic heroine of *All's Well That Ends Well* who is also deeply concerned with the value and persuasive force of language in wooing and who is faced with an equally unresponsive intended mate. But immediately after *Venus and Adonis* Shakespeare was to turn to a heroine whom, as I have argued elsewhere, he would endow with similar rhetorical qualities—verbal excess which fixes upon a need to find creational, poetic power in language itself in order to create a legacy: his Lucrece.[8] Thus the new poet's early concern with two excessively long-winded poetic heroines, both obsessed with desire for rhetorical prowess, offered a valuable proving ground for the time when he would discard once and for all the narrative voice and turn exclusively to the discourse of dramatic dialogue.

The assessment that "Shakespeare's artistic vitality is too great for the type of construction—of multiple portraits and scenes—which he inherited from Marlowe and Lodge" (Gent 728) is to an extent appropriate. And yet that artistic vitality is served quite well in this poem, for since *Venus and Adonis* is Shakespeare's first acknowledged progeny—the "first heire of my inuention"—it bears the unmistakable marks of those anxieties and desires which concern a new poet, and, significantly, a *Renaissance* new poet: to prove his poetic skill, to recast his sources, to surpass his predecessors, and to create some lasting legacy to his name. Thus Venus's apotheosis from shallow rhetorician into elegiac poet mirrors the "apotheosis" of the new poet himself, who must break the rules of poetic form and violently unmake his model in order to create his own mature expressions of his aesthetic principles. As Bloom remarks:

> Emerson, in his most idealizing temper, said of the poets that they were liberating gods, that they were free and made others free. I would amend this by saying that poets make themselves free, by their stances towards earlier Poets, and make others free only by teaching them those stances or positions of freedom. Freedom, in a poem, must mean freedom of meaning, the freedom to have a meaning of one's own. (3)

And this glance towards an earlier poet's text must necessarily be violent, for "the agon is of the essence," as Bloom suggests: "good poems must be combative" (5). In this respect, the "birth" of the new poet strongly parallels Hesiod's account of the birth of Venus, who sprang from the mixture of sea and sperm when Cronos severed the genitals of his father, Uranus, and threw them into the ocean. How appropriate, then, that this new poet would choose one of the myths of Venus, herself, as the location of his own agon with a poet-"father," Ovid, whose material Shakespeare would recast and transform again and again throughout his career.[9]

The image of the goddess who plucks the flower in an attempt to preserve forever Adonis's mortal beauty becomes an emblem of the poet's act, as well. Like Venus, seeking permanence in this impermanent mortal world, the poet constructs a poem in an attempt to leave behind a lasting legacy in a changing world—a *monumentum aere perennius,* a monument (to the poet) more lasting than bronze. And yet the attempt itself is charged with paradox, for the moment of plucking—the attempt to preserve against mortality—ensures death to the flower. So it is with the poet's attempt to transcend mortality through poetry, as well: poetic creation is, paradoxically, a death for the poet, who must release control of his "progency." Yet there remain the marks of Shakespeare's developing genius as a new poet wresting his own territory from pre-existing traditions, revealing "the ambivalent and agonistic clearing-away of [his predecessor's] poetry in order to open up a poetic space for [his] own achievement" (Bloom 18)—indeed, in order to appropriate the creational language to effect his own "apotheosis" in poetic godhead.

Notes

[1] See Asals, who offers a Neoplatonic reading which describes the change from a Venus who represents the lowest form of desire to a divine Venus who personifies the highest form of Neoplatonic desire, through a kind of life-in-death, or perhaps a rebirth through the death of Adonis. For readings which emphasize serious thematic considerations on the subject of lust, see Allen; Robert Miller; both see Venus as a representation of lust. For treatments of Adonis's "villainous" rejection of Venus Genetrix, see Bradbrook, "Beasts and Gods"; Jahn. See also Beauregard for an emphasis on the poem's representations of the concupiscible and irascible passions. Though he maintains that Shakespeare endorses the behavior of neither Venus nor Adonis, Sheidley explores the polarities of lust and chastity. A psychoanalytic reading of the passions in the poem is explored in Rothenberg.

[2] Prince cites *The Returne from Parnassus,* pt. i (1600), where the booby Gullio "wishes to sleep with *Venus and Adonis* under his pillow" (xxvi n2). Likewise, Hyder Rollins speaks of the frequent references throughout the period to the belief that "Shakespeare's poems were the favorite reading of loose and degenerate people, and that, as a consequence, they led to looseness and degeneracy" (quoted by Smith 1704). Curiously, several modern critics reveal a distaste for the erotic subject and language of *Venus and Adonis:* see, for instance, Campbell's statement that the seduction sequences are "not much to modern taste" (239); and Prince, who offers that "few English or American readers nowadays will respond to such happily wanton fancies as *Venus and Adonis*" and that Shakespeare's *Rape of Lucrece* is more to "the taste of our time" (xxv).

[3] Regarding the reversal of sexual roles in the poem, Velz writes that "one of the delights in the poem is our awareness that [Venus] is reminiscent of Apollo and other Ovidian virgin violators" (3).

[4] Although Doebler accounts for the rhetorical shifts in tone as due to the "several personalities Venus has in both the philosophy and the mythography of the Renaissance" (33), Velz says that the tone shift is "precisely Ovidian"—an "Ovidian disjunction" (3).

[5] This passage concerning the actual transformation of blood into flower is, perhaps, ambiguous. One could read the phrase, "by this the boy . . . was melted," to mean that *by this time* he was melted; Shakespeare clearly used this phrase elsewhere as a transitional device to indicate the passage of time (see, for example, *Titus Andronicus* 3.1.109). Can we not also read this as an instance of performative language? Even if we take the phrase to indicate the passage of time, it is *during* her speech that the body is transformed. In contrast, Golding's Ovid shows that Venus says,

> "In a flowre thy blood I will bestowe.
> Hadst thou the powre *Persephone* rank-scented mints to make
> Of womens limbes? and may I not like powre upon mee take
> Without disdein and spyght, to turne *Adonis* to a flowre?"
>
> (851-54)

Having said this, Venus then "sprinckled Nectar on the blood" (855), and, "before that full an howre expyred weere" (857), she finds a flower in the place of the blood. While Shakespeare's phrase, "by this," is equivocal, it may be argued that his Venus does not need to sprinkle nectar and wait nearly an hour for the transformation to take place.

[6] Gent, in fact, remarks that "if any part of Shakespeare's aim was to rival or outdo the rhetoric of Marlowe's *Hero and Leander*, it was a brilliant stroke to make the main orator a woman" (725). Critics are, however, by no means in agreement as to whether Shakespeare had read *Hero and Leander* at the time he wrote *Venus and Adonis*.

[7] For discussions of Venus as a fully tragic heroine, see Lake and Muir.

[8] An exploration of Lucrece's rhetorical excess and concerns about fame appears in French.

[9] For more material on Shakespeare's continued use of Ovid, see Velz; Klose.

Works Cited

Allen, Don Cameron. "On *Venus and Adonis*." In *Elizabethan and Jacobean Studies Presented to Frank Percy Wilson*. Ed. Herbert Davis and Helen Gardner. Oxford: Oxford UP, 1959. 100-11.

Asals, Heather. "*Venus and Adonis:* The Education of a Goddess." *SEL* 13 (1973): 31-51.

Beauregard, David N. "*Venus and Adonis:* Shakespeare's Representations of the Passions." *Shakespeare Studies* 8 (1975): 83-98.

Bloom, Harold. "The Breaking of Form." In Hartman 1-37.

Bradbrook, Muriel C. "Beasts and Gods: *Greene's Groats-worth of Witte* and the Social Purpose of *Venus and Adonis*." *Shakespeare Survey* 15 (1962): 62-72.

———. *Shakespeare and Elizabethan Poetry: A Study of His Earlier Work in Relation to the Poetry of the Time*. 1951. London: Chatto, 1964.

Campbell, Oscar James. *The Sonnets, Songs, and Poems of Shakespeare*. New York: Schocken, 1964.

Doebler, John. "The Many Faces of Love: Shakespeare's *Venus and Adonis*." *Shakespeare Studies* 16 (1983): 33-43.

French, Tita. "A 'badge of fame': Shakespeare's Rhetorical Lucrece." *Explorations in Renaissance Culture* 10 (1984): 97-106.

Gent, Lucy. "'Venus and Adonis': The Triumph of Rhetoric." *Modern Language Review* 69 (1974): 721-29.

Greenblatt, Stephen. *Shakespearean Negotiations: The Circulation of Social Energy in Renaissance England*. Berkeley: U of California P, 1988.

Hartman, Geoffrey, ed. *Deconstruction and Criticism*. New York: Continuum, 1979.

Jahn, J. D. "The Lamb of Lust: The Role of Adonis in Shakespeare's *Venus and Adonis*." *Shakespeare Studies* 6 (1970): 11-25.

Jonson, Ben. *Timber, or Discoveries*. In *Elizabethan Critical Essays*. Ed. G. Gregory Smith. Oxford: Clarendon, 1904.

Klose, Dietrich. "Shakespeare and Ovid." *Shakespeare Jahrbuch* (Heidelberg) (1968): 72-93.

Lake, James H. "Shakespeare's Venus: An Experiment in Tragedy." *Shakespeare Quarterly* 25 (1974): 351-55.

Lanham, Richard. *The Motives of Eloquence*. New Haven: Yale UP, 1976.

Miller, J. Hillis. "The Critic as Host." In Hartman 217-53.

Miller, Robert P. "Venus, Adonis, and the Horses." *English Literary History* 19 (1952): 249-64.

Muir, Kenneth. "*Venus and Adonis:* Comedy or Tragedy?" In *Shakespearean Essays*. Ed. Alwin Thaler and Norman Sanders. Knoxville: U of Tennessee P, 1964. 1-13.

Ovid. *The XV Bookes of P. Ovidius naso, entytuled Metamorphosis, translated out of Latin into English Meeter, by Arthur Golding Gentleman*. 1567. London: De la More, 1904.

Parey, Ambrose (Ambroise Pare). *The Workes of that Famous Chirurgian Ambrose Parey*. Trans. Thomas Johnson. London: Cotes, 1634.

Prince, F. T. Introduction. *The Arden Edition of the Works of William Shakespeare: The Poems.* London: Methuen, 1960. xi-xlvi.

Puttenham, George. *The Arte of English Poesie.* Ed. Baxter Hathaway. Kent: Kent State UP, 1970.

Rothenberg, Alan B. "The Oral Rape Fantasy and Rejection of Mother in the Imagery of Shakespeare's *Venus and Adonis.*" *Psychoanalytic Quarterly* 40 (1971): 447-68.

Shakespeare, William. *Venus and Adonis.* In *The Riverside Shakespeare.* Ed. G. Blakemore Evans et al. Boston: Houghton, 1974. 1705-18.

Sheidley, William E. "'Unless It Be a Boar:' Love and Wisdom in Shakespeare's *Venus and Adonis.*" *Modern Language Review* 35 (1974): 3-15.

Smith, Hallett. Introduction to *Venus and Adonis.* In *The Riverside Shakespeare.* 1703-04.

Velz, John W. "The Ovidian Soliloquy in Shakespeare." *Shakespeare Studies* 18 (1986): 1-24.

William Shakespeare's Venus and Adonis, Facsimile Edition. Menston, Engl.: Scolar, 1968.

Williams, Gordon. "The Coming of Age of Shakespeare's Adonis." *Modern Language Review* 78 (1983): 769-76.

THE RHETORIC OF DESIRE

A. D. Cousins (essay date 1996)

SOURCE: "Towards a Reconsideration of Shakespeare's Adonis: Rhetoric, Narcissus, and the Male Gaze," in *Studia Neophilologica*, Vol. 68, No. 2, 1996, pp. 195-204.

[*In the following essay, Cousins examines Shakespeare's use of rhetoric in characterizing Adonis, seeing him as an anti-Narcissus figure who is the object of a voyeuristic male sexual desire.*]

Shakespeare's Adonis, like his Venus, has been primarily studied either in terms of Renaissance thinking about myth and symbol or as if a character in a play. Study in the first mode has connected Adonis with, for example, the idea of beauty's transience, a connection that has been interestingly explored.[1] Study in the second mode has closely traced his responses to Venus' sexual aggression, examining his evasions, his defiances, and so on.[2] In what follows (and so in parallel to my discussion of Venus), both familiar critical approaches are used but new arguments about Adonis' characterization are put forward. It is initially argued that, in response to Venus' assertive (male) rhetoric of seduction, Adonis has at once an eloquent, silent, female rhetoric of rejection and a Platonic, male rhetoric of love (he also has, of course, an adolescent rhetoric of indignation and impatience at harassment). He has, that is to say, a rhetoric of chastity through which to counter the goddess's *de facto* role as *Venus Mechanitis*. Next it is argued that when Adonis refuses the goddess's seductive offer(s)—from her point of view—of metamorphosis, he does not thereby merely resemble Narcissus, with whom Venus scornfully identifies him because of his unresponsiveness to her. On the contrary, in some important respects he virtually becomes an antithesis to Narcissus, almost an anti-Narcissus figure, and in this context self-knowledge seems to be a central issue. Finally it is argued that not Venus but Adonis appears to be foregrounded as the object of sexual desire in Shakespeare's narrative. To be more specific, it is argued that the narrator, particularly through his presentation of Venus, sets up Adonis as the object of the male gaze.[3]

When confronting the unwelcome, predominantly Petrarchan language/rhetoric of seduction directed at him by Venus, and her bodily aggression, which often accompanies it, Adonis sometimes reacts with speech whose terse, sullen anger seems appropriate to his years and his situation. "Fie, no more of love! / The sun doth burn my face, I must remove" he cries when Venus tells him of his duty to breed—or else become like Narcissus (lines 185-186; see lines 157-174). At another moment, when Venus forgets what she was talking about and asks, "Where did I leave?", Adonis replies: "No matter where . . . , / Leave me, and then the story aptly ends . . ." (lines 715-716). That adolescent rhetoric of indignation and impatience has occasionally, moreover, a feminine tone to it, so that it seems appropriate not only to Adonis' years and circumstances but also to the poem's recurrent description of his beauty in female terms—for example, in terms of perfect whiteness and redness, which metonymically and immediately evoke the Petrarchan ideal of female beauty (as in line 10). When Venus strokes Adonis' cheek, then imprisons his hand, to cite one instance (lines 352-364: his cheek being "tend'rer" than her hand, his hand rivalling hers in whiteness, according to the narrator in lines 352-354 and 362-364 respectively), he cries out: "For shame," . . . "let go, and let me go . . ." (line 379; cf. line 53). The feminine tone that can be heard in such outbursts links them with a distinctly female rhetoric that Adonis at times uses, apparently not knowing that it is female, much less a cultural rhetoric.

Two episodes in the poem illustrate that clearly. In an early episode, Venus pushes Adonis to the ground (lines

40-41) and he begins "to chide" her (line 46). She silences him, stopping his lips and warning that she will not let him speak in opposition to her (lines 46-48). The narrator thereupon says: "He [Adonis] burns with bashful shame, she [Venus] with her tears / Doth quench the maiden burning of his cheeks . . ." (lines 49-50). One Renaissance commonplace about women was that they should be silent; often in early modern fictions they are simply voiceless, denied speech. It is odd, then, but not hard to understand, that in emblem books the ideal woman is figured by a tortoise, among other things. Like it she stays at home and is silent.[4] Forced into silence, like a woman but also by a female (deity) who pervasively uses a male (human) language/rhetoric of love/seduction, Adonis responds with what is recognizable at once as part of a conventionally female—and physical, silent—cultural rhetoric eloquent of sexual embarrassment and repudiation (the narrator, having said that Adonis "burns with bashful shame," goes on to specify the process as "the maiden burning of his cheeks," emphasizing that Adonis' body language is a female, necessarily silent, expressive and conventional articulation of shamefastness). Later in the narrative, Venus warily approaches Adonis and, the narrator says," [W]hat a war of looks was then between them! / Her eyes petitioners to his eyes suing, / His eyes saw her eyes, as they had not seen them, / Her eyes woo'd still, his eyes disdain'd the wooing . . ." (lines 355-358). There are some clear differences between the earlier and later episodes. In the later one Adonis' silence is voluntary; further, he seems more vigorous in rejecting Venus. Nonetheless his rhetoric appears to be broadly the same in each. The later episode presents Venus, in her role as assertive (conventionally male, Petrarchized libertine) lover aggressing Adonis in his (conventionally female, Petrarchan) role as unwilling object of desire. Like a disdainful, Petrarchan lady he repudiates his suitor's insistent gaze, expressing himself physically, tacitly, eloquently.[5]

It was mentioned above that the other important and complementary element in what seems to be Adonis' rhetoric of chastity is a Platonic, male rhetoric of love. That rhetoric, whilst idealistic and combative, appears also to be problematic.[6] Just after Venus has again informed Adonis of his duty to breed (lines 751-768) he makes the most substantial of his speeches (lines 769-810). There—as unknowingly as when using a female rhetoric—he presents himself in the guise of an armed Petrarchan object of desire, firmly and cautiously resistant to Venus' seductive discourse (lines 778-784). He unflatteringly identifies Venus as *Venus Vulgaris* trying to legitimize her desire by an appeal to her cognate function as *Venus Genetrix* (lines 790-791).[7] Then he remarks, in asserting that Venus' love is actually lust: "Call it not love, for love to heaven is fled, / Since sweating lust on earth usurp'd his name; / Under whose simple semblance he hath fed / Upon fresh beauty, blotting it with blame . . ." (lines 793-796).

Adonis distinguishes between a supplanted, original, absent Cupid of spiritual love (line 793) and a usurping, parodic Cupid of sexual desire, now present on earth (line 794). In doing so he deftly, if of course again unwittingly, evokes Pausanias' distinction in Plato's *Symposium* between two forms of love, each symbolized by a different Cupid and a different Venus: a Cupid and Venus of spiritual love (the latter being the heavenly Venus, or *Venus Urania*); a Cupid and Venus of sexual desire (the latter being the earthly Venus known as *Venus Pandemos/Venus Vulgaris*).[8] Pausanias' distinction primarily concerns how adult males should, and should not, love adolescent males—hence it is aptly evoked, given that Venus woos the adolescent Adonis as might "a bold-fac'd suitor".

Adonis' Platonic allusion functions in a range of ways; however, a couple seem particularly relevant here. First, it indicates that, in opposition to Venus' (male) Petrarchized libertine discourse of seduction, Adonis has a male, powerful, totalizing counter-discourse. On the other hand, Adonis uses that discourse only once at any length, and then some while after Venus has begun pursuing him. Next, it indicates that Adonis' view of spiritual love as having fled the earth is extreme (if not hard to understand, given his recent experience). Pausanias, in celebrating spiritual love, does not suggest that it cannot be achieved; he does not suggest that it cannot be found on earth. Adonis' Platonic rhetoric of love in this his major speech both forcefully counters Venus' discourse of seduction and reveals his intransigent belief that the world is loveless, that no human amatory experience is or will be spiritual. The male component of Adonis' rhetoric of chastity has, then, a problematic strength. Helping Adonis to demystify the sophistry of Venus, it nonetheless immerses him in an unrecognised sophistry of his own.

One of the best-known ploys in Venus' attempted seduction of Adonis is her telling him that his failure to love someone else—namely herself—may make him into another Narcissus (see lines 157-162; cf. lines 115-120). Her use of Narcissus as an example of a dangerous indifference to others' desires, of the dangers attendant on self-love, seems narcissistic in its self-interestedness and indifference to Adonis' desires. Nonetheless, her comparison has some credibility insofar as Adonis, like Narcissus, resolutely rejects love ("I know not love," quoth he, "nor will not know it . . ."—line 409; "My love to love is love but to disgrace it . . ."—line 412) and meets sexual advances with a hard unresponsiveness (Venus calls Adonis a "flint-hearted boy" and asks him if he is "obdurate, flinty, hard as steel . . ."—a parody of the *domina petrosa* motif, in lines 95 and 199 respectively; in the *Metamorphoses*, Ovid's narrator says that "[m]any lads and many girls fell in love with him [Narcissus], but his soft young body housed a pride so unyielding that none dared to touch him").[9] But whilst Adonis may be seen to resemble

Narcissus, he appears also to be significantly unlike him, in fact virtually to be his opposite.

One of the first things that Ovid's narrator relates about Narcissus is this. Just after he has been born and given a name, his mother asks the prophet Tiresias "whether [the] boy [will] live to a ripe old age." Tiresias' reported reply is: "Yes, if he does not come to know himself.'" Then the narrator says: "For a long time this pronouncement seemed to be nothing but empty words: however it was justified by the outcome of events: the strange madness which afflicted the boy and the nature of his death proved its truth."[10] Later in the tale, as Narcissus talks to his own, unrecognized image in the pool he suddenly makes the inevitable discovery and exclaims: "Alas! I am myself the boy I see. I know it: my own reflection does not deceive me. I am on fire with love for my own self. It is I who kindle the flames which I must endure."[11] Tiresias prophesied that if Narcissus were to gain self-knowledge his doing so would destroy him. Love brings the boy self-knowledge and with it comes a grief that hastens his death. The most significant dissimilarity between Ovid's Narcissus and Shakespeare's Adonis centres, I think, precisely on the issue of self-knowledge and its relation to love.

By way of explaining to Venus his refusal to love her, Adonis at one point declares: "Fair queen, . . . if any love you owe me, / Measure my strangeness with my unripe years. / Before I know myself, seek not to know me . . ." (lines 523-525). He adds: "The mellow plum doth fall, the green sticks fast, / Or being early pluck'd, is sour to taste" (lines 527-528). Venus must well understand Adonis' argument, for much earlier in the tale she has remarked: "The tender spring upon thy tempting lip / Shows thee unripe; yet mayst thou well be tasted" (lines 127-128). Subsequently, in the major speech where he asserts that true, spiritual love has fled the world, Adonis indirectly raises the "unripeness" argument again: "More I could tell, but more I dare not say: / The text is old, the orator too green" (lines 805-806). It seems reasonable to propose that Adonis' insistences on his immaturity and on true love's having fled the world shape his main arguments for rejecting Venus' advances; as has just been indicated, both occur in his speech on the difference between true love and its counterfeit, lust. Be that as it may, however, the directly relevant point here is this. Whereas Narcissus self-destructively gains self-knowledge as a result of love (self-love though of course it is), Adonis wants to have self-knowledge prior to, and quite separately from, the experience of love. He apparently wishes to know himself—and so in effect to realize the ancient imperative *"nosce te ipsum"* ("know yourself")—without gaining sexual knowledge. The play on "know" as cognition and sexual experience in his command/request, "Before I know myself, seek not to know me" (line 525), makes that much clear. Yet Adonis' wordplay there brings together self-knowledge and sexual experience, implying (despite his wish) that they are actually connected, perhaps inseparable.

When Venus offers Adonis metamorphosis via his sexual initiation (as I have argued in discussing her characterization), she in fact offers him loss of self—or identity—as someone committed to the active life and the gaining of a new, incongruously diminished identity as aesthetic/sexual object and concupiscent prize of the hunt of love. In rejecting Venus' offers of lost and gained identities, Adonis retains his self-definition as follower of the active life (hunter, servant of Diana), a self-definition that he obviously thinks incomplete or that is incompletely understood by him (again, see lines 525-528), and refuses knowledge of his sexuality. Thereby he repudiates not only Venus' proffered new identities but also an extension of his self-knowledge: he deliberately limits his acquisition of self-knowledge by his stated decision to seek it prior to, separately from, sexual experience. Moreover, retaining his incomplete and asexual identity as follower of the active life, he therefore has his parodic sexual encounter with the boar, in which his very life is lost.[12] If self-knowledge in relation to love is a key issue in the characterizations of Shakespeare's Adonis and of Ovid's Narcissus, and the textual evidence seems to support the idea, then with respect to it the two figures are virtually antithetic. Venus' forceful, slightly accurate analogy between Adonis and Narcissus elucidates through its inaccuracy Adonis' presentation in the poem.

The final aspect of Adonis' characterization that I wish now to examine concerns the male gaze. As was suggested above, not Venus but Adonis appears to be foregrounded as the object of sexual desire in Shakespeare's poem; in fact, the narrator, chiefly through his presentation of Venus, appears to set up Adonis as the object of the male gaze.[13] Perhaps the shortest way to start making that argument specific is by considering some of the poem's images of gluttony. Venus, in her role as *Venus Vulgaris,* seems appropriately (given the nature of that role) to think of Adonis as her "banquet of sense." For example, when concluding a celebration of how her senses do or would delight in Adonis, she says: "But oh what banquet wert thou to the taste, / Being nurse and feeder to the other four! / Would they not wish the feast might ever last [?]" (lines 445-447). Seemingly mindful of Venus' eagerness to gormandize on him, Adonis subsequently says in his major speech about the difference between love and lust: "Love surfeits not, lust like a glutton dies" (line 803). But whilst his allusion to gluttony denigrates, deliberately or otherwise, her picture of him as her "banquet of sense," it also echoes and condemns likewise a reference she has made to a sexual gluttony of the sight: "Who sees his true-love in her naked bed, / Teaching the sheets a whiter hue than white, / But when his glutton eye so full hath fed, / His other agents aim at like delight?" (lines 397-400).

Venus speaks those words when urging Adonis to follow the example of his horse, which has run off with "[a] breeding jennet" (line 260), and "learn to love" (line 407; cf. lines 385-408). Venus' words, that is to say, are designed to excite and to incite Adonis. They try to do so by putting before him an image of a desirable, available female subjected to a devouring, voyeuristic inspection—and of the male observer/lover's intent to follow that inspection by sexual action: she puts before him an image of the male gaze and of a consequent intent to enact its sexual power. Adonis is apparently meant to realize that he should more or less equate Venus with the desirable, available female figure in her description and that he should make himself approximate the male figure of sexual desire and power. The problem is, however, not only that Adonis does not want to become such a figure but that Venus in fact already resembles it. Adonis rather resembles the female figure in Venus' description, with the significant difference that he wishes to be neither an object of desire nor available.[14] While Venus is talking to him, uttering the words now being examined, she has him firmly by the hand and will not let him go, although he asks to be set free (see lines 361-384, especially lines 361-362 with their trope of imprisonment). More important, when Venus earlier tells Adonis about her victory over Mars (lines 97-114) she also has the boy under physical restraint, but on that occasion—in her role as assertive (male) lover—she proceeds to subject him to a version of the male gaze and to voice excitedly what that gaze reveals (lines 115-128-for an ironic counterpart see lines 211-216). Yet Venus cannot, of course, ever enact the sexual power of her masculinized gaze; in that respect, as similarly in respect of gender-reversal, she diverges from the image of the male gaze and of its consequence which she puts before Adonis.

However if Adonis is subjected at some moments of the text to the masculinized gaze of Venus, he is pervasively and primarily subjected throughout it to the male gaze of the implied reader.[15] A main factor in that would seem to be the narrator's recurrent, emphatic devaluing in the poem of Venus, the goddess of love, as an object of desire. From the first stanza he treats her ludically, introducing her as "[s]ick-thoughted Venus" who "like a bold-fac'd suitor 'gins to woo" Adonis (lines 5-6). From the start she seems a figure of comedy and of pathos. Thereafter, the narrator makes her appear not merely comic (as in lines 463-468) or pathetic (as in lines 1057-1062) but grotesque as well—veering between the poles of comedy and of pathos: in her physical power (for example, when exercizing force on Adonis; see lines 29-35); in her unreasoning and excessive passion (see lines 25-28, 61-66, 217-222, and so on). Those accord with the grotesqueness of much of her libertine rhetoric (cf. the excesses of pleading and of cajoling in lines 187-198, for instance). The narrator stresses, too, the grotesqueness/ferocity of her predatory desire (lines 54-60, 67-68, 541-576, and so on). He treats her with condescension (as notably in lines 607-610) and even celebrates her beauty only to heighten the reader's perception of Adonis' unique beauty (see, for example, lines 352-364).[16] The repeated devaluing of Venus as an object of sexual desire, for all her beauty, helps in the placement of Adonis in that role; it facilitates, that is to say, the deflection of the implied reader's male gaze from the goddess of love to the adolescent boy.

The workings and results of that deflection can, I think, be briefly and representatively illustrated. When, to cite an early instance (lines 40-84), Adonis has been pushed to the ground by Venus and is, in effect, restrained by her (see lines 40-42), her virtual imprisonment of the boy seems clearly to promote him as the implied (and male) reader's object of sexual focus. Venus "stroke[s Adonis'] cheek" and begins to kiss him (lines 45-48). His response to her doing so is represented in terms that feminize him (lines 49-50, discussed above, and line 53)—whereas, of course, her assertive sexual actions imply her masculinization. Moreover, the narrator then introduces a short, simple account of Venus' proceeding, again and again, to kiss Adonis' face (lines 59-60), by vividly and at greater length comparing the impassioned goddess to an "empty eagle" tearing at and devouring its prey (lines 55-58). To that point in the episode, Venus has arguably been imaged as desiring rather than as desirable. Her beauty has been alluded to once (line 51); her desire for Adonis has been indicated to be confining, insistent, and fiercely predatory. On the other hand, and in contrast to the (ultimately grotesque) representation of Venus, the picture of Adonis has been that of a helpless, feminized victim of sexual violence. The reader sees a sexually devalued Venus and an Adonis who is sexually foregrounded to the goddess's cost.

In what immediately follows, the narrator uses that process of devaluing and foregrounding to set up Adonis as the object of the implied reader's male gaze. The immediately subsequent description of Adonis iterates his sexual distress: "Panting he lies and breatheth in [Venus'] face" (line 62). His distress may be made to look comic in its awkward physicality but, for all that, it is nonetheless distress. If the description again conveys something of Adonis' simplicity, it likewise implies his helplessness, his role as feminized victim of sexual violence. Whether or not Venus recognizes what Adonis' "breath[ing] in her face" reveals about him, she responds to it with sexual excitement. "She feedeth on the steam as on a prey" (line 63), the narrator says. Inevitably, the narrator's word "prey" in that line evokes his preceding representation of Venus as a sexual predator, and he alludes to it once more in lines 67-68. (The picture of Adonis as her victim is evoked, in both cases, at the same time.) That continued process of devaluing and foregrounding, however, now functions differently from the way it did earlier in the episode. The narrator now uses it to focus on and to celebrate Adonis' beauty—actually, to put that beauty on display for inspection by the implied reader. Venus' excited praise of the boy's beauty is recounted (lines 64-66); her virtually limitless pleasure in it is implied (lines 77-84). And Venus' harassment of Adonis brings (the narrator relates with apparent pleasure) reactions from him which in fact heighten his feminized beauty (lines 73-78).[17] The narrator's own appreciation of Adonis' physical appeal is expressed both there and at another moment of the text (line 70). What seems to be happening here is a coercion of the female: a devaluation/suppression of Venus' attractiveness, an emphasis on her obsessive desire for and delight in Adonis' beauty, so that her beauty can be pushed into the background of the episode and thereby help to foreground his. Venus' desire for and delight in the boy's beauty, and the narrator's appreciation of it, merge in a cumulative and fairly long description—the results being that it is elaborately displayed and that Adonis is put forward as the (notional) object of sexual desire. Adonis' beauty appears to be held up by the responsive narrator and by the sexually devalued goddess of love for appreciative inspection, for visual possession, by the (notionally male and not indifferent) reader. "He" seems invited to view it with a "glutton eye" (line 399).

Whilst other instances in Shakespeare's poem could be examined (for example, in lines 241-252, after Venus has set herself on display for Adonis' male gaze and that of the implied reader, and in 349-354; 427-452; 541-572-cf. 595-606), perhaps more revealing may be to make some comparisons between how Adonis is set up as an object of the male gaze and how the male gaze is exercized/evoked in Marlowe's *Hero and Leander* and in Donne's "Elegy 19 *To his Mistress Going to Bed*."[18] In the former poem, the early and stylized descriptions of the soon-to-be lovers indicate that they are significantly alike. Hero, described in lines 5-50, is supposedly an object of irresistible sexual fascination, wooed by Apollo for the beauty of her hair alone (line 6), worthy—in his opinion—to be yielded his throne so that all men can gaze on her (lines 7-8), mistaken by Cupid for his mother Venus (lines 39-44). Leander, described in lines 51-90, supposedly complements her in attractiveness, for had his "dangling tresses that were never shorn / . . . been cut, and unto Colchos borne" (lines 55-56) they would have inspired a second, but more compelling, quest for "the Golden Fleece" (lines 57-58); moreover, Cynthia—Apollo's sister—desires him (lines 59-60). Yet the formal descriptions of Hero and of Leander indicate also that they are significantly unlike in terms of their being supposedly sexually irresistible.

The most important dissimilarity comes from the fact that whereas Marlowe's narrator describes Hero's clothing as well as her body, he subsequently pictures Leander's body but not his clothing. Such description as the narrator gives of Hero's body implies her impossible beauty; however, the account of her clothing suggests that her beauty—and the sexual desire that her beauty can generate—is linked to violence and death. The depiction of the Venus and Adonis story on her sleeves (lines 11-14), the blood on her kirtle (lines 15-16), suggest that link and foreshadow Leander's fate. It is true that, when first describing Leander, the narrator foretells/reminds the reader of Leander's death (lines 51-54). It is true, too, that some of the allusions to myth in the account of Leander's body have negative associations, linking beauty, sexual desire, and death (especially relevant here is the refiguring allusion to Narcissus, to whom Adonis in Shakespeare's poem seems a virtual antithesis). Nonetheless, even if the picture of Leander begins with a reference to his death, even if it links his beauty with sexual desire and death as does the account of Hero's clothing, it is startlingly appreciative and specific. Marlowe's narrator, seeming to delight in intimate celebration of the detail of Leander's body, puts him forward as an epitome of beauty taken too early from the world. In fact, the narrator's intimate celebration of Leander's beauty puts him forward, as an object of sexual desire, with an emotiveness and enthusiasm lacking in the description of Hero. Leander is celebrated and displayed—*by* the narrator with delight and clearly *for* the pleasure of the implied reader's male gaze:

> His body was as straight as Circe's wand;
> Jove might have sipped out nectar from his
>   hand.
> Even as delicious meat is to the taste,
> So was his neck in touching, and surpassed
> The white of Pelop's shoulder. I could tell ye
> How smooth his breast was, and how white
>   his belly,
> And whose immortal fingers did imprint
> That heavenly path with many a curious dint
> That runs along his back . . .
>
> (lines 61-69)

Marlowe's narrator may describe Hero first and he may make Hero and Leander similar as creatures who are supposed to be sexually irresistible. For all that, Leander is foregrounded to Hero's cost, as Adonis is to that of Venus in *Venus and Adonis*. Just as Shakespeare's narrator sexually devalues Venus, again and again, throughout *Venus and Adonis*, so Marlowe's narrator sexually devalues Hero throughout *Hero and Leander*. Her being constructed as the blindly, paradoxically, vulnerably virginal priestess of *Venus Vulgaris* (see 1, 131-166)—"Venus' nun"—makes her both comic and pathetic from the start; and there is the narrator's recurrent, ironic play with his characterization of her as at once beautiful and innocent (see, for example, his comparison between her and Diana seeking to evade

Actaeon, 2, 260-262, and his comparison of her to a harpy, 2, 270). The process of devaluing and foregrounding at work in Shakespeare's poem has a counterpart, though not an identical one, in Marlowe's. As has been argued above, the result of that process, in each poem, is the narrator's homoerotic celebration and display of the male protagonist for the male gaze.

In that context of devaluing/foregrounding and the male gaze, Donne's "Elegy 19 To his Mistress Going to Bed" seems both illuminatingly like and unlike the poems by Shakespeare and by Marlowe. The main similarity lies in how Donne constructs his persona and in how that persona apparently exercizes/seeks to evoke the male gaze. The chief dissimilarity lies, of course, in the aggressive heterosexuality of Donne's poem. But the comparison and the contrast are more intricate than might be thought. Donne's persona in "Elegy 19" recalls both the persona of Ovid's Elegies and, as it appears, Marlowe's recreation of that Ovidian persona in his translation of the Elegies.[19] Seeming to be wise in the ways of the world, of the flesh, and of letters, too sophisticated to take social or moral convention at face value, ingenious, ironic, fond of displaying his wit, self-assertive and self-centred, Donne's persona distinctly manifests his Ovidian and, very arguably, Marlovian lineage. This persona features, with varying emphases, in many of Donne's secular love poems; of necessity, given his lineage, he has much in common with the narrator of *Venus and Adonis* and with that of *Hero and Leander* (for although the latter poem is certainly indebted to "divine Musaeus"—1, 52—the construction of its narrator is nonetheless indebted to Ovid's earlier erotic verse).

When Donne's persona commands his fictive mistress to undress, he celebrates both her body and her clothing ("Off with that girdle, like heaven's zone glistering, / But a far fairer world encompassing," lines 5-6). His commands, as that example indicates, recreate the woman: in fact they, and almost everything else he says, reinvent and reinterpret her (to the point where she becomes, from the persona's angle of vision, his sexual/political colony, his private source of physical riches, his personal empire—see lines 27-30). Donne's persona, that is to suggest, reinvents and reinterprets the woman to her face. The silent "she" finds herself being reconstructed by her lover as she stands before him. Her appearance is celebrated and made subject to the refashioning power of his male gaze. Moreover, in refashioning her before her own eyes (as it were) the persona holds his version of her on display for the appreciative male gaze of the implied reader—a twofold exercize of power. That exercize of power is also Donne's self-display, a display of rhetorical virtuosity to his (mainly) young, male audience containing fellow poets such as his friend Christopher Brooke.[20] The fictional lady is, then, apparently foregrounded yet actually devalued because made voiceless and refashioned, in order that Donne's persona and hence Donne himself can be foregrounded for appreciation. The male is displayed—even if not homoerotically—to the cost of the female (on which it is therefore, ironically, also dependent, within the scope of libertine discourse). So perhaps the assertive heterosexuality of Donne's poem may not, finally, very greatly distinguish it from *Venus and Adonis* or from *Hero and Leander*. The process of devaluing/foregrounding, in connection with the exercize and evocation of the male gaze by Ovidian speakers, who are complicit with the implied readers in their coercing of the female, makes all three poems akin.

The calculated, flamboyant transgressiveness of Shakespeare's poem, of Marlowe's and of Donne's goes beyond issues such as the construction of narrators or of personae, and the representation of sexual politics, as one need hardly point out. Beyond them, though not separable from them, are issues such as how the relations among desire, ceremony, convention, and anarchy are represented—and what the representations of them may imply. In Marlowe's poem, ceremony and anarchy coexist: love is both ritual and disruption in a world seemingly centred on *Venus Vulgaris*. On the other hand, in Donne's poem the speaking self constructs a private world, centred on its all-subordinating desire, by means of literary/social conventions which at once shape the speaking self and allow it to reshape its surroundings.[21] Shakespeare's poem suggests love's often incongruous multiplicity and intense selfcentredness, its inability to be captured in a single definition, its ambiguous transformative power, each of which is indicated by the characterization of Venus. As in Marlowe's poem, yet not identically so, love is both ritual and disruption: ceremony and anarchy co-exist (but in a world where Venus has many aspects—to identify one of the differences between the world of *Venus and Adonis* and that of *Hero and Leander*). And the characterization of Adonis significantly complements that of Venus. His suggests, in counterpoint to hers, a link between chastity and self-ignorance, between sexual experience and self-knowledge. In rejecting sexual initiation Adonis may evade the insistence and egocentrism of sexual desire, and loss of his present, incomplete identity for the gaining of a diminished, eroticized, one, but he also evades self-knowledge, wilfully seeking to dissociate self-knowledge from sexual experience. If sexual desire is, then, problematic in its diversity, self-centredness and disorderliness, so too can chastity be in its destructive frustration of self-knowledge. Moreover, whereas Venus in her role as *Venus Mechanitis* voices a failed rhetoric of desire, excessive desire's marring the conventions of language designed to express desire, Adonis' characterization implies that chastity, desire's negation, may also flaw communication by having an intransigently idealizing, delusive rhetoric no less sophistic than that of desire. Adonis' characterization indicates as well, through its connection with a process of foregrounding/devaluing and with the exercize/evocation of the male gaze, that love's multiplicity by no means excludes homoerotic desire. Shakespeare's first poem, inventively ludic, sceptical, emphatically various in its representations of sexuality, and meta-Ovidian in its sophisticated self-awareness rather than merely Ovidian, reveals how shrewdly he understood the rhetorical possibilities of the epyllion and, in doing so, its social possibilities as a means for displaying his virtuosity as a poet in the competition for patronage.

Notes

[1] See, for example, C. Hulse, *Metamorphic Verse: The Elizabethan Minor Epic* (Princeton, N.J.: Princeton University Press, 1981), pp. 151-153. Sandys' note, "Men of excellent beauties haue likely beene subiect to miserable destinies," has a topical relevance to Buckingham (*Ovid's Metamorphoses Englished*, p. 366). Reference to Shakespeare's poem is, throughout, to *The Poems*, ed. F. T. Prince (1960; rpt. London: Methuen, 1961).

[2] See, for example, J. D. Jahn, "The Lamb of Lust: The Role of Adonis in Shakespeare's *Venus and Adonis*," *Shakespeare Studies*, 6 (1970), 11-25.

[3] On the gaze, and on the male gaze, see: Norman Bryson, *Vision and Painting: The Logic of the Gaze* (1983; rpt. London: MacMillan, 1985); Edward Snow, "Theorizing the Male Gaze: Some Problems, "*Representations*, 25 (1989), 30-41. I am grateful to Patrick Fuery for drawing my attention to the former.

[4] The emblematist Valeriano, for example, makes that point. Greville's *A Letter to an Honorable Lady* interestingly reworks/revises it.

[5] Venus is voluble but, again, *male* in her volubility (she predominately uses, after all, a Petrarchan language/rhetoric of seduction).

[6] The Platonic aspect of Adonis' rhetoric has been noted by others—but its problematic nature has not, as far as I am aware, been considered.

[7] Again, an unknowing cultural specificity.

[8] Reference to Plato's *Symposium* is from the translation by W. H. D. Rouse (ed. E. H. Warmington and P. G. Rouse) in his *Great Dialogues of Plato* (New York: New American Library, 1956), pp. 78-82. It is beyond the chosen scope of this essay to examine the characterization of Adonis in relation to the early modern discourse of homoeroticism—a subject that I shall be considering in a subsequent discussion. Thus the representation of Adonis is not considered here in the context of theorizings of that early modern discourse by writers such as Guy Poirier, E. K. Sedgwick, Joseph Cady, Jonathan Dollimore, and so on.

[9] Reference to Ovid is from Mary M. Innes, trans., *The Metamorphoses* (1955; rpt. Harmondsworth: Penguin, 1968), here at p. 83.

[10] Ovid, trans. Innes, p. 83.

[11] Ovid, trans. Innes, p. 86.

[12] Though in this he also *broadly* resembles Narcissus, because a refusal to love brings Narcissus to false love and death. The boar is clearly an antithesis to the horse: the former is unreasoning malevolence and destructiveness, the latter, innate nobility; the former, a parodic punishment for sexuality avoided, whereas the latter is "natural" sexuality exampled.

[13] In what follows, my thinking on the male gaze has been especially influenced by both Bryson and Snow (see n. 3).

[14] *Venus* sees him as available, if not as her *willing* "true-love."

[15] The assumed readership for the poem would seem to be primarily male (in kind, much the same readership as for Lodge's epyllion), and hence the male gaze seems to be evoked. I do not wish to consider here the issue of the female gaze.

[16] Venus' beauty is not always praised or displayed, of course, only to set off that of Adonis. Venus' "deer park" picture of her own body is an instance of her beauty being displayed for the implied reader's male gaze and in hope, on her part as it were, of evoking Adonis' male gaze. I am grateful to David Bevington for making me consider this point.

[17] The Petrarchan red and white being iterated, heightened even by his distress.

[18] There are not, as I read the poem, many instances at all of Venus' being displayed for the male gaze. Reference to Marlowe's verse is from S. Orgel's edition, *The Complete Poems and Translations* (Harmondsworth: Penguin, 1971). Reference to Donne's verse is from A. J. Smith's edition, *The Complete English Poems* (1971; rpt., London: Allen Lane, 1974).

[19] For similarities in rhetoric and language between Donne's persona (and the personae constructed throughout his Elegies as a whole) and Marlowe's Ovidian persona, see 3, 6 and 7 in Marlowe's translation. As S. Orgel remarks: "Donne's elegies are full of a sense of Marlowe's language . . ." (*Poems and Translations*, p. 233).

[20] See R. C. Bald, *John Donne: A Life* (Oxford: Clarendon Press, 1970), pp. 35-79.

[21] The conventions of libertinism both shape and free (in some respects) the self, helping it to create a private world of desire that subordinates all to it: the woman; politics; God, and so on.

Goran V. Stanivukovic (essay date 1997)

SOURCE: "Troping Desire in Shakespeare's 'Venus and Adonis'," in *Forum for Modern Language Studies,* Vol. XXXIII, No. 4, October, 1997, pp. 289-301.

[*In the following essay, Stanivukovic probes the rhetoric of desire in* Venus and Adonis.]

Venus and Adonis is the most rhetorical and erotic of Shakespeare's early works. Eros is the main subject of the poem's narrative and also the central topic of the rhetorical arguments in it. Hence, critics have focused on these two aspects of the poem, discussing the purpose and the tone of its rhetoric, and interpreting the representation of eros in the poem's narrative. A list of references documenting this point would be too long, and perhaps even unnecessary, because many interpretations arrive, more or less, at the same conclusion. Summarising this, Lucy Gent notices that "Rhetoric in [. . .] *Venus and Adonis* is usually thought of as remarkably plentiful, and very well done—but rather tedious, and not relevant to our understanding of the meaning of the poem."[1] Gent's view of the rhetoric-related criticism of *Venus and Adonis* still holds value. For her own part, Gent attempts to relate eloquence to meaning and to the "central issue" of the poem, which she sees in the relation between hyperbole and reality.[2] In Gent's project, hyperbole denies reality, life and sexual drive triumph over death, and she defines the theme of the poem as the antithesis between eloquence and truth. As opposed to Gent's view, the relationship between rhetoric and reality is only one aspect of the "real" issue in the poem; the other aspect concerns the reality of rhetoric, the relevance of rhetoric which prefigures the conceptualisation of eros in the poem. In *Venus and Adonis,* rhetoric reduces life to eros and, therefore, one way of understanding the theme of eros, or desire, is to analyse and interpret the structure of the rhetorical patterns which represent desire. Yet the dichotomy between the rhetoric of lust and the rhetoric of love, between the Ovidian desire for body and the Neoplatonic yearning for beauty, is not all that simple, as Richard A. Lanham argues in his rhetorical reading of *Venus and Adonis.*[3] In fact, Lanham believes that the complexity of the text lies in the rhetorical ambiguities which underlie both the representation of love and the construction of characters in this poem. He concludes his analysis of rhetoric in *Venus and Adonis* by noticing "the peculiar/serious rhetorical ambivalence toward character and language".[4] I would like to take this "rhetorical ambivalence" one step further, into semiotics of the text. Moreover, I would argue that the linguistic ambiguities and the rhetorical opacity are, in fact, functional in Shakespeare's construction of desire. I would further argue that the persuasive techniques which underlie Venus' and Adonis' rhetorical language create new expectations for our reading of desire in the poem.

Criticism of a text whose meaning depends on the rhetorical strategies which textualise that meaning should start with an interpretation of the rhetorical patterns in order to argue anything about thematic representation. A critical practice in which the move is from specific patten to representation—from argumentation to aesthetics—enables us to see a literary text in a perspective different from the one which treats rhetoric as a stylistic ornament only. An examination of sexuality as a theme of *Venus and Adonis* is further related to our interpretation of the rhetorical strategies which represent arguments about desire in the poem. I approach rhetoric as a cognitive mode which suggests the early modern conceptualisation of desire in *Venus and Adonis.* Thus in reading the poem, I employ a critical method which is not served by, but is in the service of rhetoric. We should remember that in the narrowest sense, in which both classical and the early modern culture understood it, rhetoric was considered an art of argumentation whose end is in persuasion. Therefore, instead of treating rhetoric as a stylistic ornament which supports reading—thematic criticism formulates this sort of approach as "the rhetoric of . . ."—I argue that rhetoric itself, the structure of argumentation, renders meaning. Thus I suggest that the real subject of *Venus and Adonis* is desire in rhetoric, not the rhetoric of desire. This desire is transcribed as rhetorical pattern which in itself captures the nature and the structure of desire. In this essay, I further argue that the thematic context of Venus' sexual soliciting of Adonis, expressed as ineffective rhetoric—Venus' tedious song (841)—results in Venus' failure both as an orator and as a lover. In turn, an interpretative strategy which focuses on an analysis of rhetorical arguments alters our reading of desire in the poem.

Reading *Venus and Adonis* rhetorically challenges thematic approaches to the poem. Thematic criticism of the poem, as Douglas Bush notices, centres on two main issues: First, that "The central antithesis of subject, [is] between the warm goddess and the cold youth"; and second, that "Shakespeare's representation of a chaste youth solicited by an amorous woman had precedents not only in Ovid but in the pastoral tradition derived partly from Ovid".[5] One might argue that Bush's argument is characteristic of the tendency to approach the poem in terms of binary opposites. Thus, thematic critics either examine the opposition between Venus' destructive sexuality and Adonis' amorous reluctance; or, they discuss the psychological motivations of the two characters in terms of their contrasting attitudes towards love. Moreover, discussion of the moral implication of the contrast between physical and spiritual love has been a common topic in the existing criticism of the poem.[6] Ovidian foundations of Shakespeare's poem cannot be avoided in any reading of the sexuality in *Venus and Adonis*, as Jonathan Bate so admirably demonstrates in his latest book on Ovid and Shakespeare.[7] Realised as a destructive force, the Ovidian passion in *Venus and Adonis* reflects the larger theme of Ovid's influence on the early modern erotic literature. However, Shakespeare's rhetoric in the poem is Ovidian in a very broad sense, in so far as its purpose and tone rely on the Ovidian *carpe diem* formula, an invitation to enjoy sensual love. However, Shakespeare's argumentative techniques are more diverse and functional than Ovid's eloquence. If Shakespeare borrows anything from Ovidian eloquence, it is the ornamental copiousness of its pastoral passages. In *Venus and Adonis* Shakespeare rhetorically expands on Ovid's topic of Venus' body and mind overwhelmed by passion for Adonis, rendered as "The beawty of the lad/Inflam'd hir".[8] As an early modern adaptation of Ovid, Shakespeare's poem represents a rhetorical study of that desirous flame.

Recently, John Roe has cautioned against reading the poem ethically, arguing instead that the rhetoric-related approach to the poem—his subject is wordplay—offers a more fruitful insight into the study of passions in *Venus and Adonis*. So Roe says:

> Attempting to take a consistent ethical reading of, for example, Venus's sensuality is bound to fail. The play of language in the poem sees to that. The subversions of wordplay are no trite affair, nor are they mere surface merriment. For wordplay is not [. . .] only divisive [. . .]. It provides the only solution there is—an aesthetic one, which is beyond the scope of continuous, unfinished, formless action. The language of the poem encapsulates human reality, fragmented, inconclusive, and frustrating, and submits it to the order of art.[9]

In Roe's view, the rhetoric of *Venus and Adonis* tells us much about how reality is to be critically perceived in the poem. Following up on Roe, I suggest that the pleasure of reading desire in *Venus and Adonis* textually, enhances the thematic interpretation of desire, because the uncontrollable and the irregular nature of desire is evoked in the logical and stylistic modalities which render it. As a linguistic, formal way of representing affects, rhetoric brings out what is contained in(side)—self, mind, body—and, therefore, anything external—themes, socio-cultural contexts: anything outside the realm of rhetoric—depends on the rhetorical construction.

A critical scrutiny of the commonly used rhetorical figures and tropes in *Venus and Adonis* relates my critical approach to the poem to the early modern attitudes toward the purpose of rhetoric. For the early modern humanists, ornamentation meant argumentation, and, as Bernard Weinberg and Richard Waswo remind us, the humanist poet-orators considered the poetic text to be a rhetorical construct in which literary language was an instrument for achieving moral utility.[10] While it is true that, as Thomas M. Conley notices, in the early modern period character (*ethos*) "would seem to be a more significant formal cause of work than any orderly distribution of the principles of rhetoric",[11] it can also be said that, in early modern texts, character motivation is achieved rhetorically, through strategies of argumentation. In the early modern literary culture, the character originates in the rhetorical rendering of it; it is first a rhetorical, then an ethical construct. Early modern texts demonstrate that in the quest for the self, rhetorical procedure is inseparable from an ethical endeavour.

In her discussion of humanist rhetoric, Hanna H. Gray reminds us that "humanists' own stress on form [has] not always been treated sufficiently as an integral dimension of their thought".[12] For humanists, the purpose of rhetoric is to inspire an aesthetic response by leading the mind to meaning through the rhetorical form, a process most often neglected by modern critics. By arguing for a criticism absorbed in the poetic form of the text, not the text dominated by its context, Gray and de Man argue for rhetoric as a site of meaning, not rhetoric equated with literary criticism. Those two critical paradigms provide us with tools to read Shakespeare's rhetoric not just in a new way, but also in a way closer to the early modern understanding of its purpose. Yet in the early modern treatises on style, there are numerous examples of writers' insistence on treating rhetorical patterns as vehicles for thought and tools of persuasion, and not mere stylistic ornaments. Thus, for example, in his style manual, entitled *The Garden of Eloquence* (1577), Henry Peacham discusses the relationship between ornamentation and representation, and says:

> wise men [poet-orators] remembring that many thinges were very like one to an other [. . .] declared their meaning by wordes that made a likely simillitude, of those thinges which they signifyed, and then seeing, that by this meanes, thinges were well set out, matters well expressed, and causes well commended, and that by translation they might utter their mindes largely, and set forth any matters with great perspecuity and pleasauntnesse, perceyuing also that it brought often times great delectation to the hearers, by reason of the simillitude.[13]

In suggesting that the pleasure of reading derives from both associating meaning with ornament (since this is what rhetors do in the first place) and in substituting ornaments for meaning, Peacham argues for an ornament which is the form of *knowing* the text, and subsequently, a vehicle of understanding both subjects and themes embodied in a text.

The early modern theory of *knowing* subjects (reality) in rhetorical patterns corresponds to some illuminating modern theories about the relationship between rhetorical figures and literary meaning. Thus, in an essay on the semiology of rhetorical figures, Paul de Man argues for the importance of "formalist and intrinsic criticism".[14] De Man calls for the "rhetorically conscious reading" of the literary text, arguing that rhetoric in general, and tropes in particular, constitute an epistemological system of codes whose structure shapes meaning. The act of reading then is a process of interpreting rhetoric, a process which helps us delve into the meaning of other, extrinsic (contextual) elements which shape a literary text. Paul de Man illustrates his theory with an example from Marcel Proust's novel *Swann's Way*. In the novel, the paradigmatic substitution which underlies the use of metaphor and metonymy is both crucial to our reading (*knowing*) of Proust's narrative itself, and central to our appreciation of the character of young Marcel who simultaneously takes delight in reading a text and enjoys a warm summer day, substituting one pleasure with the other in the process. Thus, for Paul de Man, interpretation represents a process of reading which is a simultaneous deconstruction and construction. Reading is an action in which analysis of the rhetorical form (an intrinsic aspect of the text) informs our *knowing* of the subject, and hence the contextual (extrinsic) aspect of the text, too. Thus deconstruction, as Paul de Man says, "is not something we have added to the text but it constituted the text in the first place".[15]

Paul de Man's epistemology of tropes, and Hanna H. Gray's idea about the relevance of the language form in the quest for meaning in our reading of humanist texts, provide a constructive theoretical framework in reopening the question of the rhetorical rendering of desire in Shakespeare's *Venus and Adonis*. Following up on Gray's and de Man's theory of interpreting meaning through rhetorical forms, and not losing from sight the humanists' attitudes toward rhetoric and meaning, I propose an approach to reading desire in *Venus and Adonis* which centres on the forms of Venus' rhetoric whose subject is desire, and I suggest that such an approach changes our perception of Venus as the powerful embodiment of desire. Arguments which Venus uses to move Adonis to love her demonstrate Venus' failure, not her mastery and dominance, as a lover-orator.

Shakespeare's insistence on rhetorically vivid articulation of sexual pleasure without satisfactory fulfilment—Venus' "hollow womb" (268)—pushes the limits of the *carpe diem* ethics and aesthetics towards conceptualisation of desire as frustration, unfulfilment, and instability. The void and anxiety created by the lack of the object of desire are rhetorically textualised in patterns of argumentation through which Venus creates an illusion of desirous possession.

Since rhetoric is always emotion-driven, the arguments through which desire is articulated in *Venus and Adonis* suggest a complex psychological situation which underlies Venus' invitation to love. Figures and tropes of anticipation, probabilities, rearrangement, displacement, suppression, and reduction, are all germane to Venus' sexual solicitations. Consider, for example, the passage in which Venus offers herself to Adonis:

> Were I hard-favoured, foul, or wrinkled-old,
> Ill-nurtured, crooked, churlish, harsh in voice,
> O'erworn, despised, rheumatic and cold,
> Thick-sighted, barren, lean, and lacking juice,
> Then mightst thou pause, for then I were not for thee;
> But having no defects, why dost thou abhor me?
>
> Thou canst not see one wrinkle in my brow;
> Mine eyes are grey and bright and quick in turning;
> My beauty as the spring doth yearly grow,
> My flesh is soft and plump, my marrow burning;
> My smooth moist hand, were it with thy hand felt,
> Would in thy palm dissolve, or seem to melt.
>   (133-44)[16]

Here, the textualisation of desire, first as denial of beauty, then as its affirmation, is inscribed in terms of the conventional use of enthymemes. Richard A. Lanham defines enthymeme as "Maintaining the truth of a Proposition from the assumed truth of its contrary. [. . .] an abridged syllogism, one of the terms being omitted as understood."[17] Venus creates an erotic self-portrait grounded in hypotheses (133-8), then, she continues to argue with a persuasion by proofs (140-2) which substitute her previous hypothetical denials, and she ends her argument with an enthymeme (143-4) expressed in the conditional mode. What Venus omits from enthymemes in the lines 133-8, she complements in the lines 139-44, thus satisfying herself as an orator, though not a good one. For Adonis' harsh snub, "Fie, no more of love!" (186), in response to Venus' oration, and his subsequent reaction to the long allegorical digression representing mating horses (193-216), whose purpose is to move him by example, but at which he only "smiles as in [. . .] disdain" (241), suggest that Venus fails as an orator. And Adonis' rejection of Venus' rhetoric as "bootless [fruitless] chat [. . .] an idle theme" (422) further suggests that her oratory is shallow. But here the question is whether we should take this—and other, similar examples in which Venus' rhetoric fails to move Adonis—as the victory of Adonis' Neoplatonism over Venus' Ovidianism. This may be relevant to a thematic reading of the poem, but there is nothing in Venus' arguments, let alone in Adonis' cryptic rejections of them, to indicate dichotomy between the two kinds of love. Yet, what the rhetorical situation indicates here—besides the subject of sexual appeal—is that Venus' argument reveals to us a character whose desire is not constructed as a stable force, but as a probability realised in the conditional mode which attempts to reshape reality.[18]

In rhetorically more precise terms, it can be said that what underlies Venus' argumentation is the Aristotelian formula of persuasion by arguments based on probabilities.[19] Venus assumes that probability is effective enough a proof to move him. But Adonis' rejection denies the possibility of persuasion by probabilities. By implying that Venus' rhetoric is shallow, Adonis denies the validity of her proofs, and consequently of her way of *knowing* desire as well. The third—narrator's—voice captures, in the form or rhetorical questions, the moment of Venus' disorientation after her failed persuasion: "Now which way shall she turn? which way shall she say?/Her words are done, her woes the more increasing;/The time is spent, her object will away" (253-5).

Similarly, Shakespeare's use of *catachresis*—an implied, extravagant, or far-fetched metaphor[20]—indicates a self-conscious end of persuasion; it pleases the speaker, but it does not move the object of desire. Thus seen in conjunction with Venus' "So shall I die with drops of hot desire" (1074), and together with the *exemplum* (a cited example) about her emasculation of Mars, "Making my arms his [Mars'] field, his tent my bed" (108), *catachresis* further transcribes Venus' desire as fantasy. As a form of vivid enthymeme, *exemplum,* as Aristotle says in *Rhetoric,* is "concerned with things which may, generally speaking, be other than they are".[21] Like enthymeme, *exemplum* only supposes reality, it does not confirm it. Since Adonis cannot love like Mars, Venus satisfies her desire by conceptualising pleasure as a vivid rhetorical possibility; here, she performs desire not as truth, but as a fantasy of sexual fulfilment, as an alternative reality. Thus, Venus' desire is localised in her mind and in her rhetoric, not realised in her body and in the narrative. In Shakespeare, Venus becomes the embodiment of desire which is, as Catherine Belsey notices, "anarchic, and its cause is not, in the end, the persuasive powers of another person, not even a goddess, but the missing *objet a*".[22]

Enthymemes, which transcribe Venus' desire as passion fantasised not realised, correspond in intention to numerous oxymora, figures of condensed paradox,[23] which Venus uses in her attempts to move Adonis. As a figure which combines opposites while affirming the impossible, oxymoron functions as a subgroup of enthymeme in *Venus and Adonis*. Oxymoron helps Shakespeare construct the erotic longing for the missing lover in terms of a logical paradox of the impossible. Thus Venus' complaint about Adonis' ability to

Frontispiece illustration to the 1714 Rowe edition of Venus and Adonis.

destabilise eros and to leave it in agony, oxymoronically realises Venus' nostalgic fashioning of Adonis as a desirable, yet unattainable, source of erotic pleasure:

> Thy mermaid's voice hath done me double wrong;
> I had my load before, now pressed with bearing:
> Melodious discord, heavenly tune harsh sounding,
> Ears' deep-sweat music, and heart's deep-sore wounding.
>
> (429-32)

The image of Adonis as a hurting mermaid, capable of harsh, hence painful tunes, on the one hand represents Adonis as a reluctant love. But on the other hand, words such as "load", "pressed", and "bearing" connote sexual charge. Venus' rhetoric suggests denial, but the narrative in which she continuously attempts to possess Adonis implies that her sexual energy cannot be reconciled with his inability to consume it. This situation, of appealing to emotions in the language of rhetorical paradox, corresponds to Quintilian's definition of enthymeme as "[an] incomplete syllogism [...] drawn from incompatibilities".[24] Quintilian's point further prefigures Venus' oxymoronic and enthymemic persuasion as the rhetorically constructed desire of the probable union with Adonis, which is the only way in which Venus conceptualises eros. Namely, Shakespeare treats enthymeme, a rhetorical figure, as if it were a representation of reality. He makes Venus believe and say it, that an unattainable object of desire is a real one.

Persuasive techniques which Shakespeare founds in the rhetoric of impossibility and logical paradox, suggest a speaker—Venus—who, though employing copious eloquence, argues, in fact, in a way which does not affect the listener. Venus' rhetoric exhausts the power of desire before this power even has a chance to possess the desired object. Hence, in the frequent use of chiasmus, a figure which in its most basic function signifies reversal, Shakespeare represents desire as a self-reflective force, thus embodying a sense of instability that suggests paradox. So, in Shakespeare's "Her eyes seen in the tears, tears in her eye" (962), the gaze, which in the early modern poetics of amorous longing has a transformative power (it represents the imagined as the real) here dissolves in its own reflection. Here, Venus' self-centred rhetoric originates in the techniques of "mirror inversion", which Richard A. Lanham identifies with chiasmus, a figure in which same elements of the verbal expression only swap places.[25] Thus chiasmus best reflects the situation in which nothing changes for Venus in her persistent quest for Adonis' body. Her rhetoric is not absorbed by the object of desire, but reflected back from it; and her pain remains the same.

In a similar fashion, antimetabole, which Lanham sees as a subgroup of chiasmus, and defines as an "inverted [...] order of repeated words [...] [which] sharpen their sense or [...] contrast the ideas they convey, or both",[26] contextualises Venus' desire as a commutative mode. So, in examples such as, "Pluck down the rich, enrich the poor with treasure" (1150) and "Make the young old, the old become a child" (1152), the opposites reshape reality into impossibility. The subjects of social distortion and of natural displacement, which constitute the two examples of antimetabole, transcribe Venus' desire in a rhetorical pattern of wrongly combined opposites. Yet, both antimetabole and chiasmus indicate a minimal persuasive effort because they do not discover new possibilities of argumentation, but only mirror the ones already established by rearranging of the existing syntactic order. Venus' rhetorical copiousness, therefore, functions not as a sign of power—it sounds more like a flurry of language—but only simulates authority and dominance in the rhetoric of paradox and impossibility. The rhetoric, whose very form limits the power of desire in the poem, also affects the body in the sense that the language of desire has the capacity, in Judith Butler's words, "to unsettle the mastery and subvert the intentionality of the subject who desires".[27]

Lack of the desired object is further transcribed as metonymy, in Venus' "I am such park" (239) and in Shakespeare's frequent comments that "She [Venus] is love" (610). As a figure of substitution,[28] metonymy can be replaced with any number of concepts which correspond to the poetic reality it contextualises. In the examples quoted, metonymy, whose subject is an "eroticized landscape",[29] enables the construction of unlimited manifestations of eros in Venus' mind and also in our imagination. As a sign of "self-willed and autonomous inventiveness"[30] metonymy satisfies Venus' fantasy of desire, constructing Venus' body as a mirage of sexual possibility. However, the tone of Venus' language changes at the sight of Adonis' dead body.

The long lamenting passage (889-1074), which opens with an evocation of "bloodless fear" (891) and ends with a tragic affirmation of loss ("So shall I die by drops of hot desire" [1074]), suggests a process by which desire evolves into the fear of loss of the desired body. As Adam Phillips remarks: "Fear of loss of love instigates a project to secure something that by definition cannot be secured. Fear thus becomes the perception of truth that inspires tenacious denial."[31] Venus' ineffective sophistry then posits a question of Shakespeare's motivation to construct her rhetoric in the way he does. Articulating desire in the forms of sophistic and probabilistic argumentation suggests that the speaker denies the possibility of affecting—moving to action—the object of desire. In turn, Venus' rhetoric transcribed as impossibility also suggests the lack of conviction in arguments whose goal is persuasion. Conviction and performance, two most important aspects of successful persuasion in the humanist rhetorical culture, do not complement one another in Venus' eloquence of desire. The real problem in the poem lies in the discrepancy between Venus' attempts to act and speak powerfully and Shakespeare's choice of rhetorical techniques which, in fact, undercut the effectiveness of her eloquence. What kind of impediment informs this discrepancy between Venus' loquaciousness and the fragile psychological foundations which underlie it?

So far, criticism of the poem has established that the dichotomy between destructive desire and chaste spirit is the central issue in *Venus and Adonis*. Yet, it seems to me that such reading of rhetoric, which helps thematic criticism but does not consider the rhetorical implication of Venus' arguments about desire, also neglects the affective foundations of rhetoric, which underly the linguistic construction of desire, and which have been implicated in the poem in the subtext of the narrative about Venus and Adonis.

The language of desire in *Venus and Adonis* is deeply entrenched in the tradition of the moralised Ovidian epyllia, in which the representation of sexual love is the main theme, and in which rhetoric both contains and subverts the display of eroticism. Yet in Shakespeare's source, Ovid's *Metamorphoses* (X. 519-651; 705-39), the emphasis is not on the rhetorical strategies through which desire is articulated, but rather on the general subject of passion, full of proverbial ruminations about love. Furthermore, in Shakespeare, the story of Venus' longing for the object of desire is also complicated by the implications of homoeroticism and incest, subjects which underlie Shakespeare's narrative, and which in Ovid provide only a larger subtext of the myth of Venus and Adonis. The complex myth of Venus and Adonis contextualises the narrative of *Venus and Adonis* and, as Jonathan Bate argues, determines the nature of love in the poem.[32] In *Metamorphoses*, the story of Venus and Adonis is told by Orpheus, who was in the early modern culture associated with homosexuality. Also, the story of Venus and Adonis cuts through two stories which contextualise homosexuality, the one of Apollo's love for a handsome boy, Cyparissus, and the other of the androgynous youth Ganymede. In Ovid, the story of Venus and Adonis also intersects with the story of Myrrha (301-63), who gave birth to Adonis in the illicit union with her father Cinyras, king of Cyprus. This story of Myrrha, Bate reminds us, contextualises incest in both Ovid and, consequently, Shakespeare, too.[33] Shakespeare's disclaimer about Adonis' birth, that he is "thing like a man, but of no woman bred" (214), realises the theme of incest in the poem. Thus the stories which contextualise the multifaceted desire in *Venus and Adonis*, and in which Venus' desire is directed to, and clashes with, an object of desire of such an ambivalent sexual history, suggest to us that the rhetoric of probability and impossibility only transcribes instabilities which constitute the thematic framework of the poem.

Adonis' own pronouncement about love, "My love to love is love but to disgrace it;/For I have heard it is a life in death" (412-13), seems not an affirmation of immature love, but a claim to scorn her desire and, therefore, to disdain her rhetoric.[34] Yet Adonis' rhetorically obfuscated expression of disdain and scorn may also suggest containment of an alternative desire, which is assumed to please him more than Venus' desire can, but which he is reluctant to define and articulate directly and clearly. Venus, however, understands well—at least her formulae are recognisable—that Adonis, "more lovely than a man" (9), is not just an idealised male figure, but an effeminate man, too. For the rhetorical formulae she uses to praise his beauty are common attributes in the conceits of praise of Petrarchan lady. So, Venus rhetorically constructs Adonis as an ideal woman with "soft bosom" (81), "soft hands, sweet lips and crystal eyne" (633), and she also rebuffs him in terms which suggest both cruelty and detachment (he is a "lifeless picture, cold and senseless stone [. . .], image dull and dead" [211-12]) of a Petrarchan mistress. The stylistic construction of femininity in Venus' praise of Adonis, and both the homoerotic and incestuous subtext of the poem, imply that Shakespeare constructs Adonis as an object of desire which cannot satisfy Venus on the grounds of his sexuality whose craving may not be for the female body. After all, he seems quite happy pursuing the boar, a symbol of overbearing masculinity. Venus' sophistic rhetoric of impossibility, therefore, may be motivated by her awareness that she desires a body which suggests subversive desire. Thus her rhetoric of failed argumentation indirectly functions as a moral controller of desire in the poem.

Venus' psychosexual situation, in which she desires the body which she cannot possess, prefigures Lacan's conceptualisation of the problematic relationship between the homoerotic jealousy and the "horror of incest" realised in "the structure of language [which] gives a clue to the function of the ego".[35] The Lacanian idea—it derives from Freud—about *knowing* the ego in the language which expresses it, correlates with Paul de Man's theory of reading content in the rhetorical form. In a similar way, in both Lacan and Paul de Man, rhetoric and language are seen as modes of consciousness. Thus reading Venus' ineffective rhetoric in psycho-rhetorical terms suggests to us that in the realm of desire, power is not stability, but, on the contrary, instability and insecurity. Instability and insecurity, which are inscribed in the rhetoric of enthymemes, constitute themes created by articulating desire not as a possession of the object of desire but as its substitute in a rhetorical fantasy. Hence the purpose of rhetoric in *Venus and Adonis* lies not in its ability to evoke themes but in its capacity to inscribe desire in linguistic terms. The aim of the poem is not to thematise eros as a subject, but to render eros in the only way it can be represented vividly, in language. And Venus' rhetorical frustration suggests both difficulties and anxieties in textualising desire and attaching to it erotic meaning.[36]

Formalist reading of the persuasive rhetoric in the poem does not only illuminate our insight into the function of rhetoric in an early modern text, but it also suggests to us one way—through rhetoric—of conceptualising desire in the literature of the sixteenth century. *Venus and Adonis* shows that the true nature of sexual pleasure is in the "pleasure of the text", in modes of its textual representation. However, such reading of desire also reopens the question of the poem's moral purpose which rhetoric had to convey according to the early modern expectations of it. Thus, if the rhetoric of probability only realises the fantasy of desire, and fashions the subject of that desire as an illusion, denying reality in the process, then the reality of desire—the subject of Venus' arguments—indicates a danger in Shakespeare's thematic project in *Venus and Adonis*. That reality is textualised as fear, pain, and the failure of the desirous performance. Thus the poem demonstrates that desiring the possession of the wrong body, the body of the one "more lovely than a man"—a handsome, effeminate youth in this case—is transcribed as an unimaginative, failed rhetoric. In turn, from both the moral and the rhetorical standpoint, an improper desire which renders bad eloquence is neither an ethical nor an eloquent ideal that Shakespeare's noble dedicatee, the allegedly licentious Earl of Southampton, should aspire to.[37]

Notes

[1] Lucy Gent, "*Venus and Adonis:* The Triumph of Rhetoric", *The Modern Language Review* 69 (1974), 721-9 (p. 721).

[2] Gent, "'Venus and Adonis'", p. 721.

[3] Richard A. Lanham, *The Motives of Eloquence: Literary Rhetoric in the Renaissance* (New Haven and London: 1976), pp. 83-94.

[4] Lanham, *The Motives*, p. 94.

[5] Douglas Bush, *Mythology & the Renaissance Tradition in English Poetry* (rev. ed. New York: 1963), p. 141.

[6] The bibliography on this subject is very long. Some of the most illuminating criticism of the poem is found in Clark Hulse, *Metamorphic Verse: The Elizabethan Minor Epic* (Princeton: 1981); William Keach, *Elizabethan Erotic Narratives: Irony and Pathos in the Ovidian Poetry of Shakespeare, Marlowe and Their Contemporaries* (New Brunswick: 1977); Coppelia Kahn, "Self and Eros in *Venus and Adonis*", *The Centennial Review* 20 (1976), 351-71; William Sheidley, "'Unless it be a boar': Love and Wisdom in Shakespeare's *Venus and Adonis*", *Modern Language Quarterly* 35 (1974), 3-15; A. C. Hamilton, "Venus and Adonis", *Studies in English Literature: 1500-1900* 1 (1961), 1-15.

[7] Jonathan Bate, *Shakespeare and Ovid* (Oxford: 1994), pp. 51-65.

[8] Arthur Golding's 1567 translation of *Metamorphoses*. Quoted in Geoffrey Bullough, ed., *Narrative and Dramatic Sources of Shakespeare* (London and New York: 1957), I, p. 167.

[9] John Roe, ed., William Shakespeare, *The Poems*, The New Cambridge Shakespeare (Cambridge: 1992), p. 5.

[10] Bernard Weinberg, *A History of Literary Criticism in the Italian Renaissance* (Chicago: 1961), I, p. 150; Richard Waswo, *Language and Meaning in the Renaissance* (Princeton: 1987), p. 228.

[11] Thomas M. Conley, *Rhetoric in the European Tradition* (Chicago and London: 1990), p. 136.

[12] Hanna H. Gray, "Renaissance Humanism: The Pursuit of Eloquence", *Journal of the History of Ideas* 34 (1963), 497-514 (p. 497).

[13] Henry Peacham, *The Garden of Eloquence* (London: 1577), Sig. B1ᵛ.

[14] Paul de Man, "Semiology and Rhetoric", *Diacritics* 3 (1973), 27-33 (p. 27).

[15] Paul de Man, "Semiology", p. 32.

[16] I quote the text of *Venus and Adonis* from: William Shakespeare, *The Narrative Poems*, ed. Maurice Evans, the New Penguin Shakespeare (Harmondsworth: 1989).

[17] Richard A. Lanham, *A Handlist of Rhetorical Terms* (Berkeley: 1991), p. 65.

[18] Here I profit from Heather Dubrow's discussion of Venus' use of conditionals. See Heather Dubrow, *Captive Victors: Shakespeare's Narrative Poems and Sonnets* (Ithaca and London: 1987), p. 19.

[19] P. Albert Duhamel, "The Function of Rhetoric as Effective Expression", *Journal of the History of Ideas* 10 (1949), 344-56 (pp. 345-9).

[20] Lanham, *A Handlist*, p. 31.

[21] Aristotle, *The Art of Rhetoric*, tr. J. H. Freese, The Loeb Classical Library (Cambridge, Mass.: 1926), I.ii.13.

[22] Catherine Belsey, "Love as Trompe-l'oeil: Taxonomies of Desire in *Venus and Adonis*", *Shakespeare Quarterly* 46 (1995), 257-76 (p. 275). Here, Belsey bases her argument on Lacan's concept of the *objet a*, "the lost object in the inextricable real, the cause of desire" (Belsey, "Love as Trompe-l'oeil", p. 258).

[23] Lanham, *A Handlist*, p. 106.

[24] Quintilian, *The Institutio Oratoria*, tr. H. E. Butler, The Loeb Classical Library (Cambridge, Mass. and London: 1921), V.xiv.2.

[25] Lanham, *A Handlist*, p. 33.

[26] Lanham, *A Handlist*, p. 14.

[27] Judith Butler, "Desire", *Critical Terms for Literary Study*, eds. Frank Lentricchia and Thomas McLaughlin (Chicago and London: 1995), 369-86 (p. 376).

[28] Kenneth Burke, "Four Master Tropes", *A Grammar of Motives* (New York: 1945), 503-17 (p. 503).

[29] Bate, *Shakespeare*, p. 65.

[30] Paul de Man, "Semiology", p. 32.

[31] Adam Phillips, "Psychoanalysis and the Future of Fear", *Raritan* 15 (1995), 51-66 (p. 56).

[32] Bate, *Shakespeare*, pp. 48-65.

[33] Bate, *Shakespeare*, pp. 51-2.

[34] Roe (*The Poems*, p. 101) glosses Adonis' "disgrace" as "to disdain", while E. T. Prince paraphrases the line 412, as "What I feel towards love is only a strong desire to scorn it". See Prince's New Arden edition of William Shakespeare, *The Poems* (Cambridge, Mass.: 1960), p. 25.

[35] Jacques Lacan, "Some Reflections on the Ego", *The International Journal of Psycho-Analysis* 34 (1953), 11-17 (p. 12).

[36] Gregory W. Bredbeck makes a similar case for Shakespeare's "boy sonnets". See his "Tradition and The Individual Sodomite: Banfield, Shakespeare, and Subjective Desire", *Homosexuality in Renaissance and Enlightenment England: Literary Representation in Historical Context*, ed. Claude J. Summers (New York and London: 1992), 41-68 (p. 54).

[37] Katherine Duncan-Jones, "Much Ado With Red and White: The Earliest Readers of Shakespeare's *Venus and Adonis*", *The Review of English Studies*, NS, 44 (1993), 479-501 (pp. 485-6); Alan Bray, "Homosexuality and the Signs of Male Friendship in Elizabethan England", *History Workshop Journal* 29 (1990), 1-19 (p. 8). G. P. V. Akrigg, *Shakespeare and the Earl of Southampton* (Cambridge, Mass.: 1968), pp. 36-7, 180-2.

Robert P. Merrix (essay date 1997)

SOURCE: "'Lo, in This Hollow Cradle Take Thy Rest': Sexual Conflict and Resolution in 'Venus and Adonis,'" in *Venus and Adonis: Critical Essays*, edited by Philip C. Kolin, Garland Publishing, Inc., 1997, pp. 341-357.

[*In the following essay, Merrix explores the conflict between domestic sexuality and the desire for what is exotic and unknown in* Venus and Adonis.]

I

Recent scholarly articles on Shakespeare's *Venus and Adonis* more and more focus on the complexity of the poem, a complexity that exposes earlier allegorical interpretations as naive or reductive. The simple allegorical interpretations have given way to more profound iconographic or mythographic analyses of the poem.[1] When allegory yields to myth or symbolism, ambivalence inevitably results. The simple one-dimensional relationship between the human attribute and its allegorical vehicle is replaced with what one scholar calls "a mystery, a complexity, even a self-contradiction."[2] Norman Rabkin also speaks of the poem as expressing the "self-contradiction implicit in a central human activity."[3] J. D. Jahn emphasizes the "sophisticated moral conception" that is similar to the complexity "underlying the great tragedies."[4] And S. Clark Hulse notes that "the debate between Venus and Adonis is never resolved"; the paradoxes of love (life and death, bliss and agony) "teeter out of sight on the even feet of oxymoron."[5]

There is, however, a residual tendency to assign allegorical categories to the main characters or to assess their conflict in neoplatonic terms, thus maintaining the traditional dualism that has provided the basis for so many interpretations of the poem. Robin Bowers and Heather Asals exemplify such allegorical treatments of the poem.[6] For Bowers, Shakespeare had a "definite" moral aim in mind in writing the poem. Venus is the "Goddess of Lust" and Adonis (apparently) the embodiment of male virtue. Bowers attempts to solve the problem of the boar, the *bête noire* of the allegorists, by calling it the "wrathful effects of lust" that "represent the fatal pains which follow the feeble pleasures of Venus." Bowers' interpretation hinges on his assertion that the sexual kiss (ll. 549-64) is actually coitus (9). Thus, by succumbing to Venus' lust Adonis is weakened and "consequently unable to succeed in the hunt of the 'savage Boare.'" Bowers sounds like the macho football coach warning his boys to avoid sexual contact with women before the big game. Bowers also ignores lines 595-600, which specifically state that though Venus is "in the very lists of love,/Her champion mounted for the hot encounter.... He will not manage her, although he mount her."[7] "Manage" (French *manege*) means literally to put a horse through its paces, thus reflecting Adonis' failure to do what his horse did.

Asals offers an interesting variation on the standard neoplatonic pattern by having Venus herself transcend her own initial earthly nature—Venus Vulgaris—to her divine one. She "purges from herself the nature of the boar" (i.e., Lust) and "by the end of the poem ... finds also the better angel, the Heavenly Venus within her soul" (48-49). Interestingly, such dualistic approaches mandate a heaven-earth dichotomy and lead both scholars to interpret Venus' mounting "through the empty skies" as a return to "heaven," rather than to Paphos, her very earthly home.[8]

There are, then, two sharply different critical approaches to *Venus and Adonis*. The first is clearly allegorical and exclusive, in which critics assign specific moral attributes to Venus and Adonis or to their "surrogates"—the boar, the horses, the eagle, and the rabbit.

The other approach, which Bowers denigrates as the "ambivalent school," is really symbolic and mythic, thus inclusive. It emphasizes the diversity and complexity of the main characters. For the allegorists, Venus is *Love*—either Venus Genetrix or Venus Vulgaris—and Adonis is *Beauty* or *Virtue*. For the symbolists, Venus is *love*, sometimes sensual,[9] sometimes maternal,[10] and Adonis is *beauty* or *virtue*, embodied, as different commentators have suggested, in an innocent adolescent boy,[11] a prig,[12] or a young nobleman and courtier.[13] Hulse reflects this inclusive approach succinctly in his summation of Venus:

> We have, in effect, not one but three Venuses—comic, sensual and violent—all embodying earthly love but differently depicted to reveal different aspects. Venus is the empty eagle, the randy jennet, the tender snail, the anguished doe and the timid hare. (98)

Both of these critical approaches tend to focus on the theme of love and beauty or the moral relationship between Venus and Adonis with little or no regard to the dramatic structure and social context of the poem within which the relationship unfolds. Dramatic structure and social context are critical to any analysis. The dialectic created by the conflicts among the main characters or their surrogates, and the bifurcated structure, revealing two radically different settings and tones for those conflicts, require a closer structural analysis of Shakespeare's poem than heretofore attempted.[14] Rather than trying to identify the allegorical absolutes or interpret the moral meanings, it may be more fruitful to analyze the sexual conflicts structurally embodied in the poem. Does Venus tempt Adonis for moral reasons—either to destroy him through lust or to preserve him by urging him to propagate his beauty? Or does she attempt to impose on him sexual or psychological norms antithetical to his own? Does Adonis reject Venus for those same moral reasons, or for other, more fundamental, ones? An analysis of the *sexual* content of the carefully patterned debate between Venus and Adonis and the psychologically and physically diverse settings in the poem will yield more personal and human reasons for their behavior, something that allegory and myth do not allow.

It is certainly true that we cannot escape some kind of allegorical or mythic meaning in the metamorphosis of Adonis at the end of the poem; but we need not imbue the entire work with one or the other critical approach. As Leonard Barkan has pointed out, Renaissance writers often employed myth and allegory to suit their own purposes without regard to the carefully structured relationship between the vehicle and its attribute.[15] Certainly numerous critics see Venus and Adonis as anything but mythological absolutes. Moreover both allegorical and mythical approaches invite and often require a purely moral or ritual interpretation of the poem. The conflict between Venus and Adonis is not moral or ritual; it is social and sexual and concerns conflicting lifestyles, one domestic, fruitful, and secure, and the other exotic, sterile, and dangerous.

These two lifestyles are reflected in Venus and the boar. Venus represents both a social and biological imperative whereby humanity domesticates and increases itself. The boar embodies all that operates against such a culture and offers instead a deadly transcendence from biological necessity. The ensuing conflict between Venus and the boar-loving Adonis adumbrates the eternal struggle of humanity to reject the ecstatic temptation of absolute freedom that leads only to narcissism and the annihilation of culture. The force represented by the boar, which historically has drawn Western man from domestic security into alien worlds, is embodied in the early tales of Actaeon, the mythic representation of the hunting frenzy. As several scholars have noted, the hunt exerts a magnetic attraction over certain men.[16] An excellent example of this transcendent quest appears in Giordano Bruno's version of Actaeon in *Gl'Eroici Furen*. Actaeon's ecstasy leads to this apotheosis as described by Bruno:

> In that divine and universal chase he comes to apprehend that it is himself who necessarily remains captured, absorbed and united. Therefore, from the vulgar, civil and ordinary man he was, he becomes free as the deer, and an inhabitant of the wilderness; he lives like a god under the protection of the woods . . . where he contemplates the sources of the great rivers . . . and converses most freely with the divinity, to which so many men have aspired.[17]

As often noted, Venus may indeed represent lust, simple procreation, sexual maternalism, or even the *femme fatale*. She may be both comic and tragic. Indeed, as Hulse suggests, she is a composite of all these roles. In order to function successfully in each role each one or, rather, the action implied by each one, must be reciprocated. Otherwise there is no moral nexus by which to judge the dynamics of a moral relationship: lust needs an object upon which to act, procreation requires two mates, the maternal female needs the willing child. Adonis' failure to reciprocate any of these sexual modes distorts all of them. Venus, the embodiment of all, runs the gamut from voluptuous mother to lusty temptress to frustrated lover to abandoned woman. Because of Adonis' failure to reciprocate these personifications, each is intensified to the point of grotesqueness. As Venus notes in her analogy: "An oven that is stop'd, or river stay'd / Burneth more hotly, swelleth with more rage" (ll. 331-32). Venus' initial sexual desire, perhaps comic, but certainly not repellant, eventually becomes ugly and frightful as reflected by the bizarre images associated with her—the "amazon," the eagle, and vulture. Whatever sexual roles Venus embodies, all require a reciprocal experience, an involvement, which is diametrically opposite to what Adonis desires. He therefore rejects the goddess for an entirely different composite—the boar.

For Shakespeare, sexual reciprocity is the sine qua non in human relationships. It is most clearly demonstrated, of course, in the "procreation" sonnets (1-17) where the poet urges the young man to "Make thee another self, for love of me, / That beauty still may live in thine and thee" (10.13-14). He accuses the young man of making a "waste in niggarding" (1.12) and "having traffic with thyself alone" (4.9); he warns him that "nothing 'gainst Time's scythe can make defence / Save breed to brave him when he takes thee hence." (12.13-14) But the theme of sexual reciprocity runs through many of the plays as well, especially the comedies. Only in *Love's Labor's Lost* does "Jack hath not Gill"; and even there the consummation will occur at a twelvemonth's end when the men are purged from their sins of "faults and perjury" (5.2.870-75).[18] In *All's Well That Ends Well,* Bertram, who, like Adonis, refuses sexual consummation, is tricked into it by Helena. In *As You Like It,* Touchstone reinforces the biological mandate when he tells Jaques: "As the ox hath his bow, sir, the horse his curb, and the falcon her bells, so wedlock would be nibbling" (3.3.79-82). Indeed, *As You Like It* provides an excellent example of two different kinds of love—the first realistic and sexual and the second "romantic" and transcendental. Touchstone's "rhyme" to Rosalind bluntly depicts the former: "Wint'red garments must be lin'd, / So must slender Rosalind / He that sweetest rose will find / Must find love's prick and Rosalind" (3.2.105-12). Fruitless transcendental love is represented by Silvius, who pines and weeps for the uncaring Phebe. Her rejection of his overtures leads him to inane protestations of love ("O Phebe, Phebe, Phebe!"), which ultimately earn him the contempt of Rosalind. She, of course, successfully embodies the romantic-realistic nexus in her relationship with Orlando.

Each of the composites in the poem—Venus and the boar—is associated with its own setting, imagery, narrative or dramatic style, and psychological imperative. The poem itself is broken into two major sections, the first 810 lines containing the sexual conflict between Venus and Adonis; and the second section of 383 lines involving Venus' search for Adonis. Venus meets Adonis at early morning in a static, pastoral setting replete with images of sensuality and a "primrose bank" upon which such sensual desire may be fulfilled. The poem here is both narrative and dramatic, the dramatic part revealing a sexual conflict between Venus and the boy. Adonis is urged to forgo his hunting trip and be "hemm'd . . . within the circle of [Venus'] ivory pale"; in short, to become ensconced in a societal structure that promises security, comfort, and physical pleasures. He refuses to accept this composite and leaves. In part two of the poem, he hunts the boar, the counter composite, in an alien environment, and is quickly killed. With the transformation of Adonis into the anemone at the end of the poem the two composites are united, forming a sexual resolution, a synthesis in which the major attributes of each are embodied in the other.[19] After plucking the flower, Venus places it in her bosom:

> Lo, in this hollow cradle take thy rest;
> My throbbing heart shall rock thee day and night:
> There shall not be one minute in an hour
> Wherein I will not kiss my sweet love's flower.
>
> (ll. 1185-88)

II

Like Ovid in *The Metamorphoses,*[20] Shakespeare does not create setting graphically. There are few specific references to scenery—the "primrose bank" with its "forceless flowers," the "copse" from which the jennet comes, the twining "bushes" and, of course, the "anemone" being the most vivid. Setting is created by allegorical episodes, such as the horses, allusions to classical figures such as Mars and Diana, and rhetorical descriptions of animals' actions or features—all of which inform the amorphous or vague terrain into psychological equivalents. Setting thus is essentially presentational, as in Shakespeare's drama, its physical or psychological manifestations emerging from actions being narrated or features being described at any given moment in the poem. Most obvious, for example, is the episode of the horses in which the setting reflects the violent sexual foreplay: Adonis' palfrey "wounds" the "bearing earth with his hard hoof" and the earth itself, described as a "hollow womb," becomes a synecdochic extension of equine sexual fruition (ll. 265-70).

Another device Shakespeare uses—again borrowed from Ovid—to create setting is time: both day and night are personified, the former by a classical equivalent—"Titan"—and the latter by epithets ("black-fac'd"; "merciless and pitchy"). Both also are associated with their symbolic birds—the larks for morning and the "shrieking" owl for night. Just as Ovid presented tales of intense sexuality during midday, "the panic hour of noon" (Segal 4), so Shakespeare presents the "sweating" couple being watched by Titan "in the midday heat," who "With burning eye did hotly overlook them" (ll. 127-178).

In the first section of the poem, various formal elements—narration, rhetorical description, dialogue—combine to reveal a world filled with fecundity, security, and domesticity in which Venus, as the major procreative and domestic force in the world, attempts to fulfill her nature. First of all, images of security or domestic taming echo throughout the first part of the poem, from the moment Venus first plucks Adonis from his horse until he leaves her. At various times Venus fastens Adonis in her arms "like a bird tangled in a net" (l. 67); she lies atop him; "her arms infold him like a band" (l. 225); she entwines her arms about him; she "hems" him in; she "prisons" his hand in "a jail of snow" (l. 362); and finally, she falls to the earth with him, "their lips together glued" (l. 546). Even the analogies reinforce the domestic imagery. Adonis is "Like a wild bird being tam'd with too much handling, / Or as the fleet-foot roe that's tir'd with chasing, / Or like the froward infant still'd with dandling" (ll. 560-562). The animals referred to in part one are associated with the benign setting. When Adonis announces that he intends to hunt the boar, Venus urges him to "uncouple at the timorous flying hare, / Or at the fox which lives by subtlety, / Or at the roe which no encounter dares" (ll. 674-76). So frightened is she of his hunting the boar that she launches into two long rhetorical descriptions of the boar and hare for contrast. The boar is a creature so fearful that even the "thorny brambles and embracing bushes . . . part" (ll. 629-30) to let him through.

Diametrically opposite and thus safe is the hare, which, unlike the boar, is torn and scratched by the "envious brier." The famous hare digression serves as the concluding face to the many-faceted icon of Venus. Though the hare, emblematic of Venus, represents fecundity and benign domesticity, it is preceded by voracious and ugly predation imagery. Earlier in part one, an epic simile ties Venus to "an empty eagle" that tears "with her beak on feathers, flesh and bone" (ll. 55-56). In the long sexual kiss (ll. 538-576) she feeds "glutton-like" on Adonis' lips, her "vulture thought" so powerful "That she will draw his lips' rich treasure dry." The hare digression also serves a second purpose. It foreshadows Venus' own pursuit of Adonis in part two and delineates the hostile environment. Like the hare in part one, Venus is encumbered by the envious brier (ll. 872-73).

Like the hare who listens fearfully for his foes and who grieves at "loud alarums" (l. 700), Venus similarly listens for the sounds of the chase. The "timorous yelping of the hounds" immediately "Appals her senses and her spirit confounds" (ll. 881-82) and she stands finally "in a trembling ecstasy" (l. 895).

These rhetorical and narrative techniques together form the composite role of Venus. She reflects the fecundity and the stultification of domestic love, but also the vulnerability of that love when it is subjected to a counterexperience more attractive to someone like Adonis.

Venus also utilizes six separate *carpe diem* motifs from society or nature in her efforts to entice Adonis to sexual union. She starts with her general physical attributes: "my eyes are grey, and bright, and quick in turning. . . . My flesh is soft and plump, my marrow burning" (ll. 140-142); she then moves to her social charms: "Bid me discourse, I will enchant thine ear, / Or like a fairy trip upon the green" (ll. 145-146). She calls attention to the secluded and sexually conducive setting: "Witness this primrose bank whereon I lie" (l. 151). She employs the traditional utilitarian argument both from society and from nature: "Torches are made to light, jewels to wear. . . . Seeds spring from seeds and beauty breedeth beauty; / Thou was begot; to get it is thy duty" (ll. 163-168). When these arguments fail, she turns to invective, calling his manhood into question: "Fie lifeless picture, cold and senseless stone. . . . Thou art no man, though of a man's complexion, / For men will kiss even by their own direction" (ll. 211-216). Finally she returns full circle with the famous sexual description of her body in traditional topographical terms, in which her breasts are "pleasant fountains" leading to "sweet bottom-grass, and high delightful plain / Round rising hillocks, brakes obscure and rough" (ll. 229-240).[21]

Adonis rejects these enticements, releases himself from Venus' "twining arms" and hastens to his horse. But at this point Shakespeare presents another image of procreation and reciprocity: the horses. The wooing action between the animals, of course, parallels that of Venus and Adonis, although in reverse. The jennet, like Adonis, "puts on outward strangeness, seems unkind" a pose that renders the courser a "melancholy malcontent." He "vails his tail . . . like a falling plume," until in his rage and sexual frustration he "stamps and bites the poor flies in his fume" (l. 316). The passage echoes Venus' own similar frustration: "Red cheeks and fiery eyes blaze forth her wrong. . . . And now she weeps and now she fain would speak, / And now her sobs do her intendments break" (ll. 219-222). The contrast between sexual fulfillment and sexual frustration is strikingly exemplified when the jennet "perceiving how [the courser] is enrag'd / Grew kinder [so that] his fury was assuag'd" (ll. 318-319). In short, the horses, a part of the world of nature, as are Venus and Adonis in the pastoral setting, mate as they should. Reciprocity thus cools the sexual rage and prevents the grotesqueness that sexual frustration leads to. Venus points this out to the sullen Adonis:

> Thy palfrey, as he should,
> Welcomes the warm approach of sweet desire:
> Affection is the coal that must be cool'd;
> Else, suffer'd it will set the heart on fire.
>
> (ll. 385-388)

Her inducements for him to imitate his horse, however, fail, and lead to Adonis' first speech, appropriately one that delineates his militant yearnings and his revulsion of domesticity:

> "I know not love," quoth he, "nor will not know it,
> Unless it be a boar, and then I chase it;

My love to love is love but to disgrace it;
For I have heard it is a life in death,
That laughs, and weeps, and all but with a
    breath."

(ll. 409-416)

With his reference to love as "life in death" Adonis firmly rejects the domestic composite embodied in Venus. "Life in death" involves social and sexual responsibility and, eventually, for the young courtier, domestic "drudgery"—what Edgar in *King Lear* terms the "dull, stale, tired marriage bed." Adonis embraces, then, not the dulling *life in death*[22] but, in the boar, its opposite, the exhilarating and dangerous *death in life*—the eternal human desire to transcend all physical and social limits, the compulsion to "immerse oneself into the destructive element"; "to pluck bright honor from the pale-fac'd moon, / Or dive into the bottom of the deep." He seeks, in short, the Romantic quest with its concomitant metaphysical aspirations. In desire he is a youthful Tamburlaine, "always moving as the restless spheres." Unfortunately, in execution, he resembles Don Quixote's Sancho Panza.

That Adonis understands the role Venus attempts to impose on him is evident in his differentiation between love and lust:

I hate not love but your device in love,
That lends embracements unto every stranger.
You do it for increase: O Strange excuse,
When reason is the bawd to lust's abuse.

(ll. 789-792)

Adonis correctly sees that the "device in love" that leads to "increase" carries with it domestic obligations antithetical to his own desires.[23] His conclusion follows the earlier sexual kiss. In that kiss, Adonis' reluctance creates in Venus the distorted image of sexual frustration earlier alluded to. In short, Adonis' refusal to reciprocate the various social and sexual roles embodied in Venus—procreator, mistress, aggressive lover, temptress—leads to the grotesque images of unfulfilled sexuality.[24] Venus' attempts in part one to fulfill her domestic function fail. From this moment on she takes on another series of roles in keeping with the new setting and narrative focus—abandoned lover (or wife), anxious mother searching for her child, or romantic heroine venturing into the unknown in search for her knight. As such Venus is related to Ovid's Oenone (as illustrated in T. H.'s *Oenone and Paris*), Virgil's Dido, Ishtar/Astarte in *Gilgamesh,* and other romantic heroines.

III

Just as various formal elements make up the domestic world of part one, such elements also inform the diametrically opposite world of part two. Adonis, having spent the morning, noon, and afternoon with Venus, "Leaves Love in darkness," such "a merciless and pitchy night" (l. 821) that Venus is confounded and loses her way. In part two she enters a sinister, demonic world similar to that portrayed by Northrop Frye in the *Anatomy of Criticism.*[25] In Frye's world a "demonic erotic relation becomes a fierce destructive passion." But the sexuality is sterile and grotesque. The animals (Frye's "animal world") are "monsters or beasts of prey" and the landscape (Frye's "vegetable world") is sinister and dangerous. It is the savage jungle of Kurtz, the Dark Tower of Childe Roland, the appropriate setting for the transcendent Faustian.

Venus searches for the doomed Adonis in this cold and alien setting. Leaving the comforting primrose bank, she struggles through unknown lands where "bushes . . . catch her about the neck" or "twine about her thigh" (ll. 871-873). Images of "adders," "blunt boar, rough bear, or lion proud" replace the benign animals in part one. The hounds, vigorous and eager like their master in part one, are now wounded, licking "venom'd sores and howling." The hostile environment adds to Venus' psychological state of mind as she stands "in a trembling ecstasy." She spies the boar "bepainted all with red, / Like milk and blood being mingled both together" (ll. 901-903).[26] Eventually she finds Adonis, his death verifying her earlier vision and justifying her warning to him. In leaving the static primrose bank, Adonis enters the deadly world of the hunt—the world of militant chivalry. In engaging the boar, the composite of all that is antithetical to Venus, he has achieved his *death in life* at last.[27] Ironically this death is also sexual. Both Ovid and Golding make clear that the death follows an erotic coupling. Ovid says the boar sank his tusks into the "groin" *(sub inguine)* of Adonis. And in Golding's translation the boar strikes Adonis in the "codds."[28] "The loving swine," says Venus, "But by a kiss thought to persuade him there / And nuzzling in his flank . . . Sheath'd unaware the tusk in his soft groin" (ll. 1114-1116).

But what does the boar in *Venus and Adonis* represent?[29] Must we view it in purely allegorical or mythic terms? As has often been noted, the boar itself is associated with the initiation of the young squire into manhood. Even more important, as Marcelle Thiébaux in his seminal article[30] shows, the boar became related in late medieval times with militant activity as dangerous and exhilarating as warfare:

Eventually, the boar as adversary becomes the object of a hunt. It is noteworthy that in romances, as in certain of the *chansons de geste,* the battles characteristic of heroic literature become increasingly replaced by, or interspersed with, hunting expeditions of a rigorous sort. Hunting itself not only ranked as a courtly accomplishment, but was also regarded by medieval theorists as a substitute for the more strenuous diversion of war, and a means by which the knight might exercise arms between campaigns. (284)

Significant also for Thiébaux is the "epic magnitude in which boars loom . . . as adversaries, even as the destroyers, directly or indirectly, of heroes." Moreover, like Adonis, "those heroes . . . are lured into danger or to their deaths once they have followed boars into the territories of their enemies." In short, the boar's role is that of "a conductor into the fateful or the unknown" (290).

It is this last role that the boar plays initially in *Venus and Adonis.* And the subsequent hunt reflects those irrational adventurous experiences that some men yearn for, a compulsion that binds them in a quest for the unknown, the search for apocalypse. The quest is chaste, exotic, an anti-life force that is set against the fruitful, domestic life by which humanity survives. In his *Love in the Western World,*[31] Denis de Rougemont characterizes this type of sterile quest as an "alien factor . . . having the power to make instinct turn away from its natural goal and to transfer desire into limitless aspiration, into something . . . which does not serve, and indeed operates against, biological ends" (62).

These two forces vying for Adonis, one domestic and procreative, and the other militant and chaste, are embodied mythically in Venus and Diana and in the two animals usually associated with them, the fecund rabbit for Venus and the boar for Diana. But sexually the two forces are reflected in the activities associated with the hearth and the hunt. In part one of *Venus and Adonis,* Venus catalogues the anti-life forces related to "modest Dian": they are "fruitless chastity, / Love-lacking vestals, and self-loving nuns, / That on the earth would breed a scarcity / And barren dearth of daughters and of sons" (ll. 751-754). When Adonis chooses to hunt the boar, then, he chooses chastity over fruitfulness, danger and death over security and long life, the mysterious over the known.[32]

IV

Following the death of Adonis and thus his failure to reciprocate the sexual love offered by Venus, the goddess makes her famous prophecy of future love. Love will be "waited on with jealousy. . . . It shall be fickle, false and full of fraud / Bud and be blasted in a breathing while." Most importantly, love shall be "the cause of war and dire events, / And set dissention twixt the son and sire" (ll. 1136-1160). Venus' prophecy is not, as some have suggested, a curse or a "law" placed on humanity by her.[33] It is simply a description of the human condition following the rise of romantic love—the love delineated by de Rougemont—which thrives on jealousy, suffering, and separation, a love that refuses reciprocity and indeed denies reciprocal relationships altogether. The new world is a postlapsarian madhouse where disunity and chaos rule. The failure to achieve sexual resolution—to propagate the race—leads to death, however glorious that death may be. If there is any truth emerging from the conflicts in *Venus and Adonis,* it is surely that humanity cannot escape its sexual nature except through constant flight into the unknown. It seems similarly true that some men cannot be satisfied with the "dull, stale, tired marriage bed" and will risk the apocalypse, that *death in life,* in order to escape. From Gottfried's *Tristan* to Byron's *Manfred* to Melville's *Moby Dick,* Faustian man, as young and pathetic as Adonis, or as old and sad as Don Quixote, has attempted to escape from what Ishmael termed the "attainable felicity" of the "wife, the bed, the table, the saddle, the fire-side." Is there, then, no reprieve for such a world of disharmony and chaos? Is there no mean to the extremes of dull domesticity and deadly exoticism?

Whatever respite comes must certainly involve the metamorphosis of Adonis, which occurs immediately after Venus' prophecy. It is here that we must include an allegorical dimension in the poem. This metamorphosis of Adonis reflects other Ovidian transformations of those who similarly rejected sexual overtures: Daphne into a tree, Picus into a bird, and Narcissus into a flower. But the transformation of Adonis into the anemone—emblematic both of fragile early love and resurrection—operates more positively. It softens Venus' harsh prophecy and provides an alternative to the earlier two choices. Just as the militant chastity of the medieval warrior was gradually transformed into more courtly and societal rituals, so the hunt itself turns from the composite exemplified by the boar and towards that exemplified by Venus. In short, the wooing ritual replaces the hunt. Such activity is now both possible and desirable, for Venus herself has undergone a change. This transformation, ignored by many critics, is interpreted by others primarily in spiritual and aesthetic terms. Asals, as earlier noted, presents a modified neoplatonic reading, as does Doebler. For them, Venus' transformation is epistemological. Doebler's Venus, moving towards knowledge, can be "mere lust in one persona and heavenly beauty in another" (34). S. Clark Hulse grounds his analysis of the "shifting character of Venus" in myth. Venus is a "sweaty muscular rapist," then a "philosopher," and finally a "grieving lover," reflecting the force of myth to overcome "seeming contradictions and improbalities" (95-96). For Tita French Baumlin, Venus' change is a "poetic apotheosis" and reflects Shakespeare's own aesthetic growth:

> Venus' apotheosis from shallow rhetorician into elegiac poet mirrors the 'apotheosis' of the new poet himself, who must break the rules of poetic

form and violently unmake his [Ovidian] model to create his own mature expression of his aesthetic principles.³⁴

A. C. Hamilton is really the only critic to evaluate Venus' change in more earthy terms:

> The bawdy, even comic, account of Venus' actions which we see through the witty and dispassionate eye of the poet gives place to a plaintive, even tragic, lament.³⁵

Finally, a recent and provocative feminist essay by Nona Fienberg emphasizes Venus' "mutability and diversity" and her ability to change roles and positions in contrast to Adonis' patriarchal fixity and absoluteness: "Venus' flexibility and ability to neogotiate [value] suggest a liberating reevaluation of the patriarchal world she both plays in and subverts."³⁶

For me, however, the major transformation is social and psychological and occurs when Venus leaves the primrose bank. From the moment she steps into the horrific world of the boar she becomes vulnerable, and is softened and humanized by the alien environment over which she has no control. Since Adonis' transformation occurs in this alien world, the flower retains elements from that world. By plucking the flower and placing it in her bosom, Venus brings the two worlds together. One could of course see the union in traditional mythic terms: the flower (Adonis) symbolizing the spirit of annual vegetation. However, one can also see the transformation in more simple social terms. In an important article on Empedocles in Rome, James Arieti speaks of the socialization of the mythic union of Mars and Venus as a cultural strategy for creating and maintaining the "tension of opposites" which kept Rome strong and vital.³⁷ That tension implies a dynamic political alternative, a mingling of the attributes of both Venus and Mars. While not an Hegelian paradigm, a similar *sexual* synthesis emerges from the transformation of Adonis. As Renaissance verse narratives like Abraham Fraunce's *The Countess of Pembrokes Yvy Church;* Marlowe's *Hero and Leander;* Thomas Edwards' two poems *Cephalus and Procris* and *Narcissus;* T. H.'s *Oenone and Paris;* and Robert Toften's *Alba,* with his "melancholy lover," all illustrate, the Renaissance attitudes about love reflect a union of these two worlds, the sexual and the "romantic." The static and stultifying sexual world of Venus is made more endurable by elevating it into the realm of physical danger and the unknown. Sexual love is now imbued with either the spirit of the chase (as in *Hero and Leander*) or with romantic suffering and separation *(Cephalus and Procris),* which, as de Rougemont notes, seem such a vital part of human love. Similarly, the chaste, dynamic world of adventure is drawn closer to the world of humanity: the quest for the boar is transformed to the quest for the mistress, from the inevitable physical death to the "little death," the sexual release so often depicted by Shakespeare, Donne, and others. In Shakespeare's mature comedies, especially, one can experience these degrees of love. As noted before, the two major extremes—domestic, sexual love and idealistic transcendental love—are humorously depicted in *As You Like It* by, respectively, Touchstone and Audrey and Phebe and Silvius. More seriously, in *All's Well That Ends Well,* the Adonis-like Bertram flees the aggressive Helena, preferring the Tuscan wars to the domestic bedding of the maid. No better parody on the Romantic Imperative exists than Parolles' subsequent apostrophe to it:

> To th' wars, my boy, to the wars!
> He wears his honor in a box unseen,
> That hugs his kicky-wicky here at home,
> Spending his manly marrow in her arms,
> Which should sustain the proud and high curvet
> Of Mars' fiery steed.
>
> (II.iii.279-283)

The chaotic romantic love with its jealousy and hate that Venus speaks of is, of course, most clearly exemplified in *Romeo and Juliet* and *Othello,* where the romantic nexus leads to just those woes listed in Venus' catalogue. But such tragedy cannot be attributed solely to the love itself. When love fails in Shakespeare, it fails because the synthesis of solid realism and transcendent romanticism is not permitted to occur. When the love succeeds, as with Rosalind and Orlando, a dynamic and fruitful future is presaged. In *A Midsummer Night's Dream* (c. 1595), written shortly after *Venus and Adonis,* Shakespeare plays with various combinations of love in four distinct subplots. Theseus, in his comments to Hippolyta, exemplifies the realistic, matter-of-fact course of love: "I wooed thee with my sword. . . . But I will wed thee in another key." The young lovers reflect the highly-charged emotional component of love—the "romantic"—which needs to be redirected into more fruitful wooing by both Oberon's and Theseus' interventions. Oberon, especially in his treatment of Titania, demonstrates a prideful narcissistic love. The rude mechanicals in the hilarious scatalogical and sexual version of *Pyramus and Thisby* are early versions of Touchstone, and proffer the necessary parodic jab in the ribs to remind us that love is both serious and comic, spiritual and sexual, logical and silly. But the lesson emerging from the plays is that love is not love when it is not reciprocated.

Venus and Adonis certainly lends itself to allegorical and mythic analyses. But the sexual conflict and its eventual resolution—suggested by the structure and the rhetorical techniques—must be considered. While I certainly would not argue that the poem has topical parallels to Shakespeare's own flight from Stratford and married love to London and its teeming excitement, I think *Venus and Adonis* exemplifies his understanding of the tension between society's strong need to procreate and fulfill its duty to nature, and its equally strong desire to escape from the bonds of that procreativeness into the exciting and mysterious world of the unknown, a romantic haven far from the burdens of husbandry. These counterimperatives can never be reconciled; but by imbuing each with the best elements of the other, a workable alternative may emerge that allows us to survive, and, more importantly, to create artistic works that reflect our struggle with and eventual acceptance of the imperatives. For me, the alternative to those two worlds emerges clearly from the sexual conflict in the poem. The synthesis of the domestic and the exotic reflects the reality of human relationships, and is as valid today as in Shakespeare's time.

Notes

[1] See Wayne A. Rebhorn for an excellent summary of the changing critical attitudes in analyses of the poem. He suggests that major critical change began during the 1960s when Venus "received more sympathetic treatment and was identified as Venus Genetrix." "Mother Venus: Temptation in Shakespeare's *Venus and Adonis*," *Shakespeare Studies* 11 (1978): 1-19.

[2] Leonard Barkan, "Diana and Actaeon: The Myth as Synthesis," *English Literary Renaissance* 10 (Autumn, 1981): 317-359.

[3] *Shakespeare and the Common Understanding* (New York: Free Press, 1967), 159.

[4] "The Lamb of Lust: The Role of Adonis in Shakespeare's *Venus and Adonis*," *Shakespeare Studies* 6 (1970): 11-25.

[5] "Shakespeare's Myth of Venus and Adonis," *PMLA* 93 (Jan 1978): 95-105.

[6] A. Robin Bowers, "'Hard Armours' and 'Delicate Amours' in Shakespeare's *Venus and Adonis*," *Shakespeare Quarterly* 12 (1979): 1-23; Heather Asals, "*Venus and Adonis*: The Education of a Goddess," *Studies in English Literature* 13 (1973): 31-51.

[7] I use the edition by Edward Hubler, *Shakespeare's Songs and Poems* (New York: McGraw-Hill, 1959) for both the sonnets and the poem.

[8] Eugene Cantelupe takes issue with the neoplatonic approach. He insists that Shakespeare is parodying the pattern. The neoplatonic conventions, "love, beauty, procreation and the spirit" are "unrealistic and absurd." The pursuit of such love leads to "propelling and repugnant lust." See "An Iconographical Interpretation of *Venus and Adonis*, Shakespeare's Ovidian Comedy," *Shakespeare Quarterly* 14 (1963): 141.

[9] Rabkin, "*Venus and Adonis* and the Myth of Love," *Pacific Coast Studies in Shakespeare*, eds. Waldo McNeir and Thelma Greenfield (Eugene, Oregon: U of Oregon P, 1966), 20-32.

[10] Rebhorn, 1.

[11] Cantelupe, 141-42.

[12] Kenneth Muir, "*Venus and Adonis:* Comedy or Tragedy?" in *Shakespearen Essays*, eds. Alwin Thaler and Norman Sanders (Knoxville: U of Tennessee P, 1964), 1-13.

[13] W.R. Streitberger, "Ideal Conduct in *Venus and Adonis*," *Shakespeare Quarterly* 26 (Summer, 1975): 285-91.

[14] David N. Beauregard interprets the two halves in terms of Renaissance faculty psychology. The first illustrates the concupiscent part of the sensitive soul and the second represents the irascible part with Venus now a "pathetic figure." "*Venus and Adonis:* Shakespeare's Representation of the Passions," *Shakespeare Studies* 8 (1975): 83-98; Donald Watson further develops this concupiscent/irascible dichotomy: "The Contrarieties of Venus and Adonis," *Studies in Philology* 75 (1978): 32-63.

[15] Barkan asserts, "The mythographers add moralistic alternatives: the norms of economic behavior, the norms of social and political behavior, and finally the recapitulation of the Christian story" (330). See also D. W. Robertson, Jr., *A Preface to Chaucer: Studies in Medieval Perspectives* (Princeton: Princeton UP, 1973), 299; and Graham Hough, *A Preface to the Faerie Queene* (New York: Norton, 1963), 100-37. Speaking of religious allegorical techniques, Robertson warns that "spiritual exegetes do not systematically make use of every detail in the texts before them." Hough asserts that pure allegory ("naive allegory") seldom occurs in the great allegorical works, especially *The Faerie Queen:* "I cannot agree with Frye, or Spenser himself for that matter, that *The Fairie Queene* as a whole is continuous allegory" (108).

[16] See Marcelle Thiébaux, *The Stag of Love: The Chase in Medieval Literature* (Ithaca: Cornell Univ. Press, 1974); Robert P. Merrix, "The 'Beste Noire': The Medieval Role of the Boar in *Venus and Adonis*," *The Upstart Crow* 11 (1991): 117-30; and Barkan, 339-44.

[17] Quoted from Barkan, 344.

[18] All references to the plays are from *The Riverside Shakespeare*, ed. G. Blakemore Evans (Boston: Houghton Mifflin, 1974).

[19] William Sheidley sees a kind of synthesis in the poem. The "sexual gluttony of Venus" and the "unnatural frigidity of Adonis" must be joined "into a creative union on the human level." In the poem, "Shakespeare distills a . . . sane and joyful spirit by raising his reader to a viewpoint from which love is revealed not to present (as it seems to Adonis) a dreary choice between lust and chastity, but to offer a welcome alternative in the 'warme effects' of charity to the self-defeating paralysis of pride" ("'Unless It Be a Boar': Love and Wisdom in Shakespeare's *Venus and Adonis,*" *Modern Language Quarterly* 35 [March 1974]: 3-15). Norman Rabkin, on the other hand, denies a synthesis: "In this romance of the self-denying Adonis whose definition of love leads him to the search for a purity attainable only in death, and of the earth-bound Venus whose love never reaches beyond apotheosized animality, Shakespeare reflects the hopelessly opposed elements of love as he found it in Renaissance neoplatonism" ("*Venus and Adonis* and the Myth of Love," 32).

[20] Charles Paul Segal, *Landscape in Ovid's Metamorphoses: A Study of the Transformation of a Literary Symbol* (Wiesbaden: Franz Steiner Verlag GMBH, 1969), 5-7.

[21] Topographical or geographical sexual imagery became a quite popular topos in Renaissance poetry. Sidney in "What Tongue Can Her Perfections Tell"; Donne in "Love's Progress"; Carew in "A Rapture"; Spenser (the undressing of Serena: VI, viii, 41-43); Nashe in the notorious *The Choice of Valentines;* and others all vividly describe the various parts of female anatomy. Most descriptions are analogical: breasts are "pommels," "rising apples," or the "Sestos and Abydos" marking the "Hellespont" of the mistress' chest (Donne); bellies are "Cupid's Hill," "a vale of Lillies" or "the mound of Venus," and so on. Donne's heroic sailor travels to his mistress' "fair Atlantic navel" and thence to the "forest [pubic hair] where many shipwrack and no further get." For a more thorough treatment of this technique see Robert P. Merrix, "'The Vale of Lillies and the Bower of Bliss': Soft-Core Pornography in Elizabethan Poetry," *Journal of Popular Culture* 19 (Spring 1986): 3-16; and David O. Frantz, "'Leud Priapians' and Renaissance Pornography," *Studies in English Literature* 12 (1972): 157-72.

[22] It is not clear whether Shakespeare was familiar with Aphrodite's classical epithet: the "Death-in-Life Goddess." See Robert Graves, *The Greek Myths* (New York: George Braziller, 1959), 71. If so, either Adonis confuses the epithets or the poet is being even more ironic in reversing the syntax.

[23] Robert P. Miller asserts that Venus seeks Adonis only for physical love. Venus abuses the "purpose" of her body (procreation), desiring Adonis only for pleasure. "Venus, Adonis and the Horses," *English Literary History* 26 (1952): 249-64; W.R. Streitberger has a similarly harsh view of Venus: "Venus presents the temptations—not merely to lust, but to neglect of duty—to succumb to the easy pleasures and endeavors of life, and exhibits in her actions the results of giving in to those temptations" (286).

[24] Both S. Clark Hulse ("Shakespeare's Myth of *Venus and Adonis*") and Jonathan Hart view Venus as rapacious. For Hulse she is a "sweaty muscular rapist" (95) and Hart asserts that "*Venus and Adonis* begins with a goddess' attempted rape of a 'mortal' boy" (37). However, J.D. Jahn ("The Lamb of Lust") denies that Adonis is a rape victim: "Adonis' brusque disdain of Venus throughout the early scenes, his childishness and physical vanity, ought to dissuade readers from the belief that he is somehow a sacrificial lamb of a lustful goddess" (13). See Jonathan Hart, "'Till Forging Nature Be Comdemned for Treason': Representational Strife in *Venus and Adonis,*" *Cahiers élisabethains* 36 (Oct 1989): 37-47.

[25] Northrop Frye, *Anatomy of Criticism* (Princeton: Princeton UP, 1973), 147-50.

[26] Hereward T. Price examines the red and white imagery in great detail. The colors are always in conflict until Adonis dies, at which time "the red and white are reconciled" ("The Function of Imagery in *Venus and Adonis,*" *Papers of the Michigan Academy of Science, Arts and Letters* 31 (1945): 275-97). Red and white imagery was often associated with sexual violation in relation to the boar, especially to the tusks which often are covered with "foam" (semen) and blood. In Grottfried's *Tristan,* Marjodoc, steward to King Mark, dreams of a boar "foaming at the mouth. . . . Arriving at Mark's chamber [where Isolde lies] he . . . tossed the king's appointed bed in all directions, and fouled the royal linen with his foam." Shortly after, Tristan (the boar in Marjodoc's dream), bloodies the bed clothes, after a vein in his arm breaks open (*Gottfried Von Strassburg: Tristan,* trans. A. T. Hatto [New York: Penguin Books, 1978] 219-42.)

[27] Rabkin ("*Venus and Adonis* and the Myth of Love") notes that "Adonis rejects the animal in himself only to be destroyed by the insentient beast he seeks" (32).

[28] Ovid, *The Metamorphoses,* trans. Frank Justus Miller, vol. 2, bk. 10 (Harvard: Cambridge Univ Press, 1984), ll. 713-16; *Shakespeare's Ovid: Arthur Golding's Translation of the Metamorphoses,* ed. W. H. D. Rouse (New York: W. W. Norton, 1961): "The Boare . . . on *Adonis* did pursew, / Who trembling and retyring back too place of refuge drew, / And hyding in his codds his tusks as farre as he could thrust / He layd him all along for dead upon the yellow dust" (ll. 836-40).

[29] Like Venus, the boar runs the gamut of meanings. On the one hand it represents lust (Miller, 294), the evil effects of lust (Bowers, 9), a surrogate of a lustful Venus (Price, 290-94) or something bent on the destruction of beauty (J. C. Maxwell, ed., *The Poems* (Boston: Cambridge UP, 1969, xiv). On the other hand, the boar is associated with strength and virility (Hatto, 41). Another time it is a "worthy adversary" (Don Cameron Allen, "On *Venus and Adonis*," in *Elizabethan and Jacobean Studies* Oxford: Clarendon Press, 1959, 100-11).

[30] Marcelle Thiébaux, "The Mouth of the Boar as a Symbol in Medieval Literature," *Romance Philology* 22 (1968): 281-99.

James Schiffer (essay date 1997)

SOURCE: "Shakespeare's *Venus and Adonis*: A Lacanian Tragicomedy of Desire," in *Venus and Adonis: Critical Essays*, edited by Philip C. Kolin, Garland Publishing, Inc., 1997, pp. 359-76.

[*In the following essay, Schiffer offers a psychoanalytic reading of* Venus and Adonis *that considers the poem's representation of phallic desire.*]

I

Why? She's neither fish nor flesh. A man knows not where to have her.
(*Henry IV, Part I*, 3.3.128-29)[1]

The subject of Shakespeare's *Venus and Adonis* is desire, its comedy and anguish, desire in all its multifaceted, paradoxical forms: "high desire" (l. 277), "sweet desire" (l. 386), "deep desire" (l. 389), "quick desire" (l. 547), but perhaps most of all "hot desire" (l. 1074), that "coal that must be cooled" (l. 387). Of the twelve uses of the word "desire" in the poem, seven come at the end of lines; of these seven, six rhyme with "fire." Venus' burning passion for Adonis powers the action. The lusty, "sick-thoughted" goddess "pants" and "sweats"; "Her face doth reek and smoke, her blood doth boil" (l. 555). Her heart is in danger of smoldering like "an oven that is stopped" (l. 331). "Enraged" with passion, "desire doth lend her force / Courageously to pluck [Adonis] from his horse" (ll. 29-30). At the end of the poem, discovering Adonis slain, the goddess laments:

> Mine eyes are turned to fire, my heart to lead.
> Heavy heart's lead, melt at mine eyes' red fire!
> So shall I die by drops of hot desire.
> (ll. 1072-74)

As important as fire's quality of searing heat is to Shakespeare's depiction of unfulfilled passion, a second quality of fire (and of desire), its constantly changing form, best describes the style of *Venus and Adonis*: fast and glowing, unpredictable, restlessly shifting throughout the work in diction, imagery, tone, mood, and distince from the protagonists. The poem's many stylistic modulations result, of course, in complex shifts and slippages in meaning, genre, and effects.

For much of its critical history, this complexity has not been appreciated. Faced with the poem's combination of so many disparate elements (Ovidian, neoplatonic, epyllionic, comic, tragic, erotic, moral, allegorical, satiric, elegiac, etc.), several scholars have tended to dismiss the work as a flawed product of Shakespeare's apprenticeship. Thus, Don Cameron Allen declares that the poem is "clearly the result of a young and unfinished artist" (101), while C. S. Lewis complains that *Venus and Adonis* fails to be successfully one thing or the other, either coherently didactic or engagingly erotic (see also Watkins 710; Smith 89; and Bush 139). According to Lewis, Shakespeare's Venus is a "very ill-conceived temptress. She is made so much larger than her victim that she can throw his horse's reins over one arm and tuck him under the other, and knows her art so badly that she threatens, almost in her first words, to 'smother him with kisses.' Certain horrible interviews with voluminous female relatives inevitably recur to mind" (498). Others have held a higher opinion of the poem but have tried to defend it by reducing its complexity, Rufus Putney by arguing the poem's comedy while ignoring its pathos, James Lake by stressing tragedy while overlooking deflating ironies after Adonis is slain. A number of recent critics, beginning with A. C. Hamilton and Kenneth Muir, have been both sensitive to and appreciative of the poem's many sudden shifts in tone and feeling. Muir finds that *Venus and Adonis* is neither "an argument against lust" nor a "straightforward eulogy of sexual love. Almost everything in the poem appears to be ambivalent" (9). This ambivalence, Muir later concludes, "is caused by the poet's own acceptance of conflicting feelings about love" (12). Muir's reading has been reinforced by a number of later critics, among them Norman Rabkin, William Keach, and Heather Dubrow.[2] In fact, Clark Hulse, who presents an iconographic reading in many ways compatible with Muir's, has used the phrase "the new orthodoxy of an ambivalent *Venus and Adonis*" to characterize the seeming consensus among critics over the past three decades (147).[3] Yet this new orthodoxy of ambivalence has left many questions about the poem unanswered. As John Doebler observes, "The problem of redeeming the poem from defectiveness by the discovery of a single 'theme' or 'unified impression,' however complex or 'ambivalent,' has been the unsolved problem of this century" (37; see also Klause 353-56).

Since the subject of *Venus and Adonis* is desire, since many of its meanings are ambiguous, and since its effect is to create a deep ambivalence in its readers, it is surprising that the poem has not received more attention from psychoanalytical critics, though there have been a few studies of this kind, the most notable by Peter Dow Webster, Alan Baer Rothenberg, Coppélia Kahn, and Wayne A. Rebhorn.[4] Webster uses the Jungian archetype of the Universal Mother to describe Venus and to make psychobiographical inferences about Shakespeare. In his opinion, Venus represents Shakespeare's "poetic version of his own infantile fantasy of his own mother" (298). Adonis' preference of the boar over Venus, according to Webster, is Adonis' "projection of his defense against a carefully concealed inner oralism" (303). Rothenberg's Freudian analysis discovers that "through Shakespeare's imagery the attempted seduction of Adonis by Venus is revealed to be substructured by a preoedipal conflict between an overactive, too-loving mother and her resistant nursing infant.... The imagery of seduction becomes the fantasy of an oral rape of a passive infant's mouth by the breast or mouth of his aggressive mother (or nurse), with results that are ultimately fatal to the infant" (3). Kahn draws on post-Freudian ego psychologists Margaret Mahler, Edith Jacobson, Erik Erikson, D. W. Winnicott, and others in her study of male psychosexual development, *Man's Estate: Masculine Identity in Shakespeare*. For her, the main conflict of the poem is "between eros and death fought within the narcissistic self" (22). Adonis' narcissism, Kahn maintains, is "a masculine defense against the fear of women—women perceived as an engulfing maternal presence by a youth not fully separated from that presence" (23). The threat that Venus poses is also the emphasis of Rebhorn, who unlike Kahn, sees Adonis' rejection of Venus not as a sign of stunted or retrograde development but as an understandable reaction to the ravenous, smothering quality of Venus' maternal love; the work "derives its comedy and pathos," he argues, "from playing with a deep-seated male fear of emasculation through infantilization at the hands of a woman" (8).

To my knowledge, no one has yet published a Lacanian reading of *Venus and Adonis*, though with the proliferation of Lacanian Shakespeareans these days, one can never be sure (not that any two Lacanian readings could be the same for long!).* In any case, there are several compelling reasons for viewing *Venus and Adonis* through the lens of Lacanian theory. First of all, like the poem, much of Lacan's work is devoted to the phenomenology of desire, its etiology, its dialectical structure, its significance, and its effects. For Lacan (and here, he could have cited Venus' pursuit of Adonis as an illustration), desire's "paradoxical, deviant, erratic, eccentric, even scandalous character" distinguishes it from need, on the one hand, and from demand (ultimately the demand for love) on the other ("Signification" 286). Desire, he writes, "is neither the appetite for satisfaction, nor the demand for love, but the difference that results from the subtraction of the first from the second, the phenomenon of their splitting *(Spaltung)*" ("Signification" 287). A related idea follows from this definition, one that has important relevance to Shakespeare's poem: the structural impossibility of desire's satisfaction. Desire, according to Lacanian interpreter Valerie Traub, can never be fulfilled because desire is always "substitutive, founded on a lack, and hence, always the desire of an other" (7). In Lacanian psychoanalysis, she explains:

> the individual is constituted simultaneously as a subject, a gender, and sexuality through the entrance into the symbolic order of language. With the insertion of the third term, the phallus, into the imaginary preoedipal relation of mother and child, the child loses its fantasized symbiosis with the mother, falling into a pre-existing order of culture that through its endlessly substitutive chain of signification, enforces an always-divided subjectivity or 'lack-in-being.' The signifier for this lack-in-being is the phallus: first, because, by breaking the imaginary dyad, it inaugurates all subsequent desire as substitutive; and, second, because all subjects, male and female, are psychically castrated, learning the meaning of separation and difference through their alienation into language. (53)

Lacan's notion that desire is governed by castration, "whether in the normal or abnormal" ("Subversion" 323), has intriguing application to *Venus and Adonis,* especially to Adonis' death by a wound to the groin. It is the threat of castration, explains Catherine Belsey, that initially "impels [the subject] to submit to the imperatives of the cultural order and renounce incest" (52). The phallus, meanwhile, is multivalent in its status as a signifier. It designates "as a whole the effects of the signified" (Lacan, "Signification" 285) and embodies "*jouissance* in the dialectic of desire" (Lacan, "Subversion" 319). It is at once "a signifier of the *fiction* of unmediated presence and integrated identity" and "the metaphor for a fragmented and precarious subjectivity" (Traub 54). It represents both the castrating agency of the symbolic order, the *Nom-du-Pere,* and "the unnameable object of desire, the desire of the Other, and it re-presents (stands in place of) the *objet a,* the lost object in the real" (Belsey 63).

II

Backward she pushed him, as she would be thrust . . .

(*Venus and Adonis,* l. 41)

In light of Lacan's notion of the phallus, one notices right away the unusual circumstance, unique in the Shakespearean canon, of the absence of a psychosexually mature, heterosexual male, human or divine, through the entire work (mature, heterosexual male animals are another matter, as we see in the examples of the stallion and the boar). Mars and Titan are alluded to, but as a way of emphasizing what is absent from the present scene, the erect penis of heterosexual male desire (Sheidley 10). Certainly this is the rhetorical context, Adonis' lack of response to her seduction, in which Venus conjures her affair with Mars:

> I have been wooed, as I entreat thee now,
> Even by the stern and direful god of war,
> Whose sinewy neck in battle ne'er did bow,
> Who conquers where he comes in every jar;
> Yet hath he been my captive and my slave,
> And begged for that which thou unasked shalt have.
>
> (ll. 97-102)

Never mind that her boast of enslaving Mars and "Leading him prisoner in a red-rose chain" (l. 110) has the unintended effect of threatening emasculation; this is not the way to win Adonis or allay his fears. She intends her account of her affair with Mars to offer Adonis a model of "normal" male response to her beauty, just as later she appeals to Adonis (again with unintended ironies) to learn from the example of his stallion:

> Thy palfrey, as he should,
> Welcomes the warm approach of sweet desire.
>
> . . . . .
>
> Who sees his true love in her naked bed,
> Teaching the sheets a whiter hue than white,
> But when his glutton eye so full hath fed,
> His other agents aim at like delight?
> Who is so faint that dares not be so bold
> To touch the fire, the weather being cold?
>
> Let me excuse thy courser, gentle boy;
> And learn of him, I heartily beseech thee,
> To take advantage on presented joy.
> Though I were dumb, yet his proceedings teach thee.
>
> (ll. 385-86; 397-406)[5]

This absence of a character embodying the masculine heterosexual response, a situation that Lacan would no doubt recognize as signifying the absence of the phallus, is responsible for many of the poem's most interesting effects and meanings. The phenomenon is similar, yet opposite to the marginalization, absence, disappearance, or destruction of the feminine in several Shakespearean history plays and tragedies. Since Shakespeare wrote his plays for an all-male, mostly adult cast, it is not surprising that each of his dramatic works features adult male characters. Despite the important presence of men in every Shakespearean play, there are scenes in several (and in certain sonnets) that recall in one way or another the dramatic situation in *Venus and Adonis*. Some scenes, for example, emphasize the impossibility of desire's satisfaction because of an inappropriate object of desire; this is the implied situation in Sonnet 20, as well as with Phebe in love with the disguised Rosalind in *As You Like It*, or the proud Countess Olivia in love with the disguised Viola in *Twelfth Night*. Other scenes in the plays remind us of *Venus and Adonis* because they depict "sexual initiatives by women" (Duncan-Jones 499). Cousins to the aggressive Venus can be found in Nell the kitchen wench in pursuit of Dromio of Syracuse in *The Comedy of Errors*, Helena in pursuit of Demetrius in *A Midsummer Night's Dream*, and that very different Helena who substitutes herself into Bertram's bed in *All's Well That Ends Well*. Cleopatra's exchange with the eunuch Mardian after Antony has departed for Rome illustrates the comic potential of a situation from which the phallus is absent, in this case, has just departed:

> *Mardian.* What's Your Highness' pleasure?
> *Cleopatra.* Not now to hear thee sing. I take no pleasure
> In aught an eunuch has. 'Tis well for thee
> That, being unseminared, thy freer thoughts
> May not fly forth of Egypt. Hast thou affections?
> *Mardian.* Yes, gracious madam.
> *Cleopatra.* Indeed?
> *Mardian.* Not in deed, madam, for I can do nothing
> But what indeed is honest to be done.
> Yet have I fierce affections, and think
> What Venus did with Mars.
> *Cleopatra.* O Charmian
> Where think'st thou he is now? Stands he or sits he?
> Or does he walk? Or is he on his horse?
> O happy horse, to bear the weight of Antony!
>
> (*Antony and Cleopatra*, 1.5.9-22)

The absence of the phallus in *Venus and Adonis* makes possible the comedy and the erotics of gender and sex role reversals, reversals that are anticipated in the antitheses and chiasmic inversion (l. 4) of the first stanza:

> Even as the sun with purple-colored face
> Had ta'en his last leave of the weeping morn,
> Rose-cheeked Adonis hied him to the chase.
> Hunting he loved, but love he laughed to scorn.
> Sick-thoughted Venus makes amain unto him,
> And like a bold-faced suitor 'gins to woo him.
>
> (ll. 1-6)

In the vacuum of the absent male, Venus takes charge, becomes the "bold fac'd suitor," while "rose-cheeked Adonis," "more lovely than a man," (l. 9) assumes the role of coy, disdainful maiden.[6] The situation, states Donald G. Watson, dramatizes the "inadequacies of the Petrarchan treatment of amorous experience. . . .

The reversal of the roles of Petrarchan *Frauendienst* in the aggressive female-passive male pattern mocks current fashion: coming at the height of the vogue in sonnets, this must have been thought marvelously witty in itself" (45-46). In changing roles, Venus does not escape the dialectic of desire; she simply occupies a different position within it. Instead of being the object of desire, self-sufficient and unmoved, she becomes the one who desires. Paradoxically, in assuming the conventionally active male role, Venus relinquishes her usual power in love to the passive, unresponsive Adonis. Not just gender but sex roles are turned topsy-turvy, a phenomenon signaled by the inverted mirroring of the letters "V" and "A," letters suggestive of the female and male genitalia. Not only does Venus push Adonis as she would be thrust, but many of the images suggest attempted phallic entry, either by breast or by the mouth as a beak (Rothenberg):

> Even as an empty eagle, sharp by fast,
> Tires with her beak on feathers, flesh, and bone,
> Shaking her wings, devouring all in haste,
> Till either gorge be stuffed or prey be gone,
> Even so she kissed his brow, his cheek, his chin,
> And where she ends she doth anew begin.
>   (ll. 55-60)

Even Venus' loquaciousness has phallic implications. She speaks 537 of the poem's 1,194 lines (Dubrow 27). She pours her rhetorical spirits into Adonis' ear, hoping to screw his courage to the sticking place. But though Venus might wish to be the phallus, she cannot ultimately succeed, no more than Adonis can. All she can do is wish: "Would thou wert as I am, and I a man" (l. 369).

The comedy of the absent phallus reaches its anticlimactic pinnacle when Venus pulls the unwilling Adonis on top of her after he says he intends to "hunt the boar with certain of his friends" (l. 588):

> She sinketh down, still hanging by his neck;
> He on her belly falls, she on her back.
> Now is she in the very lists of love,
> Her champion mounted for the hot encounter.
> All is imaginary she doth prove.
> He will not manage her, although he mount her,
> That worse than Tantalus' is her annoy,
> To clip Elysium and to lack her joy.
>   (ll. 593-600)

As Robert Sheidley explains, "The poem functions as a problem in subtraction. The equation that nicely balances for the horses, when drawn up for Venus and Adonis, obviously lacks one crucial factor which, if present, would allow Venus' hopes and those of the sympathetic reader to be fulfilled: that is, simply, an erect phallus, which Adonis will not and Venus cannot provide" (9-10). Our erotic response to this moment is not doubt a deeply personal matter, determined by our individual sexual preferences and attitudes to sex, as Heather Dubrow observes (62). Heterosexual males may fantasize "being seduced by the goddess of beauty" (Bevington 1561) and wish to provide the missing phallus.[7] In effect, they find themselves in the position of Titan, who:

> . . . tirèd in the midday heat,
> With burning eye did hotly overlook them,
> Wishing Adonis had his team to guide,
> So he were like him, and by Venus' side.
>   (ll. 177-180)

Rather than desire Venus, heterosexual women might well identify with Venus and share her passion for the "tender boy." So, in fact, might homosexual males. Though the degree to which this moment seems comic will probably vary from reader to reader as much as individual erotic responses do, there is something about the image of Tantalus—and even more about the image of an inert Adonis atop a volcanic Venus—that goes beyond comedy and titillation, that goes more deeply, to the very heart of desire, which is always absent, always, it seems, just out of reach, just around the corner, just on the other side of the glass. It is a short jump indeed from Venus' anguish of unfulfilled desire to our own.

Why Adonis does not respond to Venus is one of the unresolvable puzzles of the poem, not because Adonis fails to provide reasons, but because, Iago-like, he provides too many. The overdetermination of Adonis' motives makes it difficult to settle on a single cause: physiological, rational, moral, or unconscious, or a combination of some or all of the above. In Ovid's *Metamorphoses* revenge for his mother's horrible fate (incest with her father and transformation into a tree) apparently motivates Adonis,

> . . . and by and by a man,
> And every day more beawtifull than other he becam.
> That in the end Dame *Venus* fell in love with him: wherby
> He did revenge the outrage of his mothers villanye.
>   (Golding trans., X.602-05),

though it is unclear how he exacts his revenge in Ovid since Adonis does not spurn Venus' advances. True, he fails to listen to Venus' advice about the boar, but surely this error hurts him at lest as much as it hurts Venus. There is, perhaps, a hint of revenge in the phrase "love he laughed to scorn" (l. 4) and in Adonis' boast that his "love to love is but to disgrace it" (l. 412), but this thread is not consistently emphasized throughout the poem. Katherine Duncan-Jones notes "Shakespeare's emphasis on Adonis's youth, which appears possibly even pre-pubertal" (489). That he is still physiologically immature is Adonis' first line of defense:

> Who wears a garment shapeless and unfinished?
> Who plucks the bud before one leaf put forth?
> If springing things be any jot diminished,
> They wither in their prime, prove nothing worth.
> The colt that's backed and burdened being young
> Loseth his pride and never waxeth strong.
>
> (ll. 415-20)

> Measure my strangeness with my unripe years.
> Before I know myself, seek not to know me.
> No fisher but the ungrown fry forbears.
> The mellow plum doth fall; the green sticks fast,
> Or being early plucked is sour to taste.
>
> (ll. 524-28)

Venus' resolve to taste Adonis even though "The tender spring upon [his] tempting lip / Shows [him] unripe" (ll. 127-28) also supports the idea that Adonis is not yet physically ready for a sexual encounter.

Elsewhere Adonis seems not so much incapable of love as hostile to it for fairly rational—that is, practical—reasons. Thus he calls love "a life in death / That laughs and weeps, and all but with a breath," (ll. 413-14) and declares that his "heart longs not to groan, / But soundly sleeps, while now it sleeps alone" (ll. 785-86). Finally, he resorts to the moral argument, based upon the distinction between love and lust:

> I hate not love, but your device in love,
> That lends embracements unto every stranger,
> You do it for increase. O strange excuse,
> When reason is the bawd to lust's abuse!
>
> Call it not love, for Love to heaven is fled,
> Since sweating Lust on earth usurped his name . . .
>
> (ll. 789-94)

The problem, as Kenneth Muir points out, is that this moral argument, coming as late as it does, strikes us as an afterthought rather than a deeply held conviction (7). Then, there are the unconscious motives, or at least motives Adonis never states. Under this category comes the explanation that Adonis fails to respond because he is locked in a narcissistic desire to "grow unto himself" (l. 1180), either as a normal stage in the process of maturation or as an abnormal case of arrested development. The latter seems to be Coppélia Kahn's position: the narcissist's "primary need," she argues, "is to defend against sexual involvement in order to protect the fragile inner self. This defense is ironically self-destructive" (32-33). Jonathan Bate offers a different unconscious motive for Adonis' resistance, the fear of incest. After observing that Venus behaves as both a lover and a mother to Adonis, he argues that "such juxtapositions of sexuality and parenting suggest that Adonis is forced to re-enact, with generational roles reversed, his mother's incestuous affair" (84). Or is Adonis' motive neither narcissism nor fear of incest, but rather a quite understandable reaction to the role reversals brought on by Venus's hot pursuit? Perhaps he simply wishes to avoid sacrificing his "adult, male autonomy" (Rebhorn 9). Perhaps he chooses to be the active rather than the passive party, the hunter rather than the hunted, as a way of preserving—or even attaining—his emerging sense of manhood.

From Venus' point of view the reasons for Adonis' rejection are less important than the fact of his refusal. As with Adonis, Shakespeare does away with Ovid's explanation of Venus's motive—that she is accidentally grazed by one of Cupid's arrows; only then did the "beawty of the lad / [Inflaam] hir" (Golding trans., X.611). In Shakespeare's poem we join the action *in medias res* with Venus already "inflaamd." What Shakespeare stresses is that for Venus this is a first-time experience, the experience of the pain of mortal desire. Her love for Adonis is thus an incarnation and a submission (possibly involuntary) to her own law:

> Poor queen of love, in thy own law forlorn,
> To love a cheek that smiles at thee in scorn!
>
> (ll. 251-252)

Her law, like Lacan's, dictates that desire can never truly be satisfied, because desire is always for absence, for lack, for what is not there. The parallel has been made between Adonis and Ovid's Narcissus, but a closer comparison exists between Venus and Narcissus. A disappointed male lover prays that Narcissus "may once feele fierce *Cupids* fire / As I doe now, and yet not joy the things he doth desire" (Golding trans., III.505-06). Surely this is Venus's fate: "She's Love, she loves, and yet she is not loved" (l. 610). If Adonis were like Mars, or like his stallion, if he actually had an erect phallus and desired Venus, one doubts that he would appeal to the goddess. She is attracted to his feminine, childish qualities, to his sulking refusal, to his very inability to respond.

III

It's a question of the phallus, and that's why he will never be able to strike it, until the moment when he has made the complete sacrifice—without wanting to, moreover—of all narcissistic attachments, i.e., when he is mortally wounded and knows it.

—Lacan, "Desire and the Interpretation of Desire in *Hamlet*" (51)

We come now to the boar, that "beste noire" for critics, the "most puzzling object in the poem and the most controversial" (Merrix 117). Several critics, including Don Cameron Allen and Kenneth Muir, agree that the boar represents death, which seems reasonable enough. But death for what? In Ovid, Adonis dies after apparently consummating his relationship with Venus; therefore, in *The Metamorphoses* his death could be construed as a punishment for lust. Since Shakespeare's Adonis does not give in to Venus, however, his punishment is more often viewed as a punishment for turning away from sexuality and love (Muir 5-7; Sheidley 5; Kahn 42). For Gordon Williams, however, Adonis' death is not a punishment, but "a consummation devoutly to be wished" (770), while Hereward T. Price believes it represents "the destruction of something exquisite by what is outrageously vile" (277). In his view the boar stands for "the complete irrationality of evil" (277). Several interpreters have associated the boar with Venus, or with Adonis' projection of Venus' lust, an identification she herself invites when she imagines the boar's assault as a kind of "homosexual rape" (Barber and Wheeler 147):

> If he did see his face, why then I know
> He thought to kiss him, and hath killed him
>   so.
>
> 'Tis true, 'tis true! Thus was Adonis slain:
> He ran upon the boar with his sharp spear,
> Who did not whet his teeth at him again,
> But by a kiss thought to persuade him there;
>   And, nuzzling in his flank, the loving swine
>   Sheathed unaware the tusk in his soft groin.
>
> Had I been toothed like him, I must confess,
> With kissing him I should have killed him first.
>   (*Venus and Adonis*, ll. 1109-1118)

While this speech seems to reveal Venus' affinity with the boar, it actually shows only her affinity with the boar's desire. As A. T. Hatto correctly observes, the boar "is a symbol of overmastering virility" (354). It is Venus' masculine rival, perhaps, but not her double. Venus, to her regret, is not "toothed like him"; consequently, the "boar establishes a kind of contact such as Venus never had" (Asals 46). Peter Dow Webster also sees the boar as distinctively masculine, a version of the castrating "archetypal primal father" (300). Finally, concluding this line of phallic inquiry, William E. Sheidley contends that the boar is "the locus of [Adonis'] missing phallic impulse," the return in objective form of what Adonis has repressed (10). Instead of yielding to Venus as he should, Sheidley argues, Adonis "perversely pursues to its end a policy of self-castration" (11).

One can easily imagine Lacan delighting in the multiplicity of meanings here, the almost endless substitutions of symbol and metaphor, the almost endless play of signifier and signified. Of the serival theories about the boar, few, he would observe, are mutually exclusive. Like Webster and Alan Baer Rothenberg, he would recognize in Venus' mixture of maternal and erotic passion a clue to the preoedipal configuration of the poem. Lacan would also probably see Adonis' wound to his groin as a castration, perhaps as a punishment for threatened incest ("Signification" 282).[8] But for Lacan, the physical castration is only a metaphor for psychic castration, the result of the advent of signification, the subject's initiation into the symbolic order of language. Lacan would agree with Webster that the boar symbolizes the castrating father, though in Lacanian terms, the boar would more properly be termed the *Nom-du-Pere*, the Name-of-the-Father, representative of the symbolic order, the Other (as locus of signification), the Law. At the same time, as Sheidley points out, the boar stands for Adonis' missing phallic impulse. In Lacanian terms, the boar represents the return of the repressed phallus, signifying both the agency of castration (the *Nom-du-Pere*) and the illusion of potency and completeness which Adonis has lost:

> This is our starting point: through his relationship to the signifier, the subject is deprived of something of himself, of his very life, which has assumed the value of that which binds him to the signifier. The phallus is our term for the signifier of his alienation in signification. When the subject is deprived of this signifier, a particular object becomes for him the object of desire. (Lacan, "Desire" 28)

The object for Venus, the impossible object of desire, is Adonis; for Adonis, that object is the boar. In this "profoundly enigmatic" process, Lacan writes, "[s]omething becomes an object of desire when it takes the place of what by its very nature remains concealed from the subject: that self-sacrifice, that pound of flesh which is mortgaged *[engagé]* in his relationship to the signifier" ("Desire" 28).

Adonis' death represents his escape from the dialectic of desire. The only end of desire is death—or retreat. For Venus, her earlier inability to seduce the boy becomes the permanent impossibility of satisfaction. The prophecy she utters is interesting for a variety of reasons. First, as many have observed, her predictions are as much about the past as about the future; they describe what has just happened to her as much as they forecast the fate of love on earth. For this reason, it is possible to construe the prophecy as a mean-spirited curse on mortal love (if she cannot have her love, then no one will):

> Since thou art dead, lo, here I prophesy:
> Sorrow on love hereafter shall attend.
> It shall be waited on with jealousy,
> Find sweet beginning but unsavory end,

VENUS AND ADONIS.

Vilia miretur vulgus, mihi flavus Apollo
Pocula Castalia plenâ ministret aquâ.
          Ovid. Amor. l. 1. El. 15.

The title page to Venus and Adonis *from Rowe's 1714 edition of Shakespeare's Works.*

Ne'er settled equally, but high or low,
That all love's pleasure shall not match his
  woe.
              (ll. 1135-40)

It shall be cause of war and dire events
And set dissention twixt the son and sire,
Subject and servile to all discontents,
As dry combustious matter is to fire.
Sith in his prime Death doth my love destroy,
They that love best their loves shall not enjoy.
              (ll. 1159-64)

The words "Since" (l. 1135) and "Sith" (l. 1163) certainly suggest a causal relationship. Even more than the spirit of revenge, however, the speech expresses sad resignation, a submission to her own law, which is greater than she, beyond either her control or comprehension (which is why the speech seems more a sad prediction than a vengeful curse). It is in this spirit of resignation that she withdraws at the end of the poem from the realm of mortal desire:

Thus, weary of the world, away she hies
And yokes her silver doves, by whose swift
  aid
Their mistress mounted through the empty
  skies
In her light chariot quickly is conveyed,
Holding their course to Paphos, where their
  queen
Means to immure herself and not be seen.
              (ll. 1189-94)

Venus' prophecy-curse also reminds us of the relationship throughout the poem between language and desire. Desire makes Venus voluble—as we have seen, her speeches dominate the poem. It is through language, through rhetorical virtuosity, that she pleads her case to Adonis. Language also provides an outlet for her frustrated yearnings; as the narrator says, "Free vent of words love's fire doth assuage" (l. 334). Most important of all, language substitutes for the object of desire, who is himself merely the *petite objet a*, the lost object in the real. Yet words are a poor consolation for the loss of Adonis, even for an Adonis she never possessed. Like Caliban, Venus might well say, "You taught me language, and my profit on 't/Is I know how to curse" (*The Tempest*, 1.2.366-67). The very conditions that make language necessary make desire's fulfillment impossible.

Like the boar, the purple flower "checkered with white" that rises from Adonis' blood is rich in multivalent meanings. In Ovid, Venus causes the metamorphosis (Golding trans., X.847-863), but not in Shakespeare's poem: Venus merely discovers it on the ground. Although she later addresses the flower as the offspring of her love with Adonis, at first she compares the flower with Adonis himself, suggesting that he has been metamorphosed (of course, in the Shakespearean economy of desire, procreation is a kind of metamorphic perpetuation of the self):

She bows her head, the new-sprung flower to
  smell,
Comparing it to her Adonis' breath,
And says within her bosom it shall dwell,
Since he himself is reft from her by death.
She crops the stalk, and in the breach appears
Green drooping sap, which she compares to
  tears.
              (*Venus and Adonis,* ll. 1171-76)

The moment is rich in ironies. First of all, as Coppélia Kahn points out, "as a flower, [Adonis] can 'grow unto himself' as he wanted to in life, and Venus can possess him totally and forever as she could not before" (44-45). The irony of her plucking the flower has not been lost on earlier scholars either. This is a fulfillment of Adonis' earlier question, "Who plucks the bud before one leaf put forth?" (l. 416), as well as "a reenactment of her plucking Adonis off his horse" (Asals 49). In Hereward T. Price's opinion, "Adonis was twice butchered, once in blindness by the boar, and the second time in equal blindness but no less effectively by Venus. I know of no irony in literature so savage as this" (295). In Oedipal terms, the plucking is a second castration. The child must navigate the Scylla and Charybdis of the emasculating mother and the castrating father. Poor Adonis shipwrecks twice. The phallus thus has yet another incarnation in the flower, and this is true in the Lacanian sense of the term as well as the Freudian. The flower, itself a substitution, stands for the process of substitution and signification that is language, necessary as a means of representing what is absent or lost. The flower's difference from Adonis is the gap between signifier and signified, the gap in which we all must live. Its significance is the reality of absence, of insufficiency, of alienation in language. The flower in this phallic sense (Lacan's sense of the term) is, finally, the poem *Venus and Adonis* itself, forged in the dialectic of desire, its petals of meaning spread upon the winds of endless metaphor and metonymy, endless difference and *différance*, endless deferral of the phallocentric "right reading" (which is the reader's desire), a poem that "laughs and weeps, and all but with a breath."[9]

Notes

* Just a few months after completing this essay, I read with great interest Catherine Belsey's "Love as Tromp-l'oeil: Taxonomies of Desire in *Venus and Adonis*" in the Fall 1995 (46:3) issue of *Shakespeare Quarterly*. Belsey's essay is reprinted in this volume.

[1] All citations from Shakespeare are to *The Complete Works of Shakespeare*, 4th ed., ed. David Bevington.

[2] Rabkin states that "in portraying the genesis of love," the poem explains love's "tragicomic complementarity in the fallen world in which we live" (151); Keach argues that "Shakespeare's handling of the mythological materials is . . . deeply, at times even confusingly, ambivalent" (53) and that the poem's "seriousness—its insight into the turbulence and frustration of sexual love—is inseparable from its comedy and its entertaining eroticism" (60); Dubrow calls *Venus and Adonis* a "problem epyllion" (78). See also Rebhorn, Watson, Lindheim, and Fienberg.

[3] In a footnote, Hulse cites A. Robin Bowers and David Beauregard as two recent critics who disagree with the "new orthodoxy of an ambivalent *Venus and Adonis*" (147-48).

[4] Many studies of *Venus and Adonis*—most in fact—are *psychological* (as opposed to psychoanalytical) in their attempt to interpret the motivations of the two main characters. The studies I refer to (except perhaps for Rebhorn's), however, are grounded in the specific ideas of modern or contemporary psychoanalytical theorists.

[5] See Robert P. Miller for a view of the horses as representative of the lower appetite ungoverned by reason.

[6] See J. D. Jahn for an analysis of Adonis' coyness; in general, I think Jahn overstates the case for Adonis' *deliberate* coquetry and tends to blame the victim rather than the sexual aggressor. However, I agree with Jahn's emphasis on the way Adonis' passivity "engenders" Venus' passion (14).

[7] The original audience—the Earl of Southampton and his circle of friends—was presumably mostly male, though not necessarily heterosexual; see Smith (88) and Duncan-Jones (485-86).

[8] Lacan might observe as well that the boar's disruption of the mother-son relationship has its parallel in the murderous intrusion of Macbeth's henchmen into the scene between Lady Macduff and her son in *Macbeth* (4.2) and in the startling return of the Ghost in the closet scene of *Hamlet* (3.4). The Zeffirelli film version of *Hamlet* does a superb job of capturing Hamlet's guilty terror when the Ghost reappears (at the very moment that Hamlet kisses Gertrude on the mouth).

[9] The image of a poem as a flower was a commonplace of Elizabethan poetry. See, for example, George Gascoigne's *A Hundred Sundry Flowers* (1573).

Works Cited

Allen, Don Cameron. "On *Venus and Adonis*." *Elizabethan and Jacobean Studies Presented to Frank Percy Wilson*. Oxford: Clarendon, 1959. 100-111.

Asals, Heather. "*Venus and Adonis:* The Education of a Goddess." *Studies in English Literature* 13 (1973): 31-51.

Barber, C. L., and Richard P. Wheeler. *The Whole Journey: Shakespeare's Power of Development*. Berkeley: U of California P, 1986.

Bate, Jonathan. "Sexual Perversity in *Venus and Adonis*." *Yearbook of English Studies* 23 (1993): 80-92.

Beauregard, David N. "*Venus and Adonis:* Shakespeare's Representation of the Passions." *Shakespeare Studies* 8 (1975): 83-98.

Belsey, Catherine. *Desire: Love Stories in Western Culture*. Oxford: Blackwell, 1994.

Bevington, David. "Introduction to *Venus and Adonis*." *The Complete Works of Shakespeare*. 4th ed. New York: HarperCollins, 1992. 1560-61.

Bowers, A. Robin. "'Hard Armours' and 'Delicate Amours' in Shakespeare's *Venus and Adonis*." *Shakespeare Studies* 12 (1979): 1-23.

Bush, Douglas. *Mythology and the Renaissance Tradition*. 1932; New York: Pageant, 1957.

Doebler, John. "The Many Faces of Love: Shakespeare's *Venus and Adonis*." *Shakespeare Studies* 16 (1983): 33-43.

Dubrow, Heather. *Captive Victors: Shakespeare's Narrative Poems and Sonnets*. Ithaca: Cornell UP, 1987.

Duncan-Jones, Katherine. "Much Ado with Red and White: The Earliest Readers of Shakespeare's *Venus and Adonis*." *Review of English Studies* 44 (1993): 479-501.

Fienberg, Nona. "Thematics of Value in *Venus and Adonis*." *Criticism* 31 (1989): 21-32.

Hamilton, A. C. "*Venus and Adonis*." *Studies in English Literature* 1 (1961): 1-15.

Hatto, A. T. "*Venus and Adonis*—and the Boar." *Modern Language Review* 41 (1946): 353-61.

Hulse, S. Clark. *Metamorphic Verse: The Elizabethan Minor Epic*. Princeton: Princeton UP, 1981.

Jahn, J.D. "The Lamb of Lust: The Role of Adonis in Shakespeare's *Venus and Adonis*." *Shakespeare Studies* 6 (1970): 11-25.

Kahn, Coppélia. *Man's Estate: Masculine Identity in Shakespeare*. Berkeley: U of California P, 1981.

Keach, William. *Elizabethan Erotic Narratives: Irony and Pathos in the Ovidian Poetry of Shakespeare, Marlowe, and Their Contemporaries*. New Brunswick: Rutgers UP, 1977.

Klause, John. "*Venus and Adonis*: Can We Forgive Them?" *Studies in Philology* 85 (1988): 353-77.

Lacan, Jacques. "Desire and the Interpretation of Desire in *Hamlet*." Ed. Jacques-Alain Miller. Trans. James Hulbert. *Literature and Psychoanalysis*. Ed. Shoshana Felman. Baltimore: Johns Hopkins UP, 1982. 11-52.

———. "The Signification of the Phallus." *Écrits*. Trans. Alan Sheridan. 1966. New York: Norton, 1977. 281-91.

———. "The Subversion of the Subject and the Dialectic of Desire in the Freudian Unconscious." *Écrits*. Trans. Alan Sheridan. 1966. New York: Norton, 1977. 292-325.

Lake, James H. "Shakespeare's Venus: An Experiment in Tragedy." *Shakespeare Quarterly* 25 (1974): 351-55.

Lewis, C. S. *English Literature in the Sixteenth Century*. Oxford: Clarendon, 1954.

Lindheim, Nancy. "The Shakespearean *Venus and Adonis*." *Shakespeare Quarterly* 37 (1986): 190-203.

Merrix, Robert P. "The 'Beste Noire': The Medieval Role of the Boar in *Venus and Adonis*." *Upstart Crow* 11 (1991): 117-30.

Miller, Robert P. "Venus, Adonis, and the Horses." *English Literary History* 19 (1952): 250-64.

Muir, Kenneth. "*Venus and Adonis*: Comedy or Tragedy?" *Shakespearean Essays*. Eds. Alwin Thayer and Norman Sanders. Knoxville: U Tennessee P, 1964. 1-13.

Ovid. *Shakespeare's Ovid Being Arthur Golding's Translation of the Metamorphoses*. Ed. W. H. D. Rouse. London: Centaur, 1961.

Price, Hereward T. "The Function of Imagery in *Venus and Adonis*." *Papers of the Michigan Academy of Science, Arts, and Letters* 31 (1945): 275-297.

Putney, Rufus. "*Venus Agonistes*." *University of Colorado Studies* 4 (1953): 52-66.

Rabkin, Norman. *Shakespeare and the Common Understanding*. New York: Free Press, 1967.

Rebhorn, Wayne A. "Temptation in Shakespeare's *Venus and Adonis*." *Shakespeare Studies* 11 (1978): 1-19.

Rothenberg, Alan Baer. "The Oral Rape Fantasy and the Rejection of the Mother in the Imagery of Shakespeare's *Venus and Adonis*." *Psychoanalytic Quarterly* 40 (1971): 447-68.

Shakespeare, William. *The Complete Works of Shakespeare*. 4th ed. Ed. David Bevington. New York: HarperCollins, 1992.

Sheidley, William E. "'Unless It Be a Boar': Love and Wisdom in Shakespeare's *Venus and Adonis*." *Modern Language Quarterly* 35 (1974): 3-15.

Smith, Hallett. *Elizabethan Poetry*. 1952; Ann Arbor, Michigan: Ann Arbor Paperback, 1968.

Traub, Valerie. *Desire and Anxiety: Circulations of Sexuality in Shakespearean Drama.* London: Routledge, 1992.

Watkins, W. B. C. "Shakespeare's Banquet of Sense." *Southern Review* 7 (1942): 710.

Watson, Donald G. "The Contrarieties of *Venus and Adonis.*" *Studies in Philology* 75 (1978): 32-63.

Webster, Peter Dow. "A Critical Fantasy or Fugue." *American Imago* 6 (1949): 297-309.

Williams, Gordon. "The Coming of Age of Shakespeare's Adonis." *Modern Language Review* 78 (1983): 769-76.

Zeffirelli, Franco, dir. *Hamlet.* Los Angeles: Warner, 1990.

THEMES

John Klause (essay date 1988)

SOURCE: "*Venus and Adonis*: Can We Forgive Them?" in *Studies in Philology,* Vol. LXXXV, No. 3, Summer, 1988, pp. 353-77.

[*In the following essay, Klause discusses the theme of forgiveness in* Venus and Adonis, *tracing the related comic, ironic, and ambivalent qualities of the poem.*]

> "We may pity, though not pardon thee."
> —The Comedy of Errors
>
> "Pardon's the word to all."
> —Cymbeline
>
> "Nothing to be done."
> —Waiting for Godot

It became for Matthew Arnold a matter of regret that he had created in *Empedocles on Etna* a situation "in which there is everything to be endured, nothing to be done"[1]—his dissatisfaction arising from his belated intuition that the helpless suffering portrayed in the poem might lame the spirit that contemplated it. In these latter days we are more inclined to find some value in futility. Many critics have come to believe that poets, whatever the fate of their characters, can do no better than to lead their *readers* into a state of helplessness, to have them endure without recourse not only the finality of what passes before them, but the recalcitrance of contradiction in the meaning of facts or events. No greater compliment, it seems, may be paid to authors ancient or modern than the observation that they have discovered and portrayed an indissoluble ambiguity; for such a discovery is more likely to be closer to the complex truth of our condition than any suggestion that life or judgment might be simple. We should not be surprised, then, that the rescue of Shakespeare's *Venus and Adonis* from the critical disrepute that it once suffered has been undertaken through attempts to demonstrate that the poem embodies a multivalency of meanings leading nowhere beyond itself.

Although some readers have denied or overlooked the conflicting purposes of *Venus and Adonis,* finding the poem to be uniformly comic,[2] or satiric,[3] or tragic,[4] a majority of recent commentators has determined, with evident justice, that there is a doubleness in the tone of the work and in the assessments evoked by its characters and action. To many, this ambiguity has seemed mere confusion, an embarrassing aesthetic or moral defect. Douglas Bush, for instance, believed that the poem failed to achieve any definite literary character: "for an orgy of the senses it is too unreal, for a decorative pseudoclassic picture it has too much homely realism."[5] W. B. C. Watkins considered it "symptomatic of [a] lack of perfect control" that "the humor in *Venus and Adonis* is sporadic and incidental rather than interfused throughout: Shakespeare wavers between taking himself too seriously and not seriously enough."[6] In search of a vision, whether moral or immoral, within the poem, C. S. Lewis could find none, remarking that *Venus and Adonis* succeeds neither at titillating nor at arousing disgust.[7]

The "new orthodoxy" of "pluralism"[8] that has arisen to answer these complaints ("new," at least, as developing something of a consensus about *this* poem) transforms matter for blame into grounds for praise, insisting that the "ambivalence" in the characters of Venus and Adonis—which leads us to see them as at once types and individuals, as figures grand and gauche, sympathetic and repulsive, admirable and laughable, splendidly wholesome and horribly tainted—is but an honest reflection of things as they are. Is not love in fact a transcendental virtue and a disease? Is not beauty fire and ice? May not integrity be narcissistic? May not the maternal both nourish and kill? Cannot a goddess prove a doxy, and the object of divine attentions a somewhat odious prig? Poets who believe in the compossibility of such opposites and who in the forms of their art make provision for ambivalence may be commended. William Keach has reminded us that from Ovid, Shakespeare's predecessor and partial model, we have received examples of erotic myths treated quite convincingly with a blend of affection, cruelty, humor, horror, solemnity, and nonchalance.[9] With Norman Rabkin we can applaud Shakespeare the dramatist when his plays offer the spectacle of "absolute values contradicted by other values that paradoxically turn out to be equally absolute."[10]

The serviceableness of the pluralistic approach may be readily acknowledged. While providing a rationale for the growing consensus about the work's success, it allows *Venus and Adonis* to be read as a whole, and not just in the moments when the poem offers comedy or pathos or morality or a spectacle of frustration or a "banquet of sense." Yet a search for the complexities of ambivalence does not take us as far as we might go towards appreciating what is at stake in Shakespeare's poem. The readings of *Venus and Adonis* that point to its irresolvable tensions almost invariably assume that interpretation of the work can lead no farther than to an "awareness" of contradiction, our response thus being imprisoned in the intellect, to languish there (if we may misappropriate some words of Shakespeare) "between . . . mighty opposites," where "function / Is smothered in surmise." One may choose, of course, to stop at such an impasse; but judgment need not be defeated by contrariety, and judgment may lead to action that is more than an acquiescence of the mind.

If Venus and Adonis are part of a Nature that is (as the poem says) with itself "at strife,"[11] this fact can be welcomed insofar as it is comic, lamented or protested insofar as it is tragic. (No one has made a serious case that Shakespeare did, or that anyone else should, consider it absurd: that is, comic and tragic and neither, all in the same respect.) Should the balance between contradictions in the poem's meanings be perfect (in *Venus and Adonis* it does not appear so), the antinomies can only stand, while we may successively smile, grieve, and complain, or sit baffled, unsure how to combine responses to an ambiguous condition. When the characters themselves, however, elicit contrary judgments, perplexity need never be our ultimate reaction. To combine reproach and admiration by proffering each insofar as a character deserves it clarifies rather than confounds judgment. And even if the line separating merit from defect is not entirely clear, or if neither praise nor blame outweighs the other, there is a moral perspective, most familiar to Shakespeare, comprehensive enough to accommodate in a single definitive response the need to scorn and admire, condemn and bless. It is a perspective that countenances forgiveness.

This proposal obviously places one on the side of the moralists who believe that action in *Venus and Adonis* must be related in some way to ideals, and that, judged by a standard of perfection, reality is found wanting. At the same time, such a reading, suggesting that pressure from the ideal does not in the poem encourage a simple demand for justice, makes understandable the dissatisfaction of some critics with the poem's cloudy or less than "rigorous" morality.[12]

The uneasiness is not unlike that which many feel before Shakespeare's "comedies of forgiveness"[13] or his meditations on the quality of mercy. Indeed, plays like *The Two Gentlemen of Verona, Much Ado About Nothing, All's Well that Ends Well, Measure for Measure,* and *Cymbeline* (to name only a few in which forgiving is crucial) leave us to wonder not only about the aesthetic propriety of dramatizing a pardon quickly and almost gratuitously bestowed, but about the moral legitimacy of such acts of pardon. Shakespeare knows well that forgiveness is a discomfiting virtue, and at times, no doubt, he intends to disturb the ethical complacency of the righteous by insisting on the validity of the more radical paradoxes of mercy. Even so, it appears to be *madness* that drives Lear to the claim that "None do offend, none, I say none, I'll able 'em" (4.6.168). And although Hamlet can speak grandly about forbearance—"Use every man after his desert, and who should 'scape whipping?"—the critic's voice of common sense must be heard in opposition to the thought of a universal redemptive leveling: "We must be reminded like [Hamlet] that it is his role finally to bring about a justice in which all *are* used according to their deserts. It would be charitable to forgive Claudius the crime he so regrets; it would also be unthinkable for Hamlet to do so." At most, it seems, thoughts of pardon may produce only one of two "mighty opposites" and cannot guarantee the triumph of either. "We like to think that justice can be tempered with mercy, but in *Hamlet* Shakespeare presents the two principles as mutually irrelevant."[14] In Shakespeare's *Sonnets,* the Poet's forgiveness of the Friend is so strained as to be vexing, ultimately failing both in its strategic ends and in its continuance.[15] The absolution of Bertram in *All's Well* and of Angelo in *Measure for Measure* (not to say, of Proteus in *Two Gentlemen*) might well be thought outrageous, or at least perplexing "in the extreme." Perhaps, then, a reader who approaches *Venus and Adonis* with the will to pardon, with an inclination to "green o'er [the] bad" (Sonnet 112), should not be placed in the moral camp after all.

Before considering the problem of forgiveness in itself, however, we must first come to see why (for the answer is not immediately obvious) forgiveness is in fact at issue in Shakespeare's poem. Its presence as an issue may become evident in contrast with its absence in the work most frequently set as a foil to *Venus and Adonis,* Marlowe's *Hero and Leander.*

In Marlowe's poem, there is little to be forgiven. This is not to say that its hero and heroine remain untouched by criticism or unworthy of sympathy. Both Hero and Leander can be clumsily devious, and their love, always naive, is on occasion silly, cruel, and selfish. At the same time, their naiveté, their helplessness in the grip of forces they little understand, the frankness of their eroticism after the awkward and perhaps empty ceremonies of seduction have been abandoned, together with the sense given of the imminence of their doom— all of these things work towards pathos. Yet Marlowe, or the narrator, seems content to charge Hero and Leander with folly rather than with crime; and his sympathy merely coexists with his critical assessment of the characters—leading to no exculpation, for in this case exculpation is not especially germane. There is upon Hero's "kirtle blue" the "blood of wretched lovers slain" (1.15-16),[16] and many would-be suitors have "died" in merely "thinking" on her "scornful" denials (1.22-30). But the stains on her clothing turn out to be only blood of the turtledoves that she mindlessly sacrifices at the altar of Venus—whose chaste "nun" she is (1.45, 158), oblivious to all irony; and her scorn seems as unconscious as a child's. In his rhetorical assault on Hero's chastity Leander sounds as "bold" and "sharp" and unprincipled a "sophister" as Comus (1.177-328). But we soon learn that he presents his speech in blithe ignorance of the sexual facts of life (2.51-54), in all probability without a conscience developed enough to harbor corruption. The lovers participate in "amorous rites" that have a sinister side:

> And every kiss to her was as a charm,
> And to Leander as a fresh alarm,
> So that the truce was broke, and she alas
> (Poor silly maiden) at his mercy was.
> Love is not full of pity (as men say)
> But deaf and cruel where he means to prey.
> Even as a bird, which in our hands we wring,
> Forth plungeth, and oft flutters with her wing,
> She trembling strove; this strife of hers (like that
> Which made the world) another world begat
> Of unknown joy. Treason was in her thought,
> And cunningly to yield herself she sought.
>
> (2.283-94)

Yet whatever terror lurks in the passion here (and the "strife" is deemed creative in its violence), Hero and Leander are not condemned for submitting to it. Leander's aggression and Hero's "Treason" are hardly presented as crimes. The lovers are simply too unripe, too unaware to be thought of as sinners; and in any case we sense that the narrator has no higher hopes for them than that they "might enjoy each other, and be blest" (1.380).

The real "criminals" of the piece are the gods, whose petulance, envy, cruelty, and lust are quite adult. Divinities like Mercury (an "insolent commanding lover" [1.409]), Jove (whose reign is notable for "Murder, rape, war, lust and treachery" [1.457]), and Neptune (whose jealousy, we foresee, will produce tragedy) belong to a metaphysical sphere that places them officially beyond the need for pardon—their "incests, riots, rapes" are not horrible but "heady" (1.144)—and unofficially (because, one hopes, such critical detachment in the poet is ironical) beyond the narrator's will to absolve them.

The narrator is quite firm in his judgments. And there is a hardness, a brittleness about his poem, an intellectual and emotional toughness that finds its counterpart in the imagery. The setting is filled with stony, metallic things: Venus' temple has walls of jasper, a crystal floor, a silver altar; and Hero's tower stands upon a rock. Suggesting a kind of sclerosis in nature, the sky seems "enamell'd"; the sea is "strew'd with pearl" and with "low coral groves" that are heaped with "heavy gold." Even the body comes close to hardening: Hero's costume contains stones, silver shells, coral, pearl, and gold. Her body is "silver," her tears turn to "liquid pearl." Leander's skin and Hero's breasts are "ivory." Neptune appears "sapphire-visaged"—in color, of course, but we think of texture as well. Hero's virginity is a "gem," her nakedness reminding her lover of the gold of Dis.

We have here not the baroquely solemn passion of the Song of Solomon ("His hands are as gold rings set with beryl: his belly as bright ivory overlaid with sapphires. His legs are as pillars of marble, set upon sockets of fine gold" [5:14-15]), but the comic impassiveness of a poet more concerned with principle than with character. Marlowe's intention, we might say, is on the one hand to strip love of the falsifications of "ceremony" (as Chapman realized when he tried to restore the claims of "Ceremony" in his continuation of the poem) and on the other to remove love from the realm of the "divine" by showing divinity *so* unceremonious as to be disreputable. Love is left a diminished thing, yet an authentic reality that can survive the attack of comic irony. The lovers too can survive it, insofar as they manage to retain our admiration and sympathy. Hero and Leander do not, however, seem as important in themselves as they are as proof of the poet's superior insight.

The narrator is a constant, conspicuous, toughminded presence. He knows the characters much better than they know themselves. He fills the poem with aphorisms, clinical observations to be taken with varying degrees of seriousness, providing the dead pan that makes for comedy:

> It lies not in our power to love or hate,
> For will in us is overruled by fate.
>
> (1.167-68)

> Maids are not won by brutish force and might,
> But speeches full of pleasure and delight.
>
> (1.419-20)

> 'Tis wisdom to give much, a gift prevails
> When deep persuading oratory fails.
>
> (2.225-26)

His is the eye that winks to underscore the humor in such tricks as the slippery pronoun and the comic rhymes of:

> the more she strived,
> The more a gentle pleasing heat revived,
> Which taught him all that elder lovers know.

And now the same 'gan so to scorch and glow,
As in plain terms (yet cunningly) he craved it;
Love always makes those eloquent that have it.
She, with a kind of granting, put him by it,
And ever as he thought himself most nigh it,
Like to the tree of Tantalus she fled,
And, seeming lavish, saved her maidenhead.

(2.67-76)

The narrator's wit preserves the distance between himself and his characters, maintaining the inequality between a worldly-wise observer and the flawed, amusing, winning, and pitiable lovers whom he contemplates. The wit is of a kind to protect Hero and Leander from ignominy, while making likely that in their faults they will be accorded no more than sympathetic tolerance.

The suggestion has been made that in *Venus and Adonis* Shakespeare has given us ultimately the same kind of poem as Marlowe's, each work permeated with Ovidian ambiguity—which is conveyed in *Hero and Leander* (as in Ovid's *Amores* and *Ars Amatoria*) by an "intrusive, highly self-conscious and self-dramatizing narrator," and in *Venus and Adonis* (as in the *Metamorphoses*) by a narrator "unobtrusive [and] unselfconscious."[17] There are between the two works, however, fundamental differences in tone and vision that an appeal to Ovidian paradigms cannot resolve.

The different stories, indeed, require different settings, one urban, the other sylvan. But whereas Marlowe chooses to give special emphasis to the gem-like or metallic hardness and coolness of his scene, Shakespeare takes pains to make the world of *Venus and Adonis* softness and heat. Hero's body is a fort, Venus' is a deer-park. Instead of Marlovian torsos of ivory, silver, and gold, Shakespeare portrays warm, vibrant flesh, which cannot long stay white like snow or lilies before turning pink with blushing or red to the touch. Venus weeps, sweats, and reeks; even the cold Adonis pants steamily with anger and nervousness. Everywhere there is "melting" and "vapor," as passion plays itself out on the grassy ground. It is no petrified nature that Shakespeare describes. We find ourselves in his poem amid larks and caterpillars, snails and glowworms, deer, porcupines, horses, dogs, Wat the hare, and the fatal boar. Marlowe's sacrificial turtledoves are out of their element in a city-temple; Shakespeare's animals in their scene are absolutely at home. This fact has distressed some readers, who speculate that Shakespeare was still something of a bumpkin from Stratford when he wrote his poem—not up to the urban sophistication of Marlowe, which seems more appropriate to an Ovidian narrative (despite Ovid's fondness for woodland settings in his myth-telling) than a nostalgia for forests and fauna.[18] But Shakespeare must, surely, be allowed his own ends. His concerns are not at all the same as Marlowe's, and the images and settings he draws are right for his purpose.

Venus and Adonis is a "soft" poem not only in its images, not only because its intellectual element is strongly qualified by sensual appeal, but in the unusual sense that its ironies preserve neither the hard lines that separate just assessment from merciful allowance nor the strict hierarchies that maintain the narrator's (and reader's) superiority to his characters.[19] The narrator does not fail to criticize the goddess of love and the stubbornly resistant boy whom she craves and cannot have; but the apportioning of blame from a position of high intellectual and ethical distance is hardly the storyteller's final act.

We do not, of course, find much to "forgive" in mere silliness, and at times the poet appears content to expose his characters to ridicule without any significant concern for their culpability. Beginning with something of Marlowe's rapidity, detachment, and humor, he draws comedy from the rhyme of the first stanza's concluding couplet:

Sick thoughted Venus makes amain unto him,
And like a bold-fac'd suitor gins to woo him.

Stanzas 5 and 6 might seem to prepare for a precious farce:

With this she seizeth on his sweating palm,
The president of pith and livelihood,
And trembling in her passion, calls it balm,
Earth's sovereign salve, to do a goddess good.
Being so enrag'd, desire doth lend her force
Courageously to pluck him from his horse.

Over one arm the lusty courser's rein,
Under her other was the tender boy,
Who blush'd, and pouted in a dull disdain,
With leaden appetite, unapt to toy;
She red and hot as coals of glowing fire,
He red for shame, but frosty in desire.

We cannot be solemn about a phrase (with its sexual implication) like "to do a goddess good"; or the rhyme of "force" and "horse"; or the picture of Adonis trapped like a giant beagle under his mistress' arm. As the story proceeds, the ridiculous is never entirely absent. Sometimes it stands on its own in sharp relief:

He wrings her nose, he strikes her on the cheeks,
He bends her fingers, holds her pulses hard,
He chafes her lips, a thousand ways he seeks
To mend the hurt that his unkindness marr'd.

(475-78)

Sometimes it follows hard upon premonitions of tragedy:

> "The boar!" quoth she, whereat a sudden pale,
> Like lawn being spread upon the blushing rose,
> Usurps her cheek; she trembles at his tale,
> And on his neck her yoking arms she throws.
> She sinketh down, still hanging by his neck,
> He on her belly falls, she on her back.
>
> (589-94)

Sometimes it is so mingled with pathos that we may scarcely distinguish the absurd from the pitiable:

> "Tis true, 'tis true, thus was Adonis slain:
> He ran upon the boar with his sharp spear,
> Who did not whet his teeth at him again,
> But by a kiss thought to persuade him there;
> And nousling in his flank, the loving swine
> Sheath'd unaware the tusk in his soft groin.
>
> "Had I been tooth'd like him, I must confess,
> With kissing him I should have kill'd him first.
> But he is dead, and never did he bless
> My youth with his, the more am I accurs'd."
> With this she falleth in the place she stood,
> And stains her face with his congealed blood.
>
> (1111-22)

We may also, however, encounter in the poem matter enough for clear reproach. The suffocating, devouring lust of Venus is too "vicious" (in both the antique and the modern senses) to escape censure:

> Even as an empty eagle, sharp by fast,
> Tires with her beak on feathers, flesh, and bone,
> Shaking her wings, devouring all in haste,
> Till either gorge be stuff'd, or prey be gone;
> Even so she kiss'd his brow, his cheek, his chin,
> And where she ends, she doth anew begin.
>
> Forc'd to content, but never to obey,
> Panting he lies, and breatheth in her face.
> She feedeth on the steam, as on a prey,
> And calls it heavenly moisture, air of grace. . . .
>
> (55-64)
>
> He with her plenty press'd, she faint with death,
> Their lips together glued, fall to the earth.
>
> Now quick desire hath caught the yielding prey,
> And glutton-like she feeds, yet never filleth;
> Her lips are conquerors, his lips obey,
> Paying what ransom the insulter willeth;
> Whose vultur thought doth pitch the price so high
> That she will draw his lips' rich treasure dry.
>
> And having felt the sweetness of the spoil,
> With blindfold fury she begins to forage;
> Her face doth reek and smoke, her blood doth boil,
> And careless lust stirs up a desperate courage,
> Planting oblivion, beating reason back,
> Forgetting shame's pure blush and honor's wrack.
>
> Hot, faint, and weary, with her hard embracing,
> Like a wild bird being tam'd with too much handling,
> Or as the fleet-foot roe that's tir'd with chasing,
> Or like the froward infant still'd with dandling,
> He now obeys, and now no more resisteth,
> While she takes all she can, not all she listeth.
>
> (545-64)

On the other hand, the insensitivity and self-absorption of Adonis—

> "No, lady, no, my heart longs not to groan,
> But soundly sleeps, while now it sleeps alone"
>
> (785-86)

are enough to lend some credence to Venus' complaint that he is another Narcissus (157-62). Although like Hero and Leander he lacks the gift of a mature conscience, his faults, however venial, are real and made to appear morally unattractive. There is certainly, then, in both Venus and Adonis enough that might be absolved, if absolution is to be given. But who might grant forgiveness? And on what grounds?

Unlike Shakespeare's plays, *Venus and Adonis* has no figure like Helena or Duke Vincentio or Cordelia or Prospero to speak the word of pardon. The narrator of the poem could have played the pardoner; but he seems, as critics since Coleridge have noted, conspicuous by his silence: we "seem to be told nothing, but to see everything." When the narrator does become momentarily visible, he can be found aloof and lacking in sympathy.[20] If, however, he tends to refrain from explicit comment, he speaks enough in his own person that his words, along with inferences that can be made from the shape of his story, along, indeed, with his silences, suggest that he is not an indifferent spectator.

The epithets that he chooses are rarely ever condescending or derisive. When he calls Venus "good queen," "Poor queen" (607, 251), or Adonis "poor fool" (578), he speaks, one feels, with as much genuine sympathy as he does when imagining the "poor birds" or the "world's poor people" (601, 925)—or as Venus herself does when describing the torments of "poor Wat," the "dew-bedabbled wretch" (697, 703). His aphorisms are considerably more ingenuous than Marlowe's. Some of these, given their contexts, may offer amusement and proverbial wisdom in equal measure (although the one does not annul the other):

> All swoll'n with chafing, down Adonis sits,
> Banning his boist'rous and unruly beast;
> And now the happy season once more fits
> That love-sick Love by pleading may be blest;
> For lovers say, the heart hath treble wrong
> When it is barr'd the aidance of the tongue.
>
> (325-30)

Contexts make equally clear, however, that other maxims have in themselves very little irony:

> Her song was tedious, and outwore the night,
> For lovers' hours are long, though seeming short;
> If pleas'd themselves, others they think delight
> In such-like circumstance, with such-like sport.
> Their copious stories, oftentimes begun,
> End without audience, and are never done.
>
> (841-46)

Furthermore, the narrator of *Venus and Adonis*, never blind to faults, through his words and in his plot manages skillfully to extenuate them. We sense that he cannot be wholly insincere, for example, when he explicitly affirms that Venus has some right on her side:

> She hath assay'd as much as may be prov'd.
> Her pleading hath deserv'd a greater fee;
> She's Love, she loves, and yet she is not lov'd.
>
> (608-10)

He makes sure that the exorbitantly selfish passion of Venus is seen to have its limits, checked not only by Adonis' stubborn denial of her importunities but by her own elementary concern for the "other":

> For pity now she can no more detain him;
> The poor fool prays her that he may depart.
> She is resolv'd no longer to restrain him,
> Bids him farewell, and look well to her heart. . . .
>
> (577-80)

Venus' maternal instinct, which is present to some extent even in her lust,[21] becomes more (though by no means entirely) altruistic in the second half of the poem—as the narrator emphasizes by changing the image of a sexually voracious goddess with "vultur" thoughts ("glutton-like she feeds, yet never filleth" [548, 511]) into that of a mother who runs to offer food ("Like a milch doe, whose swelling dugs do ache, / Hasting to feed her fawn hid in some brake" [875-6]). For Adonis, too, excuses are offered in mitigation of his faults. He protests, Venus acknowledges, and the story proves that he is indeed "unripe" (128, 524) for love. Like his knowledge of the soul's passions (which derives mostly from hearsay: "I have heard [love] is a life in death" [413]), his narcissism is only incipient; and his coldness can turn to warmth before the distress of Venus in her "swoon" (463-80). His plea to the overbearing goddess to forbear has ample justice in it:

> "Fair queen," quoth he, "if any love you owe me,
> Measure my strangeness with my unripe years;
> Before I know myself, seek not to know me. . . ."
>
> (523-25)

The narrator rarely comes to the fore to *demand* sympathy for Venus and Adonis; but his reticence often has the effect of allowing the sufferings of his characters to plead for them. Venus' confusion and grief in the second half of the poem are as wonderfully dramatized as her desire and frustration in the first. After she learns of the boar, we hear a different kind of desperation in her voice, a new pitch and purpose, as she attempts to seduce Adonis and save him from destruction:

> "What is thy body but a swallowing grave,
> Seeming to bury that posterity
> Which by the rights of time thou needs must have,
> If thou destroy them not in dark obscurity?
>
> . . . . .
>
> So in thyself thyself art made away. . . ."
>
> (757-63)

We see her running about in her perplexity, searching, fearing, coming suddenly to believe signs that her Adonis is dead, just as abruptly being teased back into hope, then stumbling by accident across the boy's bleeding corpse. The narrator tactfully presents images that convey an exquisite sense of Venus' amazement and pain:

> Whereat amaz'd as one that unaware
> Hath dropp'd a precious jewel in the flood,
> Or stonish'd as night-wand'rers often are,
> Their light blown out in some mistrustful wood,
> Even so confounded in the dark she lay,
> Having lost the fair discovery of her way.
>
> (823-28)

> Or as the snail, whose tender horns being hit,
> Shrinks backward in his shelly cave with pain,

> And there, all smoth'red up, in shade doth sit,
> Long after fearing to creep forth again;
> So at his bloody view her eyes are fled
> Into the deep-dark cabins of her head. . . .
> (1033-38)

In the second half of the poem, when the characters are more clearly pitiable victims, our sympathy for them increases. The wild obsessiveness of Venus and the petulant coldness of Adonis seem less significant as she anticipates his death and he marches off in all callowness to meet it. Sympathy does not, however, accumulate to such an extent that its mass and weight finally expel criticism. The voice of comic and sometimes critical irony is resilient, able to coexist on its own terms with the swelling tones of pity, even to the end. Thus in a number of the work's most promisingly affecting stanzas, the archness of rhyme, rhythm, and diction (in the couplets especially) cools the temperature of the warmest pathos:

> And with that word, she spied the hunted boar,
>
> Whose frothy mouth bepainted all with red,
> Like milk and blood being mingled both together,
> A second fear through all her sinews spread,
> Which madly hurries her she knows not whither;
> This way she runs, and now she will no further,
> But back retires to rate the boar for murther.
> (900-906)
>
> Upon his hurt she looks so steadfastly,
> That her sight dazzling makes the wound seem three,
> And then she reprehends her mangling eye,
> That makes more gashes where no breach should be.
> His face seems twain, each several limb is doubled,
> For oft the eye mistakes, the brain being troubled.
> (1063-68)

The goddess' frantic search for the boy whom she believes to have died is punctuated by the "scowling" and "howling" of hounds, who, "Clapping their proud tails to the ground below," amuse even as they bleed (916-24).

Venus' lecture to Adonis about his "javeling's" or "spear's point," although ominous in its context, also comically suggests her jealousy of the boar whom the point would "enter" (616, 626); and her later imaginative identification with the animal who had attacked her beloved boy is touching, sinister, and ludicrous: "Had I been tooth'd like him . . . , / With kissing him I should have killed him first" (1112-22).

There is comic hyperbole in Venus' ascription to Adonis of preternatural gifts (1087-1104), comic hysteria as well as poignancy in her speeches to Death (931-54; 991-1008). And if she is a "milch doe" in her motherly concern, her love yet retains in itself something of the predatory. "As falcons to the lure" she flies after Adonis in the hope that he still lives (1027); and after the dead boy has been transformed into an anemone, she kills the flower by cropping it, to give it a home in a breast that is maternal, sexual, killing, and kind. As for Adonis, even after he is marked for slaughter, he does not allow us to forget his fatuousness:

> "from my ear the tempting tune is blown;
> For know my heart stands armed in mine ear,
> And will not let a false sound enter there.
>
> "Lest the deceiving harmony should run
> Into the quiet closure of my breast,
> And then my little heart were quite undone,
> In his bedchamber to be barr'd of rest."
> (778-84)

In the last glimpse given of him while he is alive, his ears "burn themselves" in trite and somewhat ridiculous indignation (810).

What, then, is the irony's purpose? It is not, as in *Hero and Leander*, to establish, wittily and entertainingly, a principle of authenticity by which to parcel out judgments and keep them separate, but in fact to legitimize a sympathetic response to characters who seem as important, in themselves and in what they represent, as any narrow principle of truth or justice. *Venus and Adonis* helps to establish the paradox that criticism may sanction charity.

The implorations of a pure, pathetic melodrama tend, of course, to arouse resistance rather than compassion. Even in melodramatic literature, however, if we find that a critical irony has put what is foolish and what is blameworthy in their place, we need not be, are less likely to be chary with our sympathy for the good that is bound up with what Shakespeare terms "impure defeature" (736). To be sure, not all irony works to authorize this generosity. Much comedy, like Marlowe's, places special emphasis on the superior intellectual and ethical stations of author and audience. Aristotle's remark that comedy portrays "men worse than the average" (*Poetics* 1449a) stands at the head of a critical tradition to which writers like Hobbes, Baudelaire, Bergson, and Freud have contributed—a tradition whose motto might be Puck's "What fools these mortals be!" A different perspective, offered by the "genial" Romantic Charles Lamb, finds room in the comic for a laughter that is "an overflow of sympathy, [a] feeling of identity with what is disreputably human"[22]—and its motto might read: "What fools *we* mortals be!" The comedy in *Venus and Adonis* is closer to this latter kind than to the former. Shakespeare does not abolish the distinction between the praiseworthy and the disreputable, but he indicates how forgiveness can mediate between them. In Shakespeare's poem, ironic diminishment of the characters works with an ironic turn towards their rehabilitation, for it seems more legitimate to show them good will after the exposure of their faults removes the possibility that our estimate of them may be blind.

The indignities that Venus suffers are many and severe. In her helplessness she can prove her divinity only by a limp assertion of past glories (her triumph over Mars) and by an appeal to her miraculous "lightness," which has a double meaning (97-114, 145-56). Her fortunes are subject not only to the omnipotent "Destinies" but to "Nature" (733-34). She is so untranscendent a goddess that Wat the hare can serve as her proper analogue: she imagines the "dew-bedabbled wretch" to

> "Turn, and return, indenting with the way;
> Each envious brier his weary legs do scratch,
> Each shadow makes him stop, each murmur stay,
> For misery is trodden on by many,
> And being low, never reliev'd by any—"
>
> (703-8)

not long before she herself runs about in panicked misery, as (with some deference to her divinity) bushes "catch her by the neck" and "kiss her face" and twine "about her thigh" (871-73). The palfrey of Adonis and the finally compliant mare (259-322) seem to Venus almost enviable in their simple compatibility.

We should not conclude, however, that the poet is out to give Venus her comeuppance (what fools these immortals be!), that this proud goddess who so blithely victimizes poor, helpless mortals by making them her slaves will now be placed in thrall herself and deprived of her beloved, so that we her victims can have a good if slightly cruel laugh at her. To mock Venus, the poem suggests, is in some sense to mock ourselves. As the narrator says, "She's Love" (610): not the Platonic ideal that is "fled" to "heaven" (793)—or into *Il Cortegiano*—but the drastically imperfect amalgam of lust and caring that is likely to be found in all lovers, in whom also passion's "leave exceeds commission" (568). And Adonis, we hear in almost annoying repetition, is "Beauty": the object of desire that, except in Neoplatonic idealisms, is at random too limited, too cold, too green, too distant, or too self-complacent to satisfy the love that yearns for it. In *Venus and Adonis*, then, the denigration of a goddess leads to her identification with a flawed humanity; the exposure of beauty's shortcomings impoverishes our own ideals—unless sympathy should find a way to redeem them. The narrator is neither visible nor satirical enough to insist on the distance between himself (or his readers) and his characters.

But even if there is no explicit voice in the poem demanding justice, it is not clear why we should not in all righteousness be cruel to love, to beauty, and to ourselves, since such treatment seems to be deserved; or if we offer sympathy, why pity should not stop short of forgiveness. We might wonder whether *Venus and Adonis* asks us to pardon the failings that it exposes.

Forgiveness of itself has no logic by which it can be compelled. Although extrinsic grounds, such as *raisons d'état* or public edification, may be found to prompt or even "justify" a granting of pardon (as well, of course, as to discourage it), there are no reasons intrinsic to a condition which can make the grant necessary. It may be claimed that a private act of mercy has in fact no relationship at all to truth, since in this view God, the model for all who forgive, absolves sinners freely, spontaneously, arbitrarily, responding to nothing in sinful souls that deserves to be forgiven.[23] Even the medieval systematization of the "steps" to forgiveness—contribution, confession, satisfaction[24]—did not constitute a rationale that could force God's hand, for it was by a free act of love that he promised to reward with pardon those who underwent this process of conversion. Aquinas observed that mercy is something "more than" justice.[25] If no truth can require forgiveness, the only truth to which it might be said to answer is, as Augustine suggested, that in every guilty soul *in via* there is a good that *can* become definitive, if through pardon it is given another chance or, according to the strict predestinarians, is made definitive by God.[26]

Whatever the philosophical or theological arguments that make forgiveness independent of logic and render it understandable only as an unconstrained act of love, common experience suggests that such an act can be, at least among us finite creatures, invited and encouraged. In *Venus and Adonis*, not of course a "godly" poem in any other sense, there are a number of encouragements.

As we have seen, the poem provides may warrants for sympathy, which is made legitimate in part through the very criticism that qualifies it. Pity (although the term seems on occasion merely a standard code-word for sexual surrender [95, 257]) is endorsed in the story as a value: when Venus "For pity" checks her assault (577); when Adonis attempts to revive a fallen Venus (473-80); when, in contrast, the boar is shown to know "no pity" (1000); whenever the poet without embarrassment allows the pain of goddess, mortal man, or animal to ask for compassion. We might also note that an appeal to "smallness" has often been used in pleas for forgiveness—in the understanding that the need of the humble, or humiliated, for mercy is most frank and provocative.

> And it came to pass, that when they had made an end of eating the grass of the land, then I said, O Lord God, forgive, I beseech thee: by whom shall Jacob rise? for he is small.
>
> The Lord repented for this: it shall not be, saith the Lord.
>
> (Amos 7:2-3)

In *Venus and Adonis* a very strong impression is conveyed that its characters are diminutive and helpless before the large forces that finally defeat them. The poem offers reasons enough to believe that the "Destinies" have worked "To cross the curious workmanship of Nature" (734). Like Marvell's parallels that never meet, Venus and Adonis in acting out what they are seem doomed to the most flagrant incompatibility. And for a goddess, Venus is remarkably uninformed and powerless. She can "prophesy" (671, 1135) but is helpless in the face of prophecy. Her ignorance of Adonis' whereabouts and condition allows her to be toyed with by "Death," whom she first vainly excoriates then humbly tries to appease. When Adonis disappears, dissolving into the night—

> Look how a bright star shooteth from the sky,
> So glides he in the night from Venus' eye,
>
> Which after him she darts, as one on shore
> Gazing upon a late embarked friend,
> Till the wild waves will have him seen no more,
> Whose ridges with the meeting clouds contend;
> So did the merciless and pitchy night
> Fold in the object that did feed her sight—
>
> (815-22)

we are given an acute sense of how massively formidable the darkness can be, and how puny are those who try to resist it.

The lowly may be pitied; ultimately, however, the most persuasive invitation in this stanza to proceed beyond sympathy to forgiveness lies not in the fact that the "night" is overwhelmingly large, but that it is characteristically "merciless" (821). Will the good, in order to be itself, have to match in ruthlessness its adversary? Although pardon is moved by nothing so much as by the generosity of the one who grants it, the refusal to forgive does not necessarily place one among the forces of unloving darkness. Yet by showing these powers to be without mercy, Shakespeare at least suggests that the opportunity to oppose them through an act of charity is a salutary temptation. Yielding to it may not be for a reader a terribly formal or conscious act, but it would be in light of the poem's whole truth a crucial one.

Forgiveness of Venus and Adonis must in a way be more radical than usual, because the characters do not conveniently confess and repent. Adonis remains shallow and obstinate to the end. Venus never questions the legitimacy of her passions, never regrets her onslaughts, and never quite attains a self-abnegating respect for the rights and privileges of another. Indeed, in her sour leavetaking after Adonis' death, she may seem extravagantly mean-spirited, hardly of a disposition to inspire in an accommodating observer a sympathetic attitude:

> Sith in his prime death doth my life destroy,
> They that love best their loves shall not enjoy.
>
> (1163-64)

A scrupulous reading of the poem, however, and a consideration of the ideal of forgiveness in itself suggest that these "obstacles" to pardon are not insuperable. In the first place, when Venus catalogues the woes that love will suffer in the wake of her disappointment, she is not uttering a curse but a prophecy ("Since thou art dead, lo here I prophesy . . ." [1135]). She does not in her grief blindly revenge herself on subsequent generations of lovers (she has in fact been shown to be quite powerless), any more than she contributes to Adonis' death by predicting it (671). Love shall be attended by "sorrow," shall "Bud, and be blasted, in a breathing while," shall "be sparing, and too full of riot," shall cause "dissension" and a host of other ills (1135-64)—not because Venus will maliciously produce them but because as an archetypal and imperfect Love she has already suffered them, or something like them. We should not hold her bitterness against her. In the second place, even if from the moral point of view Venus and Adonis are not wholly admirable, they are not by that fact excluded from the beneficence of mercy. As Augustine pointed out (believing with St. Paul in a God who forgives sinners not because they have become virtuous but because they are redeemable: "Christ died for the ungodly. . . . While we were yet sinners, Christ died for us" [Rom. 5:8]), pardon does not have to wait for reform. As long as wickedness is not in characters an absolutely final state, forgiveness does not irresponsibly or perversely sanction "the evil that men do."

Since this is the aspect of forgiveness that most painfully violates a conventional sense of justice, it is understandable that when Shakespeare seems to make it plausible, he may be suspected of moral or aesthetic foul play. Lear's cry for a universal pardon must be (we may think) very madness, not truth spoken by the mad (and of course that cry is inconsistent with the old king's subsequent actions). The Poet's pardon of the Friend in the *Sonnets*, Helena's of Bertram, the Duke's and Isabella's of Angelo are at the least disturbing, for these acts have, in spite of some official and problematical repentances, no real grounds, "no cause," except the pardoner's conviction of the value of mercy in itself, belief in a potential goodness in the pardoned, and anticipation that forgiveness may help to realize a good that would be impossible without it.

Venus and Adonis does not seem to present even as much a "justification" of mercy, for if in the poem there are inducements enough to such conviction and faith, there are no obvious grounds for such hope. Adonis, after all, dies with no new knowledge and essentially unchanged. Venus retreats into what appears to be a permanent malaise, certain, as her prophecy indicates, to remain what she is. Are not the follies and iniquities of these characters "final"? Not if Venus and Adonis can be seen as part of ourselves and our world—not, that is, if the poet has succeeded in creating characters who are at once sufficiently distant from us to allow criticism and sufficiently close (as mythical embodiments of possibilities in human character or in the world of values) to warrant the acknowledgment that their imperfections and dilemmas are our own. Venus and Adonis, then, would be "hopeless" cases only were we so; and as long as we are not, *they* may be forgiven, even as we may have mercy on ourselves.

It has been noted that in Falstaff, Shakespeare created a comic character whose faults, like those of Venus and Adonis, audiences often pardon in the warmth of the benevolence inspired by comedy and out of a sense that the rogue, for better and worse, is somehow too much a part of us to abandon to the impersonal strictures of principle.

> Nobody exactly likes Mrs Gamp: we all love Falstaff. Why? Not only because Falstaff is greater than Mrs Gamp, but because she is a figure which we see in the street and he is a figure we find in the looking-glass. It is a magnifying glass, no doubt, but still what it shows us is ourselves.[27]

This liberality may be viewed with alarm, not as high-mindedness but as the unthinking yet irresponsible use by an audience of "Shakespeare's characters as a means of personal purgation."[28] It may also be considered by the wise a banal sentimentality, a simplistic response to a character whose faults are too dangerous to ignore or forget. Yet Shakespeare seems willing to risk inspiring good will towards Monsieur Vice, surely because Falstaff is much more than a villain, and perhaps because poor, degenerate, splendid Jack, with his overplus of flesh, frailty, and genius, reminds his maker of a truth that seems never far from his mind, that there is value in imperfection:

> The web of our life is of a mingled yarn, good and ill together: our virtues would be proud, if our faults whipped them not, and our crimes would despair, if they were not cherished by our virtues. (*All's Well*, 4.70-74.)

William James thought that one of the greatest discouragements of religious belief was a small-minded "horror of being duped."[29] An analogous fear might as easily impede the will to pardon, a dread that "chaos" might "come again" if crime, which can find ways to escape many kinds of retribution, be allowed as well to escape the punishment of an apodictic critical judgment. It might be that Shakespeare is criminally subversive to embarrass the ethical calculus that protects us from such fear. But logic cannot try him, for "the quality of mercy is not strained," not even, ultimately, by logic.[30]

Yet we must remember that pardon is not acquittal, that forgiveness goes beyond truth without ignoring it, taking into account all the complexities and contrarieties that a "pluralist" can discover and yet finding a way to avoid a final aporia. The act of forgiveness is an affirmation (of at least potential worth) and an abstention (from punishment). As such it can be so generous as to seem wicked. Yet Shakespeare dared to flirt with wickedness by dramatizing, implicitly in his early narrative poem, explicitly and more searchingly in his plays, two momentous ideas: that the mixed fabric of good and evil may call for something other than contemplative perplexity and just estimation; that the guilty might be treated with an extraordinary temperance, since faced with a chance to condemn them (or ourselves) with truth on our side, we "might see, and know, and yet abstain." This forbearance is more than Aristotelian or Senecan moderation, and thus a paradox of the kind which Shakespeare often establishes—to the consternation of those who understand him to be in his ethical views a "conservative," as well as of those who would have him sit, whether comfortably or anxiously, in the no-man's-land of contradiction.

Notes

[1] Preface to *Poems* (1853), in *The Complete Prose Works of Matthew Arnold*, vol. 1, ed. R. H. Super (Ann Arbor: University of Michigan Press, 1960), 3.

[2] See Rufus Putney, "*Venus and Adonis*: Amour with Humor," *PQ* 20 (1941): 533-48; the same author's "Venus Agonistes," *University of Colorado Studies in Language and Literature* 4 (1953): 51-66; the Introduction to F. T. Prince's Arden edition of *The Poems* (London: Methuen, 1960), xxvi-xxxiii; Huntington Brown, "*Venus and Adonis*: The Action, the Narrator, and the Critics," *Michigan Academician* 2 (1969): 73-87.

[3] See Lu Emily Pearson, *Elizabethan Love Conventions* (Berkeley: University of California Press, 1933), 285; R. P. Miller, "Venus, Adonis, and the Horses," *ELH* 19 (1952): 249-64, and "The Myth of Mars' Hot Minion in 'Venus and Adonis,'" *ELH* 26 (1959): 470-81; Don Cameron Allen, "On *Venus and Adonis*," in *Elizabethan and Jacobean Studies Presented to Frank Percy Wilson* (Oxford: Clarendon Press, 1959), 100-

111; Eugene B. Canteloupe, "An Iconographical Interpretation of *Venus and Adonis,* Shakespeare's Ovidian Comedy," *SQ* 14 (1963): 141-51; A. Robin Bowers, "'Hard Armours' and 'Delicate Amours' in Shakespeare's *Venus and Adonis,*" *ShakS* 12 (1979): 1-23.

[4] See James H. Lake, "Shakespeare's Venus: An Experiment in Tragedy," *SQ* 25 (1974): 351-55.

[5] *Mythology and the Renaissance Tradition in English Poetry* (Minneapolis: University of Minnesota Press, 1932), 149.

[6] "Shakespeare's Banquet of Sense," in *Shakespeare and Spenser* (Princeton: Princeton University Press, 1950), 12.

[7] *English Literature in the Sixteenth Century, Excluding Drama* (Oxford: Clarendon Press, 1954), 498-99. See also Hallett Smith, *Elizabethan Poetry* (Cambridge: Harvard University Press, 1952), 84-90; and Hyder Rollins' summary of criticism on *Venus and Adonis* in his Variorum edition of *The Poems* (Philadelphia: Lipincott, 1938), 476-523.

[8] The terms are those used by Clark Hulse in *Metamorphic Verse: The Elizabethan Minor Epic* (Princeton: Princeton University Press, 1981), 147. In a note Professor Hulse refers to a number of essays written by like-minded colleagues: A. C. Hamilton, Kenneth Muir, Norman Rabkin, and William Keach. See also Coppélia Kahn, "Self and Eros in *Venus and Adonis,*" *Centennial Review* 20 (1976): 351-71; Donald G. Watson, "The Contrarieties of *Venus and Adonis,*" *SP* 75 (1978): 32-63; Wayne A. Rebhorn, "Mother Venus: Temptation in Shakespeare's *Venus and Adonis,*" *ShakS* 11 (1978): 1-16; John Doebler, "The Many Faces of Love: Shakespeare's *Venus and Adonis,*" *ShakS* 16 (1983): 33-43.

[9] See *Elizabethan Erotic Narratives* (New Brunswick: Rutgers University Press, 1978), 3-35.

[10] *Shakespeare and the Common Understanding* (New York: Free Press, 1967), 9. One would like to have seen Professor Rabkin elaborate on his reasons for believing that this theory of double-truth is "strangely affirmative." See also Robert Grudin, *Mighty Opposites: Shakespeare and Renaissance Contrarieties* (Berkeley: University of California Press, 1979) and Rabkin's *Shakespeare and the Problem of Meaning* (Chicago: University of Chicago Press, 1981).

[11] Line 11. All quotations from Shakespeare's works are taken from *The Riverside Shakespeare,* ed. G. B. Evans, et al. (Boston: Houghton Mifflin, 1974).

[12] In *Likenesses of Truth in Elizabethan and Restoration Drama* (Oxford: Clarendon Press, 1972), Harriett Hawkins attacks the "detached, derisive," and "condescending" analyses of "satirical-moralistic" critics who judge characters in Renaissance literature merely against "traditional moral or social codes" and thereby fail to account for the complex responses that the "wicked" may evoke in an audience. Professor Hawkins' quarrel seems to be more with an excessively narrow moralism than with morality itself. At any rate, in attempting to explain how some plays may encourage us to transcend "moral" judgments, she appeals to A. H. Maslow's theory about a "divinely impersonal" relationship to the world that can lead to "strange heights of acceptance." This response is "aesthetic" rather than ethical, and it is not one that I find invited by Shakespeare. (See especially pp. 14-19, 47-49.)

[13] See Robert G. Hunter, *Shakespeare's Comedies of Forgiveness* (New York: Columbia University Press, 1965). It is the thesis of Ernst Theodor Sehrt's *Vergebung und Gnade bei Shakespeare* (Stuttgart, 1952) that Shakespeare in treating the theme of forgiveness in his plays enlarges the conception of that virtue, which had been narrowed by the playwright's time through the influence of Seneca and of Renaissance humanists indebted to the classical tradition. See also Elizabeth M. Pope, "The Renaissance Background of *Measure for Measure,*" *ShS* 2 (1949): 66-82.

[14] Rabkin, *Common Understanding,* 7.

[15] See my essay, "Shakespeare's *Sonnets:* Age in Love and the Goring of Thoughts," *SP* 80 (1983): 300-24.

[16] *Hero and Leander* is quoted from the edition of Stephen Orgel in *Christopher Marlowe: The Complete Poems and Translations* (Harmondsworth: Penguin, 1971).

[17] Keach, *Erotic Narratives,* 28.

[18] See, for example, Hallett Smith, *Elizabethan Poetry,* 88-89.

[19] Hazlitt judged both *Venus and Adonis* and *Lucrece* to be anything but "soft," remarking that the poems "appear to us like a couple of ice-houses. They are about as hard, as glittering, and as cold" (*Characters of Shakespeare's Plays* [1817], quoted in Rollins, *Variorum,* 466).

[20] See *Biographia Literaria,* II, quoted in Rollins, *Variorum,* 476-78.

[21] See Rebhorn, "Mother Venus."

[22] This is Wylie Sypher's summary of Lamb's views. See "The Meanings of Comedy," in *Comedy,* ed. Wylie Sypher (New York: Anchor, 1956), 204. For an in-

stance of Lamb's generosity towards the "disreputable," see his essay "Hogarth," in Roy Park, ed., *Lamb as Critic* (London: Routledge and Kegan Paul, 1980), 315-34.

[23] See Anders Nygren, *Agape and Eros* (1932), trans. Philip Watson (Philadelphia: Westminster Press, 1953).

[24] See R. G. Hunter, *Comedies of Forgiveness*, 19.

[25] See *ST* 1.21.3. Also, Marion D. H. Parker, *The Slave of Life: A Study of Shakespeare and the Idea of Justice* (London: Chatto and Windus, 1955), 231-32.

[26] See Nygren, *Agape and Eros*, 550. Strictly speaking, in the passages referred to by Nygren, Augustine speaks of love rather than forgiveness; but the transition is, I think, a legitimate one.

[27] John Bailey, "A Note on Falstaff," quoted in J. Dover Wilson, *The Fortunes of Falstaff* (Cambridge: Cambridge University Press, 1944), 9. Bailey also speaks of the tendency of comedy to "dissolve morality" and of the "forgiveness" that Falstaff inspires. See the entire essay in Israel Gollancz, ed., *A Book of Homage to Shakespeare* (Oxford: Humphrey Milford, 1916), 149-53.

[28] Wilson, *Fortunes of Falstaff*, 10.

[29] "The Will to Believe," in *The Works of William James*, ed. Frederick H. Burkhardt, et al. (Cambridge: Harvard University Press, 1979), 25.

[30] Darryl Gless's detailed study of *Measure for Measure* demonstrates that the absolutions at the play's end are not preposterous either as dramatic or as moral actions, while at the same time they are, like much that is counseled in the Sermon on the Mount, "unreasonable" (see *Measure for Measure, the Law, and the Convent* [Princeton: Princeton University Press, 1979], 210-11).

Nona Fienberg (essay date 1989)

SOURCE: "Thematics of Value in *Venus and Adonis*," in *Criticism*, Vol. XXXI, No. 1, Winter, 1989, pp. 21-32.

[*In the following essay, Fienberg studies the dynamically shifting marketplace of value operating in* Venus and Adonis.]

When Venus finds Adonis able to resist her love, she wonders of course what his nature is, "Art thou a woman's son and canst not feel/What 'tis to love" (201-02).[1] But her energies and the interest of the poem engage the question of her nature. We seem to know so much more about Venus than about Adonis. As Coppélia Kahn points out, however, what we know about Venus is severely limited, "We know Venus as a character only through the demands she makes on Adonis; the overwhelming impression we have of her is of a mouth, pressing insistently on or toward him."[2] Since Venus' representation in all its mutability and variety so dominates the poem that she threatens to consume it quite, that representation of a woman rewards further investigation. What is this creature whom Shakespeare found to offer to the Earl of Southampton as "the first heire of my invention"? What is the representation of the female limned in the "unpolished lines" through which Shakespeare first presented his published self? Venus' power extends beyond Adonis to readers of the poem who are challenged to reevaluate a fixed and stable set of standards against her dynamic and shifting self-evaluation.

Venus' mutability and diversity contrast with Adonis' fixity and absoluteness. Her productivity contrasts with his fearful solipsism. In her confrontation of Adonis' value system with her own more dynamic sense of multiplicity, she provides a way to reevaluate patriarchy. Because the question of value and evaluation is central to my argument, I want to provide a theoretical framework for the issues. My theoretical beliefs are articulated by Barbara Herrnstein Smith's powerful assertion, "All value is radically contingent, being neither an inherent property of objects nor an arbitrary projection of subjects, but, rather, the product of the dynamics of an economic system. . . . Like its price in the marketplace, the value of an entity to an individual subject is *also* the product of the dynamics of an economic system, specifically the personal economy constituted by the subject's needs, interests, and resources—biological, psychological, material, and experiential."[3] Smith's argument frees readers from bondage either to the value system of the Renaissance world in which Shakespeare writes or to the contemporary world in which we fix the worth of texts. Instead, Smith's argument invites a new kind of cultural investigation of the contingencies in diverse local conditions of evaluation. An examination of the thematics of value can be particularly powerful for the study of the representation of females in historical texts. Without a sense both of the distance of historical texts and of the values we use texts to produce, we may be bound by oppressive absolutism.

As Smith notes, and as Venus enacts, the marketplace of value is continuously shifting, changing, dynamic, not fixed, absolute, or subject to predictable natural law. Such relativism proves liberating, since it frees women's representation from biological and social determinism. Instead of responding with alarm to Venus' range of self-representation, to her power and dynamism, we are enabled to identify her mutability, her risk-taking, and her appropriation of a system of rhetorical display with the changing cultural conditions of the early 1590s in England.[4] Venus becomes, then, a part of the cultural work of her own time and of ours.

In one stanza she addresses the economic, sexual, and epistemological range of the reevaluation of the patriarchy which she invites her audience to engage in:

> What am I that thou shouldst contemn me this?
> Or what great danger dwells upon my suit?
> What were thy lips the worse for one poor kiss?
> Speak, fair, but speak fair words, or else be mute.
> Give me one kiss, I'll give it thee again,
> And one for int'rest, if thou wilt have twain.
> (205-10)

In her first question, "What am I that thou shouldst contemn me this?", she poses the question of knowledge of selfhood that engages her and her readers throughout her poem. The next question offers an alternative formulation of the epistemological issue by introducing the possibility that she poses a danger to those she entices. For Adonis, the dangers are multiple and various. They range from the sexual, through the epistemological, and finally to the economic. In her final lines Venus poses the social and economic dimension of this dynamic interplay of the forces of reevaluation. She offers Adonis a good bargain, as a self-confident, somewhat prodigal entrepreneur, "Give me one kiss, I'll give it thee again,/And one for int'rest, if thou wilt have twain." While Adonis remains an unresponsive audience throughout Venus' powerful display, Venus succeeds in winning assent to her subversion of an oppressive dominant group.

At times, the Venus of Shakespeare's poem represents the misogynist phenomenon Neil Hertz exposes in "Medusa's Head: Male Hysteria under Political Pressure."[5] Hertz argues that under political pressure male hysteria creates representations of female sexuality and power which carry all the male fears: "The dangers to be avoided here are indeterminately political, sexual and epistemological. Enslavement, seduction, the loss of manhood and the unfixing of determinate ideas of what things mean are held up as equivalent threats" (Hertz 47). Hertz illustrates his argument using verbal and visual representations of women's part in particular moments of French Revolutionary activity. In Hertz' view, the primary fears posed by the vision of Medusa's head are fears of castration. Powerful women in the particular moment of danger, flux, and change he chooses, then, pose a threat to male potency, a threat to patriarchy, and to an authority structure. But, as Joel Fineman points out, the issues might be seen as less particular, more perennial, indeed, a commonplace. He notes "the self-conscious way that Astrophil, at the beginning of Sidney's sonnet sequence, looks into his heart to write, and finds there pre-engraved or stelled upon it the image or *imago* of the Stella whom he loves" (Hertz 57). In freeing the Medusa's head argument from the particular historical circumstances of the French Revolution, Fineman suggests that the fascination with and terror of female difference impells, for example, Sidney, in late Elizabethan England, when the patriarchal court circle expressed its profound anxiety about the question of succession. This anxiety moved Sidney to write his ill-received Letter to Elizabeth in 1582, and increased in the 1590s, as Queen Elizabeth aged without a dynastic heir.[6]

The dynamic interaction of political and sexual exigencies is especially pertinent, then, to the patriarchal anxiety and poetic productivity of the Elizabethan 1590s. In this age of primogeniture, the female's power is socially and historically tied to her ability to produce a child. If uncertainty prevails regarding the reproduction of children, of goods, and of systems of value of all kinds, then the representation of women will bear the fears of society. In Venus, male fears of the female combine with wonder at her strength. A feminist reading, however, notes that in Venus Shakespeare portrays a woman engaged in the reevaluation demanded by a marketplace world. Her conflict is with the naive Adonis, himself a relic of the time before the commercial and humanist revolutions, when value was a given, not a measure of achieved and mutable standing.

Written in late 1592, when the theaters were closed because of the plague, *Venus and Adonis* marks Shakespeare's entry into the world of publication. As such, he presents the poem to the Earl of Southampton as his first claim to authorship, in a sense, his first assumption of the power to create life. Shakespeare calls the poem his "first heire," the claimant to his goods, or, in this context, his value. Despite the patriarchal family, in Shakespeare's social and economic world, such value rested in the biological power of the mother, for through her reproductive power came the name, the goods, and the value of the child.[7] If the woman's sexuality is not contained, then the social world loses knowledge of who and what it is. When Shakespeare leaves for the first time the world of the theater to enter into the different literary realm of publishing poetry, he portrays in Venus a multiple, a various selfhood, which cannot be predicted or controlled. Through the dynamic interplay of economic, sexual, and epistemological dangers, Shakespeare's Venus links "what is politically dangerous to feelings of sexual horror and fascination" (Hertz 32). While it is revealing to expose this part of Venus' representation, it is important to note that Venus controls the rhetorical medium. When your name is Venus, the stakes are high in the game of love. She is willing to risk her name in winning over an unresponsive audience. The bargains she offers are asymmetrical, like the risks involved in the modern commercial world, and like the risks Shakespeare takes in presenting the "first heire of my invention" to the "Right Honorable Henrie Wriothesley, Earle of Southampton, and Baron of Titchfield." The asymmetry between the poet's name and his prospective patron's names measures the social distance between them, and thus the danger inherent in the gift of the poem. Similarly, Venus' willingness to take great risks involves danger, but also creativity. She uses the very rhetorical tools of the patriarchy to subvert its fixed values.

Venus' rhetorical displays have irritated some readers, like Hallett Smith, who complains, "instead of realizing evoked physical beauty we are listening to a lecture."[8] The rhetorical foundation of value in Elizabethan England is, however, particularly pertinent to her representation. In a recent book, *Ambition and Privilege: The Social Tropes of Elizabethan Courtesy Theory*,[9] Frank Whigham analyzes the central trope of the court world of the period. That trope, *paradiastole,* governs evaluation, and involves the ability to turn praise to blame and reverse as needed, thus bringing to this opposition the "potential for awareness of relativized multiplicity." Its importance lies in "positing a matrix in which praise and blame, flattery and slander, interpenetrate absolutely." The trope becomes central to an analysis of thematics of value in the first work Shakespeare published for a member of the court world. Moreover, the rhetorical foundation of value serves a central role for Venus' particular persuasive strategies. Her rhetorical versatility frees her to determine her own nature as a female.

The power struggle between Venus and Adonis is imagined as that between courtier and courted: "O what a war of looks was then between them!/Her eyes petitioners to his eyes suing" (355-57). We measure her success with the immediate audience she addresses by such small gains as might flatter a favor-seeker. Even his objections to her forwardness become material for her rhetorical play. Adonis protests, "Give me my hand, . . . why dost thou feel it?" And Venus responds with an asymmetrical offer, "Give me my heart, saith she, "and thou shalt have it" (373-74). In this exchange, Venus seizes the advantage he gives her by meeting his words one by one, an echo, but with the difference of a heart replacing a hand. Here, for the only time in the poem, Adonis addresses Venus with the familiar "thou." While she retains the "thou" in her speeches to him, he immediately corrects himself to call her the more distant "you," "And 'tis your fault I am bereft him so" (381). Through that shift he fixes on her status as "other."

While Adonis remains tied to a single sense of selfhood, characterized by epistemological, social, and sexual fears, Venus engages in play, exchange, and risk. Their first debate might be seen as a rhetorical display on the subject of love. Adonis' speech of blame exposes his fear of economic risk-taking: "'Tis much to borrow, and I will not owe it" (411). Like a parsimonious peasant, he is out-shone by the liberal Venus. Economic fear is homologous to the sexual fear he reveals, "If springing things be any jot diminish'd,/They wither in their prime, prove nothing worth" (417-18). While the immediate context refers to botanical "things," Adonis also fears phallic exhaustion and impotence. His phallocentric sense of himself leads him to associate ejaculation with annihilation: springing things that wither in their prime prove worth nothing. In contrast to Adonis' single-minded desire, "For all my mind, my thought, my busy care,/Is how to get my palfrey from the mare" (383-84), Venus' desire is unlimited, multiple, "The sea hath bounds, but deep desire hath none" (389).[10] Not annihilation and impotence, but expansion and power characterize Venus.

She subverts Adonis' absolutism through playful comic "supposes." In each of her supposes, Venus, whose imagination is not limited by a single focus, tests the value of one of the senses to love. She toys with various contingencies to discover different ways of measuring love:

> "Had I no eyes but ears, my ears would love
> That inward beauty and invisible,
> Or were I deaf, thy outward part would move
> Each part in me that were but sensible;
> Though neither eyes nor ears to hear nor see,
> Yet should I be in love by touching thee."
>
> (433-38)

Venus' rhetorical versatility creates a number of erotic pleasures despite Adonis' limitations. For example, she brings the subjunctive supposes into action in her comic pretense of a dead faint at Adonis' harsh look, "For on the grass she lies as she were slain,/Till his breath breatheth life in her again" (473-74). Later, she translates Adonis' simple offer of an exchange of salutations, into a more complex transaction:

> "Now let me say 'Good night,' and so say
>   you;
> If you will say so, you shall have a kiss."
> "Good night," quoth she, and ere he says
>   "Adieu,"
> The honey fee of parting tend'red is,
> Her arms do lend his neck a sweet embrace;
> Incorporate then they seem, face grows to
>   face.
>
> (535-40)

Venus does not settle for the meager reward he proposes. Instead, she takes the intiative, plays the entrepreneur, lends the capital she deals in, and creates a new "corporate" entity.

So often in *Venus and Adonis* does Venus employ the language of the marketplace as language of seduction, that she seems to have come to earth to learn to speak commercial jargon. In the market-place, where the values of goods, like the value of words, were, as Bacon would soon articulate, unpredictable, uncertainty pervades communication between humans. Such uncertainty informs the humorous language of love with which she presents Adonis the economics of sexuality:

> Pure lips, sweet seals in my soft lips
>   imprinted,
> What bargains may I make, still to be sealing?
> To sell myself I can be well contented,
> So thou wilt buy, and pay, and use good
>   dealing,
> Which purchase if thou make, for fear of
>   slips,
> Set thy seal manual on my wax-red lips.
>
> A thousand kisses buys my heart from me,
> And pay them at thy leisure, one by one.
> What is ten hundred touches unto thee?
> Are they not quickly told, and quickly gone?
> Say for non-payment that the debt should
>   double,
> Is twenty hundred kisses such a trouble?
>
> (511-22)

We are, here, in a commercial world gone haywire. If she sounds like a prodigal spender, expecting a return in prodigality from her partner in exchange, she soon hears her language countered by the language of the natural world. The system Adonis operates in obeys natural, orderly, predictable laws:

> The mellow plum doth fall, the green sticks
>   fast,
> Or being early pluck'd, is sour to taste.
>
> (527-28)

Like a country boy come to late sixteenth century London, he holds on to his old ways of measuring time, growth, maturity, and value. But his simple world of just price, natural time, and seasonal development is being replaced. Not only does the economic language indicate such change, but the physical description by the narrative voice suggests Venus' overturning of conventional values. She responds to the transition from a late-Medieval feudal order to a pre-capitalist society by adjusting her personal economy to a new set of contingencies.

Venus' rhetoric adjusts the flexibility of language to her changing personal economy. The complex mixture of sexual and political language in these stanzas suggests her subversion of patriarchy through parody. The comic hyperbole undermines the chivalric old order being mocked:

> Now quick desire hath caught the yielding
>   prey,
> And glutton-like she feeds, yet never filleth;
> Her lips are conquerors, his lips obey,
> Paying what ransom the insulter willeth;
> Whose vultur thought doth pitch the price so
>   high
> That she will draw his lips' rich treasure dry.
> And having felt the sweetness of the spoil,
> With blindfold fury she begins to forage;
> Her face doth reek and smoke, her blood doth
>   boil,
> And careless lust stirs up a desperate courage,
> Planting oblivion, beating reason back,
> Forgetting shame's pure blush and honor's
>   wrack.
>
> (547-58)

It is easy, at first, to judge Venus' aggression harshly. This is the devouring mouth Kahn has spoken of. And the threat extends to the political realm, as her lips are conquerors, demanding ransom, sucking his treasure dry. She is like an invader in the sovereign realm of his body. Moreover, she is so full of the signs of her physical selfhood, "Her face doth reek and smoke, her blood doth boil," that those abstractions which once determined fixed, controlled behavior, "reason," "shame," and "honor" are now subverted. Even those very words like "reason" soon placed in Adonis' mouth come to seem diminished. Adonis' few speeches are in relatively child-like language, "Fie, fie," he says, "you crush me, let me go,/You have no reason to withhold me so" (611-12). In this context, his infantile objections contrast with her impressive claims:

> But all in vain, good queen, it will not be;
> She hath assay'd as much as may be prov'd.
> Her pleading hath deserv'd a greater fee;
> She's Love, she loves, and yet she is not
>   lov'd.
>
> (607-10)

The value of "reason" slips, while Venus' mutable, flexible sense of self meets the contingencies of a newly commercial world. Moreover, her use of parody aligns her with the humanist effort to attain power through language, rather than force.

The question of danger has been implicit throughout the poem, but once the prospect of the boar is introduced, the theme of danger becomes explicit. Venus first associated herself with danger in the passage we began with, "Or what great danger dwells upon my suit?" (206). When Adonis reveals his plan to hunt the boar with his friends, Venus pleads with him, "Come not within his danger by thy will." Here, the phrase "within his danger" places her plea and Adonis' choice of dangers in a social and economic context. The *OED* tells us that danger can involve the power of a lord or master, involving jurisdiction, dominion, and the power to dispose of or to hurt or harm, specifically at times in his debt or under obligation to him. Venus, therefore, speaks to Adonis in the old feudal terms he favors, presenting the boar as a competing claimant to the dominance of Adonis. She would dominate him and keep him "within her danger," through physical, economic, and epistemological claims. But Adonis prefers the hunt of the boar to the hunt of love. Death is simpler than the reevaluation she offers.

But for Venus, the possibility of Adonis' death provokes a confusion that tests even her variable and flexible sense of self. In her range of emotions as she first fears, then curses, then hopes, and again laments, Venus is presented as maternal, infantile, and again maternal. The changes she undergoes suggest the flexibility of her nature. When she hears the cry of the hounds, a sign of Adonis' presence, she races, "Like a milch doe, whose swelling dugs do ache,/Hasting to feed her fawn hid in some brake" (875-76). Here, her nurturing maternal love is so physically drawn that the maternal and the sexual are powerfully intermingled. We remember the association of liquidity and female sexuality from her earlier offer to Adonis:

> I'll be a park, and thou shalt be my deer:
> Feed where thou wilt, on mountain, or in dale;
> Graze on my lips, and if those hills be dry,
> Stray lower, where the pleasant fountains lie.
>
> (231-34)

Soon after her fears of the hunt are realized, it is not the soothing flow of milk that conveys her love, but the flow of tears, when she is sure Adonis has died. Even then, the shout of a huntsman overcomes her tears, and she responds, "A nurse's song ne'er pleas'd her babe so well" (974). But when we read this line we pause and make mental adjustments, for we expect her now to be the nurse, and Adonis the babe. Instead, she is the babe pleased by a nurse's song. The change is a quick and surprising one, from mother to child, but one that undermines any fixed and inflexible sense of selfhood. When she finally takes the broken flower into her bosom, she again plays the nurse, "Lo in this hollow cradle take thy rest,/My throbbing heart shall rock thee day and night" (1185-86). But she has not finished either as nurturing mother, or as sexual partner, or as child. The "wide wound the boar had trench'd/In his soft flank" (1052-53) is figuratively reopened when she decapitates the purple flower. The fear of the castrating female is transferred to the imagery of a metamorphosed flower.

In this dissolving of the usual distinctions between maternal and infantile roles, between generation and castration, Venus prepares us for her range of responses to Adonis' death. But we must again add the political to the dimensions of her representation. As she tucks the flower in her bosom, she says:

> "Here was thy father's bed, here in my breast;
> Thou art the next of blood, and 'tis thy right.
> Lo in this hollow cradle take thy rest,
> My throbbing heart shall rock thee day and
>   night;"
>
> (1182-86)

She speaks as the mother to an infant, or as the nurse to a baby. But she also alludes to the rights of inheritance and succession according to primogeniture. In the late Elizabethan world, to speak of the issue of succession was to risk physical and emotional danger. For Venus to speak of the purple flower as "next of blood" is for her to broach the political dimension of generativity. This queen, however, retreats as soon as she has engaged the dispute, when she mounts to Paphos, where she "means to immure herself, and not be seen" (1194). In this final act of walling herself up not to be seen, Venus retreats from the marketplace realm which the poem has impinged upon. But she has not internalized the values of her silly dead Adonis; instead, she leaves her legacy of reevaluation in the thematics of value we produce through the poem.

Thus, although Venus becomes silent, after all that eloquence, her prophecy enters into the marketplace of poetry. She prophesies that in love all fixed, stable values shall be made unpredictable and uncertain. Communication between humans will be as inadequate and incomplete as was communication between herself and her beloved. All measures of an orderly society will become contingencies, subject to psychological, biological, economic needs. All lovers will confront the problematics of desire that she has met; but not all will face these circumstances with the flexible personal economy Venus can bring to them:

> "Since thou art dead, lo here I prophesy,
> Sorrow on love hereafter shall attend;
> It shall be waited on with jealousy,
> Find sweet beginning, but unsavory end;
> Ne'er settled equally, but high or low,
> That all love's pleasure shall not match his woe."
>
> (1135-40)

The asymmetrical bargains which we have seen Venus offer in love to her unresponsive audience become the very conditions of love itself. But when we read her words, we need not see love as a terror, any more than her presence is a terror. Venus articulates the conditions of love willingly undertaken by most humans. Whether willing or not, humans are impelled by the desires she articulates.

A feminist reading of *Venus and Adonis* reveals an analogy between the bargains Venus continuously re-enacts in operating on earth, and the dynamic renegotiating we do in creating our understanding of her. Such bargains may, in turn, be analogous to the strategies Shakespeare, already a man of the theater, would employ as he both "immures" that multiple, shifting, subversive theatrical talent between the fixed covers of a published poem, and risks exposing his poetry to the commodification of the court marketplace. Then Venus represents the politically, sexually, and epistemologically subversive realm of the theater invading the realm of published poetry. But she also suggests a liberating reevaluation of the patriarchal world she both plays in and subverts, as she demonstrates the usefulness of the thematics of value to expose the limitations of absolutist perspectives.

Notes

[1] William Shakespeare, *The Riverside Shakespeare*, edited by G. Blakemore Evans (Boston: Houghton Mifflin, 1974). All line references to this edition of *Venus and Adonis* will be provided in parentheses following the quotation.

[2] Coppélia Kahn, *Man's Estate: Masculine Identity in Shakespeare* (Berkeley: Univ. of California Press, 1981). Kahn provided a generous critical response to an early version of this paper presented at the 1986 Shakespeare Association of America meeting.

[3] Barbara Herrnstein Smith, "Contingencies of Value," in *Critical Inquiry*, 10 (1983), 1-35.

[4] For an admirable reading of the poem and an able review of the critical debate over the moral perspective "readers" are to take on the poem, see, Clark Hulse, *Metamorphic Verse: The Elizabethan Minor Epic* (Princeton: Princeton Univ. Press, 1981), pp. 147-148. In n.7, Hulse refers to "the new orthodoxy of an ambivalent *Venus and Adonis*," and argues that "such pluralism is perfectly consonant with an informed understanding of Renaissance poetics." The present paper intends to advance such a reading.

[5] Neil Hertz, "Medusa's Head: Male Hysteria under Political Pressure," *Representations*, 4 (1983), 27-54, and Gallagher, Fineman, Hertz, "More about 'Medusa's Head,'" 55-71.

[6] In a series of articles, Louis Adrian Montrose has been analyzing the uses of power by Queen Elizabeth. See, for example, "'Eliza, Queene of shepheardes,' and the Pastoral of Power," *ELR*, 10 (1980), 153-82.

For an important collection of essays using a historical materialist approach to Shakespeare, see Jonathan Dollimore and Alan Sinfield, eds., *Political Shakespeare: New Essays in Cultural Materialism* (Manchester: Manchester Univ. Press, 1985). In particular, see, Kathleen McLuskie, "The Patriarchal Bard: Feminist Criticism and Shakespeare: *King Lear* and *Measure for Measure*," pp. 88-108.

[7] Lawrence Stone, "The Rise of the Nuclear Family in Early Modern England: The Patriarchal Stage," in Charles E. Rosenberg, ed., *The Family in History* (Philadelphia: Univ. of Pennsylvania Press, 1975).

[8] *The Riverside Shakespeare*, p. 1704.

[9] Frank Whigham, *Ambition and Privilege: The Social Tropes of Elizabethan Courtesy Theory* (Berkeley: Univ. of California Press, 1984). The discussion of *paradiastole* begins on p. 40. This book illuminates the context for the poem. Whigham's approach also provides an opportunity for feminist criticism, since he declares in note 36 to p. 11, "my concern in this book is with courtesy for *men* at court. I have chosen to bracket for the moment issues regarding courtesy and women, whose situations were distinctly different, both in life and in the literature, owing to complex interactions of social and gender codes. I hope to treat these matters elsewhere." This essay begins, I hope, to treat such matters.

[10] In her helpful comments on an early version of this paper, Heather Dubrow cites John Donne's "The Apparition": "he, whose thou art then, being tyr'd before,/Will, if thou stirre, or pinch to wake him, thinke/Thou call'st for more,/And in false sleepe will from thee shrinke."

FURTHER READING

Belsey, Catherine. "Love as Trompe-l'oeil: Taxonomies of Desire in *Venus and Adonis*." *Shakespeare Quarterly* 46, No. 3 (Fall 1995): 257-76.

    Views *Venus and Adonis* as a work that performs a literary illusion by promising a "definitive account of love" but withholding it.

Blythe, David-Everett. "Shakespeare's *Venus and Adonis*." *The Explicator* 53, No. 2 (Winter 1995): 68-70.

    Argues that the phrase "vails his tail" in *Venus and Adonis* means "to lift" rather than "to lower" as it is commonly interpreted.

Bradbrook, M. C. "Beasts and Gods: The Social Purpose of *Venus and Adonis*." In *Muriel Bradbrook on Shakespeare*, pp. 43-56. Sussex: The Harvester Press, 1984.

    Sees the poem *Venus and Adonis* as a claim to social dignity by Shakespeare in an era when drama and dramatists were frequently disparaged.

Duncan-Jones, Katherine. "Much Ado with Red and White: The Earliest Readers of Shakespeare's *Venus and Adonis* (1593)." *Review of English Studies* XLIV, No. 176 (November 1993): 479-501.

Considers the early popularity of *Venus and Adonis* as an erotic courtship poem.

Dundas, Judith. "Wat the Hare, or Shakespearean Decorum." *Shakespeare Studies* XIX (1987): 1-15.

Examines Shakespeare's altering of his classical sources by tempering Venus's ideal perfection with human traits in *Venus and Adonis*.

Kolin, Philip C., ed. *'Venus and Adonis': Critical Essays*. New York: Garland Publishing, 1997, 429 p.

Collection of nineteenth- and twentieth-century essays on *Venus and Adonis* by various contributors, preceded by a survey of critical reaction to the work.

Martindale, Charles and Colin Burrow. "Clapham's *Narcissus*: A Pre-Text for Shakespeare's *Venus and Adonis*?" *English Literary Renaissance* 22, No. 2 (Spring 1992): 147-76.

Forwards the poem *Narcissus* by the little-known Elizabethan John Clapham as a source for *Venus and Adonis*.

Roberts, Jeanne Addison. "The Wild Landscape: Women and Nature." In *The Skakespearean Wild: Geography, Genus, and Gender*, pp. 23-53. Lincoln: University of Nebraska Press, 1991.

Mentions *Venus and Adonis* as part of a discussion of male entry into the feminized wilds of nature in Shakespeare's plays.

Guide to *Shakespearean Criticism* Series

VOLUMES 1-10	Provides an historical overview of the critical response to each Shakespearean work. Includes criticism from the seventeenth century to the present.
VOLUMES 11, 12, 14, 15, 17, 18, 20, 21, 23, 24, 26	Examines the performance history of Shakespeare's plays on the stage and screen through eyewitness reviews and retrospective evaluations of individual productions. Also provides comparisons of major interpretations and discusses staging issues.
VOLUMES 27, 29-31, 33-36, 38-41, 43-51	Focuses on criticism published after 1960. Each volume is ordered around a theme, such as politics, religion, or sexuality, with a topic entry that introduces the volume and several entries devoted to individual works.
Yearbooks: **VOLUMES 13, 16, 19, 22, 25, 28, 32, 37, 42, 48**	Compiled annually beginning in 1989. Includes the most noteworthy essays of the year published on Shakespeare as recommended by an international advisory board of distinguished Shakespearean scholars.

Cumulative Character Index

The Cumulative Character Index identifies the principal characters of discussion in the criticism of each play and non-dramatic poem. The characters are arranged alphabetically. Page references indicate the beginning page number of each essay containing substantial commentary on that character.

Aaron
Titus Andronicus **4:** 632, 637, 650, 651, 653, 668, 672, 675; **27:** 255; **28:** 249, 330; **43:** 176

Adonis
Venus and Adonis **10:** 411, 420, 424, 427, 429, 434, 439, 442, 451, 454, 459, 466, 473, 489; **25:** 305, 328; **28:** 355; **33:** 309, 321, 330, 347, 352, 357, 363, 370, 377; **51:** 345, 377

Adriana
The Comedy of Errors **16:** 3; **34:** 211, 220, 238

Albany
King Lear **32:** 308

Alcibiades
Timon of Athens **25:** 198; **27:** 191

Angelo
Measure for Measure
   anxiety **16:** 114
   authoritarian portrayal of **23:** 307; **49:** 274
   characterization **2:** 388, 390, 397, 402, 418, 427, 432, 434, 463, 484, 495, 503, 511; **13:** 84; **23:** 297; **32:** 81; **33:** 77; **49:** 274, 293, 379
   hypocrisy **2:** 396, 399, 402, 406, 414, 421; **23:** 345, 358, 362
   repentance or pardon **2:** 388, 390, 397, 402, 434, 463, 511, 524

Anne (Anne Boleyn)
Henry VIII See **Boleyn**

Anne (Anne Page)
The Merry Wives of Windsor See **Page**

Antigonus
The Winter's Tale
   characterization **7:** 394, 451, 464
   death (Act III, scene iii) **7:** 377, 414, 464, 483; **15:** 518, 532; **19:** 366

Antonio
The Merchant of Venice
   excessive or destructive love **4:** 279, 284, 336, 344; **12:** 54; **37:** 86
   love for Bassanio **40:** 156
   melancholy **4:** 221, 238, 279, 284, 300, 321, 328; **22:** 69; **25:** 22
   pitiless **4:** 254
   as pivotal figure **12:** 25, 129
Twelfth Night **22:** 69

Antonio and Sebastian
The Tempest **8:** 295, 299, 304, 328, 370, 396, 429, 454; **13:** 440; **29:** 278, 297, 343, 362, 368, 377; **45:** 200

Antony
Antony and Cleopatra
   characterization **6:** 22, 23, 24, 31, 38, 41, 172, 181, 211; **16:** 342; **19:** 270; **22:** 217; **27:** 117; **47:** 77, 124, 142
   Caesar, relationship with **48:** 206
   Cleopatra, relationship with **6:** 25, 27, 37, 39, 48, 52, 53, 62, 67, 71, 76, 85, 100, 125, 131, 133, 136, 142, 151, 161, 163, 165, 180, 192; **27:** 82; **47:** 107, 124, 165, 174
   death scene **25:** 245; **47:** 142
   dotage **6:** 22, 23, 38, 41, 48, 52, 62, 107, 136, 146, 175; **17:** 28
   nobility **6:** 22, 24, 33, 48, 94, 103, 136, 142, 159, 172, 202; **25:** 245
   political conduct **6:** 33, 38, 53, 107, 111, 146, 181
   public vs. private personae **6:** 165; **47:** 107
   self-knowledge **6:** 120, 131, 175, 181, 192; **47:** 77
   as superhuman figure **6:** 37, 51, 71, 92, 94, 178, 192; **27:** 110; **47:** 71
   as tragic hero **6:** 38, 39, 52, 53, 60, 104, 120, 151, 155, 165, 178, 192, 202, 211; **22:** 217; **27:** 90
Julius Caesar
   characterization **7:** 160, 179, 189, 221, 233, 284, 320, 333; **17:** 269, 271, 272, 284, 298, 306, 313, 315, 358, 398; **25:** 272; **30:** 316
   funeral oration **7:** 148, 154, 159, 204, 210, 221, 238, 259, 350; **25:** 280; **30:** 316, 333, 362

Apemantus
Timon of Athens **1:** 453, 467, 483; **20:** 476, 493; **25:** 198; **27:** 166, 223, 235

Arcite
The Two Noble Kinsmen See **Palamon and Arcite**

Ariel
The Tempest **8:** 289, 293, 294, 295, 297, 304, 307, 315, 320, 326, 328, 336, 340, 345, 356, 364, 420, 458; **22:** 302; **29:** 278, 297, 362, 368, 377

CUMULATIVE CHARACTER INDEX

Armado
Love's Labour's Lost **23:** 207

Arthur
King John **9:** 215, 216, 218, 219, 229, 240, 267, 275; **22:** 120; **25:** 98; **41:** 251, 277

Arviragus
Cymbeline See **Guiderius and Arviragus**

Audrey
As You Like It **46:** 122

Aufidius
Coriolanus **9:** 9, 12, 17, 19, 53, 121, 148, 153, 157, 169, 180, 193; **19:** 287; **25:** 263, 296; **30:** 58, 67, 89, 96, 133; **50:** 99

Autolycus
The Winter's Tale **7:** 375, 380, 382, 387, 389, 395, 396, 414; **15:** 524; **22:** 302; **37:** 31; **45:** 333; **46:** 14, 33; **50:** 45

Banquo
Macbeth **3:** 183, 199, 208, 213, 278, 289; **20:** 279, 283, 406, 413; **25:** 235; **28:** 339

Baptista
The Taming of the Shrew **9:** 325, 344, 345, 375, 386, 393, 413

Barnardine
Measure for Measure **13:** 112

Bassanio
The Merchant of Venice **25:** 257; **37:** 86; **40:** 156

the Bastard
King John See **Faulconbridge (Philip) the Bastard**

Beatrice and Benedick
Much Ado about Nothing
Beatrice's femininity **8:** 14, 16, 17, 24, 29, 38, 41, 91; **31:** 222, 245
Beatrice's request to "kill Claudio" (Act IV, scene i) **8:** 14, 17, 33, 41, 55, 63, 75, 79, 91, 108, 115; **18:** 119, 120, 136, 161, 245, 257
Benedick's challenge of Claudio (Act V, scene i) **8:** 48, 63, 79, 91; **31:** 231
Claudio and Hero, compared with **8:** 19, 28, 29, 75, 82, 115; **31:** 171, 216
marriage and the opposite sex, attitudes toward **8:** 9, 13, 14, 16, 19, 29, 36, 48, 63, 77, 91, 95, 115, 121; **16:** 45; **31:** 216; **48:** 14
mutual attraction **8:** 13, 14, 19, 24, 29, 33, 41, 75; **48:** 14
nobility **8:** 13, 19, 24, 29, 36, 39, 41, 47, 82, 91, 108
popularity **8:** 13, 38, 41, 53, 79
transformed by love **8:** 19, 29, 36, 48, 75, 91, 95, 115; **31:** 209, 216
unconventionality **8:** 48, 91, 95, 108, 115, 121
vulgarity **8:** 11, 12, 33, 38, 41, 47
wit and charm **8:** 9, 12, 13, 14, 19, 24, 27, 28, 29, 33, 36, 38, 41, 47, 55, 69, 95, 108, 115; **31:** 241

Belarius
Cymbeline **4:** 48, 89, 141

Benedick
Much Ado about Nothing See **Beatrice and Benedick**

Berowne
Love's Labour's Lost **2:** 308, 324, 327; **22:** 12; **23:** 184, 187; **38:** 194; **47:** 35

Bertram
All's Well That Ends Well
characterization **7:** 15, 27, 29, 32, 39, 41, 43, 98, 113; **26:** 48; **26:** 117; **48:** 65
conduct **7:** 9, 10, 12, 16, 19, 21, 51, 62, 104; **50:** 59
physical desire **22:** 78
transformation or redemption **7:** 10, 19, 21, 26, 29, 32, 54, 62, 81, 90, 93, 98, 109, 113, 116, 126; **13:** 84

Bianca
The Taming of the Shrew **9:** 325, 342, 344, 345, 360, 362, 370, 375
Bianca-Lucentio subplot **9:** 365, 370, 375, 390, 393, 401, 407, 413, 430; **16:** 13; **31:** 339

the boar
Venus and Adonis **10:** 416, 451, 454, 466, 473; **33:** 339, 347, 370

Boleyn (Anne Boleyn)
Henry VIII **2:** 21, 24, 31; **41:** 180

Bolingbroke
Richard II See **Henry (King Henry IV, previously known as Bolingbroke)**

Borachio and Conrade
Much Ado about Nothing **8:** 24, 69, 82, 88, 111, 115

Bottom
A Midsummer Night's Dream
awakening speech (Act IV, scene i) **3:** 406, 412, 450, 457, 486, 516; **16:** 34
folly of **46:** 1, 14, 29, 60
imagination **3:** 376, 393, 406, 432, 486; **29:** 175, 190; **45:** 147
self-possession **3:** 365, 376, 395, 402, 406, 480; **45:** 158
Titania, relationship with **3:** 377, 406, 441, 445, 450, 457, 491, 497; **16:** 34; **19:** 21; **22:** 93; **29:** 216; **45:** 160
transformation **3:** 365, 377, 432; **13:** 27; **22:** 93; **29:** 216; **45:** 147, 160

Brabantio
Othello **25:** 189

Brutus
Coriolanus See **the tribunes**
Julius Caesar **50:** 194, 258
arrogance **7:** 160, 169, 204, 207, 264, 277, 292, 350; **25:** 280; **30:** 351
as chief protagonist or tragic hero **7:** 152, 159, 189, 191, 200, 204, 242, 250, 253, 264, 268, 279, 284, 298, 333; **17:** 272, 372, 387
citizenship **25:** 272
funeral oration **7:** 154, 155, 204, 210, 350
motives **7:** 150, 156, 161, 179, 191, 200, 221, 227, 233, 245, 292, 303, 310, 320, 333, 350; **25:** 272; **30:** 321, 358
nobility or idealism **7:** 150, 152, 156, 159, 161, 179, 189, 191, 200, 221, 242, 250, 253, 259, 264, 277, 303, 320; **17:** 269, 271, 273, 279, 280, 284, 306, 308, 321, 323, 324, 345, 358; **25:** 272, 280; **30:** 351, 362
political ineptitude or lack of judgment **7:** 169, 188, 200, 205, 221, 245, 252, 264, 277, 282, 310, 316, 331, 333, 343; **17:** 323, 358, 375, 380; **50:** 13
self-knowledge or self-deception **7:** 191, 200, 221, 242, 259, 264, 268, 279, 310, 333, 336, 350; **25:** 272; **30:** 316
soliloquy (Act II, scene i) **7:** 156, 160, 161, 191, 221, 245, 250, 253, 264, 268, 279, 282, 292, 303, 343, 350; **25:** 280; **30:** 333
The Rape of Lucrece **10:** 96, 106, 109, 116, 121, 125, 128, 135

Buckingham
Henry VIII **22:** 182; **24:** 129, 140; **37:** 109

Cade (Jack [John] Cade)
Henry VI, Parts 1, 2, and 3 **3:** 35, 67, 92, 97, 109; **16:** 183; **22:** 156; **25:** 102; **28:** 112; **37:** 97; **39:** 160, 196, 205

Caesar
Antony and Cleopatra
Antony, relationship with as leader **48:** 206
Julius Caesar **50:** 189, 230, 234
ambiguous nature **7:** 191, 233, 242, 250, 272, 298, 316, 320
ambitious nature **50:** 234
arrogance **7:** 160, 207, 218, 253, 272, 279, 298; **25:** 280
idolatry **22:** 137
leadership qualities **7:** 161, 179, 189, 191, 200, 207, 233, 245, 253, 257, 264, 272, 279, 284, 298, 310, 333; **17:** 317, 358; **22:** 280; **30:** 316, 326; **50:** 234
as tragic hero **7:** 152, 200, 221, 279; **17:** 321, 377, 384
weakness **7:** 161, 167, 169, 179, 187, 188, 191, 207, 218, 221, 233, 250, 253, 298; **17:** 358; **25:** 280

Caius, Doctor
The Merry Wives of Windsor **47:** 354

Caliban
The Tempest **8:** 286, 287, 289, 292, 294, 295, 297, 302, 304, 307, 309, 315, 326,

328, 336, 353, 364, 370, 380, 390, 396, 401, 414, 420, 423, 429, 435, 454; **13:** 424, 440; **15:** 189, 312, 322, 374, 379; **22:** 302; **25:** 382; **28:** 249; **29:** 278, 292, 297, 343, 368, 377, 396; **32:** 367; **45:** 211, 219, 226, 259

Calphurnia
Julius Caesar
    Calphurnia's dream **45:** 10

Cambridge
Henry V See **traitors**

Canterbury and the churchmen
Henry V **5:** 193, 203, 205, 213, 219, 225, 252, 260; **22:** 137; **30:** 215, 262

Cardinal Wolsey
Henry VIII See **Wolsey**

Casca
Julius Caesar
    as Cynic **50:** 249
    as proto-Christian **50:** 249

Cassio
Othello **25:** 189

Cassius
Julius Caesar **7:** 156, 159, 160, 161, 169, 179, 189, 221, 233, 303, 310, 320, 333, 343; **17:** 272, 282, 284, 344, 345, 358; **25:** 272, 280; **30:** 351; **37:** 203

Celia
As You Like It **46:** 94

Chorus
Henry V
    role of **5:** 186, 192, 226, 228, 230, 252, 264, 269, 281, 293; **14:** 301, 319, 336; **19:** 133; **25:** 116, 131; **30:** 163, 202, 220

the churchmen
Henry V See **Canterbury and the churchmen**

Cinna
Julius Caesar
    as poet **48:** 240

Claudio
Much Ado about Nothing
    boorish behavior **8:** 9, 24, 33, 36, 39, 44, 48, 63, 79, 82, 95, 100, 111, 115; **31:** 209
    credulity **8:** 9, 17, 19, 24, 29, 36, 41, 47, 58, 63, 75, 77, 82, 95, 100, 104, 111, 115, 121; **31:** 241; **47:** 25
    mercenary traits **8:** 24, 44, 58, 82, 91, 95
    noble qualities **8:** 17, 19, 29, 41, 44, 58, 75
    reconciliation with Hero **8:** 33, 36, 39, 44, 47, 82, 95, 100, 111, 115, 121
    repentance **8:** 33, 63, 82, 95, 100, 111, 115, 121; **31:** 245
    sexual insecurities **8:** 75, 100, 111, 115, 121

Claudius
Hamlet **13:** 502; **16:** 246; **21:** 259, 347, 361, 371; **28:** 232, 290; **35:** 104, 182; **44:** 119, 241

Cleopatra
Antony and Cleopatra
    Antony, relationship with **6:** 25, 27, 37, 39, 48, 52, 53, 62, 67, 71, 76, 85, 100, 125, 131, 133, 136, 142, 151, 161, 163, 165, 180, 192; **25:** 257; **27:** 82; **47:** 107, 124, 165, 174
    characterization **47:** 77, 96, 113, 124
    contradictory or inconsistent nature **6:** 23, 24, 27, 67, 76, 100, 104, 115, 136, 151, 159, 202; **17:** 94, 113; **27:** 135
    costume **17:** 94
    creativity **6:** 197; **47:** 96, 113
    death **6:** 23, 25, 27, 41, 43, 52, 60, 64, 76, 94, 100, 103, 120, 131, 133, 136, 140, 146, 161, 165, 180, 181, 192, 197, 208; **13:** 383; **17:** 48, 94; **25:** 245; **27:** 135; **47:** 71
    personal attraction of **6:** 24, 38, 40, 43, 48, 53, 76, 104, 115, 155; **17:** 113
    self-knowledge **47:** 77, 96
    staging issues **17:** 94, 113
    as subverter of social order **6:** 146, 165; **47:** 113
    as superhuman figure **6:** 37, 51, 71, 92, 94, 178, 192; **27:** 110; **47:** 71, 174, 192
    as tragic heroine **6:** 53, 120, 151, 192, 208; **27:** 144
    as voluptuary or courtesan **6:** 21, 22, 25, 41, 43, 52, 53, 62, 64, 76, 146, 161; **47:** 107, 174

Cloten
Cymbeline **4:** 20, 116, 127, 155; **22:** 302, 365; **25:** 245; **36:** 99, 125, 142, 155; **47:** 228

Collatine
The Rape of Lucrece **10:** 98, 131; **43:** 102; **48:** 291

Cominius
Coriolanus **25:** 245

Conrade
Much Ado about Nothing See **Borachio and Conrade**

Constance
King John **9:** 208, 210, 211, 215, 219, 220, 224, 229, 240, 251, 254; **16:** 161; **24:** 177, 184, 196

Cordelia
King Lear
    attack on Britain **25:** 202
    characterization **2:** 110, 116, 125, 170; **16:** 311; **25:** 218; **28:** 223, 325; **31:** 117, 149, 155, 162; **46:** 218, 225, 231, 242
    as Christ figure **2:** 116, 170, 179, 188, 222, 286
    gender identity **48:** 222

    rebelliousness **13:** 352; **25:** 202
    on stage **11:** 158
    transcendent power **2:** 137, 207, 218, 265, 269, 273
    women, the Christian ideal of **48:** 222

Corin
As You Like It See **pastoral characters**

Coriolanus
Coriolanus
    anger or passion **9:** 19, 26, 45, 80, 92, 157, 164, 177, 189; **30:** 79, 96
    as complementary figure to Aufidius **19:** 287
    death scene (Act V, scene vi) **9:** 12, 80, 100, 117, 125, 144, 164, 198; **25:** 245, 263; **50:** 110
    as epic hero **9:** 130, 164, 177; **25:** 245; **50:** 119
    immaturity **9:** 62, 80, 84, 110, 117, 142; **30:** 140
    inhuman attributes **9:** 65, 73, 139, 157, 164, 169, 189, 198; **25:** 263
    internal struggle **9:** 31, 43, 45, 53, 72, 117, 121, 130; **44:** 93
    introspection or self-knowledge, lack of **9:** 53, 80, 84, 112, 117, 130; **25:** 296; **30:** 133
    isolation or autonomy **9:** 53, 65, 142, 144, 153, 157, 164, 180, 183, 189, 198; **30:** 58, 89, 111; **50:** 128
    manipulation by others **9:** 33, 45, 62, 80; **25:** 296
    as military leader **48:** 230
    modesty **9:** 8, 12, 19, 26, 53, 78, 92, 117, 121, 144, 183; **25:** 296; **30:** 79, 96, 129, 133, 149
    narcissism **30:** 111
    noble or aristocratic attributes **9:** 15, 18, 19, 26, 31, 33, 52, 53, 62, 65, 84, 92, 100, 121, 148, 157, 169; **25:** 263; **30:** 67, 74, 96; **50:** 113
    pride or arrogance **9:** 8, 11, 12, 19, 26, 31, 33, 43, 45, 65, 78, 92, 121, 148, 153, 177; **30:** 58, 67, 74, 89, 96, 129
    punishment of **48:** 230
    reconciliation with society **9:** 33, 43, 45, 65, 139, 169; **25:** 296
    as socially destructive force **9:** 62, 65, 73, 78, 110, 142, 144, 153; **25:** 296
    soliloquy (Act IV, scene iv) **9:** 84, 112, 117, 130
    as tragic figure **9:** 8, 12, 13, 18, 25, 45, 52, 53, 72, 80, 92, 106, 112, 117, 130, 148, 164, 169, 177; **25:** 296; **30:** 67, 74, 79, 96, 111, 129; **37:** 283; **50:** 99
    traitorous actions **9:** 9, 12, 19, 45, 84, 92, 148; **25:** 296; **30:** 133
    as unsympathetic character **9:** 12, 13, 62, 78, 80, 84, 112, 130, 157

the courser and the jennet
Venus and Adonis **10:** 418, 439, 466; **33:** 309, 339, 347, 352

Cranmer
Henry VIII
prophesy of **2:** 25, 31, 46, 56, 64, 68, 72; **24:** 146; **32:** 148; **41:** 120, 190

Cressida
Troilus and Cressida
as ambiguous figure **43:** 305
inconsistency **3:** 538; **13:** 53; **16:** 70; **22:** 339; **27:** 362
individual will vs. social values **3:** 549, 561, 571, 590, 604, 617, 626; **13:** 53; **27:** 396
infidelity **3:** 536, 537, 544, 554, 555; **18:** 277, 284, 286; **22:** 58, 339; **27:** 400; **43:** 298
lack of punishment **3:** 536, 537
as mother figure **22:** 339
objectification of **43:** 329
as sympathetic figure **3:** 557, 560, 604, 609; **18:** 284, 423; **22:** 58; **27:** 396, 400; **43:** 305

Dark Lady
Sonnets **10:** 161, 167, 176, 216, 217, 218, 226, 240, 302, 342, 377, 394; **25:** 374; **37:** 374; **40:** 273; **48:** 346; **51:** 284, 288, 292, 321

the Dauphin
Henry V See **French aristocrats and the Dauphin**

Desdemona
Othello
as Christ figure **4:** 506, 525, 573; **35:** 360
culpability **4:** 408, 415, 422, 427; **13:** 313; **19:** 253, 276; **35:** 265, 352, 380
innocence **35:** 360; **43:** 32; **47:** 25
as mother figure **22:** 339; **35:** 282
passivity **4:** 402, 406, 421, 440, 457, 470, 582, 587; **25:** 189; **35:** 380
spiritual nature of her love **4:** 462, 530, 559
staging issues **11:** 350, 354, 359; **13:** 327; **32:** 201

Diana
Pericles
as symbol of nature **22:** 315; **36:** 233; **51:** 71

Dogberry and the Watch
Much Ado about Nothing **8:** 9, 12, 13, 17, 24, 28, 29, 33, 39, 48, 55, 69, 79, 82, 88, 95, 104, 108, 115; **18:** 138, 152, 205, 208, 210, 213, 231; **22:** 85; **31:** 171, 229; **46:** 60

Don John
Much Ado about Nothing See **John (Don John)**

Don Pedro
Much Ado about Nothing See **Pedro (Don Pedro)**

Dromio Brothers
Comedy of Errors **42:** 80

Duke
Measure for Measure
as authoritarian figure **23:** 314, 317, 347; **33:** 85; **49:** 274, 300, 358
characterization **2:** 388, 395, 402, 406, 411, 421, 429, 456, 466, 470, 498, 511; **13:** 84, 94, 104; **23:** 363, 416; **32:** 81; **42:** 1; **44:** 89; **49:** 274, 293, 300, 358
as dramatic failure **2:** 420, 429, 441, 479, 495, 505, 514, 522
godlike portrayal of **23:** 320
noble portrayal of **23:** 301
speech on death (Act III, scene i) **2:** 390, 391, 395
Othello **25:** 189

Edgar
King Lear **28:** 223; **32:** 212; **32:** 308; **37:** 295; **47:** 9; **50:** 24, 45
Edgar-Edmund duel **22:** 365

Edmund
King Lear **25:** 218; **28:** 223
Edmund's forged letter **16:** 372

Edmund of Langley, Duke of York
Richard II See **York**

Elbow
Measure for Measure **22:** 85; **25:** 12

Elbow (Mistress Elbow)
Measure for Measure **33:** 90

elder characters
All's Well That Ends Well **7:** 9, 37, 39, 43, 45, 54, 62, 104

Elizabeth I
Love's Labour's Lost **38:** 239

Emilia
Othello **4:** 386, 391, 392, 415, 587; **35:** 352, 380; **43:** 32
The Two Noble Kinsmen **9:** 460, 470, 471, 479, 481; **19:** 394; **41:** 372, 385; **42:** 361

Enobarbus
Antony and Cleopatra **6:** 22, 23, 27, 43, 94, 120, 142; **16:** 342; **17:** 36; **22:** 217; **27:** 135

Evans, Sir Hugh
The Merry Wives of Windsor **47:** 354

fairies
A Midsummer Night's Dream **3:** 361, 362, 372, 377, 395, 400, 423, 450, 459, 486; **12:** 287, 291, 294, 295; **19:** 21; **29:** 183, 190; **45:** 147

Falstaff
Henry IV, Parts 1 and 2
characterization **1:** 287, 298, 312, 333; **25:** 245; **28:** 203; **39:** 72, 134, 137, 143; **48:** 117, 151
as comic figure **1:** 287, 311, 327, 344, 351, 354, 357, 410, 434; **39:** 89; **46:** 1, 48, 52
as comic versus tragic figure **49:** 178
as coward or rogue **1:** 285, 290, 296, 298, 306, 307, 313, 317, 323, 336, 337, 338, 342, 354, 366, 374, 391, 396, 401, 433; **14:** 7, 111, 125, 130, 133; **32:** 166
as deceiver deceived **47:** 308
diminishing powers of **47:** 363
dual personality **1:** 397, 401, 406, 434; **49:** 162
female attributes **13:** 183; **44:** 44; **47:** 325
Iago, compared with **1:** 341, 351
as Jack-a-Lent **47:** 363
Marxist interpretation **1:** 358, 361
as outlaw **49:** 133
as parody of the historical plot **1:** 314, 354, 359; **39:** 143
as positive character **1:** 286, 287, 290, 296, 298, 311, 312, 321, 325, 333, 344, 355, 357, 389, 401, 408, 434
rejection by Hal **1:** 286, 287, 290, 312, 314, 317, 324, 333, 338, 344, 357, 366, 372, 374, 379, 380, 389, 414; **13:** 183; **25:** 109; **39:** 72, 89; **48:** 95
as satire of feudal society **1:** 314, 328, 361; **32:** 103
as scapegoat **1:** 389, 414; **47:** 358, 363, 375
stage interpretations **14:** 4, 6, 7, 9, 15, 116, 130, 146; **47:** 1
as subversive figure **16:** 183; **25:** 109
Henry V **5:** 185, 186, 187, 189, 192, 195, 198, 210, 226, 257, 269, 271, 276, 293, 299; **28:** 146; **46:** 48
The Merry Wives of Windsor
characterization in *1* and *2 Henry IV*, compared with **5:** 333, 335, 336, 337, 339, 346, 347, 348, 350, 373, 400; **18:** 5, 7, 75, 86; **22:** 93
diminishing powers **5:** 337, 339, 343, 347, 350, 351, 392
as Herne the Hunter **38:** 256, 286; **47:** 358
incapability of love **5:** 335, 336, 339, 346, 348; **22:** 93
personification of comic principle or as Vice figure **1:** 342, 361, 366, 374; **5:** 332, 338, 369, 400; **38:** 273
recognition and repentance of follies **5:** 338, 341, 343, 348, 369, 374, 376, 397
sensuality **5:** 339, 343, 353, 369, 392
shrewdness **5:** 332, 336, 346, 355
threat to community **5:** 343, 369, 379, 392, 395, 400; **38:** 297
as unifying force **47:** 358
vanity **5:** 332, 339
victimization **5:** 336, 338, 341, 347, 348, 353, 355, 360, 369, 373, 374, 376, 392, 397, 400
as villain **47:** 358

Faulconbridge, (Philip) the Bastard
King John **41:** 205, 228, 251, 260, 277; **48:** 132
as chorus or commentator **9:** 212, 218, 229, 248, 251, 260, 271, 284, 297, 300; **22:** 120
as comic figure **9:** 219, 271, 297

development **9:** 216, 224, 229, 248, 263, 271, 275, 280, 297; **13:** 158, 163
  as embodiment of England **9:** 222, 224, 240, 244, 248, 271
  heroic qualities **9:** 208, 245, 248, 254, 263, 271, 275; **25:** 98
  political conduct **9:** 224, 240, 250, 260, 280, 297; **13:** 147, 158; **22:** 120

Fenton
  The Merry Wives of Windsor
  Anne Page-Fenton plot **5:** 334, 336, 343, 353, 376, 390, 395, 402; **22:** 93

Ferdinand
  The Tempest **8:** 328, 336, 359, 454; **19:** 357; **22:** 302; **29:** 362, 339, 377

Feste
  Twelfth Night
  characterization **1:** 558, 655, 658; **26:** 233, 364; **46:** 1, 14, 18, 33, 52, 60, 303, 310
  role in play **1:** 546, 551, 553, 566, 570, 571, 579, 635, 658; **46:** 297, 303, 310
  song **1:** 543, 548, 561, 563, 566, 570, 572, 603, 620, 642; **46:** 297
  gender issues **19:** 78; **34:** 344; **37:** 59

Flavius and Murellus
  Julius Caesar **50:** 64

Fluellen
  Henry V **30:** 278; **37:** 105

Fool
  King Lear **2:** 108, 112, 125, 156, 162, 245, 278, 284; **11:** 17, 158, 169; **22:** 227; **25:** 202; **28:** 223; **46:** 1, 14, 18, 24, 33, 52, 191, 205, 210, 218, 225

Ford, Francis
  The Merry Wives of Windsor **5:** 332, 334, 343, 355, 363, 374, 379, 390; **38:** 273; **47:** 321

Ford, Mistress Alice
  The Merry Wives of Windsor **47:** 321

Fortinbras
  Hamlet **21:** 136, 347; **28:** 290

French aristocrats and the Dauphin
  Henry V **5:** 188, 191, 199, 205, 213, 281; **22:** 137; **28:** 121

Friar
  Much Ado about Nothing **8:** 24, 29, 41, 55, 63, 79, 111

Friar John
  Romeo and Juliet See **John (Friar John)**

Friar Lawrence
  Romeo and Juliet See **Lawrence (Friar Lawrence)**

the **Friend**
  Sonnets **10:** 279, 302, 309, 379, 385, 391, 394; **51:** 284, 292, 300, 304, 316, 321

Ganymede
  A Winter's Tale **48:** 309

Gardiner (Stephen Gardiner)
  Henry VIII **24:** 129

Gaunt
  Richard II **6:** 255, 287, 374, 388, 402, 414; **24:** 274, 322, 325, 414, 423; **39:** 263, 279

Gertrude
  Hamlet **21:** 259, 347, 392; **28:** 311; **32:** 238; **35:** 182, 204, 229; **43:** 12; **44:** 119, 160, 189, 195, 237, 247
  death monologue **48:** 255

Ghost
  Hamlet **1:** 75, 76, 84, 85, 128, 134, 138, 154, 171, 218, 231, 254; **16:** 246; **21:** 17, 44, 112, 151, 334, 371, 377, 392; **25:** 288; **35:** 152, 157, 174, 237; **44:** 119

Gloucester
  King Lear **46:** 254

Gobbo, Launcelot
  The Merchant of Venice **46:** 24, 60

Goneril
  King Lear **31:** 151; **46:** 231, 242

Gonzalo
  The Tempest **22:** 302; **29:** 278, 343, 362, 368; **45:** 280

Gower chorus
  Pericles **2:** 548, 575; **15:** 134, 141, 143, 145, 149, 152, 177; **36:** 279; **42:** 352

Grey
  Henry V See **traitors**

Guiderius and Arviragus
  Cymbeline **4:** 21, 22, 89, 129, 141, 148; **25:** 319; **36:** 125, 158

Hal
  See **Henry (King Henry V, formerly known as Prince Henry [Hal] of Wales)**

Hamlet
  Hamlet
  as a fool **46:** 1, 29, 52, 74
  delay **1:** 76, 83, 88, 90, 94, 98, 102, 103, 106, 114, 115, 116, 119, 120, 148, 151, 166, 171, 179, 188, 191, 194, 198, 221, 268; **13:** 296, 502; **21:** 81; **25:** 209, 288; **28:** 223; **35:** 82, 174, 212, 215, 237; **44:** 180, 209, 219, 229
  divided nature **16:** 246; **28:** 223; **32:** 288; **35:** 182, 215; **37:** 241
  elocution of the character's speeches **21:** 96, 104, 112, 127, 132, 172, 177, 179, 194, 245, 254, 257

madness **1:** 76, 81, 83, 95, 102, 106, 128, 144, 154, 160, 234; **21:** 35, 50, 72, 81, 99, 112, 311, 339, 355, 361, 371, 377, 384; **35:** 117, 132, 134, 140, 144, 212; **44:** 107, 119, 152, 209, 219, 229
melancholy **21:** 99, 112, 177, 194; **35:** 82, 95, 117; **44:** 209, 219
as negative character **1:** 86, 92, 111, 171, 218; **21:** 386; **25:** 209; **35:** 167
reaction to his father's death **22:** 339; **35:** 104, 174; **44:** 133, 160, 180, 189
reaction to Gertrude's marriage **1:** 74, 120, 154, 179; **16:** 259; **21:** 371; **22:** 339; **35:** 104, 117; **44:** 133, 160, 189, 195
religion **48:** 195
romantic aspects of the character **21:** 96; **44:** 198
as scourge or purifying figure **1:** 144, 209, 242; **25:** 288; **35:** 157
sentimentality vs. intellectuality **1:** 75, 83, 88, 91, 93, 94, 96, 102, 103, 115, 116, 120, 166, 191; **13:** 296; **21:** 35, 41, 44, 72, 81, 89, 99, 129, 132, 136, 172, 213, 225, 339, 355, 361, 371, 377, 379, 381, 386; **25:** 209; **44:** 198
soliloquies **1:** 76, 82, 83, 148, 166, 169, 176, 191; **21:** 17, 31, 44, 53, 89, 112, 268, 311, 334, 347, 361, 384, 392; **25:** 209; **28:** 223; **44:** 107, 119, 229
theatrical interpretations **21:** 11, 31, 78, 101, 104, 107, 160, 177, 179, 182, 183, 192, 194, 197, 202, 203, 208, 213, 225, 232, 237, 249, 253, 254, 257, 259, 274, 311, 339, 347, 355, 361, 371, 377, 380; **44:** 198
virility **21:** 213, 301, 355

Helena
  All's Well That Ends Well
  as agent of reconciliation, renewal, or grace **7:** 67, 76, 81, 90, 93, 98, 109, 116
  as dualistic or enigmatic character **7:** 15, 27, 29, 39, 54, 58, 62, 67, 76, 81, 98, 113, 126; **13:** 66; **22:** 78; **26:** 117; **48:** 65
  as "female achiever" **19:** 113; **38:** 89
  desire **38:** 96; **44:** 35
  pursuit of Bertram **7:** 9, 12, 15, 16, 19, 21, 26, 27, 29, 32, 43, 54, 76, 116; **13:** 77; **22:** 78; **49:** 46
  virginity **38:** 65
  virtue and nobility **7:** 9, 10, 12, 16, 19, 21, 27, 32, 41, 51, 58, 67, 76, 86, 126; **13:** 77; **50:** 59
  A Midsummer Night's Dream **29:** 269

Henry (King Henry IV, previously known as Bolingbroke)
  Henry IV, Parts 1 and 2 **39:** 123, 137
  effectiveness as ruler **49:** 116
  guilt **49:** 112
  historical context **49:** 139
  illegitimacy of rule **49:** 112, 133, 137
  power **49:** 139
  as tragic figure **49:** 186
  as usurper **49:** 116, 137

Richard II
  Bolingbroke and Richard as opposites **24:** 423
  Bolingbroke-Mowbray dispute **22:** 137
  comic elements **28:** 134
  guilt **24:** 423; **39:** 279
  language and imagery **6:** 310, 315, 331, 347, 374, 381, 397; **32:** 189
  as Machiavellian figure **6:** 305, 307, 315, 331, 347, 388, 393, 397; **24:** 428
  as politician **6:** 255, 263, 264, 272, 277, 294, 364, 368, 391; **24:** 330, 333, 405, 414, 423, 428; **39:** 256
  Richard, compared with **6:** 307, 315, 347, 374, 391, 393, 409; **24:** 346, 349, 351, 352, 356, 395, 419, 423, 428
  seizure of Gaunt's estate **49:** 60
  his silence **24:** 423
  structure, compared with **39:** 235
  usurpation of crown, nature of **6:** 255, 272, 289, 307, 310, 347, 354, 359, 381, 385, 393; **13:** 172; **24:** 322, 356, 383, 419; **28:** 178

Henry (King Henry V, formerly known as Prince Henry [Hal] of Wales)
  Henry IV, Parts 1 and 2
    and betrayal **49:** 123
    as the central character **1:** 286, 290, 314, 317, 326, 338, 354, 366, 374, 396; **39:** 72, 100
    dual personality **1:** 397, 406; **25:** 109, 151; **48:** 95; **49:** 112, 139, 153, 162
    as Everyman **1:** 342, 366, 374
    from audience's perspective **49:** 153
    from Henry's perspective **49:** 153
    fall from humanity **1:** 379, 380, 383
    general assessment **1:** 286, 287, 289, 290, 314, 317, 326, 327, 332, 357, 397; **25:** 245; **32:** 212; **39:** 134; **48:** 151
    as ideal ruler **1:** 289, 309, 317, 321, 326, 337, 342, 344, 374, 389, 391, 434; **25:** 109; **39:** 123; **47:** 60
    as Machiavellian ruler **47:** 60
    as negative character **1:** 312, 332, 333, 357; **32:** 212
    as outlaw **49:** 112
    preparation for rule **49:** 112
    as restorer of law **49:** 133
    Richard II, compared with **1:** 332, 337; **39:** 72
  Henry V
    brutality and cunning **5:** 193, 203, 209, 210, 213, 219, 233, 239, 252, 260, 271, 287, 293, 302, 304; **30:** 159; **43:** 24
    characterization in *1* and *2 Henry IV* contrasted **5:** 189, 190, 241, 304, 310; **19:** 133; **25:** 131; **32:** 157
    chivalry **37:** 187
    courage **5:** 191, 195, 210, 213, 228, 246, 257, 267
    disguise **30:** 169, 259
    education **5:** 246, 267, 271, 289; **14:** 297, 328, 342; **30:** 259
    emotion, lack of **5:** 209, 212, 233, 244, 264, 267, 287, 293, 310
    as heroic figure **5:** 192, 205, 209, 223, 244, 252, 257, 260, 269, 271, 299, 304; **28:** 121, 146; **30:** 237, 244, 252; **37:** 187; **49:** 194, 200, 236, 247
    humor **5:** 189, 191, 212, 217, 239, 240, 276
    intellectual and social limitations **5:** 189, 191, 203, 209, 210, 225, 226, 230, 293; **30:** 220
    interpersonal relations **5:** 209, 233, 267, 269, 276, 287, 293, 302, 318; **19:** 133; **28:** 146
    mercy **5:** 213, 267, 289, 293
    mixture of good and bad qualities **5:** 199, 205, 209, 210, 213, 244, 260, 304, 314; **30:** 262, 273; **49:** 211
    piety **5:** 191, 199, 209, 217, 223, 239, 257, 260, 271, 289, 310, 318; **30:** 244; **32:** 126
    public vs. private selves **22:** 137; **30:** 169, 207
    self-doubt **5:** 281, 310
    slaughter of prisoners **5:** 189, 205, 246, 293, 318; **28:** 146
    speech **5:** 212, 230, 233, 246, 264, 276, 287, 302; **28:** 146; **30:** 163, 227

Henry (King Henry VI)
  Henry VI, Parts 1, 2, and 3
    characterization **3:** 64, 77, 151; **39:** 160, 177; **47:** 32
    source of social disorder **3:** 25, 31, 41, 115; **39:** 154, 187
    as sympathetic figure **3:** 73, 143, 154; **24:** 32

Henry (King Henry VIII)
  Henry VIII
    as agent of divine retribution **2:** 49
    characterization **2:** 23, 39, 51, 58, 60, 65, 66, 75; **28:** 184; **37:** 109
    incomplete portrait **2:** 15, 16, 19, 35; **41:** 120
    as realistic figure **2:** 21, 22, 23, 25, 32

Henry (Prince Henry)
  King John **41:** 277

Hermia
  A Midsummer Night's Dream **29:** 225, 269; **45:** 117

Hermione
  The Winter's Tale
    characterization **7:** 385, 395, 402, 412, 414, 506; **15:** 495, 532; **22:** 302, 324; **25:** 347; **32:** 388; **36:** 311; **47:** 25; **49:** 18
    restoration (Act V, scene iii) **7:** 377, 379, 384, 385, 387, 389, 394, 396, 412, 425, 436, 451, 452, 456, 464, 483, 501; **15:** 411, 412, 413, 518, 528, 532; **49:** 18
    sex as identity **48:** 309
    supposed death **25:** 339; **47:** 25
    trial of **49:** 18

Hero
  Much Ado about Nothing **8:** 13, 14, 16, 19, 28, 29, 44, 48, 53, 55, 82, 95, 104, 111, 115, 121; **31:** 231, 245; **47:** 25

Hippolyta
  A Midsummer Night's Dream **48:** 23

Holofernes
  Love's Labour's Lost **23:** 207

Horatio
  Hamlet **44:** 189
  stoic perfection, example of **48:** 195

Hotspur
  Henry IV, Parts 1 and 2 **25:** 151; **28:** 101; **39:** 72, 134, 137; **42:** 99
  and prisoners of war **49:** 137
  versus Henry **49:** 137
  Henry V **5:** 189, 199, 228, 271, 302

Humphrey
  Henry VI, Parts 1, 2, and 3 **13:** 131

Iachimo
  Cymbeline **25:** 245, 319; **36:** 166; **47:** 274

Iago
  Othello
    affinity with Othello **4:** 400, 427, 468, 470, 477, 500, 506; **25:** 189; **44:** 57
    as conventional dramatic villain **4:** 440, 527, 545, 582
    as homosexual **4:** 503
    Machiavellian elements **4:** 440, 455, 457, 517, 545; **35:** 336, 347
    motives **4:** 389, 390, 397, 399, 402, 409, 423, 424, 427, 434, 451, 462, 545, 564; **13:** 304; **25:** 189; **28:** 344; **32:** 201; **35:** 265, 276, 310, 336, 347; **42:** 273
    revenge scheme **4:** 392, 409, 424, 451
    as scapegoat **4:** 506
    as victim **4:** 402, 409, 434, 451, 457, 470

Imogen
  Cymbeline **4:** 21, 22, 24, 29, 37, 45, 46, 52, 56, 78, 89, 108; **15:** 23, 32, 105, 121; **19:** 411; **25:** 245, 319; **28:** 398; **32:** 373; **36:** 129, 142, 148; **47:** 25, 205, 228, 245, 274, 277
    reawakening of (Act IV, scene ii) **4:** 37, 56, 89, 103, 108, 116, 150; **15:** 23; **25:** 245; **47:** 252

Isabella
  Measure for Measure **2:** 388, 390, 395, 396, 397, 401, 402, 406, 409, 410, 411, 418, 420, 421, 432, 437, 441, 466, 475, 491, 495, 524; **16:** 114; **23:** 278, 279, 280, 281, 282, 296, 344, 357, 363, 405; **28:** 102; **33:** 77, 85

Jack [John] Cade
  Henry VI, Parts 1, 2, and 3 See **Cade**

the jailer's daughter
  The Two Noble Kinsmen **9:** 457, 460, 479, 481, 486, 502; **41:** 340; **50:** 295, 305, 310, 348, 361

Jaques
As You Like It
love-theme, relation to **5**: 103; **23**: 7, 37, 118, 128
as malcontent **5**: 59, 70, 84
melancholy **5**: 20, 28, 32, 36, 39, 43, 50, 59, 63, 68, 77, 82, 86, 135; **23**: 20, 26, 103, 104, 107, 109; **34**: 85; **46**: 88, 94
pastoral convention, relation to **5**: 61, 63, 65, 79, 93, 98, 114, 118
Seven Ages of Man speech (Act II, scene vii) **5**: 28, 52, 136; **23**: 48, 103, 105, 126, 138, 152; **46**: 88, 156, 164, 169
Shakespeare, relation to **5**: 35, 50, 154; **48**: 42
as superficial critic **5**: 28, 30, 43, 54, 55, 63, 65, 68, 75, 77, 82, 86, 88, 98, 138; **34**: 85

the jennet
Venus and Adonis See **the courser and the jennet**

Jessica
The Merchant of Venice **4**: 196, 200, 228, 293, 342; **48**: 54, 77

Joan of Arc
Henry VI, Parts 1, 2, and 3 **16**: 131; **32**: 212

John (Don John)
Much Ado about Nothing **8**: 9, 12, 16, 17, 19, 28, 29, 36, 39, 41, 47, 48, 55, 58, 63, 82, 104, 108, 111, 121

John (Friar John)
Romeo and Juliet
detention of **5**: 448, 467, 470

John (King John)
King John **41**: 205, 260
death **9**: 212, 215, 216, 240
decline **9**: 224, 235, 240, 263, 275
Hubert, scene with (Act III, scene iii) **9**: 210, 212, 216, 218, 219, 280
moral insensibility **13**: 147, 163
negative qualities **9**: 209, 212, 218, 219, 229, 234, 235, 244, 245, 246, 250, 254, 275, 280, 297
positive qualities **9**: 209, 224, 235, 240, 244, 245, 263

John of Lancaster, Prince
Henry IV **49**: 123
and betrayal **49**: 123

Julia
The Two Gentlemen of Verona **6**: 450, 453, 458, 476, 494, 499, 516, 519, 549, 564; **40**: 312, 327, 374

Juliet
Romeo and Juliet See **Romeo and Juliet**

Launcelot Gobbo
The Merchant of Venice See **Gobbo**

Kate
The Taming of the Shrew
characterization **32**: 1; **43**: 61
final speech (Act V, scene ii) **9**: 318, 319, 329, 330, 338, 340, 341, 345, 347, 353, 355, 360, 365, 381, 386, 401, 404, 413, 426, 430; **19**: 3; **22**: 48
love for Petruchio **9**: 338, 340, 353, 430; **12**: 435
portrayals of **31**: 282
shrewishness **9**: 322, 323, 325, 332, 344, 345, 360, 365, 370, 375, 386, 393, 398, 404, 413
transformation **9**: 323, 341, 355, 370, 386, 393, 401, 404, 407, 419, 424, 426, 430; **16**: 13; **19**: 34; **22**: 48; **31**: 288, 295, 339, 351

Katherine
Henry V **5**: 186, 188, 189, 190, 192, 260, 269, 299, 302; **13**: 183; **19**: 217; **30**: 278; **44**: 44
Henry VIII
characterization **2**: 18, 19, 23, 24, 38; **24**: 129; **37**: 109; **41**: 180
Hermione, compared with **2**: 24, 51, 58, 76
politeness strategies **22**: 182
religious discourse **22**: 182
as tragic figure **2**: 16, 18

Kent
King Lear **25**: 202; **28**: 223; **32**: 212; **47**: 9

King
All's Well That Ends Well **38**: 150

King Richard II
Richard II See **Richard**

King Richard III, formerly Richard, Duke of Gloucester
Richard III See **Richard**

Lady Macbeth
Macbeth See **Macbeth (Lady Macbeth)**

Laertes
Hamlet **21**: 347, 386; **28**: 290; **35**: 182

Launce and Speed
The Two Gentlemen of Verona
comic function of **6**: 438, 439, 442, 456, 458, 460, 462, 472, 476, 478, 484, 502, 504, 507, 509, 516, 519, 549; **40**: 312, 320

Lavatch
All's Well That Ends Well **26**: 64; **46**: 33, 52, 68

Lavinia
Titus Andronicus **27**: 266; **28**: 249; **32**: 212; **43**: 1, 170, 239, 247, 255, 262

Lawrence (Friar Lawrence)
Romeo and Juliet
contribution to catastrophe **5**: 437, 444, 470; **33**: 300; **51**: 253
philosophy of moderation **5**: 427, 431, 437, 438, 443, 444, 445, 458, 467, 479, 505, 538
as Shakespeare's spokesman **5**: 427, 431, 437, 458, 467

Lear
King Lear
curse on Goneril **11**: 5, 7, 12, 114, 116
love-test and division of kingdom **2**: 100, 106, 111, 124, 131, 137, 147, 149, 151, 168, 186, 208, 216, 281; **16**: 351; **25**: 202; **31**: 84, 92, 107, 117, 149, 155; **46**: 231, 242
madness **2**: 94, 95, 98, 99, 100, 101, 102, 103, 111, 116, 120, 124, 125, 149, 156, 191, 208, 216, 281; **46**: 264
as scapegoat **2**: 241, 253
self-knowledge **2**: 103, 151, 188, 191, 213, 218, 222, 241, 249, 262; **25**: 218; **37**: 213; **46**: 191, 205, 225, 254, 264

Leontes
The Winter's Tale
characterization **19**: 431; **43**: 39; **45**: 366
jealousy **7**: 377, 379, 382, 383, 384, 387, 389, 394, 395, 402, 407, 412, 414, 425, 429, 432, 436, 464, 480, 483, 497; **15**: 514, 518, 532; **22**: 324; **25**: 339; **36**: 334, 344, 349; **44**: 66; **45**: 295, 297, 344, 358; **47**: 25
Othello, compared with **7**: 383, 390, 412; **15**: 514; **36**: 334; **44**: 66; **47**: 25
repentance **7**: 381, 389, 394, 396, 402, 414, 497; **36**: 318, 362; **44**: 66

Lord Chief Justice
Henry IV
as keeper of law and justice **49**: 133

Lucentio
The Taming of the Shrew **9**: 325, 342, 362, 375, 393

Lucio
Measure for Measure **13**: 104; **49**: 379

Lucrece
The Rape of Lucrece
chastity **33**: 131, 138; **43**: 92
as example of Renaissance *virtù* **22**: 289; **43**: 148
heroic **10**: 84, 93, 109, 121, 128
patriarchal woman, model of **10**: 109, 131; **33**: 169, 200
self-perception **48**: 291
self-responsibility **10**: 89, 96, 98, 106, 125; **33**: 195; **43**: 85, 92, 158
unrealistic **10**: 64, 65, 66, 121
verbose **10**: 64, 81, 116; **25**: 305; **33**: 169
as victim **22**: 294; **25**: 305; **32**: 321; **33**: 131, 195; **43**: 102, 158

Macbeth
Macbeth
ambition **44**: 284, 324
characterization **20**: 20, 42, 73, 107, 113, 130, 146, 151, 279, 283, 312, 338, 343,

379, 406, 413; **29:** 139, 152, 155, 165; **44:** 289
courage **3:** 172, 177, 181, 182, 183, 186, 234, 312, 333; **20:** 107; **44:** 315
disposition **3:** 173, 175, 177, 182, 186; **20:** 245, 376
imagination **3:** 196, 208, 213, 250, 312, 345; **20:** 245, 376; **44:** 351
as "inauthentic" king **3:** 245, 302, 321, 345
inconsistencies **3:** 202
as Machiavellian villain **3:** 280
manliness **20:** 113; **29:** 127, 133; **44:** 315
psychoanalytic interpretations **20:** 42, 73, 238, 376; **44:** 284, 289, 297, 324; **45:** 48, 58
Richard III, compared with **3:** 177, 182, 186, 345; **20:** 86, 92; **22:** 365; **44:** 269
as Satan figure **3:** 229, 269, 275, 289, 318
self-awareness **3:** 312, 329, 338; **16:** 317; **44:** 361
as sympathetic figure **3:** 229, 306, 314, 338; **29:** 139, 152; **44:** 269, 306, 337
as tragic hero **44:** 269, 306, 315, 324, 337

Macbeth (Lady Macbeth)
Macbeth
ambition **3:** 185, 219; **20:** 279, 345
characterization **20:** 56, 60, 65, 73, 140, 148, 151, 241, 279, 283, 338, 350, 406, 413; **29:** 109, 146
childlessness **3:** 219, 223; **48:** 214
good and evil, combined traits of **3:** 173, 191, 213; **20:** 60, 107
inconsistencies **3:** 202; **20:** 54, 137
influence on Macbeth **3:** 171, 185, 191, 193, 199, 262, 289, 312, 318; **13:** 502; **20:** 345; **25:** 235; **29:** 133
psychoanalytic interpretations **20:** 345; **44:** 289, 297; **45:** 58
sleepwalking scene **44:** 261
as sympathetic figure **3:** 191, 193, 203

Macduff
Macbeth **3:** 226, 231, 253, 262,; **25:** 235; **29:** 127, 133, 155

MacMorris
Henry V **22:** 103; **28:** 159; **30:** 278

Malcolm
Macbeth **25:** 235
fatherhood **48:** 214

Malvolio
Twelfth Night
characterization **1:** 540, 544, 545, 548, 550, 554, 558, 567, 575, 577, 615; **26:** 207, 233, 273; **46:** 286
forged letter **16:** 372; **28:** 1
punishment **1:** 539, 544, 548, 549, 554, 555, 558, 563, 577, 590, 632, 645; **46:** 291, 297, 338
as Puritan **1:** 549, 551, 555, 558, 561, 563; **25:** 47

role in play **1:** 545, 548, 549, 553, 555, 563, 567, 575, 577, 588, 610, 615, 632, 645; **26:** 337, 374; **46:** 347

Mamillius
The Winter's Tale **7:** 394, 396, 451; **22:** 324

Margaret
Henry VI, Parts 1, 2, and 3
characterization **3:** 18, 26, 35, 51, 103, 109, 140, 157; **24:** 48
Suffolk, relationship with **3:** 18, 24, 26, 157; **39:** 213
Richard III **8:** 153, 154, 159, 162, 163, 170, 193, 201, 206, 210, 218, 223, 228, 243, 248, 262; **39:** 345

Marina
Pericles **37:** 361; **51:** 118

Menenius
Coriolanus **9:** 8, 9, 11, 14, 19, 26, 78, 80, 106, 148, 157; **25:** 263, 296; **30:** 67, 79, 89, 96, 111, 133

Mercutio
Romeo and Juliet
bawdy **5:** 463, 525, 550, 575
death **5:** 415, 418, 419, 547; **33:** 290
as worldly counterpart to Romeo **5:** 425, 464, 542; **33:** 290; **51:** 195

minor characters
Richard III **8:** 154, 159, 162, 163, 168, 170, 177, 184, 186, 201, 206, 210, 218, 223, 228, 232, 239, 248, 262, 267

Miranda
The Tempest **8:** 289, 301, 304, 328, 336, 370, 454; **19:** 357; **22:** 302; **28:** 249; **29:** 278, 297, 362, 368, 377, 396

Mistress Elbow
Measure for Measure See **Elbow (Mistress Elbow)**

Mistress Quickly
Henry V See **Quickly**

Mortimer
Henry IV, Parts 1 and 2 **25:** 151

Norfolk
Henry VIII **22:** 182

Northumberland
Richard II **24:** 423

Nurse
Romeo and Juliet **5:** 419, 425, 463, 464, 575; **33:** 294

Oberon
A Midsummer Night's Dream
as controlling force **3:** 434, 459, 477, 502; **29:** 175

Octavius
Antony and Cleopatra **6:** 22, 24, 31, 38, 43, 53, 62, 107, 125, 146, 178, 181, 219; **25:** 257
Julius Caesar **30:** 316

Olivia
Twelfth Night **1:** 540, 543, 545; **46:** 286, 324, 369; **47:** 45

Ophelia
Hamlet **1:** 73, 76, 81, 82, 91, 96, 97, 154, 166, 169, 171, 218, 270; **13:** 268; **16:** 246; **19:** 330; **21:** 17, 41, 44, 72, 81, 101, 104, 107, 112, 136, 203, 259, 347, 381, 386, 392, 416; **28:** 232, 325; **35:** 104, 126, 140, 144, 182, 238; **44:** 189, 195, 248
in art **48:** 255
death **48:** 255
as icon **48:** 255
influence on popular culture **48:** 255

Orlando
As You Like It
as ideal man **5:** 32, 36, 39, 162; **34:** 161; **46:** 94
as younger brother **5:** 66, 158; **46:** 94

Orsino
Twelfth Night **46:** 286, 333; **47:** 45

Othello
Othello
affinity with Iago **4:** 400, 427, 468, 470, 477, 500, 506; **25:** 189; **35:** 276, 320, 327
as conventional "blameless hero" **4:** 445, 486, 500
credulity **4:** 384, 385, 388, 390, 396, 402, 434, 440, 455; **13:** 327; **32:** 302; **47:** 25, 51
Desdemona, relationship with **22:** 339; **35:** 301, 317; **37:** 269; **43:** 32
divided nature **4:** 400, 412, 462, 470, 477, 493, 500, 582, 592; **16:** 293; **19:** 276; **25:** 189; **35:** 320
egotism **4:** 427, 470, 477, 493, 522, 536, 541, 573, 597; **13:** 304; **35:** 247, 253
self-destructive anger **16:** 283
self-dramatizing or self-deluding **4:** 454, 457, 477, 592; **13:** 313; **16:** 293; **35:** 317
self-knowledge **4:** 462, 470, 477, 483, 508, 522, 530, 564, 580, 591, 596; **13:** 304, 313; **16:** 283; **28:** 243; **35:** 253, 317
spiritual state **4:** 483, 488, 517, 525, 527, 544, 559, 564, 573; **28:** 243; **35:** 253

Page, Anne
The Merry Wives of Windsor **47:** 321
Anne Page-Fenton plot **5:** 334, 336, 343, 353, 376, 390, 395, 402; **22:** 93; **47:** 308

Page, Mistress Margaret
The Merry Wives of Windsor **47:** 321

Painter
Timon of Athens See **Poet and Painter**

Palamon and Arcite
The Two Noble Kinsmen **9**: 474, 481, 490, 492, 502; **50**: 295, 305, 348, 361

Parolles
All's Well That Ends Well
    characterization **7**: 8, 9, 43, 76, 81, 98, 109, 113, 116, 126; **22**: 78; **26**: 48, 73, 97; **26**: 117; **46**: 68
    exposure **7**: 9, 27, 81, 98, 109, 113, 116, 121, 126
    Falstaff, compared with **7**: 8, 9, 16

pastoral characters (Silvius, Phebe, and Corin)
As You Like It **23**: 37, 97, 98, 99, 108, 110, 118, 122, 138; **34**: 147

Paulina
The Winter's Tale **7**: 385, 412, 506; **15**: 528; **22**: 324; **25**: 339; **36**: 311

Pedro (Don Pedro)
Much Ado about Nothing **8**: 17, 19, 48, 58, 63, 82, 111, 121

Perdita
The Winter's Tale
    characterization **7**: 395, 412, 414, 419, 429, 432, 452, 506; **22**: 324; **25**: 339; **36**: 328; **43**: 39
    reunion with Leontes (Act V, scene ii) **7**: 377, 379, 381, 390, 432, 464, 480

Pericles
Pericles
    characterization **36**: 251; **37**: 361
    patience **2**: 572, 573, 578, 579
    suit of Antiochus's daughter **2**: 547, 565, 578, 579; **51**: 126
    Ulysses, compared with **2**: 551

Petruchio
The Taming of the Shrew
    admirable qualities **9**: 320, 332, 341, 344, 345, 370, 375, 386
    as lord of misrule **50**: 64
    audacity or vigor **9**: 325, 337, 355, 375, 386, 404
    characterization **32**: 1
    coarseness or brutality **9**: 325, 329, 365, 390, 393, 398, 407; **19**: 122; **43**: 61
    as lord of misrule **9**: 393
    love for Kate **9**: 338, 340, 343, 344, 386; **12**: 435
    portrayals of **31**: 282
    pragmatism **9**: 329, 334, 375, 398, 424; **13**: 3; **31**: 345, 351
    taming method **9**: 320, 323, 329, 340, 341, 343, 345, 355, 369, 370, 375, 390, 398, 407, 413, 419, 424; **19**: 3, 12, 21 **31**: 269, 295, 326, 335, 339

Phebe
As You Like It See **pastoral characters**

Pistol
Henry V **28**: 146

plebeians
Coriolanus **9**: 8, 9, 11, 12, 15, 18, 19, 26, 33, 39, 53, 92, 125, 153, 183, 189; **25**: 296; **30**: 58, 79, 96, 111

Poet and Painter
Timon of Athens **25**: 198

the poets
Julius Caesar **7**: 179, 320, 350

Polixenes
The Winter's Tale
    Leontes, relationship with **48**: 309

Polonius
Hamlet **21**: 259, 334, 347, 386, 416; **35**: 182

Porter
Henry VIII **24**: 155
Macbeth **3**: 173, 175, 184, 190, 196, 203, 205, 225, 260, 271, 297, 300; **20**: 283

Portia
The Merchant of Venice **4**: 194, 195, 196, 215, 254, 263, 336, 356; **12**: 104, 107, 114; **13**: 37; **22**: 3, 69; **25**: 22; **32**: 294; **37**: 86; **40**: 142, 156, 197, 208

Posthumus
Cymbeline **4**: 24, 30, 53, 78, 116, 127, 141, 155, 159, 167; **15**: 89; **19**: 411; **25**: 245, 319; **36**: 142; **44**: 28; **45**: 67, 75; **47**: 25, 205, 228

Prince Henry
King John See **Henry (Prince Henry)**

Prospero
The Tempest
    characterization **8**: 312, 348, 370, 458; **16**: 442; **22**: 302; **45**: 188, 272
    as God or Providence **8**: 311, 328, 364, 380, 429, 435
    magic, nature of **8**: 301, 340, 356, 396, 414, 423, 458; **25**: 382; **28**: 391; **29**: 278, 292, 368, 377, 396; **32**: 338, 343
    psychoanalytic interpretation **45**: 259
    redemptive powers **8**: 302, 320, 353, 370, 390, 429, 439, 447; **29**: 297
    as ruler **8**: 304, 308, 309, 420, 423; **13**: 424; **22**: 302; **29**: 278, 362, 377, 396
    self-control **8**: 312, 414, 420; **22**: 302; **44**: 11
    self-knowledge **16**: 442; **22**: 302; **29**: 278, 292, 362, 377, 396
    as Shakespeare or creative artist **8**: 299, 302, 308, 312, 320, 324, 353, 364, 435, 447
    as tragic hero **8**: 359, 370, 464; **29**: 292

Proteus
The Two Gentlemen of Verona **6**: 439, 450, 458, 480, 490, 511; **40**: 312, 327, 330, 335, 359; **42**: 18

Puck
A Midsummer Night's Dream **45**: 96, 158

Quickly (Mistress Quickly)
Henry V **5**: 186, 187, 210, 276, 293; **30**: 278

Regan
King Lear **31**: 151; **46**: 231, 242

Richard (King Richard II)
Richard II
    artistic temperament **6**: 264, 267, 270, 272, 277, 292, 294, 298, 315, 331, 334, 347, 368, 374, 393, 409; **24**: 298, 301, 304, 315, 322, 390, 405, 408, 411, 414, 419; **39**: 289
    Bolingbroke, compared with **24**: 346, 349, 351, 352, 356, 419; **39**: 256
    characterization **6**: 250, 252, 253, 254, 255, 258, 262, 263, 267, 270, 272, 282, 283, 304, 343, 347, 364, 368; **24**: 262, 263, 267, 269, 270, 271, 272, 273, 274, 278, 280, 315, 322, 325, 330, 333, 390, 395, 402, 405, 423; **28**: 134; **39**: 279, 289
    dangerous aspects **24**: 405
    delusion **6**: 267, 298, 334, 368, 409; **24**: 329, 336, 405
    homosexuality **24**: 405
    kingship **6**: 253, 254, 263, 272, 327, 331, 334, 338, 364, 402, 414; **24**: 278, 295, 336, 337, 339, 356, 419; **28**: 134, 178; **39**: 256, 263
    loss of identity **6**: 267, 338, 368, 374, 381, 388, 391, 409; **24**: 298, 414, 428
    as martyr-king **6**: 289, 307, 321; **19**: 209; **24**: 289, 291; **28**: 134
    nobility **6**: 255, 258, 259, 262, 263, 391; **24**: 260, 263, 274, 280, 289, 291, 402, 408, 411
    political acumen **6**: 263, 264, 272, 292, 310, 327, 334, 364, 368, 374, 388, 391, 397, 402, 409; **24**: 405; **39**: 256
    private vs. public persona **6**: 317, 327, 364, 368, 391, 409; **24**: 428
    role-playing **24**: 419, 423; **28**: 178
    seizure of Gaunt's estate **6**: 250, 338, 388
    self-dramatization **6**: 264, 267, 307, 310, 315, 317, 331, 334, 368, 393, 409; **24**: 339; **28**: 178
    self-hatred **13**: 172; **24**: 383; **39**: 289
    self-knowledge **6**: 255, 267, 331, 334, 338, 352, 354, 368, 388, 391; **24**: 273, 289, 411, 414; **39**: 263, 289
    spiritual redemption **6**: 255, 267, 331, 334, 338, 352, 354, 368, 388, 391; **24**: 273, 289, 411, 414

Richard (King Richard III, formerly Richard, Duke of Gloucester)
Henry VI, Parts 1, 2, and 3
    characterization **3**: 35, 48, 57, 64, 77, 143, 151; **22**: 193; **39**: 160, 177
    as revenger **22**: 193
    soliloquy (*3 Henry VI*, Act III, scene ii) **3**: 17, 48
Richard III
    ambition **8**: 148, 154, 165, 168, 170,

177, 182, 213, 218, 228, 232, 239, 252, 258, 267; **39:** 308, 341, 360, 370, 383
attractive qualities **8:** 145, 148, 152, 154, 159, 161, 162, 165, 168, 170, 181, 182, 184, 185, 197, 201, 206, 213, 228, 243, 252, 258; **16:** 150; **39:** 370, 383
credibility, question of **8:** 145, 147, 154, 159, 165, 193; **13:** 142
death **8:** 145, 148, 154, 159, 165, 168, 170, 177, 182, 197, 210, 223, 228, 232, 243, 248, 252, 258, 267
deformity as symbol **8:** 146, 147, 148, 152, 154, 159, 161, 165, 170, 177, 184, 185, 193, 218, 248, 252, 267; **19:** 164
inversion of moral order **8:** 159, 168, 177, 182, 184, 185, 197, 201, 213, 218, 223, 232, 239, 243, 248, 252, 258, 262, 267; **39:** 360
as Machiavellian villain **8:** 165, 182, 190, 201, 218, 232, 239, 243, 248; **39:** 308, 326, 360, 387
as monster or symbol of diabolic **8:** 145, 147, 159, 162, 168, 170, 177, 182, 193, 197, 201, 228, 239, 248, 258; **13:** 142; **37:** 144; **39:** 326, 349
other literary villains, compared with **8:** 148, 161, 162, 165, 181, 182, 206, 213, 239, 267
role-playing, hypocrisy, and dissimulation **8:** 145, 148, 154, 159, 162, 165, 168, 170, 182, 190, 206, 213, 218, 228, 239, 243, 252, 258, 267; **25:** 141, 164, 245; **39:** 335, 341, 387
as scourge or instrument of God **8:** 163, 177, 193, 201, 218, 228, 248, 267; **39:** 308
as Vice figure **8:** 190, 201, 213, 228, 243, 248, 252; **16:** 150; **39:** 383, 387

Richard Plantagenet, Duke of York
Henry VI, Parts 1, 2, and 3 See **York**

Richmond
Richard III **8:** 154, 158, 163, 168, 177, 182, 193, 210, 218, 223, 228, 243, 248, 252; **13:** 142; **25:** 141; **39:** 349

the Rival Poet
Sonnets **10:** 169, 233, 334, 337, 385; **48:** 352

Roman citizenry
Julius Caesar
portrayal of **7:** 169, 179, 210, 221, 245, 279, 282, 310, 320, 333; **17:** 271, 279, 288, 291, 292, 298, 323, 334, 351, 367, 374, 375, 378; **22:** 280; **30:** 285, 297, 316, 321, 374, 379; **37:** 229

Romeo and Juliet
Romeo and Juliet
death-wish **5:** 431, 489, 505, 528, 530, 538, 542, 550, 566, 571, 575; **32:** 212
first meeting (Act I scene v) **51:** 212
immortality **5:** 536
Juliet's epithalamium speech (Act III, scene ii) **5:** 431, 477, 492
Juliet's innocence **5:** 421, 423, 450, 454; **33:** 257
maturation **5:** 437, 454, 467, 493, 498, 509, 520, 565; **33:** 249, 257
rebellion **25:** 257
reckless passion **5:** 419, 427, 431, 438, 443, 444, 448, 467, 479, 485, 505, 533, 538, 542; **33:** 241
Romeo's dream (Act V, scene i) **5:** 513, 536, 556; **45:** 40; **51:** 203
Rosaline, Romeo's relationship with **5:** 419, 423, 425, 427, 438, 498, 542, 575

Rosalind
As You Like It **46:** 94, 122
Beatrice, compared with **5:** 26, 36, 50, 75
charm **5:** 55, 75; **23:** 17, 18, 20, 41, 89, 111
disguise, role of **5:** 75, 107, 118, 122, 128, 130, 133, 138, 141, 146, 148, 164, 168; **13:** 502; **23:** 35, 42, 106, 119, 123, 146; **34:** 130; **46:** 127, 134, 142
femininity **5:** 26, 36, 52, 75; **23:** 24, 29, 46, 54, 103, 108, 121, 146
love-theme, relation to **5:** 79, 88, 103, 116, 122, 138, 141; **23:** 114, 115; **34:** 85, 177

rustic characters
As You Like It **5:** 24, 60, 72, 84; **23:** 127; **34:** 78, 161
A Midsummer Night's Dream **3:** 376, 397, 432; **12:** 291, 293; **45:** 147, 160

Scroop
Henry V See **traitors**

Sebastian
The Tempest See **Antonio and Sebastian**

Shylock
The Merchant of Venice
alienation **4:** 279, 312; **40:** 175; **48:** 77; **49:** 23, 37
ambiguity **4:** 247, 254, 315, 319, 331; **12:** 31, 35, 36, 50, 51, 52, 56, 81, 124; **40:** 175
forced conversion **4:** 209, 252, 268, 282, 289, 321
Jewishness **4:** 193, 194, 195, 200, 201, 213, 214, 279; **22:** 69; **25:** 257; **40:** 142, 175, 181; **48:** 65, 77
motives in making the bond **4:** 252, 263, 266, 268; **22:** 69; **25:** 22
as Puritan **40:** 127, 166
as scapegoat figure **4:** 254, 300; **40:** 166; **49:** 27
as traditional comic villain **4:** 230, 243, 261, 263, 315; **12:** 40, 62, 124; **40:** 175
as tragic figure **12:** 6, 9, 10, 16, 21, 23, 25, 40, 44, 66, 67, 81, 97; **40:** 175

Sicinius
Coriolanus See **the tribunes**

Silvia
The Two Gentlemen of Verona **6:** 450, 453, 458, 476, 494, 499, 516, 519, 549, 564; **40:** 312, 327, 374

Silvius
As You Like It See **pastoral characters**

Sly
The Taming of the Shrew **9:** 320, 322, 350, 370, 381, 390, 398, 430; **12:** 316, 335, 416, 427, 441; **16:** 13; **19:** 34, 122; **22:** 48; **37:** 31; **50:** 74

soldiers
Henry V **5:** 203, 239, 267, 276, 281, 287, 293, 318; **28:** 146; **30:** 169.

Speed
The Two Gentlemen of Verona See **Launce and Speed**

Stephano and Trinculo
The Tempest
comic subplot of **8:** 292, 297, 299, 304, 309, 324, 328, 353, 370; **25:** 382; **29:** 377; **46:** 14, 33

Stephen Gardiner
Henry VIII See **Gardiner**

Talbot
Henry VI, Parts 1, 2, and 3 **39:** 160, 213, 222

Tamora
Titus Andronicus **4:** 632, 662, 672, 675; **27:** 266; **43:** 170

Tarquin
The Rape of Lucrece **10:** 80, 93, 98, 116, 125; **22:** 294; **25:** 305; **32:** 321; **33:** 190; **43:** 102
Petrarchan lover **48:** 291
platonic tyrant **48:** 291
Satan role **48:** 291

Thersites
Troilus and Cressida **13:** 53; **25:** 56; **27:** 381

Theseus
A Midsummer Night's Dream
characterization **3:** 363
Hippolyta, relationship with **3:** 381, 412, 421, 423, 450, 468, 520; **29:** 175, 216, 243, 256; **45:** 84
as ideal **3:** 379, 391
"lovers, lunatics, and poets" speech (Act V, scene i) **3:** 365, 371, 379, 381, 391, 402, 411, 412, 421, 423, 441, 498, 506; **29:** 175
as representative of institutional life **3:** 381, 403; **51:** 1

Time-Chorus
The Winter's Tale **7:** 377, 380, 412, 464, 476, 501; **15:** 518

Timon
Timon of Athens
comic traits **25:** 198
as flawed hero **1:** 456, 459, 462, 472, 495, 503, 507, 515; **16:** 351; **20:** 429,

433, 476; **25:** 198; **27:** 157, 161
misanthropy **13:** 392; **20:** 431, 464, 476, 481, 491, 492, 493; **27:** 161, 175, 184, 196; **37:** 222
as noble figure **1:** 467, 473, 483, 499; **20:** 493; **27:** 212

Titania
A Midsummer Night's Dream **29:** 243

Titus
Titus Andronicus **4:** 632, 637, 640, 644, 647, 653, 656, 662; **25:** 245; **27:** 255

Touchstone
As You Like It
callousness **5:** 88
comic and farcical elements **46:** 117
as philosopher-fool **5:** 24, 28, 30, 32, 36, 63, 75, 98; **23:** 152; **34:** 85; **46:** 1, 14, 18, 24, 33, 52, 60, 88, 105
relation to pastoral convention **5:** 54, 61, 63, 72, 75, 77, 79, 84, 86, 93, 98, 114, 118, 135, 138, 166; **34:** 72, 147, 161
satire or parody of pastoral conventions **46:** 122
selflessness **5:** 30, 36, 39, 76

traitors (Scroop, Grey, and Cambridge)
Henry V **16:** 202; **30:** 220, 278

the tribunes (Brutus and Sicinius)
Coriolanus **9:** 9, 11, 14, 19, 33, 169, 180

Trinculo
The Tempest See **Stephano and Trinculo**

Troilus
Troilus and Cressida
contradictory behavior **3:** 596, 602, 635; **27:** 362

Cressida, relationship with **3:** 594, 596, 606; **22:** 58
integrity **3:** 617
opposition to Ulysses **3:** 561, 584, 590
as unsympathetic figure **18:** 423; **22:** 58, 339; **43:** 317
as warrior **3:** 596; **22:** 339

Ulysses
Troilus and Cressida
speech on degree (Act I, scene iii) **3:** 549, 599, 609, 642; **27:** 396

Venetians
The Merchant of Venice **4:** 195, 200, 228, 254, 273, 300, 321, 331

Venus
Venus and Adonis **10:** 427, 429, 434, 439, 442, 448, 449, 451, 454, 466, 473, 480, 486, 489; **16:** 452; **25:** 305, 328; **28:** 355; **33:** 309, 321, 330, 347, 352, 357, 363, 370, 377; **51:** 335, 352, 377, 388

Viola
Twelfth Night **26:** 308; **46:** 286, 324, 347, 369

Virgilia
Coriolanus **9:** 11, 19, 26, 33, 58, 100, 121, 125; **25:** 263; **30:** 79, 96, 133; **50:** 99

Volumnia
Coriolanus
Coriolanus's subservience to **9:** 16, 26, 33, 53, 62, 80, 92, 100, 117, 125, 142, 177, 183; **30:** 140, 149; **44:** 79
influence on Coriolanus **9:** 45, 62, 65, 78, 92, 100, 110, 117, 121, 125, 130, 148, 157, 183, 189, 193; **25:** 263, 296; **30:** 79, 96, 125, 133, 140, 142, 149; **44:** 93
as noble Roman matron **9:** 16, 19, 26, 31, 33
personification of Rome **9:** 125, 183; **50:** 119

Wat the hare
Venus and Adonis **10:** 424, 451

the Watch
Much Ado about Nothing See **Dogberry and the Watch**

Williams
Henry V **13:** 502; **16:** 183; **28:** 146; **30:** 169, 259, 278

witches
Macbeth
and supernaturalism **3:** 171, 172, 173, 175, 177, 182, 183, 184, 185, 194, 196, 198, 202, 207, 208, 213, 219, 229, 239; **16:** 317; **19:** 245; **20:** 92, 175, 213, 279, 283, 374, 387, 406, 413; **25:** 235; **28:** 339; **29:** 91, 101, 109, 120

Wolsey (Cardinal Wolsey)
Henry VIII **2:** 15, 18, 19, 23, 24, 38; **22:** 182; **24:** 80, 91, 112, 113, 129, 140; **37:** 109; **41:** 129

York (Edmund of Langley, Duke of York)
Richard II **6:** 287, 364, 368, 388, 402, 414; **24:** 263, 320, 322, 364, 395, 414; **39:** 243, 279

York (Richard Plantagenet, Duke of York)
Henry VI, Parts 1, 2, and 3
death of **13:** 131

Cumulative Critic Index

Abel, Lionel
Hamlet **1**: 237

Abrams, Richard
Authorship Controversy (topic entry) **41**: 98
King Lear **46**: 218
The Two Noble Kinsmen **41**: 385; **50**: 295

Adams, Howard C.
Troilus and Cressida **27**: 400

Adams, John C.
Romeo and Juliet **11**: 507
The Tempest **15**: 346

Adams, John F.
All's Well That Ends Well **7**: 86

Adams, John Quincy
Othello **4**: 408
Romeo and Juliet **5**: 426

Adams, Joseph Quincy
The Phoenix and Turtle **10**: 16

Adams, Robert M.
The Tempest **29**: 303

Adamson, Jane
Othello **4**: 591

Adamson, W. D.
Othello **35**: 360

Addenbrooke, David
Macbeth **20**: 263

Addison, Joseph
Hamlet **1**: 75
Henry IV, 1 and 2 **1**: 287
King Lear **2**: 93

Adelman, Janet
All's Well That Ends Well **13**: 84
Antony and Cleopatra **6**: 211; **27**: 110; **47**: 77
Coriolanus **9**: 183
Hamlet **44**: 160
Measure for Measure **13**: 84
Othello **22**: 339; **42**: 203
Psychoanalytic Interpretations (topic entry) **44**: 79
Troilus and Cressida **22**: 339

Adler, Doris
Antony and Cleopatra **17**: 94

Agate, James
Coriolanus **17**: 157
Hamlet **21**: 155, 167, 169, 177, 194
Henry IV, 1 and 2 **14**: 25
King Lear **11**: 46, 51
Macbeth **20**: 182, 184
Othello **11**: 262, 266
Richard II **24**: 298
Romeo and Juliet **11**: 444
Troilus and Cressida **18**: 300
The Two Noble Kinsmen **9**: 462

Agee, James
Henry V **14**: 213, 214

Aggeler, Geoffrey
Hamlet **48**: 195

Aichinger, C. P.
Hamlet **35**: 212

Aire, Sally
As You Like It **23**: 131
The Merry Wives of Windsor **18**: 56
A Midsummer Night's Dream **12**: 271
Pericles **15**: 165
Twelfth Night **26**: 294

Akrigg, G. P. V.
Henry V **30**: 252

Alden, Barbara
Othello **11**: 212

Alden, Raymond Macdonald
Sonnets **10**: 247

Aldus, P. J.
Hamlet **35**: 134

Alexander, Bill
The Merry Wives of Windsor **18**: 64

Alexander, Peter
Henry VIII **2**: 43

Alger, William Rounseville
Othello **11**: 208

Allen, Don Cameron
The Rape of Lucrece **10**: 89
Venus and Adonis **10**: 451

Allen, John A.
A Midsummer Night's Dream **3**: 457

Allen, Shirley
Pericles **15**: 135

Allen, Shirley S.
Antony and Cleopatra **17**: 20
A Midsummer Night's Dream **12**: 175
The Winter's Tale **15**: 419

Alleva, Richard
Hamlet **21**: 321

Alleyn, Henry
Cymbeline **15**: 50

Almeida, Barbara Heliodora C. de M. F. de
Troilus and Cressida **3**: 604

Alpert, Hollis
Hamlet **21**: 160

Altemus, Jameson Torr
As You Like It **23**: 41

Altick, Richard D.
Richard II **6**: 298

Altieri, Joanne
Henry V **5**: 314

Altman, Joel B.
Henry V **19**: 133

Aulis, Joseph
As You Like It **46**: 94

Alvarez, A.
All's Well That Ends Well **26**: 26

Coriolanus **17**: 166
Hamlet **21**: 268
King Lear **11**: 74
The Merchant of Venice **12**: 66
Othello **11**: 286
The Phoenix and Turtle **10**: 31
The Taming of the Shrew **12**: 356
Troilus and Cressida **18**: 322
Twelfth Night **26**: 253
The Two Gentlemen of Verona **12**: 473

Alvis, John
Politics and Power (topic entry) **30**: 11

Amhurst, Nicholas
Henry VIII **2**: 15

Amory, Mark
All's Well That Ends Well **26**: 58
Macbeth **20**: 309

Anderson, Linda
The Merry Wives of Windsor **38**: 264

Anderson, Mary
The Winter's Tale **15**: 443

Andreasen, Nancy J. C.
Madness (topic entry) **35**: 34

Andres, Michael Cameron
Hamlet **35**: 167

Andrews, Nigel
The Tempest **15**: 294

Anson, John
Julius Caesar **7**: 324

Ansorge, Peter
All's Well That Ends Well **26**: 46
Coriolanus **17**: 193
Cymbeline **15**: 75
Julius Caesar **17**: 382
The Merchant of Venice **12**: 74
A Midsummer Night's Dream **12**: 259
Richard II **24**: 349
The Tempest **15**: 280

Anstey, Edgar
Henry V **14**: 202

Anthony, Earl of Shaftesbury
Hamlet **1**: 75

Appelbaum, Robert
Romeo and Juliet **51**: 253

Appleton, William W.
Macbeth **20**: 48

Archer, William
All's Well That Ends Well **26**: 8
Henry IV, 1 and 2 **14**: 16, 20, 21
Measure for Measure **23**: 284
A Midsummer Night's Dream **12**: 196
Richard III **14**: 400
The Tempest **15**: 222
Twelfth Night **1**: 558; **26**: 201, 216
The Winter's Tale **15**: 437

Arden, John
Henry V **14**: 336

Arditti, Michael
Macbeth **20**: 315

Armstrong, William A.
Hamlet **21**: 136

Arnold, Aerol
Richard III **8**: 210

Aronson, Alex
Appearance vs. Reality (topic entry) **34**: 12

Arthos, John
All's Well That Ends Well **7**: 58
Macbeth **3**: 250
Othello **4**: 541
The Phoenix and Turtle **10**: 50
Shakespeare and Classical Civilization (topic entry) **27**: 1
The Two Gentlemen of Verona **6**: 532
The Tempest **45**: 247

Ashcroft, Peggy
Antony and Cleopatra **17**: 113
Romeo and Juliet **11**: 516

Asnani, Shyam M.
Clowns and Fools (topic entry) **46**: 14

Asp, Carolyn
Love's Labour's Lost **38**: 200
Macbeth **29**: 133
Psychoanalytic Interpretations (topic entry) **44**: 35
Troilus and Cressida **27**: 396

Asquith, Ros
Richard III **14**: 490
Troilus and Cressida **18**: 382

Astington, John
Twelfth Night **28**: 1; **46**: 338

Aston, Anthony
Hamlet **21**: 10

Atkinson, Brooks
As You Like It **23**: 72, 75
Hamlet **21**: 219
Henry IV, 1 and 2 **14**: 60, 63, 64
Julius Caesar **17**: 318
King John **24**: 209
King Lear **11**: 58
Macbeth **20**: 200, 224, 232, 240
The Merchant of Venice **12**: 53
A Midsummer Night's Dream **12**: 209, 239
Much Ado about Nothing **18**: 171, 172, 175
The Taming of the Shrew **12**: 341, 345, 348
Troilus and Cressida **18**: 313
Twelfth Night **26**: 246

Auberlen, Eckhard
Henry VIII **2**: 78

Auden, W. H.
Henry IV, 1 and 2 **1**: 410
Much Ado about Nothing **8**: 77
Sonnets **10**: 325
Twelfth Night **1**: 599

Austin, L. F.
The Merry Wives of Windsor **18**: 26

Axton, Marie
The Phoenix and Turtle **38**: 378

Bache, William B.
Fathers and Daughters (topic entry) **36**: 51

Bacon, Lord Francis
Richard II **6**: 250

Baddeley, V. C. Clinton
Troilus and Cressida **18**: 394

Badeau, Adam
Hamlet **21**: 62

Bagehot, Walter
Measure for Measure **2**: 406

Baildon, H. Bellyse
Titus Andronicus **4**: 632

Baines, Barbara J.
Henry IV, 1 and 2 **39**: 123

Baker, David J.
Henry V **22**: 103

Baker, Donald
As You Like It **23**: 132

Baker, Felix
Antony and Cleopatra **17**: 26

Baker, George Pierce
Romeo and Juliet **5**: 448

Baker, H. Barton
Romeo and Juliet **11**: 378, 399, 422

Baker, Harry T.
Henry IV, 1 and 2 **1**: 347

Baker, Herschel
Macbeth **20**: 64

Baker, Nick
Pericles **15**: 173

Baker, Susan
Appearance vs. Reality (topic entry) **34**: 45

Baldwin, Thomas Whitfield
The Comedy of Errors **1**: 21; **34**: 215

Balk, Wes
The Taming of the Shrew **12**: 366

Bamber, Linda
Gender Identity (topic entry) **40**: 15

Bamford, Karen
Cymbeline **36**: 148

Banks-Smith, Nancy
Richard II **24**: 364

Barber, C. L.
As You Like It **5**: 79
The Comedy of Errors **34**: 190
Hamlet **44**: 152
Henry IV, 1 and 2 **1**: 414
Love's Labour's Lost **2**: 335
The Merchant of Venice **4**: 273
A Midsummer Night's Dream **3**: 427
Pericles **2**: 582
Sonnets **10**: 302
Twelfth Night **1**: 620
The Winter's Tale **7**: 480

Barish, Jonas
As You Like It **28**: 9
Measure for Measure **28**: 9
The Merchant of Venice **28**: 9
The Merry Wives of Windsor **28**: 9
A Midsummer Night's Dream **28**: 9
Violence in Shakespeare's Works (topic entry) **43**: 1

Barkan, Leonard
Titus Andronicus **43**: 203

Barker, Frank Granville
Coriolanus **17**: 168
Hamlet **21**: 216

Barker, Kathleen M. D.
Richard II **24**: 402

Barker, Ronald
Twelfth Night **26**: 245

Barnaby, Andrew
As You Like It **34**: 120; **37**: 1

Barnes, Clive
As You Like It **23**: 101
The Comedy of Errors **26**: 154
Hamlet **21**: 231, 269
Measure for Measure **23**: 330
The Merchant of Venice **12**: 80
A Midsummer Night's Dream **12**: 252
Pericles **15**: 158
Twelfth Night **26**: 290
The Winter's Tale **15**: 482

Barnes, Howard
King Lear **11**: 56

Barnes, Thomas
Hamlet **21**: 40

Barnet, Sylvan
As You Like It **5**: 125
Twelfth Night **1**: 588

Barnfield, Richard
Venus and Adonis **10**: 410

Barnstorff, D.
Sonnets **10**: 190

Barry, Gerald
A Midsummer Night's Dream **12**: 249

Bartels, Emily C.
Hamlet **28**: 223
King Lear **28**: 223
Titus Andronicus **43**: 176

Bartholomeusz, Dennis
The Winter's Tale **15**: 401, 465, 503, 507

Barton, Anne
Antony and Cleopatra **6**: 208
The Comedy of Errors **1**: 61
Henry V **30**: 169
The Merry Wives of Windsor **5**: 400
Twelfth Night **1**: 656

Barton, John
All's Well That Ends Well **26**: 48
Troilus and Cressida **18**: 403

Baskervill, Charles Read
The Merchant of Venice **4**: 226

Bate, Jonathan
Shakespeare and Classical Civilization (topic entry) **27**: 46
Sonnets **16**: 472
Venus and Adonis **25**: 305

Bates, Ronald
The Phoenix and Turtle **10**: 27

Bateson, F. W.
Sonnets **10**: 277

Battenhouse, Roy W.
Antony and Cleopatra **6**: 192
Henry IV, 1 and 2 **1**: 434
Henry V **5**: 260
King Lear **31**: 149
Macbeth **3**: 269
Measure for Measure **2**: 466
Othello **4**: 573
The Rape of Lucrece **10**: 98
Richard II **6**: 402
Romeo and Juliet **5**: 542

Baumlin, Tita French
Venus and Adonis **16**: 452; **51**: 335

Bawcutt, N. W.
Measure for Measure **23**: 400; **49**: 293
The Two Noble Kinsmen **9**: 492

Baxter, John
Cymbeline **25**: 319

Bayley, John
Coriolanus **30**: 133
King Lear **31**: 162
Othello **4**: 552
Timon of Athens **27**: 175
Troilus and Cressida **3**: 634; **27**: 381

Bayley, P. C.
Henry VI, 1, 2, and 3 **24**: 25

Bean, John C.
The Taming of the Shrew **9**: 426

Beauchamp, Gorman
Henry V **14**: 242

Beaufort, John
As You Like It **23**: 73
Measure for Measure **23**: 352
Much Ado about Nothing **18**: 219
Richard III **14**: 480
The Taming of the Shrew **12**: 347
Twelfth Night **26**: 313

Beauman, Sally
As You Like It **23**: 66
Henry V **14**: 287, 295, 297, 301
Love's Labour's Lost **23**: 186
Macbeth **20**: 197
Pericles **15**: 138
Titus Andronicus **17**: 459
Troilus and Cressida **18**: 292

Beaurline, L. A.
King John **41**: 228

Beckman, Margaret Boerner
As You Like It **34**: 172

Beckwith, Sarah
Macbeth **19**: 245

Beerbohm, Max
Hamlet **21**: 140
King John **24**: 201
Macbeth **20**: 164
A Midsummer Night's Dream **12**: 203
Much Ado about Nothing **18**: 145

Belsey, Catherine
Desire (topic entry) **38**: 19
The Merchant of Venice **22**: 3
A Midsummer Night's Dream **28**: 15
Romeo and Juliet **25**: 181; **51**: 227
Shakespeare's Representation of Women (topic entry) **31**: 43

Bennett, H. S.
Pericles **15**: 139
Romeo and Juliet **11**: 458

Bennett, Josephine Waters
All's Well That Ends Well **7**: 104

Bennetts, Leslie
Much Ado about Nothing **18**: 223

Benson, Frank
Twelfth Night **26**: 207

Benson, John
Sonnets **10**: 153

Benston, Alice N.
The Merchant of Venice **4**: 336

Bentley, Eric
Julius Caesar **17**: 350

Berek, Peter
The Taming of the Shrew **31**: 276

Berge, Mark
King Lear **46**: 225

Berger, Harry, Jr.
General Commentary **13**: 457
Henry IV, 1 and 2 **28**: 101; **42**: 101; **48**: 95
King Lear **46**: 242
Macbeth **3**: 340
Much Ado about Nothing **8**: 121
Othello **35**: 380
Richard II **13**: 172
The Tempest **29**: 278

Berger, Thomas L.
Henry V **13**: 183

Bergeron, David M.
Cymbeline **4**: 170
Henry IV, 1 and 2 **19**: 157; **39**: 143
Henry VI, 1, 2, and 3 **3**: 149
Richard II **19**: 151
The Winter's Tale **49**: 18

Berggren, Paula S.
Gender Identity (topic entry) **40**: 1
The Two Noble Kinsmen **9**: 502

Berkeley, David S.
General Commentary **50**: 1
All's Well That Ends Well **38**: 155

Berkowitz, Gerald M.
Antony and Cleopatra **17**: 82
Hamlet **21**: 301
Much Ado about Nothing **18**: 211

Berlin, Normand
Macbeth **20**: 279

Berman, Ronald
Henry VI, 1, 2, and 3 **3**: 89
Love's Labour's Lost **2**: 348
Measure for Measure **33**: 52

Bermann, Sandra L.
Sonnets **40**: 303

Bernard, John
Othello **11**: 190; **32**: 201

Berry, Edward
Othello **16**: 293

Berry, Edward I.
Henry V **30**: 220
Henry VI, 1, 2, and 3 **39**: 177
Henry VIII **41**: 120

Berry, Philippa
Hamlet **42**: 217
The Rape of Lucrece **22**: 289

Berry, Ralph
All's Well That Ends Well **26**: 114
As You Like It **23**: 118; **34**: 72
Coriolanus **9**: 174; **17**: 248; **50**: 13
Hamlet **21**: 361
Henry V **14**: 328
Julius Caesar **7**: 356; **17**: 317, 421; **50**: 13, 194
Love's Labour's Lost **2**: 348
Measure for Measure **23**: 335, 375; **33**: 69
The Merchant of Venice **12**: 48
The Merry Wives of Windsor **5**: 373; **18**: 52, 64
A Midsummer Night's Dream **12**: 207
Much Ado about Nothing **31**: 184
The Taming of the Shrew **9**: 401
The Tempest **15**: 338
Timon of Athens **20**: 470; **50**: 13
Titus Andronicus **17**: 472; **50**: 13
Troilus and Cressida **18**: 406
Twelfth Night **26**: 342, 374
The Two Gentlemen of Verona **6**: 529; **12**: 488

Bertin, Michael
Twelfth Night **26**: 299

Bertram, Joseph L.
King Lear **11**: 93
Much Ado about Nothing **18**: 182

Bertram, Paul
Henry VIII **2**: 60

Bethell, S. L.
Antony and Cleopatra **6**: 115
Henry VI, 1, 2, and 3 **3**: 67
Othello **4**: 517
The Winter's Tale **7**: 446

Bethell, Tom
Authorship Controversy (topic entry) **41**: 48, 61

Bevington, David
Antony and Cleopatra **17**: 101
Love's Labour's Lost **16**: 17; **38**: 209
The Merry Wives of Windsor **18**: 71
Politics and Power (topic entry) **30**: 29
The Winter's Tale **45**: 295

Bevington, David M.
Henry VI, 1, 2, and 3 **3**: 103
A Midsummer Night's Dream **3**: 491

Bickerstaff, Isaac
See also Steele, Sir Richard
Julius Caesar **7**: 152

Bickersteth, Geoffrey L.
King Lear **2**: 179

Billington, Michael
All's Well That Ends Well **26**: 57
Antony and Cleopatra **17**: 40, 54
As You Like It **23**: 103, 120, 145
The Comedy of Errors **26**: 149, 157, 158
Cymbeline **15**: 60
Hamlet **21**: 323, 329
Henry V **14**: 307
Julius Caesar **17**: 372, 382
King John **24**: 215, 221, 236
Love's Labour's Lost **23**: 207, 231

Macbeth **20**: 298, 317
The Merchant of Venice **12**: 82
The Merry Wives of Windsor **18**: 49, 54
Pericles **15**: 174, 176
Richard II **24**: 336, 337, 380
The Tempest **15**: 271
Titus Andronicus **17**: 465
Twelfth Night **26**: 282, 346
The Winter's Tale **15**: 474

Bingham, Madeleine
Julius Caesar **17**: 315

Bishop, T. G.
The Comedy of Errors **37**: 12
The Winter's Tale **45**: 297

Black, James
Henry IV, 1 and 2 **14**: 150; **39**: 89
Measure for Measure **2**: 519
The Tempest **19**: 357

Blackmur, R. P.
Sonnets **10**: 315

Paula Blank
Richard II **42**: 120

Blau, Herbert
King Lear **11**: 154

Bliss, Lee
Henry VIII **2**: 72

Bloom, Allan
Julius Caesar **7**: 310
Politics and Power (topic entry) **30**: 1

Bloom, Harold
A Midsummer Night's Dream **45**: 158

Bluestone, Max
Henry IV, 1 and 2 **14**: 67
Troilus and Cressida **18**: 338

Blumenthal, Eileen
Antony and Cleopatra **17**: 67

Bly, Mary
All's Well That Ends Well **38**: 118

Boaden, James
Hamlet **21**: 31
Henry V **14**: 180
Henry VIII **24**: 68
King John **24**: 175, 176
Macbeth **20**: 59
Sonnets **10**: 169

Boas, Frederick S.
As You Like It **5**: 54
King John **9**: 240
Measure for Measure **2**: 416
The Merry Wives of Windsor **5**: 347
A Midsummer Night's Dream **3**: 391
The Phoenix and Turtle **10**: 8
The Rape of Lucrece **10**: 68
Romeo and Juliet **5**: 443
Timon of Athens **1**: 476
Titus Andronicus **4**: 631
Troilus and Cressida **3**: 555
The Two Gentlemen of Verona **6**: 451

Bock, Philip K.
The Phoenix and the Turtle **51**: 155

Bodenstedt, Friedrich
Othello **4**: 422

Bodkin, Maud
Othello **4**: 468

Bogard, Travis
Richard II **6**: 317

Bolton, Joseph S. G.
Titus Andronicus **4**: 635

Bolton, W. F.
Richard II **49**: 60

Bonaventure, Sister Mary
The Phoenix and Turtle **38**: 326; **51**: 143

Bonazza, Blaze Odell
The Comedy of Errors **1**: 50

Bond, R. Warwick
Cymbeline **15**: 36
The Two Gentlemen of Verona **6**: 46

Bond, Ronald B.
Romeo and Juliet **33**: 241

Bonheim, Helmut
Richard II **6**: 385

Bonheim, Jean
Richard II **6**: 385

Bonjour, Adrien
Julius Caesar **7**: 284
King John **9**: 263; **41**: 260
The Winter's Tale **7**: 456

Bonnard, George A.
A Midsummer Night's Dream **3**: 42
The Phoenix and Turtle **10**: 17
Richard II **6**: 310

Bono, Barbara J.
Gender Identity (topic entry) **40**: 90

Boose, Lynda E.
As You Like It **19**: 3
The Comedy of Errors **19**: 3
Fathers and Daughters (topic entry) **36**: 78
The Merchant of Venice **13**: 37
The Merry Wives of Windsor **19**: 3
The Taming of the Shrew **19**: 3; **28**: 24; **31**: 351

Booth, Michael R.
Henry VIII **24**: 91

Booth, Stephen
Hamlet **44**: 107
Macbeth **3**: 349
Sonnets **10**: 349

Booth, Wayne
Macbeth **3**: 306

Boothroyd, Basil
Richard II **24**: 331
Troilus and Cressida **18**: 346, 347

Boothroyd, J. B.
Measure for Measure **23**: 309
The Tempest **15**: 258
Titus Andronicus **17**: 440

Borot, Luc
Titus Andronicus **17**: 481

Bost, James S.
The Taming of the Shrew **12**: 396

Boswell, James
King Lear **11**: 6
Sonnets **10**: 166

Bowers, A. Robin
Rape of Lucrece **43**: 148

Bowers, Fredson Thayer
Hamlet **1**: 209
Titus Andronicus **4**: 637

Bowers, Rick
Antony and Cleopatra **48**: 206

Bowman, James
Hamlet **21**: 322

Boxer, Setphen
Julius Caesar **17**: 407

Boxill, Roger
All's Well That Ends Well **26**: 62
Richard III **14**: 484

Boyd, Brian
King John **32**: 93; **41**: 251

Bradbrook, M. C.
Appearance vs. Reality (topic entry) **34**: 1
Timon of Athens **20**: 492; **27**: 203

Bradbrook, Muriel C.
All's Well That Ends Well **7**: 51
Henry IV, 1 and 2 **1**: 418
Henry VI, 1, 2, and 3 **3**: 75
Love's Labour's Lost **2**: 321, 330
Measure for Measure **2**: 443
The Merchant of Venice **4**: 261
The Merry Wives of Windsor **5**: 366; **18**: 44
The Rape of Lucrece **10**: 78
Romeo and Juliet **5**: 479; **11**: 488
The Taming of the Shrew **9**: 355
Titus Andronicus **4**: 646
Twelfth Night **1**: 655
The Two Gentlemen of Verona **6**: 486
The Two Noble Kinsmen **9**: 490

Bradby, G. F.
As You Like It **5**: 65

Braddock, M. C.
Romeo and Juliet **11**: 488

Bradley, A. C.
Antony and Cleopatra **6**: 53
Coriolanus **9**: 43, 53
Hamlet **1**: 120
Henry IV, 1 and 2 **1**: 333
Henry V **5**: 209
Julius Caesar **7**: 188
King Lear **2**: 137; **11**: 137
Macbeth **3**: 213
The Merry Wives of Windsor **5**: 348
Othello **4**: 434
Sonnets **10**: 238
Twelfth Night **1**: 566

Bradley, Marshall C.
Julius Caesar **50**: 249

Bradshaw, Graham
Henry V **49**: 260
Othello **22**: 207; **25**: 189
Sonnets **25**: 189

Brady, Owen E.
Macbeth **20**: 308
The Merry Wives of Windsor **18**: 35

Brahms, Caryl
Julius Caesar **17**: 368
King Lear **11**: 76
Measure for Measure **23**: 317
Othello **11**: 292
The Taming of the Shrew **12**: 361
The Tempest **15**: 263
Timon of Athens **20**: 448
Titus Andronicus **17**: 447
Troilus and Cressida **18**: 325
Twelfth Night **26**: 254
The Two Gentlemen of Verona **12**: 463, 475

Brandes, George
As You Like It **5**: 50
Coriolanus **9**: 39
Hamlet **1**: 116
Henry IV, 1 and 2 **1**: 329
King Lear **2**: 136
Love's Labour's Lost **2**: 315
Measure for Measure **2**: 414
The Merry Wives of Windsor **5**: 346
A Midsummer Night's Dream **3**: 389
Much Ado about Nothing **8**: 36
Pericles **2**: 551
Timon of Athens **1**: 474
Troilus and Cressida **3**: 554
The Two Gentlemen of Verona **6**: 456
The Two Noble Kinsmen **9**: 460

Brathwait, Richard
Venus and Adonis **10**: 411

Braunmuller, A. R.
King John **24**: 245; **41**: 243

Bredbeck, Gregory W.
Sonnets **40**: 268

Breight, Curt
The Tempest **16**: 426

Breitenberg, Mark
Love's Labour's Lost **22**: 12

Brewer, Derek
The Merry Wives of Windsor **38**: 278

Brennan, Anthony S.
Antony and Cleopatra **47**: 107
Henry V **49**: 194

Brewster, Dorothy
Henry V **14**: 177

Bridie, James
Othello **11**: 268

Brien, Alan
All's Well That Ends Well **26**: 25
Coriolanus **17**: 165
Hamlet **21**: 223
King Lear **11**: 73, 91
The Merchant of Venice **12**: 65
Much Ado about Nothing **18**: 184
Othello **11**: 283
Pericles **15**: 141
The Taming of the Shrew **12**: 356
Troilus and Cressida **18**: 320
Twelfth Night **26**: 250
The Two Gentlemen of Verona **12**: 472

Briggs, Julia
All's Well That Ends Well **28**: 38
Measure for Measure **28**: 38

Brigham, A.
King Lear **2**: 116

Brill, Lesley W.
Timon of Athens **1**: 526

Brink, Bernhard Ten
Antony and Cleopatra **6**: 52

Brink, Jean R.
Shakespeare's Representation of Women (topic entry) **31**: 53

Brissenden, Alan
A Midsummer Night's Dream **3**: 513

Bristol, Michael D.
The Winter's Tale **19**: 366

Brittin, Norman A.
Twelfth Night **1**: 594

Broadbent, J. B.
Sonnets **10**: 322

Brockbank, Philip
All's Well That Ends Well **26**: 87
Coriolanus **17**: 227
General Commentary **13**: 476
Henry VIII **24**: 118
Julius Caesar **13**: 252
Troilus and Cressida **13**: 53

Brodwin, Leonora Leet
Romeo and Juliet **33**: 233

Bromley, John C.
Richard III **39**: 341

Bromley, Laura G.
Rape of Lucrece **43**: 85

Bronson, Bertrand H.
Love's Labour's Lost **2**: 326

Brook, Peter
Antony and Cleopatra **17**: 65
As You Like It **23**: 173
King Lear **11**: 84
A Midsummer Night's Dream **12**: 254, 259
Romeo and Juliet **11**: 459
The Winter's Tale **15**: 528

Brooke, C. F. Tucker
Henry IV, 1 and 2 **1**: 337, 341
Othello **4**: 451
Troilus and Cressida **3**: 560
The Two Noble Kinsmen **9**: 461

Brooke, Nicholas
All's Well That Ends Well **7**: 121
Richard III **8**: 243
Romeo and Juliet **5**: 528
Titus Andronicus **27**: 246

Brooke, Stopford A.
As You Like It **5**: 57
Henry V **5**: 213
Julius Caesar **7**: 205
King Lear **2**: 149
Othello **4**: 444
Romeo and Juliet **5**: 447

Brooks, Charles
The Taming of the Shrew **9**: 360

Brooks, Cleanth
Henry IV, 1 and 2 **1**: 380
Macbeth **3**: 253

Brooks, Douglas A.
Henry IV, 1 and 2 **48**: 117

Brooks, Harold F.
The Comedy of Errors **1**: 40
The Two Gentlemen of Verona **6**: 504

Brooks, Jeremy
Romeo and Juliet **11**: 462
The Winter's Tale **15**: 470

Broude, Ronald
Titus Andronicus **4**: 680; **27**: 282

Broun, Heywood
Julius Caesar **17**: 324

Brower, Reuben Arthur
Coriolanus **9**: 164
Hamlet **1**: 259
The Tempest **8**: 384

Brown, Carolyn E.
The Taming of the Shrew **32**: 1
Measure for Measure **42**: 1

Brown, Charles Armitage
Sonnets **10**: 176
The Two Gentlemen of Verona **6**: 439

Brown, Constance A.
Richard III **14**: 435

Brown, Ivor
All's Well That Ends Well **26**: 13
As You Like It **23**: 78, 87
Hamlet **21**: 156, 178, 196, 218
Henry IV, 1 and 2 **14**: 29
King John **24**: 203
King Lear **11**: 48
Macbeth **20**: 232, 244
The Merchant of Venice **12**: 47, 52
Much Ado about Nothing **18**: 159
Richard III **14**: 409
Romeo and Juliet **11**: 443
The Taming of the Shrew **12**: 351
Titus Andronicus **17**: 445
The Two Gentlemen of Verona **12**: 459

Brown, Jane K.
A Midsummer Night's Dream **45**: 126

Brown, Jeffrey
Othello **35**: 276

Brown, John Mason
As You Like It **23**: 76
Julius Caesar **17**: 319
Macbeth **20**: 227
The Tempest **15**: 242

Brown, John Russell
All's Well That Ends Well **26**: 34
As You Like It **5**: 103
The Comedy of Errors **1**: 36
Cymbeline **4**: 113; **15**: 70, 122
Hamlet **21**: 217
Macbeth **20**: 254, 265
Measure for Measure **23**: 312
The Merchant of Venice **4**: 270; **12**: 67
The Merry Wives of Windsor **5**: 354
A Midsummer Night's Dream **3**: 425 **12**: 244, 262
Much Ado about Nothing **8**: 75; **18**: 261
Othello **11**: 305
Richard II **24**: 414
Romeo and Juliet **11**: 466
The Taming of the Shrew **9**: 353; **12**: 363
The Tempest **15**: 193
Troilus and Cressida **18**: 329
Twelfth Night **1**: 600; **26**: 366, 371
The Two Gentlemen of Verona **12**: 478
The Winter's Tale **7**: 469; **15**: 524

Browne, Junius Henri
Othello **11**: 323

Browne, Martin E.
Coriolanus **17**: 182

Brownell, Arthur
Measure for Measure **23**: 280

Browning, I. R.
Coriolanus **9**: 117

Browning, Robert
Sonnets **10**: 213

Brownlow, F. W.
The Two Noble Kinsmen **9**: 498

Brubaker, Edward S.
King John **24**: 249

Bruce, Brenda
Romeo and Juliet **11**: 519

Brucher, Richard T.
Titus Andronicus **27**: 255

Brustein, Robert
The Comedy of Errors **26**: 176
Coriolanus **17**: 180, 221
Henry IV, 1 and 2 **14**: 66
Much Ado about Nothing **18**: 228
Othello **11**: 321

Bruster, Douglas
The Two Noble Kinsmen **41**: 340; **50**: 310

Bryan, George B.
Richard II **24**: 291

Bryant, J. A., Jr.
Cymbeline **4**: 105
The Merry Wives of Windsor **5**: 376
Twelfth Night **46**: 291
Richard II **6**: 323

Bryant, James C.
Romeo and Juliet **33**: 300

Bryden, Ronald
Hamlet **21**: 253
Henry IV, 1 and 2 **14**: 72, 81
Henry V **14**: 277
King John **24**: 221
The Merry Wives of Windsor **18**: 38
Othello **11**: 296

Buckle, Richard
King Lear **11**: 63
The Merry Wives of Windsor **18**: 33
Much Ado about Nothing **18**: 162

Buckmann-de Villegas, Sabine
Julius Caesar **17**: 411

Bucknill, John Charles
King Lear **2**: 120

Buhler, Stephen M.
Julius Caesar **37**: 203

Bullen, A. H.
Titus Andronicus **4**: 631

Bullogh, Geoffrey
King John **41**: 234

Bulthaupt, Heinrich
The Winter's Tale **7**: 396

Burckhardt, Sigurd
Henry IV, 1 and 2 **1**: 421
Julius Caesar **7**: 331
King John **9**: 284
King Lear **2**: 257
The Merchant of Venice **4**: 293

Burke, Kenneth
Coriolanus **9**: 148; **30**: 67
Julius Caesar **7**: 238
Othello **4**: 506

Burkhardt, Louis
Measure for Measure **32**: 16

Burnett, Mark Thornton
Hamlet **28**: 232
Love's Labour's Lost **25**: 1

Burnim, Kalman
Macbeth **20**: 32

Burrows, Jill
The Comedy of Errors **26**: 164
Measure for Measure **23**: 347

Burt, Richard A.
The Taming of the Shrew **31**: 269

Burton, Richard
Hamlet **21**: 245

Bush, Douglas
The Rape of Lucrece **10**: 73
Venus and Adonis **10**: 424

Bush, Geoffrey
As You Like It **5**: 102
King Lear **2**: 207

Bushnell, Nelson Sherwin
The Tempest **8**: 340

Butler, Francelia
Timon of Athens **20**: 433

Butler, Guy
As You Like It **46**: 117

Buxton, John
The Phoenix and Turtle **38**: 329

Byles, Joanna Montgomery
Hamlet **44**: 180

Byrne, Muriel St. Clare
All's Well That Ends Well **26**: 28
As You Like It **23**: 85
Cymbeline **15**: 100
Henry VIII **24**: 106
Othello **11**: 287
Pericles **15**: 145
The Tempest **15**: 261
Timon of Athens **20**: 449
The Two Gentlemen of Verona **12**: 464

Calderwood, James L.
All's Well That Ends Well **7**: 93; **38**: 65
Coriolanus **9**: 144, 198
Hamlet **35**: 215
Henry IV, 1 and 2 **39**: 117; **47**: 1
Henry V **5**: 310; **30**: 181
Henry VI, 1, 2, and 3 **3**: 105
King John **9**: 275; **41**: 269
Love's Labour's Lost **2**: 356; **38**: 219
A Midsummer Night's Dream **3**: 477; **19**: 21; **22**: 23

Othello **13**: 304
Romeo and Juliet **5**: 550
Titus Andronicus **4**: 664

Callaghan, Dympna
Henry IV, 1 and 2 **25**: 89
Richard II **25**: 89

Camden, Carroll
Hamlet **35**: 126

Campbell, K. T. S.
The Phoenix and Turtle **10**: 42

Campbell, Mrs. Patrick
Macbeth **20**: 165

Campbell, Oscar James
As You Like It **5**: 70
Coriolanus **9**: 80
King Lear **2**: 188
Measure for Measure **2**: 456
The Tempest **15**: 247
Troilus and Cressida **3**: 574
Twelfth Night **1**: 577
The Two Gentlemen of Verona **6**: 468

Campbell, Thomas
Coriolanus **17**: 131
Hamlet **1**: 97
King John **24**: 177
Much Ado about Nothing **8**: 16
The Tempest **8**: 302
The Winter's Tale **7**: 387; **15**: 400

Candido, Joseph
The Comedy of Errors **16**: 3; **34**: 220
Henry VI, 1, 2, and 3 **39**: 213
King John **13**: 147

Cantor, Paul A.
King Lear **37**: 213

Capell, Edward
Henry VI, 1, 2, and 3 **3**: 20
Henry VIII **2**: 21
Love's Labour's Lost **2**: 300
Measure for Measure **2**: 394
Richard III **8**: 153
The Taming of the Shrew **9**: 318
Titus Andronicus **4**: 614

Carducci, Jane S.
Titus Andronicus **43**: 222

Carlisle, Carol J.
As You Like It **23**: 28
Cymbeline **15**: 11
King Lear **11**: 158
Romeo and Juliet **11**: 407
Two Gentlemen of Verona **42**: 18

Carlson, Harry
Coriolanus **17**: 183

Carlson, Marvin
Othello **11**: 235

Carlson, Susan
As You Like It **34**: 177
Measure for Measure **49**: 338

Carlyle, Thomas
Henry V **5**: 197

Carr, Joan
Cymbeline **36**: 142

Carroll, Lewis
Henry VIII **24**: 76
The Tempest **15**: 205

Carroll, William C.
Love's Labour's Lost **2**: 367
Henry VI, 1, 2, and 3 **50**: 45
King Lear **50**: 45
The Merry Wives of Windsor **5**: 379; **47**: 314
Richard III **19**: 164
Romeo and Juliet **51**: 219
Sexuality (topic entry) **33**: 28
The Taming of the Shrew **9**: 430; **37**: 31
The Winter's Tale **37**: 31; **50**: 45

Cartelli, Thomas
All's Well That Ends Well **38**: 142
Henry VI, 1, 2, and 3 **28**: 112
Macbeth **20**: 406

Carter, Albert Howard
All's Well That Ends Well **7**: 62

Carter, Stephen
The Rape of Lucrece **32**: 321

Case, Arthur E.
All's Well That Ends Well **26**: 94

Case, R. H.
Antony and Cleopatra **6**: 60

Cavell, Stanley
Coriolanus **30**: 111
King Lear **31**: 155
Macbeth **29**: 91

Cazemian, Louis
Henry IV, 1 and 2 **1**: 355

Cecil, David
Antony and Cleopatra **6**: 111

Cerasano, S. P.
Richard III **14**: 490

Cespedes, Frank V.
Henry VIII **2**: 81

Chaillet, Ned
The Comedy of Errors **26**: 158
Hamlet **21**: 308
Richard III **14**: 474
The Two Gentlemen of Verona **12**: 490

Challinor, A. M.
Authorship Controversy (topic entry) **41**: 42

Chalmers, George
Measure for Measure **2**: 394
Sonnets **10**: 156, 158

Chambers, Colin
Richard III **14**: 475

Chambers, E. K.
All's Well That Ends Well **7**: 27
Antony and Cleopatra **6**: 64
As You Like It **5**: 55
The Comedy of Errors **1**: 16
Coriolanus **9**: 43
Cymbeline **4**: 46
Henry IV, 1 and 2 **1**: 336
Henry V **5**: 210
Henry VIII **2**: 42
Julius Caesar **7**: 189
King John **9**: 244
King Lear **2**: 143
Love's Labour's Lost **2**: 316
The Merchant of Venice **4**: 221
The Merry Wives of Windsor **5**: 350
A Midsummer Night's Dream **3**: 395
Much Ado about Nothing **8**: 39
Othello **4**: 440
Pericles **2**: 554
Richard II **6**: 277
Richard III **8**: 182
Romeo and Juliet **5**: 445
The Taming of the Shrew **9**: 330
The Tempest **8**: 326
Timon of Athens **1**: 478
Troilus and Cressida **3**: 557
Twelfth Night **1**: 561
The Two Gentlemen of Verona **6**: 460
The Winter's Tale **7**: 410

Chambers, R. W.
King Lear **2**: 170
Measure for Measure **2**: 437

Champion, Larry S.
The Comedy of Errors **1**: 56
Henry IV, 1 and 2 **49**: 93
Henry V **30**: 227
Henry VI, 1, 2, and 3 **3**: 154; **39**: 187
King John **13**: 152
Much Ado about Nothing **31**: 216
Othello **35**: 253
Titus Andronicus **4**: 662

Chaney, Joseph
Love's Labour's Lost **38**: 172

Chapman, John
King Lear **11**: 55

Charles, Casey
Twelfth Night **42**: 32

Charlton, H. B.
All's Well That Ends Well **7**: 37
The Comedy of Errors **1**: 23
Hamlet **1**: 166
Henry IV, 1 and 2 **1**: 357
Henry V **5**: 225
Julius Caesar **7**: 218
Love's Labour's Lost **2**: 322
Measure for Measure **2**: 434
The Merry Wives of Windsor **5**: 350
A Midsummer Night's Dream **3**: 402

Richard II **6**: 304
Richard III **8**: 197
Romeo and Juliet **5**: 464
The Taming of the Shrew **9**: 334
Titus Andronicus **4**: 640
Troilus and Cressida **3**: 571
Twelfth Night **1**: 573
The Two Gentlemen of Verona **6**: 472

Charnes, Linda
Troilus and Cressida **43**: 340

Charney, Hanna
Madness (topic entry) **35**: 49

Charney, Maurice
Antony and Cleopatra **6**: 155, 161
Coriolanus **9**: 136
Henry V **14**: 303
Julius Caesar **7**: 296
King John **25**: 98
Madness (topic entry) **35**: 49
Timon of Athens **25**: 198
Titus Andronicus **16**: 225
Troilus and Cressida **27**: 366

Chateaubriand
Romeo and Juliet **5**: 420

Chaudhuri, Sukanta
Kingship (topic entry) **39**: 20

Cheney, Donald
The Rape of Lucrece **10**: 125

Chesterton, C. K.
A Midsummer Night's Dream **3**: 393

Child, Harold
All's Well That Ends Well **26**: 72
The Comedy of Errors **26**: 182
Coriolanus **17**: 34
Henry IV, 1 and 2 **14**: 120
The Merry Wives of Windsor **18**: 67
A Midsummer Night's Dream **12**: 282
Much Ado about Nothing **18**: 232
Richard II **24**: 390
The Winter's Tale **15**: 500

Chillington, Carol A.
Coriolanus **17**: 194
Henry VI, 1, 2, and 3 **24**: 38

Chinoy, Helen Krich
The Merchant of Venice **12**: 91

Christensen, Ann C.
Coriolanus **42**: 223

Church, Tony
Hamlet **21**: 416

Cibber, Colley
Hamlet **21**: 19
King John **9**: 209

Cibber, Theophilus
King Lear **11**: 114
Romeo and Juliet **11**: 379

Cirillo, Albert R.
As You Like It **5**: 130
Romeo and Juliet **11**: 475

Clapp, Henry A.
As You Like It **5**: 44
A Midsummer Night's Dream **3**: 380

Clark, Cumberland
A Midsummer Night's Dream **3**: 400

Clarke, Asia Booth
Hamlet **21**: 70

Clarke, Charles Cowden
As You Like It **5**: 36
Henry IV, 1 and 2 **1**: 321
King John **9**: 229; **24**: 186
A Midsummer Night's Dream **3**: 376
Much Ado about Nothing **8**: 24
Romeo and Juliet **11**: 400
The Tempest **8**: 308

Clarke, Mary
All's Well That Ends Well **26**: 37
Cymbeline **15**: 51
Henry V **14**: 260
King John **24**: 203
Othello **11**: 280
Timon of Athens **20**: 450
Troilus and Cressida **18**: 314
The Two Gentlemen of Verona **12**: 465

Clarke, Mary Cowden
Romeo and Juliet **11**: 400

Clary, F. Nick
Henry IV, 1 and 2 **49**: 153

Clayton, Thomas
Macbeth **48**: 214
Othello **28**: 243

Clemen, Wolfgang H.
Hamlet **1**: 188
Henry VI, 1, 2, and 3 **3**: 71
King Lear **2**: 199
Richard III **8**: 206
Romeo and Juliet **5**: 477
Titus Andronicus **4**: 644

Clements, John
The Tempest **15**: 366

Clurman, Harold
All's Well That Ends Well **26**: 27
King Lear **11**: 92, 103
The Merchant of Venice **12**: 78
A Midsummer Night's Dream **12**: 240
The Two Gentlemen of Verona **12**: 471

Coates, John
Antony and Cleopatra **27**: 117

Cochrane, Claire
Timon of Athens **20**: 475

Coddon, Karin S.
Madness (topic entry) **35**: 68
Macbeth **13**: 361
Twelfth Night **34**: 330

Coffey, Denise
Much Ado about Nothing **18**: 254

Coghill, Nevill
Measure for Measure **2**: 491
The Merchant of Venice **4**: 250
The Taming of the Shrew **9**: 344
The Winter's Tale **7**: 464; **15**: 518

Cohen, D. M.
The Merchant of Venice **40**: 175

Cohen, Stephen A.
The Merchant of Venice **49**: 37

Cohen, Derek
Henry VI, 1, 2, and 3 **25**: 102, 109; **50**: 51
King Lear **25**: 202
Titus Andronicus **43**: 255
Violence in Shakespeare's Works (topic entry) **43**: 24

Cohn, Ruby
Coriolanus **17**: 188

Cole, Douglas
Troilus and Cressida **27**: 376

Cole, John William
Henry V **14**: 186
King John **24**: 196
A Midsummer Night's Dream **12**: 185
Richard II **24**: 280
The Tempest **15**: 210

Coleman, John
As You Like It **23**: 18
Hamlet **21**: 59
Macbeth **20**: 105
The Taming of the Shrew **12**: 371

Coleman, Robert
The Two Gentlemen of Verona **12**: 467

Coleridge, Hartley
Antony and Cleopatra **6**: 32
The Merry Wives of Windsor **5**: 339
Much Ado about Nothing **8**: 19
The Two Noble Kinsmen **9**: 455
The Winter's Tale **7**: 389

Coleridge, Samuel Taylor
All's Well That Ends Well **7**: 15
Antony and Cleopatra **6**: 25
As You Like It **5**: 23
The Comedy of Errors **1**: 14
Coriolanus **9**: 17
Hamlet **1**: 94, 95
Henry IV, 1 and 2 **1**: 310, 311
Henry VI, 1, 2, and 3 **3**: 27
Julius Caesar **7**: 160
King Lear **2**: 106
Love's Labour's Lost **2**: 302
Macbeth **3**: 184
Measure for Measure **2**: 397
A Midsummer Night's Dream **3**: 365
Much Ado about Nothing **8**: 16
Othello **4**: 399, 402, 405, 406
Pericles **2**: 544
Richard II **6**: 255, 262
Richard III **8**: 161
Romeo and Juliet **5**: 425
Sonnets **10**: 159, 173
The Tempest **8**: 295, 299
Timon of Athens **1**: 459
Titus Andronicus **4**: 617
Troilus and Cressida **3**: 541
The Two Noble Kinsmen **9**: 447
Venus and Adonis **10**: 414
The Winter's Tale **7**: 383, 387

Colie, Rosalie L.
As You Like It **34**: 147
Cymbeline **4**: 148
King Lear **31**: 92
Romeo and Juliet **5**: 559
Sonnets **40**: 247
Troilus and Cressida **43**: 293

Colley, John Scott
Cymbeline **47**: 228

Collier, Jeremy
See also Steevens, George; Hic et Ubique; Longinus; and Lorenzo
Hamlet **1**: 73
Henry IV, 1 and 2 **1**: 286
Henry V **5**: 185
Timon of Athens **1**: 456

Collins, A. S.
Timon of Athens **1**: 492

Collins, Glenn
The Comedy of Errors **26**: 172
Julius Caesar **17**: 398

Colman, E. A. M.
Cymbeline **36**: 155
Sexuality (topic entry) **33**: 1

Colman, George
King Lear **2**: 102
The Merchant of Venice **4**: 192

Colvin, Clare
Julius Caesar **17**: 394
Richard III **14**: 473

Conklin, Paul
Hamlet **21**: 339

Conrad, Hermann
Sonnets **10**: 214

Cook, Ann Jennalie
All's Well That Ends Well **51**: 44
Antony and Cleopatra **51**: 44
As You Like It **51**: 44
Hamlet **51**: 44
Love's Labour's Lost **51**: 44
Measure for Measure **51**: 44
The Merchant of Venice **12**: 95; **55**: 44
Merry Wives of Windsor **51**: 44
Midsummer Night's Dream **51**: 44

Much Ado About Nothing **51**: 44
Othello **51**: 44
Romeo and Juliet **51**: 44
Taming of the Shrew **51**: 44
Troilus and Cressida **51**: 44
Two Gentlemen of Verona **51**: 44
Winter's Tale **51**: 44

Cook, Carol
Much Ado about Nothing **31**: 245
Troilus and Cressida **43**: 329

Cook, Dorothy
Henry V **5**: 289

Cook, Dutton
The Merchant of Venice **12**: 16
Othello **11**: 244
Richard III **14**: 397
The Tempest **15**: 217

Cook, Judith
Antony and Cleopatra **17**: 113
Julius Caesar **17**: 387
Macbeth **20**: 294
Much Ado about Nothing **18**: 235, 236
Richard III **14**: 511

Cooke, William
The Merchant of Venice **12**: 4
Othello **11**: 189

Cookman, A. V.
Romeo and Juliet **11**: 447

Cope, Walter
Love's Labour's Lost **2**: 299

Copland, Murray
The Phoenix and Turtle **10**: 40; **51**: 184

Corballis, Richard
Madness (topic entry) **35**: 7

Corbet, Richard
Richard III **8**: 144

Corfield, Coano
The Tempest **8**: 458

Coriat, Isador H.
Macbeth **3**: 219
Romeo and Juliet **5**: 425

Corliss, Richard
Much Ado about Nothing **18**: 221

Cornwallis, Sir William
Richard III **8**: 144

Cotton, Nancy
The Merry Wives of Windsor **47**: 321

Cottrell, John
Coriolanus **17**: 161
Hamlet **21**: 203
Henry V **14**: 232
The Merchant of Venice **12**: 90
Othello **11**: 311

Coursen, H. R.
Hamlet **44**: 133
Macbeth **44**: 289
Much Ado about Nothing **18**: 201

Coursen, Herbert R., Jr.
Macbeth **3**: 318
The Tempest **8**: 429

Courthope, W. J.
The Two Gentlemen of Verona **6**: 460

Courtney, W. L.
A Midsummer Night's Dream **12**: 206

Cousins, A. D.
The Rape of Lucrece **48**: 291
Venus and Adonis **28**: 355; **51**: 345

Coveney, Michael
All's Well That Ends Well **26**: 71
As You Like It **23**: 139, 146
Hamlet **21**: 292, 326
Henry IV, 1 and 2 **14**: 88
Henry VIII **24**: 126
King Lear **11**: 111
Love's Labour's Lost **23**: 230
Macbeth **20**: 291
Much Ado about Nothing **18**: 208
Twelfth Night **26**: 285, 329, 337
The Winter's Tale **15**: 488

Cox, Catherine I.
Clowns and Fools (topic entry) **46**: 78

Cox, Catherine S.
King Lear **48**: 222

Cox, Francis
Troilus and Cressida **18**: 353

Cox, Frank
Henry VI, 1, 2, and 3 **24**: 27

Cox, J. F.
Much Ado about Nothing **18**: 257

Cox, John D.
All's Well That Ends Well **13**: 66
Henry V **30**: 215
Henry VI, 1, 2, and 3 **3**: 151; **13**: 131
Richard III **13**: 131

Cox, Majore Kolb
Romeo and Juliet **33**: 249

Cox, Roger L.
The Comedy of Errors **19**: 34
Henry IV, 1 and 2 **1**: 438
The Taming of the Shrew **19**: 34
The Two Gentlemen of Verona **19**: 34

Craig, Edward
Much Ado about Nothing **18**: 147

Craig, H. A. L.
Much Ado about Nothing **18**: 178

Craig, Hardin
The Comedy of Errors **1**: 31
Coriolanus **30**: 74
Pericles **2**: 564
The Taming of the Shrew **9**: 341

Craik, T. W.
Much Ado about Nothing **8**: 63
Twelfth Night **26**: 337

Cran, Mrs. George
The Merry Wives of Windsor **18**: 26
Much Ado about Nothing **18**: 156

Crane, Milton
As You Like It **5**: 92
Twelfth Night **1**: 590

Crewe, Jonathan
Rape of Lucrece **43**: 158

Crick, Bernard
Antony and Cleopatra **17**: 61
Twelfth Night **26**: 286

Crist, Judith
The Merchant of Venice **12**: 69

Crockett, Bryan
The Tempest **45**: 211

Crosman, Robert
Sonnets **16**: 461

Crowley, Richard C.
Coriolanus **9**: 177

Crowne, John
Henry VI, 1, 2, and 3 **3**: 16

Crowther, Bosley
Henry V **14**: 209, 211
Macbeth **20**: 199

Cruttwell, Patrick
Hamlet **1**: 234

Csengeri, Karen
Pericles **16**: 391

Cumberland, Richard
Henry IV, 1 and 2 **1**: 305
Henry V **5**: 192

Cummings, Peter
Sexuality (topic entry) **33**: 12

Cunliffe, John William
Henry V **5**: 217

Cunningham, James
Hamlet **42**: 234
King Lear **42**: 234
Macbeth **42**: 234
Othello **42**: 234

Cunningham, John
Macbeth **44**: 337

Cunningham, J. V.
The Phoenix and Turtle **10**: 24

Cunningham, Karen
Titus Andronicus **43**: 247

Curry, Walter Clyde
Macbeth **3**: 239
The Tempest **8**: 356

Curtis, Anthony
The Comedy of Errors **26**: 160
The Winter's Tale **15**: 484

Curtis, Jared R.
Othello **4**: 580

Curtis, Nick
Macbeth **20**: 315

Cusack, Sinead
The Merchant of Venice **12**: 104

Cushman, Robert
The Comedy of Errors **26**: 162
Henry IV, 1 and 2 **14**: 101
Macbeth **20**: 301
Measure for Measure **23**: 344
A Midsummer Night's Dream **12**: 269, 274
Twelfth Night **26**: 268
The Two Gentlemen of Verona **12**: 481

Cutts, John P.
The Comedy of Errors **34**: 211
Cymbeline **47**: 205
The Two Gentlemen of Verona **40**: 327

Daigle, Lennett J.
Venus and Adonis **33**: 330

Daly, Joseph Francis
As You Like It **23**: 52
The Merry Wives of Windsor **18**: 19

D'Amico, Jack
Madness (topic entry) **35**: 62
Politics and Power (topic entry) **30**: 49

Danby, David
Hamlet **21**: 319

Danby, John F.
Antony and Cleopatra **6**: 125
Henry IV, 1 and 2 **1**: 391
Pericles **2**: 573
The Two Gentlemen of Verona **6**: 492

Daniel, George
As You Like It **5**: 25

Daniell, David
Coriolanus **17**: 201

Danson, Lawrence
Desire (topic entry) **38**: 48
Hamlet **44**: 198
Julius Caesar **50**: 258
Henry V **49**: 200
The Merchant of Venice **4**: 328
Titus Andronicus **27**: 318

Darlington, W. A.
Cymbeline **15**: 59
King Lear **11**: 53
The Merchant of Venice **12**: 65
Othello **11**: 284
The Taming of the Shrew **12**: 354

Dash, Irene G.
A Midsummer Night's Dream **42**: 46
Othello **35**: 369
Romeo and Juliet **33**: 257
Shakespeare's Representation of Women (topic entry) **31**: 1
Twelfth Night **46**: 369

David, Richard
All's Well That Ends Well **26**: 40
As You Like It **23**: 109
Cymbeline **15**: 83
Hamlet **21**: 355
Henry IV, 1 and 2 **14**: 49
Henry V **14**: 259
Julius Caesar **17**: 384
King John **24**: 206, 228
Love's Labour's Lost **23**: 191, 207
Macbeth **20**: 302, 318
Measure for Measure **23**: 299
Richard II **24**: 325, 419
The Taming of the Shrew **12**: 352
Titus Andronicus **17**: 448
Troilus and Cressida **18**: 307, 314
Twelfth Night **26**: 231
The Winter's Tale **15**: 490

Davidson, Clifford
Timon of Athens **27**: 196

Davidson, Frank
The Tempest **8**: 420

Davies, H. Neville
The Phoenix and Turtle **51**: 181

Davies, John
Henry VIII **24**: 127
Venus and Adonis **10**: 411

Davies, Robertson
Henry V **14**: 263
The Merchant of Venice **12**: 56

Davies, Thomas
All's Well That Ends Well **26**: 92
Antony and Cleopatra **6**: 23; **17**: 5
Hamlet **21**: 21, 29, 334
Henry IV, 1 and 2 **14**: 111
Julius Caesar **7**: 159
King John **9**: 216; **24**: 162, 167, 168
King Lear **11**: 116
Macbeth **3**: 181; **20**: 12, 25, 22
Richard III **14**: 365
Romeo and Juliet **11**: 377
The Taming of the Shrew **12**: 309
Troilus and Cressida **18**: 278
The Winter's Tale **15**: 396

Davis, Lloyd
Appearance vs. Reality (topic entry) **34**: 23

Desire (topic entry) **38**: 31
Romeo and Juliet **51**: 236

Davis, Michael
Macbeth **44**: 315

Dawes, James
Sonnets **32**: 327

Dawson, Anthony B.
As You Like It **23**: 162
Hamlet **21**: 371
Henry IV, 1 and 2 **14**: 160
Henry V **14**: 342
Julius Caesar **17**: 426
Macbeth **20**: 413
Measure for Measure **23**: 395
Richard II **24**: 428
The Tempest **15**: 385
The Winter's Tale **15**: 532

Dawson, Helen
Love's Labour's Lost **23**: 201
A Midsummer Night's Dream **12**: 256

de Grazia, Margareta
General Commentary **13**: 487
Sonnets **28**: 363; **40**: 273

de Jongh, Nicholas
As You Like It **23**: 141, 148
King John **24**: 239
Twelfth Night **26**: 334

de Sousa, Geraldo U.
Henry VI, 1, 2, and 3 **37**: 97

De Quincey, Thomas
Macbeth **3**: 190
The Two Noble Kinsmen **9**: 447

Dean, John
Pericles **51**: 71

Dean, Leonard F.
Henry IV, 1 and 2 **1**: 370
Richard II **6**: 315

Dean, Paul
General Commentary **13**: 481

Deats, Sara Munson
Violence in Shakespeare's Works (topic entry) **43**: 32

Deighton, K.
Pericles **2**: 553

Demaray, John G.
The Tempest **48**: 299

Dench, Judi
Antony and Cleopatra **17**: 82

Dennis, Carl
Twelfth Night **47**: 45

Dennis, John
Coriolanus **9**: 9
Julius Caesar **7**: 151
The Merry Wives of Windsor **5**: 333; **18**: 5, 7

Dent, Alan
All's Well That Ends Well **26**: 13
As You Like It **23**: 69
Julius Caesar **17**: 370
Macbeth **20**: 166
Richard II **24**: 329

Dent, R. W.
A Midsummer Night's Dream **3**: 441

Derrick, Patty S.
Two Gentlemen of Verona **42**: 18

Desai, R. W.
The Winter's Tale **37**: 305

Desmet, Christy
Appearance vs. Reality (topic entry) **34**: 54
Cymbeline **47**: 286

Dessen, Allan C.
As You Like It **32**: 212
Henry IV, 1 and 2 **32**: 212
King Lear **32**: 212
Macbeth **32**: 212
Romeo and Juliet **32**: 212
Titus Andronicus **17**: 483, 492

Detmer, Emily
Violence in Shakespeare's Works (topic entry) **43**: 61

DeVine, Lawrence
Titus Andronicus **17**: 473

DeWilde, G. J.
Macbeth **20**: 89

Dexter, John
As You Like It **23**: 124

Di Biase, Carmine
Cymbeline **28**: 373

Dibdin, Charles
Richard II **6**: 255
Romeo and Juliet **5**: 419
The Two Gentlemen of Verona **6**: 438

DiGangi, Mario
As You Like It **46**: 142

Dick Bernard F.
Julius Caesar **17**: 364

Dickey, Franklin M.
Romeo and Juliet **5**: 485
Troilus and Cressida **3**: 594
Venus and Adonis **10**: 449

Dickey, Stephen
Pericles **36**: 279
Twelfth Night **19**: 42

Dickinson, Hugh
Henry VI, Parts 1, 2, and 3 **47**: 32

Diehl, Huston
Measure for Measure **48**: 1; **49**: 325

DiGangi, Mario
Measure for Measure **25**: 12; **33**: 90

Digges, Leonard
Julius Caesar **7**: 149
Twelfth Night **1**: 539

Dillon, Janette
Sonnets **10**: 372

Disch, Thomas M.
Julius Caesar **17**: 403
Love's Labour's Lost **23**: 228

Dithmar, E. A.
The Merry Wives of Windsor **18**: 16
Twelfth Night **26**: 214

Dobranski, Stephen B.
Much Ado about Nothing **48**: 14

Dodds, W. M. T.
Measure for Measure **2**: 463

Dodsworth, Martin
All's Well That Ends Well **26**: 72
Hamlet **21**: 334
Julius Caesar **17**: 389
Love's Labour's Lost **23**: 215

Doebler, John
Venus and Adonis **10**: 486

Dolan, Frances E.
Violence in Shakespeare's Works (topic entry) **43**: 39

Donaldson, E. Talbot
Troilus and Cressida **43**: 305

Donaldson, Ian
All's Well That Ends Well **38**: 123
The Rape of Lucrece **33**: 131

Donnellan, Declan
The Tempest **15**: 338

Donno, Elizabeth Story
Twelfth Night **46**: 286

Donohue, Joseph
Macbeth **20**: 376

Donohue, Joseph W., Jr.
Macbeth **20**: 32, 70, 73

Doone, Rupert
Richard III **14**: 420

Doran, John
The Merchant of Venice **12**: 6

Doran, Madeleine
Antony and Cleopatra **27**: 96

Dorsch, T. S.
The Comedy of Errors **26**: 142, 186
Julius Caesar **7**: 277

Dowden, Edward
All's Well That Ends Well **7**: 26

Antony and Cleopatra 6: 41
As You Like It 5: 43
The Comedy of Errors 1: 16
Coriolanus 9: 31
Hamlet 1: 115
Henry IV, 1 and 2 1: 326
Henry VI, 1, 2, and 3 3: 41
Julius Caesar 7: 174
King John 9: 234
King Lear 2: 131
Love's Labour's Lost 2: 308
Macbeth 3: 207
Measure for Measure 2: 410
A Midsummer Night's Dream 3: 379
Much Ado about Nothing 8: 28
Pericles 2: 549
The Phoenix and Turtle 10: 9
The Rape of Lucrece 10: 68
Richard II 6: 267
Richard III 8: 168
Romeo and Juliet 5: 437
Sonnets 10: 215
The Taming of the Shrew 9: 325
The Tempest 8: 312
Timon of Athens 1: 470
Titus Andronicus 4: 625
Troilus and Cressida 3: 548
Twelfth Night 1: 561
The Two Gentlemen of Verona 6: 449
The Two Noble Kinsmen 9: 456
Venus and Adonis 10: 419
The Winter's Tale 7: 395

Dowling, Ellen
The Taming of the Shrew 12: 441

Downer, Alan S.
Macbeth 20: 107
Romeo and Juliet 11: 463

Downes, John
Hamlet 21: 9
Macbeth 20: 12
A Midsummer Night's Dream 12: 144
Romeo and Juliet 11: 377
The Tempest 15: 195

Downs-Gamble, Margaret
The Taming of the Shrew 31: 339

Drake, James
Hamlet 1: 73

Drake, Nathan
Richard II 6: 259
Richard III 8: 162
Sonnets 10: 158, 161
Venus and Adonis 10: 416

Draper, John W.
As You Like It 5: 66
King Lear 2: 168
Shakespeare's Representation of Women (topic entry) 31: 12
Timon of Athens 1: 487, 489
Twelfth Night 1: 581

Draper, R. P.
Richard II 39: 289

Dreher, Diane Elizabeth
Fathers and Daughters (topic entry) 36: 12

Drew, John
Richard II 24: 291
The Taming of the Shrew 12: 330

Driver, Tom F.
King Lear 11: 97
Macbeth 3: 293
Richard III 8: 223
Romeo and Juliet 5: 518

Dromey, Mary Jane Scholtes
Coriolanus 17: 148

Dronke, Peter
The Phoenix and Turtle 38: 367

Drury, Alan
As You Like It 23: 129
The Merry Wives of Windsor 18: 54
Pericles 15: 164

Dryden, John
Henry IV, 1 and 2 1: 285
Julius Caesar 7: 149
Macbeth 3: 170
The Merry Wives of Windsor 5: 332
A Midsummer Night's Dream 3: 361
Pericles 2: 537
Richard II 6: 250
Romeo and Juliet 5: 415
The Tempest 8: 286; 15: 189, 343
Troilus and Cressida 3: 536; 18: 276, 277
The Winter's Tale 7: 376

Dubrow, Heather
The Rape of Lucrece 10: 135
Sonnets 10: 367; 40: 238

Duff, William
A Midsummer Night's Dream 3: 362

Dukes, Ashley
Richard II 24: 302
Romeo and Juliet 11: 447

Dunbar, Mary Judith
Pericles 36: 251

Duncan-Jones, Katherine
Authorship Controversy (topic entry) 41: 110
Richard II 24: 382
Sonnets 42: 303
Venus and Adonis 25: 328

Dundas, Judith
Rape of Lucrece 10: 128

Dunkel, Wilbur
Henry VIII 24: 80

Dunkley, Chris
The Taming of the Shrew 12: 397

Dunn, Allen
A Midsummer Night's Dream 13: 19

Dunn, Esther Cloudman
The Rape of Lucrece 10: 74

Dusinberre, Juliet
As You Like It 28: 46
Gender Identity (topic entry) 40: 51
King John 16: 161
The Taming of the Shrew 31: 307

Duthie, George Ian
Romeo and Juliet 5: 480
The Taming of the Shrew 9: 347

Dyboski, Roman
Coriolanus 9: 62

Dyson, H. V. D.
Henry VI, 1, 2, and 3 3: 64

Dyson, J. P.
Macbeth 3: 302

Eagleton, Terence
Coriolanus 9: 153
Macbeth 3: 321
Measure for Measure 2: 507
Troilus and Cressida 3: 617
Twelfth Night 34: 293

Edelman, Charles
Cymbeline 22: 365
King Lear 22: 365
Macbeth 22: 365

Eder, Richard
Antony and Cleopatra 17: 71
As You Like It 23: 119
Henry V 14: 325
Macbeth 20: 306
Richard III 14: 468

Edinborough, Arnold
Antony and Cleopatra 17: 47
Hamlet 21: 222
Henry V 14: 265, 269
Much Ado about Nothing 18: 176
The Taming of the Shrew 12: 368
Timon of Athens 20: 458
Twelfth Night 26: 248

Edwards, Christopher
As You Like It 23: 138
Coriolanus 17: 212
Hamlet 21: 314, 315
Henry VI, 1, 2, and 3 24: 48
Love's Labour's Lost 23: 216
The Taming of the Shrew 12: 409
Troilus and Cressida 18: 385, 390
Twelfth Night 26: 305, 330
The Two Gentlemen of Verona 12: 493

Edwards, Philip
Hamlet 44: 119
Pericles 2: 586
Romeo and Juliet 33: 272
Sonnets 10: 342
Twelfth Night 1: 654
The Two Noble Kinsmen 9: 481

Egan, Robert
The Tempest 8: 435

Eggert, Katherine
Henry V 28: 121

Eliot, T. S.
Coriolanus 9: 58
Hamlet 1: 142
Othello 4: 454

Ellen, Terry
Henry VIII 24: 82
Much Ado about Nothing 18: 133

Elliot, John R., Jr.
Richard II 39: 235

Elliott, G. R.
The Comedy of Errors 1: 27
Macbeth 3: 286
Othello 4: 470, 522

Elliott, Michael
The Winter's Tale 15: 449

Ellis, David
Clowns and Fools (topic entry) 46: 68

Ellis, Roger
Clowns and Fools (topic entry) 46: 1

Ellis-Fermor, Una
Coriolanus 9: 121
Henry IV, 1 and 2 1: 379
Henry V 5: 244
Julius Caesar 7: 252
Measure for Measure 2: 432
Timon of Athens 1: 490
Troilus and Cressida 3: 578; 18: 412

Ellrodt, Robert
The Phoenix and Turtle 38: 350
Sonnets 28: 380

Elsom, John
All's Well That Ends Well 26: 54
Antony and Cleopatra 17: 66
As You Like It 23: 112, 122
Henry IV, 1 and 2 14: 86
King John 24: 220
Measure for Measure 23: 338
A Midsummer Night's Dream 12: 271
Pericles 15: 159
Richard II 24: 345, 371
The Taming of the Shrew 12: 389
The Tempest 15: 279
Troilus and Cressida 18: 357
The Two Gentlemen of Verona 12: 491

Elze, Karl
All's Well That Ends Well 7: 21
Henry VIII 2: 35
The Merchant of Venice 4: 209

Emerson, Ralph Waldo
The Phoenix and Turtle 10: 7

Emerson, Sally
The Comedy of Errors **26**: 157
Henry VI, 1, 2, and 3 **24**: 34

Empson, William
Hamlet **1**: 202
Henry IV, 1 and 2 **1**: 359
Measure for Measure **2**: 486
The Rape of Lucrece **10**: 96
Sonnets **10**: 256
Troilus and Cressida **3**: 569

Engle, Lars
The Merchant of Venice **25**: 22; **40**: 197
Sonnets **13**: 445

Enright, D. J.
Coriolanus **9**: 112

Enterline, Lynn
The Winter's Tale **42**: 308

Erickson, Peter
As You Like It **5**: 168
Hamlet **44**: 189
King Lear **31**: 137
Love's Labour's Lost **38**: 232
The Merry Wives of Windsor **5**: 402

Erskine, John
Romeo and Juliet **5**: 450

Ervine, St. John
The Two Gentlemen of Verona **12**: 459

Esslin, Martin
As You Like It **23**: 98
The Winter's Tale **15**: 480

Estrin, Barbara L.
Romeo and Juliet **51**: 203

Ettin, Andrew V.
Titus Andronicus **27**: 275

Eure, John D.
King Lear **49**: 1
Measure for Measure **49**: 1
The Merchant of Venice **49**: 1

Evans, B. Ifor
The Merchant of Venice **4**: 267
A Midsummer Night's Dream **3**: 415

Evans, Bertrand
All's Well That Ends Well **7**: 81
As You Like It **5**: 107
The Comedy of Errors **1**: 37
Love's Labour's Lost **2**: 338
Macbeth **3**: 338
Measure for Measure **2**: 498
The Merry Wives of Windsor **5**: 355
A Midsummer Night's Dream **3**: 434
Much Ado about Nothing **8**: 82
Pericles **2**: 575
Romeo and Juliet **5**: 470
Twelfth Night **1**: 625
The Two Gentlemen of Verona **6**: 499

Evans, G. Blakemore
Romeo and Juliet **11**: 517; **33**: 210

Evans, Gareth Lloyd
All's Well That Ends Well **26**: 48
As You Like It **23**: 132
Clowns and Fools (topic entry) **46**: 52
Henry IV, 1 and 2 **14**: 81
King Lear **11**: 112
Macbeth **20**: 262, 296, 329, 379
The Merry Wives of Windsor **18**: 46
A Midsummer Night's Dream **12**: 276
Richard III **14**: 490
The Taming of the Shrew **12**: 358
Troilus and Cressida **18**: 349, 403
Twelfth Night **26**: 272
The Two Gentlemen of Verona **12**: 480

Evans, Malcolm
Love's Labour's Lost **2**: 365

Evans, Peter
The Merry Wives of Windsor **18**: 90

Evans, Robert O.
Romeo and Juliet **5**: 530

Everett, Barbara
Antony and Cleopatra **17**: 79
Hamlet **1**: 268
King Lear **2**: 229
Much Ado about Nothing **8**: 91; **28**: 56
Romeo and Juliet **33**: 294
Sonnets **28**: 385
Troilus and Cressida **27**: 347

Ewbank, Inga-Stina
Hamlet **1**: 270
The Tempest **19**: 379
The Two Gentlemen of Verona **6**: 541
The Winter's Tale **7**: 476; **13**: 409

Eyres, Harry
Richard II **24**: 385

Faber, M. D.
A Midsummer Night's Dream **3**: 483
Othello **35**: 282
Romeo and Juliet **5**: 556

Fairchild, Arthur H. R.
The Phoenix and Turtle **10**: 9

Fairchild, Hoxie N.
Measure for Measure **2**: 427

Falk, Florence
A Midsummer Night's Dream **3**: 502

Farber, Manny
Henry V **14**: 212

Farber, Stephen
The Taming of the Shrew **12**: 373

Farjeon, Herbert
All's Well That Ends Well **26**: 14
As You Like It **23**: 68
Henry IV, 1 and 2 **14**: 28
King Lear **11**: 47, 52
A Midsummer Night's Dream **12**: 235, 294
Othello **11**: 264
Richard II **24**: 300, 303
Richard III **14**: 410
The Tempest **15**: 233
Twelfth Night **26**: 359

Farley-Hills, David
The Taming of the Shrew **31**: 261
Timon of Athens **16**: 351

Farmer, Richard
Henry V **5**: 190
Pericles **2**: 538

Farnham, Willard
Antony and Cleopatra **6**: 136
Coriolanus **9**: 92

Farrah
Henry V **14**: 295

Farrell, Kirby
Fathers and Daughters (topic entry) **36**: 25
Romeo and Juliet **13**: 235
Venus and Adonis **33**: 370

Faucit, Helena (Lady Martin)
As You Like It **5**: 44
Cymbeline **4**: 37
Hamlet **21**: 386
Othello **11**: 334
The Winter's Tale **15**: 413

Fawcett, Mary Laughlin
Titus Andronicus **43**: 239

Fehrenbach, Robert J.
Henry IV, 1 and 2 **39**: 137

Feingold, Michael
Measure for Measure **23**: 353
Much Ado about Nothing **18**: 222
Richard III **14**: 483

Felheim, Marvin
The Merry Wives of Windsor **18**: 21; **38**: 313
A Midsummer Night's Dream **12**: 198
The Taming of the Shrew **12**: 331
The Two Gentlemen of Verona **12**: 456; **40**: 330

Felperin, Howard
Henry VIII **2**: 66
Macbeth **44**: 341
Pericles **2**: 581

Feltham, Owen
Pericles **2**: 537

Felton, Felix
A Midsummer Night's Dream **12**: 213

Felver, Charles
Clowns and Fools (topic entry) **46**: 33

Fender, Stephen
A Midsummer Night's Dream **3**: 459

Fenton, James
The Comedy of Errors **26**: 162
Much Ado about Nothing **18**: 211
Twelfth Night **26**: 302

Fenwick, Henry
Richard II **24**: 364

Ferber, Michael
The Merchant of Venice **40**: 127

Ferguson, Otis
A Midsummer Night's Dream **12**: 212

Fergusson, Francis
The Comedy of Errors **1**: 35
Hamlet **1**: 184
Macbeth **3**: 267
Richard III **39**: 305
Troilus and Cressida **18**: 298

Ferry, Anne
Sonnets **40**: 292

Fichter, Andrew
Antony and Cleopatra **6**: 224

Fiedler, Leslie A.
Henry VI, 1, 2, and 3 **3**: 140

Field, Kate
Hamlet **21**: 81

Fielding, Henry
Hamlet **21**: 15

Fienberg, Nona
Pericles **2**: 590; **36**: 274
Venus and Adonis **51**: 388

Figes, Eva
Kingship (topic entry) **39**: 62

Findlater, Richard
Antony and Cleopatra **17**: 37
The Comedy of Errors **26**: 164
Henry IV, 1 and 2 **14**: 37
The Taming of the Shrew **12**: 358
Twelfth Night **26**: 304
The Two Gentlemen of Verona **12**: 476
The Winter's Tale **15**: 469

Findlay, Alison
Hamlet **35**: 144

Fineman, Joel
Rape of Lucrece **43**: 113

Fink, Joel G.
The Comedy of Errors **26**: 171

Fink, Z. S.
As You Like It **5**: 68

Finkelpearl, Philip J.
The Two Noble Kinsmen **37**: 312

Finkelstein, Sidney
Julius Caesar **50**: 189

Fisch, Harold
Antony and Cleopatra **47**: 71

Fisher, James E.
Othello **11**: 306

Fisher, Sandra K.
Henry IV, 1 and 2 **13**: 213
Henry V **13**: 213
Richard II **13**: 213

Fitz, L. T.
Antony and Cleopatra **27**: 144

Fitzgerald, Percy
Henry VIII **24**: 70
A Midsummer Night's Dream **12**: 287
Othello **11**: 253
The Tempest **15**: 343

Fitzpatrick, Thomas
King Lear **2**: 99

Fitzsimons, Raymond
The Merchant of Venice **12**: 14

Flathe, J. L. F.
Macbeth **3**: 199

Fleming, Peter
Antony and Cleopatra **17**: 30
As You Like It **23**: 79, 83
Macbeth **20**: 188
Measure for Measure **23**: 297
The Merchant of Venice **12**: 52
Othello **11**: 275
Richard II **24**: 319
Romeo and Juliet **11**: 446
Twelfth Night **26**: 243
The Winter's Tale **15**: 461

Flesy, F. G.
Measure for Measure **2**: 548
Timon of Athens **1**: 469

Fletcher, George
King John **24**: 184

Flint, Stella
The Taming of the Shrew **12**: 408

Fly, Richard D.
King Lear **2**: 271
Timon of Athens **1**: 522
Troilus and Cressida **3**: 630; **27**: 354

Foakes, R. A.
The Comedy of Errors **26**: 183; **34**: 208
Cymbeline **4**: 134
Hamlet **25**: 209
Henry VIII **2**: 51
King Lear **25**: 218
Measure for Measure **2**: 516
The Tempest **45**: 188
Troilus and Cressida **27**: 341

Folland, Harold F.
Richard II **6**: 393

Foote, Samuel
King Lear **11**: 5

Forbes-Robinson, John
King Lear **11**: 21

Ford-Davies, Oliver
Coriolanus **17**: 195

Forker, Charles R.
Henry VI, 1, 2, and 3 **3**: 97

Forman, Simon
Cymbeline **4**: 17
The Winter's Tale **7**: 375

Forster, John
Hamlet **21**: 22, 51
King Lear **11**: 17
Macbeth **20**: 98

Fortin, Rene E.
Julius Caesar **7**: 336
King Lear **2**: 286
The Merchant of Venice **4**: 324

Foster, Charles J.
Henry IV, 1 and 2 **14**: 4
The Merry Wives of Windsor **18**: 12

Foster, Donald W.
Authorship Controversy (topic entry) **41**: 85

Foster, Verna A.
The Winter's Tale **25**: 339

Foulkes, Richard
The Merchant of Venice **12**: 43, 107
A Midsummer Night's Dream **12**: 172
Richard II **24**: 283

Fowler, Alastair
The Winter's Tale **36**: 362

Fowler, William Warde
Julius Caesar **7**: 200

Fox-Good, Jacquelyn
The Tempest **37**: 320

Frail, David
As You Like It **46**: 105

France, Richard
Julius Caesar **17**: 334
Macbeth **20**: 213

Fraser, Russell
All's Well That Ends Well **26**: 87

Freedman, Barbara
The Comedy of Errors **19**: 54
The Merry Wives of Windsor **5**: 392

Freedman, Gerald
Titus Andronicus **17**: 463

Freer, Coburn
Cymbeline **36**: 166

French, A. L.
Antony and Cleopatra **6**: 202
Richard II **6**: 359

French, Marilyn
Henry VI, 1, 2, and 3 **3**: 157
Macbeth **3**: 333
The Merry Wives of Windsor **5**: 395
Othello **35**: 327

French, Philip
Henry V **14**: 308
Julius Caesar **17**: 372
The Merry Wives of Windsor **18**: 41
Romeo and Juliet **11**: 473

Frenzel, Karl
Antony and Cleopatra **6**: 39

Freud, Sigmund
Hamlet **1**: 119
King Lear **2**: 147
Macbeth **3**: 223
Richard III **8**: 185

Frey, Charles
Fathers and Daughters (topic entry) **36**: 37
The Tempest **29**: 373
The Two Gentlemen of Verona **12**: 488
The Winter's Tale **7**: 497

Friedman, Michael D.
Much Ado about Nothing **16**: 45; **31**: 222

Fripp, Edgar I.
Henry VIII **2**: 46

Frost, William
King Lear **2**: 216

Frye, Northrop
Antony and Cleopatra **6**: 178
The Comedy of Errors **1**: 32
Coriolanus **9**: 142
Cymbeline **4**: 115
Henry V **5**: 269
Henry VIII **2**: 65
King Lear **2**: 253
The Merry Wives of Windsor **5**: 353
Pericles **2**: 580
Romeo and Juliet **5**: 575
Sonnets **10**: 309
The Tempest **8**: 401
Timon of Athens **1**: 512
Troilus and Cressida **3**: 642
The Winter's Tale **7**: 479; **36**: 289

Fuchs, Barbara
The Tempest **42**: 327

Fujimura, Thomas H.
The Merchant of Venice **4**: 308

Fuller, Edward
Measure for Measure **23**: 279

Fuller, Thomas
Henry IV, 1 and 2 **1**: 285

Funke, Lewis
The Two Gentlemen of Verona **12**: 470

Furness, Horace Howard
Antony and Cleopatra **6**: 62
As You Like It **5**: 45
Cymbeline **4**: 48
A Midsummer Night's Dream **3**: 386

Furness, Horace Howard, Jr.
Hamlet **21**: 151

Furnivall, F. J.
Sonnets **10**: 213
Twelfth Night **1**: 557

Furse, Roger
Richard III **14**: 515

Fuxier, J.
A Midsummer Night's Dream **12**: 272
Much Ado about Nothing **18**: 215
Richard III **14**: 489

Gajowski, Evelyn
Antony and Cleopatra **47**: 174; **51**: 25
Othello **19**: 253; **51**: 25
Romeo and Juliet **51**: 25

Gallenca, Christiane
The Merry Wives of Windsor **38**: 256

Ganz, Arthur
All's Well That Ends Well **26**: 62
Richard III **14**: 484

Garber, Marjorie
Antony and Cleopatra **45**: 28
Hamlet **45**: 28
Julius Caesar **50**: 265
A Midsummer Night's Dream **45**: 96
Romeo and Juliet **33**: 246
The Tempest **45**: 236
The Winter's Tale **45**: 366

Gardiner, Judith Kegan
Sonnets **10**: 379

Gardner, Helen
As You Like It **5**: 98
Hamlet **1**: 224

Gardner, Lyn
Antony and Cleopatra **17**: 82

Garebian, Keith
Macbeth **20**: 307
The Merry Wives of Windsor **18**: 51

Garland, Robert
King Lear **11**: 56

Garner, Shirley Nelson
Cymbeline **47**: 25

Garner, Stanton B., Jr.
Much Ado about Nothing **47:** 25
Othello **47:** 25
The Winter's Tale **47:** 25

Garner, Stanton B., Jr.
The Tempest **8:** 454
The Winter's Tale **36:** 301; **45:** 374

Garnett, Edward
Troilus and Cressida **18:** 286

Garnett, Richard
The Two Gentlemen of Verona **6:** 464

Garrick, David
Romeo and Juliet **5:** 378; **11:** 382

Gascoigne, Bamber
As You Like It **23:** 89
Cymbeline **15:** 65
King Lear **11:** 87
Macbeth **20:** 251
Measure for Measure **23:** 316
Much Ado about Nothing **18:** 179
Othello **11:** 290
Richard III **14:** 454
The Taming of the Shrew **12:** 360

Gaw, Allison
The Comedy of Errors **1:** 19

Geduld, Harry M.
Henry V **14:** 225

Gelb, Arthur
The Merchant of Venice **12:** 70

Gelb, Hal
Measure for Measure **2:** 514

Geller, Lila
Cymbeline **36:** 158

Gellert, Roger
Hamlet **21:** 229
Henry VI, 1, 2, and 3 **24:** 20
Julius Caesar **17:** 368
King Lear **11:** 87
Measure for Measure **23:** 315
A Midsummer Night's Dream **12:** 248

Genster, Julia
Othello **16:** 272

Gent, Lucy
Venus and Adonis **33:** 357

Gentleman, Francis
Antony and Cleopatra **6:** 22
As You Like It **5:** 19
Coriolanus **9:** 12
Cymbeline **15:** 94
Hamlet **21:** 16
Henry IV, 1 and 2 **1:** 295
Henry V **5:** 190
Henry VI, 1, 2, and 3 **3:** 21
Julius Caesar **7:** 158
King John **9:** 212; **24:** 167
Love's Labour's Lost **2:** 301
Macbeth **3:** 175; **20:** 21
The Merchant of Venice **12:** 4

A Midsummer Night's Dream **3:** 363
Much Ado about Nothing **18:** 230
Richard II **6:** 253
Romeo and Juliet **11:** 384, 495
Titus Andronicus **4:** 615
Troilus and Cressida **3:** 538

Gerard, Albert
Troilus and Cressida **3:** 596
Twelfth Night **1:** 638

Gerard, Alexander
Measure for Measure **2:** 394

Gervinus, G. G.
All's Well That Ends Well **7:** 19; **26:** 93
Antony and Cleopatra **6:** 33
As You Like It **5:** 32
Coriolanus **9:** 19
Cymbeline **4:** 29
Hamlet **1:** 103
Henry IV, 1 and 2 **1:** 317
Henry V **5:** 199
Henry VI, 1, 2, and 3 **3:** 31
Henry VIII **2:** 31
Julius Caesar **7:** 161
King John **9:** 224
King Lear **2:** 116
Love's Labour's Lost **2:** 305
Macbeth **3:** 196
Measure for Measure **2:** 402
The Merchant of Venice **4:** 204
The Merry Wives of Windsor **5:** 339
A Midsummer Night's Dream **3:** 372
Much Ado about Nothing **8:** 19
Othello **4:** 415
Pericles **2:** 546
The Rape of Lucrece **10:** 66
Richard II **6:** 264
Richard III **8:** 165
Romeo and Juliet **5:** 431
Sonnets **10:** 185
The Taming of the Shrew **9:** 323
The Tempest **8:** 304
Timon of Athens **1:** 467
Titus Andronicus **4:** 623
Troilus and Cressida **3:** 544
Twelfth Night **1:** 551
The Two Gentlemen of Verona **6:** 445
The Two Noble Kinsmen **9:** 455
Venus and Adonis **10:** 418
The Winter's Tale **7:** 390

Ghose, Zulfikar
Macbeth **25:** 235

Gibbons, Brian
Coriolanus **25:** 245
Henry VI, 1, 2, and 3 **25:** 245
Richard III **25:** 245
Romeo and Juliet **25:** 245
The Tempest **28:** 391
Titus Andronicus **25:** 245

Gibson, H. N.
Authorship Controversy (topic entry) **41:** 66

Gibbs, Patrick
All's Well That Ends Well **26:** 24

Gibbs, Wolcott
As You Like It **23:** 73
King Lear **11:** 71
Macbeth **20:** 225, 226
The Tempest **15:** 240

Gibson, Joy Leslie
Richard II **24:** 339

Gielgud, John
Hamlet **21:** 182, 192, 237
Julius Caesar **17:** 344, 356
King Lear **11:** 50
Much Ado about Nothing **18:** 168, 170
Othello **11:** 295
Richard II **24:** 411
Romeo and Juliet **11:** 448
The Tempest **15:** 311

Gieskes, Edward
King John **48:** 132

Gilbert, Miriam
Richard II **24:** 423

Gilbert, W. Stephen
Henry IV, 1 and 2 **14:** 85
Henry V **14:** 283

Gilder, Jeanette
As You Like It **23:** 40, 46
Twelfth Night **26:** 215

Gilder, Rosamond
Hamlet **21:** 172
Macbeth **20:** 230
Othello **11:** 272
Richard III **14:** 413
The Tempest **15:** 246
Twelfth Night **26:** 226

Gildon, Charles
All's Well That Ends Well **7:** 8
Antony and Cleopatra **6:** 20
As You Like It **5:** 18
The Comedy of Errors **1:** 13
Coriolanus **9:** 8
Cymbeline **4:** 17
Hamlet **1:** 75, 76
Henry IV, 1 and 2 **1:** 286
Henry V **5:** 186
Henry VI, 1, 2, and 3 **3:** 17
Julius Caesar **7:** 152
King John **9:** 208
King Lear **2:** 93
Love's Labour's Lost **2:** 299
Macbeth **3:** 171
Measure for Measure **2:** 387
The Merchant of Venice **4:** 192
The Merry Wives of Windsor **5:** 334
A Midsummer Night's Dream **3:** 362
Much Ado about Nothing **8:** 9
Othello **3:** 380, 384
The Rape of Lucrece **10:** 64
Richard II **6:** 252
Richard III **8:** 145
Romeo and Juliet **5:** 416

Sonnets **10:** 153
The Taming of the Shrew **9:** 318
The Tempest **8:** 287
Timon of Athens **1:** 454
Titus Andronicus **4:** 613
Troilus and Cressida **18:** 277
Twelfth Night **1:** 539
The Two Gentlemen of Verona **6:** 435
The Winter's Tale **7:** 377

Gilliatt, Penelope
Much Ado about Nothing **18:** 188

Gillies, John
Antony and Cleopatra **28:** 249
Othello **28:** 249
The Tempest **29:** 343
Titus Andronicus **28:** 249

Girard, René
The Merchant of Venice **4:** 331
A Midsummer Night's Dream **29:** 234; **45:** 147
Troilus and Cressida **43:** 317
Twelfth Night **46:** 333
The Two Gentlemen of Verona **13:** 12; **40:** 335
The Winter's Tale **36:** 334

Giroux, Robert
Love's Labour's Lost **23:** 224

Glavin, John
Romeo and Juliet **19:** 261

Glaz, A. Andre
Othello **35:** 265

Glazov-Corrigan, Elena
Cymbeline **28:** 398; **36:** 186; **47:** 296
Pericles **19:** 387

Glick, Claris
Hamlet **21:** 347

Glover, Julian
Coriolanus **17:** 195

Goddard, Harold C.
As You Like It **5:** 88
Coriolanus **9:** 100
Cymbeline **4:** 89
Hamlet **1:** 194
Henry IV, 1 and 2 **1:** 397
Henry V **5:** 252
Henry VI, 1, 2, and 3 **3:** 73
The Merchant of Venice **4:** 254
A Midsummer Night's Dream **3:** 412
Much Ado about Nothing **8:** 55
The Taming of the Shrew **9:** 345
The Two Gentlemen of Verona **6:** 484

Godfrey, D. R.
Othello **35:** 310

Godshalk, William Leigh
All's Well That Ends Well **7:** 113
Henry V **30:** 273
Measure for Measure **33:** 61

The Merry Wives of Windsor **5:** 374
The Two Gentlemen of Verona **6:** 526

Godwin, William
Troilus and Cressida **3:** 539

Goethe, Johann Wolfgang von
Hamlet **1:** 91; **21:** 379
Henry IV, 1 and 2 **1:** 311
Troilus and Cressida **3:** 541

Goldberg, Jonathan
Henry IV, 1 and 2 **22:** 114

Goldman, Michael
Henry IV, 1 and 2 **48:** 143
Henry V **30:** 163
Othello **11:** 362

Goldstein, Neal L.
Love's Labour's Lost **38:** 185

Gollanez, Sir Israel
The Merchant of Venice **4:** 224

Gomme, Andor
Timon of Athens **1:** 503

Gordon, D. J.
Coriolanus **30:** 58

Gordon, Giles
Julius Caesar **17:** 390
Measure for Measure **23:** 344
Pericles **15:** 173
Richard III **14:** 487, 488

Gorfain, Phyllis
Pericles **2:** 588

Gottfried, Martin
As You Like It **23:** 101
Love's Labour's Lost **23:** 206

Gould, Gerald
Henry V **5:** 219

Gould, Robert
Timon of Athens **1:** 453

Gourlay, Patricia Southard
The Winter's Tale **36:** 311

Gow, Gordon
As You Like It **23:** 124

Goy-Blanquet, Dominique
Henry VI, 1, 2, and 3 **24:** 48
Julius Caesar **17:** 393

Grady, Hugh
As You Like It **37:** 43

Graham, Virginia
Richard III **14:** 422

Grangier, Derek
Measure for Measure **23:** 307

Granville-Barker, F.
As You Like It **23:** 84

Granville-Barker, Harley
Antony and Cleopatra **6:** 80; **17:** 104
Coriolanus **9:** 84
Cymbeline **4:** 56; **15:** 111
Hamlet **1:** 160
Henry V **5:** 226
Julius Caesar **7:** 210; **17:** 416
King Lear **2:** 154; **11:** 145
Love's Labour's Lost **2:** 317; **23:** 237
Macbeth **20:** 353
The Merchant of Venice **4:** 232; **12:** 115
A Midsummer Night's Dream **12:** 291
Othello **4:** 488
Richard II **24:** 301
Romeo and Juliet **5:** 454; **11:** 505
Twelfth Night **1:** 562; **26:** 357
The Winter's Tale **7:** 412; **15:** 514

Gray, Henry David
Pericles **2:** 558

Gray, Simon
Twelfth Night **26:** 265

Grebanier, Bernard
Hamlet **35:** 182

Green, Andrew J.
Hamlet **1:** 207

Green, Brian
The Phoenix and Turtle **38:** 345; **51:** 188

Green, Douglas E.
Twelfth Night **46:** 362
Titus Andronicus **43:** 170

Green, Harris
Much Ado about Nothing **18:** 197

Green, Janet M.
King Lear **46:** 276; **49:** 67

Green, London
Richard III **14:** 383, 390

Greenblatt, Stephen
Henry IV, 1 and 2 **49:** 139
King Lear **31:** 107

Greene, Gayle
Julius Caesar **7:** 350; **30:** 333
Othello **4:** 587
Troilus and Cressida **43:** 298

Greene, Robert
Henry VI, 1, 2, and 3 **3:** 16

Greene, Thomas M.
Love's Labour's Lost **2:** 351
Sonnets **10:** 385

Greenfield, Thelma Nelson
The Taming of the Shrew **9:** 350

Germaine Greer
General Commentary **50:** 34

Greg, Walter W.
As You Like It **5:** 60
Hamlet **1:** 134

Greif, Karen
Twelfth Night **34:** 316; **46:** 310

Grene, Nicholas
Antony and Cleopatra **22:** 217
Coriolanus **30:** 79

Grennan, Eamon
As You Like It **34:** 155
The Comedy of Errors **34:** 238
Henry V **30:** 202

Grey, Zachary
The Tempest **8:** 292

Griffin, Alice
Macbeth **20:** 234
The Merchant of Venice **12:** 55, 64, 72
Richard III **14:** 426

Griffith, Elizabeth
Antony and Cleopatra **6:** 22
As You Like It **5:** 20
Coriolanus **9:** 12
Henry IV, 1 and 2 **1:** 296
Henry V **5:** 191
Henry VIII **2:** 19
Richard II **6:** 254
Richard III **8:** 152
Romeo and Juliet **5:** 418
The Taming of the Shrew **9:** 319
Titus Andronicus **4:** 615
Troilus and Cressida **3:** 538
The Two Gentlemen of Verona **6:** 438
The Winter's Tale **7:** 381

Griffiths, G. S.
Antony and Cleopatra **6:** 120

Griffiths, L. M.
Titus Andronicus **4:** 626

Griffiths, Trevor R.
The Tempest **15:** 312

Grindon, Mrs. Rosa Leo
The Merry Wives of Windsor **5:** 349

Gross, Gerard J.
All's Well That Ends Well **38:** 132

Gross, John
Henry VIII **24:** 126

Gross, Kenneth
Othello **13:** 313

Grossman, Marc
Henry IV, 1 and 2 **49:** 162

Guinness, Alec
Richard II **24:** 318

Guizot, M.
Romeo and Juliet **5:** 436

Gunderode, Freiherr von
Hamlet **21:** 17

Gurr, Andrew
General Commentary **13:** 494
Coriolanus **50:** 140
Hamlet **44:** 241
Henry V **30:** 234
Sonnets **10:** 358

Gussow, Mel
Henry IV, 1 and 2 **14:** 87
King John **24:** 237
Love's Labour's Lost **23:** 226
Macbeth **20:** 312
Much Ado about Nothing **18:** 191, 214
Pericles **15:** 162
Timon of Athens **20:** 468
Titus Andronicus **17:** 473, 480
Twelfth Night **26:** 297, 313

Guthrie, Tyrone
All's Well That Ends Well **26:** 15, 19
The Merchant of Venice **12:** 129
The Tempest **15:** 364

Guthrie, William
Hamlet **1:** 79

Gutierrez, Nancy A.
Henry VI, 1, 2, and 3 **16:** 131

Hackett, James Henry
Hamlet **21:** 53
Henry IV, 1 and 2 **14:** 4

Hager, Alan
The Taming of the Shrew **16:** 13

Hale, David George
Coriolanus **30:** 105

Hale, Lionel
Love's Labour's Lost **23:** 187

Hales, John W.
Macbeth **3:** 205

Halio, Jay L.
As You Like It **5:** 112
Coriolanus **9:** 169
A Midsummer Night's Dream **29:** 263; **45:** 169
The Merchant of Venice **49:** 23

Hall, Joan Lord
Antony and Cleopatra **19:** 270

Hall, Jonathan
Desire (topic entry) **38:** 56
Henry IV, 1 and 2 **32:** 103

Hall, Peter
Hamlet **21:** 251
Macbeth **20:** 265
The Tempest **15:** 274, 338
Twelfth Night **26:** 257

Hallam, Henry
Hamlet **1:** 98
King Lear **2:** 111

Romeo and Juliet **5:** 426
Sonnets **10:** 175

Hallinan, Tim
The Taming of the Shrew **12:** 400

Halliwell-Phillipps, J. O.
Love's Labour's Lost **2:** 307
A Midsummer Night's Dream **3:** 370
The Phoenix and Turtle **10:** 7
Sonnets **10:** 217

Halmstrom, John
Othello **11:** 300

Halpern, Richard
The Tempest **45:** 280

Halverson, John
Richard II **28:** 134; **39:** 243

Hamer, Mary
Julius Caesar **50:** 230

Hamilton, A. C.
Henry VI, 1, 2, and 3 **3:** 83
Titus Andronicus **4:** 659; **43:** 195
Venus and Adonis **10:** 454

Hamilton, Donna B.
King John **22:** 120
The Winter's Tale **25:** 347

Hamlin, William M.
The Tempest **45:** 226

Hammersmith, James P.
Richard III **13:** 142

Hammond, Anthony
Henry V **49:** 211

Hammond, Gerald
Sonnets **40:** 228

Hampton, Timothy
Julius Caesar **50:** 196

Handelman, Susan
Timon of Athens **1:** 529

Hands, Terry
Coriolanus **17:** 190
Henry V **14:** 293

Hankey, Julie
Richard II **24:** 371

Hankin, St. John
Julius Caesar **17:** 308

Hanmer, Sir Thomas
Hamlet **1:** 76
Henry V **5:** 188

Hapgood, Norman
Henry V **14:** 199

Hapgood, Robert
General Commentary **13:** 502
King Lear **13:** 343
Othello **11:** 332; **35:** 247

Harbage, Alfred
King Lear **11:** 101

Harcourt, John B.
Macbeth **3:** 297

Hardin, Richard F.
Henry V **22:** 137
Julius Caesar **22:** 137
Kingship (topic entry) **39:** 45
The Merry Wives of Windsor **5:** 390
Richard II **22:** 137

Harding, D. W.
Shakespeare's Representation of Women (topic entry) **31:** 16

Haring-Smith, Tori
The Taming of the Shrew **12:** 416

Harrier, Richard C.
Troilus and Cressida **3:** 602

Harris, Anthony
Magic and the Supernatural (topic entry) **29:** 65

Harris, Arthur J.
Measure for Measure **23:** 291

Harris, Bernard
Henry VIII **2:** 67

Harris, Diana
The Tempest **42:** 339

Harris, Frank
The Comedy of Errors **1:** 18
Pericles **2:** 555
Richard II **6:** 279
Sonnets **10:** 240
Timon of Athens **1:** 480

Harris, Jonathan Gil
Antony and Cleopatra **47:** 192

Harrison, Carey
The Taming of the Shrew **12:** 372

Harrison, G. B.
Timon of Athens **1:** 499

Harrison, W. A.
Sonnets **10:** 216

Harron, Mary
Titus Andronicus **17:** 477

Hart, John
The Tempest **37:** 335

Hart, John A.
As You Like It **34:** 78
Clowns and Fools (topic entry) **46:** 60
Fathers and Daughters (topic entry) **36:** 32

Hart, Jonathan
The Rape of Lucrece **22:** 294
Venus and Adonis **33:** 363

Hart, Lynda
Henry IV, 1 and 2 **14:** 109

Hart-Davis, Rupert
A Midsummer Night's Dream **12:** 210

Hartley, Anthony
King Lear **11:** 64

Hartsock, Mildred E.
Julius Caesar **7:** 320

Hartwig, Joan
Cymbeline **36:** 99
The Taming of the Shrew **31:** 335
Twelfth Night **1:** 658; **46:** 297

Harvey, Gabriel
The Rape of Lucrece **10:** 63
Venus and Adonis **10:** 410

Harvey, John Martin
The Taming of the Shrew **12:** 335

Harwood, Ellen Aprill
Venus and Adonis **33:** 339

Hassel, R. Chris
As You Like It **34:** 85

Hassel, R. Chris, Jr.
The Merchant of Venice **4:** 321
A Midsummer Night's Dream **3:** 506
Richard III **14:** 497

Hassell, Graham
Hamlet **21:** 328

Hatch, Robert
Hamlet **21:** 200
The Merchant of Venice **12:** 70
Richard III **14:** 424

Hatlen, Burton
Coriolanus **42:** 248

Hattaway, Michael
Henry VI, 1, 2, and 3 **39:** 222
Sexuality (topic entry) **33:** 39

Hatton, Joseph
The Merchant of Venice **12:** 31

Hawkes, Terence
Love's Labour's Lost **2:** 359
Richard II **6:** 374

Hawkins, C. Halford
Julius Caesar **17:** 289

Hawkins, F. W.
King John **24:** 179
Macbeth **20:** 92
Richard II **24:** 267
Romeo and Juliet **11:** 397

Hawkins, Harriet
Antony and Cleopatra **25:** 257
Measure for Measure **49:** 358
Othello **25:** 257
Romeo and Juliet **25:** 257

Hawkins, Sherman H.
Henry IV, 1 and 2 **39:** 100

Hawkins, William
Cymbeline **4:** 19

Hawley, William M.
Coriolanus **48:** 230

Hayes, Richard
Much Ado about Nothing **18:** 166

Hayles, Nancy K.
Appearance vs. Reality (topic entry) **34:** 5
As You Like It **5:** 146
Cymbeline **4:** 162

Hayman, Ronald
Hamlet **21:** 183
Julius Caesar **17:** 357
King Lear **11:** 67
A Midsummer Night's Dream **12:** 254
Othello **11:** 295
Romeo and Juliet **11:** 474

Hays, Janice
Much Ado about Nothing **8:** 111

Hazlitt, William
All's Well That Ends Well **7:** 9
Antony and Cleopatra **6:** 25
As You Like It **5:** 24
The Comedy of Errors **1:** 14
Coriolanus **9:** 15; **17:** 129
Cymbeline **4:** 22
Hamlet **1:** 96; **21:** 30, 41
Henry IV, 1 and 2 **1:** 312
Henry V **5:** 193
Henry VI, 1, 2, and 3 **3:** 25
Henry VIII **2:** 23
Julius Caesar **17:** 273
King John **9:** 219; **24:** 174
King Lear **2:** 108; **11:** 12, 16
Love's Labour's Lost **2:** 303
Macbeth **3:** 185; **20:** 58, 59, 86
Measure for Measure **2:** 396
The Merchant of Venice **4:** 195; **12:** 9, 10, 11
The Merry Wives of Windsor **5:** 337
A Midsummer Night's Dream **3:** 364; **12:** 152
Much Ado about Nothing **8:** 13
Othello **4:** 402; **11:** 191, 195, 196, 197, 198
Pericles **2:** 544
The Rape of Lucrece **10:** 65
Richard II **6:** 258; **24:** 267
Richard III **8:** 161, **14:** 376, 377, 380
Romeo and Juliet **5:** 421; **11:** 393, 395
Sonnets **10:** 160
The Taming of the Shrew **9:** 320
The Tempest **8:** 297
Timon of Athens **1:** 460
Titus Andronicus **4:** 617
Troilus and Cressida **3:** 540
Twelfth Night **1:** 544
The Two Gentlemen of Verona **6:** 439

Venus and Adonis **10**: 415
The Winter's Tale **7**: 384

Heath, Benjamin
The Tempest **8**: 292
Titus Andronicus **4**: 614

Hecht, Anthony
Sonnets **37**: 346

Hecht, Anthony B.
Sonnets **51**: 270
The Tempest **25**: 357

Hedley, Jane
Sonnets **51**: 304

Heffernan, Carol F.
The Taming of the Shrew **31**: 345

Heilbrun, Carolyn G.
Hamlet **44**: 237

Heilman, Robert
Politics and Power (topic entry) **30**: 22

Heilman, Robert Bechtold
Antony and Cleopatra **6**: 175
Henry IV, 1 and 2 **1**: 380
King Lear **2**: 191
Macbeth **3**: 312, 314; **29**: 139; **44**: 306
Othello **4**: 508, 530
Richard III **8**: 239
The Taming of the Shrew **9**: 386

Heine, Heinrich
The Merchant of Venice **4**: 200
Richard III **8**: 164
Troilus and Cressida **3**: 542

Heinemann, Margot
King Lear **22**: 227; **46**: 269

Helgerson, Richard
Henry VI, 1, 2, and 3 **22**: 156

Helms, Lorraine
Gender Identity (topic entry) **40**: 27
Pericles **51**: 118
Shakespeare's Representation of Women (topic entry) **31**: 68
Troilus and Cressida **43**: 357

Hemingway, Samuel B.
Henry IV, 1 and 2 **1**: 401; **14**: 130
A Midsummer Night's Dream **3**: 396

Henneman, John Bell
Henry VI, 1, 2, and 3 **3**: 46

Henze, Richard
The Comedy of Errors **1**: 57
Julius Caesar **30**: 321
The Taming of the Shrew **9**: 398
Twelfth Night **34**: 287

Heraud, J. A.
Antony and Cleopatra **6**: 37

Othello **4**: 421
Sonnets **10**: 191

Herbert, T. Walter
A Midsummer Night's Dream **3**: 447

Herford, C. H.
Antony and Cleopatra **6**: 76
The Phoenix and Turtle **10**: 16

Herman, Peter C.
The Two Noble Kinsmen **50**: 348

Herring, Robert
Cymbeline **15**: 46
Henry VIII **24**: 105

Hethmon, Robert H.
Measure for Measure **23**: 407

Hewes, Henry
Antony and Cleopatra **17**: 43
Hamlet **21**: 232, 239, 288
King John **24**: 210
King Lear **11**: 72, 89, 103
The Merchant of Venice **12**: 54, 62, 71, 79
A Midsummer Night's Dream **12**: 240
Much Ado about Nothing **18**: 173
Othello **11**: 314
The Taming of the Shrew **12**: 365
Timon of Athens **20**: 456
Troilus and Cressida **18**: 337
Twelfth Night **26**: 247

Hewison, Robert
Coriolanus **17**: 208
A Midsummer Night's Dream **12**: 274
Twelfth Night **26**: 316

Heyse, Paul
Antony and Cleopatra **6**: 38

Hibbard, George R.
Antony and Cleopatra **27**: 105
Love's Labour's Lost **23**: 233
Othello **4**: 569
The Taming of the Shrew **9**: 375

Hic et Ubique
See also Steevens, George; Collier, Jeremy; Longinus, and Lorenzo
Hamlet **1**: 87
Twelfth Night **1**: 542

Hieatt, A. Kent
Cymbeline **13**: 401

Hieatt, Charles W.
The Winter's Tale **36**: 374

Higgins, John
Antony and Cleopatra **17**: 65
Coriolanus **17**: 190
The Merry Wives of Windsor **18**: 42
The Taming of the Shrew **12**: 386
The Two Gentlemen of Verona **12**: 490

Hignett, Sean
Richard III **14**: 473

Hill, Aaron
Hamlet **1**: 76; **21**: 377

Hill, Errol G.
The Tempest **15**: 322

Hill, R. F.
Richard II **6**: 347
Romeo and Juliet **5**: 492

Hill, Sir John
Antony and Cleopatra **6**: 21
Romeo and Juliet **11**: 494

Hill, William
Henry V **14**: 174

Hillebrand, Harold Newcomb
Richard II **24**: 272

Hillman, David
Troilus and Cressida **42**: 66

Hillman, Richard
Hamlet **44**: 219
Henry IV, 1 and 2 **19**: 170
Henry V **19**: 170
Measure for Measure **22**: 302
Richard II **19**: 170
The Tempest **8**: 464; **22**: 302
The Two Noble Kinsmen **19**: 394; **41**: 301
The Winter's Tale **22**: 302

Hinely, Jan Lawson
The Merry Wives of Windsor **5**: 397
A Midsummer Night's Dream **45**: 107

Hinman, Charlton
Timon of Athens **1**: 518

Hirsch, Foster
Richard III **14**: 447

Hirsh, James
Othello **19**: 276

Hirst, David L.
The Tempest **15**: 327

Hirvela, David P.
King John **24**: 241

Hobday, C. H.
Henry V **30**: 159
The Two Noble Kinsmen **41**: 317

Hobson, Harold
Antony and Cleopatra **17**: 33
Henry IV, 1 and 2 **14**: 54, 84
Henry V **14**: 281
Much Ado about Nothing **18**: 205
Troilus and Cressida **18**: 362
The Winter's Tale **15**: 486

Hoby, Sir Edward
Richard II **6**: 249

Hockey, Dorothy C.
Much Ado about Nothing **8**: 73

Hodgdon, Barbara
Henry IV, 1 and 2 **49**: 102
King John **19**: 182
Romeo and Juliet **13**: 243
Troilus and Cressida **16**: 70

Hodgson, Moira
Measure for Measure **23**: 354

Hoeniger, F. David
Cymbeline **4**: 103
Pericles **2**: 576, 578
The Winter's Tale **7**: 452

Hofling, Charles K.
Coriolanus **9**: 125
Cymbeline **36**: 134

Holbrook, Peter
A Midsummer Night's Dream **50**: 74
The Taming of the Shrew **50**: 74
The Two Noble Kinsmen **50**: 305

Holden, Anthony
Coriolanus **17**: 163
Hamlet **21**: 213

Holden, Stephen
The Tempest **15**: 288

Holderness, Graham
Henry V **14**: 247
King Lear **31**: 84
Richard II **6**: 414
The Taming of the Shrew **12**: 404
The Winter's Tale **16**: 410

Holding, Edith
As You Like It **23**: 10

Hole, Richard
Othello **4**: 397

Holland, Norman N.
A Midsummer Night's Dream **29**: 225
Psychoanalytic Interpretations (topic entry) **44**: 11
Romeo and Juliet **5**: 513, 525

Holland, Peter
As You Like It **23**: 151
Measure for Measure **23**: 362
A Midsummer Night's Dream **29**: 216; **45**: 117
The Tempest **32**: 334

Hollander, John
Twelfth Night **1**: 596, 615

Holleran, James V.
Hamlet **13**: 268

Holloway, John
Coriolanus **9**: 139
King Lear **2**: 241

Holmer, Joan Ozark
Romeo and Juliet **32**: 222; **45**: 40

Holmes, Martin
Henry IV, 1 and 2 **14**: 146
The Merry Wives of Windsor **18**: 86

Holmstrom, John
Othello **11**: 300

Holt, John
The Comedy of Errors **1**: 13

Homan, Sidney
Antony and Cleopatra **47**: 103
Henry V **30**: 207
The Merry Wives of Windsor **18**: 95

Homan, Sidney R.
The Comedy of Errors **34**: 194
A Midsummer Night's Dream **3**: 466; **48**: 23
Richard II **6**: 391

Home, Henry, Lord Kames
Romeo and Juliet **5**: 418

Honigmann, E. A. J.
All's Well That Ends Well **13**: 77; **38**: 89
Julius Caesar **30**: 342
Macbeth **29**: 146
Timon of Athens **1**: 507

Hope, John Francis
All's Well That Ends Well **26**: 11

Hope-Wallace, Philip
As You Like It **23**: 80, 81
Cymbeline **15**: 47
Hamlet **21**: 181
Henry VI, 1, 2, and 3 **24**: 16
Julius Caesar **17**: 343
King John **24**: 214
Macbeth **20**: 221
Richard III **14**: 461
Troilus and Cressida **18**: 305
The Two Gentlemen of Verona **12**: 462

Hopkins, Lisa
As You Like It **48**: 32
Henry V **37**: 105
Macbeth **42**: 263
A Midsummer Night's Dream **48**: 32
The Two Gentlemen of Verona **48**: 32

Horn, Franz
Coriolanus **9**: 16
Macbeth **3**: 190
Romeo and Juliet **5**: 423

Hornby, Richard
Julius Caesar **17**: 403

Horwich, Richard
The Merchant of Venice **4**: 326

Hosley, Richard
Othello **11**: 359

Hotson, Leslie
Sonnets **10**: 270

Houseman, John
Julius Caesar **17**: 326, 347, 348
King John **24**: 211

Houston, Penelope
Romeo and Juliet **11**: 472
The Taming of the Shrew **12**: 372

Howard, Alan
Coriolanus **17**: 195
Henry V **14**: 297

Howard, Jean E.
Gender Identity (topic entry) **40**: 61

Howard, Skiles
A Midsummer Night's Dream **25**: 36

Hoy, Cyrus
Fathers and Daughters (topic entry) **36**: 45
Timon of Athens **1**: 523
The Two Noble Kinsmen **41**: 308
Love's Labour's Lost **47**: 35

Hoyle, Martin
The Comedy of Errors **26**: 168
Julius Caesar **17**: 391
Troilus and Cressida **18**: 389
Twelfth Night **26**: 322

Hubert, Judd D.
Much Ado about Nothing **19**: 68

Hubler, Edward
Othello **4**: 544
Sonnets **10**: 279

Hudson, Rev. H. N.
As You Like It **5**: 39
Coriolanus **9**: 26
Henry VI, 1 and 2 **1**: 323, 324
Henry VI, 1, 2, and 3 **3**: 35
Henry VIII **3**: 32
Julius Caesar **7**: 167
King Lear **2**: 125
Macbeth **3**: 203
Measure for Measure **2**: 406
The Merry Wives of Windsor **5**: 341
A Midsummer Night's Dream **3**: 377
Twelfth Night **1**: 555

Huebert, Ronald
The Merry Wives of Windsor **5**: 385

Hughes, Alan
Coriolanus **17**: 144
Hamlet **21**: 112
Macbeth **20**: 151
Much Ado about Nothing **18**: 138
Othello **11**: 259
Richard III **14**: 405

Hughes, John
Othello **4**: 384

Hugo, François-Victor
Coriolanus **9**: 25

Hugo, Victor
Antony and Cleopatra **6**: 37
Henry IV, 1 and 2 **1**: 323
King Lear **2**: 124

Othello **4**: 421
The Winter's Tale **7**: 394

Hulse, Clark
The Rape of Lucrece **10**: 121
Venus and Adonis **10**: 480

Hulse, S. Clark
Titus Andronicus **27**: 325

Humphreys, A. R.
Henry IV, 1 and 2 **1**: 419

Humphreys, Arthur
Julius Caesar **30**: 297

Hunt, Hugh
Julius Caesar **17**: 418
The Merchant of Venice **12**: 119
The Merry Wives of Windsor **18**: 75
Twelfth Night **26**: 233

Hunt, Leigh
Hamlet **21**: 50
Julius Caesar **17**: 272
King John **24**: 180
King Lear **11**: 10, 136
Much Ado about Nothing **18**: 231
Othello **11**: 198
Richard III **14**: 379, 389
Timon of Athens **1**: 460; **20**: 439

Hunt, Maurice
Comedy of Errors **42**: 80
Coriolanus **19**: 287
Cymbeline **36**: 115
Henry IV, 1 and 2 **48**: 151
Henry VIII **41**: 190
Love's Labour's Lost **38**: 239
A Midsummer Night's Dream **22**: 39
Pericles **51**: 86
Richard III **39**: 349; **42**: 132
Titus Andronicus **27**: 299
Twelfth Night **25**: 47
The Two Gentlemen of Verona **6**: 564

Hunter, G. K.
All's Well That Ends Well **7**: 76; **26**: 52
As You Like It **5**: 116
Henry IV, 1 and 2 **1**: 402
Henry V **16**: 217
Henry VI, 1, 2, and 3 **16**: 217; **24**: 55
King Lear **16**: 217
Politics and Power (topic entry) **30**: 39
Richard II **16**: 217
Richard III **16**: 217
Shakespeare and Classical Civilization (topic entry) **27**: 21
Sonnets **10**: 283
The Taming of the Shrew **16**: 217
Troilus and Cressida **16**: 217
Twelfth Night **1**: 635

Hunter, Joseph
Twelfth Night **1**: 549

Hunter, Mark
Julius Caesar **7**: 221

Hunter, Robert Grams
All's Well That Ends Well **7**: 98
Cymbeline **4**: 116
Macbeth **44**: 351
Othello **4**: 582
The Two Gentlemen of Verona **6**: 514

Hurd, Richard
As You Like It **5**: 18

Hurdis, James
Coriolanus **9**: 13

Hurrell, John D.
The Merchant of Venice **4**: 284

Hurren, Kenneth
Antony and Cleopatra **17**: 56
As You Like It **23**: 106
Hamlet **21**: 298
Love's Labour's Lost **23**: 204
A Midsummer Night's Dream **12**: 251
Much Ado about Nothing **18**: 206
Titus Andronicus **17**: 467
Troilus and Cressida **18**: 357
Twelfth Night **26**: 326
The Winter's Tale **15**: 487

Huston, J. Dennis
Love's Labour's Lost **2**: 375
A Midsummer Night's Dream **3**: 516
The Taming of the Shrew **9**: 419

Hutchings, Geoffrey
All's Well That Ends Well **26**: 64
Romeo and Juliet **51**: 195

Hutson, Lorna
Twelfth Night **34**: 344; **37**: 59

Hyde, Mary Crapo
As You Like It **23**: 71

Hyland, Peter
As You Like It **34**: 130
Troilus and Cressida **25**: 56

Hyman, Lawrence W.
Measure for Measure **2**: 524

Hynes, Sam
The Rape of Lucrece **10**: 80

Ide, Richard S.
Measure for Measure **13**: 94

Ihering, Rudolf von
The Merchant of Venice **4**: 213

Inchbald, Elizabeth
Henry IV, 1 and 2 **1**: 309
Much Ado about Nothing **8**: 12

Inglis, Brian
Troilus and Cressida **18**: 311

Irving, Henry
Hamlet **21**: 381

Irving, Laurence
Henry VIII **24**: 87**

Much Ado about Nothing **18:** 136
Othello **11:** 255
Twelfth Night **26:** 210

Isaacs, Edith J. R.
Richard II **24:** 308

Isaacs, Hermine Rich
The Taming of the Shrew **12:** 346
The Tempest **15:** 237

Iser, Wolfgang
As You Like It **34:** 131

Itzin, Catherine
Macbeth **20:** 17

Jackson, Barry
Henry VI, 1, 2, and 3 **24:** 12

Jackson, Berners W.
Pericles **15:** 155, 158
The Taming of the Shrew **12:** 485
Twelfth Night **26:** 292

Jackson, Glenda
Antony and Cleopatra **17:** 113

Jackson, MacDonald
The Tempest **42:** 339

Jackson, Russell
All's Well That Ends Well **26:** 58
As You Like It **23:** 158
Love's Labour's Lost **23:** 217
Richard II **24:** 373

Jackson, T. A.
Henry IV, 1 and 2 **1:** 361

Jacobson, Gerald F.
A Midsummer Night's Dream **3:** 44

Jaffa, Harry V.
King Lear **2:** 208
Measure for Measure **33:** 101

Jagendorf, Zvi
Coriolanus **50:** 110

Jahn, J. D.
Venus and Adonis **10:** 466

James, D. G.
Hamlet **1:** 191
King Lear **2:** 201
Pericles **2:** 561
The Tempest **8:** 423

James, Emrys
Henry IV, 1 and 2 **14:** 92
Henry V **14:** 301

James, Heather
Titus Andronicus **27:** 306

James, Henry
Cymbeline **15:** 41
Henry V **14:** 194
Henry VIII **24:** 77
King Lear **11:** 27
Macbeth **20:** 135

The Merchant of Venice **12:** 29
The Merry Wives of Windsor **18:** 25
Othello **11:** 225
Richard III **14:** 405
Romeo and Juliet **11:** 424, 426

James, John
Antony and Cleopatra **17:** 80
The Comedy of Errors **26:** 161

Jameson, Anna Brownell
All's Well That Ends Well **7:** 12
Antony and Cleopatra **6:** 27
As You Like It **5:** 26
Coriolanus **9:** 16
Cymbeline **4:** 24
Henry VI, 1, 2, and 3 **3:** 26
Henry VIII **2:** 24
King John **9:** 220
King Lear **2:** 110
Macbeth **3:** 191
Measure for Measure **2:** 397
The Merchant of Venice **4:** 196
Much Ado about Nothing **8:** 14
Othello **4:** 406
Romeo and Juliet **5:** 423
Sonnets **10:** 167
The Tempest **8:** 301
Twelfth Night **1:** 545
The Winter's Tale **7:** 385

Jamieson, Michael
As You Like It **23:** 176
Shakespeare's Representation of Women (topic entry) **31:** 60

Janakiram, A.
The Rape of Lucrece **33:** 195

Jarman, Derik
The Tempest **15:** 299

Jayne, Sears
The Taming of the Shrew **9:** 381

Jefford, Barbara
Antony and Cleopatra **17:** 113

Jekels, Ludwig
Macbeth **3:** 226

Jenkins, Harold
As You Like It **5:** 93
Hamlet **44:** 229
Henry VI, 1 and 2 **1:** 404
Twelfth Night **1:** 610

Jenkins, Peter
The Taming of the Shrew **12:** 394

Jennings, H. J.
King Lear **11:** 39

Jennings, Richard
Othello **11:** 264

Jensen, Ejner J.
Love's Labour's Lost **28:** 63
The Merchant of Venice **28:** 63
The Merry Wives of Windsor **28:** 63
Much Ado about Nothing **28:** 63

Joffee, Linda
Henry V **14:** 312

John, Lord Chedworth
Measure for Measure **2:** 395

Johnson, Nora
The Winter's Tale **48:** 309

Johnson, Robert Carl
Romeo and Juliet **33:** 290

Johnson, Samuel
All's Well That Ends Well **7:** 8
Antony and Cleopatra **6:** 21
As You Like It **5:** 19
Coriolanus **9:** 11
Cymbeline **4:** 20
Hamlet **1:** 83
Henry IV, 1 and 2 **1:** 290
Henry V **5:** 189
Henry VI, 1, 2, and 3 **3:** 19
Henry VIII **2:** 18
Julius Caesar **7:** 156
King John **9:** 211
King Lear **2:** 101
Love's Labour's Lost **2:** 300
Macbeth **3:** 171, 172
Measure for Measure **2:** 390
The Merchant of Venice **4:** 193
The Merry Wives of Windsor **5:** 335
Othello **4:** 390
Richard II **6:** 253
Richard III **8:** 146
Romeo and Juliet **5:** 418
The Taming of the Shrew **9:** 318
The Tempest **8:** 292
Timon of Athens **1:** 454
Titus Andronicus **4:** 614
Troilus and Cressida **3:** 538
Twelfth Night **1:** 542
The Two Gentlemen of Verona **6:** 437
The Winter's Tale **7:** 380

Jonassen, Frederick B.
The Merry Wives of Windsor **47:** 363

Jones, D. A. N.
King John **24:** 216
Macbeth **20:** 258
Measure for Measure **23:** 320
The Merry Wives of Windsor **18:** 43
Pericles **15:** 151
Richard III **14:** 463
Troilus and Cressida **18:** 342

Jones, David E.
Henry IV, 1 and 2 **14:** 78
Timon of Athens **20:** 458

Jones, Emrys
Measure for Measure **23:** 345
Much Ado about Nothing **18:** 212
Titus Andronicus **27:** 285

Jones, Ernest
Hamlet **1:** 179

Jones, Gemma
The Winter's Tale **15:** 495

Jones, Gordon P.
Love's Labour's Lost **23:** 223

Jones, James Earl
Othello **11:** 319

Jones, Robert C.
Richard II **39:** 263

Jonson, Ben
Julius Caesar **7:** 148
Pericles **2:** 536
Titus Andronicus **4:** 612
The Winter's Tale **7:** 376

Jorgens, Jack
Richard II **24:** 379

Jorgens, Jack J.
Hamlet **21:** 208
Henry V **14:** 238
Julius Caesar **17:** 358
Macbeth **20:** 283
Pericles **15:** 163
Richard III **14:** 443
The Taming of the Shrew **12:** 374

Jorgensen, Paul A.
The Comedy of Errors **1:** 55
Hamlet **35:** 117
King Lear **2:** 262; **31:** 133
Macbeth **3:** 327

Joseph, Bertram L.
Cymbeline **15:** 67

Joseph, Sister Miriam, C.S.C.
Hamlet **1:** 231

Jump, John
Julius Caesar **30:** 369

Kael, Pauline
Macbeth **20:** 276

Kahn, Coppélia
Coriolanus **30:** 149
Gender Identity (topic entry) **40:** 33
The Merchant of Venice **40:** 151
The Rape of Lucrece **10:** 109; **33:** 200
Romeo and Juliet **5:** 566
The Taming of the Shrew **9:** 413
Timon of Athens **27:** 212
Venus and Adonis **10:** 473

Kaison, Albert E.
Richard III **14:** 358

Kaiser, Walter
Clowns and Fools (topic entry) **46:** 48

Kalem, T. E.
Richard III **14:** 482

Kalson, Albert E.
The Comedy of Errors **26:** 170

Kaminsky, Judith
Rape of Lucrece **43:** 141

Kamps, Ivo
 Henry VIII **37**: 109

Kantorowicz, Ernst H.
 Richard II **6**: 327

Karhl, George M.
 Much Ado about Nothing **18**: 116
 Richard III **14**: 366

Kastan, David Scott
 Antony and Cleopatra **17**: 101
 Henry IV, 1 and 2 **19**: 195
 Henry V **49**: 236
 King Lear **50**: 24
 The Merry Wives of Windsor **18**: 71

Katz, Leslie S.
 The Merry Wives of Windsor **32**: 31; **47**: 344

Kauffman, Stanley
 Hamlet **21**: 321
 Henry V **14**: 291, 313
 Much Ado about Nothing **18**: 195
 Othello **11**: 322

Kaufman, Gerald
 The Taming of the Shrew **12**: 371

Kaufmann, R. J.
 Troilus and Cressida **3**: 611

Kautsky, Karl
 The Merry Wives of Windsor **5**: 343

Kay, Carol McGinnis
 Henry VI, 1, 2, and 3 **3**: 131
 Othello **4**: 596

Kay, Dennis
 The Phoenix and Turtle **51**: 138

Keach, William
 Desire (topic entry) **38**: 1

Kean, Charles
 A Midsummer Night's Dream **12**: 184
 Richard II **24**: 279

Keatman, Martin
 Authorship Controversy (topic entry) **41**: 76

Keats, John
 King Lear **2**: 109
 Sonnets **10**: 160

Kee, Robert
 Henry VI, 1, 2, and 3 **24**: 29

Keesee, Donald
 All's Well That Ends Well **38**: 155

Keevak, Michael
 Sonnets **48**: 325

Kegl, Rosemary
 The Merry Wives of Windsor **28**: 69; **47**: 331

Kehler, Dorothea
 The Comedy of Errors **34**: 251
 Hamlet **32**: 238

Keith, W. J.
 Henry V **14**: 270

Kellaway, Kate
 Twelfth Night **26**: 324

Kelly, Henry Ansgar
 Henry IV, 1 and 2 **1**: 429

Kelly, Hugh
 Richard III **14**: 364

Kelly, Katherine E.
 The Two Gentlemen of Verona **16**: 122

Kemble, Frances Anne
 Henry VIII **2**: 38
 Othello **11**: 227
 Romeo and Juliet **11**: 401

Kemble, John Philip
 Macbeth **3**: 186

Kemp, Peter
 As You Like It **23**: 147
 King John **24**: 231
 Love's Labour's Lost **23**: 221
 Twelfth Night **26**: 323

Kemp, T. C.
 Henry V **14**: 259
 Henry VI, 1, 2, and 3 **24**: 15
 Henry VIII **24**: 112
 Julius Caesar **17**: 344
 The Taming of the Shrew **12**: 350

Kendall, Gillian Murray
 Titus Andronicus **13**: 225

Kendall, Paul M.
 Troilus and Cressida **3**: 587

Kennedy, Dennis
 Antony and Cleopatra **17**: 73
 A Midsummer Night's Dream **12**: 231
 The Winter's Tale **15**: 454

Kenny, Thomas
 Cymbeline **4**: 35
 Hamlet **1**: 113
 Twelfth Night **1**: 554

Kenrick, William
 Measure for Measure **2**: 391
 Much Ado about Nothing **8**: 11
 Othello **4**: 392
 The Winter's Tale **7**: 380

Keown, Eric
 Antony and Cleopatra **17**: 32, 36
 As You Like It **23**: 80, 89
 Cymbeline **15**: 55, 65
 Henry IV, 1 and 2 **14**: 58
 King John **24**: 215
 Macbeth **20**: 189, 222, 251
 Measure for Measure **23**: 315

The Merry Wives of Windsor **18**: 34
 Much Ado about Nothing **18**: 160, 163, 179, 185
 Othello **11**: 277
 The Taming of the Shrew **12**: 355
 Troilus and Cressida **18**: 305, 324, 331
 Twelfth Night **26**: 242, 253
 The Two Gentlemen of Verona **12**: 474

Keown, Roger
 All's Well That Ends Well **26**: 37

Kermode, Frank
 Cymbeline **15**: 75
 Henry VIII **2**: 49
 King Lear **11**: 104
 The Tempest **8**: 396; **15**: 295
 The Two Noble Kinsmen **9**: 480

Kernan, Alvin
 Measure for Measure **33**: 58
 The Tempest **32**: 343
 Timon of Athens **27**: 155

Kernan, Alvin B.
 Henry IV, 1 and 2 **1**: 427
 Henry V **5**: 287
 Henry VI, 1, 2, and 3 **3**: 76
 King Lear **2**: 255
 The Taming of the Shrew **9**: 424

Kernodle, George R.
 King Lear **2**: 177

Kerr, Heather B.
 Titus Andronicus **43**: 186

Kerr, Walter
 Antony and Cleopatra **17**: 23, 45
 The Merchant of Venice **12**: 124
 Much Ado about Nothing **18**: 192; 219
 Othello **11**: 315
 Richard III **14**: 469
 The Taming of the Shrew **12**: 364
 The Two Gentlemen of Verona **12**: 469

Kerrigan, John
 Henry IV, 1 and 2 **16**: 161
 Sonnets **10**: 394; **28**: 407

Kerrigan, William
 As You Like It **34**: 109
 General Commentary **13**: 523
 Hamlet **28**: 280

Keyishian, Harry
 Hamlet **35**: 174
 Othello **35**: 261

Kezar, Dennis
 Julius Caesar **48**: 240

Kiasashvili, Nico
 Richard III **14**: 477

Kiberd, Declan
 Shakespeare's Representation of Women (topic entry) **31**: 8

Kiefer, Frederick
 Pericles **22**: 315; **36**: 233
 Romeo and Juliet **5**: 573

Kierkegaard, Soren
 See Taciturnus, Frater

Kiernan, Pauline
 Sonnets **32**: 352
 Venus and Adonis **32**: 352; **33**: 377

Kiernan, Thomas
 Coriolanus **17**: 162

Kiernan, Victor
 Timon of Athens **37**: 222

Kilbourne, Frederick W.
 As You Like It **23**: 6
 Henry VI, 1, 2, and 3 **24**: 3
 King John **24**: 163
 Measure for Measure **23**: 267, 274
 The Merry Wives of Windsor **18**: 8
 Much Ado about Nothing **18**: 112
 Pericles **15**: 129
 Richard II **24**: 261
 The Tempest **15**: 190
 Troilus and Cressida **18**: 278

Kimbrough, Robert
 As You Like It **5**: 164
 Cymbeline **16**: 442
 Macbeth **29**: 127
 Pericles **16**: 442
 The Tempest **16**: 442
 Troilus and Cressida **27**: 374
 The Winter's Tale **16**: 442

King, Bruce
 Coriolanus **30**: 140

King, Walter N.
 Much Ado about Nothing **8**: 95
 Twelfth Night **34**: 301

Kingston, Jeremy
 As You Like It **23**: 105
 The Comedy of Errors **26**: 149, 150
 Cymbeline **15**: 18
 Hamlet **21**: 281, 324
 Henry VI, 1, 2, and 3 **24**: 50
 Julius Caesar **17**: 375
 Macbeth **20**: 257
 The Merry Wives of Windsor **18**: 37, 41, 61
 Pericles **15**: 150
 Richard III **14**: 463
 The Taming of the Shrew **12**: 384
 Timon of Athens **20**: 474
 Titus Andronicus **17**: 469
 Troilus and Cressida **18**: 392
 Twelfth Night **26**: 262, 267
 The Two Gentlemen of Verona **12**: 482
 The Winter's Tale **15**: 479

Kinney, Arthur F.
 The Comedy of Errors **34**: 258

Kirk, John Foster
 Hamlet **21**: 58

Kirkman, Francis
  A Midsummer Night's Dream **3**: 361

Kirkman, Rev. J.
  King Lear **2**: 129

Kirsch, Arthur
  Hamlet **16**: 381; **35**: 85; **44**: 209
  Macbeth **16**: 381
  Othello **16**: 381
  The Tempest **42**: 346

Kirsch, Arthur C.
  All's Well That Ends Well **7**: 109
  Cymbeline **4**: 138
  Macbeth **44**: 324
  Much Ado about Nothing **8**: 115

Kirschbaum, Leo
  Julius Caesar **7**: 255
  Macbeth **3**: 278
  The Merchant of Venice **40**: 166

Kirstein, Lincoln
  A Midsummer Night's Dream **12**: 295

Kitchin, Laurence
  Coriolanus **17**: 169

Kitto, H. D. F.
  Hamlet **1**: 212

Kittredge, George Lyman
  Macbeth **3**: 225

Klause, John
  Sonnets **51**: 321
  Venus and Adonis **51**: 377

Kleinstuck, Johannes
  Troilus and Cressida **3**: 599

Kliman, Bernice W.
  Hamlet **21**: 311

Kline, Herbert W.
  The Merchant of Venice **12**: 40

Knapp, Jeffrey
  Henry V **25**: 116
  Henry VI, 1, 2, and 3 **25**: 116

Knapp, Margaret
  The Comedy of Errors **26**: 138

Knight, Charles
  All's Well That Ends Well **7**: 16
  Henry V **5**: 198
  Henry VI, 1, 2 and 3 **3**: 29
  Henry VIII **2**: 27
  Love's Labour's Lost **2**: 304
  Measure for Measure **2**: 401
  A Midsummer Night's Dream **3**: 371
  Sonnets **10**: 182
  Timon of Athens **1**: 464
  Titus Andronicus **4**: 619
  Twelfth Night **1**: 548
  The Two Gentlemen of Verona **6**: 442

Knight, G. Wilson
  All's Well That Ends Well **7**: 67
  Antony and Cleopatra **6**: 85
  The Comedy of Errors **1**: 25
  Coriolanus **9**: 65
  Cymbeline **4**: 78
  Hamlet **1**: 144
  Henry VIII **2**: 51
  Julius Caesar **7**: 227, 233
  King Lear **2**: 156; **11**: 127, 130, 150
  Macbeth **3**: 231, 234
  Measure for Measure **2**: 421
  The Merchant of Venice **12**: 117
  A Midsummer Night's Dream **3**: 401
  Much Ado about Nothing **8**: 43
  Othello **4**: 462; **11**: 339
  Pericles **2**: 559, 565
  Phoenix and Turtle **51**: 145
  Romeo and Juliet **11**: 509
  Sonnets **10**: 290
  The Tempest **8**: 364
  Timon of Athens **1**: 483, 499
  Troilus and Cressida **3**: 561
  Twelfth Night **1**: 570
  Venus and Adonis **10**: 428
  The Winter's Tale **7**: 417, 436

Knight, Joseph
  The Merchant of Venice **12**: 21
  Othello **11**: 223, 245
  Richard III **14**: 398
  Romeo and Juliet **11**: 421, 422

Knights, L. C.
  Antony and Cleopatra **6**: 131
  Coriolanus **9**: 110
  Hamlet **1**: 221
  Henry IV, 1 and 2 **1**: 354, 411
  Julius Caesar **7**: 262
  King Lear **2**: 222
  Macbeth **3**: 241
  Measure for Measure **2**: 446
  Sonnets **10**: 251
  The Tempest **29**: 292
  Timon of Athens **1**: 515
  Troilus and Cressida **3**: 584
  The Winter's Tale **7**: 493

Knoepflmacher, U. C.
  Henry IV, 1 and 2 **1**: 413

Knowles, James Sheridan
  Romeo and Juliet **11**: 413

Kobialka, Michael
  The Comedy of Errors **26**: 138

Kolin, Philip C.
  Titus Andronicus **32**: 249

Koller, Ann Marie
  Julius Caesar **17**: 302

Komisarjevsky, Theodore
  Macbeth **20**: 192

Kornstein, Daniel J.
  Henry IV, 1 and 2 **49**: 133
  The Merchant of Venice **49**: 27

Kott, Jan
  As You Like It **5**: 118
  Gender Identity (topic entry) **40**: 65
  Hamlet **1**: 247
  Henry IV, 1 and 2 **1**: 418
  King Lear **2**: 245; **11**: 151
  Macbeth **3**: 309
  A Midsummer Night's Dream **3**: 445
  Richard II **6**: 354
  Richard III **8**: 232; **39**: 308
  The Tempest **8**: 408; **15**: 361; **29**: 368
  Titus Andronicus **17**: 449
  Troilus and Cressida **3**: 609
  Twelfth Night **1**: 639

Kowsar, Mohammad
  Richard III **14**: 477

Kramer, Jerome A.
  Rape of Lucrece **43**: 141

Kramer, Mimi
  Coriolanus **17**: 220
  Much Ado about Nothing **18**: 227

Kreider, P. V.
  As You Like It **5**: 72

Krempel, Daniel
  Henry V **14**: 222

Kreyssig, Friedrich
  King Lear **2**: 124
  The Merchant of Venice **4**: 208
  Twelfth Night **1**: 553

Krieger, Elliot
  As You Like It **5**: 148
  Much Ado about Nothing **31**: 191

Krieger, Murray
  Measure for Measure **2**: 482
  Richard III **8**: 218
  Sonnets **10**: 329; **40**: 284

Kroll, Jack
  Antony and Cleopatra **17**: 68
  As You Like It **23**: 121
  Othello **11**: 316
  Richard III **14**: 471

Kronenfeld, Judy
  King Lear **22**: 233

Kronenfeld, Judy Z.
  As You Like It **34**: 161

Krutch, Joseph Wood
  Hamlet **21**: 171
  Julius Caesar **17**: 321
  Macbeth **20**: 229
  Richard III **14**: 411
  The Taming of the Shrew **12**: 344
  The Tempest **15**: 241
  Troilus and Cressida **18**: 297
  Twelfth Night **26**: 223

Kuhl, Ernest P.
  The Taming of the Shrew **12**: 427

Kuner, Mildred C.
  Titus Andronicus **17**: 462

Kurland, Stuart M.
  Hamlet **28**: 290
  Pericles **37**: 360
  The Winter's Tale **19**: 401

Kurtz, Martha
  Henry IV, 1 and 2 **37**: 122
  Henry V **37**: 122
  Henry VI, 1, 2, and 3 **37**: 122
  Richard II **37**: 122
  Richard III **37**: 122

Kyle, Howard
  Henry VIII **24**: 85

Lady Martin
  See Faucit, Helena

LaGuardia, Eric
  All's Well That Ends Well **7**: 90

Laird, David
  Romeo and Juliet **5**: 520

Lamb, Charles
  Hamlet **1**: 93
  King Lear **2**: 106; **11**: 136
  Macbeth **3**: 184
  Othello **4**: 401; **11**: 334
  Richard III **8**: 159; **14**: 368, 369
  Timon of Athens **1**: 459
  Twelfth Night **1**: 545
  The Two Noble Kinsmen **9**: 446

Lamb, Margaret
  Antony and Cleopatra **17**: 12, 84

Lamb, Mary Ellen
  Measure for Measure **13**: 104
  A Midsummer Night's Dream **3**: 498

Lambert, J. W.
  Antony and Cleopatra **17**: 58
  As You Like It **23**: 99, 105
  Hamlet **21**: 293
  Love's Labour's Lost **23**: 202, 210
  Macbeth **20**: 293
  The Merchant of Venice **12**: 93
  Richard II **24**: 355
  The Taming of the Shrew **12**: 393
  The Tempest **15**: 272
  Troilus and Cressida **18**: 356
  Twelfth Night **26**: 283

Lamont, Rosette
  The Tempest **15**: 292

Lamont, Rosette C.
  The Tempest **15**: 287

Lancashire, Anne
  Timon of Athens **1**: 518

Lancaster, Osbert
  All's Well That Ends Well **26**: 95

Landor, Walter Savage
  Sonnets **10**: 167

Landry, D. E.
  Cymbeline **4**: 167; **45**: 67

Landstone, Charles
King Lear 11: 124

Lane, John Francis
The Tempest 15: 285

Lane, Robert
Henry V 28: 146
King John 32: 114

Lang, Andrew
Much Ado about Nothing 8: 33

Lang, David Marshall
Richard III 14: 476

Langbaine, Gerard
Antony and Cleopatra 6: 20
Cymbeline 4: 17
Henry V 5: 185
Henry VI, 1, 2, and 3 3: 17
The Merry Wives of Windsor 5: 332
Much Ado about Nothing 8: 9
Pericles 2: 538

Langbaum, Robert
Henry IV, 1 and 2 1: 408

Langham, Michael
Antony and Cleopatra 17: 48

Langton, Robert Gore
Antony and Cleopatra 17: 74

Lanham, Richard A.
The Rape of Lucrece 10: 116; 33: 190
Sonnets 40: 221

Lanier, Douglas
The Comedy of Errors 25: 63; 34: 201

Lanier, Sidney
The Phoenix and Turtle 10: 7

Lardner, James
Hamlet 21: 309

Laroque, Francois
Henry VI, 1, 2, and 3 39: 205
Macbeth 29: 109
The Merry Wives of Windsor 18: 56
Romeo and Juliet 32: 256
Titus Andronicus 17: 481
Twelfth Night 26: 318

Larson, Orville K.
Richard III 14: 516

Latham, Grace
The Two Gentlemen of Verona 6: 453

Laver, James
Macbeth 20: 52

Law, Robert Adger
Henry IV, 1 and 2 1: 348

Lawlor, John
Romeo and Juliet 5: 509

Lawrence, W. J.
Henry VIII 24: 150
The Tempest 15: 196

Lawrence, William Witherle
All's Well That Ends Well 7: 32
Cymbeline 4: 53
Measure for Measure 2: 429
Troilus and Cressida 3: 566

Laws, Jennifer
Sonnets 48: 336

Leavis, F. R.
Cymbeline 4: 77
Measure for Measure 2: 449
Othello 4: 477
The Winter's Tale 7: 436

Lecter-Siegal Amy
Measure for Measure 33: 85

Lee, Jane
Henry VI, 1, 2, and 3 3: 39

Lee, Sidney
Henry V 14: 334
Pericles 2: 553
The Phoenix and Turtle 10: 8
The Rape of Lucrece 10: 69
Sonnets 10: 233

Leech, Clifford
All's Well That Ends Well 7: 54
Antony and Cleopatra 17: 34
Henry IV, 1 and 2 1: 393
Henry VIII 2: 64
Macbeth 29: 152
Measure for Measure 2: 479
Pericles 2: 571
Romeo and Juliet 5: 562
Shakespeare and Classical Civilization (topic entry) 27: 60
The Taming of the Shrew 12: 350
The Tempest 8: 380
Twelfth Night 1: 645
The Two Noble Kinsmen 9: 479, 486

Leggatt, Alexander
As You Like It 5: 141; 46: 254
The Comedy of Errors 1: 63
Cymbeline 4: 159
Henry V 49: 247
Henry VI, 1, 2, and 3 39: 160
King John 41: 205
Love's Labour's Lost 2: 362
Measure for Measure 49: 313
Pericles 36: 257
The Taming of the Shrew 9: 407
Twelfth Night 1: 660
The Two Gentlemen of Verona 6: 549

Leibler, Naomi Conn
Julius Caesar 50: 269

Lejeune, C. A.
Henry V 14: 204

Lelyveld, Toby
The Merchant of Venice 12: 6

Lemmon, Jeremy
Macbeth 20: 382

Lennox, Charlotte
Cymbeline 4: 18
Hamlet 1: 81
Henry IV, 1 and 2 1: 289
Henry V 5: 188
Henry VI, 1, 2, and 3 3: 18
Henry VIII 2: 16
King Lear 2: 100
Macbeth 3: 172
Measure for Measure 2: 388
Much Ado about Nothing 8: 9
Othello 4: 386
Richard II 6: 252
Richard III 8: 145
Romeo and Juliet 5: 416
Troilus and Cressida 3: 537
Twelfth Night 1: 540
The Two Gentlemen of Verona 6: 436
The Winter's Tale 7: 377

Lenz, Joseph M.
The Winter's Tale 36: 380

Leonard, Hugh
Henry V 14: 278
Twelfth Night 26: 262

Lesser, Simon O.
Macbeth 45: 48

Lessing, Gotthold Ephraim
Hamlet 1: 84

Levenson, Jill L.
Romeo and Juliet 11: 451

Lever, J. W.
Measure for Measure 2: 505
The Merchant of Venice 4: 263
Sonnets 10: 293

Levett, Karl
Much Ado about Nothing 18: 229

Levin, Bernard
As You Like It 23: 89, 115, 120
Cymbeline 15: 62
Henry VI, 1, 2, and 3 24: 31
King Lear 11: 110
A Midsummer Night's Dream 12: 270
Twelfth Night 26: 330

Levin, Harry
Hamlet 1: 227
Henry IV, 1 and 2 49: 178
Macbeth 44: 261
Othello 4: 562
Romeo and Juliet 5: 496
Timon of Athens 1: 520

Levin, Richard A.
Julius Caesar 30: 362
Merchant of Venice 51: 15
Much Ado About Nothing 51: 15
The Rape of Lucrece 33: 138
Twelfth Night 46: 324; 51: 15

Levine, Nina S.
Richard III 39: 345

Lewalski, B. K.
Much Ado about Nothing 31: 209

Lewalski, Barbara K.
The Merchant of Venice 4: 289
Twelfth Night 1: 642

Lewes, George Henry
Hamlet 21: 384
Othello 11: 201, 219

Lewis, Anthony J.
Pericles 36: 264

Lewis, C. S.
The Phoenix and Turtle 10: 20
The Rape of Lucrece 10: 77
Sonnets 10: 287
Venus and Adonis 10: 448

Lewis, Chariton M.
Hamlet 1: 125

Lewis, Cynthia
Cymbeline 19: 411

Lewis, Majorie Dunlavy
The Merry Wives of Windsor 47: 354

Lewis, Wyndham
Coriolanus 9: 62
Henry VI, 1 and 2 1: 351
Othello 4: 455
Timon of Athens 1: 481

Lewsen, Charles
Antony and Cleopatra 17: 55
Henry V 14: 280
Pericles 15: 161

Lezra, Jacques
Measure for Measure 13: 112

Lictenberg, Georg Christoph
Hamlet 21: 17

Lidz, Theodore
Hamlet 35: 132

Lieber, Naomi Conn
Titus Andronicus 32: 265

Lief, Madelon
The Two Noble Kinsmen 41: 326

Lillo, George
Pericles 2: 538

Lindenbaum, Peter
The Two Gentlemen of Verona 6: 555

Lindheim, Nancy
Venus and Adonis 10: 489

Linville, Susan E.
King Lear 16: 311

Liston, William T.
A Midsummer Night's Dream 45: 143

Littledale, Harold
The Two Noble Kinsmen **9**: 457

Lloyd, William Watkiss
Henry V **5**: 203
Pericles **2**: 547
The Two Gentlemen of Verona **6**: 447

Lockridge, Richard
Romeo and Juliet **11**: 418

Loewenstein, Joseph
Hamlet **13**: 282

Loggins, Vernon P.
Troilus and Cressida **43**: 377

Lolleran, James V.
Hamlet **13**: 268

Londre, Felicia Hardison
Coriolanus **17**: 151

Loney, Glenn
As You Like It **23**: 117

Long, John H.
A Midsummer Night's Dream **3**: 418

Long, Michael
Antony and Cleopatra **6**: 219

Longinus
See also Steevens, George; Collier, Jeremy; Hic et Ubique; Lorenzo
Hamlet **1**: 86

Longstaffe, Steve
King John **37**: 132

Lorenzo
See also Steevens, George; Collier, Jeremy; Hic et Ubique; Longinus
Othello **4**: 391
Richard III **8**: 147

Love, John M.
All's Well That Ends Well **50**: 59

Lowe, Lisa
Coriolanus **30**: 125

Lowell, James Russell
The Tempest **8**: 308

Lowenthal, David
Julius Caesar **50**: 234
King Lear **46**: 177

Lubbock, Tom
Pericles **15**: 174

Lucas, Walter
The Taming of the Shrew **12**: 369

Lucking, David
The Merchant of Venice **13**: 43
Romeo and Juliet **32**: 276; **42**: 271

Luders, Charles Henry
The Winter's Tale **15**: 440

Lusardi, James P.
King Lear **19**: 295

Lustig, Vera
Julius Caesar **17**: 406

Lyons, Charles R.
A Midsummer Night's Dream **3**: 474

Mabie, Hamilton Wright
Antony and Cleopatra **6**: 53

Mac Liammoir, Micheal
Othello **11**: 285

Macauly, Alastair
Twelfth Night **26**: 335

MacCallum, M. W.
Coriolanus **9**: 45
Julius Caesar **7**: 191

MacCarthy, Desmond
Hamlet **21**: 157, 179
A Midsummer Night's Dream **12**: 223
Richard III **14**: 416
Troilus and Cressida **18**: 302

MacCary, W. Thomas
Love's Labour's Lost **38**: 194
Much Ado about Nothing **31**: 241
The Two Gentlemen of Verona **40**: 365

Macdonald, Dwight
Hamlet **21**: 242

MacDonald, Jan
The Taming of the Shrew **12**: 338

MacDonald, Joyce Green
The Rape of Lucrece **33**: 155

MacDonald, Ronald R.
Antony and Cleopatra **6**: 228
Measure for Measure **16**: 114
A Midsummer Night's Dream **29**: 210

MacIntyre, Jean
King Lear **47**: 9

Mack, Maynard
Antony and Cleopatra **6**: 163; **27**: 90
Hamlet **1**: 198
Julius Caesar **7**: 298
King Lear **2**: 249; **11**: 132
The Taming of the Shrew **9**: 369

Mack, Maynard, Jr.
Hamlet **1**: 264
Macbeth **29**: 155

Mackail, J. W.
Sonnets **10**: 243

Mackenzie, Henry
Hamlet **1**: 88
Henry IV, 1 and 2 **1**: 304

Mackenzie, Suzie
As You Like It **23**: 142

Macklin, Charles
Othello **11**: 185

MacLeish, Archibald
Julius Caesar **17**: 323

Macready, William Charles
King John **24**: 181
King Lear **11**: 15
Macbeth **20**: 100, 101, 103
Romeo and Juliet **11**: 398

Madariaga, Salvador de
Hamlet **1**: 171

Maginn, William
As You Like It **5**: 28
Macbeth **3**: 193
A Midsummer Night's Dream **3**: 365
Othello **4**: 409

Magnusson, Lynne A.
Henry VIII **22**: 182
Othello **42**: 278

Maguin, J. M.
Henry V **14**: 284
Henry VI, 1, 2, and 3 **24**: 36
Julius Caesar **17**: 396
King John **24**: 238
Much Ado about Nothing **18**: 215
Pericles **15**: 166
The Taming of the Shrew **12**: 410
Titus Andronicus **17**: 481

Maguin, Jean Marie
Julius Caesar **30**: 293
The Merry Wives of Windsor **18**: 60
The Tempest **32**: 367

Mahood, M. M.
Macbeth **3**: 283
Richard II **6**: 331
Romeo and Juliet **5**: 489
Sonnets **10**: 296
The Winter's Tale **7**: 460

Mairowitz, David Zane
Troilus and Cressida **18**: 359

Majors, G. W.
The Rape of Lucrece **10**: 106

Malcolm, Donald
Henry IV, 1 and 2 **14**: 62, 65

Malcolmson, Cristina
Twelfth Night **19**: 78; **46**: 347

Mallett, Phillip
Richard III **39**: 387

Mallin, Eric S.
Troilus and Cressida **16**: 84; **43**: 365

Malone, Edmond
Henry VI, 1, 2, and 3 **3**: 21
Henry VIII **2**: 19
King John **9**: 218
A Midsummer Night's Dream **3**: 363
Pericles **2**: 538, 543
The Rape of Lucrece **10**: 64
Richard III **8**: 158
Sonnets **10**: 155, 156
Titus Andronicus **4**: 616
Venus and Adonis **10**: 412

Manheim, Leonard F.
Twelfth Night **34**: 338

Manheim, Michael
Henry VI, 1, 2, and 3 **3**: 143
King John **9**: 297; **13**: 158

Manningham, John
Richard III **8**: 144
Twelfth Night **1**: 539

Mantel, Hilary
Henry V **14**: 309

Manvell, Roger
Henry V **14**: 203
Macbeth **20**: 148, 203
A Midsummer Night's Dream **12**: 214
Richard III **14**: 442

Manzoni, Alessandro
Richard II **6**: 260

Marchitello, Howard
The Merchant of Venice **32**: 41

Marcus, Frank
As You Like It **23**: 99
The Taming of the Shrew **12**: 387

Marcus, Leah
The Taming of the Shrew **22**: 48

Marcus, Mordecai
A Midsummer Night's Dream **3**: 511

Marder, Louis
Authorship Controversy (topic entry) **41**: 5

Mares, F. H.
Much Ado about Nothing **18**: 239

Margeson, John
Henry VIII **24**: 146; **41**: 129

Markels, Julian
Antony and Cleopatra **6**: 181; **27**: 121

Marowitz, Charles
Hamlet **21**: 256
King Lear **11**: 78
Love's Labour's Lost **23**: 200

Marriott, J. A. R.
Henry VI, 1, 2, and 3 **3**: 51

Marsh, Derick R. C.
Romeo and Juliet **5**: 565

Marsh, Henry
A Midsummer Night's Dream **3**: 361

Marsh, Ngaio
Twelfth Night **26**: 364

Marshall, Cynthia
As You Like It **48**: 42
Coriolanus **50**: 128

Marshall, David
A Midsummer Night's Dream **3**: 520

Marshall, Margaret
Hamlet **21**: 201
Othello **11**: 268

Marston, Westland
King Lear **11**: 18
Romeo and Juliet **11**: 404

Martin, Philip
Sonnets **51**: 300

Martin, Theodore
As You Like It **23**: 47
The Merchant of Venice **12**: 25

Martindale, Charles
Shakespeare and Classical Civilization (topic entry) **27**: 67

Martindale, Michelle
Shakespeare and Classical Civilization (topic entry) **27**: 67

Marx, Joan C.
Cymbeline **36**: 125

Marx, Karl
Timon of Athens **1**: 466

Marx, Leo
The Tempest **8**: 404

Marx, Steven
Henry V **32**: 126

Masefield, John
Coriolanus **9**: 52
Henry V **5**: 212
King John **9**: 245
Macbeth **20**: 363
The Phoenix and Turtle **10**: 14
Richard III **8**: 184

Mason, John Monck
Sonnets **10**: 156

Massey, Daniel
Measure for Measure **23**: 416

Massey, Gerald
Sonnets **10**: 196
Titus Andronicus **4**: 624

Masters, Anthony
A Midsummer Night's Dream **12**: 277
Timon of Athens **20**: 471

Matchett, William H.
King John **41**: 277

The Phoenix and Turtle **38**: 357
The Winter's Tale **7**: 483

Matheson, Mark
Hamlet **32**: 284
Othello **32**: 294

Matthews, Brander
Cymbeline **4**: 52
Henry V **5**: 213
Julius Caesar **7**: 204; **17**: 296
Romeo and Juliet **5**: 448

Matthews, C. M.
Othello **4**: 564

Matthews, Harold
As You Like It **23**: 85
Coriolanus **17**: 167
Henry VI, 1, 2, and 3 **24**: 24
King Lear **11**: 75
Love's Labour's Lost **23**: 197
Measure for Measure **23**: 311, 317
Much Ado about Nothing **18**: 180
Othello **11**: 294
Richard III **14**: 460

Matthews, Harold G.
Troilus and Cressida **18**: 307, 323

Matthews, William
Love's Labour's Lost **2**: 345

Matus, Irvin
Authorship Controversy (topic entry) **41**: 57, 63

Maus, Katharine Eisaman
Love's Labour's Lost **19**: 92
Measure for Measure **33**: 112
The Rape of Lucrece **33**: 144

Maxwell, Baldwin
Hamlet **35**: 204

Maxwell, J. C.
Timon of Athens **1**: 495

Mayer, Jean-Christophe
Henry IV, Parts 1 and 2 **42**: 143
Henry V **42**: 143

Mazer, Cary M.
Much Ado about Nothing **18**: 148
The Taming of the Shrew **12**: 337

McAleer, John J.
Henry IV, and 1 and 2 **14**: 13

McAlindon, T.
Hamlet **1**: 249
Julius Caesar **50**: 280
Richard II **6**: 397
Troilus and Cressida **3**: 624

McAlindon, Tom
Antony and Cleopatra **19**: 304
Coriolanus **25**: 263
Henry IV, 1 and 2 **32**: 136

McBride, Tom
Henry VIII **2**: 75
Measure for Measure **2**: 522

McCarten, John
Hamlet **21**: 199
Henry V **14**: 210

McClain, John
The Two Gentlemen of Verona **12**: 469

McCloskey, John C.
Henry V **5**: 239

McCollom, William G.
Much Ado about Nothing **31**: 178

McConnell, Stanlie
Henry V **14**: 219

McCourt, James
The Tempest **15**: 298

McCoy, Richard C.
Kingship (topic entry) **39**: 34
The Phoenix and Turtle **51**: 162

McCreadie, Marsha
Henry V **14**: 326

McDonald, Jan
The Taming of the Shrew **12**: 317

McDonald, Russ
The Tempest **19**: 421
Richard III **47**: 15

McElroy, Bernard
King Lear **2**: 273
Macbeth **3**: 329

McEwan, Ian
As You Like It **23**: 123

McFarland, Thomas
King Lear **46**: 231

McGlinchee, Claire
The Merchant of Venice **12**: 63
A Midsummer Night's Dream **12**: 241
Much Ado about Nothing **18**: 174
Troilus and Cressida **18**: 338

McGrath, John
Macbeth **20**: 259

McGuire, Philip C.
A Midsummer Night's Dream **29**: 256
The Tempest **45**: 200

McKellan, Ian
Richard II **24**: 337

McKenzie, Stanley D.
Coriolanus **9**: 193
Henry IV, 1 and 2 **49**: 123

McLaughlin, John J.
Richard III **39**: 383

McLaughlin, John
Hamlet **21**: 249

McLuhan, Herbert Marshall
Henry IV, 1 and 2 **1**: 385

McLuskie, Kathleen
King Lear **31**: 123
Shakespeare's Representation of Women (topic entry) **31**: 35

McMullan, Gordon
Henry VIII **32**: 148

McMullen, Glenys
Clowns and Fools (topic entry) **46**: 18

McNeely, Trevor
Othello **47**: 51

McPeek, James A. S.
Much Ado about Nothing **8**: 88
Richard II **6**: 334

Meadowcroft, J. R. W.
King Lear **11**: 165

Mebane, John S.
Magic and the Supernatural (topic entry) **29**: 12

Mehl, Dieter
Macbeth **44**: 269

Merchant, Moelwyn W.
Henry VIII **24**: 71

Merchant, W. M.
Timon of Athens **1**: 500

Meres, Francis
The Rape of Lucrece **10**: 63
Sonnets **10**: 153
Venus and Adonis **10**: 410

Merrix, Robert P.
Venus and Adonis **51**: 359

Merryn, Anthony
Measure for Measure **23**: 312

Meryman, Richard
Othello **11**: 297

Meszaros, Patricia K.
Coriolanus **9**: 180

Metzger, Mary Jane
The Merchant of Venice **48**: 54

Mezieres, Alfred J. F.
Macbeth **3**: 198
Romeo and Juliet **5**: 437

Micheli, Linda McJ.
Henry VIII **24**: 101; **41**: 180

Michell, John
Authorship Controversy (topic entry) **41**: 2

Michener, Charles
Othello **11**: 321
Pericles **15**: 162

Midgley, Graham
The Merchant of Venice **4**: 279

Mikalachki, Jodi
Cymbeline **32**: 373

Miko, Stephen J.
The Tempest **29**: 297
The Winter's Tale **13**: 417

Miles, Geoffrey
Julius Caesar **37**: 229

Millard, Barbara C.
Fathers and Daughters (topic entry) **36**: 60
King Lear **13**: 352

Miller, J. Hillis
Troilus and Cressida **3**: 635

Miller, Jonathan
The Merchant of Venice **12**: 92
The Taming of the Shrew **12**: 400, 402
The Tempest **15**: 338

Miller, Robert P.
Venus and Adonis **10**: 439

Miller, Ronald F.
King Lear **2**: 278
A Midsummer Night's Dream **3**: 486

Miller, Shannon
Coriolanus **50**: 172

Miller, Tice L.
The Taming of the Shrew **12**: 425

Mills, John A.
Hamlet **21**: 89, 44, 274

Milne, Tom
The Taming of the Shrew **12**: 359

Miola, Robert S.
Othello **16**: 283
Julius Caesar **30**: 326
Shakespeare and Classical Civilization (topic entry) **27**: 39
Titus Andronicus **43**: 206

Milton, John
Richard III **8**: 145

Mincoff, M.
The Two Noble Kinsmen **9**: 471

Mincoff, Marco
Henry VIII **41**: 158

Miner, Madonne M.
Richard III **8**: 262

Mizener, Arthur
Sonnets **10**: 265

Modjeska, Helena
As You Like It **23**: 42

Moffet, Robin
Cymbeline **4**: 108

Moglen, Helene
Twelfth Night **34**: 311

Moisan, Thomas
Julius Caesar **50**: 64
The Merchant of Venice **50**: 64
The Taming of the Shrew **32**: 56; **50**: 64

Monsey, Derek
All's Well That Ends Well **26**: 36

Montagu, Elizabeth
Hamlet **1**: 85
Henry IV, 1 and 2 **1**: 293
Julius Caesar **7**: 156
Macbeth **3**: 173

Montague, C. E.
Measure for Measure **23**: 286
Richard II **24**: 408

Montegut, Emile
Love's Labour's Lost **2**: 306
Twelfth Night **1**: 554
The Winter's Tale **7**: 394

Montrose, Louis Adrian
As You Like It **5**: 158
Love's Labour's Lost **2**: 371
A Midsummer Night's Dream **29**: 243; **45**: 84; **50**: 86

Moody, A. D.
The Merchant of Venice **4**: 300

Mooney, Michael E.
Antony and Cleopatra **16**: 342
Julius Caesar **19**: 321
Richard III **16**: 150

Moore, Dan
The Merchant of Venice **12**: 80

Moore, Don D.
Much Ado about Nothing **18**: 216

Moore, Edward M.
Measure for Measure **23**: 293
The Merchant of Venice **12**: 44

Moore, Hannah
Hamlet **21**: 20

Moore, Jeanie Grant
Richard II **39**: 295

Morgann, Maurice
Henry IV, 1 and 2 **1**: 298
The Tempest **8**: 293

Morley, Henry
As You Like It **23**: 26
Cymbeline **15**: 19, 20
Henry IV, 1 and 2 **14**: 15
King John **24**: 194
King Lear **11**: 20
Macbeth **20**: 121
A Midsummer Night's Dream **12**: 169, 183
Othello **11**: 217
Richard II **24**: 273
The Taming of the Shrew **12**: 323
Timon of Athens **20**: 444

Morley, Sheridan
All's Well That Ends Well **26**: 57
Coriolanus **17**: 213
Cymbeline **15**: 86
Hamlet **21**: 314, 333
Henry V **14**: 282
Henry VIII **24**: 123
Julius Caesar **17**: 388
The Merry Wives of Windsor **18**: 62
Much Ado about Nothing **18**: 207
Romeo and Juliet **11**: 483
The Taming of the Shrew **12**: 410
Titus Andronicus **17**: 485
Troilus and Cressida **18**: 363
Twelfth Night **26**: 293, 306, 317, 325
The Two Gentlemen of Verona **12**: 492
The Winter's Tale **15**: 488

Morris, Brian
Macbeth **3**: 345

Morris, Corbyn
Henry IV, 1 and 2 **1**: 287

Morris, Harry
As You Like It **46**: 164

Morris, Mowbray
Othello **11**: 249

Morrisey, LeRoy J.
As You Like It **23**: 9

Morse, Ruth
The Two Gentlemen of Verona **40**: 359

Morse, William R.
The Winter's Tale **19**: 431

Mortimer, Anthony
Venus and Adonis **42**: 354

Mortimer, Raymond
Hamlet **21**: 197
Othello **11**: 267

Morton, Richard
Timon of Athens **20**: 431

Mosdell, D.
Henry V **14**: 215

Moseley, Charles
Macbeth **44**: 361

Moss, Roger
The Merry Wives of Windsor **47**: 325

Motohashi, Tetsuya
Coriolanus **50**: 119

Moulton, Ian Frederick
Richard III **37**: 144

Moulton, Richard G.
Henry VI, 1, 2, and 3 **3**: 48
Julius Caesar **7**: 179
Richard III **8**: 170
Romeo and Juliet **5**: 444
The Tempest **8**: 315
The Winter's Tale **7**: 407

Mowat, Barbara A.
Cymbeline **4**: 124
Shakespeare's Representation of Women (topic entry) **31**: 29
The Winter's Tale **45**: 333

Mueller, Martin
King Lear **28**: 301

Muir, Edwin
King Lear **2**: 183

Muir, Kenneth
As You Like It **5**: 154
Macbeth **3**: 300; **29**: 76
The Merchant of Venice **12**: 81
Pericles **2**: 568; **36**: 199
The Phoenix and Turtle **10**: 18
Shakespeare and Classical Civilization (topic entry) **27**: 15
Timon of Athens **1**: 495; **27**: 161
Troilus and Cressida **3**: 589
The Two Noble Kinsmen **9**: 474
Venus and Adonis **10**: 459

Mukherji, Subha
All's Well That Ends Well **49**: 46

Mullaney, Steven
Hamlet **28**: 311

Muller, Wolfgang G.
Richard III **39**: 360

Mullin, Michael
Hamlet **21**: 270
Henry IV, 1 and 2 **14**: 92
Macbeth **20**: 175, 192, 210, 245, 324
A Midsummer Night's Dream **12**: 250

Mullini, Roberta
Clowns and Fools (topic entry) **46**: 24

Mulryne, J. R.
Coriolanus **17**: 195
Much Ado about Nothing **18**: 252
Pericles **15**: 167

Munoz, Marie-Christine
The Comedy of Errors **26**: 178

Murphy, Arthur
All's Well That Ends Well **7**: 8
Hamlet **1**: 82; **21**: 21
Henry IV, 1 and 2 **1**: 290
Henry VIII **2**: 17
King Lear **2**: 98
Macbeth **3**: 172; **20**: 23
Measure for Measure **2**: 390
Much Ado about Nothing **18**: 114
Richard III **14**: 364
Romeo and Juliet **11**: 382, 385
The Tempest **15**: 200
The Winter's Tale **7**: 379; **15**: 397

Murphy, Gerard
Henry IV, 1 and 2 **14:** 98

Murray, Gilbert
Hamlet **1:** 130

Murray, Peter B.
Hamlet **37:** 241

Murry, John Middleton
Antony and Cleopatra **6:** 94
Coriolanus **9:** 58
Henry IV, 1 and 2 **1:** 365
Henry VI, 1, 2, and 3 **3:** 55
King John **9:** 248
King Lear **2:** 165
The Merchant of Venice **4:** 247
The Phoenix and Turtle **10:** 14
Richard II **6:** 287
The Tempest **8:** 353
Twelfth Night **1:** 572
The Winter's Tale **7:** 419

Myrick, Kenneth O.
Othello **4:** 483

Nagarajan, S.
Twelfth Night **1:** 609

Nagler, A. M.
Romeo and Juliet **11:** 514
The Tempest **15:** 303

Nardo, Anna K.
Hamlet **35:** 104
Romeo and Juliet **33:** 255

Naremore, James
Macbeth **20:** 206

Nashe, Thomas
Henry VI, 1, 2, and 3 **3:** 16

Nathan, George Jean
Henry VIII **24:** 100
Macbeth **20:** 222
Richard III **14:** 414
The Tempest **15:** 251

Nathan, Norman
The Merchant of Venice **4:** 252, 266

Nechkina, M.
Henry IV, 1 and 2 **1:** 358

Neely, Carol Thomas
All's Well That Ends Well **38:** 99; **51:** 33
Antony and Cleopatra **51:** 33
Gender Identity (topic entry) **40:** 75
Hamlet **19:** 330
King Lear **19:** 330
Macbeth **19:** 330
Madness (topic entry) **35:** 8
Much Ado about Nothing **31:** 231; **51:** 33
The Winter's Tale **7:** 506; **51:** 33

Neill, Kerby
Much Ado about Nothing **8:** 58

Neill, Michael
Henry IV, 1 and 2 **28:** 159

Henry V **28:** 159
Henry VI, 1, 2, and 3 **28:** 159
Othello **13:** 327
Richard II **28:** 159

Nemerov, Howard
A Midsummer Night's Dream **3:** 421
The Two Gentlemen of Verona **6:** 509

Nemirovich-Danchenko, V. I.
Julius Caesar **17:** 295

Nesbitt, Cathleen
The Winter's Tale **15:** 449

Nevo, Ruth
All's Well That Ends Well **48:** 65
The Comedy of Errors **34:** 245
Pericles **36:** 214
The Two Gentlemen of Verona **6:** 560
The Winter's Tale **45:** 344

Newlin, Jeanne T.
Troilus and Cressida **18:** 395, 437

Newman, Karen
Henry V **19:** 203
The Merchant of Venice **40:** 208

Nice, David
Troilus and Cressida **18:** 387

Nicholls, Graham
Measure for Measure **23:** 379

Nichols, Lewis
The Tempest **15:** 237, 240

Nicoll, Allardyce
Othello **4:** 457

Nietzsche, Friedrich
Hamlet **1:** 114
Julius Caesar **7:** 179

Nightingale, Benedict
All's Well That Ends Well **26:** 55, 71
Antony and Cleopatra **17:** 57
As You Like It **23:** 128, 148
The Comedy of Errors **26:** 150
Coriolanus **17:** 192, 207
Cymbeline **15:** 73
Hamlet **21:** 267, 297, 330
Henry IV, 1 and 2 **14:** 90
Henry V **14:** 282
Henry VI, 1, 2, and 3 **24:** 32
Henry VIII **24:** 115, 124
Julius Caesar **17:** 380
King John **24:** 216
King Lear **11:** 109
Macbeth **20:** 289, 314
Measure for Measure **23:** 321, 327, 339, 355
The Merchant of Venice **12:** 95
The Merry Wives of Windsor **18:** 55
A Midsummer Night's Dream **12:** 257, 275
Much Ado about Nothing **18:** 205

Pericles **15:** 148, 160, 175
Richard II **24:** 345, 374, 381
Richard III **14:** 464
Romeo and Juliet **11:** 485
The Taming of the Shrew **12:** 389
The Tempest **15:** 269, 289
Titus Andronicus **17:** 466
Troilus and Cressida **18:** 343, 389
Twelfth Night **26:** 270, 327, 336
The Winter's Tale **15:** 477, 485, 486

Nilan, Mary M.
The Tempest **15:** 215, 305

Noble, James Ashcroft
Sonnets **10:** 214

Noble, Richmond
Love's Labour's Lost **2:** 316

Nokes, David
Troilus and Cressida **18:** 364

North, Richard
Much Ado about Nothing **18:** 200

Norton, Elliot
Antony and Cleopatra **17:** 52

Novick, Julius
Hamlet **21:** 287
Henry V **14:** 304
Measure for Measure **23:** 331
Titus Andronicus **17:** 461, 474

Novy, Marianne
Fathers and Daughters (topic entry) **36:** 54
Gender Identity (topic entry) **40:** 9
King Lear **31:** 117
The Merchant of Venice **40:** 142
Shakespeare's Representation of Women (topic entry) **31:** 3
Troilus and Cressida **27:** 362; **43:** 351

Novy, Marianne L.
The Taming of the Shrew **31:** 288

Nowottny, Winifred M. T.
King Lear **2:** 213, 235
Othello **4:** 512
Romeo and Juliet **5:** 522
Timon of Athens **1:** 505
Troilus and Cressida **3:** 590

Nunn, Trevor
Julius Caesar **17:** 421

Nuttall, A. D.
Measure for Measure **2:** 511; **49:** 274
The Tempest **29:** 313
Timon of Athens **13:** 392; **27:** 184

O'Loughlin, Sean
The Phoenix and Turtle **10:** 18

Odell, George C. D.
Antony and Cleopatra **17:** 5
As You Like It **23:** 8, 19

Henry V **14:** 178, 182, 188, 189, 194, 195
Henry VI, 1, 2, and 3 **24:** 4
Henry VIII **24:** 70, 77, 84
King John **24:** 165
Measure for Measure **23:** 267
The Merry Wives of Windsor **18:** 9
A Midsummer Night's Dream **12:** 144, 146, 155, 180
Much Ado about Nothing **18:** 113
Pericles **15:** 130
Richard II **24:** 262, 271
The Tempest **15:** 199, 201
Timon of Athens **20:** 428, 442, 445
Troilus and Cressida **18:** 280
The Winter's Tale **15:** 397, 431, 444

Ogawa, Yasuhiro
Hamlet **42:** 284

Ogburn, Charlton
Authorship Controversy (topic entry) **41:** 32

Ogden, Dunbar H.
The Comedy of Errors **26:** 154

Oliver, Edith
The Comedy of Errors **26:** 175
Hamlet **21:** 288
Julius Caesar **17:** 401
Othello **11:** 314
Twelfth Night **26:** 299

Oliver, H. J.
Coriolanus **30:** 129
Timon of Athens **27:** 157

Olivier, Laurence
Antony and Cleopatra **17:** 28
Hamlet **21:** 202
Henry V **14:** 252
Othello **11:** 297

Ong, Walter J.
The Phoenix and Turtle **10:** 31

Orgel, Stephen
Sexuality (topic entry) **33:** 18
The Tempest **29:** 396
The Winter's Tale **19:** 441; **45:** 329

Orgel, Stephen Kitay
The Tempest **8:** 414

Ormerod, David
A Midsummer Night's Dream **3:** 497

Ornstein, Robert
Antony and Cleopatra **47:** 96
Hamlet **1:** 230
Henry IV, 1 and 2 **1:** 431
Henry V **5:** 293
Henry VI, 1, 2, and 3 **3:** 136
Henry VIII **2:** 68
Julius Caesar **7:** 282
King John **9:** 292
King Lear **2:** 238

Measure for Measure **2**: 495
A Midsummer Night's Dream **29**: 175
Troilus and Cressida **27**: 370
The Two Gentlemen of Verona **40**: 312

Orwell, George
King Lear **2**: 186

Osborne, Laurie
Twelfth Night **37**: 78

Osborne, Laurie E.
The Merry Wives of Windsor **38**: 273

Over, William
Coriolanus **17**: 225

Overholser, Winfred
Madness (topic entry) **35**: 24

Owens, Margaret E.
Henry VI, 1, 2, and 3 **37**: 157

O'Connor, Garry
Julius Caesar **17**: 394
King John **24**: 223
Love's Labour's Lost **23**: 204
Richard II **24**: 383
Titus Andronicus **17**: 479
Twelfth Night **26**: 318

O'Connor, John J.
Hamlet **21**: 310
King John **24**: 232
Richard II **24**: 368
Troilus and Cressida **18**: 370

O'Dair, Sharon
Julius Caesar **25**: 272

O'Rourke, James
Macbeth **44**: 366
Troilus and Cressida **22**: 58

Pack, Robert
Macbeth **3**: 275

Page, Malcolm
Richard II **24**: 405

Page, Nadine
Much Ado about Nothing **8**: 44

Palmer, D. J.
As You Like It **5**: 128; **46**: 88
Julius Caesar **7**: 343
Macbeth **20**: 400
The Merchant of Venice **40**: 106
Titus Andronicus **4**: 668
Twelfth Night **1**: 648

Palmer, Daryl W.
The Winter's Tale **32**: 388

Palmer, John
Coriolanus **17**: 147
King John **9**: 260
Love's Labour's Lost **2**: 324
A Midsummer Night's Dream **3**: 406; **12**: 220

The Taming of the Shrew **12**: 333
Troilus and Cressida **18**: 284
The Winter's Tale **15**: 446

Pansinetti, P. M.
Julius Caesar **17**: 354

Panter-Downes, Mollie
Richard II **24**: 331

Paolucci, Anne
A Midsummer Night's Dream **3**: 494

Papp, Joseph
Troilus and Cressida **18**: 423

Paris, Bernard J.
Psychoanalytic Interpretations (topic entry) **44**: 89
Richard II **19**: 209

Parker, A. A.
Henry VIII **2**: 56

Parker, Barbara L.
Julius Caesar **25**: 280
Macbeth **47**: 41

Parker, Brian
Richard III **14**: 523

Parker, David
Sonnets **10**: 346

Parker, Patricia
Cymbeline **47**: 265
General Commentary **22**: 378

Parker, R. B.
All's Well That Ends Well **7**: 126
Coriolanus **50**: 145
King Lear **19**: 344

Parr, Wolstenholme
Coriolanus **9**: 13
Othello **4**: 396

Parrott, Thomas Marc
As You Like It **5**: 84
Love's Labour's Lost **2**: 327
A Midsummer Night's Dream **3**: 410
Timon of Athens **1**: 481
The Two Gentlemen of Verona **6**: 476

Parsons, Philip
Love's Labour's Lost **2**: 344

Parten, Anne
The Merchant of Venice **4**: 356
The Merry Wives of Windsor **38**: 300

Pasco, Richard
Richard II **24**: 346
Timon of Athens **20**: 494

Paster, Gail Kern
Julius Caesar **13**: 260

Pater, Walter
Love's Labour's Lost **2**: 308

Measure for Measure **2**: 409
Richard II **6**: 270

Patterson, Annabel
Henry V **13**: 194
A Midsummer Night's Dream **13**: 27

Paulin, Bernard
Timon of Athens **1**: 510

Payne, Ben Iden
Measure for Measure **23**: 294
The Merchant of Venice **12**: 131

Payne, Michael
The Tempest **45**: 272

Pearce, Edward
Twelfth Night **26**: 320

Pearce, Frances M.
All's Well That Ends Well **7**: 116

Pearce, G. M.
All's Well That Ends Well **26**: 51
Antony and Cleopatra **17**: 73
As You Like It **23**: 116, 124
Henry IV, 1 and 2 **14**: 104
King John **24**: 233
Love's Labour's Lost **23**: 222
Richard II **24**: 370
The Taming of the Shrew **12**: 395
Timon of Athens **20**: 473
Troilus and Cressida **18**: 365, 369

Pearce, Jill
Troilus and Cressida **18**: 388
Twelfth Night **26**: 326

Pearlman, E.
Henry V **32**: 157
Henry VI, 1, 2, and 3 **22**: 193; **37**: 165; **42**: 155
Richard III **22**: 193; **39**: 370
Romeo and Juliet **33**: 287

Pearson, Lu Emily
Venus and Adonis **10**: 427

Pearson, Norman Holmes
Antony and Cleopatra **6**: 142

Pechter, Edward
Henry IV, 1 and 2 **1**: 441
Othello **37**: 269

Pedicord, Harry William
King John **24**: 171

Pendelbury, B. J.
Cymbeline **51**: 30
Midsummer Night's Dream **51**: 30
Much Ado About Nothing **51**: 30
Othello **51**: 30
Twelfth Night **51**: 30
Two Gentlemen of Verona **51**: 30
Winter's Tale **51**: 30

Pepys, Samuel
Hamlet **21**: 9
Henry VIII **2**: 15
Macbeth **3**: 170; **20**: 11

Measure for Measure **23**: 267
The Merry Wives of Windsor **5**: 332
A Midsummer Night's Dream **3**: 361; **12**: 144
Romeo and Juliet **5**: 415; **11**: 377
The Tempest **15**: 189

Pequigney, Joseph
Desire (topic entry) **38**: 40
The Merchant of Venice **22**: 69
Sonnets **10**: 391
Twelfth Night **22**: 69

Percival, John
A Midsummer Night's Dream **12**: 250

Perret, Marion D.
The Taming of the Shrew **31**: 295

Perry, Ruth
Madness (topic entry) **35**: 1

Perry, Thomas A.
The Two Gentlemen of Verona **6**: 490

Peter, John
All's Well That Ends Well **26**: 44
Antony and Cleopatra **17**: 76
As You Like It **23**: 112
The Comedy of Errors **26**: 177
Hamlet **21**: 327
Henry VI, 1, 2, and 3 **24**: 47
Henry VIII **24**: 122
Julius Caesar **17**: 392, 406
King John **24**: 235
Measure for Measure **23**: 356
The Merry Wives of Windsor **18**: 58
Much Ado about Nothing **18**: 209
Richard III **14**: 486
The Taming of the Shrew **12**: 387
Titus Andronicus **17**: 477
Troilus and Cressida **18**: 361, 382
Twelfth Night **26**: 329

Peterson, Douglas L.
Cymbeline **4**: 141
Romeo and Juliet **5**: 533
The Tempest **8**: 439

Peterson, Kaara
Hamlet **48**: 255

Petronella, Vincent
The Comedy of Errors **34**: 233
The Phoenix and Turtle **10**: 45; **51**: 171

Pettet, E. C.
All's Well That Ends Well **7**: 43
King John **9**: 267
Measure for Measure **2**: 474
A Midsummer Night's Dream **3**: 408
Much Ado about Nothing **8**: 53
Romeo and Juliet **5**: 467
The Taming of the Shrew **9**: 342
Twelfth Night **1**: 580
The Two Gentlemen of Verona **6**: 478
The Two Noble Kinsmen **9**: 470

Pettigrew, John
  The Comedy of Errors 26: 155
  Henry V 14: 267
  Measure for Measure 23: 333
  Pericles 15: 156
  Timon of Athens 20: 459
  Twelfth Night 26: 290
  The Two Gentlemen of Verona 12: 486

Phelps, Samuel
  As You Like It 23: 18

Phelps, W. May
  King Lear 11: 21

Phialas, Peter G.
  As You Like It 5: 122
  The Comedy of Errors 1: 53
  Henry V 5: 267
  Love's Labour's Lost 38: 163
  The Merchant of Venice 4: 312
  A Midsummer Night's Dream 3: 450
  Much Ado about Nothing 31: 198
  Richard II 6: 352
  Twelfth Night 34: 270
  The Two Gentlemen of Verona 6: 516

Philip, Duke of Wharton
  Henry V 14: 175

Phillabaum, Corliss E.
  Timon of Athens 20: 446

Phillipps, Augustine
  Richard II 6: 249

Phillips, Graham
  Authorship Controversy (topic entry) 41: 76

Phillips, James E.
  Julius Caesar 17: 351

Phillips, James Emerson, Jr.
  Antony and Cleopatra 6: 107
  Henry V 14: 216
  Julius Caesar 7: 245
  Richard III 14: 429

Phillips, Robin
  Measure for Measure 23: 335

Pierce, Robert B.
  Henry VI, 1, 2, and 3 3: 126
  Richard II 6: 388
  Richard III 8: 248

Pietscher, A.
  The Merchant of Venice 4: 214

Pilkington, Ace G.
  Henry V 19: 217

Piper, William Bowman
  Sonnets 10: 360

Pitcher, John
  The Tempest 29: 355

Pittenger, Elizabeth
  The Merry Wives of Windsor 19: 101

Planche, James Robinson
  The Taming of the Shrew 12: 316

Platt, Peter G.
  Cymbeline 47: 252
  Pericles 42: 359

Playfair, Giles
  Macbeth 20: 95

Playfair, Nigel
  As You Like It 23: 60

Plotz, John
  Coriolanus 37: 283

Poel, William
  Henry V 14: 336
  King Lear 11: 142
  Macbeth 20: 350
  Measure for Measure 23: 405
  The Merchant of Venice 12: 111
  Romeo and Juliet 11: 499

Pollock, Lady
  As You Like It 23: 17
  Hamlet 21: 58

Poole, Adrian
  Richard II 28: 178

Poole, Kristen
  Henry IV, 1 and 2 32: 166

Pope, Alexander
  Cymbeline 4: 17
  Henry V 5: 187
  Richard II 6: 252
  Troilus and Cressida 3: 536
  The Two Gentlemen of Verona 6: 435
  The Two Noble Kinsmen 9: 444
  The Winter's Tale 7: 377

Pope, Elizabeth Marie
  Measure for Measure 2: 470

Popkin, Henry
  All's Well That Ends Well 26: 48
  Measure for Measure 23: 332
  Richard II 24: 378
  Timon of Athens 20: 469

Porter, Joseph A.
  Henry IV, 1 and 2 1: 439

Potter, John
  Cymbeline 4: 20
  The Merchant of Venice 4: 193
  The Merry Wives of Windsor 5: 335
  Othello 4: 390
  Timon of Athens 1: 455
  Twelfth Night 1: 543

Potter, Lois
  Julius Caesar 17: 405
  Love's Labour's Lost 23: 230
  Timon of Athens 20: 474

Potter, Nick
  As You Like It 16: 53
  King Lear 31: 84
  Twelfth Night 16: 53

Potter, Stephen
  Henry IV, 1 and 2 14: 30, 36
  Richard II 24: 314

Powell, Raymond
  Othello 32: 302

Prendergast, Maria Teresa Micaela
  Pericles 51: 126

Preston, Dennis R.
  Twelfth Night 34: 281

Price, Hereward T.
  Henry VI, 1, 2, and 3 3: 69
  Venus and Adonis 10: 434

Price, Jonathan Reeve
  King John 9: 290

Price, Joseph G.
  All's Well That Ends Well 26: 73, 97; 38: 72

Price, Thomas R.
  Love's Labour's Lost 2: 310
  The Winter's Tale 7: 399

Priestley, J. B.
  As You Like It 5: 63
  Henry IV, 1 and 2 1: 344
  Twelfth Night 1: 567

Priestley, Joseph
  King John 9: 215

Prince, F. T.
  The Phoenix and Turtle 10: 35
  The Rape of Lucrece 10: 81

Prior, Moody E.
  Henry V 5: 299
  Henry VI, 1, 2, and 3 39: 154

Pritchett, V. S.
  Much Ado about Nothing 18: 184
  Richard III 14: 453
  The Taming of the Shrew 12: 360

Procter, Bryan Waller
  Hamlet 21: 44
  Macbeth 20: 91
  The Merchant of Venice 12: 13
  Othello 11: 199
  Romeo and Juliet 11: 396

Prosser, Eleanor
  Hamlet 1: 254; 35: 152

Proudfoot, Richard
  A Midsummer Night's Dream 12: 268

Prouse, Derek
  Richard III 14: 423

Prouty, Charles Tyler
  Twelfth Night 34: 323

Pryce-Jones, Alan
  The Comedy of Errors 26: 153
  The Two Gentlemen of Verona 12: 473

Pryce-Jones, David
  Henry VI, 1, 2, and 3 24: 21
  Othello 11: 298

Puckler-Muskau, Prince
  Macbeth 20: 96

Pugliatti, Paolo
  Henry IV, 1 and 2 48: 167
  Henry V 25: 131

Puknat, Elisabeth M.
  Romeo and Juliet 11: 414

Purdom, C. B.
  Henry VIII 2: 65

Pursell, Michael
  The Taming of the Shrew 12: 378

Pushkin, A. S.
  Henry VI, 1 and 2 1: 313
  Measure for Measure 2: 399

Putney, Rufus
  Venus and Adonis 10: 442

Pye, Christopher
  Henry V 16: 202
  King Lear 16: 202
  Macbeth 16: 328
  Richard II 16: 202

Quayle, Anthony
  Henry IV, 1 and 2 14: 38

Quiller-Couch, Sir Arthur
  All's Well That Ends Well 7: 29
  Antony and Cleopatra 6: 71
  As You Like It 5: 61
  The Comedy of Errors 1: 19
  Cymbeline 15: 105
  Macbeth 3: 229
  Measure for Measure 2: 420
  The Merchant of Venice 4: 228
  Much Ado about Nothing 8: 41
  The Taming of the Shrew 9: 332
  The Tempest 8: 334
  Twelfth Night 1: 569
  The Two Gentlemen of Verona 6: 466
  The Winter's Tale 7: 414

Quinn, Michael
  Richard II 6: 338

Rabkin, Leslie Y.
  Othello 35: 276

Rabkin, Norman
  Antony and Cleopatra 6: 180
  Coriolanus 30: 96
  Henry V 5: 304
  Julius Caesar 7: 316
  The Merchant of Venice 4: 350
  Richard II 6: 364
  Romeo and Juliet 5: 538
  Troilus and Cressida 3: 613
  Venus and Adonis 10: 462

Rackin, Phyllis
  Antony and Cleopatra 6: 197; 27: 135

Coriolanus **9**: 189
Henry IV, 1 and 2 **16**: 183
Henry V **16**: 183
Henry VI, 1, 2, and 3 **16**: 183; **39**: 196
King John **9**: 303; **41**: 215
King Lear **2**: 269
Politics and Power (topic entry) **30**: 46
Richard III **25**: 141
Shakespeare's Representation of Women (topic entry) **31**: 48

Radel, Nicholas F.
The Two Noble Kinsmen **41**: 326

Raleigh, Walter
Cymbeline **4**: 48
Measure for Measure **2**: 417
Pericles **2**: 554
Rape of Lucrece **10**: 70
Timon of Athens **1**: 477
Venus and Adonis **10**: 423

Ramsey, Jarold W.
Timon of Athens **1**: 513

Ranald, Margaret Loftus
The Comedy of Errors **26**: 180
The Taming of the Shrew **31**: 282, 326

Ransley, Peter
Twelfth Night **26**: 284

Ransom, John Crowe
Sonnets **10**: 260

Ratcliffe, Michael
Antony and Cleopatra **17**: 78
As You Like It **23**: 138
Coriolanus **17**: 209
Henry VI, 1, 2, and 3 **24**: 45
Julius Caesar **17**: 392, 405
King John **24**: 235
Love's Labour's Lost **23**: 214
Pericles **15**: 175
Richard III **14**: 485
Romeo and Juliet **11**: 483
The Taming of the Shrew **12**: 398
Titus Andronicus **17**: 485
Twelfth Night **26**: 315

Rauchut, E. A.
Henry IV, 1 and 2 **49**: 137

Ravenscroft, Edward
Titus Andronicus **4**: 613

Ravich, Robert A.
Psychoanalytic Interpretations (topic entry) **44**: 1

Ray, Robin
Antony and Cleopatra **17**: 78

Ray, Sid
Titus Andronicus **48**: 264

Read, David
Henry IV, Parts 1 and 2 **42**: 164
Henry V **42**: 164

Rebhorn, Wayne A.
Henry IV, 1 and 2 **39**: 130
Julius Caesar **16**: 231; **30**: 379; **50**: 211
Venus and Adonis **33**: 321

Rede, W. L.
The Merchant of Venice **12**: 12

Redfern, James
Hamlet **21**: 181

Redfern, Stephen
Henry IV, 1 and 2 **14**: 31

Redgrave, Michael
Antony and Cleopatra **17**: 38

Reed, Robert Rentoul, Jr.
Magic and the Supernatural (topic entry) **29**: 53

Rees, Roger
Cymbeline **15**: 88

Reese, Jack E.
Titus Andronicus **17**: 501

Reese, M. M.
Henry IV, 1 and 2 **39**: 134
Henry V **30**: 237
Henry VI, 1, 2, and 3 **3**: 77
King John **9**: 280
Richard III **8**: 228

Reibetanz, John
King Lear **2**: 281

Reid, B. L.
Hamlet **1**: 242

Reid, Stephen
Othello **35**: 301

Reik, Theodor
The Merchant of Venice **4**: 268

Reynolds, Frederick
Much Ado about Nothing **18**: 115

Reynolds, George F.
Hamlet **21**: 407

Reynolds, Sir Joshua
Macbeth **3**: 181

Ribner, Irving
Henry VI, 1, 2, and 3 **3**: 100
Julius Caesar **7**: 279
King Lear **2**: 218
Macbeth **3**: 289
Othello **4**: 527, 559
Richard II **6**: 305
Romeo and Juliet **5**: 493
The Taming of the Shrew **9**: 390
Titus Andronicus **4**: 656

Rice, Julian
Othello **35**: 352

Rich, Alan
Henry V **14**: 290

Rich, Frank
Coriolanus **17**: 217
Julius Caesar **17**: 401
Measure for Measure **23**: 351
Much Ado about Nothing **18**: 217
Othello **11**: 319
Richard II **24**: 375
Richard III **14**: 479

Richard, David
Henry V **14**: 337
Othello **11**: 317

Richardson, D. L.
Sonnets **10**: 174

Richardson, Ian
Richard II **24**: 346

Richardson, Jack
Richard III **14**: 471

Richardson, Ralph
A Midsummer Night's Dream **12**: 284

Richardson, William
As You Like It **5**: 20
Hamlet **1**: 88
Henry IV, 1 and 2 **1**: 307
King Lear **2**: 103
Richard III **8**: 154
Timon of Athens **1**: 456

Richman, David
Much Ado about Nothing **18**: 264

Richmond, H. M.
Henry VIII **41**: 171

Richmond, Hugh M.
As You Like It **5**: 133
Cymbeline **47**: 260
Henry V **5**: 271
Henry VI, 1, 2, and 3 **3**: 109
Henry VIII **2**: 76; **28**: 184
Julius Caesar **7**: 333
A Midsummer Night's Dream **3**: 480
Richard II **39**: 256
Richard III **16**: 137

Ridley, M. R.
Antony and Cleopatra **6**: 140
King John **9**: 250
The Taming of the Shrew **9**: 337

Riemer, A. P.
Antony and Cleopatra **6**: 189
As You Like It **5**: 156
Love's Labour's Lost **2**: 374
Much Ado about Nothing **8**: 108

Riggs, David
Henry VI, 1, 2, and 3 **3**: 119
Richard III **39**: 335

Ripley, John
Coriolanus **17**: 232, 248
Julius Caesar **17**: 345

Riss, Arthur
Coriolanus **22**: 248

Rissik, Andrew
Antony and Cleopatra **17**: 80

Ristori, Adelaide
Macbeth **20**: 345

Ritchey, David
Richard III **14**: 527

Ritson, Joseph
Hamlet **1**: 90
Julius Caesar **7**: 158

Rives, Amelie
The Taming of the Shrew **12**: 325

Roberts, Jeanne Addison
The Merry Wives of Windsor **5**: 369; **38**: 297; **47**: 358, 375

Roberts, Josephine A.
Sonnets **37**: 373

Roberts, Peter
The Comedy of Errors **26**: 147
Cymbeline **15**: 60
Hamlet **21**: 283
Henry IV, 1 and 2 **14**: 74
Henry V **14**: 273
Henry VI, 1, 2, and 3 **24**: 22
Julius Caesar **17**: 375
King Lear **11**: 84, 97
Measure for Measure **23**: 347
The Merchant of Venice **12**: 67
The Merry Wives of Windsor **18**: 43
Much Ado about Nothing **18**: 179, 189, 213, 216
Othello **11**: 304
Pericles **15**: 152
Richard II **24**: 332, 338
Richard III **14**: 459, 465
The Taming of the Shrew **12**: 385
Troilus and Cressida **18**: 332
Twelfth Night **26**: 271
The Two Gentlemen of Verona **12**: 483
The Winter's Tale **15**: 473, 480

Robertson, John M.
The Rape of Lucrece **10**: 70

Robertson, W. Graham
The Merchant of Venice **12**: 35

Robinson, David
The Taming of the Shrew **12**: 370
The Tempest **15**: 294

Robinson, Henry Crabb
Hamlet **21**: 43
King Lear **11**: 12, 18
A Midsummer Night's Dream **12**: 153
Othello **11**: 193
Pericles **15**: 135
Richard II **24**: 269
The Taming of the Shrew **12**: 316
The Tempest **15**: 210
The Two Gentlemen of Verona **12**: 452

Robson, Flora
The Winter's Tale **15**: 528

Roche, Thomas P.
Sonnets 10: 353

Roderick, Richard
Henry VIII 2: 16

Roe, John
The Phoenix and Turtle 38: 334
Rape of Lucrece 43: 92

Roesen, Bobbyann
Love's Labour's Lost 2: 331

Rogers, Paul
A Midsummer Night's Dream 12: 238

Rogers, Robert
Othello 35: 320

Rogoff, Gordon
Hamlet 21: 240
Julius Caesar 17: 402
Richard II 24: 377

Ronk, Martha
Hamlet 44: 248
Psychoanalytic Interpretations (topic entry) 44: 66
The Winter's Tale 36: 349

Rose, Mark
Julius Caesar 30: 374

Rosen, William
Antony and Cleopatra 6: 165

Rosenberg, Marvin
King Lear 11: 161
Macbeth 20: 297, 338, 387
Othello 11: 344

Rosenfeld, Megan
Love's Labour's Lost 23: 221

Rosenfeld, Sybil
Coriolanus 17: 140
The Two Gentlemen of Verona 12: 453

Ross, Daniel W.
Hamlet 13: 296

Ross, Lawrence J.
Othello 11: 354

Ross, T. A.
The Merchant of Venice 4: 238

Rossi, Alfred
A Midsummer Night's Dream 12: 238

Rossiter, A. P.
Coriolanus 9: 106; 30: 89
Henry V 30: 193
Much Ado about Nothing 8: 69
Richard II 6: 343
Richard III 8: 201

Rossky, William
The Two Gentlemen of Verona 40: 354

Rostron, David
Henry V 14: 180
Henry VIII 24: 74
Julius Caesar 17: 274

Rothschild, Herbert B., Jr.
Henry IV, 1 and 2 1: 433
Richard II 6: 381

Rothwell, Kenneth
Henry V 14: 315
The Taming of the Shrew 12: 402

Rothwell, Kenneth S.
All's Well That Ends Well 26: 51
Macbeth 20: 277

Rougement, Denis de
Romeo and Juliet 5: 484

Rowe, Katherine A.
Titus Andronicus 43: 262

Rowe, Nicholas
Hamlet 1: 74; 21: 9
Henry IV, 1 and 2 1: 286
Henry V 5: 186
Henry VI, 1, 2, and 3 3: 17
Henry VIII 2: 15
The Merchant of Venice 4: 191
The Merry Wives of Windsor 5: 334
Romeo and Juliet 5: 415
The Tempest 8: 287
Timon of Athens 1: 453
The Winter's Tale 7: 376

Rowse, A. L.
Sonnets 10: 377

Roy, Emil
Troilus and Cressida 43: 287

Rozett, Martha Tuck
Antony and Cleopatra 47: 165

Rozmovits, Linda
The Merchant of Venice 48: 77

Rubenstein, Frankie
Dreams in Shakespeare (topic entry) 45: 1

Rudnytsky, Peter L.
Henry VIII 41: 146

Ruskin, John
The Tempest 8: 307

Russell, Edward R.
King Lear 11: 42
The Tempest 8: 311

Russell, Robert
The Taming of the Shrew 12: 365

Rustin, Michael
Romeo and Juliet 33: 225

Rutherford, Malcolm
All's Well That Ends Well 26: 70
Hamlet 21: 324, 331
Julius Caesar 17: 369
Macbeth 20: 314

Troilus and Cressida 18: 391
Twelfth Night 26: 328

Rutter, Carol
All's Well That Ends Well 19: 113

Rylands, George
Antony and Cleopatra 17: 24
Othello 11: 295
Pericles 15: 139
Romeo and Juliet 11: 458

Rylands, George H. W.
The Rape of Lucrece 10: 71
Sonnets 10: 255

Rymer, Thomas
Julius Caesar 7: 150
Othello 4: 370

Sacharoff, Mark
Julius Caesar 30: 358

Sage, Lorna
The Taming of the Shrew 12: 390

Salgaudo, Gaumini
Magic and the Supernatural (topic entry) 29: 46

Salingar, L. G.
Twelfth Night 1: 603

Salinger, Leo
King Lear 31: 77
The Merry Wives of Windsor 47: 308

Salkeld, Duncan
Hamlet 35: 140

Salomon, Patricia P.
Henry V 32: 185

Salvini, Tommaso
King Lear 11: 29
Othello 11: 229

Sampson, Martin W.
The Two Gentlemen of Verona 6: 465

Sams, Eric
Twelfth Night 26: 332

Sanders, Norman
Henry IV, 1 and 2 49: 112
Julius Caesar 30: 316
The Two Gentlemen of Verona 6: 519

Sanderson, James L.
The Comedy of Errors 1: 66

Sanfield, Keith
Macbeth 20: 315

Santayana, George
Hamlet 1: 128

Sargent, Ralph M.
The Two Gentlemen of Verona 6: 480

Sarkar, Malabika
Sonnets 48: 346

Sasayama, Takashi
Hamlet 28: 325
King Lear 28: 325

Saunders, J. G.
King Lear 37: 295

Saunders, J. W.
Antony and Cleopatra 17: 110
Henry VIII 24: 155

Schalkwyk, David
Sonnets 48: 352
The Winter's Tale 22: 324

Schanzer, Ernest
Antony and Cleopatra 27: 32
Julius Caesar 7: 268, 272
Measure for Measure 2: 503
A Midsummer Night's Dream 3: 411
Pericles 2: 579
The Winter's Tale 7: 473

Schein, Harry
Richard III 14: 432

Scheye, Thomas E.
The Two Gentlemen of Verona 6: 547

Schiffer, James
Venus and Adonis 51: 368

Schiffhorst, Gerald J.
Pericles 36: 244

Schlegel, August Wilhelm
All's Well That Ends Well 7: 9
Antony and Cleopatra 6: 24
As You Like It 5: 24
The Comedy of Errors 1: 13
Coriolanus 9: 14
Cymbeline 4: 21
Hamlet 1: 92
Henry IV, 1 and 2 1: 309
Henry V 5: 192
Henry VI, 1, 2, and 3 3: 24
Henry VIII 2: 22
Julius Caesar 7: 159
King John 9: 218
King Lear 2: 104
Love's Labour's Lost 2: 301
Macbeth 3: 183
Measure for Measure 2: 395
The Merchant of Venice 4: 194
The Merry Wives of Windsor 5: 336
A Midsummer Night's Dream 3: 364
Much Ado about Nothing 8: 13
Othello 4: 400
Richard II 6: 255
Richard III 8: 159
Romeo and Juliet 5: 421
Sonnets 10: 159
The Taming of the Shrew 9: 320
The Tempest 8: 294
Timon of Athens 1: 459
Titus Andronicus 4: 616

Troilus and Cressida **3**: 539
Twelfth Night **1**: 543
The Two Gentlemen of Verona **6**: 439
The Two Noble Kinsmen **9**: 446
The Winter's Tale **7**: 382

Schlegel, Frederick
Sonnets **10**: 160

Schlueter, June
King Lear **19**: 295

Schlueter, Kurt
The Two Gentlemen of Verona **40**: 320

Schmidt, Dana Adams
As You Like It **23**: 96

Schneider, Michael
A Midsummer Night's Dream **45**: 160

Schneider, Pierre
Timon of Athens **20**: 466

Schoen, Elin
Othello **11**: 319

Schoenbaum, S.
Authorship Controversy (topic entry) **41**: 18
Love's Labour's Lost **23**: 211
The Merchant of Venice **12**: 94
The Taming of the Shrew **12**: 393

Schork, R. J.
Cymbeline **47**: 274

Schucking, Levin L.
Antony and Cleopatra **6**: 67
Julius Caesar **7**: 207
King Lear **2**: 151
The Tempest **8**: 336

Schwartz, Elias
The Phoenix and Turtle **38**: 342

Schwartz, Kathryn
Henry IV, 1 and 2 **48**: 175

Scofield, Martin
King Lear **48**: 277
Measure for Measure **48**: 277
Othello **48**: 277
Titus Andronicus **48**: 277

Scofield, Paul
Timon of Athens **20**: 464

Scott, Clement
Hamlet **21**: 96, 132
King Lear **11**: 34
Macbeth **20**: 130
The Merchant of Venice **12**: 17
Much Ado about Nothing **18**: 120
Othello **11**: 243
Romeo and Juliet **11**: 427

Scott, Margaret
Measure for Measure **49**: 286

Scott, William O.
The Two Gentlemen of Verona **6**: 511

Scuro, Daniel
Titus Andronicus **17**: 452

Sedgwick, Eve Kosofsky
Sonnets **40**: 254

Sedulus
Much Ado about Nothing **18**: 198

Seelig, Sharon Cadman
Richard II **32**: 189; **39**: 279

Seiden, Melvin
King Lear **2**: 284
Measure for Measure **49**: 300
Twelfth Night **1**: 632

Seltzer, Daniel
Othello **11**: 350
The Phoenix and Turtle **10**: 37

Sen Gupta, S. C.
As You Like It **5**: 86
The Comedy of Errors **1**: 34
Henry VI, 1, 2, and 3 **3**: 92
Love's Labour's Lost **2**: 328
Troilus and Cressida **3**: 583

Sen, Sailendra Kumar
Coriolanus **9**: 130

Seoufos, Alice-Lyle
As You Like It **5**: 162

Seronsy, Cecil C.
The Taming of the Shrew **9**: 370

Sewall, Richard B.
King Lear **2**: 226

Seward, Thomas
Antony and Cleopatra **6**: 21

Sewell, Arthur
Henry IV, 1 and 2 **1**: 396
King Lear **2**: 197
Measure for Measure **2**: 484

Sewell, Elizabeth
A Midsummer Night's Dream **3**: 432

Sewell, George
Sonnets **10**: 154

Sexton, Joyce H.
Cymbeline **47**: 277
Shakespeare's Representation of Women (topic entry) **31**: 34

Sexton, Joyce Hengerer
Much Ado about Nothing **8**: 104

Seymour, Alan
Othello **11**: 301

Shaaber, M. A.
Henry IV, 1 and 2 **1**: 387

Shabani, Ranjee G.
The Phoenix and Turtle **10**: 21

Shakespeare, William
Venus and Adonis **10**: 409

Shannon, Laurie J.
The Two Noble Kinsmen **41**: 372; **42**: 368

Shapiro, James
Henry IV, 1 and 2 **19**: 233
Henry V **19**: 233
The Merchant of Venice **32**: 66
Richard II **19**: 233

Shapiro, Michael
Cymbeline **47**: 245
The Merchant of Venice **40**: 156
The Taming of the Shrew **31**: 315
The Two Gentlemen of Verona **40**: 374

Shapiro, Stephen A.
Othello **35**: 317
Romeo and Juliet **5**: 516

Sharp, Cecil
A Midsummer Night's Dream **12**: 289

Shattuck, Charles H.
Julius Caesar **17**: 277, 287
As You Like It **23**: 20, 54
Hamlet **21**: 72, 145
Henry V **14**: 200
King John **24**: 187
Measure for Measure **23**: 282
A Midsummer Night's Dream **12**: 199
The Merry Wives of Windsor **18**: 15, 22, 31
Othello **11**: 327
Twelfth Night **26**: 211, 219

Shaw, Bernard
Antony and Cleopatra **6**: 52
All's Well That Ends Well **26**: 9
As You Like It **5**: 52; **23**: 51
Coriolanus **9**: 42
Cymbeline **4**: 45; **15**: 23, 32
Hamlet **21**: 129, 154
Henry IV, 1 and 2 **1**: 328, 332; **14**: 24
Henry V **5**: 209
Julius Caesar **7**: 187, 188; **17**: 306
The Merchant of Venice **12**: 33
A Midsummer Night's Dream **12**: 194
Much Ado about Nothing **8**: 38; **18**: 146, 152
Othello **4**: 433, 442; **11**: 335
Richard III **8**: 181, 182, **14**: 402
Romeo and Juliet **11**: 438
The Taming of the Shrew **9**: 329
The Tempest **15**: 223
The Two Gentlemen of Verona **12**: 454

Shaw, Catherine M.
Henry IV, 1 and 2 **49**: 186

Shaw, Glen Byam
Julius Caesar **17**: 419
Macbeth **20**: 242

Shaw, William P.
Troilus and Cressida **18**: 332

Shebbeare, John
Othello **4**: 388

Shelley, Percy Bysshe
King Lear **2**: 110
The Two Noble Kinsmen **9**: 447

Sheppard, Samuel
Pericles **2**: 537

Sher, Antony
King Lear **11**: 169

Sheridan, Thomas
Hamlet **1**: 83

Shewey, Don
Coriolanus **17**: 238

Shickman, Allan R.
King Lear **46**: 205

Shindler, Robert
Sonnets **10**: 230

Shorter, Eric
As You Like It **23**: 141
Timon of Athens **20**: 466

Showalter, Elaine
Madness (topic entry) **35**: 54

Shrimpton, Nicholas
All's Well That Ends Well **26**: 63
As You Like It **23**: 143
The Comedy of Errors **26**: 169
Coriolanus **17**: 215
Hamlet **21**: 317
Henry IV, 1 and 2 **14**: 110
Henry VIII **24**: 124
King John **24**: 230
Love's Labour's Lost **23**: 220
Macbeth **20**: 312
Measure for Measure **23**: 350
The Merry Wives of Windsor **18**: 63
A Midsummer Night's Dream **12**: 275
Richard III **14**: 488
Romeo and Juliet **11**: 486
The Tempest **15**: 368
Troilus and Cressida **18**: 383
Twelfth Night **26**: 307

Shulman, Jeffrey
A Midsummer Night's Dream **45**: 136

Shumaker, Wayne
Magic and the Supernatural (topic entry) **29**: 28

Shurgot, Michael W.
The Taming of the Shrew **12**: 435
Troilus and Cressida **18**: 451

Shuttleworth, Betram
Macbeth **20**: 146

Siddons, Sarah
Macbeth **20**: 60
The Winter's Tale **15**: 400

Siegel, Paul N.
  Hamlet 25: 288
  Macbeth 3: 280
  A Midsummer Night's Dream 3: 417
  Othello 4: 525
  Romeo and Juliet 5: 505

Siemon, James Edward
  Cymbeline 4: 155
  The Merchant of Venice 4: 319

Sierz, Alex
  Macbeth 20: 318

Simeon, James R.
  Richard II 28: 188

Simmons, J. L.
  Coriolanus 50: 105
  Henry IV, 1 and 2 25: 151
  Henry V 25: 151
  Henry VI, 1, 2, and 3 25: 151
  The Two Gentlemen of Verona 40: 343

Simon, Francesca
  Henry IV, 1 and 2 14: 98

Simon, John
  All's Well That Ends Well 26: 59
  The Comedy of Errors 26: 175, 182
  Coriolanus 17: 219
  Hamlet 21: 243, 290
  Henry V 14: 292, 305
  King Lear 11: 106
  Love's Labour's Lost 23: 227
  Measure for Measure 23: 353
  A Midsummer Night's Dream 12: 298
  Much Ado about Nothing 18: 193, 221, 225
  Richard II 24: 354, 376
  Richard III 14: 480, 14: 470
  Twelfth Night 26: 314

Simpson, Percy
  Julius Caesar 17: 311

Simpson, Richard
  Sonnets 10: 205

Sinclair, Andrew
  The Taming of the Shrew 12: 398

Sinden, Donald
  King Lear 11: 165
  Twelfth Night 26: 273

Sinfield, Alan
  The Merchant of Venice 37: 86

Singh, Jyotsna
  Antony and Cleopatra 47: 113

Singleton, Mary
  King Lear 11: 8

Sirluck, Katherine A.
  The Taming of the Shrew 19: 122

Sisk, John P.
  The Merchant of Venice 4: 317

Sisson, C. J.
  The Taming of the Shrew 12: 430

Sitwell, Edith
  Macbeth 3: 256

Skeele, David
  Pericles 48: 364; 51: 99

Skinner, Richard Dana
  Troilus and Cressida 18: 296

Skura, Meredith Anne
  Clowns and Fools (topic entry) 46: 29
  Psychoanalytic Interpretations (topic entry) 44: 28
  Richard II 42: 175
  Richard III 25: 164
  The Tempest 13: 425

Slater, Ann Pasternak
  Twelfth Night 26: 303

Slights, Camille Wells
  The Merchant of Venice 4: 342
  Much Ado about Nothing 25: 77
  The Taming of the Shrew 13: 3
  The Two Gentlemen of Verona 6: 568

Slights, William W. E.
  Timon of Athens 1: 525

Slulsky, Harold
  Hamlet 35: 157

Small, S. Asa
  Henry IV, 1 and 2 1: 353

Smallwood, R. L.
  Henry IV, 1 and 2 14: 105

Smallwood, Robert
  As You Like It 23: 149
  Love's Labour's Lost 23: 232
  Measure for Measure 23: 359
  Pericles 15: 177
  Richard II 24: 383
  Troilus and Cressida 18: 392

Smidt, Kristian
  Hamlet 16: 259
  Pericles 25: 365

Smith, Bruce R.
  Sonnets 40: 264

Smith, Gordon Ross
  Henry V 30: 262
  Julius Caesar 7: 292; 30: 351

Smith, Hallett
  Sonnets 51: 316

Smith, James
  Much Ado about Nothing 8: 48; 31: 229

Smith, Lisa Gordon
  The Taming of the Shrew 12: 357

Smith, Marion Bodwell
  The Comedy of Errors 1: 49

Smith, Peter D.
  The Taming of the Shrew 12: 367

Smith, Peter J.
  Twelfth Night 26: 332

Smith, Rebecca
  Hamlet 35: 229

Smith, Warren D.
  Romeo and Juliet 5: 536

Smith, William
  Julius Caesar 7: 155

Smollett, Tobias
  Hamlet 1: 82

Snider, Denton J.
  Antony and Cleopatra 6: 43
  As You Like It 5: 46
  Coriolanus 9: 33
  Cymbeline 4: 38
  Henry V 5: 205
  Henry VI, 1, 2, and 3 3: 42
  Henry VIII 2: 39
  King John 9: 235
  King Lear 2: 133
  Love's Labour's Lost 2: 312
  Macbeth 3: 208
  Measure for Measure 2: 411
  The Merchant of Venice 4: 215
  The Merry Wives of Windsor 5: 343
  A Midsummer Night's Dream 3: 381
  Much Ado about Nothing 8: 29
  Othello 4: 427
  Richard II 6: 272
  Richard III 8: 177
  Romeo and Juliet 5: 438
  The Taming of the Shrew 9: 325
  The Tempest 8: 320
  Timon of Athens 1: 472
  Troilus and Cressida 3: 549
  The Two Gentlemen of Verona 6: 450
  The Winter's Tale 7: 402

Snyder, Susan
  All's Well That Ends Well 22: 78
  Macbeth 44: 373
  Othello 4: 575
  Romeo and Juliet 5: 547; 51: 245

Soellner, Rolf
  Timon of Athens 1: 531; 27: 191

Solomon, Alisa
  Love's Labour's Lost 23: 228
  Much Ado about Nothing 18: 226
  The Tempest 15: 290

Solway, David
  Pericles 51: 97

Solway, Diane
  Twelfth Night 26: 312

Sommers, Alan
  Titus Andronicus 4: 653

Southall, Raymond
  Troilus and Cressida 3: 606

Spalding, William
  The Two Noble Kinsmen 9: 448

Spanabel, Robert R.
  Henry V 14: 189

Spargo, John Webster
  Henry IV, 1 and 2 1: 342

Speaight, Robert
  All's Well That Ends Well 26: 47
  Antony and Cleopatra 17: 60
  As You Like It 23: 92, 107
  The Comedy of Errors 26: 148
  Cymbeline 15: 79
  Hamlet 21: 254, 257, 284
  Henry IV, 1 and 2 14: 75, 79, 88
  Henry V 14: 274
  Henry VIII 24: 117
  Julius Caesar 17: 370, 378, 383
  King Lear 11: 77, 99
  Love's Labour's Lost 23: 198, 202
  Macbeth 20: 260, 294
  Measure for Measure 23: 287, 324, 328
  Much Ado about Nothing 18: 181, 190
  Othello 11: 304
  Richard II 24: 296, 333, 351
  Richard III 14: 455, 466
  Romeo and Juliet 11: 463
  The Taming of the Shrew 12: 357
  The Tempest 8: 390; 15: 224, 273, 283
  Timon of Athens 20: 463
  Troilus and Cressida 18: 289, 327, 347
  Twelfth Night 26: 255, 263, 269, 284
  The Two Gentlemen of Verona 12: 457, 478, 484
  The Winter's Tale 15: 427, 482, 489

Speaight, Robert W.
  Pericles 15: 154

Spedding, James
  Henry VIII 2: 28

Spencer, Anthony
  Richard III 14: 357

Spencer, Benjamin T.
  Antony and Cleopatra 6: 159
  Henry IV, 1 and 2 1: 372

Spencer, Hazelton
  Henry IV, 1 and 2 14: 116
  Henry VI, 1, 2, and 3 24: 6
  Macbeth 20: 12
  Measure for Measure 23: 269, 276
  The Merry Wives of Windsor 18: 10
  Much Ado about Nothing 8: 47
  Richard II 24: 263
  Timon of Athens 20: 429
  Troilus and Cressida 18: 281

Spencer, Janet M.
  Henry V 37: 175

Spencer, T. J. B.
  Julius Caesar 30: 285

Shakespeare and Classical Civilization (topic entry) 27: 56

Spencer, Theodore
Hamlet 1: 169
Henry IV, 1 and 2 1: 366
King Lear 2: 174
Macbeth 3: 248
Pericles 2: 564
The Two Noble Kinsmen 9: 463

Spender, Stephen
Macbeth 3: 246

Spinrad, Phoebe S.
King Lear 46: 264
Measure for Measure 22: 85; 49: 370
Much Ado about Nothing 22: 85

Spivack, Bernard
Othello 4: 545
Richard III 8: 213
Titus Andronicus 4: 650

Sprague, Arthur Colby
Hamlet 21: 11, 35, 392
Henry IV, 1 and 2 14: 10, 133
Henry V 14: 319
Henry VI, 1, 2, and 3 24: 51
Henry VIII 24: 140, 152
Macbeth 20: 65, 113
The Merchant of Venice 12: 36
The Merry Wives of Windsor 18: 68
Othello 11: 202, 257
Richard II 24: 395
Richard III 14: 517
Twelfth Night 26: 360
The Winter's Tale 15: 517

Sprengnether, Madelon
Antony and Cleopatra 13: 368
Coriolanus 30: 142
Psychoanalytic Interpretations (topic entry) 44: 93

Sprigg, Douglas C.
Troilus and Cressida 18: 442

Spurgeon, Caroline F. E.
Antony and Cleopatra 6: 92
Coriolanus 9: 64
Cymbeline 4: 61
Hamlet 1: 153
Henry IV, 1 and 2 1: 358
Henry VI, 1, 2, and 3 3: 52
Henry VIII 2: 45
Julius Caesar 7: 242
King John 9: 246
King Lear 2: 161
Love's Labour's Lost 2: 320
Macbeth 3: 245
Measure for Measure 2: 431
The Merchant of Venice 4: 241
Much Ado about Nothing 8: 46
Pericles 2: 560
Richard II 6: 283
Richard III 8: 186
Romeo and Juliet 5: 456
The Taming of the Shrew 9: 336
Timon of Athens 1: 488
The Winter's Tale 7: 418

Spurling, Hilary
All's Well That Ends Well 26: 45
As You Like It 23: 97
Hamlet 21: 281
Henry VIII 24: 116
Julius Caesar 17: 372, 377
King John 24: 217
Macbeth 20: 259
Measure for Measure 23: 323
The Merry Wives of Windsor 18: 38
Pericles 15: 149
The Tempest 15: 270
Troilus and Cressida 18: 344, 351
Twelfth Night 26: 260, 267
The Winter's Tale 15: 478

Squire, Jack Collings
Macbeth 20: 172

Squire, Sir John
Henry VIII 2: 44

St. George, Andrew
Love's Labour's Lost 23: 229
Measure for Measure 23: 356
Richard II 24: 379

St. John, Christopher
The Merry Wives of Windsor 18: 27

Stack, Rev. Richard
Henry IV, 1 and 2 1: 306

Staebler, Warren
As You Like It 5: 82

Stallybrass, Peter
Macbeth 29: 120

Stamm, R.
Romeo and Juliet 51: 212

Stampfer, Judah
Julius Caesar 7: 339
King Lear 2: 231

Stanhope, Lord
Much Ado about Nothing 8: 8

Stanislavski, Constantin
Othello 11: 233

Stanivukovic, Goran
Venus and Adonis 51: 352

Stapfer, Paul
Julius Caesar 7: 169

Stapleton, M. L.
Sonnets 25: 374

Starkey, David
Henry VIII 24: 120

Stauffer, Donald A.
Cymbeline 4: 87
Julius Caesar 7: 257
The Merry Wives of Windsor 5: 353
Pericles 2: 569
Romeo and Juliet 5: 469

The Taming of the Shrew 9: 343
The Two Gentlemen of Verona 6: 479

Steadman, John M.
The Merry Wives of Windsor 38: 286

Stedman, Jane W.
Pericles 15: 161
The Tempest 15: 283

Steele, Richard
Hamlet 21: 9

Steele, Sir Richard
See also Bickerstaff, Isaac
Hamlet 1: 74
Twelfth Night 1: 540

Steevens, George
See also Collier, Jeremy; Hic et Ubique; Longinus; Lorenzo
Antony and Cleopatra 6: 24
The Comedy of Errors 1: 13
Cymbeline 4: 20, 21
King Lear 11: 7, 8
Macbeth 3: 182
Measure for Measure 2: 393
Much Ado about Nothing 8: 12
Pericles 2: 540
Richard III 8: 159
Sonnets 10: 155, 156
Titus Andronicus 4: 616
Troilus and Cressida 3: 538
Twelfth Night 1: 543
The Two Noble Kinsmen 9: 445
Venus and Adonis 10: 411

Stein, Arnold
Macbeth 3: 263
Troilus and Cressida 43: 277

Stein, Rita
Richard II 24: 353

Steinberg, Theodore L.
Venus and Adonis 33: 352

Stempel, Daniel
Antony and Cleopatra 6: 146
Othello 35: 336

Stephenson, A. A., S.J.
Cymbeline 4: 73

Stephenson, William E.
The Two Gentlemen of Verona 6: 514

Sterne, Richard L.
Hamlet 21: 237, 245

Sternroyd, Vincent
Much Ado about Nothing 18: 134

Sterrit, David
The Taming of the Shrew 12: 399

Stewart, J. I. M.
Henry IV, 1 and 2 1: 389
Julius Caesar 7: 250
Othello 4: 500

Stewart, Patrick
The Merchant of Venice 12: 97

Still, Colin
The Tempest 8: 328

Stirling, Brents
Antony and Cleopatra 6: 151
Julius Caesar 7: 259
Macbeth 3: 271
Othello 4: 486, 536
Richard II 6: 307

Stockard, Emily E.
Sonnets 42: 382

Stockholder, Kay
Macbeth 44: 297; 45: 58
The Merchant of Venice 45: 17
Pericles 51: 110
The Winter's Tale 45: 358

Stoker, Bram
Much Ado about Nothing 18: 132
Romeo and Juliet 11: 433

Stokes, Margaret
As You Like It 23: 26
Romeo and Juliet 11: 406

Stokes, Sewell
King Lear 11: 53

Stoll, Elmer Edgar
All's Well That Ends Well 7: 41
Antony and Cleopatra 6: 76
As You Like It 5: 59, 75
Coriolanus 9: 72
Hamlet 1: 151
Henry IV, 1 and 2 1: 338
Henry V 5: 223
Measure for Measure 2: 460
The Merchant of Venice 4: 230, 445
Romeo and Juliet 5: 458
The Tempest 8: 345

Stone, George Winchester, Jr.
Antony and Cleopatra 17: 6
Cymbeline 15: 6
Hamlet 21: 23
Macbeth 20: 25
A Midsummer Night's Dream 12: 147
Much Ado about Nothing 18: 116
Othello 11: 183
Richard III 14: 366
Romeo and Juliet 11: 386
The Tempest 15: 203

Storey, Graham
Much Ado about Nothing 8: 79

Strachey, Edward
Hamlet 1: 102

Strachey, Lytton
The Tempest 8: 324

Straumann, Heinrich
The Phoenix and Turtle 10: 48; 51: 151

Strehler, Giorgio
 The Tempest **15**: 338

Stribrny, Zdenek
 Henry V **30**: 244

Stroud, T. A.
 Measure for Measure **49**: 379

Stubbes, George
 Hamlet **1**: 76

Styan, J. L.
 All's Well That Ends Well **26**: 85, 117
 As You Like It **23**: 64, 118
 A Midsummer Night's Dream **12**: 215, 228, 264
 The Winter's Tale **15**: 451

Suchet, David
 The Tempest **15**: 374

Suddard, Mary, S.J.
 Measure for Measure **2**: 418

Suhamy, Henri
 Hamlet **35**: 241

Sullivan, Dan
 Antony and Cleopatra **17**: 43
 Titus Andronicus **17**: 460

Sullivan, Patrick
 The Merchant of Venice **12**: 83

Summers, Joseph H.
 Twelfth Night **1**: 591

Summers, Montague
 Troilus and Cressida **18**: 283

Sundelson, David
 Measure for Measure **2**: 528
 The Tempest **29**: 377

Suzman, Janet
 Antony and Cleopatra **17**: 113

Swan, Christopher
 King John **24**: 232

Swander, Homer
 A Midsummer Night's Dream **16**: 34

Swander, Homer D.
 Cymbeline **4**: 127

Sweeney, Louise
 Macbeth **20**: 273

Swinarski, Konrad
 All's Well That Ends Well **26**: 114

Swinburne, Algernon Charles
 Antony and Cleopatra **6**: 40
 As You Like It **5**: 42
 The Comedy of Errors **1**: 16
 Coriolanus **9**: 31
 Cymbeline **4**: 37
 Henry IV, 1 and 2 **1**: 325
 Henry V **5**: 205
 Henry VIII **2**: 36
 King Lear **2**: 129
 Love's Labour's Lost **2**: 307
 Much Ado about Nothing **8**: 28
 Othello **4**: 423
 Pericles **2**: 550
 The Rape of Lucrece **10**: 69
 Richard II **6**: 282
 Richard III **8**: 167
 Romeo and Juliet **5**: 437
 Troilus and Cressida **3**: 548
 The Two Gentlemen of Verona **6**: 449
 The Two Noble Kinsmen **9**: 456
 Venus and Adonis **10**: 419
 The Winter's Tale **7**: 396

Swinden, Patrick
 As You Like It **5**: 138

Sykes, H. Dugdale
 Pericles **2**: 556

Sylvester, Bickford
 The Rape of Lucrece **10**: 93

Symonds, John Addington
 Titus Andronicus **4**: 627

Symons, Arthur
 Antony and Cleopatra **6**: 48
 Coriolanus **17**: 140
 Titus Andronicus **4**: 628

Taciturnus, Frater (Kierkegaard, Seren)
 Hamlet **1**: 102

Taine, Nippolyte A.
 As You Like It **5**: 35
 Much Ado about Nothing **8**: 27

Talbert, Ernest William
 The Comedy of Errors **1**: 43

Tate, Nahum
 Julius Caesar **7**: 149
 King Lear **2**: 92
 Richard II **6**: 250; **24**: 260

Tatham, John
 Pericles **2**: 537

Tatlock, John S. P.
 Troilus and Cressida **3**: 558

Taubman, Howard
 The Comedy of Errors **26**: 153
 Cymbeline **15**: 62
 Hamlet **21**: 236
 Othello **11**: 313
 Timon of Athens **20**: 455
 Troilus and Cressida **18**: 336

Tave, Stuart M.
 A Midsummer Night's Dream **45**: 175

Tayler, Edward W.
 King Lear **16**: 301

Taylor, Anthony Brian
 A Midsummer Night's Dream **16**: 25

Taylor, Donn Ervin
 As You Like It **34**: 102

Taylor, Gary
 Henry V **30**: 278
 Authorship Controversy (topic entry) **41**: 81

Taylor, John Russell
 Macbeth **20**: 272
 Romeo and Juliet **11**: 471
 The Taming of the Shrew **12**: 369

Taylor, Mark
 Cymbeline **15**: 66
 Fathers and Daughters (topic entry) **36**: 1
 King Lear **16**: 372
 Macbeth **16**: 372
 A Midsummer Night's Dream **29**: 269
 The Tempest **25**: 382
 Twelfth Night **16**: 372

Taylor, Michael
 Cymbeline **4**: 172
 Pericles **36**: 226

Taylor, Paul
 Hamlet **21**: 325, 332
 Macbeth **20**: 316
 Richard II **24**: 381
 Twelfth Night **26**: 335

Teague, Frances
 Love's Labour's Lost **23**: 222

Tennenhouse, Leonard
 Kingship (topic entry) **39**: 1
 Violence in Shakespeare's Works (topic entry) **43**: 12

Tenschert, Joachim
 Coriolanus **17**: 185

Terry, Ellen
 Cymbeline **15**: 23
 Hamlet **21**: 107
 King John **24**: 198
 Macbeth **20**: 144
 The Merchant of Venice **12**: 34, 114
 The Merry Wives of Windsor **18**: 27
 A Midsummer Night's Dream **12**: 187
 Much Ado about Nothing **18**: 245
 Othello **11**: 336
 Romeo and Juliet **11**: 434
 The Winter's Tale **15**: 429

Thaler, Alwin
 The Two Gentlemen of Verona **6**: 471

Thatcher, David
 Measure for Measure **32**: 81; **33**: 117

Thayer, C. G.
 Henry V **5**: 318

Theobald, Lewis
 Henry V **5**: 187
 Henry VI, 1, 2, and 3 **3**: 18
 Julius Caesar **7**: 153
 King John **9**: 209
 King Lear **2**: 94
 Love's Labour's Lost **2**: 299
 Measure for Measure **2**: 388
 Othello **4**: 385
 Timon of Athens **1**: 454
 Titus Andronicus **4**: 613
 Troilus and Cressida **3**: 537
 Twelfth Night **1**: 540

Thomas, Brook
 Cymbeline **47**: 237

Thomas, Ceridwen
 Measure for Measure **23**: 358

Thomas, Moy
 Hamlet **21**: 101

Thomas, Sidney
 King Lear **32**: 308
 Richard III **8**: 190

Thompson, Ann
 Comedy of Errors **42**: 93
 Cymbeline **36**: 129
 Love's Labour's Lost **42**: 93

Thompson, Karl F.
 Richard II **6**: 321
 Twelfth Night **1**: 587
 The Two Gentlemen of Verona **6**: 488

Thomson, Ann
 The Two Noble Kinsmen **50**: 326

Thomson, Leslie
 Antony and Cleopatra **13**: 374

Thomson, Patricia
 Troilus and Cressida **27**: 332

Thomson, Peter
 Antony and Cleopatra **17**: 62
 As You Like It **23**: 108
 Cymbeline **15**: 81
 Hamlet **21**: 294
 Henry IV, 1 and 2 **14**: 91
 King John **24**: 218, 225
 Measure for Measure **23**: 328
 A Midsummer Night's Dream **12**: 260
 Richard III **14**: 467
 The Taming of the Shrew **12**: 484
 Twelfth Night **26**: 288

Thomson, Richard
 Richard II **24**: 352

Thomson, Virgil
 Much Ado about Nothing **18**: 249

Thorne, W. B.
 Cymbeline **4**: 129
 Pericles **2**: 584
 The Taming of the Shrew **9**: 393

Thorp, Joseph
 Macbeth **20**: 191

Thorpe, Thomas
 Sonnets **10**: 153

Tice, Terrence N.
 Julius Caesar **45**: 10

Tieck, Ludwig
Hamlet **21**: 30

Tierney, Margaret
Antony and Cleopatra **17**: 58

Tiffany, Grace
The Merry Wives of Windsor **22**: 93; **38**: 319

Tilley, Morris P.
Twelfth Night **1**: 563

Tillyard, E. M. W.
All's Well That Ends Well **7**: 45
Antony and Cleopatra **6**: 103
The Comedy of Errors **1**: 46
Cymbeline **4**: 68
Hamlet **1**: 176
Henry IV, 1 and 2 **1**: 378
Henry V **5**: 241
Henry VI, 1, 2, and 3 **3**: 59
King John **9**: 254
Love's Labour's Lost **2**: 340
Measure for Measure **2**: 475
The Merchant of Venice **4**: 282
Othello **4**: 483
Pericles **2**: 563
Richard II **6**: 294
Richard III **8**: 193
The Taming of the Shrew **9**: 365
The Tempest **8**: 359
Titus Andronicus **4**: 639
The Winter's Tale **7**: 429

Tinker, Jack
As You Like It **23**: 140

Tinkler, F. C.
Cymbeline **4**: 64
The Winter's Tale **7**: 420

Tofte, Robert
Love's Labour's Lost **2**: 299

Toliver, Harold
Antony and Cleopatra **13**: 383

Tolstoy, Leo
Henry IV, 1 and 2 **1**: 337
King Lear **2**: 145

Tompkins, J. M. S.
Pericles **2**: 572

Toole, William B.
Richard III **8**: 252

Totten, Eileen
Richard II **24**: 346

Tovey, Barbara
The Merchant of Venice **4**: 344

Towse, John Ranken
Hamlet **21**: 107
Henry VIII **24**: 83
King Lear **11**: 26, 31
Measure for Measure **23**: 281
The Merry Wives of Windsor **18**: 28
Othello **11**: 231
Richard II **24**: 291

Traci, Philip
Antony and Cleopatra **47**: 124
As You Like It **46**: 127
The Merry Wives of Windsor **38**: 313
The Two Gentlemen of Verona **40**: 330

Tracy, Robert
Hamlet **35**: 163

Trafton, Dain A.
Henry IV, 1 and 2 **49**: 116

Traister, Barbara Howard
Kingship (topic entry) **39**: 16
Magic and the Supernatural (topic entry) **29**: 1

Traub, Valerie
Hamlet **44**: 195
Henry IV, 1 and 2 **13**: 183
Henry V **13**: 183
Psychoanalytic Interpretations (topic entry) **44**: 44

Traversi, Derek A.
Antony and Cleopatra **6**: 100
The Comedy of Errors **1**: 39
Coriolanus **9**: 73, 157
Cymbeline **4**: 93
Henry IV, 1 and 2 **1**: 383
Henry V **5**: 233
Julius Caesar **7**: 303
Macbeth **3**: 323
Measure for Measure **2**: 452
The Merchant of Venice **4**: 315
Othello **4**: 493
The Taming of the Shrew **9**: 362
The Tempest **8**: 370
Troilus and Cressida **3**: 621
The Two Gentlemen of Verona **6**: 502
The Winter's Tale **7**: 425

Tree, Herbert Beerbohm
Henry IV, 1 and 2 **14**: 19
Henry VIII **24**: 89
Julius Caesar **17**: 310
The Tempest **15**: 228

Tree, Maud
Julius Caesar **17**: 313
The Merry Wives of Windsor **18**: 30

Treglown, Jeremy
All's Well That Ends Well **26**: 50
Antony and Cleopatra **17**: 69
As You Like It **23**: 129
Cymbeline **15**: 87

Trench, Richard Chenevix
Antony and Cleopatra **6**: 39

Trewin, J. C.
All's Well That Ends Well **26**: 46
Antony and Cleopatra **17**: 33, 70
As You Like It **23**: 20, 70, 82, 91, 95, 114, 126, 135
The Comedy of Errors **26**: 146
Coriolanus **17**: 160
Cymbeline **15**: 48, 57, 68, 77, 87
Hamlet **21**: 216, 224, 230, 293, 300
Henry IV, 1 and 2 **14**: 28, 58, 73
Henry V **14**: 77, 318
Henry VI, 1, 2, and 3 **24**: 11, 21, 41
Henry VIII **24**: 91, 118
Julius Caesar **17**: 374
King Lear **11**: 61, 66, 88, 110
Love's Labour's Lost **23**: 184, 212
Macbeth **20**: 187, 241, 252, 292, 311
Measure for Measure **23**: 301, 309, 316, 322
A Midsummer Night's Dream **12**: 236, 242, 248, 258
The Merry Wives of Windsor **18**: 34, 47, 70
Much Ado about Nothing **18**: 160, 163
Othello **11**: 285, 291, 300
Pericles **15**: 136, 142, 152, 160
Richard II **24**: 335, 372
Richard III **14**: 416, 419, 455, 457
Romeo and Juliet **11**: 441
The Taming of the Shrew **12**: 355, 385
The Tempest **15**: 259, 266, 267, 282
Timon of Athens **20**: 462
Titus Andronicus **17**: 442, 456, 469
Troilus and Cressida **18**: 306, 331, 345, 352, 358
Twelfth Night **26**: 230, 244, 261, 295
The Two Gentlemen of Verona **12**: 461, 474, 482
The Winter's Tale **15**: 462, 464, 471

Tricomi, Albert H.
Titus Andronicus **4**: 672; **27**: 313

Trotter, Stewart
The Comedy of Errors **26**: 151

Truax, Elizabeth
Rape of Lucrece **43**: 77

Turgenieff, Ivan
Hamlet **1**: 111

Turner, Frederick
As You Like It **46**: 156
The Tempest **15**: 335

Turner, John
Hamlet **16**: 246
King Lear **31**: 84

Tyler, Thomas
Sonnets **10**: 226

Tynan, Kenneth
King John **24**: 213
Measure for Measure **23**: 298
The Merchant of Venice **12**: 50
A Midsummer Night's Dream **12**: 247
Othello **11**: 278, 288, 289
Pericles **15**: 141
Richard II **24**: 317
Richard III **14**: 420
Romeo and Juliet **11**: 460

The Taming of the Shrew **12**: 354
The Tempest **15**: 257
Titus Andronicus **17**: 439

Ulrici, Hermann
All's Well That Ends Well **7**: 15
Antony and Cleopatra **6**: 31
As You Like It **5**: 30
The Comedy of Errors **1**: 14
Coriolanus **9**: 18
Cymbeline **4**: 28
Hamlet **1**: 98
Henry IV, 1 and 2 **1**: 314
Henry V **5**: 195
Henry VI, 1, 2, and 3 **3**: 27
Henry VIII **3**: 25
Julius Caesar **7**: 160
King John **9**: 222
King Lear **2**: 112
Love's Labour's Lost **2**: 303
Macbeth **3**: 194
Measure for Measure **2**: 399
The Merchant of Venice **4**: 201
The Merry Wives of Windsor **5**: 338
A Midsummer Night's Dream **3**: 368
Much Ado about Nothing **8**: 17
Othello **4**: 412
Pericles **2**: 544
Richard II **6**: 263
Richard III **8**: 163
Romeo and Juliet **5**: 427
Sonnets **10**: 182
The Taming of the Shrew **9**: 322
The Tempest **8**: 302
Timon of Athens **1**: 462
Titus Andronicus **4**: 618
Troilus and Cressida **3**: 543
Twelfth Night **1**: 546
The Two Gentlemen of Verona **6**: 442
The Winter's Tale **7**: 387

Underwood, Richard Allan
The Two Noble Kinsmen **50**: 361

Unger, Leonard
Henry IV, 1 and 2 **1**: 406

Uphaus, Robert W.
The Winter's Tale **7**: 501

Upton, John
Coriolanus **9**: 11
Henry IV, 1 and 2 **1**: 289
Julius Caesar **7**: 155
Titus Andronicus **4**: 613
The Two Gentlemen of Verona **6**: 436

Ure, Peter
Timon of Athens **1**: 511

Vache, Jean
Coriolanus **17**: 201

Valesio, Paolo
Madness (topic entry) **35**: 40

Van de Water, Julia C.
King John **9**: 271

Van Doren, Mark
　All's Well That Ends Well **7**: 39
　Antony and Cleopatra **6**: 104
　As You Like It **5**: 77
　The Comedy of Errors **1**: 30
　Coriolanus **9**: 78
　Cymbeline **4**: 70
　Henry IV, 1 and 2 **1**: 365
　Henry V **5**: 230
　Henry VI, 1, 2, and 3 **3**: 57
　Henry VIII **2**: 48
　Julius Caesar **7**: 242
　King John **9**: 251
　Measure for Measure **2**: 441
　The Merry Wives of Windsor **5**: 351
　Richard II **6**: 292
　Richard III **8**: 187
　Romeo and Juliet **5**: 463
　The Taming of the Shrew **9**: 338
　Timon of Athens **1**: 489
　Twelfth Night **1**: 575
　The Two Noble Kinsmen **9**: 469
　The Winter's Tale **7**: 432

Van Laan, Thomas F.
　Richard II **6**: 409
　Richard III **8**: 258

Vandenbroucke, Russell
　Cymbeline **15**: 78
　King John **24**: 224

Vandenhoff, George
　Romeo and Juliet **11**: 413

Vaughan, Alden T.
　The Tempest **45**: 219

Vaughan, James N.
　Richard III **14**: 411

Vaughan, Stuart
　Julius Caesar **50**: 186

Vaughan, Virgina Mason
　King John **41**: 221
　Othello **28**: 330
　The Tempest **15**: 379; **45**: 219

Velie, Alan R.
　Pericles **2**: 585

Velz, John W.
　Coriolanus **50**: 99
　Julius Caesar **7**: 346
　Shakespeare and Classical Civilization (topic entry) **27**: 9

Venezky, Alice
　Henry VIII **24**: 112
　King Lear **11**: 62
　Much Ado about Nothing **18**: 157
　The Winter's Tale **15**: 463

Vernon, Grenville
　Julius Caesar **17**: 323
　Richard II **24**: 306, 309
　Twelfth Night **26**: 225

Verplanck, Gulian C.
　Pericles **2**: 545
　Timon of Athens **1**: 466
　Twelfth Night **1**: 550

Vickers, Brian
　Henry V **5**: 276
　The Merry Wives of Windsor **5**: 363
　Twelfth Night **1**: 650

Vickers, Nancy J.
　The Rape of Lucrece **10**: 131; **43**: 102

Victor, Benjamin
　The Two Gentlemen of Verona **6**: 437; **12**: 450

Vidal, Gore
　Much Ado about Nothing **18**: 164

Videbaek, Bente A.
　As You Like It **46**: 122, 210

Vincent, Barbara C.
　Antony and Cleopatra **47**: 149

Voltaire, Francois-Marie Arouet de
　Hamlet **1**: 80
　Julius Caesar **7**: 154

Von Rumelin, Gustav
　Macbeth **3**: 202

Vyvyan, John
　A Midsummer Night's Dream **3**: 437
　Romeo and Juliet **5**: 498
　The Two Gentlemen of Verona **6**: 494

Waddington, Raymond B.
　The Merchant of Venice **40**: 117

Wade, Nicholas
　Henry V **14**: 314

Wain, John
　Much Ado about Nothing **8**: 100
　Romeo and Juliet **5**: 524
　Twelfth Night **26**: 249

Waith, Eugene M.
　Antony and Cleopatra **6**: 172
　Macbeth **3**: 262; **20**: 367
　Titus Andronicus **4**: 647; **17**: 487; **27**: 261
　The Two Noble Kinsmen **41**: 355

Walch, Günther
　Henry V **49**: 219

Walcutt, Charles C.
　Hamlet **35**: 82

Waldock, A. J. A.
　Hamlet **1**: 148

Walker, Roy
　As You Like It **23**: 87
　Henry V **14**: 266
　King John **24**: 215
　Macbeth **3**: 260
　The Merchant of Venice **12**: 51
　Timon of Athens **20**: 452
　Twelfth Night **26**: 251

Walkley, A. B.
　As You Like It **23**: 46

Much Ado about Nothing **18**: 151
The Two Gentlemen of Verona **12**: 457
The Winter's Tale **15**: 445

Wall, Stephen
　Coriolanus **17**: 210
　Henry IV, 1 and 2 **14**: 102
　Macbeth **20**: 310
　Measure for Measure **23**: 340, 357
　Troilus and Cressida **18**: 384
　The Winter's Tale **15**: 493

Wallace, John M.
　Coriolanus **25**: 296
　Timon of Athens **27**: 235

Walley, Harold R.
　The Merchant of Venice **4**: 243
　The Rape of Lucrece **10**: 84

Walpole, Horace
　The Winter's Tale **7**: 381

Walter, J. H.
　Henry V **5**: 257

Walwyn, B.
　The Merchant of Venice **4**: 193

Wanamaker, Zoe
　Twelfth Night **26**: 308

Wangh, Martin
　Othello **4**: 503

Wapshott, Nicholas
　Hamlet **21**: 232

Warburton, William
　As You Like It **5**: 18
　Henry IV, 1 and 2 **1**: 287
　Julius Caesar **7**: 155
　Love's Labour's Lost **2**: 300
　Othello **4**: 386
　The Tempest **8**: 289
　The Two Noble Kinsmen **9**: 445

Ward, Adolphus William
　Henry VI, 1, 2, and 3 **3**: 50

Ward, David
　Hamlet **22**: 258

Ward, John Paul
　As You Like It **46**: 134

Warde, Frederick
　Henry V **14**: 195

Wardle, Irving
　Antony and Cleopatra **17**: 76
　As You Like It **23**: 96, 110, 114, 128, 137
　The Comedy of Errors **26**: 157
　Coriolanus **17**: 191
　Cymbeline **15**: 72, 80
　Hamlet **21**: 267, 280, 291, 296, 328, 330
　Henry IV, 1 and 2 **14**: 84, 89, 101
　Henry V **14**: 286
　Henry VI, 1, 2, and 3 **24**: 45
　Henry VIII **24**: 125

　Julius Caesar **17**: 379, 405
　King John **24**: 219, 234
　King Lear **11**: 90, 108
　Love's Labour's Lost **23**: 200, 203
　Macbeth **20**: 256, 289, 299, 317
　Measure for Measure **23**: 319, 326, 343
　The Merchant of Venice **12**: 72
　The Merry Wives of Windsor **18**: 48, 49
　A Midsummer Night's Dream **12**: 253, 277
　Much Ado about Nothing **18**: 177, 204
　Richard II **24**: 335
　Richard III **14**: 452, 462, 475
　The Taming of the Shrew **12**: 384, 389, 409
　The Tempest **15**: 269, 278
　Titus Andronicus **17**: 465
　Troilus and Cressida **18**: 341, 355, 350, 363, 381
　Twelfth Night **26**: 265, 282, 301, 321, 336
　The Two Gentlemen of Verona **12**: 481
　The Winter's Tale **15**: 475, 492

Warner, Beverley E.
　Henry IV, 1 and 2 **1**: 328

Warren, Roger
　All's Well That Ends Well **26**: 61; **38**: 80
　Antony and Cleopatra **17**: 81
　As You Like It **23**: 115, 126, 136, 143
　The Comedy of Errors **26**: 161, 167
　Coriolanus **17**: 214
　Cymbeline **4**: 150; **15**: 88
　Hamlet **21**: 316
　Henry IV, 1 and 2 **14**: 108
　Henry VI, 1, 2, and 3 **24**: 42
　Henry VIII **24**: 121
　Julius Caesar **17**: 390
　Love's Labour's Lost **23**: 212
　Macbeth **20**: 299, 312
　Measure for Measure **23**: 342, 348
　The Merchant of Venice **12**: 96
　The Merry Wives of Windsor **18**: 62
　A Midsummer Night's Dream **12**: 273, 285
　Much Ado about Nothing **18**: 210
　Pericles **15**: 172, 180; **16**: 399
　Romeo and Juliet **11**: 485
　The Taming of the Shrew **12**: 396
　Titus Andronicus **17**: 475
　Troilus and Cressida **18**: 366, 386
　Twelfth Night **26**: 295, 305
　The Two Gentlemen of Verona **12**: 495
　The Winter's Tale **15**: 494

Warton, Joseph
　King Lear **2**: 95
　The Tempest **8**: 289

Warton, Thomas
　Romeo and Juliet **5**: 419

Wasson, John
Measure for Measure 23: 413

Watkins, Ronald
Macbeth 20: 382

Watkins, W. B. C.
Venus and Adonis 10: 429

Watson, Donald G.
Venus and Adonis 33: 309

Watson, Robert N.
Measure for Measure 16: 102
Richard III 8: 267
The Winter's Tale 36: 318

Watt, David
Henry VI, 1, 2, and 3 24: 16
The Tempest 15: 265

Watters, Tammie
Antony and Cleopatra 17: 67

Watts, Richard, Jr.
As You Like It 23: 72
King Lear 11: 57

Waugh, Evelyn
Titus Andronicus 17: 443

Weales, Gerald
The Comedy of Errors 26: 177

Webster, Margaret
Cymbeline 15: 121
Henry IV, 1 and 2 14: 118
Love's Labour's Lost 23: 250
Macbeth 20: 374
The Merry Wives of Windsor 18: 74
A Midsummer Night's Dream 12: 293
Much Ado about Nothing 18: 247
Othello 11: 273, 342
Richard II 24: 310
Romeo and Juliet 11: 512
The Taming of the Shrew 9: 340
The Tempest 15: 253
Timon of Athens 20: 491

Wedmore, Frederick
King Lear 11: 33
Macbeth 20: 142
Othello 11: 222
Romeo and Juliet 11: 425

Weever, John
Julius Caesar 7: 148
Venus and Adonis 10: 410

Wehl, Feodor
A Midsummer Night's Dream 12: 167

Weightman, J. G.
Henry V 14: 264

Weightman, John
The Merchant of Venice 12: 76

Weil, Herbert S.
Measure for Measure 23: 301; 49: 349

Weimann, Robert
The Two Gentlemen of Verona 6: 524

Weiner, Albert B.
Macbeth 20: 123

Weinraub, Bernard
Macbeth 20: 273

Weinstein, Philip M.
The Winter's Tale 7: 490

Weiser, David K.
Sonnets 51: 292

Weiss, Theodore
The Comedy of Errors 1: 59

Wekwerth, Manfred
Coriolanus 17: 185

Weller, Barry
The Two Noble Kinsmen 41: 363

Wells, Charles
Antony and Cleopatra 27: 126
Shakespeare and Classical Civilization (topic entry) 27: 35

Wells, Robert Headlam
Henry V 37: 187
Politics and Power (topic entry) 30: 42

Wells, Stanley
All's Well That Ends Well 26: 56
Antony and Cleopatra 17: 83
The Comedy of Errors 26: 163; 179
Coriolanus 17: 172
Hamlet 21: 259
Julius Caesar 17: 397
King John 24: 235; 240
Macbeth 29: 101
Measure for Measure 23: 372
The Merry Wives of Windsor 18: 59
A Midsummer Night's Dream 12: 188; 29: 183
Richard II 24: 356
Richard III 14: 486
The Taming of the Shrew 12: 398
Timon of Athens 20: 472
Titus Andronicus 17: 486
Troilus and Cressida 18: 368
Twelfth Night 26: 317
The Two Gentlemen of Verona 6: 507; 12: 492

Wells, Stanley W.
The Tempest 28: 415

Welsford, Enid
As You Like It 5: 75
King Lear 2: 162
A Midsummer Night's Dream 3: 397
Twelfth Night 1: 571

Welsh, Andrew
Pericles 36: 205

Wendell, Barrett
Cymbeline 4: 43
Twelfth Night 1: 560

Wendlandt, Wilhelm
Timon of Athens 1: 473

Wentersdorf, Karl P.
Henry V 49: 223
The Taming of the Shrew 12: 431

Werder, Karl
Hamlet 1: 106

Wesley, Samuel
Antony and Cleopatra 6: 20

West, E. J.
Twelfth Night 1: 579

West, Fred
Othello 35: 347

West, Grace Starry
Titus Andronicus 27: 293

West, Michael
The Taming of the Shrew 9: 404

West, Rebecca
Hamlet 1: 218

West, Robert H.
King Lear 2: 265; 31: 129

West, Thomas G.
Troilus and Cressida 3: 638

Westlund, Joseph
All's Well That Ends Well 38: 96
Cymbeline 45: 75
The Tempest 32: 400

Whately, Thomas
Macbeth 3: 177
Richard III 8: 148

Wheeler, Richard P.
Fathers and Daughters (topic entry) 36: 70
Hamlet 44: 152
Psychoanalytic Interpretations (topic entry) 44: 18
Richard III 39: 326
The Tempest 45: 259

Whitaker, Virgil K.
Julius Caesar 7: 264

White, Antonia
The Taming of the Shrew 12: 349

White, Howard B.
Timon of Athens 27: 223

White, R. S.
As You Like It 51: 1
King Lear 49: 73
Love's Labour's Lost 51: 1
Merchant of Venice 51: 1
The Merry Wives of Windsor 38: 307
Midsummer Night's Dream 51: 1
Pericles 51: 79
Twelfth Night 51: 1

White, Richard Grant
As You Like It 23: 167
Henry IV, 1 and 2 1: 327
Much Ado about Nothing 8: 23
Othello 4: 424

Whitebait, William
Hamlet 21: 198
Richard III 14: 422

Whitehead, Frank
King Lear 22: 271

Whitehead, Ted
Hamlet 21: 308

Whiter, Walter
As You Like It 5: 21

Whitney, Charles
Henry VIII 28: 203

Whittaker, Herbert
All's Well That Ends Well 26: 22
A Midsummer Night's Dream 12: 239

Whittier, Gayle
General Commentary 13: 530

Whitworth, C. W.
The Comedy of Errors 26: 165

Wickham, Glynn
The Tempest 29: 339
The Two Noble Kinsmen 41: 289

Wiess, Theodore
Henry IV, 1 and 2 39: 72

Wigston, W. F. C.
The Phoenix and Turtle 10: 7
The Winter's Tale 7: 397

Wilcher, Robert
Twelfth Night 46: 303

Willbern, David
The Rape of Lucrece 33: 179

Willems, Michèle
Henry IV, Parts 1 and 2 47: 60

Wilcher, Robert
As You Like It 5: 166

Wilcox, Helen
Gender Identity (topic entry) 40: 99

Wilde, Oscar
Sonnets 10: 218

Wilkes, Thomas
Macbeth 20: 20
Othello 4: 389
Richard III 14: 363

Willbern, David
Henry IV, Parts 1 and 2 42: 187
Titus Andronicus 4: 675

Willcock, Gladys Doidge
  Love's Labour's Lost **2:** 319

Willeford, William
  Clowns and Fools (topic entry) **46:** 74

William, David
  The Merry Wives of Windsor **18:** 84
  The Tempest **15:** 352

Williams, Charles
  Henry V **5:** 228
  Troilus and Cressida **3:** 568

Williams, Clifford
  The Comedy of Errors **26:** 188

Williams, Gary Jay
  A Midsummer Night's Dream **12:** 153, 161, 278
  Timon of Athens **20:** 481

Williams, George Walton
  Macbeth **28:** 339

Williams, Gordon
  Macbeth **20:** 343
  Venus and Adonis **33:** 347

Williams, Gwyn
  The Comedy of Errors **1:** 45; **34:** 229

Williams, Harcourt
  Macbeth **20:** 186
  Much Ado about Nothing **18:** 134

Williams, John T.
  Richard III **14:** 528
  The Tempest **15:** 371

Williams, Mary C.
  Much Ado about Nothing **8:** 125

Williams, Simon
  A Midsummer Night's Dream **12:** 168

Williams, Stanley T.
  Timon of Athens **20:** 476

Williamson, Audrey
  All's Well That Ends Well **26:** 41
  Coriolanus **17:** 159
  Henry IV, 1 and 2 **14:** 35
  Henry VIII **24:** 113
  King John **24:** 206
  Macbeth **20:** 186, 234
  Othello **11:** 279
  Richard II **24:** 304, 315
  The Tempest **15:** 234
  Troilus and Cressida **18:** 318

Williamson, Jane
  Measure for Measure **23:** 363

Williamson, Marilyn L.
  All's Well That Ends Well **38:** 99
  Henry V **5:** 302; **30:** 259
  Romeo and Juliet **5:** 571

Williamson, Nicol
  Hamlet **21:** 268

Willis, Deborah
  The Tempest **13:** 440

Willis, Susan
  Troilus and Cressida **18:** 371

Wills, Garry
  Coriolanus **17:** 223
  Hamlet **21:** 244

Wilmeth, Don B.
  Richard III **14:** 370

Wilson, Daniel
  The Tempest **8:** 309

Wilson, Edmund
  Henry IV, 1 and 2 **1:** 393

Wilson, Harold S.
  Measure for Measure **2:** 490
  Romeo and Juliet **5:** 487

Wilson, John Dover
  Antony and Cleopatra **6:** 133
  As You Like It **5:** 114
  Hamlet **1:** 138, 154
  Henry IV, 1 and 2 **1:** 125, 366, 373
  Henry V **5:** 246
  Henry VI, 1, 2, and 3 **3:** 66
  Julius Caesar **7:** 253
  King Lear **2:** 160
  Love's Labour's Lost **2:** 342; **23:** 252
  The Merry Wives of Windsor **5:** 360
  Much Ado about Nothing **31:** 171
  Richard II **6:** 289
  Sonnets **10:** 334; **51:** 284
  The Tempest **8:** 348
  Titus Andronicus **4:** 642
  Venus and Adonis **10:** 427

Wilson, Milton
  Hamlet **21:** 220

Wilson, Rawdon R.
  As You Like It **46:** 169
  The Rape of Lucrece **33:** 169

Wilson, Richard
  Coriolanus **50:** 152
  Julius Caesar **22:** 280

Wilson, Rob
  Psychoanalytic Interpretations (topic entry) **44:** 57

Wincor, Richard
  Pericles **2:** 570
  The Winter's Tale **7:** 451

Wingate, Charles E. L.
  King Lear **11:** 119
  Macbeth **20:** 103
  Much Ado about Nothing **18:** 115
  The Taming of the Shrew **12:** 411

Winny, James
  Henry IV, 1 and 2 **1:** 424
  Henry V **5:** 281
  Henry VI, 1, 2, and 3 **3:** 115
  Richard II **6:** 368
  Sonnets **10:** 337

Winstanley, William
  Richard III **8:** 145

Winter, Jack
  The Taming of the Shrew **12:** 366

Winter, William
  Antony and Cleopatra **6:** 51
  As You Like It **23:** 27
  Coriolanus **17:** 132
  Cymbeline **15:** 21, 43, 96
  Hamlet **21:** 64, 143
  Henry IV, 1 and 2 **14:** 9
  Henry VIII **24:** 129
  Julius Caesar **17:** 284, 286
  King Lear **11:** 25
  Measure for Measure **23:** 281
  The Merry Wives of Windsor **18:** 14, 17, 18, 29, 66, 126
  A Midsummer Night's Dream **12:** 192, 225, 280
  Richard II **24:** 289
  Richard III **14:** 503
  Romeo and Juliet **11:** 416, 423
  The Taming of the Shrew **12:** 414
  Twelfth Night **26:** 207, 212
  The Winter's Tale **15:** 442

Winton, Calhoun
  Henry V **14:** 178

Witt, Robert W.
  Sonnets **51:** 288

Wittenburg, Robert
  The Tempest **29:** 362

Witts, Noel
  As You Like It **23:** 113

Wixson, Douglas C.
  King John **9:** 300

Wofford, Susanne L.
  As You Like It **28:** 82

Wolf, Matt
  Antony and Cleopatra **17:** 81

Womersley, David
  King John **13:** 163

Wood, Glena D.
  King Lear **46:** 191

Wood, James O.
  Pericles **2:** 583

Wood, Robert E.
  The Comedy of Errors **26:** 190

Wood, Roger
  All's Well That Ends Well **26:** 37
  Henry V **14:** 260
  King John **24:** 203
  Othello **11:** 280
  Troilus and Cressida **18:** 314

Woodbridge, Linda
  Shakespeare's Representation of Women (topic entry) **31:** 41

Woods, George B.
  Hamlet **21:** 78

Woollcott, Alexander
  A Midsummer Night's Dream **12:** 224

Worden, Blair
  General Commentary **22:** 395

Wordsworth, William
  Sonnets **10:** 159, 160, 167

Worsley, T. C.
  Antony and Cleopatra **17:** 31
  As You Like It **23:** 94
  The Comedy of Errors **26:** 145
  Cymbeline **15:** 45, 58, 64
  Hamlet **21:** 225
  Henry IV, 1 and 2 **14:** 38, 39, 56
  Henry V **14:** 256
  Henry VI, 1, 2, and 3 **24:** 17
  Julius Caesar **17:** 366
  King Lear **11:** 58, 60, 65
  Macbeth **20:** 188, 221, 239
  Measure for Measure **23:** 297, 311, 313
  The Merchant of Venice **12:** 52
  The Merry Wives of Windsor **18:** 36
  Much Ado about Nothing **18:** 157, 177
  Othello **11:** 276
  Pericles **15:** 143
  Richard II **24:** 305, 320, 322
  The Taming of the Shrew **12:** 353
  Titus Andronicus **17:** 441
  Troilus and Cressida **18:** 313, 319, 330
  Twelfth Night **26:** 229, 245, 256

Worthen W. B.
  Antony and Cleopatra **47:** 142

Wotton, Sir Henry
  Henry VIII **2:** 14

Woudhuysen, H. R.
  Titus Andronicus **17:** 478
  Twelfth Night **26:** 325

Wright, Abraham
  Othello **4:** 370

Wright, Laurence
  The Winter's Tale **36:** 344

Wright, Neil H.
  The Tempest **8:** 447

Wyatt, Euphemia Van Rensselaer
  Julius Caesar **17:** 325
  Macbeth **20:** 201, 230, 233
  The Merchant of Venice **12:** 63
  Much Ado about Nothing **18:** 174
  The Tempest **15:** 245
  Twelfth Night **26:** 228
  The Two Gentlemen of Verona **12:** 471

Wylie, Betty Jane
  Pericles **15:** 181

Wyndham, George
  Sonnets **10**: 236
  Venus and Adonis **10**: 420

Wynne-David, Marion
  Titus Andronicus **27**: 266

Yates, Frances A.
  Henry VIII **2**: 71
  Cymbeline **47**: 219

Yearling, Elizabeth M.
  Twelfth Night **1**: 664

Yeats, W. B.
  Henry IV, 1 and 2 **1**: 332
  Henry V **5**: 210
  Richard II **6**: 277

Yoder, R. A.
  Troilus and Cressida **3**: 626

Young, B. A.
  All's Well That Ends Well **26**: 43
  Antony and Cleopatra **17**: 55

  As You Like It **23**: 104, 112, 121
  Hamlet **21**: 252
  Henry V **14**: 271, 275, 279
  Henry VI, 1, 2, and 3 **24**: 19, 30
  Julius Caesar **17**: 377, 379
  King John **24**: 220
  Love's Labour's Lost **23**: 196, 203, 207
  Macbeth **20**: 256, 292, 307
  Measure for Measure **23**: 319, 326
  The Merry Wives of Windsor **18**: 40, 46, 47
  Much Ado about Nothing **18**: 187, 203, 209
  Pericles **15**: 147
  Richard III **14**: 462
  The Taming of the Shrew **12**: 382, 388
  The Tempest **15**: 268
  Timon of Athens **20**: 461
  Titus Andronicus **17**: 464
  Troilus and Cressida **18**: 340, 354
  Twelfth Night **26**: 281

Young, Bruce W.
  The Winter's Tale **36**: 328

Young, C. B.
  Cymbeline **15**: 102
  Henry VIII **24**: 136
  Julius Caesar **17**: 408
  Pericles **15**: 178
  Richard III **14**: 507

Young, David
  As You Like It **23**: 102
  Macbeth **16**: 317
  The Tempest **29**: 323

Young, David P.
  As You Like It **5**: 135
  A Midsummer Night's Dream **3**: 453; **29**: 190

Young, Julian Charles
  Coriolanus **17**: 132
  Julius Caesar **17**: 273

Young, Stark
  Hamlet **21**: 148

  Julius Caesar **17**: 321
  Othello **11**: 270
  Richard II **24**: 307
  Richard III **14**: 412
  The Taming of the Shrew **12**: 344
  Troilus and Cressida **18**: 295
  Twelfth Night **26**: 224

Zarkin, Robert
  The Tempest **15**: 297

Zender, Karl F.
  Macbeth **3**: 336
  Measure for Measure **28**: 92; **33**: 77
  Othello **28**: 344

Zimbardo, Rose A.
  Henry V **5**: 264
  A Midsummer Night's Dream **3**: 468

Zinter, Sheldon P.
  All's Well That Ends Well **26**: 91, 128; **38**: 150
  Henry IV, 1 and 2 **14**: 156

Cumulative Topic Index

The Cumulative Topic Index identifies the principal topics of discussion in the criticism of each play and non-dramatic poem. The topics are arranged alphabetically. Page references indicate the beginning page number of each essay containing substantial commentary on that topic. A parenthetical reference after a topic indicates that the topic is extensively discussed in that volume.

absurdities, inconsistencies, and shortcomings
 The Two Gentlemen of Verona **6:** 435, 436, 437, 439, 464, 507, 541, 560

accident or chance
 Romeo and Juliet **5:** 418, 444, 448, 467, 470, 487, 573

acting and dissimulation
 Richard II **6:** 264, 267, 307, 310, 315, 368, 393, 409; **24:** 339, 345, 346, 349, 352, 356

adolescence
 Romeo and Juliet **33:** 249, 255, 257

adultery
 The Comedy of Errors **34:** 215

aggression
 Coriolanus **9:** 112, 142, 174, 183, 189, 198; **30:** 79, 111, 125, 142; **44:** 11, 79

alienation
 Timon of Athens **1:** 523; **27:** 161

allegorical elements
 King Lear **16:** 311
 The Merchant of Venice **4:** 224, 250, 261, 268, 270, 273, 282, 289, 324, 336, 344, 350
 The Phoenix and Turtle **10:** 7, 8, 9, 16, 17, 48; **38:** 334, 378; **51:** 138, 188
 The Rape of Lucrece **10:** 89, 93
 Richard II **6:** 264, 283, 323, 385
 The Tempest **8:** 294, 295, 302, 307, 308, 312,

326, 328, 336, 345, 364; **42:** 320
 Venus and Adonis **10:** 427, 434, 439, 449, 454, 462, 480; **28:** 355; **33:** 309, 330

ambiguity
 Antony and Cleopatra **6:** 53, 111, 161, 163, 180, 189, 208, 211, 228; **13:** 368
 Hamlet **1:** 92, 160, 198, 227, 230, 234, 247, 249; **21:** 72; **35:** 241
 King John **13:** 152; **41:** 243
 Measure for Measure **2:** 417, 420, 432, 446, 449, 452, 474, 479, 482, 486, 495, 505
 A Midsummer Night's Dream **3:** 401, 459, 486; **45:** 169
 Richard III **44:** 11; **47:** 15
 Sonnets **10:** 251, 256; **28:** 385; **40:** 221, 228, 268
 Troilus and Cressida **3:** 544, 568, 583, 587, 589, 599, 611, 621; **27:** 400; **43:** 305
 Twelfth Night **1:** 554, 639; **34:** 287, 316
 Venus and Adonis **10:** 434, 454, 459, 462, 466, 473, 480, 486, 489; **33:** 352; **51:** 368, 377, 388

ambition or pride
 Henry VIII **2:** 15, 38, 67
 Macbeth **44:** 284, 324

ambivalent or ironic elements
 Henry VI, Parts 1, 2, and 3 **3:** 69, 151, 154; **39:** 160
 Richard III **44:** 11
 Troilus and Cressida **43:** 340

amorality, question of
 The Two Noble Kinsmen **9:** 447, 460, 492

amour-passion or *Liebestod* myth
 Romeo and Juliet **5:** 484, 489, 528, 530, 542, 550, 575; **32:** 256; **51:** 195, 219, 236

amputations, significance of
 Titus Andronicus **48:** 264

anachronisms
 Julius Caesar **7:** 331

androgyny
 Antony and Cleopatra **13:** 530
 As You Like It **23:** 98, 100, 122, 138, 143, 144; **34:** 172, 177; **46:** 134
 Romeo and Juliet **13:** 530

anti-Catholic rhetoric
 King John **22:** 120; **25:** 98

anti-romantic elements
 As You Like It **34:** 72

antithetical or contradictory elements
 Macbeth **3:** 185, 213, 271, 302; **25:** 235; **29:** 76, 127; **47:** 41

anxiety
 Romeo and Juliet **13:** 235

appearance, perception, and illusion
 A Midsummer Night's Dream **3:** 368, 411, 425, 427, 434, 447, 459, 466, 474, 477, 486, 497, 516; **19:** 21; **22:** 39; **28:** 15; **29:** 175, 190; **45:** 136

Appearance versus Reality (Volume 34: 1, 5, 12, 23, 45, 54)
   All's Well That Ends Well **7**: 37, 76, 93; **26**: 117
   As You Like It **34**: 130, 131; **46**: 105
   The Comedy of Errors **34**: 194, 201
   Coriolanus **30**: 142
   Cymbeline **4**: 87, 93, 103, 162; **36**: 99; **47**: 228, 286
   Hamlet **1**: 95, 116, 166, 169, 198; **35**: 82, 126, 132, 144, 238; **44**: 248; **45**: 28
   Macbeth **3**: 241, 248; **25**: 235
   The Merchant of Venice **4**: 209, 261, 344; **12**: 65; **22**: 69
   Much Ado about Nothing **8**: 17, 18, 48, 63, 69, 73, 75, 79, 88, 95, 115; **31**: 198, 209
   The Taming of the Shrew **9**: 343, 350, 353, 365, 369, 370, 381, 390, 430; **12**: 416; **31**: 326
   Timon of Athens **1**: 495, 500, 515, 523
   The Two Gentlemen of Verona **6**: 494, 502, 511, 519, 529, 532, 549, 560
   Twelfth Night **34**: 293, 301, 311, 316
   The Winter's Tale **7**: 429, 446, 479

appetite
   Twelfth Night **1**: 563, 596, 609, 615

archetypal or mythic elements
   Macbeth **16**: 317

archetypal structure
   Pericles **2**: 570, 580, 582, 584, 588; **25**: 365; **51**: 71, 79

aristocracy and aristocratic values
   As You Like It **34**: 120
   Hamlet **42**: 212
   Julius Caesar **16**: 231; **22**: 280; **30**: 379; **50**: 194, 196, 211

art and nature
   See also **nature**
   Pericles **22**: 315; **36**: 233
   The Phoenix and Turtle **10**: 7, 42

art versus nature
   See also **nature**
   As You Like It **5**: 128, 130, 148; **34**: 147
   The Tempest **8**: 396, 404; **29**: 278, 297, 362
   The Winter's Tale **7**: 377, 381, 397, 419, 452; **36**: 289, 318; **45**: 329

artificial nature
   Love's Labour's Lost **2**: 315, 317, 324, 330; **23**: 207, 233

Athens
   Timon of Athens **27**: 223, 230

Athens and the forest, contrast between
   A Midsummer Night's Dream **3**: 381, 427, 459, 466, 497, 502; **29**: 175

assassination
   Julius Caesar **7**: 156, 161, 179, 191, 200, 221, 264, 272, 279, 284, 350; **25**: 272; **30**: 326

audience interpretation
   Julius Caesar **48**: 240

audience perception
   The Comedy of Errors **1**: 37, 50, 56; **19**: 54; **34**: 258
   King Lear **19**: 295; **28**: 325
   Richard II **24**: 414, 423; **39**: 295
   Pericles **42**: 352; **48**: 364

audience perception, Shakespeare's manipulation of
   The Winter's Tale **7**: 394, 429, 456, 483, 501; **13**: 417; **19**: 401, 431, 441; **25**: 339; **45**: 374

audience perspective
   All's Well That Ends Well **7**: 81, 104, 109, 116, 121

audience response
   Antony and Cleopatra **48**: 206
   Hamlet **28**: 325; **32**: 238; **35**: 167; **44**: 107
   Julius Caesar **7**: 179, 238, 253, 255, 272, 316, 320, 336, 350; **19**: 321; **48**: 240
   Macbeth **20**: 17, 400, 406; **29**: 139, 146, 155, 165; **44**: 306
   Measure for Measure **48**: 1

audience versus character perceptions
   The Two Gentlemen of Verona **6**: 499, 519, 524

authenticity
   The Phoenix and Turtle **10**: 7, 8, 16
   Sonnets **10**: 153, 154, 230, 243; **48**: 325

Authorship Controversy (Volume 41: 2, 5, 18, 32, 42, 48, 57, 61, 63, 66, 76, 81, 85, 98, 110)
   Cymbeline **4**: 17, 21, 35, 48, 56, 78
   Henry VI, Parts 1, 2, and 3 **3**: 16, 18, 19, 20, 21, 26, 27, 29, 31, 35, 39, 41, 55, 66; **24**: 51
   Henry VIII **2**: 16, 18, 19, 22, 23, 27, 28, 31, 35, 36, 42, 43, 44, 46, 48, 51, 58, 64, 68; **41**: 129, 146, 158, 171
   Love's Labour's Lost **2**: 299, 300; **32**: 308
   Pericles **2**: 538, 540, 543, 544, 545, 546, 548, 550, 551, 553, 556, 558, 564, 565, 568, 576, 586; **15**: 132, 141, 148, 152; **16**: 391, 399; **25**: 365; **36**: 198, 244
   Timon of Athens **1**: 464, 466, 467, 469, 474, 477, 478, 480, 490, 499, 507, 518; **16**: 351; **20**: 433
   Titus Andronicus **4**: 613, 614, 615, 616, 617, 619, 623, 624, 625, 626, 628, 631, 632, 635, 642
   The Two Gentlemen of Verona **6**: 435, 436, 437, 438, 439, 449, 466, 476
   The Two Noble Kinsmen
     Shakespeare not a co-author **9**: 445, 447, 455, 461
     Shakespearean portions of the text **9**: 446, 447, 448, 455, 456, 457, 460, 462, 463, 471, 479, 486; **41**: 308, 317, 355
     Shakespeare's part in the overall conception or design **9**: 444, 446, 448, 456, 457, 460, 480, 481, 486, 490; **37**: 313; **41**: 326; **50**: 326

autobiographical elements
   As You Like It **5**: 25, 35, 43, 50, 55, 61
   The Comedy of Errors **1**: 16, 18
   Cymbeline **4**: 43, 46; **36**: 134
   Hamlet **1**: 98, 115, 119; **13**: 487
   Henry VI, Parts 1, 2, and 3 **3**: 41, 55

King John **9**: 209, 218, 245, 248, 260, 292
King Lear **2**: 131, 136, 149, 165
Measure for Measure **2**: 406, 410, 414, 431, 434, 437
A Midsummer Night's Dream **3**: 365, 371, 379, 381, 389, 391, 396, 402, 432
Othello **4**: 440, 444
Pericles **2**: 551, 554, 555, 563, 581
The Phoenix and Turtle **10**: 14, 18, 42, 48; **51**: 155
Sonnets **10**: 159, 160, 166, 167, 175, 176, 182, 196, 205, 213, 215, 226, 233, 238, 240, 251, 279, 283, 302, 309, 325, 337, 377; **13**: 487; **16**: 461; **28**: 363, 385; **42**: 296; **48**: 325
The Tempest **8**: 302, 308, 312, 324, 326, 345, 348, 353, 364, 380
Timon of Athens **1**: 462, 467, 470, 473, 474, 478, 480; **27**: 166, 175
Titus Andronicus **4**: 619, 624, 625, 664
Troilus and Cressida **3**: 548, 554, 557, 558, 574, 606, 630
Twelfth Night **1**: 557, 561, 599; **34**: 338
The Winter's Tale **7**: 395, 397, 410, 419

avarice
   The Merry Wives of Windsor **5**: 335, 353, 369, 376, 390, 395, 402

battle of Agincourt
   Henry V **5**: 197, 199, 213, 246, 257, 281, 287, 289, 293, 310, 318; **19**: 217; **30**: 181

battle of the sexes
   Much Ado about Nothing **8**: 14, 16, 19, 48, 91, 95, 111, 121, 125; **31**: 231, 245

bawdy elements
   As You Like It **46**: 122
   Cymbeline **36**: 155

bear-baiting
   Twelfth Night **19**: 42

beauty
   Sonnets **10**: 247; **51**: 288
   Venus and Adonis **10**: 420, 423, 427, 434, 454, 480; **33**: 330, 352

bed-trick
   All's Well That Ends Well **7**: 8, 26, 27, 29, 32, 41, 86, 93, 98, 113, 116, 126; **13**: 84; **26**: 117; **28**: 38; **38**: 65, 118; **49**: 46
   Measure for Measure **13**: 84; **49**: 313

bird imagery
   The Phoenix and Turtle **10**: 21, 27; **38**: 329, 350, 367; **51**: 145, 181, 184

body, role of
   Troilus and Cressida **42**: 66

body politic, metaphor of
   Coriolanus **22**: 248; **30**: 67, 96, 105, 125; **50**: 105, 110, 119, 140, 145, 152

bonding
   The Merchant of Venice **4**: 293, 317, 336; **13**: 37

British nationalism
See also **nationalism and patriotism**
Cymbeline **4**: 19, 78, 89, 93, 129, 141, 159, 167; **32**: 373; **36**: 129; **45**: 6; **47**: 219, 265

brutal elements
A Midsummer Night's Dream **3**: 445, 491, 497, 511; **12**: 259, 262, 298; **16**: 34; **19**: 21; **29**: 183, 225, 263, 269; **45**: 169

Cade scenes
Henry VI, Parts 1, 2, and 3 **50**: 45, 51

Caesarism
Julius Caesar **7**: 159, 160, 161, 167, 169, 174, 191, 205, 218, 253, 310; **30**: 316, 321; **50**: 196, 234

Calvinist implications
Hamlet **48**: 195

capriciousness of the young lovers
A Midsummer Night's Dream **3**: 372, 395, 402, 411, 423, 437, 441, 450, 497, 498; **29**: 175, 269; **45**: 107

caricature
The Merry Wives of Windsor **5**: 343, 347, 348, 350, 385, 397

carnival elements
Henry IV, Parts 1 and 2 **28**: 203; **32**: 103
Henry VI, Parts 1, 2, and 3 **22**: 156
Richard II **19**: 151; **39**: 273

casket scenes
The Merchant of Venice **49**: 27

censorship
Richard II **24**: 260, 261, 262, 263, 386; **42**: 118

ceremonies, rites, and rituals, importance of
See also **pageantry**
Coriolanus **9**: 139, 148, 169
Hamlet **13**: 268; **28**: 232
Julius Caesar **7**: 150, 210, 255, 259, 268, 284, 316, 331, 339, 356; **13**: 260; **22**: 137; **30**: 374; **50**: 258, 269.
Richard II **6**: 270, 294, 315, 368, 381, 397, 409, 414; **24**: 274, 356, 411, 414, 419
Titus Andronicus **27**: 261; **32**: 265; **48**: 264
The Two Noble Kinsmen **9**: 492, 498

change
Henry VIII **2**: 27, 65, 72, 81

characterization
As You Like It **5**: 19, 24, 25, 36, 39, 54, 82, 86, 116, 148; **34**: 72; **48**: 42
The Comedy of Errors **1**: 13, 21, 31, 34, 46, 49, 50, 55, 56; **19**: 54; **25**: 63; **34**: 194, 201, 208, 245
Henry IV, Parts 1 and 2 **1**: 321, 328, 332, 333, 336, 344, 365, 383, 385, 389, 391, 397, 401; **19**: 195; **39**: 123, 137; **42**: 99, 162; **49**: 93
Henry V **5**: 186, 189, 192, 193, 199, 219, 230, 233, 252, 276, 293; **30**: 227, 278; **42**: 162
Henry VI, Parts 1, 2, and 3 **3**: 18, 20, 24, 25, 31, 57, 64, 73, 77, 109, 119, 151; **24**: 22, 28, 38, 42, 45, 47; **39**: 160; **47**: 32
Henry VIII **2**: 17, 23, 25, 32, 35, 39; **24**: 106
King John **9**: 222, 224, 229, 240, 250, 292; **41**: 205, 215
King Lear **2**: 108, 125, 145, 162, 191; **16**: 311; **28**: 223; **46**: 177, 210
Love's Labour's Lost **2**: 303, 310, 317, 322, 328, 342; **23**: 237, 250, 252; **38**: 232; **47**: 35
Macbeth **20**: 12, 318, 324, 329, 353, 363, 367, 374, 387; **28**: 339; **29**: 101, 109, 146, 155, 165; **45**: 67; **47**: 41
Measure for Measure **2**: 388, 390, 391, 396, 406, 420, 421, 446, 466, 475, 484, 505, 516, 524; **23**: 299, 405; **33**:
The Merry Wives of Windsor **5**: 332, 334, 335, 337, 338, 351, 360, 363, 366, 374, 379, 392; **18**: 74, 75; **38**: 264, 273, 313, 319
The Tempest **8**: 287, 289, 292, 294, 295, 308, 326, 334, 336; **28**: 415; **42**: 332; **45**: 219
Titus Andronicus **4**: 613, 628, 632, 635, 640, 644, 647, 650, 675; **27**: 293; **43**: 170, 176,
Troilus and Cressida **3**: 538, 539, 540, 541, 548, 566, 571, 604, 611, 621; **27**: 381, 391
Twelfth Night **1**: 539, 540, 543, 545, 550, 554, 581, 594; **26**: 257, 337, 342, 346, 364, 366, 371, 374; **34**: 281, 293, 311, 338; **46**: 286, 324
The Two Gentlemen of Verona **6**: 438, 442, 445, 447, 449, 458, 462, 560; **12**: 458; **40**: 312, 327, 330, 365
The Two Noble Kinsmen **9**: 457, 461, 471, 474; **41**: 340, 385; **50**: 305, 326
The Winter's Tale **47**: 25

chastity
A Midsummer Night's Dream **45**: 143

Chaucer's Criseyde, compared with
Troilus and Cressida **43**: 305

chivalry
Troilus and Cressida **16**: 84; **27**: 370, 374
The Two Noble Kinsmen **50**: 305, 348

Christian elements
See also **religious, mythic, or spiritual content**
As You Like It **5**: 39, 98, 162
Coriolanus **30**: 111
King Lear **2**: 137, 170, 179, 188, 191, 197, 207, 218, 222, 226, 229, 238, 249, 265, 286; **22**: 233, 271; **25**: 218; **46**: 276
Macbeth **3**: 194, 239, 260, 269, 275, 286, 293, 297, 318; **20**: 203, 206, 210, 256, 262, 289, 291, 294; **44**: 341, 366; **47**: 41
Measure for Measure **2**: 391, 394, 399, 421, 437, 449, 466, 479, 491, 511, 522; **48**: 1; **49**: 325
Much Ado about Nothing **8**: 17, 19, 29, 55, 95, 104, 111, 115; **31**: 209
The Phoenix and Turtle **10**: 21, 24, 31; **38**: 326; **51**: 162, 171, 181
The Rape of Lucrece **10**: 77, 80, 89, 96, 98, 109
Sonnets **10**: 191, 256
Titus Andronicus **4**: 656, 680
Twelfth Night **46**: 338
The Two Gentlemen of Verona **6**: 438, 494, 514, 532, 555, 564
The Winter's Tale **7**: 381, 387, 402, 410, 417, 419, 425, 429, 436, 452, 460, 501; **36**: 318

as Christian play
King Lear **48**: 222

Chorus, role of
Henry V **49**: 194, 200, 211, 219, 260

church versus state
King John **9**: 209, 212, 222, 235, 240; **22**: 120

civilization versus barbarism
Titus Andronicus **4**: 653; **27**: 293; **28**: 249; **32**: 265

***Clarissa*, (Samuel Richardson), compared with**
King Lear **48**: 277
Measure for Measure **48**: 277
Othello **48**: 277
Titus Andronicus **48**: 277

class distinctions, conflict, and relations
General Commentary **50**: 1, 34
Henry V **28**: 146
Henry VI, Parts 1, 2, and 3 **37**: 97; **39**: 187; **50**: 45, 51
The Merry Wives of Windsor **5**: 338, 343, 346, 347, 366, 390, 395, 400, 402; **22**: 93; **28**: 69
A Midsummer Night's Dream **22**: 23; **25**: 36; **45**: 160; **50**: 74, 86
The Taming of the Shrew **31**: 300, 351; **50**: 64, 74
The Two Noble Kinsmen **50**: 295, 305, 310

classical influence and sources
The Comedy of Errors **1**: 13, 14, 16, 31, 32, 43, 61
The Tempest **29**: 278, 343, 362, 368

Clowns and Fools (Volume **46**: 1, 14, 18, 24, 29, 33, 48, 52, 60)
As You Like It **5**: 24, 28, 30, 32, 36, 39, 54, 61, 63, 72, 75, 76, 77, 79, 84, 86, 93, 98, 114, 118, 135, 138, 166; **23**: 152; **34**: 72, 85, 147, 161; **46**: 88, 105, 117, 122
King Lear **2**: 108, 112, 125, 156, 162, 245, 278, 284; **11**: 17, 158, 169; **22**: 227; **25**: 202; **28**: 223; **46**: 191, 205, 210, 218, 225
Twelfth Night **1**: 543, 548, 558, 561, 563, 566, 570, 572, 603, 620, 642, 655, 658; **26**: 233, 364; **46**: 297, 303, 310

colonialism
Henry V **22**: 103
The Tempest **13**: 424, 440; **15**: 228, 268, 269, 270, 271, 272, 273; **19**: 421; **25**: 357, 382; **28**: 249; **29**: 343, 368; **32**: 338, 367, 400; **42**: 320; **45**: 200, 280

combat
King Lear **22**: 365
Macbeth **22**: 365

comedy of affectation
Love's Labour's Lost **2**: 302, 303, 304; **23**: 191, 224, 226, 228, 233

comic and tragic elements, combination of
King Lear **2**: 108, 110, 112, 125, 156, 162, 245, 278, 284; **46**: 191

Measure for Measure **16**: 102
Romeo and Juliet **5**: 496, 524, 528, 547, 559; **46**: 78
Troilus and Cressida **43**: 351

comic and farcical elements
All's Well That Ends Well **26**: 97, 114; **48**: 65
Antony and Cleopatra **6**: 52, 85, 104, 125, 131, 151, 192, 202, 219; **47**: 77, 124, 149, 165
The Comedy of Errors **1**: 14, 16, 19, 23, 30, 34, 35, 43, 46, 50, 55, 56, 59, 61; **19**: 54; **26**: 183, 186, 188, 190; **34**: 190, 245
Coriolanus **9**: 8, 9, 14, 53, 80, 106
Cymbeline **4**: 35, 56, 113, 141; **15**: 111, 122; **47**: 296
Henry IV, Parts 1 and 2 **1**: 286, 290, 314, 327, 328, 336, 353; **19**: 195; **25**: 109; **39**: 72
Henry V **5**: 185, 188, 191, 192, 217, 230, 233, 241, 252, 260, 276; **19**: 217; **28**: 121; **30**: 193, 202
The Merry Wives of Windsor **5**: 336, 338, 346, 350, 360, 369, 373; **18**: 74, 75, 84
Richard II **24**: 262, 263, 395; **39**: 243
Twelfth Night **26**: 233, 257, 337, 342, 371; **51**: 1
Venus and Adonis **10**: 429, 434, 439, 442, 459, 462, 489; **33**: 352; **51**: 377

comic form
As You Like It **46**: 105; **51**: 1
Measure for Measure **2**: 456, 460, 479, 482, 491, 514, 516; **13**: 94, 104; **23**: 309, 326, 327; **49**: 349

comic resolution
Love's Labour's Lost **2**: 335, 340; **16**: 17; **19**: 92; **38**: 209; **51**: 1

comic, tragic, and romantic elements, fusion of
The Winter's Tale **7**: 390, 394, 396, 399, 410, 412, 414, 429, 436, 479, 483, 490, 501; **13**: 417; **15**: 514, 524, 532; **25**: 339; **36**: 295, 380

commodity
King John **9**: 224, 229, 245, 260, 275, 280, 297; **19**: 182; **25**: 98; **41**: 228, 269

communication, failure of
Troilus and Cressida **43**: 277

compassion, theme of
The Tempest **42**: 339

complex or enigmatic nature
The Phoenix and Turtle **10**: 7, 14, 35, 42; **38**: 326, 357; **51**: 145, 162

composition date
The Comedy of Errors **1**: 18, 23, 34, 55
Henry VIII **2**: 19, 22, 35; **24**: 129
Pericles **2**: 537, 544
Sonnets **10**: 153, 154, 161, 166, 196, 217, 226, 270, 277; **28**: 363, 385
Twelfth Night **37**: 78

conclusion
All's Well That Ends Well **38**: 123, 132, 142
Love's Labour's Lost **38**: 172

Troilus and Cressida **3**: 538, 549, 558, 566, 574, 583, 594
comedy vs. tragedy **43**: 351

conflict between Christianity and Judaism
The Merchant of Venice **4**: 224, 250, 268, 289, 324, 344; **12**: 67, 70, 72, 76; **22**: 69; **25**: 257 **40**: 117, 127, 166, 181; **48**: 54, 77

conscience
Richard III **8**: 148, 152, 162, 165, 190, 197, 201, 206, 210, 228, 232, 239, 243, 252, 258; **39**: 341

as consciously philosophical
The Phoenix and Turtle **10**: 7, 21, 24, 31, 48; **38**: 342, 378

conspiracy or treason
The Tempest **16**: 426; **19**: 357; **25**: 382; **29**: 377
Henry V **49**: 223

constancy and faithfulness
The Phoenix and Turtle **10**: 18, 20, 21, 48; **38**: 329

construing the truth
Julius Caesar **7**: 320, 336, 343, 350; **37**: 229

consummation of marriage
Othello **22**: 207

contemptus mundi
Antony and Cleopatra **6**: 85, 133

contractual and economic relations
Henry IV, Parts 1 and 2 **13**: 213
Richard II **13**: 213; **49**: 602

contradiction, paradox, and opposition
As You Like It **46**: 105
Romeo and Juliet **5**: 421, 427, 431, 496, 509, 513, 516, 520, 525, 528, 538; **33**: 287; **44**: 11
Troilus and Cressida **43**: 377

contrasting dramatic worlds
Henry IV, Parts 1 and 2 **14**: 56, 60, 61, 84, 105; **48**: 95; **49**: 162
The Merchant of Venice **44**: 11

contrasts and oppositions
Othello **4**: 421, 455, 457, 462, 508; **25**: 189

corruption in society
As You Like It **46**: 94
King John **9**: 222, 234, 280, 297

costume
As You Like It **46**: 117
Hamlet **21**: 81
Henry VIII **24**: 82, 87; **28**: 184
Richard II **24**: 274, 278, 291, 304, 325, 356, 364, 423
Romeo and Juliet **11**: 505, 509
Troilus and Cressida **18**: 289, 371, 406, 419

counsel
The Winter's Tale **19**: 401

Court of Love
The Phoenix and Turtle **10**: 9, 24, 50

court society
The Winter's Tale **16**: 410

courtly love
Troilus and Cressida **22**: 58

courtly love tradition, influence of
Romeo and Juliet **5**: 505, 542, 575; **33**: 233

courtship and marriage
See also marriage
As You Like It **34**: 109, 177; **48**: 32; **51**: 44
Much Ado about Nothing **8**: 29, 44, 48, 95, 115, 121, 125; **31**: 191, 231; **51**: 33, 44

credibility
Twelfth Night **1**: 540, 542, 543, 554, 562, 581, 587

critical history
Henry IV, Parts 1 and 2 **42**: 185; **48**: 167

cynicism
Troilus and Cressida **43**: 298

dance
Henry VI, Parts 1, 2, and 3 **22**: 156

dance and patterned action
Love's Labour's Lost **2**: 308, 342; **23**: 191, 237

dark elements
All's Well That Ends Well **7**: 27, 37, 39, 43, 54, 109, 113, 116; **26**: 85; **48**: 65; **50**: 59
Twelfth Night **46**: 310

death, decay, nature's destructiveness
Antony and Cleopatra **47**: 71
As You Like It **46**: 169
Hamlet **1**: 144, 153, 188, 198, 221, 242; **13**: 502; **28**: 280, 311; **35**: 241; **42**: 279
King Lear **2**: 93, 94, 101, 104, 106, 109, 112, 116, 129, 131, 137, 143, 147, 149, 156, 160, 170, 179, 188, 197, 207, 218, 222, 226, 231, 238, 241, 245, 249, 253, 265, 269, 273; **16**: 301; **25**: 202, 218; **31**: 77, 117, 137, 142; **46**: 264
Love's Labour's Lost **2**: 305, 331, 344, 348
Measure for Measure **2**: 394, 452, 516; **25**: 12; **49**: 370
Venus and Adonis **10**: 419, 427, 434, 451, 454, 462, 466, 473, 480, 489; **25**: 305; **33**: 309, 321, 347, 352, 363, 370

decay of heroic ideals
Henry VI, Parts 1, 2, and 3 **3**: 119, 126

deception, disguise, and duplicity
As You Like It **46**: 134
Henry IV, Parts 1 and 2 **1**: 397, 406, 425; **42**: 99; **47**: 1, 60; **48**: 95
The Merry Wives of Windsor **5**: 332, 334, 336, 354, 355, 379; **22**: 93; **47**: 308, 314, 321, 325, 344
Much Ado about Nothing **8**: 29, 55, 63, 69, 79, 82, 88, 108, 115; **31**: 191, 198

Sonnets **25**: 374; **40**: 221
The Taming of the Shrew **12**: 416

Deconstructionist interpretation of
Pericles **48**: 364

deposition scene
Richard II **42**: 118

Desire (Volume 38: 1, 19, 31, 40, 48, 56)
All's Well That Ends Well **38**: 96, 99, 109, 118
As You Like It **37**: 43
Love's Labour's Lost **38**: 185, 194, 200, 209
The Merchant of Venice **22**: 3; **40**: 142; **45**: 17
The Merry Wives of Windsor **38**: 286, 297, 300
Romeo and Juliet **51**: 227, 236
Troilus and Cressida **43**: 317, 329, 340,

discrepancy between prophetic ending and preceding action
Henry VIII **2**: 22, 25, 31, 46, 49, 56, 60, 65, 68, 75, 81; **32**: 148; **41**: 190

disillusioned or cynical tone
Troilus and Cressida **3**: 544, 548, 554, 557, 558, 571, 574, 630, 642; **18**: 284, 332, 403, 406, 423; **27**: 376

disorder
Troilus and Cressida **3**: 578, 589, 599, 604, 609; **18**: 332, 406, 412, 423; **27**: 366

disorder and civil dissension
Henry VI, Parts 1, 2, and 3 **3**: 59, 67, 76, 92, 103, 126; **13**: 131; **16**: 183; **24**: 11, 17, 28, 31, 47; **25**: 102; **28**: 112; **39**: 154, 177, 187, 196, 205

displacement
All's Well That Ends Well **22**: 78
Measure for Measure **22**: 78

divine right versus justice
Henry IV **49**: 116

divine vs. worldly
King Lear **49**: 1

divine will, role of
Romeo and Juliet **5**: 485, 493, 505, 533, 573

domestic elements
As You Like It **46**: 142
Coriolanus **42**: 218; **50**: 145
Venus and Adonis **51**: 359

double-plot
King Lear **2**: 94, 95, 100, 101, 104, 112, 116, 124, 131, 133, 156, 253, 257; **46**: 254
Troilus and Cressida **3**: 569, 613

doubling of roles
Pericles **15**: 150, 152, 167, 173, 180

dramatic elements
Sonnets **10**: 155, 182, 240, 251, 283, 367
Venus and Adonis **10**: 459, 462, 486

dramatic shortcomings or failure
As You Like It **5**: 19, 42, 52, 61, 65
Love's Labour's Lost **2**: 299, 301, 303, 322
Romeo and Juliet **5**: 416, 418, 420, 426, 436, 437, 448, 464, 467, 469, 480, 487, 524, 562

dramatic structure
The Comedy of Errors **1**: 19, 27, 40, 43, 46, 50; **26**: 186, 190; **34**: 190, 229, 233; **37**: 12
Cymbeline **4**: 17, 18, 19, 20, 21, 22, 24, 38, 43, 48, 53, 64, 68, 89, 116, 129, 141; **22**: 302, 365; **25**: 319; **36**: 115, 125
Othello **4**: 370, 390, 399, 427, 488, 506, 517, 569; **22**: 207; **28**: 243
The Winter's Tale **7**: 382, 390, 396, 399, 402, 407, 414, 429, 432, 473, 479, 493, 497, 501; **15**: 528; **25**: 339; **36**: 289, 295, 362, 380; **45**: 297, 344, 358, 366

as dream-play
A Midsummer Night's Dream **3**: 365, 370, 372, 377, 389, 391; **29**: 190; **45**: 117

Dreams in Shakespeare (Volume 45: 1, 10, 17, 28, 40, 48, 58, 67, 75)
Antony and Cleopatra **45**: 28
Cymbeline **4**: 162, 167; **44**: 28; **45**: 67, 75
Hamlet **45**: 28
Julius Caesar **45**: 10
A Midsummer Night's Dream **45**: 96, 107, 117
Romeo and Juliet **45**: 40
The Tempest **45**: 236, 247, 259

dualisms
Antony and Cleopatra **19**: 304; **27**: 82
Cymbeline **4**: 29, 64, 73

duration of time
As You Like It **5**: 44, 45
A Midsummer Night's Dream **3**: 362, 370, 380, 386, 494; **45**: 175

economic relations
Henry V **13**: 213

economics and exchange
Coriolanus **50**: 152
The Merchant of Venice **40**: 197, 208

editorial and textual issues
Sonnets **28**: 363; **40**: 273; **42**: 296

education
All's Well That Ends Well **7**: 62, 86, 90, 93, 98, 104, 116, 126
The Two Gentlemen of Verona **6**: 490, 494, 504, 526, 532, 555, 568

education or nurturing
The Tempest **8**: 353, 370, 384, 396; **29**: 292, 368, 377

egotism or narcissism
Much Ado about Nothing **8**: 19, 24, 28, 29, 55, 69, 95, 115

Elizabeth, audience of
Sonnets **48**: 325

Elizabeth's influence
The Merry Wives of Windsor **5**: 333, 334, 335, 336, 339, 346, 355, 366, 402; **18**: 5, 86; **38**: 278; **47**: 344

Elizabethan and Jacobean politics, relation to
Hamlet **28**: 232; **28**: 290, 311; **35**: 140

Elizabethan attitudes, influence of
Richard II **6**: 287, 292, 294, 305, 321, 327, 364, 402, 414; **13**: 494; **24**: 325; **28**: 188; **39**: 273; **42**: 118

Elizabethan betrothal and marriage customs
Measure for Measure **2**: 429, 437, 443, 503; **49**: 286

Elizabethan culture, relation to
General Commentary **50**: 34
Antony and Cleopatra **47**: 103
As You Like It **5**: 21, 59, 66, 68, 70, 158; **16**: 53; **28**: 46; **34**: 120; **37**: 1; **46**: 142
The Comedy of Errors **26**: 138, 142; **34**: 201, 215, 233, 238, 258; **42**: 80
Hamlet **1**: 76, 148, 151, 154, 160, 166, 169, 171, 176, 184, 202, 209, 254; **13**: 282, 494; **19**: 330; **21**: 407, 416; **22**: 258
Henry IV, Parts 1 and 2 **19**: 195; **48**: 117, 143, 151, 175
Henry V **5**: 210, 213, 217, 223, 257, 299, 310; **16**: 202; **19**: 133, 233; **28**: 121, 159; **30**: 215, 262; **37**: 187; **49**: 260
Julius Caesar **16**: 231; **30**: 342, 379; **50**: 13, 211, 269, 280
King Lear **2**: 168, 174, 177, 183, 226, 241; **19**: 330; **22**: 227, 233, 365; **25**: 218; **46**: 276; **47**: 9; **49**: 67
Measure for Measure **2**: 394, 418, 429, 432, 437, 460, 470, 482, 503
The Merchant of Venice **32**: 66; **40**: 117, 127, 142, 166, 181, 197, 208; **48**: 54, 77; **49**: 37
A Midsummer Night's Dream **50**: 86
Much Ado about Nothing **8**: 23, 33, 44, 55, 58, 79, 88, 104, 111, 115; **51**: 15
The Rape of Lucrece **33**: 195; **43**: 77
The Taming of the Shrew **31**: 288, 295, 300, 315, 326, 345, 351
Timon of Athens **1**: 487, 489, 495, 500; **20**: 433; **27**: 203, 212, 230; **50**: 13
Titus Andronicus **27**: 282
Troilus and Cressida **3**: 560, 574, 606; **25**: 56
Twelfth Night **1**: 549, 553, 555, 563, 581, 587, 620; **16**: 53; **19**: 42, 78; **26**: 357; **28**: 1; **34**: 323, 330; **46**: 291; **51**: 15

Elizabethan dramatic conventions
Cymbeline **4**: 53, 124
Henry VIII **24**: 155

Elizabethan literary influences
Henry VI, Parts 1, 2, and 3 **3**: 75, 97, 100, 119, 143; **22**: 156; **28**: 112; **37**: 97

Elizabethan love poetry
Love's Labour's Lost **38**: 232

Elizabethan poetics, influence of
Romeo and Juliet **5**: 416, 520, 522, 528, 550, 559, 575

Elizabethan politics, relation to
  Henry IV, Parts 1 and 2 **22:** 395; **28:** 203; **47:** 60; **48:** 117, 143, 167, 175
  Henry VIII **22:** 395; **24:** 115, 129, 140; **32:** 148
  King John **48:** 132
  Richard III **22:** 395; **25:** 141; **37:** 144; **39:** 345, 349; **42:** 130

Elizabethan setting
  The Two Gentlemen of Verona **12:** 463, 485

Elizabethan society
  The Merry Wives of Windsor **47:** 331

Epicureanism 50: 249

emulation or rivalry
  Julius Caesar **16:** 231; **50:** 211

England and Rome, parallels between
  Coriolanus **9:** 39, 43, 106, 148, 180, 193; **25:** 296; **30:** 67, 105

English language and colonialism
  Henry V **22:** 103; **28:** 159

English Reformation, influence of
  Henry VIII **2:** 25, 35, 39, 51, 67; **24:** 89

epic elements
  Henry V **5:** 192, 197, 246, 257, 314; **30:** 181, 220, 237, 252

erotic elements
  A Midsummer Night's Dream **3:** 445, 491, 497, 511; **12:** 259, 262, 298; **16:** 34; **19:** 21; **29:** 183, 225, 269
  Venus and Adonis **10:** 410, 411, 418, 419, 427, 428, 429, 442, 448, 454, 459, 466, 473; **25:** 305, 328; **28:** 355; **33:** 321, 339, 347, 352, 363, 370; **51:** 345, 352, 359, 368

as experimental play
  Romeo and Juliet **5:** 464, 509, 528

Essex Rebellion, relation to
  Richard II **6:** 249, 250; **24:** 356

ethical or moral issues
  King John **9:** 212, 222, 224, 229, 235, 240, 263, 275, 280

ethnicity
  The Winter's Tale **37:** 306

Euripides, influence of
  Titus Andronicus **27:** 285

evil
  See also **good versus evil**
  Macbeth **3:** 194, 208, 231, 234, 239, 241, 267, 289; **20:** 203, 206, 210, 374
  Romeo and Juliet **5:** 485, 493, 505

excess
  King John **9:** 251

fable of the belly
  Coriolanus **50:** 13, 110, 140

fame
  Coriolanus **30:** 58

family honor, structure, and inheritance
  Richard II **6:** 338, 368, 388, 397, 414; **39:** 263, 279
  Richard III **8:** 177, 248, 252, 263, 267; **25:** 141; **39:** 335, 341, 349, 370

family, theme of
  Cymbeline **44:** 28

fancy
  Twelfth Night **1:** 543, 546

as farce
  The Taming of the Shrew **9:** 330, 337, 338, 341, 342, 365, 381, 386, 413, 426

farcical elements
  See **comic and farcical elements**

fate
  Richard II **6:** 289, 294, 304, 352, 354, 385
  Romeo and Juliet **5:** 431, 444, 464, 469, 470, 479, 480, 485, 487, 493, 509, 530, 533, 562, 565, 571, 573; **33:** 249

Fathers and Daughters (Volume 36: 1, 12, 25, 32, 37, 45, 70, 78)
  As You Like It **46:** 94
  Cymbeline **34:** 134
  King Lear **34:** 51, 54, 60
    cruelty of daughters **2:** 101, 102, 106; **31:** 84, 123, 137, 142
  Pericles **34:** 226, 233
  The Winter's Tale **34:** 311, 318, 328

Feast of the Lupercal
  Julius Caesar **50:** 269

feminist criticism
  As You Like It **23:** 107, 108
  Comedy of Errors **42:** 93
  Love's Labour's Lost **42:** 93
  Measure for Measure **23:** 320

feminist interpretation
  A Midsummer Night's Dream **48:** 23

festive or folklore elements
  Twelfth Night **46:** 338; **51:** 15

feud
  Romeo and Juliet **5:** 415, 419, 425, 447, 458, 464, 469, 479, 480, 493, 509, 522, 556, 565, 566, 571, 575; **25:** 181; **51:** 245

fire and water
  Coriolanus **25:** 263

flattery
  Coriolanus **9:** 26, 45, 92, 100, 110, 121, 130, 144, 157, 183, 193; **25:** 296

  Henry IV, Parts 1 and 2 **22:** 395
  Henry VIII **22:** 395
  Richard III **22:** 395

folk drama, relation to
  The Winter's Tale **7:** 420, 451

folk elements
  The Taming of the Shrew **9:** 381, 393, 404, 426

folk rituals, elements and influence of
  Henry VI, Parts 1, 2, and 3 **39:** 205
  The Merry Wives of Windsor **5:** 353, 369, 376, 392, 397, 400; **38:** 256, 300

food, meaning of
  The Comedy of Errors **34:** 220
  Troilus and Cressida **43:** 298

forest
  The Two Gentlemen of Verona **6:** 450, 456, 492, 514, 547, 555, 564, 568

Forest of Arden
  As You Like It
    as "bitter" Arcadia **5:** 98, 118, 162; **23:** 97, 98, 99, 100, 122, 139
    Duke Frederick's court, contrast with **5:** 46, 102, 103, 112, 130, 156; **16:** 53; **23:** 126, 128, 129, 131, 134; **34:** 78, 102, 131; **46:** 164
    pastoral elements **5:** 18, 20, 24, 32, 35, 47, 50, 54, 55, 57, 60, 77, 128, 135, 156; **23:** 17, 20, 27, 46, 137; **34:** 78, 147; **46:** 88
    as patriarchal society **5:** 168; **23:** 150; **34:** 177
    as source of self-knowledge **5:** 98, 102, 103, 128, 130, 135, 148, 158, 162; **23:** 17; **34:** 102
    as timeless, mythical world **5:** 112, 130, 141; **23:** 132; **34:** 78; **37:** 43; **46:** 88
    theme of play **46:** 88

forgiveness or redemption
  Venus and Adonis **51:** 377
  The Winter's Tale **7:** 381, 389, 395, 402, 407, 436, 456, 460, 483; **36:** 318

free will versus fate
  Macbeth **3:** 177, 183, 184, 190, 196, 198, 202, 207, 208, 213; **13:** 361; **44:** 351, 361, , 366, 373
  The Two Noble Kinsmen **9:** 474, 481, 486, 492, 498

freedom and servitude
  The Tempest **8:** 304, 307, 312, 429; **22:** 302; **29:** 278, 368, 377; **37:** 336

French language, Shakespeare's use of
  Henry V **5:** 186, 188, 190; **25:** 131

Freudian analysis
  A Midsummer Night's Dream **44:** 1

friendship
  See also **love and friendship** *and* **love versus friendship**

Coriolanus **30**: 125, 142
Sonnets **10**: 185, 279; **28**: 380; **51**: 284, 288;
The Two Noble Kinsmen **9**: 448, 463, 470, 474, 479, 481, 486, 490; **19**: 394; **41**: 363, 372; **42**: 361

Gender Identity and Issues (Volume **40**: 1, 9, 15, 27, 33, 51, 61, 65, 75, 90, 99)
All's Well That Ends Well **7**: 9, 10, 67, 126; **13**: 77, 84; **19**: 113; **26**: 128; **38**: 89, 99, 118; **44**: 35
Antony and Cleopatra **13**: 368; **25**: 257; **27**: 144; **47**: 174, 192
As You Like It **46**: 127, 134
The Comedy of Errors **34**: 215, 220
Coriolanus **30**: 79, 125, 142; **44**: 93; **50**: 128
Hamlet **35**: 144; **44**: 189, 195, 198
Henry IV, Parts 1 and 2 **13**: 183; **25**: 151; **44**: 44; **48**: 175
Henry V **13**: 183; **28**: 121, 146, 159; **44**: 44
Julius Caesar **13**: 260
The Merchant of Venice **40**: 142, 151, 156
Othello **32**: 294; **35**: 327
Richard II **25**: 89; **39**: 295
Richard III **25**: 141; **37**: 144; **39**: 345
Romeo and Juliet **32**: 256; **51**: 253
Sonnets **37**: 374; **40**: 238, 247, 254, 264, 268, 273
The Taming of the Shrew **28**: 24; **31**: 261, 268, 276, 282, 288, 295, 300, 335, 351
Twelfth Night **19**: 78; **34**: 344; **37**: 59; **42**: 32; **46**: 347, 362, 369
The Two Gentlemen of Verona **40**: 374
The Two Noble Kinsmen **42**: 361

genre
All's Well That Ends Well **48**: 65
As You Like It **5**: 46, 55, 79
The Comedy of Errors **34**: 251, 258
Coriolanus **9**: 42, 43, 53, 80, 106, 112, 117, 130, 164, 177; **30**: 67, 74, 79, 89, 111, 125; **50**: 99
Hamlet **1**: 176, 212, 237
Love's Labour's Lost **38**: 163
The Merchant of Venice **4**: 191, 200, 201, 209, 215, 221, 232, 238, 247; **12**: 48, 54, 62
Much Ado about Nothing **8**: 9, 18, 19, 28, 29, 39, 41, 44, 53, 63, 69, 73, 79, 82, 95, 100, 104; **48**: 14
Richard III **8**: 181, 182, 197, 206, 218, 228, 239, 243, 252, 258; **13**: 142; **39**: 383
The Taming of the Shrew **9**: 329, 334, 362, 375; **22**: 48; **31**: 261, 269, 276
Timon of Athens **1**: 454, 456, 459, 460, 462, 483, 492, 499, 503, 509, 511, 512, 515, 518, 525, 531; **27**: 203
Troilus and Cressida **3**: 541, 542, 549, 558, 566, 571, 574, 587, 594, 604, 630, 642; **27**: 366
The Two Gentlemen of Verona **6**: 460, 468, 472, 516; **40**: 320

genres, mixture of
Timon of Athens **16**: 351; **25**: 198

gift exchange
Love's Labour's Lost **25**: 1

good versus evil
See also evil
Measure for Measure **2**: 432, 452, 524; **33**: 52, 61
The Tempest **8**: 302, 311, 315, 370, 423, 439; **29**: 278; 297

grace
The Winter's Tale **7**: 420, 425, 460, 493; **36**: 328

grace and civility
Love's Labour's Lost **2**: 351

Greece
Troilus and Cressida **43**: 287

grotesque or absurd elements
Hamlet **42**: 279
King Lear **2**: 136, 156, 245; **13**: 343

handkerchief, significance of
Othello **4**: 370, 384, 385, 396, 503, 530, 562; **35**: 265, 282, 380

Hercules Furens (Seneca) as source
Othello **16**: 283

heroism
Henry V **49**: 194, 200, 211, 236

Hippolytus, myth of
A Midsummer Night's Dream **29**: 216; **45**: 84

historical accuracy
Henry VI, Parts 1, 2, and 3 **3**: 18, 21, 35, 46, 51; **16**: 217; **24**: 16, 18, 25, 31, 45, 48
Richard III **8**: 144, 145, 153, 159, 163, 165, 168, 213, 223, 228, 232; **39**: 305, 308, 326, 383

historical allegory
The Winter's Tale **7**: 381; **15**: 528

historical elements
Cymbeline **47**: 260

historical and dramatic elements
Henry IV **49**: 93

historical and romantic elements, combination of
Henry VIII **2**: 46, 49, 51, 75, 76, 78; **24**: 71, 80, 146; **41**: 129, 146, 180

historical content
Henry IV, Parts 1 and 2 **1**: 310, 328, 365, 366, 370, 374, 380, 387, 421, 424, 427, 431; **16**: 172; **19**: 157; **25**: 151; **32**: 136; **39**: 143; **48**: 143, 167
Henry V **5**: 185, 188, 190, 192, 193, 198, 246, 314; **13**: 201; **19**: 133; **25**: 131; **30**: 193, 202, 207, 215, 252
King John **9**: 216, 219, 220, 222, 235, 240, 254, 284, 290, 292, 297, 300, 303; **13**: 163; **32**: 93, 114; **41**: 234, 243
The Tempest **8**: 364, 408, 420; **16**: 426; **25**: 382; **29**: 278, 339, 343, 368; **45**: 226

historical determinism versus free will
Julius Caesar **7**: 160, 298, 316, 333, 346, 356; **13**: 252

historical epic, as epilogue to Shakespeare's
Henry VIII **2**: 22, 25, 27, 39, 51, 60, 65

historical epic, place in or relation to Shakespeare's
Henry IV, Parts 1 and 2 **1**: 309, 314, 328, 374, 379, 424, 427
Henry V **5**: 195, 198, 205, 212, 225, 241, 244, 287, 304, 310; **14**: 337, 342; **30**: 215
Henry VI, Parts 1, 2, and 3 **3**: 24, 59; **24**: 51; **48**: 167

historical principles
Richard III **39**: 308, 326, 387

historical relativity, theme of **41**: 146

historical sources, compared with
Richard II **6**: 252, 279, 343; **28**: 134; **39**: 235; **49**: 60

historiography
Henry VIII **37**: 109

homoerotic elements
As You Like It **46**: 127, 142
Henry V **16**: 202
Sonnets **10**: 155, 156, 159, 161, 175, 213, 391; **16**: 461; **28**: 363, 380; **37**: 347; **40**: 254, 264, 273; **51**: 270, 284

homosexuality
As You Like It **46**: 127, 142
Measure for Measure **42**: 1
The Merchant of Venice **22**: 3, 69; **37**: 86; **40**: 142, 156, 197
Twelfth Night **22**: 69; **42**: 32; **46**: 362
The Winter's Tale **48**: 309

honor or integrity
Coriolanus **9**: 43, 65, 73, 92, 106, 110, 121, 144, 153, 157, 164, 177, 183, 189; **30**: 89, 96, 133

hospitality
The Winter's Tale **19**: 366

as humanistic play
Henry VI, Parts 1, 2, and 3 **3**: 83, 92, 109, 115, 119, 131, 136, 143

hunt motif
Venus and Adonis **10**: 434, 451, 466, 473; **33**: 357, 370

hypocrisy
Henry V **5**: 203, 213, 219, 223, 233, 260, 271, 302

ideal love
See also love
Romeo and Juliet **5**: 421, 427, 431, 436, 437, 450, 463, 469, 498, 505, 575; **25**: 257; **33**: 210, 225, 272; **51**: 25; **51**: 44, 195, 203, 219

idealism versus pragmatism
  Hamlet **16**: 246; **28**: 325

idealism versus realism
  See also realism
  Love's Labour's Lost **38**: 163
  Othello **4**: 457, 508, 517; **13**: 313; **25**: 189

identities of persons
  Sonnets **10**: 154, 155, 156, 161, 166, 167, 169, 173, 174, 175, 185, 190, 191, 196, 218, 226, 230, 233, 240; **40**: 238

identity
  The Comedy of Errors **34**: 201, 208, 211
  Coriolanus **42**: 243; **50**: 128
  A Midsummer Night's Dream **29**: 269
  The Two Gentlemen of Verona **6**: 494, 511, 529, 532, 547, 560, 564, 568; **19**: 34

illusion
  The Comedy of Errors **1**: 13, 14, 27, 37, 40, 45, 59, 63; **26**: 188; **34**: 194, 211

illusion versus reality
  Love's Labour's Lost **2**: 303, 308, 331, 340, 344, 348, 356, 359, 367, 371, 375; **23**: 230, 231

imagery
  Venus and Adonis **10**: 414, 415, 416, 420, 429, 434, 449, 459, 466, 473, 480; **25**: 328; **28**: 355; **33**: 321, 339, 352, 363, 370, 377; **42**: 347; **51**: 335, 388

imagination and art
  A Midsummer Night's Dream **3**: 365, 371, 381, 402, 412, 417, 421, 423, 441, 459, 468, 506, 516, 520; **22**: 39; **45**: 96, 126, 136, 147

immortality
  Measure for Measure **16**: 102

imperialism
  Henry V **22**: 103; **28**: 159

implausibility of plot, characters, or events
  All's Well That Ends Well **7**: 8, 45
  King Lear **2**: 100, 136, 145, 278; **13**: 343
  The Merchant of Venice **4**: 191, 192, 193; **12**: 52, 56, 76, 119
  Much Ado about Nothing **8**: 9, 12, 16, 19, 33, 36, 39, 44, 53, 100, 104
  Othello **4**: 370, 380, 391, 442, 444; **47**: 51

inaction
  Troilus and Cressida **3**: 587, 621; **27**: 347

incest, motif of
  Pericles **2**: 582, 588; **22**: 315; **36**: 257, 264; **51**: 97, 110

inconsistencies
  Henry VIII **2**: 16, 27, 28, 31, 60

inconsistency between first and second halves
  Measure for Measure **2**: 474, 475, 505, 514, 524; **49**: 349, 358

induction
  The Taming of the Shrew **9**: 320, 322, 332, 337, 345, 350, 362, 365, 369, 370, 381, 390, 393, 407, 419, 424, 430; **12**: 416, 427, 430, 431, 441; **19**: 34, 122; **22**: 48; **31**: 269, 315, 351

as inferior or flawed play
  Henry VI, Parts 1, 2, and 3 **3**: 20, 21, 25, 26, 35
  Pericles **2**: 537, 546, 553, 563, 564; **15**: 139, 143, 156, 167, 176; **36**: 198; **51**: 79
  Timon of Athens **1**: 476, 481, 489, 499, 520; **20**: 433, 439, 491; **25**: 198; **27**: 157, 175

infidelity
  Troilus and Cressida **43**: 298

innocence
  Macbeth **3**: 234, 241, 327
  Othello **47**: 25
  Pericles **36**: 226, 274

innocence to experience
  The Two Noble Kinsmen **9**: 481, 502; **19**: 394

Ireland, William Henry, forgeries of
  Sonnets **48**: 325

Irish affairs
  Henry V **22**: 103; **28**: 159

ironic or parodic elements
  The Two Gentlemen of Verona **6**: 447, 472, 478, 484, 502, 504, 509, 516, 529, 549; **13**: 12
  Henry VIII **41**: 129

irony
  All's Well That Ends Well **7**: 27, 32, 58, 62, 67, 81, 86, 109, 116
  Antony and Cleopatra **6**: 53, 136, 146, 151, 159, 161, 189, 192, 211, 224
  As You Like It **5**: 30, 32, 154
  Coriolanus **9**: 65, 73, 80, 92, 106, 153, 157, 164, 193; **30**: 67, 89, 133
  Cymbeline **4**: 64, 77, 103
  Henry V **5**: 192, 210, 213, 219, 223, 226, 233, 252, 260, 269, 281, 299, 304; **14**: 336; **30**: 159, 193
  Julius Caesar **7**: 167, 257, 259, 262, 268, 282, 316, 320, 333, 336, 346, 350
  The Merchant of Venice **4**: 254, 300, 321, 331, 350; **28**: 63
  Much Ado about Nothing **8**: 14, 63, 79, 82; **28**: 63
  The Rape of Lucrece **10**: 93, 98, 128
  Richard II **6**: 270, 307, 364, 368, 391; **24**: 383; **28**: 188
  Sonnets **10**: 256, 293, 334, 337, 346; **51**: 300
  The Taming of the Shrew **9**: 340, 375, 398, 407, 413; **13**: 3; **19**: 122
  The Two Noble Kinsmen **9**: 463, 481, 486; **41**: 301; **50**: 348
  The Winter's Tale **7**: 419, 420

the island
  The Tempest **8**: 308, 315, 447; **25**: 357, 382; **29**: 278, 343

Italian influences
  Sonnets **28**: 407

Jacobean culture, relation to
  Coriolanus **22**: 248
  Macbeth **19**: 330; **22**: 365
  Pericles **37**: 361; **51**: 86, 110
  The Winter's Tale **19**: 366, 401, 431; **25**: 347; **32**: 388; **37**: 306

jealousy
  The Merry Wives of Windsor **5**: 334, 339, 343, 353, 355, 363; **22**: 93; **38**: 273, 307
  Othello **4**: 384, 488, 527; **35**: 253, 265, 282, 301, 310; **44**: 57, 66; **51**: 30
  The Winter's Tale **44**: 66; **47**: 25

Jonsonian humors comedy, influence of
  The Merry Wives of Windsor **38**: 319

judicial versus natural law
  Measure for Measure **2**: 446, 507, 516, 519; **22**: 85; **33**: 58, 117; **49**: 1, 293

justice
  As You Like It **46**: 94
  Henry IV **49**: 112, 123
  King Lear **49**: 1
  Othello **35**: 247

justice and mercy
  Measure for Measure **2**: 391, 395, 399, 402, 406, 409, 411, 416, 421, 437, 443, 463, 466, 470, 491, 495, 522, 524; **22**: 85; **33**: 52, 61, 101; **49**: 1, 274, 293, 300
  The Merchant of Venice **4**: 213, 214, 224, 250, 261, 273, 282, 289, 336; **12**: 80, 129; **40**: 127; **49**: 1, 23, 27, 37
  Much Ado about Nothing **22**: 85

justice, divine vs. worldly
  King Lear **49**: 67, 73

juxtaposition of opposing perspectives
  As You Like It **5**: 86, 93, 98, 141; **16**: 53; **23**: 119; **34**: 72, 78, 131

Kingship (Volume 39: 1, 16, 20, 34, 45, 62)
  Henry IV, Parts 1 and 2 **1**: 314, 318, 337, 366, 370, 374, 379, 380, 383, 424; **16**: 172; **19**: 195; **28**: 101; **39**: 100, 116, 123, 130; **42**: 141; **48**: 143
  Henry V **5**: 205, 223, 225, 233, 239, 244, 257, 264, 267, 271, 287, 289, 299, 302, 304, 314, 318; **16**: 202; **22**: 137; **30**: 169, 202, 259, 273; **42**: 141; **49**: 200
  Henry VI, Parts 1, 2, and 3 **3**: 69, 73, 77, 109, 115, 136, 143; **24**: 32; **39**: 154, 177, 187; **47**: 32
  Henry VIII **2**: 49, 58, 60, 65, 75, 78; **24**: 113; **41**: 129, 171
  King John **9**: 235, 254, 263, 275, 297; **13**: 158; **19**: 182; **22**: 120
  Richard II **6**: 263, 264, 272, 277, 289, 294, 327, 354, 364, 381, 388, 391, 402, 409, 414; **19**: 151, 209; **24**: 260, 289, 291, 322, 325, 333, 339, 345, 346, 349, 351, 352, 356, 395, 408, 419, 428; **28**: 134; **39**: 235, 243, 256, 263, 273, 279, 289; **42**: 173
  Richard III **39**: 335, 341, 345, 349

knighthood
  The Merry Wives of Windsor **5:** 338, 343, 390, 397, 402; **47:** 354

knowledge
  Love's Labour's Lost **22:** 12; **47:** 35

language and imagery
  All's Well That Ends Well **7:** 12, 29, 45, 104, 109, 121; **38:** 132, 65
  Antony and Cleopatra **6:** 21, 25, 39, 64, 80, 85, 92, 94, 100, 104, 142, 146, 155, 159, 161, 165, 189, 192, 202, 211; **13:** 374, 383; **25:** 245, 257; **27:** 96, 105, 135
  As You Like It **5:** 19, 21, 35, 52, 75, 82, 92, 138; **23:** 15, 21, 26; **28:** 9; **34:** 131; **37:** 43; **48:** 42
  The Comedy of Errors **1:** 16, 25, 39, 40, 43, 57, 59; **34:** 233
  Coriolanus **9:** 8, 9, 13, 53, 64, 65, 73, 78, 84, 100, 112, 121, 136, 139, 142, 144, 153, 157, 174, 183, 193, 198; **22:** 248; **25:** 245, 263; **30:** 111, 125, 142; **37:** 283; **44:** 79
  Cymbeline **4:** 43, 48, 61, 64, 70, 73, 93, 108; **13:** 401; **25:** 245; **28:** 373, 398; **36:** 115, 158, 166, 186; **47:** 205, 286, 296
  Hamlet **1:** 95, 144, 153, 154, 160, 188, 198, 221, 227, 249, 259, 270; **22:** 258, 378; **28:** 311; **35:** 144, 152, 238, 241; **42:** 212; **44:** 248
  Henry IV, Parts 1 and 2 **13:** 213; **16:** 172; **25:** 245; **28:** 101; **39:** 116, 130; **42:** 153; **47:** 1
  Henry V **5:** 188, 230, 233, 241, 264, 276; **9:** 203; **19:** 203; **25:** 131; **30:** 159, 181, 207, 234
  30: 159, 181, 207, 234
  Henry VI, Parts 1, 2, and 3 **3:** 21, 50, 52, 55, 57, 66, 67, 71, 75, 76, 97, 105, 109, 119, 126, 131; **24:** 28; **37:** 157; **39:**213, 222
  Henry VIII **41:** 180, 190
  Julius Caesar **7:** 148, 155, 159, 188, 204, 207, 227, 242, 250, 277, 296, 303, 324, 346, 350; **13:** 260; **17:** 347, 348, 350, 356, 358; **19:** 321; **22:** 280; **25:** 280; **30:** 333, 342; **50:** 196, 258
  King Lear **2:** 129, 137, 161, 191, 199, 237, 257, 271; **16:** 301; **19:** 344; **22:** 233; **46:** 177
  King John **9:** 212, 215, 220, 246, 251, 254, 267, 280, 284, 292, 297, 300; **13:** 147, 158; **22:** 120; **37:** 132; **48:** 132
  Love's Labour's Lost **2:** 301, 302, 303, 306, 307, 308, 315, 319, 320, 330, 335, 344, 345, 348, 356, 359, 362, 365, 371, 374, 375; **19:** 92; **22:** 12, 378; **23:** 184, 187, 196, 197, 202, 207, 211, 221, 227, 231, 233, 237, 252; **28:** 9, 63; **38:** 219, 226
  Macbeth **3:** 170, 193, 213, 231, 234, 241, 245, 250, 253, 256, 263, 271, 283, 300, 302, 306, 323, 327, 338, 340, 349; **13:** 476; **16:** 317; **20:** 241, 279, 283, 367, 379, 400; **25:** 235; **28:** 339; **29:** 76, 91; **42:** 258; **44:** 366; **45:** 58
  Measure for Measure **2:** 394, 421, 431, 466, 486, 505; **13:** 112; **28:** 9; **33:** 69; **49:** 370
  The Merry Wives of Windsor **5:** 335, 337, 343, 347, 351, 363, 374, 379; **19:** 101; **22:** 93, 378; **28:** 9, 69; **38:** 313, 319
  The Merchant of Venice **4:** 241, 267, 293; **22:** 3; **25:** 257; **28:** 9, 63; **32:** 41; **40:** 106
  A Midsummer Night's Dream **3:** 397, 401, 410, 412, 415, 432, 453, 459, 468, 494; **22:** 23, 39, 93, 378; **28:** 9; **29:** 263; **45:** 143, 169, 175; **48:** 23, 32
  Much Ado about Nothing **8:** 9, 38, 43, 46, 55, 69, 73, 88, 95, 100, 115, 125; **19:** 68; **25:** 77; **28:** 63; **31:** 178, 184, 222, 241, 245; **48:** 14
  Othello **4:** 433, 442, 445, 462, 493, 508, 517, 552, 587, 596; **13:** 304; **16:** 272; **22:** 378; **25:** 189, 257; **28:** 243, 344; **42:** 273; **47:** 51
  Pericles **2:** 559, 560, 565, 583; **16:** 391; **19:** 387; **22:** 315; **36:** 198, 214, 233, 244, 251, 264; **51:** 86, 99
  The Rape of Lucrece **10:** 64, 65, 66, 71, 78, 80, 89, 93, 116, 109, 125, 131; **22:** 289, 294; **25:** 305; **32:** 321; **33:** 144, 155, 179, 200; **43:** 102, 113, 141
  Richard II **6:** 252, 282, 283, 294, 298, 315, 323, 331, 347, 368, 374, 381, 385, 397, 409; **13:** 213, 494; **24:** 269, 270, 298, 301, 304, 315, 325, 329, 333, 339, 356, 364, 395, 405, 408, 411, 414, 419; **28:** 134, 188; **39:** 243, 273, 289, 295; **42:** 173
  Richard III **8:** 159, 161, 165, 167, 168, 170, 177, 182, 184, 186, 193, 197, 201, 206, 218, 223, 243, 248, 252, 258, 262, 267; **16:** 150; **25:** 141, 245; **39:** 360, 370, 383; **47:** 15
  Romeo and Juliet **5:** 420, 426, 431, 436, 437, 456, 477, 479, 489, 492, 496, 509, 520, 522, 528, 538, 542, 550, 559; **25:** 181, 245, 257; **32:** 276; **33:** 210, 272, 274, 287; **42:** 266; **51:** 203, 212, 227
  Sonnets **10:** 247, 251, 255, 256, 290, 353, 372, 385; **13:** 445; **28:** 380, 385; **32:** 327, 352; **40:** 228, 247, 284, 292, 303; **51:** 270, 304
  The Taming of the Shrew **9:** 336, 338, 393, 401, 404, 407, 413; **22:** 378; **28:** 9; **31:** 261, 288, 300, 326, 335, 339; **32:** 56
  The Tempest **8:** 324, 348, 384, 390, 404, 454; **19:** 421; **29:** 278; **29:** 297, 343, 368, 377
  Timon of Athens **1:** 488; **13:** 392; **25:** 198; **27:** 166, 184, 235
  Titus Andronicus **4:** 617, 624, 635, 642, 644, 646, 659, 664, 668, 672, 675; **13:** 225; **16:** 225; **25:** 245; **27:** 246, 293, 313, 318, 325; **43:** 186, 222, 227, 239, 247, 262
  Troilus and Cressida **3:** 561, 569, 596, 599, 606, 624, 630, 635; **22:** 58, 339; **27:** 332; **366; 42:** 66
  Twelfth Night **1:** 570, 650, 664; **22:** 12; **28:** 9; **34:** 293; **37:** 59
  The Two Gentlemen of Verona **6:** 437, 438, 439, 445, 449, 490, 504, 519, 529, 541; **28:** 9; **40:** 343
  The Two Noble Kinsmen **9:** 445, 446, 447, 448, 456, 461, 462, 463, 469, 471, 498, 502; **41:** 289, 301, 308, 317, 326; **50:** 310
  The Winter's Tale **7:** 382, 384, 417, 418, 420, 425, 460, 506; **13:** 409; **19:** 431; **22:** 324; **25:** 347; **36:** 295; **42:** 301; **45:** 297, 344, 333; **50:** 45

language versus action
  Titus Andronicus **4:** 642, 644, 647, 664, 668; **13:** 225; **27:** 293, 313, 325; **43:** 186

law and justice
  Henry V **49:** 223, 236, 260

law versus passion for freedom
  Much Ado about Nothing **22:** 85

laws of nature, violation of
  Macbeth **3:** 234, 241, 280, 323; **29:** 120

legal issues
  King Lear **46:** 276

legitimacy
  Henry VI, Parts 1, 2, and 3 **3:** 89, 157; **39:** 154; *Henry VIII* **37:** 109

legitimacy or inheritance
  King John **9:** 224, 235, 254, 303; **13:** 147; **19:** 182; **37:** 132; **41:** 215

liberty versus tyranny
  Julius Caesar **7:** 158, 179, 189, 205, 221, 253; **25:** 272

love
  See also **ideal love**
  All's Well That Ends Well **7:** 12, 15, 16, 51, 58, 67, 90, 93, 116; **38:** 80; **51:** 33, 44
  As You Like It **5:** 24, 44, 46, 57, 79, 88, 103, 116, 122, 138, 141, 162; **28:** 46, 82; **34:** 85
  King Lear **2:** 109, 112, 131, 160, 162, 170, 179, 188, 197, 218, 222, 238, 265; **25:** 202; **31:** 77, 149, 151, 155, 162
  Love's Labour's Lost **2:** 312, 315, 340, 344; **22:** 12; **23:** 252; **38:** 194; **51:** 44
  The Merchant of Venice **4:** 221, 226, 270, 284, 312, 344; **22:** 3, 69; **25:** 257; **40:** 156; **51:** 1, 44
    sacrificial love **13:** 43; **22:** 69; **40:** 142
  A Midsummer Night's Dream
    passionate or romantic love **3:** 372, 389, 395, 396, 402, 408, 411, 423, 441, 450, 480, 497, 498, 511; **29:** 175, 225, 263, 269; **45:** 126, 136; **51:** 44
  Much Ado about Nothing **8:** 24, 55, 75, 95, 111, 115; **28:** 56; **51:** 30
  Othello **4:** 412, 493, 506, 512, 530, 545, 552, 569, 570, 575, 580, 591; **19:** 253; **22:** 207; **25:** 257; **28:** 243, 344; **32:** 201; **35:** 261, 317; **51:** 25, 30
  The Phoenix and Turtle **10:** 31, 37, 40, 50; **38:** 342, 345, 367; **51:** 145, 151, 155
  Sonnets **10:** 173, 247, 287, 290, 293, 302, 309, 322, 325, 329, 394; **28:** 380; **37:** 347; **51:** 270, 284, 288, 292
  The Tempest **8:** 435, 439; **29:** 297, 339, 377, 396
  Twelfth Night **1:** 543, 546, 573, 580, 587, 595, 600, 603, 610, 660; **19:** 78; **26:** 257, 364; **34:** 270, 293, 323; **46:** 291, 333, 347, 362; **51:** 30
  The Two Gentlemen of Verona **6:** 442, 445, 456, 479, 488, 492, 494, 502, 509, 516, 519, 549; **13:** 12; **40:** 327, 335, 343, 354, 365; **51:** 30, 44
  The Two Noble Kinsmen **9:** 479, 481, 490, 498; **41:** 289, 301, 355, 363, 372, 385; **50:** 295, 361
  The Winter's Tale **7:** 417, 425, 469, 490; **51:** 30, 33, 44

love and friendship
  See also **friendship**
  Julius Caesar **7:** 233, 262, 268; **25:** 272

love and honor
  Troilus and Cressida **3:** 555, 604; **27:** 370, 374

love and passion
  Antony and Cleopatra **6:** 51, 64, 71, 80, 85, 100, 115, 159, 165, 180; **25:** 257; **27:** 126; **47:** 71, 124., 174, 192; **51:** 25, 33, 44

love and reason
See also **reason**
Othello **4:** 512, 530, 580; **19:** 253

Love and Romance (Volume **51:** 1, 15, 25, 30, 33, 44)
Pericles **51:** 71
The Phoenix and Turtle **51:** 145, 151, 155
Romeo and Juliet **51:** 195, 203, 212
Sonnets **51:** 284, 288, 292
Venus and Adonis
The Rhetoric of Desire **51:** 345, 352, 359, 368

love, lechery, or rape
Troilus and Cressida **43:** 357

love versus fate
Romeo and Juliet **5:** 421, 437, 438, 443, 445, 458; **33:** 249

love versus friendship
See also **friendship**
The Two Gentlemen of Verona **6:** 439, 449, 450, 458, 460, 465, 468, 471, 476, 480; **40:** 354, 365

love versus lust
Venus and Adonis **10:** 418, 420, 427, 434, 439, 448, 449, 454, 462, 466, 473, 480, 489; **25:** 305; **28:** 355; **33:** 309, 330, 339, 347, 357, 363, 370; **51:** 359

love versus reason
See also **reason**
Sonnets **10:** 329

love versus war
Troilus and Cressida **18:** 332, 371, 406, 423; **22:** 339; **27:** 376

Machiavellianism
Henry V **5:** 203, 225, 233, 252, 287, 304; **25:** 131; **30:** 273
Henry VI, Parts 1, 2, and 3 **22:** 193

Madness (Volume **35:** 1, 7, 8, 24, 34, 49, 54, 62, 68)
Hamlet **19:** 330; **35:** 104, 117, 126, 132, 134, 140, 144
King Lear **19:** 330
Macbeth **19:** 330
Othello **35:** 265, 276, 282
Twelfth Night **1:** 554, 639, 656; **26:** 371

Magic and the Supernatural (Volume **29:** 1, 12, 28, 46, 53, 65)
The Comedy of Errors **1:** 27, 30
Macbeth
supernatural grace versus evil or chaos **3:** 241, 286, 323
witchcraft and supernaturalism **3:** 171, 172, 173, 175, 177, 182, 183, 184, 185, 194, 196, 198, 202, 207, 208, 213, 219, 229, 239; **16:** 317; **19:** 245; **20:** 92, 175, 213, 279, 283, 374, 387, 406, 413; **25:** 235; **28:** 339; **29:** 91, 101, 109, 120; **44:** 351, 373
A Midsummer Night's Dream **29:** 190, 201, 210, 216

The Tempest **8:** 287, 293, 304, 315, 340, 356, 396, 401, 404, 408, 435, 458; **28:** 391, 415; **29:** 297, 343, 377; **45:** 272
Sonnets
occult **48:** 346
The Winter's Tale
witchcraft **22:** 324

male discontent
The Merry Wives of Windsor **5:** 392, 402

male domination
Love's Labour's Lost **22:** 12
A Midsummer Night's Dream **3:** 483, 520; **13:** 19; **25:** 36; **29:** 216, 225, 243, 256, 269; **42:** 46; **45:** 84

male/female relationships
As You Like It **46:** 134
The Comedy of Errors **16:** 3
The Rape of Lucrece **10:** 109, 121, 131; **22:** 289; **25:** 305; **43:** 113, 141
Troilus and Cressida **16:** 70; **22:** 339; **27:** 362

male sexual anxiety
Love's Labour's Lost **16:** 17

manhood
Macbeth **3:** 262, 309, 333; **29:** 127, 133

Marlowe's works, compared with
Richard II **42:** 173

marriage
See also **courtship and marriage**
The Comedy of Errors **34:** 251
Hamlet **22:** 339; **51:** 44
Love's Labour's Lost **2:** 335, 340; **19:** 92; **38:** 209, 232; **51:** 1, 44
Measure for Measure **2:** 443, 507, 516, 519, 524, 528; **25:** 12; **33:** 61, 90; **49:** 286; **51:** 44
The Merry Wives of Windsor **5:** 343, 369, 376, 390, 392, 400; **22:** 93; **38:** 297; **51:** 44
A Midsummer Night's Dream **3:** 402, 423, 450, 483, 520; **29:** 243, 256; **45:** 136, 143; **48:** 32; **51:** 1, 30, 44
Othello **35:** 369; **51:** 44
The Taming of the Shrew **9:** 322, 325, 329, 332, 329, 332, 334, 341, 342, 343, 344, 345, 347, 353, 360, 362, 375, 381, 390, 398, 401, 404, 413, 426, 430; **13:** 3; **19:** 3; **28:** 24; **31:** 288; **51:** 44
Titus Andronicus
marriage as political tyranny **48:** 264
Troilus and Cressida **22:** 339; **51:** 44
The Two Gentlemen of Verona **48:** 32

martial vs. civil law
Coriolanus **48:** 230

Marxist criticism
Hamlet **42:** 229
King Lear **42:** 229
Macbeth **42:** 229
Othello **42:** 229

masque elements
The Two Noble Kinsmen **9:** 490
The Tempest **42:** 332

master-slave relationship
Troilus and Cressida **22:** 58

mediation
The Merry Wives of Windsor **5:** 343, 392

as medieval allegory or morality play
Henry IV, Parts 1 and 2 **1:** 323, 324, 342, 361, 366, 373, 374; **32:** 166; **39:** 89; **47:** 60
Measure for Measure **2:** 409, 421, 443, 466, 475, 491, 505, 511, 522; **13:** 94
Timon of Athens **1:** 492, 511, 518; **27:** 155

medieval chivalry
Richard II **6:** 258, 277, 294, 327, 338, 388, 397, 414; **24:** 274, 278, 279, 280, 283; **39:** 256
Troilus and Cressida **3:** 539, 543, 544, 555, 606; **27:** 376

medieval dramatic influence
All's Well That Ends Well **7:** 29, 41, 51, 98, 113; **13:** 66
King Lear **2:** 177, 188, 201; **25:** 218
Othello **4:** 440, 527, 545, 559, 582

medieval homilies, influence of
The Merchant of Venice **4:** 224, 250, 289

medieval influence
Romeo and Juliet **5:** 480, 505, 509, 573

medieval literary influence
Henry VI, Parts 1, 2, and 3 **3:** 59, 67, 75, 100, 109, 136, 151; **13:** 131
Titus Andronicus **4:** 646, 650; **27:** 299

medieval mystery plays, relation to
Macbeth **44:** 341

medieval physiology
Julius Caesar **13:** 260

mercantilism and feudalism
Richard II **13:** 213

merit versus rank
All's Well That Ends Well **7:** 9, 10, 19, 37, 51, 76; **38:** 155; **50:** 59

Messina
Much Ado about Nothing **8:** 19, 29, 48, 69, 82, 91, 95, 108, 111, 121, 125; **31:** 191, 209, 229, 241, 245

metadramatic elements
As You Like It **5:** 128, 130, 146; **34:** 130
Henry V **13:** 194; **30:** 181; **49:** 200, 211
Love's Labour's Lost **2:** 356, 359, 362
Measure for Measure **13:** 104
A Midsummer Night's Dream **3:** 427, 468, 477, 516, 520; **29:** 190, 225, 243; **50:** 86
The Taming of the Shrew **9:** 350, 419, 424; **31:** 300, 315
The Winter's Tale **16:** 410

metamorphosis or transformation
The Merry Wives of Windsor **47:** 314

Much Ado about Nothing **8**: 88, 104, 111, 115
The Taming of the Shrew **9**: 370, 430

metaphysical poem
The Phoenix and Turtle **10**: 7, 8, 9, 20, 31, 35, 37, 40, 45, 50; **51**: 143, 171, 184

Midlands Revolt, influence of
Coriolanus **22**: 248; **30**: 79; **50**: 140, 172

military and sexual hierarchies
Othello **16**: 272

mimetic rivalry
The Two Gentlemen of Verona **13**: 12; **40**: 335

as "mingled yarn"
All's Well That Ends Well **7**: 62, 93, 109, 126; **38**: 65

Minotaur, myth of
A Midsummer Night's Dream **3**: 497, 498; **29**: 216

as miracle play
Pericles **2**: 569, 581; **36**: 205; **51**: 97

misgovernment
Measure for Measure **2**: 401, 432, 511; **22**: 85
Much Ado about Nothing **22**: 85

misogyny
King Lear **31**: 123
Measure for Measure **23**: 358

misperception
Cymbeline **19**: 411; **36**: 99, 115; **47**: 228, 237, 252, 277, 286, 296

mistaken identity
The Comedy of Errors **1**: 13, 14, 27, 37, 40, 45, 49, 55, 57, 61, 63; **19**: 34, 54; **25**: 63; **34**: 194

modernization
Richard III **14**: 523

Montaigne's *Essais***, relation to**
Sonnets **42**: 375
The Tempest **42**: 339

moral choice
Julius Caesar **7**: 179, 264, 279, 343

moral corruption
Troilus and Cressida **3**: 578, 589, 599, 604, 609; **18**: 332, 406, 412, 423; **27**: 366

moral corruption of English society
Richard III **8**: 154, 163, 165, 177, 193, 201, 218, 228, 232, 243, 248, 252, 267; **39**: 308

moral inheritance
Henry VI, Parts 1, 2, and 3 **3**: 89, 126

moral intent
Henry VIII **2**: 15, 19, 25; **24**: 140

moral lesson
Macbeth **20**: 23

moral relativism
Antony and Cleopatra **22**: 217; **27**: 121

moral seriousness, question of
Measure for Measure **2**: 387, 388, 396, 409, 417, 421, 452, 460, 495; **23**: 316, 321

morality
Henry V **5**: 195, 203, 213, 223, 225, 239, 246, 260, 271, 293
The Merry Wives of Windsor **5**: 335, 339, 347, 349, 353, 397
The Two Gentlemen of Verona **6**: 438, 492, 494, 514, 532, 555, 564
Venus and Adonis **10**: 411, 412, 414, 416, 418, 419, 420, 423, 427, 428, 439, 442, 448, 449, 454, 459, 466; **33**: 330

multiple endings
Henry IV **49**: 102

multiple perspectives of characters
Henry VI, Parts 1, 2, and 3 **3**: 69, 154

music
The Tempest **8**: 390, 404; **29**: 292; **37**: 321; **42**: 332
Twelfth Night **1**: 543, 566, 596

music and dance
A Midsummer Night's Dream **3**: 397, 400, 418, 513; **12**: 287, 289; **25**: 36
Much Ado about Nothing **19**: 68; **31**: 222

mutability, theme of
Sonnets **42**: 375

mythic elements
See **religious, mythic, or spiritual content**

mythological allusions
As You Like It **46**: 142
Antony and Cleopatra **16**: 342; **19**: 304; **27**: 110, 117; **47**: 71, 192

naming, significance of
Coriolanus **30**: 58, 96, 111, 125

narrative strategies
The Rape of Lucrece **22**: 294

nationalism and patriotism
See also **British nationalism**
Henry V **5**: 198, 205, 209, 210, 213, 219, 223, 233, 246, 252, 257, 269, 299; **19**: 133, 217; **30**: 227, 262; **49**: 219, 247
Henry VI, Parts 1, 2, and 3 **24**: 25, 45, 47
King John **9**: 209, 218, 222, 224, 235, 240, 244, 275; **25**: 98; **37**: 132
The Merry Wives of Windsor **47**: 344
The Winter's Tale **32**: 388

nature
See also **art and nature** and **art versus nature**
As You Like It **46**: 94
The Tempest **8**: 315, 370, 390, 408, 414; **29**: 343, 362, 368, 377

The Winter's Tale **7**: 397, 418, 419, 420, 425, 432, 436, 451, 452, 473, 479; **19**: 366; **45**: 329

nature as book
Pericles **22**: 315; **36**: 233

nature, philosophy of
Coriolanus **30**: 74

negative appraisals
Cymbeline **4**: 20, 35, 43, 45, 48, 53, 56, 68; **15**: 32, 105, 121
Richard II **6**: 250, 252, 253, 255, 282, 307, 317, 343, 359
Venus and Adonis **10**: 410, 411, 415, 418, 419, 424, 429

Neoclassical rules
As You Like It **5**: 19, 20
Henry IV, Parts 1 and 2 **1**: 286, 287, 290, 293
Henry VI, Parts 1, 2, and 3 **3**: 17, 18
King John **9**: 208, 209, 210, 212
Love's Labour's Lost **2**: 299, 300
Macbeth **3**: 170, 171, 173, 175; **20**: 17
Measure for Measure **2**: 387, 388, 390, 394; **23**: 269
The Merry Wives of Windsor **5**: 332, 334
Romeo and Juliet **5**: 416, 418, 426
The Tempest **8**: 287, 292, 293, 334; **25**: 357; **29**: 292; **45**: 200
Troilus and Cressida **3**: 537, 538; **18**: 276, 278, 281
The Winter's Tale **7**: 376, 377, 379, 380, 383, 410; **15**: 397

Neoplatonism
The Phoenix and Turtle **10**: 7, 9, 21, 24, 40, 45, 50; **38**: 345, 350, 367; **51**: 184
Sonnets **10**: 191, 205

nightmarish quality
Macbeth **3**: 231, 309; **20**: 210, 242; **44**: 261

nihilistic elements
King Lear **2**: 130, 143, 149, 156, 165, 231, 238, 245, 253; **22**: 271; **25**: 218; **28**: 325
Timon of Athens **1**: 481, 513, 529; **13**: 392; **20**: 481
Troilus and Cressida **27**: 354

nihilistic or pessimistic vision
King Lear **49**: 67

"nothing," significance of
Much Ado about Nothing **8**: 17, 18, 23, 55, 73, 95; **19**: 68

nurturing or feeding
Coriolanus **9**: 65, 73, 136, 183, 189; **30**: 111; **44**: 79; **50**: 110

oaths, importance of
Pericles **19**: 387

obscenity
Henry V **5**: 188, 190, 260

Oldcastle, references to
  Henry IV, Parts 1 and 2 **48**: 117

omens
  Julius Caesar **22**: 137; **45**: 10; **50**: 265, 280

oppositions or dualisms
  King John **9**: 224, 240, 263, 275, 284, 290, 300

order
  Henry V **5**: 205, 257, 264, 310, 314; **30**: 193.
  Twelfth Night **1**: 563, 596; **34**: 330; **46**: 291, 347

order versus disintegration
  Titus Andronicus **4**: 618, 647; **43**: 186, 195

other sonnet writers, Shakespeare compared with
  Sonnets **42**: 296

Ovid, compared with
  Venus and Adonis **51**: 335, 352

Ovid, influence of
  A Midsummer Night's Dream **3**: 362, 427, 497, 498; **22**: 23; **29**: 175, 190, 216
  Titus Andronicus **4**: 647, 659, 664, 668; **13**: 225; **27**: 246, 275, 285, 293, 299, 306; **28**: 249; **43**: 195, 203, 206

Ovid's *Metamorphoses*, relation to
  The Winter's Tale **42**: 301
  Venus and Adonis **42**: 347

pagan elements
  King Lear **25**: 218

pageantry
  See also ceremonies, rites, and rituals, importance of
  Henry VIII **2**: 14, 15, 18, 51, 58; **24**: 77, 83, 84, 85, 89, 91, 106, 113, 118, 120, 126, 127, 140, 146, 150; **41**: 120, 129, 190

paradoxical elements
  Coriolanus **9**: 73, 92, 106, 121, 153, 157, 164, 169, 193

parent-child relations
  A Midsummer Night's Dream **13**: 19; **29**: 216, 225, 243

pastoral convention, parodies of
  As You Like It **5**: 54, 57, 72

pastoral convention, relation to
  As You Like It **5**: 72, 77, 122; **34**: 161; **37**: 1

pastoral tradition, compared with
  A Lover's Complaint **48**: 336

patience
  Henry VIII **2**: 58, 76, 78
  Pericles **2**: 572, 573, 578, 579; **36**: 251

patriarchal claims
  Henry VI, Parts 1, 2, and 3 **16**: 131 **25**: 102

patriarchal or monarchical order
  King Lear **13**: 353, 457; **16**: 351; **22**: 227, 233; **25**: 218; **31**: 84, 92, 107, 117, 123, 137, 142; **46**: 269

patriarchy
  Cymbeline **32**: 373; **36**: 134; **47**: 237; **51**: 25
  Henry V **37**: 105; **44**: 44
  Titus Andronicus **50**: 13
  Troilus and Cressida **22**: 58

patriotism
  See nationalism and patriotism

***Pattern of Painful Adventures* (Lawrence Twine), compared with**
  Pericles **48**: 364

Pauline doctrine
  A Midsummer Night's Dream **3**: 457, 486, 506

pedagogy
  Sonnets **37**: 374
  The Taming of the Shrew **19**: 122

perception
  Othello **19**: 276; **25**: 189, 257

performance history
  The Taming of the Shrew **31**: 282

performance issues
  See also staging issues
  Julius Caesar **50**: 186
  King Lear **2**: 106, 137, 154, 160; **11**: 10, 20, 27, 56, 57, 132, 136, 137, 145, 150, 154; **19**: 295, 344; **25**: 218
  Much Ado about Nothing **18**: 173, 174, 183, 184, 185, 186, 187, 188, 189, 190, 191, 192, 193, 195, 197, 199, 201, 204, 206, 207, 208, 209, 210, 254
  Sonnets **48**: 352
  The Taming of the Shrew **12**: 313, 314, 316, 317, 337, 338; **31**: 315

pessimistic elements
  Timon of Athens **1**: 462, 467, 470, 473, 478, 480; **20**: 433, 481; **27**: 155, 191

Petrarchan poetics, influence of
  Romeo and Juliet **5**: 416, 520, 522, 528, 550, 559, 575; **32**: 276; **51**: 212, 236

philosophical elements
  Julius Caesar **7**: 310, 324; **37**: 203
  Twelfth Night **1**: 560, 563, 596; **34**: 301, 316; **46**: 297

physical versus intellectual world
  Love's Labour's Lost **2**: 331, 348, 367

pictorial elements
  Venus and Adonis **10**: 414, 415, 419, 420, 423, 480; **33**: 339

Platonic elements
  A Midsummer Night's Dream **3**: 368, 437, 450, 497; **45**: 126

play-within-the-play, convention of
  Henry VI, Parts 1, 2, and 3 **3**: 75, 149
  The Merry Wives of Windsor **5**: 354, 355, 369, 402
  The Taming of the Shrew **12**: 416; **22**: 48

plebians
  Coriolanus **50**: 13, 105; **50**: 189, 196, 230

plot
  The Winter's Tale **7**: 376, 377, 379, 382, 387, 390, 396, 452; **13**: 417; **15**: 518; **45**: 374

plot and incident
  Richard III **8**: 146, 152, 159; **25**: 164

Plutarch and historical sources
  Coriolanus **9**: 8, 9, 13, 14, 16, 26, 39, 92, 106, 130, 142, 164; **30**: 74, 79, 105; **50**: 99

poet-patron relationship
  Sonnets **48**: 352

poetic justice, question of
  King Lear **2**: 92, 93, 94, 101, 129, 137, 231, 245; **49**: 73
  Othello **4**: 370, 412, 415, 427

poetic style
  Sonnets **10**: 153, 155, 156, 158, 159, 160, 161, 173, 175, 182, 214, 247, 251, 255, 260, 265, 283, 287, 296, 302, 315, 322, 325, 337, 346, 349, 360, 367, 385; **16**: 472; **40**: 221, 228; **51**: 270

political and social disintegration
  Antony and Cleopatra **6**: 31, 43, 53, 60, 71, 80, 100, 107, 111, 146; 180, 197, 219; **22**: 217; **25**: 257; **27**: 121

political content
  Titus Andronicus **43**: 262

Politics (Volume 30: 1, 4, 11, 22, 29, 39, 42, 46, 49)
  Coriolanus **9**: 15, 17, 18, 19, 26, 33, 43, 53, 62, 65, 73, 80, 92, 106, 110, 112, 121, 144, 153, 157, 164, 180; **22**: 248; **25**: 296; **30**: 58, 67, 79, 89, 96, 105, 111, 125; **37**: 283; **42**: 218; **48**: 230; **50**: 13, 140, 172
  Hamlet **44**: 241
  Henry V **49**: 219, 247, 260
  Henry IV, Parts 1 and 2 **28**: 101; **39**: 130; **42**: 141; **48**: 143, 175
  Henry VIII **2**: 39, 49, 51, 58, 60, 65, 67, 71, 72, 75, 78, 81; **24**: 74, 121, 124; **41**: 146
  Julius Caesar **7**: 161, 169, 191, 205, 218, 221, 245, 262, 264, 279, 282, 310, 324, 333, 346; **17**: 317, 318, 321, 323, 334, 350, 351, 358, 378, 382, 394, 406; **22**: 137, 280; **25**: 272, 280; **30**: 285, 297, 316, 321, 342, 374, 379; **37**: 203; **50**: 13
  King John **9**: 218, 224, 260, 280; **13**: 163; **22**: 120; **37**: 132; **41**: 221, 228
  King Lear **46**: 269; **50**: 45
  Measure for Measure **23**: 379; **49**: 274
  A Midsummer Night's Dream **29**: 243
  Pericles **37**: 361

The Tempest **8**: 304, 307, 315, 353, 359, 364, 401, 408; **16**: 426; **19**: 421; **29**: 339; **37**: 336; **42**: 320; **45**: 272, 280
Timon of Athens **27**: 223, 230; **50**: 13
Titus Andronicus **27**: 282; **48**: 264
Troilus and Cressida **3**: 536, 560, 606; **16**: 84

popularity
Pericles **2**: 536, 538, 546; **37**: 361
Richard III **8**: 144, 146, 154, 158, 159, 162, 181, 228; **39**: 383
The Taming of the Shrew **9**: 318, 338, 404
Venus and Adonis **10**: 410, 412, 418, 427; **25**: 328

Portia
The Merchant of Venice **49**: 27

power
Henry V **37**: 175
Measure for Measure **13**: 112; **22**: 85; **23**: 327, 330, 339, 352; **33**: 85
A Midsummer Night's Dream **42**: 46; **45**: 84
Much Ado about Nothing **22**: 85; **25**: 77; **31**: 231, 245

pride and rightful self-esteem
Othello **4**: 522, 536, 541; **35**: 352

primitivism
Macbeth **20**: 206, 213; **45**: 48

primogeniture
As You Like It **5**: 66, 158; **34**: 109, 120
Titus Andronicus **50**: 13

as "problem" plays
The Comedy of Errors **34**: 251
Julius Caesar **7**: 272, 320
Measure for Measure **2**: 416, 429, 434, 474, 475, 503, 514, 519; **16**: 102; **23**: 313, 328, 351; **49**: 358, 370
Troilus and Cressida **3**: 555, 566
  lack of resolution **43**: 277

procreation
Sonnets **10**: 379, 385; **16**: 461
Venus and Adonis **10**: 439, 449, 466; **33**: 321, 377

providential order
King Lear **2**: 112, 116, 137, 168, 170, 174, 177, 218, 226, 241, 253; **22**: 271; **49**: 1, 73
Macbeth **3**: 208, 289, 329, 336
Measure for Measure **48**: 1

Psychoanalytic Interpretations of Shakespeare's Works (Volume **44**: 1, 11, 18, 28, 35, 44, 57, 66, 79, 89, 93)
As You Like It **5**: 146, 158; **23**: 141, 142; **34**: 109; **48**: 42
Coriolanus **44**: 93
Cymbeline **45**: 67, 75
Hamlet **1**: 119, 148, 154, 179, 202; **21**: 197, 213, 361; **25**: 209; **28**: 223; **35**: 95, 104, 134, 237; **37**: 241; **44**: 133, 152, 160, 180, 209, 219
Henry IV, Parts 1 and 2 **13**: 457; **28**: 101; **42**: 185; **44**: 44

Henry V **13**: 457; **44**: 44
Julius Caesar **45**: 10
Macbeth **3**: 219, 223, 226; **44**: 11, 284, 289, 297; **45**: 48, 58
Measure for Measure **23**: 331, 332, 333, 334, 335, 340, 355, 356, 359, 379, 395; **44**: 89
Merchant of Venice **45**: 17
A Midsummer Night's Dream **3**: 440, 483; **28**: 15; **29**: 225; **44**: 1; **45**: 107, 117
Othello **4**: 468, 503; **35**: 265, 276, 282, 301, 317, 320, 347; **42**: 198; **44**: 57
Romeo and Juliet **5**: 513, 556; **51**: 253
The Tempest **45**: 259
Troilus and Cressida **43**: 287
Twelfth Night **46**: 333

psychological elements
Cymbeline **36**: 134; **44**: 28

public versus private principles
Julius Caesar **7**: 161, 179, 252, 262, 268, 284, 298; **13**: 252

public versus private speech
Love's Labour's Lost **2**: 356, 362, 371

public versus private worlds
As You Like It **46**: 164
Coriolanus **37**: 283; **42**: 218
Romeo and Juliet **5**: 520, 550; **25**: 181; **33**: 274

as "pure" poetry
The Phoenix and Turtle **10**: 14, 31, 35; **38**: 329

Puritanism
Measure for Measure **2**: 414, 418, 434; **49**: 325
Twelfth Night **1**: 549, 553, 555, 632; **16**: 53; **25**: 47; **46**: 338

Pyramus and Thisbe interlude
A Midsummer Night's Dream **50**: 74

racial issues
Othello **4**: 370, 380, 384, 385, 392, 399, 401, 402, 408, 427, 564; **13**: 327; **16**: 293; **25**: 189, 257; **28**: 249, 330; **35**: 369; **42**: 198

rape
Titus Andronicus **43**: 227, 255; **48**: 277

realism
See also **idealism versus realism**
The Merry Wives of Windsor **38**: 313
The Tempest **8**: 340, 359, 464
Troilus and Cressida **43**: 357

reality and illusion
The Tempest **8**: 287, 315, 359, 401, 435, 439, 447, 454; **22**: 302; **45**: 236, 247

reason
See also **love and reason** and **love versus reason**
Venus and Adonis **10**: 427, 439, 449, 459, 462, 466; **28**: 355; **33**: 309, 330

reason versus imagination
Antony and Cleopatra **6**: 107, 115, 142, 197, 228; **45**: 28

A Midsummer Night's Dream **3**: 381, 389, 423, 441, 466, 506; **22**: 23; **29**: 190; **45**: 96

rebellion
See also **usurpation**
Henry IV, Parts 1 and 2 **22**: 395; **28**: 101
Henry VIII **22**: 395
King John **9**: 218, 254, 263, 280, 297
Richard III **22**: 395

rebirth, regeneration, resurrection, or immortality
All's Well That Ends Well **7**: 90, 93, 98
Antony and Cleopatra **6**: 100, 103, 125, 131, 159, 181
Cymbeline **4**: 38, 64, 73, 93, 105, 113, 116, 129, 138, 141, 162, 170
Measure for Measure **13**: 84; **16**: 102, 114; **23**: 321, 327, 335, 340, 352; **25**: 12
Pericles **2**: 555, 564, 584, 586, 588; **36**: 205
The Tempest **8**: 302, 312, 320, 334, 348, 359, 370, 384, 401, 404, 414, 429, 439, 447, 454; **16**: 442; **22**: 302; **29**: 297; **37**: 336
The Winter's Tale **7**: 397, 414, 417, 419, 429, 436, 451, 452, 456, 480, 490, 497, 506; **25**: 339, 452, 480, 490, 497, 506; **45**: 366

reconciliation
As You Like It **46**: 156
All's Well That Ends Well **7**: 90, 93, 98; **51**: 33
Antony and Cleopatra **6**: 100, 103, 125, 131, 159, 181
Cymbeline **4**: 38, 64, 73, 93, 105, 113, 116, 129, 138, 141, 162, 170
The Merry Wives of Windsor **5**: 343, 369, 374, 397, 402
A Midsummer Night's Dream **3**: 412, 418, 437, 459, 468, 491, 497, 502, 513; **13**: 27; **29**: 190
Romeo and Juliet **5**: 415, 419, 427, 439, 447, 480, 487, 493, 505, 533, 536, 562
The Tempest **8**: 302, 312, 320, 334, 348, 359, 370, 384, 401, 404, 414, 429, 439, 447, 454; **16**: 442; **22**: 302; **29**: 297; **37**: 336; **45**: 236

reconciliation of opposites
As You Like It **5**: 79, 88, 103, 116, 122, 138; **23**: 127, 143; **34**: 161, 172; **46**: 156

redemption
The Comedy of Errors **19**: 54; **26**: 188

regicide
Macbeth **3**: 248, 275, 312; **16**: 317, 328

relation to tetralogy
Henry V **49**: 223

relationship to other Shakespearean plays
Twelfth Night **46**: 303
Henry IV, Parts 1 and 2 **42**: 99, 153; **48**: 167; **49**: 93, 186

relationship between Parts 1 and 2
Henry IV, Parts 1 and 2 **32**: 136; **39**: 100; **49**: 178

religious and theological issues
Macbeth **44**: 324, 341, 351, 361, 366, 373
Measure for Measure **48**: 1

religious, mythic, or spiritual content
See also **Christian elements**
All's Well That Ends Well **7**: 15, 45, 54, 67, 76, 98, 109, 116
Antony and Cleopatra **6**: 53, 94, 111, 115, 178, 192, 224; **47**: 71
Cymbeline **4**: 22, 29, 78, 93, 105, 108, 115, 116, 127, 134, 138, 141, 159; **28**: 373; **36**: 142, 158, 186; **47**: 219, 260, 274
Hamlet **1**: 98, 102, 130, 184, 191, 209, 212, 231, 234, 254; **21**: 361; **22**: 258; **28**: 280; **32**: 238; **35**: 134
Henry IV, Parts 1 and 2 **1**: 314, 374, 414, 421, 429, 431, 434; **32**: 103; **48**: 151
Henry V **25**: 116; **32**: 126
King Lear **49**: 67
Macbeth **3**: 208, 269, 275, 318; **29**: 109
Measure for Measure **48**: 1
Othello **4**: 483, 517, 522, 525, 559, 573; **22**: 207; **28**: 330
Pericles **2**: 559, 561, 565, 570, 580, 584, 588; **22**: 315; **25**: 365; **51**: 97
The Tempest **8**: 328, 390, 423, 429, 435; **45**: 211, 247
Timon of Athens **1**: 505, 512, 513, 523; **20**: 493

repentance and forgiveness
Much Ado about Nothing **8**: 24, 29, 111
The Two Gentlemen of Verona **6**: 450, 514, 516, 555, 564
The Winter's Tale **44**: 66

resolution
Measure for Measure **2**: 449, 475, 495, 514, 516; **16**: 102, 114
The Merchant of Venice **4**: 263, 266, 300, 319, 321; **13**: 37; **51**: 1
The Two Gentlemen of Verona **6**: 435, 436, 439, 445, 449, 453, 458, 460, 462, 465, 466, 468, 471, 476, 480, 486, 494, 509, 514, 516, 519, 529, 532, 541, 549; **19**: 34

retribution
Henry VI, Parts 1, 2, and 3 **3**: 27, 42, 51, 59, 77, 83, 92, 100, 109, 115, 119, 131, 136, 151
Julius Caesar **7**: 160, 167, 200
Macbeth **3**: 194, 208, 318; **48**: 214
Richard III **8**: 163, 170, 177, 182, 184, 193, 197, 201, 206, 210, 218, 223, 228, 243, 248, 267

revenge
Hamlet **1**: 74, 194, 209, 224, 234, 254; **16**: 246; **22**: 258; **25**: 288; **28**: 280; **35**: 152, 157, 167, 174, 212; **44**: 180, 209, 219, 229
The Merry Wives of Windsor **5**: 349, 350, 392; **38**: 264, 307
Othello **35**: 261

revenge tragedy elements
Julius Caesar **7**: 316
Titus Andronicus **4**: 618, 627, 628, 636, 639, 644, 646, 664, 672, 680; **16**: 225; **27**: 275, 318

reversal
A Midsummer Night's Dream **29**: 225

rhetoric
Venus and Adonis **33**: 377; **51**: 335, 345, 352
Romeo and Juliet **42**: 266

rhetoric of consolation
Sonnets **42**: 375

rhetoric of politeness
Henry VIII **22**: 182

rhetorical style
King Lear **16**: 301; **47**: 9

riddle motif
Pericles **22**: 315; **36**: 205, 214

rightful succession
Titus Andronicus **4**: 638

rings episode
The Merchant of Venice **22**: 3; **40**: 106, 151, 156

role-playing
Julius Caesar **7**: 356; **37**: 229
The Taming of the Shrew **9**: 322, 353, 355, 360, 369, 370, 398, 401, 407, 413, 419, 424; **13**: 3; **31**: 288, 295, 315

as romance play
As You Like It **5**: 55, 79; **23**: 27, 28, 40, 43

romance or chivalric tradition, influence of
Much Ado about Nothing **8**: 53, 125; **51**: 15

romance or folktale elements
All's Well That Ends Well **7**: 32, 41, 43, 45, 54, 76, 104, 116, 121; **26**: 117

romance or pastoral tradition, influence of
The Tempest **8**: 336, 348, 396, 404; **37**: 336

Roman citizenry, portrayal of
Julius Caesar **50**: 64, 230

romantic and courtly conventions
The Two Gentlemen of Verona **6**: 438, 460, 472, 478, 484, 486, 488, 502, 507, 509, 529, 541, 549, 560, 568; **12**: 460, 462; **40**: 354, 374

romantic elements
The Comedy of Errors **1**: 13, 16, 19, 23, 25, 30, 31, 36, 39, 53
Cymbeline **4**: 17, 20, 46, 68, 77, 141, 148, 172; **15**: 111; **25**: 319; **28**: 373
King Lear **31**: 77, 84
The Taming of the Shrew **9**: 334, 342, 362, 375, 407

royalty
Antony and Cleopatra **6**: 94

Salic Law
Henry V **5**: 219, 252, 260; **28**: 121

as satire or parody
Love's Labour's Lost **2**: 300, 302, 303, 307, 308, 315, 321, 324, 327; **23**: 237, 252
The Merry Wives of Windsor **5**: 338, 350, 360, 385; **38**: 278, 319; **47**: 354, 363,

satire or parody of pastoral conventions
As You Like It **5**: 46, 55, 60, 72, 77, 79, 84, 114, 118, 128, 130, 154

satirical elements
The Phoenix and Turtle **10**: 8, 16, 17, 27, 35, 40, 45, 48
Timon of Athens **27**: 155, 235
Troilus and Cressida **3**: 539, 543, 544, 555, 558, 574; **27**: 341

Saturnalian elements
Twelfth Night **1**: 554, 571, 603, 620, 642; **16**: 53

schemes and intrigues
The Merry Wives of Windsor **5**: 334, 336, 339, 341, 343, 349, 355, 379

Scholasticism
The Phoenix and Turtle **10**: 21, 24, 31; **51**: 188

School of Night, allusions to
Love's Labour's Lost **2**: 321, 327, 328

self-conscious or artificial nature of play
Cymbeline **4**: 43, 52, 56, 68, 124, 134, 138; **36**: 99

self-deception
Twelfth Night **1**: 554, 561, 591, 625; **47**: 45

self-indulgence
Twelfth Night **1**: 563, 615, 635

self-interest or expediency
Henry V **5**: 189, 193, 205, 213, 217, 233, 260, 287, 302, 304; **30**: 273; **49**: 223

self-knowledge
As You Like It **5**: 32, 82, 102, 116, 122, 133, 164
Much Ado about Nothing **8**: 69, 95, 100
Timon of Athens **1**: 456, 459, 462, 495, 503, 507, 515, 518, 526; **20**: 493; **27**: 166

self-love
Sonnets **10**: 372; **25**: 374; **51**: 270, 300, 304

Senecan or revenge tragedy elements
Timon of Athens **27**: 235
Titus Andronicus **4**: 618, 627, 628, 636, 639, 644, 646, 664, 672, 680; **16**: 225; **27**: 275, 318; **43**: 170, 206, 227

servitude
See also **freedom and servitude**
Comedy of Errors **42**: 80

setting
The Merry Wives of Windsor **47**: 375
Much Ado about Nothing **18**: 173, 174, 183, 184, 185, 186, 187, 188, 189, 190, 191, 192, 193, 195, 197, 199, 201, 204, 206, 207, 208, 209, 210, 254
Richard III **14**: 516, 528
The Two Gentlemen of Verona **12**: 463, 465, 485

sexual ambiguity and sexual deception
  As You Like It **46:** 134, 142
  Twelfth Night **1:** 540, 562, 620, 621, 639, 645; **22:** 69; **34:** 311, 344; **37:** 59; **42:** 32
  Troilus and Cressida **43:** 365

sexual anxiety
  Macbeth **16:** 328; **20:** 283

sexual politics
  The Merchant of Venice **22:** 3; **51:** 44
  The Merry Wives of Windsor **19:** 101; **38:** 307

Sexuality in Shakespeare (Volume 33: 1, 12, 18, 28, 39)
  As You Like It **46:** 122, 127, 134, 142
  All's Well That Ends Well **7:** 67, 86, 90, 93, 98, 126; **13:** 84; **19:** 113; **22:** 78; **28:** 38; **44:** 35; **49:** 46; **51:** 44
  Coriolanus **9:** 112, 142, 174, 183; **189, 198;** **30:** 79, 111, 125, 142
  Cymbeline **4:** 170, 172; **25:** 319; **32:** 373; **47:** 245
  King Lear **25:** 202; **31:** 133, 137, 142
  Love's Labour's Lost **22:** 12; **51:** 44
  Measure for Measure **13:** 84; **16:** 102, 114; **23:** 321, 327, 335, 340, 352; **25:** 12; **33:** 85, 90, 112; **49:** 286, 338; **51:** 44
  A Midsummer Night's Dream **22:** 23, 93; **29:** 225, 243, 256, 269; **42:** 46; **45:** 107
  Othello **22:** 339; **28:** 330, 344; **35:** 352, 360; **37:** 269; **44:** 57, 66; **51:** 44
  Romeo and Juliet **25:** 181; **33:** 225, 233, 241, 246, 274, 300; **51:** 227, 236
  Sonnets **25:** 374; **48:** 325
  Troilus and Cressida **22:** 58, 339; **25:** 56; **27:** 362; **43:** 365

Shakespeare and Classical Civilization (Volume 27: 1, 9, 15, 21, 30, 35, 39, 46, 56, 60, 67)
  Antony and Cleopatra
    Egyptian versus Roman values **6:** 31, 33, 43, 53, 104, 111, 115, 125, 142, 155, 159, 178, 181, 211, 219; **17:** 48; **19:** 270; **27:** 82, 121, 126; **28:** 249; **47:** 96, 103, 113, 149
  The Rape of Lucrece
    Roman history, relation to **10:** 84, 89, 93, 96, 98, 109, 116, 125, 135; **22:** 289; **25:** 305; **33:** 155, 190
  Timon of Athens **27:** 223, 230, 325
  Titus Andronicus **27:** 275, 282, 293, 299, 306
    Roman elements **43:** 206, 222
  Troilus and Cressida
    Trojan versus Greek values **3:** 541, 561, 574, 584, 590, 596, 621, 638; **27:** 370

Shakespeare's artistic growth, *Richard III*'s contribution to
  Richard III **8:** 165, 167, 182, 193, 197, 206, 210, 228, 239, 267; **25:** 164; **39:** 305, 326, 370

Shakespeare's canon, place in
  Titus Andronicus **4:** 614, 616, 618, 619, 637, 639, 646, 659, 664, 668; **43:** 195
  Twelfth Night **1:** 543, 548, 557, 569, 575, 580, 621, 635, 638

Shakespeare's dramas, compared with
  The Phoenix and Turtle **51:** 151, 155
  The Rape of Lucrece **43:** 92

Shakespeare's moral judgment
  Antony and Cleopatra **6:** 33, 37, 38, 41, 48, 51, 64, 76, 111, 125, 136, 140, 146, 163, 175, 189, 202, 211, 228; **13:** 368, 523; **25:** 257

Shakespeare's other plays, compared with
  The Taming of the Shrew **50:** 74

Shakespeare's political sympathies
  Coriolanus **9:** 8, 11, 15, 17, 19, 26, 39, 52, 53, 62, 80, 92, 142; **25:** 296; **30:** 74, 79, 89, 96, 105, 133; **50:** 172
  Richard II **6:** 277, 279, 287, 347, 359, 364, 391, 393, 402
  Richard III **8:** 147, 163, 177, 193, 197, 201, 223, 228, 232, 243, 248, 267; **39:** 349; **42:** 130

Shakespeare's Representation of Women (Volume 31: 1, 3, 8, 12, 16, 21, 29, 34, 35, 41, 43, 48, 53, 60, 68)
  Henry VI, Parts 1, 2, and 3 **3:** 103, 109, 126, 140, 157; **16:** 183; **39:** 196
  King John **9:** 222, 303; **16:** 161; **19:** 182; **41:** 215, 221
  King Lear **31:** 117, 123, 133
  Love's Labour's Lost **19:** 92; **22:** 12; **23:** 215; **25:** 1
  The Merry Wives of Windsor **5:** 335, 341, 343, 349, 369, 379, 390, 392, 402; **19:** 101; **38:** 307
  Much Ado about Nothing **31:** 222, 231, 241, 245
  Othello **19:** 253; **28:** 344
  The Taming of the Shrew **31:** 288, 300, 307, 315
  The Winter's Tale **22:** 324; **36:** 311; **42:** 301; **51:** 30

Shakespeare's romances, compared with
  Henry VIII **41:** 171

shame
  Coriolanus **42:** 243

sibling rivalry
  As You Like It **34:** 109
  Henry VI, Parts 1, 2, and 3 **22:** 193

slander or hearsay, importance of
  Coriolanus **48:** 230
  Much Ado about Nothing **8:** 58, 69, 82, 95, 104

social action
  Sonnets **48:** 352

social and moral corruption
  King Lear **2:** 116, 133, 174, 177, 241, 271; **22:** 227; **31:** 84, 92; **46:** 269

social and political context
  All's Well That Ends Well **13:** 66; **22:** 78; **38:** 99, 109, 150, 155; **49:** 46

social aspects
  Measure for Measure **23:** 316, 375, 379, 395

Social Class (Volume 50: 1, 13, 24, 34, 45, 51, 59, 64, 74, 86)
  General Commentary **50:** 1, 34
  Coriolanus **50:** 105, 110, 119
  Julius Caesar **50:** 189, 194, 196, 211, 230
  Timon of Athens **1:** 466, 487, 495; **25:** 198; **27:** 184, 196, 212
  The Two Noble Kinsmen **50:** 295, 305, 310

social milieu
  The Merry Wives of Windsor **18:** 75, 84; **38:** 297, 300

social order
  As You Like It **37:** 1; **46:** 94
  The Comedy of Errors **34:** 238

society
  Coriolanus **9:** 15, 17, 18, 19, 26, 33, 43, 53, 62, 65, 73, 80, 92, 106, 110, 112, 121, 144, 153, 157, 164, 180; **22:** 248; **25:** 296; **30:** 58, 67, 79, 89, 96, 105, 111, 125; **50:** 13, 105, 119, 152
  Troilus and Cressida **43:** 298

soldiers
  Henry V **49:** 194

songs, role of
  Love's Labour's Lost **2:** 303, 304, 316, 326, 335, 362, 367, 371, 375

sonnet arrangement
  Sonnets **10:** 174, 176, 182, 205, 226, 230, 236, 315, 353; **28:** 363; **40:** 238

sonnet form
  Sonnets **10:** 255, 325, 367; **37:** 347; **40:** 284, 303; **51:** 270

sonnets, compared with
  A Lover's Complaint **48:** 336

source of tragic catastrophe
  Romeo and Juliet **5:** 418, 427, 431, 448, 458, 469, 479, 480, 485, 487, 493, 509, 522, 528, 530, 533, 542, 565, 571, 573; **33:** 210; **51:** 245

sources
  Antony and Cleopatra **6:** 20, 39; **19:** 304; **27:** 96, 126; **28:** 249
  As You Like It **5:** 18, 32, 54, 59, 66, 84; **34:** 155; **46:** 117
  The Comedy of Errors **1:** 13, 14, 16, 19, 31, 32, 39; **16:** 3; **34:** 190, 215, 258
  Cymbeline **4:** 17, 18; **13:** 401; **28:** 373; **47:** 245, 265, 277
  Hamlet **1:** 76, 81, 113, 125, 128, 130, 151, 191, 202, 224, 259
  Henry VI, Parts 1, 2, and 3 **3:** 18, 21, 29, 31, 35, 39, 46, 51; **13:** 131; **16:** 217; **39:** 196
  Henry VIII **2:** 16, 17; **24:** 71, 80
  Julius Caesar **7:** 149, 150, 156, 187, 200, 264, 272, 282, 284, 320; **30:** 285, 297, 326, 358
  King John **9:** 216, 222, 300; **32:** 93, 114; **41:** 234, 243, 251
  King Lear **2:** 94, 100, 143, 145, 170, 186; **13:** 352; **16:** 351; **28:** 301

Love's Labour's Lost **16:** 17
Measure for Measure **2:** 388, 393, 427, 429, 437, 475; **13:** 94; **49:** 349
The Merry Wives of Windsor **5:** 332, 350, 360, 366, 385; **32:** 31
A Midsummer Night's Dream **29:** 216
Much Ado about Nothing **8:** 9, 19, 53, 58, 104
Othello **28:** 330
Pericles **2:** 538, 568, 572, 575; **25:** 365; **36:** 198, 205; **51:** 118, 126,
The Phoenix and Turtle **10:** 7, 9, 18, 24, 45; **38:** 326, 334, 350, 367; **51:** 138
The Rape of Lucrece **10:** 63, 64, 65, 66, 68, 74, 77, 78, 89, 98, 109, 121, 125; **25:** 305; **33:** 155, 190; **43:** 77, 92, 148
Richard III
   chronicles **8:** 145, 165, 193, 197, 201, 206, 210, 213, 228, 232
   Marlowe, Christopher **8:** 167, 168, 182, 201, 206, 218
   morality plays **8:** 182, 190, 201, 213, 239
   Seneca, other classical writers **8:** 165, 190, 201, 206, 228, 248
Romeo and Juliet **5:** 416, 419, 423, 450; **32:** 222; **33:** 210; **45:** 40
Sonnets **10:** 153, 154, 156, 158, 233, 251, 255, 293, 353; **16:** 472; **28:** 407; **42:** 375
The Taming of the Shrew
   folk tales **9:** 332, 390, 393
   Old and New Comedy **9:** 419
   Ovid **9:** 318, 370, 430
   Plautus **9:** 334, 341, 342
   shrew tradition **9:** 355; **19:** 3; **32:** 1, 56
The Tempest **45:** 226
Timon of Athens **16:** 351; **27:** 191
Troilus and Cressida **3:** 537, 539, 540, 541, 544, 549, 558, 566, 574, 587; **27:** 376, 381, 391, 400
Twelfth Night **1:** 539, 540, 603; **34:** 301, 323, 344; **46:** 291
The Two Gentlemen of Verona **6:** 436, 460, 462, 468, 476, 480, 490, 511, 547; **19:** 34; **40:** 320
The Two Noble Kinsmen **19:** 394; **41:** 289, 301, 363, 385; **50:** 326, 348
Venus and Adonis **10:** 410, 412, 420, 424, 429, 434, 439, 451, 454, 466, 473, 480, 486, 489; **16:** 452; **25:** 305; **28:** 355; **33:** 309, 321, 330, 339, 347, 352, 357, 370, 377; **42:** 347

spectacle
   Love's Labour's Lost **38:** 226
   Macbeth **42:** 258
   Pericles **42:** 352

spectacle versus simple staging
   The Tempest **15:** 206, 207, 208, 210, 217, 219, 222, 223, 224, 225, 227, 228, 305, 352; **28:** 415

stage history
   As You Like It **46:** 117
   Antony and Cleopatra **17:** 84, 94, 101
   The Merry Wives of Windsor **18:** 66, 67, 68, 70, 71

staging issues
   See also **performance issues**
   All's Well That Ends Well **19:** 113; **26:** 15, 19, 48, 52, 64, 73, 85, 92, 93, 94, 95, 97, 114, 117, 128

Antony and Cleopatra **17:** 6, 12, 84, 94, 101, 104, 110; **27:** 90; **47:** 142
As You Like It **13:** 502; **23:** 7, 17, 19, 22, 58, 96, 97, 98, 99, 101, 110, 137; **28:** 82; **32:** 212
The Comedy of Errors **26:** 182, 183, 186, 188, 190
Coriolanus **17:** 172, 242, 248
Cymbeline **15:** 6, 23, 75, 105, 111, 121, 122; **22:** 365
Hamlet **13:** 494, 502; **21:** 11, 17, 31, 35, 41, 44, 50, 53, 78, 81, 89, 101, 112, 127, 139, 142, 145, 148, 151, 157, 160, 172, 182, 183, 202, 203, 208, 225, 232, 237, 242, 245, 249, 251, 259, 268, 270, 274, 283, 284, 301, 311, 334, 347, 355, 361, 371, 377, 379, 380, 381, 384, 386, 392, 407, 410, 416; **44:** 198
Henry IV, Parts 1 and 2 **32:** 212; **47:** 1; **49:** 102
Henry V **5:** 186, 189, 192, 193, 198, 205, 226, 230, 241, 281, 314; **13:** 194, 502; **14:** 293, 295, 297, 301, 310, 319, 328, 334, 336, 342; **19:** 217; **32:** 185
Henry VI, Parts 1, 2, and 3 **24:** 21, 22, 27, 31, 32, 36, 38, 41, 45, 48, 55; **32:** 212
Henry VIII **24:** 67, 70, 71, 75, 77, 83, 84, 85, 87, 89, 91, 101, 106, 113, 120, 127, 129, 136, 140, 146, 150, 152, 155; **28:** 184
Julius Caesar **48:** 240; **50:** 186
King John **16:** 161; **19:** 182; **24:** 171, 187, 203, 206, 211, 225, 228, 241, 245, 249
King Lear **11:** 136, 137, 142, 145, 150, 151, 154, 158, 161, 165, 169; **32:** 212; **46:** 205, 218
Love's Labour's Lost **23:** 184, 187, 191, 196, 198, 200, 201, 202, 207, 212, 215, 216, 217, 229, 230, 232, 233, 237, 252
Macbeth **13:** 502; **20:** 12, 17, 32, 64, 65, 70, 73, 107, 113, 151, 175, 203, 206, 210, 213, 245, 279, 283, 312, 318, 324, 329, 343, 345, 350, 353, 363, 367, 374, 376, 379, 382, 387, 400, 406, 413; **22:** 365; **32:** 212
Measure for Measure **2:** 427, 429, 437, 441, 443, 456, 460, 482, 491, 519; **23:** 283, 284, 285, 286, 287, 291, 293, 294, 298, 299, 311, 315, 327, 338, 339, 340, 342, 344, 347, 363, 372, 375, 395, 400, 405, 406, 413; **32:** 16
The Merchant of Venice **12:** 111, 114, 115, 117, 119, 124, 129, 131
The Merry Wives of Windsor **18:** 74, 75, 84, 86, 90, 95
A Midsummer Night's Dream **3:** 364, 365, 371, 372, 377; **12:** 151, 152, 154, 158, 159, 280, 284, 291, 295; **16:** 34; **19:** 21; **29:** 183, 256; **48:** 23
Much Ado about Nothing **8:** 18, 33, 41, 75, 79, 82, 108; **16:** 45; **18:** 245, 247, 249, 252, 254, 257, 261, 264; **28:** 63
Othello **11:** 273, 334, 335, 339, 342, 350, 354, 359, 362
Pericles **16:** 399; **48:** 364; **51:** 99
Richard II **13:** 494; **24:** 273, 274, 278, 279, 280, 283, 291, 295, 296, 301, 303, 304, 310, 315, 317, 320, 325, 333, 338, 346, 351, 352, 356, 364, 383, 386, 395, 402, 405, 411, 414, 419, 423, 428; **25:** 89
Richard III **14:** 515, 527, 528, 537; **16:** 137
Romeo and Juliet **11:** 499, 505, 507, 514, 517; **13:** 243; **25:** 181; **32:** 212
The Tempest **15:** 343, 346, 352, 361, 364, 366,
368, 371, 385; **28:** 391, 415; **29:** 339; **32:** 338, 343; **42:** 332; **45:** 200
Timon of Athens **20:** 445, 446, 481, 491, 492, 493
Titus Andronicus **17:** 449, 452, 456, 487; **25:** 245; **32:** 212, 249
Troilus and Cressida **16:** 70; **18:** 289, 332, 371, 395, 403, 406, 412, 419, 423, 442, 447, 451
Twelfth Night **26:** 219, 233, 257, 337, 342, 346, 357, 359, 360, 364, 366, 371, 374; **46:** 310, 369
The Two Gentlemen of Verona **12:** 457, 464; **42:** 18
The Winter's Tale **7:** 414, 425, 429, 446, 464, 480, 483, 497; **13:** 409; **15:** 518; **48:** 309

Stoicism
   Hamlet **48:** 195
   Julius Caesar **50:** 249

strategic analysis
   Antony and Cleopatra **48:** 206

structure
   All's Well That Ends Well **7:** 21, 29, 32, 45, 51, 76, 81, 93, 98, 116; **22:** 78; **26:** 128; **38:** 72, 123, 142
   As You Like It **5:** 19, 24, 25, 35, 44, 45, 46, 86, 93, 116, 138, 158; **23:** 7, 8, 9, 10, 11; **34:** 72, 78, 131, 147, 155
   Coriolanus **9:** 8, 9, 11, 12, 13, 14, 16, 26, 33, 45, 53, 58, 72, 78, 80, 84, 92, 112, 139, 148; **25:** 263; **30:** 79, 96
   Hamlet **22:** 378; **28:** 280, 325; **35:** 82, 104, 215; **44:** 152
   Henry IV **49:** 93
   Henry V **5:** 186, 189, 205, 213, 230, 241, 264, 289, 310, 314; **30:** 220, 227, 234, 244
   Henry VI, Parts 1, 2, and 3 **3:** 31, 43, 46, 69, 83, 103, 109, 119, 136, 149, 154; **39:** 213
   Henry VIII **2:** 16, 25, 27, 28, 31, 36, 44, 46, 51, 56, 68, 75; **24:** 106, 112, 113, 120
   Julius Caesar **7:** 152, 155, 159, 160, 179, 200, 210, 238, 264, 284, 298, 316, 346; **13:** 252; **30:** 374
   King John **9:** 208, 212, 222, 224, 229, 240, 244, 245, 254, 260, 263, 275, 284, 290, 292, 300; **24:** 228, 241; **41:** 260, 269, 277
   King Lear **28:** 325; **32:** 308; **46:** 177
   Love's Labour's Lost **22:** 378; **23:** 191, 237, 252; **38:** 163, 172
   Macbeth **16:** 317; **20:** 12, 245
   Measure for Measure **2:** 390, 411, 449, 456, 466, 474, 482, 490, 491; **33:** 69; **49:** 379
   The Merchant of Venice **4:** 201, 215, 230, 232, 243, 247, 254, 261, 263, 308, 321; **12:** 115; **28:** 63
   The Merry Wives of Windsor **5:** 332, 333, 334, 335, 343, 349, 355, 369, 374; **18:** 86; **22:** 378
   A Midsummer Night's Dream **3:** 364, 368, 381, 402, 406, 427, 450, 513; **13:** 19; **22:** 378; **29:** 175; **45:** 126, 175
   Much Ado about Nothing **8:** 9, 16, 17, 19, 28, 29, 33, 39, 48, 63, 69, 73, 75, 79, 82, 115; **31:** 178, 184, 198, 231
   Othello **22:** 378; **28:** 325
   The Phoenix and Turtle **10:** 27, 31, 37, 45, 50; **38:** 342, 345, 357; **51:** 138, 143

The Rape of Lucrece **10**: 84, 89, 93, 98, 135; **22**: 294; **25**: 305; **43**: 102, 141
Richard II **6**: 282, 304, 317, 343, 352, 359, 364, 39; **24**: 307, 322, 325, 356, 395
Richard III **8**: 154, 161, 163, 167, 168, 170, 177, 184, 193, 197, 201, 206, 210, 218, 223, 228, 232, 243, 252, 262, 267; **16**: 150
Romeo and Juliet **5**: 438, 448, 464, 469, 470, 477, 480, 496, 518, 524, 525, 528, 547, 559; **33**: 210, 246
Sonnets **10**: 175, 176, 182, 205, 230, 260, 296, 302, 309, 315, 337, 349, 353; **40**: 238
The Taming of the Shrew **9**: 318, 322, 325, 332, 334, 341, 362, 370, 390, 426; **22**: 48, 378; **31**: 269
The Tempest **8**: 294, 295, 299, 320, 384, 439; **28**: 391, 415; **29**: 292, 297; **45**: 188
Timon of Athens **27**: 157, 175, 235
Titus Andronicus **4**: 618, 619, 624, 631, 635, 640, 644, 646, 647, 653, 656, 659, 662, 664, 668, 672; **27**: 246, 285
Troilus and Cressida **3**: 536, 538, 549, 568, 569, 578, 583, 589, 611, 613; **27**: 341, 347, 354, 391
Twelfth Night **1**: 539, 542, 543, 546, 551, 553, 563, 570, 571, 590, 600, 660; **26**: 374; **34**: 281, 287; **46**: 286
The Two Gentlemen of Verona **6**: 445, 450, 460, 462, 504, 526
The Two Noble Kinsmen **37**: 313; **50**: 326, 361
Venus and Adonis **10**: 434, 442, 480, 486, 489; **33**: 357, 377

style
Henry VIII **41**: 158
The Phoenix and Turtle **10**: 8, 20, 24, 27, 31, 35, 45, 50; **38**: 334, 345, 357; **51**: 171, 188
The Rape of Lucrece **10**: 64, 65, 66, 68, 69, 70, 71, 73, 74, 77, 78, 81, 84, 98, 116, 131, 135; **43**: 113, 158
Venus and Adonis **10**: 411, 412, 414, 415, 416, 418, 419, 420, 423, 424, 428, 429, 439, 442, 480, 486, 489; **16**: 452

subjectivity
Hamlet **45**: 28
Sonnets **37**: 374

substitution of identities
Measure for Measure **2**: 507, 511, 519; **13**: 112; **49**: 313, 325

subversiveness
Cymbeline **22**: 302
The Tempest **22**: 302
The Winter's Tale **22**: 302

supernatural grace versus evil or chaos
Measure for Measure **48**: 1

suffering
King Lear **2**: 137, 160, 188, 201, 218, 222, 226, 231, 238, 241, 249, 265; **13**: 343; **22**: 271; **25**: 218; **50**: 24
Pericles **2**: 546, 573, 578, 579; **25**: 365; **36**: 279

symbolism
The Winter's Tale **7**: 425, 429, 436, 452, 456, 469, 490, 493

textual arrangement
Henry VI, Parts 1, 2, and 3 **24**: 3, 4, 6, 12, 17, 18, 19, 20, 21, 24, 27, 42, 45; **37**: 165
Richard II **24**: 260, 261, 262, 263, 271, 273, 291, 296, 356, 390

textual issues
Henry IV, Parts 1 and 2 **22**: 114
King Lear **22**: 271; **37**: 295; **49**: 73
A Midsummer Night's Dream **16**: 34; **29**: 216
The Taming of the Shrew **22**: 48; **31**: 261, 276; **31**: 276
The Winter's Tale **19**: 441, **45**: 333

textual problems
Henry V **5**: 187, 189, 190; **13**: 201

textual revisions
Pericles **15**: 129, 130, 132, 134, 135, 136, 138, 152, 155, 167, 181; **16**: 399; **25**: 365; **51**: 99

textual variants
Hamlet **13**: 282; **16**: 259; **21**: 11, 23, 72, 101, 127, 129, 139, 140, 142, 145, 202, 208, 259, 270, 284, 347, 361, 384; **22**: 258; **32**: 238

theatrical viability
Henry VI, Parts 1, 2, and 3 **24**: 31, 32, 34

theatricality
Antony and Cleopatra **47**: 96, 103, 107, 113
Macbeth **16**: 328
Measure for Measure **23**: 285, 286, 294, 372, 406; **49**: 358
The Merry Wives of Windsor **47**: 325

thematic disparity
Henry VIII **2**: 25, 31, 56, 68, 75; **41**: 146

time
As You Like It **5**: 18, 82, 112, 141; **23**: 146, 150; **34**: 102; **46**: 88, 156, 164, 169
Macbeth **3**: 234, 246, 283, 293; **20**: 245
Richard II **22**: 137
Sonnets **10**: 265, 302, 309, 322, 329, 337, 360, 379; **13**: 445; **40**: 292
The Tempest **8**: 401, 439, 464; **25**: 357; **29**: 278, 292; **45**: 236
Troilus and Cressida **3**: 561, 571, 583, 584, 613, 621, 626, 634
Twelfth Night **37**: 78; **46**: 297
The Winter's Tale **7**: 397, 425, 436, 476, 490; **19**: 366; **36**: 301, 349; **45**: 297, 329, 366, 374

time and change, motif of
Henry IV, Parts 1 and 2 **1**: 372, 393, 411; **39**: 89; **48**: 143
As You Like It **46**: 156, 164, 169

time scheme
Othello **4**: 370, 384, 390, 488; **22**: 207; **35**: 310; **47**: 51

topical allusions or content
Hamlet **13**: 282
Henry V **5**: 185, 186; **13**: 201
Love's Labour's Lost **2**: 300, 303, 307, 315, 316, 317, 319, 321, 327, 328; **23**: 187, 191, 197, 203, 221, 233, 237, 252; **25**: 1
Macbeth **13**: 361; **20**: 17, 350; **29**: 101

traditional values
Richard III **39**: 335

tragedies of major characters
Henry VIII **2**: 16, 39, 46, 48, 49, 51, 56, 58, 68, 81; **41**: 120

tragic elements
The Comedy of Errors **1**: 16, 25, 27, 45, 50, 59; **34**: 229
Cymbeline **25**: 319; **28**: 373; **36**: 129; **47**: 296
Henry V **5**: 228, 233, 267, 269, 271

Julius Caesar **50**: 258, 265
King John **9**: 208, 209, 244
A Midsummer Night's Dream **3**: 393, 400, 401, 410, 445, 474, 480, 491, 498, 511; **29**: 175; **45**: 169
The Rape of Lucrece **10**: 78, 80, 81, 84, 98, 109; **43**: 85, 148
The Tempest **8**: 324, 348, 359, 370, 380, 408, 414, 439, 458, 464
Twelfth Night **1**: 557, 569, 572, 575, 580, 599, 621, 635, 638, 639, 645, 654, 656; **26**: 342

treachery
Coriolanus **30**: 89
King John **9**: 245

treason and punishment
Macbeth **13**: 361; **16**: 328

trial scene
The Merchant of Venice **49**: 1, 23, 37

trickster, motif of
Cymbeline **22**: 302
The Tempest **22**: 302; **29**: 297
The Winter's Tale **22**: 302; **45**: 333

triumph over death or fate
Romeo and Juliet **5**: 421, 423, 427, 505, 509, 520, 530, 536, 565, 566; **51**: 219

Trojan War
Troilus and Cressida
as myth **43**: 293

The Troublesome Reign (anonymous), compared with
King John **41**: 205, 221, 260, 269; **48**: 132

Troy
Troilus and Cressida **43**: 287

Troy passage
The Rape of Lucrece **43**: 77, 85

Tudor doctrine
King John **9**: 254, 284, 297; **41**: 221

Tudor myth
Henry VI, Parts 1, 2, and 3 **3**: 51, 59, 77, 92, 100, 109, 115, 119, 131; **39**: 222

Richard III **8:** 163, 165, 177, 184, 193, 201, 218, 228, 232, 243, 248, 252, 267; **39:** 305, 308, 326, 387; **42:** 130

Turkish elements
Henry IV, Parts 1 and 2 **19:** 170
Henry V **19:** 170

two fathers
Henry IV, Parts 1 and 2 **14:** 86, 101, 105, 108; **39:** 89, 100; **49:** 102

tyranny
King John **9:** 218

unity
Antony and Cleopatra **6:** 20, 21, 22, 24, 25, 32, 33, 39, 43, 53, 60, 67, 111, 125, 146, 151, 165, 208, 211, 219; **13:** 374; **27:** 82, 90, 135
Hamlet **1:** 75, 76, 87, 103, 113, 125, 128, 142, 148, 160, 184, 188, 198, 264; **16:** 259; **35:** 82, 215
Henry VI, Parts 1, 2, and 3 **39:** 177, 222
A Midsummer Night's Dream **3:** 364, 368, 381, 402, 406, 427, 450, 513; **13:** 19; **22:** 378; **29:** 175, 263

unity of double plot
The Merchant of Venice **4:** 193, 194, 201, 232; **12:** 16, 67, 80, 115; **40:** 151

unnatural ordering
Hamlet **22:** 378
Love's Labour's Lost **22:** 378
The Merry Wives of Windsor **22:** 378
A Midsummer Night's Dream **22:** 378
Othello **22:** 378

as unsuccessful play
Measure for Measure **2:** 397, 441, 474, 482; **23:** 287

usurpation
See also **rebellion**
Richard II **6:** 263, 264, 272, 287, 289, 315, 323, 331, 343, 354, 364, 381, 388, 393, 397; **24:** 383
The Tempest **8:** 304, 370, 408, 420; **25:** 357, 382; **29:** 278, 362, 377; **37:** 336

utopia
The Tempest **45:** 280

value systems
Troilus and Cressida **3:** 578, 583, 589, 602, 613, 617; **13:** 53; **27:** 370, 396, 400

Venetian politics
Othello **32:** 294

Venice, Elizabethan perceptions of
The Merchant of Venice **28:** 249; **32:** 294; **40:** 127

Venus and Adonis
The Rape of Lucrece **43:** 148

Vergil, influence of
Titus Andronicus **27:** 306; **28:** 249

verisimilitude
As You Like It **5:** 18, 23, 28, 30, 32, 39, 125; **23:** 107

Verona society
Romeo and Juliet **5:** 556, 566; **13:** 235; **33:** 255; **51:** 245

Violence in Shakespeare's Works (Volume 43: 1, 12, 24, 32, 39, 61)
Henry IV, Parts 1 and 2 **25:** 109
Henry VI, Parts 1, 2, and 3 **24:** 25, 31; **37:** 157
Julius Caesar **48:** 240
Love's Labour's Lost **22:** 12
Macbeth **20:** 273, 279, 283; **45:** 58
Othello **22:** 12
The Rape of Lucrece **43:** 148, 158
Titus Andronicus **13:** 225; **25:** 245; **27:** 255; **28:** 249; **32:** 249, 265; **43:** 186, 203, 227, 239, 247, 255, 262
Troilus and Cressida **43:** 329, 340, 351, 357, 365, 377

virginity or chastity, importance of
Much Ado about Nothing **8:** 44, 75, 95, 111, 121, 125; **31:** 222

Virgo vs. Virago
King Lear **48:** 222

visual arts, relation to
Sonnets **28:** 407

visual humor
Love's Labour's Lost **23:** 207, 217

war
Coriolanus **25:** 263; **30:** 79, 96, 125, 149
Henry V **5:** 193, 195, 197, 198, 210, 213, 219, 230, 233, 246, 281, 293; **28:** 121, 146; **30:** 262; **32:** 126; **37:** 175, 187; **42:** 141; **49:** 194, 236, 247, 260

Wars of the Roses
Richard III **8:** 163, 165, 177, 184, 193, 201, 218, 228, 232, 243, 248, 252, 267; **39:** 308

Watteau, influence on staging
Love's Labour's Lost **23:** 184, 186

wealth
The Merchant of Venice **4:** 209, 261, 270, 273, 317; **12:** 80, 117; **22:** 69; **25:** 22; **28:** 249; **40:** 117, 197, 208; **45:** 17; **49:** 1; **51:** 15

wealth and social class
Timon of Athens **1:** 466, 487, 495; **25:** 198; **27:** 184, 196, 212; **50:** 13

wheel of fortune, motif of
Antony and Cleopatra **6:** 25, 178; **19:** 304
Henry VIII **2:** 27, 65, 72, 81

widowhood and remarriage, themes of
Hamlet **32:** 238

wisdom
King Lear **37:** 213; **46:** 210

wit
The Merry Wives of Windsor **5:** 335, 336, 337, 339, 343, 351
Much Ado about Nothing **8:** 27, 29, 38, 69, 79, 91, 95; **31:** 178, 191

witchcraft
See **Magic and the Supernatural**

women, role of
See **Shakespeare's Representation of Women**

wonder, dynamic of
The Comedy of Errors **37:** 12

wordplay
As You Like It **46:** 105
Romeo and Juliet **32:** 256

written versus oral communication
Love's Labour's Lost **2:** 359, 365; **28:** 63

youth
The Two Gentlemen of Verona **6:** 439, 450, 464, 514, 568

youth versus age
All's Well That Ends Well **7:** 9, 45, 58, 62, 76, 81, 86, 93, 98, 104, 116, 126; **26:** 117; **38:** 109

Cumulative Topic Index, by Play

The Cumulative Topic Index, by Play identifies the principal topics of discussion in the criticism of each play and non-dramatic poem. The topics are arranged alphabetically by play. Page references indicate the beginning page number of each essay containing substantial commentary on that topic. A parenthetical reference after a play indicates which volumes discuss the play extensively.

All's Well That Ends Well (Volumes 7, 26, 38)

appearance versus reality **7:** 37, 76, 93; **26:** 117
audience perspective **7:** 81, 104, 109, 116, 121
bed-trick **7:** 8, 26, 27, 29, 32, 41, 86, 93, 98, 113, 116, 126; **13:** 84; **26:** 117; **28:** 38; **38:** 65, 118; **49:** 46
Bertram
  characterization **7:** 15, 27, 29, 32, 39, 41, 43, 98, 113; **26:** 48; **26:** 117
  conduct **7:** 9, 10, 12, 16, 19, 21, 51, 62, 104; **50:** 59
  desire **22:** 78
  transformation or redemption **7:** 10, 19, 21, 26, 29, 32, 54, 62, 81, 90, 93, 98, 109, 113, 116, 126; **13:** 84
comic elements **26:** 97, 114; **48:** 65
dark elements **7:** 27, 37, 39, 43, 54, 109, 113, 116; **26:** 85; **48:** 65; **50:** 59
Decameron (Boccaccio), compared with **7:** 29, 43
desire **38:** 99, 109, 118
displacement **22:** 78
education **7:** 62, 86, 90, 93, 98, 104, 116, 126
elder characters **7:** 9, 37, 39, 43, 45, 54, 62, 104
conclusion **38:** 123, 132, 142
gender issues **7:** 9, 10, 67, 126; **13:** 77, 84; **19:** 113; **26:** 128; **38:** 89, 99, 118; **44:** 35
genre **48:** 65
Helena
  as agent of reconciliation, renewal, or grace **7:** 67, 76, 81, 90, 93, 98, 109, 116

as dualistic or enigmatic character **7:** 15, 27, 29, 39, 54, 58, 62, 67, 76, 81, 98, 113, 126; **13:** 66; **22:** 78; **26:** 117
  as "female achiever" **19:** 113; **38:** 89
  desire **38:** 96; **44:** 35
  pursuit of Bertram **7:** 9, 12, 15, 16, 19, 21, 26, 27, 29, 32, 43, 54, 76, 116; **13:** 77; **22:** 78; **49:** 46
  virginity **38:** 65
  virtue and nobility **7:** 9, 10, 12, 16, 19, 21, 27, 32, 41, 51, 58, 67, 76, 86, 126; **13:** 77; **50:** 59
implausibility of plot, characters, or events **7:** 8, 45
irony, paradox, and ambiguity **7:** 27, 32, 58, 62, 67, 81, 86, 109, 116
King **38:** 150
language and imagery **7:** 12, 29, 45, 104, 109, 121; **38:** 132; **48:** 65
Lavatch **26:** 64; **46:** 33, 52, 68
love **7:** 12, 15, 16, 51, 58, 67, 90, 93, 116; **38:** 80; **51:** 33, 44
merit versus rank **7:** 9, 10, 19, 37, 51, 76; **38:** 155; **50:** 59
"mingled yarn" **7:** 62, 93, 109, 126; **38:** 65
morality plays, influence of **7:** 29, 41, 51, 98, 113; **13:** 66
Parolles
  characterization **7:** 8, 9, 43, 76, 81, 98, 109, 113, 116, 126; **22:** 78; **26:** 48, 73, 97; **26:** 117; **46:** 68
  exposure **7:** 9, 27, 81, 98, 109, 113, 116, 121, 126
  Falstaff, compared with **7:** 8, 9, 16

reconciliation **7:** 90, 93, 98; **51:** 33
religious, mythic, or spiritual content **7:** 15, 45, 54, 67, 76, 98, 109, 116
romance or folktale elements **7:** 32, 41, 43, 45, 54, 76, 104, 116, 121; **26:** 117
sexuality **7:** 67, 86, 90, 93, 98, 126; **13:** 84; **19:** 113; **22:** 78; **28:** 38; **44:** 35; **49:** 46; **51:** 44
social and political context **13:** 66; **22:** 78; **38:** 99, 109, 150, 155; **49:** 46
staging issues **19:** 113; **26:** 15, 19, 48, 52, 64, 73, 85, 92, 93, 94, 95, 97, 114, 117, 128
structure **7:** 21, 29, 32, 45, 51, 76, 81, 93, 98, 116; **22:** 78; **26:** 128; **38:** 72, 123, 142
youth versus age **7:** 9, 45, 58, 62, 76, 81, 86, 93, 98, 104, 116, 126; **26:** 117; **38:** 109

Antony and Cleopatra (Volumes 6, 17, 27, 47)

All for Love (John Dryden), compared with **6:** 20, 21; **17:** 12, 94, 101
ambiguity **6:** 53, 111, 161, 163, 180, 189, 208, 211, 228; **13:** 368
androgyny **13:** 530
Antony
  characterization **6:** 22, 23, 24, 31, 38, 41, 172, 181, 211; **16:** 342; **19:** 270; **22:** 217; **27:** 117; **47:** 77, 124, 142
  Cleopatra, relationship with **6:** 25, 27, 37, 39, 48, 52, 53, 62, 67, 71, 76, 85, 100, 125, 131, 133, 136, 142, 151, 161, 163, 165, 180, 192; **27:** 82; **47:** 107, 124, 165, 174
death scene **25:** 245; **47:** 142

dotage **6:** 22, 23, 38, 41, 48, 52, 62, 107, 136, 146, 175; **17:** 28
nobility **6:** 22, 24, 33, 48, 94, 103, 136, 142, 159, 172, 202; **25:** 245
political conduct **6:** 33, 38, 53, 107, 111, 146, 181
public versus private personae **6:** 165; **47:** 107
self-knowledge **6:** 120, 131, 175, 181, 192; **47:** 77
as superhuman figure **6:** 37, 51, 71, 92, 94, 178, 192; **27:** 110; **47:** 71
as tragic hero **6:** 38, 39, 52, 53, 60, 104, 120, 151, 155, 165, 178, 192, 202, 211; **22:** 217; **27:** 90
audience response **48:** 206
Cleopatra
Antony, relationship with **6:** 25, 27, 37, 39, 48, 52, 53, 62, 67, 71, 76, 85, 100, 125, 131, 133, 136, 142, 151, 161, 163, 165, 180, 192; **25:** 257; **27:** 82; **47:** 107, 124, 165, 174
characterization **47:** 77, 96, 113, 124
contradictory or inconsistent nature **6:** 23, 24, 27, 67, 76, 100, 104, 115, 136, 151, 159, 202; **17:** 94, 113; **27:** 135
costume **17:** 94
creativity **6:** 197; **47:** 96, 113
death, decay, and nature's destructiveness **6:** 23, 25, 27, 41, 43, 52, 60, 64, 76, 94, 100, 103, 120, 131, 133, 136, 140, 146, 161, 165, 180, 181, 192, 197, 208; **13:** 383; **17:** 48, 94; **25:** 245; **27:** 135; **47:** 71
personal attraction of **6:** 24, 38, 40, 43, 48, 53, 76, 104, 115, 155; **17:** 113
self-knowledge **47:** 77, 96
staging issues **17:** 94, 113
as subverter of social order **6:** 146, 165; **47:** 113
as superhuman figure **6:** 37, 51, 71, 92, 94, 178, 192; **27:** 110; **47:** 71, 174, 192
as tragic heroine **6:** 53, 120, 151, 192, 208; **27:** 144
as voluptuary or courtesan **6:** 21, 22, 25, 41, 43, 52, 53, 62, 64, 67, 76, 146, 161; **47:** 107, 174
comic elements **6:** 52, 85, 104, 125, 131, 151, 192, 202, 219; **47:** 77, 124, 149, 165
contemptus mundi **6:** 85, 133
dreams **45:** 28
dualisms **19:** 304; **27:** 82
Egyptian versus Roman values **6:** 31, 33, 43, 53, 104, 111, 115, 125, 142, 155, 159, 178, 181, 211, 219; **17:** 48; **19:** 270; **27:** 82, 121, 126; **28:** 249; **47:** 96, 103, 113, 149
Elizabethan culture, relation to **47:** 103
Enobarbus **6:** 22, 23, 27, 43, 94, 120, 142; **16:** 342; **17:** 36; **22:** 217; **27:** 135
gender issues **13:** 368; **25:** 257; **27:** 144; **47:** 174, 192
irony or paradox **6:** 53, 136, 146, 151, 159, 161, 189, 192, 211, 224
language and imagery **6:** 21, 25, 39, 64, 80, 85, 92, 94, 100, 104, 142, 146, 155, 159, 161, 165, 189, 192, 202, 211; **13:** 374, 383; **25:** 245, 257; **27:** 96, 105, 135
love and passion **6:** 51, 64, 71, 80, 85, 100, 115, 159, 165, 180; **25:** 257; **27:** 126; **47:** 71, 124, 174, 192; **51:** 25, 33, 44

monument scene **13:** 374; **16:** 342; **17:** 104, 110; **22:** 217; **47:** 142, 165
moral relativism **22:** 217; **27:** 121
mythological allusions **16:** 342; **19:** 304; **27:** 110, 117; **47:** 71, 192
Octavius **6:** 22, 24, 31, 38, 43, 53, 62, 107, 125, 146, 178, 181, 219; **25:** 257
political and social disintegration **6:** 31, 43, 53, 60, 71, 80, 100, 107, 111, 146, 180, 197, 219; **22:** 217; **25:** 257; **27:** 121
reason versus imagination **6:** 107, 115, 142, 197, 228; **45:** 28
reconciliation **6:** 100, 103, 125, 131, 159, 181
religious, mythic, or spiritual content **6:** 53, 94, 111, 115, 178, 192, 224; **47:** 71
royalty **6:** 94
Seleucus episode (Act V, scene ii) **6:** 39, 41, 62, 133, 140, 151; **27:** 135
Shakespeare's major tragedies, compared with **6:** 25, 53, 60, 71, 120, 181, 189, 202; **22:** 217; **47:** 77
Shakespeare's moral judgment **6:** 33, 37, 38, 41, 48, 51, 64, 76, 111, 125, 136, 140, 146, 163, 175, 189, 202, 211, 228; **13:** 368, 523; **25:** 257
sources **6:** 20, 39; **19:** 304; **27:** 96, 126; **28:** 249
stage history **17:** 84, 94, 101
staging issues **17:** 6, 12, 84, 94, 101, 104, 110; **27:** 90; **47:** 142
strategic analysis **48:** 206
theatricality and role-playing **47:** 96, 103, 107, 113
unity **6:** 20, 21, 22, 24, 25, 32, 33, 39, 43, 53, 60, 67, 111, 125, 146, 151, 165, 208, 211, 219; **13:** 374; **27:** 82, 90, 135
wheel of fortune, motif of **6:** 25, 178; **19:** 304

As You Like It (Volumes 5, 23, 34, 46)
Appearance versus Reality **46:** 105
androgyny **23:** 98, 100, 122, 138, 143, 144; **34:** 172, 177; **46:** 134
anti-romantic elements **34:** 72
aristocracy **34:** 120
art versus nature **5:** 128, 130, 148; **34:** 147
Audrey **46:** 122
autobiographical elements **5:** 25, 35, 43, 50, 55, 61
bawdy elements **46:** 122
Celia **46:** 94
characterization **5:** 19, 24, 25, 36, 39, 54, 82, 86, 116, 148; **34:** 72; **48:** 42
Christian elements **5:** 39, 98, 162
contradiction, paradox, and opposition **46:** 105
comic form **46:** 105; **51:** 1
corruption in society **46:** 94
costume **46:** 117
courtship and marriage **34:** 109, 177; **48:** 32; **51:** 44
death, decay, nature's destructiveness **46:** 169
deception, disguise, and duplicity **46:** 134
desire **37:** 43
domestic elements **46:** 142
dramatic shortcomings or failure **5:** 19, 42, 52, 61, 65
duration of time **5:** 44, 45
Elizabethan culture, relation to **5:** 21, 59, 66, 68, 70, 158; **16:** 53; **28:** 46; **34:** 120; **37:** 1; **46:** 142
Fathers and Daughters **46:** 94
feminism **23:** 107, 108
Forest of Arden
as "bitter" Arcadia **5:** 98, 118, 162; **23:** 97, 98, 99, 100, 122, 139
Duke Frederick's court, contrast with **5:** 46, 102, 103, 112, 130, 156; **16:** 53; **23:** 126, 128, 129, 131, 134; **34:** 78, 102, 131; **46:** 164
pastoral elements **5:** 18, 20, 24, 32, 35, 47, 50, 54, 55, 57, 60, 77, 128, 135, 156; **23:** 17, 20, 27, 46, 137; **34:** 78, 147; **46:** 88
as patriarchal society **5:** 168; **23:** 150; **34:** 177
as source of self-knowledge **5:** 98, 102, 103, 128, 130, 135, 148, 158, 162; **23:** 17; **34:** 102
as timeless, mythical world **5:** 112, 130, 141; **23:** 132; **34:** 78; **37:** 43; **46:** 88
theme of play **46:** 88
gender identity **46:** 127, 134,
genre **5:** 46, 55, 79
homoerotic elements **46:** 127, 142
homosexuality **46:** 127, 142
Hymen episode **5:** 61, 116, 130; **23:** 22, 48, 54, 109, 111, 112, 113, 115, 146, 147
irony **5:** 30, 32, 154
Jaques
love-theme, relation to **5:** 103; **23:** 7, 37, 118, 128
as malcontent **5:** 59, 70, 84
melancholy **5:** 20, 28, 32, 36, 39, 43, 50, 59, 63, 68, 77, 82, 86, 135; **23:** 20, 26, 103, 104, 107, 109; **34:** 85; **46:** 88, 94
pastoral convention, relation to **5:** 61, 63, 65, 79, 93, 98, 114, 118
Seven Ages of Man speech (Act II, scene vii) **5:** 28, 52, 156; **23:** 48, 103, 105, 126, 138, 152; **46:** 88, 156, 164, 169
Shakespeare, relation to **5:** 35, 50, 154
as superficial critic **5:** 28, 30, 43, 54, 55, 63, 65, 68, 75, 77, 82, 86, 88, 98, 138; **34:** 85
justice **46:** 94
juxtaposition of opposing perspectives **5:** 86, 93, 98, 141; **16:** 53; **23:** 119; **34:** 72, 78, 131
language and imagery **5:** 19, 21, 35, 52, 75, 82, 92, 138; **23:** 15, 21, 26; **28:** 9; **34:** 131; **37:** 43; **48:** 42
love **5:** 24, 44, 46, 57, 79, 88, 103, 116, 122, 138, 141, 162; **28:** 46, 82; **34:** 85
Love in a Forest (Charles Johnson adaptation) **23:** 7, 8, 9, 10
male/female relationships
metadramatic elements **5:** 128, 130, 146; **34:** 130
mythological allusions **46:** 142
nature **46:** 94
Neoclassical rules **5:** 19, 20
Orlando
as ideal man **5:** 32, 36, 39, 162; **34:** 161; **46:** 94
as younger brother **5:** 66, 158; **46:** 94
pastoral characters (Silvius, Phebe, and Corin) **23:** 37, 97, 98, 99, 108, 110, 118, 122, 138; **34:** 147

pastoral convention, parodies of **5:** 54, 57, 72
pastoral convention, relation to **5:** 72, 77, 122; **34:** 161; **37:** 1
primogeniture **5:** 66, 158; **34:** 109, 120
psychoanalytic interpretation **5:** 146, 158; **23:** 141, 142; **34:** 109; **48:** 42
public versus private worlds **46:** 164
reconciliation of opposites **5:** 79, 88, 103, 116, 122, 138; **23:** 127, 143; **34:** 161, 172; **46:** 156
as romance **5:** 55, 79; **23:** 27, 28, 40, 43
Rosalind **46:** 94, 122,
   Beatrice, compared with **5:** 26, 36, 50, 75
   charm **5:** 55, 75; **23:** 17, 18, 20, 41, 89, 111
   disguise, role of **5:** 75, 107, 118, 122, 128, 130, 133, 138, 141, 146, 148, 164, 168; **13:** 502; **23:** 35, 42, 106, 119, 123, 146; **34:** 130; **46:** 134
   femininity **5:** 26, 36, 52, 75; **23:** 24, 29, 46, 54, 103, 108, 121, 146
   as Ganymede **46:** 127, 142
   love-theme, relation to **5:** 79, 88, 103, 116, 122, 138, 141; **23:** 114, 115; **34:** 85, 177
rustic characters **5:** 24, 60, 72, 84; **23:** 127; **34:** 78, 161
sexual ambiguity and sexual deception **46:** 134, 142
Sexuality in Shakespeare **46:** 122, 127, 134, 142
as satire or parody of pastoral conventions **5:** 46, 55, 60, 72, 77, 79, 84, 114, 118, 128, 130, 154
self-knowledge **5:** 32, 82, 102, 116, 122, 133, 164
sibling rivalry **34:** 109
social order **37:** 1; **46:** 94
sources **5:** 18, 32, 54, 59, 66, 84; **34:** 155; **46:** 117
stage history **46:** 117
staging issues **13:** 502; **23:** 7, 17, 19, 22, 58, 96, 97, 98, 99, 101, 110, 137; **28:** 82; **32:** 212
structure **5:** 19, 24, 25, 35, 44, 45, 46, 86, 93, 116, 138, 158; **23:** 7, 8, 9, 10, 11; **34:** 72, 78, 131, 147, 155
time **5:** 18, 82, 112, 141; **23:** 146, 150; **34:** 102; **46:** 88, 156, 164, 169
Touchstone
   callousness **5:** 88
   comic and farcical elements **46:** 117
   as philosopher-fool **5:** 24, 28, 30, 32, 36, 63, 75, 98; **23:** 152; **34:** 85; **46:** 1, 14, 18, 24, 33, 52, 60, 88, 105,
   relation to pastoral convention **5:** 54, 61, 63, 72, 75, 77, 79, 84, 86, 93, 98, 114, 118, 135, 138, 166; **34:** 72, 147, 161
   selflessness **5:** 30, 36, 39, 76
verisimilitude **5:** 18, 23, 28, 30, 32, 39, 125; **23:** 107
wordplay **46:** 105

The Comedy of Errors (Volumes 1, 26, 34)

Adriana **16:** 3; **34:** 211, 220, 238
adultery **34:** 215
audience perception **1:** 37, 50, 56; **19:** 54; **34:** 258
autobiographical elements **1:** 16, 18
characterization **1:** 13, 21, 31, 34, 46, 49, 50, 55, 56; **19:** 54; **25:** 63; **34:** 194, 201, 208, 245

classical influence and sources **1:** 13, 14, 16, 31, 32, 43, 61
comic elements **1:** 43, 46, 55, 56, 59; **26:** 183, 186, 188, 190; **34:** 190, 245
composition date **1:** 18, 23, 34, 55
dramatic structure **1:** 19, 27, 40, 43, 46, 50; **26:** 186, 190; **34:** 190, 229, 233; **37:** 12
Elizabethan culture, relation to **26:** 138, 142; **34:** 201, 215, 233, 238, 258; **42:** 80
Dromio brothers **42:** 80
farcical elements **1:** 14, 16, 19, 23, 30, 34, 35, 46, 50, 59, 61; **19:** 54; **26:** 188, 190; **34:** 245
feminist criticism **42:** 93
food, meaning of **34:** 220
gender issues **34:** 215, 220
genre **34:** 251, 258
identity **34:** 201, 208, 211
illusion **1:** 13, 14, 27, 37, 40, 45, 59, 63; **26:** 188; **34:** 194, 211
language and imagery **1:** 16, 25, 39, 40, 43, 57, 59; **34:** 233
male/female relationships **16:** 3
marriage **34:** 251
mistaken identity **1:** 13, 14, 27, 37, 40, 45, 49, 55, 57, 61, 63; **19:** 34, 54; **25:** 63; **34:** 194
Plautus's works, compared with **1:** 13, 14, 16, 53, 61; **16:** 3; **19:** 34
problem comedy **34:** 251
redemption **19:** 54; **26:** 188
romantic elements **1:** 13, 16, 19, 23, 25, 30, 31, 36, 39, 53
servitude **42:** 80
social order **34:** 238
sources **1:** 13, 14, 16, 19, 31, 32, 39; **16:** 3; **34:** 190, 215, 258
staging issues **26:** 182, 183, 186, 188, 190
supernatural, role of **1:** 27, 30
tragic elements **1:** 16, 25, 27, 45, 50, 59; **34:** 229
wonder, dynamic of **37:** 12

Coriolanus (9, 17, 30, 50)

aggression **9:** 112, 142, 174, 183, 189, 198; **30:** 79, 111, 125, 142; **44:** 11, 79
Anthony and Cleopatra, compared with **30:** 79, 96; **50:** 105
appearance versus reality **30:** 142
Aufidius **9:** 9, 12, 17, 19, 53, 121, 148, 153, 157, 169, 180, 193; **19:** 287; **25:** 263, 296; **30:** 58, 67, 89, 96, 133; **50:** 99
body politic, metaphor of **22:** 248; **30:** 67, 96, 105, 125; **50:** 105, 110, 119, 140, 145, 152
butterfly episode (Act I, scene iii) **9:** 19, 45, 62, 65, 73, 100, 125, 153, 157
capitulation scene (Act V, scene iii) **9:** 19, 26, 53, 65, 100, 117, 125, 130, 157, 164, 183
ceremonies, rites, and rituals, importance of **9:** 139, 148, 169
Christian elements **30:** 111
comic elements **9:** 8, 9, 14, 53, 80, 106
Cominius **25:** 245
Cominius's tribute (Act II, scene ii) **9:** 80, 100, 117, 125, 144, 164, 198; **25:** 296
Coriolanus
   anger or passion **9:** 19, 26, 45, 80, 92, 157, 164, 177, 189; **30:** 79, 96

   as complementary figure to Aufidius **19:** 287
   death scene (Act V, scene vi) **9:** 12, 80, 100, 117, 125, 144, 164, 198; **25:** 245, 263; **50:** 110
   as epic hero **9:** 130, 164, 177; **25:** 245; **50:** 119
   immaturity **9:** 62, 80, 84, 110, 117, 142; **30:** 140
   inhuman attributes **9:** 65, 73, 139, 157, 164, 169, 189, 198; **25:** 263
   internal struggle **9:** 31, 43, 45, 53, 72, 117, 121, 130; **44:** 93
   introspection or self-knowledge, lack of **9:** 53, 80, 84, 112, 117, 130; **25:** 296; **30:** 133
   isolation or autonomy **9:** 53, 65, 142, 144, 153, 157, 164, 180, 183, 189, 198; **30:** 58, 89, 111; **50:** 128
   manipulation by others **9:** 33, 45, 62, 80; **25:** 296
   modesty **9:** 8, 12, 19, 26, 53, 78, 92, 117, 121, 144, 183; **25:** 296; **30:** 79, 96, 129, 133, 149
   narcissism **30:** 111
   noble or aristocratic attributes **9:** 15, 18, 19, 26, 31, 33, 52, 53, 62, 65, 84, 92, 100, 121, 148, 157, 169; **25:** 263; **30:** 67, 74, 96; **50:** 13
   pride or arrogance **9:** 8, 11, 12, 19, 26, 31, 33, 43, 45, 65, 78, 92, 121, 148, 153, 177; **30:** 58, 67, 74, 89, 96, 129
   reconciliation with society **9:** 33, 43, 45, 65, 139, 169; **25:** 296
   as socially destructive force **9:** 62, 65, 73, 78, 110, 142, 144, 153; **25:** 296
   soliloquy (Act IV, scene iv) **9:** 84, 112, 117, 130
   as tragic figure **9:** 8, 12, 13, 18, 25, 45, 52, 53, 72, 80, 92, 106, 112, 117, 130, 148, 164, 169, 177; **25:** 296; **30:** 67, 74, 79, 96, 111, 129; **37:** 283; **50:** 99
   traitorous actions **9:** 9, 12, 19, 45, 84, 92, 148; **25:** 296; **30:** 133
   as unsympathetic character **9:** 12, 13, 62, 78, 80, 84, 112, 130, 157
domestic elements **42:** 223; **50:** 145
economics **50:** 152
England and Rome, parallels between **9:** 39, 43, 106, 148, 180, 193; **25:** 296; **30:** 67, 105; **50:** 172
fable of the belly (Act I, scene i) **9:** 8, 65, 73, 80, 136, 153, 157, 164, 180, 183, 189; **25:** 296; **30:** 79, 105, 111; **50:** 13, 110, 140
fame **30:** 58
fire and water **25:** 263
flattery or dissimulation **9:** 26, 45, 92, 100, 110, 121, 130, 144, 157, 183, 193; **25:** 296
friendship **30:** 125, 142
gender issues **30:** 79, 125, 142; **44:** 93; **50:** 128
genre **9:** 42, 43, 53, 80, 106, 112, 117, 130, 164, 177; **30:** 67, 74, 79, 89, 111, 125; **50:** 99
honor or integrity **9:** 43, 65, 73, 92, 106, 110, 121, 144, 153, 157, 164, 177, 183, 189; **30:** 89, 96, 133
identity **42:** 248; **50:** 128
irony or satire **9:** 65, 73, 80, 92, 106, 153, 157, 164, 193; **30:** 67, 89, 133
Jacobean culture, relation to **22:** 248

language and imagery **9:** 8, 9, 13, 53, 64, 65, 73, 78, 84, 100, 112, 121, 136, 139, 142, 144, 153, 157, 174, 183, 193, 198; **22:** 248; **25:** 245, 263; **30:** 111, 125, 142; **37:** 283; **44:** 79
Macbeth, compared with **30:** 79
martial vs. civil law **48:** 230
Menenius **9:** 8, 9, 11, 14, 19, 26, 78, 80, 106, 148, 157; **25:** 263, 296; **30:** 67, 79, 89, 96, 111, 133
Midlands Revolt, influence of **22:** 248; **30:** 79; **50:** 140, 172
naming, significance of **30:** 58, 96, 111, 125
nature, philosophy of **30:** 74
nurturing or feeding **9:** 65, 73, 136, 183, 189; **30:** 111; **44:** 79; **50:** 110
paradoxical elements **9:** 73, 92, 106, 121, 153, 157, 164, 169, 193
plebeians **9:** 8, 9, 11, 12, 15, 18, 19, 26, 33, 39, 53, 92, 125, 153, 183, 189; **25:** 296; **30:** 58, 79, 96, 111; **50:** 13, 105
Plutarch and historical sources **9:** 8, 9, 13, 14, 16, 26, 39, 92, 106, 130, 142, 164; **30:** 74, 79, 105; **50:** 99
politics **9:** 15, 17, 18, 19, 26, 33, 43, 53, 62, 65, 73, 80, 92, 106, 110, 112, 121, 144, 153, 157, 164, 180; **22:** 248; **25:** 296; **30:** 58, 67, 79, 89, 96, 105, 111, 125; **37:** 283; **42:** 223; **48:** 230; **50:** 13, 140, 172
psychoanalytic interpretations **44:** 93
public versus private worlds **37:** 283; **42:** 223
sexuality **9:** 112, 142, 174, 183, 189, 198; **30:** 79, 111, 125, 142
shame **42:** 248
Shakespeare's political sympathies **9:** 8, 11, 15, 17, 19, 26, 39, 52, 53, 62, 80, 92, 142; **25:** 296; **30:** 74, 79, 89, 96, 105, 133; **50:** 145, 172
slander **48:** 230
society **9:** 15, 17, 18, 19, 26, 33, 43, 53, 62, 65, 73, 80, 92, 106, 110, 112, 121, 144, 153, 157, 164, 180; **22:** 248; **25:** 296; **30:** 58, 67, 79, 89, 96, 105, 111, 125; **50:** 13, 105, 119, 152
staging issues **17:** 172, 242, 248
structure **9:** 8, 9, 11, 12, 13, 14, 16, 26, 33, 45, 53, 58, 72, 78, 80, 84, 92, 112, 139, 148; **25:** 263; **30:** 79, 96
treachery **30:** 89
the tribunes (Brutus and Sicinius) **9:** 9, 11, 14, 19, 33, 169, 180
Virgilia **9:** 11, 19, 26, 33, 58, 100, 121, 125; **25:** 263; **30:** 79, 96, 133; **50:** 99
Volumnia
  Coriolanus's subservience to **9:** 16, 26, 33, 53, 62, 80, 92, 100, 117, 125, 142, 177, 183; **30:** 140, 149; **44:** 79
  influence on Coriolanus **9:** 45, 62, 65, 78, 92, 100, 110, 117, 121, 125, 130, 148, 157, 183, 189, 193; **25:** 263, 296; **30:** 79, 96, 125, 133, 140, 142, 149; **44:** 93
  as noble Roman matron **9:** 16, 19, 26, 31, 33
  personification of Rome **9:** 125, 183; **50:** 119
war **25:** 263; **30:** 79, 96, 125, 149

Cymbeline (Volumes 4, 15, 36, 47)

appearance versus reality **4:** 87, 93, 103, 162; **36:** 99; **47:** 228, 286
authorship controversy **4:** 17, 21, 35, 48, 56, 78
autobiographical elements **4:** 43, 46; **36:** 134
bawdy elements **36:** 155
Beaumont and Fletcher's romances, compared with **4:** 46, 52, 138
Belarius **4:** 48, 89, 141
British nationalism **4:** 19, 78, 89, 93, 129, 141, 159, 167; **32:** 373; **36:** 129; **45:** 67; **47:** 219, 265
Cloten **4:** 20, 116, 127, 155; **22:** 302, 365; **25:** 245; **36:** 99, 125, 142, 155; **47:** 228
combat scenes **22:** 365
comic elements **4:** 35, 56, 113, 141; **15:** 111, 122; **47:** 296
dramatic structure **4:** 17, 18, 19, 20, 21, 22, 24, 38, 43, 48, 53, 64, 68, 89, 116, 129, 141; **22:** 302, 365; **25:** 319; **36:** 115, 125
dreams **4:** 162, 167; **44:** 28; **45:** 67, 75
dualisms **4:** 29, 64, 73
Elizabethan dramatic conventions **4:** 53, 124
family, theme of **44:** 28
Guiderius and Arviragus **4:** 21, 22, 89, 129, 141, 148; **25:** 319; **36:** 125, 158
historical elements **47:** 260
Iachimo **25:** 245, 319; **36:** 166
Imogen **4:** 21, 22, 24, 29, 37, 45, 46, 52, 56, 78, 89, 108; **15:** 23, 32, 105, 121; **19:** 411; **25:** 245, 319; **28:** 398; **32:** 373; **36:** 129, 142, 148; **47:** 25, 205, 228, 245, 274, 277
Imogen's reawakening (Act IV, scene ii) **4:** 37, 56, 89, 103, 108, 116, 150; **15:** 23; **25:** 245; **47:** 252
irony **4:** 64, 77, 103
language and imagery **4:** 43, 48, 61, 64, 70, 73, 93, 108; **13:** 401; **25:** 245; **28:** 373, 398; **36:** 115, 158, 166, 186; **47:** 205, 286, 296
Lucretia, analogies to **36:** 148
misperception **19:** 411; **36:** 99, 115; **47:** 228, 237, 252, 277, 286, 296,
negative appraisals **4:** 20, 35, 43, 45, 48, 53, 56, 68; **15:** 32, 105, 121
patriarchy **32:** 373; **36:** 134; **47:** 237; **51:** 30
Posthumus **4:** 24, 30, 53, 78, 116, 127, 141, 155, 159, 167; **15:** 89; **19:** 411; **25:** 245, 319; **36:** 142; **44:** 28; **45:** 67, 75; **47:** 25, 205, 228
psychological elements **36:** 134; **44:** 28; **45:** 67, 75
reconciliation **4:** 38, 64, 73, 93, 105, 113, 116, 129, 138, 141, 162, 170
religious, mythical, or spiritual content **4:** 22, 29, 78, 93, 105, 108, 115, 116, 127, 134, 138, 141, 159; **28:** 373; **36:** 142, 158, 186; **47:** 219, 260, 274
romantic elements **4:** 17, 20, 46, 68, 77, 141, 148, 172; **15:** 111; **25:** 319; **28:** 373
self-conscious or artificial nature of play **4:** 43, 52, 56, 68, 124, 134, 138; **36:** 99
sexuality **4:** 170, 172; **25:** 319; **32:** 373; **47:** 245
Shakespeare's lyric poetry, compared with **13:** 401
sources **4:** 17, 18; **13:** 401; **28:** 373; **47:** 245, 265, 277
staging issues **15:** 6, 23, 75, 105, 111, 121, 122; **22:** 365
subversiveness **22:** 302
tragic elements **25:** 319; **28:** 373; **36:** 129; **47:** 296
trickster, motif of **22:** 302

vision scene (Act V, scene iv) **4:** 17, 21, 28, 29, 35, 38, 78, 105, 108, 134, 150, 167; **47:** 205
wager plot **4:** 18, 24, 29, 53, 78, 155; **22:** 365; **25:** 319; **47:** 205, 277

Hamlet (1, 21, 35, 44)

ambiguity **1:** 92, 160, 198, 227, 230, 234, 247, 249; **21:** 72; **35:** 241
appearance versus reality **1:** 95, 116, 166, 169, 198; **35:** 82, 126, 132, 144, 238; **44:** 248; **45:** 28
aristocracy **42:** 217
audience response **28:** 325; **32:** 238; **35:** 167; **44:** 107
autobiographical elements **1:** 98, 115, 119; **13:** 487
Calvinist implications **48:** 195
classical Greek tragedies, compared with **1:** 74, 75, 130, 184, 212; **13:** 296; **22:** 339
Claudius **13:** 502; **16** 246; **21:** 259, 347, 361, 371; **28:** 232, 290; **35:** 104, 182; **44:** 119, 241
closet scene (Act III, scene iv) **16:** 259; **21:** 151, 334, 392; **35:** 204, 229; **44:** 119, 237
costume **21:** 81
death, decay, and nature's destructiveness **1:** 144, 153, 188, 198, 221, 242; **13:** 502; **28:** 280, 311; **35:** 241; **42:** 284
dreams **45:** 28
dumbshow and play scene (Act III, scene ii) **1:** 76, 86, 134, 138, 154, 160, 207; **13:** 502; **21:** 392; **35:** 82; **44:** 241; **46:** 74
Elizabethan culture, relation to **1:** 76, 148, 151, 154, 160, 166, 169, 171, 176, 184, 202, 209, 254; **13:** 282, 494; **19:** 330; **21:** 407, 416; **22:** 258
Elizabethan and Jacobean politics, relation to **28:** 232; **28:** 290, 311; **35:** 140
fencing scene (Act V, scene ii) **21:** 392
Fortinbras **21:** 136, 347; **28:** 290
gender issues **35:** 144; **44:** 189, 195, 198,
genre **1:** 176, 212, 237
Gertrude **21:** 259, 347, 392; **28:** 311; **32:** 238; **35:** 182, 204, 229; **44:** 119, 160, 189, 195, 237, 248
Ghost **1:** 75, 76, 84, 85, 128, 134, 138, 154, 171, 218, 231, 254; **16:** 246; **21:** 17, 44, 112, 151, 334, 371, 377, 392; **25:** 288; **35:** 152, 157, 174, 237; **44:** 119
gravedigger scene (Act V, scene i) **21:** 392; **28:** 280; **46:** 74
grotesque elements **42:** 284
Hamlet
  delay **1:** 76, 83, 88, 90, 94, 98, 102, 103, 106, 114, 115, 116, 119, 120, 148, 151, 166, 171, 179, 188, 191, 194, 198, 221, 268; **13:** 296, 502; **21:** 81; **25:** 209, 288; **28:** 223; **35:** 82, 174, 212, 215, 237; **44:** 180, 209, 219, 229
  divided nature **16:** 246; **28:** 223; **32:** 288; **35:** 182, 215; **37:** 241
  elocution of the character's speeches **21:** 96, 104, 112, 127, 132, 172, 177, 179, 194, 245, 254, 257
  as a fool **46:** 1, 29, 52, 74
  madness **1:** 76, 81, 83, 95, 102, 106, 128,

144, 154, 160, 234; **21:** 35, 50, 72, 81, 99, 112. 311, 339, 355, 361, 371, 377, 384; **35:** 117, 132, 134, 140, 144, 212; **44:** 107, 119, 152, 209, 219, 229

melancholy **21:** 99, 112, 177. 194; **35:** 82, 95, 117; **44:** 209, 219

as negative character **1:** 86, 92, 111, 171, 218; **21:** 386; **25:** 209; **35:** 167

reaction to his father's death **22:** 339; **35:** 104, 174; **44:** 133, 160, 180, 189

reaction to Gertrude's marriage **1:** 74, 120, 154, 179; **16:** 259; **21:** 371; **22:** 339; **35:** 104, 117; **44:** 133, 160, 189, 195

romantic aspects of the character **21:** 96; **44:** 198

as scourge or purifying figure **1:** 144, 209, 242; **25:** 288; **35:** 157

sentimentality versus intellectuality **1:** 75, 83, 88, 91, 93, 94, 96, 102, 103, 115, 116, 120, 166, 191; **13:** 296; **21:** 35, 41, 44, 72, 81, 89, 99, 129, 132, 136, 172, 213, 225, 339, 355, 361, 371, 377, 379, 381, 386; **25:** 209; **44:** 198

soliloquies **1:** 76, 82, 83, 148, 166, 169, 176, 191; **21:** 17, 31, 44, 53, 89, 112, 268, 311, 334, 347, 361, 384, 392; **25:** 209; **28:** 223; **44:** 107, 119, 229

theatrical interpretations **21:** 11, 31, 78, 101, 104, 107, 160, 177, 179, 182, 183, 192, 194, 197, 202, 203, 208, 213, 225, 232, 237, 249, 253, 254, 257, 259, 274, 311, 339, 347, 355, 361, 371, 377, 380

virility **21:** 213, 301, 355; **44:** 198

Hamlet with Alterations (David Garrick adaptation) **21:** 23, 334, 347

Horatio **44:** 189

idealism versus pragmatism **16** 246; **28:** 325

Laertes **21:** 347, 386; **28:** 290; **35:** 182

language and imagery **1:** 95, 144, 153, 154, 160, 188, 198, 221, 227, 249, 259, 270; **22:** 258, 378; **28:** 311; **35:** 144, 152, 238, 241; **42:** 217; **44:** 248

madness **19:** 330; **35:** 104, 126, 134, 140, 144; **44:** 107, 119, 152, 209, 219, 229

marriage **22:** 339; **51:** 44

Marxist criticism **42:** 234

nunnery scene (Act III, scene i) **21:** 157, 381, 410

Ophelia **1:** 73, 76, 81, 82, 91, 96, 97, 154, 166, 169, 171, 218, 270; **13:** 268; **16:** 246; **19:** 330; **21:** 17, 41, 44, 72, 81, 101, 104, 107, 112, 136, 203, 259, 347, 381, 386, 392, 416; **28:** 232, 325; **35:** 104, 126, 140, 144, 182, 238; **44:** 189, 195, 248

Polonius **21:** 259, 334, 347, 386, 416; **35:** 182

prayer scene (Act III, scene iii) **1:** 76, 106, 160, 212, 231; **44:** 119

psychoanalytic interpretations **1:** 119, 148, 154, 179, 202; **21:** 197, 213, 361; **25:** 209; **28:** 223; **35:** 95, 104, 134, 237; **37:** 241; **44:** 133, 152. 160, 180, 209, 219

religious, mythic, or spiritual content **1:** 98, 102, 130, 184, 191, 209, 212, 231, 234, 254; **21:** 361; **22:** 258; **28:** 280; **32:** 238; **35:** 134

revenge **1:** 74, 194, 209, 224, 234, 254; **16:** 246; **22:** 258; **25:** 288; **28:** 280; **35:** 152, 157, 167, 174, 212; **44:** 180, 209, 219, 229

Richard II, compared with **1:** 264

ceremonies, rites, and rituals, importance of **13:** 268; **28:** 232

sources **1:** 76, 81, 113, 125, 128, 130, 151, 191, 202, 224, 259

staging issues **13:** 494, 502; **21:** 11, 17, 31, 35, 41, 44, 50, 53, 78, 81, 89, 101, 112, 127, 139, 142, 145, 148, 151, 157, 160, 172, 182, 183, 202, 203, 208, 225, 232, 237, 242, 245, 249, 251, 259, 268, 270, 274, 283, 284, 301, 311, 334, 347, 355, 361, 371, 377, 379, 380, 381, 384, 386, 392, 407, 410, 416; **44:** 198

Stoicism **48:** 195

structure **22:** 378; **28:** 280, 325; **35:** 82, 104, 215; **44:** 152

subjectivity **45:** 28

textual variants **13:** 282; **16:** 259; **21:** 11, 23, 72, 101, 127, 129, 139, 140, 142, 145, 202, 208, 259, 270, 284, 347, 361, 384; **22:** 258; **32:** 238

topical allusions or content **13:** 282

unity **1:** 75, 76, 87, 103, 113, 125, 128, 142, 148, 160, 184, 188, 198, 264; **16:** 259; **35:** 82, 215

unnatural ordering **22:** 378

widowhood and remarriage, themes of **32:** 238

Henry IV, Parts 1 and 2 (Volumes 1, 14, 39, 49)

carnival elements **28:** 203; **32:** 103

characterization **1:** 321, 328, 332, 333, 336, 344, 365, 383, 385, 389, 391, 397, 401; **19:** 195; **39:** 123, 137; **42:** 101, 164; **49:** 93

comic elements **1:** 286, 290, 314, 327, 328, 336, 353; **19:** 195; **25:** 109; **39:** 72

contractual and economic relations **13:** 213

contrasting dramatic worlds **14:** 56, 60, 61, 84, 105; **48:** 95; **49:** 162

critical history **42:** 187; **48:** 167

deception, disguise, and duplicity **1:** 397, 406, 425; **42:** 101; **47:** 1, 60; **48:** 95

divine right versus justice **49:** 116

Elizabethan culture, relation to **19:** 195; **48:** 117, 143, 151, 175

Elizabethan politics, relation to **22:** 395; **28:** 203; **47:** 60; **48:** 117, 143, 167, 175

Falstaff

characterization **1:** 287, 298, 312, 333; **25:** 245; **28:** 203; **39:** 72, 134, 137, 143

as comic figure **1:** 287, 311, 327, 344, 351, 354, 357, 410, 434; **39:** 89; **46:** 1, 48, 52; **49:** 178

as coward or rogue **1:** 285, 290, 296, 298, 306, 307, 313, 317, 323, 336, 337, 338, 342, 354, 366, 374, 391, 396, 401, 433; **14:** 7, 111, 125, 130, 133; **32:** 166

dual personality **1:** 397, 401, 406, 434; **49:** 162

female attributes **13:** 183; **44:** 44

Iago, compared with **1:** 341, 351

Marxist interpretation **1:** 358, 361

as outlaw **49:** 133

as parody of the historical plot **1:** 314, 354, 359; **39:** 143

as positive character **1:** 286, 287, 290, 296, 298, 311, 312, 321, 325, 333, 344, 355, 357, 389, 401, 408, 434

rejection by Hal **1:** 286, 287, 290, 312, 314, 317, 324, 333, 338, 344, 357, 366, 372, 374, 379, 380, 389, 414; **13:** 183; **25:** 109; **39:** 72, 89

as satire of feudal society **1:** 314, 328, 361; **32:** 103

as scapegoat **1:** 389, 414

stage interpretations **14:** 4, 6, 7, 9, 15, 116, 130, 146; **47:** 1

as subversive figure **16:** 183; **25:** 109

as Vice figure **1:** 342, 361, 366, 374

flattery **22:** 395

gender issues **13:** 183; **25:** 151; **44:** 44; **48:** 175

Hal

audience's perspective of **49:** 153

and betrayal **49:** 123

as the central character **1:** 286, 290, 314, 317, 326, 338, 354, 366, 374, 396; **39:** 72, 100

dual personality **1:** 397, 406; **25:** 109, 151; **49:** 112, 139, 153, 162

as Everyman **1:** 342, 366, 374

fall from humanity **1:** 379, 380, 383

general assessment **1:** 286, 287, 289, 290, 314, 317, 326, 327, 332, 357, 397; **25:** 245; **32:** 212; **39:** 134

Henry's perspective of **49:** 153

as ideal ruler **1:** 289, 309, 317, 321, 326, 337, 342, 344, 374, 389, 391, 434; **25:** 109; **39:** 123; **47:** 60

as Machiavellian ruler **47:** 60

as negative character **1:** 312, 332, 333, 357; **32:** 212

as outlaw **49:** 112

preparation for rule **49:** 112

Richard II, compared with **1:** 332, 337; **39:** 72

as restorer of law **49:** 133

Henry **39:** 123, 137; **49:** 139

effectiveness as ruler **49:** 116

guilt **49:** 112

illegitimacy of rule **49:** 112, 133, 137

as tragic figure **49:** 186

as usurper **49:** 116, 137

historical content **1:** 310, 328, 365, 366, 370, 374, 380, 387, 421, 424, 427, 431; **16:** 172; **19:** 157; **25:** 151; **32:** 136; **39:** 143; **48:** 143, 167; **49:** 139

historical and dramatic elements **49:** 93

historical epic, place in or relation to Shakespeare's **1:** 309, 314, 328, 374, 379, 424, 427; **48:** 167

Hotspur **25:** 151; **28:** 101; **39:** 72, 134, 137; **42:** 101; **49:** 137

and prisoners of war **49:** 137

versus Henry **49:** 137

John of Lancaster, Prince

and betrayal **49:** 123

justice **49:** 112, 123

kingship **1:** 314, 318, 337, 366, 370, 374, 379, 380, 383, 424; **16:** 172; **19:** 195; **28:** 101; **39:** 100, 116, 123, 130; **42:** 143; **48:** 143

language and imagery **13:** 213; **16:** 172; **25:** 245; **28:** 101; **39:** 116, 130; **42:** 155; **47:** 1

Lord Chief Justice

as keeper of law and justice **49:** 133

as medieval allegory or morality play **1:** 323, 324, 342, 361, 366, 373, 374; **32:** 166; **39:** 89; **47:** 60

Mortimer **25**: 151
multiple endings **49**: 102
Neoclassical rules **1**: 286, 287, 290, 29
politics **28**: 101; **39**: 130; **42**: 143; **48**: 143, 175
power **49**: 139
psychoanalytic interpretations **13**: 457; **28**: 101; **42**: 187; **44**: 44
rebellion **22**: 395; **28**: 101
references to **22**: 114; **32**: 166; **48**: 117
relationship to other Shakespearean plays **1**: 286, 290, 309, 329, 365, 396; **28**: 101; **42**: 101, 155; **48**: 167; **49**: 93, 186
relationship of Parts 1 and 2 **32**: 136; **39**: 100; **49**: 178
religious, mythic, or spiritual content **1**: 314, 374, 414, 421, 429, 431, 434; **32**: 103; **48**: 151
   as autonomous works **1**: 289, 337, 338, 347, 348, 373, 387, 393, 411, 418, 424
   comparison **1**: 290, 295, 329, 348, 358, 393, 411, 419, 429, 431, 441
   unity of both parts **1**: 286, 290, 309, 314, 317, 329, 365, 373, 374, 396, 402, 404, 419
staging issues **32**: 212; **47**: 1; **49**: 102
structure **49**: 93
textual issues **22**: 114
time and change, motif of **1**: 372, 393, 411; **39**: 89; **48**: 143
Turkish elements **19**: 170
two fathers **14**: 86, 101, 105, 108; **39**: 89, 100; **49**: 102
violence **25**: 109

Henry V (Volumes 5, 14, 30, 49)

battle of Agincourt **5**: 197, 199, 213, 246, 257, 281, 287, 289, 293, 310, 318; **19**: 217; **30**: 181
Canterbury and churchmen **5**: 193, 203, 205, 213, 219, 225, 252, 260; **22**: 137; **30**: 215, 262
characterization **5**: 186, 189, 192, 193, 199, 219, 230, 233, 252, 276, 293; **30**: 227, 278
Chorus, role of **5**: 186, 192, 226, 228, 230, 252, 264, 269, 281, 293; **14**: 301, 319, 336; **19**: 133; **25**: 116, 131; **30**: 163, 202, 220; **49**: 194, 200, 211, 219, 260
class distinctions, conflict, and relations **28**: 146
colonialism **22**: 103
comic elements **5**: 185, 188, 191, 192, 217, 230, 233, 241, 252, 260, 276; **19**: 217; **28**: 121; **30**: 193, 202,
economic relations **13**: 213
Elizabethan culture, relation to **5**: 210, 213, 217, 223, 257, 299, 310; **16**: 202; **19**: 133, 233; **28**: 121, 159; **30**: 215, 262; **37**: 187; **49**: 260
English language and colonialism **22**: 103; **28**: 159
epic elements **5**: 192, 197, 246, 257, 314; **30**: 181, 220, 237, 252
Falstaff **5**: 185, 186, 187, 189, 192, 195, 198, 210, 226, 257, 269, 271, 276, 293, 299; **28**: 146; **46**: 48

Fluellen **30**: 278; **37**: 105
French aristocrats and the Dauphin **5**: 188, 191, 199, 205, 213, 281; **22**: 137; **28**: 121
French language, Shakespeare's use of **5**: 186, 188, 190; **25**: 131
gender issues **13**: 183; **28**: 121, 146, 159; **44**: 44
Henry
   brutality and cunning **5**: 193, 203, 209, 210, 213, 219, 233, 239, 252, 260, 271, 287, 293, 302, 304; **30**: 159
   characterization in *1* and *2 Henry IV* contrasted **5**: 189, 190, 241, 304, 310; **19**: 133; **25**: 131; **32**: 157
   chivalry **37**: 187
   courage **5**: 191, 195, 210, 213, 228, 246, 257, 267
   disguise **30**: 169, 259
   education **5**: 246, 267, 271, 289; **14**: 297, 328, 342; **30**: 259
   emotion, lack of **5**: 209, 212, 233, 244, 264, 267, 287, 293, 310
   as heroic figure **5**: 192, 205, 209, 223, 244, 252, 257, 260, 269, 271, 299, 304; **28**: 121, 146; **30**: 237, 244, 252; **37**: 187; **49**: 194, 200, 236, 247
   humor **5**: 189, 191, 212, 217, 239, 240, 276
   intellectual and social limitations **5**: 189, 191, 203, 209, 210, 225, 226, 230, 293; **30**: 220
   interpersonal relations **5**: 209, 233, 267, 269, 276, 287, 293, 302, 318; **19**: 133; **28**: 146
   mercy **5**: 213, 267, 289, 293
   mixture of good and bad qualities **5**: 199, 205, 209, 210, 213, 244, 260, 304, 314; **30**: 262, 273; **49**: 211
   piety **5**: 191, 199, 209, 217, 223, 239, 257, 260, 271, 289, 310, 318; **30**: 244; **32**: 126
   public versus private selves **22**: 137; **30**: 169, 207
   self-doubt **5**: 281, 310
   slaughter of prisoners **5**: 189, 205, 246, 293, 318; **28**: 146
   speech **5**: 212, 230, 233, 246, 264, 276, 287, 302; **28**: 146; **30**: 163, 227
heroism **49**: 194, 200, 211, 236
historical content **5**: 185, 188, 190, 192, 193, 198, 246, 314; **13**: 201; **19**: 133; **25**: 131; **30**: 193, 202, 207, 215, 252; **49**: 223
historical epic, place in or relation to Shakespeare's **5**: 195, 198, 205, 212, 225, 241, 244, 287, 304, 310; **14**: 337, 342; **30**: 215
homoerotic elements **16**: 202
Hotspur **5**: 189, 199, 228, 271, 302
hypocrisy **5**: 203, 213, 219, 223, 233, 260, 271, 302
imperialism **22**: 103; **28**: 159
Irish affairs **22**: 103; **28**: 159
irony **5**: 192, 210, 213, 219, 223, 226, 233, 252, 260, 269, 281, 299, 304; **14**: 336; **30**: 159, 193,
Katherine **5**: 186, 188, 189, 190, 192, 260, 269, 299, 302; **13**: 183; **19**: 217; **30**: 278; **44**: 44
kingship **5**: 205, 223, 225, 233, 239, 244, 257, 264, 267, 271, 287, 289, 299, 302, 304, 314, 318; **16**: 202; **22**: 137; **30**: 169, 202, 259, 273; **49**: 200

language and imagery **5**: 188, 230, 233, 241, 264, 276; **19**: 203; **25**: 131; **30**: 159, 181, 207, 234
law and justice **49**: 223, 226, 260
Machiavellianism **5**: 203, 225, 233, 252, 287, 304; **25**: 131; **30**: 273
MacMorris **22**: 103; **28**: 159; **30**: 278
Marlowe's works, compared with **19**: 233
metadramatic elements **13**: 194; **30**: 181; **49**: 200, 211
Mistress Quickly **5**: 186, 187, 210, 276, 293; **30**: 278
morality **5**: 195, 203, 213, 223, 225, 239, 246, 260, 271, 293
obscenity **5**: 188, 190, 260
order **5**: 205, 257, 264, 310, 314; **30**: 193,
patriarchy **37**: 105; **44**: 44
politics and ideology **49**: 219, 247, 260
nationalism and patriotism **5**: 198, 205, 209, 210, 213, 219, 223, 233, 246, 252, 257, 269, 299; **19**: 133, 217; **30**: 227, 262; **49**: 219, 247
Pistol **28**: 146
power **37**: 175
psychoanalytic interpretations **13**: 457; **44**: 44
religious, mythic, or religious content **25**: 116; **32**: 126
Salic Law **5**: 219, 252, 260; **28**: 121
self-interest or expediency **5**: 189, 193, 205, 213, 217, 233, 260, 287, 302, 304; **30**: 273; **49**: 223
soldiers **5**: 203, 239, 267, 276, 281, 287, 293, 318; **28**: 146; **30**: 169; **49**: 194
staging issues **5**: 186, 189, 192, 193, 198, 205, 226, 230, 241, 281, 314; **13**: 194, 502; **14**: 293, 295, 297, 301, 310, 319, 328, 334, 336, 342; **19**: 217; **32**: 185
structure **5**: 186, 189, 205, 213, 230, 241, 264, 289, 310, 314; **30**: 220, 227, 234, 244
tetralogy, relation to **49**: 223
textual problems **5**: 187, 189, 190; **13**: 201
topical allusions or content **5**: 185, 186; **13**: 201
tragic elements **5**: 228, 233, 267, 269, 271
traitors (Scroop, Grey, and Cambridge) **16**: 202; **30**: 220, 278
   Southampton conspiracy **49**: 223
Turkish elements **19**: 170
violence **43**: 24
war **5**: 193, 195, 197, 198, 210, 213, 219, 230, 233, 246, 281, 293; **28**: 121, 146; **30**: 262; **32**: 126; **37**: 175, 187; **42**: 143; **49**: 194, 236, 247, 260
Williams **13**: 502; **16**: 183; **28**: 146; **30**: 169, 259, 278
wooing scene (Act V, scene ii) **5**: 186, 188, 189, 191, 193, 195, 260, 276, 299, 302; **14**: 297; **28**: 121, 159; **30**: 163, 207

Henry VI, Parts 1, 2, and 3 (Volumes 3, 24, 39)

ambivalent or ironic elements **3**: 69, 151, 154; **39**: 160
authorship controversy **3**: 16, 18, 19, 20, 21, 26, 27, 29, 31, 35, 39, 41, 55, 66; **24**: 51
autobiographical elements **3**: 41, 55
Bordeaux sequence **37**: 165
Cade scenes **3**: 35, 67, 92, 97, 109; **16**: 183;

22: 156; **25:** 102; **28:** 112; **37:** 97; **39:** 160, 196, 205; **50:** 45, 51
carnival elements **22:** 156
characterization **3:** 18, 20, 24, 25, 31, 57, 64, 73, 77, 109, 119, 151; **24:** 22, 28, 38, 42, 45, 47; **39:** 160
class distinctions, conflict, and relations **37:** 97; **39:** 187; **50:** 45, 51
dance **22:** 156
decay of heroic ideals **3:** 119, 126
disorder and civil dissension **3:** 59, 67, 76, 92, 103, 126; **13:** 131; **16:** 183; **24:** 11, 17, 28, 31, 47; **25:** 102; **28:** 112; **39:** 154, 177, 187, 196, 205
Elizabethan literary and cultural influences **3:** 75, 97, 100, 119, 143; **22:** 156; **28:** 112; **37:** 97
Folk rituals, elements and influence of **39:** 205
Henry
   characterization **3:** 64, 77, 151; **39:** 160, 177; **47:** 32
   source of social disorder **3:** 25, 31, 41, 115; **39:** 154, 187
   as sympathetic figure **3:** 73, 143, 154; **24:** 32
historical accuracy **3:** 18, 21, 35, 46, 51; **16:** 217; **24:** 16, 18, 25, 31, 45, 48
historical epic, place in or relation to Shakespeare's **3:** 24, 59; **24:** 51
as humanistic play **3:** 83, 92, 109, 115, 119, 131, 136, 143
Humphrey **13:** 131
as inferior or flawed plays **3:** 20, 21, 25, 26, 35
Joan of Arc **16:** 131; **32:** 212
kingship **3:** 69, 73, 77, 109, 115, 136, 143; **24:** 32; **39:** 154, 177, 187; **47:** 32
language and imagery **3:** 21, 50, 52, 55, 57, 66, 67, 71, 75, 76, 97, 105, 109, 119, 126, 131; **24:** 28; **37:** 157; **39:** 213, 222
legitimacy **3:** 89, 157; **39:** 154,
Machiavellianism **22:** 193
Margaret
   characterization **3:** 18, 26, 35, 51, 103, 109, 140, 157; **24:** 48
   Suffolk, relationship with **3:** 18, 24, 26, 157; **39:** 213
Marlowe's works, compared with **19:** 233
medieval literary influence **3:** 59, 67, 75, 100, 109, 136, 151; **13:** 131
molehill scene (*3 Henry VI*, Act III, scene ii) **3:** 75, 97, 126, 149
moral inheritance **3:** 89, 126
multiple perspectives of characters **3:** 69, 154
Neoclassical rules **3:** 17, 18
patriarchal claims **16:** 131 **25:** 102
nationalism and patriotism **24:** 25, 45, 47
play-within-the-play, convention of **3:** 75, 149
retribution **3:** 27, 42, 51, 59, 77, 83, 92, 100, 109, 115, 119, 131, 136, 151
Richard of Gloucester
   characterization **3:** 35, 48, 57, 64, 77, 143, 151; **22:** 193; **39:** 160, 177
   as revenger **22:** 193
   soliloquy (*3 Henry VI*, Act III, scene ii) **3:** 17, 48
sibling rivalry **22:** 193
sources **3:** 18, 21, 29, 31, 35, 39, 46, 51; **13:** 131; **16:** 217; **39:** 196
staging issues **24:** 21, 22, 27, 31, 32, 36, 38, 41, 45, 48, 55; **32:** 212

structure **3:** 31, 43, 46, 69, 83, 103, 109, 119, 136, 149, 154; **39:** 213
Talbot **39:** 160, 213, 222
textual arrangement **24:** 3, 4, 6, 12, 17, 18, 19, 20, 21, 24, 27, 42, 45; **37:** 165
theatrical viability **24:** 31, 32, 34
Tudor myth **3:** 51, 59, 77, 92, 100, 109, 115, 119, 131; **39:** 222
Unity **39:** 177, 222
violence **24:** 25, 31; **37:** 157
women, role of **3:** 103, 109, 126, 140, 157; **16:** 183; **39:** 196
York's death **13:** 131

Henry VIII (Volumes 2, 24, 41)

   ambition or pride **2:** 15, 38, 67
   authorship controversy **2:** 16, 18, 19, 22, 23, 27, 28, 31, 35, 36, 42, 43, 44, 46, 48, 51, 58, 64, 68; **41:** 129, 146, 158, 171,
   Anne Boleyn **2:** 21, 24, 31; **41:** 180
   Buckingham **22:** 182; **24:** 129, 140; **37:** 109
   change **2:** 27, 65, 72, 81
   characterization **2:** 17, 23, 25, 32, 35, 39; **24:** 106
   composition date **2:** 19, 22, 35; **24:** 129
   costumes **24:** 82, 87; **28:** 184
   Cranmer's prophecy **2:** 25, 31, 46, 56, 64, 68, 72; **24:** 146; **32:** 148; **41:** 120, 190
   Cymbeline, compared with **2:** 67, 71
   discrepancy between prophetic ending and preceding action **2:** 22, 25, 31, 46, 49, 56, 60, 65, 68, 75, 81; **32:** 148; **41:** 190
   Elizabethan politics, relation to **22:** 395; **24:** 115, 129, 140; **32:** 148
   Elizabethan dramatic conventions **24:** 155
   English Reformation, influence of **2:** 25, 35, 39, 51, 67; **24:** 89
   flattery **22:** 395
   historical and romantic elements, combination of **41:** 129, 146, 180
   historical epic, as epilogue to Shakespeare's **2:** 22, 25, 27, 39, 51, 60, 65
   historical relativity, theme of **41:** 146
   King Henry
      as agent of divine retribution **2:** 49
      characterization **2:** 23, 39, 51, 58, 60, 65, 66, 75; **28:** 184; **37:** 109
      incomplete portrait **2:** 15, 16, 19, 35; **41:** 120
      as realistic figure **2:** 21, 22, 23, 25, 32
   historical and romantic elements, combination of **2:** 46, 49, 51, 75, 76, 78; **24:** 71, 80, 146
   historiography **37:** 109
   inconsistencies **2:** 16, 27, 28, 31, 60
   ironic aspects **41:** 129
   Katherine
      characterization **2:** 18, 19, 23, 24, 38; **24:** 129; **37:** 109; **41:** 180
      Hermione, compared with **2:** 24, 51, 58, 76
      politeness strategies **22:** 182
      religious discourse **22:** 182
      as tragic figure **2:** 16, 18
   kingship **2:** 49, 58, 60, 65, 75, 78; **24:** 113; **41:** 129, 171
   language and imagery **41:** 180, 190
   legitimacy **37:** 109

moral intent **2:** 15, 19, 25; **24:** 140
Norfolk **22:** 182
pageantry **2:** 14, 15, 18, 51, 58; **24:** 77, 83, 84, 85, 89, 91, 106, 113, 118, 120, 126, 127, 140, 146, 150; **41:** 120, 129, 190
patience **2:** 58, 76, 78
politics **2:** 39, 49, 51, 58, 60, 65, 67, 71, 72, 75, 78, 81; **24:** 74, 121, 124; **41:** 146
Porter **24:** 155
rebellion **22:** 395
rhetoric of politeness **22:** 182
Shakespeare's romances, compared with **2:** 46, 51, 58, 66, 67, 71, 76; **41:** 171
sources **2:** 16, 17; **24:** 71, 80
staging issues **24:** 67, 70, 71, 75, 77, 83, 84, 85, 87, 89, 91, 101, 106, 113, 120, 127, 129, 136, 140, 146, 150, 152, 155; **28:** 184
Stephen Gardiner **24:** 129
structure **2:** 16, 25, 27, 28, 31, 36, 44, 46, 51, 56, 68, 75; **24:** 106, 112, 113, 120
style **41:** 158
thematic disparity **2:** 25, 31, 56, 68, 75; **41:** 146
tragedies of major characters **2:** 16, 39, 46, 48, 49, 51, 56, 58, 68, 81; **41:** 120
wheel of fortune, motif of **2:** 27, 65, 72, 81
Cardinal Wolsey **2:** 15, 18, 19, 23, 24, 38; **22:** 182; **24:** 80, 91, 112, 113, 129, 140; **37:** 109; **41:** 129

Julius Caesar (Volumes 7, 17, 30, 50)

   anachronisms **7:** 331
   Antony
      characterization **7:** 160, 179, 189, 221, 233, 284, 320, 333; **17:** 269, 271, 272, 284, 298, 306, 313, 315, 358, 398; **25:** 272; **30:** 316
      funeral oration **7:** 148, 154, 159, 204, 210, 221, 238, 259, 350; **25:** 280; **30:** 316, 333, 362
   aristocratic values **16:** 231; **22:** 280; **30:** 379; **50:** 194, 196, 211
   the assassination **7:** 156, 161, 179, 191, 200, 221, 264, 272, 279, 284, 350; **25:** 272; **30:** 326
   audience interpretation **48:** 240
   audience response **7:** 179, 238, 253, 255, 272, 316, 320, 336, 350; **19:** 321; **48:** 240
   Brutus **50:** 194, 258
      arrogance **7:** 160, 169, 204, 207, 264, 277, 292, 350; **25:** 280; **30:** 351
      as chief protagonist or tragic hero **7:** 152, 159, 189, 191, 200, 204, 242, 250, 253, 264, 268, 279, 284, 298, 333; **17:** 272, 372, 387
      citizenship **25:** 272
      funeral oration **7:** 154, 155, 204, 210, 350
      motives **7:** 150, 156, 161, 179, 191, 200, 221, 227, 233, 245, 292, 303, 310, 320, 333, 350; **25:** 272; **30:** 321, 358
      nobility or idealism **7:** 150, 152, 156, 159, 161, 179, 189, 191, 200, 221, 242, 250, 253, 259, 264, 277, 303, 320; **17:** 269, 271, 273, 279, 280, 284, 306, 308, 321, 323, 324, 345, 358; **25:** 272, 280; **30:** 351, 362; **50:** 194
      political ineptitude or lack of judgment **7:**

169, 188, 200, 205, 221, 245, 252, 264, 277, 282, 310, 316, 331, 333, 343; **17:** 323, 358, 375, 380; **50:** 13
  self-knowledge or self-deception **7:** 191, 200, 221, 242, 259, 264, 268, 279, 310, 333, 336, 350; **25:** 272; **30:** 316
  soliloquy (Act II, scene i) **7:** 156, 160, 161, 191, 221, 245, 250, 253, 264, 268, 279, 282, 292, 303, 343, 350; **25:** 280; **30:** 333
Caesar **50:** 189, 230, 234
  ambiguous nature **7:** 191, 233, 242, 250, 272, 298, 316, 320
  ambitious nature **50:** 234
  arrogance **7:** 160, 207, 218, 253, 272, 279, 298; **25:** 280
  idolatry **22:** 137
  leadership qualities **7:** 161, 179, 189, 191, 200, 207, 233, 245, 253, 257, 264, 272, 279, 284, 298, 310, 333; **17:** 317, 358; **22:** 280; **30:** 316, 326; **50:** 234
  as tragic hero **7:** 152, 200, 221, 279; **17:** 321, 377, 384
  weakness **7:** 161, 167, 169, 179, 187, 188, 191, 207, 218, 221, 233, 250, 253, 298; **17:** 358; **25:** 280
Caesarism **7:** 159, 160, 161, 167, 169, 174, 191, 205, 218, 253, 310; **30:** 316, 321; **50:** 196, 234
Calphurnia
  dream **45:** 10
Casca
  as Cynic **50:** 249
  as proto-Christian **50:** 249
Cassius **7:** 156, 159, 160, 161, 169, 179, 189, 221, 233, 303, 310, 320, 333, 343; **17:** 272, 282, 284, 344, 345, 358; **25:** 272, 280; **30:** 351; **37:** 203
ceremonies, rites, and rituals, importance of **7:** 150, 210, 255, 259, 268, 284, 316, 331, 339, 356; **13:** 260; **22:** 137; **30:** 374; **50:** 258, 269
construing the truth **7:** 320, 336, 343, 350; **37:** 229
Elizabethan culture, relation to **16:** 231; **30:** 342, 379; **50:** 13, 211, 269, 280
emulation or rivalry **16:** 231
Epicureanism **50:** 249
Flavius and Murellus **50:** 64
gender issues **13:** 260
historical determinism versus free will **7:** 160, 298, 316, 333, 346, 356; **13:** 252
irony or ambiguity **7:** 167, 257, 259, 262, 268, 282, 316, 320, 333, 336, 346, 350
language and imagery **7:** 148, 155, 159, 188, 204, 207, 227, 242, 250, 277, 296, 303, 324, 346, 350; **13:** 260; **17:** 347, 348, 350, 356, 358; **19:** 321; **22:** 280; **25:** 280; **30:** 333, 342; **50:** 196, 258
liberty versus tyranny **7:** 158, 179, 189, 205, 221, 253; **25:** 272
love and friendship **7:** 233, 262, 268; **25:** 272
medieval physiology **13:** 260
moral choice **7:** 179, 264, 279, 343
Octavius **30:** 316
omens **22:** 137; **45:** 10; **50:** 265, 280
patricians versus plebeians **50:** 189, 196
philosophical elements **7:** 310, 324; **37:** 203
plebeians versus tribunes **50:** 230
the poets **7:** 179, 320, 350

politics **7:** 161, 169, 191, 205, 218, 221, 245, 262, 264, 279, 282, 310, 324, 333, 346; **17:** 317, 318, 321, 323, 334, 350, 351, 358, 378, 382, 394, 406; **22:** 137, 280; **25:** 272, 280; **30:** 285, 297, 316, 321, 342, 374, 379; **37:** 203; **50:** 13
as "problem play" **7:** 272, 320
psychoanalytic interpretation **45:** 10
public versus private principles **7:** 161, 179, 252, 262, 268, 284, 298; **13:** 252
quarrel scene (Act IV, scene iii) **7:** 149, 150, 152, 153, 155, 160, 169, 188, 191, 204, 268, 296, 303, 310
retribution **7:** 160, 167, 200
revenge tragedy elements **7:** 316
role-playing **7:** 356; **37:** 229
Roman citizenry, portrayal of **7:** 169, 179, 210, 221, 245, 279, 282, 310, 320, 333; **17:** 271, 279, 288, 291, 292, 298, 323, 334, 351, 367, 374, 375, 378; **22:** 280; **30:** 285, 297, 316, 321, 374, 379; **37:** 229; **50:** 230
Senecan elements **37:** 229
Shakespeare's English history plays, compared with **7:** 161, 189, 218, 221, 252; **22:** 137; **30:** 369
Shakespeare's major tragedies, compared with **7:** 161, 188, 227, 242, 264, 268
sources **7:** 149, 150, 156, 187, 200, 264, 272, 282, 284, 320; **30:** 285, 297, 326, 358
staging **48:** 240; **50:** 186
Stoicism **50:** 249
structure **7:** 152, 155, 159, 160, 179, 200, 210, 238, 264, 284, 298, 316, 346; **13:** 252; **30:** 374
tragic elements **50:** 258, 265
violence **48:** 240

King John (Volumes 9, 24, 41)

ambiguity **13:** 152; **41:** 243
anti-catholic rhetoric **22:** 120; **25:** 98
Arthur **9:** 215, 216, 218, 219, 229, 240, 267, 275; **22:** 120; **25:** 98; **41:** 251, 277
autobiographical elements **9:** 209, 218, 245, 248, 260, 292
characterization **9:** 222, 224, 229, 240, 250, 292; **41:** 205, 215
church versus state **9:** 209, 212, 222, 235, 240; **22:** 120
commodity or self-interest **9:** 224, 229, 245, 260, 275, 280, 297; **19:** 182; **25:** 98; **41:** 228
commodity versus honor **41:** 269
Constance **9:** 208, 210, 211, 215, 219, 220, 224, 229, 240, 251, 254; **16:** 161; **24:** 177, 184, 196
corruption in society **9:** 222, 234, 280, 297
Elizabethan politics, relation to **48:** 132
ethical or moral issues **9:** 212, 222, 224, 229, 235, 240, 263, 275, 280
excess **9:** 251
Faulconbridge, the Bastard **41:** 205, 228, 251, 260, 277
  as chorus or commentator **9:** 212, 218, 229, 248, 251, 260, 271, 284, 297, 300; **22:** 120
  as comic figure **9:** 219, 271, 297
  development **9:** 216, 224, 229, 248, 263, 271, 275, 280, 297; **13:** 158, 163

  as embodiment of England **9:** 222, 224, 240, 244, 248, 271
  heroic qualities **9:** 208, 245, 248, 254, 263, 271, 275; **25:** 98
  political conduct **9:** 224, 240, 250, 260, 280, 297; **13:** 147, 158; **22:** 120
Henry **41:** 277
historical content **9:** 216, 219, 220, 222, 235, 240, 254, 284, 290, 292, 297, 300, 303; **13:** 163; **32:** 93, 114; **41:** 234, 243
John **41:** 205, 260
  death, decay, and nature's destructiveness **9:** 212, 215, 216, 240
  decline **9:** 224, 235, 240, 263, 275
  Hubert, scene with (Act III, scene iii) **9:** 210, 212, 216, 218, 219, 280
  moral insensibility **13:** 147, 163
  negative qualities **9:** 209, 212, 218, 219, 229, 234, 235, 244, 245, 246, 250, 254, 275, 280, 297
  positive qualities **9:** 209, 224, 235, 240, 244, 245, 263
kingship **9:** 235, 254, 263, 275, 297; **13:** 158; **19:** 182; **22:** 120
language and imagery **9:** 212, 215, 220, 246, 251, 254, 267, 280, 284, 292, 297, 300; **13:** 147, 158; **22:** 120; **37:** 132; **48:** 132
legitimacy or inheritance **9:** 224, 235, 254, 303; **13:** 147; **19:** 182; **37:** 132; **41:** 215
Neoclassical rules **9:** 208, 209, 210, 212
oppositions or dualisms **9:** 224, 240, 263, 275, 284, 290, 300
Papal Tyranny in the Reign of King John (Colley Cibber adaptation) **24:** 162, 163, 165
nationalism and patriotism **9:** 209, 218, 222, 224, 235, 240, 244, 275; **25:** 98; **37:** 132
politics **9:** 218, 224, 260, 280; **13:** 163; **22:** 120; **37:** 132; **41:** 221, 228
rebellion **9:** 218, 254, 263, 280, 297
Roman citizenry, portrayal of **50:** 64
Shakespeare's other history plays, compared with **9:** 218, 254; **13:** 152, 158; **25:** 98
sources **9:** 216, 222, 300; **32:** 93, 114; **41:** 234, 243, 251
staging issues **16:** 161; **19:** 182; **24:** 171, 187, 203, 206, 211, 225, 228, 241, 245, 249
structure **9:** 208, 212, 222, 224, 229, 240, 244, 245, 254, 260, 263, 275, 284, 290, 292, 300; **24:** 228, 241; **41:** 260, 269, 277
tragic elements **9:** 208, 209, 244
treachery **9:** 245
The Troublesome Reign (anonymous), compared with **9:** 216, 244, 260, 292; **22:** 120; **32:** 93; **41:** 205, 221, 260, 269; **48:** 132
Tudor doctrine **9:** 254, 284, 297; **41:** 221
tyranny **9:** 218
women, role of **9:** 222, 303; **16:** 161; **19:** 182; **41:** 205, 221

King Lear (Volumes 2, 11, 31, 46)

Albany **32:** 308
allegorical elements **16:** 311
audience perception **19:** 295; **28:** 325
autobiographical elements **2:** 131, 136, 149, 165
characterization **2:** 108, 125, 145, 162, 191; **16:** 311; **28:** 223; **46:** 177, 210

Christian elements **2:** 137, 170, 179, 188, 191, 197, 207, 218, 222, 226, 229, 238, 249, 265, 286; **22:** 233, 271; **25:** 218; **46:** 276; **49:** 67
as Christian play **48:** 222
Clarissa (Samuel Richardson), compared with **48:** 277
combat scenes **22:** 365
comic and tragic elements, combination of **2:** 108, 110, 112, 125, 156, 162, 245, 278, 284; **46:** 191
Cordelia
   attack on Britain **25:** 202
   characterization **2:** 110, 116, 125, 170; **16:** 311; **25:** 218; **28:** 223, 325; **31:** 117, 149, 155, 162; **46:** 225, 231, 242
   as Christ figure **2:** 116, 170, 179, 188, 222, 286
   rebelliousness **13:** 352; **25:** 202
   self-knowledge **46:** 218
   on stage **11:** 158
   transcendent power **2:** 137, 207, 218, 265, 269, 273
cruelty of daughters **2:** 101, 102, 106; **31:** 84, 123, 137, 142
death, decay, and nature's destructiveness **2:** 93, 94, 101, 104, 106, 109, 112, 116, 129, 131, 137, 143, 147, 149, 156, 160, 170, 179, 188, 197, 207, 218, 222, 226, 231, 238, 241, 245, 249, 253, 265, 269, 273; **16:** 301; **25:** 202, 218; **31:** 77, 117, 137, 142; **46:** 264
double-plot **2:** 94, 95, 100, 101, 104, 112, 116, 124, 131, 133, 156, 253, 257; **46:** 254
Dover Cliff scene **2:** 156, 229, 255, 269; **11:** 8, 151
Edgar **28:** 223; **32:** 212; **32:** 308; **37:** 295; **47:** 9; **50:** 24, 45
Edgar-Edmund duel **22:** 365
Edmund **25:** 218; **28:** 223
Edmund's forged letter **16:** 372
Elizabethan culture, relation to **2:** 168, 174, 177, 183, 226, 241; **19:** 330; **22:** 227, 233, 365; **25:** 218; **46:** 276; **47:** 9; **49:** 67
Fool **2:** 108, 112, 125, 156, 162, 245, 278, 284; **11:** 17, 158, 169; **22:** 227; **25:** 202; **28:** 223; **46:** 1, 14, 18, 24, 33, 52, 191, 205, 210, 218, 225
Gloucester **46:** 254
Goneril **31:** 151; **46:** 231, 242
grotesque or absurd elements **2:** 136, 156, 245; **13:** 343
implausibility or plot, characters, or events **2:** 100, 136, 145, 278; **13:** 343
Job, compared with **2:** 226, 241, 245; **25:** 218
justice, divine vs. worldly **49:** 1, 67, 73
Kent **25:** 202; **28:** 223; **32:** 212; **47:** 9
language and imagery **2:** 129, 137, 161, 191, 199, 237, 257, 271; **16:** 301; **19:** 344; **22:** 233; **46:** 177
Lear
   curse on Goneril **11:** 5, 7, 12, 114, 116
   love-test and division of kingdom **2:** 100, 106, 111, 124, 131, 137, 147, 149, 151, 168, 186, 208, 216, 281; **16:** 351; **25:** 202; **31:** 84, 92, 107, 117, 149, 155; **46:** 231, 242
   madness **2:** 94, 95, 98, 99, 100, 101, 102, 103, 111, 116, 120, 124, 125, 149, 156, 191, 208, 216, 281; **46:** 264

   as scapegoat **2:** 241, 253
   self-knowledge **2:** 103, 151, 188, 191, 213, 218, 222, 241, 249, 262; **25:** 218; **37:** 213; **46:** 191, 205, 225, 254, 264,
legal issues **46:** 276
love **2:** 109, 112, 131, 160, 162, 170, 179, 188, 197, 218, 222, 238, 265; **25:** 202; **31:** 77, 149, 151, 155, 162
madness **19:** 330
Marxist criticism **42:** 234
medieval or morality drama, influence of **2:** 177, 188, 201; **25:** 218
misogyny **31:** 123
nihilistic or pessimistic vision **2:** 130, 143, 149, 156, 165, 231, 238, 245, 253; **22:** 271; **25:** 218; **28:** 325; **49:** 67
pagan elements **25:** 218
patriarchal or monarchical order **13:** 353, 457; **16:** 351; **22:** 227, 233; **25:** 218; **31:** 84, 92, 107, 117, 123, 137, 142; **46:** 269
performance issues **2:** 106, 137, 154, 160; **11:** 10, 20, 27, 56, 57, 132, 136, 137, 145, 150, 154; **19:** 295, 344; **25:** 218
poetic justice, question of **2:** 92, 93, 94, 101, 129, 137, 231, 245; **49:** 73
politics **46:** 269; **50:** 45
providential order **2:** 112, 116, 137, 168, 170, 174, 177, 218, 226, 241, 253; **22:** 271; **49:** 1, 73
Regan **31:** 151; **46:** 231, 242
rhetorical style **16:** 301; **47:** 9
romantic elements **31:** 77, 84
sexuality **25:** 202; **31:** 133, 137, 142
social and moral corruption **2:** 116, 133, 174, 177, 241, 271; **22:** 227; **31:** 84, 92; **46:** 269
sources **2:** 94, 100, 143, 145, 170, 186; **13:** 352; **16:** 351; **28:** 301
staging issues **11:** 1-178; **32:** 212; **46:** 205, 218
structure **28:** 325; **32:** 308; **46:** 177
suffering **2:** 137, 160, 188, 201, 218, 222, 226, 231, 238, 241, 249, 265; **13:** 343; **22:** 271; **25:** 218; **50:** 24
Tate's adaptation **2:** 92, 93, 94, 101, 102, 104, 106, 110, 112, 116, 137; **11:** 10, 136; **25:** 218; **31:** 162
textual issues **22:** 271; **37:** 295; **49:** 73
Timon of Athens, relation to **16:** 351
Virgo vs. Virago **48:** 222
wisdom **37:** 213; **46:** 210

Love's Labour's Lost (Volumes 2, 23, 38)

Armado **23:** 207
artificial nature **2:** 315, 317, 324, 330; **23:** 207, 233
authorship controversy **2:** 299, 300; **32:** 308
Berowne **2:** 308, 324, 327; **22:** 12; **23:** 184, 187; **38:** 194; **47:** 35
characterization **2:** 303, 310, 317, 322, 328, 342; **23:** 237, 250, 252; **38:** 232; **47:** 35
as comedy of affectation **2:** 302, 303, 304; **23:** 191, 224, 226, 228, 233
comic resolution **2:** 335, 340; **16:** 17; **19:** 92; **38:** 209; **51:** 1
conclusion **38:** 172
dance and patterned action **2:** 308, 342; **23:** 191, 237

death, decay, and nature's destructiveness **2:** 305, 331, 344, 348
desire **38:** 185, 194, 200, 209
dramatic shortcomings or failure **2:** 299, 301, 303, 322
Elizabeth I **38:** 239
Elizabethan love poetry **38:** 232
feminist criticism **42:** 93
genre **38:** 163
gift exchange **25:** 1
grace and civility **2:** 351
Holofernes **23:** 207
illusion versus reality **2:** 303, 308, 331, 340, 344, 348, 356, 359, 367, 371, 375; **23:** 230, 231
knowledge **22:** 12; **47:** 35
language and imagery **2:** 301, 302, 303, 306, 307, 308, 315, 319, 320, 330, 335, 344, 345, 348, 356, 359, 362, 365, 371, 374, 375; **19:** 92; **22:** 12, 378; **23:** 184, 187, 196, 197, 202, 207, 211, 221, 227, 231, 233, 237, 252; **28:** 9, 63; **38:** 219, 226
love **2:** 312, 315, 340, 344; **22:** 12; **23:** 252; **38:** 194; **51:** 44
male domination **22:** 12
male sexual anxiety **16:** 17
marriage **2:** 335, 340; **19:** 92; **38:** 209, 232; **51:** 1, 44
metadramatic elements **2:** 356, 359, 362
Neoclassical rules **2:** 299, 300
as satire or parody **2:** 300, 302, 303, 307, 308, 315, 321, 324, 327; **23:** 237, 252
physical versus intellectual world **2:** 331, 348, 367
public versus private speech **2:** 356, 362, 371
School of Night, allusions to **2:** 321, 327, 328
sexuality **22:** 12; **51:** 44
songs, role of **2:** 303, 304, 316, 326, 335, 362, 367, 371, 375
sources **16:** 17
spectacle **38:** 226
staging issues **23:** 184, 187, 191, 196, 198, 200, 201, 202, 207, 212, 215, 216, 217, 229, 230, 232, 233, 237, 252
structure **22:** 378; **23:** 191, 237, 252; **38:** 163, 172
theme
   idealism versus realism **38:** 163
topical allusions or content **2:** 300, 303, 307, 315, 316, 317, 319, 321, 327, 328; **23:** 187, 191, 197, 203, 221, 233, 237, 252; **25:** 1
unnatural ordering **22:** 378
violence **22:** 12
visual humor **23:** 207, 217
Watteau, influence on staging **23:** 184, 186
women, role of **19:** 92; **22:** 12; **23:** 215; **25:** 1
written versus oral communication **2:** 359, 365; **28:** 63

Macbeth (Volumes 3, 20, 29, 44)

antithetical or contradictory elements **3:** 185, 213, 271, 302; **25:** 235; **29:** 76, 127; **47:** 41
appearance versus reality **3:** 241, 248; **25:** 235
archetypal or mythic elements **16:** 317
audience response **20:** 17, 400, 406; **29:** 139, 146, 155, 165; **44:** 306

banquet scene (Act III, scene iv) **20:** 22, 32, 175
Banquo **3:** 183, 199, 208, 213, 278, 289; **20:** 279, 283, 406, 413; **25:** 235; **28:** 339
characterization **20:** 12, 318, 324, 329, 353, 363, 367, 374, 387; **28:** 339; **29:** 101, 109, 146, 155, 165; **44:** 289; **47:** 41
Christian elements **3:** 194, 239, 260, 269, 275, 286, 293, 297, 318; **20:** 203, 206, 210, 256, 262, 289, 291, 294; **44:** 341, 366; **47:** 41
combat scenes **22:** 365
dagger scene (Act III, scene i), staging of **20:** 406
evil **3:** 194, 208, 231, 234, 239, 241, 267, 289; **20:** 203, 206, 210, 374
free will versus fate **3:** 177, 183, 184, 190, 196, 198, 202, 207, 208, 213; **13:** 361; **44:** 351, 361, 366, 373
innocence **3:** 234, 241, 327
Jacobean culture, relation to **19:** 330; **22:** 365
Lady Macbeth
 ambition **3:** 185, 219; **20:** 279, 345
 characterization **20:** 56, 60, 65, 73, 140, 148, 151, 241, 279, 283, 338, 350, 406, 413; **29:** 109, 146
 childlessness **3:** 219, 223
 good and evil, combined traits of **3:** 173, 191, 213; **20:** 60, 107
 inconsistencies **3:** 202; **20:** 54, 137
 influence on Macbeth **3:** 171, 185, 191, 193, 199, 262, 289, 312, 318; **13:** 502; **20:** 345; **25:** 235; **29:** 133
 psychoanalytic interpretations **20:** 345; **44:** 289, 297, 324; **45:** 58
 as sympathetic figure **3:** 191, 193, 203
language and imagery **3:** 170, 193, 213, 231, 234, 241, 245, 250, 253, 256, 263, 271, 283, 300, 302, 306, 323, 327, 338, 340, 349; **13:** 476; **16:** 317; **20:** 241, 279, 283, 367, 379, 400; **25:** 235; **28:** 339; **29:** 76, 91; **42:** 263; **44:** 366; **45:** 58
laws of nature, violation of **3:** 234, 241, 280, 323; **29:** 120
letter to Lady Macbeth **16:** 372; **20:** 345; **25:** 235
Macbeth
 ambition **44:** 284, 324
 characterization **20:** 20, 42, 73, 107, 113, 130, 146, 151, 279, 283, 312, 338, 343, 379, 406, 413; **29:** 139, 152, 155, 165; **44:** 289
 courage **3:** 172, 177, 181, 182, 183, 186, 234, 312, 333; **20:** 107; **44:** 315
 disposition **3:** 173, 175, 177, 182, 186; **20:** 245, 376
 imagination **3:** 196, 208, 213, 250, 312, 345; **20:** 245, 376; **44:** 351
 as "inauthentic" king **3:** 245, 302, 321, 345
 inconsistencies **3:** 202
 as Machiavellian villain **3:** 280
 manliness **20:** 113; **29:** 127, 133; **44:** 315
 psychoanalytic interpretations **20:** 42, 73, 238, 376; **44:** 284, 289, 297, 324; **45:** 48, 58
 Richard III, compared with **3:** 177, 182, 186, 345; **20:** 86, 92; **22:** 365; **44:** 269
 as Satan figure **3:** 229, 269, 275, 289, 318
 self-awareness **3:** 312, 329, 338; **16:** 317; **44:** 361

as sympathetic figure **3:** 229, 306, 314, 338; **29:** 139, 152; **44:** 269, 306, 337
 as tragic hero **44:** 269, 306, 315, 324, 337
Macduff **3:** 226, 231, 253, 262,; **25:** 235; **29:** 127, 133, 155
madness **19:** 330
major tragedies, relation to Shakespeare's other **3:** 171, 173, 213; **44:** 269
Malcolm **25:** 235
manhood **3:** 262, 309, 333; **29:** 127, 133
Marxist criticism **42:** 234
medieval mystery plays, relation to **44:** 341
moral lesson **20:** 23
murder scene (Act II, scene ii) **20:** 175
Neoclassical rules **3:** 170, 171, 173, 175; **20:** 17
nightmarish quality **3:** 231, 309; **20:** 210, 242; **44:** 261
Porter scene (Act II, scene iii) **3:** 173, 175, 184, 190, 196, 203, 205, 225, 260, 271, 297, 300; **20:** 283; **44:** 261; **46:** 29, 78
primitivism **20:** 206, 213; **45:** 48
providential order **3:** 208, 289, 329, 336
psychoanalytic interpretations **3:** 219, 223, 226; **44:** 11, 284, 289, 297
regicide **16:** 317, 328; **45:** 48, 248, 275, 312
religious and theological issues **44:** 324, 341, 351, 361, 366, 373
religious, mythic, or spiritual content **3:** 208, 269, 275, 318; **29:** 109
retribution **3:** 194, 208, 318; **48:** 214
sexual anxiety **16:** 328; **20:** 283
sleepwalking scene (Act V, scene i) **3:** 191, 203, 219; **20:** 175; **44:** 261
staging issues **13:** 502; **20:** 12, 17, 32, 64, 65, 70, 73, 107, 113, 151, 175, 203, 206, 210, 213, 245, 279, 283, 312, 318, 324, 329, 343, 345, 350, 353, 363, 367, 374, 376, 379, 382, 387, 400, 406, 413; **22:** 365; **32:** 212
structure **16:** 317; **20:** 12, 245
supernatural grace versus evil or chaos **3:** 241, 286, 323
theatricality **16:** 328
time **3:** 234, 246, 283, 293; **20:** 245
topical allusions or content **13:** 361; **20:** 17, 350; **29:** 101
treason and punishment **13:** 361; **16:** 328
violence **20:** 273, 279, 283; **45:** 58
witches and supernaturalism **3:** 171, 172, 173, 175, 177, 182, 183, 184, 185, 194, 196, 198, 202, 207, 208, 213, 219, 229, 239; **16:** 317; **19:** 245; **20:** 92, 175, 213, 279, 283, 374, 387, 406, 413; **25:** 235; **28:** 339; **29:** 91, 101, 109, 120; **44:** 351, 373

Measure for Measure (Volumes 2, 23, 33, 49)

ambiguity **2:** 417, 420, 432, 446, 449, 452, 474, 479, 482, 486, 495, 505
Angelo
 anxiety **16:** 114
 authoritarian portrayal of **23:** 307; **49:** 274
 characterization **2:** 388, 390, 397, 402, 418, 427, 432, 434, 463, 484, 495, 503, 511; **13:** 84; **23:** 297; **32:** 81; **33:** 77; **49:** 274, 293, 379

 hypocrisy **2:** 396, 399, 402, 406, 414, 421; **23:** 345, 358, 362
 repentance or pardon **2:** 388, 390, 397, 402, 434, 463, 511, 524
audience response **48:** 1
autobiographical elements **2:** 406, 410, 414, 431, 434, 437
Barnardine **13:** 112
bed-trick **13:** 84; **49:** 313
characterization **2:** 388, 390, 391, 396, 406, 420, 421, 446, 466, 475, 484, 505, 516, 524; **23:** 299, 405; **33:** 77
Christian elements **2:** 391, 394, 399, 421, 437, 449, 466, 479, 491, 511, 522; **48:** 1; **49:** 325
Clarissa (Samuel Richardson), compared with **48:** 277
comic form **2:** 456, 460, 479, 482, 491, 514, 516; **13:** 94, 104; **23:** 309, 326, 327; **49:** 349
death, decay, and nature's destructiveness **2:** 394, 452, 516; **25:** 12; **49:** 370
displacement **22:** 78
Duke
 as authoritarian figure **23:** 314, 317, 347; **33:** 85; **49:** 274, 300, 358
 characterization **2:** 388, 395, 402, 406, 411, 421, 429, 456, 466, 470, 498, 511; **13:** 84, 94, 104; **23:** 363, 416; **32:** 81; **42:** 1; **44:** 89; **49:** 274, 293, 300, 358
 dramatic shortcomings or failure **2:** 420, 429, 441, 479, 495, 505, 514, 522
 godlike portrayal of **23:** 320
 noble portrayal of **23:** 301
 speech on death (Act III, scene i) **2:** 390, 391, 395
Elbow **22:** 85; **25:** 12
Elbow, Mistress **33:** 90
Elizabethan betrothal and marriage customs **2:** 429, 437, 443, 503; **49:** 286
Elizabethan culture, relation to **2:** 394, 418, 429, 432, 437, 460, 470, 482, 503
feminist interpretation **23:** 320
good and evil **2:** 432, 452, 524; **33:** 52, 61
homosexuality **42:** 1
immortality **16:** 102
inconsistency between first and second halves **2:** 474, 475, 505, 514, 524; **49:** 349, 358
Isabella **2:** 388, 390, 395, 396, 397, 401, 402, 406, 409, 410, 411, 418, 420, 421, 432, 437, 441, 466, 475, 491, 495, 524; **16:** 114; **23:** 278, 279, 280, 281, 282, 296, 344, 357, 363, 405; **28:** 92; **33:** 77, 85
judicial versus natural law **2:** 446, 507, 516, 519; **22:** 85; **33:** 58, 117; **49:** 293
justice and mercy **2:** 391, 395, 399, 402, 406, 409, 411, 416, 421, 437, 443, 463, 466, 470, 491, 495, 522, 524; **22:** 85; **33:** 52, 61, 101; **49:** 274, 293, 300
judicial vs. natural law **49:** 1
justice and mercy **49:** 1
language and imagery **2:** 394, 421, 431, 466, 486, 505; **13:** 112; **28:** 9; **33:** 69; **49:** 370
Lucio **13:** 104; **49:** 379
marriage **2:** 443, 507, 516, 519, 524, 528; **25:** 12; **33:** 61, 90; **49:** 286; **51:** 44
as medieval allegory or morality play **2:** 409, 421, 443, 466, 475, 491, 505, 511, 522; **13:** 94
metadramatic elements **13:** 104
misgovernment **2:** 401, 432, 511; **22:** 85

misogyny **23:** 358;
moral seriousness, question of **2:** 387, 388, 396, 409, 417, 421, 452, 460, 495; **23:** 316, 321
Neoclassical rules **2:** 387, 388, 390, 394; **23:** 269
politics **23:** 379; **49:** 274
power **13:** 112; **22:** 85; **23:** 327, 330, 339, 352; **33:** 85
as "problem play" **2:** 416, 429, 434, 474, 475, 503, 514, 519; **16:** 102; **23:** 313, 328, 351; **49:** 358, 370
providential order **48:** 1
psychoanalytic interpretations **23:** 331, 332, 333, 334, 335, 340, 355, 356, 359, 379, 395; **44:** 79
Puritanism **2:** 414, 418, 434; **49:** 325
rebirth, regeneration, resurrection, or immortality **13:** 84; **16:** 102, 114; **23:** 321, 327, 335, 340, 352; **25:** 12
religious and theological issues **48:** 1
religious, mythic, or spiritual content **48:** 1
resolution **2:** 449, 475, 495, 514, 516; **16:** 102, 114
sexuality **13:** 84; **16:** 102, 114; **23:** 321, 327, 335, 340, 352; **25:** 12; **33:** 85, 90, 112; **49:** 286, 338; **51:** 44
social aspects **23:** 316, 375, 379, 395; **49:** 338
sources **2:** 388, 393, 427, 429, 437, 475; **13:** 94; **49:** 349
staging issues **2:** 427, 429, 437, 441, 443, 456, 460, 482, 491, 519; **23:** 283, 284, 285, 286, 287, 291, 293, 294, 298, 299, 311, 315, 327, 338, 339, 340, 342, 344, 347, 363, 372, 375, 395, 400, 405, 406, 413; **32:** 16
structure **2:** 390, 411, 449, 456, 466, 474, 482, 490, 491; **33:** 69; **49:** 379
substitution of identities **2:** 507, 511, 519; **13:** 112; **49:** 313, 325
supernatural grace vs. evil or chaos **48:** 1
theatricality **23:** 285, 286, 294, 372, 406; **49:** 358
comic and tragic elements, combination of **16:** 102
as unsuccessful play **2:** 397, 441, 474, 482; **23:** 287

The Merchant of Venice **(Volumes 4, 12, 40)**

Act V, relation to Acts I through IV **4:** 193, 194, 195, 196, 204, 232, 270, 273, 289, 300, 319, 321, 326, 336, 356
allegorical elements **4:** 224, 250, 261, 268, 270, 273, 282, 289, 324, 336, 344, 350
Antonio
    excessive or destructive love **4:** 279, 284, 336, 344; **12:** 54; **37:** 86
    love for Bassanio **40:** 156
    melancholy **4:** 221, 238, 279, 284, 300, 321, 328; **22:** 69; **25:** 22
    pitiless **4:** 254
    as pivotal figure **12:** 25, 129
appearance versus reality **4:** 209, 261, 344; **12:** 65; **22:** 69
Bassanio **25:** 257; **37:** 86; **40:** 156
bonding **4:** 293, 317, 336; **13:** 37
casket scenes **4:** 226, 241, 308, 344; **12:** 23, 46, 47, 65, 117; **13:** 43; **22:** 3; **40:** 106; **49:** 27
contrasting dramatic worlds **44:** 11
conflict between Christianity and Judaism **4:** 224, 250, 268, 289, 324, 344; **12:** 67, 70, 72, 76; **22:** 69; **25:** 257; **40:** 117, 127, 166, 181; **48:** 54, 77
desire **22:** 3; **40:** 142; **45:** 17
Economics and exchange **40:** 197, 208
Elizabethan culture, relation to **32:** 66; **40:** 117, 127, 142, 166, 181, 197, 208; **48:** 54, 77; **49:** 37
genre **4:** 191, 200, 201, 209, 215, 221, 232, 238, 247; **12:** 48, 54, 62
homosexuality **22:** 3, 69; **37:** 86; **40:** 142, 156, 197
implausibility of plot, characters, or events **4:** 191, 192, 193; **12:** 52, 56, 76, 119
irony **4:** 254, 300, 321, 331, 350; **28:** 63
Jessica **4:** 196, 200, 228, 293, 342
justice and mercy **4:** 213, 214, 224, 250, 261, 273, 282, 289, 336; **12:** 80, 129; **40:** 127; **49:** 1, 23, 27, 37
language and imagery **4:** 241, 267, 293; **22:** 3; **25:** 257; **28:** 9, 63; **32:** 41; **40:** 106
Launcelot Gobbo **46:** 24, 60; **50:** 64
love **4:** 221, 226, 270, 284, 312, 344; **22:** 3, 69; **25:** 257; **40:** 156; **51:** 1, 44
medieval homilies, influence of **4:** 224, 250, 289
Portia **4:** 194, 195, 196, 215, 254, 263, 336, 356; **12:** 104, 107, 114; **13:** 37; **22:** 3, 69; **25:** 22; **32:** 294; **37:** 86; **40:** 142, 156, 197, 208; **49:** 27
psychoanalytic interpretation **45:** 17
resolution **4:** 263, 266, 300, 319, 321; **13:** 37; **51:** 1
rings episode **22:** 3; **40:** 106, 151, 156
sacrificial love **13:** 43; **22:** 69; **40:** 142
sexual politics **22:** 3; **51:** 44
Shylock
    alienation **4:** 279, 312; **40:** 175; **49:** 23, 37
    ambiguity **4:** 247, 254, 315, 319, 331; **12:** 31, 35, 36, 50, 51, 52, 56, 81, 124; **40:** 175
    as scapegoat figure **49:** 27
    forced conversion **4:** 209, 252, 268, 282, 289, 321
    Jewishness **4:** 193, 194, 195, 200, 201, 213, 214, 279; **22:** 69; **25:** 257; **40:** 142, 175, 181
    motives in making the bond **4:** 252, 263, 266, 268; **22:** 69; **25:** 22
    as Puritan **40:** 127, 166
    as scapegoat figure **4:** 254, 300; **40:** 166
    as traditional comic villain **4:** 230, 243, 261, 263, 315; **12:** 40, 62, 124; **40:** 175
    as tragic figure **12:** 6, 9, 10, 16, 21, 23, 25, 40, 44, 66, 67, 81, 97; **40:** 175
staging issues **12:** 111, 114, 115, 117, 119, 124, 129, 131
structure **4:** 201, 215, 230, 232, 243, 247, 254, 261, 263, 308, 321; **12:** 115; **28:** 63
trial scene **13:** 43; **25:** 22; **40:** 106, 156; **49:** 1, 23, 27, 37
unity of double plot **4:** 193, 194, 201, 232; **12:** 16, 67, 80, 115, 40: 151
Venetians **4:** 195, 200, 228, 254, 273, 300, 321, 331
Venice, Elizabethan perceptions of **28:** 249; **32:** 294; **40:** 127
wealth **4:** 209, 261, 270, 273, 317; **12:** 80, 117; **22:** 69; **25:** 22; **28:** 249; **40:** 117, 197, 208; **45:** 17; **49:** 1; **51:** 15

The Merry Wives of Windsor **(Volumes 5, 18, 38, 47)**

Anne Page-Fenton plot **5:** 334, 336, 343, 353, 376, 390, 395, 402; **22:** 93; **47:** 308
avarice **5:** 335, 353, 369, 376, 390, 395, 402
Caius, Doctor **47:** 354
caricature **5:** 343, 347, 348, 350, 385, 397
characterization **5:** 332, 334, 335, 337, 338, 351, 360, 363, 366, 374, 379, 392; **18:** 74, 75; **18:** 264, 273, 313, 319
class distinctions, conflict, and relations **5:** 338, 343, 346, 347, 366, 390, 395, 400, 402; **22:** 93; **28:** 69
comic and farcical elements **5:** 336, 338, 346, 350, 360, 369, 373; **18:** 74, 75, 84
The Comical Gallant (John Dennis adaptation) **18:** 5, 7, 8, 9, 10
deception, disguise, and duplicity **5:** 332, 334, 336, 354, 355, 379; **22:** 93; **47:** 308, 314, 321, 325, 344
desire **38:** 286, 297, 300
Elizabethan society **47:** 331
Elizabeth's influence **5:** 333, 334, 335, 336, 339, 346, 355, 366, 402; **18:** 5, 86; **38:** 278; **47:** 344
Evans, Sir Hugh **47:** 354
Falstaff
    characterization in *1* and *2 Henry IV*, compared with **5:** 333, 335, 336, 337, 339, 346, 347, 348, 350, 373, 400; **18:** 5, 7, 75, 86; **22:** 93
    diminishing powers **5:** 337, 339, 343, 347, 350, 351, 392; **28:** 373; **47:** 363
    as Herne the Hunter **38:** 256, 286; **47:** 358
    incapability of love **5:** 335, 336, 339, 346, 348; **22:** 93
    as Jack-a-Lent **47:** 363
    personification of comic principle or Vice figure **5:** 332, 338, 369, 400; **38:** 273
    recognition and repentance of follies **5:** 338, 341, 343, 348, 369, 374, 376, 397
    as scapegoat **47:** 358, 363, 375
    sensuality **5:** 339, 343, 353, 369, 392
    shrewdness **5:** 332, 336, 346, 355
    threat to community **5:** 343, 369, 379, 392, 395, 400; **38:** 297
    as unifying force **47:** 358
    vanity **5:** 332, 339
    victimization **5:** 336, 338, 341, 347, 348, 353, 355, 360, 369, 373, 374, 376, 392, 397, 400
    as villain **47:** 358
    as a woman **47:** 325
folk rituals, elements and influence of **5:** 353, 369, 376, 392, 397, 400; **38:** 256, 300
Ford, Francis **5:** 332, 334, 343, 355, 363, 374, 379, 390; **38:** 273; **47:** 321
Ford, Mistress Alice **47:** 321
insults **47:** 331
jealousy **5:** 334, 339, 343, 353, 355, 363; **22:** 93; **38:** 273, 307
Jonsonian humors comedy, influence of **38:** 319

knighthood **5:** 338, 343, 390, 397, 402; **47:** 354
language and imagery **5:** 335, 337, 343, 347, 351, 363, 374, 379; **19:** 101; **22:** 93, 378; **28:** 9, 69; **38:** 313, 319
male discontent **5:** 392, 402
marriage **5:** 343, 369, 376, 390, 392, 400; **22:** 93; **38:** 297; **51:** 44
mediation **5:** 343, 392
morality **5:** 335, 339, 347, 349, 353, 397
Neoclassical rules **5:** 332, 334
Page, Anne **47:** 321
Page, Mistress Margaret **47:** 321
play and theatricality **47:** 325
play-within-the-play, convention of **5:** 354, 355, 369, 402
realism **38:** 313
reconciliation **5:** 343, 369, 374, 397, 402
revenge **5:** 349, 350, 392; **38:** 264, 307
as satire or parody **5:** 338, 350, 360, 385; **38:** 278, 319; **47:** 354, 363
schemes and intrigues **5:** 334, 336, 339, 341, 343, 349, 355, 379
setting **47:** 375
sexual politics **19:** 101; **38:** 307
social milieu **18:** 75, 84; **38:** 297, 300
sources **5:** 332, 350, 360, 366, 385; **32:** 31
stage history **18:** 66, 67, 68, 70, 71
staging issues **18:** 74, 75, 84, 86, 90, 95
structure **5:** 332, 333, 334, 335, 343, 349, 355, 369, 374; **18:** 86; **22:** 378
unnatural ordering **22:** 378
wit **5:** 335, 336, 337, 339, 343, 351
women, role of **5:** 335, 341, 343, 349, 369, 379, 390, 392, 402; **19:** 101; **38:** 307

A Midsummer Night's Dream (Volumes 3, 12, 29, 45)

adaptations **12:** 144, 146, 147, 153, 280, 282
ambiguity **3:** 401, 459, 486; **45:** 169
appearance, perception, and illusion **3:** 368, 411, 425, 427, 434, 447, 459, 466, 474, 477, 486, 497, 516; **19:** 21; **22:** 39; **28:** 15; **29:** 175,190; **45:** 136
Athens and the forest, contrast between **3:** 381, 427, 459, 466, 497, 502; **29:** 175
autobiographical elements **3:** 365, 371, 379, 381, 389, 391, 396, 402, 432
Bottom
  awakening speech (Act IV, scene i) **3:** 406, 412, 450, 457, 486, 516; **16:** 34
  folly of **46:** 1, 14, 29, 60
  imagination **3:** 376, 393, 406, 432, 486; **29:** 175, 190; **45:** 147
  self-possession **3:** 365, 376, 395, 402, 406, 480; **45:** 158
  Titania, relationship with **3:** 377, 406, 441, 445, 450, 457, 491, 497; **16:** 34; **19:** 21; **22:** 93; **29:** 216; **45:** 160
  transformation **3:** 365, 377, 432; **13:** 27; **22:** 93; **29:** 216; **45:** 147, 160
brutal elements **3:** 445, 491, 497, 511; **12:** 259, 262, 298; **16:** 34; **19:** 21; **29:** 183, 225, 263, 269; **45:** 169
capriciousness of the young lovers **3:** 372, 395, 402, 411, 423, 437, 441, 450, 497, 498; **29:** 175, 269; **45:** 107

chastity **45:** 143
class distinctions, conflict, and relations **22:** 23; **25:** 36; **45:** 160; **50:** 74, 86
as dream-play **3:** 365, 370, 372, 377, 389, 391; **29:** 190; **45:** 117
dreams **45:** 96, 107, 117
duration of time **3:** 362, 370, 380, 386, 494; **45:** 175
Elizabethan culture, relation to **50:** 86
erotic elements **3:** 445, 491, 497, 511; **12:** 259, 262, 298; **16:** 34; **19:** 21; **29:** 183, 225, 269
fairies **3:** 361, 362, 372, 377, 395, 400, 423, 450, 459, 486; **12:** 287, 291, 294, 295; **19:** 21; **29:** 183, 190; **45:** 147
feminist interpretation **48:** 23
Helena **29:** 269
Hermia **29:** 225, 269; **45:** 117
Hippolytus, myth of **29:** 216; **45:** 84
identity **29:** 269
imagination and art **3:** 365, 371, 381, 402, 412, 417, 421, 423, 441, 459, 468, 506, 516, 520; **22:** 39
language and imagery **3:** 397, 401, 410, 412, 415, 432, 453, 459, 468, 494; **22:** 23, 39, 93, 378; **28:** 9; **29:** 263; **45:** 96, 126, 136, 147; **45:** 143, 169, 175; **48:** 23, 32
male domination **3:** 483, 520; **13:** 19; **25:** 36; **29:** 216, 225, 243, 256, 269; **42:** 46; **45:** 84
marriage **3:** 402, 423, 450, 483, 520; **29:** 243, 256; **45:** 136, 143; **48:** 32; **51:** 1, 30, 44
metadramatic elements **3:** 427, 468, 477, 516, 520; **29:** 190, 225, 243; **50:** 86
Metamorphoses (Golding translation of Ovid) **16:** 25
Minotaur, myth of **3:** 497, 498; **29:** 216
music and dance **3:** 397, 400, 418, 513; **12:** 287, 289; **25:** 36
Oberon as controlling force **3:** 434, 459, 477, 502; **29:** 175
Ovid, influence of **3:** 362, 427, 497, 498; **22:** 23; **29:** 175, 190, 216
parent-child relations **13:** 19; **29:** 216, 225, 243
passionate or romantic love **3:** 372, 389, 395, 396, 402, 408, 411, 423, 441, 450, 480, 497, 498, 511; **29:** 175, 225, 263, 269; **45:** 126, 136; **51:** 44
Pauline doctrine **3:** 457, 486, 506
Platonic elements **3:** 368, 437, 450, 497; **45:** 126
politics **29:** 243
power **42:** 46; **45:** 84
psychoanalytic interpretations **3:** 440, 483; **28:** 15; **29:** 225; **44:** 1; **45:** 107, 117
Puck **45:** 96, 158
Pyramus and Thisbe interlude **3:** 364, 368, 379, 381, 389, 391, 396, 408, 411, 412, 417, 425, 427, 433, 441, 447, 457, 468, 474, 511; **12:** 254; **13:** 27; **16:** 25; **22:** 23; **29:** 263; **45:** 107, 175; **50:** 74
reason versus imagination **3:** 381, 389, 423, 441, 466, 506; **22:** 23; **29:** 190; **45:** 96
reconciliation **3:** 412, 418, 437, 459, 468, 491, 497, 502, 513; **13:** 27; **29:** 190
reversal **29:** 225
Romeo and Juliet, compared with **3:** 396, 480
rustic characters **3:** 376, 397, 432; **12:** 291, 293; **45:** 147, 160
sexuality **22:** 23, 93; **29:** 225, 243, 256, 269; **42:** 46; **45:** 107

sources **29:** 216
staging issues **3:** 364, 365, 371, 372, 377; **12:** 151, 152, 154, 158, 159, 280, 284, 291, 295; **16:** 34; **19:** 21; **29:** 183, 256; **48:** 23
structure **3:** 364, 368, 381, 402, 406, 427, 450, 513; **13:** 19; **22:** 378; **29:** 175; **45:** 126, 175
textual issues **16:** 34; **29:** 216
Theseus **51:** 1
  characterization **3:** 363
  Hippolyta, relationship with **3:** 381, 412, 421, 423, 450, 468, 520; **29:** 175, 216, 243, 256; **45:** 84
  as ideal **3:** 379, 391
  "lovers, lunatics, and poets" speech (Act V, scene i) **3:** 365, 371, 379, 381, 391, 402, 411, 412, 421, 423, 441, 498, 506; **29:** 175
  as representative of institutional life **3:** 381, 403
Titania **29:** 243
tragic elements **3:** 393, 400, 401, 410, 445, 474, 480, 491, 498, 511; **29:** 175; **45:** 169
unity **3:** 364, 368, 381, 402, 406, 427, 450, 513; **13:** 19; **22:** 378; **29:** 175, 263
unnatural ordering **22:** 378

Much Ado about Nothing (Volumes 8, 18, 31)

appearance versus reality **8:** 17, 18, 48, 63, 69, 73, 75, 79, 88, 95, 115; **31:** 198, 209
battle of the sexes **8:** 14, 16, 19, 48, 91, 95, 111, 121, 125; **31:** 231, 245
Beatrice and Benedick
  Beatrice's femininity **8:** 14, 16, 17, 24, 29, 38, 41, 91; **31:** 222, 245
  Beatrice's request to "kill Claudio" (Act IV, scene i) **8:** 14, 17, 33, 41, 55, 63, 75, 79, 91, 108, 115; **18:** 119, 120, 136, 161, 245, 257
  Benedick's challenge of Claudio (Act V, scene i) **8:** 48, 63, 79, 91; **31:** 231
  Claudio and Hero, compared with **8:** 19, 28, 29, 75, 82, 115; **31:** 171, 216
  marriage and the opposite sex, attitudes toward **8:** 9, 13, 14, 16, 19, 29, 36, 48, 63, 77, 91, 95, 115, 121; **16:** 45; **31:** 216
  mutual attraction **8:** 13, 14, 19, 24, 29, 33, 41, 75
  nobility **8:** 13, 19, 24, 29, 36, 39, 41, 47, 82, 91, 108
  popularity **8:** 13, 38, 41, 53, 79
  transformed by love **8:** 19, 29, 36, 48, 75, 91, 95, 115; **31:** 209, 216
  unconventionality **8:** 48, 91, 95, 108, 115, 121
  vulgarity **8:** 11, 12, 33, 38, 41, 47
  wit and charm **8:** 9, 12, 13, 14, 19, 24, 27, 28, 29, 33, 36, 38, 41, 47, 55, 69, 95, 108, 115; **31:** 241
Borachio and Conrade **8:** 24, 69, 82, 88, 111, 115
Christian elements **8:** 17, 19, 29, 55, 95, 104, 111, 115; **31:** 209
church scene (Act IV, scene i) **8:** 13, 14, 16, 19, 33, 44, 47, 48, 58, 63, 69, 75, 79, 82, 91, 95, 100, 104, 111, 115; **18:** 120, 130, 138, 145, 146, 148, 192; **31:** 191, 198, 245
Claudio
  boorish behavior **8:** 9, 24, 33, 36, 39, 44, 48, 63, 79, 82, 95, 100, 111, 115; **31:** 209

credulity **8:** 9, 17, 19, 24, 29, 36, 41, 47, 58, 63, 75, 77, 82, 95, 100, 104, 111, 115, 121; **31:** 241; **47:** 25
mercenary traits **8:** 24, 44, 58, 82, 91, 95
noble qualities **8:** 17, 19, 29, 41, 44, 58, 75
reconciliation with Hero **8:** 33, 36, 39, 44, 47, 82, 95, 100, 111, 115, 121
repentance **8:** 33, 63, 82, 95, 100, 111, 115, 121; **31:** 245
sexual insecurities **8:** 75, 100, 111, 115, 121
courtship and marriage **8:** 29, 44, 48, 95, 115, 121, 125; **31:** 191, 231; **51:** 33, 44
deception, disguise, and duplicity **8:** 29, 55, 63, 69, 79, 82, 88, 108, 115; **31:** 191, 198
Dogberry and the Watch **8:** 9, 12, 13, 17, 24, 28, 29, 33, 39, 48, 55, 69, 79, 82, 88, 95, 104, 108, 115; **18:** 138, 152, 205, 208, 210, 213, 231; **22:** 85; **31:** 171, 229; **46:** 60
Don John **8:** 9, 12, 16, 17, 19, 28, 29, 36, 39, 41, 47, 48, 55, 58, 63, 82, 104, 108, 111, 121
Don Pedro **8:** 17, 19, 48, 58, 63, 82, 111, 121
eavesdropping scenes (Act II, scene iii and Act III, scene i) **8:** 12, 13, 17, 19, 28, 29, 33, 36, 48, 55, 63, 73, 75, 82, 121; **18:** 120, 138, 208, 215, 245, 264; **31:** 171, 184
egotism or narcissism **8:** 19, 24, 28, 29, 55, 69, 95, 115
Elizabethan culture, relation to **8:** 23, 33, 44, 55, 58, 79, 88, 104, 111, 115; **51:** 15
Friar **8:** 24, 29, 41, 55, 63, 79, 111
genre **8:** 9, 18, 19, 28, 29, 39, 41, 44, 53, 63, 69, 73, 79, 82, 95, 100, 104; **48:** 14
Hero **8:** 13, 14, 16, 19, 28, 29, 44, 48, 53, 55, 82, 95, 104, 111, 115, 121; **31:** 231, 245; **47:** 25
implausibility of plot, characters, or events **8:** 9, 12, 16, 19, 33, 36, 39, 44, 53, 100, 104
irony **8:** 14, 63, 79, 82; **28:** 63
justice and mercy **22:** 85
language and imagery **8:** 9, 38, 43, 46, 55, 69, 73, 88, 95, 100, 115, 125; **19:** 68; **25:** 77; **28:** 63; **31:** 178, 184, 222, 241, 245; **48:** 14
law versus passion for freedom **22:** 85
love **8:** 24, 55, 75, 95, 111, 115; **28:** 56; **51:** 30
Messina **8:** 19, 29, 48, 69, 82, 91, 95, 108, 111, 121, 125; **31:** 191, 209, 229, 241, 245
misgovernment **22:** 85
music and dance **19:** 68; **31:** 222
"nothing," significance of **8:** 17, 18, 23, 55, 73, 95; **19:** 68
performance issues **18:** 173, 174, 183, 184, 185, 186, 187, 188, 189, 190, 191, 192, 193, 195, 197, 199, 201, 204, 206, 207, 208, 209, 210, 254
power **22:** 85; **25:** 77; **31:** 231, 245
repentance or forgiveness **8:** 24, 29, 111
resurrection, metamorphosis, or transformation **8:** 88, 104, 111, 115
romance or chivalric tradition, influence of **8:** 53, 125; **51:** 15
self-knowledge **8:** 69, 95, 100
setting **18:** 173, 174, 183, 184, 185, 186, 187, 188, 189, 190, 191, 192, 193, 195, 197, 199, 201, 204, 206, 207, 208, 209, 210, 254
slander or hearsay, importance of **8:** 58, 69, 82, 95, 104
sources **8:** 9, 19, 53, 58, 104
staging issues **8:** 18, 33, 41, 75, 79, 82, 108; **16:** 45; **18:** 245, 247, 249, 252, 254, 257, 261, 264; **28:** 63

structure **8:** 9, 16, 17, 19, 28, 29, 33, 39, 48, 63, 69, 73, 75, 79, 82, 115; **31:** 178, 184, 198, 231
virginity or chastity, importance of **8:** 44, 75, 95, 111, 121, 125; **31:** 222
wit **8:** 27, 29, 38, 69, 79, 91, 95; **31:** 178, 191
works by Shakespeare or other authors, compared with **8:** 16, 19, 27, 28, 33, 38, 39, 41, 53, 69, 79, 91, 104, 108; **31:** 231

Othello (Volumes 4, 11, 35)

autobiographical elements **4:** 440, 444
Brabantio **25:** 189
Cassio **25:** 189
Clarissa (Samuel Richardson), compared with **48:** 277
consummation of marriage **22:** 207
contrasts and oppositions **4:** 421, 455, 457, 462, 508; **25:** 189
Desdemona
    as Christ figure **4:** 506, 525, 573; **35:** 360
    culpability **4:** 408, 415, 422, 427; **13:** 313; **19:** 253, 276; **35:** 265, 352, 380
    innocence **35:** 360; **47:** 25
    as mother figure **22:** 339; **35:** 282
    passivity **4:** 402, 406, 421, 440, 457, 470, 582, 587; **25:** 189; **35:** 380
    spiritual nature of her love **4:** 462, 530, 559
    staging issues **11:** 350, 354, 359; **13:** 327; **32:** 201
dramatic structure **4:** 370, 390, 399, 427, 488, 506, 517, 569; **22:** 207; **28:** 243
Duke **25:** 189
Emilia **4:** 386, 391, 392, 415, 587; **35:** 352, 380
gender issues **32:** 294; **35:** 327
handkerchief, significance of **4:** 370, 384, 385, 396, 503, 530, 562; **35:** 265, 282, 380
Hercules Furens (Seneca) as source **16:** 283
Iago
    affinity with Othello **4:** 400, 427, 468, 470, 477, 500, 506; **25:** 189; **44:** 57
    as conventional dramatic villain **4:** 440, 527, 545, 582
    as homosexual **4:** 503
    Machiavellian elements **4:** 440, 455, 457, 517, 545; **35:** 336, 347
    motives **4:** 389, 390, 397, 399, 402, 409, 423, 424, 427, 434, 451, 462, 545, 564; **13:** 304; **25:** 189; **28:** 344; **32:** 201; **35:** 265, 276, 310, 336, 347; **42:** 278
    revenge scheme **4:** 392, 409, 424, 451
    as scapegoat **4:** 506
    as victim **4:** 402, 409, 434, 451, 457, 470
idealism versus realism **4:** 457, 508, 517; **13:** 313; **25:** 189
implausibility of plot, characters, or events **4:** 370, 380, 391, 442, 444; **47:** 51
jealousy **4:** 384, 488, 527; **35:** 253, 265, 282, 301, 310; **44:** 57, 66; **51:** 30
justice **35:** 247
language and imagery **4:** 433, 442, 445, 462, 493, 508, 517, 552, 587, 596; **13:** 304; **16:** 272; **22:** 378; **25:** 189, 257; **28:** 243, 344; **42:** 278; **47:** 51
love **4:** 412, 493, 506, 512, 530, 545, 552, 569,

570, 575, 580, 591; **19:** 253; **22:** 207; **25:** 257; **28:** 243, 344; **32:** 201; **35:** 261, 317; **51:** 25, 30
love and reason **4:** 512, 530, 580; **19:** 253
madness **35:** 265, 276, 282
marriage **35:** 369; **51:** 44
Marxist criticism **42:** 234
Measure for Measure, compared with **25:** 189
medieval dramatic conventions, influence of **4:** 440, 527, 545, 559, 582
military and sexual hierarchies **16:** 272
Othello
    affinity with Iago **4:** 400, 427, 468, 470, 477, 500, 506; **25:** 189; **35:** 276, 320, 327
    as conventional "blameless hero" **4:** 445, 486, 500
    credulity **4:** 384, 385, 388, 390, 396, 402, 434, 440, 455; **13:** 327; **32:** 302; **47:** 25, 51
    Desdemona, relationship with **22:** 339; **35:** 301, 317; **37:** 269
    divided nature **4:** 400, 412, 462, 470, 477, 493, 500, 582, 592; **16:** 293; **19:** 276; **25:** 189; **35:** 320
    egotism **4:** 427, 470, 477, 493, 522, 536, 541, 573, 597; **13:** 304; **35:** 247, 253
    self-destructive anger **16:** 283
    self-dramatizing or self-deluding **4:** 454, 457, 477, 592; **13:** 313; **16:** 293; **35:** 317
    self-knowledge **4:** 462, 470, 477, 483, 508, 522, 530, 564, 580, 591, 596; **13:** 304, 313; **16:** 283; **28:** 243; **35:** 253, 317
    spiritual state **4:** 483, 488, 517, 525, 527, 544, 559, 564, 573; **28:** 243; **35:** 253
perception **19:** 276; **25:** 189, 257
poetic justice, question of **4:** 370, 412, 415, 427
pride and rightful self-esteem **4:** 522, 536, 541; **35:** 352
psychoanalytic interpretations **4:** 468, 503; **35:** 265, 276, 282, 301, 317, 320, 347; **42:** 203; **44:** 57
racial issues **4:** 370, 380, 384, 385, 392, 399, 401, 402, 408, 427, 564; **13:** 327; **16:** 293; **25:** 189, 257; **28:** 249, 330; **35:** 369; **42:** 203
religious, mythic, or spiritual content **4:** 483, 517, 522, 525, 559, 573; **22:** 207; **28:** 330
revenge **35:** 261
Romeo and Juliet, compared with **32:** 302
sexuality **22:** 339; **28:** 330, 344; **35:** 352, 360; **37:** 269; **44:** 57, 66; **51:** 44
sources **28:** 330
staging issues **11:** 273, 334, 335, 339, 342, 350, 354, 359, 362
structure **22:** 378; **28:** 325
time scheme **4:** 370, 384, 390, 488; **22:** 207; **35:** 310; **47:** 51
'Tis Pity She's a Whore (John Ford), compared with
unnatural ordering **22:** 378
Venetian politics **32:** 294
violence **22:** 12; **43:** 32
The Winter's Tale, compared with **35:** 310
women, role of **19:** 253; **28:** 344

Pericles (Volumes 2, 15, 36, 51)

archetypal structure **2:** 570, 580, 582, 584, 588; **25:** 365; **51:** 71, 79

art and nature **22:** 315; **36:** 233
audience perception **42:** 359; **48:** 364
authorship controversy **2:** 538, 540, 543, 544, 545, 546, 548, 550, 551, 553, 556, 558, 564, 565, 568, 576, 586; **15:** 132, 141, 148, 152; **16:** 391, 399; **25:** 365; **36:** 198, 244
autobiographical elements **2:** 551, 554, 555, 563, 581
brothel scenes (Act IV, scenes ii and vi) **2:** 548, 550, 551, 553, 554, 586, 590; **15:** 134, 145, 154, 166, 172, 177; **36:** 274; **51:** 118
composition date **2:** 537, 544
Deconstructionist interpretation of **48:** 364
Diana, as symbol of nature **22:** 315; **36:** 233; **51:** 71
doubling of roles **15:** 150, 152, 167, 173, 180
Gower chorus **2:** 548, 575; **15:** 134, 141, 143, 145, 149, 152, 177; **36:** 279; **42:** 359
incest, motif of **2:** 582, 588; **22:** 315; **36:** 257, 264; **51:** 110, 97
as inferior or flawed plays **2:** 537, 546, 553, 563, 564; **15:** 139, 143, 156, 167, 176; **36:** 198; **51:** 79
innocence **36:** 226, 274
Jacobean culture, relation to **37:** 361; **51:** 110, 86
language and imagery **2:** 559, 560, 565, 583; **16:** 391; **19:** 387; **22:** 315; **36:** 198, 214, 233, 244, 251, 264; **51:** 86, 99
Marina **37:** 361; **51:** 118
as miracle play **2:** 569, 581; **36:** 205; **51:** 97
nature as book **22:** 315; **36:** 233
oaths, importance of **19:** 387
patience **2:** 572, 573, 578, 579; **36:** 251
Pericles
  characterization **36:** 251; **37:** 361
  patience **2:** 572, 573, 578, 579
  suit of Antiochus's daughter **2:** 547, 565, 578, 579; **51:** 126
  Ulysses, compared with **2:** 551
politics **37:** 361
popularity **2:** 536, 538, 546; **37:** 361
recognition scene (Act V, scene i) **15:** 138, 139, 141, 145, 161, 162, 167, 172, 175
reconciliation **2:** 555, 564, 584, 586, 588; **36:** 205
religious, mythic, or spiritual content **2:** 559, 561, 565, 570, 580, 584, 588; **22:** 315; **25:** 365; **51:** 97
riddle motif **22:** 315; **36:** 205, 214
Shakespeare's other romances, relation to **2:** 547, 549, 551, 559, 564, 570, 571, 584, 585; **15:** 139; **16:** 391, 399; **36:** 226, 257; **51:** 71, 79
spectacle **42:** 359
sources **2:** 538, 568, 572, 575; **25:** 365; **36:** 198, 205; **51:** 118, 126
staging issues **16:** 399; **48:** 364; **51:** 99
suffering **2:** 546, 573, 578, 579; **25:** 365; **36:** 279
textual revisions **15:** 129, 130, 132, 134, 135, 136, 138, 152, 155, 167, 181; **16:** 399; **25:** 365; **51:** 99

The Phoenix and Turtle (Volumes 10, 38, 51)

allegorical elements **10:** 7, 8, 9, 16, 17, 48; **38:** 334, 378; **51:** 138, 188

art and nature **10:** 7, 42
authenticity **10:** 7, 8, 16
autobiographical elements **10:** 14, 18, 42, 48; **51:** 155
bird imagery **10:** 21, 27; **38:** 329, 350, 367; **51:** 145, 181, 184
Christian elements **10:** 21, 24, 31; **38:** 326; **51:** 162, 171, 181
complex or enigmatic nature **10:** 7, 14, 35, 42; **38:** 326, 357; **51:** 145, 162
consciously philosophical **10:** 7, 21, 24, 31, 48; **38:** 342, 378
constancy and faithfulness **10:** 18, 20, 21, 48; **38:** 329
Court of Love **10:** 9, 24, 50
Donne, John, compared with **10:** 20, 31, 35, 37, 40; **51:** 143
satiric elements **10:** 8, 16, 17, 27, 35, 40, 45, 48
love **10:** 31, 37, 40, 50; **38:** 342, 345, 367; **51:** 145, 151, 155
as metaphysical poem **10:** 7, 8, 9, 20, 31, 35, 37, 40, 45, 50; **51:** 143, 171, 184
Neoplatonism **10:** 7, 9, 21, 24, 40, 45, 50; **38:** 345, 350, 367, 184
as "pure" poetry **10:** 14, 31, 35; **38:** 329
Scholasticism **10:** 21, 24, 31; **51:** 188
Shakespeare's dramas, compared with **10:** 9, 14, 17, 18, 20, 27, 37, 40, 42, 48; **38:** 342; **51:** 151, 155
sources **10:** 7, 9, 18, 24, 45; **38:** 326, 334, 350, 367; **51:** 138
structure **10:** 27, 31, 37, 45, 50; **38:** 342, 345, 357; **51:** 138, 143
style **10:** 8, 20, 24, 27, 31, 35, 45, 50; **38:** 334, 345, 357, 171; **51:** 188

The Rape of Lucrece (Volumes 10, 33, 43)

allegorical elements **10:** 89, 93
Brutus **10:** 96, 106, 109, 116, 121, 125, 128, 135
Christian elements **10:** 77, 80, 89, 96, 98, 109
Collatine **10:** 98, 131; **43:** 102
Elizabethan culture, relation to **33:** 195; **43:** 77
irony or paradox **10:** 93, 98, 128
language and imagery **10:** 64, 65, 66, 71, 78, 80, 89, 93, 116, 109, 125, 131; **22:** 289, 294; **25:** 305; **32:** 321; **33:** 144, 155, 179, 200; **43:** 102, 113, 141
Lucrece
  chastity **33:** 131, 138; **43:** 92
  as example of Renaissance *virtù* **22:** 289; **43:** 148
  heroic **10:** 84, 93, 109, 121, 128
  patriarchal woman, model of **10:** 109, 131; **33:** 169, 200
  self-responsibility **10:** 89, 96, 98, 106, 125; **33:** 195; **43:** 85, 92, 158
  unrealistic **10:** 64, 65, 66, 121
  verbose **10:** 64, 81, 116; **25:** 305; **33:** 169
  as victim **22:** 294; **25:** 305; **32:** 321; **33:** 131, 195; **43:** 102, 158
male/female relationships **10:** 109, 121, 131; **22:** 289; **25:** 305; **43:** 113, 141
narrative strategies **22:** 294

Roman history, relation to **10:** 84, 89, 93, 96, 98, 109, 116, 125, 135; **22:** 289; **25:** 305; **33:** 155, 190
Shakespeare's dramas, compared with **10:** 63, 64, 65, 66, 68, 71, 73, 74, 78, 80, 81, 84, 98, 116, 121, 125; **43:** 92
sources **10:** 63, 64, 65, 66, 68, 74, 77, 78, 89, 98, 109, 121, 125; **25:** 305; **33:** 155, 190; **43:** 77, 92, 148
structure **10:** 84, 89, 93, 98, 135; **22:** 294; **25:** 305; **43:** 102, 141
style **10:** 64, 65, 66, 68, 69, 70, 71, 73, 74, 77, 78, 81, 84, 98, 116, 131, 135; **43:** 113, 158
Tarquin **10:** 80, 93, 98, 116, 125; **22:** 294; **25:** 305; **32:** 321; **33:** 190; **43:** 102
tragic elements **10:** 78, 80, 81, 84, 98, 109; **43:** 85, 148
the Troy passage **10:** 74, 89, 98, 116, 121, 128; **22:** 289; **32:** 321; **33:** 144, 179; **43:** 77, 85
Venus and Adonis, compared with **10:** 63, 66, 68, 69, 70, 73, 81; **22:** 294; **43:** 148
violence **43:** 148, 158

Richard II (Volumes 6, 24, 39, 49)

abdication scene (Act IV, scene i) **6:** 270, 307, 317, 327, 354, 359, 381, 393, 409; **13:** 172; **19:** 151; **24:** 274, 414
acting and dissimulation **6:** 264, 267, 307, 310, 315, 368, 393, 409; **24:** 339, 345, 346, 349, 352, 356
allegorical elements **6:** 264, 283, 323, 385
audience perception **24:** 414, 423; **39:** 295
Bolingbroke
  comic elements **28:** 134
  guilt **24:** 423; **39:** 279
  language and imagery **6:** 310, 315, 331, 347, 374, 381, 397; **32:** 189
  as Machiavellian figure **6:** 305, 307, 315, 331, 347, 388, 393, 397; **24:** 428
  as politician **6:** 255, 263, 264, 272, 277, 294, 364, 368, 391; **24:** 330, 333, 405, 414, 423, 428; **39:** 256
  Richard, compared with **6:** 307, 315, 347, 374, 391, 393, 409; **24:** 346, 349, 351, 352, 356, 395, 419, 423, 428
  his silence **24:** 423
  structure, compared with **39:** 235
  usurpation of crown, nature of **6:** 255, 272, 289, 307, 310, 347, 354, 359, 381, 385, 393; **13:** 172; **24:** 322, 356, 383, 419; **28:** 178
Bolingbroke and Richard as opposites **24:** 423
Bolingbroke-Mowbray dispute **22:** 137
carnival elements **19:** 151; **39:** 273
censorship **24:** 260, 261, 262, 263, 386; **42:** 120
ceremonies, rites, and rituals, importance of **6:** 270, 294, 315, 368, 381, 397, 409, 414; **24:** 274, 356, 411, 414, 419
comic elements **24:** 262, 263, 395; **39:** 243
contractual and economic relations **13:** 213; **49:** 60
costumes **24:** 274, 278, 291, 304, 325, 356, 364, 423
deposition scene (Act III, scene iii) **24:** 298, 395, 423; **42:** 120

Elizabethan attitudes, influence of **6**: 287, 292, 294, 305, 321, 327, 364, 402, 414; **13**: 494; **24**: 325; **28**: 188; **39**: 273; **42**: 120
Essex Rebellion, relation to **6**: 249, 250; **24**: 356
family honor, structure, and inheritance **6**: 338, 368, 388, 397, 414; **39**: 263, 279
fate **6**: 289, 294, 304, 352, 354, 385
garden scene (Act III, scene iv) **6**: 264, 283, 323, 385; **24**: 307, 356, 414
Gaunt **6**: 255, 287, 374, 388, 402, 414; **24**: 274, 322, 325, 414, 423; **39**: 263, 279
gender issues **25**: 89; **39**: 295
historical sources, compared with **6**: 252, 279, 343; **28**: 134; **39**: 235; **49**: 60
irony **6**: 270, 307, 364, 368, 391; **24**: 383; **28**: 188
King of Misrule **19**: 151; **39**: 273
kingship **6**: 263, 264, 272, 277, 289, 294, 327, 354, 364, 381, 388, 391, 402, 409, 414; **19**: 151, 209; **24**: 260, 289, 291, 322, 325, 333, 339, 345, 346, 349, 351, 352, 356, 395, 408, 419, 428; **28**: 134; **39**: 235, 243, 256, 273, 279, 289; **42**: 175
language and imagery **6**: 252, 282, 283, 294, 298, 315, 323, 331, 347, 368, 374, 381, 385, 397, 409; **13**: 213, 494; **24**: 269, 270, 298, 301, 304, 315, 325, 329, 333, 339, 356, 364, 395, 405, 408, 411, 414, 419; **28**: 134, 188; **39**: 243, 273, 289, 295; **42**: 175
Marlowe's works, compared with **19**: 233; **24**: 307, 336; **42**: 175
medievalism and chivalry, presentation of **6**: 258, 277, 294, 327, 338, 388, 397, 414; **24**: 274, 278, 279, 280, 283; **39**: 256
mercantilism and feudalism **13**: 213
mirror scene (Act IV, scene i) **6**: 317, 327, 374, 381, 393, 409; **24**: 267, 356, 408, 414, 419, 423; **28**: 134, 178; **39**: 295
negative assessments **6**: 250, 252, 253, 255, 282, 307, 317, 343, 359
Northumberland **24**: 423
Richard
  artistic temperament **6**: 264, 267, 270, 272, 277, 292, 294, 298, 315, 331, 334, 347, 368, 374, 393, 409; **24**: 298, 301, 304, 315, 322, 390, 405, 408, 411, 414, 419; **39**: 289
  Bolingbroke, compared with **24**: 346, 349, 351, 352, 356, 419; **39**: 256
  characterization **6**: 250, 252, 253, 254, 255, 258, 262, 263, 267, 270, 272, 282, 283, 304, 343, 347, 364, 368; **24**: 262, 263, 267, 269, 270, 271, 272, 273, 274, 278, 280, 315, 322, 325, 330, 333, 390, 395, 402, 405, 423; **28**: 134; **39**: 279, 289
  dangerous aspects **24**: 405
  delusion **6**: 267, 298, 334, 368, 409; **24**: 329, 336, 405
  homosexuality **24**: 405
  kingship **6**: 253, 254, 263, 272, 327, 331, 334, 338, 364, 402, 414; **24**: 278, 295, 336, 337, 339, 356, 419; **28**: 134, 178; **39**: 256, 263
  loss of identity **6**: 267, 338, 368, 374, 381, 388, 391, 409; **24**: 298, 414, 428
  as martyr-king **6**: 289, 307, 321; **19**: 209; **24**: 289, 291; **28**: 134
  nobility **6**: 255, 258, 259, 262, 263, 391; **24**: 260, 263, 274, 280, 289, 291, 402, 408, 411
  political acumen **6**: 263, 264, 272, 292, 310, 327, 334, 364, 368, 374, 388, 391, 397, 402, 409; **24**: 405; **39**: 256
  private versus public persona **6**: 317, 327, 364, 368, 391, 409; **24**: 428
  role-playing **24**: 419, 423; **28**: 178
  seizure of Gaunt's estate **6**: 250, 338, 388; **49**: 60
  self-dramatization **6**: 264, 267, 307, 310, 315, 317, 331, 334, 368, 393, 409; **24**: 339; **28**: 178
  self-hatred **13**: 172; **24**: 383; **39**: 289
  self-knowledge **6**: 255, 267, 331, 334, 338, 352, 354, 368, 388, 391; **24**: 273, 289, 411, 414; **39**: 263, 289
  spiritual redemption **6**: 255, 267, 331, 334, 338, 352, 354, 368, 388, 391; **24**: 273, 289, 411, 414
Shakespeare's other histories, compared with **6**: 255, 264, 272, 294, 304, 310, 317, 343, 354, 359; **24**: 320, 325, 330, 331, 332, 333; **28**: 178
Shakespeare's sympathies, question of **6**: 277, 279, 287, 347, 359, 364, 391, 393, 402
Sicilian Usurper (Nahum Tate adaptation) **24**: 260, 261, 262, 263, 386, 390
staging issues **13**: 494; **24**: 273, 274, 278, 279, 280, 283, 291, 295, 296, 301, 303, 304, 310, 315, 317, 320, 325, 333, 338, 346, 351, 352, 356, 364, 383, 386, 395, 402, 405, 411, 414, 419, 423, 428; **25**: 89
structure **6**: 282, 304, 317, 343, 352, 359, 364, 39; **24**: 307, 322, 325, 356, 395
textual arrangement **24**: 260, 261, 262, 263, 271, 273, 291, 296, 356, 390
time **22**: 137
usurpation **6**: 263, 264, 272, 287, 289, 315, 323, 331, 343, 354, 364, 381, 388, 393, 397; **24**: 383
York **6**: 287, 364, 368, 388, 402, 414; **24**: 263, 320, 322, 364, 395, 414; **39**: 243, 279

Richard III (Volumes 8, 14, 39)

ambivalence and ambiguity **44**: 11; **47**: 15
conscience **8**: 148, 152, 162, 165, 190, 197, 201, 206, 210, 228, 232, 239, 243, 252, 258; **39**: 341
Elizabethan politics, relation to **22**: 395; **25**: 141; **37**: 144; **39**: 345, 349; **42**: 132
family honor, structure and inheritance **8**: 177, 248, 252, 263, 267; **25**: 141; **39**: 335, 341, 349, 370
flattery **22**: 395
gender issues **25**: 141; **37**: 144; **39**: 345
genre **8**: 181, 182, 197, 206, 218, 228, 239, 243, 252, 258; **13**: 142; **39**: 383
ghost scene (Act V, scene iii) **8**: 152, 154, 159, 162, 163, 165, 170, 177, 193, 197, 210, 228, 239, 243, 252, 258, 267
Henry VI, relation to **8**: 159, 165, 177, 182, 193, 201, 210, 213, 218, 228, 243, 248, 252, 267; **25**: 164; **39**: 370
historical accuracy **8**: 144, 145, 153, 159, 163, 165, 168, 213, 223, 228, 232; **39**: 305, 308, 326, 383
historical principles **39**: 308, 326, 387
language and imagery **8**: 159, 161, 165, 167, 168, 170, 177, 182, 184, 186, 193, 197, 201, 206, 218, 223, 243, 248, 252, 258, 262, 267; **16**: 150; **25**: 141, 245; **39**: 360, 370, 383; **47**: 15
Margaret **8**: 153, 154, 159, 162, 163, 170, 193, 201, 206, 210, 218, 223, 228, 243, 248, 262; **39**: 345
Christopher Marlowe's works, compared with **19**: 233
minor characters **8**: 154, 159, 162, 163, 168, 170, 177, 184, 186, 201, 206, 210, 218, 223, 228, 232, 239, 248, 262, 267
modernization **14**: 523
moral corruption of English society **8**: 154, 163, 165, 177, 193, 201, 218, 228, 232, 243, 248, 252, 267; **39**: 308
plot and incident **8**: 146, 152, 159; **25**: 164
popularity **8**: 144, 146, 154, 158, 159, 162, 181, 228; **39**: 383
rebellion **22**: 395
retribution **8**: 163, 170, 177, 182, 184, 193, 197, 201, 206, 210, 218, 223, 228, 243, 248, 267
Richard III
  ambition **8**: 148, 154, 165, 168, 170, 177, 182, 213, 218, 228, 232, 239, 252, 258, 267; **39**: 308, 341, 360, 370, 383
  attractive qualities **8**: 145, 148, 152, 154, 159, 161, 162, 165, 168, 170, 181, 182, 184, 185, 197, 201, 206, 213, 228, 243, 252, 258; **16**: 150; **39**: 370, 383
  credibility, question of **8**: 145, 147, 154, 159, 165, 193; **13**: 142
  death, decay, and nature's destructiveness **8**: 145, 148, 154, 159, 165, 168, 170, 177, 182, 197, 210, 223, 228, 232, 243, 248, 252, 258, 267
  deformity as symbol **8**: 146, 147, 148, 152, 154, 159, 161, 165, 170, 177, 184, 185, 193, 218, 248, 252, 267; **19**: 164
  inversion of moral order **8**: 159, 168, 177, 182, 184, 185, 197, 201, 213, 218, 223, 232, 239, 243, 248, 252, 258, 262, 267; **39**: 360
  as Machiavellian villain **8**: 165, 182, 190, 201, 218, 232, 239, 243, 248; **39**: 308, 326, 360, 387
  as monster or symbol of diabolic **8**: 145, 147, 159, 162, 168, 170, 177, 182, 193, 197, 201, 228, 239, 248, 258; **13**: 142; **37**: 144; **39**: 326, 349
  other literary villains, compared with **8**: 148, 161, 162, 165, 181, 182, 206, 213, 239, 267
  role-playing, hypocrisy, and dissimulation **8**: 145, 148, 154, 159, 162, 165, 168, 170, 182, 190, 206, 213, 218, 228, 239, 243, 252, 258, 267; **25**: 141, 164, 245; **39**: 335, 341, 387
  as scourge or instrument of God **8**: 163, 177, 193, 201, 218, 228, 248, 267; **39**: 308
  as Vice figure **8**: 190, 201, 213, 228, 243, 248, 252; **16**: 150; **39**: 383, 387
Richmond **8**: 154, 158, 163, 168, 177, 182, 193, 210, 218, 223, 228, 243, 248, 252; **13**: 142; **25**: 141; **39**: 349
settings **14**: 516, 528
Shakespeare's artistic growth, *Richard III*'s contribution to **8**: 165, 167, 182, 193, 197, 206, 210, 228, 239, 267; **25**: 164; **39**: 305, 326, 370

Shakespeare's political sympathies 8: 147, 163, 177, 193, 197, 201, 223, 228, 232, 243, 248, 267; 39: 349; 42: 132
sources
chronicles 8: 145, 165, 193, 197, 201, 206, 210, 213, 228, 232
Marlowe, Christopher 8: 167, 168, 182, 201, 206, 218
morality plays 8: 182, 190, 201, 213, 239
Seneca, other classical writers 8: 165, 190, 201, 206, 228, 248
staging issues 14: 515, 527, 528, 537; 16: 137
structure 8: 154, 161, 163, 167, 168, 170, 177, 184, 193, 197, 201, 206, 210, 218, 223, 228, 232, 243, 252, 262, 267; 16: 150
The Tragical History of King Richard III (Colley Cibber adaptation), compared with 8: 159, 161, 243
traditional values 39: 335
Tudor myth 8: 163, 165, 177, 184, 193, 201, 218, 228, 232, 243, 248, 252, 267; 39: 305, 308, 326, 387; 42: 132
Wars of the Roses 8: 163, 165, 177, 184, 193, 201, 218, 228, 232, 243, 248, 252, 267; 39: 308
wooing scenes (Act I, scene ii and Act IV, scene iv) 8: 145, 147, 152, 153, 154, 159, 161, 164, 170, 190, 197, 206, 213, 218, 223, 232, 239, 243, 252, 258, 267; 16: 150; 19: 164; 25: 141, 164; 39: 308, 326, 360, 387

Romeo and Juliet (Volumes 5, 11, 33, 51)

accident or chance 5: 418, 444, 448, 467, 470, 487, 573
adolescence 33: 249, 255, 257
amour-passion or *Liebestod* myth 5: 484, 489, 528, 530, 542, 550, 575; 32: 256; 51: 195, 219, 236
androgyny 13: 530
anxiety 13: 235
balcony scene 32: 276; 51: 219
Caius Marius (Thomas Otway adaptation) 11: 377, 378, 488, 495
comic and tragic elements, combination of 46: 78
contradiction, paradox, and opposition 5: 421, 427, 431, 496, 509, 513, 516, 520, 525, 528, 538; 33: 287; 44: 11
costuming 11: 505, 509
courtly love tradition, influence of 5: 505, 542, 575; 33: 233
desire 51: 227, 236
detention of Friar John 5: 448, 467, 470
divine will, role of 5: 485, 493, 505, 533, 573
dramatic shortcomings or failure 5: 416, 418, 420, 426, 436, 437, 448, 464, 467, 469, 480, 487, 524, 562
Elizabethan poetics, influence of 5: 416, 520, 522, 528, 550, 559, 575
evil 5: 485, 493, 505
as experimental play 5: 464, 509, 528
fate 5: 431, 444, 464, 469, 470, 479, 480, 485, 487, 493, 509, 530, 533, 562, 565, 571, 573; 33: 249
feud 5: 415, 419, 425, 447, 458, 464, 469, 479, 480, 493, 509, 522, 556, 565, 566, 571, 575; 25: 181; 51: 245
Friar Lawrence
contribution to catastrophe 5: 437, 444, 470; 33: 300; 51: 253
philosophy of moderation 5: 427, 431, 437, 438, 443, 444, 445, 458, 467, 479, 505, 538
as Shakespeare's spokesman 5: 427, 431, 437, 458, 467
ideal love 5: 421, 427, 431, 436, 437, 450, 463, 469, 498, 505, 575; 25: 257; 33: 210, 225, 272; 51: 25, 44, 195, 203, 219
gender issues 32: 256; 51: 253
lamentation scene (Act IV, scene v) 5: 425, 492, 538
language and imagery 5: 420, 426, 431, 436, 437, 456, 477, 479, 489, 492, 496, 509, 520, 522, 528, 538, 542, 550, 559; 25: 181, 245, 257; 32: 276; 33: 210, 272, 274, 287; 42: 271; 51: 203, 212, 227
love versus fate 5: 421, 437, 438, 443, 445, 458; 33: 249
medieval influence 5: 480, 505, 509, 573
Mercutio
bawdy 5: 463, 525, 550, 575
death, decay, and nature's destructiveness 5: 415, 418, 419, 547; 33: 290
as worldly counterpoint to Romeo 5: 425, 464, 542; 33: 290; 51: 195
comic and tragic elements, combination of 5: 496, 524, 528, 547, 559
Neoclassical rules 5: 416, 418, 426
Nurse 5: 419, 425, 463, 464, 575; 33: 294
Othello, compared with 32: 302
Petrarchian poetics, influence of 5: 416, 520, 522, 528, 550, 559, 575; 32: 276; 51: 212, 236
prose adaptations of Juliet's character 19: 261
psychoanalytic interpretation 5: 513, 556; 51: 253
public versus private worlds 5: 520, 550; 25: 181; 33: 274
reconciliation 5: 415, 419, 427, 439, 447, 480, 487, 493, 505, 533, 536, 562
rhetoric 42: 271
rival productions 11: 381, 382, 384, 385, 386, 487
Romeo and Juliet
death-wish 5: 431, 489, 505, 528, 530, 538, 542, 550, 566, 571, 575; 32: 212
first meeting (Act I, scene v) 51: 212
immortality 5: 536
Juliet's epithalamium speech (Act III, scene ii) 5: 431, 477, 492
Juliet's innocence 5: 421, 423, 450, 454; 33: 257
maturation 5: 437, 454, 467, 493, 498, 509, 520, 565; 33: 249, 257
rebellion 25: 257
reckless passion 5: 419, 427, 431, 438, 443, 444, 448, 467, 479, 485, 505, 533, 538, 542; 33: 241
Romeo's dream (Act V, scene i) 5: 513, 536, 556; 45: 40; 51: 203
Rosaline, Romeo's relationship with 5: 419, 423, 425, 427, 438, 498, 542, 575
sexuality 25: 181; 33: 225, 233, 241, 246, 274, 300; 51: 227, 236
source of tragic catastrophe 5: 418, 427, 431, 448, 458, 469, 479, 480, 485, 487, 493, 509, 522, 528, 530, 533, 542, 565, 571, 573; 33: 210; 51: 245
sources 5: 416, 419, 423, 450; 32: 222; 33: 210; 45: 40
staging issues 11: 499, 505, 507, 514, 517; 13: 243; 25: 181; 32: 212
structure 5: 438, 448, 464, 469, 470, 477, 480, 496, 518, 524, 525, 528, 547, 559; 33: 210, 246
tomb scene (Act V, scene iii) 5: 416, 419, 423; 13: 243; 25: 181, 245; 51: 219
triumph over death or fate 5: 421, 423, 427, 505, 509, 520, 530, 536, 565, 566; 51: 219
Verona society 5: 556, 566; 13: 235; 33: 255; 51: 245
wordplay 32: 256

Sonnets (Volumes 10, 40, 51)

ambiguity 10: 251, 256; 28: 385; 40: 221, 228, 268
audience 51: 316
authenticity 10: 153, 154, 230, 243; 48: 325
autobiographical elements 10: 159, 160, 166, 167, 175, 176, 182, 196, 205, 213, 215, 226, 233, 238, 240, 251, 279, 283, 302, 309, 325, 337, 377; 13: 487; 16: 461; 28: 363, 385; 42: 303; 48: 325
beauty 10: 247; 51: 288
Christian elements 10: 191, 256
composition date 10: 153, 154, 161, 166, 196, 217, 226, 270, 277; 28: 363, 385
Dark Lady 10: 161, 167, 176, 216, 217, 218, 226, 240, 302, 342, 377, 394; 25: 374; 37: 374; 40: 273; 48: 346; 51: 284, 288, 292, 321
deception, disguise, and duplicity 25: 374; 40: 221
dramatic elements 10: 155, 182, 240, 251, 283, 367
editorial and textual issues 28: 363; 40: 273; 42: 303
Elizabeth, audience of 48: 325
the Friend 10: 279, 302, 309, 379, 385, 391, 394; 51: 284, 288, 292, 300, 304, 316, 321
friendship 10: 185, 279; 28: 380; 51: 284
gender issues 37: 374; 40: 238, 247, 254, 264, 268, 273
homoerotic elements 10: 155, 156, 159, 161, 175, 213, 391; 16: 461; 28: 363, 380; 37: 347; 40: 254, 264, 273; 51: 270, 284
identities of persons 10: 154, 155, 156, 161, 166, 167, 169, 173, 174, 175, 185, 190, 191, 196, 218, 226, 230, 233, 240; 40: 238
Ireland, William Henry, forgeries of 48: 325
irony or satire 10: 256, 293, 334, 337, 346; 51: 300
Italian influences 28: 407
language and imagery 10: 247, 251, 255, 256, 290, 353, 372, 385; 13: 445; 28: 380, 385; 32: 327, 352; 40: 228, 247, 284, 292, 303; 51: 270, 304
love 10: 173, 247, 287, 290, 293, 302, 309, 322, 325, 329, 394; 28: 380; 37: 347; 51: 270, 284, 288, 292
love versus reason 10: 329
A Lover's Complaint (the Rival Poet) 10: 243, 353

gender issues **48**: 336
pastoral tradition, compared with **48**: 336
sonnets, compared with **48**: 336
lust **51**: 292
lust versus reason **51**: 288
magic **48**: 346
Mr. W. H. **10**: 153, 155, 161, 169, 174, 182, 190, 196, 217, 218, 377
Montaigne's *Essais*, relation to **42**: 382
mutability, theme of **42**: 382
Neoplatonism **10**: 191, 205
occult **48**: 346
other sonnet writers, Shakespeare compared with **10**: 247, 260, 265, 283, 290, 293, 309, 353, 367; **28**: 380, 385, 407; **37**: 374; **40**: 247, 264, 303; **42**: 303
pedagogy **37**: 374
performative issues **48**: 352
poet-patron relationship **48**: 352
poetic style **10**: 153, 155, 156, 158, 159, 160, 161, 173, 175, 182, 214, 247, 251, 255, 260, 265, 283, 287, 296, 302, 315, 322, 325, 337, 346, 349, 360, 367, 385; **16**: 472; **40**: 221, 228; **51**: 270
procreation **10**: 379, 385; **16**: 461
rhetoric of consolation **42**: 382
the Rival Poet **10**: 169, 233, 334, 337, 385; **48**: 352
self-love **10**: 372; **25**: 374; **51**: 270, 300, 304
selfishness versus self-knowledge **51**: 292
sexuality **25**: 374
as social action **48**: 352
sonnet arrangement **10**: 174, 176, 182, 205, 226, 230, 236, 315, 353; **28**: 363; **40**: 238
sonnet form **10**: 255, 325, 367; **37**: 347; **40**: 284, 303; **51**: 270
sonnets (individual):
3 **10**: 346
12 **10**: 360
15 **40**: 292
18 **40**: 292
20 **10**: 391; **13**: 530
21 **32**: 352
26 **10**: 161
30 **10**: 296
35 **10**: 251
49 **10**: 296
53 **10**: 349; **32**: 327, 352
54 **32**: 352
55 **13**: 445
57 **10**: 296
59 **16**: 472
60 **10**: 296; **16**: 472
64 **10**: 329, 360
65 **10**: 296; **40**: 292
66 **10**: 315
68 **32**: 327
71 **10**: 167
73 **10**: 315, 353, 360
76 **10**: 334
79 **32**: 352
82 **32**: 352
86 **32**: 352
87 **10**: 296; **40**: 303
93 **13**: 487
94 **10**: 256, 296; **32**: 327
95 **32**: 327
98 **32**: 352
99 **32**: 352
104 **10**: 360
105 **32**: 327
107 **10**: 270, 277
116 **10**: 329, 379; **13**: 445
117 **10**: 337
119 **10**: 337
121 **10**: 346
123 **10**: 270
124 **10**: 265, 270, 329
126 **10**: 161
129 **10**: 353, 394; **22**: 12
130 **10**: 346
138 **10**: 296
144 **10**: 394
145 **10**: 358; **40**: 254
146 **10**: 353
sonnets (groups):
1-17 **10**: 296, 315, 379, 385; **16**: 461; **40**: 228
1-21 **40**: 268
1-26 **10**: 176
1-126 **10**: 161, 176, 185, 191, 196, 205, 213, 226, 236, 279, 309, 315, 372
18-22 **10**: 315
18-126 **10**: 379
23-40 **10**: 315
27-55 **10**: 176
33-9 **10**: 329
56-77 **10**: 176
76-86 **10**: 315
78-80 **10**: 334, 385
78-101 **10**: 176
82-6 **10**: 334
100-12 **10**: 337
102-26 **10**: 176
123-25 **10**: 385
127-52 **10**: 293, 385
127-54 **10**: 161, 176, 185, 190, 196, 213, 226, 236, 309, 315, 342, 394
151-52 **10**: 315
sources **10**: 153, 154, 156, 158, 233, 251, 255, 293, 353; **16**: 472; **28**: 407; **42**: 382
structure **10**: 175, 176, 182, 205, 230, 260, 296, 302, 309, 315, 337, 349, 353; **40**: 238
subjectivity **37**: 374
time **10**: 265, 302, 309, 322, 329, 337, 360, 379; **13**: 445; **40**: 292
visual arts, relation to **28**: 407
voice **51**: 316
apparent inconsistencies in **51**: 321

The Taming of the Shrew (Volumes 9, 12, 31)

appearance versus reality **9**: 343, 350, 353, 365, 369, 370, 381, 390, 430; **12**: 416; **31**: 326
Baptista **9**: 325, 344, 345, 375, 386, 393, 413
Bianca **9**: 325, 342, 344, 345, 360, 362, 370, 375
Bianca-Lucentio subplot **9**: 365, 370, 375, 390, 393, 401, 407, 413, 430; **16**: 13; **31**: 339
Catherine and Petruchio (David Garrick adaptation) **12**: 309, 310, 311, 416
class distinctions, conflict, and relations **31**: 300, 351; **50**: 64, 74
deception, disguise, and duplicity **12**: 416
Elizabethan culture, relation to **31**: 288, 295, 300, 315, 326, 345, 351
as farce **9**: 330, 337, 338, 341, 342, 365, 381, 386, 413, 426
folk elements **9**: 381, 393, 404, 426
gender issues **28**: 24; **31**: 261, 268, 276, 282, 288, 295, 300, 335, 351
genre **9**: 329, 334, 362, 375; **22**: 48; **31**: 261, 269, 276
induction **9**: 320, 322, 332, 337, 345, 350, 362, 365, 369, 370, 381, 390, 393, 407, 419, 424, 430; **12**: 416, 427, 430, 431, 441; **19**: 34, 122; **22**: 48; **31**: 269, 315, 351
irony or satire **9**: 340, 375, 398, 407, 413; **13**: 3; **19**: 122
Kate
characterization **32**: 1
final speech (Act V, scene ii) **9**: 318, 319, 329, 330, 338, 340, 341, 345, 347, 353, 355, 360, 365, 381, 386, 401, 404, 413, 426, 430; **19**: 3; **22**: 48
love for Petruchio **9**: 338, 340, 353, 430; **12**: 435
portrayals of **31**: 282
shrewishness **9**: 322, 323, 325, 332, 344, 345, 360, 365, 370, 375, 386, 393, 398, 404, 413
transformation **9**: 323, 341, 355, 370, 386, 393, 401, 404, 407, 419, 424, 426, 430; **16**: 13; **19**: 34; **22**: 48; **31**: 288, 295, 339, 351
Kiss Me, Kate (Cole Porter adaptation) **31**: 282
language and imagery **9**: 336, 338, 393, 401, 404, 407, 413; **22**: 378; **28**: 9; **31**: 261, 288, 300, 326, 335, 339; **32**: 56
Lucentio **9**: 325, 342, 362, 375, 393
marriage **9**: 322, 325, 329, 332, 329, 332, 334, 341, 342, 343, 344, 345, 347, 353, 360, 362, 375, 381, 390, 398, 401, 404, 413, 426, 430; **13**: 3; **19**: 3; **28**: 24; **31**: 288; **51**: 44
metadramatic elements **9**: 350, 419, 424; **31**: 300, 315
metamorphosis or transformation **9**: 370, 430
pedagogy **19**: 122
performance history **31**: 282
performance issues **12**: 313, 314, 316, 317, 337, 338; **31**: 315
Petruchio
admirable qualities **9**: 320, 332, 341, 344, 345, 370, 375, 386
as lord of misrule **50**: 64
audacity or vigor **9**: 325, 337, 355, 375, 386, 404
characterization **32**: 1
coarseness or brutality **9**: 325, 329, 365, 390, 393, 398, 407; **19**: 122
as lord of misrule **9**: 393
love for Kate **9**: 338, 340, 343, 344, 386; **12**: 435
portrayals of **31**: 282
pragmatism **9**: 329, 334, 375, 398, 424; **13**: 3; **31**: 345, 351
taming method **9**: 320, 323, 329, 340, 341, 343, 345, 355, 369, 370, 375, 390, 398, 407, 413, 419, 424; **19**: 3, 12, 21; **31**: 269, 295, 326, 335, 339
popularity **9**: 318, 338, 404
role-playing **9**: 322, 353, 355, 360, 369, 370, 398, 401, 407, 413, 419, 424; **13**: 3; **31**: 288, 295, 315

romantic elements **9:** 334, 342, 362, 375, 407
Shakespeare's other plays, compared with **9:** 334, 342, 360, 393, 426, 430; **31:** 261; **50:** 74
Sly **9:** 320, 322, 350, 370, 381, 390, 398, 430; **12:** 316, 335, 416, 427, 441; **16:** 13; **19:** 34, 122; **22:** 48; **37:** 31; **50:** 74
sources
    Ariosto **9:** 320, 334, 341, 342, 370
    folk tales **9:** 332, 390, 393
    Gascoigne **9:** 370, 390
    Old and New Comedy **9:** 419
    Ovid **9:** 318, 370, 430
    Plautus **9:** 334, 341, 342
    shrew tradition **9:** 355; **19:** 3; **32:** 1, 56
structure **9:** 318, 322, 325, 332, 334, 341, 362, 370, 390, 426; **22:** 48, 378; **31:** 269
    play-within-a-play **12:** 416; **22:** 48
The Taming of a Shrew (anonymous), compared with **9:** 334, 350, 426; **12:** 312; **22:** 48; **31:** 261, 276, 339
textual issues **22:** 48; **31:** 261, 276; **31:** 276
violence **43:** 61

The Tempest (Volumes 8, 15, 29, 45)

allegorical elements **8:** 294, 295, 302, 307, 308, 312, 326, 328, 336, 345, 364; **42:** 327
Antonio and Sebastian **8:** 295, 299, 304, 328, 370, 396, 429, 454; **13:** 440; **29:** 278, 297, 343, 362, 368, 377
Ariel **8:** 289, 293, 294, 295, 297, 304, 307, 315, 320, 326, 328, 336, 340, 345, 356, 364, 420, 458; **22:** 302; **29:** 278, 297, 362, 368, 377
art versus nature **8:** 396, 404; **29:** 278, 297, 362
autobiographical elements **8:** 302, 308, 312, 324, 326, 345, 348, 353, 364, 380
Caliban **8:** 286, 287, 289, 292, 294, 295, 297, 302, 304, 307, 309, 315, 326, 328, 336, 353, 364, 370, 380, 390, 396, 401, 414, 420, 423, 429, 435, 454; **13:** 424, 440; **15:** 189, 312, 322, 374, 379; **22:** 302; **25:** 382; **28:** 249; **29:** 278, 292, 297, 343, 368, 377, 396; **32:** 367; **45:** 211, 219, 226, 259
characterization **8:** 287, 289, 292, 294, 295, 308, 326, 334, 336; **28:** 415; **42:** 339; **45:** 219
classical influence and sources **29:** 278, 343, 362, 368
colonialism **13:** 424, 440; **15:** 228, 268, 269, 270, 271, 272, 273; **19:** 421; **25:** 357, 382; **28:** 249; **29:** 343, 368; **32:** 338, 367, 400; **42:** 327; **45:** 200, 280
compassion, theme of **42:** 346
conspiracy or treason **16:** 426; **19:** 357; **25:** 382; **29:** 377
dreams **45:** 236, 247, 259
education or nurturing **8:** 353, 370, 384, 396; **29:** 292, 368, 377
exposition scene (Act I, scene ii) **8:** 287, 289, 293, 299, 334
Ferdinand **8:** 328, 336, 359, 454; **19:** 357; **22:** 302; **29:** 362, 339, 377
freedom and servitude **8:** 304, 307, 312, 429; **22:** 302; **29:** 278, 368, 377; **37:** 336
Gonzalo **22:** 302; **29:** 278, 343, 362, 368

Gonzalo's commonwealth **8:** 312, 336, 370, 390, 396, 404; **19:** 357; **29:** 368; **45:** 280
good versus evil **8:** 302, 311, 315, 370, 423, 439; **29:** 278; 297
historical content **8:** 364, 408, 420; **16:** 426; **25:** 382; **29:** 278, 339, 343, 368; **45:** 226
the island **8:** 308, 315, 447; **25:** 357, 382; **29:** 278, 343
language and imagery **8:** 324, 348, 384, 390, 404, 454; **19:** 421; **29:** 278; **29:** 297, 343, 368, 377
love **8:** 435, 439; **29:** 297, 339, 377, 396
magic or supernatural elements **8:** 287, 293, 304, 315, 340, 356, 396, 401, 404, 408, 435, 458; **28:** 391, 415; **29:** 297, 343, 377; **45:** 272
the masque (Act IV, scene i) **8:** 404, 414, 423, 435, 439; **25:** 357; **28:** 391, 415; **29:** 278, 292, 339, 343, 368; **42:** 339; **45:** 188
Miranda **8:** 289, 301, 304, 328, 336, 370, 454; **19:** 357; **22:** 302; **28:** 249; **29:** 278, 297, 362, 368, 377, 396
Montaigne's *Essais*, relation to **42:** 346
music **8:** 390, 404; **29:** 292; **37:** 321; **42:** 339
nature **8:** 315, 370, 390, 408, 414; **29:** 343, 362, 368, 377
Neoclassical rules **8:** 287, 292, 293, 334; **25:** 357; **29:** 292; **45:** 200
politics **8:** 304, 307, 315, 353, 359, 364, 401, 408; **16:** 426; **19:** 421; **29:** 339; **37:** 336; **42:** 327; **45:** 272, 280
Prospero
    characterization **8:** 312, 348, 370, 458; **16:** 442; **22:** 302; **45:** 188, 272
    as God or Providence **8:** 311, 328, 364, 380, 429, 435
    magic, nature of **8:** 301, 340, 356, 396, 414, 423, 458; **25:** 382; **28:** 391; **29:** 278, 292, 368, 377, 396; **32:** 338, 343
    psychoanalytic interpretation **45:** 259
    redemptive powers **8:** 302, 320, 353, 370, 390, 429, 439, 447; **29:** 297
    as ruler **8:** 304, 308, 309, 420, 423; **13:** 424; **22:** 302; **29:** 278, 362, 377, 396
    self-control **8:** 312, 414, 420; **22:** 302; **44:** 11
    self-knowledge **16:** 442; **22:** 302; **29:** 278, 292, 362, 377, 396
    as Shakespeare or creative artist **8:** 299, 302, 308, 312, 320, 324, 353, 364, 435, 447
    as tragic hero **8:** 359, 370, 464; **29:** 292
realism **8:** 340, 359, 464
reality and illusion **8:** 287, 315, 359, 401, 435, 439, 447, 454; **22:** 302; **45:** 236, 247
reconciliation **8:** 302, 312, 320, 334, 348, 359, 370, 384, 401, 404, 414, 429, 439, 447, 454; **16:** 442; **22:** 302; **29:** 297; **37:** 336; **45:** 236
religious, mythic, or spiritual content **8:** 328, 390, 423, 429, 435; **45:** 211, 247
romance or pastoral tradition, influence of **8:** 336, 348, 396, 404; **37:** 336
Shakespeare's other plays, compared with **8:** 294, 302, 324, 326, 348, 353, 380, 401, 464; **13:** 424
spectacle versus simple staging **15:** 206, 207, 208, 210, 217, 219, 222, 223, 224, 225, 227, 228, 305, 352; **28:** 415
sources **45:** 226
staging issues **15:** 343, 346, 352, 361, 364, 366, 368, 371, 385; **28:** 391, 415; **29:** 339; **32:** 338, 343; **42:** 339; **45:** 200

Stephano and Trinculo, comic subplot of **8:** 292, 297, 299, 304, 309, 324, 328, 353, 370; **25:** 382; **29:** 377; **46:** 14, 33
structure **8:** 294, 295, 299, 320, 384, 439; **28:** 391, 415; **29:** 292, 297; **45:** 188
subversiveness **22:** 302
The Tempest; or, The Enchanted Island (William Davenant/John Dryden adaptation) **15:** 189, 190, 192, 193
The Tempest; or, The Enchanted Island (Thomas Shadwell adaptation) **15:** 195, 196, 199
time **8:** 401, 439, 464; **25:** 357; **29:** 278, 292; **45:** 236
tragic elements **8:** 324, 348, 359, 370, 380, 408, 414, 439, 458, 464
trickster, motif of **22:** 302; **29:** 297
usurpation or rebellion **8:** 304, 370, 408, 420; **25:** 357, 382; **29:** 278, 362, 377; **37:** 336
utopia **45:** 280

Timon of Athens (Volumes 1, 20, 27)

Alcibiades **25:** 198; **27:** 191
alienation **1:** 523; **27:** 161
Apemantus **1:** 453, 467, 483; **20:** 476, 493; **25:** 198; **27:** 166, 223, 235
appearance versus reality **1:** 495, 500, 515, 523
Athens **27:** 223, 230
authorship controversy **1:** 464, 466, 467, 469, 474, 477, 478, 480, 490, 499, 507, 518; **16:** 351; **20:** 433
autobiographical elements **1:** 462, 467, 470, 473, 474, 478, 480; **27:** 166, 175
Elizabethan culture, relation to **1:** 487, 489, 495, 500; **20:** 433; **27:** 203, 212, 230; **50:** 13
as inferior or flawed plays **1:** 476, 481, 489, 499, 520; **20:** 433, 439, 491; **25:** 198; **27:** 157, 175
genre **1:** 454, 456, 459, 460, 462, 483, 492, 499, 503, 509, 511, 512, 515, 518, 525, 531; **27:** 203
King Lear, relation to **1:** 453, 459, 511; **16:** 351; **27:** 161; **37:** 222
language and imagery **1:** 488; **13:** 392; **25:** 198; **27:** 166, 184, 235
as medieval allegory or morality play **1:** 492, 511, 518; **27:** 155
mixture of genres **16:** 351; **25:** 198
nihilistic elements **1:** 481, 513, 529; **13:** 392; **20:** 481
pessimistic elements **1:** 462, 467, 470, 473, 478, 480; **20:** 433, 481; **27:** 155, 191
Poet and Painter **25:** 198
politics **27:** 223, 230; **50:** 13
religious, mythic, or spiritual content **1:** 505, 512, 513, 523; **20:** 493
satirical elements **27:** 155, 235
self-knowledge **1:** 456, 459, 462, 495, 503, 507, 515, 518, 526; **20:** 493; **27:** 166
Senecan elements **27:** 235
Shakespeare's other tragedies, compared with **27:** 166
sources **16:** 351; **27:** 191
staging issues **20:** 445, 446, 481, 491, 492, 493
structure **27:** 157, 175, 235
Timon
    comic traits **25:** 198

as flawed hero **1**: 456, 459, 462, 472, 495, 503, 507, 515; **16**: 351; **20**: 429, 433, 476; **25**: 198; **27**: 157, 161
misanthropy **13**: 392; **20**: 431, 464, 476, 481, 491, 492, 493; **27**: 161, 175, 184, 196; **37**: 222
as noble figure **1**: 467, 473, 483, 499; **20**: 493; **27**: 212
wealth and social class **1**: 466, 487, 495; **25**: 198; **27**: 184, 196, 212; **50**: 13

Titus Andronicus (Volumes 4, 17, 27, 43)

Aaron **4**: 632, 637, 650, 651, 653, 668, 672, 675; **27**: 255; **28**: 249, 330; **43**: 176
amputations, significance of **48**: 264
authorship controversy **4**: 613, 614, 615, 616, 617, 619, 623, 624, 625, 626, 628, 631, 632, 635, 642
autobiographical elements **4**: 619, 624, 625, 664
banquet scene **25**: 245; **27**: 255; **32**: 212
ceremonies, rites, and rituals, importance of **27**: 261; **32**: 265; **48**: 264
characterization **4**: 613, 628, 632, 635, 640, 644, 647, 650, 675; **27**: 293; **43**: 170, 176
Christian elements **4**: 656, 680
civilization versus barbarism **4**: 653; **27**: 293; **28**: 249; **32**: 265
Clarissa (Samuel Richardson), compared with **48**: 277
Elizabethan culture, relation to **27**: 282
Euripides, influence of **27**: 285
language and imagery **4**: 617, 624, 635, 642, 644, 646, 659, 664, 668, 672, 675; **13**: 225; **16**: 225; **25**: 245; **27**: 246, 293, 313, 318, 325; **43**: 186, 222, 227, 239, 247, 262,
language versus action **4**: 642, 644, 647, 664, 668; **13**: 225; **27**: 293, 313, 325; **43**: 186
Lavinia **27**: 266; **28**: 249; **32**: 212; **43**: 170, 239, 247, 255, 262
marriage as political tyranny **48**: 264
medieval literary influence **4**: 646, 650; **27**: 299
order versus disintegration **4**: 618, 647; **43**: 186, 195
Ovid, influence of **4**: 647, 659, 664, 668; **13**: 225; **27**: 246, 275, 285, 293, 299, 306; **28**: 249; **43**: 195, 203, 206
partiarchy **50**: 13
political content **43**: 262
politics **27**: 282; **48**: 264
primogeniture **50**: 13
rape **43**: 227, 255; **48**: 277
rightful succession **4**: 638
Roman elements **43**: 206, 222
Romans versus Goths **27**: 282
Senecan or revenge tragedy elements **4**: 618, 627, 628, 636, 639, 644, 646, 664, 672, 680; **16**: 225; **27**: 275, 318; **43**: 170, 206, 227
Shakespeare's canon, place in **4**: 614, 616, 618, 619, 637, 639, 646, 659, 664, 668; **43**: 195
Shakespeare's other tragedies, compared with **16**: 225; **27**: 275, 325
staging issues **17**: 449, 452, 456, 487; **25**: 245; **32**: 212, 249
structure **4**: 618, 619, 624, 631, 635, 640, 644, 646, 647, 653, 656, 659, 662, 664, 668, 672; **27**: 246, 285

Tamora **4**: 632, 662, 672, 675; **27**: 266; **43**: 170
Titus **4**: 632, 637, 640, 644, 647, 653, 656, 662; **25**: 245; **27**: 255
Vergil, influence of **27**: 306; **28**: 249
violence **13**: 225; **25**: 245; **27**: 255; **28**: 249; **32**: 249, 265; **43**: 1, 186, 203, 227, 239, 247, 255, 262

Troilus and Cressida (Volumes 3, 18, 27, 43)

ambiguity **3**: 544, 568, 583, 587, 589, 599, 611, 621; **27**: 400; **43**: 365
ambivalence **43**: 340
assignation scene (Act V, scene ii) **18**: 442, 451
autobiographical elements **3**: 548, 554, 557, 558, 574, 606, 630
body, role of **42**: 66
characterization **3**: 538, 539, 540, 541, 548, 566, 571, 604, 611, 621; **27**: 381, 391
Chaucer's Criseyde, compared with **43**: 305
chivalry, decline of **16**: 84; **27**: 370, 374
communication, failure of **43**: 277
conclusion **3**: 538, 549, 558, 566, 574, 583, 594
comedy vs. tragedy **43**: 351
contradictions **43**: 377
costumes **18**: 289, 371, 406, 419
courtly love **22**: 58
Cressida
as ambiguous figure **43**: 305
inconsistency **3**: 538; **13**: 53; **16**: 70; **22**: 339; **27**: 362
individual will versus social values **3**: 549, 561, 571, 590, 604, 617, 626; **13**: 53; **27**: 396
infidelity **3**: 536, 537, 544, 554, 555; **18**: 277, 284, 286; **22**: 58, 339; **27**: 400; **43**: 298
lack of punishment **3**: 536, 537
as mother figure **22**: 339
objectification of **43**: 329
as sympathetic figure **3**: 557, 560, 604, 609; **18**: 284, 423; **22**: 58; **27**: 396, 400; **43**: 305
cynicism **43**: 298
desire **43**: 317, 329, 340
disillusioned or cynical tone **3**: 544, 548, 554, 557, 558, 571, 574, 630, 642; **18**: 284, 332, 403, 406, 423; **27**: 376
disorder **3**: 578, 589, 599, 604, 609; **18**: 332, 406, 412, 423; **27**: 366
double plot **3**: 569, 613
Elizabeth I
waning power **43**: 365
Elizabethan culture, relation to **3**: 560, 574, 606; **25**: 56
food imagery **43**: 298
genre **3**: 541, 542, 549, 558, 566, 571, 574, 587, 594, 604, 630, 642; **27**: 366
Greece **43**: 287
inaction **3**: 587, 621; **27**: 347
language and imagery **3**: 561, 569, 596, 599, 606, 624, 630, 635; **22**: 58, 339; **27**: 332, 366; **42**: 66
love and honor **3**: 555, 604; **27**: 370, 374
love versus war **18**: 332, 371, 406, 423; **22**: 339; **27**: 376; **43**: 377
male/female relationships **16**: 70; **22**: 339; **27**: 362
marriage **22**: 339; **51**: 44

master-slave relationship **22**: 58
medieval chivalry **3**: 539, 543, 544, 555, 606; **27**: 376
moral corruption **3**: 578, 589, 599, 604, 609; **18**: 332, 406, 412, 423; **27**: 366; **43**: 298
Neoclassical rules **3**: 537, 538; **18**: 276, 278, 281
nihilistic elements **27**: 354
patriarchy **22**: 58
politics **3**: 536, 560, 606; **16**: 84
as "problem play" **3**: 555, 566
lack of resolution **43**: 277
psychoanalytical criticism **43**: 287
rape **43**: 357
satirical elements **3**: 539, 543, 544, 555, 558, 574; **27**: 341
sexuality **22**: 58, 339; **25**: 56; **27**: 362; **43**: 365
sources **3**: 537, 539, 540, 541, 544, 549, 558, 566, 574, 587; **27**: 376, 381, 391, 400
staging issues **16**: 70; **18**: 289, 332, 371, 395, 403, 406, 412, 419, 423, 442, 447, 451
structure **3**: 536, 538, 549, 568, 569, 578, 583, 589, 611, 613; **27**: 341, 347, 354, 391
Thersites **13**: 53; **25**: 56; **27**: 381
time **3**: 561, 571, 583, 584, 613, 621, 626, 634
Troilus
contradictory behavior **3**: 596, 602, 635; **27**: 362
Cressida, relationship with **3**: 594, 596, 606; **22**: 58
integrity **3**: 617
opposition to Ulysses **3**: 561, 584, 590
as unsympathetic figure **18**: 423; **22**: 58, 339; **43**: 317
as warrior **3**: 596; **22**: 339
Troilus and Cressida, or Truth Found too late (John Dryden adaptation) **18**: 276, 277, 278, 280, 281, 283
Trojan versus Greek values **3**: 541, 561, 574, 584, 590, 596, 621, 638; **27**: 370
Trojan War
as myth **43**: 293
Troy **43**: 287
Ulysses's speech on degree (Act I, scene iii) **3**: 549, 599, 609, 642; **27**: 396
value systems **3**: 578, 583, 589, 602, 613, 617; **13**: 53; **27**: 370, 396, 400
violence **43**: 329, 351, 357, 365, 377
through satire **43**: 293

Twelfth Night (Volumes 1, 26, 34, 46)

ambiguity **1**: 554, 639; **34**: 287, 316
Antonio **22**: 69
appetite **1**: 563, 596, 609, 615
autobiographical elements **1**: 557, 561, 599; **34**: 338
bear-baiting **19**: 42
characterization **1**: 539, 540, 543, 545, 550, 554, 581, 594; **26**: 257, 337, 342, 346, 364, 366, 371, 374; **34**: 281, 293, 311, 338; **46**: 286, 324
Christian elements **46**: 338
comic elements **26**: 233, 257, 337, 342, 371; **51**: 1
composition date **37**: 78
credibility **1**: 540, 542, 543, 554, 562, 581, 587

dark or tragic elements **46:** 310
Elizabethan culture, relation to **1:** 549, 553, 555, 563, 581, 587, 620; **16:** 53; **19:** 42, 78; **26:** 357; **28:** 1; **34:** 323, 330; **46:** 291; **51:** 15
fancy **1:** 543, 546
Feste
  characterization **1:** 558, 655, 658; **26:** 233, 364; **46:** 1, 14, 18, 33, 52, 60, 303, 310
  role in play **1:** 546, 551, 553, 566, 570, 571, 579, 635, 658; **46:** 297, 303, 310
  song **1:** 543, 548, 561, 563, 566, 570, 572, 603, 620, 642; **46:** 297
festive or folklore elements **46:** 338; **51:** 15
gender issues **19:** 78; **34:** 344; **37:** 59; **42:** 32; **46:** 347, 362, 369
homosexuality **22:** 69; **42:** 32; **46:** 362
language and imagery **1:** 570, 650, 664; **22:** 12; **28:** 9; **34:** 293; **37:** 59
love **1:** 543, 546, 573, 580, 587, 595, 600, 603, 610, 660; **19:** 78; **26:** 257, 364; **34:** 270, 293, 323; **46:** 291, 333, 347, 362; **51:** 30
madness **1:** 554, 639, 656; **26:** 371
Malvolio
  characterization **1:** 540, 544, 545, 548, 550, 554, 558, 567, 575, 577, 615; **26:** 207, 233, 273; **46:** 286
  forged letter **16:** 372; **28:** 1
  punishment **1:** 539, 544, 548, 549, 554, 555, 558, 563, 577, 590, 632, 645; **46:** 291, 297, 338
  as Puritan **1:** 549, 551, 555, 558, 561, 563; **25:** 47
  role in play **1:** 545, 548, 549, 553, 555, 563, 567, 575, 577, 588, 610, 615, 632, 645; **26:** 337, 374; **46:** 347
music **1:** 543, 566, 596
Olivia **1:** 540, 543, 545; **46:** 286, 333, 369; **47:** 45
order **1:** 563, 596; **34:** 330; **46:** 291, 347
Orsino **46:** 286, 333; **47:** 45
philosophical elements **1:** 560, 563, 596; **34:** 301, 316; **46:** 297
Puritanism **1:** 549, 553, 555, 632; **16:** 53; **25:** 47; **46:** 338
psychoanalytic criticism **46:** 333
Saturnalian elements **1:** 554, 571, 603, 620, 642; **16:** 53
self-deception **1:** 554, 561, 591, 625; **47:** 45
self-indulgence **1:** 563, 615, 635
sexual ambiguity and sexual deception **1:** 540, 562, 620, 621, 639, 645; **22:** 69; **34:** 311, 344; **37:** 59; **42:** 32
Shakespeare's canon, place in **1:** 543, 548, 557, 569, 575, 580, 621, 635, 638
Shakespeare's other plays, relation to **34:** 270; **46:** 303
sources **1:** 539, 540, 603; **34:** 301, 323, 344; **46:** 291
staging issues **26:** 219, 233, 257, 337, 342, 346, 357, 359, 360, 364, 366, 371, 374; **46:** 310, 369
structure **1:** 539, 542, 543, 546, 551, 553, 563, 570, 571, 590, 600, 660; **26:** 374; **34:** 281, 287; **46:** 286
time **37:** 78; **46:** 297
tragic elements **1:** 557, 569, 572, 575, 580, 599, 621, 635, 638, 639, 645, 654, 656; **26:** 342
Viola **26:** 308; **46:** 286, 324, 347, 369

The Two Gentlemen of Verona (Volumes 6, 12, 40)

absurdities, inconsistencies, and shortcomings **6:** 435, 436, 437, 439, 464, 507, 541, 560
appearance versus reality **6:** 494, 502, 511, 519, 529, 532, 549, 560
audience versus character perceptions **6:** 499, 519, 524
authorship controversy **6:** 435, 436, 437, 438, 439, 449, 466, 476
characterization **6:** 438, 442, 445, 447, 449, 458, 462, 560; **12:** 458; **40:** 312, 327, 330, 365
Christian elements **6:** 438, 494, 514, 532, 555, 564
education **6:** 490, 494, 504, 526, 532, 555, 568
Elizabethan setting **12:** 463, 485
forest **6:** 450, 456, 492, 514, 547, 555, 564, 568
genre **6:** 460, 468, 472, 516; **40:** 320
identity **6:** 494, 511, 529, 532, 547, 560, 564, 568; **19:** 34
ironic or parodic elements **6:** 447, 472, 478, 484, 502, 504, 509, 516, 529, 549; **13:** 12
Julia or Silvia **6:** 450, 453, 458, 476, 494, 499, 516, 519, 549, 564; **40:** 312, 327, 374
language and imagery **6:** 437, 438, 439, 445, 449, 490, 504, 519, 529, 541; **28:** 9; **40:** 343
Launce and Speed, comic function of **6:** 438, 439, 442, 456, 458, 460, 462, 472, 476, 478, 484, 502, 504, 507, 509, 516, 519, 549; **40:** 312, 320
love **6:** 442, 445, 456, 479, 488, 492, 494, 502, 509, 516, 519, 549; **13:** 12; **40:** 327, 335, 343, 354, 365; **51:** 30, 44
love versus friendship **6:** 439, 449, 450, 458, 460, 465, 468, 471, 476, 480; **40:** 354, 359, 365
marriage **48:** 32
mimetic rivalry **13:** 12; **40:** 335
morality **6:** 438, 492, 494, 514, 532, 555, 564
Proteus **6:** 439, 450, 458, 480, 490, 511; **40:** 312, 327, 330, 335, 359; **42:** 18
repentance and forgiveness **6:** 450, 514, 516, 555, 564
resolution **6:** 435, 436, 439, 445, 449, 453, 458, 460, 462, 465, 466, 468, 471, 476, 480, 486, 494, 509, 514, 516, 519, 529, 532, 541, 549; **19:** 34
romantic and courtly conventions **6:** 438, 460, 472, 478, 484, 486, 488, 502, 507, 509, 529, 541, 549, 560, 568; **12:** 460, 462; **40:** 354, 374
setting **12:** 463, 465, 485
sources **6:** 436, 460, 462, 468, 476, 480, 490, 511, 547; **19:** 34; **40:** 320
staging issues **12:** 457, 464; **42:** 18
structure **6:** 445, 450, 460, 462, 504, 526
youth **6:** 439, 450, 464, 514, 568

The Two Noble Kinsmen (Volumes 9, 41, 50)

amorality, question of **9:** 447, 460, 492
authorship controversy
  Shakespeare not a co-author **9:** 445, 447, 455, 461
  Shakespearean portions of the text **9:** 446, 447, 448, 455, 456, 457, 460, 462, 463, 471, 479, 486; **41:** 308, 317, 355
  Shakespeare's part in the overall conception or design **9:** 444, 446, 448, 456, 457, 460, 480, 481, 486, 490; **37:** 313; **41:** 326; **50:** 326
ceremonies, rites, and rituals, importance of **9:** 492, 498
characterization **9:** 457, 461, 471, 474; **41:** 340, 385; **50:** 305, 326
chivalry **50:** 305, 348
class distinctions, conflict and relations **50:** 295, 305, 310
Emilia **9:** 460, 470, 471, 479, 481; **19:** 394; **41:** 372, 385; **42:** 368
free will versus fate **9:** 474, 481, 486, 492, 498
friendship **9:** 448, 463, 470, 474, 479, 481, 486, 490; **19:** 394; **41:** 355, 363, 372; **42:** 368
gender issues **42:** 368; **50:** 310
innocence to experience **9:** 481, 502; **19:** 394
irony or satire **9:** 463, 481, 486; **41:** 301; **50:** 348
the jailer's daughter **9:** 457, 460, 479, 481, 486, 502; **41:** 340; **50:** 295, 305, 310, 348, 361
language and imagery **9:** 445, 446, 447, 448, 456, 461, 462, 463, 469, 471, 498, 502; **41:** 289, 301, 308, 317, 326; **50:** 310
love **9:** 479, 481, 490, 498; **41:** 289, 355, 301, 363, 372, 385; **50:** 295, 361
masque elements **9:** 490
Palamon and Arcite **9:** 474, 481, 490, 492, 502; **50:** 295, 305, 348, 361
sexuality **50:** 361
sources **19:** 394; **41:** 289, 301, 363, 385; **50:** 326, 348
structure **37:** 313; **50:** 326, 361

Venus and Adonis (Volumes 10, 33, 51)

Adonis **10:** 411, 420, 424, 427, 429, 434, 439, 442, 451, 454, 459, 466, 473, 489; **25:** 305, 328; **28:** 355; **33:** 309, 321, 330, 347, 352, 357, 363, 370, 377; **51:** 345, 377
allegorical elements **10:** 427, 434, 439, 449, 454, 462, 480; **28:** 355; **33:** 309, 330
ambiguity **10:** 434, 454, 459, 462, 466, 473, 480, 486, 489; **33:** 352; **51:** 368, 377, 388
beauty **10:** 420, 423, 427, 434, 454, 480; **33:** 330, 352
the boar **10:** 416, 451, 454, 466, 473; **33:** 339, 347, 370; **51:** 359, 368
comic elements **51:** 377
the courser and the jennet **10:** 418, 439, 466; **33:** 309, 339, 347, 352
death, decay, and nature's destructiveness **10:** 419, 427, 434, 451, 454, 462, 466, 473, 480, 489; **25:** 305; **33:** 309, 321, 347, 352, 363, 370
dramatic elements **10:** 459, 462, 486
domesticity **51:** 359
eroticism or sensuality **10:** 410, 411, 418, 419, 427, 428, 429, 442, 448, 454, 459, 466, 473; **25:** 305, 328; **28:** 355; **33:** 321, 339, 347, 352, 363, 370; **51:** 345, 352, 359, 368
Faerie Queene (Edmund Spenser), compared with **33:** 339

forgiveness **51**: 377
Hero and Leander (Christopher Marlowe), compared with **10**: 419, 424, 429; **33**: 309, 357; **51**: 345, 377
comic elements **10**: 429, 434, 439, 442, 459, 462, 489; **33**: 352
hunt motif **10**: 434, 451, 466, 473; **33**: 357, 370
imagery **10**: 414, 415, 416, 420, 429, 434, 449, 459, 466, 473, 480; **25**: 328; **28**: 355; **33**: 321, 339, 352, 363, 370, 377; **42**: 348; **51**: 335, 388
love versus lust **10**: 418, 420, 427, 434, 439, 448, 449, 454, 462, 466, 473, 480, 489; **25**: 305; **28**: 355; **33**: 309, 330, 339, 347, 357, 363, 370; **51**: 359
morality **10**: 411, 412, 414, 416, 418, 419, 420, 423, 427, 428, 439, 442, 448, 449, 454, 459, 466; **33**: 330
negative appraisals **10**: 410, 411, 415, 418, 419, 424, 429
Ovid, compared with **32**: 352; **42**: 348; **51**: 335, 352
pictorial elements **10**: 414, 415, 419, 420, 423, 480; **33**: 339
popularity **10**: 410, 412, 418, 427; **25**: 328
procreation **10**: 439, 449, 466; **33**: 321, 377
reason **10**: 427, 439, 449, 459, 462, 466; **28**: 355; **33**: 309, 330
rhetoric **33**: 377; **51**: 335, 345, 352
Shakespeare's plays, compared with **10**: 412, 414, 415, 434, 459, 462
Shakespeare's sonnets, compared with **33**: 377
sources **10**: 410, 412, 420, 424, 429, 434, 439, 451, 454, 466, 473, 480, 486, 489; **16**: 452; **25**: 305; **28**: 355; **33**: 309, 321, 330, 339, 347, 352, 357, 370, 377; **42**: 348; **51**: 335
structure **10**: 434, 442, 480, 486, 489; **33**: 357, 377
style **10**: 411, 412, 414, 415, 416, 418, 419, 420, 423, 424, 428, 429, 439, 442, 480, 486, 489; **16**: 452
Venus **10**: 427, 429, 434, 439, 442, 448, 449, 451, 454, 466, 473, 480, 486, 489; **16**: 452; **25**: 305, 328; **28**: 355; **33**: 309, 321, 330, 347, 352, 357, 363, 370, 377; **51**: 335, 352, 377, 388
Wat the hare **10**: 424, 451

The Winter's Tale (Volumes 7, 15, 36, 45)

Antigonus
  characterization **7**: 394, 451, 464
  death scene (Act III, scene iii) **7**: 377, 414, 464, 483; **15**: 518, 532; **19**: 366
appearance versus reality **7**: 429, 446, 479
art versus nature **7**: 377, 381, 397, 419, 452; **36**: 289, 318; **45**: 329
audience perception, Shakespeare's manipulation of **7**: 394, 429, 456, 483, 501; **13**: 417; **19**: 401, 431, 441; **25**: 339; **45**: 374
autobiographical elements **7**: 395, 397, 410, 419
Autolycus **7**: 375, 380, 382, 387, 389, 395, 396, 414; **15**: 524; **22**: 302; **37**: 31; **45**: 333; **46**: 14, 33; **50**: 45
Christian elements **7**: 381, 387, 402, 410, 417, 419, 425, 429, 436, 452, 460, 501; **36**: 318
counsel **19**: 401
court society **16**: 410
dramatic structure **7**: 382, 390, 396, 399, 402, 407, 414, 429, 432, 473, 479, 493, 497, 501; **15**: 528; **25**: 339; **36**: 289, 295, 362, 380; **45**: 297, 344, 358, 366
ethnicity **37**: 306
folk drama, relation to **7**: 420, 451
forgiveness or redemption **7**: 381, 389, 395, 402, 407, 436, 456, 460, 483; **36**: 318
fusion of comic, tragic, and romantic elements **7**: 390, 394, 396, 399, 410, 412, 414, 429, 436, 479, 483, 490, 501; **13**: 417; **15**: 514, 524, 532; **25**: 339; **36**: 295, 380; **45**: 295, 329
grace **7**: 420, 425, 460, 493; **36**: 328
Hermione
  characterization **7**: 385, 395, 402, 412, 414, 506; **15**: 495, 532; **22**: 302, 324; **25**: 347; **32**: 388; **36**: 311; **47**: 25; **49**: 18
  restoration (Act V, scene iii) **7**: 377, 379, 384, 385, 387, 389, 394, 396, 412, 425, 436, 451, 452, 456, 464, 483, 501; **15**: 411, 412, 413, 518, 528, 532; **49**: 18
  supposed death **25**: 339; **47**: 25
  trial of **49**: 18
as historical allegory **7**: 381; **15**: 528
homosexuality **48**: 309
hospitality **19**: 366
irony **7**: 419, 420
Jacobean culture, relation to **19**: 366, 401, 431; **25**: 347; **32**: 388; **37**: 306
language and imagery **7**: 382, 384, 417, 418, 420, 425, 460, 506; **13**: 409; **19**: 431; **22**: 324; **25**: 347; **36**: 295; **42**: 308; **45**: 297, 333, 344; **50**: 45
Leontes
  characterization **19**: 431; **45**: 366
  jealousy **7**: 377, 379, 382, 383, 384, 387, 389, 394, 395, 402, 407, 412, 414, 425, 429, 432, 436, 464, 480, 483, 497; **15**: 514, 518, 532; **22**: 324; **25**: 339; **36**: 334, 344, 349; **44**: 66; **45**: 295, 297, 344, 358, 366; **47**: 25
Othello, compared with **7**: 383, 390, 412; **15**: 514; **36**: 334; **44**: 66; **47**: 25
repentance **7**: 381, 389, 394, 396, 402, 414, 497; **36**: 318, 362; **44**: 66
love **7**: 417, 425, 469, 490; **51**: 30, 33, 44
Mamillius **7**: 394, 396, 451; **22**: 324
metadramatic elements **16**: 410
myth of Demeter and Persephone, relation to **7**: 397, 436
nationalism and patriotism **32**: 388
nature **7**: 397, 418, 419, 420, 425, 432, 436, 451, 452, 473, 479; **19**: 366; **45**: 329
Neoclassical rules **7**: 376, 377, 379, 380, 383, 410; **15**: 397
Ovid's *Metamorphoses*, relation to **42**: 308
Pandosto, compared with **7**: 376, 377, 390, 412, 446; **13**: 409; **25**: 347; **36**: 344, 374
Paulina **7**: 385, 412, 506; **15**: 528; **22**: 324; **25**: 339; **36**: 311
Perdita
  characterization **7**: 395, 412, 414, 419, 429, 432, 452, 506; **22**: 324; **25**: 339; **36**: 328
  reunion with Leontes (Act V, scene ii) **7**: 377, 379, 381, 390, 432, 464, 480
plot **7**: 376, 377, 379, 382, 387, 390, 396, 452; **13**: 417; **15**: 518; **45**: 374
rebirth, regeneration, resurrection, or immortality **7**: 397, 414, 417, 419, 429, 436, 451, 452, 456, 480, 490, 497, 506; **25**: 339 452, 480, 490, 497, 506; **45**: 366
sheep-shearing scene (Act IV, scene iv) **7**: 379, 387, 395, 396, 407, 410, 412, 414, 419, 420, 429, 432, 436, 451, 479, 490; **16**: 410; **19**: 366; **25**: 339; **36**: 362, 374; **45**: 374
staging issues **7**: 414, 425, 429, 446, 464, 480, 483, 497; **13**: 409; **15**: 518; **48**: 309
statue scene (Act V, scene iii) **7**: 377, 379, 384, 385, 387, 389, 394, 396, 412, 425, 436, 451, 456, 464, 483, 501; **15**: 411, 412, 518, 528, 532; **25**: 339, 347; **36**: 301
subversiveness **22**: 302
symbolism **7**: 425, 429, 436, 452, 456, 469, 490, 493
textual issues **19**: 441; **45**: 333
Time-Chorus **7**: 377, 380, 412, 464, 476, 501; **15**: 518
time **7**: 397, 425, 436, 476, 490; **19**: 366; **36**: 301, 349; **45**: 297, 329, 366, 374
trickster, motif of **22**: 302; **45**: 333
Union debate, relation to **25**: 347
violence **43**: 39
witchcraft **22**: 324
women, role of **22**: 324; **36**: 311; **42**: 308; **51**: 30

ISBN 0-7876-3146-9

90000